THE EDITORS

DUANE HEATH has been co-editor of the *South African Rugby Annual* since 2010. He has been a journalist and editor since 1994, having worked at the *Guardian* and *Observer* newspapers in London and for the *Sunday Times* and *Rugby World* magazine in South Africa. He wrote the best-selling and award-winning cookbook *Springbok Kitchen*, which raised over half a million rand for the Chris Burger Petro Jackson Fund for rugby players who have suffered catastrophic injuries. He works for the South African Rugby Union as manager of special projects. Duane lives in Cape Town with his wife Aisling, and children, Kian and Emma.

EDDIE GRIEB has been the official statistician of the South African Rugby Union since 2006 and co-editor of the *South African Rugby Annual* since 2008. A former representative flyhalf and fullback for the now defunct provincial unions of Far North and Eastern Free State, he worked for SuperSport from 2006-2012 and has written a number of books on the sport, including *Far North Rugby 1968-1992*; *Eastern Free State Rugby 1968-1997* (with Heinrich Schulze), *Pumas Rugby 1969-2008* (with Heinrich Schulze), *Springbok Miscellany* (with Stuart Farmer); and *The Springbok Handbook* (with Stuart Farmer). Eddie lives in Pretoria with his wife Alida, and children, Lee and Edrich.

SOUTH AFRICAN RUGBY ANNUAL 2017

Edited by Duane Heath & Eddie Grieb

Contributing Editors:
Kobus Smit & Stephen Nell
Design: Ryan Manning

SOUTH AFRICAN RUGBY UNION
CAPE TOWN

ISBN: 978-0-620-74427-0

Designer: Ryan Manning
Text by the Editor, Stephen Nell, or as credited
Photographs by Gallo Images or as credited

Printed & bound by Creda Communications, Eliot Ave, Eppindust II, Cape Town

Disclaimer: The views expressed in this *Annual* are those of the editors & contributors and not necessarily those of the South African Rugby Union.

The Editors welcome suggestions and notification of any errors or omissions.
Duane Heath: PO Box 22643 Fish Hoek 7974; 021 928 7055 (office); duaneh@sarugby.co.za
Eddie Grieb: PO Box 989 Olifantsfontein 1665; 086 559 0744 (fax); eddieg@sarugby.co.za

Contents

SOUTH AFRICAN RUGBY ANNUAL 2017

CONTENTS

CONTENTS

Notes

KEY TO TEAM APPEARANCE LISTS:

R = Replacement

X = Unused replacement

c = Captain

A dash (–) denotes player not named in match-day squad for that particular match.

1. All records are correct as at 1 January 2017, unless otherwise stated.

2. All teams listed are in the order of fullback (15) to loosehead prop (1).

3. For record purposes, team names at the time of the establishment of the record have been used.

4. Union names and the names of their senior teams in 2015 were as follows:

Blue Bulls Rugby Union (formerly Northern Transvaal) – playing as Blue Bulls.

Boland Rugby Union – playing as Boland Cavaliers.

Border Rugby Football Union – playing as Border Bulldogs.

Eastern Province Rugby Union – playing as Eastern Province Kings.

Free State Rugby Union (formerly Orange Free State) – playing as Free State Cheetahs or Free State XV.

Golden Lions Rugby Union (formerly Transvaal & Gauteng Lions) – playing as Golden Lions.

Griffons Rugby Union (formerly Northern Free State) – playing as Griffons.

Griqualand West Rugby Union – playing as Griquas.

Leopards Rugby Union (formerly Western Transvaal & North West) – playing as Leopards or Leopards XV.

Mpumalanga Rugby Union (formerly South Eastern Transvaal) – playing as Pumas.

KwaZulu-Natal Rugby Union (formerly Natal) – playing as Sharks or Sharks XV.

South Western Districts Rugby Football Union – playing as SWD Eagles.

Falcons Rugby Union (formerly Eastern Transvaal, Gauteng Falcons & Falcons) – playing as the Falcons.

Western Province Rugby Football Union – playing as Western Province.

5. Definition of a 'first-class match' and 'first-class appearance':

i) To qualify as a first-class match, it must be played strictly according to the Laws of the game (no more than seven or eight players on the bench, depending on the tournament or match).

ii) The following categories of matches qualify for first-class status if point i) is fulfilled:

   a) All matches featuring the South African national team (Springboks) and the South African national under-20 team (Junior Springboks);

   b) All matches in senior tournaments sanctioned by SARU;

   c) All matches against touring international teams;

   d) All matches between senior provincial teams & touring teams of the same or a higher status;

   e) All matches between senior provincial teams outside of SARU tournaments where the strongest possible teams are fielded;

   f) All matches played by senior teams carrying the name of a South African national team;

   g) All matches played by senior composite teams in World Rugby-approved tournaments.

iii) Any player appearing in one of the above matches (either in the starting XV or as a replacement – blood replacements and yellow-card replacements included) will be deemed to have made a first-class appearance.

Team Abbreviations

SOUTH AFRICAN TEAMS: *BB – Blue Bulls; Bol – Boland; Bor – Border; EP – Eastern Province; ETvl – Eastern Transvaal; F – Falcons; FS – Free State; GF – Gauteng Falcons; GL – Golden Lions; GW – Griqualand West; MPU – Mpumalanga; NEC – North Eastern Cape; NED – North Eastern Districts; NNtl – Northern Natal; NOFS – Northern Orange Free State; NTvl – Northern Transvaal; OFS – Orange Free State; SWD – South Western Districts; SETvl – South Eastern Transvaal; Tvl – Transvaal; WP – Western Province; WTvl – Western Transvaal.*
INTERNATIONAL TEAMS: *Arg – Argentina; A – Australia; B – Brazil; Bot – Botswana; BI – British & Irish Lions; C – Canada; Cam – Cameroon; Ch – Chile; Cze – Czechoslovakia; E – England; Fj – Fiji; F – France; G – Germany; Geo – Georgia; Gulf – Gulf States; I – Ireland; IC – Ivory Coast; It - Italy; J – Japan; Ken – Kenya; Mad – Madagascar; Mor – Morocco; Nam – Namibia; Net – Netherlands; NZ – New Zealand; NZC – New Zealand Cavaliers; NZM – New Zealand Maoris; Nor – Norway; Par – Paraguay; Per – Peru; PI – Pacific Islands; Pol – Poland; Por – Portugal; R – Romania; Rus – Russia; S – Scotland; Sm – Samoa; SAm – South America; SAm&Sp – South America & Spain; SA – South Africa; SK – South Korea; SWA - South West Africa; Sp – Spain; Swa – Swaziland; Tan – Tanzania; Tun – Tunisia; T – Tonga; US – United States of America; Ug – Uganda; Ur – Uruguay; Ven- Venezuela; W – Wales; WS – Western Samoa; WT – World Team; Zam – Zambia; Zim - Zimbabwe.*
COUNTRIES/TOWNS – SEVENS RUGBY CURCUITS: *A – Australia; Arg – Argentina; C – Canada; CG – Commonwealth Games; Ch – Chile; Chi – China; Dub – Dubai; E – England; F – France; Fj – Fiji; HK – Hong Kong; J – Japan; Mal – Malaysia; NZ – New Zealand; OG – Olympic Games; RWC – Rugby World Cup; S – Scotland; SA – South Africa; Sin – Singapore; Ur – Uruguay; US – United States of America; W – Wales; WG – World Games.*

FOREWORD

Challenging but exciting times ahead

SOUTH African rugby is nothing if not durable and resilient and, as we look ahead to the 2017 season, I have no doubt that our historical ability to bounce back from adversity will once again come to the fore.

The 125 years that the Springboks have played international rugby have been characterised by memorable highs but also low points – such is the cycle of life in any sport, especially at the sharp end of Test rugby.

The year 2016 may well be remembered as one during which our national team – the pride of our nation – lost more matches than they won. But it would be worth remembering that such an occurrence has happened before – just think of 1965, for instance – and sometime in the future it may happen again.

But Springbok rugby is built on solid foundations over a century in the making and it is this foundation that has always stood us in good stead whenever the going got tough. Results might not have gone our way in 2016 but I am positive that, having learnt from these experiences, the players and coaching staff will bounce back as only the Springboks can.

It may be tempting to paint a generally gloomy picture of South African rugby circa 2017 by viewing circumstances solely through the lens of the Springbok team. To be sure, the national side are our flagship brand but the Springboks are just a part of a larger rugby movement, brilliantly epitomised in 2016 by our #LoveRugby campaign, which reached into the hearts of rugby supporters in every corner of our country.

Truth be told, there is so much to be positive about when it comes to our beloved game. New Zealand's All Blacks may be setting the pace at Test level but elsewhere it is South African rugby that continues to push the boundaries of excellence and innovation.

Our Springbok Sevens team encapsulates everything that is good about South Africa.

These young, passionate South Africans won bronze at the 2016 Olympic Games in Rio de Janeiro and, at the time of writing, were setting new standards in sevens rugby in the 2016/17 HSBC World Series, winning their third tournament in four attempts and surging ahead of the chasing pack. Where once the All Blacks and Fijians set the benchmark, now it is Neil Powell and his wonderfully transformed Blitzboks who are reshaping the sport.

The Cape Town Sevens has also, within the space of a year, established itself as the best sevens tournament on the planet. It is a truly world-class event held in a world-class city.

At the other end of the rugby spectrum, let us also not forget that our Coca-Cola Youth Weeks – with the Under-18 Craven Week as its focal point – remain the envy of the schoolboy rugby world.

And club rugby, thanks to the successful Gold Cup, continues its amazing resurgence as amateur players from across the land are given a platform to display their talents to a national audience. The Gold Cup has, like the Cape Town Sevens, very quickly established itself as an international tournament that no other country can boast of, while at the provincial level, our big club derbies frequently draw bigger crowds than most professional club leagues around the world.

As we kick off the 2017 rugby season, I am confident that South African rugby stands poised to raise the bar even further when it comes to these world-class events I have mentioned. A century of heritage and pride will also no doubt ensure that our flagship Springbok team will bounce back as well, as they have done countless times in the past.

These are challenging but exciting times for our sport.

Mark Alexander
South African Rugby Union President

ACKNOWLEDGEMENTS

THE *South African Rugby Annual* is, as always, a labour of love made possible by the enduring passion of all who contribute to its creation: colleagues, contributors and ordinary readers – all of whom are united by a love of history, and of documenting the constantly unfolding history of South African rugby for future generations.

Without them, quite frankly, this publication would no longer be the so-called 'bible' of the game on which so many associated with this marvellous game depend for facts and insights.

Thank you to our friends at the provincial unions: Saartjie Olivier (Blue Bulls), Jaco van Wyk (Boland), Trevor Barnes (KZN), Marius van Rensburg (Mpumalanga), Luvuyo Matsha & Gesie van der Merwe (Valke), Revenne Maritz (WP), Rynhardt van As (SWD), Karen Crafford (Leopards), Leah van Wyk & Michael Herbert (Griffons), Debbie Ellis (EP), Lizette Viviers (Free State), David Ruiters (Border) and Martin Coetzee (Griquas).

Thanks once again go to my co-editor Eddie Grieb's statistical team made up of Piet Landman, Paul Dobson, Heinrich Schulze, Gideon Nieman, Ashley Berry, Johanna de Vos, Frikkie van Rensburg, Herman le Roux and our overseas stalwarts – John Griffiths (World Rugby statistician), Geoff Miller (New Zealand Rugby Union), Matthew Alvarez (Australian Rugby Union) and Stuart Farmer (Stuart Farmer Media Services Ltd, England).

Thank you to Gallo Images for their superb efforts to once again visually document our sport, and to the writers whose words make the *Annual* the respected document of record it is: John Bishop, Paul Dobson, Vata Ngobeni, Craig Ray and Stephen Nell. JJ Harmse and Zeena Isaacs of SARU also deserve thanks for their contributions, as does Andy Colquhoun, the *Annual's* editor for many years and now, in his position as general manager of Communications at SARU, the person who continues, with the admirable support of the organisation, to ensure its continued survival.

Thanks once again also to Lesley Ackermann of Creda Communications, who always goes beyond the call of duty, as well as Mark Hackney and everyone at Blue Weaver.

Finally, a very special thanks to Eddie Grieb and designer Ryan Manning, who together have once again burnt more midnight oil than the rest of the names mentioned here put together.

And, for the eighth year running, on behalf of them I extend a heartfelt thanks to our family members whose patience seemingly knows no limits: Alida Grieb and Lee & Edrich; Vanessa Manning and Hannah & Joshua; and, finally, to my wife Aisling, our son Kian and daughter Emma.

Duane Heath
Cape Town
January 2017

Emirates Lions captain Jaco Kriel accepts the Super Rugby South African conference trophy.

2016 Season Award Winners

SA Rugby Player of the Year:
Pieter-Steph du Toit
Nominees: *Ruan Combrinck, Eben Etzebeth, Jaco Kriel, Warren Whiteley*

Young Player of the Year:
Malcolm Marx
Nominees: *Curwin Bosch, Rohan Janse van Rensburg, Seabelo Senatla, RG Snyman*

Players' Player of the Year, presented by MyPlayers:
Jean-Luc du Preez *(Cell C Sharks)*

Team of the Year:
Emirates Lions *(Vodacom Super Rugby)*
Nominees: *Springbok Sevens, Toyota Free State Cheetahs (Currie Cup Premier Division)*

Coach of the Year:
Johan Ackermann *(Emirates Lions, Xerox Golden Lions)*
Nominees: *Brent Janse van Rensburg (Boland), Neil Powell (Springbok Sevens)*

Junior Springbok Player of the Year:
Curwin Bosch
Nominees: *Manie Libbok, Jeremy Ward*

SA Sevens Player of the Year:
Seabelo Senatla
Nominees: *Kyle Brown, Rosko Specman*

Vodacom Super Rugby Player of Year:
Elton Jantjies (Emirates Lions)
Nominees: *Ruan Combrinck (Emirates Lions), Warren Whiteley (Emirates Lions)*

Currie Cup Premier Division Player of the Year:
Ox Nche *(Toyota Free State Cheetahs)*
Nominees: *Huw Jones (DHL Western Province), Nico Lee (Toyota Free State Cheetahs)*

Currie Cup First Division Player of the Year:
Masixole Banda (Border)
Nominees: *Johan Deysel (Leopards), George Whitehead (Griffons)*

Club Player of the Year:
Leon du Plessis* (Rustenburg Impala)
* Du Plessis won the award for the second year running

Supersport Try of the Year:
Jacques Nel *(Xerox Golden Lions v DHL Western Province, Currie Cup Premier Division)*

Coca-Cola Craven Week Player of the Year:
Damian Willemse (DHL Western Province)

Outsurance Referee Award: Rasta Rasivhenge

Springbok Women's Achiever Award:
Marithy Pienaar

Best Development Programme Award:
Blue Bulls Rugby Union
Nominees: *KwaZulu-Natal Rugby Union, Western Province Rugby Football Union*

PLAYER OF THE YEAR

Pieter-Steph du Toit

(DHL Stormers, South Africa)

IT was a windy day in Cape Town on 15 April 2013 when former Springbok coach Heyneke Meyer, speaking after a training session at the Westerford High School, predicted that Pieter-Steph du Toit was destined for greatness.

Big words, but no one was better qualified to deliver a judgement than Meyer, who brought second-row greats such as Bakkies Botha and Victor Matfield through the South African system.

Du Toit's development was disrupted by injuries, but three and a half years later he would be named South Africa's Rugby Player of the Year after splendid performances for the Stormers and Springboks.

We're not quite ready to declare him one of the 'greatest Springboks of all time', but barring serious misfortune on the injury front, one can safely say he's going to achieve very big things.

For the DHL Stormers he and Eben Etzebeth were a pillar of strength on the way to the Cape side winning their Vodacom Super Rugby conference. Du Toit also stood out in a struggling Springbok team – a sure sign of undoubted class.

While ticking the all-important box of lineout prowess for a No 5 lock, Du Toit is a robust player who adds significant muscle to the pack. He also distinguished himself as a ball-carrier and a player with a keen sense of anticipation, as was evident with the intercept try he scored against Ireland at Newlands.

Du Toit, as Player of the Year, was preferred over Etzebeth, his lock partner at the Stormers and Springboks, and the Lions trio of Ruan Combrinck, Jaco Kriel and Warren Whiteley.

Combrinck's performances were highlighted by the superb try that he scored in South Africa's sensational fightback victory against Ireland in Johannesburg, while alongside him Kriel and Whiteley were standout performers for the Lions in their march to the Super Rugby final.

Whiteley's leadership, in particular, made him a strong contender.

But ultimately Du Toit was an easy choice as his performances in the Green and Gold were as compelling as when he played for the Stormers.

Du Toit had, of course, made his debut as long ago as 2013 when the Springboks edged Wales in Cardiff, but was powerless to do anything about the knee and shoulder injuries that would halt his progress.

In 2016, however, he seized the moment in the wake of Victor Matfield's eventual retirement and is equally considered South Africa's best option for the No 5 jersey as his predecessor was in his prime. – *Stephen Nell*

Previous Players of the Year

2015: Lood de Jager (Winner, FS), Damian de Allende (WP), Schalk Burger (WP), Eben Etzebeth (WP), Jaco Kriel (GL).

2014: Duane Vermeulen (Winner, WP), Nizaam Carr (WP), Marcell Coetzee (KZN), Willie le Roux (FS), Handré Pollard (BB).

2013: Jean de Villiers (Winner, WP), Bismarck du Plessis (KZN), Eben Etzebeth (WP), Willie le Roux (FS), Duane Vermeulen (WP).

2012: Bryan Habana (Winner, WP), Keegan Daniel (KZN), Patrick Lambie (KZN), Eben Etzebeth (WP), JP Pietersen (KZN).

2011: Schalk Burger (Winner, WP), Bismarck du Plessis (KZN), Patrick Lambie (KZN), Francois Hogaard (BB), Victor Matfield (BB).

2010: Gurthrö Steenkamp (Winner, BB), Gio Aplon (WP), Schalk Burger (WP), Juan de Jongh (WP), Francois Hougaard (BB).

2009: Fourie du Preez (Winner, BB), Heinrich Brüssow (FS), Victor Matfield (BB), John Smit (KZN), Morné Steyn (BB).

2008: Jean de Villiers (Winner, WP), Tendai Mtawarira, Bismarck du Plessis, Ryan Kankowski, Adrian Jacobs (all KZN).

2007: Bryan Habana (Winner, Fourie du Preez, Victor Matfield (all BB), Percy Montgomery (KZN), Juan Smith (FS).

2006: Fourie du Preez (Winner, BB), Os du Randt (FS), Victor Matfield (BB), Pierre Spies (BB), Luke Watson (WP).

2005: Bryan Habana (Winner), Bakkies Botha, Victor Matfield (all BB), Jean de Villiers (WP), Ricky Januarie (GL).

2004: Schalk Burger (Winner, WP), Os du Randt (FS), De Wet Barry, Marius

Joubert (WP), Bakkies Botha (BB).

2003: Ashwin Willemse (Winner, GL), Juan Smith (FS), Richard Bands, Bakkies Botha (BB), Joe van Niekerk (GL).

2002: Joe van Niekerk (Winner), Jannes Labuschagne, André Pretorius, Lawrence Sephaka (all GL), Werner Greeff (WP).

2001: André Vos (Winner, GL), Braam van Straaten (WP), Victor Matfield (BB), Lukas van Biljon (Natal), Conrad Jantjes (GL).

2000: Breyton Paulse (Winner, WP), Thinus Delport, Rassie Erasmus (both GL), Kennedy Tsimba (FS), Corné Krige (WP).

1999: André Venter (Winner, FS), Breyton Paulse, Cobus Visagie (both WP), Joost van der Westhuizen (BB), Hennie le Roux (GL).

1998: Gary Teichmann (Winner, Natal), Joost van der Westhuizen, Krynauw Otto (BB), Gaffie du Toit (GW), Bobby Skinstad (WP).

1997: Os du Randt (Winner, FS), Pieter Rossouw, Percy Montgomery, Dick Muir (all WP), Johan Roux (GL).

1996: André Joubert (Winner, Natal), Henry Honiball, Gary Teichmann (both Natal), Ruben Kruger, Joost van der Westhuizen (both NTvl).

1995: Ruben Kruger (Winner), Joost van der Westhuizen (both NTvl), Francois Pienaar (Tvl), Joel Stransky (WP), André Joubert (Natal).

1994: Chester Williams (Winner, WP), Mark Andrews, André Joubert (both Natal), Ruben Kruger, Joost vd Westhuizen (both NTvl).

1993: Gavin Johnson (Winner), Francois Pienaar (both Tvl), James Small (Natal), Tiaan Strauss (WP), Joost vd Westhuizen (NTvl).

1992: Tiaan Strauss (Winner), Danie Gerber (both WP), Jacques Olivier, Naas Botha, Adriaan Richter (all NTvl).

1991: Uli Schmidt (Winner), Naas Botha, Gerbrand Grobler (all NTvl), André Joubert (OFS), Wahl Bartmann (Natal).

1990: Uli Schmidt (Winner), Robert du Preez (both NTvl), Wahl Bartmann, Joel Stransky (both Natal), Tiaan Strauss (WP).

1989: Johan Heunis (Winner), Robert du Preez, Burger Geldenhuys (all NTvl), André Joubert (OFS), Carel du Plessis (WP).

1988: Calla Scholtz (Winner), Tiaan Strauss (both WP), Naas Botha, Adolf Malan (both NTvl), Gerhard Mans (SWA).

1987: Naas Botha (Winner), Adri Geldenhuys (both NTvl), Gysie Pienaar (OFS), John Robbie, Jannie Breedt (both Tvl).

1986: Jannie Breedt (Winner), Wahl Bartmann (both Tvl), Carel du Plessis (WP), Uli Schmidt (NTvl), Garth Wright (EP).

1985: Naas Botha (Winner, NTvl), Jannie Breedt (Tvl), Schalk (SWP) Burger (WP), Danie Gerber (EP), Gerrie Sonnekus (OFS).

1984: Danie Gerber (Winner, EP), Rob Louw, Calla Scholtz (both WP), Ray Mordt (NTvl), Errol Tobias (Bol).

1983: Hennie Bekker (Winner), Divan Serfontein, Carel du Plessis (all WP), Liaan Kirkham (Tvl), Ray Mordt (NTvl).

1982: Divan Serfontein (Winner), Colin Beck, Hennie Bekker (all WP), Naas Botha, Johan Heunis (both NTvl).

1981: Naas Botha (Winner), Johan Heunis (both NTvl), Ray Mordt (Tvl), Divan Serfontein, De Villiers Visser (both WP).

1980: Gysie Pienaar (Winner, OFS), Naas Botha, Louis Moolman (both NTvl), Morné du Plessis (WP), Gerrie Germishuys (Tvl).

1979: Naas Botha (Winner), Louis Moolman (both NTvl), Morné du Plessis, Rob Louw, De Villiers Visser (all WP).

1978: Thys Lourens (Winner), Tommy du Plessis, Pierre Edwards (all NTvl), De Wet Ras (OFS), Ian Robertson (Rhodesia).

1977: Moaner van Heerden (Winner), Thys Lourens (both NTvl), Morné du Plessis (WP), Hermanus Potgieter, Theuns Stofberg (both OFS).

*1976: Morné du Plessis (WP), Moaner van Heerden (NTvl), Bryan Williams, Sid Going, Peter Whiting (all NZ).

*1975: Gerald Bosch (Tvl), Gerrie Germishuys (OFS), Pierre Spies, Thys Lourens (both NTvl), Johan Oosthuizen (WP).

*1974: Gareth Edwards, Willie John McBride, JPR Williams (all British Lions), Willem Stapelberg, John Williams (both NTvl).

*1973: Gerald Bosch (Tvl), Dirk de Vos, Moaner van Heerden, Pierre Spies (all NTvl), Johan Oosthuizen (WP).

*1972: Kevin de Klerk (Tvl), Sam Doble (England), Jan Ellis (SWA), Carel Fourie (NE Cape) John Pullin (England).

*1971: Benoit Dauga (France), Frik du Preez (NTvl), Jan Ellis (SWA), Hannes Marais (EP), Hannes Viljoen (Natal).

*1970: Piet Greyling (Tvl), Joggie Jansen (OFS), Ian McCallum (WP), Alan Sutherland, Bryan Williams (both NZ).

* Before 1977, no single player of the year was named.

1994 Player of the Year, Chester Williams

YOUNG PLAYER OF THE YEAR

Malcolm Marx

(Emirates Lions, South Africa)

THERE was a hint of Bismarck du Plessis about Malcolm Marx as the Emirates Lions hooker set purposefully about his task during the 2016 season.

Like the former Springbok hooker, Marx is the quintessential South African forward - a hulking, no-nonsense fellow who revels in imposing himself on a luckless opponent.

A converted loose forward, Marx is also an outstanding carrier of the ball, more so than Du Plessis because he's a little quicker. To go with his powerful scrummaging ability, it's quite a package.

Of course, it's quite another thing to impose oneself at Test level in the way Du Plessis did in his prime. In fact, it will be an achievement just to get close to that.

But with Adriaan Strauss also having moved on, Marx showed with his performances in 2016 that he's ready to step up to compete alongside Bongi Mbonambi and others for the Springboks' No 2 jersey.

Marx, a former SA under-20 international, made his Test debut as a substitute in a lost cause against the All Blacks in Christchurch.

The opportunity of playing at the highest level was richly deserved after his contribution for the Lions, who on another day might have beaten the Hurricanes in the Vodacom Super Rugby final in Wellington, New Zealand.

In being named as South Africa's Young Player of the Year, Marx eclipsed other outstanding contenders in flyhalf-cum-fullback Curwin Bosch, wing and sevens star Seabelo Senatla, lock RG Snyman and inside centre Rohan Janse van Rensburg.

The latter, of course, shone with Marx at the Lions, regularly crossing the advantage line thanks to the physical impetus Marx and co. were providing from up front.

Bosch looks ready to take it to the next level in 2017, but still needs to deliver in the cauldron of Super Rugby.

Snyman showed definite signs of being destined for bigger things and Test rugby is probably also beckoning him in spite of South Africa already boasting a handful of world-class locks

But even in that company one cannot but feel Marx was a deserved winner of the award.

Apart from his natural ability, Marx is also appreciated for his humility. He's a young man who talks through his deeds - a much-loved *soutie* among a large grouping of *boerseuns*!

Make no mistake, though, this is a young man who has found his voice. Not as a chatterbox, but certainly through the quality of his performances. – *Stephen Nell*

Previous Young Players of the Year

2015: Jesse Kriel (Winner, BB), Lood de Jager (FS), Handré Pollard (BB), Warrick Gelant (BB), Seabelo Senatla (WP).

2014: Handré Pollard (Winner, BB), Nizaam Carr (WP), Cheslin Kolbe (WP), Seabelo Senatla (WP), Jan Serfontein (BB).

2013: Eben Etzebeth (Winner, WP), Pieter-Steph du Toit (KZN), Cheslin Kolbe (WP), Siya Kolisi (WP), Jan Serfontein (BB).

2012: Eben Etzebeth (Winner, WP), Elton Jantjies (GL), Marcell Coetzee (KZN), Johan Goosen (FS), Raymond Rhule (FS).

2011: Patrick Lambie (Winner, KZN), Elton Jantjies (GL), Johan Goosen (FS), Jaco Taute (GL), Francois Hougaard (BB).

2010: Elton Jantjies (Winner, GL), Bjorn Basson (BB), Juan de Jongh (WP), Francois Hougaard (BB), Patrick Lambie (KZN).

2009: Heinrich Brüssow (Winner, FS), Juan de Jongh (WP), Francois Hougaard (BB), Lionel Mapoe (FS), Frans Steyn (KZN).

2008: Robert Ebersohn (Winner, FS), Heinrich Brüssow (FS), Nick Koster (WP), Tendai Mtawarira, Bismarck du Plessis (both KZN).

2007: Francois Steyn (Winner), JP Pietersen, Ryan Kankowski (all KwaZulu-Natal), Heinke van der Merwe (GL), Richardt Strauss (FS).

2006: Pierre Spies (Winner, BB), JP Pietersen, Keegan Daniel (KwaZulu-Natal), Hilton Lobberts (Blue Buls), Gio Aplon (Western Province).

2005: Jongi Nokwe (Winner, Boland), Wynand Olivier, Morné Steyn (BB), Ruan Pienaar, JP Pietersen (KwaZulu-Natal).

2004: Bryan Habana (Winner, GL),

Schalk Burger (WP), Schalk Brits (GL), Fourie du Preez (BB), Luke Watson (Natal).

2003: Ashwin Willemse (Winner, GL), Schalk Burger (WP), John Mametsa (BB), Jaque Fourie (GL), Fourie du Preez (BB).

2002: Pedrie Wannenburg (Winner, BB), Brent Russell (Pumas), Hanyani Shimange (FS), Jaque Fourie (GL), Derick Hougaard (BB).

2001: Conrad Jantjes (Winner), Gcobani Bobo, Joe van Niekerk (all GL), Adi Jacobs (Falcons), Wylie Human (FS).

2000: Marius Joubert (Bol), Conrad Jantjes (GL), De Wet Barry, Adri Badenhorst (both WP), Wylie Human (FS).

1999: John Smit (Natal), Kaya Malotana (Border), Jannes Labuschagne (GL), Wayne Julies (Boland), Torros Pretorius (Pumas).

1998: Lourens Venter, Robert Markram (both Griquas), Grant Esterhuizen, Nicky van der Walt (both BB), André Vos (GL).

1997: Thinus Delport (Gauteng GL), Breyton Paulse, Louis Koen, Bobby Skinstad (all WP), Jan-Harm van Wyk (FS).

1996: Dawie du Toit, Hannes Venter (both NTvl), Marius Goosen (Boland), MJ Smith (FS), André Vos (EP).

1995: Stephen Brink, Jorrie Kruger (both OFS), Robbie Kempson (Natal), Danie van Schalkwyk, Joggie Viljoen (both NTvl).

1994: Frikkie Bosman (ETvl), Braam Els (OFS), Harold Karele (EP), André Snyman (NTvl), Justin Swart (WP).

1993: Krynauw Otto, FP Naude (both NTvl), Ryno Oppermann (OFS), Johan Roux (Tvl), Christiaan Scholtz (WP).

1992: Jannie de Beer, Hentie Martens, Brendan Venter, André Venter (all OFS), Joost van der Westhuizen (NTvl).

1991: Pieter Hendriks (Tvl), Hennie le Roux (EP), Pieter Müller (OFS), Johan Nel, Jacques Olivier (both NTvl).

1990: Andrew Aitken (Natal), Jannie Claassens, Theo van Rensburg (both NTvl), Bernard Fourie (WTvl), Ian Macdonald (Tvl).

1989: Stompie Fourie (OFS), Pieter Nel, Verwoerd Roodt (both NTvl), Joel Stransky, Jeremy Thomson (both Natal).

1988: Kobus Burger, Christian Stewart (WP), Jacques du Plessis (EP), André Joubert (OFS), JJ van der Walt (NTvl).

1987: Chris Badenhorst (OFS), Robert du Preez (WTvl), Jan Lock, Charles Rossouw (both NTvl), Andrew Paterson (EP).

1986: Keith Andrews, Tiaan Strauss (both WP), Martin Knoetze (WTvl), Hendrik Kruger (NTvl), Frans Wessels (OFS).

1985: Schalk (SW) Burger, Faffa Knoetze (both WP), Deon Coetzee (Tvl), Christo Ferreira (OFS), Giepie Nel (NTvl).

1984: Paul Botes, Uli Schmidt (both NTvl), Niel Burger (WP), Wessel Lightfoot, Helgard Müller (both OFS).

1983: Wahl Bartmann (Tvl), Jannie Dreyer, Adolf Malan (both NTvl), Calla Scholtz (WP), Gert Smal (WTvl).

1982: Wilfred Cupido (South African Rugby Federation), Michael du Plessis (WP), Liaan Kirkham (Tvl), Piet Kruger (NTvl), Rudi Visagie (OFS).

1981: Harry Viljoen, Jannie Breedt, André Skinner (all NTvl), Jan du Toit, Ernest Viljoen (both OFS).

1980: Colin Beck (WP), Cliffie Brown (Natal), Johan Marais (NTvl), Chris Rogers (Zimbabwe), Japie Wessels (OFS).

1979: Darius Botha (NTvl), Willie du Plessis (WP), Doug Jeffrey (OFS), André Markgraaff (WTvl), Gawie Visagie (Griquas).

1978: Burger Geldenhuys, Okkie Oosthuizen (both NTvl), Eben Jansen (OFS), Ray Mordt, David Smith (both Rhodesia).

1977: Naas Botha, Thys Burger (both NTvl), Agie Koch, Flippie van der Merwe (both WP), Gysie Pienaar (OFS).

1976: Dirk Froneman, Wouter Hugo (both OFS), Divan Serfontein, Nick Mallet (both WP), LM Rossouw (NTvl).

1975: Tommy du Plessis, Christo Wagenaar (both NTvl), Corrie Pypers (Tvl),

Hermanus Potgieter, De Wet Ras (both OFS).

1974: Gavin Cowley (EP), Peter Kirsten (WP), John Knox, Louis Moolman (both NTvl), Johan Strauss (Tvl).

1973: Dave Frederickson (Tvl), Wilhelm Landman (WP), Martiens le Roux (OFS), Keith Thoresson (Natal), Barry Wolmarans (Boland).

1972: Paul Bayvel, Gerald Bosch (both Tvl), Pikkie du Toit (OFS), Dugald Mac-

donald (WP), Jackie Snyman (OFS).

1971: Kevin de Klerk, Gert Schutte (both Tvl), Piet du Plessis (NTvl), Buddy Swartz (Griquas), Johan Wagenaar (OFS).

1970: Francois de Villiers, Johan Walters (both WP), Peter Cronje (Tvl), Jannie van Aswegen (Griquas), John Williams (NTvl).

* Before 2001, no single young player of the year was named.

2002 Young Player of the Year, Springbok loose forward Pedrie Wannenburg

SECTION 2:
THE 2016 SEASON

FIRST-CLASS TEAMS BY WINNING PERCENTAGE

TEAM	TOURNAMENT	P	W	L	D	PF	PA	TF	TA	Win %
Free State Cheetahs	Currie Cup	10	10	0	0	457	214	57	22	100%
Western Province	CC Qualifiers/Currie Cup	23	18	5	0	844	589	115	66	78,3%
Lions	Super Rugby	18	13	5	0	622	424	81	51	72,2%
Griquas	CC Qualifiers/Currie Cup	22	15	7	0	750	656	96	88	68,2%
Stormers	Super Rugby	16	10	1	1	461	334	52	36	62,5%
Sharks	Currie Cup	8	5	3	0	272	173	33	21	62,5%
Bulls	Super Rugby	15	9	5	1	399	339	47	37	60,0%
Boland Cavaliers	CC Qualifiers/Currie Cup	22	13	9	0	679	591	91	79	59,1%
Blue Bulls	CC Qualifiers/Currie Cup	24	14	10	0	821	649	109	76	58,3%
Golden Lions XV	CC Qualifiers	14	8	5	1	594	353	83	45	57,1%
Free State XV	CC Qualifiers	14	8	6	0	372	337	52	41	57,1%
Leopards	CC Qualifiers/First Division	21	12	9	0	727	673	97	93	57,1%
Griffons	CC Qualifiers/First Division	21	12	9	0	812	702	104	97	57,1%
Sharks	Super Rugby	16	9	6	1	360	310	40	36	56,3%
Golden Lions	Currie Cup	9	5	4	0	372	246	52	29	55,6%
Pumas	CC Qualifiers/Currie Cup	22	11	11	0	595	582	79	75	50,0%
Border Bulldogs	CC Qualifiers/First Division	20	9	11	0	591	424	81	55	45,0%
Sharks XV	CC Qualifiers	14	6	8	0	338	399	53	58	42,9%
SA Under-20	IRB JWC	5	2	3	0	148	157	19	20	40,0%
Falcons	CC Qualifiers/First Division	20	7	13	0	596	711	86	96	35,0%
Springboks (Tests)	Incoming/Rugby Champs/EOY	12	4	8	0	240	329	20	35	33,3%
SWD Eagles	CC Qualifiers/First Division	19	6	13	0	577	535	75	66	31,6%
Cheetahs	Super Rugby	15	4	11	0	377	425	47	48	26,7%
Southern Kings	Super Rugby	15	2	13	0	282	684	34	95	13,3%
Eastern Province Kings	CC Qualifiers/Currie Cup	22	2	19	1	415	892	51	131	9,1%
Springbok XV	Tour match	1	0	0	1	31	31	5	5	0,0%
Welwitschias	CC Qualifiers/First Division	19	0	19	0	288	1239	40	186	0%

LEADING SCORERS IN SOUTH AFRICAN FIRST-CLASS RUGBY

100 POINTS OR MORE

PLAYER	TEAM	M	T	C	P	DG	Pts
George Whitehead	Griffons, Cheetahs	21	5	83	32	2	293
Elton Jantjies	Lions, SA	25	3	56	43	2	262
Tian Schoeman	Bulls, Blue Bulls	25	2	47	33	1	206
Robert du Preez	Stormers, WP	20	3	59	21	0	196
Niel Marais	Cheetahs, Free State	21	4	43	26	0	184
Masixole Banda	Border	20	10	41	17	0	183
Clinton Swart	Griquas	19	5	45	22	0	181
Curwin Bosch	Sharks XV, Sharks, SA U20	17	5	35	27	1	179
Francois Brummer	Bulls, Pumas, SA A	23	2	35	28	2	170
Fred Zeilinga	Cheetahs, Free State	24	0	41	29	0	169
Nico Scheepers	Boland	181	5	46	17	0	168
Rhyno Smith	Leopards, Sharks	16	6	33	17	2	153
Marnitz Boshoff	Lions, Golden Lions XV	12	1	47	11	0	132
Jean-Luc du Plessis	Stormers	12	2	26	22	0	128
Johan Deysel	Leopards	13	10	29	6	0	126
Karlo Aspeling	Valke	17	2	38	13	0	125
Justin van Staden	Pumas	15	1	30	19	0	122
Hansie Graaff	SWD	16	0	28	16	0	104
André Swarts	Griquas	15	4	21	14	0	104

TRIES – 10 OR MORE

PLAYER	TEAM	Matches	Tries
Selvyn Davids	Griffons	20	19
Sergeal Petersen	Cheetahs, FS, SA A, Springbok XV	21	17
Makazole Mapimpi	Border	20	16
AJ Coertzen	Griquas	20	15
Warren Williams	Griffons	18	15
Leolin Zas	Stormers, WP, SA A	26	14
Rohan Janse van Rensburg	Lions, Golden Lions, SA, Springbok XV	27	14
Ryan Nell	Boland	18	13
Etienne Taljaard	Valke	18	13
Anthony Volmink	Lions, Golden Lions	21	13
Jamba Ulengo	Bulls, Blue Bulls, SA	20	12
Frank Herne	Pumas	21	12
Uzair Cassiem	Cheetahs, Free State, SA	26	11
Christopher Bosch	Boland	21	11
Huw Jones	Stormers, WP	15	11
Courtnall Skosan	Lions, Golden Lions	21	10
Ruan Combrinck	Lions, Golden Lions, SA	24	10
Danwel Demas	Boland	22	10
Mark Pretorius	SWD	16	10
Alshaun Bock	Griquas	18	10
Sylvian Mahuza	Lions, Golden Lions	14	10
Gene Willemse	Leopards	19	10
Johan Deysel	Leopards	13	10
Masixole Banda	Border	20	10
JP Lewis	WP, Pumas	19	10

28 Appearances or more

Ruan Ackermann	Lions, Golden Lions, Barbarians	30
Faf de Klerk	Lions, Golden Lions, South Africa	29
Howard Mnisi	Lions, Golden Lions	28

Players who recorded a 100th appearance for their province in 2016

Player	*Against*	*Date*
Kyle Hendricks	Valke vs Welwitschias	11/06/2016

Players who recorded a 100th appearance for their franchise in 2016
None

Youngest and oldest first-class players in 2016

Ruben van Heerden	Blue Bulls vs Free State XV	18 years 172 days
Danwel Demas	Boland vs WP	34 years 350 days

Tallest, shortest, heaviest and lightest players in 2016

Jean-Pierre du Preez	Lions	2.09m
Percy Williams	Leopards	1.60m
Dean Hopp	SWD	138kg
Bangi Kobese	Border	63kg

FIRST-CLASS CAREER POINTS - PLAYERS ACTIVE IN 2016

500 POINTS OR MORE*

PLAYER	TEAM/S	Matches	Tries	Conversions	Penalties	Drop Goals	Total
M Steyn	Blue Bulls	292	50	544	546	47	3117
PJ Lambie	Sharks	164	26	205	258	7	1335
ET Jantjies	Golden Lions	147	10	205	248	5	1219
F Brummer	Pumas	158	18	182	169	25	1036
ML Boshoff	Golden Lions	116	9	207	161	19	999
EG Watts	EP Kings	158	42	157	88	1	791
BG Habana	WP	294	158	0	0	0	790
FJ Zeilinga	Cheetahs	84	7	128	124	3	672
JM Ebersohn	Cheetahs	115	13	134	80	9	600
JL Goosen	Cheetahs	64	10	96	108	7	587
KK Coleman	WP	100	9	82	96	1	500

50 TRIES OR MORE*

PLAYER	TEAM	Tries	PLAYER	TEAM	Tries
BG Habana	WP	158	LN Mvovo	Sharks	72
AG Bock	SWD	109	D Demas	Boland	66
BA Basson	Blue Bulls	107	M Schoeman	Pumas	61
OM Ndungane	Sharks	99	JW Jonker	Griquas	59
NT Nelson	Griffons	90	J Nel	Griffons	51
RS Benjamin	Cheetahs	85	J Vermaak	WP	51
J-PR Pietersen	Sharks	82	M Steyn	Blue Bulls	50

250 APPEARANCES OR MORE*

PLAYER	TEAM	Matches	PLAYER	TEAM	Matches
OM Ndungane	Sharks	310	SWP Burger	WP	261
BG Habana	WP	294	JP-R Pietersen	Sharks	258
M Steyn	Blue Bulls	292	KR Daniel	Sharks	251
JA Strauss	Blue Bulls	288			

for South African teams only

MATCH FEATURES

Most points scored by a team (75 or more)

110	Boland vs Welwitschias (110-10)	CC Qualifiers
101	Griffons vs Welwitschias (101-0)	CC Qualifiers
96	SWD vs Welwitschias (96-5)	CC Qualifiers
95	Blue Bulls vs Welwitschias (95-12)	CC Qualifiers
92	Cheetahs vs Sunwolves (92-17)	Super Rugby
84	Griffons vs Welwitschias (84-25)	CC First Division
76	Griffons vs Leopards (76-26)	CC Qualifiers
76	Border vs Welwitschias (76-18)	CC Qualifiers
75	Golden Lions XV vs Valke (75-14)	CC Qualifiers

Most tries scored by a team (10 or more)

16	Boland vs Welwitschias	CC Qualifiers
15	Griffons vs Welwitschias	CC Qualifiers
15	Blue Bulls vs Welwitschias	CC Qualifiers
14	Cheetahs vs Sunwolves	Super Rugby
14	SWD vs Welwitschias	CC Qualifiers
12	Border vs Welwitschias	CC Qualifiers
11	Golden Lions XV vs Valke	CC Qualifiers
11	Griffons vs Leopards	CC Qualifiers
11	WP vs Welwitschias	CC Qualifiers
11	Golden Lions vs EP Kings	CC Premier Div
10	Golden Lions XV vs Welwitschias	CC Qualifiers
10	Golden Lions XV vs Leopards	CC Qualifiers
10	Golden Lions XV vs Griffons	CC Qualifiers
10	Valke vs Welwitschias	CC Qualifiers
10	Golden Lions vs Pumas	CC Premier Div

Biggest winning margin (50 points or more)

101	Griffons vs Welwitschias (101-0)	CC Qualifiers
100	Boland vs Welwitschias (110-10)	CC Qualifiers
91	SWD vs Welwitschias (96-5)	CC Qualifiers
83	Blue Bulls vs Welwitschias (95-12)	CC Qualifiers
75	Cheetahs vs Sunwolves (92-17)	Super Rugby
61	Golden Lions XV vs Valke (75-14)	CC Qualifiers
59	Griffons vs Welwitschias (84-25)	CC First Division
58	Border vs Welwitschias (76-18)	CC Qualifiers
53	Sharks vs Kings (53-0)	Super Rugby
50	Griffons vs Leopards (76-26)	CC Qualifiers

Most points scored in a match by a player (25 points or more)

45	Nico Scheepers	Boland vs Welwitschias	CC Qualifiers
34	George Whitehead	Griffons vs Leopards	CC Qualifiers
26	George Whitehead	Griffons vs Welwitschias	CC Qualifiers

Most tries scored in a match by a player (3 tries or more)

4	Huw Jones	Stormers vs Kings	Super Rugby
4	Ryan Nell	Boland vs Welwitschias	CC Qualifiers
4	Christopher Bosch	Boland vs Welwitschias	CC Qualifiers
4	Jade Stiglingh	Blue Bulls vs Welwitschias	CC Qualifiers
4	Makazole Mapimpi	Border vs Sharks XV	CC Qualifiers
4	Makazole Mapimpi	Border vs Welwitschias	CC Qualifiers
4	Warren Williams	Griffons vs Welwitschias	CC First Division
3	Nico Scheepers	Boland vs Welwitschias	CC Qualifiers
3	Sergeal Petersen	Cheetahs vs Sunwolves	Super Rugby
3	Bjorn Basson	Bulls vs Rebels	Super Rugby
3	Lionel Mapoe	Lions vs Blues	Super Rugby
3	Selom Gavor	Golden Lions XV vs Welwitschias	CC Qualifiers
3	Stokkies Hanekom	Golden Lions XV vs Griquas	CC Qualifiers
3	Anthony Volmink	Goldens Lions XV vs Valke	CC Qualifiers
3	George Whitehead	Griffons vs Leopards	CC Qualifiers
3	Selvyn Davids	Griffons vs Leopards	CC Qualifiers
3	Warren Williams	Griffons vs Valke	CC Qualifiers
3	Warren Williams	Griffons vs Welwitschias	CC Qualifiers
3	Marius Louw	Sharks XV vs Welwitschias	CC Qualifiers
3	Martin du Toit	SWD vs Welwitschias	CC Qualifiers
3	Etienne Taljaard	Valke vs Griquas	CC Qualifiers
3	Reg Muller	Valke vs Welwitschias	CC Qualifiers
3	JP Lewis	WP vs Valke	CC Qualifiers
3	Vuyo Mbotho	Griffons vs Valke	CC First Division
3	De Wet Kruger	Griffons vs Welwitschias	CC First Division
3	Gene Willemse	Leopards vs Welwitschias	CC First Division
3	HP Swart	Leopards vs Griffons	CC First Division
3	Ryno Benjamin	Free State vs Pumas	CC Premier Div
3	Sergeal Petersen	Free State vs Golden Lions	CC Premier Div
3	Kwagga Smith	Golden Lions vs EP Kings	CC Premier Div
3	Frank Herne	Pumas vs EP Kings	CC Premier Div
3	Huw Jones	WP vs EP Kings	CC Premier Div

Most conversions in a match by a player (7 or more)

15	Nico Scheepers	Boland vs Welwitschias	CC Qualifiers
13	George Whitehead	Griffons vs Welwitschias	CC Qualifiers
12	George Whitehead	Griffons vs Welwitschias	CC First Division
8	Niel Marais	Cheetahs vs Sunwolves	Super Rugby
8	George Whitehead	Griffons vs Leopards	CC Qualifiers
8	Curwin Bosch	SA U20 vs Japan U20	World U20 Champs
8	Grant Hermanus	WP vs Welwitschias	CC Qualifiers
8	Masixole Banda	Border vs Welwitschias	CC First Division
7	Marnitz Boshoff	Golden Lions XV vs Griquas	CC Qualifiers
7	Marnitz Boshoff	Golden Lions XV vs Leopards	CC Qualifiers

7	Tony Jantjies	Blue Bulls vs Welwitschias	CC Qualifiers
7	Logan Basson	Border vs Welwitschias	CC Qualifiers
7	Clinton Swart	Griquas vs Valke	CC Qualifiers
7	Jaquin Jansen	SWD vs Welwitschias	CC Qualifiers
7	Karlo Aspeling	Valke vs Welwitschias	CC Qualifiers
7	Robert du Preez	WP vs Valke	CC Qualifiers
7	Masixole Banda	Border vs Valke	CC First Division
7	Johan Deysel	Leopards vs Welwitschias	CC First Division
7	Hansie Graaff	SWD vs Welwitschias	CC First Division
7	Tian Schoeman	Blue Bulls vs EP Kings	CC Premier Div
7	Tian Schoeman	Blue Bulls vs Griquas	CC Premier Div

Most penalties in a match by a player (7 or more)

7	Niel Marais	Free State vs Blue Bulls	CC Premier Div

Two drop goals

None

Scored in all four ways

19 Pts	Rhyno Smith [1T, 4C, 1P, 1DG]	Leopards vs Border	CC Qualifiers
24 Pts	Rhyno Smith [2T, 4C, 1P, 1DG]	Leopards vs WP	CC Qualifiers
21 Pts	Curwin Bosch [1T, 2C, 3P, 1DG]	Sharks vs Blue Bulls	CC Premier Div

Leopards fullback Rhyno Smith.

FIRST-CLASS MATCHES

A list of all 255 first-class matches played by South African teams during 2016

#	Date	Home		Away		Competition	Venue	Referee
1	26/02/2016	Cheetahs	33	Jaguares	34	Super Rugby	Bloemfontein	Stuart Berry
2	27/02/2016	Sunwolves	13	Lions	26	Super Rugby	Tokyo	Ben O'Keeffe
3	27/02/2016	Kings	8	Sharks	43	Super Rugby	Port Elizabeth	Jaco van Heerden
4	27/02/2016	Stormers	33	Bulls	9	Super Rugby	Cape Town	Craig Joubert
5	05/03/2016	Chiefs	32	Lions	36	Super Rugby	Hamilton	Andrew Lees
6	05/03/2016	Bulls	45	Rebels	25	Super Rugby	Pretoria	Ben O'Keeffe
7	05/03/2016	Cheetahs	10	Stormers	20	Super Rugby	Bloemfontein	Craig Joubert
8	05/03/2016	Sharks	19	Jaguares	15	Super Rugby	Durban	Jaco Peyper
9	12/03/2016	Highlanders	34	Lions	15	Super Rugby	Dunedin	Chris Pollock
10	12/03/2016	Sunwolves	31	Cheetahs	32	Super Rugby	Singapore	Quinton Immelman
11	12/03/2016	Kings	24	Chiefs	58	Super Rugby	Port Elizabeth	Jaco van Heerden
12	12/03/2016	Stormers	13	Sharks	18	Super Rugby	Cape Town	Mike Fraser
13	18/03/2016	Bulls	16	Sharks	16	Super Rugby	Pretoria	Glen Jackson
14	18/03/2016	Crusaders	57	Kings	24	Super Rugby	Christchurch	Will Houston
15	19/03/2016	Lions	39	Cheetahs	22	Super Rugby	Johannesburg	Stuart Berry
16	19/03/2016	Stormers	31	Brumbies	11	Super Rugby	Cape Town	Jaco Peyper
17	25/03/2016	Hurricanes	42	Kings	20	Super Rugby	Wellington	Brendon Pickerill
18	26/03/2016	Sunwolves	27	Bulls	30	Super Rugby	Singapore	Will Houston
19	26/03/2016	Cheetahs	18	Brumbies	25	Super Rugby	Bloemfontein	Glen Jackson
20	26/03/2016	Sharks	14	Crusaders	19	Super Rugby	Durban	Jaco Peyper
21	26/03/2016	Jaguares	8	Stormers	13	Super Rugby	Buenos Aires	Chris Pollock
22	01/04/2016	Lions	37	Crusaders	43	Super Rugby	Johannesburg	Stuart Berry
23	02/04/2016	Kings	33	Sunwolves	38	Super Rugby	Port Elizabeth	Rasta Rasivhenge
24	02/04/2016	Bulls	23	Cheetahs	18	Super Rugby	Pretoria	Craig Joubert
25	07/08/2016	Griquas	34	Griffons	14	Provincial Cup	Kimberley	Jaco Peyper
26	08/04/2016	Golden Lions XV	23	Border	27	Provincial Cup	Johannesburg	Jaco van Heerden
27	08/04/2016	WP	30	Blue Bulls	16	Provincial Cup	Cape Town	AJ Jacobs
28	08/04/2016	Stormers	46	Sunwolves	19	Super Rugby	Cape Town	Nic Berry
29	08/04/2016	Sharks XV	25	Boland	37	Provincial Cup	Durban	Rodney Bonaparte
30	08/04/2016	Pumas	9	Valke	12	Provincial Cup	Nelspruit	Cwengile Jadezweni
31	09/04/2016	Free State XV	32	Welwitschias	17	Provincial Cup	Bloemfontein	Quinton Immelman
32	09/04/2016	EP Kings	14	SWD Eagles	37	Provincial Cup	Port Elizabeth	Craig Joubert
33	09/04/2016	Sharks	9	Lions	24	Super Rugby	Durban	Angus Gardner
34	09/04/2016	Kings	6	Bulls	38	Super Rugby	Port Elizabeth	Shuhei Kubo
35	15/04/2016	Valke	29	Griquas	56	Provincial Cup	Kempton Park	Stephan Geldenhuys
36	15/04/2016	SWD Eagles	25	Pumas	21	Provincial Cup	George	Rodney Bonaparte
37	15/04/2016	Cheetahs	92	Sunwolves	17	Super Rugby	Bloemfontein	Nic Berry
38	15/04/2016	Border	37	Sharks XV	32	Provincial Cup	East London	Lesego Legoete
39	16/04/2016	Blues	23	Sharks	18	Super Rugby	Auckland	Jaco Peyper
40	16/04/2016	Blue Bulls	20	Free State XV	17	Provincial Cup	Pretoria	Quinton Immelman
41	16/04/2016	Griffons	76	Leopards	26	Provincial Cup	Welkom	Lourens vd Merwe
42	16/04/2016	Welwitschias	12	Golden Lions XV	66	Provincial Cup	Windhoek	Archie Sehlako
43	16/04/2016	Boland	37	EP Kings	18	Provincial Cup	Wellington	Francois Pretorius
44	16/04/2016	Bulls	41	Reds	22	Super Rugby	Pretoria	Angus Gardner
45	16/04/2016	Lions	29	Stormers	22	Super Rugby	Johannesburg	Stuart Berry
46	22/04/2016	Highlanders	14	Sharks	15	Super Rugby	Dunedin	Ben O'Keeffe
47	22/04/2016	Rebels	36	Cheetahs	14	Super Rugby	Melbourne	Glen Jackson
48	22/04/2016	Free State XV	31	WP	36	Provincial Cup	Bloemfontein	Ben Crouse

FIRST-CLASS MATCHES IN 2016

49	22/04/2016	Pumas	12	Boland	10	Provincial Cup	Nelspruit	Stephan Geldenhuys
50	22/04/2016	Leopards	26	Valke	24	Provincial Cup	Potchefstroom	Cwengile Jadezweni
51	23/04/2016	EP Kings	14	Border	26	Provincial Cup	Port Elizabeth	AJ Jacobs
52	23/04/2016	Stormers	40	Reds	22	Super Rugby	Cape Town	Marius vd Westhuizen
53	23/04/2016	Golden Lions XV	38	Blue Bulls	17	Provincial Cup	Alberton	Lourens vd Merwe
54	23/04/2016	Sharks XV	48	Welwitschias	18	Provincial Cup	Durban	Rodney Bonaparte
55	23/04/2016	Griquas	27	SWD Eagles	17	Provincial Cup	Kimberley	Lesego Legoete
56	23/04/2016	Kings	10	Lions	45	Super Rugby	Port Elizabeth	Rasta Rasivhenge
57	27/04/2016	Valke	26	Griffons	49	Provincial Cup	Kempton Park	Lourens vd Merwe
58	27/04/2016	SWD Eagles	26	Leopards	21	Provincial Cup	Outeniqua Park	Rodney Bonaparte
59	29/04/2016	Chiefs	24	Sharks	22	Super Rugby	New Plymouth	Chris Pollock
60	29/04/2016	Force	20	Bulls	42	Super Rugby	Perth	Jaco van Heerden
61	29/04/2016	Boland	14	Griquas	30	Provincial Cup	Wellington	Cwengile Jadezweni
62	30/04/2016	Reds	30	Cheetahs	17	Super Rugby	Brisbane	Ben O'Keeffe
63	30/04/2016	Border	3	Pumas	28	Provincial Cup	East London	Christie du Preez
64	30/04/2016	Welwitschias	18	EP Kings	31	Provincial Cup	Windhoek	Lesego Legoete
65	30/04/2016	WP	27	Golden Lions XV	24	Provincial Cup	Cape Town	Rasta Rasivhenge
66	30/04/2016	Lions	17	Hurricanes	50	Super Rugby	Johannesburg	Marius vd Westhuizen
67	30/04/2016	Stormers	30	Waratahs	32	Super Rugby	Cape Town	Mike Fraser
68	30/04/2016	Jaguares	73	Kings	27	Super Rugby	Buenos Aires	Stuart Berry
69	06/05/2016	Brumbies	23	Bulls	6	Super Rugby	Canberra	Ben O'Keeffe
70	06/05/2016	Griffons	30	SWD Eagles	14	Provincial Cup	Welkom	Stephan Geldenhuys
71	07/05/2016	Waratahs	21	Cheetahs	6	Super Rugby	Sydney	Nic Berry
72	07/05/2016	EP Kings	19	Blue Bulls	14	Provincial Cup	Port Elizabeth	Rasta Rasivhenge
73	07/05/2016	Leopards	31	Boland	43	Provincial Cup	Potchefstroom	Jaco van Heerden
74	07/05/2016	Sharks	32	Hurricanes	15	Super Rugby	Durban	Marius vd Westhuizen
75	07/05/2016	Golden Lions XV	15	Free State XV	29	Provincial Cup	Randburg	Francois Pretorius
76	07/05/2016	Pumas	47	Welwitschias	7	Provincial Cup	Ermelo	Egon Seconds
77	07/05/2016	Griquas	21	Border	12	Provincial Cup	Kimberley	Lesego Legoete
78	07/05/2016	Kings	18	Blues	34	Super Rugby	Port Elizabeth	Federico Anselmi
79	07/05/2016	Sharks XV	24	WP	16	Provincial Cup	Durban	Quinton Immelman
80	13/05/2016	Blue Bulls	13	Pumas	25	Provincial Cup	Pretoria	Jaco Peyper
81	13/05/2016	Boland	56	Griffons	17	Provincial Cup	Wellington	Lourens vd Merwe
82	13/05/2016	SWD Eagles	32	Valke	30	Provincial Cup	George	Quinton Immelman
83	13/05/2016	Border	22	Leopards	34	Provincial Cup	East London	Lesego Legoete
84	14/05/2016	Waratahs	31	Bulls	8	Super Rugby	Sydney	Glen Jackson
85	14/05/2016	Sunwolves	17	Stormers	17	Super Rugby	Singapore	Paul Williams
86	14/05/2016	Free State XV	19	Sharks XV	13	Provincial Cup	Bloemfontein	Stuart Berry
87	14/05/2016	WP	50	EP Kings	10	Provincial Cup	Cape Town	Stephan Geldenhuys
88	14/05/2016	Welwitschias	25	Griquas	55	Provincial Cup	Windhoek	Egon Seconds
89	14/05/2016	Cheetahs	34	Kings	20	Super Rugby	Bloemfontein	Federico Anselmi
90	14/05/2016	Lions	43	Blues	5	Super Rugby	Johannesburg	Jaco van Heerden
91	14/05/2016	Jaguares	22	Sharks	25	Super Rugby	Buenos Aires	Marius vd Westhuizen
92	20/05/2016	Valke	22	Boland	24	Provincial Cup	Kempton Park	AJ Jacobs
93	20/05/2016	EP Kings	15	Free State XV	35	Provincial Cup	Port Elizabeth	Rodney Bonaparte
94	20/05/2016	Sharks XV	16	Golden Lions XV	53	Provincial Cup	Durban	Egon Seconds
95	20/05/2016	Pumas	20	WP	27	Provincial Cup	Nelspruit	Marius vd Westhuizen
96	20/05/2016	Leopards	42	Welwitschias	17	Provincial Cup	Potchefstroom	Sindile Ngcese

FIRST-CLASS MATCHES IN 2016

97	21/05/2016	Lions	52	Jaguares	24	Super Rugby	Johannesburg	Stuart Berry
98	21/05/2016	Griquas	39	Blue Bulls	38	Provincial Cup	Kimberley	Lesego Legoete
99	21/05/2016	Griffons	34	Border	23	Provincial Cup	Welkom	Jaco Kotze
100	21/05/2016	Sharks	53	Kings	0	Super Rugby	Durban	Quinton Immelman
101	21/05/2016	Bulls	17	Stormers	13	Super Rugby	Pretoria	Ben O'Keeffe
102	27/05/2016	Free State XV	26	Pumas	29	Provincial Cup	Bloemfontein	Marius vd Westhuizen
103	27/05/2016	Boland	32	SWD Eagles	16	Provincial Cup	Wellington	AJ Jacobs
104	27/05/2016	Kings	29	Jaguares	22	Super Rugby	Port Elizabeth	Nick Briant
105	27/05/2016	Border	29	Valke	24	Provincial Cup	East London	Rodney Bonaparte
106	28/05/2016	WP	24	Griquas	23	Provincial Cup	Cape Town	Quinton Immelman
107	28/05/2016	Blue Bulls	26	Leopards	51	Provincial Cup	Pretoria	Archie Sehlako
108	28/05/2016	Stormers	31	Cheetahs	24	Super Rugby	Cape Town	Glen Jackson
109	28/05/2016	Golden Lions XV	35	EP Kings	35	Provincial Cup	Johannesburg	Lourens vd Merwe
110	28/05/2016	Welwitschias	0	Griffons	101	Provincial Cup	Windhoek	Lesego Legoete
111	28/05/2016	Bulls	20	Lions	56	Super Rugby	Pretoria	Craig Joubert
112	03/06/2016	EP Kings	26	Sharks XV	34	Provincial Cup	Port Elizabeth	Marius vd Westhuizen
113	04/06/2016	Pumas	35	Golden Lions XV	24	Provincial Cup	KaNyamazane	Jaco van Heerden
114	04/06/2016	Griffons	28	Blue Bulls	57	Provincial Cup	Welkom	Ben Crouse
115	04/06/2016	Griquas	44	Free State XV	31	Provincial Cup	Kimberley	Rasta Rasivhenge
116	04/06/2016	Leopards	34	WP	43	Provincial Cup	Potchefstroom	Egon Seconds
117	07/06/2016	South Africa U20	59	Japan U20	19	World U20 Champs	Manchester (UK)	Elia Rizzo
118	10/06/2016	Blue Bulls	22	Sharks XV	18	Provincial Cup	Pretoria	Egon Seconds
119	10/06/2016	SWD Eagles	39	Border	22	Provincial Cup	George	Marius vd Westhuizen
120	10/06/2016	South Africa A	24	England Saxons	32	International	Bloemfontein	Rasta Rasivhenge
121	11/06/2016	Valke	66	Welwitschias	5	Provincial Cup	Kempton Park	Rodney Bonaparte
122	11/06/2016	Golden Lions XV	52	Griquas	37	Provincial Cup	Johannesburg	Quinton Immelman
123	11/06/2016	South Africa	20	Ireland	26	International	Cape Town	Mathieu Raynal
124	11/06/2016	South Africa U20	13	Argentina U20	19	World U20 Champs	Salford	Craig Evans
125	15/06/2016	South Africa U20	40	France U20	31	World U20 Champs	Manchester (UK)	Craig Maxwell-Keys
126	16/06/2016	Border	17	Boland	38	Provincial Cup	East London	Quinton Immelman
127	17/06/2016	Blue Bulls	42	Valke	15	Provincial Cup	Pretoria	AJ Jacobs
128	17/06/2016	Free State XV	23	Leopards	14	Provincial Cup	Bloemfontein	Rodney Bonaparte
129	17/06/2016	South Africa A	26	England Saxons	29	International	George	Jaco van Heerden
130	18/06/2016	WP	43	Griffons	26	Provincial Cup	Cape Town	Sindile Ngcese
131	18/06/2016	Welwitschias	5	SWD Eagles	96	Provincial Cup	Windhoek	Francois Pretorius
132	18/06/2016	South Africa	32	Ireland	26	International	Johannesburg	Angus Gardner
133	18/06/2016	Sharks XV	13	Pumas	35	Provincial Cup	Newcastle	Egon Seconds
134	20/06/2016	South Africa U20	17	England U20	39	World U20 Champs	Manchester (UK)	Paul Williams
135	24/06/2016	Pumas	53	EP Kings	20	Provincial Cup	Nelspruit	Lourens vd Merwe
136	24/06/2016	Leopards	28	Golden Lions XV	64	Provincial Cup	Potchefstroom	Stuart Berry
137	24/06/2016	Valke	31	WP	59	Provincial Cup	Kempton Park	Quinton Immelman
138	24/06/2016	SWD Eagles	23	Blue Bulls	28	Provincial Cup	George	Sindile Ngcese
139	25/06/2016	Griffons	49	Free State XV	33	Provincial Cup	Welkom	Lesego Legoete
140	25/06/2016	Griquas	36	Sharks XV	14	Provincial Cup	Upington	Jaco van Heerden
141	25/06/2016	Boland	110	Welwitschias	10	Provincial Cup	Wellington	AJ Jacobs
142	25/06/2016	South Africa U20	19	Argentina U20	49	World U20 Champs	Salford	Andrew Brace
143	25/06/2016	South Africa	19	Ireland	13	International	Port Elizabeth	Glen Jackson
144	01/07/2016	Sharks XV	26	Leopards	23	Provincial Cup	Durban	Rodney Bonaparte

FIRST-CLASS MATCHES IN 2016

145	01/07/2016	Blue Bulls	26	Boland	35	Provincial Cup	Pretoria	Quinton Immelman
146	02/07/2016	Rebels	31	Stormers	57	Super Rugby	Melbourne	Angus Gardner
147	02/07/2016	Free State XV	33	Valke	27	Provincial Cup	Bloemfontein	AJ Jacobs
148	02/07/2016	Golden Lions XV	66	Griffons	19	Provincial Cup	Johannesburg	Lesego Legoete
149	02/07/2016	Cheetahs	30	Force	29	Super Rugby	Bloemfontein	Shuhei Kubo
150	02/07/2016	WP	45	SWD Eagles	17	Provincial Cup	Cape Town	Ben Crouse
151	02/07/2016	EP Kings	12	Griquas	29	Provincial Cup	Port Elizabeth	Jaco van Heerden
152	02/07/2016	Welwitschias	18	Border	76	Provincial Cup	Windhoek	Egon Seconds
153	02/07/2016	Lions	37	Sharks	10	Super Rugby	Johannesburg	Jaco Peyper
154	02/07/2016	Kings	18	Highlanders	48	Super Rugby	Port Elizabeth	Marius vd Westhuizen
155	02/07/2016	Jaguares	29	Bulls	11	Super Rugby	Buenos Aires	Craig Joubert
156	07/07/2016	Griquas	37	Pumas	14	Provincial Cup	Kimberley	Rasta Rasivhenge
157	08/07/2016	Leopards	54	EP Kings	14	Provincial Cup	Potchefstroom	Juan Sylvestre
158	08/07/2016	Lions	57	Kings	21	Super Rugby	Johannesburg	Jaco van Heerden
159	08/07/2016	SWD Eagles	16	Free State XV	24	Provincial Cup	George	Lesego Legoete
160	09/07/2016	Valke	14	Golden Lions XV	75	Provincial Cup	Kempton Park	Ben Crouse
161	09/07/2016	Griffons	27	Sharks XV	36	Provincial Cup	Welkom	Jaco Peyper
162	09/07/2016	Boland	14	WP	25	Provincial Cup	Piketberg	Rodney Bonaparte
163	09/07/2016	Border	26	Blue Bulls	45	Provincial Cup	East London	Cwengile Jadezweni
164	09/07/2016	Bulls	50	Sunwolves	3	Super Rugby	Pretoria	Quinton Immelman
165	09/07/2016	Sharks	26	Cheetahs	10	Super Rugby	Durban	Stuart Berry
166	15/07/2016	EP Kings	24	Griffons	32	Provincial Cup	Port Elizabeth	Lesego Legoete
167	15/07/2016	Sharks XV	10	Valke	26	Provincial Cup	Durban	Juan Sylvestre
168	15/07/2016	Blue Bulls	95	Welwitschias	12	Provincial Cup	Pretoria	Rodney Bonaparte
169	15/07/2016	Sharks	40	Sunwolves	29	Super Rugby	Durban	Rasta Rasivhenge
170	15/07/2016	Pumas	29	Leopards	27	Provincial Cup	Nelspruit	Jaco van Heerden
171	16/07/2016	WP	52	Border	26	Provincial Cup	Cape Town	Pierre Brousset
172	16/07/2016	Golden Lions XV	35	SWD Eagles	29	Provincial Cup	Johannesburg	Cwengile Jadezweni
173	16/07/2016	Free State XV	17	Boland	24	Provincial Cup	Bloemfontein	AJ Jacobs
174	16/07/2016	Stormers	52	Kings	24	Super Rugby	Cape Town	Jaco Peyper
175	16/07/2016	Cheetahs	17	Bulls	43	Super Rugby	Bloemfontein	Craig Joubert
176	16/07/2016	Jaguares	34	Lions	22	Super Rugby	Buenos Aires	Rohan Hoffman
177	22/07/2016	Valke	59	EP Kings	26	Provincial Cup	Kempton Park	Marius vd Westhuizen
178	22/07/2016	SWD Eagles	24	Sharks XV	29	Provincial Cup	George	Sindile Ngcese
179	22/07/2016	Leopards	37	Griquas	17	Provincial Cup	Potchefstroom	Egon Seconds
180	22/07/2016	Border	18	Free State XV	22	Provincial Cup	East London	Lourens vd Merwe
181	23/07/2016	Hurricanes	41	Sharks	0	Super Rugby	Wellington	Glen Jackson
182	23/07/2016	Griffons	17	Pumas	60	Provincial Cup	Welkom	Rodney Bonaparte
183	23/07/2016	Boland	28	Golden Lions XV	24	Provincial Cup	Grabouw	Pierre Brousset
184	23/07/2016	Welwitschias	7	WP	71	Provincial Cup	Windhoek	Archie Sehlako
185	23/07/2016	Lions	42	Crusaders	25	Super Rugby	Johannesburg	Craig Joubert
186	23/07/2016	Stormers	21	Chiefs	60	Super Rugby	Cape Town	Jaco Peyper
187	30/07/2016	Lions	42	Highlanders	30	Super Rugby	Johannesburg	Jaco Peyper
188	05/08/2016	Blue Bulls	45	WP	26	CC Premier Div	Pretoria	Stuart Berry
189	05/08/2016	Pumas	10	Sharks	33	CC Premier Div	Nelspruit	Lesego Legoete
190	06/08/2016	Hurricanes	20	Lions	3	Super Rugby	Wellington	Glen Jackson
191	06/08/2016	Boland	16	Free State	44	CC Premier Div	Wellington	Rodney Bonaparte
192	12/08/2016	Griffons	50	Valke	27	CC First Div	Welkom	Quinton Immelman

FIRST-CLASS MATCHES IN 2016

193	12/08/2016	EP Kings	10	Boland	28	CC Premier Div	Port Elizabeth	Rodney Bonaparte
194	12/08/2016	SWD Eagles	54	Welwitschias	23	CC First Div	George	Sindile Ngcese
195	12/08/2016	Leopards	26	Border	24	CC First Div	Potchefstroom	AJ Jacobs
196	12/08/2016	Sharks	46	Griquas	24	CC Premier Div	Durban	Jaco van Heerden
197	13/08/2016	Golden Lions	68	Pumas	26	CC Premier Div	Johannesburg	Stuart Berry
198	13/08/2016	Free State	43	Blue Bulls	20	CC Premier Div	Bloemfontein	Lesego Legoete
199	19/08/2016	Boland	20	Sharks	41	CC Premier Div	Wellington	Marius vd Westhuizen
200	19/08/2016	SWD Eagles	27	Griffons	33	CC First Div	George	Egon Seconds
201	19/08/2016	WP	25	Free State	32	CC Premier Div	Cape Town	Craig Joubert
202	19/08/2016	Blue Bulls	49	EP Kings	35	CC Premier Div	Pretoria	Rasta Rasivhenge
203	20/08/2016	Griquas	30	Golden Lions	24	CC Premier Div	Kimberley	Quinton Immelman
204	20/08/2016	Welwitschias	42	Leopards	54	CC First Div	Windhoek	AJ Jacobs
205	20/08/2016	South Africa	30	Argentina	23	Rugby Champs	Nelspruit	Glen Jackson
206	26/08/2016	Golden Lions	60	Boland	12	CC Premier Div	Johannesburg	Rasta Rasivhenge
207	26/08/2016	Leopards	43	Griffons	33	CC First Div	Potchefstroom	Rodney Bonaparte
208	26/08/2016	Border	61	Welwitschias	7	CC First Div	East London	Egon Seconds
209	26/08/2016	Pumas	35	Griquas	41	CC Premier Div	Nelspruit	Stuart Berry
210	27/08/2016	Valke	34	SWD Eagles	32	CC First Div	Kempton Park	Jaco van Heerden
211	27/08/2016	EP Kings	6	WP	36	CC Premier Div	Port Elizabeth	Lesego Legoete
212	27/08/2016	Sharks	26	Blue Bulls	19	CC Premier Div	Durban	Marius vd Westhuizen
213	27/08/2016	Argentina	26	South Africa	24	Rugby Champs	Salta	Jérôme Garcès
214	31/08/2016	Griquas	47	EP Kings	24	CC Premier Div	Kimberley	AJ Jacobs
215	02/09/2016	Boland	25	Pumas	22	CC Premier Div	Wellington	Marius vd Westhuizen
216	02/09/2016	Blue Bulls	31	Golden Lions	17	CC Premier Div	Pretoria	Craig Joubert
217	02/09/2016	Border	41	Griffons	24	CC First Div	East London	Jaco Peyper
218	03/09/2016	Free State	57	EP Kings	25	CC Premier Div	Bloemfontein	Jaco van Heerden
219	03/09/2016	Valke	19	Leopards	42	CC First Div	Kempton Park	AJ Jacobs
220	03/09/2016	WP	34	Sharks	27	CC Premier Div	Cape Town	Rasta Rasivhenge
221	08/09/2016	Griquas	46	Boland	22	CC Premier Div	Kimberley	Jaco van Heerden
222	09/09/2016	Valke	29	Border	54	CC First Div	Kempton Park	Cwengile Jadezweni
223	09/09/2016	Golden Lions	58	WP	32	CC Premier Div	Johannesburg	Jaco Peyper
224	10/09/2016	Australia	23	South Africa	17	Rugby Champs	Brisbane	Nigel Owens
225	10/09/2016	Leopards	49	SWD Eagles	31	CC First Div	Potchefstroom	Alexandre Ruiz
226	10/09/2016	Griffons	84	Welwitschias	25	CC First Div	Welkom	Quinton Immelman
227	10/09/2016	Sharks	30	Free State	38	CC Premier Div	Durban	Rasta Rasivhenge
228	10/09/2016	Pumas	14	Blue Bulls	41	CC Premier Div	Nelspruit	Stuart Berry
229	15/09/2016	Free State	37	Golden Lions	29	CC Premier Div	Bloemfontein	Jaco van Heerden
230	16/09/2016	Blue Bulls	57	Griquas	20	CC Premier Div	Pretoria	Quinton Immelman
231	16/09/2016	Border	31	SWD Eagles	24	CC First Div	East London	Mike Adamson
232	17/09/2016	New Zealand	41	South Africa	13	Rugby Champs	Christchurch	Angus Gardner
233	17/09/2016	Sharks	53	EP Kings	0	CC Premier Div	Durban	Cwengile Jadezweni
234	17/09/2016	Welwitschias	20	Valke	50	CC First Div	Windhoek	Rodney Bonaparte
235	17/09/2016	WP	31	Pumas	23	CC Premier Div	Cape Town	Alexandre Ruiz
236	23/09/2016	Boland	26	Blue Bulls	48	CC Premier Div	Wellington	Shuhei Kubo
237	23/09/2016	Pumas	10	Free State	52	CC Premier Div	Nelspruit	Lesego Legoete
238	23/09/2016	Griquas	31	WP	52	CC Premier Div	Kimberley	Jaco Peyper
239	24/09/2016	EP Kings	7	Golden Lions	71	CC Premier Div	Port Elizabeth	Cwengile Jadezweni
240	30/09/2016	Golden Lions	28	Sharks	16	CC Premier Div	Johannesburg	Craig Joubert

FIRST-CLASS MATCHES IN 2016

241	30/09/2016	Leopards	40	Valke	30	CC First Div	Potchefstroom	Jaco van Heerden
242	30/09/2016	EP Kings	30	Pumas	38	CC Premier Div	Port Elizabeth	Quinton Immelman
243	30/09/2016	Border	16	Griffons	25	CC First Div	East London	Lesego Legoete
244	30/09/2016	WP	30	Boland	28	CC Premier Div	Cape Town	AJ Jacobs
245	01/10/2016	Free State	63	Griquas	26	CC Premier Div	Bloemfontein	Cwengile Jadezweni
246	01/10/2016	South Africa	18	Australia	10	Rugby Champs	Pretoria	Wayne Barnes
247	07/10/2016	Leopards	25	Griffons	44	CC First Div Final	Potchefstroom	Quinton Immelman
248	08/10/2016	South Africa	15	New Zealand	57	Rugby Champs	Durban	Jérôme Garcès
249	15/10/2016	Free State	55	Golden Lions	17	CC Premier Div	Bloemfontein	Rasta Rasivhenge
250	15/10/2016	Blue Bulls	36	WP	30	CC Premier Div	Pretoria	Marius v/dWesthuizen
251	22/10/2016	Free State	36	Blue Bulls	16	CC Premier Div Fin	Bloemfontein	Jaco Peyper
252	05/11/2016	British Barbarians	31	Springbok XV	31	International Friendly	London	Mike Fraser
253	12/11/2016	England	37	South Africa	21	Outgoing Tour	London	Jérôme Garcès
254	19/11/2016	Italy	20	South Africa	18	Outgoing Tour	Florence	George Clancy
255	26/11/2016	Wales	27	South Africa	13	Outgoing Tour	Cardiff	Romain Poite

The Toyota Free State Cheetahs celebrate winning the Currie Cup.

South Africans Playing Abroad

Compiled by Stuart Farmer

South Africans appearing for leading clubs overseas at some point during the 2016 calendar year.
*Springbok   + Overseas international

	Player	Club	Country
+	NJ (Nick) Abendanon	Clermont Auvergne	France
	HJ (Heini) Adams	Bordeaux-Bègles	France
	T (Tythan) Adams	Selkirk	Scotland
*	WS (Willem) Alberts	Stade Français Paris	France
	LE (Louis) Albertse	Provence Rugby	France
	CG (Chris) Alcock	Western Force	Australia
		Sydney Rays	Australia
*	GG (Gio) Aplon	Grenoble	France
	JC (JC) Astle	Mont-de-Marsan	France
+	BM (Brad) Barritt	Saracens	England
*	BA (Bjorn) Basson	Honda Heat	Japan
	CJ (Coenie) Basson	Lyon O.U.	France
	S (Stefan) Basson	Femi CZ Rovigo	Italy
	GP (Greg) Bauer	Lafert San Donà	Italy
*	A (Andries) Bekker	Kobe Kobelco Steelers	Japan
	RM (Rynier) Bernardo	Ospreys	Wales
		Scarlets	Wales
		Scarlets Premiership Select	Wales
	U (Ulrich) Beyers	Zebre	Italy
	JDB (Jannie) Bornman	Provence Rugby	France
*	ML (Marnitz) Boshoff	Connacht	Ireland
*	HM (Meyer) Bosman	Stade Français Paris	France
	BJ (Berend) Botha	Bordeaux-Bègles	France
*	BJ (BJ) Botha	Munster	Ireland
		Lyon O.U.	France
+	MJ (Mouritz) Botha	Newcastle Falcons	England
+	R (Renaldo) Bothma	Toyota Verblitz	Japan
	JJ (JJ) Breet	Rugby Viadana	Italy
*	SB (Schalk) Brits	Saracens	England
	WS (Willie) Britz	NTT Shining Arcs	Japan
*	HW (Heinrich) Brüssow	NTT Docomo Red Hurricanes	Japan
	AM (Albertus) Buckle	Lyon O.U.	France
	DJ (David) Bulbring	Scarlets	Wales
	CB (Craig) Burden	Stade Français Paris	France
*	SWP (Schalk) Burger	Suntory Sungoliath	Japan
		Saracens	England
	K (Kevin) Buys	Brive	France
	J (Jake) Carter	Sheffield Tigers	England
	D (Demetri) Catrakilis	Montpellier	France
	DM (Dale) Chadwick	Narbonne	France
+	D (Dario) Chistolini	Zebre	Italy
*	PM (Pat) Cilliers	Montpellier	France
		Nottingham Rugby	England
		Leicester Tigers	England
+	AD (Antonie) Claassen	Racing 92	France
*	MC (Marcell) Coetzee	Honda Heat	Japan
	JG (Jean) Cook	Zebre	Italy
		Kintetsu Liners	Japan
	KL (Kyle) Cooper	Newcastle Falcons	England
	B (Brendan) Cope	Jersey Reds	England
*	KR (Keegan) Daniel	Kubota Spears	Japan
+	S (Shaun) Davies	Ohio Aviators	United States
	A (Aidon) Davis	Toulon	France
	JM (Johan) de Bruin	Vannes	France
	SJ (Sebastian) de Chaves	Leicester Tigers	England
		London Irish	England
+	B (Ben) de Jager	Pataro Calvisano	Italy
	RP (Rossouw) de Klerk	Grenoble	France
*	NA (Neil) de Kock	Saracens	England
*	AME (Allan) Dell	Edinburgh Rugby	Scotland
	M (Marius) Delport	Rugby Viadana	Italy
*	J (Jean) de Villiers	Leicester Tigers	England
+	RJE (Robbie) Diack	Ulster	Ireland
+	MC (Mike) Dias	Hull Ionians	England
	WJ (Hanno) Dirksen	Ospreys	Wales
	J (Justin) Downey	Suntory Sungoliath	Japan
	MC (Martin) Dreyer	Dax	France
*	BW (Bismarck) du Plessis	Montpellier	France
	CJ (Chris) du Plessis	Rugby Viadana	Italy
		Zebre	Italy
*	JN (Jannie) du Plessis	Montpellier	France
	PVW (Petrus) du Plessis	Saracens	England
	WHJ (Jacques) du Plessis	Montpellier	France
	WNF (Willie) du Plessis	Bayonne	France
	AE (Armand) du Preez	Conad Reggio Emilia	Italy
	CG (Cornell) du Preez	Edinburgh Rugby	Scotland
	P (Philip) du Preez	Mont-de-Marsan	France
*	PF (Fourie) du Preez	Suntory Sungoliath	Japan
	R (Ruaan) du Preez	Agen	France
	RE (Ruan) du Preez	Béziers	France
*	WH (Wian) du Preez	Lyon O.U.	France
	TJ (Thomas) du Toit	Munster	Ireland
	DO (Dewaldt) Duvenage	Perpignan	France
	GW (George) Earle	Scarlets	Wales
		Cardiff Blues	Wales
	RT (Robert) Ebersohn	Montpellier	France
		Castres Olympique	France
+	JP (Jean-Pierre) Eloff	Ohio Aviators	United States
	JW (Jarrid) Els	Heidelberger RK	Germany
	C (Carlo) Engelbrecht	Zebre	Italy
	JJ (Jacques) Engelbrecht	Montauban	France
*	JJ (JJ) Engelbrecht	Toyota Shokki Shuttles	Japan
		Ospreys	Wales
+	J (Jaco) Erasmus	Lafert San Dona	Italy
	JM (Mees) Erasmus	Perth Spirit	Australia

Victor Matfield in action for Northampton Saints in the Aviva Premiership.

* E (Eben) Etzebeth	NTT Docomo	
	Red Hurricanes	Japan
+ IR (Ian) Evans	Bristol Rugby	England
DC (Danie) Faasen	L'Aquila Rugby	Italy
NS (Nick) Fenton-Wells	Bedford Blues	England
	Bristol Rugby	England
AS (Andries) Ferreira	Toulon	France
SR (Sebastian) Ferreira	Darlington Mowden	
	Park	England
	Heidelberger RK	Germany
S (Sam) Figg	Country Eagles	Australia
LDvZ (Louis) Fouché	Kubota Spears	Japan
DA (Deon) Fourie	Lyon O.U.	France
* J (Jaque) Fourie	Kobe Kobelco Steelers	Japan
BK (Burton) Francis	Agen	France
SE (Shane) Gates	NTT Shining Arcs	Japan
+ Q (Quintin) Geldenhuys	Zebre	Italy
R (Ross) Geldenhuys	Highlanders	New Zealand
	Tasman Makos	New Zealand
D (Danré) Gerber	Beziers	France
	Mont-de-Marsan	France
NR (Reggie) Goodes	Hurricanes	New Zealand
	Wellington Lions	New Zealand
* JL (Johan) Goosen	Racing 92	France
WT (Wes) Goosen	Hurricanes	New Zealand
	Wellington Lions	New Zealand

K (Kieran) Goss	Cornish Pirates	England
	Chinnor	England
JPJ (Hansie) Graaff	Cetransa El Salvador	Spain
* PJ (Peter) Grant	Western Force	Australia
LD (Lloyd) Greeff	Zebre	Italy
* MD (Dean) Greyling	Oyonnax	France
AJ (Abrie) Griesel	Munster	Ireland
DG (Gerbrandt) Grobler	Racing 92	France
JH (Hans) Grobler	Tarbes	France
NJ (Nic) Groom	Northampton Saints	England
* BG (Bryan) Habana	Toulon	France
JR (James) Hall	Oyonnax	France
T (Thor) Halvorsen	Mogliano	Italy
D (Dean) Hammond	Worcester Warriors	England
AJ (Alistair) Hargreaves	Saracens	England
J (Brok) Harris	Newport Gwent Dragons	Wales
GN (Grant) Hattingh	Kubota Spears	Japan
R (Riekert) Hattingh	Ohio Aviators	United States
PJ (Petrus) Hauman	Brive	France
+ DS (Dane) Haylett-Petty	Western Force	Australia
RB (Ross) Haylett-Petty	Western Force	Australia
	Perth Spirit	Australia
C (Chris) Heiberg	Western Force	Australia
	Perth Spirit	Australia
WJ (Wiehahn) Herbst	Ulster	Ireland
+ RW (Rob) Herring	Ulster	Ireland

	Player	Club	Country
	BW (Brett) Herron	Rosslyn Park	England
		Ulster	Ireland
	EW (Edwin) Hewitt	Biarritz Olympique	France
	CO (Cliffie) Hodgson	Coventry	England
	C (Cameron) Holenstein	Pau	France
+	TT (Tyrone) Holmes	Glasgow Warriors	Scotland
		Newcastle Falcons	England
	D (Devlin) Hope	Coventry	England
		London Scottish	England
		Darlington Mowden Park	England
	JP (Joubert) Horn	Bayonne	France
*	F (Francois) Hougaard	Worcester Warriors	England
	A (André) Hough	Albi	France
	PB (Pat) Howard	Newport Gwent Dragons	Wales
	H (Henry) Immelman	Montpellier	France
	EA (Rassie) Jansen van Vuuren	Bayonne	France
	NJ (Nicolaas) Janse van Rensburg	Montpellier	France
*	ET (Elton) Jantjies	NTT Shining Arcs	Japan
*	ER (Ricky) Januarie	La Rochelle	France
	J (Jody) Jenneker	Oyonnax	France
		Castres Olympique	France
*	AF (Ashley) Johnson	Wasps	England
	G (Gavin) Jones	Blaydon	England
	R (Ross) Jones-Davies	Richmond	England
	PA (Paul) Jordaan	La Rochelle	France
*	R (Ryan) Kankowski	Toyota Shokki Shuttles	Japan
	JB (Kobus) Kemp	Aurillac	France
	S (Simon) Kerrod	Jersey Reds	England
*	Z (Zane) Kirchner	Leinster	Ireland
*	S (Steven) Kitshoff	Bordeaux-Bègles	France
	J (Jean) Kleyn	Munster	Ireland
	M (Martin) Knoetze	Denver Stampede	United States
*	VP (Vincent) Koch	Saracens	England
+	RM (Rory) Kockott	Castres Olympique	France
	G (Gideon) Koegelenberg	Zebre	Italy
	RN (Nick) Koster	Bristol Rugby	England
+	DM (Dan) Kotze	Clermont Auvergne	France
		Castres Olympique	France
	J (Juan) Kotze	Lazio	Italy
	M (Marco) Kotze	Agen	France
*	JA (Jaco) Kriel	Kubota Spears	Japan
*	JA (Jesse) Kriel	NTT Docomo Red Hurricanes	Japan
	AG (Andries) Kruger	Soyaux Angouleme	France
+	NA (Niku) Kruger	Denver Stampede	United States
*	PJJ (Juandré) Kruger	Racing 92	France
		Toulon	France
*	W (Werner) Kruger	Scarlets	Wales
	PHC (Lappies) Labuschagne	Kubota Spears	Japan
	B (Brad) Lacey	Brisbane City	Australia
	RJ (Rynard) Landman	Newport Gwent Dragons	Wales
+	B (Bernard) le Roux	Racing 92	France
+	JE (Jacques) le Roux	Coventry	England
		Birmingham Moseley	England
*	WJ (Willie) le Roux	Canon Eagles	Japan
	PL (Vickus) Liebenberg	Mont-de-Marsan	France
		Dax	France
	WA (Wian) Liebenberg	Montpellier	France
+	CJ (Chad) London	Denver Stampede	United States
*	L-FP (Francois) Louw	Bath Rugby	England
	R (Ryan) Louwrens	Western Force	Australia
		Perth Spirit	Australia
	L (Louis) Ludik	Ulster	Ireland
	G (Gino) Lupini	Mogliano	Italy
		Lafert San Donà	Italy
	ML (Luhandre) Luus	Pataro Calvisano	Italy
	A (Ali) Lyon	Richmond	England
*	C (Charl) McLeod	Grenoble	France
	SJ (Shaun) Malton	Exeter Chiefs	England
*	LG (Lionel) Mapoe	Kubota Spears	Japan
	JA (Jandré) Marais	Bordeaux-Bègles	France
	PC (Peet) Marais	Brive	France
	L (Lynton) Mare	Denver Stampede	United States
	LR (Lorenzo Robin) Masselli	Sitav Lyons Piacenza	Italy
*	V (Victor) Matfield	Northampton Saints	England
+	K (Kotaro) Matsushima	Suntory Sungoliath	Japan
		Melbourne Rebels	Australia
	HC (Carl) Meyer	Newport Gwent Dragons	Wales
	JG (Johan) Meyer	Zebre	Italy
	GR (Gareth) Milasinovich	Worcester Warriors	England
	GP (Guy) Millar	Western Force	Australia
		Southland Stags	New Zealand
	DJ (Derick) Minnie	Zebre	Italy
	C (Conor) Mitchell	Queensland Country	Australia
	CJ (Jacques) Momberg	Femi CZ Rovigo	Italy
	DS (Devin) Montgomery	Blackheath	England
+	RA (Randall) Morrison	Timisoara Saracens	Romania
*	FJ (Franco) Mostert	Ricoh Black Rams	Japan
	G (Gerhard) Mostert	Stade Français Paris	France
	GH (Gert) Muller	Toulouse	France
		Perpignan	France
	RD (Duncan) Naudé	Benetton Rugby Treviso	Italy
	DM (Dylan) Nel	Canterbury	New Zealand
+	WP (Willem) Nel	Edinburgh Rugby	Scotland
	SW (Schalk) Oelofse	Mont-de-Marsan	France
*	W (Wynand) Olivier	Worcester Warriors	England
	AI (Ian) Oosthuizen	Selkirk	Scotland
	J (Jaco) Otto	Heidelberger RK	Germany
	RJ (Richard) Palframan	London Irish	England
	BJM (Ben) Pienaar	London Welsh	England
*	R (Ruan) Pienaar	Ulster	Ireland
*	J-PR (JP) Pietersen	Panasonic Wild Knights	Japan
		Leicester Tigers	England
*	H (Handré) Pollard	NTT Docomo Red Hurricanes	Japan
	DJ (Danie) Poolman	Connacht	Ireland
	M (Michael) Poppmeier	Heidelberger RK	Germany
*	DJ (Dewald) Potgieter	Worcester Warriors	England
	JL (Jacques-Louis) Potgieter	Lyon O.U.	France
	P (Phil) Potgieter	Queensland Country	Australia
*	UJ (Jacques) Potgieter	Munakata Sanix Blues	Japan
	SJ (Sarel) Pretorius	Newport Gwent Dragons	Wales
	CA (Charlie) Purdon	San Diego Breakers	United States

	Player	Club	Country
	M (Mike) Reid	San Francisco Rush	United States
	MK (Mike) Rhodes	Saracens	England
	JR (Ricky) Riccitelli	Hurricanes	New Zealand
		Hawke's Bay Magpies	New Zealand
	SMK (Shannon) Rick	Albi	France
	SJ (Sean) Robinson	Racing 92	France
		Colomiers	France
	NG (Nemo) Roelofse	Albi	France
	HL (Hendrik) Roodt	Grenoble	France
	DW (De Wet) Roos	Sydney Rays	Australia
	JC (JC) Roos	Canon Eagles	Japan
+	JG (Jody) Rose	Timisoara Saracens	Romania
	JM (Jono) Ross	Stade Français Paris	France
	A (Armand) Roux	Dorking	England
+	Q (Quinn) Roux	Connacht	Ireland
	J (Johann) Sadie	Agen	France
	JJ (Jared) Saunders	Saracens	England
	K (Kurt) Schonert	London Scottish	England
	NP (Nick) Schonert	Worcester Warriors	England
	L (Louis) Schreuder	Kubota Spears	Japan
	WJ (Warren) Seals	Darlington Mowden Park	England
		Yorkshire Carnegie	England
	RC (Ross) Skeate	Provence Rugby	France
	R (Rayn) Smid	Bristol Rugby	England
		Ealing Trailfinders	England
	AJ (Riaan) Smit	Tarbes	France
*	JH (Juan) Smith	Toulon	France
	RH (Ruan) Smith	Toyota Verblitz	Japan
		ACT Brumbies	Australia
	BM (Brendon) Snyman	Rosslyn Park	England
		London Welsh	England
		Coventry	England
	J (Joe) Snyman	Brive	France
+	SL (Scott) Spedding	Clermont Auvergne	France
*	PJ (Pierre) Spies	Kintetsu Liners	Japan
		Montpellier	France
	B (Brynard) Stander	Western Force	Australia
		Perth Spirit	Australia
+	CJ Stander	Munster	Ireland
	B (Brandon) Staples	Darlington Mowden Park	England
		Yorkshire Carnegie	England
*	GG (Gurthrö) Steenkamp	Toulouse	France
	JWA (Wilhelm) Steenkamp	Brive	France
*	GJ (Deon) Stegmann	Honda Heat	Japan
*	MJH (Matt) Stevens	Toulon	England
+	AJ (Braam) Steyn	Benetton Rugby Treviso	Italy
*	FPL (Frans) Steyn	Toshiba Brave Lupus	Japan
		Montpellier	France
*	M (Morné) Steyn	Stade Français Paris	France
	AJ (Andries) Strauss	Edinburgh Rugby	Scotland
+	CR (Richardt) Strauss	Leinster	Ireland
+	JZ (Josh) Strauss	Glasgow Warriors	Scotland
	NJ (Nic) Strauss	Narbonne	France
	PA (Piet Louw) Strauss	Perpignan	France
	R (Riaan) Swanepoel	Provence Rugby	France
		Montauban	France

	Player	Club	Country
	SR (Steven) Sykes	Oyonnax	France
*	JJ (Jaco) Taute	Munster	Ireland
	JE (Jarrod) Taylor	Cambridge	England
	DJ (De-Jay) Terblanche	Mont-de-Marsan	France
	MJ (Morgan) Thompson	Old Albanians	England
+	GA (Greig) Tonks	Edinburgh Rugby	Scotland
		London Irish	England
	F (Francois) Uys	Toyota Verblitz	Japan
	JF (Jan) Uys	Brive	France
	GJ (Gerhard) van den Heever	Munster	Ireland
		Yamaha Jubilo	Japan
	D (Duhan) van der Merwe	Montpellier	France
+	DTH (DTH) van der Merwe	Scarlets	Wales
*	F (Franco) van der Merwe	Ulster	Ireland
	FC (Francois) van der Merwe	Racing 92	France
	HJ (Hendrik) van der Merwe	Heidelberger RK	Germany
*	HS (Heinke) van der Merwe	Stade Français Paris	France
*	M (Marcel) van der Merwe	Toulon	France
*	PR (Flip) van der Merwe	Clermont Auvergne	France
	W (Wilhelm) van der Sluys	Worcester Warriors	England
		Rotherham Titans	England
	PW (Wimpie) van der Walt	NTT Docomo Red Hurricanes	Japan
	MRS (Pellow) van der Westhuizen	Clermont Auvergne	France
		Montauban	France
	NJJ (Maks) van Dyk	Toulouse	France
	R (Ruahan) van Jaarsveld	Vannes	France
	J (Joe) van Niekerk	Femi CZ Rovigo	Italy
+	AJ (Dries) van Schalkwyk	Zebre	Italy
	E (Eugene) van Staden	Biarritz Olympique	France
	GJ (GJ) van Velze	Worcester Warriors	England
	M (Michael) van Vuuren	Mogliano	Italy
		Benetton Rugby Treviso	Italy
	MT (Mike) van Vuuren	Leicester Tigers	England
		Bath Rugby	England
		London Scottish	England
	A (Arno) van Wyk	Montpellier	France
	CG (Coenie) van Wyk	Toshiba Brave Lupus	Japan
	FD (Francois) van Wyk	Western Force	Australia
	HJ (Hencus) van Wyk	Munakata Sanix Blues	Japan
	JP (Kobus) van Wyk	Bordeaux-Bègles	France
	KD (Kayle) van Zyl	Zebre	Italy
	D (Darryl) Veenendaal	Nottingham Rugby	England
*	DJ (Duane) Vermeulen	Toulon	France
	R (Riaan) Viljoen	Sunwolves	Japan
	R (Robert) Visagie	Conad Reggio Emilia	Italy
*	PJ (Pedrie) Wannenburg	Oyonnax	France
		Denver Stampede	United States
	A (Adam) Wessels	Lafert San Donà	Italy
	G (Gerhard) Wessels	Cambridge	England
	KJ (Kyle) Whyte	Edinburgh Rugby	Scotland
	P (Paul) Willemse	Montpellier	France
	JI (Jeff) Williams	Bath Rugby	England
	MJ (Matti) Williams	Northampton Saints	England
		Worcester Warriors	England
	CR (Cameron) Wright	Montpellier	France
	S (Stephan) Zaayman	Conad Reggio Emilia	Italy
	C (Cameron) Zeiss	Esher	England

Who's Who of First-Class Rugby

A complete list of all players who appeared in a first-class* match for a South African team in 2016.
* For a definition of what constitutes a first-class match, please see page 8.

Abrahams, Yuseph William's (Boela) (Hentie Cilliers HS, Virginia) b 23/07/1988, Port Elizabeth. 1.63m. 65kg. Scrumhalf. FC DEBUT: 2007. PROV CAREER: Griffons 2007-08 & 14-16 51-8-0-0-2-46. EP Kings 2011-13 20-0-0-0-0-0. REP Honours: SA Kings 2011 2-0-0-0-0-0. SA Barbarians 2012 1-0-0-0-0-0. FC RECORD: 74-8-0-0-2-46. RECORD IN 2016: (Griffons) 18-1-0-0-1-8.

Ackerman, Justin (Paarl Boys'HS) b 17/03/1992, Johannesburg. 1.83m. 112kg. Prop. FC DEBUT: 2014. PROV CAREER: WP 2014 2-0-0-0-0-0. Lions 2016 1-0-0-0-0-0. Golden Lions XV 2016 5-0-0-0-0-0. SUPERRUGBY: Southern Kings 8-0-0-0-0-0. FC RECORD: 16-0-0-0-0-0. RECORD IN 2016: (Southern Kings, Lions, Golden Lions XV) 14-0-0-0-0-0.

Ackermann, Ruan (Garsfontein HS, Pretoria) b 29/12/1995, Pretoria. 1.93m. 108kg. Flank. FC DEBUT: 2015. PROV CAREER: Golden Lions XV 2015-16 8-2-0-0-0-10. Lions 2016 9-1-0-0-0-5. SUPERRUGBY: Lions 2016 16-3-0-0-0-15. REP Honours: British Barbarians 2016 3-0-0-0-0-0. MISC INFO: Son of former Springbok Johan Ackermann. FC RECORD: 36-6-0-0-0-30. RECORD IN 2016: (Lions S18, Lions, Golden Lions XV, British Barbarians) 30-5-0-0-0-25.

Adendorff, Jonathan Wallis (Napier HS & US) b 23/08/1985, Napier. 1.91m. 102kg. Flank. FC DEBUT: 2011. PROV CAREER: Pumas 2011 5-0-0-0-0-0. Griquas 2012-16 64-6-0-0-0-30. FC RECORD: 69-6-0-0-0-30. RECORD IN 2016: (Griquas) 12-1-0-0-0-5.

Adendorff, Shaun (Glenwood HS, Durban & UP) b 28/05/1992, Durban. 1.85m. 100kg. Flank. FC DEBUT: 2012. PROV CAREER: Blue Bulls 2013 3-0-0-0-0-0. Boland 2016 17-5-0-0-0-25. REP Honours: SA U20 2012 3-2-0-0-0-10. SA Sevens 2014. FC RECORD: 23-7-0-0-0-35. RECORD IN 2016: (Boland) 17-5-0-0-0-25.

Adriaanse, Jacobus Petrus (Jacobie) (Paarl Gym.) b 19/07/1985, Cape Town. 1.78m 112kg. Prop. FC DEBUT: 2008. PROV CAREER: Boland 2008-09 23-0-0-0-0-0. Griquas 2010 21-1-0-0-0-5. Lions 2011-12 24-3-0-0-0-15. Golden Lions XV 2011-12 9-0-0-0-0-0. Blue Bulls 2016 7-0-0-0-0-0. SUPERRUGBY: Lions 2011-12 14-0-0-0-0-0. Southern Kings 2016 12-0-0-0-0-0. REP Honours: Emerging Springboks 2008 1-0-0-0-0-0. MISC INFO: Brother of Lourens Adriaanse. FC RECORD: 111-4-0-0-0-20. RECORD IN 2016: (Southern Kings, Blue Bulls) 19-0-0-0-0-0.

Adriaanse, Lourens Cornelius (Paarl Gym. & US) b 05/02/1988, Cape Town. 1.80m. 115kg. Prop. FC DEBUT: 2009. PROV CAREER: Griquas 2011-13 37-3-0-0-0-15. Sharks 2014-16 14-3-0-0-0-15. SUPERRUGBY: Cheetahs 2011-13 30-0-0-0-0-0. Sharks 2014-16 46-0-0-0-0-0. REP Honours: SA 2013 & 16 TESTS: 6-0-0-0-0-0. Springbok XV 2016 1-0-0-0-0-0. SA Students 2009 2-0-0-0-0-0. British Barbarians 2014 2-0-0-0-0-0. MISC INFO: Brother of Jacobie Adriaanse. FC RECORD: 138-6-0-0-0-30. RECORD IN 2016: (SA, Springbok XV, Sharks S18, Sharks) 23-0-0-0-0-0.

Afrika, Cecil Sebastian (Hentie Cilliers HS, Virginia) b 03/03/1988, Port Elizabeth. 1.77m. 65kg. Fullback. FC DEBUT: 2006. PROV CAREER: Griffons 2006-09 48-36-2-0-1-187. REP Honours: SA U20 2008 4-1-0-0-0-5. SA Sevens 2009-16. SA Schools 2006. MISC INFO: IRB Sevens PoY2010 -11. SARU Sevens PoY2012. FC RECORD: 52-37-2-0-1-192. RECORD IN 2016: (SA Sevens).

Agaba, Timothy Ernest Victor Kwizera (Stirling HS, East London & NMMU) b 23/07/1989, Kampala. 1.93m. 106kg. Eighthman. FC DEBUT: 2013. PROV CAREER: EP Kings 2013-15 28-4-0-0-0-20. REP Honours: SA Univ 2013 1-0-0-0-0-0. SA Sevens 2016. FC RECORD: 29-4-0-0-0-20. RECORD IN 2016: (SA Sevens).

Alberts, Gert Dirk Jacobus (Jacques) (Helpmekaar HS, Johannesburg) b 17/01/1991, Johannesburg. 2.02.00m. 98kg. Lock. FC DEBUT: 2011. PROV CAREER: Valke 2011-16 67-2-0-0-0-10. FC RECORD: 67-2-0-0-0-10. RECORD IN 2016: (Valke) 4-0-0-0-0-0.

Alberts, Willem Schalk (Monument HS, Krugersdorp) b 05/11/1984, Pretoria. 1.91m. 119kg. Lock. FC DEBUT: 2005. PROV CAREER: Lions 2005 & 07-09 35-7-0-0-0-35. Lions XV 2007-08 2-1-0-0-0-5. Golden Lions XV 2005 3-0-0-0-0-0. Sharks 2010-13 19-4-0-0-0-20. Sharks XV 2013 2-2-0-0-0-10. SUPERRUGBY: Lions 2007-09 37-4-0-0-0-20. Sharks 2010-15 73-8-0-0-0-40. REP Honours: SA 2010-16 TESTS: 43-7-0-0-0-35. Tour: 1-0-0-0-0-0. Springboks 2014 1-0-0-0-0-0. Total: 45-7-0-0-0-35. FC RECORD: 216-33-0-0-0-165. RECORD IN 2016 (SA) 5-0-0-0-0-0.

Albertse, Louis Erasmus (Michaelhouse, Balgowan & UJ) b 02/04/1990, Ermelo. 1.81m. 100kg. Prop. FC DEBUT: 2013. PROV CAREER: Blue Bulls 2013 6-0-0-0-0-0. EP Kings 2016 9-0-0-0-0-0. Pumas 2016 6-0-0-0-0-0. SUPERRUGBY: Southern Kings 2016 2-0-0-0-0-0. FC RECORD: 23-0-0-0-0-0. RECORD IN 2016: (Southern Kings, EP Kings, Pumas) 17-0-0-0-0-0.

Allerston, Ruan (Port Natal HS & NMMU) b 20/08/1992, Empangeni. 1.78m. 89kg. Centre. FC DEBUT: 2016. PROV CAREER: Valke 2016 4-0-0-0-0-0. FC RECORD: 4-0-0-0-0-0. RECORD IN 2016: (Valke) 4-0-0-0-0-0.

Am, Lukhanyo (De Vos Malan HS, King William's Town) b 28/11/1993, King William's Town. 1.86m. 93kg. Centre. FC DEBUT: 2013. PROV CAREER: Bulldogs 2013 & 15 20-1-0-0-0-5. Valke 2014 2-1-0-0-0-5. Sharks 2016 7-0-0-0-0-0. SUPERRUGBY: Southern Kings 2016 10-1-0-0-0-5. REP Honours: SA A 2016 2-0-0-0-0-0. FC RECORD: 41-3-0-0-0-15. RECORD IN 2016: (SA A, Southern Kings, Sharks) 19-1-0-0-0-5.

Andrews, Hyron Diego (Garsfontein HS, Pretoria) b 06/07/1995, Paarl. 2.02.00m. 104kg. Lock. FC DEBUT: 2015. PROV CAREER: Sharks XV 2015-16 13-0-0-0-0-0. SUPERRUGBY: Sharks 2016 9-0-0-0-0-0. REP Honours: SAU20 2015 2-0-0-0-0-0. FC RECORD: 24-0-0-0-0-0. RECORD IN 2016: (Sharks S18, Sharks XV) 17-0-0-0-0-0.

Annandale, Gavin Barnard (Brandwag HS, Benoni) b 27/04/1989, Welkom. 1.94m. 112kg. Lock. FC DEBUT: 2009. PROV CAREER: Valke 2009 5-0-0-0-0-0. Griffons 2010-12 & 16 48-4-0-0-0-20. Golden Lions XV 2013 2-0-0-0-0-0. Leopards 2013 1-0-0-0-0-0. Boland 2014-15 27-1-0-0-0-5. WP 2014 1-0-0-0-0-0. FC RECORD: 84-5-0-0-0-25. RECORD IN 2016: (Griffons) 21-2-0-0-0-10.

Antonites, David Alexander (President HS, Johannesburg & UJ) b 25/03/1991, Johannesburg. 1.97m. 117kg. Lock. FC DEBUT: 2016.

PROV CAREER: EP Kings 2016 3-0-0-0-0-0. Griquas 2016 2-0-0-0-0-0. FC RECORD: 5-0-0-0-0-0. RECORD IN 2016: (EP Kings, Griquas) 5-0-0-0-0-0.

April, Garth Graham (Bergrivier HS, Wellington) b 16/07/1991, Cape Town. 1.70m. 74kg. Fullback/Flyhalf. FC DEBUT: 2012. PROV CAREER: Golden Lions XV 2012 5-2-0-0-0-10. Boland 2013-14 6-0-2-0-0-4. Sharks 2015-16 9-2-1-0-0-12. Sharks XV 2015 2-0-0-1-0-3. WP 2015 2-1-0-0-0-5. SUPERRUGBY: Sharks 2016 12-2-11-11-0-65. REP Honours: SA A 2016 1-0-0-1-0-3. FC RECORD: 37-7-14-13-0-102. RECORD IN 2016: (SA A, Sharks S18, Sharks) 15-2-12-12-0-70.

April, Zungisa Nelson (Ithembelihle HS, Port Elizabeth) b 19/06/1990, Port Elizabeth. 1.80m. 100kg. Flank. FC DEBUT: 2014. PROV CAREER: Free State XV 2014-15 12-8-0-0-0-40. Griffons 2016 4-0-0-0-0-0. FC RECORD: 16-8-0-0-0-40. RECORD IN 2016: (Griffons) 4-0-0-0-0-0.

Arends, Riaan Allister (Brandwag HS, Uitenhage, UJ & Wits) b 31/01/1989, Uitenhage. 1.86m. 86kg. Wing. FC DEBUT: 2012. PROV CAREER: Valke 2014-15 16-12-0-0-0-60. Eagles 2016 8-1-0-0-0-5. REP Honours: SA Students 2012 2-0-0-0-0-0. FC RECORD: 26-13-0-0-0-65. RECORD IN 2016: (Eagles) 8-1-0-0-0-5.

Arendse, Ederies (Aloe HS, Cape Town) b 25/11/1987, Cape Town. 1.84m. 78kg. Wing. FC DEBUT: 2009. PROV CAREER: Valke 2009 6-3-0-0-0-15. WP 2011-13 15-5-0-0-0-25. Griquas 2014-16 49-20-0-0-0-100. FC RECORD: 70-28-0-0-0-140. RECORD IN 2016: (Griquas) 16-6-0-0-0-30.

Arnoldi, Wilmar (Ermelo HS & UP) b 21/10/1994, Pretoria. 1.81m. 105kg. Hooker. FC DEBUT: 2015. PROV CAREER: Leopards 2015-16 21-5-0-0-0-25. Leopards XV 2015 3-1-0-0-0-5. FC RECORD: 24-6-0-0-0-30. RECORD IN 2016: (Leopards) 14-4-0-0-0-20.

Aspeling, Karlo Gericke (Outeniqua HS, George & TUT) b 13/12/1987, George. 1.79m. 88kg. Flyhalf. FC DEBUT: 2012. PROV CAREER: Valke 2012 & 16 31-6-63-23-2-231. Bulldogs 2013 20-1-11-23-1-99. Eagles 2014 13-0-33-14-2-114. EP Kings 2015 10-0-3-0-0-6. FC RECORD: 74-7-110-60-5-450. RECORD IN 2016: (Valke) 17-2-38-13-0-125.

Astle, John-Charles (Pionier HS, Vryheid & UFS) b 30/08/1990, Queen'stown. 1.98m. 92kg. Lock. FC DEBUT: 2010. PROV CAREER: Cheetahs 2010-11 12-0-0-0-0-0. Free State XV 2012 4-0-0-0-0-0. Boland 2013-14 25-2-0-0-0-10. Sharks 2014-16 12-0-0-0-0-0. Sharks XV 2015 4-0-0-0-0-0. SUPERRUGBY: Southern Kings 2016 15-0-0-0-0-0. FC RECORD: 72-2-0-0-0-10. RECORD IN 2016: (Southern Kings, Sharks) 17-0-0-0-0-0.

Baard, Gerard (Outeniqua HS, George) b 29/01/1991, Moorreesburg. 1.83m. 105kg. Prop. FC DEBUT: 2014. PROV CAREER: Griffons 2014-16 23-0-0-0-0-0. FC RECORD: 23-0-0-0-0-0. RECORD IN 2016: (Griffons) 7-0-0-0-0-0.

Baard, Le Roux (Outeniqua HS, George & UJ) b 27/02/1996, Belville. 1.76m. 93kg. Hooker. FC DEBUT: 2016. PROV CAREER: Golden Lions XV 2016 1-0-0-0-0-0. FC RECORD: 1-0-0-0-0-0. RECORD IN 2016: (Golden Lions XV) 1-0-0-0-0-0.

Badiyana, Lusanda (Cambridge HS & NMMU) b 01/09/1996, East London. 1.80m. 98kg. Eighthman. FC DEBUT: 2016. PROV CAREER: EP Kings 2016 9-2-0-0-0-10. FC RECORD: 9-2-0-0-0-10. RECORD IN 2016: (EP Kings) 9-2-0-0-0-10.

Balekile, Tango (Selborne College, East London & NMMU) b 07/03/1996, East London. 1.81m. 100kg. Hooker. FC DEBUT: 2016.

PROV CAREER: EP Kings 2016 3-0-0-0-0-0. REP Honours: SAU20 2016 5-0-0-0-0-0. FC RECORD: 8-0-0-0-0-0. RECORD IN 2016: (EP Kings, SAU20) 8-0-0-0-0-0.

Banda, Masixole (Etembelihle HS, Port Elizabeth & UFH) b 11/06/1988, Port Elizabeth. 1.65m. 69kg. Fullback. FC DEBUT: 2014. PROV CAREER: EP Kings 2014 5-2-3-1-0-19. Bulldogs 2014-16 46-15-65-46-0-343. MISC INFO: CC First Div PoY2016. FC RECORD: 51-17-68-47-0-362. RECORD IN 2016: (Bulldogs) 20-10-41-17-0-183.

Baron, Darren Marc (Paarl Gym. & CUT) b 25/05/1995, Ceres. 1.80m. 91kg. Flyhalf. FC DEBUT: 2016. PROV CAREER: Free State XV 2016 9-0-1-0-0-2. FC RECORD: 9-0-1-0-0-2. RECORD IN 2016: (Free State XV) 9-0-1-0-0-2.

Bashiya, Yves Mulengi Tshiumbi (Capricorn HS) b 13/02/1987, Kinshasa. 1.85m. 107kg. Flank. FC DEBUT: 2009. PROV CAREER: Valke 2009-10 14-2-0-0-0-10. EP Kings 2009-10 12-1-0-0-0-5. EP Inv XV 2010 1-0-0-0-0-0. Boland 2014-16 25-1-0-0-0-5. FC RECORD: 52-4-0-0-0-20. RECORD IN 2016: (Boland) 2-0-0-0-0-0.

Basson, Bjorn Alberic (Dale College, King William's Town) b 11/02/1987, King William's Town. 1.87m. 82kg. Wing. FC DEBUT: 2008. PROV CAREER: Griquas 2008-10 56-47-0-0-0-235. Blue Bulls 2011-14 & 16 27-21-0-0-0-105. SUPERRUGBY: Cheetahs 2009-10 9-6-0-0-0-30. Bulls 2011-16 86-29-0-0-0-145. REP Honours: SA 2010-13 TESTS: 11-3-0-0-0-15. Emerging Springboks 2008-09 4-1-0-0-0-5. Royal XV 2009 1-0-0-0-0-0. MISC INFO: Holds SA record for most tries in a Currie Cup season (21 in 2010 for Griquas). Brother of Logan Basson. Holds Bulls record for most tries in a season (10 in 2012). FC RECORD: 195-107-0-0-0-535. RECORD IN 2016: (Bulls, Blue Bulls) 17-7-0-0-0-35.

Basson, Justin Johan (Boland Agric. HS, Paarl) b 10/02/1994, Cape Town. 1.94m. 116kg. Lock. FC DEBUT: 2015. PROV CAREER: Free State XV 2015-16 14-0-0-0-0-0. Cheetahs 2016 9-0-0-0-0-0. FC RECORD: 23-0-0-0-0-0. RECORD IN 2016: (Cheetahs, Free State XV) 17-0-0-0-0-0.

Basson, Logan Andrew (Dale College, King William's Town) b 09/03/1989, King William'stown. 1.91m. 77kg. Flyhalf. FC DEBUT: 2010. PROV CAREER: Bulldogs 2010 & 12 & 15-16 38-11-28-31-0-204. Griquas 2010-11 & 13 12-2-8-1-0-29. Eagles 2011 2-0-0-0-0-0. Free State XV 2014 3-1-0-0-0-5. Boland 2016 3-0-0-0-0-0. MISC INFO: Brother of Bjorn Basson. FC RECORD: 58-14-36-32-0-238. RECORD IN 2016: (Bulldogs) 10-2-12-4-0-46.

Beerwinkel, Andrew (Porterville HS) b 05/03/1993, Saron. 1.86m. 115kg. Prop. FC DEBUT: 2013. PROV CAREER: Blue Bulls 2015-16 10-0-0-0-0-0. REP Honours: SA U20 2013 4-1-0-0-0-5. FC RECORD: 14-1-0-0-0-5. RECORD IN 2016: (Blue Bulls) 6-0-0-0-0-0.

Bell, John-Wessel (JW) (Eldoraigne HS, Pretoria & UP) b 18/01/1990, Cape Town. 1.75m. 73kg. Fullback. FC DEBUT: 2011. PROV CAREER: Valke 2011-12 29-12-0-0-0-60. Pumas 2013-15 55-19-0-0-0-95. Lions 2016 1-1-0-0-0-5. Golden Lions XV 2016 10-8-0-0-0-40. SUPERRUGBY: Lions 2016 2-0-0-0-0-0. FC RECORD: 97-40-0-0-0-200. RECORD IN 2016: (Lions S18, Lions, Golden Lions XV) 13-9-0-0-0-45.

Benjamin, Rayno Shannon (Weston HS, Vredenburg) b 03/08/1983, St Helena Bay. 1.84m. 83kg. Wing. FC DEBUT: 2004. PROV CAREER: Boland 2004-06 42-35-0-0-0-175. Lions 2007-08 23-13-0-0-0-65. Lions XV 2008 1-1-0-0-0-5. Cheetahs 2011-16 47-17-0-0-0-85. Emerging Cheetahs 2011 1-1-0-0-0-5. Free State XV 2016 1-0-0-0-0-0. SUPERRUGBY: Stormers 2006 11-2-0-0-0-10. Lions 2008 12-2-0-0-0-10. Cheetahs 2011-16 54-14-0-0-0-70. REP Honours: SA Sevens 2005-07 & 13 & 15. FC RECORD: 192-85-0-0-0-425. RECORD IN

2016: (Cheetahs S18, Cheetahs, Free State XV) 12-6-0-0-0-30.

Bester, Adriaan Andries Jacobus (Driaan) (Middelburg HTS & UJ) b 25/05/1996, Middelburg, Mpumalanga. 1.93m. 103kg. Lock. FC DEBUT: 2016. PROV CAREER: Golden Lions XV 2016 2-0-0-0-0-0. FC RECORD: 2-0-0-0-0-0. RECORD IN 2016: (Golden Lions XV) 2-0-0-0-0-0.

Beukman, Rowayne Elrich (Outeniqua HS, George & NWU) b 05/03/1992, Mossel Bay. 1.77m. 88kg. Wing. FC DEBUT: 2014. PROV CAREER: Leopards 2014-16 22-5-0-0-0-25. Leopards XV 2014-15 9-3-0-0-0-15. FC RECORD: 31-8-0-0-0-40. RECORD IN 2016: (Leopards) 12-5-0-0-0-25.

Beyers, Ulrich (Ermelo HS) b 22/01/1991, Pretoria. 1.89m. 87kg. Fullback. FC DEBUT: 2011. PROV CAREER: Blue Bulls 2011-14 & 16 42-7-1-0-1-40. SUPERRUGBY: Bulls 2013-14 10-0-0-0-0-0. REP Honours: SAU20 2011 4-0-0-0-0-0. FC RECORD: 56-7-1-0-1-40. RECORD IN 2016: (Blue Bulls) 8-3-0-0-0-15.

Bezuidenhout, Martin Johannes (Klerksdorp HS & UJ) b 21/08/1989, Orkney. 1.82.00m. 102kg. Hooker. FC DEBUT: 2010. PROV CAREER: Golden Lions 2010-13 33-1-0-0-0-5. Golden Lions XV 2010-11 10-1-0-0-0-5. Griquas 2014-15 42-8-0-0-0-40. EP Kings 2016 11-1-0-0-0-5. SUPERRUGBY: Lions 2011-12 24-3-0-0-0-15. Lions P/R 2013 2-0-0-0-0-0. Stormers 2013 8-0-0-0-0-0. Southern Kings 2016 8-0-0-0-0-0. FC RECORD: 138-14-0-0-0-70. RECORD IN 2016: (Southern Kings, EP Kings) 19-1-0-0-0-5.

Bholi, Thembelani (Jamangile HS, Maclear) b 18/01/1990, East London. 1.95m. 92kg. Eighthman. FC DEBUT: 2013. PROV CAREER: EP Kings 2013-15 34-2-0-0-0-10. SUPERRUGBY: Southern Kings 2016 9-1-0-0-0-5. FC RECORD: 43-3-0-0-0-15. RECORD IN 2016: (Southern Kings) 9-1-0-0-0-5.

Blaauw, Phumlani (Woodridge HS) b 16/03/1994, Port Elizabeth. 1.83m. 122kg. Prop. FC DEBUT: 2016. PROV CAREER: Bulldogs 2016 2-0-0-0-0-0. FC RECORD: 2-0-0-0-0-0. RECORD IN 2016: (Bulldogs) 2-0-0-0-0-0.

Blewett, Tristan James (Hilton College & UKZN) b 26/08/1996, Johannesburg. 1.79m. 89kg. Centre. FC DEBUT: 2016. PROV CAREER: Sharks XV 2016 2-0-0-0-0-0. FC RECORD: 2-0-0-0-0-0. RECORD IN 2016: (Sharks XV) 2-0-0-0-0-0.

Blommetjies, Clayton (New Orleans SSS, Paarl & UP) b 30/08/1990, Paarl. 1.85m. 75kg. Wing. FC DEBUT: 2009. PROV CAREER: Blue Bulls 2011-14 41-12-0-0-0-60. Cheetahs 2014-16 28-7-1-0-0-37. Free State XV 2015 1-0-0-0-0-0. SUPERRUGBY: Cheetahs 2015-16 24-6-0-0-0-30. REP Honours: SA Students 2009 1-2-0-0-0-10. SAU20 2009 2-0-0-0-0-0. SA Sevens 2012. British Barbarians 2016 1-0-0-0-0-0. FC RECORD: 98-27-1-0-0-137. RECORD IN 2016: (Cheetahs S18, Cheetahs, British Barbarians) 25-7-0-0-0-35.

Blose, Kwenzokuhle Ndumiso (Glenwood HS, Durban & UFS) b 12/05/1997, Paulpietersburg. 1.87m. 110kg. Prop. FC DEBUT: 2016. REP Honours: SAU20 2016 2-0-0-0-0-0. FC RECORD: 2-0-0-0-0-0. RECORD IN 2016: (SAU20) 2-0-0-0-0-0.

Bock, Alshaun Gerswon (Weltevrede HS, Wellington) b 16/05/1982, Wellington. 1.79m. 78kg. Wing. FC DEBUT: 2002. PROV CAREER: Boland 2002-04 & 07-08 38-19-0-0-0-95. Griquas 2005-06 & 16 40-23-0-0-0-115. WP 2009 1-1-0-0-0-5. Eagles 2012-15 64-55-0-0-0-275. REP Honours: SA Pres XV 2013 3-2-0-0-0-10. SA Sevens 2003; SA U21 2003 5-9-0-0-0-45. FC RECORD: 151-109-0-0-0-545. RECORD IN 2016: (Griquas) 18-10-0-0-0-50.

Bolze, Simon Nord (Queen's College, Queen'stown & NMMU) b 30/07/1995, Queen'stown. 1.79m. 84kg. Flyhalf. FC DEBUT: 2016. PROV

CAREER: EP Kings 2016 7-1-9-1-0-26. FC RECORD: 7-1-9-1-0-26. RECORD IN 2016: (EP Kings) 7-1-9-1-0-26.

Booi, Ayabonga Ludwe (Pretoria THS & UFH) b 14/05/1987, Butterworth. 1.79m. 90kg. Wing. FC DEBUT: 2010. PROV CAREER: Bulldogs 2010 & 14-16 35-2-0-0-0-10. FC RECORD: 35-2-0-0-0-10. RECORD IN 2016: (Bulldogs) 13-1-0-0-0-5.

Booysen, Brianton Justin (Outeniqua HS, George) b 27/04/1993, Riversdale. 1.77m. 92kg. Hooker. FC DEBUT: 2016. PROV CAREER: Eagles 2016 6-0-0-0-0-0. FC RECORD: 6-0-0-0-0-0. RECORD IN 2016: (Eagles) 6-0-0-0-0-0.

Booysen, Fabian Connal Frazer (Florida HS & UJ) b 21/03/1992, Caledon. 1.90m. 103kg. Eighthman. FC DEBUT: 2012. PROV CAREER: Golden Lions XV 2012-13 & 15-16 12-1-0-0-0-5. Lions 2015-16 16-0-0-0-0-0. SUPERRUGBY: Lions 2016 2-0-0-0-0-0. REP Honours: SA Univ 2013 1-0-0-0-0-0. SAU20 2012 5-0-0-0-0-0. FC RECORD: 36-1-0-0-0-5. RECORD IN 2016: (Lions S18, Lions, Golden Lions XV) 16-1-0-0-0-5.

Bosch, Christopher (Paarl Gym.) b 27/03/1992, Pretoria. 1.83m. 90kg. Centre. FC DEBUT: 2013. PROV CAREER: Blue Bulls 2013 1-0-0-0-0-0. Boland 2014 & 16 31-11-0-0-0-55. Valke 2015 8-1-0-0-0-5. FC RECORD: 40-12-0-0-0-60. RECORD IN 2016: (Boland) 21-11-0-0-0-55.

Bosch, Curwin Dominique (Grey HS, Port Elizabeth & UKZN) b 25/06/1997, Port Elizabeth. 1.80m. 80kg. Flyhalf. FC DEBUT: 2016. PROV CAREER: Sharks 2016 8-1-19-20-1-106. Sharks XV 2016 1-1-0-0-0-5. SUPERRUGBY: Sharks 2016 3-1-0-0-0-5. REP Honours: SAU20 2016 5-2-16-7-0-63. MISC INFO: SARU YPoYnominee 2016. FC RECORD: 17-5-35-27-1-179. RECORD IN 2016: (Sharks S18, Sharks, Sharks XV, SAU20) 17-5-35-27-1-179.

Boshoff, Henri Bossau (Nelspruit HS & UJ) b 08/02/1992, Nelspruit. 1.86m. 110kg. Hooker. FC DEBUT: 2013. PROV CAREER: Golden Lions XV 2013 2-1-0-0-0-5. Boland 2015 5-0-0-0-0-0. Valke 2016 17-1-0-0-0-5. FC RECORD: 24-2-0-0-0-10. RECORD IN 2016: (Valke) 17-1-0-0-0-5.

Boshoff, Marnitz Louis (Nelspruit HS & UP) b 11/01/1989, Nelspruit. 1.76m. 78kg. Flyhalf. FC DEBUT: 2009. PROV CAREER: Blue Bulls 2009-11 24-3-23-21-2-130. Griquas 2012 13-0-11-5-0-37. Lions 2013-16 32-4-91-57-4-385. Golden Lions XV 2013 & 15-16 14-0-49-26-5-191. SUPERRUGBY: Lions 2014-16 29-1-25-52-8-235. Lions P/R 2013 1-0-0-0-0-0. REP Honours: SA 2014 TESTS: 1-0-1-0-0-2. British Barbarians 2014 2-1-7-0-0-19. FC RECORD: 116-9-207-161-19-999. RECORD IN 2016: (Lions S18, Lions, Golden Lions XV) 12-1-47-11-0-132.

Botha, Arnoldus Francois (Arno) (Nylstroom HS & UP) b 26/10/1991, Modimolle. 1.90m. 102kg. Flank. FC DEBUT: 2011. PROV CAREER: Blue Bulls 2011-12 & 15-16 34-6-0-0-0-30. SUPERRUGBY: Bulls 2012-13 & 15-16 46-1-0-0-0-5. REP Honours: SA TESTS: 2012-13 2-0-0-0-0-0. SA A 2016 1-0-0-0-0-0. SAU20 2011 5-7-0-0-0-35. Misc: SA U20 PoY2011. FC RECORD: 88-14-0-0-0-70. RECORD IN 2016: (SA A, Bulls, Blue Bulls) 21-0-0-0-0-0.

Botha, Bernardo Carl (Florida HS, Roodepoort) b 04/07/1988, Oudtshoorn. 1.81m. 86kg. Wing. FC DEBUT: 2009. PROV CAREER: Young Lions 2009-10 8-4-0-0-0-20. Griffons 2013 5-0-0-0-0-0. Pumas 2014-16 39-8-1-0-0-42. SUPERRUGBY: Lions 2010 2-0-0-0-0-0. Rep. honours: SA Sevens 2010-13. FC RECORD: 54-12-1-0-0-62. RECORD IN 2016: (Pumas) 15-1-0-0-0-5.

Botha. Pieter Willem (PW) (Ficksburg HS) b 24/05/1991, Durban. 1.85m. 105kg. Prop. FC DEBUT: 2014. PROV CAREER: Griffons 2014-16 19-0-0-0-0-0. FC RECORD: 19-0-0-0-0-0. RECORD IN 2016: (Griffons)

4-0-0-0-0-0.

Botha, Renier (Diamantveld HS, Kimberley) b 28/09/1992, Bloemfontein. 1.73m. 73kg. Scrumhalf. FC DEBUT: 2014. PROV CAREER: Free State XV 2014-16 14-3-0-0-0-15. Griquas 2016 9-1-0-0-0-5. SUPERRUGBY: Cheetahs 2015 1-0-0-0-0-0. FC RECORD: 24-4-0-0-0-20. RECORD IN 2016: (Griquas, Free State XV) 14-1-0-0-0-5.

Botha, Ruan (Jeugland HS, Kempton Park) b 10/01/1992, Brakpan. 2.03m. 113kg. Lock. FC DEBUT: 2012. PROV CAREER: Golden Lions XV 2012 1-0-0-0-0-0. WP 2013-15 19-1-0-0-0-5. Sharks 2016 8-2-0-0-0-10. Sharks XV 2016 4-1-0-0-0-5. SUPERRUGBY: Lions 2012 5-0-0-0-0-0. Stormers 2014-15 21-1-0-0-0-5. Sharks 2016 3-0-0-0-0-0. REP Honours: SAU20 2012 5-0-0-0-0-0. FC RECORD: 66-5-0-0-0-25. RECORD IN 2016: (Sharks S18, Sharks, Sharks XV) 15-3-0-0-0-15.

Botha, Tom (Paul Roos Gym., Stellenbosch) b 31/08/1990, Belville. 1.79m. 110kg. Prop. FC DEBUT: 2011. PROV CAREER: WP 2011-12 17-0-0-0-0-0. EP Kings 2014-15 15-0-0-0-0-0. Cheetahs 2016 6-1-0-0-0-5. SUPERRUGBY: Southern Kings 2016 15-0-0-0-0-0. FC RECORD: 53-1-0-0-0-5. RECORD IN 2016: (Southern Kings, Cheetahs, EP Kings) 21-1-0-0-0-5.

Bothma, Petrus Lodewikus (Rikus) (Paarl Gym.) b 17/10/1995, Keimoes. 1.87m. 107kg. Eighthman. FC DEBUT: 2015. PROV CAREER: WP 2016 2-0-0-0-0-0. REP Honours: SAU20 2015 2-1-0-0-0-5. FC RECORD: 4-1-0-0-0-5. RECORD IN 2016: (WP) 2-0-0-0-0-0.

Bothma, Renaldo (Volkskool Heidelberg) b 18/09/1989, Alberton. 1.87m. 100kg. Flank. FC DEBUT: 2010. PROV CAREER: Golden Lions 2010 7-2-0-0-0-10. Golden Lions XV 2011 6-1-0-0-0-5. Leopards 2011 1-0-0-0-0-0. Pumas 2012-14 & 16 61-24-0-0-0-120. Blue Bulls 2016 3-2-0-0-0-10. SUPERRUGBY: Sharks 2015 15-1-0-0-0-5. Bulls 2016 3-2-0-0-0-10. REP Honours: SA Pres XV 2013 2-1-0-0-0-5. MISC INFO: Namibia international. FC RECORD: 98-33-0-0-0-165. RECORD IN 2016: (Bulls, Blue Bulls, Pumas) 13-6-0-0-0-30.

Bouwer, Molotsi Elias (Potchefstroom HS & NWU) b 11/08/1991, Potchefstroom. 1.90m. 109kg. Flank. FC DEBUT: 2014. PROV CAREER: Leopards 2014-16 13-0-0-0-0-0. Leopards XV 2014-15 12-1-0-0-0-5. FC RECORD: 25-1-0-0-0-5. RECORD IN 2016: (Leopards) 7-0-0-0-0-0.

Brandt, Alvin b 30/09/1991. Wing. FC DEBUT: 2014. PROV CAREER: Free State XV 2014-15 10-3-0-0-0-15. Griffons 2015 5-4-0-0-0-20. WP 2016 1-0-0-0-0-0. FC RECORD: 16-7-0-0-0-35. RECORD IN 2016: (WP) 1-0-0-0-0-0.

Bredenkamp, Eital (Affies, Pretoria) b 28/01/1993, Pretoria. 1.79m. 92kg. Flank. FC DEBUT: 2014. PROV CAREER: WP 2014 & 16 19-3-0-0-0-15. EP Kings 2015 4-1-0-0-0-5. FC RECORD: 23-4-0-0-0-20. RECORD IN 2016: (WP) 13-3-0-0-0-15.

Briers, Johannes Albertus Myburgh (Oakdale Agric. HS, Riversdale & NWU) b 02/04/1994, Riversdale. 1.80m. 90kg. Fullback. FC DEBUT: 2015. PROV CAREER: Leopards XV 2015 5-1-0-0-0-5. Leopards 2016 3-0-0-0-0-0. FC RECORD: 8-1-0-0-0-5. RECORD IN 2016: (Leopards) 3-0-0-0-0-0.

Brink, Cyle Justin (KES, Johannesburg) b 16/01/1994, Johannesburg. 1.83m. 112kg. Flank. FC DEBUT: 2014. PROV CAREER: Golden Lions XV 2014-16 16-5-0-0-0-25. Lions 2016 9-2-0-0-0-10. SUPERRUGBY: Lions 2016 13-1-0-0-0-5. REP Honours: SAU20 2014 5-0-0-0-0-0. FC RECORD: 43-8-0-0-0-40. RECORD IN 2016: (Lions S18, Lions, Golden Lions XV) 24-4-0-0-0-20.

Brink, Michael Muller (Grens HS, East London) b 24/09/1996, Pretoria. 1.82.00m. 91kg. Centre. FC DEBUT: 2016. PROV CAREER: EP Kings 2016 7-0-4-2-14. FC RECORD: 7-0-4-2-0-14. RECORD IN 2016: (EP Kings) 7-0-4-2-0-14.

Britz, Rudolph Martinus (Rudi) (Hentie Cilliers HS, Virginia) b 03/03/1989, Virginia. 1.89m. 126kg. Prop. FC DEBUT: 2012. PROV CAREER: Griffons 2012-16 52-3-0-0-0-15. FC RECORD: 52-3-0-0-0-15. RECORD IN 2016: (Griffons) 2-0-0-0-0-0.

Britz, Willem Stephanus (Willie) (Diamantveld HS, Kimberley & UFS) b 31/08/1988, Cape Town. 1.91m. 98kg. FC DEBUT: 2009. PROV CAREER: Cheetahs 2009 & 2011 5-2-0-0-0-10. Griffons 2010-12 28-8-0-0-0-40. Lions 2012-14 32-4-0-0-0-20. Golden Lions XV 2013 7-1-0-0-0-5. Emerging Cheetahs 2011 1-0-0-0-0-0. Free State XV 2016 1-0-0-0-0-0. SUPERRUGBY: Lions 2014 13-0-0-0-0-0. Lions P/R 2013 2-0-0-0-0-0. Cheetahs 2015-16 12-0-0-0-0-0. FC RECORD: 101-15-0-0-0-75. RECORD IN 2016: (Cheetahs S18, Free State XV) 3-0-0-0-0-0.

Brown, Henry Brandon (Grey HS, Port Elizabeth & NMMU) b 16/11/1994, Port Elizabeth. 1.85m. 102kg. Flank. FC DEBUT: 2016. PROV CAREER: EP Kings 2016 8-1-0-0-0-5. FC RECORD: 8-1-0-0-0-5. RECORD IN 2016: (EP Kings) 8-1-0-0-0-5.

Brown, Kyle Gie (SACS, Cape Town & UCT) b 06/02/1987, Cape Town. 1.82.00m. 96kg. Rep. Honours: SA Sevens 2008-16. RECORD IN 2016: (SA Sevens).

Brummer, Francois (Waterkloof HS, Pretoria) b 17/05/1989, Pretoria. 1.82.00m. 90kg. Flyhalf. FC DEBUT: 2008. PROV CAREER: Blue Bulls 2008-11 49-6-66-91-15-480. Griquas 2012-15 72-7-52-34-7-262. Pumas 2016 7-0-8-9-1-46. SUPERRUGBY: Bulls 2010 & 16 15-1-23-19-1-111. Cheetahs 2013 & 15 4-0-4-3-0-17. REP Honours: SA A 2016 2-1-5-0-0-15. SAU20 2008-09 9-3-24-13-1-105. FC RECORD: 158-18-182-169-25-1036. RECORD IN 2016: (SA A, Bulls, Pumas) 23-2-35-28-2-170.

Burger, Martinus Abraham (Grey College, Bloemfontein & UFS) b 01/11/1993, Rosendal. 1.93m. 104kg. Flank. FC DEBUT: 2014. PROV CAREER: Cheetahs 2014-16 16-2-0-0-0-10. Free State XV 2014 & 16 11-2-0-0-0-10. SUPERRUGBY: Cheetahs 2015 11-0-0-0-0-0. FC RECORD: 38-4-0-0-0-20. RECORD IN 2016: (Cheetahs, Free State XV) 12-1-0-0-0-5.

Burger, Schalk Willem Petrus (Paarl Gym.) b 13/04/1983, Port Elizabeth. 1.93m. 114kg. Flank. FC DEBUT: 2002. PROV CAREER: WP 2003-05 & 08-11 & 13 37-7-0-0-0-35. SUPERRUGBY: Stormers 2004-12 & 14-16 123-9-0-0-0-45. REP Honours: SA 2003-11 & 14-15 TESTS: 86-16-0-0-0-80. Springboks 2014-15 2-0-0-0-0-0. Total: 88-16-0-0-0-80. SA U21 2002-03 8-4-0-0-0-20; British Barbarians 2004 & 08,09,13 4-0-0-0-0-0. S Hemisphere XV 2005 1-1-0-0-0-5. MISC INFO: SA PoY 2004. IRB PoY 2004. IRPA PoY& YPoY 2004. Super PoYnominee 2011. SARU PoY 2011. SA YPoY nominee 2003, 2004; Holds SA record for most Tests as a Flank - 79 (also seven at No. 8). Son of 1984-86 Springbok SWP (Schalk) Burger. FC RECORD: 261-37-0-0-0-185. RECORD IN 2016: (Stormers): 15-1-0-0-0-5.

Cameron, Davron Austin (Kingswood College, Grahamstown & NMMU) b 08/06/1996, George. 1.68m. 73kg. Scrumhalf. FC DEBUT: 2016. PROV CAREER: EP Kings 2016 3-0-0-0-0-0. FC RECORD: 3-0-0-0-0-0. RECORD IN 2016: (EP Kings) 3-0-0-0-0-0.

Campbell, Duncan (Westville Boys' HS & Varsity College) b 13/02/1992, Westville. 1.78m. 83kg. Flyhalf. FC DEBUT: 2014. PROV CAREER: Sharks XV 2014 & 16 4-0-2-1-0-7. FC RECORD: 4-0-2-1-0-7. RECORD IN 2016: (Sharks XV) 3-0-1-1-0-5.

Campher, Jan-Henning (Garsfontein HS & UP) b 10/12/1996,

Pretoria. 1.86m. 103kg. Hooker. FC DEBUT: 2016. PROV CAREER: Blue Bulls 2016 4-0-0-0-0-0. REP Honours: SAU20 2016 5-1-0-0-0-5. FC RECORD: 9-1-0-0-0-5. RECORD IN 2016: (Blue Bulls, SAU20) 9-1-0-0-0-5.

Carelse, Adriaan John (Hottentots Holland HS, Somerset West) b 08/02/1995, Somerset WeSt 1.73m. 72kg. Flyhalf. FC DEBUT: 2015. PROV CAREER: Boland 2015-16 31-5-6-1-1-43. FC RECORD: 31-5-6-1-1-43. RECORD IN 2016: (Boland) 22-4-6-0-0-32.

Carr, Nizaam (Bishops HS, Rondebosch) b 04/04/1991, Cape Town. 1.84m. 93kg. Flank. FC DEBUT: 2011. PROV CAREER: WP 2011-16 43-11-0-0-0-55. SUPERRUGBY: Stormers 2012-16 67-6-0-0-0-30. REP Honours: SA 2014 & 16 TESTS: 5-0-0-0-0-0. Springbok XV 2016 1-0-0-0-0-0. SA A 2016 2-0-0-0-0-0. SAU20 2011 4-2-0-0-0-10. MISC INFO: PoYnominee 2014. FC RECORD: 122-19-0-0-0-95. RECORD IN 2016: (SA, Springbok XV, SA A, Stormers, WP) 24-3-0-0-0-15.

Cassiem, Uzair (Strand HS, Cape Town & Boland College) b 17/03/1990, Strand. 1.89m. 98kg. Flank. FC DEBUT: 2011. PROV CAREER: Lions 2012 4-0-0-0-0-0. Golden Lions XV 2011 1-1-0-0-0-5. Valke 2012 3-2-0-0-0-10. Pumas 2012-15 71-13-0-0-0-65. Cheetahs 2016 10-4-0-0-0-20. SUPERRUGBY: Cheetahs 2016 15-6-0-0-0-30. REP Honours: SA 2016 TESTS: 1-1-0-0-0-5. SA Pres XV 2013 4-2-0-0-0-10. FC RECORD: 109-29-0-0-0-145. RECORD IN 2016: (SA, Cheetahs S18, Cheetahs) 26-11-0-0-0-55.

Cele, Malcolm Malusi (Greytown HS) b 10/01/1995, Greytown. 1.85m. 85kg. Wing. FC DEBUT: 2016. PROV CAREER: Sharks XV 2016 4-2-0-0-0-10. FC RECORD: 4-2-0-0-0-10. RECORD IN 2016: (Sharks XV) 4-2-0-0-0-10.

Chadwick, Dale Michael (Westville Boys"HS) b 20/06/1989, Westville. 1.83m. 105kg. Prop. FC DEBUT: 2009. PROV CAREER: Sharks 2009 & 2011-16 51-2-0-0-0-10. Sharks XV 2010-12 & 15-16 15-2-0-0-0-10. Sharks Inv XV 2009 1-0-0-0-0-0. SUPERRUGBY: Sharks 2012 & 14-16 44-1-0-0-0-5. FC RECORD: 111-5-0-0-0-25. RECORD IN 2016: (Sharks S18, Sharks, Sharks XV) 10-0-0-0-0-0.

Chetty, Wesley (Rondebosch HS, Bishops HS & UCT) b 05/02/1987, Cape Town. 1.75m. 106kg. Prop. FC DEBUT: 2012. PROV CAREER: WP 2016 2-0-0-0-0-0. REP Honours: SA Students 2012 2-0-0-0-0-0. FC RECORD: 4-0-0-0-0-0. RECORD IN 2016: (WP) 2-0-0-0-0-0.

Claassen, Neil (Daniel Pienaar HS, Uitenhage) b 26/09/1992, Pretoria. 1.94m. 85kg. Lock/Flank. FC DEBUT: 2012. PROV CAREER: Free State XV 2012-14 & 16 16-2-0-0-0-10. Cheetahs 2014 10-0-0-0-0-0. FC RECORD: 26-2-0-0-0-10. RECORD IN 2016: (Free State XV) 4-0-0-0-0-0.

Claassens, Michael (Kroonstad HS) b 28/10/1982, Kroonstad. 1.78m. 85kg. Scrumhalf. FC DEBUT: 2003. PROV CAREER: Cheetahs 2003-06 64-16-0-0-0-80. Sharks 2015-16 15-3-0-0-0-15. SUPERRUGBY: Cats 2005 9-0-0-0-0-0. Cheetahs 2006-07 20-0-0-0-0-0. Sharks 2016 15-1-0-0-0-5. REP Honours: SA TESTS: 2004-05 & 07 8-0-0-0-0-0. SA'A' 2004. SA U21 2003 1-1-0-0-0-5. British Barbarians 2008 2-0-0-0-0-0. CW NFS 1999-2000. FC RECORD: 135-21-0-0-0-105. RECORD IN 2016: (Sharks S18, Sharks) 21-3-0-0-0-15.

Cloete, Christopher Anthony (Selbourne College, East London) b 15/02/1991, East London. 1.76m. 91kg. Flank. FC DEBUT: 2012. PROV CAREER: Sharks XV 2012 7-1-0-0-0-5. WP 2013 & 15 12-5-0-0-0-25. SUPERRUGBY: Southern Kings 2016 9-4-0-0-0-20. FC RECORD: 28-10-0-0-0-50. RECORD IN 2016: (Southern Kings) 9-4-0-0-0-20.

Coertzen, Adriaan Jacobus Van der Berg (AJ) (Jim Fouche HS, Bloemfontein & UFS) b 16/10/1990, Bethlehem. 1.85m. 85kg. Fullback/Wing. FC DEBUT: 2011. PROV CAREER: Cheetahs 2011 & 14-15

10-1-0-0-0-5. Griquas 2015-16 26-18-0-0-0-90. FC RECORD: 36-19-0-0-0-95. RECORD IN 2016: (Griquas) 20-15-0-0-0-75.

Coetzee, Andries (Middelburg THS) b 01/03/1990, Bethal. 1.81m. 86kg. Fullback. FC DEBUT: 2011. PROV CAREER: Lions 2012-16 40-8-6-3-0-61. Golden Lions XV 2011-14 & 16 5-2-5-0-0-20. SUPERRUGBY: Lions 2012 & 14-16 42-3-0-0-1-18. Sharks 2013 1-0-0-0-0-0. FC RECORD: 88-13-11-3-1-99. RECORD IN 2016: (Lions S18, Lions, Golden Lions XV) 19-2-5-3-0-29.

Coetzee, Carel-Jan Wynand (Jim Fouche HS, Bloemfontein & UFS) b 23/01/1995, Bloemfontein. 1.83m. 92kg. Centre. FC DEBUT: 2016. PROV CAREER: Free State XV 2016 8-1-0-0-0-5. FC RECORD: 8-1-0-0-0-5. RECORD IN 2016: (Free State XV) 8-1-0-0-0-5.

Coetzee, Christo (Henneman HS) b 13/09/1994, Bloemfontein. 1.91m. 91kg. Fullback. FC DEBUT: 2016. PROV CAREER: Valke 2016 7-1-5-0-0-15. FC RECORD: 7-1-5-0-0-15. RECORD IN 2016: (Valke) 7-1-5-0-0-15.

Coetzee, Jean-Pierre Morgan Alrich (Oakdale HS, Riversdale) b 24/03/1995, Somerset WeSt 1.90m. 90kg. Wing. FC DEBUT: 2016. PROV CAREER: Free State XV 2016 11-3-0-0-0-15. FC RECORD: 11-3-0-0-0-15. RECORD IN 2016: (Free State XV) 11-3-0-0-0-15.

Coetzee, Johan Voges (Aranos) (Boland Agric. College, Paarl) b 14/03/1988, Windhoek. 1.87m. 122kg. Prop. FC DEBUT: 2010. PROV CAREER: Leopards 2010 11-0-0-0-0-0. Cheetahs 2016 5-0-0-0-0-0. Free State XV 2016 4-1-0-0-0-5. SUPERRUGBY: Cheetahs 2016 8-0-0-0-0-0. FC RECORD: 28-1-0-0-0-5. RECORD IN 2016: (Cheetahs S18, Cheetahs, Free State XV) 17-1-0-0-0-5.

Coetzee, Marcel Saayman (Maritzburg College & UKZN) b 14/12/1995, Harare. 1.81m. 93kg. Wing. FC DEBUT: 2016. PROV CAREER: Sharks XV 2016 4-0-3-3-0-15. FC RECORD: 4-0-3-3-0-15. RECORD IN 2016: (Sharks XV) 4-0-3-3-0-15.

Coetzee, Marcell Cornelius (Port Natal HS, Durban) b 08/05/1991, Potchefstroom. 1.90m. 106kg. Loose Forward. FC DEBUT: 2011. PROV CAREER: Sharks 2011-13 24-1-0-0-0-5. Sharks XV 2011 8-3-0-0-0-15. SUPERRUGBY: Sharks 2011-16 74-14-0-0-0-70. REP Honours: SA 2012-15 TESTS: 28-6-0-0-0-30. Springboks 2015 1-0-0-0-0-0. Total: 29-6-0-0-0-30. MISC INFO: YPoY2012 nominee. Super PoY2012 nominee. PoY nominee 2014. FC RECORD: 135-24-0-0-0-120. RECORD IN 2016: (Sharks S18) 6-1-0-0-0-5.

Coetzee, Marné (Waterkloof HS, Pretoria & Glenwood HS, Durban) b 17/09/1993, Pretoria. 1.83m. 114kg. Prop. FC DEBUT: 2015. PROV CAREER: Sharks XV 2015 7-0-0-0-0-0. Pumas 2015-16 11-0-0-0-0-0. FC RECORD: 18-0-0-0-0-0. RECORD IN 2016: (Pumas) 10-0-0-0-0-0.

Coetzee, Robin Leendert (Robbie) (Eldoraigne HS, Pretoria) b 02/05/1989, Pretoria. 1.85m. 105kg. Hooker. FC DEBUT: 2012. PROV CAREER: Blue Bulls 2012 11-1-0-0-0-5. Lions 2013-16 34-4-0-0-0-20. Golden Lions XV 2013 6-1-0-0-0-5. SUPERRUGBY: Lions 2014-16 28-2-0-0-0-10. Lions P/R 2013 2-0-0-0-0-0. FC RECORD: 81-8-0-0-0-40. RECORD IN 2016: (Lions S18, Lions) 8-3-0-0-0-15.

Coetzee, Stephanus Hendrik (Paarl Boys'HS) b 09/01/1992, Worcester. 1.85m. 105kg. Hooker. FC DEBUT: 2013. PROV CAREER: WP 2013-14 17-0-0-0-0-0. Griquas 2015 1-0-0-0-0-0. Sharks XV 2016 14-3-0-0-0-15. SUPERRUGBY: Stormers 2014 7-0-0-0-0-0. Cheetahs 2015 11-0-0-0-0-0. FC RECORD: 50-3-0-0-0-15. RECORD IN 2016: (Sharks XV) 14-3-0-0-0-15.

Coetzer, Wihan (Framesby HS, Port Elizabeth) b 30/08/1996, Port Elizabeth. 1.96m. 90kg. Lock. FC DEBUT: 2016. PROV CAREER: EP Kings 2016 1-0-0-0-0-0. FC RECORD: 1-0-0-0-0-0. RECORD IN 2016: (EP

Kings) 1-0-0-0-0-0.

Coleman, Kurt Kendall (Grey HS, Port Elizabeth & US) b 29/01/1990, Knysna. 1.77m. 82kg. Flyhalf. FC DEBUT: 2011. PROV CAREER: WP 2011-15 61-7-50-55-0-300. Eagles 2012 4-0-7-7-0-35. SUPERRUGBY: Stormers 2011 & 13-16 35-2-25-34-1-165. FC RECORD: 100-9-82-96-1-500. RECORD IN 2016: (Stormers) 5-0-4-10-0-38.

Collopy, Cullen Troy (Kearsney College, Botha's Hill & UCT) b 12/01/1993, Cape Town. 1.78m. 100kg. Hooker. FC DEBUT: 2016. PROV CAREER: WP 2016 7-2-0-0-0-10. EP Kings 2016 2-1-0-0-0-5. FC RECORD: 9-3-0-0-0-15. RECORD IN 2016: (WP, EP Kings) 9-3-0-0-0-15.

Combrink, Ruan Jacobus (Michaelhouse HS, Balgowan) b 10/05/1990, Vryheid. 1.83m. 96kg. Wing. FC DEBUT: 2010. PROV CAREER: WP 2010 1-0-0-0-0-0. Lions 2012 & 14-15 29-12-20-15-0-145. Golden Lions XV 2012 & 14 6-3-0-0-0-15. SUPERRUGBY: Lions 2012 & 14-16 45-13-4-4-0-85. P/R 2013 2-0-0-0-0-0. REP Honours: SA 2016 TESTS: 7-2-1-1-0-15. Springbok XV 2016 1-0-0-0-0-0. MISC INFO: SARU PoYnominee 2016. FC RECORD: 91-30-25-20-0-260. RECORD IN 2016: (SA, Springbok XV, Lions S18) 25-10-5-3-0-69.

Cooper, Kyle Lorran (Glenwood HS, Durban) b 10/02/1989, Johannesburg. 1.77m. 107kg. Hooker. FC DEBUT: 2010. PROV CAREER: Sharks 2010-15 52-2-0-0-0-10. Sharks XV 2010-12 & 15 28-2-0-0-0-10. Sharks Inv XV 2010 1-1-0-0-0-5. SUPERRUGBY: Sharks 2012-16 48-3-0-0-0-15. REP Honours: SAU20 2009 5-0-0-0-0-0. FC RECORD: 134-8-0-0-0-40. RECORD IN 2016: (Sharks S18) 10-1-0-0-0-5.

Cox, Dennis Clive (Excelsior HS) b 01/02/1995, Cape Town. 1.75m. 78kg. Fullback. FC DEBUT: 2016. PROV CAREER: WP 2016 5-1-1-0-0-7. FC RECORD: 5-1-1-0-0-7. RECORD IN 2016: (WP) 5-1-1-0-0-7.

Cronjé, Coert Frederick (Jeugland HS, Kempton Park & UJ) b 11/05/1988, Vereeniging. 1.82.00m. 86kg. Centre. FC DEBUT: 2010. PROV CAREER: Valke 2010-16 99-36-0-0-0-180. FC RECORD: 99-36-0-0-0-180. RECORD IN 2016: (Valke) 14-2-0-0-0-10.

Cronjé, Kenan (Montana HS) b 29/04/1995, Worcester. 1.89m 97kg. Prop. FC DEBUT: 2015. PROV CAREER: Boland 2015-16 19-4-0-0-0-20. FC RECORD: 19-4-0-0-0-20. RECORD IN 2016: (Boland) 14-2-0-0-0-10.

Cronjé, Ross (Michaelhouse HS, Balgowan) b 26/7/1989, Johannesburg. 1.81m. 79kg. Scrumhalf. FC DEBUT: 2009. PROV CAREER: Sharks 2009 & 2011 14-0-0-0-0-0. Sharks XV 2009-11 22-3-11-4-0-49. Lions 2012-16 45-4-0-0-0-20. Golden Lions XV 2012-13 & 16 8-0-3-0-0-6. SUPERRUGBY: Sharks 2009 1-0-0-0-0-0. Lions 2012 & 14-16 48-2-0-0-0-10. Lions P/R 2013 1-0-0-0-0-0. REP Honours: SAU20 2009 5-1-0-0-0-5. MISC INFO: Twin brother of Guy Cronjé. FC RECORD: 144-10-14-4-0-90. RECORD IN 2016: (Lions S18, Lions, Golden Lions XV) 23-1-0-0-0-5.

Cronjé, Xander (Dr EG Jansen HS, Boksburg & UJ) b 09/08/1995, Kempton Park. 1.89m. 98kg. Centre. FC DEBUT: 2016. PROV CAREER: Valke 2016 5-1-0-0-0-5. FC RECORD: 5-1-0-0-0-5. RECORD IN 2016: (Valke) 5-1-0-0-0-5.

Cupido, Lucien Ronwil (Paarl Boys'HS & NWU) b 21/11/1991, Paarl. 1.74m. 80kg. Wing. FC DEBUT: 2014. PROV CAREER: Leopards 2014-16 11-1-0-0-0-5. Leopards XV 2014 2-0-0-0-0-0. FC RECORD: 13-1-0-0-0-5. RECORD IN 2016: (Leopards) 5-0-0-0-0-0.

Daniel, Keegan Rhys (Dale College, King William's Town) b 05/03/1985, Humansdorp. 1.85m. 100kg. Flank. FC DEBUT: 2006. PROV CAREER: Sharks 2006-13 & 16 110-33-0-0-0-165. Sharks XV 2006-09 & 14 11-7-0-0-0-35. Sharks Inv XV 2009-10 2-2-1-0-0-12. SUPER-RUGBY: Sharks 2006-14 & 16 117-16-0-0-0-80. REP Honours: SA

2010 & 12 TESTS: 5-0-0-0-0-0. Tour: 1-0-0-0-0-0. Total: 6-0-0-0-0-0. SA U21 2006 5-3-0-0-0-15. MISC INFO: U21 PoY2006, VC PoY2006, YPoYnominee 2006, IRB YPoYnominee 2006. SARU PoY2012 nominee. Super PoY2012. FC RECORD: 251-61-1-0-0-307. RECORD IN 2016: (Sharks S18, Sharks) 18-0-0-0-0-0.

Daniller, Tertius (Paarl Gym.) b 04/08/1989, Paarl. 1.94m. 88kg. Eighthman. FC DEBUT: 2010. PROV CAREER: WP 2010-11 & 16 20-1-0-0-0-5. Griffons 2013 11-2-0-0-0-10. Free State XV 2013 7-2-0-0-0-10. MISC INFO: Brother of Hennie Daniller. FC RECORD: 38-5-0-0-0-25. RECORD IN 2016: (WP) 3-0-0-0-0-0.

Davids, Ashlon (Schoonspruit HS, Malmesbury) b 24/06/1993, Malmesbury. 1.70m. 85kg. Flyhalf. FC DEBUT: 2013. PROV CAREER: Golden Lions XV 2013 & 15-16 20-7-24-4-0-95. Lions 2015-16 2-0-0-0-0-0. Leopards 2015 3-1-0-0-0-5. SUPERRUGBY: Lions 2016 1-0-0-0-0-0. FC RECORD: 26-8-24-4-0-100. RECORD IN 2016: (Lions S18, Lions, Golden Lions XV) 12-1-7-0-0-19.

Davids, Clyde Eathan (Paarl Gym. & UP) b 17/04/1993, Paarl. 1.94m. 105kg. Eighthman. FC DEBUT: 2014. PROV CAREER: Blue Bulls 2014-16 17-2-0-0-0-10. FC RECORD: 17-2-0-0-0-10. RECORD IN 2016: (Blue Bulls) 2-0-0-0-0-0.

Davids, Mogamat Zain (Rondebosch HS) b 04/05/1997, Cape Town. 1.81m. 104kg. Flank. FC DEBUT: 2016. REP Honours: SAU20 2016 5-3-0-0-0-15. FC RECORD: 5-3-0-0-0-15. RECORD IN 2016: (SAU20) 5-3-0-0-0-15.

Davids, Selvyn (Nico Malan HS, Humansdorp) b 26/03/1994, Jeffreys Bay. 1.69m. 70kg. Fullback. FC DEBUT: 2014. PROV CAREER: EP Kings 2014 4-2-0-0-0-10. Griffons 2016 20-19-0-0-0-95. FC RECORD: 24-21-0-0-0-105. RECORD IN 2016: (Griffons) 20-19-0-0-0-95.

Davis, Aidon (Daniel Pienaar THS, Uitenhage) b 29/04/1994, Uitenhage. 1.89m. 102kg. Flank. FC DEBUT: 2013. PROV CAREER: EP Kings 2013-15 19-6-0-0-0-30. SUPERRUGBY: Southern Kings 2013 & 16 10-0-0-0-0-0. REP Honours: SA U20 2013-14 8-2-0-0-0-10. FC RECORD: 37-8-0-0-0-40. RECORD IN 2016: (Southern Kings) 9-0-0-0-0-0.

De Allende, Damian (Milnerton HS) b 25/11/1991, Cape Town. 1.89m. 96kg. Centre. FC DEBUT: 2012. PROV CAREER: WP 2012-13 & 16 25-6-0-0-0-30. SUPERRUGBY: Stormers 2013-16 55-10-0-0-0-50. REP Honours: SA 2014-16 TESTS: 22-3-0-0-0-15. Springboks 2015 1-2-0-0-0-10. Total: 23-5-0-0-0-25. FC RECORD: 103-21-0-0-0-105. RECORD IN 2016: (SA, Stormers, WP) 21-4-0-0-0-20.

De Beer, Christopher Timothy (Hilton College) b 12/04/1994, Westville. 1.86m. 109kg. Hooker. FC DEBUT: 2015. PROV CAREER: Sharks XV 2015-16 4-0-0-0-0-0. FC RECORD: 4-0-0-0-0-0. RECORD IN 2016: (Sharks XV) 1-0-0-0-0-0.

De Beer, Marthinus Herbert (Tinus) (Waterkloof HS, Pretoria) b 24/01/1996, Pretoria. 1.76m. 87kg. Flyhalf. FC DEBUT: 2015. PROV CAREER: Blue Bulls 2015-16 4-0-4-1-0-11. REP Honours: SAU20 2015 4-0-3-0-0-6. FC RECORD: 8-0-7-1-0-17. RECORD IN 2016: (Blue Bulls) 2-0-1-0-0-2.

De Bruin, Christiaan Pieter (Waterkloof HS, Pretoria) b 20/01/1993, Centurion. 1.98m. 107kg. Flank. FC DEBUT: 2014. PROV CAREER: Blue Bulls 2014 4-0-0-0-0-0. Sharks 2015 3-0-0-0-0-0. Sharks XV 2015-16 10-0-0-0-0-0. EP Kings 2016 7-0-0-0-0-0. FC RECORD: 24-0-0-0-0-0. RECORD IN 2016: (EP Kings, Sharks XV) 14-0-0-0-0-0.

De Bruin, Luan (Affies, Pretoria) b 13/02/1993, Pretoria. 1.83m. 124kg. Prop. FC DEBUT: 2013. PROV CAREER: Cheetahs 2014-15 13-0-0-0-0-0. Free State XV 2014-16 9-0-0-0-0-0. SUPERRUGBY: Cheetahs 2014 & 16 9-0-0-0-0-0. REP Honours: SA U20 2013 4-1-0-0-0-5. FC

RECORD: 35-1-0-0-0-5. RECORD IN 2016: (Cheetahs S18, Free State XV) 11-0-0-0-0-0.

De Jager, Erich Estiaan (Brandwag HS, Uitenhage & UFS) b 29/02/1996, Port Elizabeth. 1.86m. 119kg. Prop. FC DEBUT: 2016. PROV CAREER: Free State XV 2016 4-0-0-0-0-0. FC RECORD: 4-0-0-0-0-0. RECORD IN 2016: (Free State XV) 4-0-0-0-0-0.

De Jager, Lodewyk (Huguenote HS, Springs & NWU) b 17/12/1992, Alberton. 2.05m. 118kg. Lock. FC DEBUT: 2013. PROV CAREER: Cheetahs 2013-14 11-0-0-0-0-5. SUPERRUGBY: Cheetahs 2013-16 40-1-0-0-0-5. REP Honours: SA 2014-16 TESTS: 28-4-0-0-0-20. British Barbarians 2015 2-1-0-0-0-5. FC RECORD: 81-6-0-0-0-30. RECORD IN 2016: (SA, Cheetahs S15) 20-0-0-0-0-0.

De Jager, Nicholas John Konrad (Nick) (St John's College, Johannesburg & US) b 07/02/1990, Johannesburg. 1.93m. 111kg. Eighthman. FC DEBUT: 2015. PROV CAREER: Blue Bulls 2015-16 14-2-0-0-0-10. SUPERRUGBY: Bulls 2015-16 19-3-0-0-0-15. FC RECORD: 19-3-0-0-0-15. RECORD IN 2016: (Bulls, Blue Bulls) 18-3-0-0-0-15.

De Jongh, Juan Leon (Huguenot HS, Wellington) b 15/04/1988, Paarl. 1.77m. 85kg. Centre. FC DEBUT: 2009. PROV CAREER: WP 2009-16 58-23-0-0-0-115. SUPERRUGBY: Stormers 2010-16 93-15-0-0-0-75. REP Honours: SA 2009-12 & 16 TESTS: 19-3-0-0-0-15. Tour 2009 2-1-0-0-0-5. Total: 21-4-0-0-0-20. British Barbarians 2014 2-2-0-0-0-10. SA Sevens 2008 & 15-16. MISC INFO: YPoYNominee 2009. FC RECORD: 174-44-0-0-0-220. RECORD IN 2016: (SA, Stormers, WP, SA Sevens) 16-2-0-0-0-10.

De Klerk, Francois (Waterkloof HS, Pretoria) b 19/10/1991, Nelspruit. 1.69m. 66kg. Scrumhalf. FC DEBUT: 2012. PROV CAREER: Pumas 2012-13 & 15 56-4-0-0-0-20. Lions 2016 1-0-0-0-0-0. SUPERRUGBY: Lions 2014-16 49-12-0-0-0-60. REP Honours: SA 2016 TESTS: 11-0-0-0-0-0. FC RECORD: 115-16-0-0-0-80. RECORD IN 2016: (SA, Lions S18, Lions) 29-4-0-0-0-20.

De Klerk, Johannes Cornélis (Jan) (Pietersburg HS, Waterkloof HS, Pretoria & US) b 10/02/1991, Polokwane. 1.98m. 110kg. Lock. FC DEBUT: 2014. PROV CAREER: WP 2014-16 25-3-0-0-0-15. SUPERRUGBY: Stormers 2015-16 2-0-0-0-0-0. FC RECORD: 27-3-0-0-0-15. RECORD IN 2016: (Stormers, WP) 9-2-0-0-0-10.

De Koker, Jovelian (Worcester Gym. & CPUT) b 28/02/1992, Worcester. 74kg. Scrumhalf. FC DEBUT: 2014. PROV CAREER: Boland 2014-16 35-1-0-0-0-5. FC RECORD: 35-1-0-0-0-5. RECORD IN 2016: (Boland) 9-0-0-0-0-0.

De Villiers, Beyers Johannes (Paarl Boys' HS & US) b 06/01/1992, Pretoria. 1.85m. 100kg. Flank. FC DEBUT: 2016. PROV CAREER: WP 2016 7-2-0-0-0-10. FC RECORD: 7-2-0-0-0-10. RECORD IN 2016: (WP) 7-2-0-0-0-10.

De Villiers, Jo-Hanco (Eldoraigne HS, Pretoria & UJ) b 28/04/1996, Bloemfontein. 1.92.00m. 110kg. Eighthman. FC DEBUT: 2016. PROV CAREER: Golden Lions XV 2016 1-1-0-0-0-5. FC RECORD: 1-1-0-0-0-5. RECORD IN 2016: (Golden Lions XV) 1-1-0-0-0-5.

De Villiers, Ruben Christiaan (Paarl Boys" HS) b 22/03/1997, Pretoria. 1.97m. 103kg. Lock. FC DEBUT: 2016. REP Honours: SAU20 2016 5-0-0-0-0-0. FC RECORD: 5-0-0-0-0-0. RECORD IN 2016: (SAU20) 5-0-0-0-0-0.

De Wee, Artur Bobby (Southdowns College, Centurion & UP) b 04/02/1994, Klerksdorp. 1.96m. 95kg. Flank. FC DEBUT: 2014. PROV CAREER: Golden Lions XV 2014-16 20-5-0-0-0-25. Lions 2015-16 6-0-0-0-0-0. FC RECORD: 26-5-0-0-0-25. RECORD IN 2016: (Lions, Golden Lions XV) 13-3-0-0-0-15.

De Wet, Pieter-Steyn (Paarl Gym.) b 08/01/1991, Caledon. 1.75m. 83kg. Flyhalf. FC DEBUT: 2012. PROV CAREER: Cheetahs 2014 4-0-6-1-0-15. Free State XV 2012 & 14 & 16 8-0-7-1-0-17. Griquas 2013 5-0-13-6-1-47. Griffons 2014 & 16 5-0-7-2-0-20. EP Kings 2016 5-0-6-4-1-27. FC RECORD: 27-0-39-14-2-126. RECORD IN 2016: (EP Kings, Griffons, Free State XV) 7-0-8-5-1-34

De Wit, Allen Stephan (Transvalia HS, Vanderbijlpark & UJ) b 01/01/1992, Vereeniging. 1.86m. 104kg. Flank. FC DEBUT: 2012. PROV CAREER: Golden Lions XV 2012 & 14-16 29-11-0-0-0-55. Lions 2015-16 16-2-0-0-0-10. SUPERRUGBY: Lions 2014 & 16 4-0-0-0-0-0. FC RECORD: 49-13-0-0-0-65. RECORD IN 2016: (Lions S18, Lions, Golden Lions XV) 16-1-0-0-0-5.

Deetlefs, Isak Petrus (Noordheuwel HS, Krugersdorp & TUT) b 24/11/1992, Krugersdorp. 2.05m. 115kg. Lock. FC DEBUT: 2015. PROV CAREER: Limpopo 2015 7-0-0-0-0-0. Valke 2015-16 20-0-0-0-0-0. FC RECORD: 27-0-0-0-0-0. RECORD IN 2016: (Valke) 12-0-0-0-0-0.

Dekker, Dewald (Outeniqua HS, George & NWU) b 10/10/1993, Sasolburg. 1.77m. 110kg. Prop. FC DEBUT: 2016. PROV CAREER: Leopards 2016 6-0-0-0-0-0. FC RECORD: 6-0-0-0-0-0. RECORD IN 2016: (Leopards) 6-0-0-0-0-0.

Delo, Layle Antonio (Outeniqua HS, George) b 28/10/1989, George. 1.86m. 115kg. Hooker. FC DEBUT: 2011. PROV CAREER: Eagles 2011-16 64-4-0-0-0-20. FC RECORD: 64-4-0-0-0-20. RECORD IN 2016: (Eagles) 14-2-0-0-0-10.

Demas, Danwel (New Orleans HS, Paarl) b 15/10/1981, Paarl. 1.86m. 79kg. Wing. FC DEBUT: 2004. PROV CAREER: Pumas 2004 & 12-13 19-8-0-0-0-40. Blue Bulls 2005-08 27-8-0-0-0-40. Boland 2008 & 2011 & 14-16 60-43-0-0-0-215. Cheetahs 2009 12-3-0-0-0-15. Cheetahs XV 2010 1-0-0-0-0-0. Griffons 2013 2-1-0-0-0-5. SUPERRUGBY: Bulls 2006 & 08 4-0-0-0-0-0. Cheetahs 2009-10 21-2-0-0-0-10. REP Honours: Emerging Springboks 2009 1-1-0-0-0-5. SA Barbarians 2012 1-0-0-0-0-0. SA Sevens 2003-06. FC RECORD: 148-66-0-0-0-330. RECORD IN 2016: (Boland) 22-10-0-0-0-50.

Deysel, Jean Roy (Hentie Cilliers HS, Virginia) b 05/03/1985, Virginia. 1.92.00m. 103kg. Flank. FC DEBUT: 2005. PROV CAREER: Lions 2005-07 21-1-0-0-0-5. Sharks 2007-13 & 15-16 70-8-0-0-0-40. Sharks XV 2007-08 & 2011-12 8-1-0-0-0-5. Sharks Inv XV 2007,09 2-3-0-0-0-15. SUPERRUGBY: Sharks 2008-16 78-1-0-0-0-5. REP Honours: SA 2009,2011 Tests 4-0-0-0-0-0. Tour: 2009 2-0-0-0-0-0. Total: 6-0-0-0-0-0. Emerging Springboks 2009 1-0-0-0-0-0. SA Students 2007 1-0-0-0-0-0. MISC INFO: Absa CC PoY2008. FC RECORD: 187-14-0-0-0-70. RECORD IN 2016: (Sharks S18, Sharks) 10-1-0-0-0-5.

Deysel, Johan (Windhoek HS & NWU) b 26/09/1991, Windhoek. 1.84m. 92kg. Centre. FC DEBUT: 2014. PROV CAREER: Leopards 2014-16 22-14-29-6-0-146. Leopards XV 2014-15 6-1-0-0-0-5. REP Honours: Namibia RWC 2015. FC RECORD: 28-15-29-6-0-151. RECORD IN 2016: (Leopards) 13-10-29-6-0-126.

Deyzel, Stephan (Brandwag HS, Uitenhage) b 24/04/1992, Uiten-hage. 1.92.00m. 118kg. Eighthman. FC DEBUT: 2016. PROV CAREER: EP Kings 2016 2-0-0-0-0-0. FC RECORD: 2-0-0-0-0-0. RECORD IN 2016: (EP Kings) 2-0-0-0-0-0.

Digue, Juandré Christiaan (Oakdale Agric. HS, Riversdale & NMMU) b 09/05/1995, Somerset-WeSt 1.85m. 109kg. Prop. FC DEBUT: 2015. PROV CAREER: Eagles 2015-16 16-1-0-0-0-5. FC RECORD: 16-1-0-0-0-5. RECORD IN 2016: (Eagles) 6-1-0-0-0-5.

Dippenaar, Stephanus Christiaan (Stephan) (Paul Roos Gym., Stellenbosch) b 03/01/1988, Moorreesburg. 1.88m. 88kg. Centre.

FC DEBUT: 2008. PROV CAREER: Blue Bulls 2008-11 32-6-0-0-0-30. SUPERRUGBY: Bulls 2008 & 10-11 21-1-0-0-0-5. REP Honours: SAU20 2008 2-1-0-0-0-5. SA Sevens 2012-16. FC RECORD: 55-8-0-0-0-40. RECORD IN 2016: (SA Sevens).

Dolo, Maputhla Stephen (Ben Vorster HS, Tzaneen & UFS) b 13/03/1992, Polokwane. 1.78m. 82kg. Fullback. FC DEBUT: 2013. PROV CAREER: Free State XV 2013-16 22-4-0-0-0-20. Cheetahs 2014-16 3-0-0-0-0-0. FC RECORD: 25-4-0-0-0-20. RECORD IN 2016: (Cheetahs, Free State XV) 13-2-0-0-0-10.

Dorfling, Tiaan Arno (Framesby HS & NWU) b 26/07/1990, Port Elizabeth. 1.75m. 80kg. Scrumhalf. FC DEBUT: 2010. PROV CAREER: Leopards 2010 & 12-13 & 15 15-1-1-0-0-7. Leopard XV 2013 4-0-0-0-0-0. Griquas 2016 12-4-0-0-0-20. FC RECORD: 31-5-1-0-0-27. RECORD IN 2016: (Griquas) 12-4-0-0-0-20.

Dreyer, Marthinus Christoffel (Martin) (Wonderboom HS, Pretoria & NWU) b 25/08/1988, Rustenburg. 1.85m. 112kg. Prop. FC DEBUT: 2011. PROV CAREER: Leopards 2011 & 13 13-1-0-0-0-5. Leopard XV 2013 4-0-0-0-0-0. Boland 2014-15 19-1-0-0-0-5. Blue Bulls 2016 10-0-0-0-0-0. SUPERRUGBY: Stormers 2014 5-0-0-0-0-0. REP Honours: SA Univ 2013 1-0-0-0-0-0. SA Pres XV 2013 4-0-0-0-0-0. FC RECORD: 56-2-0-0-0-10. RECORD IN 2016: (Blue Bulls) 10-0-0-0-0-0.

Dreyer, Ruan Martin (Ruan)((Monument HS, Krugersdorp) b 16/09/1990, Carletonville. 1.86m. 113kg. Prop. FC DEBUT: 2010. PROV CAREER: Lions 2012-16 41-4-0-0-0-20. Golden Lions XV 2010-13 18-1-0-0-0-5. SUPERRUGBY: Lions 2012 & 14-16 43-1-0-0-0-5. Lions P/R 2013 2-0-0-0-0-0. REP Honours: SAU20 2010 5-0-0-0-0-0. FC RECORD: 109-6-0-0-0-30. RECORD IN 2016: (Lions S18, Lions) 13-0-0-0-0-0.

Droste, Jean (Affies, Pretoria) b 21/01/1994, Pretoria. 1.90m. 95kg. Lock. FC DEBUT: 2015. PROV CAREER: Sharks XV 2015-16 4-0-0-0-0-0. Sharks 2016 2-0-0-0-0-0. FC RECORD: 6-0-0-0-0-0. RECORD IN 2016: (Sharks, Sharks XV) 5-0-0-0-0-0.

Dry, Christopher Adriaan (Grey College, Bloemfontein & CUT.) b 13/02/1988, Cape Town. 1.91m. 95kg. FC DEBUT: 2009. PROV CAREER: Cheetahs 2009-10 5-0-0-0-0-0. Rep. Honours: SA Sevens 2010-16. FC RECORD: 5-0-0-0-0-0. RECORD IN 2016: (SA Sevens).

Du Plessis, Andrew Terblanche (Grey College, Bloemfontein) b 14/01/1995, Welkom. 1.79m. 104kg. Hooker. FC DEBUT: 2015. PROV CAREER: Shark XV 2015-16 3-0-0-0-0-0. FC RECORD: 3-0-0-0-0-0. RECORD IN 2016: (Sharks XV) 2-0-0-0-0-0.

Du Plessis, Christo John (George HS) b 02/06/1989, George. 1.86m. 92kg. Flank. FC DEBUT: 2010. PROV CAREER: Eagles 2010 & 12-16 82-17-0-0-0-85. FC RECORD: 82-17-0-0-0-85. RECORD IN 2016: (Eagles) 18-6-0-0-0-30.

Du Plessis, Daniel Michael (Paul Roos Gym., Stellenbosch) b 17/03/1995, Port Elizabeth. 1.87m. 97kg. Centre. FC DEBUT: 2015. PROV CAREER: WP 2016 8-4-0-0-0-20. SUPERRUGBY: Stormers 2016 3-1-0-0-0-5. REP Honours: SAU20 2015 5-1-0-0-0-5. MISC INFO: Son of former Springbok Michael du Plessis. FC RECORD: 16-6-0-0-0-30. RECORD IN 2016: (Stormers, WP) 11-5-0-0-0-25.

Du Plessis, Jean-Luc (Paarl Boys' HS & Varsity College) b 07/05/1994, Cape Town. 1.79m. 87kg. Flyhalf. FC DEBUT: 2014. PROV CAREER: Sharks XV 2014 2-1-1-2-0-13. WP 2015 9-0-15-13-0-69. SUPERRUGBY: Stormers 2016 12-2-26-22-0-128. REP Honours: SAU20 2014 2-0-1-0-0-2. MISC INFO: Son of former Springbok Carel du Plessis. FC RECORD: 25-3-43-37-0-212. RECORD IN 2016: (Stormers) 12-2-26-22-0-128.

Du Plessis, Jean-Pierre (JP) (HTS Middelburg) B 06/05/1992,

VolksruSt 1.85m. 105kg. Centre. FC DEBUT: 2012. PROV CAREER: Golden Lions XV 2012-13 3-1-0-0-0-5. Limpopo 2015 2-0-0-0-0-0. Valke 2016 4-0-0-0-0-0. FC RECORD: 9-1-0-0-0-5. RECORD IN 2016: (Valke) 4-0-0-0-0-0.

Du Plessis, Leon Andries (Port Rex HS) b 29/12/1989, East London. 1.87m. 108kg. Flank. FC DEBUT: 2016. PROV CAREER: Leopards 2016 1-1-0-0-0-5. FC RECORD: 1-1-0-0-0-5. RECORD IN 2016: (Leopards) 1-1-0-0-0-5.

Du Plessis, Nico Visser (Florida HS & UJ) b 22/09/1993, Pretoria. 1.86m. 116kg. Prop. FC DEBUT: 2014. PROV CAREER: Golden Lions XV 2014 & 16 8-2-0-0-0-10. FC RECORD: 8-2-0-0-0-10. RECORD IN 2016: (Golden Lions XV) 5-0-0-0-0-0.

Du Plessis, Phillipus Jacobus Snyman (JP) (Paul Roos Gym., Stellenbosch) b 29/04/1991, Kroonstad. 1.84m. 89kg. Centre. FC DEBUT: 2012. PROV CAREER: WP 2012 16-3-0-0-0-15. Cheetahs 2014 10-1-0-0-0-5. Free State XV 2015 4-1-0-0-0-5. EP Kings 2015-16 15-1-0-0-0-5. SUPERRUGBY: Stormers 2012 2-0-0-0-0-0. Southern Kings 2016 8-1-0-0-0-5. MISC INFO: Son of former Transvaal & Eastern Free State utility back Charl du Plessis. FC RECORD: 55-7-0-0-0-35. RECORD IN 2016: (Southern Kings, EP Kings) 13-1-0-0-0-5.

Du Preez, Branco Bewinn Nazeem (PW Botha College, George) b 08/05/1990, George. 1.66m. 72kg. Flyhalf. REP Honours: SAU20 2010 4-1-0-0-0-5. SA Sevens 2010-16. FC RECORD: 4-1-0-0-0-5. RECORD IN 2016: (SA Sevens).

Du Preez, Daniel (Kearsney College, Botha's Hill) b 05/08/1995, Durban. 1.96m. 112kg. Loose Forward. FC DEBUT: 2015. PROV CAREER: Sharks 2015 5-3-0-0-0-15. Sharks XV 2015 3-1-0-0-0-5. SUPERRUGBY: Sharks 2015-16 13-2-0-0-0-10. REP Honours: SAU20 2015 5-2-0-0-0-10. MISC INFO: Son of former Springbok Robert du Preez. Twin brother of Jean-Luc du Preez. Brother of Robert du Preez (jnr). FC RECORD: 26-8-0-0-0-40. RECORD IN 2016: (Sharks S18) 11-2-0-0-0-10.

Du Preez, Hermanus Carel (Noordkaap HS, Kimberley.) b 30/04/1983, Hartswater. 1.98m. 100kg. Eighthman. FC DEBUT: 2013. PROV CAREER: WP 2013-14 10-2-0-0-0-10. REP Honours: SA Sevens 2015-16. FC RECORD: 10-2-0-0-0-10. RECORD IN 2016: (SA Sevens) .

Du Preez, Ivan-John (Brandwag HS, Uitenhage) b 23/06/1994, Port Elizabeth. 1.87m. 94kg. Flank. FC DEBUT: 2014. PROV CAREER: EP Kings 2014 & 16 7-2-0-0-0-10. FC RECORD: 7-2-0-0-0-10. RECORD IN 2016: (EP Kings) 2-0-0-0-0-0.

Du Preez, Jean-Luc (Kearsney College, Botha's Hill) b 05/08/1995, Durban. 1.93m. 110kg. Flank. FC DEBUT: 2014. PROV CAREER: Sharks 2015-16 12-2-0-0-0-10. Sharks XV 2015 4-0-0-0-0-0. SUPERRUGBY: Sharks 2016 13-1-0-0-0-5. REP Honours: SA 2016 TESTS: 1-0-0-0-0-0. Springbok XV 2016 1-0-0-0-0-0. SA A 2016 2-1-0-0-0-5. SAU20 2014-15 8-0-0-0-0-0. MISC INFO: Son of former Springbok Robert du Preez. Twin brother of Daniel du Preez. Brother of Robert du Preez (jnr). FC RECORD: 41-4-0-0-0-20. RECORD IN 2016: (SA, Springbok XV, SA A, Sharks S18, Sharks) 23-4-0-0-0-20.

Du Preez, Jean-Pierre (Dr. EG Jansen HS, Boksburg) b 09/11/1994, Florida. 2.09m. 115kg. Lock. FC DEBUT: 2015. PROV CAREER: Golden Lions XV 2015-16 11-0-0-0-0-0. Lions 2016 4-1-0-0-0-5. SUPER-RUGBY: Lions 2015 1-0-0-0-0-0. FC RECORD: 16-1-0-0-0-5. RECORD IN 2016: (Lions, Golden Lions XV) 7-1-0-0-0-5.

Du Preez, Phillip (Monument HS, Krugersdorp) b 01/08/1993, Roodepoort. 1.99m. 112kg. Lock. FC DEBUT: 2014. PROV CAREER: Free State XV 2014 3-0-0-0-0-0. EP Kings 2016 6-0-0-0-0-0. FC RECORD:

9-0-0-0-0-0. RECORD IN 2016: (EP Kings) 6-0-0-0-0-0.

Du Preez, Robert James (Kearsney College, Botha's Hill) b 30/07/1993, Durban. 1.92.00m. 95kg. Flyhalf. FC DEBUT: 2013. PROV CAREER: WP 2014-16 34-9-69-34-0-285. SUPERRUGBY: Stormers 2015-16 4-1-6-4-0-29. REP Honours: SA U20 2013 4-0-8-4-0-28. British Barbarians 2016 3-0-12-0-0-24. Misc info. Son of former Springbok Robert du Preez (snr). Brother of the twins Daniel and Jean-Luc du Preez. FC RECORD: 45-10-95-42-0-366. RECORD IN 2016: (Stormers, WP, British Barbarians) 20-3-59-21-0-196.

Du Toit, Francois (Florida HS, Roodepoort & UJ) b 17/08/1990, Johannesburg. 1.78m. 103kg. Hooker. FC DEBUT: 2011. PROV CAREER: Lions 2012-13 3-0-0-0-0-0. Golden Lions XV 2011-13 14-3-0-0-0-15. Pumas 2013-16 46-6-0-0-0-30. REP Honours: SA Students 2012 2-0-0-0-0-0. SAU20 2010 4-0-0-0-0-0. FC RECORD: 69-9-0-0-0-45. RECORD IN 2016: (Pumas) 16-4-0-0-0-20.

Du Toit, Francois Cornelius (Franna) (Grey College, Bloemfontein & UFS) b 16/03/1990, Vryburg. 1.83m. 84kg. Flyhalf. FC DEBUT: 2011. PROV CAREER: Cheetahs 2011 1-1-0-0-0-5. Griffons 2013-16 29-1-44-20-0-153. REP Honours: SA Students 2012 2-0-2-1-0-7. FC RECORD: 32-2-46-21-0-165. RECORD IN 2016: (Griffons) 1-0-0-0-0-0.

Du Toit, Johannes Willem (Johan) (Swartland HS, Malmesbury & UKZN) b 08/09/1995, Cape Town. 1.95m. 108kg. Lock. FC DEBUT: 2015. PROV CAREER: Sharks XV 2015-16 9-1-0-0-0-5. FC RECORD: 9-1-0-0-0-5. RECORD IN 2016: (Sharks XV) 6-1-0-0-0-5.

Du Toit, Ockert Jacobus Jacques (Grey College, Bloemfontein & UFS) b 19/11/1993, Bloemfontein. 1.86m. 102kg. Hooker. FC debut: 2013. PROV CAREER: Free State XV 2014-16 11-1-0-0-0-5. Cheetahs 2015-16 19-0-0-0-0-0. SUPERRUGBY: Cheetahs 2016 8-2-0-0-0-10. REP Honours: SA U20 2013 5-1-0-0-0-5. FC RECORD: 43-4-0-0-0-20. RECORD IN 2016: (Cheetahs S18, Cheetahs, Free State XV) 24-3-0-0-0-15.

Du Toit, Ozard Martin (Hottentots Holland HS, Somerset West) b 27/06/1989, Welkom. 1.82.00m. 80kg. Fullback. FC DEBUT: 2012. PROV CAREER: Eagles 2012-16 68-16-0-0-0-80. FC RECORD: 68-16-0-0-0-80. RECORD IN 2016: (Eagles) 12-7-0-0-0-35.

Du Toit, Pieter Stephanus (Swartland HS, Malmesbury) b 20/08/1992, Cape Town. 2.00m. 115kg. Lock. FC DEBUT: 2012. PROV CAREER: Sharks XV 2012 5-1-0-0-0-5. Sharks 2013 5-0-0-0-0-0. SUPERRUGBY: Sharks 2012-15 27-0-0-0-0-0. Stormers 2016 14-3-0-0-0-15. REP Honours: SA 2013 & 15-16 TESTS: 20-3-0-0-0-15. Springbok XV 2016 1-1-0-0-0-5. SAU20 2012 5-1-0-0-0-5. MISC INFO: SA Rugby Player of the Year in 2016. FC RECORD: 77-9-0-0-0-45. RECORD IN 2016: (SA, Springbok XV, Stormers) 27-7-0-0-0-35.

Du Toit, Thomas Joubert (Paarl Boys' HS) b 05/05/1995, Cape Town. 1.89m. 130kg. Prop. FC DEBUT: 2014. PROV CAREER: Sharks 2014-16 25-2-0-0-0-10. Sharks XV 2014-16 10-2-0-0-0-10. SUPERRUGBY: Sharks 2014-16 20-2-0-0-0-10. REP Honours: SA A 2016 2-0-0-0-0-0. SAU20 2014-15 9-2-0-0-0-10. British Barbarians 2014-15 4-1-0-0-0-5. FC RECORD: 70-9-0-0-0-45. RECORD IN 2016: (SA A, Sharks S18, Sharks, Sharks XV) 21-2-0-0-0-10.

Dubase, Onke Sydwell (Hudson Park HS, East London & UFH) b 06/08/1989, East London. 1.80m. 94kg. Flank. FC DEBUT: 2010. PROV CAREER: Bulldogs 2010-11 & 14-16 50-7-0-0-0-35. FC RECORD: 50-7-0-0-0-35. RECORD IN 2016: (Bulldogs) 8-3-0-0-0-15.

Dukisa, Ntabeni (Loyolo HS) b 25/07/1988. Wing. FC DEBUT: 2010. PROV CAREER: Bulldogs 2010-12 26-5-19-34-0-165. Griffons 2012 5-0-0-0-0-0. EP Kings 2013-14 32-6-17-14-1-109. Griquas 2015-16

29-13-4-5-0-88. REP Honours: SA Barbarians 2012 1-1-0-0-0-5. FC RECORD: 93-25-40-53-1-367. RECORD IN 2016: (Griquas) 10-4-2-0-0-24.

Dumezweni, Lunga (Hector Peterson HS, Kraaifontein & Walter Sisulu Univ. & UFH) b 20/06/1987, King William's Town. 1.80m. 92kg. Centre. FC DEBUT: 2011. PROV CAREER: Bulldogs 2011 & 16 17-3-0-0-0-15. FC RECORD: 17-3-0-0-0-15. RECORD IN 2016: (Bulldogs) 15-3-0-0-0-15.

Dumond, Cecil (Orkney HS) b 08/04/1987, Klerksdorp. 1.82.00m. 84kg. Flyhalf. FC DEBUT: 2007. PROV CAREER: Leopards 2007 & 09-11 & 16 28-2-18-29-2-139. Eagles 2011-12 13-1-1-4-0-19. Bulldogs 2013 7-0-2-1-0-7. Valke 2014 9-1-2-4-0-21. MISC INFO: Brother of Monty Dumond. FC RECORD: 57-4-23-38-1-186. RECORD IN 2016: (Leopards) 2-0-0-0-0-0.

Dutton, Billy (Cambridge HS) b 09/06/1989, Transkei. 1.85m. 93kg. Flank. FC DEBUT: 2010. PROV CAREER: Bulldogs 2010-11 & 15-16 30-1-0-0-0-5. FC RECORD: 30-1-0-0-0-5. RECORD IN 2016: (Bulldogs) 15-1-0-0-0-5.

Duvenage, Dewaldt Otto (Paarl Gym.) b 22/05/1988, Bellville. 1.76m. 75kg. Scrumhalf. FC DEBUT: 2007. PROV CAREER: Boland 2007-08 24-3-0-0-0-15. WP 2008-12 & 16 56-6-2-1-0-37. SUPER-RUGBY: Stormers 2009-13 67-2-4-4-0-30. REP Honours: SAU20 2008 4-0-0-0-0-0. FC RECORD: 151-11-6-5-0-82. RECORD IN 2016: (WP) 5-1-0-0-0-5.

Dweba, Joseph (Florida HS, Roodepoort & HTS Louis Botha, Bloemfontein) b 25/10/1995, Carletonville. 1.72.00m. 103kg. Hooker. FC DEBUT: 2014. PROV CAREER: Free State XV 2015-16 13-6-0-0-0-30. Cheetahs 2016 1-0-0-0-0-0. SUPERRUGBY: Cheetahs 2016 3-0-0-0-0-0. REP Honours: SAU20 2014-15 6-0-0-0-0-0. FC RECORD: 23-6-0-0-0-30. RECORD IN 2016: (Cheetahs S18, Cheetahs, Free State XV) 13-6-0-0-0-30.

Dyantyi, Mzoxolo (Willie) (Kwezi Lomso HS, Port Elizabeth) b 10/10/1985, Port Elizabeth. 1.65m. 75kg. Scrumhalf. FC DEBUT: 2006. PROV CAREER: Griffons 2006 11-0-0-0-0-0. Eagles 2007-09 & 2011-16 78-8-0-0-0-40. FC RECORD: 89-8-0-0-0-40. RECORD IN 2016: (Eagles) 11-0-0-0-0-0.

Dyantyi, Aphiwe Odwa (Dale College, King William's Town & UJ) b 26/08/1994, East London. 1.82.00m. 87kg. Wing. FC DEBUT: 2016. PROV CAREER: Golden Lions XV 2016 1-0-0-0-0-0. FC RECORD: 1-0-0-0-0-0. RECORD IN 2016: (Golden Lions XV) 1-0-0-0-0-0.

Ebersohn, Josias Mathiem (Sias) (Grey College, Bloemfontein) b 23/02/1989, Bloemfontein. 1.75m. 81kg. Flyhalf. FC DEBUT: 2008. PROV CAREER: Cheetahs 2008-12 & 15-16 67-6-56-26-5-235. Cheetahs XV 2010 1-0-0-0-0-0. Free State XV 2016 10-1-26-6-0-75. SUPERRUGBY: Cheetahs 2010-12 & 16 31-2-36-44-2-220. REP Honours: SAU20 2008-09 6-4-16-4-2-70. MISC INFO: Twin brother of Robert Ebersohn. FC RECORD: 115-13-134-80-9-600. RECORD IN 2016: (Cheetahs S18, Cheetahs, Free State XV) 12-1-26-6-0-75.

Eksteen, Alrin Edgar (Robertson HS & Varsity College) b 12/04/1994, Robertson. 1.88m. 96kg. Fullback. FC DEBUT: 2016. PROV CAREER: Sharks XV 2016 12-2-0-0-0-10. FC RECORD: 12-2-0-0-0-10. RECORD IN 2016: (Sharks XV) 12-2-0-0-0-10.

Eksteen, Leighton (Outeniqua HS, George) b 15/09/1994, Riversdale. 1.70m. 70kg. Flyhalf. FC DEBUT: 2014. PROV CAREER: Eagles 2014-16 33-8-19-21-0-141. SUPERRUGBY: Southern Kings 2016 5-0-0-0-0-0. FC RECORD: 38-8-19-21-0-141. RECORD IN 2016: (Southern

Kings, Eagles) 12-3-3-1-0-24.

Elder, Kelvin (Maritzburg College & Varsity College) b 20/01/1995, Amanzimtoti. 1.85m. 89kg. Fullback. FC DEBUT: 2016. PROV CAREER: Sharks XV 2016 4-0-0-0-0-0. FC RECORD: 4-0-0-0-0-0. RECORD IN 2016: (Sharks XV) 4-0-0-0-0-0.

Els, Cornelius Wilhelmus (Corniel) (Grey College, Bloemfontein) b 19/01/1994, Polokwane. 1.83m. 102kg. Hooker. FC DEBUT: 2014. PROV CAREER: Blue Bulls 2015-16 17-4-0-0-0-20. REP Honours: SAU20 2014 4-1-0-0-0-5. FC RECORD: 21-5-0-0-0-25. RECORD IN 2016: (Blue Bulls) 7-2-0-0-0-10.

Els, Heinrich (Jim Fouche HS, Bloemfontein & UP) b 25/03/1992, Bloemfontein. 1.89m. 118kg. Prop. FC DEBUT: 2015. PROV CAREER: Limpopo 2015 7-1-0-0-0-5. Valke 2016 1-0-0-0-0-0. FC RECORD: 8-1-0-0-0-5. RECORD IN 2016: (Valke) 1-0-0-0-0-0.

Elstadt, Rynhardt (Montagu HS) b 02/12/1989, Johannesburg. 1.98m. 112kg. Lock. FC DEBUT: 2010. PROV CAREER: WP 2010 & 12-16 46-4-0-0-0-20. SUPERRUGBY: Stormers 2011-16 52-0-0-0-0-0. REP Honours: SAU20 2009 3-0-0-0-0-0. FC RECORD: 101-4-0-0-0-20. RECORD IN 2016: (Stormers, WP) 17-0-0-0-0-0.

Engelbrecht, Gabriel Joubert (Upington HS & NWU) b 27/06/1989, Kimberley. 1.89m. 90kg. Centre. FC DEBUT: 2010. PROV CAREER: Leopards 2010-12 36-14-0-0-0-70. Griffons 2013-14 & 16 25-2-5-1-0-23. Cheetahs 2013-14 10-1-0-0-0-5. Free State XV 2013-15 19-7-0-0-0-35. SUPERRUGBY: Cheetahs 2016 1-0-0-0-0-0. REP Honours: SA Students 2012 1-0-0-0-0-0. SA Barbarians 2012 1-1-0-0-0-5. FC RECORD: 93-25-5-1-0-138. RECORD IN 2016: (Cheetahs S18, Griffons) 12-0-0-0-0-0.

Engelbrecht, Gerhardus Petrus (Affies, Pretoria & UP) b 30/05/1991, Pretoria. 1.90m. 118kg. Prop. FC DEBUT: 2014. PROV CAREER: Valke 2014 3-0-0-0-0-0. Sharks 2015 9-0-0-0-0-0. Sharks XV 2016 11-1-0-0-0-5. Griffons 2016 7-0-0-0-0-0. FC RECORD: 30-1-0-0-0-5. RECORD IN 2016: (Griffons, Sharks XV) 18-1-0-0-0-5.

Engelbrecht, Jacques Jacobus (Monument HS, Krugersdorp) b 10/06/1985, Cape Town. 1.94m. 105kg. Flank. FC DEBUT: 2007. PROV CAREER: WP 2007-08 2-0-0-0-0-0. Eagles 2008-10 48-3-0-0-0-15. EP Kings 2011-12 & 15-16 35-5-0-0-0-25. Blue Bulls 2013-15 21-0-0-0-0-0. Boland 2016 7-1-0-0-0-5. SUPERRUGBY: Southern Kings 2013 & 16 25-1-0-0-0-5. P/R 2013 2-0-0-0-0-0. Bulls 2014 13-0-0-0-0-0. REP Honours: SA Kings 2011 2-0-0-0-0-0. SA Barbarians 2012 1-1-0-0-0-5. SA Sevens 2010-11. FC RECORD: 156-11-0-0-0-55. RECORD IN 2016: (Southern Kings, EP Kings, Boland) 21-1-0-0-0-5.

Engelbrecht, Wilneth Renaldo b 29/05/1993. Centre. FC DEBUT: 2015. PROV CAREER: Boland 2015 13-4-0-0-0-20. Eagles 2016 13-1-0-0-0-5. FC RECORD: 26-5-0-0-0-25. RECORD IN 2016: (Eagles) 13-1-0-0-0-5.

Engledoe, Damien Courtney (New Orleans HS, Paarl) b 07/03/1993, Paarl. 1.72.00m. 63kg. Wing/Fullback. FC DEBUT: 2013. PROV CAREER: Golden Lions XV 2013 & 15 8-2-2-0-0-14. Leopards 2015 11-4-0-0-0-20. Valke 2016 13-1-1-0-0-7. FC RECORD: 32-7-3-0-0-41. RECORD IN 2016: (Valke) 13-1-1-0-0-7.

Enslin, Jan-Frederik (Grey HS, Bloemfontein & UP) b 06/10/1993, Port Elizabeth. 1.87m. 110kg. Prop. FC DEBUT: 2015. PROV CAREER: Blue Bulls 2015 1-0-0-0-0-0. Valke 2016 4-1-0-0-0-5. FC RECORD: 5-1-0-0-0-5. RECORD IN 2016: (Valke) 4-1-0-0-0-5.

Erasmus, Albertus Bernardus (Waterkloof HS & UFS) b 15/03/1995, Pretoria. 1.91m. 104kg. Flank. FC DEBUT: 2016. PROV CAREER: Free State XV 2016 2-1-0-0-0-5. FC RECORD: 2-1-0-0-0-5.

RECORD IN 2016: (Free State XV) 2-1-0-0-0-5.

Erasmus, Lourens Jacobus (Garsfontein HS, Pretoria & UJ) b 14/06/1993, Pretoria. 2.00m. 105kg. Lock. FC DEBUT: 2014. PROV CAREER: Golden Lions XV 2014-16 17-6-0-0-0-30. Lions 2015-16 11-4-0-0-0-20. SUPERRUGBY: Lions 2016 8-2-0-0-0-10. FC RECORD: 36-12-0-0-0-60. RECORD IN 2016: (Lions S18, Lions, Golden Lions XV) 17-7-0-0-0-35.

Erwee, Reinhardt (Jim Fouche HS, Bloemfontein & UFS) b 20/01/1988, Bloemfontein. 1.81m. 85kg. Flyhalf. FC DEBUT: 2011. PROV CAREER: Griffons 2011-13 & 16 26-6-20-12-0-106. Boland 2013 3-0-0-0-0-0. Free State XV 2015-16 14-6-0-0-0-30. FC RECORD: 43-12-20-12-0-136. RECORD IN 2016: (Griffons, Free State XV) 15-8-0-0-0-40.

Esterhuizen, Adriaan Pieter (Andre) (Klerksdorp HS) b 30/03/1994, Potchefstroom. 1.91m. 106kg. Centre. FC DEBUT: 2013. PROV CAREER: Sharks XV 2013-14 9-2-0-0-0-10. Sharks 2014-16 24-10-0-0-0-50. SUPERRUGBY: Sharks 2014-16 29-2-0-0-0-10. REP Honours: SAU20 2014 4-2-0-0-0-10. FC RECORD: 66-16-0-0-0-80. RECORD IN 2016: (Sharks S18, Sharks) 23-6-0-0-0-30.

Esterhuizen, Riaan Etienne (Brandwag HS, Uitenhage & NMMU) b 08/08/1994, Stellenbosch. 1.84m. 94kg. Centre. FC DEBUT: 2016. PROV CAREER: EP Kings 2016 4-0-0-0-0-0. FC RECORD: 4-0-0-0-0-0. RECORD IN 2016: (EP Kings) 4-0-0-0-0-0.

Esterhuyzen, Francois (Overberg & Tygerberg HS) b 16/11/1994, Somerset WeSt 1.87m, 104kg. Hooker. FC DEBUT: 2016. PROV CAREER: Boland 2016 10-0-0-0-0-0. FC RECORD: 10-0-0-0-0-0. RECORD IN 2016: (Boland) 10-0-0-0-0-0.

Etzebeth, Eben (Tygerberg HS, Cape Town) b 29/10/1991, Cape Town. 2.03m. 117kg. Lock. FC DEBUT: 2012. PROV CAREER: WP 2012-14 7-0-0-0-0-0. SUPERRUGBY: Stormers 2012-13 & 15-16 42-4-0-0-0-20. REP Honours: SA 2012-16 TESTS: 54-2-0-0-0-10. Springboks 2015 1-1-0-0-0-5. Total: 55-3-0-0-0-15. Springbok XV 2016 1-0-0-0-0-0. SAU20 2011 5-1-0-0-0-5. MISC INFO: SARU PoY2012 nominee. YPoY2012. Super PoY2012 nominee, SARU PoYnominee 2016. FC RECORD: 110-7-0-0-0-35. RECORD IN 2016: (SA, Springbok XV, Stormers) 21-2-0-0-0-10.

Faas, Chuma Sean Kenosi (Grey HS, Port Elizabeth & UJ) b 22/01/1990, Port Elizabeth. 1.69m. 74kg. Scrumhalf. FC DEBUT: 2016. PROV CAREER: EP Kings 2016 4-0-0-0-0-0. FC RECORD: 4-0-0-0-0-0. RECORD IN 2016: (EP Kings) 4-0-0-0-0-0.

Ferreira, Andries Stephanus (Affies, Pretoria & TUT) b 29/03/1990, Despatch. 1.97m. 117kg. Lock. FC DEBUT: 2012. PROV CAREER: Cheetahs 2012 3-1-0-0-0-5. Griffons 2013 1-0-0-0-0-0. Free State XV 2013 3-0-0-0-0-0. Lions 2016 2-0-0-0-0-0. Golden Lions XV 2016 1-0-0-0-0-0. SUPERRUGBY: Cheetahs 2012 & 14 20-1-0-0-0-5. Lions 2015-16 22-1-0-0-0-5. FC RECORD: 52-3-0-0-0-15. RECORD IN 2016: (Lions S18, Lions, Golden Lions XV) 18-1-0-0-0-5.

Ferreira, Martin (Grey HS, PE & NMMU & UFS) b 24/01/1989, Port Elizabeth. 1.88m. 115kg. Hooker. FC DEBUT: 2011. PROV CAREER: Eagles 2011 & 13 22-6-0-0-0-30. EP Kings 2014-15 16-0-0-0-0-0. Bulldogs 2014 1-0-0-0-0-0. WP 2016 1-0-0-0-0-0. SUPERRUGBY: Southern Kings 2016 9-0-0-0-0-0. REP Honours: SA Univ 2013 1-2-0-0-0-10. FC RECORD: 50-8-0-0-0-40. RECORD IN 2016: (Southern Kings, WP) 10-0-0-0-0-0.

Ferreira, Schalk Jakobus Petrus (Paul Roos Gym., Stellenbosch) b 09/02/1984, Pretoria. 1.88m. 107kg. Prop. FC DEBUT: 2004. PROV

CAREER: WP 2005-09 & 12 58-2-0-0-0-10. Boland 2009 1-0-0-0-0-0.
EP Kings 2012 & 15-16 22-1-0-0-0-5. SUPERRUGBY: Stormers 2007-
09 16-0-0-0-0-0. Southern Kings 2013 & 16 27-3-0-0-0-15. P/R 2013
2-1-0-0-0-5. REP Honours: SA U21 2004 3-0-0-0-0-0. SA U19 2003.
SA Schools 2002. CW WP 2002. FC RECORD: 129-7-0-0-0-35. RECORD
IN 2016: (Southern Kings, EP Kings) 13-2-0-0-0-10.

Ferreira, Sebastian Roche (Paarl Boys' HS) b 10/02/1994, Cape
Town. 1.94m. 110kg. Lock. FC DEBUT: 2016. PROV CAREER: EP Kings
2016 7-0-0-0-0-0. FC RECORD: 7-0-0-0-0-0. RECORD IN 2016: (EP
Kings) 7-0-0-0-0-0.

Fick, Jacques (Huguenote HS, Springs & UJ) b 29/03/1994, Springs.
1.90m. 91kg. Scrumhalf. FC DEBUT: 2016. PROV CAREER: EP Kings 2016
2-0-0-0-0-0. FC RECORD: 2-0-0-0-0-0. RECORD IN 2016: (EP Kings)
2-0-0-0-0-0.

Fihlani, Lwazi Samora (Lumnko HS) b 14/05/1985, East London.
1.98m. 104kg. Lock. FC DEBUT: 2008. PROV CAREER: Bulldogs 2008-12
61-5-0-0-0-25. Griffons 2012 & 16 21-0-0-0-0-0. EP Kings 2013
17-3-0-0-0-15. REP Honours: SA Barbarians 2012 1-0-0-0-0-0. FC
RECORD: 100-8-0-0-0-40. RECORD IN 2016: (Griffons) 14-0-0-0-0-0.

Fisher, Tyler Luke (Westville Boys' HS) b 19/11/1993, Westville.
1.89m. 93kg. Centre. FC DEBUT: 2013. PROV CAREER: Sharks XV 2013
& 15 9-3-0-0-0-15. Leopards 2015 10-7-0-0-0-35. Pumas 2016 15-
6-0-0-0-30. FC RECORD: 34-16-0-0-0-80. RECORD IN 2016: (Pumas)
15-6-0-0-0-30.

Fortuin, Aston Brad (Southdowns College & UP) b 16/04/1996,
Cape Town. 1.97m. 114kg. Lock. FC DEBUT: 2016. PROV CAREER: Blue
Bulls 2016 9-0-0-0-0-0. FC RECORD: 9-0-0-0-0-0. RECORD IN 2016:
(Blue Bulls) 9-0-0-0-0-0.

Forwood, Justin (Waterkloof HS & UP) b 19/09/1993, Pretoria.
1.92.00m. 125kg. Prop. FC DEBUT: 2015. PROV CAREER: Blue Bulls
2015-16 2-0-0-0-0-0. EP Kings 2016 6-0-0-0-0-0. FC RECORD: 8-0-0-
0-0-0. RECORD IN 2016: (Blue Bulls, EP Kings) 7-0-0-0-0-0.

Fouche, Johan Neethling (Rustenburg HS, Grey College, Bloemfontein & UP) b 10/01/1993, Rustenburg. 1.87m. 114kg. Prop. FC DEBUT:
2014. PROV CAREER: Blue Bulls 2014 & 16 3-0-0-0-0-0. FC RECORD:
3-0-0-0-0-0. RECORD IN 2016: (Blue Bulls) 2-0-0-0-0-0.

Fouche, Louis Daniel van Zyl (Rustenburg HS) b 04/01/1990,
Pretoria. 1.86m. 92kg. Flyhalf. FC DEBUT: 2011. PROV CAREER: Blue
Bulls 2011-12 & 14-15 36-3-50-70-5-340. SUPERRUGBY: Bulls
2012-14 23-2-5-8-1-47. Southern Kings 2016 14-1-17-14-0-81.
FC RECORD: 73-6-72-92-6-468. RECORD IN 2016: (Southern Kings)
14-1-17-14-0-81.

Fourie, Corné (Waterkloof HS, Pretoria) b 02/09/1988, Roodepoort.
1.87m. 116kg. Prop. FC DEBUT: 2010. PROV CAREER: Blue Bulls 2010-11
16-3-0-0-0-15. Pumas 2015-12 72-6-0-0-0-30. Lions 2016 5-1-0-0-
0-5. Golden Lions XV 2016 2-0-0-0-0-0. SUPERRUGBY: Lions 2014-16
40-3-0-0-0-15. REP Honours: SA Barbarians 2012 1-0-0-0-0-0. SAU20
2008 4-0-0-0-0-0. FC RECORD: 140-13-0-0-0-65. RECORD IN 2016:
(Lions S18, Lions, Golden Lions XV) 24-3-0-0-0-15.

Fourie, Marius (Outeniqua HS, George & NWU) b 15/10/1990, Cape
Town. 1.83m. 108kg. Hooker. FC DEBUT: 2011. PROV CAREER: Leopards
2011-12 & 14 30-2-0-0-0-10. WP 2015 2-0-0-0-0-0. Eagles 2015 18-
0-0-0-0-0. Griquas 2016 19-1-0-0-0-5. FC RECORD: 69-3-0-0-0-15.
RECORD IN 2016: (Griquas) 19-1-0-0-0-5.

Francke, Jonathan Charles (Strand HS, Cape Town & Boland
College) b 17/05/1986, Strand. 1.80m. 92kg. Fullback. FC DEBUT: 2011.
PROV CAREER: Boland 2011-13 55-16-0-0-0-80. Griquas 2013-16

62-13-0-0-0-65. FC RECORD: 117-29-0-0-0-145. RECORD IN 2016:
(Griquas) 17-6-0-0-0-30.

Fraser, Jason-Collin (Sutherland HS) b 15/04/1991, Amanzimtoti.
1.96m. 100kg. Eighthman. FC DEBUT: 2014. PROV CAREER: Boland
2014 8-0-0-0-0-0. Pumas 2015 18-3-0-0-0-15. Griquas 2016 21-
6-0-0-0-30. FC RECORD: 47-9-0-0-0-45. RECORD IN 2016: (Griquas)
21-6-0-0-0-30.

Fuzani, Mthetheleli Godfrey (Bellville HS) b 18/01/1991,
Uitenhage. 1.97m. 118kg. Lock. FC DEBUT: 2013. PROV CAREER: WP
2013-14 15-0-0-0-0-0. EP Kings 2015-16 21-1-0-0-0-5. FC RECORD:
36-1-0-0-0-5. RECORD IN 2016: (EP Kings) 15-1-0-0-0-5.

Gans, Stedman-Ghee Rivett (Waterkloof HS, Pretoria & UP) b
19/03/1997, Vredenburg. 1.80m. 85kg. Centre. FC DEBUT: 2016. REP
Honours: SAU20 2016 1-0-0-0-0-0. FC RECORD: 1-0-0-0-0-0. RECORD
IN 2016: (SAU20) 1-0-0-0-0-0.

Gates, Shane Edward (Muir College, Uitenhage & Boys' HS) b
27/09/1993, Port Elizabeth. 1.82.00m. 91kg. Flyhalf. FC DEBUT: 2011.
PROV CAREER: EP Kings 2012-15 24-7-0-0-0-35. SUPERRUGBY:
Southern Kings 2013 & 16 19-1-0-0-0-5. P/R 2013 2-0-0-0-0-0. REP
Honours: SA Kings 2011 1-0-0-0-0-0. FC RECORD: 46-8-0-0-0-40.
RECORD IN 2016: (Southern Kings) 14-1-0-0-0-5.

Gavor, Selom (Rondebosch HS) b 18/09/1993. 1.92.00m. 90kg. Wing.
FC DEBUT: 2014. PROV CAREER: Golden Lions XV 2014-16 19-8-0-
0-0-40. Lions 2015-16 4-2-0-0-0-10. FC RECORD: 23-10-0-0-0-50.
RECORD IN 2016: (Lions, Golden Lions XV) 15-7-0-0-0-35.

Geduld, Justin Gilberto (Tygerberg HS, Cape Town) b 01/10/1993,
Cape Town. 1.75m. 70kg. Centre. FC DEBUT: 2013. PROV CAREER: WP
2014 4-2-0-0-0-10. REP Honours: SA U20 2013 3-2-0-0-0-10. SA
Sevens 2013-16. FC RECORD: 7-4-0-0-0-20. RECORD IN 2016: (SA
Sevens).

Gelant, Warrick Wayne (Outeniqua HS, George) b 20/05/1995,
Knysna. 1.79m. 86kg. Fullback. FC DEBUT: 2014. PROV CAREER: Blue
Bulls 2015-16 16-3-0-0-0-15. SUPERRUGBY: Bulls 2016 4-1-0-0-0-5.
REP Honours: SAU20 2014-15 10-2-0-0-0-10. FC RECORD: 30-6-0-0-
0-30. RECORD IN 2016: (Bulls, Blue Bulls) 5-1-0-0-0-5.

Geldenhuys, Graham Henri (Rondebosch Boys' HS) b 09/08/1995,
Cape Town. 1.91m. 108kg. Eighthman. FC DEBUT: 2016. PROV CAREER:
Sharks XV 2016 2-0-0-0-0-0. FC RECORD: 2-0-0-0-0-0. RECORD IN
2016: (Sharks XV) 2-0-0-0-0-0.

Gemashe, Ndzondelelo (Khalile HS & Walter Sisulu Univ.) b
02/07/1991, King William's Town. 1.93m. 100kg. Flank. FC DEBUT:
2016. PROV CAREER: Bulldogs 2016 1-1-0-0-0-5. FC RECORD: 1-1-0-0-
0-5. RECORD IN 2016: (Bulldogs) 1-1-0-0-0-5.

Genade, Jacobus Cornelius (JC) (Augsberg Agric. HS, Clanwilliam)
b 09/06/1995, Durbanville. 1.82.00m. 115kg. Hooker. FC DEBUT: 2015.
PROV CAREER: Boland 2015-15 8-1-0-0-0-5. FC RECORD: 8-1-0-0-0-5.
RECORD IN 2016: (Boland) 5-1-0-0-0-5.

Goosen, Johannes Lodewikus (Johan) (Grey College, Bloemfontein)
b 27/07/1992, Burgersdorp. 1.85m. 85kg. Flyhalf. FC DEBUT: 2011.
PROV CAREER: Cheetahs 2011-13 17-2-3-26-3-143. Emerging
Cheetahs 2011 1-0-0-0-0-0. SUPERRUGBY: Cheetahs 2012-14 27-4-
46-70-3-331. REP Honours: SA 2012 & 14 & 16 TESTS: 13-3-2-2-0-25.
SAU20 2011 5-0-23-10-1-79. Springbok XV 2014 1-1-2-0-0-9. MISC
INFO: YPoY2011 and 2012 nominee. FC RECORD: 64-10-96-108-7-587.
RECORD IN 2016: (SA) 7-3-1-0-0-17

Gordon, Dean (St John's College, Johannesburg & UJ) b 21/01/1993,

Kempton Park. 1.85m. 95kg. Wing. FC DEBUT: 2015. PROV CAREER: Limpopo 2015 6-1-0-0-0-5. Leopards 2016 3-3-0-0-0-15. FC RECORD: 9-4-0-0-0-20. RECORD IN 2016: (Leopards) 3-3-0-0-0-15.

Gordon, Lorenzo Trevor Isaac (Oakdale Agric. HS, Riversdale & UFS) b 19/05/1995, Tygerberg. 1.83m. 83kg. Wing. FC DEBUT: 2015. PROV CAREER: Free State XV 2015-16 11-2-0-0-0-10. FC RECORD: 11-2-0-0-0-10. RECORD IN 2016: (Free State XV) 9-2-0-0-0-10.

Gosa, Lungelo (Selborne College, East London) b 31/01/1995, King William's Town. 1.78m. 80kg. Flyhalf. FC DEBUT: 2016. PROV CAREER: EP Kings 2016 7-0-3-1-0-9. FC RECORD: 7-0-3-1-0-9. RECORD IN 2016: (EP Kings) 7-0-3-1-0-9.

Gouws, Rowan Petrus Christiaan (HTS Middelburg & UKZN) b 06/08/1995, Richards Bay. 1.77m. 80kg. Scrumhalf. FC DEBUT: 2016. PROV CAREER: Sharks XV 2016 1-0-0-0-0-0. FC RECORD: 1-0-0-0-0-0. RECORD IN 2016: (Sharks XV) 1-0-0-0-0-0.

Gqoboka, Lizo Pumzile (Ntabankuku HS, Butterworth) b 24/03/1990, Mount Frere. 1.83m. 115kg. Prop. FC DEBUT: 2012. PROV CAREER: EP Kings 2012-15 58-4-0-0-0-20. Blue Bulls 2016 6-1-0-0-0-5. SUPERRUGBY: Bulls 2016 12-0-0-0-0-0. REP Honours: Springbok XV 2016 1-0-0-0-0-0. SA A 2016 2-0-0-0-0-0. FC RECORD: 79-5-0-0-0-25. RECORD IN 2016: (Springbok XV, SA A, Bulls, Blue Bulls) 21-1-0-0-0-5.

Graaff, Johannes Petrus Jacobus (Hansie) (Wonderboom HS, Pretoria & TUT) b 10/09/1989, Pretoria. 1.90m. 94kg. Wing/Fullback. FC DEBUT: 2012. PROV CAREER: Griffons 2012-13 27-7-46-15-2-178. Sharks XV 2014 2-1-0-0-0-5. EP Kings 2014-15 9-1-3-2-0-17. Bulldogs 2014 1-0-1-1-0-5. Eagles 2016 16-0-28-16-0-104. MISC INFO: CC First Div PoY 2012. FC RECORD: 55-9-78-34-2-309. RECORD IN 2016: (Eagles) 16-0-28-16-0-104.

Grassmann, Wynand (Despatch HS & NMMU) b 19/01/1995, Port Elizabeth. 1.93m. 104kg. Lock. FC DEBUT: 2016. PROV CAREER: EP Kings 2016 2-0-0-0-0-0. FC RECORD: 2-0-0-0-0-0. RECORD IN 2016: (EP Kings) 2-0-0-0-0-0.

Greeff, Carel Fredrick Kirstein (Schoonspruit HS, Malmesbury) b 20/05/1990, Klerksdorp. 1.83m. 99kg. Flank. FC DEBUT: 2011. PROV CAREER: Golden Lions XV 2011 1-0-0-0-0-0. Griquas 2013-15 50-32-0-0-0-160. Pumas 2016 19-4-0-0-0-20. SUPERRUGBY: Cheetahs 2014-15 6-2-0-0-0-10. FC RECORD: 76-38-0-0-0-190. RECORD IN 2016: (Pumas) 19-4-0-0-0-20.

Greeff, Lloyd Dirk (Transvalia HS, Vanderbijlpark & NWU) b 03/01/1994, Vanderbijlpark. 1.93m. 103kg. Wing. FC DEBUT: 2014. PROV CAREER: Golden Lions XV 2016 1-0-0-0-0-0. REP Honours: SAU20 2014 3-3-0-0-0-15. FC RECORD: 4-3-0-0-0-15. RECORD IN 2016: (Golden Lions V) 1-0-0-0-0-0.

Greeff, Stephan (Gill College, Somerset East) b 24/12/1989, Cape Town. 1.98m. 103kg. Lock. FC DEBUT: 2010. PROV CAREER: WP 2010-11 6-0-0-0-0-0. Lions 2013 2-0-0-0-0-0. Golden Lions XV 2012-13 2-0-0-0-0-0. Leopards 2013 2-0-0-0-0-0. Griquas 2014-15 23-0-0-0-0-0. Pumas 2016 16-0-0-0-0-0. SUPERRUGBY: Lions 2012 5-0-0-0-0-0. FC RECORD: 56-0-0-0-0-0. RECORD IN 2016: (Pumas) 16-0-0-0-0-0.

Grey, Siyanda (Hlumani HS, Komga) b 16/08/1989, Komga. 1.79m. 79kg. Centre. FC DEBUT: 2010. PROV CAREER: EP Kings 2010-15 46-17-0-0-0-85. SUPERRUGBY: Southern Kings 2013 & 16 5-0-0-0-0-0. REP Honours: SA Kings 2011 3-6-0-0-0-30. FC RECORD: 54-23-0-0-0-115. RECORD IN 2016: (Southern Kings) 1-0-0-0-0-0.

Greyling, Johan Corné (Klerksdorp HS) b 21/06/1991, Okahandja.

1.87m. 93kg. Centre. SA FC debut: 2016. PROV CAREER: EP Kings 2016 4-1-0-0-0-5. FC RECORD: 4-1-0-0-0-5. REP Honours: Namibia RWC 2015. Welwitchias 2015-16. RECORD IN 2016: (EP Kings) 4-1-0-0-0-5.

Greyling, MacGuyver Dean (Affies, Pretoria) b 01/01/1986, Potgietersrus. 1.92.00m, 122kg. Prop. FC DEBUT: 2005. PROV CAREER: Blue Bulls 2005,07-16 85-10-0-0-0-50. SUPERRUGBY: Bulls 2008 & 10-15 67-6-0-0-0-30. REP Honours: SA 2011-12 TESTS: 3-0-0-0-0-0. S/Kings 2009 1-0-0-0-0-0. FC RECORD: 156-16-0-0-0-80. RECORD IN 2016 (Blue Bulls) 1-1-0-0-0-5.

Grobbelaar, Hendrik (Dirk) (Hans Strijdom HS, Naboomspruit) b 08/02/1992, Benoni. 1.89m. 106kg. Flank. FC DEBUT: 2013. PROV CAREER: Griffons 2013-16 15-2-0-0-0-10. EP Kings 2016 2-0-0-0-0-0. FC RECORD: 17-2-0-0-0-10. RECORD IN 2016: (EP Kings, Griffons) 8-2-0-0-0-10.

Grobbelaar, Roan (Helpmekaar HS, Johannesburg & NWU) b 06/03/1995, Germiston. 1.80m. 118kg. Prop. FC DEBUT: 2016. PROV CAREER: Leopards 2016 16-1-0-0-0-5. FC RECORD: 16-1-0-0-0-5. RECORD IN 2016: (Leopards) 16-1-0-0-0-5.

Groenewald, Lambert Smith (Paul Roos Gym., Stellenbosch) b 01/02/1989, Worcester. 1.89m. 106kg. Flank. FC DEBUT: 2010. PROV CAREER: Sharks XV 2010-11 14-1-0-0-0-5. Lions 2013 6-0-0-0-0-0. Golden Lions XV 2014 1-0-0-0-0-0. Pumas 2015-16 28-7-0-0-0-35. SUPERRUGBY: Sharks 2011 1-0-0-0-0-0. FC RECORD: 50-8-0-0-0-40. RECORD IN 2016: (Pumas) 18-5-0-0-0-25.

Groenewald, Wilmar Romano (Hentie Cilliers HS, Virginia) b 30/04/1990, George. 1.84m. 81kg. Flank. FC DEBUT: 2010. PROV CAREER: Griffons 2010-16 37-5-0-0-0-25. FC RECORD: 37-5-0-0-0-25. RECORD IN 2016: (Griffons) 4-0-0-0-0-0.

Groom, Nicholas James (Rondebosch Boys' HS & UCT) b 21/02/1990, King William's Town. 1.71m. 81kg. Scrumhalf. FC DEBUT: 2011. PROV CAREER: WP 2011-15 69-10-0-0-0-50. SUPERRUGBY: Stormers 2011 & 13-16 57-5-0-0-0-25. REP Honours: SA A 2016 1-0-0-0-0-0. British Barbarians 2015 1-0-0-0-0-0. FC RECORD: 128-16-0-0-0-80. RECORD IN 2016: (SA A, Stormers) 15-2-0-0-0-10.

Grundlingh, Johann Alfonso (Transvalia HS, Vanderbijlpark & CUT) b 27/09/1995, Vanderbijlpark. 1.94m. 109kg. Lock. FC DEBUT: 2015. PROV CAREER: Free State XV 2015-16 9-0-0-0-0-0. FC RECORD: 9-0-0-0-0-0. RECORD IN 2016: (Free State XV) 7-0-0-0-0-0.

Gumede, Njabula (Maritzburg College) b 03/01/1995, Eshowe. 1.80m. 105kg. Hooker. FC DEBUT: 2015. PROV CAREER: Blue Bulls 2016 6-0-0-0-0-0. REP Honours: SAU20 2015 1-0-0-0-0-0. FC RECORD: 7-0-0-0-0-0. RECORD IN 2016: (Blue Bulls) 6-0-0-0-0-0.

Habana, Bryan Gary (KES, Johannesburg & RAU) b 12/06/1983, Johannesburg. 1.80m. 93kg. Wing. FC DEBUT: 2003. PROV CAREER: Lions 2003-04 21-17-0-0-0-85. Blue Bulls 2005 & 08-09 14-9-0-0-0-45. WP 2010-12 8-2-0-0-0-10. SUPERRUGBY: Bulls 2005-09 61-37-0-0-0-185. Stormers 2010-13 57-19-0-0-0-95. REP Honours: SA TESTS: 2004-16 124-67-0-0-0-335. Tour: 2007 2-0-0-0-0-0. Springboks 2014-15 2-1-0-0-0-5. Total: 128-68-0-0-0-340. SA Sevens 2004 & 16. SA U21 2004 3-3-0-0-0-15. British Barbarians 2008,09,11 3-3-0-0-0-15. MISC INFO: SARU PoY2005, 2007, 2012 . YPoY2004, S12 PoY2005. IRB PoY2007. IRB PoYnominee 2005. IRPA YPoY2005. Try of the year 2012 (SA vs All Blacks). Leading FC try-scorer 2004, 2005, 2007. Holds SA record for most tries in a season (13 in 2007) Holds SA record for most tries in Tests - 67. Holds SA record for most Tests as a wing - 123 (also one at centre). Holds SA record for most tries in Superrugby (56 - Bulls 37 & Stormers 19) FC RECORD: 294-158-0-0-0-790. RECORD IN 2016: (SA, SA Sevens) 7-3-0-0-0-15.

Hall, James Robert (Kearsney College, Durban) b 02/01/1996, Durban. 1.73m. 82kg. Scrumhalf. FC DEBUT: 2016. SUPERRUGBY: Southern Kings 2016 7-2-0-0-0-10. REP Honours: SAU20 2016 5-0-0-0-0-0. FC RECORD: 12-2-0-0-0-10. RECORD IN 2016: (Southern Kings, SAU20) 12-2-0-0-0-10.

Halvorsen, Thorleif (Boland Agric. HS, Paarl) b 09/05/1988, Cape Town. 1.93m. 107kg. Eighthman. FC DEBUT: 2010. PROV CAREER: Boland 2010-13 39-3-0-0-0-15. Eagles 2016 10-2-0-0-0-10. FC RECORD: 49-5-0-0-0-25. RECORD IN 2016: (Eagles) 10-2-0-0-0-10.

Hanekom, Nicolaas Johannes (Stokkies) (Paarl Gym.) b 17/05/1989, Citrusdal. 1.93m. 101kg. Centre. FC DEBUT: 2012. PROV CAREER: Eagles 2012 14-5-0-0-0-25. Lions 2013-16 24-9-0-0-0-45. Golden Lions XV 2013-16 23-11-0-0-0-55. SUPERRUGBY: Lions 2014-16 6-0-0-0-0-0. Lions P/R 2013 2-2-0-0-0-10. REP Honours: SAU20 2009 5-2-0-0-0-10. FC RECORD: 74-29-0-0-0-145. RECORD IN 2016: (Lions S18, Lions, Golden Lions XV) 13-7-0-0-0-35.

Hanekom, Pierre Francois (Marlow Agric. HS, Cradock & UFS) b 06/02/1989, Port Elizabeth. 1.86m. 120kg. Prop. FC DEBUT: 2012. PROV CAREER: Boland 2012-14 & 16 65-2-0-0-0-10. Sharks XV 2012 1-0-0-0-0-0. FC RECORD: 66-2-0-0-0-10. RECORD IN 2016 (Boland) 20-2-0-0-0-10.

Hartnick, Lyndon Lee (Kairos HS, Johannesburg) b 08/07/1986, Heidelberg. 1.90m. 97kg. Flank. FC DEBUT: 2008. PROV CAREER: Bulldogs 2008 6-0-0-0-0-0. Eagles 2010-16 88-10-0-0-0-50. FC RECORD: 94-10-0-0-0-50. RECORD IN 2016: (Eagles) 11-1-0-0-0-5.

Hattingh, Grant Neil (Kingswood College, Grahamstown) b 03/10/1990, Johannesburg. 2.01m. 105kg. Lock. FC DEBUT: 2011. PROV CAREER: WP 2011-12 2-0-0-0-0-0. Blue Bulls 2012-14 29-2-0-0-0-10. SUPERRUGBY: Lions 2012 9-1-0-0-0-5. Bulls 2013-16 46-1-0-0-0-5. FC RECORD: 86-4-0-0-0-20. RECORD IN 2016: (Bulls) 7-0-0-0-0-0.

Haupt, Kurt Stanley (St Albans College, Pretoria & UP) b 17/01/1989, Johannesburg. 1.90m. 112kg. Hooker. FC DEBUT: 2013. PROV CAREER: Blue Bulls 2013 2-0-0-0-0-0. Eagles 2014-16 39-14-0-0-0-70. FC RECORD: 41-14-0-0-0-70. RECORD IN 2016: (Eagles) 13-8-0-0-0-40.

Hauptfleisch, Gavin (Paarl Boys' HS) b 11/02/1992, Belville. 1.85m. 85kg. Flyhalf. FC DEBUT: 2012. PROV CAREER: Sharks XV 2012 1-0-0-0-0-0. Boland 2016 1-0-0-0-0-0. FC RECORD: 2-0-0-0-0-0. RECORD IN 2016: (Boland) 1-0-0-0-0-0.

Hay, Wiehan (Jeugland HS, Kempton Park) b 02/02/1992, Kempton Park. 1.96m. 122kg. Lock. FC DEBUT: 2013. PROV CAREER: Sharks XV 2013 1-0-0-0-0-0. Sharks 2014 1-0-0-0-0-0. Pumas 2016 9-0-0-0-0-0. FC RECORD: 11-0-0-0-0-0. RECORD IN 2016: (Pumas) 9-0-0-0-0-0.

Hayward, Jacobus (Centurion & Lichtenburg HS) b 06/06/1994, Bloemfontein. 1.84m. 94kg. Wing. FC DEBUT: 2015. PROV CAREER: Leopards 2015-16 17-6-0-0-0-30. Leopards XV 2015 6-5-0-0-0-25. FC RECORD: 23-11-0-0-0-55. RECORD IN 2016: (Leopards) 15-6-0-0-0-30.

Helberg, Gideon Gerhardus (Middelburg THS) b 27/09/1989, Lichtenburg. 1.87m. 91kg. Wing. FC DEBUT: 2010. PROV CAREER: Blue Bulls 2010 10-4-0-0-0-20. Lions 2012-13 18-5-0-0-0-25. Golden Lions XV 2013-14 10-2-0-0-0-10. Pumas 2015-16 11-1-0-0-0-5. SUPERRUGBY: Bulls 2010 1-0-0-0-0-0. Lions P/R 2013 1-0-0-0-0-0. FC RECORD: 51-12-0-0-0-60. RECORD IN 2016: (Pumas) 9-1-0-0-0-5.

Hendricks, Carlyle (Kyle) (Excelsior HS) b 12/12/1986, Cape Town.

1.74m. 70kg. Wing. FC DEBUT: 2009. PROV CAREER: Valke 2009-16 102-48-19-10-0-308. FC RECORD: 102-48-19-10-0-308. RECORD IN 2016: (Valke) 9-4-0-0-0-20.

Hendricks, Liam Chad (Paarl Boys' HS & US) b 31/05/1994, Belville. 1.80m. 111kg. Prop. FC DEBUT: 2016. PROV CAREER: EP Kings 2016 8-1-0-0-0-5. Griquas 2016 5-0-0-0-0-0. SUPERRUGBY: Southern Kings 2016 1-0-0-0-0-0. REP Honours: SA Schools 2012. FC RECORD: 14-1-0-0-0-5. RECORD IN 2016: (Southern Kings, Griquas, EP Kings) 14-1-0-0-0-5.

Herbert, Colin (Goudveld HS, Welkom) b 19/03/1992, Welkom. 1.90m. 85kg. Flyhalf. FC DEBUT: 2012. PROV CAREER: Griffons 2012-16 25-1-6-1-0-20. MISC INFO: Son of former Free State and Griffons flyhalf Eric Herbert. FC RECORD: 25-1-6-1-0-20. RECORD IN 2016: (Griffons) 2-0-2-0-0-4.

Herbst, Irné Philip (Waterkloof HS, Pretoria) b 04/05/1993, Witbank. 1.97m. 117kg. Lock. FC DEBUT: 2013. PROV CAREER: Blue Bulls 2016 3-0-0-0-0-0. REP Honours: SA U20 2013 5-1-0-0-0-5. FC RECORD: 8-1-0-0-0-5. RECORD IN 2016: (Blue Bulls) 3-0-0-0-0-0.

Herbst, Johan David (Boland Agric. HS, Paarl & US) b 18/05/1987, Stellenbosch. 1.77m. 93kg. Scrumhalf. FC DEBUT: 2011. PROV CAREER: Griquas 2011 4-3-0-0-0-15. Eagles 2012-13 23-10-0-0-0-50. Pumas 2015-16 9-1-0-0-0-5. SUPERRUGBY: Southern Kings 2013 1-0-0-0-0-0. FC RECORD: 37-14-0-0-0-70. RECORD IN 2016: (Pumas) 1-0-0-0-0-0.

Hermanus, Grant Hagan (Paarl Gym.) b 11/11/1995, Durbanville. 1.79m. 83kg. Wing. FC DEBUT: 2015. PROV CAREER: WP 2015-16 14-4-16-4-0-64. REP Honours: SAU20 2015 3-0-0-0-0-0. FC RECORD: 17-4-16-4-0-64. RECORD IN 2016: (WP) 12-3-16-4-0-59.

Herne, Frank (Grey College, Bloemfontein & UOFS) b 31/10/1989, Ficksburg. 1.78m. 101kg. Hooker. FC DEBUT: 2011. PROV CAREER: EP Kings 2011-12 39-4-0-0-0-20. Pumas 2013-16 71-22-0-0-0-110. REP Honours: SA Kings 2011 3-0-0-0-0-0. SA Pres XV 2013 4-0-0-0-0-0. FC RECORD: 117-26-0-0-0-130. RECORD IN 2016: (Pumas) 21-12-0-0-0-60.

Hess, Cornéll Norman (Affies, Pretoria) b 01/03/1989, Wynberg. 2.0m. 106kg. Lock. FC DEBUT: 2010. PROV CAREER: Blue Bulls 2010-13 39-0-0-0-0-0. EP Kings 2015-16 23-0-0-0-0-0. SUPERRUGBY: Southern Kings 2016 1-0-0-0-0-0. REP Honours: SAU20 2008 5-0-0-0-0-0. FC RECORD: 68-0-0-0-0-0. RECORD IN 2016: (Southern Kings, EP Kings) 12-0-0-0-0-0.

Heyns, Kirsten Ralph (Hentie Cilliers HS, Virginia) b 31/07/1993, George. 1.81m. 81kg. Centre. FC DEBUT: 2015. PROV CAREER: Eagles 2015-16 26-4-0-0-0-20. FC RECORD: 26-4-0-0-0-20. RECORD IN 2016: (Eagles) 10-1-0-0-0-5.

Hill, Denzel Frederick (Jeppe HS, Johannesburg & UP) b 17/01/1996, Lusaka. 1.90m. 99kg. Eighthman. FC DEBUT: 2016. REP Honours: SAU20 2016 2-0-0-0-0-0. FC RECORD: 2-0-0-0-0-0. RECORD IN 2016: (SAU20) 2-0-0-0-0-0.

Hollis, Justin Warren (Queen's College, Queen'stown) b 17/10/1995, Tarkastad. 1.86m. 92kg. Eighthman. FC DEBUT: 2016. PROV CAREER: EP Kings 2016 1-0-0-0-0-0. FC RECORD: 1-0-0-0-0-0. RECORD IN 2016: (EP Kings) 1-0-0-0-0-0.

Holtzhausen, Jacobus Johannes (Monument HS, Krugersdorp & UP) b 12/01/1996, Pretoria. 1.81m. 117kg. Prop. FC DEBUT: 2016. REP Honours: SAU20 2016 3-0-0-0-0-0. FC RECORD: 3-0-0-0-0-0. RECORD IN 2016: (SAU20) 3-0-0-0-0-0.

Hopp, Dean Lionel John (Kairos SS) b 07/09/82, Heidelberg. 1.76m.

138kg. Hooker. FC DEBUT: 2002. PROV CAREER: Eagles 2002-03 & 2011-13 & 15-16 66-5-0-0-0-25. Elephants 2005 19-1-0-0-0-5. Griquas 2006-08 21-3-0-0-0-15. REP Honours: SA U21 2002 2-0-0-0-0-0. SA Barbarians 2012 1-0-0-0-0-0. FC RECORD: 109-9-0-0-0-45. RECORD IN 2016: (Eagles) 13-1-0-0-0-5

Horn, Jakobus Ferdinand (Glenwood HS, Durban & UP) b 30/06/1993, Empangeni. 1.92.00m. 100kg. Lock. FC DEBUT: 2016. PROV CAREER: Boland 2016 10-0-0-0-0-0. FC RECORD: 10-0-0-0-0-0. RECORD IN 2016: (Boland) 10-0-0-0-0-0.

Horn, Joubert Prinsloo (Burgersdorp HS & Grey College, Bloemfontein & UFS) b 08/10/1988, Welkom. 1.95m. 100kg. Lock. FC DEBUT: 2010. PROV CAREER: Griffons 2010-12 30-2-0-0-0-10. Griquas 2013 5-0-0-0-0-0. Free State XV 2014 2-0-0-0-0-0. Boland 2016 8-1-0-0-0-5. FC RECORD: 45-3-0-0-0-15. RECORD IN 2016: (Boland) 8-1-0-0-0-5.

Hougaard, Francois (Paul Roos Gym., Stellenbosch) b 06/04/1988, Paarl. 1.79m. 92kg. Scrumhalf. FC DEBUT: 2007. PROV CAREER: WP 2007 3-0-0-0-0-0. Blue Bulls 2008-10 & 12 & 15 48-16-0-0-0-80. SUPER-RUGBY: Bulls 2008-15 88-26-0-0-0-130. REP Honours: SA 2009-12 & 14 & 16 TESTS: 39-5-0-0-0-25. Tour: 2009-10 3-0-0-0-0-0. Total: 42-5-0-0-0-25. SAU20 2008 3-0-0-0-0-0. S/Kings 2009 1-0-0-0-0-0. SA Sevens 2015-16. MISC INFO: PoYnominee 2011. YPoYnominee 2009, 2011. IRPA try of the year 2014 (vs All Blacks). FC RECORD: 185-47-0-0-0-235. RECORD IN 2016: (SA, SA Sevens) 4-0-0-0-0-0.

Huggett, Elandré (Premier HS, Johannesburg) b 05/10/1991, Cape Town. 1.76m. 93kg. Hooker. FC DEBUT: 2011. PROV CAREER: Cheetahs 2011-12 & 15-16 8-1-0-0-0-5. Free State XV 2012-13 & 16 18-3-0-0-0-15. Griffons 2013-16 25-3-0-0-0-15. SUPERRUGBY: Cheetahs 2015-16 3-0-0-0-0-0. FC RECORD: 54-7-0-0-0-35. RECORD IN 2016: (Cheetahs S18, Cheetahs, Griffons, Free State XV) 14-3-0-0-0-15.

Hugo, Abraham Pieter Marnus (Paarl Gym.) b 24/09/1986, Paarl. 1.70m. 84kg. Scrumhalf. FC DEBUT: 2006. PROV CAREER: Boland 2006 & 08-09 & 2011 & 14-16 76-5-0-0-0-25. Griquas 2010-13 57-1-0-0-0-5. SUPERRUGBY: Cheetahs 2010 2-0-0-0-0-0. FC RECORD: 135-6-0-0-0-30. RECORD IN 2016: (Boland) 21-1-0-0-0-5.

Hugo, Daniel Pieter (Reniel) (Paul Roos Gym., Stellenbosch & US) b 19/07/1990, Belville. 1.97m. 112kg. Lock. FC DEBUT: 2011. PROV CAREER: WP 2011 2-0-0-0-0-0. Blue Bulls 2014-15 7-2-0-0-0-10. Free State XV 2015-16 11-3-0-0-0-15. Cheetahs 2015-16 21-1-0-0-0-5. SUPERRUGBY: Cheetahs 2016 4-0-0-0-0-0. REP Honours: SA Univ 2013 1-0-0-0-0-0. MISC INFO: Son of former Springbok Niel Hugo. FC RECORD: 46-6-0-0-0-30. RECORD IN 2016: (Cheetahs S18, Cheetahs, Free State XV) 23-4-0-0-0-20.

Hugo, Schalk Burger (Worcester Gym.) b 17/08/1994, Oudtshoorn. 1.78m. 80kg. Centre. FC DEBUT: 2015. PROV CAREER: Leopards 2015-16 11-3-7-1-0-32. Leopards XV 2015 1-0-0-0-0-0. FC RECORD: 12-3-7-1-0-32. RECORD IN 2016: (Leopards) 5-0-4-1-0-11.

Huisamen, Gerrit (Grey HS, Port Elizabeth & NMMU) b 07/03/1995, Port Elizabeth. 1.94m. 103kg. Lock. FC DEBUT: 2016. PROV CAREER: EP Kings 2016 4-0-0-0-0-0. FC RECORD: 4-0-0-0-0-0. RECORD IN 2016: (EP Kings) 4-0-0-0-0-0.

Huisamen, Johannes Frederik (Brandwag HS, Uitenhage, US & NMMU) b 09/04/1989, Malmesbury. 1.98m. 107kg. Lock. FC DEBUT: 2016. PROV CAREER: EP Kings 2016 2-0-0-0-0-0. FC RECORD: 2-0-0-0-0-0. RECORD IN 2016: (EP Kings) 2-0-0-0-0-0.

Human, Dewald Dawid (Outeniqua HS, George) b 19/05/1995, Un-iondale. 1.68m. 70kg. Flyhalf. FC DEBUT: 2016. SUPERRUGBY: Southern

Kings 2016 3-1-1-1-0-10. REP Honours: SA Schools 2013. FC RECORD: 3-1-1-1-0-10. RECORD IN 2016: (Southern Kings) 3-1-1-1-0-10.

Isbell, Ruwellyn Miguel (Grey College, Bloemfontein) b 17/02/1993, Somerset EaSt 1.78m. 88kg. Wing. FC DEBUT: 2014. PROV CAREER: Pumas 2014-16 21-8-0-0-0-40. FC RECORD: 21-8-0-0-0-40. REP Honours: SA Sevens 2012. RECORD IN 2016: (Pumas) 6-1-0-0-0-5.

Ismaiel, Travis Keenan (Tygerberg HS, Cape Town & UP) b 02/06/1992, Cape Town. 1.83m. 92kg. Wing. FC DEBUT: 2012. PROV CAREER: Blue Bulls 2013-16 37-18-0-0-0-90. SUPERRUGBY: Bulls 2015-16 17-6-0-0-0-30. REP Honours: SA A 2016 2-0-0-0-0-0. SA U20 2012 1-0-0-0-0-0. FC RECORD: 57-24-0-0-0-120. RECORD IN 2016: (SA A, Bulls, Blue Bulls) 19-9-0-0-0-45.

Izaacs, Alcino Marchioni (Namib HS) b 16/11/1993, Windhoek. 1.89m. 84kg. Wing. FC DEBUT: 2014. PROV CAREER: Sharks XV 2014-15 14-1-0-0-0-5. EP Kings 2016 4-2-0-0-0-10. Blue Bulls 2016 11-3-0-0-0-15. FC RECORD: 29-6-0-0-0-30. RECORD IN 2016: (Blue Bulls, EP Kings) 15-5-0-0-0-25.

Jackson, Gregory Angus Shaw (Michaelhouse, Balgowan & NMMU) b 07/03/1996, Pietermaritzburg. 1.84m. 108kg. Hooker. FC DEBUT: 2016. PROV CAREER: EP Kings 2016 2-1-0-0-0-5. FC RECORD: 2-1-0-0-0-5. RECORD IN 2016: (EP Kings) 2-1-0-0-0-5.

Jackson, John Thomas (JT) (Oakdale HTS, Riversdale) b 10/07/1996, Calvinia. 1.89m. 96kg. Centre. FC DEBUT: 2015. PROV CAREER: Blue Bulls 2016 3-0-0-0-0-0. REP Honours: SAU20 2015-16 7-1-0-0-0-5. FC RECORD: 10-1-0-0-0-5. RECORD IN 2016: (Blue Bulls, SAU20) 8-1-0-0-0-5.

Jacobs, Wiehan Heinrich (Monument HS, Krugersdorp) b 18/04/1995, Louis Trichardt. 1.90m. 102kg. Eighthman. FC DEBUT: 2016. PROV CAREER: Golden Lions XV 2016 2-0-0-0-0-0. FC RECORD: 2-0-0-0-0-0. RECORD IN 2016: (Golden Lions XV) 2-0-0-0-0-0.

Jaer, Malcolm Adrian Emile (Brandwag HS, Uitenhage) b 29/06/1995, Uitenhage. 1.74m. 72kg. Fullback. FC DEBUT: 2014. PROV CAREER: EP Kings 2014 1-0-0-0-0-0. SUPERRUGBY: Southern Kings 2016 10-2-0-0-0-10. REP Honours: SAU20 2015 3-1-0-0-0-5. FC RECORD: 14-3-0-0-0-15. RECORD IN 2016: (Southern Kings) 10-2-0-0-0-10.

Jamieson, Jean-Pierre (Grey HS, Port Elizabeth & NMMU) b 15/02/1995, Port Elizabeth. 1.80m. 104kg. Hooker. FC DEBUT: 2016. PROV CAREER: EP Kings 2016 11-1-0-0-0-5. FC RECORD: 11-1-0-0-0-5. RECORD IN 2016: (EP Kings) 11-1-0-0-0-5.

Janke, Grant Donovan (Welkom HS) b 02/11/1990, Cape Town. 1.78m. 87kg. Wing. FC DEBUT: 2011. PROV CAREER: Griffons 2011-12 9-0-0-0-0-0. Leopards 2012 3-0-0-0-0-0. Lions 2013 1-0-0-0-0-0. Golden Lions XV 2013 1-0-0-0-0-0. Valke 2014-16 43-11-0-0-0-55. FC RECORD: 57-11-0-0-0-55. RECORD IN 2016: (Valke) 18-5-0-0-0-25.

Janse van Rensburg, Barend Johannes (Benhard) (Frikkie Meyer HS, Thabazimbi & NWU) b 14/01/1997, Pretoria. 1.86m. 86kg. Flyhalf. FC DEBUT: 2016. PROV CAREER: Leopards 2016 10-2-8-2-0-32. REP Honours: SAU20 2016 1-0-0-0-0-0. FC RECORD: 11-2-8-2-0-32. RECORD IN 2016: (Leopards, SAU20) 11-2-8-2-0-32.

Janse van Rensburg, Johannes Christiaan (Port Rex HS, East London, Tom Naudé HS, Polokwane & UP) b 25/07/1995, Uitenhage. 1.92.00m. 95kg. Eighthman. FC DEBUT: 2016. PROV CAREER: Bulldogs 2016 9-0-0-0-0-0. FC RECORD: 9-0-0-0-0-0. RECORD IN 2016: (Bulldogs) 9-0-0-0-0-0.

Janse van Rensburg, Jonathan Barry (Jono) (Maritzburg College

& UP) b 27/02/1989, Pietermaritzburg. 1.90m. 106kg. Eighthman. FC DEBUT: 2015. PROV CAREER: Griquas 2015-16 37-6-0-0-0-30. FC RECORD: 37-6-0-0-0-30. RECORD IN 2016: (Griquas) 20-2-0-0-0-10.

Janse van Rensburg, Jakobus Christo (JC) (Oakdale HS) b 09/01/1986, Prins Albert. 1.85m. 109kg. Prop. FC DEBUT: 2006. PROV CAREER: Lions 2006-12 67-0-0-0-0-0. Golden Lions XV 2006-09 & 13 12-1-0-0-0-5. WP 2016 8-0-0-0-0-0. SUPERRUGBY: Lions 2008-12 50-1-0-0-0-5. Lions P/R 2013 2-0-0-0-0-0. Sharks 2013 3-0-0-0-0-0. Stormers 2016 11-0-0-0-0-0. REP Honours: SA2 2012 no tests. SA U19 2005. MISC INFO: CC PoY2012 nominee. FC RECORD: 153-2-0-0-0-10. RECORD IN 2016: (Stormers, WP) 19-0-0-0-0-0.

Janse van Rensburg, Nicolaas Jacobus (Nico) (Affies, Pretoria) b 06/05/1994, Pretoria. 1.99m. 109kg. Lock. FC DEBUT: 2014. PROV CAREER: Blue Bulls 2014-16 26-0-0-0-0-0. SUPERRUGBY: Bulls 2014-16 5-0-0-0-0-0. REP Honours: SAU20 2014 5-0-0-0-0-0. FC RECORD: 36-0-0-0-0-0. RECORD IN 2016: (Bulls, Blue Bulls) 7-0-0-0-0-0.

Janse van Rensburg, Rohan (Waterkloof HS, Pretoria) b 11/09/1994, Welkom. 1.86m. 100kg. Centre. FC DEBUT: 2013. PROV CAREER: Blue Bulls 2013-14 7-4-0-0-0-20. Golden Lions XV 2015-16 6-2-0-0-0-10. Lions 2015-16 13-3-0-0-0-15. SUPERRUGBY: Lions 2016 17-10-0-0-0-50. REP Honours: SA 2016 TESTS: 1-0-0-0-0-0. Springbok XV 2016 1-1-0-0-0-5. SA U20 2013-14 3-0-0-0-0-0. MISC INFO: SARU YPoYnominee 2016. FC RECORD: 48-20-0-0-0-100. RECORD IN 2016: (SA, Springbok XV, Lions S18, Lions, Golden Lions XV) 27-14-0-0-0-70.

Janse van Vuuren, Gunther (Monument HS, Krugersdorp & UFS) b 24/08/1995, Pretoria. 1.86m. 120kg. Prop. FC DEBUT: 2015. PROV CAREER: Free State XV 2015-16 11-0-0-0-0-0. FC RECORD: 11-0-0-0-0-0. RECORD IN 2016: (Free State XV) 7-0-0-0-0-0.

Jansen, Jaquin (Bergrivier HS, Wellington) b 27/05/1986, Paarl. 1.75m. 83kg. Flyhalf. FC DEBUT: 2008. PROV CAREER: Boland 2008-13 66-21-60-39-0-342. Griquas 2014-15 20-1-6-6-0-35. Eagles 2016 12-1-11-2-0-33. REP Honours: SA Barbarians 2012 1-0-0-0-0-0. SA Pres XV 2013 2-0-0-0-0-0. FC RECORD: 101-23-77-47-0-410. RECORD IN 2016: (Eagles) 12-1-11-2-0-33.

Jansen, Pieter (Dr EG Jansen HS, Boksburg) b 21/03/1995, Springs. 1.83m. 103kg. Hooker. FC DEBUT: 2016. PROV CAREER: Golden Lions XV 2016 12-1-0-0-0-5. FC RECORD: 12-1-0-0-0-5. RECORD IN 2016: (Golden Lions XV) 12-1-0-0-0-5.

Jansen van Rensburg, Damien (Monument HS, Krugersdorp & Unisa) b 11/01/1989, Johannesburg. 1.75m. 92kg. Centre. FC DEBUT: 2016. PROV CAREER: Pumas 2016 4-1-0-0-0-5. FC RECORD: 4-1-0-0-0-5. RECORD IN 2016: (Pumas) 4-1-0-0-0-5.

Jansen van Vuuren, Erasmus Albertus (Rassie) (Nelspruit HS) b 23/05/1985, Potgietersrus. 1.89m. 125kg. Prop. FC DEBUT: 2007. PROV CAREER: Pumas 2007 & 16 21-5-0-0-0-25. Blue Bulls 2008 9-2-0-0-0-10. Valke 2008 5-1-0-0-0-5. FC RECORD: 35-8-0-0-0-40. RECORD IN 2016: (Pumas) 1-0-0-0-0-0.

Jansen van Vuuren, Marco (Transvalia HS, Vanderbijlpark) b 14/06/1996, Vanderbijlpark. 1.86m. 87kg. Scrumhalf. FC DEBUT: 2015. PROV CAREER: Golden Lions XV 2015-16 4-0-0-0-0-0. REP Honours: SAU20 2015-16 6-0-0-0-0-0. FC RECORD: 10-0-0-0-0-0. RECORD IN 2016: (SAU20, Golden Lions XV) 6-0-0-0-0-0.

Jantjies, Altonio (Tony) (Menlopark HS, Pretoria) b 19/04/1992, Cape Town. 1.78m. 90kg. Flyhalf. FC DEBUT: 2012. PROV CAREER: Blue Bulls 2012-14 & 16 29-6-52-37-0-245. EP Kings 2015 2-0-0-0-0-0. REP Honours: SAU20 2012 3-0-2-5-0-19. MISC INFO: Brother of Elton

Jantjies. FC RECORD: 34-6-54-42-0-264. RECORD IN 2016: (Blue Bulls) 9-3-16-6-0-65.

Jantjies, Elton Thomas (Florida HS, Johannesburg & UJ) b 01/08/1990, Graaff Reinet. 1.76m. 84kg. Flyhalf. FC DEBUT: 2010. PROV CAREER: Golden Lions 2010-13 42-4-75-101-2-479. Golden Lions XV 2010-11 & 14 3-0-3-2-0-12. SUPERRUGBY: Lions 2011-12 & 14-16 70-4-109-117-3-598. Lions P/R 2013 2-0-3-6-0-24. Stormers 2013 13-0-1-3-0-11. REP Honours: SA 2012 & 16 TESTS: 11-0-12-18-0-78. 2010 Tour: 1-0-1-1-0-5. Total: 12-0-13-19-0-83. SAU20 2010 5-2-1-0-0-12. MISC INFO: YPoY2011 and 2012 nominee. CC PoY2012 nominee, Super rugby PoY2016, Brother of Tony Jantjies. FC RECORD: 147-10-205-248-5-1219. RECORD IN 2016: (SA, Lions S18) 25-3-56-43-2-262.

Jantjies, Herschel Jerome (Paul Roos Gym., Stellenbosch) b 22/04/1996, Stellenbosch. 1.67m. 75kg. Scrumhalf. FC DEBUT: 2016. PROV CAREER: WP 2016 1-0-0-0-0-0. FC RECORD: 1-0-0-0-0-0. RECORD IN 2016: (WP) 1-0-0-0-0-0.

Jenkins, Jason Howell (St Albans College, Pretoria) b 02/12/1995, Pretoria. 2.01m. 121kg. Lock. FC DEBUT: 2015. PROV CAREER: Blue Bulls 2015-16 8-2-0-0-0-10. SUPERRUGBY: Bulls 2016 13-1-0-0-0-5. REP Honours: SA A 2016 1-0-0-0-0-0. SAU20 2015 5-3-0-0-0-15. FC RECORD: 27-6-0-0-0-30. RECORD IN 2016: (SA A, Bulls, Blue Bulls) 20-3-0-0-0-15.

Jenkinson, John-Roy (Glenwood HS, Durban & NWU) b 26/03/1991, Worcester. 1.77m. 127kg. Prop. FC DEBUT: 2011. PROV CAREER: Leopards 2011-15 40-3-0-0-0-15. Cheetahs 2013 2-0-0-0-0-0. Leopards XV 2014-15 3-1-0-0-0-5. Blue Bulls 2016 1-0-0-0-0-0. REP Honours: SA Students 2012 2-1-0-0-0-5. SA U20 2011 5-0-0-0-0-0. FC RECORD: 53-5-0-0-0-25. RECORD IN 2016: (Blue Bulls) 1-0-0-0-0-0.

Jho, Andile (Dale College, King William's Town & NMMU) b 21/04/1992, King William's Town. 1.73m. 83kg. Centre. FC DEBUT: 2013. PROV CAREER: EP Kings 2013-16 11-1-0-0-0-5. FC RECORD: 11-1-0-0-0-5. RECORD IN 2016: (EP Kings) 11-1-0-0-0-5.

Jho, Somila (Kingswood College, Grahamstown & NMMU) b 25/08/1995, King William's Town. 1.80m. 90kg. Centre. FC DEBUT: 2016. PROV CAREER: EP Kings 2016. 13-5-0-0-0-25. FC RECORD: 13-5-0-0-0-25. RECORD IN 2016: (EP Kings) 13-5-0-0-0-25.

Jobo, Vincent Thabiso (KES, Johannesburg, UJ & UCT) b 01/02/1991, Krugersdorp. 1.86m. 104kg. Eighthman. FC DEBUT: 2013. PROV CAREER: WP 2013 1-0-0-0-0-0. Cheetahs 2014-15 5-3-0-0-0-15. Free State XV 2014-15 6-2-0-0-0-10. Valke 2016 6-0-0-0-0-0. EP Kings 2016 6-1-0-0-0-5. FC RECORD: 24-6-0-0-0-30. RECORD IN 2016: (EP Kings, Valke) 12-1-0-0-0-5.

Johannes, Reuben Benjamin (Paul Roos Gym., Stellenbosch & US) b 05/10/1990, Belville. 1.83m, 96kg, Flank. FC DEBUT: 2011. PROV CAREER: WP 2011-12 & 14 11-3-0-0-0-15. Free State XV 2015 4-2-0-0-0-10. Pumas 2016 5-1-0-0-0-5. REP Honours: SA Sevens 2012-13. FC RECORD: 20-6-0-0-0-30. RECORD IN 2016: (Pumas) 5-1-0-0-0-5.

Jonas, Curtis (Glenwood HS, Durban & UJ) b 27/08/1996, Swellendam. 1.72.00m. 74kg. Scrumhalf. FC DEBUT: 2016. PROV CAREER: Golden Lions XV 2016 1-0-0-0-0-0. FC RECORD: 1-0-0-0-0-0. RECORD IN 2016: (Golden Lions XV) 1-0-0-0-0-0.

Jonck, Juan-Pierre (Roodepoort HS & NMMU) b 07/12/1991, Roodepoort. 1.82.00m. 101kg. Flank. FC DEBUT: 2014. PROV CAREER: Valke 2014 8-0-0-0-0-0. EP Kings 2016 9-2-0-0-0-10. SUPERRUGBY: Southern Kings 2016 1-0-0-0-0-0. FC RECORD: 18-2-0-0-0-10. RECORD IN 2016: (Southern Kings, EP Kings) 10-2-0-0-0-10.

Jones, Huw Richard Forbes (Milfield HS, UK) b 17/12/1993, Edinburgh. 1.86m. 91kg. Centre. FC DEBUT: 2014. PROV CAREER: WP 2014-16 16-9-0-0-0-45. SUPERRUGBY: Stormers 2015-16 23-5-0-0-0-25. FC RECORD: 39-14-0-0-0-70. RECORD IN 2016: (Stormers, WP) 15-11-0-0-0-55.

Jonker, Jacobus Willem (JW) (Grey College, Bloemfontein) b 19/03/1987, Bloemfontein. 1.81m. 85kg. Centre. FC DEBUT: 2006. PROV CAREER: Cheetahs 2006-10 65-18-0-0-0-90. Griffons 2010 4-6-0-0-0-30. Pumas 2011-12 & 14 56-23-0-0-0-115. Griquas 2015-16 19-6-0-0-0-30. SUPERRUGBY: Cheetahs 2008-09 16-6-0-0-0-30. Lions 2014 11-0-0-0-0-0. REP Honours: SA Students 2007 1-0-0-0-0-0. SA Barbarians 2012 1-0-0-0-0-0. MISC INFO: CC First Div PoY2012 nominee. FC RECORD: 173-59-0-0-0-295. RECORD IN 2016: (Griquas) 16-4-0-0-0-20.

Jonker, Johannes Gideon Andries (Hudson Park HS, East London) b 22/08/1994, East London. 1.84m. 118kg. Prop. FC DEBUT: 2014. PROV CAREER: Bulldogs 2014-16 43-5-0-0-0-25. FC RECORD: 43-5-0-0-0-25. RECORD IN 2016: (Bulldogs) 18-2-0-0-0-10.

Jordaan, Daniel Barend (Fochville HS & NWU) b 25/01/1991, Johannesburg. 1.96m. 104kg. Lock. FC DEBUT: 2012. PROV CAREER: Leopards 2012-16 15-0-0-0-0-0. Leopards XV 2014-15 5-0-0-0-0-0. FC RECORD: 20-0-0-0-0-0. RECORD IN 2016: (Leopards) 6-0-0-0-0-0.

Jordaan, Daniel Niell (Grey College, Bloemfontein) b 13/01/1992, Newcastle. 1.90m. 103kg. Eighthman. FC DEBUT: 2013. PROV CAREER: Free State XV 2013 & 16 7-0-0-0-0-0. Griffons 2014 3-0-0-0-0-0. Cheetahs 2015-16 19-2-0-0-0-10. SUPERRUGBY: Cheetahs 2015-16 5-1-0-0-0-5. FC RECORD: 34-3-0-0-0-15. RECORD IN 2016: (Cheetahs S18, Cheetahs, Free State XV) 16-1-0-0-0-5.

Jordaan, Gerhard Johan (Boland Agric., Wellington & US) b 10/04/1992, Kempton Park. 1.80m. 83kg. Scrumhalf. FC DEBUT: 2014. PROV CAREER: WP 2014 1-0-0-0-0-0. Boland 2016 12-0-0-0-0-0. FC RECORD: 13-0-0-0-0-0. RECORD IN 2016: (Boland) 12-0-0-0-0-0.

Jordaan, Jaco (Paarl Gym. & NWU) b 27/09/1993, Belville. 1.87m. 103kg. Flank. FC DEBUT: 2015. PROV CAREER: Leopards 2015-16 22-2-0-0-0-10. Leopards XV 2015 7-1-0-0-0-5. FC RECORD: 29-3-0-0-0-15. RECORD IN 2016: (Leopards) 15-2-0-0-0-10.

Jordaan, Jeremy (Fichardtpark HS, Bloemfontein & UJ) b 06/01/1991, Bloemfontein. 1.96m. 121kg. Lock. FC DEBUT: 2013. PROV CAREER: Griffons 2013 14-2-0-0-0-10. Pumas 2016 2-0-0-0-0-0. FC RECORD: 16-2-0-0-0-10. RECORD IN 2016: (Pumas) 2-0-0-0-0-0.

Jordaan, Paul Abraham (Grey College, Bloemfontein) b 04/01/1992, Somerset EaSt 1.80m. 88kg. Centre. FC DEBUT: 2011. PROV CAREER: Sharks 2012 & 14-15 28-10-0-0-0-50. Sharks XV 2011-12 & 15 5-1-0-0-0-5. SUPERRUGBY: Sharks 2012-14 & 16 43-9-0-0-0-45. Rep. Honours: SAU20 2011-12 8-1-0-0-0-5. SA Sevens 2010-11. FC RECORD: 84-21-0-0-0-105. RECORD IN 2016: (Sharks S18) 13-4-0-0-0-20.

Jordaan, Zandré (Paarl Boys' HS) b 24/09/1987, Empangeni. 1.91m. 93kg. FC DEBUT: 2009. PROV CAREER: Boland 2009-14 & 16 94-28-0-0-0-140. WP 2009 4-2-0-0-0-10. Eagles 2015 15-4-0-0-0-20. REP Honours: SA Barbarians 2012 1-0-0-0-0-0. SA Pres XV 2013 2-1-0-0-0-5. FC RECORD: 116-35-0-0-0-175. RECORD IN 2016: (Boland) 20-5-0-0-0-25.

Joubert, Morné (Glenwood HS, Durban & UKZN) b 19/01/1996, Pretoria. 1.80m. 85kg. Wing. FC DEBUT: 2016. PROV CAREER: Sharks XV 2016 6-2-1-0-0-12. FC RECORD: 6-2-1-0-0-12. RECORD IN 2016: (Sharks XV) 6-2-1-0-0-12.

Juries, Jaywin Angelo (Hentie Cilliers HS, Virginia & UKZN) b

09/10/1996, Great Brak River. 1.70m. 75kg. Scrumhalf. FC DEBUT: 2016. PROV CAREER: Sharks XV 2016 4-0-0-0-0-0. FC RECORD: 4-0-0-0-0-0. RECORD IN 2016: (Sharks XV) 4-0-0-0-0-0.

Kankowski, Ryan (St Andrew's College, Grahamstown) b 14/10/1985, Port Elizabeth. 1.93m. 103kg. Eighthman. FC DEBUT: 2006. PROV CAREER: KZN 2006-11 59-16-0-0-0-80. Sharks XV 2009 & 12-13 3-0-0-0-0-0. SUPERRUGBY: Sharks 2007-15 104-19-0-0-0-95. REP Honours: SA 2007-12 TESTS: 20-1-0-0-0-5. Tour: 2-0-0-0-0-0. Total: 22-1-0-0-0-5. SA Sevens 2006 & 16. MISC INFO: PoYnominee 2008. YPoYnominee 2008. Son of former EP, Border & Griquas wing Tino Kankowski. FC RECORD: 188-36-0-0-0-180. RECORD IN 2016: (SA Sevens).

Kean, Thomas Michael (Michaelhouse, Balgowan & NMMU) b 25/11/1992, Pietermaritzburg. 1.89m. 90kg. Fullback. FC DEBUT: 2015. PROV CAREER: Eagles 2015-16 17-0-14-21-0-61. FC RECORD: 17-0-14-21-0-61. RECORD IN 2016: (Eagles) 14-0-14-21-0-91.

Kebble, Oliver Ralph (Bishops HS, Rondebosch) b 18/06/1992, Durban. 1.91m. 124kg. Prop. FC DEBUT: 2012. PROV CAREER: WP 2012 & 14-16 18-0-0-0-0-0. SUPERRUGBY: Stormers 2014-16 34-1-0-0-0-5. Rep honours: SAU20 2012 4-0-0-0-0-0. MISC INFO: Son of former Springbok Guy Kebble. FC RECORD: 56-1-0-0-0-5. RECORD IN 2016: (Stormers, WP) 16-0-0-0-0-0.

Kebe, Ntando Lucky (Thubalethu HS, Fort Beaufort & UFH) b 19/08/1988, East London. 1.79m. 80kg. Scrumhalf. FC DEBUT: 2010. PROV CAREER: Bulldogs 2010-12 & 14-15 69-7-0-0-0-35. Boland 2013 21-1-0-0-0-5. Griquas 2014 2-1-0-0-0-5. SUPERRUGBY: Southern Kings 2016 13-0-0-0-0-0. REP Honours: SA A 2016 1-0-0-0-0-0. SA Barbarians 2012 1-0-0-0-0-0. SA Pres XV 2013 4-0-0-0-0-0. FC RECORD: 111-9-0-0-0-45. RECORD IN 2016: (SA A, Southern Kings) 14-0-0-0-0-0.

Khetani, Athenkosi Ernest (Lukhozi HS, Nkomkobe, Eastern Cape & Walter Sisulu Univ.) b 01/12/1992, Cape Town. 1.95m. 102kg. Lock. FC DEBUT: 2016. PROV CAREER: Bulldogs 2016 10-3-0-0-0-15. FC RECORD: 10-3-0-0-0-15. RECORD IN 2016: (Bulldogs) 10-3-0-0-0-15.

Kirkwood, Shane Monro (Marais Viljoen HS, Alberton) b 06/09/89, Alberton. 1.94m. 113kg. Lock. FC DEBUT: 2009. PROV CAREER: Valke 2013-16 63-13-0-0-0-65. Golden Lions XV 2009 3-1-0-0-0-5. FC RECORD: 66-14-0-0-0-70. RECORD IN 2016: (Valke) 19-6-0-0-0-30.

Kirsten, Johannes Casper (Jannes) (Affies, Pretoria & UP) b 01/12/1993, Johannesburg. 1.96m. 107kg. Lock. FC DEBUT: 2013. PROV CAREER: Blue Bulls 2013 & 15-16 12-2-0-0-0-10. SUPERRUGBY: Bulls 2016 15-2-0-0-0-10. REP Honours: SA U20 2013 1-0-0-0-0-0. MISC INFO: Brother of Frik Kirsten. FC RECORD: 28-4-0-0-0-20. RECORD IN 2016: (Bulls, Blue Bulls) 23-4-0-0-0-20.

Kitshoff, Johannes Jakobus (Hanno) (Worcester Gym.) b 25/01/1984, George. 1.91m. 92kg. Flank. FC DEBUT: 2012. PROV CAREER: Boland 2012-16 62-4-0-0-0-20. FC RECORD: 62-4-0-0-0-20. RECORD IN 2016: (Boland) 22-2-0-0-0-10.

Kitshoff, Steven (Paul Roos Gym., Stellenbosch) b 10/02/1992, Somerset WeSt 1.83m. 114kg. Prop. FC DEBUT: 2011. PROV CAREER: WP 2011-13 & 15 39-1-0-0-0-5. SUPERRUGBY: Stormers 2011-15 60-0-0-0-0-0. REP Honours: SA 2016 TESTS: 10-0-0-0-0-0. SA U20 2012 5-1-0-0-0-5. FC RECORD: 114-2-0-0-0-10. RECORD IN 2016: (SA) 10-0-0-0-0-0.

Klaasen, Berton Wesley (Somerset West HS) b 24/01/1990, Somerset WeSt 1.87m. 92kg. Centre. FC DEBUT: 2011. PROV CAREER:

WP 2011-13 & 16 28-2-0-0-0-10. EP Kings 2016 7-2-0-0-0-10. FC RECORD: 35-4-0-0-0-20. RECORD IN 2016: (WP, EP Kings) 11-2-0-0-0-10.

Kleinhans, Francois (Glenwood HS, Durban) b 07/01/1991, Parklands. 1.84m. 96kg. Flank. FC DEBUT: 2011. PROV CAREER: Sharks 2011-12 & 14-16 24-5-0-0-0-25. Sharks XV 2011-16 30-3-0-0-0-15. REP Honours: SAU20 2011 3-1-0-0-0-5. FC RECORD: 57-9-0-0-0-45. RECORD IN 2016: (Sharks, Sharks XV) 6-2-0-0-0-10.

Kleyn, Jean (Linden HS, Johannesburg & US) b 26/08/1993, Krugersdorp. 2.02.00m. 110kg. Lock. FC DEBUT: 2014. PROV CAREER: WP 2014-16 24-1-0-0-0-5. SUPERRUGBY: Stormers 2014-16 18-0-0-0-0-0. FC RECORD: 42-1-0-0-0-5. RECORD IN 2016: (Stormers, WP) 3-1-0-0-0-5.

Kloppers, Pieter Hugo (Worcester Gym. & US) b 14/10/1988, Worcester. 1.97m. 99kg. Lock. FC DEBUT: 2010. PROV CAREER: WP 2010 4-0-0-0-0-0. Lions 2013 4-0-0-0-0-0. Golden Lions XV 2013-14 12-1-0-0-0-5. Griquas 2014-15 32-2-0-0-0-10. Pumas 2016 18-0-0-0-0-0. REP Honours: SA Students 2012 2-1-0-0-0-5. FC RECORD: 72-4-0-0-0-20. RECORD IN 2016: (Pumas) 18-0-0-0-0-0.

Kobese, Bangihlombe (Dale College, King William's Town & UFH) b 19/01/1992, Mdantsane. 1.68m. 63kg. Scrumhalf. FC DEBUT: 2014. PROV CAREER: Bulldogs 2014-16 45-1-5-1-0-18. FC RECORD: 45-1-5-1-0-18. RECORD IN 2016: (Bulldogs) 19-0-0-0-0-0.

Koch, Vincent Philip (Huguenote HS, Springs) b 13/03/1990, Empangeni. 1.85m. 118kg. Prop. FC DEBUT: 2012. PROV CAREER: Blue Bulls 2012 3-1-0-0-0-5. Pumas 2012-15 51-8-0-0-0-40. SUPERRUGBY: Stormers 2015-16 33-7-0-0-0-35. REP Honours: SA 2015-16 TESTS: 9-0-0-0-0-0. Springboks 2015 1-0-0-0-0-0. Total: 10-0-0-0-0-0. SA A 2016 1-0-0-0-0-0. SA Pres XV 2013 2-0-0-0-0-0. FC RECORD: 100-16-0-0-0-80. RECORD IN 2016: (SA, SA A, Stormers) 24-6-0-0-0-30.

Koekemoer, Jordan (Maritzburg College & NMMU) b 20/06/1996, Westville. 1.74m. 79kg. Flyhalf. FC DEBUT: 2016. PROV CAREER: EP Kings 2016 3-0-0-0-0-0. FC RECORD: 3-0-0-0-0-0. RECORD IN 2016: (EP Kings) 3-0-0-0-0-0.

Koen, Sias (Klerksdorp HS) b 01/01/1994, Bloemfontein. 1.90m. 108kg. Flank. FC DEBUT: 2015. Sharks XV 2015 5-0-0-0-0-0. Griquas 2016 18-1-0-0-0-5. FC RECORD: 23-1-0-0-0-5. RECORD IN 2016: (Griquas) 18-1-0-0-0-5.

Kok, Werner (Nelspruit HS) b 17/01/1993, Nelspruit. 1.79m. 88kg. Wing. FC DEBUT: 2016. PROV CAREER: WP 2016 7-4-0-0-0-20. FC RECORD: 7-4-0-0-0-20. REP Honours: SA Sevens 2013-15. RECORD IN 2016: (WP) 7-4-0-0-0-20.

Kolbe, Cheslin (Brackenfell HS, Cape Town) b 28/10/1993, Kraaifontein. 1.70m. 69kg. Utility back. FC DEBUT: 2013. PROV CAREER: WP 2013-16 47-13-1-0-0-67. SUPERRUGBY: Stormers 2014-16 35-3-0-0-0-15. REP Honours: SA U20 2013 5-2-0-0-0-10. SA Sevens 2012-16. FC RECORD: 87-18-1-0-0-92. RECORD IN 2016: (Stormers, WP, SA Sevens) 20-1-0-0-0-5.

Kolisi, Siya (Grey HS, PE) b 16/06/1991, Port Elizabeth. 1.86m. 96kg. Eighthman. FC DEBUT: 2011. PROV CAREER: WP 2011-14 29-7-0-0-0-35. SUPERRUGBY: Stormers 2012-16 76-8-0-0-0-40. REP Honours: SA 2013 & 15-16 TESTS: 16-0-0-0-0-0. SAU20 2010-11 8-2-0-0-0-10. FC RECORD: 129-17-0-0-0-85. RECORD IN 2016: (SA, Stormers) 19-3-0-0-0-15.

Koster, Armandt (Pionier HS, Vryheid & UFS) b 20/01/1990, Vryheid. 1.92.00m. 105kg. Flank/Lock. FC DEBUT: 2012. PROV CAREER: Griffons 2012-15 28-3-0-0-0-15. Free State XV 2012 & 16 9-0-0-0-0-0.

Cheetahs 2015-16 13-0-0-0-0-0. SUPERRUGBY: Cheetahs 2016 3-0-0-0-0-0. FC RECORD: 53-3-0-0-0-15. RECORD IN 2016: (Cheetahs S18, Cheetahs, Free State XV) 15-0-0-0-0-0.

Kota, Mbeko (Itembelihle HS) b 23/09/1987, Port Elizabeth. 1.80m. 89kg. Hooker. FC DEBUT: 2015. PROV CAREER: Bulldogs 2015-16 10-1-0-0-0-5. FC RECORD: 10-1-0-0-0-5. RECORD IN 2016: (Bulldogs) 6-1-0-0-0-5.

Kotze, Andre Jacques (Nelspruit HS) b 17/06/1991, Vredendal. 1.83m. 124kg. Prop. FC DEBUT: 2013. PROV CAREER: Boland 2013 13-0-0-0-0-0. Golden Lions XV 2013 1-0-0-0-0-0. Pumas 2016 12-2-0-0-0-10. FC RECORD: 26-2-0-0-0-10. RECORD IN 2016: (Pumas) 12-2-0-0-0-10.

Kotze, Gert Johannes (Grey College, Bloemfontein & UFS) b 13/01/1995, Upington. 1.77m. 107kg. Prop. FC DEBUT: 2016. PROV CAREER: Free State XV 2016 4-0-0-0-0-0. FC RECORD: 4-0-0-0-0-0. RECORD IN 2016: (Free State XV) 4-0-0-0-0-0.

Kotze, John-Ben (Johnny) (Bishops College, Cape Town) b 24/01/1993, Carletonville. 1.85m. 89kg. Centre. FC DEBUT: 2014. PROV CAREER: WP 2014-16 27-5-0-0-0-25. SUPERRUGBY: Stormers 2015-16 19-1-0-0-0-5. FC RECORD: 46-6-0-0-0-30. RECORD IN 2016: (Stormers, WP) 21-3-0-0-0-15.

Kotze, Stephan Clyde (Grey College, Bloemfontein) b 21/01/1991, Kimberley. 1.88m. 119kg. Prop. FC DEBUT: 2011. PROV CAREER: Cheetahs 2011 3-0-0-0-0-0. Free State XV 2012 2-0-0-0-0-0. Pumas 2013-14 6-0-0-0-0-0. Griquas 2015-16 39-4-0-0-0-20. REP Honours: SAU20 2011 2-0-0-0-0-0. FC RECORD: 52-4-0-0-0-20. RECORD IN 2016: (Griquas) 17-3-0-0-0-15.

Kotze, Theuns Andries Willem (Upington HS & NWU) b 16/07/1987, Karasburg. 1.81m. 88kg. Flyhalf. FC DEBUT: 2010. PROV CAREER: Leopards 2010 3-0-0-0-0-0. Eagles 2012 7-1-10-4-0-37. Boland 2016 14-3-24-8-1-90. MISC INFO: Namibia RWC 2011 & 2015. FC RECORD: 24-4-34-12-1-127. RECORD IN 2016: (Boland) 14-3-24-8-1-90.

Koza, Luxolo (Muir Boys' HS, Uitenhage) b 18/09/1994, Uitenhage. 1.89m. 101kg. Flank. FC DEBUT: 2014. PROV CAREER: Griquas 2014-16 12-0-0-0-0-0. FC RECORD: 12-0-0-0-0-0. RECORD IN 2016: (Griquas) 3-0-0-0-0-0.

Kramer, Ruan Cornelius Adriaan (Grey College, Bloemfontein & UKZN) b 03/08/1995, Bloemfontein. 1.85m. 123kg. Prop. FC DEBUT: 2016. PROV CAREER: Sharks XV 2016 12-0-0-0-0-0. FC RECORD: 12-0-0-0-0-0. RECORD IN 2016: (Sharks XV) 12-0-0-0-0-0.

Kriel, Daniel David (Maritzburg College) b 15/02/1994, Cape Town. 1.93m. 103kg. Centre. FC DEBUT: 2014. PROV CAREER: Blue Bulls 2015-16 15-1-0-0-0-5. SUPERRUGBY: Bulls 2016 3-0-0-0-0-0. REP Honours: SAU20 2014 4-0-0-0-0-0. MISC INFO: Twin brother of Jesse Kriel. FC RECORD: 22-1-0-0-0-5. RECORD IN 2016: (Bulls, Blue Bulls) 11-1-0-0-0-5.

Kriel, Jacobus Albertus (Jaco) (Standerton HS & UJ) b 21/08/1989, Standerton. 1.83m. 86kg. Flank. FC DEBUT: 2010. PROV CAREER: Golden Lions 2010-15 44-20-0-0-0-100. Golden Lions XV 2010-13 26-7-0-0-0-35. SUPERRUGBY: Lions 2011-12 & 14-16 55-13-0-0-0-65. P/R 2013 2-1-0-0-0-5. REP Honours: SA 2016 TESTS: 7-0-0-0-0-0. MISC INFO: VC PoY 2012 nominee. SARU PoY nominee 2016. FC RECORD: 134-41-0-0-0-205. RECORD IN 2016: (SA, Lions S18) 24-6-0-0-0-30.

Kriel, Jesse Andre (Maritzburg College & UP) b 15/02/1994, Cape Town. 1.86m. 95kg. Fullback. FC DEBUT: 2013. PROV CAREER: Blue Bulls 2014 16-4-0-0-0-20. SUPERRUGBY: 2014-16 Bulls 31-2-0-0-0-10.

REP Honours: SA 2015-16 TESTS: 17-3-0-0-0-15. Springboks 2015 1-0-0-0-0-0. Total: 18-3-0-0-0-15. Springbok XV 2016 1-0-0-0-0-0. SA U20 2013-14 9-7-0-0-0-35. MISC INFO: Twin brother of Daniel Kriel. FC RECORD: 75-16-0-0-0-80. RECORD IN 2016: (SA, Springbok XV, Bulls) 21-1-0-0-0-5.

Kruger, De Wet (Oudtshoorn HS & UFS) b 18/11/1991, Randfontein. 1.91m. 112kg. Flank. FC DEBUT: 2015. PROV CAREER: Cheetahs 2015 2-1-0-0-0-5. Griffons 2016 18-8-0-0-0-40. MISC INFO: Brother of Tertius Kruger. FC RECORD: 20-9-0-0-0-45. RECORD IN 2016: (Griffons) 18-8-0-0-0-40.

Kruger, Kyle Hercules (Florida & Linden HS, Johannesburg & UJ) b 05/08/1995, Johannesburg. 1.80m. 116kg. Prop. FC DEBUT: 2016. PROV CAREER: Golden Lions XV 2016 1-0-0-0-0-0. FC RECORD: 1-0-0-0-0-0. RECORD IN 2016: (Golden Lions XV) 1-0-0-0-0-0.

Kruger, Marco (Nelspruit HS) b 20/08/1992, Nelspruit. 1.94m. 113kg. Lock. FC DEBUT: 2014. PROV CAREER: Pumas 2014 1-0-0-0-0-0. Griffons 2015 11-0-0-0-0-0. Eagles 2016 11-0-0-0-0-0. FC RECORD: 23-0-0-0-0-0. RECORD IN 2016: (Eagles) 11-0-0-0-0-0.

Kruger, Robert Albertus (Standerton HS & NWU) b 28/04/1988, Johannesburg. 1.94m. 106kg. FC DEBUT: 2009. PROV CAREER: Lions 2009-10 4-0-0-0-0-0. Golden Lions XV 2009-11 & 16 13-1-0-0-0-5. Leopards 2011-15 48-4-0-0-0-20. Leopard XV 2013-14 13-2-0-0-0-10. SUPERRUGBY: Lions 2009-10 & 15-16 28-0-0-0-0-0. FC RECORD: 106-7-0-0-0-35. RECORD IN 2016: (Lions S18, Golden Lions XV) 13-0-0-0-0-0.

Kruger, Tertius (Outeniqua HS, George) b 09/08/1993, Randfontein. 1.79m. 90kg. Centre. FC DEBUT: 2015. PROV CAREER: Cheetahs 2015 2-0-0-0-0-0. Free State XV 2016 12-4-0-0-0-20. Griffons 2016 7-2-0-0-0-10. MISC INFO: Brother of De Wet Kruger. FC RECORD: 21-6-0-0-0-30. RECORD IN 2016: (Griffons, Free State XV) 19-6-0-0-0-30.

Kruger, Werner (Kempton Park HS) b 23/01/1985, Kempton Park. 1.90m. 107kg. Prop. FC DEBUT: 2003. PROV CAREER: Blue Bulls 2003 & 05-07-16 134-7-0-0-0-35. Blue Bulls XV 2007 1-0-0-0-0-0. SUPERRUGBY: Bulls 2008-16 120-8-0-0-0-40. REP Honours: SA 2011-12 TESTS: 4-0-0-0-0-0. Tour: 2010 1-0-0-0-0-0. Total: 5-0-0-0-0-0. Emerging Springboks 2009 1-0-0-0-0-0. SA U21 2005-06 6-0-0-0-0-0. FC RECORD: 267-15-0-0-0-75. RECORD IN 2016: (Bulls, Blue Bulls) 8-0-0-0-0-0.

Kubekha, Sandile Mlungisi (Kearsney College, Botha's Hill) b 03/07/1994, Durban. 1.76m. 86kg. Centre. FC DEBUT: 2014. PROV CAREER: Sharks XV 2014-16 10-1-3-0-0-11. Leopards 2016 5-0-0-0-0-0. FC RECORD: 15-1-3-0-0-11. RECORD IN 2016: (Leopards, Sharks XV) 8-1-0-0-0-5.

Kyd, Blake Jonathan (Maritzburg College) b 10/06/1988, Pietermaritzburg. 1.78m. 94kg. Prop. FC DEBUT: 2012. PROV CAREER: Bulldogs 2012-16 86-2-0-0-0-10. FC RECORD: 86-2-0-0-0-10. RECORD IN 2016: (Bulldogs) 20-0-0-0-0-0.

Labuschagne, Gerhardus Jacobus (Die Anker HS, Brakpan & UFS) b 05/12/1995, Springs. 1.94m. 95kg. Wing. FC DEBUT: 2015. PROV CAREER: Free State XV 2015-16 5-0-2-0-0-4. FC RECORD: 5-0-2-0-0-4. RECORD IN 2016: (Free State XV) 2-0-2-0-0-4.

Labuschagne, Pieter Hermias Cornelius (Grey College, Bloemfontein & UFS) b 11/01/1989, Pretoria. 1.89m. 103kg. Flank. FC DEBUT: 2011. PROV CAREER: Cheetahs 2011-14 44-11-0-0-0-55. Free State XV 2012 2-0-0-0-0-0. Emerging Cheetahs 2011 1-0-0-0-0-0. Blue Bulls 2015 11-2-0-0-0-10. SUPERRUGBY: Cheetahs 2012-14 27-2-0-0-0-

10. Bulls 2015-16 22-5-0-0-0-25. FC RECORD: 107-20-0-0-0-100. RECORD IN 2016: (Bulls) 11-2-0-0-0-10.

Ladendorf Ernst (Marais Viljoen HS, Alberton) b 05/02/1992, Alberton. 2.0m. 103kg. Flank. FC DEBUT: 2013. PROV CAREER: Bulldogs 2013 3-0-0-0-0-0. Valke 2014-16 41-3-0-0-0-15. FC RECORD: 44-3-0-0-0-15. RECORD IN 2016: (Valke) 15-0-0-0-0-0.

Lambie, Patrick Jonathan (Michaelhouse, Balgowan) b 17/10/90, Durban. 1.77m. 90kg. Flyhalf. FC DEBUT: 2009. PROV CAREER: Sharks 2009-14 & 16 30-6-52-63-2-329. Sharks Inv XV 2009 1-0-1-1-0-5. SUPERRUGBY: Sharks 2010-16 66-13-86-158-1-714. REP Honours: SA 2010-16 TESTS: 56-2-25-27-4-153. Tour: 1-0-0-0-0-0. Springboks 2015 1-0-2-0-0-4. Total: 58-2-27-27-4-157. Springbok XV 2016 1-0-3-0-0-6. SAU20 2010 5-4-17-7-0-75. British Barbarians 2013 & 15 3-1-8-0-0-21. MISC INFO: SARU PoY2011 and 2012 nominee. SA Rugby YPoY2011. MISC INFO: Son of former Natal utility back Ian Lambie. Grandson of Nic Labuschagne (England and Natal) and former President of the KZNRU. FC RECORD: 164-26-194-258-7-1313. RECORD IN 2016: (SA, Springbok XV, Sharks S18, Sharks) 11-2-14-12-1-77.

Language, Juan Michael (Framesby HS, Port Elizabeth) b 19/04/1989, Port Elizabeth. 1.83m. 97kg. Flank. FC DEBUT: 2014. PROV CAREER: Leopards 2014-16 29-15-0-0-0-75. Leopards XV 2015 8-2-0-0-0-10. FC RECORD: 37-17-0-0-0-85. RECORD IN 2016: (Leopards) 8-2-0-0-0-10.

Lee, Nicolaas Jacobus (Affies, Pretoria & UFS) b 13/03/1994, Pretoria. 1.80m. 89kg. Centre. FC DEBUT: 2014. PROV CAREER: Free State XV 2014-15 12-6-0-0-0-30. Cheetahs 2016 8-4-0-0-0-20. SUPERRUGBY: Cheetahs 2016 7-0-0-0-0-0. FC RECORD: 27-10-0-0-0-50. RECORD IN 2016: (Cheetahs S18, Cheetahs) 15-4-0-0-0-20.

Le Roux, Abraham Jacobus (AJ) (Overkruin HS, Pretoria) b 12/12/1990, Pretoria. 1.80m. 108kg. Hooker. FC DEBUT: 2010. PROV CAREER: Blue Bulls 2010 2-0-0-0-0-0. Cheetahs 2012-14 11-1-0-0-0-5. Golden Lions XV 2011-12 10-0-0-0-0-0. Griffons 2013-14 13-5-0-0-0-25. Griquas 2015-16 42-6-0-0-0-30. FC RECORD: 78-12-0-0-0-60. RECORD IN 2016: (Griquas) 18-2-0-0-0-10.

Le Roux, Bartholomeus Gabriel (Bart) (Framesby HS, Port Elizabeth) b 28/01/1994, Pretoria. 1.89m. 122kg. Prop. FC DEBUT: 2015. PROV CAREER: Leopards 2015-16 19-5-0-0-0-25. FC RECORD: 19-5-0-0-0-25. RECORD IN 2016: (Leopards) 13-3-0-0-0-15.

Le Roux, Grant (Flippie) (Vereeniging THS & NWU) b 13/01/1986, Sasolburg. 1.97m. 110kg. Lock. FC DEBUT: 2009. PROV CAREER: Boland 2009-11 44-1-0-0-0-5. Eagles 2012-16 68-4-0-0-0-20. FC RECORD: 112-5-0-0-0-25. RECORD IN 2016: (Eagles) 10-0-0-0-0-0.

Le Roux, Willem Jacobus (Willie) (Paul Roos Gym., Stellenbosch) b 18/08/1989, Cape Town. 1.86m. 88kg. Fullback. FC DEBUT: 2010. PROV CAREER: Boland 2010-11 39-27-31-6-2-221. Griquas 2012-13 11-1-0-0-0-5. SUPERRUGBY: Cheetahs 2012-15 58-18-0-0-0-90. Sharks 2016 13-3-0-0-0-15. REP Honours: SA 2013-16 TESTS: 41-10-0-0-0-50. Springboks 2014-15 2-4-0-0-0-20. Total: 43-14-0-0-0-70. British Barbarians 2013 1-0-0-0-0-0. MISC INFO: IRB PoYnominee 2014. PoY2014 nominee. FC RECORD: 165-63-31-6-2-401. RECORD IN 2016: (SA, Sharks S18) 20-4-0-0-0-20.

Lerm, Ruaan Stephan (Dr. EG Jansen HS, Boksburg) b 25/03/1992, Kempton Park. 1.92.00m. 93kg. Eighthman. FC DEBUT: 2012. PROV CAREER: Golden Lions XV 2012-16 35-18-0-0-0-90. Griquas 2014 8-1-0-0-0-5. Lions 2015-16 11-1-0-0-0-5. SUPERRUGBY: Lions 2015-16 3-0-0-0-0-0. FC RECORD: 57-20-0-0-0-100. RECORD IN 2016: (Lions S18, Lions, Golden Lions XV) 19-9-0-0-0-45.

Lewies, Joseph Stephanus Theuns (Stephan) (Eldoraigne HS, Pretoria) b 27/01/1992, Pretoria. 2.00m. 114kg. Lock. FC DEBUT: 2012. PROV CAREER: Sharks XV 2012-13 & 15 3-0-0-0-0-0. Sharks 2013-14 & 16 17-1-0-0-0-5. SUPERRUGBY: Sharks 2014-16 35-0-0-0-0-0. REP Honours: SA 2014 TESTS: 1-0-0-0-0-0. SA A 2016 1-0-0-0-0-0. FC RECORD: 57-1-0-0-0-5. RECORD IN 2016: (SA A, Sharks S18, Sharks) 18-0-0-0-0-0.

Lewis, Clemen (Boland Agric. HS, Paarl) b 10/10/1983. 1.75m. 90kg. Hooker. FC DEBUT: 2006. PROV CAREER: Boland 2006-16 144-11-0-0-0-55. REP Honours: SA Barbarians 2012 1-0-0-0-0-0. FC RECORD: 145-11-0-0-0-55. RECORD IN 2016: (Boland) 10-1-0-0-0-5.

Lewis, Jean-Paul (Paul Roos Gym., Stellenbosch & US) b 20/10/1993, Stellenbosch. 1.76m. 72kg. Centre. FC DEBUT: 2013. PROV CAREER: WP 2014-16 23-8-0-0-0-40. Pumas 2016 9-5-0-0-0-25. REP Honours: SA Univ 2013 1-3-0-0-0-15. FC RECORD: 33-16-0-0-0-80. RECORD IN 2016: (WP, Pumas) 19-10-0-0-0-50.

Leyds, Dillyn Yullrich (Bishops College, Rondebosch & UCT) b 12/09/1992, Somerset WeSt 1.85m. 78kg. Wing. FC DEBUT: 2012. PROV CAREER: WP 2013-15 15-6-1-1-0-35. SUPERRUGBY: Stormers 2015-16 19-7-0-0-0-35. REP Honours: SA U20 2012 4-0-0-0-0-0. FC RECORD: 38-13-1-1-0-70. RECORD IN 2016: (Stormers) 4-1-0-0-0-5.

Libbok, Immanuel (Manie) (Daniel Pienaar THS, Uitenhage & Outeniqua HS, George) b 15/07/1997, Humansdorp. 1.82.00m. 80kg. Fullback. FC DEBUT: 2016. PROV CAREER: Blue Bulls 2016 4-1-0-1-0-8. REP Honours: SAU20 2016 5-3-0-0-0-15. FC RECORD: 9-4-0-1-0-23. RECORD IN 2016: (Blue Bulls, SAU20) 9-4-0-1-0-23.

Liebenberg, Christiaan Rudolph (Tiaan) (Grey College, Bloemfontein) b 18/12/1981, Kimberley. 1.85m. 107kg. Hooker. FC DEBUT: 2002. PROV CAREER: Sharks 2002 2-0-0-0-0-0. Griquas 2003-06 64-4-1-0-0-22. WP 2006-07,09-14 62-6-0-0-0-30. Free State XV 2016 5-2-0-0-0-10. SUPERRUGBY: Cheetahs 2006 13-1-0-0-0-5. Stormers 2007-14 73-5-0-0-0-25. REP Honours: SA 2012 TESTS: 5-0-0-0-0-0. SA 2007 Tour: 1-0-0-0-0-0. Total: 6-0-0-0-0-0. Emerging Springboks 2009 1-0-0-0-0-0. MISC INFO: Brother of FS hooker Hercu. Son of former GW & FS flyhalf & fullback Henning Liebenberg. FC RECORD: 226-18-1-0-0-92. RECORD IN 2016: (Free State XV) 5-2-0-0-0-10.

Liebenberg, Christiaan Rudolph (Tiaan) (Monument HS, Krugersdorp & Jan Viljoen HS, Randfontein) b 06/10/1993, Krugersdorp. 1.93m. 108kg. Flank. FC DEBUT: 2015. PROV CAREER: Leopards XV 2015 1-0-0-0-0-0. Leopards 2016 2-1-0-0-0-5. FC RECORD: 3-1-0-0-0-5. RECORD IN 2016: (Leopards) 2-1-0-0-0-5.

Liebenberg, Hanro (Drostdy HS, Worcester) b 10/10/1995, Brackenfell. 1.96m. 103kg. Eighthman. FC DEBUT: 2015. PROV CAREER: Blue Bulls 2015-16 22-6-0-0-0-30. SUPERRUGBY: Bulls 2015-16 8-1-0-0-0-5. REP Honours: SAU20 2015 5-2-0-0-0-10. FC RECORD: 35-9-0-0-0-45. RECORD IN 2016: (Bulls, Blue Bulls) 21-7-0-0-0-35.

Liebenberg, RJ (Voortrekker HS, Bethlehem) b 11/12/1990, Bethlehem. 1.84m. 101kg. Flank. FC DEBUT: 2011. PROV CAREER: Golden Lions XV 2011 1-0-0-0-0-0. Griquas 2013-16 54-1-0-0-0-5. REP Honours: SA Univ 2013 1-0-0-0-0-0. FC RECORD: 56-1-0-0-0-5. RECORD IN 2016: (Griquas) 12-0-0-0-0-0.

Lobberts, Hilton (New Orleans SS, Paarl) b 11/06/1986, Paarl. 1.90m. 102kg. Flank. FC DEBUT: 2005. PROV CAREER: Blue Bulls 2006-08 37-5-0-0-0-25. Boland 2009-10 17-0-0-0-0-0. WP 2009 & 2011-12 34-3-0-0-0-15. Griquas 2013-16 27-2-0-0-0-10. SUPERRUGBY: Bulls 2007-08 7-0-0-0-0-0. Stormers 2009 5-0-0-0-0-0. Cheetahs 2014 & 16 7-1-0-0-0-5. REP Honours: SA 2006-07 TESTS:

2-0-0-0-0-0. Tour: 2006,07 2-0-0-0-0-0. Total: 4-0-0-0-0-0. Emerging Springboks 2007 1-0-0-0-0-0. SA U21 2005-06 10-1-0-0-0-5. SA U19s 2004-05. FC RECORD: 149-12-0-0-0-60. RECORD IN 2016: (Cheetahs S18, Griquas) 8-1-0-0-0-5.

Lombard, Kyle (Paul Roos Gym., Stellenbosch) b 16/03/1993, Port Elizabeth. 1.76m. 87kg. Centre. FC DEBUT: 2014. PROV CAREER: WP 2014-15 14-3-0-0-0-15. Griquas 2016 5-0-0-0-0-0. FC RECORD: 19-3-0-0-0-15. RECORD IN 2016: (Griquas) 5-0-0-0-0-0.

Louw, Louis-Francois Pickard (Francois) (Bishops, Rondebosch) b 15/06/1985, Cape Town. 1.90m. 114kg. Flank. FC DEBUT: 2006. PROV CAREER: WP 2006-10 65-13-0-0-0-65. SUPERRUGBY: Stormers 2008-11 52-4-0-0-0-20. REP Honours: SA 2010-16 TESTS: 52-8-0-0-0-40. Springboks 2014-15 2-0-0-0-0-0. Total: 54-8-0-0-0-40. British Barbarians 2013 1-0-0-0-0-0. MISC INFO: Grandson of former Springbok Jan Pickard. FC RECORD: 172-25-0-0-0-125. RECORD IN 2016: (SA) 9-0-0-0-0-0.

Louw, Marius (Grey College, Bloemfontein & UKZN) b 24/10/1995, Bloemfontein. 1.81m. 94kg. Centre. FC DEBUT: 2015. PROV CAREER: Sharks XV 2015-16 10-8-0-0-0-40. FC RECORD: 10-8-0-0-0-40. RECORD IN 2016: (Sharks XV) 6-5-0-0-0-25.

Louw, Robert Mathew Mark (Paul Roos Gym., Stellenbosch) b 19/11/1992, Cape Town. 1.88m. 95kg. Centre. FC DEBUT: 2016. PROV CAREER: Boland 2016 4-2-0-0-0-10. MISC INFO: Son of former Springbok Rob Louw. FC RECORD: 4-2-0-0-0-10. RECORD IN 2016: (Boland) 4-2-0-0-0-10.

Louw, Wilco Mario (HTS Drostdy, Worcester & UP) b 20/07/1994, Ceres. 1,85m. 130kg. Prop. FC DEBUT: 2014. PROV CAREER: WP 2015-16 36-1-0-0-0-5. SUPERRUGBY: Stormers 2015-16 3-0-0-0-0-0. REP Honours: SAU20 2014 5-0-0-0-0-0. FC RECORD: 44-1-0-0-0-5. RECORD IN 2016: (Stormers, WP) 15-0-0-0-0-0.

Louw, Wilmaure Derrick (Carlton van Heerden HS, Upington) b 02/02/1987, Upington. 1.83m. 86kg. Centre. FC DEBUT: 2009. PROV CAREER: Griquas 2009-12 63-11-0-0-0-55. Pumas 2013-16 51-3-0-0-0-15. SUPERRUGBY: Cheetahs 2010-11 6-0-0-0-0-0. REP Honours: SA Pres XV 2013 3-1-0-0-0-5. FC RECORD: 123-15-0-0-0-75. RECORD IN 2016: (Pumas) 6-0-0-0-0-0.

Lubbe, Lohan (Paarl Gym. & ETA College) b 06/04/1995, Strand. 1.91m. 92kg. Fullback. FC DEBUT: 2016. PROV CAREER: Griffons 2016 2-0-0-0-0-0. FC RECORD: 2-0-0-0-0-0. RECORD IN 2016: (Griffons) 2-0-0-0-0-0.

Ludick, Wayne (Riebeeckstad HS) b 26/01/1992, Welkom. 1.96m. 87kg. Lock. FC DEBUT: 2016. PROV CAREER: Griffons 2016 4-0-0-0-0-0. FC RECORD: 4-0-0-0-0-0. RECORD IN 2016: (Griffons) 4-0-0-0-0-0.

Luiters, Kevin (Grey College, Bloemfontein & UFS) b 02/07/1992, Port Elizabeth. 1.72.00m. 75kg. Scrumhalf. FC DEBUT: 2011. PROV CAREER: Cheetahs 2011 & 13 6-1-0-0-0-5. Free State XV 2012-13 6-0-0-0-0-0. EP Kings 2014-15 15-2-0-0-0-10. Pumas 2016 6-2-0-0-0-10. SUPERRUGBY: Southern Kings 2016 8-0-0-0-0-0. REP Honours: SA Sevens 2012-13. FC RECORD: 41-5-0-0-0-25. RECORD IN 2016: (Southern Kings, Pumas) 14-2-0-0-0-10.

Lusaseni, Luvuyiso (Selborne College, East London & Ethekwini College) b 16/12/1988, East London. 1.96m. 102kg. FC DEBUT: 2009. PROV CAREER: Sharks XV 2009-10 11-1-0-0-0-5. Griquas 2010 3-0-0-0-0-0. Leopards 2011-13 43-2-0-0-0-10. Leopard XV 2013 4-0-0-0-0-0. Lions 2014-16 16-0-0-0-0-0. Golden Lions XV 2015-16 17-1-0-0-0-5. SUPERRUGBY: Lions 2014-15 14-0-0-0-0-0. REP Honours: SA Barbarians 2012 1-0-0-0-0-0. SAU20 2008 1-0-0-0-0-0.

SA Univ 2013 1-0-0-0-0-0. FC RECORD: 111-4-0-0-0-20. RECORD IN 2016: (Lions, Golden Lions XV) 13-1-0-0-0-5.

Lyons, Robert James (Selborne College, East London) b 26/06/1996, East London. 1.88m. 106kg. Lock. FC DEBUT: 2016. PROV CAREER: EP Kings 2016 4-0-0-0-0-0. FC RECORD: 4-0-0-0-0-0. RECORD IN 2016: (EP Kings) 4-0-0-0-0-0.

Maarman, Tertius (Hentie Cilliers HS, Virginia) b 14/04/1987, Port Elizabeth. 1.69m. 79kg. Utility back. FC DEBUT: 2008. PROV CAREER: Griffons 2008-16 120-37-5-0-0-195. FC RECORD: 120-37-5-0-0-195. RECORD IN 2016: (Griffons) 12-4-0-0-0-20.

Mabuza, Sikhumbuzo Thabo (Centurion HS) b 01/03/1994, Nelspruit. 1.82.00m. 90kg. Flank. FC DEBUT: 2014. PROV CAREER: Golden Lions XV 2014-15 7-3-0-0-0-15. Griquas 2016 7-1-0-0-0-5. REP Honours: SAU20 2014 1-0-0-0-0-0. FC RECORD: 15-4-0-0-0-20. RECORD IN 2016: (Griquas) 7-1-0-0-0-5.

Maebane, Adrian (Ben Vorster HS, Tzaneen & UP) b 09/08/1995, Acornhoek. 1.78m. 94kg. Centre. FC DEBUT: 2016. PROV CAREER: Blue Bulls 2016 2-0-0-0-0-0. FC RECORD: 2-0-0-0-0-0. RECORD IN 2016: (Blue Bulls) 2-0-0-0-0-0.

Mafela, Mashudu Cornelius (Merensky HS, Tzaneen & NWU) b 16/06/1991, Vierfontein, Limpopo. 1.83m. 118kg. Prop. FC DEBUT: 2014. PROV CAREER: Leopards 2014 & 16 16-0-0-0-0-0. FC RECORD: 16-0-0-0-0-0. RECORD IN 2016: (Leopards) 10-0-0-0-0-0.

Mafuma, Mosolwa Mashudu (St Benedict's College, Johannesburg) b 13/02/1996, Germiston. 1.83m. 89kg. Wing. FC DEBUT: 2016. PROV CAREER: Free State XV 2016 3-3-0-0-0-15. REP Honours: SAU20 2016 3-1-0-0-0-5. FC RECORD: 6-4-0-0-0-20. RECORD IN 2016: (Free State XV, SAU20) 6-4-0-0-0-20.

Mahlasela, Musa (Cambridge HS & UFS) b 26/07/1996, East London. 1.86m. 91kg. Flank. FC DEBUT: 2016. PROV CAREER: Free State XV 2016 1-0-0-0-0-0. FC RECORD: 1-0-0-0-0-0. RECORD IN 2016: (Free State XV) 1-0-0-0-0-0.

Mahlo, Kefentse Seshego (Ben Vorster HS, Tzaneen & UP) b 31/03/1993, Tzaneen. 1.78m. 78kg. Wing. FC DEBUT: 2014. PROV CAREER: Blue Bulls 2014-16 23-12-0-0-0-60. FC RECORD: 23-12-0-0-0-60. RECORD IN 2016: (Blue Bulls) 11-5-0-0-0-25.

Mahuza, Sylvian (Outeniqua HS, George & NWU) b 29/07/1993, George. 1.78m. 80kg. Wing. FC DEBUT: 2013. PROV CAREER: Leopards 2013-14 14-15-0-0-0-75. EP Kings 2015 7-2-0-0-0-10. Lions 2016 5-5-0-0-0-25. Golden Lions XV 2016 3-3-0-0-0-15. SUPERRUGBY: Lions 2016 6-2-0-0-0-10. REP Honours: SA U20 2013 no appearances. FC RECORD: 35-27-0-0-0-135. RECORD IN 2016: (Lions S18, Lions, Golden Lions XV) 14-10-0-0-0-50.

Majola, Khaya (Westville Boys'HS) b 13/03/1992, Kokstad. 1.85m. 98kg. Flank. FC DEBUT: 2012. PROV CAREER: Sharks XV 2012-16 35-8-0-0-0-40. Sharks 2014-16 9-1-0-0-0-5. SUPERRUGBY: Sharks 2015 2-0-0-0-0-0. REP Honours: SAU20 2012 1-0-0-0-0-0. FC RECORD: 47-9-0-0-0-45. RECORD IN 2016: (Sharks, Sharks XV) 15-4-0-0-0-20.

Majola, Mzamo (Westville Boys'HS, Pinetown & Varsity College) b 20/02/1995, Durban. 1.82.00m. 115kg. Prop. FC DEBUT: 2015. PROV CAREER: Sharks 2015 3-0-0-0-0-0. Sharks XV 2015-16 12-0-0-0-0-0. REP Honours: SAU20 2015 4-0-0-0-0-0. FC RECORD: 19-0-0-0-0-0. RECORD IN 2016: (Sharks XV) 10-0-0-0-0-0.

Makase, Michael (Luxolo HS) b 20/11/1990, Keiskammahoek. 1.90m. 90kg. Wing. FC DEBUT: 2014. PROV CAREER: Bulldogs 2014-16 45-11-0-0-0-55. FC RECORD: 45-11-0-0-0-55. RECORD IN 2016:

(Bulldogs) 15-6-0-0-0-30.

Maku, Bandise Grey (Dale College, King William's Town) b 24/06/1986, King William's Town. 1.87m. 111kg. Hooker. FC DEBUT: 2006. PROV CAREER: Blue Bulls 2006-10 & 13-16 93-3-0-0-0-15. Lions 2011-12 23-1-0-0-0-5. SUPERRUGBY: Bulls 2008 & 10 & 14 & 16 28-0-0-0-0-0. Lions 2011 14-0-0-0-0-0. Southern Kings 2013 16-0-0-0-0-0. P/R 2013 2-0-0-0-0-0. REP Honours: SA 2010 TESTS: 1-0-0-0-0-0. Tour: 2009-10 3-1-0-0-0-5. Total: 4-1-0-0-0-5. Emerging Springboks 2007,09 2-0-0-0-0-0. SA U21 2006 3-0-0-0-0-0. FC RECORD: 185-5-0-0-0-25. RECORD IN 2016: (Bulls, Blue Bulls) 15-0-0-0-0-0.

Malherbe, Arnout (Transvalia HS, Vanderbijlpark) b 28/08/1995, Sasolburg. 1.82.00m. 108kg. Prop. FC DEBUT: 2016. PROV CAREER: Golden Lions XV 2016 4-1-0-0-0-5. FC RECORD: 4-1-0-0-0-5. RECORD IN 2016: (Golden Lions XV) 4-1-0-0-0-5.

Malherbe, Jozua Francois (Paarl Boys'HS) b 14/03/1991, Paarl. 1.90m. 124kg. Prop. FC DEBUT: 2011. PROV CAREER: WP 2011-14 34-0-0-0-0-0. SUPERRUGBY: Stormers 2011-16 66-2-0-0-0-10. REP Honours: SA 2012-16 TESTS: 15-0-0-0-0-0. FC RECORD: 115-2-0-0-0-10. RECORD IN 2016: (SA, Stormers) 15-0-0-0-0-0.

Mamojele, Thabo (Patriot HS, Witbank) b 29/07/1986, Witbank. 1.95m. 104kg. Flank. FC DEBUT: 2007. PROV CAREER: Sharks 2007 2-2-0-0-0-10. Valke 2008 & 16 17-2-0-0-0-10. Leopards 2009 & 2011 16-0-0-0-0-0. EP Kings 2012-13 16-2-0-0-0-10. Golden Lions XV 2014 5-0-0-0-0-0. SUPERRUGBY: Southern Kings 2013 1-0-0-0-0-0. FC RECORD: 57-6-0-0-0-30. RECORD IN 2016: (Valke) 12-0-0-0-0-0.

Manentsa, Athenkosi (Khwazi Lomso HS, Port Elizabeth) b 20/05/1990, Keiskammahoek. 1.70m. 90kg. Eighthman. FC DEBUT: 2014. PROV CAREER: Bulldogs 2014-16 15-1-0-0-0-5. FC RECORD: 15-1-0-0-0-5. RECORD IN 2016: (Bulldogs) 8-1-0-0-0-5.

Manjezi, Sintu (St Andrews College, Grahamstown & NMMU) b 07/04/1995, East London. 1.96m. 113kg. Lock. FC DEBUT: 2016. PROV CAREER: EP Kings 2016 11-0-0-0-0-0. SUPERRUGBY: Southern Kings 2016 2-0-0-0-0-0. FC RECORD: 13-0-0-0-0-0. RECORD IN 2016: (Southern Kings, EP Kings) 13-0-0-0-0-0.

Mapimpi, Makazole (Jim Mvabaza HS) b 26/07/1990, Mdantsane. 1.87m. 90kg. Wing. FC DEBUT: 2014. PROV CAREER: Bulldogs 2014-16 54-28-3-1-0-149. FC RECORD: 54-28-3-1-0-149. RECORD IN 2016: (Bulldogs) 20-16-0-0-0-80.

Mapoe, Lionel Granton (Fichardtpark HS, Bloemfontein) b 13/07/1988, Port Elizabeth. 1.82.00m. 84kg. Wing. FC DEBUT: 2008. PROV CAREER: Cheetahs 2008-09 12-6-0-0-0-30. Cheetahs XV 2010 1-0-0-0-0-0. Lions 2011-14 32-6-0-0-0-30. SUPERRUGBY: Cheetahs 2010 5-1-0-0-0-5. Lions 2011-12 & 14-16 62-20-0-0-0-100. Bulls 2013 12-2-0-0-0-10. REP Honours: SA 2012 & 15-16 TESTS: 11-0-0-0-0-0. SAU20 2008 4-5-0-0-0-25. MISC INFO: YP0YNominee 2009. FC RECORD: 139-40-0-0-0-200. RECORD IN 2016: (SA, Lions S18) 26-9-0-0-0-45.

Marais, Charles Maclean (Paarl Boys'HS & UFS) b 29/08/1988, Paarl. 1.91m. 114kg. Prop. FC DEBUT: 2010. PROV CAREER: Cheetahs 2010-11 & 16 17-2-0-0-0-10. Free State XV 2012-13 8-0-0-0-0-0. Griffons 2012-13 6-1-0-0-0-5. Golden Lions XV 2014 10-0-0-0-0-0. EP Kings 2014-15 7-0-0-0-0-0. SUPERRUGBY: Lions 2014 1-0-0-0-0-0. Cheetahs 2016 14-0-0-0-0-0. FC RECORD: 63-3-0-0-0-15. RECORD IN 2016: (Cheetahs S18, Cheetahs) 24-2-0-0-0-10.

Marais, Daniel Rudolf (Niel) (Grey College, Bloemfontein & UFS) b 21/01/1992, Bloemfontein. 1.81m. 97kg. Flyhalf. FC DEBUT: 2013.

PROV CAREER: Free State XV 2013-16 19-1-24-13-0-92. Griquas 2014 1-0-0-0-0-0. Cheetahs 2015-16 12-3-24-17-0-114. SUPERRUGBY: Cheetahs 2015-16 13-2-24-9-0-85. FC RECORD: 45-6-72-39-0-291. RECORD IN 2016: (Cheetahs S18, Cheetahs, Free State XV) 21-4-43-26-0-184.

Marais, Franco Stephan (Transvalia HS, Vanderbijlpark) b 23/09/1992, Vereeniging. 1.86m. 94kg. Hooker. FC DEBUT: 2012. PROV CAREER: Sharks 2012 & 14-16 21-2-0-0-0-10. Sharks XV 2013-15 17-1-0-0-0-5. SUPERRUGBY: Sharks 2014-16 21-0-0-0-0-0. SAU20 2012 1-0-0-0-0-0. FC RECORD: 60-3-0-0-0-15. RECORD IN 2016: (Sharks S18, Sharks) 21-2-0-0-0-10.

Marais, Hendrik Jacobus (Henko) (Volkskool, Potchefstroom & NWU) b 18/06/1993, Lichtenburg. 1.86m. 99kg. Centre. FC DEBUT: 2015. PROV CAREER: Leopards XV 2015 1-0-0-0-0-0. Leopards 2016 9-4-0-0-0-20. FC RECORD: 10-4-0-0-0-20. RECORD IN 2016: (Leopards) 9-4-0-0-0-20.

Marais, Jacobus Johannes (Kobus) (Waterkloof HS, Pretoria) b 05/07/1994, Richards Bay. 1.83m. 92kg. Flyhalf. FC DEBUT: 2013. PROV CAREER: Blue Bulls 2013 & 15 11-2-21-11-0-85. EP Kings 2016 4-0-3-5-0-21. FC RECORD: 15-2-24-16-0-106. RECORD IN 2016: (EP Kings) 4-0-3-5-0-21.

Marais, Philip Retief (Welkom Gym. & UKZN) b 20/07/1995, Welkom. 1.91m. 105kg. Eighthman. FC DEBUT: 2016. PROV CAREER: Sharks XV 2016 8-0-0-0-0-0. FC RECORD: 8-0-0-0-0-0. RECORD IN 2016: (Sharks XV) 8-0-0-0-0-0.

Marais, Sarel Petrus (Paarl Boys' HS) b 16/03/1989. 1.84m. 80kg. Wing/Fullback. PROV CAREER: Leopards 2010 2-3-1-0-0-17. EP Kings 2011-12 36-18-4-0-0-98. Sharks 2013-15 24-7-0-2-0-41. SUPERRUGBY: Southern Kings 2013 8-0-0-0-0-0. P/R 2013 2-0-0-0-0-0. Sharks 2014-15 27-1-0-1-0-8. Bulls 2016 11-2-0-0-0-10. REP Honours: SA Kings 2011 3-0-0-0-0-0. FC RECORD: 113-31-5-3-0-174. RECORD IN 2016: (Bulls) 11-2-0-0-0-10.

Marcus, Dylan (Westville Boys' HS) b 12/09/1993, Westville. 1.76m. 87kg. Scrumhalf. FC DEBUT: 2016. PROV CAREER: Sharks XV 2016 11-0-0-0-0-0. FC RECORD: 11-0-0-0-0-0. RECORD IN 2016: (Sharks XV) 11-0-0-0-0-0.

Maree, Theodorus Daniel (Ben Vorster HS, Tzaneen & UP) b 02/03/1995, Tzaneen. 1.81m. 79kg. Scrumhalf. FC DEBUT: 2016. PROV CAREER: Blue Bulls 2016 3-1-0-0-0-5. FC RECORD: 3-1-0-0-0-5. RECORD IN 2016: (Blue Bulls) 3-1-0-0-0-5.

Marich, George (Afrikaanse HS, Kroonstad) b 11/07/1992, Kroonstad. 1.83m. 120kg. Prop. FC DEBUT: 2014. PROV CAREER: Cheetahs 2014 8-0-0-0-0-0. Free State XV 2015 1-0-0-0-0-0. Griffons 2016 7-0-0-0-0-0. FC RECORD: 16-0-0-0-0-0. RECORD IN 2016: (Griffons) 7-0-0-0-0-0.

Maritz, Hoffman Van Heerden (Voortrekker HS, Bethlehem) b 29/03/1989, Bethlehem. 1.85m. 93kg. Wing. FC DEBUT: 2011. PROV CAREER: Golden Lions XV 2011 5-0-0-0-0-0. Leopards 2011-12 & 14 37-16-0-0-0-80. Leopard XV 2013 4-1-0-0-0-5. Pumas 2015-16 20-3-0-0-0-15. REP Honours: SA Barbarians 2012 1-0-0-0-0-0. SA Pres XV 2013 1-1-0-0-0-5. SA Univ 2013 1-0-0-0-0-0. FC RECORD: 69-21-0-0-0-105. RECORD IN 2016: (Pumas) 12-3-0-0-0-15.

Maritz, Neil Kobus (Paarl Boys' HS) b 22/02/1994, Worcester. 1.83m. 94kg. Centre. FC DEBUT: 2014. PROV CAREER: Sharks XV 2014-16 17-5-0-0-0-25. Sharks 2016 4-0-0-0-0-0. FC RECORD: 21-5-0-0-0-25. RECORD IN 2016: (Sharks, Sharks XV) 12-2-0-0-0-10.

Martinus, Devon Roy (Bredasdorp HS & UWC) b 28/01/1993, Bre-

dasdorp. 1.86m. 114kg. Prop. FC DEBUT: 2013. PROV CAREER: Golden Lions XV 2013 3-0-0-0-0-0. Leopards 2015 4-0-0-0-0-0. Leopards XV 2015 8-0-0-0-0-0. Griquas 2016 19-1-0-0-0-5. REP Honours: SA U20 2013 1-0-0-0-0-0. FC RECORD: 35-1-0-0-0-5. RECORD IN 2016: (Griquas) 19-1-0-0-0-5.

Maruping, Mosoeu Vincent (HTS Louis Botha, Bloemfontein) b 25/11/1993, Virginia. 1.92.00m. 90kg. Flank. FC DEBUT: 2014. PROV CAREER: Free State XV 2014 1-0-0-0-0-0. Griffons 2015-16 24-3-0-0-0-15. FC RECORD: 25-3-0-0-0-15. RECORD IN 2016: (Griffons) 19-0-0-0-0-0.

Maruping, Thamaha Victor (HTS Louis Botha, Bloemfontein & CUT) b 24/08/1996, Welkom. 1.88m. 89kg. Flank. FC DEBUT: 2016. PROV CAREER: Free State XV 2016 1-0-0-0-0-0. FC RECORD: 1-0-0-0-0-0. RECORD IN 2016: (Free State XV) 1-0-0-0-0-0.

Marutlulle, Edgar (Potchefstroom HS) b 20/12/1987, Boksburg. 1.77m. 91kg. Hooker. FC DEBUT: 2007. PROV CAREER: Golden Lions 2010 13-1-0-0-0-5. Golden Lions XV 2011-12 11-3-0-0-0-15. Leopards 2012-13 26-10-0-0-0-50. Leopard XV 2013-14 8-0-0-0-0-0. EP Kings 2014-15 23-0-0-0-0-0. Blue Bulls 2016 2-0-0-0-0-0. SUPERRUGBY: Lions 2011 8-0-0-0-0-0. Southern Kings: 2013 & 16 17-4-0-0-0-20. REP Honours: SA A 2016 1-0-0-0-0-0. SA Students 2007-09 4-0-0-0-0-0. FC RECORD: 113-18-0-0-0-90. RECORD IN 2016: (SA A, Southern Kings, Blue Bulls) 16-4-0-0-0-20.

Marwana, Nkululeko (Glenwood HS, Durban) b 26/04/1994, Port Elizabeth. 1.76m. 88kg. Centre. FC DEBUT: 2015. PROV CAREER: Sharks XV 2015-16 16-3-0-0-0-15. FC RECORD: 16-3-0-0-0-15. RECORD IN 2016: (Sharks XV) 13-3-0-0-0-15.

Marx, Koch Peter (Alberton HS) b 21/01/1994, Johannesburg. 1.91m. 94kg. Wing. FC DEBUT: 2016. PROV CAREER: Lions 2016 4-2-0-0-0-10. Golden Lions XV 2016 9-4-0-0-0-20. SUPERRUGBY: Lions 2016 1-0-0-0-0-0. FC RECORD: 14-6-0-0-0-30. RECORD IN 2016: (Lions S18, Lions, Golden Lions XV) 14-6-0-0-0-30.

Marx, Malcolm Justin (KES, Johannesburg) b 13/07/1994, Germiston. 1.88m. 119kg. Hooker. FC DEBUT: 2014. PROV CAREER: Lions 2014-16 15-1-0-0-0-5. Golden Lions XV 2014-15 12-2-0-0-0-10. SUPERRUGBY: Lions 2014-16 20-5-0-0-0-25. REP Honours: SA 2016 TESTS: 2-0-0-0-0-0. Springbok XV 2016 1-0-0-0-0-0. SA A 2016 2-0-0-0-0-0. SAU20 2014 1-1-0-0-0-5. MISC INFO: SARU YPoY2016. FC RECORD: 53-9-0-0-0-45. RECORD IN 2016: (SA, Springbok XV, SA A, Lions S18, Lions) 22-4-0-0-0-20.

Masimla, Godlen Herschelle Derrick (Huguenote HS, Wellington & UWC) b 11/08/1992, Wellington. 1.77m. 80kg. Scrumhalf. FC DEBUT: 2013. PROV CAREER: WP 2013-16 39-5-0-0-0-25. SUPERRUGBY: Stormers 2015-16 2-0-0-0-0-0. FC RECORD: 41-5-0-0-0-25. RECORD IN 2016: (Stormers, WP) 13-2-0-0-0-10.

Mastriet, Sampie (Drostdy HS, Worcester) b 03/08/1990, Mairsdas. 1.80m. 84kg. Wing. FC DEBUT: 2011. PROV CAREER: Blue Bulls 2011-14 49-31-0-0-0-155. Golden Lions XV 2015 3-0-0-0-0-0. Lions 2015 6-1-0-0-0-5. EP Kings 2016 7-1-0-0-0-5. SUPERRUGBY: Bulls 2013-14 2-1-0-0-0-5. Lions 2015 5-0-0-0-0-0. REP Honours: SAU20 2009-10 6-4-0-0-0-20. SA Sevens 2013-14. FC RECORD: 78-38-0-0-0-190. RECORD IN 2016: (EP Kings) 7-1-0-0-0-5.

Masuku, Siyabonga Praisegod (Piet Retief HS) b 01/08/1996, Paulpietersburg. 1.89m. 85kg. Flyhalf. FC DEBUT: 2016. PROV CAREER: Golden Lions 2016 2-0-3-3-0-15. FC RECORD: 2-0-3-3-0-15. RECORD IN 2016: (Golden Lions XV) 2-0-3-3-0-15.

Mattheus, Garrick Frederick (Grey HS, Port Elizabeth & NMMU) b 23/03/1996, Port Elizabeth. 1.84m. 89kg. Flyhalf. FC DEBUT: 2016. PROV CAREER: EP Kings 2016 8-2-10-12-0-66. FC RECORD: 8-2-10-12-0-66. RECORD IN 2016: (EP Kings) 8-2-10-12-0-66.

Matthews, Duncan Victor (Swartland HS, Malmesbury & UP) b 24/02/1994, Atlantis. 1.82.00m. 88kg. Fullback. FC DEBUT: 2016. PROV CAREER: Blue Bulls 2016 7-1-0-0-0-5. FC RECORD: 7-1-0-0-0-5. RECORD IN 2016: (Blue Bulls) 7-1-0-0-0-5.

Mavundla, Thato Siward (Jeppe HS, Johannesburg & UJ) b 15/05/1989, Welkom. 1.72.00m. 94kg, Flank. FC DEBUT: 2016. PROV CAREER: Griffons 2016 11-1-0-0-0-5. FC RECORD: 11-1-0-0-0-5. RECORD IN 2016: (Griffons) 11-1-0-0-0-5.

Maxwane, Sibahle Ndiphiwe (Dale College, King William's Town) b 14/08/1995, Queen'stown. 1.81m. 83kg. Centre. FC DEBUT: 2016. PROV CAREER: WP 2016 8-2-0-0-0-10. FC RECORD: 8-2-0-0-0-10. RECORD IN 2016: (WP) 8-2-0-0-0-10.

May, Ganfried (Oudtshoorn HS & UP) b 25/07/1994, Oudtshoorn. 1.88m. 88kg. Centre. FC DEBUT: 2015. PROV CAREER: Blue Bulls 2015-16 3-1-0-0-0-5. EP Kings 2016 3-0-0-0-0-0. FC RECORD: 6-1-0-0-0-5. RECORD IN 2016: (Blue Bulls, EP Kings) 4-0-0-0-0-0.

Mayeza, Charles Ndumiso (Glenwood HS, Durban & Varsity College) b 16/05/1990, Durban. 1.83m. 90kg. Wing. FC DEBUT: 2015. PROV CAREER: Sharks XV 2015 3-0-0-0-0-0. Valke 2016 7-4-0-0-0-20. FC RECORD: 10-4-0-0-0-20. RECORD IN 2016: (Valke) 7-4-0-0-0-20.

Mayinje, Athenkosi (Grey HS, Port Elizabeth & NMMU) b 18/01/1996, Port Elizabeth. 1.74m. 84kg. Wing. FC DEBUT: 2016. PROV CAREER: EP Kings 2016 10-2-2-0-0-14. FC RECORD: 10-2-2-0-0-14. RECORD IN 2016: (EP Kings) 10-2-2-0-0-14.

Mbonambi, Mbongeni Theo (Bongi) (Voortrekker HS, Bethlehem, St Albans HS & TUT) b 07/01/1991, Bethlehem. 1.80m. 97kg. Hooker. FC DEBUT: 2012. PROV CAREER: Blue Bulls 2012-14 30-1-0-0-0-5. WP 2015-16 14-2-0-0-0-10. SUPERRUGBY: Bulls 2012 & 14 15-0-0-0-0-0. Stormers: 2015-16 30-0-0-0-0-0. REP Honours: SA 2016 TESTS: 5-0-0-0-0-0. Springbok XV 2016 1-0-0-0-0-0. SAU20 2011 5-0-0-0-0-0. FC RECORD: 100-3-0-0-0-15. RECORD IN 2016: (SA, Springbok XV, Stormers, WP) 24-1-0-0-0-5.

Mbotho, Vuyo (Lukhozi HS, Debenek). b 28/09/1988. Wing. FC DEBUT: 2010. PROV CAREER: Bulldogs 2010-12 26-7-0-0-0-35. Griffons 2013-16 70-23-0-0-0-115. FC RECORD: 96-30-0-0-0-150. RECORD IN 2016: (Griffons) 19-7-0-0-0-35.

McDonald, Shaun (Tygerberg HS, Cape Town) b 09/02/1989, Goodwood. 1.92.00m. 117kg. Flank. FC DEBUT: 2014. PROV CAREER: EP Kings 2014 5-0-0-0-0-0. Boland 2016 22-2-0-0-0-10. FC RECORD: 27-2-0-0-0-10. RECORD IN 2016: (Boland) 22-2-0-0-0-10.

McDuling, David b 08/06/1989. 1.96m. 115kg. Lock. SA FC DEBUT: 2015. PROV CAREER: Sharks 2015 8-0-0-0-0-0. Sharks XV 2016 11-1-0-0-0-5. SUPERRUGBY: Reds 2012-15. Sharks 2016 1-0-0-0-0-0. SA FC RECORD: 20-1-0-0-0-5. RECORD IN 2016: (Sharks S18, Sharks XV) 12-1-0-0-0-5.

Mdaka, Siyabulela (George Campbell HS, Durban & NWU) b 14/02/1988, Umtata. 1.88m. 102kg. Flank. FC DEBUT: 2011. PROV CAREER: Leopards 2011 4-0-0-0-0-0. Bulldogs 2012-16 70-2-0-0-0-10. FC RECORD: 74-2-0-0-0-10. RECORD IN 2016: (Bulldogs) 16-1-0-0-0-5.

Meiring, Steven (Affies, Pretoria) b 02/01/1994, Boksburg. 1.88m. 100kg. Flank. FC DEBUT: 2016. PROV CAREER: Griquas 2016 13-0-0-0-0-0. FC RECORD: 13-0-0-0-0-0. RECORD IN 2016: (Griquas) 13-0-0-0-0-0.

Meyer, Christiaan Jan Petrus (Dr. EG Jansen HS, Boksburg) b 16/05/1994, Springs. 1.76m. 65kg. Scrumhalf. FC DEBUT: 2015. PROV CAREER: Golden Lions XV 2015 1-1-0-0-0-5. Griquas 2016 5-1-0-0-0-5. FC RECORD: 6-2-0-0-0-10. RECORD IN 2016: (Griquas) 5-1-0-0-0-5.

Meyer, John-Hubert (Paul Roos Gym., Stellenbosch, US & UKZN) b 19/09/1993, Cape Town. 1.89m. 119kg. Prop. FC DEBUT: 2016. PROV CAREER: Sharks 2016 7-0-0-0-0-0. Sharks XV 2016 5-0-0-0-0-0. FC RECORD: 12-0-0-0-0-0. RECORD IN 2016: (Sharks, Sharks XV) 12-0-0-0-0-0.

Meyer, Tian Carel (Westville HS) b 20/09/1988, Pietermaritzburg. 1.76m. 71kg. Scrumhalf/Centre. FC DEBUT: 2010. PROV CAREER: Pumas 2010-11 36-10-0-0-0-50. Sharks XV 2013 4-0-0-0-0-0. Lions 2013 6-0-0-0-0-0. Griquas 2014-15 40-12-0-0-0-60. Cheetahs 2016 8-3-0-0-0-15. SUPERRUGBY: Lions 2012 11-2-0-0-0-10. Cheetahs 2014-16 29-1-0-0-0-5. FC RECORD: 134-28-0-0-0-140. RECORD IN 2016: (Cheetahs S18, Cheetahs) 22-4-0-0-0-20.

Mgijima, Aliqhayiya (HTS Louis Botha, Bloemfontein & CUT) b 11/02/1995, Adelaide. 1.78m. 97kg. Centre. FC DEBUT: 2016. PROV CAREER: Free State XV 2016 6-1-0-0-0-5. FC RECORD: 6-1-0-0-0-5. RECORD IN 2016: (Free State XV) 6-1-0-0-0-5.

Mhlongo, Sthembiso Santo (Siyahomula HS, Wartburg & UP) b 13/05/1987, Pietermaritzburg. 2.01m. 112kg. Lock. FC DEBUT: 2013. PROV CAREER: Bulldogs 2013 9-1-0-0-0-5. Leopards 2014-16 26-1-0-0-0-5. Leopards XV 2014-15 8-2-0-0-0-10. FC RECORD: 43-4-0-0-0-20. RECORD IN 2016: (Leopards) 14-0-0-0-0-0.

Mienie, Daniel Jacobus (Danie) (Merensky HS, Tzaneen) b 01/03/1991, Polokwane. 1.78m. 104kg. Prop. FC DEBUT: 2012. PROV CAREER: Sharks 2013-14 9-0-0-0-0-0. Sharks XV 2012-14 15-0-0-0-0-0. Griquas 2015 12-0-0-0-0-0. Free State XV 2016 1-0-0-0-0-0. SUPERRUGBY: Sharks 2013 1-0-0-0-0-0. Cheetahs 2015-16 17-0-0-0-0-0. FC RECORD: 55-0-0-0-0-0. RECORD IN 2016: (Cheetahs S18, Free State XV) 3-0-0-0-0-0.

Minnie, Derick Johannes (Marais Viljoen HS, Alberton) b 29/10/1986, Alberton. 1.86m. 95kg. Flank. FC DEBUT: 2006. PROV CAREER: Golden Lions 2006-14 70-22-0-0-0-110. Golden Lions XV 2006-09 & 13 & 16 28-6-0-0-0-30. Lions XV 2007 1-0-0-0-0-0. SUPERRUGBY: Lions 2010-12 & 14-15 61-6-0-0-0-30. Lions P/R 2013 2-1-0-0-0-5. Sharks 2013 3-3-0-0-0-15. FC RECORD: 165-38-0-0-0-190. RECORD IN 2016: (Golden Lions XV) 6-1-0-0-0-5.

Mjekevu, Wandile Gabada (KES, Johannesburg & UJ) b 07/01/1991, Houghton. 1.90m. 87kg. Wing. FC DEBUT: 2010. PROV CAREER: Golden Lions XV 2011 4-1-0-0-0-5. Sharks XV 2012 & 16 9-5-0-0-0-25. Sharks 2015-16 13-3-0-0-0-15. SUPERRUGBY: Lions 2010 10-4-0-0-0-20. Southern Kings 2016 4-3-0-0-0-15. REP Honours: SAU20 2010-11 10-7-0-0-0-35. FC RECORD: 50-23-0-0-0-115. RECORD IN 2016: (Southern Kings, Sharks, Sharks XV) 11-8-0-0-0-40.

Mkhabela, Mthokozisi Cyprial (Glenwood HS, Durban) b 15/10/1994, Empangeni. 1.68m. 73kg. Scrumhalf. FC DEBUT: 2014. PROV CAREER: Cheetahs 2015-16 5-1-0-0-0-5. Free State XV 2016 3-0-0-0-0-0. REP Honours: SAU20 2014 1-0-0-0-0-0. FC RECORD: 9-1-0-0-0-5. RECORD IN 2016: (Cheetahs, Free State XV) 5-0-0-0-0-0.

Mkhafu, Khwezilokusa (Kwezi) (Lebogang HS, Welkom) b 17/06/1988, Engcobo. 1.77m. 97kg. Hooker. FC DEBUT: 2010. PROV CAREER: Bulldogs 2010-13 70-6-0-0-0-30. Boland 2014 18-1-0-0-5. Griffons 2015-16 36-1-0-0-0-5. REP Honours: SA Pres XV 2013 2-1-0-0-0-5. FC RECORD: 126-9-0-0-0-45. RECORD IN 2016: (Griffons) 19-0-0-0-0-0.

Mkhize, Sipho George (Greytown HS) b 14/05/1994, Greytown. 1.78m. 98kg. Wing. FC DEBUT: 2016. PROV CAREER: Sharks XV 2016 2-0-0-0-0-0. FC RECORD: 2-0-0-0-0-0. RECORD IN 2016: (Sharks XV) 2-0-0-0-0-0.

Mkokeli, Thembani Moeren (Msobumvu HS) b 12/03/1984, East London. 1.79m. 77kg. Flyhalf. FC DEBUT: 2003. PROV CAREER: Bulldogs 2003-06 & 08-12 & 14-16 120-18-0-1-0-93. REP Honours: SA U19 2003. SA Schools 2001-02. CW Border 2001-02. FC RECORD: 120-18-0-1-0-93. RECORD IN 2016: (Bulldogs) 3-0-0-0-0-0.

Mngadi, Siphesihle Percy (Glenwood HS, Durban) b 19/01/1996, Durban. 1.74m. 112kg. Hooker. FC DEBUT: 2016. PROV CAREER: WP 2016 1-0-0-0-0-0. FC RECORD: 1-0-0-0-0-0. RECORD IN 2016: (WP) 1-0-0-0-0-0.

Mnisi, Xolane Howard (Standerton HS & NMMU) b 13/07/1989, Elukwatini. 1.86m. 96kg. Centre. FC DEBUT: 2011. PROV CAREER: Sharks XV 2011 3-1-0-0-0-5. Griquas 2013-14 20-3-0-0-0-15. Lions 2014-16 31-13-0-0-0-65. SUPERRUGBY: Cheetahs 2013-14 3-0-0-0-0-0. Lions 2015-16 32-2-0-0-0-10. REP Honours: SA A 2016 2-0-0-0-0-0. SA Students 2012 1-0-0-0-0-0. SA Univ 2013 1-0-0-0-0-0. FC RECORD: 93-19-0-0-0-95. RECORD IN 2016: (SA A, Lions S18, Lions) 28-8-0-0-0-40.

Mnyaka, Abongile Enoch. b 18/10/1993. Prop. FC DEBUT: 2013. PROV CAREER: EP Kings 2013 & 15 3-0-0-0-0-0. Boland 2016 6-0-0-0-0-0. FC RECORD: 9-0-0-0-0-0. RECORD IN 2016: (Boland) 6-0-0-0-0-0.

Mohoje, Teboho Stephen (Oupa) (Louis Botha THS, Bloemfontein & UFS) b 03/08/1990, Qwa Qwa. 1.92.00m. 103kg. Lock. FC DEBUT: 2012. PROV CAREER: Griffons 2012-13 6-0-0-0-0-0. Cheetahs 2013-15 18-1-0-0-0-5. Free State XV 2013-14 & 16 8-4-0-0-0-20. SUPERRUGBY: Cheetahs 2014-16 25-1-0-0-0-5. REP Honours: SA 2014-16 TESTS: 15-0-0-0-0-0. Springboks 2015 1-0-0-0-0-0. Total: 16-0-0-0-0-0. Springbok XV 2016 1-0-0-0-0-0. SA A 2016 2-0-0-0-0-0. FC RECORD: 76-6-0-0-0-30. RECORD IN 2016: (SA, Springbok XV, SA A, Cheetahs S18, Free State XV) 20-1-0-0-0-5.

Moir, Steven Andrew (Pretoria Boys' HS & Unisa) b 16/08/1991, Johannesburg. 1.78m. 88kg. Flyhalf. FC DEBUT: 2016. PROV CAREER: Griquas 2016 3-0-0-0-0-0. FC RECORD: 3-0-0-0-0-0. RECORD IN 2016: (Griquas) 3-0-0-0-0-0.

Molapo, Matjikinyane Jixie Nkosinathi (Jixie) (Ben Voster HS, Tzaneen & NMMU) b 02/01/1995, Middelburg, Mpumalanga. 1.83m. 95kg. Wing. FC DEBUT: 2016. PROV CAREER: EP Kings 2016 3-0-0-0-0-0. FC RECORD: 3-0-0-0-0-0. RECORD IN 2016: (EP Kings) 3-0-0-0-0-0.

Molefe, Gopolang (HTS Louis Botha, Bloemfontein) b 18/10/1995, Rustenburg. 1.98m. 93kg. Lock. FC DEBUT: 2016. PROV CAREER: Free State XV 2016 3-0-0-0-0-0. FC RECORD: 3-0-0-0-0-0. RECORD IN 2016: (Free State XV) 3-0-0-0-0-0.

Mona, Khwezi Jongamazizi (Selborne College, East London) b 08/10/1992, East London. 1.81m. 112kg. Prop. FC DEBUT: 2014. PROV CAREER: Sharks XV 2014 4-0-0-0-0-0. Pumas 2015-16 30-2-0-0-0-10. FC RECORD: 34-2-0-0-0-10. RECORD IN 2016: (Pumas) 13-1-0-0-0-5.

Moolman, Bradley Johannes (Monument HS, Krugersdorp) b 18/01/1991, Welkom. 1.80m. 90kg. Centre. FC DEBUT: 2011. PROV CAREER: Blue Bulls 2011 4-0-0-0-0-0. Golden Lions XV 2012-13 8-4-0-0-0-20. Leopards 2016 20-7-0-0-0-35. REP Honours: SAU20 2011 2-0-0-0-0-0. FC RECORD: 34-11-0-0-0-55. RECORD IN 2016: (Leopards) 20-7-0-0-0-35.

Moos, Leegan Viano (PW Botha College, George & Florida HS,

Johannesburg) b 16/04/1991, George. 1.75m. 73kg. Flyhalf. FC DEBUT: 2016. PROV CAREER: Eagles 2016 1-0-0-0-0-0. FC RECORD: 1-0-0-0-0-0. RECORD IN 2016: (Eagles) 1-0-0-0-0-0.

Morison, Chase Wayne (Selborne College, East London) b 37/11/1992, Germiston. 1.81m. 105kg. Prop. FC DEBUT: 2014. PROV CAREER: Free State XV 2014 & 16 13-0-0-0-0-0. Cheetahs 2015 2-0-0-0-0-0. Griffons 2015 2-0-0-0-0-0. Griquas 2016 1-0-0-0-0-0. FC RECORD: 18-0-0-0-0-0. RECORD IN 2016: (Griquas, Free State XV) 10-0-0-0-0-0.

Morrison, Neil Loftus (Witteberg HS & NWU) b 25/04/1993, Bethlehem. 1.95m. 115kg. Lock. FC DEBUT: 2015. PROV CAREER: Leopards 2015-16 28-10-0-0-0-50. Leopards XV 2015 2-0-0-0-0-0. FC RECORD: 30-10-0-0-0-50. RECORD IN 2016: (Leopards) 15-6-0-0-0-30.

Mostert, Francois John (Franco) (Brits HS & UP) b 27/11/1990, Bloemfontein. 1.98m. 103kg. Lock. FC DEBUT: 2012. PROV CAREER: Blue Bulls 2012 12-2-0-0-0-10. Golden Lions XV 2013 3-0-0-0-0-0. Lions 2014-15 22-6-0-0-0-30. SUPERRUGBY: Lions 2014-16 47-1-0-0-0-5. REP Honours: SA 2016 TESTS: 7-0-0-0-0-0. MISC INFO: Brother of JP Mostert. FC RECORD: 91-9-0-0-0-45. RECORD IN 2016: (SA, Lions S18) 24-1-0-0-0-5.

Mostert, Juan-Pierre Francois (JP) (Brits HS & US) b 22/01/1988, Brits. 1.93m. 106kg. Flank. FC DEBUT: 2011. PROV CAREER: Pumas 2011-12 21-1-0-0-0-5. Valke 2012-16 75-13-0-0-0-65. MISC INFO: Brother of Franco Mostert. FC RECORD: 96-14-0-0-0-70. RECORD IN 2016: (Valke) 19-0-0-0-0-0.

Motloung, Kabelo Martin (Riverside HS & Northwood HS) b 26/07/1996, Bethlehem. 1.80m. 122kg. Prop. FC DEBUT: 2016. PROV CAREER: Leopards 2016 3-0-0-0-0-0. FC RECORD: 3-0-0-0-0-0. RECORD IN 2016: (Leopards) 3-0-0-0-0-0.

Mpafi, Mihlali (Hudson Park HS, East London & CUT) b 17/06/1992, East London. 1.78m. 94kg. Hooker. FC DEBUT: 2014. PROV CAREER: Bulldogs 2014-16 50-3-0-0-0-15. FC RECORD: 50-3-0-0-0-15. RECORD IN 2016: (Bulldogs) 19-1-0-0-0-5.

Mqalo, Sonwabiso (Nzuluwazi HS, Alice) b 06/06/1986, Cape Town. 1.80m. Centre. FC DEBUT: 2016. PROV CAREER: Bulldogs 2016 14-6-0-0-0-30. FC RECORD: 14-6-0-0-0-30. RECORD IN 2016: (Bulldogs) 14-6-0-0-0-30.

Msutwana, Siphumelele Nkosikhona Petros (Siphu) (Dale College, King William's Town) b 31/10/1993, Fort Beaufort. 1.73m. 85kg. Wing. FC DEBUT: 2014. PROV CAREER: EP Kings 2014-16 19-1-0-0-0-5. FC RECORD: 19-1-0-0-0-5. RECORD IN 2016: (EP Kings) 13-1-0-0-0-5.

Mtawarira, Tendai (Beast) (Peterhouse, Zimbabwe) b 01/07/1985, Harare. 1.88m. 118kg. Prop. FC DEBUT: 2006. PROV CAREER: Sharks 2006-13 37-3-0-0-0-15. Sharks XV 2006-08 & 12 9-0-0-0-0-0. Sharks Inv XV 2010 1-1-0-0-0-5. SUPERRUGBY: Sharks 2007-16 126-4-0-0-0-20. REP Honours: SA 2008-16 Tests 87-2-0-0-0-10. 2010 Tour: 1-0-0-0-0-0. Springboks 2014-15 2-0-0-0-0-0. Total: 90-2-0-0-0-10. Springbok XV 2016 1-0-0-0-0-0. British Barbarians 2009 & 13 2-0-0-0-0-0. MISC INFO: PoYnominee 2008. YPoYnominee 2008. FC RECORD:266-10-0-0-0-50. RECORD IN 2016: (SA, Springbok XV, Sharks S18) 26-1-0-0-0-5.

Mtembu, Lubabalo Siphosethu (Dale College, King William's Town) b 09/12/1990, East London. 1.87m. Eighthman. FC DEBUT: 2011. PROV CAREER: Sharks XV 2011-16 23-4-0-0-0-20. Sharks 2012-14 & 16 25-5-0-0-0-25. SUPERRUGBY: Sharks 2012-16 24-1-0-0-0-5. Rep. honours: SAU20 2010 4-0-0-0-0-0. SA Sevens 2010-11. FC RECORD: 76-10-0-0-0-50. RECORD IN 2016: (Sharks S18, Sharks, Sharks XV)

13-1-0-0-0-5.

Mthethwa, Mimenthie Lithuxolo (Eshowe HS & UWC) b
05/08/1991, Empangeni. 1.77m. 88kg. Wing. FC DEBUT: 2016. PROV
CAREER: EP Kings 2016 3-0-0-0-0-0. FC RECORD: 3-0-0-0-0-0.
RECORD IN 2016: (EP Kings) 3-0-0-0-0-0.

Mtsulwana, Sibabalwe (Breidbach HS, King William's Town & UFH)
b 06/06/1989, Mount Cote. 1.73m. 70kg. Flank. FC DEBUT: 2016.
PROV CAREER: Bulldogs 2016 1-0-0-0-0-0. FC RECORD: 1-0-0-0-0-0.
RECORD IN 2016: (Bulldogs) 1-0-0-0-0-0.

Mtyanda, Lubabalo (Cowan HS, Hilton) b 19/03/1986, Port Elizabeth. 1.99m. 116kg. Lock. FC DEBUT: 2006. PROV CAREER: Elephants
2006 13-0-0-0-0-0. Lions 2007 4-0-0-0-0-0. Eagles 2010-13
70-8-0-0-0-40. Pumas 2013-16 47-4-0-0-0-20. SUPERRUGBY: Sharks
2015-16 13-0-0-0-0-0. REP Honours: SA Pres XV 2013 4-0-0-0-0-0.
FC RECORD: 151-12-0-0-0-60. RECORD IN 2016: (Sharks S18, Pumas)
4-0-0-0-0-0.

Muir, Dean (Glenwood HS, Durban) b 06/02/1989, Durban. 1.81m.
102kg. Hooker. FC DEBUT: 2012. PROV CAREER: Bulldogs 2012-13 31-4-
0-0-0-20. Valke 2014-16 39-4-0-0-0-20. FC RECORD: 70-8-0-0-0-40.
RECORD IN 2016: (Valke) 14-3-0-0-0-15.

Muller, Bruce (Klerksdorp HS) b 24/02/1989, Klerksdorp. 1.76m.
116kg. Prop. FC DEBUT: 2012. PROV CAREER: Valke 2012-14 29-7-0-
0-0-35. Leopards 2016 1-1-0-0-0-5. FC RECORD: 30-8-0-0-0-40.
RECORD IN 2016: (Leopards) 1-1-0-0-0-5.

Muller, Frederick Jacobus (Huguenote HS, Wellington & UWC) b
03/02/1990, Belville. 1.68m. 78kg. Scrumhalf. FC DEBUT: 2013. PROV
CAREER: WP 2014 & 16 5-1-0-0-0-5. REP Honours: SA U20 2010 no
appearances. SA Univ 2013 1-0-0-0-0-0. FC RECORD: 6-1-0-0-0-5.
RECORD IN 2016: (WP) 1-1-0-0-0-5.

Muller, Gideon Pieter (Florida HS) b 24/11/1992, Johannesburg.
1.85m. 120kg. Prop. FC DEBUT: 2015. PROV CAREER: Eagles 2015-16
5-0-0-0-0-0. FC RECORD: 5-0-0-0-0-0. RECORD IN 2016: (Eagles)
4-0-0-0-0-0.

Muller, Martin Dirk (Bishops HS, Rondebosch & UCT) b 23/03/1988,
Cape Town. 1.98m. 105kg. Lock. FC DEBUT: 2009. PROV CAREER:
WP 2009-10 22-1-0-0-0-5. Griquas 2011-12 23-1-0-0-0-5. Lions
2014-16 20-1-0-0-0-5. Golden Lions XV 2014-15 12-0-0-0-0-0.
SUPERRUGBY: Stormers 2009 3-0-0-0-0-0. Cheetahs 2011 11-0-0-
0-0-0. Lions 2014-16 16-0-0-0-0-0. REP Honours: SA Students 2009
2-0-0-0-0-0. SAU20 2008 5-1-0-0-0-5. British Barbarians 2016
3-0-0-0-0-0. FC RECORD: 117-4-0-0-0-20. RECORD IN 2016: (Lions
S18, Lions, Golden Lions XV, British Barbarians) 17-0-0-0-0-0.

Muller, Reg-Hack (Marais Viljoen HS, Alberton) b 06/03/1986,
Johannesburg. 1.89m. 104kg. Eighthman. FC DEBUT: 2007. PROV
CAREER: Sharks 2007 3-0-0-0-0-0. Valke 2008-13 & 15-16 94-33-
0-0-0-165. FC RECORD: 97-33-0-0-0-165. RECORD IN 2016: (Valke)
16-6-0-0-0-30.

Murray, David George (St Andrew's College, Grahamstown) b
07/03/1995, Port Elizabeth. 1.80m. 100kg. Prop. FC DEBUT: 2016.
PROV CAREER: EP Kings 2016 8-1-0-0-0-5. FC RECORD: 8-1-0-0-0-5.
RECORD IN 2016: (EP Kings) 8-1-0-0-0-5.

Murray, Waylon Michael (Westville Boys" HS) b 27/04/1986,
Durban. 1.90m. 105kg. Centre. FC DEBUT: 2005. PROV CAREER: Sharks
2005-09 & 15 53-18-0-0-0-90. Sharks XV 2005-10 8-0-0-0-0-0.
Golden Lions 2010-12 19-5-0-0-0-25. Blue Bulls 2013-14 14-2-0-0-
0-10. EP Kings 2013 & 16 6-0-0-0-0-0. SUPERRUGBY: Sharks 2006-10
& 15 49-5-0-0-0-25. Lions 2011-12 14-3-0-0-0-15. Southern Kings

2013 7-0-0-0-0-0. P/R 2013 1-0-0-0-0-0. REP Honours: SA TESTS:
2007 3-0-0-0-0-0. Tour: 1-0-0-0-0-0. Total: 4-0-0-0-0-0. SA U21
2006 5-3-0-0-0-15. FC RECORD: 180-36-0-0-0-180. RECORD IN 2016:
(EP Kings) 5-0-0-0-0-0.

Mvovo, Lwazi Ncedo (Maria Louw HS, Queen'stown) b 03/06/1986,
Mthatha. 1.81m. 92kg. Wing. FC DEBUT: 2007. PROV CAREER: Sharks
2007-14 & 16 63-28-0-0-0-140. Sharks XV 2007-10 20-9-0-0-0-45.
Sharks Inv XV 2009 1-0-0-0-0-0. SUPERRUGBY: Sharks 2010-16
99-29-0-0-0-145. REP Honours: SA 2010-12 & 14-16 TESTS: 17-6-
0-0-0-30. Tour: 1-0-0-0-0-0. Springboks 2014 1-0-0-0-0-0. Total:
19-6-0-0-0-30. FC RECORD: 202-72-0-0-0-360. RECORD IN 2016: (SA,
Sharks S18, Sharks) 16-6-0-0-0-30.

Mxoli, Nqobisizwe Mimentle (Westville Boys' HS & UP) b
02/02/1994, Durban. 1.83m. 112kg. Prop. FC DEBUT: 2014. PROV
CAREER: Blue Bulls 2014-16 14-3-0-0-0-15. SUPERRUGBY: Bulls 2016
2-0-0-0-0-0. REP Honours: SAU20 2014 no appearances. FC RECORD:
16-3-0-0-0-15. RECORD IN 2016: (Bulls, Blue Bulls) 13-2-0-0-0-10.

Mxunyelwa, Buhle (Stirling HS, East London) b 25/06/1986, East
London. 1.87m. 129kg. Prop. FC DEBUT: 2008. PROV CAREER: Bulldogs
2008-09 & 14-16 43-2-0-0-0-10. E/Cape XV 2008 1-0-0-0-0-0. WP
2010 8-0-0-0-0-0. Leopards 2011-12 6-0-0-0-0-0. Leopard XV 2013
3-0-0-0-0. MISC INFO: Brother of Siya Mxunyelwa. FC RECORD: 61-2-
0-0-0-10. RECORD IN 2016: (Bulldogs) 3-0-0-0-0-0.

Naudé, Dewald Donovan (Paarl Boys' HS & UP) b 24/08/1995,
Paarl. 1.79m. 87kg. Centre. FC DEBUT: 2016. PROV CAREER: Blue Bulls
2016 2-0-0-0-0-0. FC RECORD: 2-0-0-0-0-0. RECORD IN 2016: (Blue
Bulls) 2-0-0-0-0-0.

Naudé, Franco Johan (Garsfontein HS, Pretoria & UP) b 28/03/1996,
Pretoria. 1.88m. 101kg, Centre. FC DEBUT: 2016. PROV CAREER: Blue
Bulls 2016 4-1-0-0-0-5. REP Honours: SAU20 2016 5-0-0-0-0-0.
FC RECORD: 9-1-0-0-0-5. RECORD IN 2016: (Blue Bulls, SAU20)
9-1-0-0-0-5.

Ncanywa, Siyasanga (Mdibaniso HS, Middledrift, Eastern Cape)
b 08/10/1991, Middledrift. 1.78m. 81kg. Fullback. FC DEBUT: 2016.
PROV CAREER: Bulldogs 2016 2-0-0-0-0-0. FC RECORD: 2-0-0-0-0-0.
RECORD IN 2016: (Bulldogs) 2-0-0-0-0-0.

Nche, Retshegofaditswe (Ox) (Louis Botha HTS, Bloemfontein &
UFS) b 23/07/1995, Bloemfontein. 1.75m. 105kg. Prop. FC DEBUT:
2015. PROV CAREER: Cheetahs 2016 10-2-0-0-0-10. Free State XV
2016 4-1-0-0-0-5. SUPERRUGBY: Cheetahs 2016 12-0-0-0-0-0.
REP Honours: SAU20 2015 5-1-0-0-0-5. MISC INFO: CC Premier Div
PoY2016. FC RECORD: 31-4-0-0-0-20. RECORD IN 2016: (Cheetahs S18,
Cheetahs, Free State XV) 26-3-0-0-0-15.

Ndlovu, Nkululuko (Sarel Cilliers HS, Glencoe) b 29/04/1994,
Dundee. 1.78m. 82kg. Fullback. FC DEBUT: 2016. PROV CAREER:
Bulldogs 2016 6-1-0-0-0-5. FC RECORD: 6-1-0-0-0-5. RECORD IN
2016: (Bulldogs) 6-1-0-0-0-5.

Ndungane, Odwa Mzuzo (Hudson Park HS, East London & Eastern
Cape Tech.) b 20/02/1981, Umtata. 1.83m. 93kg. Wing. FC DEBUT:
2000. PROV CAREER: Bulldogs 2000-03 49-25-0-0-0-125. Blue Bulls
2004 2-0-0-0-0-0. Sharks 2005-16 97-33-1-0-0-167. Sharks XV
2005-08 & 12 4-0-0-0-0-0. SUPERRUGBY: Bulls 2004 10-3-0-0-0-15.
Sharks 2005-16 131-33-0-0-0-165. REP Honours: SA 2008-11 TESTS:
9-2-0-0-0-10. Tour: 2009-10 3-1-0-0-0-5. Total: 12-3-0-0-0-15.
SA 'A' 2004 2-2-0-0-0-10. Emerging Springboks 2007 2-0-0-0-0-0. SA
U21 2002 1-0-0-0-0-0. MISC INFO: Twin brother of Springbok and Blue

Bulls wing Akona Ndungane. FC RECORD: 310-99-1-0-0-497. RECORD IN 2016: (Sharks S18, Sharks) 19-4-0-0-0-20.

Nel, Adriaan Ruhan (Brandwag HS, Benoni) b 17/05/1991. 1.92.00m. 88kg. Wing. FC DEBUT: 2012. PROV CAREER: Lions 2013 3-1-0-0-0-5. Young Lions 2012-14 7-4-0-0-0-20. Griquas 2015 9-6-0-0-0-30. REP Honours: SA Sevens 2015-16. MISC INFO: Brother of Jacques Nel. FC RECORD: 19-11-0-0-0-55. RECORD IN 2016: (SA Sevens).

Nel, Jacques Johan (Brandwag HS, Uitenhage) b 17/03/1993, Port Elizabeth. 1.86m. 88kg. Centre. FC DEBUT: 2013. PROV CAREER: Golden Lions XV 2013 & 15-16 18-8-0-0-0-40. Lions 2015-16 11-6-0-0-0-30. SUPERRUGBY: Lions 2016 2-0-0-0-0-0. MISC INFO: Brother of Ruhan Nel. FC RECORD: 31-14-0-0-0-70. RECORD IN 2016: (Lions S18, Lions, Golden Lions XV) 19-9-0-0-0-45.

Nel, Japie (Goudveld HS, Welkom) b 20/11/1982, Welkom. 1.90m. 105kg. Wing. FC DEBUT: 2005. PROV CAREER: Griffons 2005-07 & 2011-16 126-47-0-0-0-235. Leopards 2008-10 35-4-0-0-0-20. FC RECORD: 161-51-0-0-0-255. RECORD IN 2016: (Griffons) 16-7-0-0-0-35.

Nel, Rouche (Framesby HS, Port Elizabeth) b 26/03/1996, Port Elizabeth. 1.78m. 78kg. Scrumhalf. FC DEBUT: 2016. PROV CAREER: EP Kings 2016 5-0-0-0-0-0. FC RECORD: 5-0-0-0-0-0. RECORD IN 2016: (EP Kings) 5-0-0-0-0-0.

Nell, Ryan Desmond (Paarl Gym. & US) b 04/09/1990, Port Elizabeth. 1.91m. 95kg. Utility back. PROV CAREER: WP 2013 2-0-0-0-0-0. Blue Bulls 2014 9-2-0-0-0-10. Boland 2016 18-13-0-0-0-65. REP Honours: SA Univ 2013 1-0-0-0-0-0. SA Sevens 2012. FC RECORD: 30-15-0-0-0-75. RECORD IN 2016: (Boland) 18-13-0-0-0-65.

Nelson, Norman Tsimba (Patensie HS) b 10/08/1983, Patensie. 1.75m. 81kg. Wing. FC DEBUT: 2006. PROV CAREER: EP Kings 2006-08 & 10-13 92-56-0-0-0-280. E/Cape XV 2008 1-0-0-0-0-0. Eagles 2009 20-15-1-0-0-77. Griffons 2013-16 42-18-0-0-0-90. REP Honours: SA Barbarians 2012 1-1-0-0-0-5. FC RECORD: 156-90-1-0-0-452. RECORD IN 2016: (Griffons) 6-1-0-0-0-5.

Nepgen, Jaco (Hangklip HS, Queen'stown) b 03/01/1986. 1.98m. 103kg. Lock. FC DEBUT: 2008. PROV CAREER: Griquas 2010-16 89-8-0-0-0-40. Eagles 2011 1-0-0-0-0-0. REP Honours: SA Students 2008-09 3-1-0-0-0-5. FC RECORD: 93-9-0-0-0-45. RECORD IN 2016: (Griquas) 4-0-0-0-0-0.

Ngande, Siyamthanda b 11/07/1990. Prop. FC DEBUT: 2014. PROV CAREER: Bulldogs 2014-16 23-1-0-0-0-5. FC RECORD: 23-1-0-0-0-5. RECORD IN 2016: (Bulldogs) 13-1-0-0-0-5.

Ngcamu, Nhlanhla (Maritzburg College & NWU) b 27/03/1992, Pietermaritzburg. 1.78m. 110kg. Prop. FC DEBUT: 2016. PROV CAREER: Leopards 2016 15-0-0-0-0-0. FC RECORD: 15-0-0-0-0-0. RECORD IN 2016: (Leopards) 15-0-0-0-0-0.

Ngcobo, Sandile Caleb (Stix) (Highlands North HS, Johannesburg & UJ) b 01/08/1989, Thembisa. Wing. FC DEBUT: 2012. PROV CAREER: Valke 2012-14 36-10-0-0-0-50. Griquas 2015 6-1-0-0-0-5. REP Honours: SA Sevens 2016. FC RECORD: 42-11-0-0-0-55. RECORD IN 2016: (SA Sevens).

Ngcokowane, Sibusiso (Dale College, King William's Town & NMMU) b 17/02/1996, King William's Town. 1.68m. 70kg. Scrumhalf. FC DEBUT: 2016. PROV CAREER: EP Kings 2016 6-0-0-0-0-0. FC RECORD: 6-0-0-0-0-0. RECORD IN 2016: (EP Kings) 6-0-0-0-0-0.

Ngcukana, Khanyo Templeton (Rondebosch HS) b 10/05/1995, The Hague, Netherlands. 1.78m. 80kg. Wing. FC DEBUT: 2015. PROV CAREER: WP 2016 11-6-0-0-0-30. REP Honours: SAU20 2015 3-1-0-0-0-5. FC RECORD: 14-7-0-0-0-35. RECORD IN 2016: (WP)

11-6-0-0-0-30.

Ngoma, Sanelise Aphiwe (King Edward VI (UK) & UFH) b 26/01/1989, East London. 1.84m. 86kg. Centre. FC DEBUT: 2016. PROV CAREER: Bulldogs 2016 1-0-0-0-0-0. FC RECORD: 1-0-0-0-0-0. RECORD IN 2016: (Bulldogs) 1-0-0-0-0-0.

Ngoza, Thato Frederick Ntandyenkosi (Volksrust HS & UFS) b 20/10/1991, Piet Retief. 1.90m. 105kg. Lock. FC DEBUT: 2011. PROV CAREER: Griffons 2011 & 13 13-1-0-0-0-5. Cheetahs 2013 & 15 12-1-0-0-0-5. Free State XV 2013 & 15 7-1-0-0-0-5. Blue Bulls 2016 8-1-0-0-0-5. FC RECORD: 40-4-0-0-0-20. RECORD IN 2016: (Blue Bulls) 8-1-0-0-0-5.

Nhlapo, Sabelo (Highlands North Boys' HS, Johannesburg) b 17/12/1988, Johannesburg. 1.90m. 116kg. Prop. FC DEBUT: 2009. PROV CAREER: Sharks XV 2009-11 20-0-0-0-0-0. Boland 2013 8-0-0-0-0-0. Pumas 2014-16 13-0-0-0-0-0. REP Honours: SAU20 2008 3-1-0-0-0-5. FC RECORD: 44-1-0-0-0-5. RECORD IN 2016: (Pumas) 2-0-0-0-0-0.

Nieuwoudt, Stephanus Francois (Framesby HS, Port Elizabeth & NMMU) b 27/08/1996, Port Elizabeth. 1.78m. 90kg. Flank. FC DEBUT: 2016. PROV CAREER: EP Kings 2016 9-1-0-0-0-5. FC RECORD: 9-1-0-0-0-5. RECORD IN 2016: (EP Kings) 9-1-0-0-0-5.

Nieuwoudt, Teunis (Waterkloof HS, Pretoria) b 03/12/1994, East London. 1.86m. 118kg. Prop. FC DEBUT: 2015. PROV CAREER: Cheetahs 2015 4-0-0-0-0-0. Free State XV 2015 2-1-0-0-0-5. Griquas 2016 2-0-0-0-0-0. Eagles 2016 3-0-0-0-0-0. FC RECORD: 11-1-0-0-0-5. RECORD IN 2016: (Griquas, Eagles) 5-0-0-0-0-0.

Nkosi, S'busiso Romeo. Wing. FC DEBUT: 2016. PROV CAREER: Sharks XV 2016 2-0-0-0-0-0. REP Honours: SAU20 1016 3-0-0-0-0-0. FC RECORD: 5-0-0-0-0-0. RECORD IN 2016: (Sharks XV, SAU20) 5-0-0-0-0-0.

Nofemele, Siphosenkosi (Eyabantu HS & UFH) b 12/11/1989, Fort Beaufort. 1.60m. 75kg. Wing. FC DEBUT: 2014. PROV CAREER: Bulldogs 2014-16 38-14-0-0-0-70. FC RECORD: 38-14-0-0-0-70. RECORD IN 2016: (Bulldogs) 14-6-0-0-0-30.

Nofuma, Nkosikhana (Lebogang HS, CUT & UFH) b 29/04/1988, Qumbu. 1.90m. 95kg. Flank. FC DEBUT: 2014. PROV CAREER: Bulldogs 2014-16 40-2-0-0-0-10. FC RECORD: 40-2-0-0-0-10. RECORD IN 2016: (Bulldogs) 12-2-0-0-0-10.

Nomdo, Lenesleyo (Albertina HS & NMMU) b 24/07/1995, Riversdale. 1.77m. 74kg. Utility Back. FC DEBUT: 2016. PROV CAREER: Eagles 2016 6-0-0-0-0-0. FC RECORD: 6-0-0-0-0-0. RECORD IN 2016: (Eagles) 6-0-0-0-0-0.

Nomzanga, Lukhanyo Welcome (Forbes Grant HS) b 08/10/1987, King William's Town. 1.83m. 83kg. Flank. FC DEBUT: 2014. PROV CAREER: Bulldogs 2014-16 35-0-0-0-0-0. FC RECORD: 35-0-0-0-0-0. RECORD IN 2016: (Bulldogs) 14-0-0-0-0-0.

Nonkontwana, Abongile (Selborne College, East London & St Albans College) b 10/04/1995, Port Elizabeth. 1.96m. 107kg. Lock. FC DEBUT: 2014. PROV CAREER: Blue Bulls 2016 12-1-0-0-0-5. REP Honours: SAU20 2014-15 3-0-0-0-0-0. FC RECORD: 15-1-0-0-0-5. RECORD IN 2016: (Blue Bulls) 12-1-0-0-0-5.

Nortjé, Oshwill (Hentie Cilliers HS, Virginia) b 03/12/1990, George. 1.65m. 67kg. Scrumhalf. FC DEBUT: 2011. PROV CAREER: Griffons 2011-16 51-8-0-0-0-40. FC RECORD: 51-8-0-0-0-40. RECORD IN 2016: (Griffons) 3-1-0-0-0-5.

Notshe, Sikhumbuzo (Wynberg Boys' HS) b 28/05/1993, King William's Town. 1.90m. 100kg. Eighthman. FC DEBUT: 2013. PROV CAREER: WP 2013-16 44-17-0-0-0-85. SUPERRUGBY: Stormers 2014-16 23-5-0-

0-0-25. REP Honours: SA A 2016 1-1-0-0-0-5. FC RECORD: 68-22-0-0-0-110. RECORD IN 2016: (SA A, Stormers, WP) 20-5-0-0-0-25.

Ntsila, Anidisa (Queen's College, Queen'stown & NMMU) b 07/11/1993, Queen'stown. 1.81m. 98kg. Flank. FC DEBUT: 2015. PROV CAREER: Eagles 2015-16 28-4-0-0-0-20. SUPERRUGBY: Southern Kings 2016 2-0-0-0-0-0. FC RECORD: 30-4-0-0-0-20. RECORD IN 2016: (Southern Kings, Eagles) 18-3-0-0-0-15.

Ntubeni, Siyabonga (King Edward HS, Johannesburg) b 18/02/1991, East London. 1.77m. 92kg. Hooker. FC DEBUT: 2011. PROV CAREER: WP 2011-16 47-2-0-0-0-10. SUPERRUGBY: Stormers 2011-16 45-4-0-0-0-20. REP Honours: SA 2013 no appearances. SA A 2016 1-0-0-0-0-0. FC RECORD: 93-6-0-0-0-30. RECORD IN 2016: (SA A, Stormers, WP) 19-3-0-0-0-15.

Nyakane, Trevor Ntando (Ben Vorster HS, Tzaneen) b 04/05/1989, Bushbuck Ridge. 1.78m. 109kg. Prop. FC DEBUT: 2010. PROV CAREER: Cheetahs 2010-14 38-2-0-0-0-10. Griffons 2011 1-0-0-0-0-0. Emerging Cheetahs 2011 1-0-0-0-0-0. SUPERRUGBY: Cheetahs 2012-14 42-3-0-0-0-15. Bulls 2015-16 28-0-0-0-0-0. REP Honours: SA TESTS: 2013-16 28-1-0-0-0-5. Springboks 2015 1-0-0-0-0-0. Total: 29-1-0-0-0-5. Springbok XV 2016 1-0-0-0-0-0. FC RECORD: 138-6-0-0-0-30. RECORD IN 2016: (SA, Springbok XV, Bulls) 18-0-0-0-0-0.

Nyoka, Sinovuyo (Dale College, King William's Town) b 07/08/1990, King William's Town. 1.68m. 67kg. Scrumhalf. FC DEBUT: 2010. PROV CAREER: Bulldogs 2010-13 & 16 58-3-0-0-0-15. Valke 2014 & 16 5-1-0-0-0-5. Pumas 2014-15 15-1-0-0-0-5. Griffons 2015 6-0-0-0-0-0. REP Honours: SA Pres XV 2013 3-0-0-0-0-0. FC RECORD: 87-5-0-0-0-25. RECORD IN 2016: (Bulldogs, Valke) 13-2-0-0-0-10.

Obi, Luther Banks St Charles (St Benedict's College, Johannesburg) b 29/04/1993, Aba, Nigeria. 1.75m. 86kg. Wing. FC DEBUT: 2013. PROV CAREER: Leopards 2013-14 23-18-0-0-0-90. EP Kings 2015 13-5-0-0-0-25. Blue Bulls 2016 2-0-0-0-0-0. REP Honours: SA U 20 2013 5-4-0-0-0-20. FC RECORD: 43-27-0-0-0-135. RECORD IN 2016: (Blue Bulls) 2-0-0-0-0-0.

Odendaal, Megiel Burger (Monument HS, Krugersdorp & UP) b 15/04/1993, Bloemfontein. 1.87m. 95kg. Centre. FC DEBUT: 2013. PROV CAREER: Blue Bulls 2013-16 38-8-0-0-0-40. SUPERRUGBY: Bulls 2015-16 18-2-0-0-0-10. FC RECORD: 56-10-0-0-0-50. RECORD IN 2016: (Bulls, Blue Bulls) 18-1-0-0-0-5.

Oelofse, Niel (Glenwood HS, Durban & US) b 09/05/1993, Durban. 1.77m. 117kg. Prop. FC DEBUT: 2016. PROV CAREER: Boland 2016 3-0-0-0-0-0. FC RECORD: 3-0-0-0-0-0. RECORD IN 2016: (Boland) 3-0-0-0-0-0.

Oelofse, Schalk Wentzel (Daniel Pienaar THS, Uitenhage & NMMU) b 02/11/1988, Port Elizabeth. 1.97m. 111kg. Lock. FC DEBUT: 2013. PROV CAREER: EP Kings 2013 1-0-0-0-0-0. Eagles 2013-16 40-2-0-0-0-10. SUPERRUGBY: Southern Kings 2016 13-0-0-0-0-0. REP Honours: SA Univ 2013 1-0-0-0-0-0. FC RECORD: 55-2-0-0-0-10. RECORD IN 2016: (Southern Kings, Eagles) 15-0-0-0-0-0.

Olivier, Friedle (Dr Johan Jurgens HS, Springs) b 27/05/1992, Pretoria. 1.98m. 94kg. Flank. FC DEBUT: 2013. PROV CAREER: Valke 2013-16 44-12-0-0-0-60. FC RECORD: 44-12-0-0-0-60. RECORD IN 2016: (Valke) 11-2-0-0-0-10.

Oosthuizen, Caylib Rees (Oudtshoorn HS & UJ) b 01/09/1989, Cape Town. 1.86m. 114kg. Prop. FC DEBUT: 2011. PROV CAREER: Lions 2012 2-0-0-0-0-0. Golden Lions XV 2011 2-0-0-0-0-0. Cheetahs 2013-15 13-0-0-0-0-0. Free State XV 2013 & 15 5-0-0-0-0-0. EP Kings 2016

1-0-0-0-0-0. SUPERRUGBY: Lions 2012 6-1-0-0-0-5. Cheetahs 2014-15 19-0-0-0-0-0. REP Honours: SA U20 2009 5-0-0-0-0-0. FC RECORD: 53-1-0-0-0-5. RECORD IN 2016: (EP Kings) 1-0-0-0-0-0.

Oosthuizen, Coenraad Victor (Grey College, Bloemfontein) b 22/03/89, Potchefstroom. 1.83m. 127kg. Prop. FC DEBUT: 2008. PROV CAREER: Cheetahs 2008-14 55-11-0-0-0-55. Cheetahs XV 2010 1-0-0-0-0-0. SUPERRUGBY: Cheetahs 2010-15 74-8-0-0-0-40. Sharks 2016 14-1-0-0-0-5. REP Honours: SA TESTS: 2012-15 23-3-0-0-0-15. 2010 Tour: 1-0-0-0-0-0. Springboks 2014 1-0-0-0-0-0. Total: 25-3-0-0-0-15. SA A 2016 2-0-0-0-0-0. British Barbarians 2013 1-0-0-0-0-0. SAU20 2009 5-0-0-0-0-0. FC RECORD: 177-23-0-0-0-115. RECORD IN 2016: (SA A, Sharks S18) 16-1-0-0-0-5.

Oosthuizen, Ettienne (Bergsig HS, Rustenburg) b 22/12/1992, Klerksdorp. 1.98m. 120kg. Flank. FC DEBUT: 2012. PROV CAREER: Lions 2012 3-0-0-0-0-0. Golden Lions XV 2012 3-1-0-0-0-5. Sharks 2014-16 29-3-0-0-0-15. Sharks XV 2015 2-0-0-0-0-0. SUPERRUGBY: Lions 2012 3-0-0-0-0-0. Sharks 2014-16 39-0-0-0-0-0. FC RECORD: 79-4-0-0-0-20. RECORD IN 2016: (Sharks S18, Sharks) 24-2-0-0-0-10.

Oosthuizen, Johan Etienne (Kempton Park HS & UJ) b 20/07/1994, Johannesburg. 1.98m. 99kg. Lock. FC DEBUT: 2016. PROV CAREER: EP Kings 2016 7-0-0-0-0-0. FC RECORD: 7-0-0-0-0-0. RECORD IN 2016: (EP Kings) 7-0-0-0-0-0.

Oosthuizen, Nicolaas Jacobus (Marlow Agric. HS, Cradock & NMMU) b 19/11/1996, George. 1.85m. 119kg. Prop. FC DEBUT: 2016. PROV CAREER: EP Kings 2016 3-0-0-0-0-0. REP Honours: SAU20 2016 3-0-0-0-0-0. FC RECORD: 6-0-0-0-0-0. RECORD IN 2016: (EP Kings, SAU20) 6-0-0-0-0-0.

Oosthuizen, Ryan (Paarl Gym. & US) b 22/05/1995, Stellenbosch. 1.89m. 92kg. Centre. FC DEBUT: 2016. PROV CAREER: WP 2016 2-0-0-0-0-0. FC RECORD: 2-0-0-0-0-0. RECORD IN 2016: (WP) 2-0-0-0-0-0.

Orie, Marvin (Tygerberg HS, Parow) b 15/02/1993, Cape Town. 1.98m. 104kg. Lock. FC DEBUT: 2014. PROV CAREER: Blue Bulls 2014-16 40-3-0-0-0-15. SUPERRUGBY: Bulls 2014 & 16 10-0-0-0-0-0. REP Honours: SAU20 2012 no appearances. FC RECORD: 50-3-0-0-0-15. RECORD IN 2016: (Bulls, Blue Bulls) 23-2-0-0-0-10.

Paige, Rudy (Bastion HS, Krugersdorp & UJ) b 02/08/1989, Riversdal. 1.67m. 70kg. Scrumhalf. FC DEBUT: 2010. PROV CAREER: Lions 2011 2-0-0-0-0-0. Golden Lions XV 2010-12 10-0-0-0-0-0. Blue Bulls 2012-14 & 16 36-2-0-0-0-10. SUPERRUGBY: Bulls 2013-16 34-0-0-0-0-0. REP Honours: SA 2015-16 TESTS: 7-0-0-0-0-0. Springbok XV 2016 1-0-0-0-0-0. SA Students 2012 2-0-0-0-0-0. SAU20 2009 4-0-0-0-0-0. FC RECORD: 96-2-0-0-0-10. RECORD IN 2016: (SA, Springbok XV, Bulls, Blue Bulls) 22-0-0-0-0-0.

Pansegrouw, Adriaan-Dwight (Windhoek HS, Garsfontein HS & UP) b 10/09/1992, Windhoek. 1.82.00m. 104kg. Flank/Hooker. FC DEBUT: 2016. PROV CAREER: Valke 2016 19-1-0-0-0-5. FC RECORD: 19-1-0-0-0-5. RECORD IN 2016: (Valke) 19-1-0-0-0-5.

Papier, Embrose Chelden (Garsfontein HS, Pretoria) b 25/04/1997, Clanwilliam. 1.76m. 80kg. Scrumhalf. FC DEBUT: 2016. REP Honours: SAU20 2016 2-1-0-0-0-5. FC RECORD: 2-1-0-0-0-5. RECORDIN 2016: (SAU20) 2-1-0-0-0-5.

Parks, Buran Joshua (Harmony Sports Academy, Virginia) b 27/06/1992, George. 1.80m. 85kg. Eighthman. FC DEBUT: 2011. PROV CAREER: Eagles 2011-16 52-3-0-0-0-15. FC RECORD: 52-3-0-0-0-15. RECORD IN 2016: (Eagles) 11-1-0-0-0-5.

Pedro, Hentzwill Nowellen (George HS) b 21/07/1987, George.

1.86m. 80kg. Wing. FC DEBUT: 2013. PROV CAREER: Eagles 2013-16 25-11-0-0-0-55. FC RECORD: 25-11-0-0-0-55. RECORD IN 2016: (Eagles) 7-3-0-0-0-15.

Penxe, Yaw Osei (Queen's College, Queen'stown) b 03/04/1997, Queen'stown. 1.81m. 82kg. Wing. FC DEBUT: 2016. PROV CAREER: EP Kings 2016 3-1-0-0-0-5. FC RECORD: 3-1-0-0-0-5. RECORD IN 2016: (EP Kings) 3-1-0-0-0-5.

Peter, Mabhutana (Durban HS) b 04/07/1996, Port Elizabeth. 1.75m. 80kg. Centre. FC DEBUT: 2016. PROV CAREER: EP Kings 2016 3-0-0-0-0-0. FC RECORD: 3-0-0-0-0-0. RECORD IN 2016: (EP Kings) 3-0-0-0-0-0.

Petersen, Sergeal (Grey HS, Port Elizabeth) b 01/08/1994, Port Elizabeth. 1.75m. 80kg. Wing. FC DEBUT: 2013. PROV CAREER: EP Kings 2013-14 5-1-0-0-0-5. Cheetahs 2015-16 13-10-0-0-0-50. Free State XV 2015 3-3-0-0-0-15. SUPERRUGBY: Southern Kings 2013 8-4-0-0-0-20. Cheetahs 2015-16 20-9-0-0-0-45. REP Honours: Springbok XV 2016 1-1-0-0-0-5. SA A 2016 1-2-0-0-0-10. SAU20 2014 5-3-0-0-0-15. FC RECORD: 56-33-0-0-0-165. RECORD IN 2016: (Springbok XV, SA A, Cheetahs S18, Cheetahs) 21-17-0-0-0-85.

Peterson, Dylan (KES & UJ) b 10/02/1990, Alberton. 1.90m. 102kg. Lock. FC DEBUT: 2011. PROV CAREER: Golden Lions XV 2011,13 4-0-0-0-0-0. Pumas 2015-16 5-0-0-0-0-0. FC RECORD: 9-0-0-0-0-0. RECORD IN 2016: (Pumas) 4-0-0-0-0-0.

Pheiffer, Craig Lance (Tygerberg HS & TUT) b 01/09/1991, Stellenbosch. 1.82.00m. 99kg. Wing. FC DEBUT: 2016. PROV CAREER: Boland 2016 4-1-0-0-0-5. FC RECORD: 4-1-0-0-0-5. RECORD IN 2016: (Boland) 4-1-0-0-0-5.

Phillips, Justin David (Waterkloof HS, Pretoria) b 03/02/1995, Pretoria. 1.80m. 83kg. Scrumhalf. FC DEBUT: 2015. PROV CAREER: WP 2015-16 14-5-0-0-0-25. FC RECORD: 14-5-0-0-0-25. RECORD IN 2016: (WP) 10-5-0-0-0-25.

Pieterse, Dylan John (KES, Johannesburg) b 28/01/1995, Kempton Park. 2.00m. 105kg. Lock. FC DEBUT: 2016. PROV CAREER: EP Kings 2016 5-0-0-0-0-0. FC RECORD: 5-0-0-0-0-0. RECORD IN 2016: (EP Kings) 5-0-0-0-0-0.

Pietersen, Johan Christiaan (Joe) (Grey College, Bloemfontein & US) b 18/05/1984, Vryheid. 1.80m. 81kg. Flyhalf. FC DEBUT: 2004. PROV CAREER: WP 2004-09 & 12 65-23-48-57-5-397. Sharks 2015 10-2-2-22-24-0-126. SUPERRUGBY: Stormers 2006 & 08-10 & 12-13 50-9-35-86-0-373. Cheetahs 2015 11-0-19-16-2-92. Sharks 2016 9-1-11-15-0-72. REP Honours: WP XV 2006. SA Sevens 2006. CW Free State 2002. FC RECORD: 146-35-135-198-7-1060. RECORD IN 2016: (Sharks S18) 9-1-11-15-0-72.

Pietersen, Jon-Paul Roger (JP) (General Hertzog HS, Emalahleni, Mpumalanga) b 12/07/86, Stellenbosch. 1.91m. 103kg. Wing/Fullback. FC DEBUT: 2005. PROV CAREER: Sharks 2005-06 & 08-12 42-17-0-0-0-85. SUPERRUGBY: Sharks 2006-16 137-39-0-0-0-195. REP Honours: SA 2006-16 TESTS: 70-24-0-0-0-120. Tour: 2-0-0-0-0-0. Springboks 2014-15 2-0-0-0-0-0. Total: 74-24-0-0-0-120. SA U21 2006 5-2-0-0-0-10. Misc. info: YPoYnominee 2005, 2006. SARU PoY2012 nominee. Super PoY2012 nominee. SARPA PPoY2012. FC RECORD: 258-82-0-0-0-410. RECORD IN 2016: (SA, Sharks S18) 19-6-0-0-0-30.

Pokomela, Junior Sipato (Grey HS, Port Elizabeth & NMMU) b 10/12/1996, Port Elizabeth. 1.87m. 100kg. Eighthman. FC DEBUT: 2016. PROV CAREER: EP Kings 2016 3-0-0-0-0-0. REP Honours: SAU20 2016 5-0-0-0-0-0. FC RECORD: 8-0-0-0-0-0. RECORD IN 2016: (EP Kings, SAU20) 8-0-0-0-0-0.

Potgieter, Barend Jacobus (Zwartkop HS, Centurion & Varsity College) b 28/12/1994, Pretoria. 1.86m. 118kg. Prop. FC DEBUT: 2015. PROV CAREER: Sharks XV 2015-16 7-2-0-0-0-10. EP Kings 2016 6-0-0-0-0-0. FC RECORD: 13-2-0-0-0-10. RECORD IN 2016: (EP Kings, Sharks XV) 9-0-0-0-0-0.

Potgieter, Warren Johan (Dr. EG Jansen HS, Boksburg & Glenwood HS, Durban) b 29/03/1994, Sandton. 1.79m. 88kg. Flyhalf. FC DEBUT: 2015. PROV CAREER: Golden Lions XV 2015 2-0-5-1-0-13. Valke 2016 13-0-14-3-0-37. FC RECORD: 15-0-19-4-0-50. RECORD IN 2016: (Valke) 13-0-14-3-0-37.

Pretorius, Daniel Jacobus (Duan) (Henneman HS) b 16/01/1990, Virginia. 1.86m. 80kg. Centre. FC DEBUT: 2016. PROV CAREER: Griffons 2016 16-3-5-3-0-34. FC RECORD: 16-3-5-3-0-34. RECORD IN 2016: (Griffons) 16-3-5-3-0-34.

Pretorius, Johannes Willem (Brandwag HS, Benoni & UP) b 14/01/1992, Benoni. 1.74m. 80kg. Scrumhalf. FC DEBUT: 2014. PROV CAREER: Pumas 2014 1-1-3-0-0-11. Valke 2015-16 31-13-0-0-0-65. FC RECORD: 32-14-3-0-0-76. RECORD IN 2016: (Valke) 15-8-0-0-0-40.

Pretorius, Mark (Nelspruit HS) b 09/06/1992, Nelspruit. 1.76m. 102kg. Hooker. FC DEBUT: 2013. PROV CAREER: Golden Lions XV 2013-15 10-1-0-0-0-5. Lions 2015 2-0-0-0-0-0. Eagles 2016 16-10-0-0-0-50. SUPERRUGBY: Lions 2014-15 2-0-0-0-0-0. REP Honours: SAU20 2012 4-1-0-0-0-5. FC RECORD: 34-12-0-0-0-60. RECORD IN 2016: (Eagles) 16-10-0-0-0-50.

Prinsloo, Johannes Gerhardus Pienaar (Boom) (Grey College) b 12/03/1989, Bloemfontein. 1.87m. 95kg. Flank. FC DEBUT: 2010. PROV CAREER: Cheetahs 2010-12 & 14-15 37-12-0-0-0-60. Emerging Cheetahs 2011 1-0-0-0-0-0. Free State XV 2013 3-5-0-0-0-25. SUPER-RUGBY: Cheetahs 2012-16 49-14-0-0-0-70. Rep. honours: SA Sevens 2010-12. FC RECORD: 90-31-0-0-0-155. RECORD IN 2016: (Cheetahs S18) 6-1-0-0-0-5.

Prinsloo, Johannes Gouws (Gouws) (Marlow Agric. HS, Cradock) b 19/07/1990, East London. 1.79m. 80kg. Fullback. FC DEBUT: 2011. PROV CAREER: Sharks 2011-12 4-0-0-0-0-0. Sharks XV 2011-13 21-7-28-30-0-181. Griquas 2013-16 51-4-87-58-0-368. SUPERRUGBY: Cheetahs 2014 1-0-0-0-0-0. MISC INFO: VC PoY2012 nominee. FC RECORD: 77-11-115-89-1-555. RECORD IN 2016: (GW) 6-0-8-1-0-19.

Pupuma, Luvuyo Phindile (St Benedicts College, Johannesburg & Wits) b 16/10/1992, Johannesburg. 1.76m. 116kg. Prop. FC DEBUT: 2016. PROV CAREER: Golden Lions XV 2016 2-0-0-0-0-0. FC RECORD: 2-0-0-0-0-0. RECORD IN 2016: (Golden Lions XV) 2-0-0-0-0-0.

Putuma, Wandile (Port Rex HS) b 08/08/1990, East London. 1.92.00m. 92kg. Lock. FC DEBUT: 2014. PROV CAREER: Bulldogs 2014-16 48-4-0-0-0-20. Griquas 2016 4-2-0-0-0-10. FC RECORD: 52-6-0-0-0-30. RECORD IN 2016: (Griquas, Bulldogs) 18-4-0-0-0-20.

Radebe, Charles Roger (Carlo) (Langenhoven Gym., Oudtshoorn) b 16/12/1995, Oudtshoorn. 1.76m. 76kg. Wing. FC DEBUT: 2015. PROV CAREER: Eagles 2015-16 21-7-0-0-0-35. SUPERRUGBY: Southern Kings 2016 1-0-0-0-0-0. FC RECORD: 22-7-0-0-0-35. RECORD IN 2016: (Southern Kings, Eagles) 13-2-0-0-0-10.

Radebe, Inny-Christian (Innocent) (St Stithians College, Johannesburg & UKZN) b 03/01/1995, Johannesburg. 1.76m. 83kg. Flyhalf. FC DEBUT: 2015. PROV CAREER: Sharks XV 2015-16 8-1-16-9-0-64. Sharks 2016 8-2-0-0-0-10. FC RECORD: 16-3-16-9-0-74. RECORD IN 2016: (Sharks, Sharks XV) 14-3-14-5-0-58.

Ralarala, Lundi Sinclair (Cradock HS & UFH) b 18/02/1990, Cradock.

1.82.00m. 84kg. Centre. FC DEBUT: 2014. PROV CAREER: Bulldogs 2014-16 39-9-0-0-0-45. FC RECORD: 39-9-0-0-0-45. RECORD IN 2016: (Bulldogs) 12-0-0-0-0-0.

Ralepelle, Mahlatse Chiliboy (Pretoria BHS) b 11/09/1986, Tzaneen. 1.78m. 105kg. Hooker. FC DEBUT: 2005. PROV CAREER: Blue Bulls 2006 & 08-12 35-3-0-0-0-15. Sharks 2016 8-2-0-0-0-10. Sharks XV 2016 2-0-0-0-0-0. SUPERRUGBY: Bulls 2006-07 & 09-13 69-4-0-0-0-20. Sharks 2016 9-2-0-0-0-10. Rep. honours: TESTS: SA 2006 & 08-11 & 13 22-1-0-0-0-5. Tour: 2006,09 2-0-0-0-0-0. Total: 24-1-0-0-0-5. SA U21 2005-06 9-0-0-0-0-0. SA U19 2004-05, SA Schools 2002-03. CW Blue Bulls. MISC INFO: IRB U19 PoYnominee 2005. FC RECORD: 156-12-0-0-0-60. RECORD IN 2016 (Sharks S18, Sharks, Sharks XV) 19-4-0-0-0-20.

Ramaboea, Godfrey (KES, Johannesburg & UJ) b 18/06/1995, Johannesburg. 1.74m. 81kg. Wing. FC DEBUT: 2016. PROV CAREER: Golden Lions XV 2016 1-1-0-0-0-5. FC RECORD: 1-1-0-0-0-5. RECORD IN 2016: (Golden Lions XV) 1-1-0-0-0-5.

Ramashala, Rebaballetswe Makholokoe (Kholo) (Queen's College, Queen'stown, CUT & NMMU) b 22/05/1989, Aliwal North. 1.78m. 85kg. Wing. FC DEBUT: 2010. PROV CAREER: Cheetahs 2010 8-2-0-0-0-10. Free State XV 2012 & 16 5-2-0-0-0-10. FC RECORD: 13-4-0-0-0-20. RECORD IN 2016: (Free State XV) 1-0-0-0-0-0.

Rampeta, Refuce Emmanuel (HTS Louis Botha, Bloemfontein & UFS) b 23/03/1995, Bloemfontein. 1.73m. 95kg. Flank. FC DEBUT: 2016. PROV CAREER: Free State XV 2016 10-2-0-0-0-10. FC RECORD: 10-2-0-0-0-10. RECORD IN 2016: (Free State XV) 10-2-0-0-0-10.

Raubenheimer, Davon (Pacaltsdorp SS) b 16/07/1984, Knysna. 1.94m. 92kg. Flank. FC DEBUT: 2005. PROV CAREER: Eagles 2005-08 & 14-16 98-5-0-0-0-25. Griquas 2009-11 56-4-0-0-0-20. Cheetahs 2012-13 16-0-0-0-0-0. Free State XV 2012-13 6-0-0-0-0-0. Griffons 2013 5-0-0-0-0-0. SUPERRUGBY: Cheetahs 2010-12 20-2-0-0-0-10. REP Honours: SA Tour: 2009 2-0-0-0-0-0. Emerging Springboks 2008 2-0-0-0-0-0. Royal XV 2009 1-0-0-0-0-0. SA U21 2005 3-0-0-0-0-0. FC RECORD: 209-11-0-0-0-55. RECORD IN 2016: (Eagles) 7-0-0-0-0-0.

Rautenbach, Neil (Paarl Boys' HS & UCT) b 17/05/1991, Cape Town. 1.78m. 101kg. Hooker. FC DEBUT: 2012. PROV CAREER: WP 2014-16 19-0-0-0-0-0. Cheetahs 2015 4-0-0-0-0-0. Free State XV 2016 1-1-0-0-0-5. Griffons 2016 5-1-0-0-0-5. SUPERRUGBY: Stormers 2015 3-0-0-0-0-0. REP Honours: SA Students 2012 2-0-0-0-0-0. FC RECORD: 34-2-0-0-0-10. RECORD IN 2016: (WP, Griffons, Free State XV) 10-2-0-0-0-10.

Redelinghuys, Julian (Monument HS, Krugersdorp) b 11/09/1989, Pretoria. 1.76m. 100kg. Prop. FC DEBUT: 2009. PROV CAREER: Sharks 2009 & 2011-12 9-0-0-0-0-0. Sharks XV 2010-11 8-0-0-0-0-0. Lions 2013-16 22-0-0-0-0-0. Golden Lions XV 2013 4-1-0-0-0-5. SUPERRUGBY: Lions 2014-16 45-1-0-0-0-5. Lions P/R 2013 2-0-0-0-0-0. REP Honours: SA 2014 & 16 TESTS: 8-0-0-0-0-0. SAU20 2009 4-0-0-0-0-0. FC RECORD: 102-2-0-0-0-10. RECORD IN 2016: (SA, Lions S18, Lions) 23-1-0-0-0-5.

Redelinghuys, Marno (Schoonspruit HS, Malmesbury) b 06/01/1993, Klerksdorp. 1.95m. 101kg. Flank. FC DEBUT: 2015. PROV CAREER: Leopards 2015-16 27-2-0-0-0-10. Leopards XV 2015 1-0-0-0-0-0. FC RECORD: 28-2-0-0-0-10. RECORD IN 2016: (Leopards) 14-2-0-0-0-10.

Reinach, Jacobus Meyer (Cobus) (Grey College, Bloemfontein) b 07/02/1990, Bloemfontein. 1.75m. 83kg. Scrumhalf. FC DEBUT: 2011. PROV CAREER: Sharks 2011-15 33-6-0-0-0-30. Sharks XV 2011-12

19-4-0-0-0-20. REP Honours: SA 2014-15 TESTS: 10-2-0-0-0-10. Springboks 2015 1-1-0-0-0-5. Total: 11-3-0-0-0-15. British Barbarians 2015 2-0-0-0-0-0. SUPERRUGBY: Sharks 2012-16 44-9-0-0-0-45. MISC INFO: Son of former Springbok Jaco Reinach. FC RECORD: 109-22-0-0-0-110. RECORD IN 2016: (Sharks S18) 8-0-0-0-0-0.

Reinecke, Jason Chris (Cambridge HS, East London & NMMU) b 08/12/1995, East London. 1.80m. 90kg. Hooker. FC DEBUT: 2016. PROV CAREER: EP Kings 2016 2-0-0-0-0-0. FC RECORD: 2-0-0-0-0-0. RECORD IN 2016: (EP Kings) 2-0-0-0-0-0.

Reynolds, Shaun (Goudveld HS, Welkom) b 15/06/1995, Bloemfontein. 1.87m. 91kg. Flyhalf. FC DEBUT: 2016. PROV CAREER: Golden Lions XV 2016 11-5-24-6-0-91. FC RECORD: 11-5-24-6-0-91. RECORD IN 2016: (Golden Lions XV) 11-5-24-6-0-91.

Rhule, Raymond Kofi (Louis Botha THS, Bloemfontein & UFS) b 06/11/1992, Accra (Ghana). 1.78m. 78kg. Wing. FC DEBUT: 2012. PROV CAREER: Cheetahs 2012-16 49-22-0-0-0-110. Free State XV 2012 1-0-0-0-0-0. SUPERRUGBY: Cheetahs 2013-16 52-13-0-0-0-65. MISC INFO: YPoY2012 nominee. CC PoY2012 nominee. REP Honours: SA 2012 no tests. SAU20 2012 3-2-0-0-0-10. FC RECORD: 105-37-0-0-0-185. RECORD IN 2016: (Cheetahs S18, Cheetahs) 24-7-0-0-0-35.

Ribbans, David George (Somerset College) b 29/08/1995, Somerset WeSt 2.00m. 110kg. Lock. FC DEBUT: 2015. PROV CAREER: WP 2015-16 7-1-0-0-0-5. FC RECORD: 7-1-0-0-0-5. RECORD IN 2016: (WP) 6-1-0-0-0-5.

Richter, Anrich (Dr EG Jansen HS, Boksburg) b 30/05/1991, Kempton Park. 78kg. Scrumhalf. FC DEBUT: 2011. PROV CAREER: Valke 2011-16 92-34-6-0-1-185. FC RECORD: 92-34-6-0-1-185. RECORD IN 2016: (Valke) 11-3-0-0-0-15.

Riddles, Denzel Brain (Jan Kriel HS & North Link College) b 10/08/1988, Cape Town. 1.78m. 108kg. FC DEBUT: 2009. PROV CAREER: WP 2009-10 & 16 8-0-0-0-0-0. FC RECORD: 8-0-0-0-0-0. RECORD IN 2016: (WP) 2-0-0-0-0-0.

Roberts, Daniel Cornelius (PW Botha College, George) b 20/01/1992, Riversdal. 1.85m. 73kg. Fullback. FC DEBUT: 2013. PROV CAREER: Eagles 2013-16 59-14-0-0-0-70. FC RECORD: 59-14-0-0-0-70. RECORD IN 2016: (Eagles) 18-8-0-0-0-40.

Roberts, Willem Andries Stephanus (Steph) (Grey College, Bloemfontein) b 20/03/1985, Bloemfontein. 1.80m. 108kg. Prop. FC DEBUT: 2005. PROV CAREER: Cheetahs 2005-07 15-0-0-0-0-0. Griquas 2008-16 165-6-0-0-0-30. REP Honours:Royal XV 2009 1-0-0-0-0-0. SA Students 2007 1-0-0-0-0-0. FC RECORD: 182-6-0-0-0-30. RECORD IN 2016: (Griquas) 16-0-0-0-0-0.

Robertse, Francois (George Campbell HS, Durban) b 03/03/1989, Durban. 1.97m. 118kg. Lock. FC DEBUT: 2014. PROV CAREER: Leopards 2014-16 30-7-0-0-0-35. Leopards XV 2015 7-1-0-0-0-5. FC RECORD: 37-8-0-0-0-40. RECORD IN 2016: (Leopards) 13-1-0-0-0-5.

Roelfse, Heinrich Rashid (George HS) b 25/01/1990, Mossel Bay. 1.86m. 110kg. Prop. FC DEBUT: 2012. PROV CAREER: Griffons 2012-16 63-3-0-0-0-15. FC RECORD: 63-3-0-0-0-15. RECORD IN 2016: (Griffons) 16-3-0-0-0-15.

Roelofse, Nemo Gunther (Oakdale Agric. HS, Riversdale) b 06/06/1995, Randburg. 1.80m. 115kg. Prop. FC DEBUT: 2015. PROV CAREER: Eagles 2015-16 20-1-0-0-0-5. FC RECORD: 20-1-0-0-0-5. RECORD IN 2016: (Eagles) 18-0-0-0-0-0.

Roets, Le Roux (Garsfontein HS, Pretoria & UJ) b 14/01/1995, Boksburg. 2.00m. 135kg. Lock. FC DEBUT: 2015. PROV CAREER: Golden Lions XV 2015 1-0-0-0-0-0. Blue Bulls 2016 1-0-0-0-0-0. FC RECORD:

2-0-0-0-0-0. RECORD IN 2016: (Blue Bulls) 1-0-0-0-0-0.

Rooi, Cameron Austine (Die Anker HS) b 08/06/1995, East London. 1.76m. 75kg. Centre. FC DEBUT: 2015. PROV CAREER: Golden Lions XV 2015-16 4-0-0-0-0-0. FC RECORD: 4-0-0-0-0-0. RECORD IN 2016: (Golden Lions XV) 2-0-0-0-0-0.

Rossouw, Divan (Windhoek Gym. & UP) b 12/03/1996, Windhoek. 1.83m. 89kg. Fullback. FC DEBUT: 2016. PROV CAREER: Blue Bulls 2016 12-3-1-0-0-17. FC RECORD: 12-3-1-0-0-17. RECORD IN 2016: (Blue Bulls) 12-3-1-0-0-17.

Rudolph, Jeandré (Oakdale Agric. HS, Riversdale) b 09/05/1994, Florida. 1.88m. 90kg. Eighthman. FC DEBUT: 2015. PROV CAREER: Leopards 2015-16 17-3-0-0-0-15. FC RECORD: 17-3-0-0-0-15. RECORD IN 2016: (Leopards) 16-3-0-0-0-15.

Rust, Hendri Christian (Oakdale HS, Riversdale) b 07/04/1992, Malmesbury. 1.83m. 83kg. Fullback. FC DEBUT: 2014. PROV CAREER: Boland 2014-15 27-8-12-4-0-76. Valke 2016 4-3-0-0-0-15. FC RECORD: 31-11-12-4-0-91. RECORD IN 2016: (Valke) 4-3-0-0-0-15.

Sadie, Carlo Johann (Belville HS) b 07/03/1997, Belville. 1.80m. 124kg. Prop. FC DEBUT: 2016. REP Honours: SAU20 2016 5-1-0-0-0-5. FC RECORD: 5-1-0-0-0-5. RECORD IN 2016: (SAU20) 5-1-0-0-0-5.

Sage, Dylan Michael (Wynberg Boys'HS & Varsity College) b 24/01/1992, Cape Town. 1.87m. 87kg. Wing. REP Honours: SA Sevens 2015-16. RECORD IN 2016: (SA sevens).

Sage, Jarryd Christopher (Wynberg Boys'HS) b 18/08/1995, Cape Town. 1.86m. 95kg. Centre. FC DEBUT: 2016. PROV CAREER: Golden Lions XV 2016 13-3-0-0-0-15. FC RECORD: 13-3-0-0-0-15. RECORD IN 2016: (Golden Lions XV) 13-3-0-0-0-15.

Sampson, Marcello Edward Dennis (Wynberg Boys'HS & UWC) b 27/03/1987, Cape Town. 1.83m. 85kg. Wing. FC DEBUT: 2011. PROV CAREER: EP Kings 2011-13 37 -19-0-0-0-95. Pumas 2014-16 23-7-0-0-0-35. SUPERRUGBY: Southern Kings 2013 13-0-0-0-0-0. P/R 2013 1-1-0-0-0-5. REP Honours: SA Kings 2011 1-0-0-0-0-0. FC RECORD: 75-27-0-0-0-135. RECORD IN 2016: (Pumas) 14-4-0-0-0-20.

Samuels, Ramone Christie (Paul Roos Gym., Stellenbosch) b 03/11/1994, Somerset WeSt 1.83m. 105kg. Hooker. FC DEBUT: 2015. PROV CAREER: Golden Lions XV 2015-16 18-5-0-0-0-25. Lions 2016 3-0-0-0-0-0. SUPERRUGBY: Lions 2016 3-0-0-0-0-0. FC RECORD: 24-5-0-0-0-25. RECORD IN 2016: (Lions S18, Lions, Golden Lions XV) 15-4-0-0-0-20.

Sass, Edwin (Tygerberg HS, Cape Town) b 07/02/1993, Ceres. 1.83m. 90kg. Centre. FC DEBUT: 2014. PROV CAREER: Boland 2014-16 31-5-0-0-0-25. FC RECORD: 31-5-0-0-0-25. RECORD IN 2016: (Boland) 7-2-0-0-0-10.

Scheepers, Jacobus Nicolaas (Nico) (Nico Malan HS, Humansdorp & UFS) b 27/02/1990, Port Elizabeth. 1.86m. 90kg. Wing. FC DEBUT: 2011. PROV CAREER: Cheetahs 2011-12 16-3-17-27-0-130. Free State XV 2012-13 8-3-12-5-0-54. Emerging Cheetahs 2011 1-0-0-0-0-0. Griquas 2013-14 14-2-20-17-0-101. Griffons 2015 6-2-7-7-0-45. Boland 2016 15-5-46-17-0-162. SUPERRUGBY: Cheetahs 2012 3-0-0-0-0-0. REP Honours: SAU20 2010 4-1-0-0-0-5. FC RECORD: 67-16-102-73-0-503. RECORD IN 2016: (Boland) 15-5-46-17-0-168.

Schickerling, John Dave (JD) (Paarl Gym.) b 09/05/1995, Calvinia. 2.02.00m. 108kg. Lock. FC DEBUT: 2014. PROV CAREER: WP 2014 & 16 6-0-0-0-0-0. SUPERRUGBY: Stormers 2016 13-0-0-0-0-0. REP Honours: SA A 2016 2-0-0-0-0-0. SAU20 2014 5-0-0-0-0-0. FC RECORD: 26-0-0-0-0-0. RECORD IN 2016: (SA A, Stormers, WP) 20-0-0-0-0-0.

Schoeman, Christian Francois (Tian) (John Vorster HTS, Pretoria & UP) b 23/09/1991, Pretoria. 1.82.00m. 89kg. Flyhalf. FC DEBUT: 2014. PROV CAREER: Blue Bulls 2014-16 29-5-82-60-0-369. SUPERRUGBY: Bulls 2015-16 22-0-17-12-1-73. FC RECORD: 51-5-99-72-1-442. RECORD IN 2016: (Bulls, Blue Bulls) 25-2-47-33-1-206.

Schoeman, Juan Louw (Affies, Pretoria) b 18/09/1991, Pretoria. 1.87m. 105kg. Prop. FC DEBUT: 2011. PROV CAREER: Blue Bulls 2011 & 14 9-0-0-0-0-0. Sharks 2015-16 6-0-0-0-0-0. Sharks XV 2016 9-0-0-0-0-0. SUPERRUGBY: Sharks 2016 5-0-0-0-0-0. REP Honours: SAU20 2011 3-0-0-0-0-0. FC RECORD: 32-0-0-0-0-0. RECORD IN 2016: (Sharks S18, Sharks, Sharks XV) 18-0-0-0-0-0.

Schoeman, Marnus (Waterkloof HS, Pretoria) b 09/02/1989, Edenvale. 1.78m. 95kg. FC DEBUT: 2009. PROV CAREER: Blue Bulls 2009 & 2011 12-3-0-0-0-15. Griquas 2011-14 65-42-0-0-0-210. Pumas 2015-16 29-16-0-0-0-80. REP Honours: SAU20 2009 5-0-0-0-0-0. FC RECORD: 111-61-0-0-0-305. RECORD IN 2016: (Pumas) 11-2-0-0-0-10.

Schoeman, Paul (Marlow Agric., Cradock) b 19/12/1992, Cradock. 1.90m. 97kg. Eighthman. FC DEBUT: 2013. PROV CAREER: EP Kings 2013-15 32-13-0-0-0-65. Cheetahs 2016 9-4-0-0-0-20. SUPER-RUGBY: Cheetahs 2016 14-5-0-0-0-25. FC RECORD: 55-22-0-0-0-110. RECORD IN 2016: (Cheetahs S18, Cheetahs) 23-9-0-0-0-45.

Schoeman, Pierre (Affies, Pretoria & UP) b 07/05/1994, Nelspruit. 1.84m. 118kg. Prop. FC DEBUT: 2014. PROV CAREER: Blue Bulls 2014-16 15-0-0-0-0-0. SUPERRUGBY: Bulls 2016 9-0-0-0-0-0. REP Honours: SAU20 2014 5-1-0-0-0-5. FC RECORD: 29-1-0-0-0-5. RECORD IN 2016: (Bulls, Blue Bulls) 16-0-0-0-0-0.

Scholtz, Pieter Ernst (Diamantveld HS, Kimberley) b 20/03/1994, Pretoria. 1.87m. 120kg. Prop. FC DEBUT: 2014. PROV CAREER: Golden Lions XV 2014-16 17-0-0-0-0-0. Lions 2015-16 3-0-0-0-0-0. SUPER-RUGBY: Lions 2016 2-0-0-0-0-0. FC RECORD: 22-0-0-0-0-0. RECORD IN 2016: (Lions S18, Lions, Golden Lions XV) 12-0-0-0-0-0.

Schramm, Ayron Garret (Kearsney College, Botha's Hill & UKZN) b 18/04/1995, Amanzintoti. 1.92.00m. 108kg. Eighthman. FC DEBUT: 2015. PROV CAREER: Sharks XV 2015-16 6-0-0-0-0-0. FC RECORD: 6-0-0-0-0-0. RECORD IN 2016: (Sharks XV) 4-0-0-0-0-0.

Schreuder, Louis (Paarl Gym.) b 25/04/1990, Paarl. 1.84m. 82kg. Wing. FC DEBUT: 2010. PROV CAREER: WP 2010-15 55-3-0-0-0-15. SUPERRUGBY: Stormers 2011-16 66-2-0-0-0-10. REP Honours: SA 2013 no appearances. SAU20 2010 5-0-0-0-0-0. FC RECORD: 126-5-0-0-0-25. RECORD IN 2016: (Stormers) 12-1-0-0-0-5.

Schroeder, Ricky Darryl (Paul Roos Gym., Stellenbosch & UCT) b 05/01/1991, Worcester. 1.68m. 77kg. Scrumhalf. FC DEBUT: 2012. PROV CAREER: WP 2012-13 7-0-0-0-0-0. Boland 2013 10-0-0-0-0-0. Lions 2014-15 6-0-0-0-0-0. Golden Lions XV 2014-16 28-2-0-0-0-10. EP Kings 2016 7-1-0-0-0-5. FC RECORD: 58-3 0 0 0 15. RECORD IN 2016: (EP Kings, Golden Lions XV) 17-3-0-0-0-15.

Schutte, Andries Stefanus (Hoogenhout HS) b 18/01/1994, Secunda. 1.88m. 117kg. Prop. FC DEBUT: 2014. PROV CAREER: Valke 2014-16 43-3-0-0-0-15. FC RECORD: 43-3-0-0-0-15. RECORD IN 2016: (Valke) 19-2-0-0-0-10.

Sekekete, Victor Kutlwano (Queen's HS, Sandton) b 28/01/1994, Johannesburg. 1.95m. 99kg. Flank. FC DEBUT: 2014. PROV CAREER: Golden Lions XV 2015-16 9-0-0-0-0-0. Lions 2016 3-1-0-0-0-5. REP Honours: SAU20 2016 5-1-0-0-0-5. FC RECORD: 13-1-0-0-0-5. RECORD IN 2016: (Lions, Golden Lions XV) 11-1-0-0-0-5.

Senatla, Seabelo Mohanoe (Riebeeckstad HS & CUT) b

10/02/1993, Welkom. 1.86m. 76kg. Wing. FC DEBUT: 2013. PROV CAREER: WP 2014-15 17-8-0-0-0-40. SUPERRUGBY: Stormers 2014-15 6-2-0-0-0-10. REP Honours: SA U20 2013 5-7-0-0-0-35. SA Sevens 2013-16. MISC INFO: SA Sevens PoYin 2016, YPoYnominee 2016. FC RECORD: 28-17-0-0-0-85. RECORD IN 2016: (SA Sevens).

September, Chriswill Bradley (Drostdy HS, Worcester) b 30/06/1994, Worcester. 1.72.00m. 69kg. Scrumhalf. FC DEBUT: 2014. PROV CAREER: Leopards XV 2014-15 3-0-0-0-0-0. Leopards 2016 21-0-0-0-0-0. FC RECORD: 24-0-0-0-0-0. RECORD IN 2016: (Leopards) 21-0-0-0-0-0.

September, Marquit Virgil (Garsfontein HS, Pretoria) b 19/12/1994, Riversdale. 1.85m. 94kg. Centre. FC DEBUT: 2015. PROV CAREER: Blue Bulls 2015-16 18-12-0-0-0-60. FC RECORD: 18-12-0-0-0-60. RECORD IN 2016: (Blue Bulls) 9-8-0-0-0-40.

Serfontein, Jan Lodewyk (Grey HS, PE/ Grey College, Bloemfontein) b 15/04/1993, Port Elizabeth. 1.87m. 97kg. Centre. FC DEBUT: 2012. PROV CAREER: Blue Bulls 2012-13 & 15 15-4-0-0-0-20. SUPERRUGBY: Bulls 2013-16 48-13-0-0-0-65. MISC INFO: VC PoY2012 nominee. SA U20 PoY2012. IRB U/20 PoY. Brother of Willem Serfontein. Son of former EP No. 8 Jan Serfontein. REP Honours: SA TESTS: 2013-15 26-2-0-0-0-10. SAU20 2012 5-4-0-0-0-20. FC RECORD: 94-23-0-0-0-115. RECORD IN 2016: (Bulls) 12-3-0-0-0-15.

Serfontein, Willem Jacob (Framesby HS, Port Elizabeth & Unisa) b 16/09/1988, Port Elizabeth. 1.95m. 112kg. Lock. FC DEBUT: 2009. PROV CAREER: Blue Bulls 2009 8-1-0-0-0-5. Pumas 2010-13 62-1-0-0-0-5. Griquas 2014 10-1-0-0-0-5. Cheetahs 2015-16 4-0-0-0-0-0. Griffons 2015-15 11-1-0-0-0-5. Free State XV 2016 1-0-0-0-0-0. SUPER-RUGBY: Cheetahs 2014 3-0-0-0-0-0. REP Honours: SA Barbarians 2012 1-0-0-0-0-0. MISC INFO: Brother of Jan Serfontein. Son of former EP No. 8 Jan Serfontein. FC RECORD: 100-4-0-0-0-20. RECORD IN 2016: (Cheetahs, Griffons, Free State XV) 7-0-0-0-0-0.

Shabangu, Simphiwe Brian (Glenwood HS, Durban) b 11/04/1988, Durban. 1.73m. 96kg. Flank. FC DEBUT: 2012. PROV CAREER: Bulldogs 2012-13 26-4-0-0-0-20. Valke 2014 1-0-0-0-0-0. Pumas 2014-16 25-6-0-0-0-30. REP Honours: SA Pres XV 2013 3-0-0-0-0-0. FC RECORD: 55-10-0-0-0-50. RECORD IN 2016: (Pumas) 11-3-0-0-0-15.

Short, Basil Gordon (Standerton HS & UP) b 19/05/1991, Vryheid. 1.89m. 116kg. Prop. FC DEBUT: 2012. PROV CAREER: Blue Bulls 2012-15 26-2-0-0-0-10. EP Kings 2015 3-0-0-0-0-0. Boland 2016 19-1-0-0-0-5. FC RECORD: 48-3-0-0-0-15. RECORD IN 2016: (Boland) 19-1-0-0-0-5.

Sisita, Frans Leonardo (Sand du Plessis HS, Bloemfontein & CUT) b 06/08/1990, Vryburg. 1.86m. 103kg. Wing. FC DEBUT: 2013. PROV CAREER: Griffons 2013-16 21-2-0-0-0-10. Griquas 2014 1-0-0-0-0-0. FC RECORD: 22-2-0-0-0-10. RECORD IN 2016: (Griffons) 3-0-0-0-0-0.

Sithole, Sibusiso Camagu Thokazani (Varsity College) b 14/06/1990, Queen'stown. 1.78m. 90kg. Wing/Centre. FC DEBUT: 2010. PROV CAREER: Sharks 2011-12 & 14-16 45-11-0-0-0-55. Sharks XV 2010-13 & 15-16 29-14-0-0-0-70. SUPERRUGBY: Sharks 2013-16 33-4-0-0-0-20. Rep. honours: SAU20 2010 3-4-0-0-0-20. SA Sevens 2010-11 & 13. FC RECORD: 110-33-0-0-0-165. RECORD IN 2016: (Sharks S18, Sharks, Sharks XV) 19-4-0-0-0-20.

Sithole, Simphiwe Martin (Ikusaselethu SS, Mtubatuba) b 03/02/1984, Pietermaritzburg. 1.81m. 95kg. Flank. FC DEBUT: 2005. Prov. career: Pumas 2008-11 37-6-0-0-0-30. Griffons 2011-16 89-32-0-0-0-160. Rep. honours: SA U21 2005 1-0-0-0-0-0. SA Barbarians 2012 1-0-0-0-0-0. CW Pumas 2001-02. FC RECORD: 128-38-0-0-0-190. Record in 2016 (Griffons) 18-3-0-0-0-15.

Sithole, Sithembiso Mfundo Siphesihle (Westville Boys' HS & UCT) b 31/03/1993, Durban. 1.79m. 104kg. Prop. FC DEBUT: 2013. PROV CAREER: WP 2014-16 13-0-0-0-0-0. SUPERRUGBY: Stormers 2014 3-0-0-0-0-0. Southern Kings 2016 10-0-0-0-0-0. REP Honours: SA U20 2013 4-0-0-0-0-0. FC RECORD: 30-0-0-0-0-0. RECORD IN 2016: (Southern Kings, WP) 11-0-0-0-0-0.

Skorbinski, Alfred Henry (Framesby HS, Port Elizabeth & NWU) b 25/09/1990, Port Elizabeth. 1.84m. 93kg. Centre. FC DEBUT: 2011. PROV CAREER: Leopards 2011-13 18-3-0-0-0-15. Leopard XV 2013 2-1-0-0-0-5. Pumas 2014-16 28-6-1-0-0-32. FC RECORD: 48-10-1-0-0-52. RECORD IN 2016: (Pumas) 15-2-0-0-0-10.

Skosan, Courtnall Douglas (Brackenfell HS, Cape Town) b 24/07/1991, Cape Town. 1.83m. 90kg. Wing. FC DEBUT: 2011. PROV CAREER: Blue Bulls 2011-13 12-7-0-0-0-35. Lions 2014-16 21-8-0-0-0-40. Golden Lions XV 2014 1-0-0-0-0-0. SUPERRUGBY: Lions 2014-16 36-16-0-0-0-80. REP Honours: SA A 2016 2-0-0-0-0-0. SAU20 2011 3-1-0-0-0-5. FC RECORD: 75-32-0-0-0-160. RECORD IN 2016: (SA A, Lions S18, Lions) 21-10-0-0-0-50.

Slater, Sherwin Michael (Andrew Rabie HS, Port Elizabeth) b 29/04/1994, Port Elizabeth. 1.83m. 92kg. Utility Back. FC DEBUT: 2016. PROV CAREER: Griffons 2016 3-0-0-0-0-0. FC RECORD: 3-0-0-0-0-0. RECORD IN 2016: (Griffons) 3-0-0-0-0-0.

Small-Smith, William Thomas (Grey College, Bloemfontein) b 31/03/1992, Johannesburg. 1.84m. 91kg. Centre. FC DEBUT: 2011. PROV CAREER: Blue Bulls 2011 & 13-15 24-11-0-0-0-55. Cheetahs 2016 7-2-0-0-0-10. SUPERRUGBY: Bulls 2014 7-1-0-0-0-5. Cheetahs 2016 7-1-0-0-0-5. Rep. Honours: SAU20 2012 3-2-0-0-0-10. SA Sevens 2011-12. FC RECORD: 48-17-0-0-0-85. RECORD IN 2016: (Cheetahs S18, Cheetahs) 14-3-0-0-0-15.

Smit, Barend Johannes (HTS Middelburg) b 12/02/1996, Witbank. 1.85m. 94kg. Fullback. FC DEBUT: 2015. PROV CAREER: Golden Lions XV 2015-16 3-0-0-0-0-0. FC RECORD: 3-0-0-0-0-0. RECORD IN 2016: (Golden Lions XV) 2-0-0-0-0-0.

Smit, Dillon (Middelburg HS) b 11/12/1992, Bethal. 1.75m. 83kg. Scrumhalf. FC DEBUT: 2013. PROV CAREER: Bulldogs 2013 5-0-0-0-0-0. Leopards 2014-15 15-8-0-0-0-40. Leopards XV 2014-15 2-0-0-0-0-0. Lions 2016 6-1-0-0-0-5. Golden Lions XV 2016 4-0-0-0-0-0. SUPER-RUGBY: Lions 2015-16 6-0-0-0-0-0. FC RECORD: 42-9-0-0-0-45. RECORD IN 2016: (Lions S18, Lions, Golden Lions XV) 14-1-0-0-0-5.

Smit, Hendrik Jacobus (Henco) (Garsfontein HS, Pretoria) b 06/07/1996, Pretoria. 1.85m. 109kg. Prop, FC DEBUT: 2016. PROV CAREER: Golden Lions XV 2016 4-0-0-0-0-0. FC RECORD: 4-0-0-0-0-0. RECORD IN 2016: (Golden Lions XV) 4-0-0-0-0-0.

Smit, Roelof Andries (Hangklip HS, Queen'stown) b 11/01/1993, Queen'stown. 1.90m. 90kg. Flank. FC DEBUT: 2013. PROV CAREER: Blue Bulls 2013-16 32-14-0-0-0-70. SUPERRUGBY: Bulls 2014-16 13-1-0-0-0-5. REP Honours: Springbok XV 2016 1-1-0-0-0-5. SA U20 2013 4-0-0-0-0-0. FC RECORD: 50-16-0-0-0-80. RECORD IN 2016: (Springbok XV, Bulls, Bulls) 22-8-0-0-0-40.

Smith, Albertus Stephanus (Kwagga) (HTS Middelburg) b 11/06/1993, Lydenburg. 1.80m. 80kg. Flank. FC DEBUT: 2013. PROV CAREER: Lions 2014-16 28-19-0-0-0-95. SUPERRUGBY: Lions 2015 3-0-0-0-0-0. REP Honours: SA U20 2013 3-2-0-0-0-10. SA Sevens 2014-16. British Barbarians 2016 1-2-0-0-0-10. FC RECORD: 35-23-0-0-0-115. RECORD IN 2016: (Lions, SA Sevens, British Barbarians) 7-9-0-0-0-45.

Smith, Dylan Thomas (KES, Johannesburg) b 26/02/1994, Durban. 1.81m. 102kg. Prop. FC DEBUT: 2014. PROV CAREER: Golden Lions XV 2014-16 18-0-0-0-0-0. Lions 2015-16 10-1-0-0-0-5. SUPERRUGBY: Lions 2016 16-0-0-0-0-0. FC RECORD: 44-1-0-0-0-5. RECORD IN 2016: (Lions S18, Lions, Golden Lions XV) 24-1-0-0-0-5.

Smith, Jean-Pierre (Paarl Gym.) b 24/01/1990, Vryburg. 1.86m. 117kg. Prop. FC DEBUT: 2010. PROV CAREER: WP 2010 & 15-16 22-0-0-0-0-0. SUPERRUGBY: Brumbies 2014-15. Stormers 2016 3-0-0-0-0-0. FC RECORD: 25-0-0-0-0-0. RECORD IN 2016: (Stormers, WP) 18-0-0-0-0-0.

Smith, Juan-Philip (Queen's College, Queen'stown & UP) b 30/03/1994, Bloemhof. 1.87m. 91kg. Scrumhalf. FC DEBUT: 2014. PROV CAREER: Blue Bulls 2015 4-0-0-0-0-0. Free State XV 2016 12-1-0-1-0-8. REP Honours: SAU20 2014 5-0-0-0-0-0. FC RECORD: 21-1-0-1-0-8. RECORD IN 2016: (Free State XV) 12-1-0-1-0-8.

Smith, Rhyno Christo (Paarl Boys' HS & NWU) b 11/02/1993, Paarl. 1.72.00m. 75kg. Fullback. FC DEBUT: 2014. PROV CAREER: Leopards 2014-16 27-16-49-17-4-223. Leopards XV 2015 2-1-0-0-0-5. Sharks 2016 6-1-0-0-0-5. SUPERRUGBY: Sharks 2016 3-0-0-0-0-0. FC RECORD: 38-18-40-17-4-233. RECORD IN 2016: (Sharks S18, Sharks, Leopards) 19-6-33-17-2-153.

Snell, Dilen Christo-Lee (Hillcrest HS) b 13/04/1993, Mossel Bay. 1.78m. 79kg. Centre. FC DEBUT: 2014. PROV CAREER: Eagles 2014-16 21-2-0-0-0-10. FC RECORD: 21-2-0-0-0-10. RECORD IN 2016: (Eagles) 9-1-0-0-0-5.

Snyman, Eli Colin (St John's College, Harare & UP) b 25/01/1996, Harare. 2.01m. 111kg. Lock. FC DEBUT: 2016. PROV CAREER: Blue Bulls 2016 2-0-0-0-0-0. REP Honours: SAU20 2016 5-0-0-0-0-0. FC RECORD: 7-0-0-0-0-0. RECORD IN 2016: (Blue Bulls, SAU20) 7-0-0-0-0-0.

Snyman, Johannes Hendrik (Jannes) (Kempton Park HS & UJ) b 18/08/1993, Johannesburg. 1.76m. 100kg. Hooker. FC DEBUT: 2016. PROV CAREER: Golden Lions XV 2016 5-0-0-0-0-0. FC RECORD: 5-0-0-0-0-0. RECORD IN 2016: (Golden Lions XV) 5-0-0-0-0-0.

Snyman, Phillipus Albertus Borman (Phillip) (Grey College, Bloemfontein) b 26/03/1987, Bloemfontein. 1.88m. 95kg. Centre. FC DEBUT: 2008. PROV CAREER: Griffons 2008-09 6-0-0-0-0-0. Cheetahs 2008-12 59-19-0-0-0-95. Emerging Cheetahs 2011 1-0-0-0-0-0. SUPERRUGBY: Cheetahs 2011-12 20-1-0-0-0-5. REP Honours: SA Sevens 2008 & 12-16. FC RECORD: 86-20-0-0-0-100. RECORD IN 2016: (SA Sevens).

Snyman, Rudolph Gerhardus (RG) (Affies, Pretoria) b 29/01/1995, Potchefstroom. 2.06m. 117kg. Lock. FC DEBUT: 2015. PROV CAREER: Blue Bulls 2015-16 23-1-0-0-0-5. SUPERRUGBY: Bulls 2016 12-2-0-0-0-10. REP Honours: Springbok XV 2016 1-0-0-0-0-0. SA A 2016 2-0-0-0-0-0. SAU20 2015 5-0-0-0-0-0. MISC INFO: SARU YPoYnominee 2016. FC RECORD: 43-3-0-0-0-15. RECORD IN 2016: (Springbok XV, SA A, Bulls, Blue Bulls) 24-3-0-0-0-15.

Sofisa, Mzuvukile Gift (Mzu) (Grey HS, Port Elizabeth) b 06/04/1993, Port Elizabeth. 1.81m. 110kg. Prop. FC DEBUT: 2014. PROV CAREER: EP Kings 2014 & 16 21-0-0-0-0-0. FC RECORD: 21-0-0-0-0-0. RECORD IN 2016: (EP Kings) 16-0-0-0-0-0.

Solomon, Chad (Paul Roos Gym., Stellenbosch & UCT) b 23/02/1994, Belville. 1.79m. 100kg. Hooker. FC DEBUT: 2014. PROV CAREER: WP 2014 & 16 16-6-0-0-0-30. FC RECORD: 16-6-0-0-0-30. RECORD IN 2016: (WP) 14-6-0-0-0-30.

Soyizwapi, Siviwe Sonwabile (Dale College, King William's Town)

b 07/12/1992, Mthatha. 1.72.00m. 75kg. Wing. FC DEBUT: 2012. PROV CAREER: EP Kings 2012-16 35-9-0-0-0-45. SUPERRUGBY: Southern Kings 2013 6-0-0-0-0-0. REP Honours: SA Sevens 2016. FC RECORD: 41-9-0-0-0-45. RECORD IN 2016: (EP Kings, SA Sevens) 7-1-0-0-0-5.

Speckman, Rosko Shane (Mary Waters HS, Grahamstown) b 28/04/1989, Grahamstown. 1.66m. 70kg. Wing. FC DEBUT: 2010. PROV CAREER: KZN 2012 1-0-0-0-0-0. Sharks XV 2010-12 13-5-0-0-0-25. Pumas 2013-15 45-28-0-0-0-140. REP Honours: SA Pres XV 2013 3-1-0-0-0-5. SA Sevens 2014-16. FC RECORD: 62-34-0-0-0-170. RECORD IN 2016: (SA Sevens).

Stander, Jan Hendrik (Jannie) (Monument HS, Krugersdorp) b 21/04/1993, Phalaborwa. 1.96m. 107kg. Lock. FC DEBUT: 2013. PROV CAREER: Golden Lions XV 2013-14 4-0-0-0-0-0. Pumas 2015-16 27-2-0-0-0-10. REP Honours: SA U20 2013 no appearances. FC RECORD: 31-2-0-0-0-10. RECORD IN 2016: (Pumas) 20-2-0-0-0-10.

Stander, Johannes Hendrik (Janneman) (Oakdale Agric. HS, Riversdale) b 08/09/1993, George. 1.88m. 94kg. Flank. FC DEBUT: 2013. PROV CAREER: Golden Lions XV 2013 1-0-0-0-0-0. Eagles 2014-16 32-7-0-0-0-35. MISC INFO: Brother of CJ Stander (Ireland). FC RECORD: 33-7-0-0-0-35. RECORD IN 2016: (Eagles) 14-3-0-0-0-15.

Stander, Joshua Trevor (Queen's College, Queen'stown & UP) b 01/01/1994, Cradock. 1.83m. 89kg. Flyhalf. FC DEBUT: 2014. PROV CAREER: Blue Bulls 2014-16 26-6-39-4-0-120. FC RECORD: 26-6-39-4-0-120. RECORD IN 2016: (Blue Bulls) 19-5-28-4-0-93

Steenkamp, Ruan (Monument HS & UP) b 02/02/1993, Krugersdorp. 1.83m. 100kg. Flank. FC DEBUT: 2015. PROV CAREER: Blue Bulls 2015-16 20-2-0-0-0-10. FC RECORD: 20-2-0-0-0-10. RECORD IN 2016: (Blue Bulls) 17-1-0-0-0-5.

Steenkamp, Walt (Rustenburg HS & NWU) b 21/07/1995, Rustenburg. 2.03m. 120kg. Lock. FC DEBUT: 2015. PROV CAREER: Leopards 2015-16 22-1-0-0-0-5. FC RECORD: 22-1-0-0-0-5. RECORD IN 2016: (Leopards) 17-1-0-0-0-5.

Stegmann, Gideon Johannes (Deon) (Grey College, Bloemfontein) b 22/03/1986, Cradock. 1.81m. 99kg. Flank. FC DEBUT: 2007. PROV CAREER: Blue Bulls 2007-12 & 14-16 76-17-0-0-0-85. SUPERRUGBY: Bulls 2008-16 96-9-0-0-0-45. REP Honours: SA 2010-11 TESTS: 6-0-0-0-0-0. FC RECORD: 178-26-0-0-0-130. RECORD IN 2016: (Bulls, Blue Bulls) 5-1-0-0-0-5.

Stemmet, Pieter Franz (Paul Roos Gym., Stellenbosch) b 18/02/1992, Paarl. 1.84m. 115kg. Prop. FC DEBUT: 2012. PROV CAREER: WP 2012 1-1-0-0-0-5. EP Kings 2013-14 & 16 9-1-0-0-0-5. Eagles 2015-16 11-1-0-0-0-5. FC RECORD: 21-3-0-0-0-15. RECORD IN 2016: (EP Kings, Eagles) 4-0-0-0-0-0.

Stevens, Damian Leothon (Walvis Bay HS, Paarl Boys' HS & UWC) b 02/06/1995, Walvis Bay. 1.64m. 68kg. Scrumhalf. FC DEBUT: 2016. PROV CAREER: WP 2016 4-0-0-0-0-0. REP Honours: Namibia RWC 2015. Welwitchias 2016. FC RECORD: 4-0-0-0-0-0. RECORD IN 2016: (WP) 4-0-0-0-0-0.

Steyl, Heinrich Diederick (Boland Agric. HS, Paarl & US) b 06/07/1990, Belville. 1.80m. 82kg. Fullback. FC DEBUT: 2011. PROV CAREER: WP 2011 2-0-0-0-0-0. Blue Bulls 2013 2-0-0-0-0-0. Pumas 2014-16 21-4-6-3-0-41. FC RECORD: 25-4-6-3-0-41. RECORD IN 2016: (Pumas) 15-2-6-3-0-31.

Steyn, Barend Sebastian (Carel de Wet HS) b 13/06/1990, Vereeniging. 1.90m. 110kg. Prop. FC DEBUT: 2015. PROV CAREER: Valke 2015-16 13-1-0-0-0-5. FC RECORD: 13-1-0-0-0-5. RECORD IN 2016: (Valke) 11-1-0-0-0-5.

Steyn, Johannes Hermanus (Langenhoven Gym., Oudtshoorn & NMMU) b 08/10/1995, Oudtshoorn. 1.78m. 88kg. Scrumhalf. FC DEBUT: 2015. PROV CAREER: Eagles 2015-16 31-5-0-0-0-25. FC RECORD: 31-5-0-0-0-25. RECORD IN 2016: (Eagles) 18-4-0-0-0-20.

Steyn, Morné (Sand du Plessis HS, Bloemfontein) b 11/07/1984, Bellville. 1.84m. 91kg. Flyhalf. FC DEBUT: 2003. PROV CAREER: Blue Bulls 2003-10 & 12 95-26-180-106-11-841. SUPERRUGBY: Bulls 2005-13 123-13-242-275-25-1449. REP Honours: SA 2009-16 TESTS: 66-8-102-154-10-736. Springboks 2014 1-0-2-3-0-13. Total: 67-8-104-157-10-749. SA 'A' 2004 1-0-1-0-0-2. SA U21 2005 5-3-17-7-1-73. British Barbarians 2009 1-0-0-1-0-3. CW Free State 2001-2002. MISC INFO: YPoYnominee 2005. Holds SA record for most penalty goals by a player in a test (8 vs. New Zealand in 2009). Holds SA record for most penalty goals in a season (40 in 2010). Holds SA record for most test matches as a flyhalf (64, also one at fullback and one at centre). Holds Bulls Super record for most cons in a season (38) and a career (242). Holds Bulls record for most penalties in a season (57) and a career (275). Holds Bulls record for most drop goals in a match (4), in a season (11) and a career (25). Holds Bulls and SA record for most points in a Super career (1449). SA S14 PoY 2009. PoYNominee 2009. FC RECORD: 292-50-544-546-47-3117. RECORD IN 2016: (SA) 6-0-0-12-2-42.

Stighling, Jade Kyle (Hans Moore HS, Benoni) b 27/05/1993, Johannesburg. 1.83m. 85kg. Centre. FC DEBUT: 2013. PROV CAREER: Blue Bulls 2013 & 15-16 22-7-0-0-0-35. FC RECORD: 22-7-0-0-0-35. RECORD IN 2016: (Blue Bulls) 14-6-0-0-0-30.

Stokes, Dean (Brits HS & NWU) b 03/11/1994, Pretoria. 1.84m. 88kg. Wing. FC DEBUT: 2016. PROV CAREER: Leopards 2016 5-0-0-0-0-0. FC RECORD: 5-0-0-0-0-0. RECORD IN 2016: (Leopards) 5-0-0-0-0-0.

Storm, Hendri (Outeniqua HS, George) b 08/01/1995, Welkom. 1.96m. 108kg. Lock. FC DEBUT: 2016. PROV CAREER: Bulldogs 2016 11-1-0-0-0-5. FC RECORD: 11-1-0-0-0-5. RECORD IN 2016: (Bulldogs) 11-1-0-0-0-5.

Strauss, Jan Adriaan (Grey College, Bloemfontein) b 18/11/1985, Bloemfontein. 1.84m. 102kg. Hooker. FC DEBUT: 2005. PROV CAREER: Blue Bulls 2005-06 22-3-0-0-0-15. Cheetahs 2007-13 56-9-0-0-0-45. SUPERRUGBY: Bulls 2006 & 15-16 35-6-0-0-0-30. Cheetahs 2007-14 97-8-0-0-0-40. REP Honours: SA 2008-10 & 12-16 TESTS: 66-6-0-0-0-30. Tour: 2-0-0-0-0-0. Springboks 2015 1-0-0-0-0-0. Total: 69-6-0-0-0-30. British Barbarians 2011 1-0-0-0-0-0. SA U21 2005-06 8-2-0-0-0-10. SA U19 2004. SA Schools 2003. CW Free State 2003. MISC INFO: Holds Cheetahs Super rugby record for most matches in a career (97). Cousin of Andries (SA 2010) and Richardt Strauss (Ireland). FC RECORD: 288-34-0-0-0-170. RECORD IN 2016: (SA, Bulls) 26-6-0-0-0-30.

Strauss, Jacobus Marius (Volkskool, Potchefstroom) b 26/11/1992 Vanderbijlpark. 1.89m. 126kg. Prop. FC DEBUT: 2016. PROV CAREER: Valke 2016 10-0-0-0-0-0. FC RECORD: 10-0-0-0-0-0. RECORD IN 2016: (Valke) 10-0-0-0-0-0.

Stringer, Luke Joseph (Rondebosch HS & UCT) b 12/12/1995, Cape Town. 1.92.00m. 103kg. Flank. FC DEBUT: 2016. PROV CAREER: WP 2016 13-3-0-0-0-15. FC RECORD: 13-3-0-0-0-15. RECORD IN 2016: (WP) 13-3-0-0-0-15.

Swanepoel, Andries Ebenaezer (Dries) (Grey College) b 19/02/1993, Delareyville. 1.84m. 92kg. Centre. FC DEBUT: 2013. PROV CAREER: Blue Bulls 2013 & 15-16 26-10-0-0-0-50. SUPERRUGBY: Bulls 2016 7-2-0-0-0-10. REP Honours: SA U20 2013 4-1-0-0-0-5.

FC RECORD: 37-13-0-0-0-65. RECORD IN 2016: (Bulls, Blue Bulls) 16-2-0-0-0-10.

Swanepoel, Jacobus Christoffel Entienne (Tygerberg HS, Cape Town) b 09/03/1993, Sasolburg. 1.91m. 126kg. Prop. FC DEBUT: 2014. PROV CAREER: WP 2014-15 8-0-0-0-0-0. Boland 2015 1-0-0-0-0-0. Blue Bulls 2016 13-0-0-0-0-0. FC RECORD: 22-0-0-0-0-0. RECORD IN 2016: (Blue Bulls) 13-0-0-0-0-0.

Swanepoel, Jsuan-re (Transvalia HS, Vanderbijlpark & UP) b 16/08/1995, Vereeniging. 1.84m. 95kg. Eighthman. FC DEBUT: 2016. PROV CAREER: Blue Bulls 2016 1-0-0-0-0-0. FC RECORD: 1-0-0-0-0-0. RECORD IN 2016: (Blue Bulls) 1-0-0-0-0-0.

Swanepoel, Meyer (Paul Roos Gym., Stellenbosch & ETA) b 07/05/1989, Belville. 1.96m. 114kg. Lock. FC DEBUT: 2010. PROV CAREER: Sharks XV 2010 3-0-0-0-0-0. WP 2016 5-1-0-0-0-5. FC RECORD: 8-1-0-0-0-5. RECORD IN 2016: (WP) 5-1-0-0-0-5.

Swart, Clinton Ryno (Standerton HS & UP) b 06/09/1992, Standerton. 1.84m. 91kg. Flyhalf. FC DEBUT: 2014. PROV CAREER: Valke 2014 4-0-0-0-1-3. Griquas 2015-16 39-9-58-35-0-266. FC RECORD: 43-9-58-35-1-269. RECORD IN 2016: (Griquas) 19-5-44-22-0-179.

Swart, Henro-Pierre (HP) (Framesby HS, Port Elizabeth & NWU) b 17/03/1989, Port Elizabeth. 1.89m. 108kg. Eighthman. FC DEBUT: 2012. PROV CAREER: Leopards 2012-16 39-10-0-0-0-50. Leopard XV 2013 & 15 7-2-0-0-0-10. FC RECORD: 46-12-0-0-0-60. RECORD IN 2016: (Leopards) 13-6-0-0-0-30.

Swart, Malherbe (Volkskool Potchefstroom) b 27/03/1991, Klerksdorp. 1.79m. 68kg. Scrumhalf. FC DEBUT: 2013. PROV CAREER: Leopards 2015-16 29-2-4-0-0-18. Leopard XV 2013-15 12-1-0-0-0-5. FC RECORD: 41-3-4-0-0-23. RECORD IN 2016: (Leopards) 20-1-4-0-0-13.

Swarts, Andre Schalk Wessel (Grey College, Bloemfontein) b 11/06/1995, Welkom. 1.86m. 92kg. Flyhalf. FC DEBUT: 2016. PROV CAREER: Griquas 2016 15-4-21-14-0-104. FC RECORD: 15-4-21-14-0-104. RECORD IN 2016: (Griquas) 15-4-21-14-0-104.

Sykes, Steven Robert (Marlow HS, Cradock) b 05/08/1984, Middelburg, Cape. 1.97m. 106kg. Lock. FC DEBUT: 2005. PROV CAREER: Sharks 2005-10 & 12 88-5-0-0-0-25. Sharks XV 2005-08 21-0-0-0-0-0. EP Kings 2013-15 20-4-0-0-0-20. SUPERRUGBY: Sharks 2007-12 69-9-0-0-0-45. Southern Kings 2013 & 16 26-5-0-0-0-25. P/R 2013 2-1-0-0-0-5. Cheetahs 2015 14-1-0-0-0-5. REP Honours: Emerging Springboks 2009 1-0-0-0-0-0. FC RECORD: 241-25-0-0-0-125. RECORD IN 2016: (Southern Kings) 13-4-0-0-0-20.

Taljaard, Etienne (Jim Fouche HS, Bloemfontein) b 21/07/1993, Cape Town. 1.80m. 90kg. Wing. FC DEBUT: 2014. PROV CAREER: Valke 2014-16 33-19-0-0-0-95. FC RECORD: 33-19-0-0-0-95. RECORD IN 2016: (Valke) 18-13-0-0-0-65.

Takahashi, Yosuke (Syaushilts HS) b 06/08/1991, Saitama, Japan. 1.80m. 113kg. Prop. FC DEBUT: 2016. PROV CAREER: Free State XV 2016 1-0-0-0-0-0. FC RECORD: 1-0-0-0-0-0. RECORD IN 2016: (Free State XV) 1-0-0-0-0-0.

Taute, Jacob Johannes (Jaco) (Monument HS, Krugersdorp) b 21/03/1991, Springs. 1.87m. 95kg. Fullback. FC DEBUT: 2009. PROV CAREER: Lions 2009-12 31-13-0-1-0-68. Golden Lions XV 2010 3-0-2-0-0-4. WP 2014-16 23-7-0-0-0-35. SUPERRUGBY: Lions 2010-12 31-9-0-2-0-51. Stormers 2013-16 23-1-0-0-1-8. REP Honours: SA 2012 TESTS: 3-0-0-0-0-0. SAU20 2010-11 7-4-0-0-0-20. MISC INFO: YPoYnominee 2011. FC RECORD: 121-34-2-3-1-186. RECORD IN 2016 (Stormers, WP) 7-2-0-0-0-10.

Tecklenburg, Warwick John (Uplands College, White River) b 22/01/1987, Nelspruit. 1.88m. 102kg. Flank. FC DEBUT: 2011. PROV CAREER: Blue Bulls 2011-12 22-4-0-0-0-20. Lions 2013-14 23-3-0-0-0-15. Golden Lions XV 2013 & 16 8-1-0-0-0-5. SUPERRUGBY: Lions 2014-16 45-6-0-0-0-30. Lions P/R 2013 2-0-0-0-0-0. FC RECORD: 100-14-0-0-0-70. RECORD IN 2016: (Lions S18, Golden Lions XV) 17-1-0-0-0-5.

Tedder, Tristan James (Kearsney College, Botha's Hill & UKZN) b 17/04/1996, Durban. 1.80m. 78kg. Flyhalf. FC DEBUT: 2016. PROV CAREER: Sharks XV 2016 8-2-14-10-0-68. FC RECORD: 8-2-14-10-0-68. RECORD IN 2016: (Sharks XV) 8-2-14-10-0-68.

Temperman, Emile Nicolaas George (Nelspruit HS & UP) b 05/12/1991, Nylstroom. 1.73m. 81kg. Scrumhalf. FC DEBUT: 2013. PROV CAREER: Blue Bulls 2013 1-0-0-0-0-0. Pumas 2016 21-0-0-0-0-0. FC RECORD: 22-0-0-0-0-0. RECORD IN 2016: (Pumas) 21-0-0-0-0-0.

Terblanche, De-Jay (Knysna HS) b 25/06/1985, Knysna. 1.89m. 124kg. Prop. FC DEBUT: 2008. PROV CAREER: Pumas 2008-16 157-11-0-0-0-55. FC RECORD: 157-11-0-0-0-55. RECORD IN 2016: (Pumas) 19-3-0-0-0-15.

Theron, Clinton (Florida HS, Johannesburg) b 03/11/1995, Florida. 1.80m. 108kg. Prop. FC DEBUT: 2015. PROV CAREER: Golden Lions XV 2015-16 12-2-0-0-0-10. SUPERRUGBY: Lions 2016 1-0-0-0-0-0. FC RECORD: 13-2-0-0-0-10. RECORD IN 2016: (Lions S18, Golden Lions XV) 10-2-0-0-0-10.

Thomson, Brandon Terry (Ermelo HS) b 07/03/1995, Trichardt. 1.87m. 92kg. Flyhalf. FC DEBUT: 2015. PROV CAREER: WP 2016 5-0-10-5-0-35. SUPERRUGBY: Stormers 2016 6-1-6-3-0-26. REP Honours: SAU20 2015 5-1-15-8-0 -59. FC RECORD: 16-2-31-16-0-120. RECORD IN 2016: (Stormers, WP) 11-1-16-8-0-61.

Thwala, Linda (George Campbell THS, Durban & Unisa) b 04/02/1994, Durban. 1.81m. 120kg. Prop. FC DEBUT: 2016. PROV CAREER: Boland 2016 6-0-0-0-0-0. FC RECORD: 6-0-0-0-0-0. RECORD IN 2016: (Boland) 6-0-0-0-0-0.

Till, Malcolm-Kerr (Welkom Gym.) b 04/07/1995, Klerksdorp. 1.87m. 76kg. Scrumhalf. FC DEBUT: 2015. PROV CAREER: Griffons 2015-16 7-0-0-0-0-0. FC RECORD: 7-0-0-0-0-0. RECORD IN 2016: (Griffons) 5-0-0-0-0-0.

Tobias, Sidney (Paul Roos Gym., Stellenbosch) b 20/03/1989, Caledon. 1.75m. 93kg. Hooker. FC DEBUT: 2010. PROV CAREER: WP 2010-12 22-2-0-0-0-10. Eagles 2012 13-0-0-0-0-0. Blue Bulls 2013-14 8-1-0-0-0-5. Griquas 2015-16 12-0-0-0-0-0. MISC INFO: Son of former Springbok Errol Tobias. FC RECORD: 55-3-0-0-0-15. RECORD IN 2016: (Griquas) 7-0-0-0-0-0.

Tom, Siphosethu (Grey College, Port Elizabeth) b 12/02/1992, Port Elizabeth. 1.74m. 85kg. Wing. FC DEBUT: 2012. PROV CAREER: Free State XV 2012-14 7-2-0-0-0-10. Bulldogs 2015-16 16-3-0-0-0-15. FC RECORD: 23-5-0-0-0-25. RECORD IN 2016: (Bulldogs) 13-2-0-0-0-10.

Torrens, Sergio Lorenzo (Belville South HS) b 29/01/1990, Bishop Lavis. 1.80m. 78kg. Centre. FC DEBUT: 2014. PROV CAREER: Leopards 2014-15 11-2-0-0-0-10. Leopards XV 2014-15 13-4-0-0-0-20. Boland 2016 19-9-0-0-0-45. FC RECORD: 43-15-0-0-0-75. RECORD IN 2016: (Boland) 19-9-0-0-0-45.

Tromp, Johannes Adriaan (Windhoek THS, Windhoek Gym. & UP) b 23/12/1990, Windhoek. 1.83m. 95kg. Centre. SA FC debut: 2016. PROV CAREER: EP Kings 2016 6-3-0-0-0-15. SA FC RECORD: 6-3-0-0-0-15. REP Honours: Namibia RWC 2015. Welwitchias 2015-16. RECORD IN 2016: (EP Kings) 6-3-0-0-0-15.

Truter, Jan Andries (Vredendal HS & TUT) b 29/05/1991, Vredendal. 1.82.00m. 90kg. Centre. FC DEBUT: 2013. PROV CAREER: Boland 2013 2-0-0-0-0-0. Limpopo 2015 6-1-0-0-0-5. Valke 2015-16 17-6-1-0-0-32. FC RECORD: 25-7-1-0-0-37. RECORD IN 2016: (Valke) 14-5-1-0-0-27.

Tsomondo, Tapiwa (Prince Edward HS & Dale College, King William's Town) b 05/05/1993, Harare. 1.73m. 94kg. Flank. FC DEBUT: 2015. PROV CAREER: WP 2015 4-3-0-0-0-15. Blue Bulls 2016 8-5-0-0-0-25. REP Honours: Zimbabwe Sevens 2012-13. FC RECORD: 12-8-0-0-0-40. RECORD IN 2016: (Blue Bulls) 8-5-0-0-0-25.

Tywaleni, Zukisani (Zweliyandila HS) b 26/11/1987, Frere. 1.63m. 71kg. Scrumhalf. FC DEBUT: 2015. PROV CAREER: Bulldogs 2015-16 8-0-0-0-0-0. FC RECORD: 8-0-0-0-0-0. RECORD IN 2016: (Bulldogs) 7-0-0-0-0-0.

Uanivi, Tjiuee (Academia HS & UN) b 31/12/1990, Otjiwarongo. 2.00m. 100kg. Lock. SA FC DEBUT: 2016. PROV CAREER: Sharks XV 2016 5-0-0-0-0-0. SA FC RECORD: 5-0-0-0-0-0. REP Honours: Namibia RWC 2015. RECORD IN 2016: (Sharks XV) 5-0-0-0-0-0.

Ueckermann, Francwa Johannes (Brits HS & NMMU) b 06/01/1994, Krugersdorp. 1.77m. 80kg. Scrumhalf. FC DEBUT: 2016. PROV CAREER: EP Kings 2016 8-2-0-0-0-10. FC RECORD: 8-2-0-0-0-10. RECORD IN 2016: (EP Kings) 8-2-0-0-0-10.

Ulengo, Jamba Isaac (Jim Fouche HS, Bloemfontein & UFS) b 07/01/1990, Vryburg. 1.85m. 88kg. Wing. FC DEBUT: 2012. PROV CAREER: Free State XV 2012 1-0-0-0-0-0. Blue Bulls 2014-16 31-23-0-0-0-115. SUPERRUGBY: Bulls 2016 10-5-0-0-0-25. REP Honours: SA 2016 TESTS: 1-0-0-0-0-0. Springbok XV 2016 1-0-0-0-0-0. SA Sevens 2012-14. FC RECORD: 44-28-0-0-0-140. RECORD IN 2016: (SA, Springbok XV, Bulls, Blue Bulls) 22-12-0-0-0-60.

Ungerer, Stefan (Maritzburg College) b 23/11/1993, Pietermaritzburg. 1.85m. 88kg. Scrumhalf. FC DEBUT: 2013. PROV CAREER: Sharks XV 2013-15 10-2-0-0-0-10. Sharks 2015-16 12-1-0-0-0-5. SUPER-RUGBY: Sharks 2014-16 17-5-0-0-0-25. REP Honours: SA U20 2013 4-1-0-0-0-5. FC RECORD: 43-9-0-0-0-45. RECORD IN 2016: (Sharks S18, Sharks) 15-2-0-0-0-10.

Uys, BG (Paarl Gym.) b 20/06/1988, Heidelberg (W Cape). 1.90m. 113kg. Prop. FC DEBUT: 2008. PROV CAREER: Leopards 2010-13 61-8-0-0-0-40. Leopard XV 2013 5-1-0-0-0-5. EP Kings 2014 5-0-0-0-0-0. Cheetahs 2015 9-0-0-0-0-0. Free State XV 2016 8-1-0-0-0-5. SUPERRUGBY: Cheetahs 2015 14-0-0-0-0-0. REP Honours: SA Students 2008-09 3-1-0-0-0-5. SA Barbarians 2012 1-0-0-0-0-0. FC RECORD: 106-11-0-0-0-55. RECORD IN 2016: (Free State XV) 8-1-0-0-0-5.

Uys, Francois Jacobus (Dr EG Jansen, Boksburg) b 12/03/1986, Springs. 1.91m. 103kg. Flank. FC DEBUT: 2006. PROV CAREER: Lions 2006 08 24 5 0 0 0 25. Cheetahs 2009 15 77 8 0 0-0-40. Griffons 2008 & 10 & 12 14-1-0-0-0-5. Lions XV 2008 1-0-0-0-0-0. Emerging Cheetahs 2011 1-0-0-0-0-0. Free State XV 2012 5-1-0-0-0-5. SUPER-RUGBY: Cheetahs 2009 & 2011-16 77-1-0-0-0-5. REP Honours: SA U19 2005. FC RECORD: 199-16-0-0-0-80. RECORD IN 2016: (Cheetahs S18) 14-0-0-0-0-0.

Uys, Johannes Lodewicus (Linden HS & NWU) b 11/01/1991. Johannesburg. 1.96m. 112kg. Lock. FC DEBUT: 2012. PROV CAREER: Leopards 2012 2-0-0-0-0-0. Boland 2013 7-0-0-0-0-0. Eagles 2016 14-2-0-0-0-10. FC RECORD: 23-2-0-0-0-10. RECORD IN 2016: (Eagles) 14-2-0-0-0-10.

Van den Berg, Franco (Randburg HS & UP) b 31/10/1996, Potchefstroom. 1.82.00m. 100kg. Prop. FC DEBUT: 2016. REP Honours: SAU20 2016 5-1-0-0-0-5. FC RECORD: 5-1-0-0-0-5. RECORD IN 2016: (SAU20) 5-1-0-0-0-5.

Van der Merwe, Armand Hendrik Petrus (Akker) (Outeniqua HS, George & NWU) b 17/06/1991, Vanderbijlpark. 1.78m 106kg. Hooker. FC DEBUT: 2013. PROV CAREER: Leopards 2013-14 11-0-0-0-0-0. Leopard XV 2013 6-2-0-0-0-10. Lions 2014 & 16 18-5-0-0-0-25. SUPERRUGBY: Lions 2014-16 39-6-0-0-0-30. REP Honours: British Barbarians 2016 2-2-0-0-0-10. FC RECORD: 76-15-0-0-0-75. RECORD IN 2016: (Lions S18, Lions, British Barbarians) 25-8-0-0-0-40.

Van der Merwe, Christo (Paul Roos Gym., Stellenbosch & US) b 05/01/1995, Windhoek. 1.83m. 101kg. Flank. FC DEBUT: 2016. PROV CAREER: WP 2016 4-1-0-0-0-5. FC RECORD: 4-1-0-0-0-5. RECORD IN 2016: (WP) 4-1-0-0-0-5.

Van der Merwe, Daniel Joubert (Wilgerivier HS, Frankfort) b 24/01/1989, Frankfort. 1.83m. 119kg. Prop. FC DEBUT: 2010. PROV CAREER: Golden Lions XV 2010 1-0-0-0-0-0. Griffons 2012-16 68-12-0-0-0-50. FC RECORD: 69-12-0-0-0-60. RECORD IN 2016: (Griffons) 21-6-0-0-0-30.

Van der Merwe, Duhan (Outeniqua HS, George) b 04/06/1994, George. 1.94m. 96kg. Wing. FC DEBUT: 2014. PROV CAREER: Blue Bulls 2016 2-0-0-0-0-0. REP Honours: SAU20 2014 2-0-0-0-0-0. FC RECORD: 4-0-0-0-0-0. RECORD IN 2016: (Blue Bulls) 2-0-0-0-0-0.

Van der Merwe, Edwill Charl (Paul Roos Gym., Stellenbosch & US) b 12/04/1996, Stellenbosch. 1.80m. 84kg. Wing. FC DEBUT: 2016. PROV CAREER: WP 2016 3-2-0-0-0-10. REP Honours: SAU20 2016 4-3-0-0-0-15. FC RECORD: 7-5-0-0-0-25. RECORD IN 2016: (WP, SAU20) 7-5-0-0-0-25.

Van der Merwe, Jan (Pretoria Boys"HS & UP) b 31/08/1995, Pretoria. 1.82.00m. 109kg. Hooker. FC DEBUT: 2015. PROV CAREER: Blue Bulls 2015-16 8-0-0-0-0-0. REP Honours: SAU20 2015 5-1-0-0-0-5. FC RECORD: 13-1-0-0-0-5. RECORD IN 2016: (Blue Bulls) 7-0-0-0-0-0.

Van der Merwe, Marcel (Paarl Boys'HS) b 24/10/1990, Welkom. 1.89m. 121kg. Prop. FC DEBUT: 2011. PROV CAREER: Cheetahs 2011-12 32-13-0-0-0-65. Emerging Cheetahs 2011 1-0-0-0-0-0. Free State XV 2012 6-4-0-0-0-20. Blue Bulls 2013-15 20-1-0-0-0-5. SUPERRUGBY: Cheetahs 2012 3-0-0-0-0-0. Bulls 2014-16 45-5-0-0-0-25. REP Honours: SA 2014-15 TESTS: 7-0-0-0-0-0. SA A 2016 1-0-0-0-0-0. SAU20 2010 5-2-0-0-0-10. FC RECORD: 120-25-0-0-0-125. RECORD IN 2016: (SA A, Bulls) 16-1-0-0-0-5.

Van der Smit, Luke-Kyle (SACS HS, Cape Town) b 29/06/1994, Swakopmund. 1.84m. 107kg. Flank. FC DEBUT: 2015. PROV CAREER: WP 2015 4-1-0-0-0-5. EP Kings 2016 6-0-0-0-0-0. FC RECORD: 10-1-0-0-0-5. RECORD IN 2016: (EP Kings) 6-0-0-0-0-0.

Van der Spuy, Michael George (Grey College, Bloemfontein & US) b 20/02/1991, Bethlehem. 1.80m. 86kg. Flyhalf. FC DEBUT: 2011. PROV CAREER: WP 2011-14 36-7-0-0-0-35. Griquas 2015 9-1-0-0-0-5. Free State XV 2016 4-0-0-0-0-0. Cheetahs 2016 3-1-0-0-0-5. SUPERRUGBY: Stormers 2014 4-0-0-0-0-0. Cheetahs 2015-16 17-2-0-0-0-10. FC RECORD: 70-11-0-0-0-55. RECORD IN 2016: (Cheetahs S18, Cheetahs, Free State XV) 11-2-0-0-0-10.

Van Staden, Arno Marinus (Pietersburg HS & UFS) b 05/01/1995, Nylstroom. 1.85m. 89kg. Wing. FC DEBUT: 2016. PROV CAREER: Free State XV 2016 1-0-0-0-0-0. FC RECORD: 1-0-0-0-0-0. RECORD IN 2016: (Free State XV) 1-0-0-0-0-0.

Van der Walt, Andries Petrus (Peet) (Outeniqua HS, George) b

19/09/1991, Kimberley. 1.94m. 103kg. Flank. FC DEBUT: 2013. PROV CAREER: Leopards 2013 12-0-0-0-0-0. Leopard XV 2013 5-0-0-0-0-0. Eagles 2014-16 29-1-0-0-0-5. FC RECORD: 46-1-0-0-0-5. RECORD IN 2016: (Eagles) 12-1-0-0-0-5.

Van der Walt, Christoffel Philippus (Philip) (Adelaide Gym. & UFS) b 14/07/1989, Adelaide. 1.94m. 105kg. Eighthman. FC DEBUT: 2010. PROV CAREER: Cheetahs 2010-13 31-4-0-0-0-20. Griffons 2011 1-1-0-0-0-5. Sharks 2015-16 16-0-0-0-0-0. SUPERRUGBY: Cheetahs 2010-14 49-5-0-0-0-25. Sharks 2016 11-0-0-0-0-0. FC RECORD: 108-10-0-0-0-50. RECORD IN 2016: (Sharks S18, Sharks) 17-0-0-0-0-0.

Van der Walt, Hendrik Bernardus (Nardus) (Affies, Pretoria) b 22/02/1992, Rustenburg. 1.89m. 100kg. Lock. FC DEBUT: 2013. PROV CAREER: Blue Bulls 2013 & 15 15-4-0-0-0-20. Griquas 2015 7-0-0-0-0-0. Pumas 2016 14-1-0-0-0-5. FC RECORD: 36-5-0-0-0-25. RECORD IN 2016: (Pumas) 14-1-0-0-0-5.

Van der Walt, Jako (Monument HS, Krugersdorp) b 01/02/1994, Randfontein. 1.82.00m. 84kg. Flyhalf. FC DEBUT: 2014. PROV CAREER: Lions 2014-16 29-3-35-12-1-124. Golden Lions XV 2015-16 3-1-14-3-0-42. SUPERRUGBY: Lions 2015-16 18-0-3-1-0-9. FC RECORD: 50-4-52-16-1-175. RECORD IN 2016: (Lions S18, Lions, Golden Lions XV) 23-1-27-8-0-83.

Van der Watt, Vian (Florida HS) b 18/11/1992, Springs. 1.68m. 77kg. Scrumhalf. FC DEBUT: 2011. PROV CAREER: Golden Lions XV 2011-13 4-2-0-0-0-10. Leopards 2014 6-0-0-0-0-0. EP Kings 2016 5-0-0-0-0-0. SUPERRUGBY: Lions P/R 2013 1-0-0-0-0-0. REP Honours: SAU20 2012 5-2-0-0-0-10. FC RECORD: 21-4-0-0-0-20. RECORD IN 2016: (EP Kings) 5-0-0-0-0-0.

Van der Westhuizen, Dayan Leslie (Centurion HS) b 05/04/1994, Newton. 1.82.00m. 118kg. Prop. FC DEBUT: 2014. PROV CAREER: Blue Bulls 2015-16 11-1-0-0-0-5. REP Honours: SAU20 2014 5-0-0-0-0-0. FC RECORD: 16-1-0-0-0-5. RECORD IN 2016: (Blue Bulls) 3-0-0-0-0-0.

Van der Westhuizen, Ewald (Voortrekker HS, Pietermaritzburg & UJ) b 03/04/1990, Ladysmith. 1.82.00m. 114kg. Prop. FC DEBUT: 2013. PROV CAREER: Griquas 2013-16 41-3-0-0-0-15. SUPERRUGBY: Cheetahs 2015 6-0-0-0-0-0. FC RECORD: 47-3-0-0-0-15. RECORD IN 2016: (Griquas) 7-0-0-0-0-0.

Van der Westhuizen, Louis (Windhoek HS & NWU) b 25/02/1995, Windhoek. 1.80m. 100kg. Hooker. FC DEBUT: 2016. PROV CAREER: Leopards 2016 11-0-0-0-0-0. REP Honours: Namibia RWC 2015. FC RECORD: 11-0-0-0-0-0. RECORD IN 2016: (Leopards) 11-0-0-0-0-0.

Van der Westhuyzen, Dane Robert (St Andrews College, Grahamstown) b 16/08/1992, Queen'stown. 1.80m. 95kg. Hooker. FC DEBUT: 2013. PROV CAREER: EP Kings 2013-14 14-0-0-0-0-0. Leopards 2015-16 26-3-0-0-0-15. Leopards XV 2015 5-1-0-0-0-5. FC RECORD: 45-4-0-0-0-20. RECORD IN 2016: (Leopards) 15-1-0-0-0-5.

Van Breda, Scott (Rondebosch HS) b 12/12/1991. Fullback/Wing. FC DEBUT: 2012. PROV CAREER: EP Kings 2012-15 64-10-62-77-0-405. WP 2016 15-5-17-7-0-80. SUPERRUGBY: Southern Kings 2013 1-0-0-0-0-0. P/R 2013 1-1-2-3-0-18. Stormers 2016 3-0-0-0-0-0. FC RECORD: 84-16-81-87-0-503. RECORD IN 2016: (Stormers, WP) 18-5-17-7-0-80.

Van Dyk, Jacobus Johannes (Kobus) (Overberg HS, Caledon & US) b 06/07/1994, Bredasdorp. 1.96m. 108kg. Flank. FC DEBUT: 2016. PROV CAREER: WP 2016 19-4-0-0-0-20. SUPERRUGBY: Stormers 2016 1-0-0-0-0-0. FC RECORD: 20-4-0-0-0-20. RECORD IN 2016: (Stormers, WP) 20-4-0-0-0-20.

Van Dyk, Nicolaas Johannes John (Maks) (Paarl Boys'HS) b

21/01/1992, Johannesburg. 1.86m. 118kg. Prop. FC DEBUT: 2012. PROV CAREER: Sharks XV 2012-13 10-0-0-0-0-0. Griquas 2014 14-1-0-0-0-5. Cheetahs 2015 4-0-0-0-0-0. SUPERRUGBY: Cheetahs 2014-16 39-0-0-0-0-0. REP Honours: SAU20 2012 4-0-0-0-0-0.British Barbarians 2015 1-0-0-0-0-0. FC RECORD: 82-1-0-0-0-5. RECORD IN 2016: (Cheetahs S18) 15-0-0-0-0-0.

Van Heerden, Ruben (Affies, Pretoria) b 27/10/1997, Alberton. 2.00m. 115kg. Lock. FC DEBUT: 2016. PROV CAREER: Blue Bulls 2016 9-1-0-0-0-5. FC RECORD: 9-1-0-0-0-5. RECORD IN 2016: (Blue Bulls) 9-1-0-0-0-5.

Van Jaarsveld, Torsten George (Hendrik Verwoerd HS, Pretoria) b 30/06/1987, Windhoek. 1.75m. 89kg. Hooker. FC DEBUT: 2008. PROV CAREER: Pumas 2008-12 73-8-0-0-0-40. Free State XV 2013-14 8-0-0-0-0-0. Cheetahs 2014-16 19-1-0-0-0-5. SUPERRUGBY: Cheetahs 2014-16 36-5-0-0-0-25. REP Honours: SA Barbarians 2012 1-0-0-0-0-0. MISC INFO: Namibia international. FC RECORD: 137-14-0-0-0-70. RECORD IN 2016: (Cheetahs S18, Cheetahs) 23-5-0-0-0-25.

Van Niekerk, Marlou Du Plessis (Marlow Agric.) b 19/05/1993, Douglas. 1.86m. 92kg. Flyhalf. FC DEBUT: 2013. PROV CAREER: EP Kings 2013 & 15 7-1-1-0-0-7. Pumas 2016 15-2-2-0-0-14. FC RECORD: 22-3-3-0-0-21. RECORD IN 2016: (Pumas) 15-2-2-0-0-14.

Van Rensburg, Ruan (Waterkloof HS, Pretoria) b 31/05/1993, Pretoria. 1.77m. 82kg. Scrumhalf. FC DEBUT: 2015. PROV CAREER: Leopards XV 2015 2-0-0-0-0-0. Cheetahs 2015 2-0-0-0-0-0. Free State XV 2016 8-1-1-1-0-10. FC RECORD: 12-1-1-1-0-10. RECORD IN 2016: (Free State XV) 8-1-1-1-0-10.

Van Rhyn, Ernst (Paarl Gym.) b 19/09/1997, Belville. 1.91m. 104kg. Lock. FC DEBUT: 2016. REP Honours: SAU20 2016 4-0-0-0-0-0. FC RECORD: 4-0-0-0-0-0. RECORD IN 2016: (SAU20) 4-0-0-0-0-0.

Van Rooyen, Alandre (Nico Malan HS, Humansdorp & UP) b 23/08/1996, Port Elizabeth. 1.81m. 105kg. Hooker. FC DEBUT: 2016. PROV CAREER: Blue Bulls 2016 6-1-0-0-0-5. FC RECORD: 6-1-0-0-0-5. RECORD IN 2016: (Blue Bulls) 6-1-0-0-0-5.

Van Rooyen, Jacques (Pretoria North HS & UP, TUT) b 24/10/1986, Pretoria. 1.86m. 122kg. Prop. FC DEBUT: 2013. PROV CAREER: Lions 2013-16 39-3-0-0-0-15. Golden Lions XV 2013-14 & 16 14-1-0-0-0-5. SUPERRUGBY: Lions 2014-16 31-1-0-0-0-5. FC RECORD: 84-5-0-0-0-25. RECORD IN 2016: (Lions S18, Lions, Golden Lions XV) 23-1-0-0-0-5.

Van Rooyen, Reynier (Rob Ferreira HS, White River) b 25/04/1990, Nelspruit. 1.72.00m. 74kg. Scrumhalf. FC DEBUT: 2012. PROV CAREER: EP Kings 2012 5-0-0-0-0-0. Pumas 2013-16 60-7-0-0-0-35. FC RECORD: 65-7-0-0-0-35. RECORD IN 2016: (Pumas) 15-3-0-0-0-15.

Van Rooyen, Rudi (Affies, Pretoria) b 05/01/1992, Pretoria. 1.84m. 79kg. Scrumhalf. FC DEBUT: 2012. PROV CAREER: Blue Bulls 2012 & 14 4-0-0-0-0-0. Griquas 2014-16 30-10-0-0-0-50. FC RECORD: 34-10-0-0-0-50. RECORD IN 2016: (Griquas) 12-8-0-0-0-40.

Van Staden, Justin (Merensky HS, Tzaneen) b 03/06/1990, Tzaneen. 1.79m. 86kg. Centre. FC DEBUT: 2010. PROV CAREER: Blue Bulls 2010 1-0-0-0-0-0. EP Kings 2012 7-0-6-17-1-66. Eagles 2013 12-1-25-26-2-139. Pumas 2014-16 49-4-68-55-0-321. REP Honours: SA Univ 2013 1-0-5-0-0-10. FC RECORD: 70-5-104-99-3-539. RECORD IN 2016: (Pumas) 15-1-30-19-0-122.

Van Tonder, Jaco (Outeniqua HS, George) b 07/04/1991, Cape Town. 1.86m. 95kg. Centre. FC DEBUT: 2012. PROV CAREER: Sharks XV 2012-15 14-4-1-2-0-28. Sharks 2013-14 7-0-0-0-0-0. EP Kings 2016 2-0-0-0-0-0. SUPERRUGBY: Sharks 2013-14 3-0-0-0-0-0. Southern

Kings 2016 5-0-0-0-0-0. FC RECORD: 27-3-0-0-0-15. RECORD IN 2016: (Southern Kings, EP Kings) 7-0-0-0-0-0.

Van Vuuren, Jacobus Conradus (Conrad) (Nelspruit HS & UFS) b 04/09/1995, Magaliesburg. 1.83m. 110kg. Prop. FC DEBUT: 2016. PROV CAREER: Cheetahs 2016 2-0-0-0-0-0. FC RECORD: 2-0-0-0-0-0. RECORD IN 2016: (Cheetahs) 2-0-0-0-0-0.

Van Vuuren, Jurie George (Oakdale Agric. HS, Riversdale) b 07/06/1993, Ladybrand. 1.92.00m. 100kg. Lock. FC DEBUT: 2014. PROV CAREER: WP 2014-16 35-2-0-0-0-10. SUPERRUGBY: Stormers 2014-15 8-0-0-0-0-0. FC RECORD: 43-2-0-0-0-10. RECORD IN 2016: (WP) 20-1-0-0-0-5.

Van Vuuren, Kerrod Thomas (Glenwood HS, Durban & UKZN) b 23/05/1995, Durban. 1.88m. 104kg. Hooker. FC DEBUT: 2016. PROV CAREER: Sharks XV 2016 9-1-0-0-0-5. FC RECORD: 9-1-0-0-0-5. RECORD IN 2016: (Sharks XV) 9-1-0-0-0-5.

Van Wyk, Andrew Justerine Deometrie (Diamantveld HS, Kimberley & NWU) b 04/08/1989, Prieska. 1.77m. 85kg. Wing. FC DEBUT: 2011. PROV CAREER: Leopards 2011-12 8-0-0-0-0-0. Leopard XV 2013 4-0-0-0-0-0. Bulldogs 2013 12-5-0-0-0-25. Valke 2014-16 46-11-0-0-0-55. FC RECORD: 70-16-0-0-0-80. RECORD IN 2016: (Valke) 13-4-0-0-0-20.

Van Wyk, Christo Jacques (Brackenfell HS, Cape Town) b 04/10/1988. 1.88m. 144kg. Prop. FC DEBUT: 2009. PROV CAREER: Boland 2009 5-0-0-0-0-0. WP 2014 & 16 6-1-0-0-0-5. FC RECORD: 11-1-0-0-0-5. RECORD IN 2016: (WP) 2-0-0-0-0-0.

Van Wyk, Coenraad George (Coenie) (Paul Roos Gym., Stellenbosch) b 08/01/1988, Belville. 1.83m. 80kg. FC DEBUT: 2009. PROV CAREER: WP 2009 5-0-1-0-0-2. Griquas 2010 3-2-7-1-0-27. Pumas 2011-14 73-32-35-21-0-293. Cheetahs 2015 1-0-0-0-0-0. Free State XV 2015 3-2-10-4-0-42. Griffons 2015-16 3-2-0-0-1-13. SUPERRUGBY: Lions 2014 8-1-0-0-0-5. Cheetahs 2015 6-0-5-0-0-10. REP Honours: SA Barbarians 2012 1-0-0-0-0-0. SA Pres XV 2013 3-0-0-0-0-0. FC RECORD: 106-39-58-26-1-392. RECORD IN 2016: (Griffons) 1-0-0-0-0-0.

Van Wyk, Frans Roelf Petrus (Monument HS, Krugersdorp) b 25/04/1995, Delareyville. 1.90m. 125kg. Prop. FC DEBUT: 2015. PROV CAREER: WP 2015-16 7-1-0-0-0-5. REP Honours: SAU20 2015 5-1-0-0-0-5. FC RECORD: 12-2-0-0-0-10. RECORD IN 2016: (WP) 5-1-0-0-0-5.

Van Wyk, Gerrit Jacobus (Augsberg Agric. HS, Clanwilliam) b 30/12/1993, Vredendal. 1.80m. 94kg. Centre. FC DEBUT: 2015. PROV CAREER: Boland 2015-16 13-0-0-0-0-0. FC RECORD: 13-0-0-0-0-0. RECORD IN 2016: (Boland) 9-0-0-0-0-0.

Van Wyk, Hendrik Jacobus (Hencus) (Nylstroom HS) b 02/03/1992, Nigel. 1.83m. 116kg. Prop. FC DEBUT: 2011. PROV CAREER: Blue Bulls 2011 & 13-16 22 4 0 0 0 20. SUPERRUGBY: Bulls 2013 & 16 2-0-0-0-0-0. FC RECORD: 24-4-0-0-0-20. RECORD IN 2016: (Bulls, Blue Bulls) 2-0-0-0-0-0.

Van Wyk, Jacobus Petrus (Kobus) (Paarl Gym.) b 22/01/1992, Nababeep. 1.90m. 94kg. Wing. FC DEBUT: 2012. PROV CAREER: WP 2013-16 25-10-0-0-0-50. SUPERRUGBY: Stormers 2014-16 30-9-0-0-0-45. REP Honours: SA U20 2012 1-0-0-0-0-0. FC RECORD: 56-19-0-0-0-95. RECORD IN 2016: (Stormers, WP) 15-6-0-0-0-30.

Van Wyk, Leighton-Ray Marcelino (SACS, Cape Town & UP) b 05/05/1994, George. 1.89m. 106kg. Centre. FC DEBUT: 2016. PROV CAREER: Pumas 2016 8-2-2-0-0-14. FC RECORD: 8-2-2-0-0-14. RECORD IN 2016: (Pumas) 8-2-2-0-0-14.

Van Wyk, William Andrew (Paarl Gym.) b 29/05/1991, Ceres. 1.63m. 78kg. Flyhalf. FC DEBUT: 2016. PROV CAREER: Boland 2016 7-2-0-0-0-10. FC RECORD: 7-2-0-0-0-10. RECORD IN 2016: (Boland) 7-2-0-0-0-10.

Van Zyl, Christopher Machiel (Chris) (Rondebosch HS & US) b 12/07/1986, Cape Town. 1.97m. 112kg. Lock. FC DEBUT: 2013. PROV CAREER: Lions 2013-14 8-0-0-0-0-0. Golden Lions XV 2013-14 10-0-0-0-0-0. WP 2015-16 41-1-0-0-0-5. SUPERRUGBY: Stormers 2016 1-0-0-0-0-0. FC RECORD: 60-1-0-0-0-5. RECORD IN 2016: (Stormers, WP) 23-1-0-0-0-5.

Van Zyl, Ivan (Affies, Pretoria) b 30/06/1995, Pretoria. 1.78m. 80kg. Scrumhalf. FC DEBUT: 2015. PROV CAREER: Blue Bulls 2015-16 26-2-0-0-0-10. SUPERRUGBY: Bulls 2016 2-0-0-0-0-0. REP Honours: SAU20 2015 5-0-0-0-0-0. FC RECORD: 33-2-0-0-0-10. RECORD IN 2016: (Bulls, Blue Bulls) 14-2-0-0-0-10.

Van Zyl, Ockert Petrus (Ockie) (Nelspruit HS) b 06/05/1991, Bloemfontein. 1.95m. 110kg. Flank. FC DEBUT: 2011. PROV CAREER: Griffons 2015 5-0-0-0-0-0. Cheetahs 2011 1-0-0-0-0-0. Free State XV 2012-13 9-2-0-0-0-10. Boland 2016 13-1-0-0-0-5. FC RECORD: 28-3-0-0-0-15. RECORD IN 2016: (Boland) 13-1-0-0-0-5.

Van Zyl, Petrus Erasmus (Pieter) (Grey College, Bloemfontein & UFS) b 14/09/1989, Pretoria. 1.74m. 81kg. Scrumhalf. FC DEBUT: 2010. PROV CAREER: Cheetahs 2010-13 31-6-0-0-0-30. Emerging Cheetahs 2011 1-0-0-0-0-0. Blue Bulls 2014 & 16 20-5-0-0-0-25. SUPERRUGBY: Cheetahs 2012-13 32-5-0-0-0-25. Bulls 2014-16 36-6-0-0-0-30. REP Honours: SA 2013 & 16 TESTS: 3-0-0-0-0-0. Springbok XV 2016 1-0-0-0-0-0. SA A 2016 2-1-0-0-0-5. FC RECORD: 126-23-0-0-0-115. RECORD IN 2016: (SA, Springbok XV, SA A, Bulls, Blue Bulls) 27-8-0-0-0-40.

Van Zyl, Roche Christo (Framesby HS, Port Elizabeth & NMMU) b 14/06/1996, Port Elizabeth. 1.79m. 110kg. Prop. FC DEBUT: 2016. PROV CAREER: EP Kings 2016 2-0-0-0-0-0. FC RECORD: 2-0-0-0-0-0. RECORD IN 2016: (EP Kings) 2-0-0-0-0-0.

Velleman, Cyril John (CJ) (Grey HS, Port Elizabeth & NMMU) b 24/02/1995, Somerset EaSt 1.78m. 90kg. Flank. FC DEBUT: 2014. PROV CAREER: EP Kings 2014 3-0-0-0-0-0. SUPERRUGBY: Southern Kings 2016 10-0-0-0-0-0. FC RECORD: 13-0-0-0-0-0. RECORD IN 2016: (Southern Kings) 10-0-0-0-0-0.

Venter, Hanco Charles (Monument HS, Krugersdorp) b 07/01/1993, Witbank. 1.76m. 82kg. Scrumhalf. FC DEBUT: 2012. PROV CAREER: Sharks XV 2012-16 27-5-0-0-0-25. Sharks 2014 & 16 5-1-0-0-0-5. Leopards 2015 7-2-0-0-0-10. REP Honours: SA U20 2013 3-0-0-0-0-0. FC RECORD: 42-8-0-0-0-40. RECORD IN 2016: (Sharks, Sharks XV) 10-3-0-0-0-15.

Venter, Hendrik Oswald Albertyn (Kroonstad HS) b 10/09/1992, Virginia. 1.86m. 80kg. Lock. FC DEBUT: 2015. PROV CAREER: Griffons 2015 -16 10-0-0-0-0-0. FC RECORD: 10-0-0-0-0-0. RECORD IN 2016: (Griffons) 9-0-0-0-0-0.

Venter, Hendrik Petrus (Henco) (Grey College, Bloemfontein & UFS) b 27/03/1992, Bloemfontein. 1.93m. 107kg. Flank. FC DEBUT: 2012. PROV CAREER: Cheetahs 2012 & 14-16 25-1-0-0-0-5. Free State XV 2014-16 8-1-0-0-0-5. SUPERRUGBY: Cheetahs 2014-16 18-1-0-0-0-5. MISC INFO: Nephew of former Springbok Ruben Kruger. FC RECORD: 51-3-0-0-0-15. RECORD IN 2016: (Cheetahs S18, Cheetahs, Free State XV) 24-1-0-0-0-5.

Venter, Jan Albert (Nylstroom HS & UFS) b 06/10/1994, Nylstroom. 1.93m. 105kg. Lock. FC DEBUT: 2016. PROV CAREER: Griffons 2016 16-

5-0-0-0-25. FC RECORD: 16-5-0-0-0-25. RECORD IN 2016: (Griffons) 16-5-0-0-0-25.

Venter, Jacobus Francois (Grey College, Bloemfontein & UP) b 19/04/1991, Bloemfontein. 1.85m. 91kg. Centre. FC DEBUT: 2011. PROV CAREER: Blue Bulls 2011-13 43-12-0-0-0-60. Cheetahs 2014-16 26-8-0-0-0-40. SUPERRUGBY: Bulls 2012-13 11-0-0-0-0-0. Cheetahs 2014-16 34-11-0-0-0-55. REP Honours: SA 2016 TESTS: 3-0-0-0-0-0. Springbok XV 2016 1-1-0-0-0-5. SA A 2016 2-1-0-0-0-5. SAU20 2010-11 9-7-0-0-0-35. British Barbarians 2015 2-0-0-0-0-0. FC RECORD: 131-40-0-0-0-200. RECORD IN 2016: (SA, Springbok XV, SA A, Cheetahs S18, Cheetahs) 25-8-0-0-0-40.

Venter, James (Glenwood HS & UJ) b 21/08/1996, Port Shepstone. 1.82.00m. 92kg. Flank. FC DEBUT: 2016. PROV CAREER: Golden Lions XV 2016 1-1-0-0-0-5. FC RECORD: 1-1-0-0-0-5. RECORD IN 2016: (Golden Lions XV) 1-1-0-0-0-5.

Venter, Janco (Windhoek HS & US) b 19/09/1994, Windhoek. 1.94m. 107kg. Flank. FC DEBUT: 2016. PROV CAREER: WP 2016 4-1-0-0-0-5. REP Honours: Namibia RWC 2015. Welwitchias 2015. FC RECORD: 4-1-0-0-0-5. RECORD IN 2016: (WP) 4-1-0-0-0-5.

Venter, Jano (HTS Middelburg) b 08/01/1994, Witbank. 1.92.00m. 103kg. Eighthman. FC DEBUT: 2015. PROV CAREER: Lions 2015 3-0-0-0-0-0. Golden Lions XV 2015-16 8-4-0-0-0-20. FC RECORD: 11-4-0-0-0-20. RECORD IN 2016: (Golden Lions XV) 1-0-0-0-0-0.

Venter, Louis Gideon (Affies, Pretoria & UFS) b 05/09/1994, Pretoria. 1.70m. 81kg. Scrumhalf. FC DEBUT: 2015. PROV CAREER: Free State XV 2015 2-1-0-0-0-5. Griffons 2016 12-0-0-0-0-0. FC RECORD: 14-1-0-0-0-5. RECORD IN 2016: (Griffons) 12-0-0-0-0-0.

Venter, Reinach (Waterkloof HS & UFS) b 03/01/1995, Pretoria. 1.76m. 112kg. Hooker. FC DEBUT: 2016. PROV CAREER: Free State XV 2016 1-0-0-0-0-0. FC RECORD: 1-0-0-0-0-0. RECORD IN 2016: (Free State XV) 1-0-0-0-0-0.

Venter, Ruan Christov (Monument HS, Krugersdorp) b 11/05/1992, Rustenburg. 1.98m. 108kg. Lock. FC DEBUT: 2011. PROV CAREER: Lions 2013 2-0-0-0-0-0. Golden Lions XV 2014 1-0-0-0-0-0. Pumas 2014 2-0-0-0-0-0. Leopards 2014 & 16 18-0-0-0-0-0. REP Honours: SA U20 2011 2-0-0-0-0-0. FC RECORD: 25-0-0-0-0-0. RECORD IN 2016: (Leopards) 7-0-0-0-0-0.

Venter, Shaun Harold (Affies, Pretoria) b 16/03/1987, Witbank. 1.80m. 80kg. Scrumhalf. FC DEBUT: 2007. PROV CAREER: Pumas 2007-13 105-28-0-0-0-140. Cheetahs 2014 & 16 29-9-0-0-0-45. Free State XV 2015 5-2-0-0-0-10. SUPERRUGBY: Southern Kings 2013 16-2-0-0-0-10. P/R 2013 2-0-0-0-0-0. Cheetahs 2014-16 35-1-0-0-0-5. REP Honours: SA Barbarians 2012 1-2-0-0-0-10. SA Sevens 2009. FC RECORD: 193-44-0-0-0-220. RECORD IN 2016: (Cheetahs S18, Cheetahs) 25-6-0-0-0-30.

Venter, Warrick (Selborne College, East London & NMMU) b 12/02/1993, East London. 1.79m. 105kg. Hooker. FC DEBUT: 2016. PROV CAREER: EP Kings 2016 12-0-0-0-0-0. FC RECORD: 12-0-0-0-0-0. RECORD IN 2016: (EP Kings) 12-0-0-0-0-0.

Vermaak, Alistair Fernando (Hillside HS & Hentie Cilliers HS, Virginia) b 28/04/1989, Port Elizabeth. 1.79m. 108kg. Prop. FC DEBUT: 2011. PROV CAREER: WP 2011-12 & 14-16 47-2-0-0-0-10. Boland 2013 3-0-0-0-0-0. SUPERRUGBY: Stormers 2014-16 21-0-0-0-0-0. REP Honours: SA Univ 2013 1-0-0-0-0-0. FC RECORD: 72-2-0-0-0-10. RECORD IN 2016: (Stormers, WP) 21-0-0-0-0-0.

Vermaak, Jano (THS Vereeniging) b 01/01/1985, Graaff-Reinet. 1.75m. 77kg. Scrumhalf. FC DEBUT: 2005. PROV CAREER: Lions 2005-11

74-20-3-4-0-118. Golden Lions XV 2005-08 & 10 7-1-0-0-0-5. Blue Bulls 2011-12 15-5-0-0-0-25. WP 2015-16 19-4-0-0-0-20. SUPER-RUGBY: Cats 2006 11-1-0-0-0-5. Lions 2007-11 62-10-3-4-0-68. Bulls 2012-13 31-6-0-0-0-30. Stormers 2016 4-0-0-0-0-0. REP Honours: SA 2012-13 TESTS: 3-0-0-0-0-0. Emerging Springboks 2007,09 4-2-0-0-0-10. SA U21 2006 5-2-0-0-0-10. SA Sevens 2005. MISC INFO: Son of former EP & NEC hooker Deon Vermaak. FC RECORD: 235-51-6-8-0-291. RECORD IN 2016: (Stormers, WP) 15-1-0-0-0-5.

Vermeulen, Adriaan De Wet (Monument HS, Krugersdorp) b 17/10/1990, Johannesburg. 1.87m. 95kg. Wing. FC DEBUT: 2015. PROV CAREER: Leopards 2015-16 28-10-0-0-0-50. FC RECORD: 28-10-0-0-0-50. RECORD IN 2016: (Leopards) 15-5-0-0-0-25.

Vermeulen, Daniel Johannes (Duane) (Nelspruit HS) b 03/07/1986, Nelspruit. 1.92m. 90kg. Eighthman. FC DEBUT: 2005. PROV CAREER: Pumas 2005-06 26-4-0-0-0-20. Cheetahs 2007-08 28-2-0-0-0-10. WP 2009-10 & 12-13 38-7-0-0-0-35. SUPERRUGBY: Cheetahs 2007-08 20-3-0-0-0-15. Stormers 2009-15 89-5-0-0-0-25. REP Honours: SA 2012-16 TESTS: 37-2-0-0-0-10. Springboks 2014 1-0-0-0-0-0. Total: 38-2-0-0-0-10. Emerging Springboks 2009 1-0-0-0-0-0. British Barbarians 2013 1-1-0-0-0-5. MISC INFO: Super PoYnominee 2011. IRB PoY2014 nominee. PoY2014. FC RECORD: 241-24-0-0-0-120. RECORD IN 2016: (SA, Stormers) 2-0-0-0-0-0.

Vermeulen, Johannes Frederick (Jacques) (Paarl Gym.) b 08/02/1995, Paarl. 1.94m. 107kg. Flank. FC DEBUT: 2014. PROV CAREER: WP 2015-16 12-2-0-0-0-10. REP Honours: SAU20 2014-15 7-1-0-0-0-5. FC RECORD: 19-3-0-0-0-15. RECORD IN 2016: (WP) 8-2-0-0-0-10.

Vermeulen, Petrus Jacobus (PJ) (Northern Cape HS, Kimberley) b 03/03/87, De Aar. 1.82.00m. 86kg. Centre. FC DEBUT: 2007. PROV CAREER: WP 2007-09 26-6-0-0-0-30. Boland 2009-11 & 16 40-6-0-0-0-30. Griquas 2012-13 46-8-1-0-0-42. FC RECORD: 112-20-1-0-0-102. RECORD IN 2016: (Boland) 1-0-0-0-0-0.

Vermeulen, Stephan Andre (Monument HS, Krugersdorp) b 12/04/1994, Pretoria. 1.94m. 110kg. Lock. FC DEBUT: 2016. PROV CAREER: Griquas 2016 3-0-0-0-0-0. FC RECORD: 3-0-0-0-0-0. RECORD IN 2016: (Griquas) 3-0-0-0-0-0.

Vers, Keanu Amandlo (Grey HS, Port Elizabeth & NMMU) b 04/02/1996, Middelburg (E Cape). 1.75m. 80kg. Fullback. FC DEBUT: 2016. PROV CAREER: EP Kings 2016 4-1-0-0-0-5. REP Honours: SAU20 2016 2-0-0-0-0-0. FC RECORD: 6-1-0-0-0-5. RECORD IN 2016: (EP Kings, SAU20) 6-1-0-0-0-5.

Verster, Brendan (Garsfontein HS, Pretoria) b 10/07/1996, Bloemfontein. 1.99m. 116kg. Lock. FC DEBUT: 2016. PROV CAREER: Free State XV 2016 2-0-0-0-0-0. FC RECORD: 2-0-0-0-0-0. RECORD IN 2016: (Free State XV) 2-0-0-0-0-0.

Vidima, Ntukozo Mzamomuhle (Glenwood HS, Durban & UFS) b 13/05/1995, Durban. 1.87m. 98kg. Flank. FC DEBUT: 2016. PROV CAREER: Free State XV 2016 11-2-0-0-0-10. FC RECORD: 11-2-0-0-0-10. RECORD IN 2016: (Free State XV) 11-2-0-0-0-10.

Viljoen, EW (Grey College, Bloemfontein) b 09/05/1995, Bloemfontein. 1.92.00m. 100kg. Fullback/Wing. FC DEBUT: 2014. PROV CAREER: WP 2014-16 20-10-0-0-0-50. REP Honours: SAU20 2015 3-0-0-0-0-0. FC RECORD: 23-10-0-0-0-50. RECORD IN 2016: (WP) 11-7-0-0-0-35.

Visagie, Callie-Theron (Paarl Boys' HS & US) b 09/07/1988, Paarl. 1.89m. 103kg. Hooker. FC DEBUT: 2010. PROV CAREER: WP 2010 9-0-0-0-0-0. Lions 2012 10-0-0-0-0-0. Golden Lions XV 2013 1-0-0-0-0-0. Blue Bulls 2013-14 & 16 15-2-0-0-0-10. SUPERRUGBY: Lions 2012

16-0-0-0-0-0. Bulls 2013-15 35-2-0-0-0-10. FC RECORD: 86-4-0-0-0-20. RECORD IN 2016: (Blue Bulls) 2-1-0-0-0-5.

Visagie, Gerrit Jacobus (Jaco) (Augsburg HS, Clanwilliam & UP) b 08/07/1992, Cape Town. 1.88m. 98kg. Hooker. FC DEBUT: 2013. PROV CAREER: Blue Bulls 2013-16 26-0-0-0-0-0. SUPERRUGBY: Bulls 2015-16 8-0-0-0-0-0. FC RECORD: 34-0-0-0-0-0. RECORD IN 2016: (Bulls, Blue Bulls) 16-0-0-0-0-0.

Visagie, Gihard (Helpmekaar HS, Johannesburg & Wits) b 28/05/1996, Rustenburg. 1.81m. 120kg. Hooker. FC DEBUT: 2016. PROV CAREER: Valke 2016 7-0-0-0-0-0. FC RECORD: 7-0-0-0-0-0. RECORD IN 2016: (Valke) 7-0-0-0-0-0.

Visser, Dennis (Kempton Park HS, Affies, Pretoria, UP & UFS) b 20/01/1993, Benoni. 2.00m. 120kg. Lock. FC DEBUT: 2013. PROV CAREER: Blue Bulls 2015 1-0-0-0-0-0. Griffons 2016 6-2-0-0-0-10. REP Honours: SA U20 2013 5-0-0-0-0-0. FC RECORD: 12-2-0-0-0-10. RECORD IN 2016: (Griffons) 6-2-0-0-0-10.

Visser, Petrus Jurgen (Paarl Gym.) b 13/09/1989, Paarl. 1.91m. 88kg. Flyhalf. FC DEBUT: 2009. PROV CAREER: WP 2009-10 8-1-9-4-1-38. Blue Bulls 2011-15 40-7-2-5-0-54. SUPERRUGBY: Bulls 2013-15 31-2-0-1-0-13. Southern Kings 2016 10-0-0-1-0-3. FC RECORD: 89-10-11-11-1-108. RECORD IN 2016: (Southern Kings) 10-0-0-1-0-3.

Volmink, Anthonie Alfred (HTS Bredasdorp) b 10/02/1990, Bredasdorp. 1.80m. 85kg. Wing. FC DEBUT: 2009. PROV CAREER: Boland 2009 2-1-0-0-0-5. Lions 2012-13 & 15-16 33-18-0-0-0-90. Golden Lions XV 2012-16 33-27-1-0-0-137. SUPERRUGBY: Lions 2012 & 14-16 12-3-0-0-0-15. P/R 2013 2-0-0-0-0-0. FC RECORD: 82-49-1-0-0-247. RECORD IN 2016: (Lions S18, Lions, Golden Lions XV) 21-13-0-0-0-65.

Vorster, Harold William (Frans du Toit HS, Phalaborwa) b 11/10/1993, Phalaborwa. 1.86m. 92kg. Centre. FC DEBUT: 2012. PROV CAREER: Golden Lions XV 2012-14 11-1-0-0-0-5. Lions 2014-15 8-1-0-0-0-5. SUPERRUGBY: Lions 2015-16 17-4-0-0-0-20. FC RECORD: 36-6-0-0-0-30. RECORD IN 2016: (Lions S18) 2-0-0-0-0-0.

Vorster, Quintin Trevor (Paarl Boys"HS & UFS) b 26/08/1995, Nelspruit. 1.86m. 106kg. Prop. FC DEBUT: 2016. PROV CAREER: Free State XV 2016 1-0-0-0-0-0. FC RECORD: 1-0-0-0-0-0. RECORD IN 2016: (Free State XV) 1-0-0-0-0-0.

Vosloo, Wian (Klerksdorp HS) b 15/02/1995, Paarl. 1.95m. 112kg. Flank. FC DEBUT: 2016. PROV CAREER: Sharks XV 2016 13-1-0-0-0-5. FC RECORD: 13-1-0-0-0-5. RECORD IN 2016: (Sharks XV) 13-1-0-0-0-5.

Vulindlu, Luzuko (Durban HS) b 14/11/1987, Grahamstown. 1.83m. 98kg. Centre. FC DEBUT: 2008. PROV CAREER: Sharks 2009-10 6-1-0-0-0-5. Sharks XV 2008-11 13-2-0-0-0-10. Sharks Inv XV 2009 1-0-0-0-0-0. Griquas 2012-13 11-2-0-0-0-10. Eagles 2013-16 34-5-0-0-0-25. SUPERRUGBY: Sharks 2009 9-1-0-0-0-5. Southern Kings 2016 11 2 0 0 0-10. REP Honours: Emerging Springboks 2009 1-0-0-0-0-0. FC RECORD: 86-13-0-0-0-65. RECORD IN 2016: (Southern Kings, Eagles) 16-3-0-0-0-15.

Wagman, Clinton Andrew (Florida HS) b 05/10/1990, George. 1.79m. 78kg. Wing. FC DEBUT: 2011. PROV CAREER: Eagles 2011-16 67-17-0-0-0-85. FC RECORD: 67-17-0-0-0-85. RECORD IN 2016: (Eagles) 6-1-0-0-0-5.

Ward, Jeremy Charles (Grey HS, Port Elizabeth) b 10/01/1996, Port Elizabeth. 1.87m. 86kg. Centre. FC DEBUT: 2016. PROV CAREER: EP Kings 2016 4-1-0-0-0-5. SUPERRUGBY: Southern Kings 2016 2-0-0-0-0-0. REP Honours: SAU20 2016 4-2-0-0-0-10. FC RECORD:

10-3-0-0-0-15. RECORD IN 2016: (Southern Kings, EP Kings, SAU20) 10-3-0-0-0-15.

Warner, Andre Riaan (Tygerberg HS & UP) b 02/09/1993, Cape Town. 1.84m. 85kg. Scrumhalf. FC DEBUT: 2015. PROV CAREER: Blue Bulls 2015-16 25-3-0-0-0-15. FC RECORD: 25-3-0-0-0-15. RECORD IN 2016: (Blue Bulls) 21-3-0-0-0-15.

Watermeyer, Stefan (Waterkloof HS, Pretoria) b 03/06/1988, Nelspruit. 1.85m. 95kg. FC DEBUT: 2007. PROV CAREER: Blue Bulls 2008-11 55-20-9-2-0-124. Blue Bulls XV 2007 1-0-0-0-0-0. Griquas 2012 3-0-0-0-0-0. Pumas 2013-15 50-16-0-0-0-80. SUPERRUGBY: Bulls 2010 1-0-0-0-0-0. Lions 2014 13-2-0-0-0-10. Southern Kings 2016 12-3-1-0-0-17. REP Honours: SA Pres XV 2013 3-0-0-0-0-0. SAU20 2008 4-4-0-0-0-20. FC RECORD: 142-45-10-2-0-251. RECORD IN 2016: (Southern Kings) 12-3-1-0-0-17.

Watts, Elgar Graeme (Klein Nederberg HS, Paarl) b 24/09/1985, Paarl. 1.81m. 84kg. Flyhalf. FC DEBUT: 2008. PROV CAREER: Boland 2008-09 & 2011-12 75-21-101-45-1-445. Pumas 2010 22-10-17-9-0-111. Cheetahs 2013-14 13-5-10-10-0-75. Free State XV 2013 2-0-3-1-0-9. EP Kings 2015 6-1-0-0-0-5. Griffons 2015 1-1-2-1-0-12. Griquas 2016 8-2-0-0-0-10. SUPERRUGBY: Cheetahs 2013-14 19-1-17-16-0-87. Southern Kings 2016 11-1-4-6-0-31. REP Honours: SA Barbarians 2012 1-0-3-0-0-6. Misc: First Division PoY2011. FC RECORD: 158-42-157-88-1-791. RECORD IN 2016: (Southern Kings, Griquas) 19-3-4-6-0-41.

Watts, Grant (Hans Moore HS, Benoni) b 09/10/1995. 126kg. Prop. FC DEBUT: 2016. PROV CAREER: Valke 2016 3-0-0-0-0-0. FC RECORD: 3-0-0-0-0-0. RECORD IN 2016: (Valke) 3-0-0-0-0-0.

Webster, Kurt Erwin (Durban HS & UP) b 12/01/1996, Durban. 1.74m. 85kg. Flyhalf. FC DEBUT: 2015. PROV CAREER: Blue Bulls 2015-16 7-1-6-1-0-20. FC RECORD: 7-1-6-1-0-20. RECORD IN 2016: (Blue Bulls) 4-1-6-1-0-20.

Wegner, Carl August (Grey College, Bloemfontein & CUT) b 07/02/1991, Ficksburg. 2.01m. 117kg. Lock. FC debut: 2012. PROV CAREER: Cheetahs 2012 & 14 & 16 12-0-0-0-0-0. Free State XV 2016 3-1-0-0-0-5. SUPERRUGBY: Cheetahs 2014-16 31-3-0-0-0-15. REP Honours: SAU20 2011 2-0-0-0-0-0. MISC INFO: Son of former Free State and Eastern Free State hooker Callie Wegner. FC RECORD: 48-4-0-0-0-20. RECORD IN 2016: (Cheetahs S18, Cheetahs, Free State XV) 20-2-0-0-0-10.

Wehr, Wendal Peter (Worcester SS, Boland College & UJ) b 27/12/1987, Worcester. 1.88m. 96kg. Flank. FC DEBUT: 2008. PROV CAREER: Boland 2008-09 16-2-0-0-0-10. Leopards 2012 2-0-0-0-0-0. Griquas 2014-16 34-4-0-0-0-20. FC RECORD: 52-6-0-0-0-30. RECORD IN 2016: (Griquas) 21-2-0-0-0-10.

Welemu, Lindokuhle (Cambridge HS) b 29/04/1991, East London. 1.92.00m. 113kg. Lock. FC DEBUT: 2014. PROV CAREER: Bulldogs 2014-16 47-3-0-0-0-15. FC RECORD: 47-3-0-0-0-15. RECORD IN 2016: (Bulldogs) 19-1-0-0-0-5.

Wells, Ashley David (Wynberg Boys' HS) b 29/07/1985, Carletonville. 1.87m. 119kg. Prop. FC DEBUT: 2010. PROV CAREER: WP 2010 & 13 & 16 11-0-0-0-0-0. Griquas 2011 9-1-0-0-0-5. Pumas 2012 3-0-0-0-0-0. FC RECORD: 23-1-0-0-0-5. RECORD IN 2016: (WP) 1-0-0-0-0-0.

Welthagen, John James (Johnny) (Affies, Pretoria & NWU) b 28/05/1991, Fochville. 1.88m. 90kg. Flyhalf. FC DEBUT: 2011. PROV CAREER: Leopards 2011 & 15-16 7-2-2-0-0-14. Leopard XV 2013 1-0-0-0-0-0. REP Honours: SAU20 2011 2-0-1-0-0-2. FC RECORD: 10-2-3-0-0-16. RECORD IN 2016: (Leopards) 2-2-1-0-0-12.

Wenn, Chadley (Schoonspruit HS, Malmesbury & Bolad College, Paarl) b 23/08/1993, Stellenbosch. 1.77m. 102kg. Hooker. FC DEBUT: 2015. PROV CAREER: Boland 2015-16 22-3-0-0-0-15. FC RECORD: 22-3-0-0-0-15. RECORD IN 2016: (Boland) 16-3-0-0-0-15.

Wepener, Ryno (Oakdale Agric. HS, Riversdale) b 13/05/1993, Riversdale. 1.82.00m. 81kg. Fullback. FC DEBUT: 2016. PROV CAREER: Leopards 2016 8-1-0-0-0-5. FC RECORD: 8-1-0-0-0-5. RECORD IN 2016: (Leopards) 8-1-0-0-0-5.

Wessels, Stephanus Petrus (Jan Kriel HS) b 09/11/1992, Paarl. 1.84m. 100kg. Prop. FC DEBUT: 2014. PROV CAREER: Boland 2014-16 30-0-0-0-0-0. FC RECORD: 30-0-0-0-0-0. RECORD IN 2016: (Boland) 13-0-0-0-0-0.

Westraadt, Simon (Grey HS, Port Elizabeth) b 31/03/1986, Port Elizabeth. 1.76m. 107kg. Hooker. FC DEBUT: 2007. PROV CAREER: WP 2007-08 6-0-0-0-0-0. Griquas 2009-14 68-10-0-0-0-50. Pumas 2015-16 20-0-0-0-0-0. FC RECORD: 94-10-0-0-0-50. RECORD IN 2016: (Pumas) 11-0-0-0-0-0.

Whitehead, George Alexander (Grey College, Bloemfontein) b 17/03/1989, Bloemfontein. 1.85m. 80kg. FC DEBUT: 2009. PROV CAREER: Cheetahs 2009-10 9-1-2-3-0-18. EP Kings 2011-15 50-10-62-29-1-264. Griffons 2016 18-5-82-32-2-291. SUPERRUGBY: Southern Kings 2013 15-2-6-3-0-31. P/R 2013 2-0-0-0-0-0. Cheetahs 2016 3-0-1-0-0-2. FC RECORD: 97-18-153-67-3-606. RECORD IN 2016: (Cheetahs S18, Griffons) 21-5-83-32-2-293.

Whitehead, Tim (Grey HS, Port Elizabeth & UCT) b30/05/1988. 1.86m. 88kg. Centre. FC DEBUT: 2009. PROV CAREER: WP 2010-11 & 16 33-6-0-0-0-30. Sharks 2012-13 14-1-0-0-0-5. EP Kings 2014-15 19-7-0-0-0-35. SUPERRUGBY: Stormers 2010 10-0-0-0-0-0. Sharks 2012 15-1-0-0-0-5. REP Honours: SA Students 2009 2-1-0-0-0-5. FC RECORD: 93-16-0-0-0-80. RECORD IN 2016: (WP) 10-3-0-0-0-15.

Whiteley, Warren Roger (Glenwood HS, Durban) b 18/09/1987, Durban. 1.92.00m. 97kg. Flank. FC DEBUT: 2008. PROV CAREER: Sharks XV 2008-09 13-4-0-0-0-20. Elephants 2009 5-1-0-0-0-5. Golden Lions 2010-15 52-8-0-0-0-40. Golden Lions XV 2010 & 13 11-4-0-0-0-20. SUPERRUGBY: Lions 2011-12 & 14-16 66-8-0-0-0-40. P/R 2013 2-0-0-0-0-0. REP Honours: SA 2014-16 TESTS: 15-3-0-0-0-15. Springboks 2015 1-0-0-0-0-0. Total: 16-3-0-0-0-15. SA Sevens 2013-14. MISC INFO: SARU PoY nominee 2016. FC RECORD: 165-28-0-0-0-140. RECORD IN 2016: (SA, Lions S18) 26-6-0-0-0-30.

Whyte, Kyle John (Rondebosch HS) b 03/01/1995, Cape Town. 1.91m. 116kg. Prop. FC DEBUT: 2016. PROV CAREER: WP 2016 9-0-0-0-0-0. FC RECORD: 9-0-0-0-0-0. RECORD IN 2016: (WP) 9-0-0-0-0-0.

Wiese, Jacobus Hermanus (Upington HS) b 02/06/1997, Upington. 1.97m. 103kg. Lock. FC DEBUT: 2016. REP Honours: SAU20 2016 5-0-0-0-0-0. FC RECORD: 5-0-0-0-0-0. RECORD IN 2016: (SAU20) 5-0-0-0-0-0.

Wiese, Jasper Van der Westhuizen (Upington HS & CUT) b 21/10/1995, Upington. 1.89m. 99kg. Eighthman. FC DEBUT: 2016. PROV CAREER: Free State XV 2016 9-1-0-0-0-5. FC RECORD: 9-1-0-0-0-5. RECORD IN 2016: (Free State XV) 9-1-0-0-0-5.

Willemse, Chaney (Hexriver Valley HS) b 14/02/1993, De Doorns. 1.86m. 86kg. Flank. FC DEBUT: 2014. PROV CAREER: Boland 2014-16 22-3-0-0-0-15. FC RECORD: 22-3-0-0-0-15. RECORD IN 2016: (Boland) 3-0-0-0-0-0.

Willemse, Gene Gustave (Oakdale Agric. HS, Riversdale) b 13/04/1995, George. 1.82.00m. 95kg. Flyhalf. FC DEBUT: 2016. PROV CAREER: Leopards 2016 19-10-0-0-0-50. FC RECORD: 19-10-0-0-0-50.

RECORD IN 2016: (Leopards) 19-10-0-0-0-50.

Willemse, Michael Evan (Grey HS, Port Elizabeth & UCT) b 14/02/1993, Cape Town. 1.85m. 104kg. Hooker. FC DEBUT: 2013. PROV CAREER: WP 2013-16 36-4-0-0-0-20. EP Kings 2016 4-1-0-0-0-5. SUPERRUGBY: Stormers 2014-16 4-0-0-0-0-0. FC RECORD: 49-7-0-0-0-35. RECORD IN 2016: (Stormers, WP, EP Kings) 18-4-0-0-0-20.

Willemse, Stefan (Paarl Gym. & NMMU) b 12/04/1992, Paarl. 1.94m. 114kg. Flank. FC DEBUT: 2013. PROV CAREER: EP Kings 2013-15 42-8-0-0-0-40. WP 2016 4-0-0-0-0-0. SUPERRUGBY: Southern Kings 2016 11-0-0-0-0-0. FC RECORD: 57-8-0-0-0-40. RECORD IN 2016: (Southern Kings, WP) 15-0-0-0-0-0.

Williams, Devon Frank (Paarl Boys' HS) b 16/04/1992, Stellenbosch. 1.74m. 73kg. Wing. FC DEBUT: 2013. PROV CAREER: WP 2013-14 & 16 22-13-0-0-0-65. Pumas 2016 9-1-4-0-0-13. SUPERRUGBY: Stormers 2013 3-1-0-0-0-5. FC RECORD: 34-15-4-0-0-83. RECORD IN 2016: (WP, Pumas) 15-3-4-0-0-23.

Williams, Heimar (Affies, Pretoria & Unisa) b 02/09/1991, Krugersdorp. 1.80m. 93kg. Centre. FC DEBUT: 2011. PROV CAREER: Sharks XV 2011-16 40-4-0-0-0-20. Sharks 2013-16 23-5-0-0-0-25. SUPERRUGBY: Sharks 2014-16 16-1-0-0-0-5. FC RECORD: 79-10-0-0-0-50. RECORD IN 2016: (Sharks S18, Sharks, Sharks XV) 16-2-0-0-0-10.

Williams, Kurshwill (Percy) (Oudtshoorn HS) b 05/06/1993, George. 1.60m. 70kg. Scrumhalf. FC DEBUT: 2013. PROV CAREER: Golden Lions XV 2013 3-0-0-0-0-0. Leopards 2014-16 7-0-0-0-0-0. Leopards XV 2015 5-1-0-0-0-5. REP Honours: SA U20 2013 1-0-0-0-0-0. FC RECORD: 16-1-0-0-0-5. RECORD IN 2016: (Leopards) 1-0-0-0-0-0.

Williams, Marlyn Earl (Paulus Joubert HS) b 09/01/1993, Paarl. 1.95m. 105kg. Lock. FC DEBUT: 2014. PROV CAREER: Valke 2014-16 50-6-0-0-0-30. FC RECORD: 50-6-0-0-0-30. RECORD IN 2016: (Valke) 19-4-0-0-0-20.

Williams, Warren Patrick (Noorder Paarl & New Orleans HS, Paarl) b 22/08/1995, Paarl. 1.83m. 81kg. Wing. FC DEBUT: 2016. PROV CAREER: Griffons 2016 18-15-0-0-0-75. FC RECORD: 18-15-0-0-0-75. RECORD IN 2016: (Griffons) 18-15-0-0-0-75.

Wilschut, Wayne Patrick (Worcester Gym.) b 12/06/1986, Worcester. 1.81m. 95kg. Eighthman. FC DEBUT: 2015. PROV CAREER: Boland 2015-16 35-1-0-0-0-5. FC RECORD: 35-1-0-0-0-5. RECORD IN 2016: (Boland) 17-1-0-0-0-5.

Wilson, Dale Tiaan b 16/10/1990, Cape Town. 1.92.00m. 101kg. Flank. FC DEBUT: 2016. PROV CAREER: WP 2016 2-0-0-0-0-0. FC RECORD: 2-0-0-0-0-0. RECORD IN 2016: (WP) 2-0-0-0-0-0.

Winnaar, Courtney Kreslen (Dale College, King William's Town & NMMU) b 27/03/1997, East London. 1.82.00m. 80kg. Flyhalf/Fullback. FC DEBUT: 2016. PROV CAREER: EP Kings 2016 5-4-1-2-0-28. FC RECORD: 5-4-1-2-0-28. RECORD IN 2016: (EP Kings) 5-4-1-2-0-28.

Xakalashe, Sokuphumla (Soso) (Gwaba HS, East London) b 17/03/1994, East London. 1.82.00m. 88kg. Prop. FC DEBUT: 2016. PROV CAREER: Bulldogs 2016 1-0-0-0-0-0. FC RECORD: 1-0-0-0-0-0.

RECORD IN 2016: (Bulldogs) 1-0-0-0-0-0.

Xakalashe, Yanga (Gwaba HS) b 16/08/1983, East London. 1.60m. 130kg. Prop. FC DEBUT: 2014. PROV CAREER: Bulldogs 2014-16 43-1-0-0-0-5. FC RECORD: 43-1-0-0-0-5. RECORD IN 2016: (Bulldogs) 10-0-0-0-0-0.

Zaayman, Stephan (Framesby HS, Port Elizabeth & NMMU) b 18/06/1993, Middelburg, Mpumalanga. 1.96m. 100kg. Flank. FC DEBUT: 2013. PROV CAREER: EP Kings 2013-14 & 16 12-0-0-0-0-0. FC RECORD: 12-0-0-0-0-0. RECORD IN 2016: (EP Kings) 7-0-0-0-0-0.

Zana, Eric Sydney (Outeniqua HS, George) b 25/03/1987, George. 1.76m. 70kg. Flyhalf. FC DEBUT: 2010. PROV CAREER: Eagles 2010-11 23-0-1-8-0-26. Boland 2012-15 59-17-63-32-1-310. Griquas 2016 21-1-2-0-0-9. FC RECORD: 103-18-66-40-1-345. RECORD IN 2016: (Griquas) 21-1-2-0-0-9.

Zandberg, Eduard Le Roux (Outeniqua HS, George) b 14/02/1996, George. 2.01m. 121kg. Lock. FC DEBUT: 2016. PROV CAREER: WP 2016 3-0-0-0-0-0. REP Honours: SAU20 2016 3-0-0-0-0-0. FC RECORD: 6-0-0-0-0-0. RECORD IN 2016: (WP, SAU20) 6-0-0-0-0-0.

Zas, Leolin Lucien (Hermanus HS) b 20/10/1995, Worcester. 1.84m. 88kg. Wing. FC DEBUT: 2015. PROV CAREER: WP 2015-16 10-6-0-0-0-30. SUPERRUGBY: Stormers 2016 15-8-0-0-0-40. REP Honours: SA A 2016 2-0-1-0-0-2. SAU20 2015 5-2-0-0-0-10. FC RECORD: 32-16-1-0-0-82. RECORD IN 2016: (SA A, Stormers, WP) 26-14-1-0-0-72.

Zeilinga, Frederik Johannes (Fred) (Glenwood HS, Durban) b 11/12/1992. Ladysmith. 1.75m. 82kg. Flyhalf. FC DEBUT: 2011. PROV CAREER: Sharks 2013-14 18-2-19-41-3-180. Sharks XV 2011-15 23-3-42-36-0-207. Cheetahs 2015-16 17-1-40-22-0-151. SUPERRUGBY: Sharks 2013-15 11-1-10-10-0-55. Cheetahs 2016 15-0-17-15-0-79. FC RECORD: 84-7-128-124-3-672. RECORD IN 2016: (Cheetahs S18, Cheetahs) 24-0-41-29-0-169.

Zito, Mzwanele Richman (Solomon Mahlangu HS & Bol College) b 23/11/1988, Uitenhage. 1.95m. 108kg. Lock. FC DEBUT: 2013. PROV CAREER: EP Kings 2013 1-0-0-0-0-0. Eagles 2013-15 47-6-0-0-0-30. Griquas 2016 17-2-0-0-0-10. FC RECORD: 65-8-0-0-0-40. RECORD IN 2016: (Griquas) 17-2-0-0-0-10.

Zono, Oliver (Eyabantu HS & UFH) b 26/11/1991, Fort Beaufort. 1.75m. 78kg. Flyhalf. FC DEBUT: 2014. PROV CAREER: Bulldogs 2014-16 36-9-14-6-0-91 FC RECORD: 36-9-14-6-0-91. RECORD IN 2016: (Bulldogs) 14-5-4-3-0-42.

Zungu, Lindelwe Siyanda (Piet Retief HS & NMMU) b 16/05/1995, Vryheid. 1.78m. 76kg. Wing. FC DEBUT: 2016. PROV CAREER: EP Kings 2016 13-1-0-0-0-5. FC RECORD: 13-1-0-0-0-5. RECORD IN 2016: (EP Kings) 13-1-0-0-0-5.

Leolin Zas in Currie Cup action for DHL WP against Boland.

Rasta Rasivhenge was a standout performer with the whistle in 2016.

**SA RUGBY
REFEREES**

TEST REFEREES IN 2016:
Craig Joubert:
England vs Wales, Australia vs England, New Zealand vs Argentina, Wales vs Australia, Fiji vs Japan.
He has now refereed 67 Tests.
Jaco Peyper:
France vs Ireland, Italy vs Scotland, New Zealand vs Wales, Australia vs New Zealand, Argentina vs New Zealand, Ireland vs New Zealand, England vs Australia. He has now refereed 35 Tests.
Lourens van der Merwe:
Madagascar vs Senegal.
He has now refereed 11 Tests
Stuart Berry:
Argentina vs Italy.
He has now refereed 7 Tests.
Lesego Legoete:
Zimbabwe vs Uganda.
He has now refereed 7 Tests.
Marius van der Westhuizen:
USA vs Italy, Zimbabwe vs Kenya, Namibia vs Kenya, Ireland vs Canada, Wales vs Japan.
He has now refereed 6 Tests.
Rasta Rasivhenge:
Uganda vs Namibia.
It was his first Test.
Jaco van Heerden:
Kenya vs Uganda.
It was his first Test.
Cwengile Jadezweni:
Kenya vs Hong Kong.
It was his first Test.
Aimee Barrett:
Japan and Fiji.
It was her first Test.

NOTABLE MATCHES & TOURNAMENTS:
Under-20 Junior World Championship:
Cwengile Jadezweni: *Referee*
Under-19 International Series:
Egon Seconds: *France vs England*
Ruhan Meiring: *Wales vs Italy*
Quinton Immelman: *SA Schools "A" vs England*
Vusi Msibi: *SA Schools vs Italy*
Sevens World Series:
Rasta Rasivhenge, Marius van der Westhuizen, Ben Crouse, Craig Joubert
Sevens World Series:
Aimee Barrett
2016 Rio Olympic Sevens:
Craig Joubert, Rasta Rasivhenge, Marius van der Westhuizen, Ben Crouse, Aimee Barrett.

REFEREES

REFEREES IN FINALS/MAIN MATCHES:
Currie Cup: Jaco Peyper
First Division: Quinton Immelman
Gold Cup: Jaco van Heerden
Under-21: Adriaan *(AJ)* Jacobs
Under-20: Sindile Ngcese
Under-19: Vusi Msibi
Varsity Cup: Lourens van der Merwe
Varsity Shield: Cwengile Jadezweni
Women's Section A: Aimee Barrett
Women's Section B: Ashleigh Murray
Women YTC Final: Siyanda Ketse
Under-18 Craven Week: Ruhan Meiring
Under-18 Academy Week: Johre Botha
Under-16 Grant Khomo Week: JD de Meyer
Under-13 Craven Week: Juan-Pierre Clements
LSEN Week: Sinethemba Mrulwa
Under-18 Girls: Ashleigh Murray
Under-16 Girls: Maria Mabote

REFEREE PANELS:
Elite Panel:
Stuart Berry, Rodney Bonaparte, Quinton Immelman, Cwengile Jadezweni *(new)*, Craig Joubert, Lesego Legoete, Jaco Peyper, Rasta Rasivhenge, Marius van der Westhuizen, Jaco van Heerden

National Panel:
Ben Crouse, Stephan Geldenhuys, Adriaan *(AJ)* Jacobs, Jaco Kotze, Pieter Maritz *(new)*, Mpho Matsaung *(new)*, Ruhan Meiring *(new)*, Paul Mente *(new)*, Vusi Msibi, Sindile Nqcese, Francois Pretorius, Jaco Pretorius, Oregopotse Rametsi, Egon Seconds, Archie Sehlako, Ricus van der Hoven, Lourens van der Merwe.

Women's Panel:
Aimee Barrett, Ashleigh Murray, Siyanda Belinda, Maria Mabote, Le-Ann MacClune, Bulela Qwane.

TMO Panel:
Christie du Preez, Johan Greeff, Marius Jonker, Shaun Veldsman, Willie Vos, JJ Wagner.

SARU Selectors – Elite Panel:
Dennis Immelman *(convener)*, Mark Lawrence, Balie Swart, Deon van Blommestein, Banks Yantolo *(Ref Manager)*.

SANZAAR Coach:
Mark Lawrence

Performance Reviewers – National Panel:
Pierre Oelofse, Dennis Immelman, Jacques Hugo, Thuso Mngqibisa, Kim Smit, Deon van Blommestein, Willie Roos.

Conditioning & Fitness:
Warren Adams, John Meintjies

SOUTH AFRICAN REFEREES IN FIRST-CLASS RUGBY - 2016 (ALPHABETICAL)

REFEREE	International	Super Rugby	Currie Cup Prem.	Currie Cup 1st Div	Currie Cup Qual Rounds	Total
Stuart Berry	1	7	4	0	2	14
Rodney Boneparte	0	0	2	2	12	16
Quinton Immelman	0	3	3	3	9	18
Cwengile Jadezweni	1	0	3	1	6	11
Craig Joubert	5	10	3	0	1	19
Pro Legoete	1	0	4	1	10	16
Jaco Peyper	7	11	3	1	3	25
Rasta Rasivhenge	1	3	5	0	4	13
Marius van der Westhuizen	5	7	4	0	5	21
Jaco van Heerden	1	6	4	2	6	19
Ben Crouse	0	0	0	0	4	4
Stephan Geldenhuys	0	0	0	0	4	4
AJ Jacobs	0	0	3	3	8	14
Jaco Kotze	0	0	0	0	1	1
Sindile Ngcese	0	0	0	1	4	5
Francois Pretorius	0	0	0	0	3	3
Egon Seconds	0	0	0	2	8	10
Archie Sehlako	0	0	0	0	3	3
Lourens van der Merwe	1	0	0	0	7	8
TOTAL	23	47	38	16	100	224

Jaco Peyper has his hands full against Rory Best of Ireland.

SECTION 3:
INTERNATIONAL RUGBY
IN 2016

INTERNATIONAL MATCHES IN 2016

DATE	HOME	RESULT	AWAY	VENUE	TOURNAMENT
09/01/2016	Bahamas	18-37	USA South Panthers	Nassau, Bahamas	Rugby Americas North
06/02/2016	Georgia	59-07	Germany	Avchala Stadium, Tbilisi	Six Nations B
06/02/2016	Russia	22-20	Spain	Sotchi, Russia	Six Nations B
06/02/2016	France	23-21	Italy	Stade de France, St Denis	Six Nations / Trophee Garibaldi
06/02/2016	Romania	39-14	Portugal	Cluj Arena, Cluj-Napoca, Romania	Six Nations B
06/02/2016	Scotland	09-15	England	Murrayfield, Edinburgh	Six Nations / Calcutta Cup
06/02/2016	Chile	25-22	Brazil	Mahuida Parque Reina, Santiago	Americas Rugby Championship
06/02/2016	Canada	33-17	Uruguay	Bear Mountain Stadiu, Langford	Americas Rugby Championship
07/02/2016	Ireland	16-16	Wales	AVIVA Stadium, Dublin	Six Nations
12/02/2016	Brazil	29-33	Uruguay	Athletic Club, Sao Paulo	Americas Rugby Championship
13/02/2016	Russia	46-20	Germany	Sotchi, Russia	Six Nations B
13/02/2016	France	10-09	France	Stade de France, St Denis	Six Nations
13/02/2016	Portugal	03-29	Georgia	Universitario Lisboa, Lisbon	Six Nations B
13/02/2016	Spain	18-21	Romania	Campo Universitaria, Madrid	Six Nations B
13/02/2016	Wales	27-23	Scotland	Principality Stadium, Cardiff	Six Nations
13/02/2016	Argentina	52-15	Chile	Esradio de San Juan, San Juan	Americas Rugby Championshipp
13/02/2016	USA	30-22	Canada	Dell Diamond Stadium, Texas	Americas Rugby Championship
14/02/2016	Italy	09-40	England	Olimpico Stadium, Rome	Six Nations
20/02/2016	Belgium	32-08	Netherlands	Brussels, Belgium	FIRA Championship D1
20/02/2016	USA	64-00	Chile	Lockhart Stadium, Fort Lauderdale	Americas Rugby Championship
20/02/2016	Uruguay	21-24	Argentina	Campus Municipal de, Punte de l'Este	Americas Rugby Championship
20/02/2016	Canada	52-25	Brazil	Bear Mountain Stadiu, Langford	Americas Rugby Championship
26/02/2016	Wales	19-10	France	Principality Stadium, Cardiff	Six Nations
27/02/2016	Romania	30-00	Russia	Iasi, Romania	Six Nations B
27/02/2016	Georgia	38-07	Spain	Meskhi Stadium, Tbilisi	Six Nations B
27/02/2016	Germany	50-27	Portugal	Hanover, Germany	Six Nations B
27/02/2016	Italy	20-36	Scotland	Olimpico Stadium, Rome	Six Nations
27/02/2016	England	21-10	Ireland	Twickenham Stadium, London	Six Nations / Millennium Trophy
27/02/2016	Chile	20-23	Uruguay	Mahuida Parque Reina, Santiago	Americas Rugby Championship
27/02/2016	Brazil	24-23	United States of America	Athletic Club, Sao Paulo	Americas Rugby Championship
05/03/2016	St Vincent and Grenadines	00-48	Jamaica	Kingstown, Jamaica	2019 Rugby World Cup Qualifier / Rugby Americas North
05/03/2016	Uruguay	29-25	United States of America	Estadio Charrua, Montevideo	Americas Rugby Championship
05/03/2016	Chile	13-64	Canada	La Pintana, Santiago	Americas Rugby Championship
05/03/2016	Brazil	07-42	Argentina	Sao Jose Dos Campos, Brazil	Americas Rugby Championship
12/03/2016	Moldova	09-10	Belgium	Chisinau, Moldova	FIRA Championship D1
12/03/2016	Romania	61-07	Germany	Iasi, Romania	Six Nations B
12/03/2016	Russia	07-24	Georgia	Sotchi, Russia	Six Nations B
12/03/2016	Ireland	58-15	Italy	AVIVA Stadium, Dublin	Six Nations
12/03/2016	Spain	39-07	Portugal	Campo Universitaria, Madrid	Six Nations B
12/03/2016	England	25-21	Wales	Twickenham Stadium, London	Six Nations
13/03/2016	Scotland	29-18	France	Murrayfield, Edinburgh	Six Nations
19/03/2016	Moldova	22-13	Netherlands	Chisinau, Moldova	FIRA Championship D1
19/03/2016	Georgia	38-09	Romania	National Stadium, Tbilisi	Six Nations B
19/03/2016	Germany	17-17	Spain	Cologne, Germay	Six Nations B
19/03/2016	Wales	67-14	Italy	Principality Stadium, Cardiff	Six Nations
19/03/2016	Portugal	21-53	Russia	Universitario Lisboa, Lisbon	Six Nations B
19/03/2016	Poland	11-21	Belgium	Warsaw, Poland	FIRA Championship D1
19/03/2016	Ireland	35-25	Scotland	AVIVA Stadium, Dublin	Six Nations / Centenary Quaich
19/03/2016	France	21-31	England	Stade de France, St Denis	Six Nations
26/03/2016	Andorra	10-34	Latvia	Andorra la Vella, Andorra	FIRA Championship D2

INTERNATIONAL MATCHES

DATE	HOME	RESULT	AWAY	VENUE	TOURNAMENT
02/04/2016	Israel	19-40	Czech Republic	Netanya, Israel	FIRA Championship D2
09/04/2016	Cyprus	15-03	Hungary	Paphos, Cyprus	FIRA Championship D2
09/04/2016	Czech Republic	26-05	Croatia	Havirov, Czech Republic	FIRA Championship D2
09/04/2016	Austria	12-26	Serbia and Montenegro	Vienna, Austria	FIRA Championship D2
09/04/2016	Switzerland	29-03	Malta	Zurich, Switzerland	FIRA Championship D2
16/04/2016	Malta	30-09	Israel	Paola, Malta	FIRA Championship D2
16/04/2016	Serbia and Montenegro	23-20	Denmark	Belgrade, Serbia	FIRA Championship D2
16/04/2016	Norway	17-33	Bosnia and Herzegovina	Stavanger, Norway	FIRA Championship D2
16/04/2016	Croatia	15-40	Switzerland	Zagreb, Croatia	FIRA Championship D2
16/04/2016	Latvia	37-07	Lithuania	Riga, Latvia	FIRA Championship D2
16/04/2016	Qatar	35-12	Iran	Doha, Qatar	Asian 5 Nations - Divisio
19/04/2016	Iran	12-34	Lebanon	Doha, Qatar	Asian 5 Nations - Divisio
22/04/2016	Qatar	25-19	Lebanon	Divisio, Doha	Asian 5 Nations - Divisio
23/04/2016	Turkey	45-12	Finland	Seferihisar, Turjey	FIRA Championship D2
23/04/2016	Lithuania	47-15	Cyprus	Vilnius, Lithuania	FIRA Championship D2
23/04/2016	Brazil	14-36	Uruguay	Allianz Parque, Sao Jose dos Campos	2019 Rugby World Cup Qualifier / South American Championship
23/04/2016	Guyana	48-17	Barbados	Georgetown, Guyana	2019 Rugby World Cup Qualifier / Rugby Americas North
23/04/2016	Trinidad and Tobago	34-14	Jamaica	Couva, Trinidad	2019 Rugby World Cup Qualifier / Rugby Americas North
23/04/2016	Chile	68-07	Paraguay	Old Grangonians Club, Santiago	2019 Rugby World Cup Qualifier / South American Championship
29/04/2016	Jordan	43-13	Saudi Arabia	Unknown	Saudi Arabia tour
30/04/2016	Lesotho	05-41	Botswana	Unknown	Botswana tour
30/04/2016	Turkey	21-17	Norway	Seferihisar, Turjey	FIRA Championship D2
30/04/2016	Japan	85-00	Korea	Nippatsu Mitsuzawa S, Kanagawa	Asian 5 Nations - Top 5
30/04/2016	Ukraine	23-10	Sweden	Irpin, Ukraine	FIRA Championship D1
30/04/2016	Netherlands	40-16	Poland	Amsterdam, Netherlands	FIRA Championship D1
30/04/2016	Denmark	14-19	Luxembourg	Odense, Denmark	FIRA Championship D2
30/04/2016	Brazil	20-20	Chile	Estadio do Pacaembu, Pacaembu	2019 Rugby World Cup Qualifier / South American Championship
30/04/2016	Paraguay	15-60	Uruguay	Estadio Feroes de Cu, Asuncion	2019 Rugby World Cup Qualifier / South American Championship
07/05/2016	Hong Kong	03-38	Japan	Football Club, Hong Kong	Asian 5 Nations - Top 5
07/05/2016	Bulgaria	15-23	Bosnia and Herzegovina	Sofia, Bulgaria	FIRA Championship D2
07/05/2016	Netherlands	27-30	Ukraine	Amsterdam, Netherlands	FIRA Championship D1
07/05/2016	Norway	28-24	Turkey	Stavanger, Norway	FIRA Championship D2
07/05/2016	Sovenia	38-23	Austria	Ljubliana, Slovenia	FIRA Championship D2
07/05/2016	USA South Panthers	38-05	Bermuda	Unknown	Bermuda tour
07/05/2016	Uruguay	39-14	Chile	Estadio Charrua, Montevideo	South American Championship
07/05/2016	Paraguay	21-32	Brazil	Estadio Feroes de Cu, Asuncio	2019 Rugby World Cup Qualifier / South American Championship
07/05/2016	Bahamas	03-39	Mexico	Nassau, Bahamas	2019 Rugby World Cup Qualifier / Rugby Americas North
08/05/2016	Singapore	17-33	Sri Lanka	Kuala Lampur, Malaysia	Asian 5 Nations - Divisio
08/05/2016	Malaysia	10-15	Philippines	Kuala Lampur, Malaysia	Asian 5 Nations - Divisio
11/05/2016	Philippines	24-28	Singapore	Kuala Lampur, Malaysia	Asian 5 Nations - Divisio
11/05/2016	Malaysia	42-17	Sri Lanka	Kuala Lampur, Malaysia	Asian 5 Nations - Divisio
14/05/2016	Korea	27-34	Hong Kong	Incheon, Korea	Asian 5 Nations - Top 5
14/05/2016	Philippines	21-25	Sri Lanka	Kuala Lampur, Malaysia	Asian 5 Nations - Divisio
14/05/2016	Malaysia	40-20	Singapore	Kuala Lampur, Malaysia	Asian 5 Nations - Divisio
14/05/2016	Sweden	23-25	Netherlands	Enkoping, Sweden	FIRA Championship D1

INTERNATIONAL MATCHES

DATE	HOME	RESULT	AWAY	VENUE	TOURNAMENT
14/05/2016	Luxembourg	29-10	Slovenia	Luxembourg	FIRA Championship D2
14/05/2016	Hungary	10-28	Andorra	Esztergom, Hungary	FIRA Championship D2
15/05/2016	Ukraine	36-17	Moldova	Odessa, Ukraine	FIRA Championship D1
17/05/2016	Rwanda	14-03	Burundi	Kigali, Rwanda	African CAR Championship
18/05/2016	Guam	16-25	Thailand	Unknown	Asian 5 Nations - Divisio, SEMI-FINAL
18/05/2016	Uzbekistan	13-65	United Arab Emirates	Unknown	Asian 5 Nations - Divisio, SEMI-FINAL
18/05/2016	Belarus	17-29	Slovakia	Tallinn, Estonia	FIRA Championship D3
18/05/2016	Estonia	16-13	Montenegro	Tallinn, Estonia	FIRA Championship D3
20/05/2016	Burundi	03-06	Lesotho	Kigali, Rwanda	African CAR Championship
20/05/2016	Rwanda	09-12	DR Congo	Unknown	African CAR Championship. FINAL
21/05/2016	Uzbekistan	22-23	Guam	Tashkent, Uzbekistan	Asian 5 Nations - Divisio
21/05/2016	Thailand	18-70	United Arab Emirates	Unknown	Asian 5 Nations - Divisio, FINAL
21/05/2016	Korea	03-60	Japan	Namdong Asiad Field, Incheon	Asian 5 Nations - Top 5
21/05/2016	Belarus	19-45	Montenegro	Tallinn, Estonia	FIRA Championship D3
21/05/2016	Estonia	36-29	Slovakia	Unknown	FIRA Championship D3, FINAL
21/05/2016	Mexico	75-10	Bermuda	Mexico City, Mexico	2019 Rugby World Cup Qualifier / Rugby Americas North
21/05/2016	Barbados	05-39	Trinidad and Tobago	Bridgetown, Barbados	2019 Rugby World Cup Qualifier / Rugby Americas North
21/05/2016	Guyana	23-05	Jamaica	Georgetown, Guyana	2019 Rugby World Cup Qualifier / Rugby Americas North
21/05/2016	Cayman Islands	20--08	Bahamas	Grand Caymans, Cayman Islands	2019 Rugby World Cup Qualifier / Rugby Americas North
28/05/2016	Japan	59-17	Hong Kong	Prince Chichibu Memorial Stadium	Asian 5 Nations - Top 5
28/05/2016	Finland	24-13	Bulgaria	Helsinki, Finland	FIRA Championship D2
28/05/2016	Uruguay	07-17	Argentina	Estadio Alberto Supi, Colonia del Sacramento	South American Championship
29/05/2016	England	27-13	Wales	Twickenham Stadium, London	Wales tour
04/06/2016	Hong Kong	41-15	Korea	Hong Kong	Asian 5 Nations - Top 5
04/06/2016	Uganda	10-48	Kenya	Kampala, Uganda	ELGO
04/06/2016	Bermuda	30-13	Bahamas	Hamilton, Bermuda	2019 Rugby World Cup Qualifier / Rugby Americas North
04/06/2016	Chile	12-87	Argentina	La Pintana, Santiago	South American Championship
09/06/2016	Argentina XV	38-07	Spain	Arcul de Triumf, Bucharest	Nations Cup
09/06/2016	Emerging Italy	22-21	Uruguay	Arcul de Triumf, Bucharest	Nations Cup
09/06/2016	Romania	19-05	Namibia	Arcul de Triumf, Bucharest	Nations Cup
11/06/2016	Samoa	19-19	Georgia	Apia Park, Apia	Georgia tour
11/06/2016	Fiji	23-18	Tonga	National Stadium, Suva	2019 Rugby World Cup Qualifier / Pacific Nations Cup
11/06/2016	New Zealand	39-21	Wales	Eden Park, Auckland	Wales tour
11/06/2016	Australia	28-39	England	Suncorp Stadium, Brisbane	England tour
11/06/2016	South Africa	20-26	Ireland	DHL Newlands Rugby Stadium, Cape Town	Ireland tour
11/06/2016	Argentina	30-24	Italy	Estanislao Lopez, Santa Fe	Italy tour
11/06/2016	Canada	22-26	Japan	BC Place, Vancouver	Japan tour
12/06/2016	Madagascar	25-15	Zambia	Antananarive, Madagascar	2019 Rugby World Cup Qualifier / African CAR Championship
13/06/2016	Namibia	20-28	Spain	Arcul de Triumf, Bucharest	Nations Cup
13/06/2016	Romania	37-00	Uruguay	Arcul de Triumf, Bucharest	Nations Cup
15/06/2016	Senegal	54-03	Zambia	Antananarive, Madagascar	2019 Rugby World Cup Qualifier / African CAR Championship
17/06/2016	Brazil	17-18	Kenya	Estadio Milton Corre, Macapa	Kenya tour
18/06/2016	Georgia	23-20	Tonga	Unknown	Tonga tour / Georgia tour
18/06/2016	Fiji	26-16	Samoa	National Stadium, Suva	2019 Rugby World Cup Qualifier /

INTERNATIONAL MATCHES

DATE	HOME	RESULT	AWAY	VENUE	TOURNAMENT
					Pacific Nations Cup
18/06/2016	New Zealand	36-22	Wales	Westpac Stadium, Wellington	Wales tour
18/06/2016	Australia	07-23	England	AAMI Park, Melbourne	England tour
18/06/2016	Japan	13-26	Scotland	Toyota Stadium, Aichi	Scotland tour
18/06/2016	Spain	00-10	Uruguay	Arcul de Triumf, Bucharest	Nations Cup
18/06/2016	South Africa	32-26	Ireland	Emirates Airline Park, Johannesburg	Ireland tour
18/06/2016	Romania	20-07	Argentina XV	Arcul de Triumf, Bucharest	Nations Cup
18/06/2016	Trinidad and Tobago	23-18	Guyana	Port of Spain, Trinidad and Tobago	2019 Rugby World Cup Qualifier / Rugby Americas North
18/06/2016	Canada	46-21	Russia	Kingsland, Calgary	Russia tour
18/06/2016	Cayman Islands	47-11	Bermuda	Grand Caymans, Cayman Islands	2019 Rugby World Cup Qualifier / Rugby Americas North
18/06/2016	United States of America	20-24	Italy	Avaya Stadium, San Jose	Italy tour
19/06/2016	Madagascar	24-30	Senegal	Antananarive, Madagascar	2019 Rugby World Cup Qualifier / African CAR Championship
19/06/2016	Argentina	30-19	France	Cancha Del Atletico, Tucuman	France tour
24/06/2016	Fiji	03-14	Georgia	National Stadium, Suva	Georgia tour
25/06/2016	Samoa	30-10	Tonga	Apia Park, Apia	2019 Rugby World Cup Qualifier / Pacific Nations Cup
25/06/2016	New Zealand	46-06	Wales	Forsyth Barr Stadium, Dunedin	Wales tour
25/06/2016	Australia	40-44	England	Allianz Stadium, Sydney	England tour
25/06/2016	Japan	16-21	Scotland	Ajinomoto Stadium, Tokyo	Scotland tour
25/06/2016	South Africa	19-13	Ireland	Nelson Mandela Bay Stadium, Port Elizabeth	Ireland tour
25/06/2016	Argentina	00-27	France	Cancha Del Atletico, Tucuman	France tour
25/06/2016	USA	25-00	Russia	Cal Expo Field, Sacramento	Russia tour
26/06/2016	Canada	18-20	Italy	BMO Stadium, Toronto	Italy tour
26/06/2016	Tunisia	43-10	Botswana	Monastir, Tunisia	2019 Rugby World Cup Qualifier / African CAR Championship
29/06/2016	Botswana	13-20	Ivory Coast	Monastir, Tunisia	2019 Rugby World Cup Qualifier / African CAR Championship
02/07/2016	Uganda	31-40	Namibia	Kyodondo Rugby Club, Kampala	African CAR Championship
02/07/2016	Mexico	34-17	Cayman Islands	Huixquilucan, Mexico	2019 Rugby World Cup Qualifier / Rugby Americas North
02/07/2016	Tunisia	50-05	Ivory Coast	Monastir, Tunisia	2019 Rugby World Cup Qualifier / African CAR Championship
09/07/2016	Zimbabwe	15-61	Kenya	Harare, Zimbabwe	African CAR Championship
10/07/2016	Morocco	68-03	Mauritius	Casablanca, Morocco	2019 Rugby World Cup Qualifier / African CAR Championship
13/07/2016	Mauritius	21-31	Nigeria	Casablanca, Morocco	2019 Rugby World Cup Qualifier / African CAR Championship
16/07/2016	Namibia	56-21	Kenya	Hage Geingob Rugby Stadium, Windhoek	African CAR Championship
16/07/2016	Morocco	53-10	Nigeria	Casablanca, Morocco	African CAR Championship
23/07/2016	Zimbabwe	27-34	Uganda	Harare, Zimbabwe	African CAR Championship
30/07/2016	Kenya	45-24	Uganda	Nairobi, Kenya	African CAR Championship
06/08/2016	Namibia	60-22	Zimbabwe	Hage Geingob Rugby Stadium, Windhoek	African CAR Championship
20/08/2016	Australia	08-42	New Zealand	ANZ Stadium, Sydney	Rugby Championship / Bledisloe Cup
20/08/2016	South Africa	30-23	Argentina	Mbombela Stadium, Nelspruit	Rugby Championship
23/08/2016	Kenya A	24-18	Hong Kong	Unknown	Hong Kong tour
27/08/2016	Ecuador	26-25	Guatemala	Guayaquil, Ecuador	South American Championship
27/08/2016	New Zealand	29-09	Australia	Westpac Stadium, Wellington	Rugby Championship / Bledisloe Cup

INTERNATIONAL MATCHES

DATE	HOME	RESULT	AWAY	VENUE	TOURNAMENT
27/08/2016	Kenya	34-10	Hong Kong	Unknown	Hong Kong tour
27/08/2016	Argentina	26-24	South Africa	Ernesto Maltearena, Salta	Rugby Championship
03/09/2016	Czech Republic	14-56	Czech Republic	Enkoping, Sweden	2019 Rugby World Cup Qualifier / FIRA Championship D2
10/09/2016	New Zealand	57-22	Argentina	Waikato Stadium, Hamilton	Rugby Championship
10/09/2016	Australia	23-17	South Africa	Suncorp Stadium, Brisbane	Rugby Championship
17/09/2016	New Zealand	41-13	South Africa	AMI Stadium, Christchurch	Rugby Championship / Freedom Cup
17/09/2016	Australia	36-20	Argentina	NIB Stadium, Perth	Rugby Championship
24/09/2016	Poland	22-00	Ukraine	Lublin, Poland	2019 Rugby World Cup Qualifier / FIRA Championship D1
01/10/2016	Estonia	05-53	Hungary	Tallinn, Estonia	FIRA Championship D2
01/10/2016	South Africa	18-10	Australia	Loftus Versfeld Stadium, Pretoria	Rugby Championship / Mandela Challenge Plate
01/10/2016	Mexico	32-03	Guyana	Unknown	2019 Rugby World Cup Qualifier / Rugby Americas North FINAL
01/10/2016	Argentina	17-36	New Zealand	River Plate Stadium, Buenos Aires	Rugby Championship
02/10/2016	Colombia	75-05	Ecuador	Lima, Peru	2019 Rugby World Cup Qualifier / South American Championship
02/10/2016	Peru	08-33	Venezuela	Lima, Peru	2019 Rugby World Cup Qualifier / South American Championship
05/10/2016	Ecuador	10-52	Venezuela	Unknown	2019 Rugby World Cup Qualifier / South American Championship, SEMI-FINAL
05/10/2016	Peru	14-41	Colombia	Unknown	2019 Rugby World Cup Qualifier / South American Championship, SEMI-FINAL
08/10/2016	Norway	48-31	Finland	Oslo, Norway	FIRA Championship D2
08/10/2016	Austria	29-22	Bosnia and Herzegovina	Vienna, Austria	FIRA Championship D2
08/10/2016	Hungary	25-13	Denmark	Esztergom, Hungary	FIRA Championship D2
08/10/2016	South Africa	15-57	New Zealand	Growthpoint KINGS PARK, Durban	Rugby Championship / Freedom Cup
08/10/2016	Argentina	21-33	Australia	Twickenham Stadium, London	Rugby Championship
08/10/2016	Peru	60-05	Ecuador	Lima, Peru	2019 Rugby World Cup Qualifier / South American Championship
08/10/2016	Colombia	35-10	Venezuela	Unknown	2019 Rugby World Cup Qualifier / South American Championship FINAL
22/10/2016	New Zealand	37-10	Australia	Eden Park, Auckland	Australia tour / Bledisloe Cup
22/10/2016	Finland	51-06	Estonia	Helsinki, Finland	FIRA Championship D2
22/10/2016	Latvia	31-24	Luxembourg	Jelgava, Latvia	2019 Rugby World Cup Qualifier / FIRA Championship D2
22/10/2016	Denmark	20-00	Norway	Odense, Denmark	FIRA Championship D2
22/10/2016	Andorra	15-63	Malta	Andorra la Vella, Andorra	FIRA Championship D2
29/10/2016	Slovenia	74-13	Serbia and Montenegro	Ljubliana, Slovenia	FIRA Championship D2
29/10/2016	Croatia	47-15	Andorra	Split, Croatia	FIRA Championship D2
29/10/2016	Malta	31-03	Cyprus	Paola, Malta	FIRA Championship D2
29/10/2016	Colombia	29-11	Mexico	Unknown	Unknown
02/11/2016	China	??	Brunei	Unknown	A53E, SEMI-FINAL
05/11/2016	Montenegro	07-55	Gibraltar	Unknown	Gibraltar tour
05/11/2016	Japan	20-54	Argentina	Prince Chichibu Memorial Stadium	Argentina tour
05/11/2016	Indonesia	12-48	Laos	Unknown	A53E, SEMI-FINAL
05/11/2016	Israel	23-16	Croatia	Netanya, Israel	FIRA Championship D2
05/11/2016	Lithuania	11-06	Latvia	Siauliai, Lithuania	2019 Rugby World Cup Qualifier / FIRA Championship D2
05/11/2016	Ukraine	12-54	Netherlands	Lvov, Ukraine	2019 Rugby World Cup Qualifier /

INTERNATIONAL MATCHES

DATE	HOME	RESULT	AWAY	VENUE	TOURNAMENT
05/11/2016	Wales	08-32	Wales 8 - 32 Australia	Principality Stadium, Cardiff	FIRA Championship D1 Australia tour
05/11/2016	Luxembourg	00-19	Sweden	Luxembourg City, Luxembourg	2019 Rugby World Cup Qualifier / FIRA Championship D2
05/11/2016	Ireland	40-29	New Zealand	Soldier Field, Chicago	Unknown
08/11/2016	Czech Republic	00-71	Barbarians	Prague, Czech Republic	Barbarians tour
09/11/2016	England Women	10-05	France Women	Unknown	France Women tour
11/11/2016	Russia	19-15	Zimbabwe	Football Club, Hong Kong	Cup of Nations
11/11/2016	Hong Kong	51-05	Papua New Guinea	Hong Kong	Cup of Nations
11/11/2016	Barbarians	40-07	Fiji	Ravenhill, Belfast	Fiji tour / Barbarians tour
12/11/2016	Georgia	22-28	Japan	Meskhi Stadium, Tbilisi	Japan tour
12/11/2016	Moldova	54-15	Ukraine	Anenii-Noi, Moldova	2019 Rugby World Cup Qualifier / FIRA Championship D1
12/11/2016	Cyprus	28-38	Israel	Paphos, Cyprus	FIRA Championship D2
12/11/2016	Czech Republic	15-06	Lithuania	Prague, Czech Republic	2019 Rugby World Cup Qualifier / FIRA Championship D2
12/11/2016	Italy	10-68	New Zealand	Olimpico Stadium, Rome	New Zealand tour
12/11/2016	England	37-21	South Africa	Twickenham Stadium, London	South Africa tour
12/11/2016	Scotland	22-23	Australia	Murrayfield, Edinburgh	Australia tour
12/11/2016	Portugal	26-21	Belgium	Complexo Atletismo, Setubal	Belgium tour
12/11/2016	Spain	13-28	Tonga	Campo Universitaria, Madrid	Tonga tour
12/11/2016	Romania	23-10	United States of America	Arcul de Triumf, Bucharest	United States of America tour
12/11/2016	France	52-08	Samoa	Le Stade de Toulouse, Toulouse	Samoa tour
12/11/2016	Germany	24-21	Uruguay	Volksbank Stadion, Frankfurt-am-Main	Uruguay tour
12/11/2016	Wales	24-20	Argentina	Principality Stadium, Cardiff	Argentina tour
12/11/2016	Ireland	52-21	Canada	AVIVA Stadium, Dublin	Canada tour
13/11/2016	Chile	30-12	Korea	San Carlos de Apoqui, Santiago	Korea tour
15/11/2016	Papa New Guinea	19-49	Russia	Football Club, Hong Kong	Cup of Nations
15/11/2016	Hong Kong	34-11	Zimbabwe	Hong Kong	Cup of Nations
19/11/2016	Papa New Guinea	11-38	Zimbabwe	Hong Kong	Cup of Nations
19/11/2016	Hong Kong	00-27	Russia	Football Club, Hong Kong	Cup of Nations
19/11/2016	Georgia	20-16	Samoa	Meskhi Stadium, Tbilisi	Samoa tour
19/11/2016	Germany	16-06	Brazil	Fritz Grunebaum Stadium, Heidelburg	Brazil tour
19/11/2016	Italy	20-18	South Africa	Artemio Franchi, Firenze	South Africa tour
19/11/2016	Netherlands	44-17	Moldova	Amsterdam, Netherlands	2019 Rugby World Cup Qualifier / FIRA Championship D1
19/11/2016	Switzerland	10-28	Portugal	Yverdon, Switzerland	2019 Rugby World Cup Qualifier / FIRA Championship D1
19/11/2016	England	38-15	Fiji	Twickenham Stadium, London	Fiji tour
19/11/2016	Wales	33-30	Japan	Principality Stadium, Cardiff	Japan tour
19/11/2016	Spain	33-16	Uruguay	Estadio Ciudad de Ma, Malaga	Uruguay tour
19/11/2016	Romania	21-16	Canada	Arcul de Triumf, Bucharest	Canada tour
19/11/2016	Tonga	20-17	USA	Estadio Anoeta, San Sebastian	Tonga tour / United States of America tour
19/11/2016	Scotland	19-16	Argentina	Murrayfield, Edinburgh	Argentina tour
19/11/2016	Ireland	09-21	New Zealand	AVIVA Stadium, Dublin	New Zealand tour
19/11/2016	Paraguay	39-27	Colombia	Unknown	Unknown
19/11/2016	France	23-25	Australia	Stade de France, St Denis	Australia tour
19/11/2016	Chile	36-38	Korea	Old Grangonians Club, Santiago	Korea tour
25/11/2016	Canada	23-25	Samoa	Stade des Alpes, Grenoble	Canada tour / Samoa tour
26/11/2016	Germany	36-14	Brazil	Leipzig, Germany	Brazil tour
26/11/2016	Fiji	38-25	Japan	Stade de la Rabine, Vannes	Japan tour / Fiji tour
26/11/2016	Italy	17-19	Tonga	Stadio Euganeo, Padova	Tonga tour

INTERNATIONAL MATCHES

DATE	HOME	RESULT	AWAY	VENUE	TOURNAMENT
26/11/2016	Switzerland	29-26	Moldova	Yverdon, Switzerland	2019 Rugby World Cup Qualifier / FIRA Championship D1
26/11/2016	England	27-14	Argentina	Twickenham Stadium, London	Argentina tour
26/11/2016	Scotland	43-16	Georgia	Rugby Park, Kilmarnock	Georgia tour
26/11/2016	Romania	36-10	Uruguay	Arcul de Triumf, Bucharest	Uruguay tour
26/11/2016	England Women	39-06	Canada Women	Unknown	Canada Women tour
26/11/2016	Ireland	27-24	Australia	AVIVA Stadium, Dublin	Australia tour
26/11/2016	Wales	27-13	South Africa	Principality Stadium, Cardiff	South Africa tour
26/11/2016	France	19-24	New Zealand	Stade de France, St Denis	New Zealand tour
01/12/2016	Portugal	21-17	Brazil	Sergio Conceicao, Coimbra	Brazil tour
03/12/2016	England	37-21	Australia	Twickenham Stadium, London	Australia tour

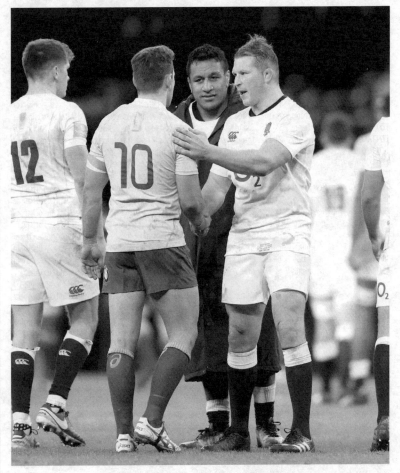

Dylan Hartley and his England team finished the year unbeaten.

South Africans Capped by Other Countries – 1879-2016

Compiled by Stuart Farmer

† *Indicates also played for South Africa*

Abbott, SRD (Stuart) - England - 9 Tests - 2003-2006

Abendanon, NJ (Nick) - England - 2 tests - 2007

†Allan, J (John) - Scotland - 9 Tests - 1990-1991

Alexander, M (Matt) - USA - 25 Tests - 1995-1998

Anderson, HJ (Henry) - Ireland - 4 Tests - 1903-1906

Andrade, MJ (Michael) - Portugal - 2 Tests - 2015

Antoni, JA (Giovani) - Italy - 2 Tests - 2001

Appleford, GN (Geoff) - England - 1 Test - 2002

Badenhorst, RS (Skipper) - Namibia - 3 Tests - 2007

Barnard, J (Barries) - Namibia - 22 Tests - 1990-1993

Barritt, BM (Brad) - England - 26 Tests - 2013-2015

Bell, PJD (Patrick) - USA - 7 Tests - 2006

Binikos, A (Andrew) - Cyprus -

Black, BH (Brian) - England - 10 Tests - 1930-1933

Blom, A (André) - USA - 13 Tests - 1998-2000

Blom, ML (Morné) - Namibia - 16 Tests - 2011-2016

Bosch, PW (Paul) - Germany - 9 Tests - 2015-2016

Botes, LW (Lu-Wayne) - Namibia - 9 Tests 2006-2007

Botes, WT (Tobias) - Italy - 22 Tests 2012-2014

Botha, MJ (Mouritz) - England - 10 Tests - 2011-2012

Bothma, R (Renaldo) - Namibia - 13 Tests - 2014-2016

Bouwer, AC (Arthur) - Namibia - 15 Tests 2012-2016

Breytenbach, CL (Conrad) - Russia - 2 Tests - 2002

Brooks, FG (Freddie) - England - 1 Test - 1906

Buchanan, JCR (Rankin) - Scotland - 16 Tests - 1921-1925

Buitendag, A (Basie) - Namibia - 22 Tests - 1990-1993

Catterall, BW (Brenton) - Zimbabwe - 7 Tests - 1991-1998

Catt, MJ (Mike) - England (75 Tests), Lions (1 Test) - 1994-2007

Chistolini, D (Dario) - Italy - 15 Tests - 2014-2016

Claassen, AD (Antonie) - France - 6 Tests - 2013-2014

Constable R (Ryan) - Australia - 1 Test - 1994

Crèmer, JAB (Beukes) - Brazil - 13 Tests - 2015-2016

Cuttitta, M (Marcello) - Italy - 54 Tests - 1987-1999

Cuttitta, M (Massimo) - Italy - 69 Tests - 1990-2000

Dalzell, K (Kevin) - USA - 42 Tests - 1996-2003

Dames, HDP (Danie) - Namibia - 8 Tests - 2011-2013

Davey, J (Jas) - England - 2 Tests - 1908-1909

Davies, MJ (Mickey) - Wales - 2 Tests - 1939

Davies, S (Shaun) - USA - 1 Test - 2013

Dell, AME (Allan) - Scotland - 3 Tests - 2016

De Jager, B (Benjamin) - Italy - 1 Test - 2006

De Jong, MG (Mike) - USA - 9 Tests - 1990-1991

De Marigny, JR (Roland) - Italy - 19 Tests - 2004-2007

De Villiers, P (Pieter) - France - 69 Tests - 1999-2007

Del Fava, CA (Carlo) - Italy - 54 Tests - 2004-2011

Diack, RJE (Robbie) - Ireland - 2 Tests - 2014

Dickson, WM (Mike) - Scotland - 7 Tests - 1912-1913

Dingley, J (Jon) - Hong Kong - 21 Tests - 1994-1998

Dirksen, C (Cornelius) - USA - 2 Tests - 2012

Downes, GT (Graham) - USA - 1 Test - 1992

Duncan, DD (Denoon) - Scotland - 4 Tests - 1920

Ehrentraut, M (Michael) - Germany - 3 Tests - 1995-1998

Elgie, MK (Kim) - Scotland - 8 Tests - 1954-1955

Eloff, JP (Jean-Pierre) - USA - 5 Tests - 2016

Eloff, PT (Phillip) - USA - 35 Tests - 2000-2007

Els, JW (Jarrid) - Germany - 8 Tests - 2015-2016

Engels, JB (Jaco) - Namibia - 8 Tests - 2013-2014

Erasmus, DJ (Danie) - Australia - 2 Tests - 1923

Erasmus, J (Jaco) - Italy - 3 Tests - 2008

Erskine, CE (Chad) - USA - 10 Tests - 2007-2008

Esterhuizen, Q (Quintin) - Namibia - 4 Tests - 2014-2016

Evans, IR (Ian) - Wales - 33 Tests - 2006-2014

Ferreira, SR (Sebastian) - Germany - 2 Tests - 2016

Forrest, JGS (John) - Scotland - 3 Tests - 1938

Fourie, CH (Hendre) - England - 8 Tests - 2010-2011

Francis, TES (Tim) - England - 4 Tests - 1926

Franken, HH (Henk) - Namibia - 3 Tests - 2011-2012

Freakes, HD (Hubert) - England - 3 Tests - 1938-1939

†Gage, JH (Jack) - Ireland - 4 Tests - 1926-1927

Gagiano, JR (JJ) - USA - 14 Tests - 2008-2011

Geldenhuys, Q (Quintin) - Italy - 67 Tests - 2009-2016

Goedeke, F (Frank) - Germany - 4 Tests - 1999-2001

Goosen, CJ (Khaki) - Namibia - 5 Tests - 1991-1993

Gouws, J (Jurie) - USA - 8 caps - 2003-2004

Grobler, J (Juan) - USA - 33 caps - 1996-2002

Hauck, A (Alexander) - Germany - 6 Tests - 2009-2010

Hall, S (Steven) - France - 2 Tests - 2002

Hands, RHM (Reg) - England - 2 Tests - 1910

Harris, SW (Stan) - England (2 Tests) Lions (2 Tests) - 1920-1924

Hauck, A (Alexander) - Germany - 6 Tests - 2009-2010

Hawkins, M (Matt) - USA - 1 Test - 2010

Haylett-Petty, DS (Dane) - Australia - 14 Tests - 2016

Heatlie, BH (Fairy) - Argentina - 1 Test - 1910

Henderson, JH (Chick) - Scotland - 9 Tests - 1953-1954

Hendriks, JHF (Tenk) - Russia - 7 Tests - 2002

Herring, RW (Rob) - Ireland - 1 Test - 2014

Hindson, RE (Ro) - Canada - 31 Tests - 1973-1990

Hofmeyr, MB (Murray) - England - 3 Tests - 1950

Holmes, T (Tyrone) - Scotland - 1 Test - 2014

Hopley, FJV (John) - England - 3 Tests - 1907-1908

Horak, MJ (Michael) - England - 1 Test - 2002

Human, P (Petrus) - Namibia - 2 Tests - 2012

Jantjies, R (Riaan) - Namibia - 15 Tests - 1994-2000

Jeffery, D (Doug) - Namibia - 1 Test - 1990

Dane Haylett-Petty.

Jones IC (Ian) - Wales - 1 Test - 1968
Jordaan PJ (Pieter) - Germany - 12 Tests - 2011-2014
Keyter, JC (Jason) - USA - 17 Tests - 2000-2003
Klerck, GS (Gerhard) - USA - 8 Tests - 2003-2004
Kockott, RM (Rory) - France - 11 Tests - 2014-2015
Kotze, DM (Dan) - France - 1 Test - 2013
Krige, JA (Jannie) - England - 1 Test - 1920
Kruger, NA (Nicu) - USA - 6 Tests - 2015-2016
Kumbier, KR (Karl) - Germany - 6 Tests - 1998-2000
Labuschagne, NA (Nick) - England - 5 Tests - 1953-1955
Lentz, O (Owen) - USA - 8 Tests - 2006-2007
Le Roux, B (Bernard) - France - 24 Tests - 2013-2016
Le Roux, JE (Jacques) - Portugal - 13 Tests - 2011-2014
Le Roux, RP (Ryan) - Spain - 4 Tests 2011-2012
Liebenberg, B (Brian) - France - 12 Tests - 2003-2005
Lipman, S (Sean) - USA - 9 Tests - 1988-1991
London, CJ (Chad) - USA - 6 Tests - 2014-2016
Losper, SJ (Sarel) - Namibia - 18 Tests - 1990-1991
Ludick, R (Ruan) - Namibia - 4 Tests - 2016
Lupini, E (Tito) - Italy - 11 Tests - 1987-1989
Luscombe, HN (Hal) - Wales - 16 Tests - 2003-2007
Macdonald, DSM (Don) - Scotland - 7 Tests - 1977-1978
MacDonald, JS (Jimmy) - Scotland - 5 Tests - 1903-1905
Marinos, AWN (Andy) - Wales - 8 Tests - 2002-2003
Maritz, WM (Willem) - Namibia - 8 Tests - 1990-1991
Marshall, KW (Kenneth) - Scotland - 8 Tests - 1934-1937
Matsushima, K (Kotaro) - Japan - 22 Tests - 2014-2016
McCowat, RH (Harold) - Scotland - 1 Test - 1905
McMillan, KHD (Keith) - Scotland - 4 Tests - 1953
Mehrtens, AP (Andrew) - New Zealand - 70 Tests - 1995-2004
Melck, RJG (Justin) - Germany - 1 Test - 2014
†Mellish, FW (Frank) - England - 6 Tests - 1920-1921
Melville, E (Eric) - France - 6 Tests - 1990-1991
Meyer, EA (Eden) - Namibia - 21 Tests - 1991-1996
Meyer, JM (Johannes) - Namibia - 16 Tests - 2003-2007
Meyer, P (Philip) - Namibia - 1 Test - 2005
Milton, HC (Cecil) - England - 1 Test - 1906
Milton, JG (Jumbo) - England - 5 Tests - 1904-1907
Morrison, RA (Randall) - Romania - 1 Test - 2015
Mulligan, PJ (Patrick) - Australia - 1 Test - 1925
Mullins, RC (Cuthbert) - British Isles - 2 Tests - 1896
Nel, WP (Willem) - Scotland - 15 Tests - 2015-2016
Newman, SC (Syd) - England - 3 Tests - 1947-1948
Newton-Thompson, JO (Ossie) - England - 2 Tests - 1947
Nieuwenhuis, J (Jacques) - Namibia - 25 Tests 2006-2011
O'Cuinneagain, D (Dion) - Ireland - 19 Tests - 1998-2000
†Oosthuizen, LT (Theo) - Namibia - 7 Tests - 1990
Openshaw, WE (William) - England - 1 Test - 1879
Osler, FL (Frank) - Scotland - 2 Tests - 1911
Otto, J (Jaco) - Germany - 10 Tests - 2015-2016
Owen-Smith, HG (Tuppy) - England - 10 Tests - 1934-1937
Peens, G (Gert) - Italy - 23 Tests - 2002-2006
Pieterse, W (Werner) - Russia - 7 Tests - 2002
Pocock, DW (David) - Australia - 66 Tests - 2008-2016
Poppmeier, M (Michael) - Germany - 20 Tests - 2009-2016

Praschma, P (Paul) - Germany - 2 Tests - 1998
Pretorius, WA (Andries) - Wales - 2 Tests - 2013
Proudfoot, MC (Matthew) - Scotland - 4 Tests - 1998-2003
Rathbone, C (Clyde) - Australia - 26 Tests - 2004-2006
Rawlinson, GP (Greg) - New Zealand - 4 Tests 2006-2007
Reid, RE (Roland) - Scotland - 2 Tests - 2001
Robertsen, JR (John) - Canada - 9 Tests - 1985-1991
Rose, JG (Jody) - Romania - 8 Tests - 2015-2016
Rosenblum, ME (Myer) - Australia - 4 Tests - 1928
Roux, Q (Quinn) - Ireland - 1 Test - 2016
Roxburgh, JR (Jim) - Australia - 9 Tests - 1968-1970
Schulze, MR (Mark) - Germany - 16 Tests - 1996-2000
Scriba, HM (Hans) - Germany - 4 Tests - 1997-1998
Small, HD (Harry) - England - 4 Tests - 1950
Smit, H (Heinrich) - Namibia - 18 Tests - 2014-2016
Smith, C (Collen) - Namibia - 6 Tests - 2012-2016
Spedding, SL (Scott) - France - 18 Tests - 2014-2016
Stander, CJ (CJ) - Ireland - 10 Tests - 2016
Stevens, MJH (Matt) - England - 44 Tests - 2004-2012
†Stewart, JC (Christian) - Canada - 14 Tests - 1991-1995
Steyn, AJ (Braam) - Italy - 6 Tests - 2016
Steyn, SSL (Stephen) - Scotland - 2 Tests - 1911-1912
Stickling, C (Conrad) - Portugal - 5 Tests - 2010
†Strauss, CP (Tiaan) - Australia - 11 Tests - 1999
Strauss, JZ (Josh) - Scotland - 9 Tests - 2015-2016
Strauss, CR (Richardt) - Ireland - 17 Tests - 2012-2016
Theisinger, AA (Adriaan) - Germany - 4 Tests - 2016
Theron, JP (Duimpie) - Namibia - 8 Tests - 1997-1999
Thomas, RM (Rhys) - Wales - 7 Tests - 2006-2009
Tonks, GA (Greig) - Scotland - 6 Tests - 2013-2015
Trenkel, N (Nick) - Canada - 1 Test - 2007
Van der Bergh, H (Henri) - Portugal - 4 Tests - 2003
Van der Merwe, AP (Arra) - Namibia - 19 Tests - 1990-1992
Van der Merwe, D (Danie) - Namibia - 1 Test - 1990
Van der Merwe, DTH - Canada - 42 Tests - 2006-2016
Van der Merwe, HJ (Hendrik) - Germany - 13 Tests - 2014-2016
Van Heerden, A (Andries) - France - 2 Tests - 1992
Van Heerden, JP (Johan) - Romania - 16 Tests - 2015-2016
Van Ryneveld, CB (Clive) - England - 4 Tests - 1949
Van Schalkwyk, AJ (Dries) - Italy - 8 Tests - 2016
Van Zyl, CC (Cornelius) - Italy - 8 Tests - 2011-2012
Van Zyl, WP (Piet) - Namibia - 19 Tests - 2007-2011
Van Zyl, R (Riaan) - USA - 13 Tests - 2003-2004
Vickerman, DJ (Dan) - Australia - 63 Tests - 2002-2011
Viljoen, F (Francois) - USA - 16 Tests - 2004-2006
Visser, W (Wim) - Italy - 22 Tests - 1999-2001
Volschenk, R (Bloues) - Russia - 9 Tests - 2002
Waters, FHH (Fraser) - England - 3 Tests - 2001-2004
White-Cooper, WRS (Steve) - England - 2 Tests - 2001
Williamson, RH (Rupert) - England - 5 Tests - 1908-1909
Wilson, AW (Andy) - Scotland - 1 Test - 2005
Wilson, DS (Tug) - England - 8 Tests - 1953-1955
Zaayman, C (Johan) - Namibia - 12 Tests - 1997-1999

RUGBY WORLD RECORDS - TIER-ONE COUNTRIES

Compiled by Kobus Smit

PLAYER RECORDS
APPEARANCES
Most Test Matches

Matches	Player	Career
148	RH McCaw *(New Zealand)*	2001-2015
141	BG O'Driscoll *(Ireland/Lions)*	1999-2014
139	GM Gregan *(Australia)*	1994-2007
134*	GD Jenkins *(Wales/Lions)*	2002-2016
132	KF Mealamu *(New Zealand)*	2002-2015
130	RJR O'Gara *(Ireland/Lions)*	2000-2013
127	V Matfield *(South Africa)*	2001-2015
124*	BG Habana *(South Africa)*	2004-2016
121*	SM Parisse *(Italy)*	2002-2016

Most Matches By Position
Fullback

Matches	Player	Career
87	PC Montgomery *(South Africa)*	1997-2008
86	JM Muliaina *(New Zealand)*	2003-2011
81	S Blanco *(France)*	1980-1991
69	JL Sadourny *(France)*	1991-2001
69	CE Latham *(Australia)*	1998-2007
67	AG Hastings *(Scotland/Lions)*	1986-1995
67*	RDJ Kearney *(Ireland/Lions)*	2008-2016

Wing

123*	BG Habana *(South Africa)*	2004-2016
91	R Underwood *(England/Lions)*	1984-1996
89	SM Williams *(Wales/Lions)*	2000-2011
85	DI Campese *(Australia)*	1982-1996
84*	SF Lamont *(Scotland)*	2004-2016

Centre

140	BG O'Driscoll *(Ireland/Lions)*	1999-2014
104	PJP Sella *(France)*	1982-1995
96	MA Nonu *(New Zealand)*	2003-2015
94	J de Villiers *(South Africa)*	2002-2015
93	CG Smith *(New Zealand)*	2004-2015
87*	JH Roberts *(Wales/Lions)*	2008-2016

Flyhalf

129	RJR O'Gara *(Ireland/Lions)*	2000-2013
100	SM Jones *(Wales/Lions)*	1998-2011
96	DW Carter *(New Zealand)*	2003-2015
90	JP Wilkinson *(England/Lions)*	1998-2011
87	SJ Larkham *(Australia)*	1996-2007

NOTE: SA's most capped flyhalf is Morné Steyn (64).

Most Matches By Position

Scrumhalf

Matches	Player	Career
139	GM Gregan *(Australia)*	1994-2007
101	A Troncon *(Italy)*	1994-2007
98	PA Stringer *(Ireland)*	2000-2011
87	JH van der Westhuizen *(SA)*	1993-2003

Prop

134*	GD Jenkins *(Wales/Lions)*	2002-2016
119*	ML Castrogiovanni *(Italy)*	2002-2016
119	J Leonard *(England/Lions)*	1990-2003
118	TD Woodcock *(New Zealand)*	2002-2015
108	JJ Hayes *(Ireland/Lions)*	2000-2010

NOTE: SA's most capped prop is Tendai Mtawarira (87).*

Hooker

131	KF Mealamu *(New Zealand)*	2002-2015
117*	ST Moore *(Australia)*	2005-2016
102*	RW Ford *(Scotland)*	2004-2016
100*	RD Best *(Ireland)*	2005-2016
96	JW Smit *(South Africa)*	2000-2011
92	SBT Fitzpatrick *(New Zealand)*	1986-1997

Lock

127	V Matfield *(South Africa)*	2001-2015
116	NC Sharpe *(Australia)*	2002-2012
113	PJ O'Connell *(Ireland/Lions)*	2002-2015
106*	AW Jones *(Wales/Lions)*	2007-2016
92	MO Johnson *(England/Lions)*	1993-2003

Flank

145	RH McCaw *(New Zealand)*	2001-2015
104	ME Williams *(Wales/Lions)*	1996-2012
101	M Bergamasco *(Italy)*	1998-2015
98	GB Smith *(Australia)*	2000-2013
79	TS Dusautoir *(France)*	2006-2015
79	SWP Burger *(South Africa)*	2003-2015

No 8

111*	SM Parisse *(Italy)*	2002-2016
94*	JPR Heaslip *(Ireland/Lions)*	2006-2016
91*	KJ Read *(New Zealand)*	2009-2016
61*	TT Faletau *(Wales/Lions)*	2011-2016
58	LBN Dallaglio *(England/Lions)*	1995-2007

NOTE: SA's most capped No 8 is Pierre Spies (48).

Substitute

55	KF Mealamu *(New Zealand)*	2002-2015
47*	SM Cronin *(Ireland)*	2009-2016
46	PAT Weepu *(New Zealand)*	2004-2013
44	EG Reddan *(Ireland)*	2006-2016
44*	JA Slipper *(Australia)*	2010-2016
43	AH le Roux *(South Africa)*	1998-2002
43	RJR O'Gara *(Ireland/Lions)*	2000-2013
43	R Pienaar *(South Africa)*	2006-2015
43*	ST Polota-Nau *(Australia)*	2005-2016
40	BJ Franks *(New Zealand)*	2010-2015

Most Matches As A Captain

Matches	Player	Career
110	RH McCaw *(New Zealand)*	2004-2015
84	BG O'Driscoll *(Ireland/Lions)*	2002-2012
83	JW Smit *(South Africa)*	2003-2011
73*	SM Parisse *(Italy)*	2008-2016
59	WDC Carling *(England)*	1988-1996
59	GM Gregan *(Australia)*	2001-2007
56	TS Dusautoir *(France)*	2009-2015

Springboks That Represented Two Countries

Player	Teams (Caps)	Career
BH Heatlie	South Africa *(6)*, Argentina *(1)*	1891-1910
WMC McEwan	Scotland *(16)*, South Africa *(2)*	1894-1903
A Frew	Scotland *(3)*, South Africa *(1)*	1901-1903
HH Ferris	Ireland *(1)*, South Africa *(1)*	1901-1903
FW Mellish	England *(6)*, South Africa *(6)*	1920-1924
JH Gage	Ireland *(4)*, South Africa *(1)*	1926-1933
AC Garvey	Zimbabwe *(10)*, South Africa *(28)*	1990-1999
J Allan	Scotland *(9)*, South Africa *(13)*	1990-1996
JC Stewart	Canada *(14)*, South Africa *(3)*	1991-1998
CP Strauss	South Africa *(15)*, Australia *(11)*	1992-1999

Longest Career

Player (Teams)	Career	Mat	From Date	To Date	Career
H Porta *(Argentina/S America)*	1971-1990	66	10/10/1971	10/11/1990	19y 31d
BH Heatlie *(South Africa/Argentina)*	1891-1910	7	29/08/1891	12/06/1910	18y 287d
M Bergamasco *(Italy)*	1998-2015	106	18/11/1998	04/10/2015	16y 320d
TH Vile *(Wales/Lions)*	1904-1921	11	23/07/1904	05/02/1921	16y 197d
A Masi *(Italy)*	1999-2015	95	26/08/1999	19/09/2015	16y 24d
MH Loffreda *(Argentina/S America)*	1978-1994	50	14/10/1978	15/10/1994	16y 1d

PLAYER RECORDS
CAREER SCORING
Most Individual Points

Points	Player	Career
1598	DW Carter (New Zealand)	2003-2015
1246	JP Wilkinson (England/Lions)	1998-2011
1090	NR Jenkins (Wales/Lions)	1991-2002
1083	RJR O'Gara (Ireland/Lions)	2000-2013
1010	D Dominguez (Argentina/Italy)	1989-2003
970	SM Jones (Wales/Lions)	1998-2011
967	AP Mehrtens (New Zealand)	1995-2004
911	MP Lynagh (Australia)	1984-1995
893	PC Montgomery (South Africa)	1997-2008
878	MC Burke (Australia)	1993-2004
809	CD Paterson (Scotland)	1999-2011
736*	M Steyn (South Africa)	2009-2016
733	AG Hastings (Scotland/Lions)	1986-1995

Most Individual Tries

Tries	Player	Career
67*	BG Habana (South Africa)	2004-2016
64	DI Campese (Australia)	1982-1996
60	SM Williams (Wales/Lions)	2000-2011
50	R Underwood (England/Lions)	1984-1996
49	DC Howlett (New Zealand)	2000-2007
47	BG O'Driscoll (Ireland/Lions)	1999-2014
46	CM Cullen (New Zealand)	1996-2002
46	JT Rokocoko (New Zealand)	2003-2010
45*	SJ Savea (New Zealand)	2012-2016
44	JW Wilson (New Zealand)	1993-2001

NOTE: Daisuku Ohata of Japan scored 69 career tries between 1996-2006.

Most Individual Tries By Position
Fullback

Tries	Player	Career
40	CM Cullen (New Zealand)	1996-2002
36	CE Latham (Australia)	1998-2007
33	S Blanco (France)	1980-1991

NOTE: Most tries for SA by Percy Montgomery (18).

Wing

67*	BG Habana (South Africa)	2004-2016
60	SM Williams (Wales/Lions)	2000-2011
52	DI Campese (Australia)	1982-1996
50	R Underwood (England/Lions)	1984-1996

Centre

47	BG O'Driscoll (Ireland/Lions)	1999-2014
31	JC Guscott (England/Lions)	1989-1999
31	WJH Greenwood (England/Lions)	1997-2005
29	MA Nonu (New Zealand)	2003-2015

NOTE: Most tries for SA by Jaque Fourie (28).

Flyhalf

25	DW Carter (New Zealand)	2003-2015
20	SJ Larkham (Australia)	1996-2007
16	RJR O'Gara (Ireland/Lions)	2000-2013
14	MP Lynagh (Australia)	1984-1995
14	CJ Spencer (New Zealand)	1997-2004

NOTE: Most tries for SA by Morné Steyn (8*).

Scrumhalf

38	JH van der Westhuizen (SA)	1993-2003
24	JW Marshall (New Zealand)	1995-2005
20	GO Edwards (Wales/Lions)	1967-1978

Prop

12*	ML Castrogiovanni (Italy)	2002-2016
10	TD Woodcock (New Zealand)	2002-2015

NOTE: Most tries for SA by Gurthrö Steenkamp (6).

Hooker

15	KGM Wood (Ireland/Lions)	1994-2003
12	SBT Fitzpatrick (New Zealand)	1986-1997
11	BW du Plessis (South Africa)	2007-2015

Most Individual Tries By Position
Lock

Tries	Player	Career
13	PL Sporleder *(Argentina)*	1990-2003
12	MG Andrews *(South Africa)*	1994-2001

NOTE: M Gorgodze (Georgia) & H Ono (Japan) scored 13 tries each in their respective careers.

Flank

26	RH McCaw *(New Zealand)*	2001-2015
20	CL Charvis *(Wales/Lions)*	1996-2007
18	RA Martin *(Argentina)*	1994-2003
17	NA Back *(England/Lions)*	1994-2005

NOTE: Most tries for SA by Schalk Burger (14).

No 8

21*	KJ Read *(New Zealand)*	2008-2016
14	MZV Brooke *(New Zealand)*	1987-1997
13*	SM Parisse *(Italy)*	2002-2016

NOTES: Most tries for SA by Pierre Spies (7). D Ormaechea of Uruguay scored 29 career tries.

Substitute

6	JA Paul *(Australia)*	1998-2006
6*	DA Mitchell *(Australia)*	2005-2016
6*	BJ Barrett *(New Zealand)*	2012-2016

NOTE: Most tries for SA by Bob Skinstad (4).

Most Individual Conversions

Conversions	Player	Career
293	DW Carter *(New Zealand)*	2003-2015
176	RJR O'Gara *(Ireland/Lions)*	2000-2013
169	AP Mehrtens *(New Zealand)*	1995-2004
169	JP Wilkinson *(England/Lions)*	1998-2011
160	SM Jones *(Wales/Lions)*	1998-2011
153	PC Montgomery *(South Africa)*	1997-2008

Most Individual Penalty Goals

Penalty Goals	Player	Career
281	DW Carter *(New Zealand)*	2003-2015
255	JP Wilkinson *(England/Lions)*	1998-2011
248	NR Jenkins *(Wales/Lions)*	1991-2002
213	D Dominguez *(Argentina/Italy)*	1989-2003
202	RJR O'Gara *(Ireland/Lions)*	2000-2013

NOTE: Most penalties for SA by Morné Steyn (154).*

Most Individual Drop Goals

DGs	Player	Career
36	JP Wilkinson *(England/Lions)*	1998-2011
28	H Porta *(Argentinia/South America)*	1971-1990
23	CR Andrew *(England/Lions)*	1985-1997
20	D Dominguez *(Argentina/Italy)*	1989-2003
18	HE Botha *(South Africa)*	1980-1992

Most Individual Yellow Cards

Y/C	Player	Career
7	M Bortolami *(Italy)*	2001-2015
7*	BG Habana *(South Africa)*	2004-2016
6	SWP Burger *(South Africa)*	2003-2015
6*	QS Cooper *(Australia)*	2008-2016
6*	JAW Haskell *(England)*	2007-2016
6*	MK Hooper *(Australia)*	2012-2016

Most Matches In A Career Without Scoring A Try

Matches	Player	Career
90*	OT Franks *(New Zealand)*	2009-2016
86*	JA Slipper *(Australia)*	2010-2016
83	S Perugini *(Italy)*	2000-2011

NOTE: *Cobus Visagie (SA) played in 29 Test matches (1999-2003) without scoring a try.*

Most Consecutive Matches Scoring A Try

Tries	Player	Start Date	Opposition	End Date	Opposition
8	JJ Kirwan *(New Zealand)*	14/06/1987	v Wales	30/07/1988	v Australia
8	CM Cullen *(New Zealand)*	16/06/2000	v Tonga	11/11/2000	v France
7	DC Howlett *(New Zealand)*	16/06/2000	v Tonga	30/06/2001	v France

NOTE: *Both Danie Gerber (1982-1984) and Chester Williams (1994-1995) of South Africa crossed the tryline in 6 consecutive Test matches.*

MOST MATCHES BEFORE SCORING A TRY

Matches	Player	Start Date	Opposition	End Date	Opposition
80	NGA Mas *(France)*	28/06/2003	v New Zealand	05/09/2015	v Scotland
61	DJ Lydiate *(Wales/Lions)*	21/11/2009	v Argentina	05/11/2016	v Australia
54	SM Kepu *(Australia)*	08/11/2008	v Italy	25/07/2015	v Argentina
50	J Leonard *(England)*	28/07/1990	v Argentina	23/11/1996	v Italy

NOTE: *It took Eben Etzebeth (SA) 33 Test matches for his first Test try.*

PLAYER RECORDS

MATCH SCORING

Most Points In a Match

Points	Player	Opposition	Venue	Date
50	ER Morgan *(Argentina)*	v Paraguay	San Pablo	14/10/1973
45	SD Culhane *(New Zealand)*	v Japan	Bloemfontein	04/06/1995
45	JM Núñez Piossek *(Argentina)*	v Paraguay	Montevideo	27/04/2003

NOTES: *T Kurihara (Japan) scored 60 points v Chinese Taipei in 2002. Percy Montgomery (SA) scored 35 points v Namibia in Cape Town in 2007.*

Most Tries In a Match

Tries	Player	Opposition	Venue	Date
11	U O'Farrell *(Argentina)*	v Brazil	Buenos Aires	13/09/1951
9	JM Núñez Piossek *(Argentina)*	v Paraguay	Montevideo	27/04/2003
8	GM Jorge *(Argentina)*	v Brazil	São Paulo	02/10/1993
6	ER Morgan *(Argentina)*	v Paraguay	São Paulo	14/10/1973
6	GM Jorge *(Argentina)*	v Brazil	Montevideo	08/10/1989
6	MCG Ellis *(New Zealand)*	v Japan	Bloemfontein	04/06/1995

| 6 | T Chavhanga *(South Africa)* | v Uruguay | East London | 11/06/2005 |
| 6 | F Barrea *(Argentina)* | v Brazil | Santiago | 23/05/2012 |

NOTE: A Billington of Hong Kong scored 10 tries v Singapore in Kuala Lumpur on 27/10/1994

Most Conversions in a Match

Cons	Player	Opposition	Venue	Date
20	SD Culhane *(New Zealand)*	v Japan	Bloemfontein	04/06/1995
16	JL Cilley *(Argentina)*	v Paraguay	Mendoza	01/05/2002
16	MS Rogers *(Australia)*	v Namibia	Adelaide	25/10/2003
15	PJ Grayson *(England)*	v Netherlands	Huddersfield	14/11/1998

NOTE: Percy Montgomery (SA) scored 12 conversions v Namibia in Cape Town in 2007.

Most Penalty Goals in a Match

Pens	Player	Opposition	Venue	Date
9	AP Mehrtens *(New Zealand)*	v Australia	Auckland	24/07/1999
9	NR Jenkins *(Wales)*	v France	Cardiff	28/08/1999
9	AP Mehrtens *(New Zealand)*	v France	Paris	11/11/2000

NOTE: Morné Steyn (SA) scored 8 penalty goals v New Zealand in Durban in 2009.

Most Drop Goals in a Match

DGs	Player	Opposition	Venue	Date
5	JH de Beer *(South Africa)*	v England	Paris	24/10/1999
4	AS Pretorius *(South Africa)*	v England	London	25/11/2006

Most Points in a Debut Match

Points	Player	Opposition	Venue	Date
45	SD Culhane *(New Zealand)*	v Japan	Bloemfontein	04/06/1995
44	CC Hodgson (England)	v Romania	London	17/11/2001
33	CJ Spencer *(New Zealand)*	v Argentina	Wellington	21/06/1997
31	E de Forteza *(Argentina)*	v Paraguay	Asunción	25/09/1975
30	T Chavhanga *(South Africa)*	v Uruguay	East London	11/06/2005

Most Tries in a Debut Match

Tries	Player	Opposition	Venue	Date
7	U O'Farrell *(Argentina)*	v Uruguay	Buenos Aires	09/09/1951
6	GM Jorge *(Argentina)*	v Brazil	Montevideo	08/10/1989
6	T Chavhanga *(South Africa)*	v Uruguay	East London	11/06/2005
5	D Lambert *(England)*	v France	Richmond	05/01/1907
5	P Grande *(Argentina)*	v Paraguay	Asunción	03/10/1998

Most Conversions in a Debut Match

Cons	Player	Opposition	Venue	Date
20	SD Culhane *(New Zealand)*	v Japan	Bloemfontein	04/06/1995
14	CC Hodgson *(England)*	v Romania	London	17/11/2001
11	E de Forteza *(Argentina)*	v Paraguay	Asunción	25/09/1975
10	P Guarrochena *(Argentina)*	v Paraguay	Tucumán	29/10/1977
10	CJ Spencer *(New Zealand)*	v Argentina	Wellington	21/06/1997
10	PF Fernández Fiant *(Argentina)*	v Chile	Montevideo	01/05/2013

NOTE: Edrich Lubbe (SA) scored 7 conversions v Tonga in Cape Town in 1997.

Most Penalty Goals in a Debut Match

Pens	Player	Opposition	Venue	Date
6	KJ Crowley *(New Zealand)*	v England	Christchurch	01/06/1985
6	AG Hastings *(Scotland)*	v France	Edinburgh	18/01/1986
5	AO Geffin *(South Africa)*	v New Zealand	Cape Town	16/07/1949
5	JF Karam *(New Zealand)*	v Wales	Cardiff	02/12/1972
5	R Blair *(South Africa)*	v World XV	Pretoria	27/08/1977
5	SP Howarth *(New Zealand)*	v South Africa	Dunedin	09/07/1994
5	PJ Grayson *(England)*	v W Samoa	London	16/12/1995
5	G Ross *(Scotland)*	v Tonga	Edinburgh	10/11/2001
5	RS Wakarua-Noema *(Italy)*	v Tonga	Canberra	15/10/2003

NOTE: R Warren of Samoa scored 8 penalty goals v Tonga in Apia in 2004

Most Drop Goals in a Debut Match

D/G's	Player	Opposition	Venue	Date
2	RC Mackenzie *(Scotland)*	v Ireland	Belfast	19/02/1877
2	TA Harris-Smith *(Argentina)*	v Scotland XV	Buenos Aires	13/09/1969
2	G Laporte *(France)*	v Ireland	Dublin	07/02/1981
2	CR Andrew *(England)*	v Romania	London	05/01/1985
2	DJ Knox *(Australia)*	v Fiji	Brisbane	10/08/1985
2	FM Botica *(New Zealand)*	v France	Christchurch	28/06/1986

NOTE: All of Bennie Osler (1924), Gerald Bosch (1974) and Naas Botha (1980) for South Africa scored one drop goal in their debut matches.

PLAYER RECORDS
BY RESULT
Most Wins by a Player

Player	Matches	Won	Career
RH McCaw *(New Zealand)*	148	131	2001-2015
KF Mealamu *(New Zealand)*	132	114	2002-2015
TD Woodcock *(New Zealand)*	118	102	2002-2015
DW Carter *(New Zealand)*	112	99	2003-2015
GM Gregan *(Australia)*	139	93	1994-2007
MA Nonu *(New Zealand)*	103	91	2003-2015

NOTE: Bryan Habana (SA) won 79 of 124 Test matches and Victor Matfield (SA) 79 of 127.

Most Losses by a Player

Player	Matches	Lost	Career
ML Castrogiovanni *(Italy)*	119	88*	2002-2016
SM Parisse *(Italy)*	121	88*	2002-2016
M Bortolami *(Italy)*	112	82	2001-2015
M Bergamasco *(Italy)*	106	75	1998-2015
A Masi *(Italy)*	95	72	1999-2015
A Zanni *(Italy)*	99	71*	2005-2016
GD Jenkins *(Wales/Lions)*	134	70*	2002-2016
A Lo Cicero Vaina *(Italy)*	103	70	2000-2013

NOTE: Victor Matfield (SA) lost 46 of 127 Test matches.

Most Draws by a Player

Player	Matches	Drawn	Carer
WJ McBride *(Ireland/Lions)*	80	13	1962-1975
CMH Gibson *(Ireland/Lions)*	81	11	1964-1979
M Crauste *(France)*	63	9	1957-1966
GO Edwards *(Wales/Lions)*	63	8	1967-1978
TJ Kiernan *(Ireland/Lions)*	59	8	1960-1973
JF Slattery *(Ireland/Lions)*	65	8	1970-1984

NOTE: Both Frik du Preez and Jan Ellis (South Africa) played in 38 Test matches with 6 draws.

Most Points in a Calender Year

Points	Player	Year	Matches
263	NR Jenkins *(Wales)*	1999	14
233	JP Wilkinson *(England)*	2003	14
219	PC Montgomery *(South Africa)*	2007	14
203	DW Carter *(NewZealand)*	2008	15
197	OA Farrell *(England)*	2016	12
196	AG Hastings *(Scotland)*	1995	10
194	DW Carter *(NewZealand)*	2010	13

Most Tries in a Calender Year

Tries	Player	Year	Matches
17	JT Rokocoko *(NewZealand)*	2003	12
16	JM Núñez Piossek *(Argentina)*	2003	9
14	U O'Farrell *(Argentina)*	1951	3
14	DC Howlett *(NewZealand)*	2003	14
13	GM Jorge *(Argentina)*	1993	7
13	BG Habana *(South Africa)*	2007	11

NOTE: D Ohata (Japan) scored 17 tries in 6 matches in 2002.

Bryan Habana.

Highest % of Matches Won (Min. 20 matches)

Player	Matches	Won	%	Span
WWV Crockett *(New Zealand)**	58	56	96,55%	2009-2016
TNJ Kerr-Barlow *(New Zealand)**	25	24	96,00%	2012-2016
AF Boric *(New Zealand)*	24	23	95,83%	2008-2011
S Williams *(New Zealand)*	33	31	93,94%	2010-2015
IJA Dagg *(New Zealand)**	61	57	93,44%	2010-2016
BA Retallick *(New Zealand)**	60	56	93,33%	2012-2016
SJ Cane *(New Zealand)**	40	37	92,50%	2012-2016
AW Cruden *(New Zealand)**	47	43	91,49%	2010-2016

NOTE: Adrian Garvey (SA) played in 28 Test matches, 24 on the winning side (85,71%)

Lowest % of Matches Won (Min. 20 matches)

Player	Matches	Won	%	Span
M Communeau *(France)*	21	1	4,76%	1906-1913
L Sarto *(Italy)**	30	4	13,33%	2013-2016
GM Garcia *(Italy)**	44	7	15,91%	2008-2016
RB Prosser *(Australia)*	25	4	16,00%	1967-1972
SJ Smith *(Ireland)*	25	4	16,00%	1988-1993
LA Cassayet-Armagnac *(France)*	31	5	16,13%	1920-1927
JW Cole *(Australia)*	24	4	16,67%	1968-1974
G Palazzani *(Italy)**	22	4	18,18%	2014-2016
F Minto *(Italy)**	31	6	19,35%	2012-2016

NOTE: Braam van Straaten (SA) played in 21 Test matches, 9 on the winning side (42,86%)

Highest % of Matches Won as a Captain (Min. 10 matches)

Player	Matches	Won	%	Span
KJ Read *(New Zealand)**	22	21	95,45%	2012-2016
WT Shelford *(New Zealand)*	14	13	92,86%	1988-1990
DM Hartley *(England)**	14	13	92,86%	2012-2016
WJA Davies *(England)*	11	10	90,91%	1921-1923
AG Dalton *(New Zealand)*	17	15	88,24%	1981-1985
RH McCaw *(New Zealand)*	110	97	88,18%	2004-2015
RD Thorne *(New Zealand)*	23	20	86,96%	2002-2007
M du Plessis *(South Africa)*	15	13	86,67%	1975-1980

Lowest % of Matches Won as a Captain (Min. 20 matches)

Player	Matches	Won	%	Span
JM Fernandez Lobbe *(Argentina)*	20	4	20,00%	2008-2013
SM Parisse *(Italy)**	73	15	20,55%	2008-2016
A Creevy *(Argentina)**	29	9	31,03%	2014-2016
A Troncon *(Italy)*	21	7	33,33%	2000-2007
M Innocenti *(Italy)*	20	7	35,00%	1985-1988
M Bortolami *(Italy)*	39	14	35,90%	2002-2014

NOTE: Dawie de Villiers (SA) played in 22 Test matches as captain, 13 on the winning side (59,09%)

Most Consecutive Wins

Player	Matches	Start Date	Opposition	End Date	Opposition
WWV Crockett *(New Zealand)*	30*	23/08/2014	v Australia	26/11/2016	v France
LBN Dallaglio *(England)*	28	24/06/2000	v South Africa	21/02/2004	v Scotland
BJ Kay *(England)*	22	23/03/2002	v Wales	21/02/2004	v Scotland
WJH Greenwood *(England)*	21	23/03/2002	v Wales	21/02/2004	v Scotland
LR MacDonald *(New Zealand)*	21	27/08/2005	v South Africa	23/09/2007	v Scotland
MA Nonu *(New Zealand)*	21	11/10/2003	v Italy	05/07/2008	v South Africa
AF Boric *(New Zealand)*	21	02/08/2008	v Australia	02/10/2011	v Canada
JT Robinson *(England)*	20	07/04/2002	v Italy	21/02/2004	v Scotland
BJ Franks *(New Zealand)*	20	09/09/2011	v Tonga	24/11/2013	v Ireland
CC Faumuina *(New Zealand)*	20	18/10/2014	v Australia	22/10/2016	v Australia
BA Retallick *(New Zealand)*	20*	15/08/2015	v Australia	26/11/2016	v France

NOTE: All of Mark Andrews, James Dalton, Pieter Rossouw, André Snyman and Gary Teichmann of South Africa played in 17 consecutive Test wins between 23/08/1997 and 28/11/1998.

Wyatt Crockett.

Most Consecutive Losses

Player	Matches	Start Date	Opposition	End Date	Opposition
MT Bosch *(Argentina)*	18	08/09/2012	v New Zealand	17/09/2014	v New Zealand
SM Parisse *(Italy)*	17	08/11/2008	v Australia	20/11/2010	v Australia
JM Fernández Lobbe *(Argentina)*	15	17/11/2012	v France	20/09/2015	v New Zealand
M Bortolami *(Italy)*	14	09/06/2012	v Argentina	21/06/2014	v Japan
ML Castrogiovanni *(Italy)*	14	23/11/2013	v Argentina	19/09/2015	v France
LA Cassayet-Armagnac *(France)*	13	18/05/1924	v USA	26/02/1927	v Wales
MRG Giacheri *(Italy)*	13	14/07/2001	v Argentina	30/08/2003	v Ireland
S Perugini *(Italy)*	13	08/11/2008	v Australia	21/11/2009	v South Africa
A Creevy *(Argentina)*	13	17/11/2012	v France	27/09/2014	v New Zealand

NOTE: All of Lionel Wilson, Jannie Engelbrecht and John Gainsford of South Africa played in 7 consecutive Test losses between 25/07/1964 and 21/08/1965.

TEAM RECORDS
MATCH SCORING
Biggest Team Win

Points (Score)	Team	Opposition	Venue	Date
152 (152-0)	Argentina	v Paraguay	Mendoza	01/05/2002
144 (144-0)	Argentina	v Paraguay	Montevideo	27/04/2003
142 (142-0)	Australia	v Namibia	Adelaide	25/10/2003
140 (147-7)	Argentina	v Venezuela	Santiago	01/05/2004
134 (134-0)	England	v Romania	London	17/11/2001
131 (134-3)	South Africa	v Uruguay	East London	11/06/2005
128 (145-17)	New Zealand	v Japan	Bloemfontein	04/06/1995

Most Team Points in a Match

Points (Score)	Team	Opposition	Venue	Date
152 (152-0)	Argentina	v Paraguay	Mendoza	01/05/2002
147 (147-7)	Argentina	v Venezuela	Santiago	01/05/2004
145 (145-17)	New Zealand	v Japan	Bloemfontein	04/06/1995
144 (144-0)	Argentina	v Paraguay	Montevideo	27/04/2003
142 (142-0)	Australia	v Namibia	Adelaide	25/10/2003
134 (134-0)	England	v Romania	London	17/11/2001
134 (134-3)	South Africa	v Uruguay	East London	11/06/2005

NOTE: Hong Kong won 164–13 v Singapore in Kuala Lumpur in 1994.

Most Team Tries in a Match

Tries	Team	Opposition	Venue	Date
24	Argentina	v Paraguay	Mendoza	01/05/2002
24	Argentina	v Paraguay	Montevideo	27/04/2003
23	Argentina	v Venezuela	Santiago	01/05/2004
22	Australia	v Namibia	Adelaide	25/10/2003
21	New Zealand	v Japan	Bloemfontein	04/06/1995
21	South Africa	v Uruguay	East London	11/06/2005
20	Argentina	v Brazil	Montevideo	08/10/1989
20	England	v Romania	London	17/11/2001

NOTE: Hong Kong scored 26 tries v Singapore in Kuala Lumpur in 1994.

Most Team Conversions in a Match

Conversions	Team	Opposition	Venue	Date
20	New Zealand	v Japan	Bloemfontein	04/06/1995
16	Argentina	v Paraguay	Mendoza	01/05/2002
16	Australia	v Namibia	Adelaide	25/10/2003
16	Argentina	v Venezuela	Santiago	01/05/2004
15	Argentina	v Brazil	Santiago	09/10/1979
15	England	v Netherlands	Huddersfield	14/11/1998
14	England	v Romania	London	17/11/2001
14	Wales	v Japan	Cardiff	26/11/2004
14	New Zealand	v Portugal	Lyon	15/09/2007

NOTE: South Africa kicked 13 conversions v Italy in Durban in 1999 and v Uruguay in East London in 2005.

Most Team Penalty Goals in a Match

Penalty goals	Team	Opposition	Venue	Date
9	New Zealand	v Australia	Auckland	24/07/1999
9	Wales	v France	Cardiff	28/08/1999
9	New Zealand	v France	Paris	11/11/2000

NOTES: Japan kicked 9 penalties v Tonga in Tokyo in 1999 and Portugal kicked 9 penalties v Georgia in Lisbon in 2000. South Africa kicked 8 penalties v Scotland in Port Elizabeth in 2006 and 8 penalties v New Zealand in Durban in 2009.

Most Team Drop Goals in a Match

Drop doals	Team	Opposition	Venue	Date
5	South Africa	v England	Paris	24/10/1999
4	South Africa	v England	London	25/11/2006
4	Argentina	v France	Paris	22/11/2014

Most Team Yellow Cards in a Match

Yellow cards	Team	Opposition	Venue	Date
4	Italy	v France	Paris	02/02/2002
4	England	v New Zealand	London	29/11/2008

NOTES: Fiji received 5 yellow cards v Italy in Cremona in 2013. South Africa received 2 yellow cards in a match on 16 occasions.

Most Team Red Cards in a Match

Red cards	Team	Opposition	Venue	Date
2	France	v England	Paris	15/02/1992

NOTE: France is the only Tier 1 country that have received two red cards in a Test match. Four other countries, Fiji (2x), Canada, Samoa and USA have also received two red cards in a Test match.

Most Team Points Without Winning the Match

Team	Result	For	Against	Opposition	Venue	Date
Wales	lost	44	50	v Argentina	Tucumán	12/06/2004
New Zealand	lost	40	46	v South Africa	Johannesburg	19/08/2001
Australia	lost	40	44	v England	Sydney	25/06/2016
South Africa	lost	39	41	v Australia	Bloemfontein	04/09/2010
Wales	lost	37	53	v New Zealand	Sydney	02/11/2003
Wales	lost	36	38	v South Africa	Cardiff	06/11/2004

NOTE: Namibia lost 54-57 v Madagascar in Antananarive in 2012.

Most Team Tries Without Winning the Match

Team	Result	Score	Tries	Opposition	Venue	Date
Australia	lost	22-25	6	v NZ Maori	Sydney	24/06/1922
South Africa	lost	35-55	5	v New Zealand	Auckland	09/08/1997
Australia	lost	35-39	5	v New Zealand	Sydney	15/07/2000
Wales	lost	44-50	5	v Argentina	Tucumán	12/06/2004
Wales	lost	34-38	5	v Fiji	Nantes	29/09/2007
France	lost	35-55	5	v England	London	21/03/2015
Australia	lost	40-44	5	v England	Sydney	25/06/2016

NOTE: Namibia scored 8 tries but lost 54-57 v Madagascar in Antananarive in 2012.

Biggest Team Lead at Half-time

Team	Half-time	H-Tdiff	Result	Opposition	Venue	Date
New Zealand	84-3	81	145-17	v Japan	Bloemfontein	04/06/1995
England	72-0	72	134-0	v Romania	London	17/11/2001
Italy	71-0	71	104-8	v Czech Republic	Viadana	18/05/1994
Australia	69-0	69	142-0	v Namibia	Adelaide	25/10/2003
Argentina	64-0	64	111-0	v Brazil	Santiago	23/05/2012
Argentina	69-7	62	147-7	v Venezuela	Santiago	01/05/2004
Wales	56-0	56	98-0	v Japan	Cardiff	26/11/2004
South Africa	56-0	56	134-3	v Uruguay	East London	11/06/2005

Most Team Points at Half-time

Team	Half-time	Result	Opposition	Venue	Date
New Zealand	84-3	145-17	v Japan	Bloemfontein	04/06/1995
England	72-0	134-0	v Romania	London	17/11/2001
Italy	71-0	104-8	v Czech Republic	Viadana	18/05/1994
Australia	69-0	142-0	v Namibia	Adelaide	25/10/2003
Argentina	69-7	147-7	v Venezuela	Santiago	01/05/2004
Argentina	64-0	111-0	v Brazil	Santiago	23/05/2012
Australia	57-3	92-10	v Spain	Madrid	01/11/2001
Wales	56-0	98-0	v Japan	Cardiff	26/11/2004
South Africa	56-0	134-3	v Uruguay	East London	11/06/2005

Biggest Team Lead at Half-time Without Winning the Match

Team	Half-time	H-Tdiff	Result	Opposition	Venue	Date
Wales	27-10	17	33-40	v France	Cardiff	25/09/1996
Australia	22-6	16	22-23	v NZ Maori	Sydney	08/07/1922
Ireland	19-3	16	26-32	v South Africa	Johannesburg	18/06/2016
Ireland	22-7	15	22-24	v New Zealand	Dublin	24/11/2013
England	23-9	14	26-26	v New Zealand	London	06/12/1997
Argentina	23-10	13	26-36	v Wales	Buenos Aires	05/06/1999
New Zealand	17-5	12	23-24	v South Africa	Durban	15/08/1998
Italy	23-11	12	30-39	v Ireland	Dublin	10/04/1999
Wales	18-6	12	28-28	v Scotland	Edinburgh	17/02/2001

NOTE: Chile led 27-0 at half-time, but lost the match 34-35 v Uruguay in Santiago in 2007. South Africa led 13-3 at half-time but lost 21-16 v British Isles in Cape Town in 1938.

Most Team Points at Half-time Without Winning the Match

Team	Half-time	Result	Opposition	Venue	Date
Australia	28-24	31-44	v South Africa	Pretoria	28/08/2010
Wales	27-10	33-40	v France	Cardiff	25/09/1996
New Zealand	27-33	40-46	v South Africa	Johannesburg	19/08/2000
Argentina	25-26	30-43	v Wales	Llanelli	21/11/1998
England	25-18	31-32	v Wales	London	11/04/1999

NOTES: Tonga led 31-10 at half-time, but lost the match 38-41 v Fiji in Apia in 2010. South Africa led 23-19 at half-time, but lost the match 32-35 v New Zealand in Johannesburg in 1997 and also led 23-17 at half-time, but lost the match v Australia in Melbourne in 2000.

TEAM RECORDS
MOST CONSECUTIVES

Most Consecutive Wins

Team	Matches	Start Date	Opposition	Venue	End Date	Opposition	Venue
New Zealand	18	15/08/2015	v Australia	Auckland	22/10/2016	v Australia	Auckland
New Zealand	17	18/09/1965	v South Africa	Auckland	14/06/1969	v Wales	Auckland
South Africa	17	23/08/1997	v Australia	Pretoria	28/11/1998	v Ireland	Dublin
New Zealand	17	08/06/2013	v France	Auckland	21/06/2014	v England	Hamilton
New Zealand	16	09/09/2011	v Tonga	Auckland	06/10/2012	v South Africa	Johannesburg
England	16*	10/10/2015	v Uruguay	Manchester	11/02/2017	v Wales	Cardiff
South Africa	15	08/10/1994	v Argentina	Port Elizabeth	02/07/1996	v Fiji	Pretoria
New Zealand	15	13/08/2005	v Australia	Sydney	26/08/2006	v South Africa	Pretoria
New Zealand	15	19/09/2009	v Australia	Wellington	11/09/2010	v Australia	Sydney
England	14	23/03/2006	v Wales	London	23/08/2003	v Wales	Cardiff

NOTE: Cyprus won 24 consecutive Test matches between 2008 and 2014.

Most Consecutive Matches Without Defeat

Team	Matches	Start Date	Opposition	Venue	End Date	Opposition	Venue
New Zealand	23	22/05/1987	v Italy	Auckland	04/08/1990	v Australia	Auckland
New Zealand	22	08/06/2013	v France	Auckland	27/09/2014	v Argentina	La Plata
New Zealand	20	09/09/2011	v Tonga	Auckland	24/11/2012	v Wales	Cardiff
New Zealand	18	15/08/2015	v Australia	Auckland	22/10/2016	v Australia	Auckland
New Zealand	17	22/07/1961	v France	Auckland	22/08/1964	v Australia	Christchurch
New Zealand	17	18/09/1965	v South Africa	Auckland	14/06/1969	v Wales	Auckland
South Africa	17	23/08/1997	v Australia	Pretoria	28/11/1998	v Ireland	Dublin
South Africa	16	06/08/1994	v New Zealand	Auckland	02/07/1996	v Fiji	Pretoria
England	16*	10/10/2015	v Uruguay	Manchester	11/02/2017	v Wales	Cardiff
South Africa	15	13/08/1960	v New Zealand	Bloemfontein	13/07/1963	v Australia	Pretoria
New Zealand	15	13/08/2005	v Australia	Sydney	26/08/2006	v South Africa	Pretoria
New Zealand	15	19/09/2009	v Australia	Wellington	11/09/2010	v Australia	Sydney

NOTE: Cyprus won 24 consecutive Test matches between 2008 and 2014.

Most Consecutive Matches Without a Win

Team	Matches	Start Date	Opposition	Venue	End Date	Opposition	Venue
France	18	28/01/1911	v England	London	17/02/1920	v Wales	Paris
Scotland	17	24/02/1951	v Ireland	Edinburgh	08/01/1955	v France	Paris
France	14	18/05/1924	v USA	Paris	26/02/1927	v Wales	Swansea
Ireland	13	28/01/1882	v Wales	Dublin	20/02/1886	v Scotland	Edinburgh
Scotland	13	05/03/1977	v France	Paris	20/02/1980	v Ireland	Dublin
Italy	13	08/11/2008	v Australia	Padova	21/11/2009	v South Africa	Udine
Australia	12	22/07/1899	v Britain	Brisbane	12/12/1908	v Wales	Cardiff
France	12	01/01/1906	v New Zealand	Paris	28/03/1910	v Ireland	Paris
Ireland	11	25/02/1961	v Scotland	Edinburgh	23/02/1963	v Scotland	Edinburgh
France	11	13/07/1968	v New Zealand	Christchurch	22/03/1969	v Wales	Paris
Ireland	11	12/10/1991	v Scotland	Edinburgh	20/02/1993	v France	Dublin

NOTES: Singapore did not win a Test match in 27 between November 1982 and July 1997. South Africa lost 7 consecutive Test matches from 25/07/1964 and 21/08/1965.

Most Consecutive Losses

Team	Matches	Start Date	Opposition	Venue	End Date	Opposition	Venue
France	18	28/01/1911	v England	London	17/02/1920	v Wales	Paris
Scotland	17	24/02/1952	v Ireland	Edinburgh	08/01/1955	v France	Paris
France	14	18/05/1924	v USA	Paris	26/02/1927	v Wales	Swansea
Italy	13	08/11/2008	v Australia	Padova	21/11/2009	v South Africa	Udine
France	12	01/01/1906	v New Zealand	Paris	28/03/1910	v Ireland	Paris
Ireland	11	18/02/1882	v Scotland	Glasgow	20/02/1886	v Scotland	Edinburgh
Ireland	11	12/10/1991	v Scotland	Edinburgh	20/02/1993	v France	Dublin

NOTES: Singapore lost 21 Test matches between November 1986 and July 1997. South Africa lost 7 consecutive Test matches from 25/07/1964 and 21/08/1965.

Most Consecutive Wins at Home

Team	Matches	Start Date	Opposition	Venue	End Date	Opposition	Venue
New Zealand	45*	19/09/2009	v Australia	Wellington	22/10/2016	v Australia	Auckland
New Zealand	30	21/06/2003	v Wales	Hamilton	05/07/2008	v South Africa	Wellington
England	22	15/10/1999	v Tonga	London	06/09/2003	v France	London
New Zealand	16	22/05/1987	v Italy	Auckland	04/08/1990	v Australia	Auckland
New Zealand	15	22/04/1995	v Canada	Auckland	27/06/1998	v England	Auckland
Wales	13	12/01/1907	v England	Swansea	25/03/1912	v France	Newport
Australia	13	15/06/1985	v Canada	Sydney	07/06/1987	v Ireland	Sydney
Scotland	13	21/01/1989	v Wales	Edinburgh	19/10/1991	v Samoa	Edinburgh
South Africa	13	11/06/1994	v England	Cape Town	03/08/1996	v Australia	Bloemfontein
Australia	12	29/08/1998	v New Zealand	Sydney	08/07/2000	v South Africa	Melbourne

Most Consecutive Matches Without Defeat at Home

Team	Matches	Start Date	Opposition	Venue	End Date	Opposition	Venue
New Zealand	45*	19/09/2009	v Australia	Wellington	22/10/2016	v Australia	Auckland
New Zealand	30	21/06/2003	v Wales	Hamilton	05/07/2008	v South Africa	Wellington
England	22	15/10/1999	v Tonga	London	06/09/2003	v France	London
New Zealand	18	09/07/1994	v South Africa	Dunedin	27/06/1998	v England	Auckland
France	17	10/11/2001	v South Africa	Paris	13/11/2004	v Australia	Paris
New Zealand	16	22/05/1987	v Italy	Auckland	04/08/1990	v Australia	Auckland
France	15	20/03/1982	v Ireland	Paris	12/04/1986	v Romania	Lille
England	14	25/01/1913	v France	London	15/03/1924	v Scotland	London
France	14	09/03/1958	v Australia	Paris	14/04/1962	v Ireland	Paris
Wales	14	20/01/1973	v England	Cardiff	18/03/1978	v France	Cardiff
Wales	13	12/01/1907	v England	Swansea	25/03/1912	v France	Newport
Australia	13	15/06/1985	v Canada	Sydney	07/06/1987	v Ireland	Sydney
Scotland	13	21/01/1989	v Wales	Edinburgh	19/10/1991	v Samoa	Edinburgh
South Africa	13	11/06/1994	v England	Cape Town	03/08/1996	v Australia	Bloemfontein
South Africa	13	12/06/2004	v Ireland	Bloemfontein	17/06/2006	v Scotland	Port Elizabeth

Most Consecutive Matches Without a Win at Home

Team	Matches	Start Date	Opposition	Venue	End Date	Opposition	Venue
Argentina	15	24/08/1952	v Ireland XV	Buenos Aires	01/10/1966	v SA Gazelles	Buenos Aires
Australia	11	22/07/1899	v Britain	Brisbane	25/06/1910	v New Zealand	Sydney
Australia	11	02/07/1910	v New Zealand	Sydney	24/06/1922	v NZ Maori	Sydney
France	10	28/02/1911	v Wales	Paris	17/02/1920	v Wales	Paris
Australia	10	25/08/1934	v New Zealand	Sydney	11/06/1949	v NZ Maori	Brisbane
Scotland	9	24/02/1951	v Ireland	Edinburgh	20/03/1954	v England	Edinburgh
Ireland	9	15/04/1961	v France	Dublin	23/01/1965	v France	Dublin
Italy	9	14/11/2014	v Argentina	Genova	12/11/2016	v New Zealand	Rome
France	8	18/05/1924	v USA	Paris	01/01/1927	v Ireland	Paris
Argentina	8	12/06/1910	v Britain XV	Flores	16/08/1936	v Britain XV	Buenos Aires
Wales	8	04/11/1989	v New Zealand	Cardiff	06/10/1991	v Samoa	Cardiff
Italy	8	08/11/2008	v Australia	Padova	21/11/2009	v South Africa	Udine
Argentina	8	24/08/2013	v South Africa	Mendoza	27/09/2014	v New Zealand	La Plata

NOTES: Japan played in 18 consecutive Test matches at home without a win between 1936 and 1967. On two occasions South Africa played in 6 consecutive home Tests without a win – 1891-1896 and 1971-1974.

Most Consecutive Losses at Home

Team	Matches	Start Date	Opposition	Venue	End Date	Opposition	Venue
Australia	11	02/07/1910	v New Zealand	Sydney	24/06/1922	v NZ Maori	Sydney
France	10	28/02/1911	v Wales	Paris	17/02/1920	v Wales	Paris
Argentina	10	31/08/1952	v Ireland XV	Buenos Aires	17/08/1960	v France	Buenos Aires
Australia	9	22/07/1899	v Britain	Brisbane	03/08/1907	v New Zealand	Brisbane
Scotland	9	24/02/1951	v Ireland	Edinburgh	20/03/1954	v England	Edinburgh
Italy	9	14/11/2014	v Argentina	Genova	12/11/2016	v New Zealand	Rome
France	8	18/05/1924	v USA	Paris	01/01/1927	v Ireland	Paris
Argentina	8	12/06/1910	v Britain XV	Flores	16/08/1936	v Britain XV	Buenos Aires
Australia	8	26/06/1937	v South Africa	Sydney	04/06/1949	v NZ Maori	Sydney
Italy	8	08/11/2008	v Australia	Padova	21/11/2009	v South Africa	Udine

Most Consecutive Losses at Home (Continued)

Team	Matches	Start Date	Opposition	End Date	Opposition	Venue
Argentina	8	24/08/2013	v South Africa	27/09/2014	v New Zealand	La Plata
South Africa	6	30/07/1891	v Britain	29/08/1896	v Britain	Kimberley
France	6	01/01/1906	v New Zealand	28/03/1910	v Ireland	Paris
Italy	6	16/11/1986	v Soviet Union	19/02/1989	v France XV	Brescia
Argentina	6	21/10/1995	v France	31/05/1997	v England	Buenos Aires
Ireland	6	12/11/1996	v Samoa	15/11/1997	v New Zealand	Dublin

Most Consecutive Wins Away from Home

Team	Matches	Start Date	Opposition	Venue	End Date	Opposition	Venue
Argentina	11	20/09/1936	v Chile	Valpariso	22/08/1964	v Chile	San Pablo
South Africa	10	08/11/1997	v Italy	Bologna	28/11/1998	v Ireland	Dublin
Australia	10	03/10/1999	v Romania	Belfast	11/11/2000	v Scotland	Edinburgh
New Zealand	10	20/09/2015	v Argentina	London	08/10/2016	v South Africa	Durban
New Zealand	9	02/07/1910	v Australia	Sydney	18/01/1925	v France	Toulouse
South Africa	9	04/09/1937	v New Zealand	Christchurch	02/06/1956	v Australia	Brisbane
Argentina	9	07/08/1971	v SA Gazelles	Pretoria	21/10/1973	v Chile	San Pablo
Australia	9	04/10/1991	v Argentina	Llanelli	21/11/1992	v Wales	Cardiff
England	9	12/10/2003	v Georgia	Perth	21/02/2004	v Scotland	Edinburgh
South Africa	9	25/08/2007	v Scotland	Edinburgh	24/11/2007	v Wales	Cardiff
New Zealand	9	22/08/2009	v Australia	Sydney	11/09/2010	v Australia	Sydney
New Zealand	8	23/11/2002	v Wales	Cardiff	08/11/2003	v South Africa	Melbourne
New Zealand	8	13/08/2005	v Australia	Sydney	26/08/2006	v South Africa	Pretoria

NOTE: Brazil won 12 consecutive Test matches away from home between 2006 and 2008.

Most Consecutive Matches Without Defeat Away From Home

Team	Matches	Start Date	Opposition	Venue	End Date	Opposition	Venue
New Zealand	13	26/05/1962	v Australia	Brisbane	22/06/1968	v Australia	Brisbane
England	12	11/03/1878	v Ireland	Dublin	08/01/1887	v Wales	Llanelli
Argentina	11	20/09/1936	v Chile	Valpariso	22/08/1964	v Chile	San Pablo

Team	Matches	Start Date	Opposition	Venue	End Date	Opposition	Venue
New Zealand	11	14/06/1987	v Wales	Brisbane	13/07/1991	v Argentina	Buenos Aires
South Africa	10	08/11/1997	v Italy	Bologna	28/11/1998	v Ireland	Dublin
Australia	10	03/10/1999	v Romania	Belfast	11/11/2000	v Scotland	Edinburgh
New Zealand	10	20/09/2015	v Argentina	London	08/10/2016	v South Africa	Durban
New Zealand	9	02/07/1910	v Australia	Sydney	18/01/1925	v France	Toulouse
South Africa	9	04/09/1937	v New Zealand	Christchurch	02/06/1956	v Australia	Brisbane
Argentina	9	07/08/1971	v SA Gazelles	Pretoria	21/10/1973	v Chile	San Pablo
South Africa	9	10/01/1970	v Ireland	Dublin	25/10/1980	v S America	Santiago
Australia	9	04/10/1991	v Argentina	Llanelli	21/11/1992	v Wales	Cardiff
New Zealand	9	16/11/2002	v France	Paris	08/11/2003	v South Africa	Melbourne
England	9	12/10/2003	v Georgia	Perth	21/02/2004	v Scotland	Edinburgh
South Africa	9	25/08/2007	v Scotland	Edinburgh	24/11/2007	v Wales	Cardiff
New Zealand	9	22/08/2009	v Australia	Sydney	11/09/2010	v Australia	Sydney
New Zealand	9	17/08/2013	v Australia	Sydney	27/09/2014	v Argentina	La Plata

Most Consecutive Matches Without a Win Away From Home

Team	Matches	Start Date	Opposition	Venue	End Date	Opposition	Venue
France	16	26/02/1921	v Wales	Cardiff	25/02/1928	v England	London
Scotland	15	19/03/1949	v England	London	25/02/1956	v Ireland	Dublin
England	15	05/02/1983	v Wales	Cardiff	23/05/1987	v Australia	Sydney
Italy	15	22/11/1998	v England	Huddersfield	17/03/2001	v Scotland	Edinburgh
Ireland	14	15/02/1875	v England	London	10/03/1888	v Scotland	Edinburgh
France	14	05/01/1907	v England	Richmond	31/01/1920	v England	London
Italy	14	07/02/2009	v England	London	11/09/2011	v Australia	North Shore City
Scotland	13	15/01/1977	v England	London	20/02/1982	v Ireland	Dublin
Ireland	13	04/03/1989	v Scotland	Edinburgh	16/01/1993	v Scotland	Edinburgh
Italy	12	09/02/2013	v Scotland	Edinburgh	14/02/2015	v England	London

NOTE: East Germany (1967–1983) and Singapore (1980–1997) played in 25 consecutive Test matches without a win away from home. South Africa (1961–1965) and (2002–2003) played in 7 consecutive Test matches without a win away from home.

Most Consecutive Losses From Home

Team	Matches	Start Date	Opposition	Venue	End Date	Opposition	Venue
Scotland	15	19/03/1949	v England	London	25/02/1956	v Ireland	Dublin
Italy	15	22/11/1998	v England	Huddersfield	17/03/2001	v Scotland	Edinburgh
Ireland	14	15/02/1875	v England	London	0/03/1888	v Scotland	Edinburgh
France	14	05/01/1907	v England	Richmond	31/01/1920	v England	London
France	14	08/04/1922	v Ireland	Dublin	25/02/1928	v England	London
England	14	19/03/1983	v Ireland	Dublin	23/05/1987	v Australia	Sydney
Italy	14	07/02/2009	v England	London	11/09/2011	v Australia	North Shore City
Italy	12	09/02/2013	v Scotland	Edinburgh	24/02/2015	v England	London
Ireland	10	14/02/1914	v England	London	23/02/1924	v Scotland	Inverleith
Wales	10	03/02/2002	v Ireland	Dublin	16/08/2003	v Ireland	Dublin
Wales	10	04/02/2006	v England	London	04/08/2007	v England	London

NOTES: East Germany had 25 consecutive losses away from home between 1967 and 1983. South Africa had 7 consecutive losses away from home between 2002 and 2003.

Most Consecutive Matches Scoring a Try

Team	Matches	Start Date	Opposition	Venue	End Date	Opposition	Venue
New Zealand	105	14/08/2004	v South Africa	Johannesburg	06/10/2012	v South Africa	Johannesburg
England	46	18/03/1911	v Scotland	London	19/03/1927	v Scotland	Edinburgh
Australia	46	16/11/2002	v England	London	15/07/2006	v South Africa	Brisbane
South Africa	44	02/09/1995	v Wales	Johannesburg	26/06/1999	v Wales	Cardiff
Argentina	41	25/04/2004	v Chile	Santiago	14/06/2008	v Scotland	Buenos Aires
France	36	18/01/1997	v Ireland	Dublin	31/10/1999	v New Zealand	London
South Africa	36	09/06/2012	v England	Durban	22/11/2014	v Italy	Padova
New Zealand	36*	23/08/2014	v Australia	Auckland	26/11/2016	v France	Paris

Most Consecutive Matches Scoring Four Tries or More

Team	Matches	Start Date	Opposition	Venue	End Date	Opposition	Venue
New Zealand	12	11/06/2016	v Wales	Auckland	12/11/2016	v Italy	Rome
South Africa	10	09/08/1997	v New Zealand	Auckland	27/06/1998	v Wales	Pretoria
England	7	03/02/2001	v Wales	Cardiff	16/06/2001	v USA	San Francisco
Argentina	6	12/10/1961	v Brazil	Montevideo	08/05/1965	v Zimbabwe	Harare
Argentina	6	08/08/1998	v Romania	Rosario	03/10/1998	v Paraguay	Asunción

Most Consecutive Matches Without Scoring a Try

Team	Matches	Start Date	Opposition	Venue	End Date	Opposition	Venue
Ireland	7	15/02/1875	v England	London	24/03/1879	v England	London
Scotland	6	05/03/1892	v England	Edinburgh	24/02/1894	v Ireland	Dublin
Argentina	5	31/07/1927	v Britain XV	Buenos Aires	16/07/1932	v Junior Boks	Buenos Aires
Italy	5	06/03/1938	v Germany	Stuttgart	05/05/1940	v Germany	Stuttgart
England	5	15/03/1958	v Scotland	Edinburgh	21/03/1959	v Scotland	London
England	5	20/03/1993	v Ireland	Dublin	05/04/1994	v France	Paris

NOTE: Singapore played in 9 consecutive Test matches between 1998 and 1992 without scoring a try. South Africa played in four consecutive Tests between 1972 and 1974 without scoring a try.

Most Consecutive Matches Conceding a Try

Team	Matches	Start Date	Opposition	Venue	End Date	Opposition	Venue
Wales	53	12/10/1994	v Italy	Cardiff	28/08/1999	v France	Cardiff
Italy	46	05/10/1996	v Wales	Rome	30/06/2001	v South Africa	Port Elizabeth
Ireland	38	07/06/1987	v Australia	Sydney	06/03/1993	v Wales	Cardiff
France	33	01/01/1906	v New Zealand	Paris	10/10/1920	v USA	Paris
South Africa	31	18/06/2005	v France	Durban	15/08/2007	v Namibia	Cape Town
Australia	30	03/09/1949	v New Zealand	Wellington	14/06/1958	v NZ Maori	Brisbane

NOTE: USA played in 66 consecutive Test matches between 1998 and 2006 conceding a try.

Most Consecutive Matches Conceding Four or More Tries

Team	Matches	Start Date	Opposition	Venue	End Date	Opposition	Venue
France	10	01/01/1906	v New Zealand	Paris	22/01/1910	v Scotland	Inverleith
Australia	8	01/08/1914	v New Zealand	Brisbane	02/07/1921	v S Africa XV	Sydney
Argentina	8	12/06/1910	v Britain XV	Flores	16/08/1936	v Britain XV	Buenos Aires
France	6	20/01/1912	v Scotland	Inverleith	25/01/1913	v England	London
Italy	6	16/06/1973	v Zimbabwe	Harare	04/07/1973	v Steval Pumas	Witbank
Italy	6	19/02/2000	v Wales	Cardiff	15/07/2000	v Fiji	Lautoka
Italy	6	22/02/2003	v Ireland	Rome	30/08/2003	v Ireland	Limerick
Scotland	5	22/03/1998	v England	Edinburgh	21/11/1998	v South Africa	Edinburgh
Wales	5	29/05/2016	v England	London	05/11/2016	v Australia	Cardiff

NOTE: The UAE conceded four or more tries in 12 consecutive matches between 2012 and 2014. S Africa conceded four or more tries in three consecutive matches on two occasions in 1997 & 2002.

Most Consecutive Matches Without Conceding a Try

Team	Matches	Start Date	Opposition	Venue	End Date	Opposition	Venue
England	10	15/02/1875	v Ireland	London	24/03/1879	v Ireland	London
Scotland	8	10/01/1885	v Wales	Glasgow	26/02/1887	v Wales	Edinburgh
Argentina	7	07/08/1971	v SA Gazelles	Pretoria	17/10/1971	v Uruguay	Montevideo
England	6	16/03/1957	v Scotland	London	15/03/1958	v Scotland	Edinburgh
France	6	13/01/1962	v Scotland	Edinburgh	11/11/1962	v Romania	Bucharest
Argentina	6	08/09/1973	v Romania	Buenos Aires	21/10/1973	v Chile	San Pablo
France	6	05/02/1977	v Wales	Paris	02/07/1977	v Argentina	Buenos Aires
Wales	5	22/03/1947	v France	Paris	07/02/1948	v Scotland	Cardiff
France	5	10/11/1984	v Romania	Bucharest	30/03/1985	v Wales	Paris
England	5	28/07/1990	v Argentina	Buenos Aires	16/02/1991	v Scotland	London
South Africa	5	10/10/1999	v Spain	Edinburgh	04/11/1999	v New Zealand	Cardiff

Most Consecutive Matches Without Scoring a Point

Team	Matches	Start Date	Opposition	End Date	Venue
South Africa	4	30/07/1891	v Britain	30/07/1896	Port Elizabeth
Ireland	3	15/03/1890	v England	21/02/1891	Belfast
Scotland	3	05/03/1892	v England	18/02/1893	Belfast
Ireland	3	04/02/1893	v England	11/03/1893	Llanelli
Ireland	3	28/02/1903	v Scotland	13/02/1904	Blackheath
Argentina	3	29/08/1948	v Oxford & Cambridge	28/08/1949	Buenos Aires
Scotland	3	09/01/1954	v France	27/02/1954	Belfast

NOTE: Mauritania played in 5 consecutive Test matches between 2003 and 2004 without scoring a point.

Most Consecutive Matches Without Conceding a Point

Team	Matches	Start Date	Opposition	End Date	Venue
Britain	4	30/07/1891	v South Africa	30/07/1896	Port Elizabeth
England	3	02/01/1892	v Wales	05/03/1892	Edinburgh
South Africa	3	23/11/1912	v Scotland	14/12/1912	Cardiff
New Zealand	3	17/09/1921	v South Africa	29/11/1924	Swansea
Wales	3	22/03/1947	v France	20/12/1947	Cardiff
France	3	09/01/1954	v Scotland	27/02/1954	Paris
England	3	18/03/1961	v Scotland	10/02/1962	London
New Zealand	3	21/12/1963	v Wales	18/01/1964	Edinburgh

www.sarugby.co.za

TEAM RECORDS
MATCH AGGREGATES
Highest Total Points in a Match

Points (Score)	Team	Opponent	Venue	Date
162 (145-17)	New Zealand	Japan	Bloemfontein	04/06/1995
154 (147-7)	Argentina	Venezuela	Santiago	01/05/2004
152 (152-0)	Argentina	Paraguay	Mendoza	01/05/2002
144 (144-0)	Argentina	Paraguay	Montevideo	27/04/2003
142 (142-0)	Australia	Namibia	Adelaide	25/10/2003
137 (134-3)	South Africa	Uruguay	East London	11/06/2005
134 (134-0)	England	Romania	London	17/11/2001
124 (111-13)	England	Uruguay	Brisbane	02/11/2003
121 (108-13)	New Zealand	Portugal	Lyon	15/09/2007
118 (105-13)	South Africa	Namibia	Cape Town	15/08/2007
115 (101-14)	New Zealand	Samoa	New Plymouth	03/09/2008

NOTE: Hong Kong won Singapore 164-13 in 1994 for a match total of 177 points.

Highest Total Tries in a Match

Tries	Team	Opponent	Venue	Date
24 (24-0)	Argentina	Paraguay	Mendoza	01/05/2002
24 (24-0)	Argentina	Paraguay	Montevideo	27/04/2003
24 (23-1)	Argentina	Venezuela	Santiago	01/05/2004
23 (21-2)	New Zealand	Japan	Bloemfontein	04/06/1995
22 (22-0)	Australia	Namibia	Adelaide	25/10/2003
21 (21-0)	South Africa	Uruguay	East London	11/06/2005
20 (20-0)	Argentina	Brazil	Montevideo	08/10/1989
20 (20-0)	England	Romania	London	17/11/2001

Highest Total Conversions in a Match

Conversions	Team	Opponent	Venue	Date
22 (20-2)	New Zealand	Japan	Bloemfontein	04/06/1995
17 (16-1)	Argentina	Venezuela	Santiago	01/05/2004
16 (16-0)	Argentina	Paraguay	Mendoza	01/05/2002
16 (16-0)	Australia	Namibia	Adelaide	25/10/2003
15 (15-0)	Argentina	Brazil	Santiago	09/10/1979
15 (15-0)	England	Netherlands	Huddersfield	14/11/1998
15 (14-1)	New Zealand	Portugal	Lyon	15/09/2007
15 (13-2)	New Zealand	Samoa	New Plymouth	03/09/2008

NOTE: South Africa was involved in three Test matches where 13 conversions were scored in the match. –
v Italy, 1999 (13-0); v Uruguay, 2005 (13-0) and v Namibia, 2007 (12-1).

Highest Total Penalty Goals in a Match

Penalty goals	Team	Opponent	Venue	Date
14 (7-7)	Argentina	Canada	Buenos Aires	22/08/1998
14 (7-7)	Argentina	Ireland	Lens	20/10/1999
14 (8-6)	Australia	South Africa	London	30/10/1999
13 (5-8)	South Africa	England	Bloemfontein	24/06/2000
13 (4-9)	France	New Zealand	Paris	11/11/2000
13 (7-6)	Argentina	Italy	Salta	11/06/2005
13 (6-7)	Scotland	Wales	Edinburgh	09/03/2013
13 (8-5)	Argentina	Georgia	San Juan	22/06/2013

Highest Total Drop Goals in a Match

Drop goals	Team	Opponent	Venue	Date
6 *(3-3)*	New Zealand	France	Christchurch	28/06/1986
5 *(0-5)*	England	South Africa	Paris	24/10/1999
4 *(3-1)*	Argentina	Australia	Buenos Aires	27/10/1979
4 *(2-2)*	France	Australia	Clermont-Ferrand	13/11/1983
4 *(1-3)*	England	France	London	02/02/1985
4 *(1-3)*	Australia	France	Sydney	30/06/1990
4 *(3-1)*	Italy	Romania	Padova	07/10/1990
4 *(3-1)*	France	Scotland	Paris	19/01/1991
4 *(2-2)*	France	England	Paris	20/01/1996
4 *(3-1)*	Italy	Scotland	Rome	05/02/2000
4 *(0-4)*	England	South Africa	London	25/11/2006
4 *(0-4)*	France	Argentina	Paris	22/11/2014

HIGHEST TOTAL YELLOW CARDS IN A MATCH

Yellow cards	Team	Opponent	Venue	Date
6 *(1-5)*	Italy	Fiji	Cremona	16/11/2013
5 *(1-4)*	France	Italy	Paris	02/02/2002
5 *(3-2)*	Argentina	Italy	Córdoba	17/06/2005
4 *(2-2)*	France	England	Paris	19/02/2000
4 *(3-1)*	Italy	England	Rome	18/03/2000
4 *(1-3)*	Italy	Canada	Rovigo	11/11/2000
4 *(2-2)*	Australia	South Africa	Brisbane	27/07/2002
4 *(2-2)*	Argentina	Samoa	Buenos Aires	03/12/2005
4 *(4-0)*	England	New Zealand	London	29/11/2008
4 *(1-3)*	Italy	Ireland	Rome	16/03/2013
4 *(2-2)*	Uruguay	Argentina	Montevideo	27/04/2013
4 *(2-2)*	South Africa	Australia	Cape Town	28/09/2013
4 *(2-2)*	England	Argentina	London	26/11/2016

NOTE: Uruguay (3) and Georgia (4) together received 7 yellow cards in 2004 in Montevideo.

Highest Total Red Cards in a Match

Red cards	Team	Opponent	Venue	Date
3 *(1-2)*	South Africa	Canada	Port Elizabeth	03/06/1995
2 *(1-1)*	Wales	Ireland	Cardiff	15/01/1977
2 *(0-2)*	England	Fiji	London	04/11/1989
2 *(1-1)*	Argentina	Samoa	Pontypridd	13/10/1991
2 *(2-0)*	France	England	Paris	15/02/1992
2 *(1-1)*	Uruguay	Argentina	Montevideo	23/10/1993
2 *(1-1)*	Canada	France	Nepean	04/06/1994
2 *(2-0)*	Samoa	France	Apia	12/06/1999
2 *(1-1)*	England	Samoa	London	26/11/2005
2 *(2-0)*	USA	Italy	Houston	23/06/2012
2 *(1-1)*	France	Tonga	Le Havre	16/11/2013
2 *(1-1)*	France	Italy	Paris	09/02/2014
2 *(1-1)*	England	Argentina	London	26/11/2016

Highest Total Points at Halftime

Points (Score)	Team	Opponent	Venue	Date
87 (3-84)	Japan	New Zealand	Bloemfontein	04/06/1995
76 (69-7)	Argentina	Venezuela	Santiago	01/05/2004
72 (72-0)	England	Romania	London	17/11/2001
71 (71-0)	Italy	Czech Republic	Viadana	18/05/1994
69 (69-0)	Australia	Namibia	Adelaide	25/10/2003
64 (64-0)	Argentina	Brazil	Santiago	23/05/2012
61 (0-61)	Chile	Argentina	Santiago	04/06/2016
60 (33-27)	South Africa	New Zealand	Johannesburg	19/08/2000
60 (3-57)	Spain	Australia	Madrid	01/11/2001

TEAM RECORDS
BY CALENDER YEAR
Most Team Wins in a Calender Year

Wins	Team	Matches	% Wins	Year
16	England	17	94,12%	2003
14	South Africa	17	82,35%	2007
14	New Zealand	14	100,00%	2013
13	New Zealand	15	86,67%	2008
13	New Zealand	14	92,86%	2010
13	England	13	100,00%	2016
13	New Zealand	14	92,86%	2016

Most Team Points in a Calender Year

Points	Team	Matches	Wins	Year
658	South Africa	17	14	2007
644	England	17	16	2003
643	Argentina	14	11	2003
602	New Zealand	14	12	2003
594	New Zealand	12	10	2007
584	New Zealand	12	10	1995
571	New Zealand	12	11	1997
568	France	18	10	2003
562	New Zealand	14	13	2016

Most Team Tries in a Calender Year

Tries	Team	Matches	Average	Year
92	Argentina	14	6,57	2003
81	New Zealand	14	5,79	2003
81	South Africa	17	4,76	2007
80	New Zealand	12	6,67	2007
80	New Zealand	14	5,71	2016
74	South Africa	13	5,69	1997
72	New Zealand	12	6,00	1997
71	New Zealand	12	5,92	1995
70	England	11	6,36	2001

Most Team Losses in a Calender Year

Lost	Team	Matches	% Lost	Year
11	Wales	16	68,75%	2003
11	Wales	15	73,33%	2007
10	Italy	13	76,92%	1973
10	Italy	12	83,33%	1999
10	Scotland	12	83,33%	2004
10	Italy	11	90,91%	2009
10	Argentina	15	66,67%	2013
10	Italy	11	90,91%	2014

NOTE: *Uruguay lost 14 of their 17 Test matches in 2015. South Africa lost 8 of their 12 Test matches in 2016 (67%).*

Most Points Conceded in a Calender Year

Points	Team	Matches	Year
627	Italy	12	1999
450	Wales	16	2003
438	Italy	12	2003
438	Argentina	15	2013
428	Wales	15	2007
415	Scotland	15	2003
413	Italy	12	2001
409	Italy	10	2000
407	Australia	15	2016

NOTES: *Chinese Taipei conceded 728 points in 13 matches during 2002. The most points conceded by South Africa were 344 in 2010.*

Most Tries Conceded in a Calender Year

Tries	Team	Matches	Year
82	Italy	12	1999
57	Italy	12	2003
55	Italy	13	1973
50	Wales	16	2003
49	Wales	15	2007
49	Argentina	15	2013
47	Italy	12	2001
46	Italy	10	2000
46	Italy	11	2016
45	Australia	15	2016

NOTE: *The most tries conceded by South Africa were 35 on three occasions – 2002 in 11 matches; 2010 in 14 matches and 2016 in 12 matches.*

SECTION 4:
SPRINGBOKS IN 2016

SPRINGBOKS

Challenging year for Springboks

By Stephen Nell

THAT old Latin expression *annus horribilis* comes to mind when telling the tale of Springbok rugby in 2016. They won only four of 12 Tests – the least by a South African team in a calendar year in the professional era.

In addition, the class of 2016 became the only Springbok team in the professional era not to win a match on their end-of-season tour. That the latter included a defeat to Italy puts into perspective the degree to which the Springboks were a team very low on confidence as the year drew to a close.

To be fair to coach Allister Coetzee, he was fighting an uphill battle from the word go: his appointment was only confirmed in April.

Ideally the national coach would be able to have some camps before the incoming series, but Coetzee had to get by without these.

Renewed hope, of course, always follows the appointment of a new national coach.

The initial preparation in Stellenbosch went well, but the magnitude of Coetzee's task was put into perspective when stock was taken of all the senior players who had called time on their international careers in the wake of the previous year's Rugby World Cup.

Victor Matfield would have a little spell at the Northampton Saints before finally calling it a day, while Jean de Villiers and Fourie du Preez retired.

Bismarck and Jannie du Plessis, both in their thirties, moved to Montpellier, while Schalk Burger declared that his priorities would lie with Saracens after one last Vodacom Super Rugby campaign with the Stormers.

Faced with this scenario, Coetzee took a conservative view of the captaincy, preferring veteran hooker Adriaan Strauss rather than charting a new course with the likes of a Patrick Lambie or Warren Whiteley.

Duane Vermeulen, of course, would have been an obvious candidate had he not decided to move to Toulon in France. Another leader, Francois Louw, played for Bath in England.

While these two still had a huge amount to

offer, their performances were arguably undermined by their conditioning, which was out of sync with the home-based players.

For Strauss's stoicism there might have been more appreciation had the team fared better. He shrugged off his initial indifferent form to become a composed and tireless leader by the end of the season. (It was telling that the Springboks became unhinged against the All Blacks in Christchurch when they lost their skipper early in the second half.)

Coetzee's reign got off to the worst possible start with a defeat to Ireland at Newlands. What made it worse was that the Springboks were a man to the good for the best part of the match following CJ Stander's red card. At one stage there were only 13 Irishmen on the field for a 10-minute spell after Robbie Henshaw landed in the sin-bin.

In Johannesburg the following week the Springboks did a Lazarus act, overturning a 19-3 half-time deficit and 26-10 shortfall going into the final quarter to win 32-26. Tellingly it was when Coetzee either placed the emphasis on, or was forced into, renewal that the Springboks sparked. Ruan Combrinck and Warren Whiteley's introductions from the substitutes' bench were vital in the stirring comeback effort.

Props Steven Kitshoff and Julian Redelinghuys also showed that, barring unforeseen circumstances, they could play for South Africa for a long time. At the time of writing, however, Redelinghuys was recovering from a serious neck injury with doubts about his future.

While there should be recognition that Coetzee had a difficult job, he also played his part in complicating it. He had a penchant for picking players out of their preferred positions. Outside centre Juan de Jongh made a few appearances as an inside centre, scrumhalf Francois Hougaard as a wing and flyhalf Johan Goosen was frequently selected as a fullback.

There was a lack of synergy in the Springboks' attack and as the pressure increased Coetzee became more conservative in his thinking during the Castle Rugby Championship. He would eventually rely on Morné Steyn's boot to get the team back on the winning track against the Wallabies at Loftus Versfeld, but there was no such luck against New Zealand in Durban the following weekend.

In fact, Growthpoint Kings Park would prove the scene of the worst Springbok defeats in history, with the world champion All Blacks showing no mercy.

Notwithstanding the Emirates Lions' good performances in Vodacom Super Rugby, Coetzee felt that South African rugby was in trouble. A very positive dialogue between coaches – a so-called 'indaba' – took place in Cape Town and the key outcome was that there would be a technical blueprint and a spirit of working together going forward.

To underline how seriously South African coaches were taking the indaba, both Vodacom Blue Bulls coach Nollis Marais and Toyota Free State coach Franco Smith attended it in the week they were preparing their teams for the Currie Cup final.

A key outcome was that the Free State Rugby Union would release Smith to assist with the Springboks' backline and skills coaching. The Golden Lions were equally generous in allowing defence coach JP Ferreira to join the team on the end-of-season tour.

However, it was a tour that demonstrated the fact that there could be no quick-fix solutions. The Springboks lost to England for the first time in a decade, though one must hasten to add it was the best English side they had played during that time.

It was rather the following weekend's loss to Italy in Florence that cut deep. Apart from a smattering of experienced players, the Azzurri was a young side that should have had no right to beat the Springboks.

However, a lack of confidence can be debilitating and South Africa consequently suffered their biggest humiliation since the defeat to Japan at the previous year's World Cup.

The following weekend's loss to Wales was less unexpected, but significantly Coetzee started to look to the future with his selections. Flank Uzair Cassiem used the stage of the Principality Stadium to show that he too can look forward to a good Springbok career.

At the time of writing, rugby bosses had a difficult choice on their hands: release Coetzee and begin the search for a new coach, or give him a chance in 2017 to right the wrongs of 2016.

Whatever is eventually decided, there can be little disagreement that Springbok rugby enters 2017 needing to chart a new direction if it hopes to emulate more successful eras.

2016 SCORERS

PLAYER	UNION/CLUB	M	T	C	P	DG	PTS
ET Jantjies	Golden Lions	9	0	12	16	0	72
M Steyn	Stade Français, France	6	0	0	12	2	42
PJ Lambie	KwaZulu-Natal	6	0	2	4	1	19
JL Goosen	Racing 92, France	7	3	1	0	0	17
PS du Toit	Western Province	12	3	0	0	0	15
WR Whiteley	Golden Lions	12	3	0	0	0	15
RJ Combrinck	Golden Lions	7	2	1	1	0	15
BG Habana	Toulon, France	7	3	0	0	0	15
D de Allende	Western Province	9	2	0	0	0	10
LN Mvovo	KwaZulu-Natal	2	1	0	0	0	5
J-PR Pietersen	KwaZulu-Natal	4	1	0	0	0	5
WJ le Roux	KwaZulu-Natal	7	1	0	0	0	5
U Cassiem	Free State	1	1	0	0	0	5
			20	16	33	3	240

SPRINGBOK MATCHES/TEST RESULTS & SCORERS

Tests Played	Won	Lost	Drawn	Points for	Points against	Tries For	Tries Against
12	4	8	0	240	329	20	35

Date	Venue	Opponent	Score	Tries	Conversions	Penalties	DG	Referee
11/06/2016	DHL Newlands, Cape Town	Ireland	20-26	Mvovo, Du Toit	Jantjies (2)	Lambie, Jantjies	-	M Raynal France
18/06/2016	Emirates Airline Park, Johannesburg	Ireland	32-26	Combrinck, Whiteley, Du Toit, De Allende	Jantjies (3)	Jantjies (2)	-	A Gardner Australia
25/06/2016	Nelson Mandela Bay Stadium, Port Elizabeth	Ireland	19-13	Pietersen	Jantjies	Jantjies (3), Combrinck	-	GW Jackson New Zealand
20/08/2016	Mbombela Stadium, Nelspruit	Argentina	30-23	Combrinck, Goosen, Whiteley	Jantjies (3)	Jantjies (3)	-	GW Jackson New Zealand
27/08/2016	Estadio Padre Ernesto Martearena, Salta	Argentina	24-26	Habana, Du Toit	Goosen	Jantjies (2), Steyn (2)	-	J Garcés France
10/09/2016	Suncorp Stadium, Brisbane	Australia	17-23	Whiteley, Goosen	Jantjies (2)	Steyn	-	N Owens Wales
17/09/2016	AMI Stadium, Christchurch	New Zealand	13-41	Habana	Jantjies	Jantjies (2)	-	A Gardner Australia
01/10/2016	Loftus Versfeld, Pretoria	Australia	18-10	-	-	Steyn (4)	Steyn (2)	W Barnes England
08/10/2016	Growthpoint Kings Park, Durban	New Zealand	15-57	-	-	Steyn (5)	-	J Garcés France
05/11/2016	Wembley Stadium, London	Barbarians (Tour match)	31-31	Du Toit, Smit, Petersen, Venter, Janse van Rensburg, Goosen, Le Roux	Lambie (3)	-	-	M Fraser New Zealand
12/11/2016	Twickenham, London	England	21-37	-	Combrinck	Lambie (2)	Lambie	J Garcés France
19/11/2016	Stadio Artemio Franchi, Florence	Italy	18-20	Habana, De Allende	Lambie	Lambie, Jantjies	-	GJ Clancy Ireland
26/11/2016	Principality Stadium, Cardiff	Wales	13-27	Cassiem	Lambie	Jantjies (2)	-	R Poite France

TEST APPEARANCES & POINTS

PLAYER	Ireland 1	Ireland 2	Ireland 3	Argentina 1	Argentina 2	Australia 1	New Zealand 1	Australia 2	New Zealand 2	England	Italy	Wales	Apps	T	C	P	DG	Pts
WJ le Roux	15	15	15	-	-	-	-	R	R	15	15	-	7	1	0	0	0	5
J-PR Pietersen	14	14	11	-	-	-	-	-	-	11	-	-	4	1	0	0	0	5
LG Mapoe	13	13	13	13	13	t+R	-	R	R	R	-	R	10	0	0	0	0	0
D de Allende	12	12	12	12	12	-	R	-	12	12	12	-	9	2	0	0	0	10
LN Mvovo	11	11	-	-	-	-	-	-	-	-	-	-	2	1	0	0	0	5
PJ Lambie	10	-	-	-	-	-	15	15	10	10	R	-	6	0	2	4	1	19
F de Klerk	9	9	9	9	9	9	9	-	9	R	R	9	11	0	0	0	0	0
DJ Vermeulen	8	8	-	-	-	-	-	-	-	-	-	-	2	0	0	0	0	0
S Kolisi	7	7	7	-	-	-	-	-	-	-	-	-	3	0	0	0	0	0
L-FP Louw	6	6	6	6	6	6	6	6	6	-	-	-	9	0	0	0	0	0
L de Jager	5	-	-	5	5	5	-	R	R	5	5	5	9	0	0	0	0	0
E Etzebeth	4	4	4	4	4	4	4	4	4	4	-	-	10	0	0	0	0	0
JF Malherbe	3	3	3	-	-	-	-	-	-	-	-	-	3	0	0	0	0	0
JA Strauss	2*	2*	2*	2*	2*	2*	2*	2*	2*	2*	2*	2*	12	0	0	0	0	0
T Mtawarira	1	1	1	1	1	1	1	1	1	1	1	1	12	0	0	0	0	0
TN Nyakane	R	R	-	-	-	R	-	-	-	-	R	R	5	0	0	0	0	0
J Redelinghuys	R	R	R	3	-	-	R	R	-	-	-	-	6	0	0	0	0	0
PS du Toit	R	5	5	R	R	R	5	5	5	7	4	4	12	3	0	0	0	15
WR Whiteley	R	R	8	8	8	8	8	8	8	8	8	8	12	3	0	0	0	15
R Paige	R	x	x	x	R	-	-	9	-	9	9	-	5	0	0	0	0	0
ET Jantjies	R	10	10	10	10	10	10	-	-	-	R	10	9	0	12	16	0	72
JA Kriel (Jesse)	R	-	-	R	R	13	13	13	-	-	-	-	6	0	0	0	0	0
MT Mbonambi	x	x	R	x	x	R	-	x	R	R	t+R	-	5	0	0	0	0	0
FJ Mostert	-	R	R	-	-	R	R	-	R	R	R	-	7	0	0	0	0	0
M Steyn	-	t	-	-	R	R	R	10	10	-	-	-	6	0	0	12	2	42
RJ Combrinck	-	R	14	14	14	-	-	-	14	14	14		7	2	1	1	0	15
S Kitshoff	-	-	R	R	R	R	R	R	R	R	R	R	10	0	0	0	0	0
JA Kriel (Jaco)	-	-	R	R	R	R	R	R	R	-	-	-	7	0	0	0	0	0
JL Goosen	-	-	-	15	15	15	15	-	-	R	R	15	7	3	1	0	0	17
BG Habana	-	-	-	11	11	14	14	14	11	-	11	-	7	3	0	0	0	15
TS Mohojé	-	-	-	7	7	7	7	7	7	7	-	-	7	0	0	0	0	0
VP Koch	-	-	-	R	3	-	3	3	3	3	3	-	7	0	0	0	0	0
JL de Jongh	-	-	-	R	-	12	12	12	13	-	-	-	5	0	0	0	0	0
LC Adriaanse	-	-	-	-	R	3	R	-	-	R	-	3	5	0	0	0	0	0
F Hougaard	-	-	-	-	-	11	11	11	14	-	-	-	4	0	0	0	0	0
WS Alberts	-	-	-	-	-	-	R	R	R	6	7	-	5	0	0	0	0	0
MJ Marx	-	-	-	-	-	-	R	-	-	-	-	R	2	0	0	0	0	0
JF Venter	-	-	-	-	-	-	-	-	-	13	13	13	3	0	0	0	0	0
N Carr	-	-	-	-	-	-	-	-	-	R	6	6	3	0	0	0	0	0
U Cassiem	-	-	-	-	-	-	-	-	-	-	-	7	1	1	0	0	0	5
JI Ulengo	-	-	-	-	-	-	-	-	-	-	-	11	1	0	0	0	0	0
R Janse v Rensburg	-	-	-	-	-	-	-	-	-	-	-	12	1	0	0	0	0	0
J-L du Preez	-	-	-	-	-	-	-	-	-	-	-	R	1	0	0	0	0	0
PE van Zyl	-	-	-	-	-	-	-	-	-	-	-	R	1	0	0	0	0	0
44 PLAYERS														20	16	33	3	240

TEST PLAYERS IN 2016 - CAREER STATS

PLAYER	Union/Club	Date of birth	Height	Weight	Tests	Tries	Conv.	Pen	DG	Pts
LC Adriaanse	KwaZulu-Natal	02/02/1988	1,80	115	6	0	0	0	0	0
WS Alberts	Stade Français, France	11/05/1984	1,92	120	43	7	0	0	0	35
N Carr	Western Province	04/04/1991	1,84	93	5	0	0	0	0	0
U Cassiem	Free State	07/03/1990	1,89	98	1	1	0	0	0	5
RJ Combrinck	Golden Lions	10/05/1990	1,83	97	7	2	1	1	0	15
D de Allende	Western Province	25/11/1991	1,89	101	22	3	0	0	0	15
L de Jager	Free State	17/12/1992	2,05	120	28	4	0	0	0	20
JL de Jongh	Western Province	15/04/1988	1,77	85	19	3	0	0	0	15
F de Klerk	Golden Lions	19/10/1991	1,72	80	11	0	0	0	0	0
J-L du Preez	KwaZulu-Natal	05/08/1995	1,93	110	1	0	0	0	0	0
PS du Toit	Western Province	20/08/1992	2,00	116	20	3	0	0	0	15
E Etzebeth	Western Province	29/10/1991	2,04	117	54	2	0	0	0	10
JL Goosen	Racing 92, France	27/07/1992	1,85	85	13	3	2	2	0	25
BG Habana	Toulon, France	12/06/1983	1,80	93	124	67	0	0	0	335
F Hougaard	Worcester Warriors, England	06/04/1988	1,79	92	39	5	0	0	0	25
R Janse van Rensburg	Golden Lions	11/09/1994	1,86	100	1	0	0	0	0	0
ET Jantjies	Golden Lions	01/08/1990	1,76	88	11	0	12	18	0	78
S Kitshoff	Bordeaux-Bègles, France	10/02/1992	1,84	125	10	0	0	0	0	0
VP Koch	Saracens, England	13/03/1990	1,85	118	9	0	0	0	0	0
S Kolisi	Western Province	16/06/1991	1,88	98	16	0	0	0	0	0
JA Kriel (Jaco)	Golden Lions	21/08/1989	1,84	97	7	0	0	0	0	0
JA Kriel (Jesse)	Blue Bulls	15/02/1994	1,86	96	17	3	0	0	0	15
PJ Lambie	KwaZulu-Natal	17/10/1990	1,78	87	56	2	25	27	4	153
WJ le Roux	KwaZulu-Natal	18/08/1989	1,86	90	41	10	0	0	0	50
L-FP Louw	Bath Rugby, England	15/06/1985	1,90	114	52	8	0	0	0	40
JF Malherbe	Western Province	14/03/1991	1,90	120	15	0	0	0	0	0
LG Mapoe	Golden Lions	13/07/1988	1,82	87	11	0	0	0	0	0
MJ Marx	Golden Lions	13/07/1994	1,88	119	2	0	0	0	0	0
MT Mbonambi	Western Province	07/01/1991	1,76	106	5	0	0	0	0	0
TS Mohojé	Free State	03/08/1990	1,92	103	15	0	0	0	0	0
FJ Mostert	Golden Lions	27/11/1990	1,98	103	7	0	0	0	0	0
T Mtawarira	KwaZulu-Natal	01/08/1985	1,83	115	87	2	0	0	0	10
LN Mvovo	KwaZulu-Natal	03/06/1986	1,85	94	17	6	0	0	0	30
TN Nyakane	Blue Bulls	04/05/1989	1,78	123	28	1	0	0	0	5
R Paige	Blue Bulls	02/08/1989	1,76	100	7	0	0	0	0	0
J-PR Pietersen	KwaZulu-Natal	12/07/1986	1,90	106	70	24	0	0	0	120
J Redelinghuys	Golden Lions	11/09/1989	1,76	100	8	0	0	0	0	0
M Steyn	Stade Français, France	11/07/1984	1,84	91	66	8	102	154	10	736
JA Strauss	Blue Bulls	18/11/1985	1,84	114	66	6	0	0	0	30
JI Ulengo	Blue Bulls	07/01/1990	1,85	88	1	0	0	0	0	0
PE van Zyl	Blue Bulls	14/09/1989	1,74	81	3	0	0	0	0	0
Venter, JF	Free State	19/04/1991	1,85	91	3	0	0	0	0	0
DJ Vermeulen	Toulon, France	03/07/1986	1,93	108	37	2	0	0	0	10
WR Whiteley	Golden Lions	18/09/1987	1,92	97	15	3	0	0	0	15

Bold letters denotes new Springbok.

CASTLE LAGER
INCOMING IRISH SERIES

Date		Score		Venue	Referee
11/06/2016	South Africa	20	Ireland	26	Newlands, Cape Town	Mathieu Raynal (France)
18/06/2016	South Africa	32	Ireland	26	Emirates Airline Park, Johannesburg	Angus Gardner (Australia)
25/06/2016	South Africa	19	Ireland	13	Nelson Mandela Bay Stadium, Port Elizabeth	Glen Jackson (New Zealand)

South Africa 20 Ireland 26
(Halftime 13-13)

Test # 453

DHL Newlands, Cape Town. Kick off: 17:00. Attendance: 42 640. June 11, 2016
Referee: M Raynal *(France)*; Ass. Ref 1: A Gardner *(Australia)*;
Ass. Ref 2: M Carley *(England)*; TMO: J Yuille *(Scotland)*

SOUTH AFRICA

Tries: Mvovo, Du Toit. Conversions: Jantjies (2). Penalty goals: Lambie, Jantjies.
SOUTH AFRICA: WJ le Roux; J-PR Pietersen, L Mapoe *(JA Kriel, 68)*, D de Allende,
LN Mvovo; PJ Lambie *(ET Jantjies, 23)*, F de Klerk *(R Paige, 68)*; DJ Vermeulen, S Kolisi,
L-FP Louw *(WR Whiteley, 56)*, L de Jager* *(PS du Toit, 56)*, E Etzebeth, JF Malherbe
(J Redelinghuys, 76), JA Strauss (C), T Mtawarira *(TN Nyakane, 59)*.
UNUSED SUBSTITUTE: MT Mbonambi. *YELLOW CARD: 11 – L de Jager.
TEST DEBUT: F de Klerk #870.

IRELAND

Tries: Payne, Murray. Conversions: Jackson (2). Penalty goals: Jackson (3). Drop goal: Jackson.
JB Payne; AD Trimble, RA Henshaw*, LD Marshall, KG Earls *(CJH Gilroy, 77)*; DPLJ Jackson,
CG Murray; JPR Heaslip, J Murphy *(RJ Ruddock, 74)*, CJ Stander**, DA Toner, WI Henderson
(U Dillane, 69), MA Ross *(TV Furlong, 59)*, RD Best (C) *(SM Cronin, 68)*, JC McGrath.
UNUSED SUBSTITUTES: FH Bealham, KD Marmion & IL Madigan.
*YELLOW CARD: 32 – RA Henshaw. **RED CARD: 23 – CJ Stander.
NOTE: This was Ireland's first win on South African soil after 7 previous attempts.

No Irish luck for Coetzee

THE clock read five seconds as Springbok wing JP Pietersen unwittingly set the tone not just for this Test match, but indeed the entire season, by taking out Ireland's towering lock Devin Toner in the air from the kick-off.

It was an unnecessary act – indicative of the unforced errors and ill discipline that would often characterise the Springboks' performances in 2016. One cannot but wonder how South Africa contrived to lose a Test that should have been theirs for the taking.

Following Ireland flank CJ Stander's red card in the 23rd minute, the hosts could look forward to being a man to the good for the rest of the match. What was to follow, however, was an exhibition of clever tactical play and stoic defence by the plucky visitors.

The Irish had some high-profile absentees, among them Lions Test flyhalf Jonathan Sexton, whose tactical kicking one thought would be badly missed.

However, Paddy Jackson gave a superb account of himself in the No 10 jersey. As did fullback Jared Payne, who filled in for another ultra-reliable Test Lion, Rob Kearney.

Apart from their defence and ability to contest possession, the Irish were very shrewd in their tactical kicking by regularly putting the ball behind the Springboks.

The one little bit of delightful rugby the South Africans produced resulted in a try for left wing Lwazi Mvovo, who took substitute flyhalf Elton Jantjies's inside pass to give them a 13-10 lead after just over half an hour played.

On top of that, Ireland's outside centre, Robbie Henshaw, was sin-binned for an illegal tackle on Jantjies, reducing the visitors to just 13 men.

In earlier drama, Payne had the Springboks reeling after scoring by running onto a grubber kick from inside centre Luke Marshall. Lood de Jager, the No 5 lock, was also sin-binned for pulling down a maul.

Ireland were 10-3 up after the first quarter, but with Stander's dismissal – he recklessly floored flyhalf Patrick Lambie with his follow-through in attempting to charge down a kick – the outcome seemed inevitable.

More so after Mvovo's try and Henshaw's yellow card, but the Springboks would be made to look increasingly ordinary as this tense Test match unfolded.

It was all square at half-time as Jackson, with the Irish down to 13 men, slotted a dropped goal. However, on the face of it there was no reason for the home supporters to panic.

That all changed early in the second half as scrumhalf Conor Murray – one of the finest halfbacks in world rugby – scored a delightful try. There was a neat build-up involving an impressive incursion by Payne before Murray tore past De Jager after a show of the ball.

The scrumhalf was chased down by the other Springbok lock, Eben Etzebeth, but rolled back onto his feet to score. Jackson converted and it was 20-13 to Ireland.

South Africa dominated possession, but their attack was lateral and generally without bite, while Ireland stood their ground impressively.

There was a potential game-changing moment when substitute lock Pieter-Steph du Toit's intercept try brought the Springboks to within three points with a touch over 10 minutes remaining. However, it was Ireland who seized the day with Jackson adding another penalty to make it 26-20.

The Springboks brought out the kitchen sink for added time, but the match appropriately ended with a double tackle by Payne and Henshaw forcing Pietersen into touch in the corner.

All in all, this was not the best of starts for new Springbok coach Allister Coetzee.

SCORING SEQUENCE (I = Ireland; SA = South Africa)

Min	Action	Score
6	Lambie missed penalty goal	0-0
11	Payne try, Jackson conversion	I 7-0
16	Lambie penalty goal	I 7-3
19	Jackson penalty goal	I 10-3
26	Jantjies penalty goal	I 10-6
32	Mvovo try, Jantjies conversion	SA 13-10
37	Jackson drop goal	13-13
43	Murray try, Jackson conversion	I 20-13
61	Jackson missed penalty goal	I 20-13
68	Jackson penalty goal	I 23-13
69	Du Toit try, Jantjies conversion	I 23-20
72	Jackson missed drop goal	I 23-20
77	Jackson penalty goal	I 26-20

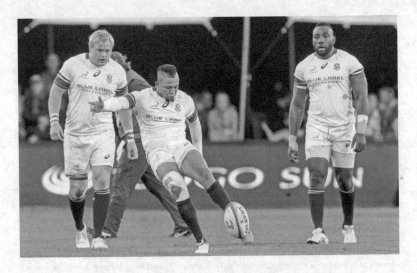

South Africa 32 Ireland 26
(Halftime 3-19)

Test # 454

Emirates Airline Park, Johannesburg. Kick-off: 17:00. Attendance: 40 468. June 18, 2016
Referee: A Gardner *(Australia)*; Ass. Ref 1: GW Jackson *(New Zealand)*;
Ass. Ref 2: BJ Whitehouse *(Wales)*; TMO: J Yuille *(Scotland)*

SOUTH AFRICA

Tries: Combrinck, Whiteley, Du Toit, De Allende. Conversions: Jantjies (3). Penalty goals: Jantjies (2).
SOUTH AFRICA - WJ le Roux; J-PR Pietersen, L Mapoe, D de Allende, LN Mvovo
(RJ Combrinck, H/T*); ET Jantjies *(M Steyn, 60-63)*, F de Klerk; DJ Vermeulen *(WR Whiteley, H/T)*,
S Kolisi *(FJ Mostert, 68**)*, L-FP Louw, PS du Toit, E Etzebeth, JF Malherbe *(J Redelinghuys, 47)*,
JA Strauss *(C)*, T Mtawarira *(TN Nyakane, 51)*.
*Combrinck to right wing, Pietersen to left wing. **Mostert to #5 lock, Du Toit to #7 flank.
UNUSED SUBSTITUTES: MT Mbonambi & R Paige. TEST DEBUTS: RJ Combrinck #871
and FJ Mostert #872.

IRELAND

Tries: Toner, Heaslip. Conversions: Jackson (2). Penalty goals: Jackson (4).
JB Payne *(T O'Halloran, 76)*; AD Trimble, RA Henshaw *(IL Madigan, 78)*, S Olding, CJH Gilroy;
DPLJ Jackson, CG Murray *(KD Marmion, 78)*; JPR Heaslip, RJ Ruddock *(S Reidy, 43-50)*,
WI Henderson *(S Reidy, 71)*, DA Toner, Q Roux *(DC Ryan, 51)*, TV Furlong *(FH Bealham, 60)*,
RD Best *(C) (CR Strauss, 66)*, JC McGrath *(D Kilcoyne, 66)*.
TEST DEBUTS: Q Roux, S Reidy & T O'Halloran.

Rear-guard rally keeps series alive

THE Springboks produced a Jekyll-and-Hyde performance in squaring the series against Ireland with a dramatic 32-26 victory at Emirates Airline Park.

By half-time a deep sense of gloom had descended on a venue that is considered a fortress for South African rugby. The Springboks had led through an early penalty by flyhalf Elton Jantjies, but thereafter it was all Ireland in the first half with Paddy Jackson's boot keeping the scoreboard ticking over.

With half-an-hour played it was 12-3 to Ireland. The Springboks had to hatch a plan, but Jantjies missed two penalty attempts in quick succession to leave a deeply patriotic crowd in disbelief.

The sense of worry then descended into deep concern after towering lock Devin Toner crashed over for a try. It was rooted in Springbok wing Lwazi Mvovo's inability on the day to master the high ball. Fullback Jared Payne latched onto a favourable bounce before the ball was recycled and travelled through the hands of scrumhalf Conor Murray and flank Rhys Ruddock to Toner. Jackson did the honours and it was 19-3.

There seemed no way back for the battered South Africans against a side emboldened by a victory over them just the previous week.

However, the match will be fondly remembered for the Springboks' comeback from the dead. The fact that the Irish ran out of steam at altitude clearly played a role, but the Springboks also deserve credit for digging deep.

Coach Allister Coetzee made some key substitutions – one shrewdly at half-time and the other through a fortunate twist of fate. Ruan Combrinck was sent on for Mvovo for the second half, while Warren Whiteley entered shortly after the break due to an injury to No 8 Duane Vermeulen.

A bright start to the second half was undone by flank Siya Kolisi knocking on a pass from Jantjies with the tryline beckoning, but the Springboks increasingly grew into the match.

The catalyst for the revival was a counter-attack launched by Willie le Roux. The nimble fullback sliced through the first line of defence before drawing his man and finding Combrinck on his right.

There was much left to do, but Combrinck smashed over Jackson in a way that made one think back to Mike Catt's misfortune of getting in the way of the late, great Jonah Lomu, albeit on a smaller scale. However, it took Ireland all of three minutes to muster a response, with No 8 Jamie Heaslip mauled over. Jackson converted and with 20 minutes left Ireland led 26-10.

A series victory seemed inevitable, but the Springboks awoke from their slumber in the nick of time. Whiteley finished by cutting inside after a neat build-up involving Jantjies, wing JP Pietersen, lock Pieter-Steph du Toit and scrumhalf Faf de Klerk.

Five minutes later the powerful Du Toit barged over the tryline after De Klerk's tap from a free kick after a visibly fatigued Irish team had conceded at a scrum.

The *coup de grace* was administered by inside centre Damian de Allende, who ran straight through scrumhalf Conor Murray and beat right wing Andrew Trimble on his way to the line.

It was 29-26 to the Springboks and four minutes remained for the Irish to regain the initiative. Instead it was the home side who built on their advantage, with Jantjies's late penalty twisting the dagger.

SCORING SEQUENCE

Min	Action	Score
4	Jantjies penalty goal	SA 3-0
11	Jackson penalty goal	3-3
15	Jackson penalty goal	I 6-3
23	Jackson penalty goal	I 9-3
28	Jackson penalty goal	I 12-3
31	Jantjies missed penalty goal.	I 12-3
33	Jantjies missed penalty goal.	I 12-3
34	Toner try, Jackson conversion	I 19-3
40	Jackson missed penalty goal.	I 19-3
47	Jackson missed penalty goal.	I 19-3
56	Combrinck try, Jantjies conversion	I 19-10
60	Heaslip try, Jackson conversion	I 26-10
64	Whiteley try, Jantjies missed conversion	I 26-15
70	Du Toit try, Jantjies conversion	I 26-22
76	De Allende try, Jantjies conversion	SA 29-26
81	Jantjies penalty goal	SA 32-26

South Africa 19 Ireland 13
(Halftime 13-10)

Test # 455

Nelson Mandela Bay Stadium, Port Elizabeth. Kick-off: 17:00. Attendance: 42 324. June 25, 2016
Referee: GW Jackson *(New Zealand)*; Ass. Ref 1: A Gardner *(Australia)*;
Ass. Ref 2: BJ Whitehouse *(Wales)*; TMO: R Kitt *(England)*

SOUTH AFRICA

Try: Pietersen. Conversion: Jantjies. Penalty goals: Jantjies (3), Combrinck.

WJ le Roux*; RJ Combrinck, LG Mapoe, D de Allende, J-PR Pietersen; ET Jantjies, F de Klerk;
WR Whiteley, S Kolisi *(JA Kriel, 61)*, L-FP Louw, PS du Toit, E Etzebeth *(FJ Mostert, 74)*,
JF Malherbe *(J Redelinghuys, 58)*, JA Straus (C) *(MT Mbonambi, 79)*, T Mtawarira *(S Kitshoff, 58)*.
*UNUSED SUBSTITUTES: R Paige, M Steyn & LN Mvovo. *YELLOW CARD: 11 – WJ le Roux*
TEST DEBUTS: S Kitshoff #873, JA Kriel #874 and MT Mbonambi #875.

IRELAND

Try: Marshall. Conversion: Jackson. Penalty goals: Jackson (2).

T O'Halloran *(M Healy, 11-19, H/T*)*; AD Trimble, LD Marshall *(KG Earls, 77-F/T)*, S Olding,
KG Earls *(IL Madigan, 73)*; DPLJ Jackson, CG Murray *(EG Reddan, 69)*; JPR Heaslip, J Murphy,
CJ Stander *(RJ Ruddock, 69)*, DA Toner, WI Henderson *(U Dillane, 69)*, MA Ross *(TV Furlong, 51)*,
RD Best (C) *(SM Cronin, 73)*, JC McGrath.
Healy to left wing, Earls to fullback. UNUSED SUBSTITUTE: FH Bealham. TEST DEBUT: M Healy.
NOTE: CG Murray played in his 50th test and EG Reddan played in his last test as
he announced his retirement from rugby.

Series secured in Bay bruiser

WHILE rugby will always be arguably the ultimate team sport, South Africa's victory in the series-deciding Test against Ireland at the Nelson Mandela Bay Stadium owed much to the defensive heroics of scrumhalf Faf de Klerk.

Twice the Springboks appeared to be on the rack and twice there was an intervention by the little man. In the first instance, with the home side leading 13-10, he leapt into the air to intercept a cut-out pass from Ireland flyhalf Paddy Jackson that was sure to find right wing Andrew Trimble with the goal-line in sight.

Then, as Ireland piled on the pressure in the dying embers looking for a converted try that could seal the victory, De Klerk shot up to catch left wing Keith Earls in possession.

The ensuing penalty allowed the Springboks to put the ball into touch and that, as they say, was that. A see-saw series that seemed utterly lost midway through the second Test had somehow been won.

Initially, South Africa looked ready to kick on from where they finished the second Test. No 8 Warren Whiteley epitomised the positive attitude with his chase to catch Ireland's fullback Jared Payne in possession from the kick-off.

In the sixth minute, flyhalf Elton Jantjies slotted a superb penalty from the right-hand touchline. However, a second attempt two minutes later faded out to the left of the uprights.

Nonetheless, the Springboks were looking good and energetic.

Unfortunately they would be robbed of their rhythm in the 11th minute by some foul play by fullback Willie le Roux, who could count himself fortunate that he only received a yellow card for taking Payne out in the air.

Ireland capitalised on their numerical advantage not long thereafter, patiently building up to a try for outside centre Luke Marshall.

There had been powerful barges by loosehead prop Jack McGrath and flank Iain Henderson through a passive Springbok defence before Marshall smashed his way through Jantjies to the tryline.

Then followed a big let-off as flyhalf Paddy Jackson fluffed an easy penalty attempt, which meant the score was 7-3 upon Le Roux's return.

It would increase to 10-3 not long thereafter when Jackson succeeded with a penalty after Whiteley had strayed offside.

The Springboks, however, were flexing their muscles in the scrums, setting up an opportunity for Jantjies to close the gap. South Africa would then take the lead on the stroke of half-time, with left wing JP Pietersen scoring after a pinpoint cross-kick by Jantjies.

It required De Klerk's first intervention to prevent Ireland from taking the lead and the Springboks then got some momentum after coach Allister Coetzee sent on props Steven Kitshoff and Julian Redelinghuys.

The first scrum with the fresh pair of props resulted in a penalty that was sent through the posts via right wing Ruan Combrinck's booming long-range boot.

Ireland then conceded a breakdown penalty, which gave the Springboks a 19-10 lead and left the Irish having to score at least twice in the last 12 minutes to win.

They very nearly did that through a combination of their own endeavour and the Springboks' poor decision-making.

With 10 minutes left, the hosts were penalised for holding on at the breakdown, giving the impressive Jackson the opportunity to reduce the deficit.

Now the Springboks had to hold out and it did little for Coetzee's heart-rate when the Irish launched a searing counter-attack after an ill-judged grubber by Le Roux.

The Irish piled on the pressure mercilessly, but were undone by De Klerk's decisive intervention. Two Tests to one does not tell the full story of a series that was as close as they came.

SCORING SEQUENCE

Min	Action	Score
6	Jantjies penalty goal	SA 3-0
9	Jantjies missed penalty goal.	SA 3-0
16	Marshall try, Marshall conversion	I 7-3
21	Jackson missed penalty goal	I 7-3
23	Jackson penalty goal	I 10-3
32	Jantjies penalty goal	I 10-6
40	Pietersen try, Jantjies conversion	SA 13-10
59	Combrinck penalty goal	SA 16-10
69	Jantjies penalty goal	SA 19-10
70	Jackson penalty goal	SA 19-13

SOUTH AFRICA – SERIES APPEARANCES & POINTS

PLAYER	Date of birth	Height	Weight	Union/Club	Ireland 1	Ireland 2	Ireland 3	Apps	T	C	P	DG	Pts
WJ le Roux	18/08/1989	1,86	90	KwaZulu-Natal	15	15	15	3	0	0	0	0	0
J-PR Pietersen	12/07/1986	1,90	106	KwaZulu-Natal	14	14	11	3	1	0	0	0	5
LG Mapoe	13/07/1988	1,82	87	Golden Lions	13	13	13	3	0	0	0	0	0
D de Allende	25/11/1991	1,89	101	Western Province	12	12	12	3	1	0	0	0	5
LN Mvovo	03/06/1986	1,85	94	KwaZulu-Natal	11	11	-	2	1	0	0	0	5
PJ Lambie	17/10/1990	1,78	87	KwaZulu-Natal	10	-	-	1	0	0	1	0	3
F de Klerk	19/10/1991	1,72	80	Golden Lions	9	9	9	3	0	0	0	0	0
DJ Vermeulen	03/07/1986	1,93	108	Toulon, France	8	8	-	2	0	0	0	0	0
S Kolisi	16/06/1991	1,88	98	Western Province	7	7	7	3	0	0	0	0	0
L-FP Louw	15/06/1985	1,90	114	Bath Rugby, England	6	6	6	3	0	0	0	0	0
L de Jager	17/12/1992	2,05	120	Free State	5	-	-	1	0	0	0	0	0
E Etzebeth	29/10/1991	2,04	117	Western Province	4	4	4	3	0	0	0	0	0
JF Malherbe	14/03/1991	1,90	120	Western Province	3	3	3	3	0	0	0	0	0
JA Strauss (c)	18/11/1985	1,84	114	Blue Bulls	2*	2*	2*	3	0	0	0	0	0
T Mtawarira	01/08/1985	1,83	115	KwaZulu-Natal	1	1	1	3	0	0	0	0	0
TN Nyakane	04/05/1989	1,78	123	Blue Bulls	R	R	-	2	0	0	0	0	0
J Redelinghuys	11/09/1989	1,76	100	Golden Lions	R	R	R	3	0	0	0	0	0
PS du Toit	20/08/1992	2,00	116	Western Province	R	5	5	3	2	0	0	0	10
WR Whiteley	18/09/1987	1,92	97	Golden Lions	R	R	8	3	1	0	0	0	5
R Paige	02/08/1989	1,69	82	Blue Bulls	R	x	x	1	0	0	0	0	0
ET Jantjies	01/08/1990	1,76	88	Golden Lions	R	10	10	3	0	6	6	0	30
JA (Jesse) Kriel	15/02/1994	1,86	96	Blue Bulls	R	-	-	1	0	0	0	0	0
MT Mbonambi	07/01/1991	1,76	106	Western Province	x	x	R	1	0	0	0	0	0
FJ Mostert	27/11/1990	1,98	103	Golden Lions	-	R	R	2	0	0	0	0	0
M Steyn	11/07/1984	1,84	87	Stade Français, France	-	t	-	1	0	0	0	0	0
RJ Combrinck	10/05/1990	1,83	97	Golden Lions	-	R	14	2	1	0	1	0	8
S Kitshoff	10/02/1992	1,84	125	Bordeaux-Bègles, France	-	-	R	1	0	0	0	0	0
JA (Jaco) Kriel	21/08/1989	1,84	97	Golden Lions	-	-	R	1	0	0	0	0	0
28 Players									7	6	8	0	71

Note: C = Captain, ▪ = Yellow Card, □ = Test Debut

Head Coach: Allister Coetzee **Forwards Coach:** Johann van Graan
Forwards Coach: Matthew Proudfoot **Backs Coach:** Mzwandile Stick
Team Doctor: Dr Konrad von Hagen **Physiotherapist:** Vivian Verwant
PR and Admin: Annelee Murray **Logistics Manager:** JJ Fredericks
Media Manager: Rayaan Adriaanse **Team Manager:** Ian Schwartz
Strength & Conditioning: Warren Adams **Physiotherapist:** Tanu Pillay
Technical Analyst: Willie Maree

IRELAND –SERIES APPEARANCES & POINTS

PLAYER	Date of birth	Height	Weight	Union/Club	South Africa 1	South Africa 2	South Africa 3	Apps	T	C	P	DG	Pts
JB Payne	13/10/1985	1,88	96	Ulster	15	15	-	2	1	0	0	0	5
AD Trimble	20/10/1984	1,85	99	Ballymena	14	14	14	3	0	0	0	0	0
RA Henshaw	12/06/1993	1,91	103	Buccaneers	13	13	-	2	0	0	0	0	0
LD Marshall	03/03/1991	1,80	100	Ulster	12	-	13	2	1	0	0	0	5
KG Earls	02/10/1987	1,78	90	Young Munster	11	-	11	2	0	0	0	0	0
DPLJ Jackson	05/01/1992	1,78	87	Dungannon	10	10	10	3	0	5	9	1	40
CG Murray	20/04/1989	1,88	94	Garryowen	9	9	9	3	1	0	0	0	5
JPR Heaslip	15/12/1983	1,93	110	Dublin University	8	8	8	3	1	0	0	0	5
J Murphy	22/04/1991	1,88	106	Lansdowne	7	-	7	2	0	0	0	0	0
CJ Stander	05/04/1990	1,88	114	Munster	6	-	6	2	0	0	0	0	0
DA Toner	29/06/1986	2,08	124	Lansdowne	5	4	5	3	1	0	0	0	5
WI Henderson	21/02/1992	1,98	121	Ballynahinch	4	6	4	3	0	0	0	0	0
MA Ross	21/12/1979	1,88	127	Clontarf	3	-	3	2	0	0	0	0	0
RD Best (c)	15/08/1982	1,80	105	Banbridge	2*	2*	2*	3	0	0	0	0	0
JC McGrath	11/10/1989	1,85	118	St Mary's College	1	1	1	3	0	0	0	0	0
SM Cronin	06/05/1986	1,80	101	St Mary's College	R	-	R	2	0	0	0	0	0
TV Furlong	14/11/1992	1,85	119	Clontarf	R	3	R	3	0	0	0	0	0
U Dillane	09/11/1993	1,98	115	Corinthians	R	-	R	2	0	0	0	0	0
RJ Ruddock	13/11/1990	1,91	111	St Mary's College	R	7	R	3	0	0	0	0	0
CJH Gilroy	11/03/1991	1,83	91	Dungannon	R	11	-	2	0	0	0	0	0
FH Bealham	09/10/1991	1,85	122	Buccaneers	x	R	x	1	0	0	0	0	0
KD Marmion	11/02/1992	1,73	86	Buccaneers	x	R	-	1	0	0	0	0	0
IL Madigan	21/03/1989	1,80	90	Blackrock College	x	R	R	2	0	0	0	0	0
S Olding	11/03/1993	1,78	94	Ulster	-	12	12	2	0	0	0	0	0
Q Roux	30/10/1990	1,96	124	Galwegians	-	5	-	1	0	0	0	0	0
CR Strauss	29/01/1986	1,73	101	Old Wesley	-	R	-	1	0	0	0	0	0
D Kilcoyne	14/12/1988	1,83	112	UL Bohemians	-	R	-	1	0	0	0	0	0
DC Ryan	11/12/1983	2,01	114	Shannon	-	R	-	1	0	0	0	0	0
S Reidy	10/05/1989	1,83	105	Belfast Harlequins	-	t+R	-	1	0	0	0	0	0
T O'Halloran	26/02/1991	1,88	98	Buccaneers	-	R	15	2	0	0	0	0	0
M Healy	14/03/1989	1,83	92	Connacht	-	-	t+R	1	0	0	0	0	0
EG Reddan	20/11/1980	1,78	83	Old Crescent	-	-	R	1	0	0	0	0	0
32 Players									5	5	9	1	65

Note: C = Captain, ▓ = Yellow Card, □ = Test Debut, ■ = Red Card, ☐ = 50 Tests, ■ = Last Test

Head Coach: Joe Schmidt **Team Manager:** Michael Kearney
Forwards Coach: Simon Easterby **Scrum Coach:** Greg Feek
Kicking Coach: Richard Murphy **Strength & Conditioning:** Jason Cowman
Technical Analyst: Mervyn Murphy **Performance Nutritionist:** Ruth Wood-Martin
Physiotherapist: James Allen **Physiotherapist:** Keith Fox
Masseur: David Revins **Masseur:** Willie Bennett
Assistant Technical Analyst: Vinny Hammond
Media & Communications Officer: David O'Siochain **Team Co-Ordinator:** Nicola Lyons

CASTLE LAGER
RUGBY CHAMPIONSHIP

South Africa 30 Argentina 23
(Halftime 10-13)

Test # 456

Mbombela Stadium, Nelspruit. Kick-off: 17:05. Attendance: 27 357. August 20, 2016
Referee: GW Jackson *(New Zealand)*; Ass. Ref 1: J Garcès *(France)*;
Ass. Ref 2: B O'Keefe *(New Zealand)*; TMO: G Newman *(New Zealand)*

SOUTH AFRICA

Tries: Combrinck, Goosen, Whiteley. Conversions: Jantjies (3). Penalty goals: Jantjies (3).

JL Goosen; RJ Combrinck, LG Mapoe *(Jesse Kriel, 72)*, D de Allende *(JL de Jongh, 72)*,
BG Habana*; ET Jantjies, F de Klerk; WR Whiteley, TS Mohojé, L-FP Louw *(Jaco Kriel, 54)*,
L de Jager *(PS du Toit, 54)*, E Etzebeth, J Redelinghuys *(VP Koch, 32)*, JA Straus *(C)*,
T Mtawarira *(S Kitshoff, 54)*.

UNUSED SUBSTITUTES: MT Mbonambi & R Paige. *YELLOW CARD: 46 – BG Habana
CHAMPIONSHIP DEBUTS: RJ Combrinck, F de Klerk, J Redelinghuys, Jaco Kriel & S Kitshoff

ARGENTINA

Tries: Orlando, Cordero. Conversions: Sánchez (2). Penalty goals: Sánchez (3).

J Tuculet; S Cordero, M Orlando *(S Gonález Iglesias, 74)*, J-M Hernández, M Montero*;
FN Sánchez, M Landajo *(TM Cubelli, 56)*; F Isa, J-M Leguizamón *(J Ortega Desio, 64)*,
PN Matera, TE Lavanini, MI Alemanno *(G Petti, 56)*, R Herrera *(E Pieretto, 79)*, A Creevy *(C)*
(JS Montoya, 63), FN Tetaz Chaparro.

UNUSED SUBSTITUTES: F Arregui & R Moyano Joya. *YELLOW CARD: 22 – M Montero.
CHAMPIONSHIP DEBUTS: M Orlando, G Petti & E Pieretto.
*NOTE: Augustín Creevy played in his 50th test. Cordero's try was the 700th try that
South Africa conceded in Test rugby.*

Springboks master art of escape

SOUTH Africa, down by 10 points with the match winding down, dug deep to score 17 points in the final 10 minutes and secure a 30-23 victory.

As was the case in the second Test against Ireland in Johannesburg, the scales were very firmly tilted in favour of the visitors as the match entered the home straight.

The early running, though, was made by South Africa. With flyhalf Elton Jantjies just having missed a penalty, lock Eben Etzebeth fielded the dropout and the Springboks mauled briefly before attacking on the open side.

Jantjies broke superbly before being caught by Pumas flank Juan-Manuel Leguizamón. However, the ball was recycled and travelled through the hands of flank Francois Louw and fullback Johan Goosen to right wing Ruan Combrinck for the try.

Jantjies and opposite number Nicolas Sánchez then exchanged penalties before the match took a twist that tilted the momentum in Argentina's favour.

In truth, the yellow card to Argentine left wing Manuel Montero – for tipping over Damian de Allende - should have been the catalyst for the Springboks to put distance between themselves and the visitors.

SCORING SEQUENCE

Min	Action	Score
7	Jantjies missed penalty goal	
7	Combrinck try, Jantjies conversion	SA 7-0
16	Sánchez penalty goal	SA 7-3
18	Jantjies penalty goal	SA 10-3
24	Sánchez penalty goal	SA 10-6
25	Orlando try, Sánchez conversion	Arg 13-10
29	Goosen missed penalty goal	Arg 13-10
39	Jantjies missed penalty goal	Arg 13-10
56	Jantjies penalty goal	13-13
63	Sánchez missed penalty goal	13-13
65	Sánchez penalty goal	Arg 16-13
67	Cordero try, Sánchez conversion	Arg 23-13
71	Goosen try, Jantjies conversion	Arg 23-20
73	Jantjies penalty goal	23-23
76	Goosen missed penalty goal	23-23
79	Whiteley try, Jantjies conversion	SA 30-23

Instead Argentina outscored the hosts 10-0 in the time that Montero spent in the sin-bin.

First there was a penalty by Sánchez after the Springboks were caught in possession behind the advantage line and then a terrific try by outside centre Matias Orlando after scrumhalf Martin Landajo had initiated an attack down the blind side.

Sánchez's conversion made the score 13-10 to Argentina, who were looking as if they were a man to the good rather than one short.

Goosen and Jantjies both missed penalty attempts that could have drawn the Springboks level, but the miss of the day comfortably belonged to outside centre Lionel Mapoe, who lost the ball over the tryline late in the first half.

It was just one episode in a comedy of errors that even saw an attempted clearance kick by Jantjies strike a bewildered captain Adriaan Strauss in the face.

Not long after half-time the home side were hamstrung when left wing Bryan Habana landed in the sin-bin for taking out Santiago Cordero's legs from under him.

Argentina couldn't make their numerical advantage count and Jantjies squared the match at 13-13 before Habana's return.

Sánchez then restored the lead before setting up Cordero for a try with a delightful chip over the Springboks' defensive line.

With the home side staring into the abyss, scrumhalf Faf de Klerk tore away from the back of the scrum. A posse of Pumas defenders followed the fleet-footed No 9 across the field before he executed a perfect switch-pass against the grain to set up Goosen for a try.

A Jantjies penalty followed soon after to square the match before the decisive try by No 8 Warren Whiteley in the 79th minute. The Springboks had played through a few phases off an attacking lineout before De Klerk switched the direction of play and Whiteley finished after some good work on attack by Etzebeth and Habana.

Heart palpitations were to follow from the kick-off. Whiteley, left with the simple task of kicking the ball out to end the match, quite incredibly didn't find touch. He caught his own kick before eventually carrying the ball into touch – an incident that perhaps best summed up the Springboks' stuttering performance.

Argentina 26 South Africa 24
(Halftime 13-3)

Test # 457

Estadio Padre Ernesto Martearena, Salta. Kick-off: 16:40. Attendance: 16 000. August 27, 2016
Referee: J Garcès *(France)*; Ass. Ref 1: GW Jackson *(New Zealand)*; Ass. Ref 2: B O'Keefe
(New Zealand); TMO: G Newman *(New Zealand)*

ARGENTINA

Tries: Tuculet, Leguizamón. Conversions: Sánchez, Hernández. Penalty goals: Sánchez (2), Hernández, González Iglesias.

J Tuculet; S Cordero, M Orlando *(TM Cubelli, 61)**, J-M Hernández *(E Pieretto, 67)***, M Montero *(LP González Amorosino, H/T)*; FN Sánchez *(S González Iglesias, 46)*, M Landajo; F Isa, J-M Leguizamón *(J Ortega Desio, 65)*, PN Matera, TE Lavanini *(G Petti, 46)*, MI Alemanno, R Herrera, A Creevy *(C)* *(JS Montoya, 61)*, FN Tetaz Chaparro *(L Noguera Paz, 65)*.
*Cubelli to scrumhalf, Landajo to outside centre. **Pieretto to tighthead prop, Herrera to #5 lock, Petti to #7 flank, Ortega Desio to back three. *YELLOW CARD: 20 - R Herrera.
NOTE: Tomas Cubelli played in his 50th Test and Leguizamón in his 70th. Argentina's first win at home against South Africa.

SOUTH AFRICA

Tries: Habana, Du Toit. Conversion: Goosen. Penalty goals: Jantjies (2), Steyn (2).

JL Goosen; RJ Combrinck *(Jesse Kriel, 33)*, LG Mapoe, D de Allende, BG Habana; ET Jantjies *(M Steyn, 46)*, F de Klerk *(R Paige, 74)*; WR Whiteley, TS Mohojé, L-FP Louw *(Jaco Kriel, 54)*, L de Jager *(PS du Toit, 46)*, E Etzebeth, VP Koch *(LC Adriaanse, 46)*, JA Straus *(C)*, T Mtawarira *(S Kitshoff, 46)*.
UNUSED SUBSTITUTE: MT Mbonambi. CHAMPIONSHIP DEBUT: LC Adriaanse & R Paige.
NOTE: Pieter-Steph du Toit scored South Africa's 100th try against Argentina and Morné Steyn's two penalty goals brought up his 700th career point for South Africa.
Tendai Mtawarira played in his 80th Test, equalling Os du Randt's record for most tests as a prop.

Springboks run out of lives

THERE was another attempt at a stirring fightback, but in Salta the Springboks' luck finally ran out.

The 26-24 defeat was South Africa's first in Argentina – another unwanted record after their first home loss to Ireland in June. Both sides struggled to find their rhythm in the first half, though Allister Coetzee would have been the most frustrated of the coaches at half-time.

Once again the Springboks failed to adequately capitalise on a numerical advantage. Ramiro Herrera, the Pumas' tighthead prop, was sin-binned in the 20th minute for a late and dangerous tackle on flank Francois Louw.

Flyhalf Elton Jantjies immediately capitalised with a three-pointer, but by the time Herrera returned Argentina led 6-3 courtesy of two penalties by Nicolas Sánchez.

There was immediate drama after Herrera's return with Pumas fullback Joaquin Tuculet scoring after a sweeping counter-attack from deep that saw the ball transferred through one pair of skilful hands after the other.

While it was all too easy for the Pumas to find space out wide, the Springboks by contrast were playing too far behind the advantage line. On top of that they could not secure enough possession to be able to put the Pumas' defence to the test. At half-time the score was 13-3 to the hosts – a generally fair reflection of their dominance.

South Africa were much better after the break and it took them just six minutes to draw level.

A penalty by Jantjies was followed by Bryan Habana's 65th Test try, which made him the world record holder of career tries for a tier-one rugby country. (He had previously shared it with Wallaby legend David Campese.)

Habana's try owed much to a sleight of hand by Louw, who passed the ball from behind his back. There was also some impressive build-up play, with the Springboks suddenly looking a lot slicker.

However, the Argentines were not to be outdone. They are now far more than the side of a decade ago that was feared for little other than their scrummaging.

This was perfectly illustrated by flank Juan-Manuel Leguizamón's try from a cross-kick by inside centre Juan-Martin Hernández.

Leguizamón and his colleagues in the Pumas' loose-forward combination, Facundo Isa and Pablo Matera, were another point of difference between the teams.

Just before Leguizamón's try, Coetzee had sent on his so-called 'insurance policy' in Morné Steyn. The reasoning was that the veteran flyhalf had the ability to decide a close match with precision kicking – out of hand and at the posts.

As it turned out, both he and Jantjies fluffed two kicks at goal, a crucial statistic in the outcome. The Springboks were down by 10 points again when Hernández added a penalty, but played themselves into a potential winning position. Steyn reduced the gap to seven points with a penalty before lock Pieter-Steph du Toit eventually crashed over through the Springboks' perseverance with the ball in hand.

Then, in the 73rd minute, the visitors took the lead. Argentina strayed off-side and Steyn, who had earlier missed a penalty and conversion attempt, edged South Africa ahead by 24-23.

Steyn, however, couldn't secure the match when offered enough space for a drop goal. The Pumas then caught the Springboks napping with a short kickoff and a counter-attack led to the penalty that made history for both sides.

SCORING SEQUENCE

Min	Action	Score
3	Jantjies missed penalty goal	
21	Jantjies penalty goal	SA 3-0
23	Sánchez penalty goal	3-3
30	Sánchez penalty goal	Arg 6-3
31	Tuculet try, Sánchez conversion	Arg 13-3
42	Jantjies missed penalty goal	Arg 13-3
43	Jantjies penalty goal	Arg 13-6
45	Habana try, Goosen conversion	13-13
48	Leguizamón try, Hernández conversion	Arg 20-13
52	Steyn missed penalty goal	Arg 20-13
54	Hernández penalty goal	Arg 23-13
64	Steyn penalty goal	Arg 23-16
68	Du Toit try, Steyn missed conversion	Arg 23-21
74	Steyn penalty goal	SA 24-23
76	Steyn missed drop goal	SA 24-23
78	González Iglesias penalty goal	Arg 26-24

Australia 23 South Africa 17
(Halftime 13-14)

Test # 458

Suncorp Stadium, Brisbane. Kick-off: 20:05. Attendance: 30 327. September 10, 2016
Referee: N Owens *(Wales)*; Ass. Ref 1: W Barnes *(England)*; Ass. Ref 2: P Gaüzère *(France)*;
TMO: B Skeen *(New Zealand)*

AUSTRALIA

Tries: Coleman, Foley. Conversions: Foley (2). Penalty goals: Foley (3).
IF Folau; DS Haylett-Petty *(DA Mitchell, 69)**, SV Kerevi *(RTRN Kuridrani, 74)*, BT Foley,
R Hodge; QS Cooper, SW Genia; DW Pocock *(SP McMahon, 74)*, MK Hooper, DW Mumm,
AP Coleman *(RW Arnold, 55)*, KP Douglas, SM Kepu *(AEA Ala'atoa, 51)*, ST Moore (C)
(SUT Polota-Nau, 55), ST Sio *(JA Slipper, 51)*.
*Mitchell to left wing, Hodge to right wing. UNUSED SUBSTITUTE: NJ Phipps.
CHAMPIONSHIP DEBUTS: RW Arnold & SP McMahon.

SOUTH AFRICA

Tries: Whiteley, Goosen. Conversion: Jantjies (2). Penalty goal: Steyn.
JL Goosen; BG Habana *(LG Mapoe, 59-64)*, Jesse Kriel, JL de Jongh, F Hougaard *(LG Mapoe,
79)***; ET Jantjies *(M Steyn, 64)*, F de Klerk; WR Whiteley, TS Mohojé *(FJ Mostert, 47)**, L-FP
Louw *(Jaco Kriel, 51)*, L de Jager *(PS du Toit, H/T)*, E Etzebeth***, LC Adriaanse *(TN Nyakane, 51)*,
JA Strauss (C) *(MT Mbonambi, 74)*, T Mtawarira *(S Kitshoff, 51)*.
*Mostert to lock, Du Toit to #7 flank. **Mapoe to outside centre, Jesse Kriel to right wing.
***YELLOW CARD: 42 - E Etzebeth. CHAMPIONSHIP DEBUTS: MT Mbonambi & FJ Mostert.
*NOTE: Eben Etzebeth became the youngest Springbok ever to reach 50 appearances in tests for
South Africa while Tendai Mtawarira became the most capped Springbok prop (81 Tests) surpassing
the record of Os du Rand.*

Wallabies show their street smarts

AN outside centre at inside centre, a flyhalf at fullback and a scrumhalf at wing. Needless to say, selection was a talking point after the Springboks' 23-17 defeat to the Wallabies at the Suncorp Stadium in Brisbane. Not to mention their decision-making and tactical approach.

It's one thing to kick a high ball, but quite another when your target is Israel Folau, the Wallaby fullback with perhaps unmatched aerial skills in world rugby.

Ironically, one such action actually led to a try for the Springboks against the run of play. Australia counter-attacked after Folau had fielded fullback Johan Goosen's kick and had the Springboks on the rack. All that was left to do was to shift the ball down the open side and finish in the corner.

However, inside centre Bernard Foley's pass was intercepted by hooker and skipper Adriaan Strauss, who immediately shifted the ball to flyhalf Elton Jantjies. He kicked downfield and Goosen ran down the ball for the try that put the Springboks 14-3 ahead.

They had earlier taken the lead through a try by No 8 Warren Whiteley, who ran a splendid line to collect scrumhalf Faf de Klerk's pass after attacking with purpose from turnover possession.

But after Goosen's try, the Springboks were comfortably second best and they conceded 20 points before substitute flyhalf Morné Steyn added a penalty 15 minutes before the end to bring them within six for a fighting chance.

South Africa also struggled to get out of their own half and couldn't command the same dominance at the scrums one has become accustomed to against the Australians.

Without the ability to physically dominate the Wallabies, the Springboks struggled to create much at the back. Of course, it didn't help that Juan de Jongh was at inside centre when he's clearly at his most comfortable at No 13. On top of that, a scrumhalf, Francois Hougaard, was playing on the left wing.

As with Goosen, who is primarily a flyhalf, it wasn't the first time that the aforementioned players had to slot into these positions. But the past has taught us not to expect much of them there, so why go down that path?

Goosen's try served only to briefly mask the Springboks' shortcomings.

Australia pulled one back in the 27th minute, with sustained pressure resulting in a comfortable try for lock Adam Coleman, who received a floating pass from scrumhalf Will Genia.

Another badly-judged kick on Folau resulted in a counter-attack that saw the Springboks concede a penalty to allow Foley to make it a one-point game.

Thereafter the visitors conspired against themselves. Jantjies missed an opportunity to edge them four points ahead and early in the second half lock Eben Etzebeth was sin-binned for infringing at a ruck with the Springboks desperately defending their line.

Foley slotted the penalty before himself making the decisive score by cutting between Jantjies and substitute lock Pieter-Steph du Toit.

It was all too easy for the streetwise Wallabies, who comfortably found space to attack out wide and on another day might have won more comfortably.

SCORING SEQUENCE

Min	Action	Score
3	Whiteley try, Jantjies conversion	SA 7-0
11	Foley penalty goal	SA 7-3
18	Goosen try, Jantjies conversion	SA 14-3
27	Coleman try, Foley conversion	SA 14-10
35	Foley penalty goal	SA 14-13
39	Jantjies missed penalty goal	SA 14-13
43	Foley penalty goal	A 16-14
62	Foley try, Foley conversion	A 23-14
66	Steyn penalty goal	A 23-17

New Zealand 41 South Africa 13
(Halftime 15-10)

Test # 459

AMI Stadium, Christchurch. Kick-off: 19:35. Attendance: 20 826. September 17, 2016
Referee: A Gardner *(Australia)*; Ass. Ref 1: P Gaüzère *(France)*; Ass. Ref 2: M Mitrea *(Italy)*;
TMO: GJP Ayoub *(Australia)*

NEW ZEALAND

Tries: Dagg, SJ Savea, BR Smith, AS Savea, Whitelock, Perenara. Conversions: Barrett (4).
Penalty goal: Barrett.

BR Smith; IJA Dagg *(LZ Sopoaga, 68)***, MF Fekitoa, RS Crotty *(AR Lienert-Brown, 66)*, SJ Savea;
BJ Barrett, AL Smith *(TTR Perenara, 64)*; KJ Read *(C)*, AS Savea *(L Romano, 60)**, J Kaino
(MB Todd, 52), SL Whitelock, BA Retallick, OT Franks *(CC Faumuina, 54)*, DS Coles
(CJD Taylor, 66), JPT Moody *(WWV Crockett, 46)*.

*Romano to #5 lock, Whitelock to #7 flank. **Sopoaga to flyhalf, Barrett to fullback, BR Smith to right wing.
NOTE: *For the first time in New Zealand Rugby history, two brothers (Savea brothers) both scored in the*
same test match. This was the All Blacks' 44th consecutive win at home.

SOUTH AFRICA

Try: Habana. Conversion: Jantjies. Penalty goals: Jantjies (2).

JL Goosen *(D de Allende, 51)**; BG Habana, Jesse Kriel, JL de Jongh, F Hougaard; ET Jantjies
(M Steyn, 60), F de Klerk; WR Whiteley, TS Mohojé *(WS Alberts, 51)*, L-FP Louw *(Jaco Kriel, 60)*,
PS du Toit *(FJ Mostert, 63)*, E Etzebeth, VP Koch *(LC Adriaanse, 72)*, JA Strauss *(C)* *(MJ Marx, 44)*,
T Mtawarira *(S Kitshoff, 60)*.

*De Allende to inside centre, De Jongh to outside centre, Jesse Kriel to fullback. Whiteley wore #26 from the
53rd minute. TEST AND CHAMPIONSHIP DEBUT: MJ Marx #876.
NOTE: *Francois Louw played in his 50th Test match. Bryan Habana scored his 66th try, now only*
3 tries short of the record for most tries ever scored in a Test match career. Eben Etzebeth equalled
Victor Matfield's record for most consecutive tests (28) as a lock.

All Blacks expose shortcomings

ANY rugby supporter will know that feeling, when their team is well beaten and the final whistle cannot come quickly enough.

That was pretty much the story of the Springboks as they were battered by the All Blacks in Christchurch.

Initially the visitors gave as good as they got. They even led 7-3 after Bryan Habana's try in the 19th minute, with the great wing running a terrific angle as he collected No 8 Warren Whiteley's pass to finish.

It was 7-3 to the Springboks and they looked a side determined to go toe to toe with the world champions.

Sadly, the advantage they held would dissipate within a matter of minutes, with flyhalf Elton Jantjies knocking the ball on in the Springboks' 22-metre area from the kick-off following Habana's score.

The All Blacks set the scrum and as early as the second phase right wing Israel Dagg rounded off after the ball had travelled quickly through the hands of their dynamic hooker Dane Coles.

There was a large amount of space in the wide channel and this match would be characterised by the Springboks' lack of defensive organisation. It was particularly problematic at the scrums where the Kiwi scrumhalf Aaron Smith, arguably the most dangerous player in his position in the world, could comfortably make metres when unmarked.

On top of that, the Springboks shifted the ball to one another far behind the advantage line, which meant their attack was mostly inef-

fective. It also did not help matters that coach Allister Coetzee was also persevering with his decision to pick Johan Goosen, Juan de Jongh and Francois Hougaard out of position in the backline.

The set-piece also offered little reason for cheer. Not too far in the distant past, the Springboks could still rely on a bit of dominance in the scrums and lineouts when playing the All Blacks. No more.

New Zealand have tightened up those aspects of their game and put a dominant scrum to good use. It served as a solid platform for their second try, with Coles again joining the line before offloading to left wing Julian Savea.

Jantjies struck a penalty a few minutes before half-time and at 15-10 to the All Blacks it appeared to be still anyone's game.

However, the second half highlighted the All Black' class and exposed the Springboks' shortcomings. Even at the lineouts they were out of sorts, though there were extenuating circumstances after losing captain Adriaan Strauss to injury early in the second half.

The All Blacks are never more dangerous than when they are gifted possession. That was the case when Jantjies hoofed the ball downfield and All Black fullback Ben Smith finished a sweeping counter-attack underneath South Africa's posts.

Next to score was flank Ardie Savea, a move that had its roots in pilfering the ball at a ruck.

Coles's good hands was again evident as he delivered the pass that saw lock Sam Whitelock finish in the corner.

The humiliation was completed in the 71st minute when the All Blacks' replacement scrumhalf, TJ Perenara, must have thought that it was Christmas in September with the amount of space he was afforded after collecting the ball at the back of a dominant scrum.

SCORING SEQUENCE

Min	Action	Score
9	Barrett penalty goal.	NZ 3-0
19	Habana try, Jantjies conversion.	SA 7-3
22	Dagg try, Barrett missed conversion.	NZ 8-7
28	SJ Savea try, Barrett conversion.	NZ 15-7
37	Jantjies penalty goal.	NZ 15-10
49	BR Smith try, Barrett conversion.	NZ 22-10
53	Jantjies penalty goal.	NZ 22-13
56	AS Savea try, Barrett conversion	NZ 29-13
65	Whitelock try, Barrett missed conversion.	NZ 34-13
71	Perenara try, Barrett conversion.	NZ 41-13

South Africa 18 Australia 10
(Halftime 12-10)

Test # 460

Loftus Versfeld, Pretoria. Kick-off: 17:05. Attendance: 38 704. October 1, 2016
Referee: W Barnes *(England)*; Ass. Ref 1: J Lacey *(Ireland)*; Ass. Ref 2: GJ Clancy *(Ireland)*;
TMO: J Yuille *(Scotland)*

SOUTH AFRICA

Penalty goals: Steyn (4). Drop goals: Steyn (2).

PJ Lambie; BG Habana *(WJ le Roux, 46)**, Jesse Kriel *(LG Mapoe, 39)*, JL de Jongh, F Hougaard;
M Steyn, R Paige *(WS Alberts, 57)***; WR Whiteley, TS Mohojé *(Jaco Kriel, 55)*, L-FP Louw,
PS du Toit *(L de Jager, 45)*, E Etzebeth, VP Koch *(J Redelinghuys, 45)*, JA Strauss *(C)*,
T Mtawarira *(S Kitshoff, 45)*.

*Le Roux to fullback, Lambie to right wing. **Alberts to flank, Jaco Kriel to left wing,
Hougaard to scrumhalf. UNUSED SUBSTITUTE: MT Mbonambi.
NOTE: For the third time in his career Morné Steyn scored all points in a Test match with a total of
18 points or more and as a result he also surpassed Percy Montgomery's career record for most career
penalty goals (149).

AUSTRALIA

Try: Sio. Conversion: Foley. Penalty goal: Foley.

IF Folau*; DS Haylett-Petty *(S Naivalu, 69)*, SV Kerevi *(RTRN Kuridrani, 54)*, BT Foley, R Hodge;
QS Cooper, SW Genia *(NJ Phipps, 77)*; SP McMahon *(SM Fardy, H/T)*, MK Hooper, DW Mumm,
AP Coleman, RA Simmons *(KP Douglas, 46)*, SM Kepu *(T Robertson, 56)*, ST Moore *(C)*,
ST Sio *(JA Slipper, 56)*.

UNUSED SUBSTITUTE: JE Hanson. *YELLOW CARD: 34 - IF Folau.
TEST AND CHAMPIONSHIP DEBUT: S Naivalu.
NOTE: After seven Test matches at Loftus Versfeld, Australia is still winless at this venue.

Steyn steps up to sink Wallabies

SOUTH Africans haven't always been kind to Morné Steyn, but the veteran flyhalf underlined his value by booting all the Springboks' points in their victory over Australia at Loftus Versfeld.

The selection of Steyn, with Rudy Paige as his halfback partner, was a clear indicator towards a more pragmatic approach by coach Allister Coetzee.

He had taken on the job with public expectation high that Springbok rugby would break free of its shackles on the back of the Emirates Lions' impressive Vodacom Super Rugby campaign, which saw their free-flowing style take them all the way to the final.

However, when the Lions' celebrated halfback pairing of Faf de Klerk and Elton Jantjies were shown up when the pressure was really on, Coetzee went back to basics.

The Springboks might even have added a few tries to Steyn's four penalties and two dropped goals had they been more clinical. However, passes were sometimes rushed when in Australia's red zone, while there was also a smattering of unforced errors.

One such mistake – Bryan Habana not clearing into touch – resulted in a passage of play that led to Scott Sio scoring under the Springbok posts and the Wallabies leading 10-3 inside the first 15 minutes.

South Africa conceded the advantage line all too easily and their defence might have been a talking point had they not managed to get out of jail through good breakdown play.

Francois Louw, in particular, was hugely influential, while the likes of skipper Adriaan Strauss and even scrumhalf-cum-wing Francois Hougaard chipped in to ensure that Australia could not make their territorial advantage count where it mattered.

As the match to'd and fro'd, the Springboks patiently wore down the Wallabies, with Steyn keeping the scoreboard ticking over.

By half-time it was 12-10 and the second half produced over a half an hour of uninspired rugby before being settled with another penalty and dropped goal by Steyn in the final five minutes of normal time.

The Springboks had ground their way to that point, with the substitute props Steven Kitshoff and Julian Redelinghuys playing a big part in turning the screws through impressive scrum dominance.

Yet for the man of the match one couldn't look further than Strauss, who had led by example. He covered every inch of ground and his influence extended to the Springboks' attack with some splendid ball carries.

He was clearly determined to leave Springbok rugby on a high after announcing in September that he would be retiring from international rugby at the end of the season.

Strauss had copped some public and media criticism for his performances earlier in the year, but his influence was best summed up by All Black hooker Dane Coles before the following week's match against the All Blacks in Durban.

"Adriaan was leading from the front. The best way for a team to improve is for a captain to perform like that," Coles said.

Significantly, this also marked the point where the Springboks stopped falling between tactical stools. The pressure to reinvent the wheel was cast aside and a very necessary victory was achieved in a manner which was pragmatic, familar and comforting.

Yes, it wasn't pretty, but in the modern era of professionalism and added pressures from all corners, the Springboks have seldom been a team renowned for its subtleties.

Nick Mallett's class of 1997-98 might have won with style and panache but as anyone will tell you, winning ugly is pretty enough if you're on the right side of the scoreboard.

SCORING SEQUENCE

Min	Action	Score
4	Steyn drop goal.	SA 3-0
8	Foley penalty goal.	3-3
14	Sio try, Foley conversion.	A 10-3
23	Hodge missed penalty goal.	A 10-3
26	Steyn penalty goal.	A 10-6
35	Steyn penalty goal.	A 10-9
41	Steyn penalty goal.	SA 12-10
52	Hodge missed penalty goal.	SA 12-10
61	Steyn missed penalty goal.	SA 12-10
76	Steyn penalty goal.	SA 15-10
80	Steyn drop goal.	SA 18-10

South Africa 15 New Zealand 57
(Halftime 9-12)

Test # 461

Growthpoint Kings Park, Durban. Kick-off: 17:05. Attendance: 52 595. October 8, 2016
Referee: J Garcès *(France)*; Ass. Ref 1: J Lacey *(Ireland)*; Ass. Ref 2: GJ Clancy *(Ireland)*;
TMO: J Yuille *(Scotland)*

SOUTH AFRICA
Penalty goals: Steyn (5).
PJ Lambie; F Hougaard, JL de Jongh, D de Allende, BG Habana; M Steyn *(WJ le Roux, 64)**,
F de Klerk *(LG Mapoe, 68)***; WR Whiteley, TS Mohojé *(WS Alberts, 46)*, L-FP Louw *(Jaco Kriel, 12)*, PS du Toit, E Etzebeth *(L de Jager, 46)*, VP Koch *(J Redelinghuys, 46)*, JA Strauss *(C)* *(MT Mbonambi, 75)*, T Mtawarira *(S Kitshoff, 51)*.
*Le Roux to fullback, Lambie to flyhalf. **Mapoe to outside centre, De Jongh to right wing, Hougaard to scrumhalf. YELLOW CARD: 72 - L de Jager,
NOTE: This was the biggest defeat ever for South Africa at home and the nine tries conceded the most ever in a Test match anywhere.

NEW ZEALAND
Tries: Dagg (2), Perenara (2), Barrett (2), Taylor, Smith, Squire. Conversions: Barrett (3), Sopoaga (3).
BR Smith; IJA Dagg, AR Lienert-Brown, RS Crotty *(G Moala, 66)***, WR Naholo *(LZ Sopoaga, 62)**; BR Barrett, TTR Perenara *(TNJ Kerr-Barlow, 68)*; KJ Read *(C)*, MB Todd *(AS Savea, 56)*, J Kaino *(LIJ Squire, 62)*, SL Whitelock, BA Retallick, OT Franks *(CC Faumuina, 66)*, DS Coles *(CJD Taylor, 68)*, JPT Moody *(WWV Crockett, 51)*. **Sopoaga to flyhalf, Barrett to fullback, Smith to left wing. **Moala to left wing (for Smith), Smith to outside centre, Lienert-Brown to inside centre.*
*YELLOW CARD: 81 - CJD Taylor.
NOTE: This was the biggest ever win for New Zealand against South Africa and the nine tries scored the most ever against South Africa. This was the All Blacks' 17th consecutive win, thereby equalling the record for most consecutive wins by a Tier 1 country..

Barrett puts Springboks to sword

WITH 20 minutes gone of a quite remarkable Test match, the smell of expectation permeated the early evening Durban air.

It was all going according to script: the Springboks were defending courageously and, while outgunned in terms of territory and possession, were up 6-0 courtesy of two penalties by veteran flyhalf Morné Steyn.

Could this be the scene of one of the most famous and satisfying Springbok victories of the modern era, the day they prevented the world champions from equalling the record of 17 consecutive Test wins for a tier-one country?

Alas, it was not to be. Not by a long shot. By the time referee Jérôme Garcès sounded the final whistle, it is an understatement to say that the Springboks were well beaten.

New Zealand 57, South Africa 15 – a record loss to the old foe and to any opponent on home soil.

The only impressive thing about the Springboks was their guts. New Zealand found easy routes through the first line of defence, but the South Africans scrambled as if their lives depended on it.

However, character can take you only so far. The All Blacks can pounce on the smallest error and that was indeed the case when Juan de Jongh missed a tackle deep in Kiwi territory.

A counter-attack followed and several phases later Israel Dagg trotted over for a try. Another by TJ Perenara followed after Anton Lienert-Brown broke the line to give the All Blacks a 12-9 lead.

In the minutes before half-time the Springboks were feverishly plugging leaks. One increasingly got the sense the dam wall would break and a deep sense of dread turned into relief as the half-time whistle sounded.

The television match official had just ruled that there was obstruction when the Kiwis crossed the tryline from a lineout move. It was 12-9 to New Zealand. The Springboks were hanging in there.

Flyhalf Beauden Barrett's missed conversion from Dagg's and then his own try inside the first 15 minutes of the second half meant that the Springboks remained in the game.

Steyn added two penalties and with a touch over 20 minutes left it was anyone's game at 22-15 to the All Blacks.

Ominously, however, a four-tries-to-nil statistic at that point told its own story. The All Blacks' lead would have been comfortable had Barrett not left his kicking boots in the Land of the Long White Cloud.

That said, no one was more influential than him as it rained tries in a forgettable second half. Four of the visitors' match haul of nine were scored from the 71st minute onwards as the floodgates opened.

Barrett showed a tremendous turn of pace to the tryline after substitute flank Liam Squire's offload – a move that was rooted in turnover possession.

Lood de Jager, the Springboks' replacement lock, then made their task of now simply avoiding embarrassment decidedly more difficult by storming recklessly into a ruck.

For his troubles he landed in the sin-bin – a spectator as his team-mates were mercilessly put to the sword with three more All Black tries for substitute hooker Codie Taylor, fullback Ben Smith and Squire.

The result reverberated around the rugby world. New Zealand had reached a fresh high, while Springbok rugby found itself, not for the first time in 125 years of history, at a crossroads.

SCORING SEQUENCE

Min	Action	Score
5	Steyn penalty goal	SA 3-0
7	Barrett missed penalty goal	SA 3-0
18	Steyn penalty goal	SA 6-0
22	Dagg try, Barrett missed conversion	SA 6-5
27	Steyn penalty goal	SA 9-5
31	Perenara try, Barrett conversion	NZ 12-9
37	Steyn missed drop goal	NZ 12-9
44	Dagg try, Barrett missed conversion	NZ 17-9
50	Steyn penalty goal	NZ 17-12
55	Barrett try, Barrett missed conversion	NZ 22-12
59	Steyn penalty goal	NZ 22-15
61	Perenara try, Barrett conversion	NZ 29-15
71	Barrett try, Barrett conversion	NZ 36-15
73	Taylor try, Sopoaga conversion	NZ 43-15
76	Smith try, Sopoaga conversion	NZ 50-15
82	Squire try, Sopoaga conversion	NZ 57-15

CASTLE LAGER RUGBY CHAMPIONSHIP

Date	Venue	Home Team		Away Team	
20/08/2016	Sydney	Australia	8	New Zealand	42
20/08/2016	Nelspruit	South Africa	30	Argentina	23
27/08/2016	Wellington	New Zealand	29	Australia	9
27/08/2016	Salta	Argentina	26	South Africa	24
10/09/2016	Hamilton	New Zealand	57	Argentina	22
10/09/2016	Brisbane	Australia	23	South Africa	17
17/09/2016	Christchurch	New Zealand	41	South Africa	13
17/09/2016	Perth	Australia	36	Argentina	20
01/10/2016	Pretoria	South Africa	18	Australia	10
01/10/2016	Buenos Aires	Argentina	17	New Zealand	36
08/10/2016	Durban	South Africa	15	New Zealand	57
08/10/2016	London	Argentina	21	Australia	33

LOG

Team	P	W	L	D	PF	PA	PD	TF	TA	BP	PTS
New Zealand	6	6	0	0	262	84	178	38	5	6	30
Australia	6	3	3	0	119	147	-28	13	16	2	14
South Africa	6	2	4	0	117	180	-63	8	22	2	10
Argentina	6	1	5	0	129	216	-87	11	27	1	5

Note: *BP = Bonus point*

Warren Whiteley and Teboho Mohojé.

2016 CHAMPIONSHIP – ALL SCORERS

PLAYER	Country	Apps	T	C	P	DG	Pts
BJ Barrett	New Zealand	6	4	23	5	0	81
FN Sánchez	Argentina	5	0	7	13	0	53
BT Foley	Australia	6	1	9	10	0	53
M Steyn	South Africa	5	0	0	12	2	42
ET Jantjies	South Africa	4	0	6	7	0	33
IJA Dagg	New Zealand	6	5	0	1	0	28
BR Smith	New Zealand	6	5	0	0	0	25
SJ Savea	New Zealand	5	4	0	0	0	20
RS Crotty	New Zealand	5	4	0	0	0	20
TTR Perenara	New Zealand	6	4	0	0	0	20
S González Iglesias	Argentina	6	0	2	4	0	16
S Cordero	Argentina	5	3	0	0	0	15
SV Kerevi	Australia	5	3	0	0	0	15
JL Goosen	South Africa	4	2	1	0	0	12
WR Whiteley	South Africa	6	2	0	0	0	10
DS Coles	New Zealand	6	2	0	0	0	10
J Tuculet	Argentina	6	2	0	0	0	10
BG Habana	South Africa	6	2	0	0	0	10
F Isa	Argentina	5	2	0	0	0	10
SW Genia	Australia	6	2	0	0	0	10
AP Coleman	Australia	5	2	0	0	0	10
R Hodge	Australia	5	0	0	2	0	6
LZ Sopoaga	New Zealand	3	0	3	0	0	6
RJ Combrinck	South Africa	2	1	0	0	0	5
M Orlando	Argentina	6	1	0	0	0	5
NJ Phipps	Australia	4	1	0	0	0	5
WR Naholo	New Zealand	2	1	0	0	0	5
J Kaino	New Zealand	5	1	0	0	0	5
J-M Leguizamón	Argentina	5	1	0	0	0	5
J-M Hernández	Argentina	3	0	1	1	0	5
PS du Toit	South Africa	6	1	0	0	0	5
SJ Cane	New Zealand	3	1	0	0	0	5
DS Haylett-Petty	Australia	6	1	0	0	0	5
CC Faumuina	New Zealand	5	1	0	0	0	5
MK Hooper	Australia	6	1	0	0	0	5
AR Lienert-Brown	New Zealand	5	1	0	0	0	5
L Romano	New Zealand	2	1	0	0	0	5
AS Savea	New Zealand	6	1	0	0	0	5
SL Whitelock	New Zealand	6	1	0	0	0	5
ST Sio	Australia	6	1	0	0	0	5
MI Alemanno	Argentina	6	1	0	0	0	5
J de la Fuente	Argentina	2	1	0	0	0	5
DW Mumm	Australia	6	1	0	0	0	5
CJD Taylor	New Zealand	5	1	0	0	0	5
LIJ Squire	New Zealand	4	1	0	0	0	5
AW Cruden	New Zealand	3	0	1	0	0	2

SOUTH AFRICA APPEARANCES & POINTS

PLAYER	Union/Club	Date of birth	Height	Weight	Arg1	Arg2	Aus1	NZ1	Aus2	NZ2	Apps	T	C	P	DG	Pts
JL Goosen	Racing 92[1]	27/07/1992	1,85	85	15	15	15	15	-	-	4	2	1	0	0	12
RJ Combrinck	Golden Lions	10/05/1990	1,83	97	14	14	-	-	-	-	2	1	0	0	0	5
LG Mapoe	Golden Lions	13/07/1988	1,82	87	13	13	t+R	-	R	R	5	0	0	0	0	0
D de Allende	Western Province	25/11/1991	1,89	101	12	12	-	R	-	12	4	0	0	0	0	0
BG Habana	Toulon[1]	12/06/1983	1,80	93	11	11	14	14	14	11	6	2	0	0	0	10
ET Jantjies	Golden Lions	01/08/1990	1,76	88	10	10	10	10	-	-	4	0	6	7	0	33
F de Klerk	Golden Lions	19/10/1991	1,72	80	9	9	9	9	-	9	5	0	0	0	0	0
WR Whiteley	Golden Lions	18/09/1987	1,92	97	8	8	8	8	8	8	6	2	0	0	0	10
TS Mohojé	Free State	03/08/1990	1,92	103	7	7	7	7	7	7	6	0	0	0	0	0
L-FP Louw	Bath Rugby[2]	15/06/1985	1,90	114	6	6	6	6	6	6	6	0	0	0	0	0
L de Jager	Free State	17/12/1992	2,05	120	5	5	5	-	R	R	5	0	0	0	0	0
E Etzebeth	Western Province	29/10/1991	2,04	117	4	4	4	4	4	4	6	0	0	0	0	0
J Redelinghuys	Golden Lions	11/09/1989	1,76	100	3	-	-	-	R	R	3	0	0	0	0	0
JA Strauss (C)	Blue Bulls	18/11/1985	1,84	114	2*	2*	2*	2*	2*	2*	6	0	0	0	0	0
T Mtawarira	KwaZulu-Natal	01/08/1985	1,83	115	1	1	1	1	1	1	6	0	0	0	0	0
S Kitshoff	Bordeaux-Bègles[1]	10/02/1992	1,84	125	R	R	R	R	R	R	6	0	0	0	0	0
VP Koch	Mpumalanga	13/03/1990	1,85	118	R	3	-	3	3	3	5	0	0	0	0	0
PS du Toit	Western Province	20/08/1992	2,00	116	R	R	R	5	5	5	6	1	0	0	0	5
JA Kriel (Jaco)	Golden Lions	21/08/1989	1,84	97	R	R	R	R	R	R	6	0	0	0	0	0
JL de Jongh	Western Province	15/04/1988	1,77	85	R	-	12	12	12	13	5	0	0	0	0	0
JA Kriel (Jesse)	Blue Bulls	15/02/1994	1,86	96	R	R	13	13	13	-	5	0	0	0	0	0
R Paige	Blue Bulls	02/08/1989	1,76	100	x	R	-	-	9	-	2	0	0	0	0	0
MT Mbonambi	Western Province	07/01/1991	1,76	106	x	x	R	-	x	R	2	0	0	0	0	0
LC Adriaanse	KwaZulu-Natal	02/02/1988	1,80	115	-	R	3	R	-	-	3	0	0	0	0	0
M Steyn	Stade Français[1]	11/07/1984	1,84	91	-	R	R	R	10	10	5	0	0	12	2	42
F Hougaard	Worcester Warriors[2]	06/04/1988	1,79	92	-	-	11	11	11	14	4	0	0	0	0	0
FJ Mostert	Golden Lions	27/11/1990	1,98	103	-	-	R	R	-	-	2	0	0	0	0	0
TN Nyakane	Blue Bulls	04/05/1989	1,78	123	-	-	R	-	-	-	1	0	0	0	0	0
MJ Marx	Golden Lions	13/07/1994	1,88	119	-	-	-	R	-	-	1	0	0	0	0	0
WS Alberts	Stade Français[1]	11/05/1984	1,92	120	-	-	-	R	R	R	3	0	0	0	0	0
PJ Lambie	KwaZulu-Natal	17/10/1990	1,78	87	-	-	-	-	15	15	2	0	0	0	0	0
WJ le Roux	KwaZulu-Natal	18/08/1989	1,86	90	-	-	-	-	R	R	2	0	0	0	0	0
LN Mvovo	KwaZulu-Natal	03/06/1986	1,85	94	-	-	-	-	-	-	0	0	0	0	0	0
S Notshe	Western Province	28/05/1993	1,90	100	-	-	-	-	-	-	0	0	0	0	0	0
DJ Vermeulen	Toulon[1]	03/07/1986	1,93	108	-	-	-	-	-	-	0	0	0	0	0	0
PE van Zyl	Blue Bulls	14/09/1989	1,74	81	-	-	-	-	-	-	0	0	0	0	0	0
36 PLAYERS												8	7	19	2	117

Note: C = Captain, [1] = France, [2] = England

Head Coach: Allister Coetzee **Assistant Coach:** Matthew Proudfoot
Assistant Coach: Johann van Graan **Assistant Coach:** Mzwandile Stick
Defence Coach: Chean Roux **Team Manager:** Ian Schwartz
Team Doctor: Jerome Mampane **Strength & Conditioning Coach:** Warren Adams
Physiotherapist: Vivian Verwant **Physiotherapist:** Tanu Pillay
Logistics Manager: JJ Fredericks **Public Relations Manager:** Annelee Murray
Media Manager: Rayaan Adriaanse **Technical Analyst:** Willie Maree

ARGENTINA APPEARANCES & POINTS

PLAYER	Union/Club	Date of birth	Height	Weight	SA1	SA2	NZ1	Aus1	NZ2	Aus2	Apps	T	C	P	DG	Pts
J Tuculet	Bordeaux-Bègles[1]	08/08/1989	1,84	92	15	15	15	15	15	15	6	2	0	0	0	10
S Cordero	Regatas de Bella Vista	06/12/1993	1,77	83	14	14	11	14	14	-	5	3	0	0	0	15
M Orlando	Huirapuca R.C.	14/11/1991	1,83	96	13	13	13	R	R	13	6	1	0	0	0	5
J-M Hernández	Toulon[1]	07/08/1982	1,87	94	12	12	12	-	-	-	3	0	1	1	0	5
M Montero	Pucurá	20/11/1991	1,94	104	11	11	-	-	-	-	2	0	0	0	0	0
FN Sánchez	Toulon[1]	26/10/1988	1,77	83	10	10	10	10	10	-	5	0	7	13	0	53
M Landajo	Club Atletico de San Isidro	14/06/1988	1,75	82	9	9	9	R	9	9	6	0	0	0	0	0
F Isa	Toulon[1]	21/09/1993	1,88	106	8	8	8	8	8	-	5	2	0	0	0	10
J-M Leguizamón	Lyon[1]	06/06/1983	1,90	105	7	7	-	7	R	R	5	1	0	0	0	5
P Matera	Leicester Tigers[2]	18/07/1993	1,93	110	6	6	6	6	6	6	6	0	0	0	0	0
TE Lavanini	Racing 92[1]	22/01/1993	2,01	130	5	5	-	-	-	-	2	0	0	0	0	0
MI Alemanno	La Tablada	05/12/1991	1,99	117	4	4	5	5	5	5	6	1	0	0	0	5
R Herrera	Castres[1]	14/02/1989	1,94	123	3	3	3	3	3	3	6	0	0	0	0	0
A Creevy (C)	Worcester Warriors[2]	15/03/1985	1,81	110	2*	2*	2*	2*	2*	2*	6	0	0	0	0	0
N Tetaz Chaparro	Lyon[1]	11/06/1988	1,88	111	1	1	1	1	1	-	5	0	0	0	0	0
JS Montoya	Club Newman	29/10/1993	1,84	102	R	R	R	R	R	R	6	0	0	0	0	0
E Pieretto	Córdoba Athletic	14/12/1994	1,89	122	R	R	R	R	R	R	6	0	0	0	0	0
G Petti	San Isidro Club	17/11/1994	1,94	108	R	R	4	-	4	4	5	0	0	0	0	0
J Ortega Desio	San Isidro Club	14/06/1990	1,93	108	R	R	7	4	7	7	6	0	0	0	0	0
TM Cubelli	Belgrano Athletic	12/06/1989	1,77	81	R	R	R	9	R	R	6	0	0	0	0	0
S González Iglesias	Asociación Alumni	16/06/1988	1,79	92	R	R	-	12	12	10	6	0	2	4	0	16
F Arregui	Duendes	09/06/1994	1,89	111	x	-	-	-	-	-	0	0	0	0	0	0
R Moyano Joya	Lince R.C.	28/05/1990	1,80	86	x	-	R	-	11	11	3	0	0	0	0	0
LP González Amorosino	Cardiff Blues[3]	02/11/1985	1,85	94	-	R	-	11	-	x	2	0	0	0	0	0
L Noguera Paz	Lince R.C.	05/10/1993	1,79	108	-	R	R	R	R	1	5	0	0	0	0	0
M Moroni	Club Universitario[5]	29/03/1991	1,85	87	-	-	14	13	13	14	4	0	0	0	0	0
LV Senatore	Worcester Warriors[2]	13/05/1984	1,91	106	-	-	R	R	R	8	3	0	0	0	0	0
M Kremer	Atlético del Rosario	30/07/1997	1,95	115	-	-	R	R	-	R	3	0	0	0	0	0
G Ascárate	Glasgow Warriors[4]	20/10/1987	1,84	96	-	-	-	t+R	-	x	1	0	0	0	0	0
J de la Fuente	Duendes	24/02/1991	1,83	97	-	-	-	-	R	12	2	1	0	0	0	5
SE Garcia Botta	Stade Français[1]	19/06/1992	1,83	109	-	-	-	-	-	R	1	0	0	0	0	0
F Bosch	Club Universitario[5]	08/08/1991	1,79	102	-	-	-	-	-	-	0	0	0	0	0	0
P Ezcurra	Hindú	15/04/1993	1,78	89	-	-	-	-	-	-	0	0	0	0	0	0
T Lezana	Santiago Lawn Tennis Club	21/09/1993	1,88	106	-	-	-	-	-	-	0	0	0	0	0	0
34 PLAYERS												11	10	18	0	129

Note: C = Captain, [1] = France, [2] = England, [3] = Wales, [4] = Scotland, [5] = Buenos Aires

Head Coach: Daniel Hourcade
Assistant Coaches: Emiliano Bergamaschi, Pablo Bouza & Germán Fernández
Doctor: Dr Guillermo Botto **Manager:** Diego Tyslak
Sports Manager: José Santamarina **Conditioning:** Gonzalo Santos
Physio: Cristian Barrea & Juan Otero **Video Analyst:** Daniel Pérez
Media Manager: Rafael Laría **Kit Manager:** Jorge Ruarte

AUSTRALIA APPEARANCES & POINTS

PLAYER	Union/Club	Date of birth	Height	Weight	NZ1	NZ2	SA1	Arg1	SA2	Arg2	Apps	T	C	P	DG	Pts
IF Folau	NSW	03/04/1989	1,93	103	15	15	15	15	15	15	6	0	0	0	0	0
DS Haylett-Petty	Western Australia	18/06/1989	1,90	100	14	14	14	14	14	14	6	1	0	0	0	5
RTRN Kuridrani	ACT	31/03/1991	1,92	102	13	R	R	R	R	R	6	0	0	0	0	0
MJ Giteau	Toulon, France	29/09/1982	1,78	85	12	-	-	-	-	-	1	0	0	0	0	0
AP Ashley-Cooper	Bordeaux-Bègles[1]	27/03/1984	1,85	98	11	11	-	-	-	-	2	0	0	0	0	0
BT Foley	NSW	08/09/1989	1,82	89	10	12	12	12	12	12	6	1	9	10	0	53
SW Genia	Stade Français[1]	17/01/1988	1,74	82	9	9	9	9	9	9	6	2	0	0	0	10
DW Pocock	ACT	23/04/1988	1,87	115	8	8	8	8	-	-	4	0	0	0	0	0
MK Hooper	NSW	29/10/1991	1,82	101	7	7	7	7	7	7	6	1	0	0	0	5
BJ McCalman	Western Australia	18/03/1988	1,92	106	6	-	-	-	-	-	1	0	0	0	0	0
RA Simmons	Queensland	19/04/1989	2,00	115	5	-	-	4	4	-	3	0	0	0	0	0
KP Douglas	Queensland	01/06/1989	2,02	123	4	4	4	-	R	R	5	0	0	0	0	0
SM Kepu	NSW	05/02/1986	1,88	118	3	3	3	3	3	3	6	0	0	0	0	0
ST Moore (C)	ACT	20/01/1983	1,86	112	2*	2*	2*	2*	2*	2*	6	0	0	0	0	0
ST Sio	ACT	16/10/1991	1,87	115	1	1	1	1	1	1	6	1	0	0	0	5
JA Slipper	Queensland	06/06/1989	1,86	117	R	R	R	R	R	-	5	0	0	0	0	0
SUT Polota-Nau	NSW	26/07/1985	1,81	114	R	t+R	R	R	-	-	4	0	0	0	0	0
AEA Ala'alatoa	ACT	28/01/1984	1,82	120	R	R	R	-	-	R	4	0	0	0	0	0
DW Mumm	NSW	05/03/1984	1,96	109	R	R	6	6	6	6	6	1	0	0	0	5
SM Fardy	ACT	05/07/1984	1,98	114	R	6	-	-	x	R	3	0	0	0	0	0
MP To'omua	ACT	02/01/1990	1,82	91	R	-	-	-	-	-	1	0	0	0	0	0
RG Horne	NSW	15/08/1989	1,86	93	R	-	-	-	-	-	1	0	0	0	0	0
NJ Phipps	NSW	09/01/1989	1,8	87	R	R	x	R	R	R	5	1	0	0	0	5
SV Kerevi	Queensland	27/09/1993	1,86	108	-	13	13	13	13	13	5	3	0	0	0	15
QS Cooper	Toulon[1]	05/04/1988	1,86	93	-	10	10	10	10	10	5	0	0	0	0	0
AP Coleman	Western Australia	07/10/1991	2,04	122	-	5	5	5	5	5	5	2	0	0	0	10
WRJ Skelton	NSW	03/05/1992	2,03	140	-	R	-	-	-	-	1	0	0	0	0	0
R Hodge	Victoria	26/08/1994	1,91	94	-	R	11	11	11	11	5	0	0	2	0	6
SP McMahon	Victoria	18/06/1994	1,86	100	-	-	R	R	8	-	3	0	0	0	0	0
DA Mitchell	Toulon[1]	26/03/1984	1,82	92	-	-	R	-	-	-	1	0	0	0	0	0
RW Arnold	ACT	01/07/1990	2,08	120	-	-	R	R	-	4	3	0	0	0	0	0
T Robertson	NSW	28/08/1994	1,80	111	-	-	-	R	R	R	3	0	0	0	0	0
L Timani	Victoria	28/09/1990	1,93	123	-	-	-	R	-	8	2	0	0	0	0	0
JE Hanson	Victoria	15/09/1988	1,83	104	-	-	-	-	x	R	1	0	0	0	0	0
S Naivalu	Victoria	07/01/1992	1,86	94	-	-	-	-	R	-	1	0	0	0	0	0
L Houston	Queensland	10/11/1986	1,91	117	-	-	-	-	-	R	1	0	0	0	0	0
K Godwin	Western Australia	30/07/1992	1,87	93	-	-	-	-	-	-	0	0	0	0	0	0
LJ Morahan	Western Australia	13/04/1990	1,88	95	-	-	-	-	-	-	0	0	0	0	0	0
HV Speight	ACT	25/03/1988	1,86	97	-	-	-	-	-	-	0	0	0	0	0	0
N Frisby	Queensland	29/10/1992	1,84	84	-	-	-	-	-	-	0	0	0	0	0	0
S Latu	NSW	23/02/1993	1,78	110	-	-	-	-	-	-	0	0	0	0	0	0
41 PLAYERS												13	9	12	0	119

Note: C = Captain, [1] = France

Head Coach: Michael Cheika **Assistant Coaches:** Stephen Larkham & Nathan Grey
Set Piece Coach: Mario Ledesma **National Skills Coach:** Mick Bryne
Team Manager: Patrick Molihan **Operations Manager:** Simon Roberts
Team Doctor: Dr Mike Cadogan **Head Physiotherapist:** Kieran Cleary
Physiotherapist: Alex Hill **Head - Wallabies Athletic Performance:** Haydn Masters
Head -Digital and Wallabies Media: Adam Freier
Digital Media & Wallabies Video Journalist: Chris Ford

NEW ZEALAND APPEARANCES & POINTS

PLAYER	Union/Club	Date of birth	Height	Weight	Aus1	Aus2	Arg1	SA1	Arg2	SA2	Apps	T	C	P	DG	Pts
IJA Dagg	Hawke's Bay	06/06/1988	1,86	96	15	14	14	14	14	14	6	5	0	1	0	28
BR Smith	Otago	01/06/1986	1,86	93	14	15	15	15	15	15	6	5	0	0	0	25
MF Fekitoa	Auckland	10/05/1992	1,87	99	13	13	13	13	-	-	4	0	0	0	0	0
RS Crotty	Canterbury	23/09/1988	1,79	91	12	-	12	12	12	12	5	4	0	0	0	20
WR Naholo	Taranaki	08/05/1991	1,86	96	11	-	-	-	-	11	2	1	0	0	0	5
BJ Barrett	Taranaki	27/05/1991	1,87	91	10	10	10	10	10	10	6	4	23	5	0	81
AL Smith	Manawatu	21/11/1988	1,71	84	9	9	9	9	-	-	4	0	0	0	0	0
KJ Reid (C)	Canterbury	26/10/1985	1,93	111	8*	8*	8*	8*	8*	8*	6	0	0	0	0	0
SJ Cane	Bay of Plenty	13/01/1992	1,89	103	7	7	7	-	-	-	3	1	0	0	0	5
J Kaino	Auckland	06/04/1983	1,96	105	6	6	6	6	-	6	5	1	0	0	0	5
SL Whitelock	Canterbury	12/10/1988	2,02	116	5	5	5	5	R	5	6	1	0	0	0	5
BA Retallick	Bay of Plenty	31/05/1991	2,04	120	4	4	4	4	5	4	6	0	0	0	0	0
OT Franks	Canterbury	23/12/1987	1,85	119	3	3	3	3	3	3	6	0	0	0	0	0
CJD Taylor	Canterbury	31/03/1991	1,83	106	2	-	R	R	R	R	5	1	0	0	0	5
WWV Crockett	Canterbury	24/01/1983	1,93	116	1	R	R	R	t+R	R	6	0	0	0	0	0
KS Hames	Tasman	28/08/1988	1,81	111	R	-	-	-	-	-	1	0	0	0	0	0
DS Coles	Wellington	10/12/1986	1,84	109	R	2	2	2	2	2	6	2	0	0	0	10
CC Faumuina	Auckland	24/12/1986	1,84	127	R	R	R	R	-	R	5	1	0	0	0	5
LIJ Squire	Tasman	20/03/1991	1,96	113	R	R	-	-	6	R	4	1	0	0	0	5
AS Savea	Wellington	14/10/1993	1,90	89	R	R	R	7	7	R	6	1	0	0	0	5
TTR Perenara	Wellington	23/01/1992	1,84	94	R	R	R	R	9	9	6	4	0	0	0	20
AW Cruden	Manawatu	08/01/1989	1,78	84	R	R	R	-	-	-	3	0	1	0	0	2
SJ Savea	Wellington	07/08/1990	1,92	108	R	11	11	11	11	-	5	4	0	0	0	20
AR Lienert-Brown	Waikato	15/04/1995	1,85	96	-	12	R	R	13	13	5	1	0	0	0	5
JPT Moody	Canterbury	18/09/1988	1,88	118	-	1	1	-	1	1	5	0	0	0	0	0
JW Parsons	North Harbour	27/11/1986	1,85	106	-	R	-	-	-	-	1	0	0	0	0	0
S Tamanivalu	Taranaki	23/06/1992	1,89	104	-	R	-	-	-	-	1	0	0	0	0	0
L Romano	Canterbury	16/02/1986	1,99	115	-	-	R	R	-	-	2	1	0	0	0	5
MB Todd	Canterbury	24/03/1988	1,85	104	-	-	-	R	-	7	2	0	0	0	0	0
LZ Sopoaga	Southland	03/02/1991	1,77	91	-	-	-	R	R	R	3	0	3	0	0	6
PT Tuipulotu	Auckland	23/01/1993	1,98	120	-	-	-	-	4	-	1	0	0	0	0	0
EC Dixon	Southland	04/09/1989	1,93	110	-	-	-	-	R	-	1	0	0	0	0	0
TNJ Kerr-Barlow	Waikato	15/08/1990	1,87	89	-	-	-	-	R	R	2	0	0	0	0	0
AOHM Tu'ungafasi	Auckland	19/04/1992	1,92	115	-	-	-	-	R	-	1	0	0	0	0	0
DS McKenzie	Waikato	20/04/1995	1,77	81	-	-	-	-	R	-	1	0	0	0	0	0
G Moala	Auckland	05/11/1990	1,88	104	-	-	-	-	-	R	1	0	0	0	0	0
NP Harris	Bay of Plenty	08/03/1992	1,86	105	-	-	-	-	-	-	0	0	0	0	0	0
LJ Coltman	Otago	25/01/1990	1,85	109	-	-	-	-	-	-	0	0	0	0	0	0
38 PLAYERS											38	27	6		0	262

Note: C = Captain

Head Coach / Selector: Steve Hansen **Assistant Head Coach / Selector:** Ian Foster
Selector: Grant Fox **Manager - Business & Operations:** Darren Shand
Manager - Leadership: Gilbert Enoka **Assistant Coach - Forwards:** Mike Cron
Assistant Coach - Defence: Wayne Smith **Strength & Conditioning Coach:** Dr Nic Gill
Performance Analysis Manager: Jason Healy **Performance Analyst:** Jamie Hamilton
Doctor: Dr Tony Page **Physiotherapist:** Peter Gallagher **Manual Therapist:** George Duncan
Nutritionist: Katrina Darry **Team Services Manager:** Bianca Thiel **Media Manager:** Joe Locke
Logistics Manager: Kevin "Chalky" Carr

Australia 8 New Zealand 42 (halftime 3-32)

ANZ Stadium, Sydney. Kick-off: 20:05. Attendance: 65 328. August 20, 2016

Referee: J Peyper *(South Africa)*; Ass. Ref 1: R Poite *(France)*; Ass. Ref 2: F Anselmi *(Argentina)*;
TMO: S Veldsman *(South Africa)*

AUSTRALIA

Try: Phipps. Penalty goal: Foley.

IF Folau; DS Haylett-Petty*, RTRN Kuridrani, MJ Giteau *(MP To'omua, 12) (RG Horne, 31) (NJ Phipps, 40)***, AP Ashley-Cooper*; BT Foley, SW Genia; DW Pocock, MK Hooper, BJ McCalman *(SM Fardy, 62)*, RA Simmons *(DW Mumm, 49)*, KP Douglas, SM Kepu *(AEA Ala'alatoa, 55)*, ST Moore (C) *(SUT Polota-Nau, 63)*, ST Sio *(JA Slipper, 78) (ST Sio, 75-F/T).*

*Haylett-Petty wore #11 and Ashley-Cooper wore #14. **Phipps to left wing, Ashley-Cooper to centre.

NOTE: This is the biggest loss for Australia against the All Blacks on home soil.

NEW ZEALAND

Tries: Crotty, Barrett, Kaino, Naholo, Coles, SJ Savea. Conversions: Barrett (3). Penalty goals: Barrett (2).

IJA Dagg; BR Smith, MF Fekitoa, RS Crotty *(AW Cruden, H/T)*, WR Naholo *(SJ Savea, 40)*; BJ Barrett, AL Smith *(TTR Perenara, 68)*; KJ Read (C)*, SJ Cane *(AS Savea, 64)*, J Kaino *(LIJ Squire, 58)*, SL Whitelock, BA Retallick, OT Franks *(CC Faumuina, 46)*, CJD Taylor *(DS Coles, 03)*, WWV Crockett *(KS Hames, 58).*

*YELLOW CARD: 74 - KJ Read. TEST DEBUTS: KS Hames & LIJ Squire.

CHAMPIONSHIP DEBUTS: KS Hames, LIJ Squire & AS Savea.

NOTE: The winning margin of 34 is the biggest by New Zealand against Australia away from home.

New Zealand 29 Australia 9 (halftime 15-9)

Westpac Stadium, Wellington. Kick-off: 19:35. Attendance: 35 372. August 27, 2016

Referee: R Poite *(France)*; Ass. Ref 1: J Peyper *(South Africa)*; Ass. Ref 2: F Anselmi *(Argentina)*;
TMO: S Veldsman *(South Africa)*

NEW ZEALAND

Tries: Dagg (2), SJ Savea, Cane. Conversions: Barrett (3). Penalty goal: Barrett.

BR Smith; IJA Dagg, MF Fekitoa, AR Lienert-Brown *(S Tamanivalu, 76)*, SJ Savea *(AW Cruden, 66)**; BJ Barrett, AL Smith *(TTR Perenara, 66)*; KJ Read (C), SJ Cane *(AS Savea, 72)*, J Kaino, SL Whitelock, BA Retallick *(LIJ Squire, 70)*, OT Franks *(CC Faumuina, 52)*, DS Coles *(JW Parsons, 70)*, JPT Moody *(WWV Crockett, 52).*

*Cruden to flyhalf, Barrett to fullback, BR Smith to left wing. TEST DEBUT: AR Lienert-Brown.

CHAMPIONSHIP DEBUTS: AR Lienert-Brown, JW Parsons & S Tamanivalu..

NOTE: This was the All Blacks 42nd Test match at home without a loss.

AUSTRALIA

Penalty goals: Foley (2), Hodge.

IF Folau; DS Haylett-Petty*, SV Kerevi *(RTRN Kuridrani, 68)*, BT Foley, AP Ashley-Cooper* *(R Hodge, 17)*; QS Cooper, SW Genia *(NJ Phipps, 68)*; DW Pocock *(SM Fardy, 64-70)*, MK Hooper, SM Fardy *(DW Mumm, 38)*, AP Coleman** *(WRJ Skelton, 64)*, KP Douglas, SM Kepu *(AEA Ala'alatoa, 52)*, ST Moore (C) *(SUT Polota-Nau, 39-H/T, 49-54, 64)*, ST Sio *(JA Slipper, 52).*

*Haylett-Petty wore #11 and Ashley-Cooper wore #14. **YELLOW CARD: 37 - AP Coleman

TEST DEBUT: R Hodge. CHAMPIONSHIP DEBUTS: AP Coleman, R Hodge & SV Kerevi,

NOTE: This was Australia's 19th consecutive loss in New Zealand against the All Blacks.

New Zealand 57 Argentina 22 (halftime 24-19)

FMG Stadium, Hamilton. Kick-off: 19:35. Attendance: 23 361. September 10, 2016
Referee: CP Joubert *(South Africa)*; Ass. Ref 1: A Gardner *(Australia)*; Ass. Ref 2: M Mitrea *(Italy)*;
TMO: GJP Ayoub *(Australia)*

NEW ZEALAND

Tries: SJ Savea, BR Smith (2), Barrett, Crotty (2), Faumuina, Romano. Conversions: Barrett (6), Cruden.
Penalty goal: Dagg.

BR Smith; IJA Dagg, MF Fekitoa, RS Crotty *(AR Lienert-Brown, 69)*, SJ Savea; BJ Barrett
(AW Cruden, 65), AL Smith *(TTR Perenara, 49)*; KJ Read (C), SJ Cane *(AS Savea, 46)*, J Kaino,
SL Whitelock, BA Retallick *(L Romano, 65)*, OT Franks *(CC Faumuina, 49)*, DS Coles
(CJD Taylor, 53), JPT Moody *(WWV Crockett, 53)*.

NOTE: This was the All Blacks 43rd Test match at home without a loss.

ARGENTINA

Try: Cordero. Conversion: Sánchez. Penalty goals: Sánchez (5).

J Tuculet; M Moroni, M Orlando, J-M Hernández *(S González Iglesias, 37)*, S Cordero; FN Sánchez
(R Moyano Joya, 65)***, M Landajo *(TM Cubelli, 61)*; F Isa, J Ortega Desio, PN Matera *(M Kremer,
65)***, MI Alemanno, G Petti *(LV Senatore, H/T)**, R Herrera *(E Pieretto, 66)*, A Creevy (C)
(JS Montoya, 63), FN Tetaz Chaparro *(L Noguera Paz, 63)*.

*Senatore to #7 flank, Ortega Desio to #4 lock. **Kremer to lock, Ortega Desio back to #6 flank.
***Moyano Joya to right wing, Moroni to left wing, Cordero to inside centre, González Iglesias to flyhalf.
TEST AND CHAMPIONSHIP DEBUT: M Kremer. CHAMPIONSHIP DEBUT: R Moyano Joya.
NOTE: The 22 points scored by Argentina were the most by the Pumas against the All Blacks in 23 Tests.

Australia 36 Argentina 20 (halftime 21-6)

nib Stadium, Perth. Kick-off: 18:05. Attendance: 16 202. September 17, 2016
Referee: W Barnes *(England)*; Ass. Ref 1: N Owens *(Wales)*; Ass. Ref 2: N Bryant *(New Zealand)*;
TMO: B Skeen *(New Zealand)*

AUSTRALIA

Tries: Kerevi, Haylett-Petty, Genia (2), Hooper. Conversions: Foley (4). Penalty goal: Hodge.
IF Folau; DS Haylett-Petty, SV Kerevi *(RTRN Kuridrani, 74)*, BT Foley, R Hodge; QS Cooper*,
SW Genia *(NJ Phipps, 68)*; DW Pocock *(JA Slipper, 36-45)* *(SP McMahon, 44)*, MK Hooper,
DW Mumm *(L Timani, 68)*, AP Coleman *(RW Arnold, 61)*, RA Simmons, SM Kepu *(T Robertson,
61)*, ST Moore (C) *(SUT Polota-Nau, 49)*, ST Sio* *(JA Slipper, 61)*.

*YELLOW CARDS: 33 - ST Sio and 68 - QS Cooper.
TEST AND CHAMPIONSHIP DEBUTS: T Robertson & L Timani.

ARGENTINA

Tries: Cordero, Isa. Conversions: Sánchez (2). Penalty goals: Sánchez (2).
J Tuculet; S Cordero, M Moroni, S González Iglesias *(G Ascárate, 32-37)*, LP González Amorosino
(M Orlando, 62)*; FN Sánchez *(G Ascárate, 67-72)*, TM Cubelli *(M Landajo, 62)*; F Isa
(G Ascárate, 72)***, J-M Leguizamón *(LV Senatore, 44)*, PN Matera *(M Kremer, 66)***, MI Alemanno,
J Ortega Desio, R Herrera *(E Pieretto, 66)*, A Creevy (C) *(JS Montoya, 47)*, FN Tetaz Chaparro
(L Noguera Paz, 62).

**Orlando to outside centre, Moroni to right wing, Cordero to left wing. **Kremer to #4 lock, Ortego Desio to
#6 flank. ***Ascárate to right wing, Moroni back to outside centre, Orlando to inside centre, González Iglesias
to #7 flank, Senatore to #8. CHAMPIONSHIP DEBUT: G Ascárate.*

Argentina 17 New Zealand 36 (halftime 3-29)

Vélez Sársfield, Buenos Aires. Kick-off: 19:10. Attendance: 31 257. October 1, 2016

Referee: J Peyper *(South Africa)*; Ass. Ref 1: S Berry *(South Africa)*;

Ass. Ref 2: M van der Westhuizen *(South Africa)*; TMO: J Greef *(South Africa)*

ARGENTINA

Tries: Isa, Tuculet. Conversions: Sánchez, González Iglesias. Penalty goals: Sánchez.

J Tuculet; S Cordero, M Moroni *(M Orlando, 76)*, S González Iglesias, R Moyano Joya; FN Sánchez *(J de la Fuente, 69)*, M Landajo *(TM Cubelli, 57)*; F Isa, J Ortego Desio, PN Matera *(J-M Leguizamón, 66)*, MI Alemanno *(LV Senatore, 59)*, G Petti, H Herrera *(E Pieretto, 64)*, A Creevy *(C) (JS Montoya, 49)*, FN Tetaz Chaparro *(L Noguera Paz, 52)*.

NEW ZEALAND

Tries: Lienert-Brown, Crotty, Coles, Perenara, Smith. Conversions: Barrett (4). Penalty goal: Barrett.

BR Smith; IJA Dagg, AR Lienert-Brown, RS Crotty *(DS McKenzie, 49)**, SJ Savea; BJ Barrett *(LZ Sopoaga, 76)*, TTR Perenara *(TNJ Kerr-Barlow, 69)*; KJ Read *(C) (EC Dixon, 76)***, AS Savea, LIJ Squire*** *(WWV Crockett, 52-64)*, BA Retallick *(SL Whitelock, 48)*, PT Tuipulotu, OT Franks *(AOHM Tu'ungafasi, 64)*, DS Coles *(CJD Taylor, 69)*, JPT Moody*** *(WWV Crockett, 64)*.

*McKenzie to fullback, Smith to outside centre, Lienert Brown to inside centre.**Dixon to #6 flank, Squire to #8. ***YELLOW CARDS: 52 – JPT Moody and 65 – LIJ Squire.

TEST AND CHAMPIONSHIP DEBUT: DS McKenzie.

NOTE: This was New Zealand's 16th consecutive win, now only one win short of their record of 17 consecutive wins.

Argentina 21 Australia 33 (halftime 8-18)

Twickenham, London. Kick-off: 19:30. Attendance: 48 515. October 8, 2016

Referee: M Raynal *(France)*; Ass. Ref 1: JP Doyle *(England)*; Ass. Ref 2: M Carley *(England)*; TMO: R Kitt *(England)*

ARGENTINA

Tries: Alemanno, De la Fuente. Conversion: González Iglesias. Penalty goals: González Iglesias (3).

J Tuculet; M Moroni, M Orlando, J de la Fuente, R Moyano Joya *(TM Cubelli, 58)**; S González Iglesias, M Landajo; LV Senatore *(J-M Leguizamón, 51)*, J Ortego Desio, PN Matera, MI Alemanno, G Petti *(M Kremer, 75)*, H Herrera *(E Pieretto, 68)*, A Creevy *(C) (JS Montoya, 65)*, L Noguera Paz *(SE Garcia Botta, 68)*.

UNUSED SUBSTITUTES: G Ascárate and LP González Amorosino.

AUSTRALIA

Tries: Coleman, Kerevi (2), Mumm. Conversions: Foley (2). Penalty goals: Foley (3).

IF Folau *(RTRN Kuridrani, 79)*; DS Haylett-Petty, SV Kerevi, BT Foley, R Hodge; QS Cooper, SW Genia *(NJ Phipps, 64)*; L Timani *(L Houston, 70)*, MK Hooper**, DW Mumm, AP Coleman** *(KP Douglas, 61)*, RW Arnold *(SM Fardy, 55)**, SM Kepu *(AEA Ala'atoa, 61)*, ST Moore *(C) (JE Hanson, 74)*, ST Sio *(T Robertson, 61)*.

*Fardy to #6 flank, Mumm to #4 lock. **YELLOW CARDS: 17 - MK Hooper and 31 - AP Coleman.

Pieter-Steph du Toit & Eben Etzebeth.

Tournament Records

(Incorporating old Tri–Nations records)

CHAMPIONS

1996	New Zealand	2003	New Zealand	2010	New Zealand
1997	New Zealand	**2004**	**SOUTH AFRICA**	2011	Australia
1998	**SOUTH AFRICA**	2005	New Zealand	2012	New Zealand
1999	New Zealand	2006	New Zealand	2013	New Zealand
2000	Australia	2007	New Zealand	2014	New Zealand
2001	Australia	2008	New Zealand	2015	Australia
2002	New Zealand	**2009**	**SOUTH AFRICA**	2016	New Zealand

MATCH RECORDS

Most points by a team

73-13	South Africa v Argentina	17/08/2013	Johannesburg

Biggest winning margin

60	South Africa v Argentina	17/08/2013	Johannesburg

Most points away from home

57	New Zealand v South Africa	08/10/2016	Durban

Most tries by a team

9	South Africa v Argentina	17/08/2013	Johannesburg
9	New Zealand v South Africa	08/10/2016	Durban

Most points by a player

31	M Steyn (1t, 1c, 8p), SA v NZ	01/08/2009	Durban

Most tries by a player

4	JL Nokwe, SA v Australia	30/08/2008	Johannesburg

Most conversions by a player

8	M Steyn, SA v Argentina	17/08/2013	Johannesburg

Most penalty goals by a player

9	AP Mehrtens, NZ v Australia	24/07/1999	Auckland

Most drop goals by a player

2	JH de Beer, SA v NZ	19/07/1997	Johannesburg
2	FPL Steyn, SA v Australia	16/06/2007	Cape Town
2	M Steyn, SA v Australia	01/10/2016	Pretoria

MOST DROP GOALS BY A PLAYER

2

*M Steyn,
SA v Australia*

01/10/2016, Pretoria

SEASON RECORDS BY THE TEAM

	Most points		
262	New Zealand		2016

Most points conceded

224	Argentina	2013

Most tries

38	New Zealand	2016

Most tries conceded

27	Argentina	2016

Most log points

30	New Zealand	2016

SEASON RECORDS BY A PLAYER

Most points

99	DW Carter	New Zealand	2006

Most tries

8	BR Smith	New Zealand	2013

Most conversions

23	BJ Barrett	New Zealand	2016

Most penalty goals

23	M Steyn	South Africa	2009

Most drop goals

3	M Steyn	South Africa	2009

MOST TRIES IN A CAREER BY A PLAYER — 21 — BG Habana, South Africa

CAREER RECORDS

Most points

		App	T	C	P	D	Pts
DW Carter	New Zealand	41	6	76	120	4	554

Most tries

21	BG Habana	South Africa

Most conversions

76	DW Carter	New Zealand

Most penalty goals

120	DW Carter	New Zealand

Most appearances

58	RH McCaw	New Zealand

Most drop goals

6	M Steyn	South Africa

CASTLE LAGER
OUTGOING TOUR

Date			Score		Venue	Referee
05/11/2016	Barbarians	31	South Africa	31	Wembley Stadium, London	Ml Fraser (New Zealand)
12/11/2016	England	37	South Africa	21	Twickenham, London	J Garcès (France)
19/11/2016	Italy	20	South Africa	18	Stadio Artemio Franchi, Florence	GJ Clancy (Ireland)
26/11/2016	Wales	27	South Africa	13	Principality Stadium, Cardiff	R Poite (France)

Barbarians 31 South Africa 31
(Halftime 17-12)

Tour/Non-Test Match # 342

Wembley Stadium, London. Kick-off: 15:00. Attendance: 46 646. November 5, 2016
Referee: MI Fraser *(New Zealand)*; Ass. Ref 1: PM Williams *(New Zealand)*;
Ass. Ref 2: S Kubo *(Japan)*; TMO: G Hughes *(England)*.

BRITISH BARBARIANS

Tries: Nanai, Ellis, Naiyaravoro, Morahan (2). Conversions: Du Preez, Mo'unga (2).
M Nanai; M Faddes *(LJ Morahan, 52)*, S Tamanivalu, R Buckman, T Naiyaravoro; RJ du Preez
(R Mo'unga, 52), AM Ellis *(C) (N Stirzaker, 78)*; LC Whitelock, J Taufua *(R Ackermann, 75)*,
BDF Shields, M Fatialofa, MD Muller *(STG Carter, 52)*, PJ Ryan *(SW van der Merwe, 57)*,
AHP van der Merwe *(A Ready, 78)*, R Goodes *(TJ Smith, 52)*.

SOUTH AFRICA

Tries: Du Toit, Smit, Petersen, Venter, Janse van Rensburg. Conversions: Lambie (3).
JA Kriel *(RJ Combrinck, H/T)*; SP Petersen, JF Venter, R Janse van Rensburg, JI Ulengo; PJ Lambie
(C), R Paige *(PE van Zyl, 70)*; N Carr, TS Mohojé *(J-L du Preez, 52)*, RA Smit, PS du Toit,
RG Snyman *(E Etzebeth, 52)*, LC Adriaanse *(TN Nyakane, 60)*, MJ Marx *(MT Mbonambi, 52)*,
T Mtawarira *(LP Gqoboka, 70)*.
UNUSED SUBSTITUTE: CF Schoeman.
NOTE: Eight players played in their first match in the Green & Gold for the senior Springbok team.
They were SP Petersen, JF Venter, R Janse van Rensburg, JI Ulengo, J-L du Preez, RA Smit, RG Snyman
and LP Gqoboka. This was, however, a non-Test match.

Springboks show Barbarian spirit

THE tradition is for matches against the Barbarians to be played at the end of tours, which generally excuses a disappointing finale by tired players who would rather be elsewhere.

However, this being a match to kick off the Springboks' tour and an opportunity for a number of young players to put up their hands, there would be less of a defence if they came up short. That very nearly happened and it took two tries in the last 10 minutes for the Springboks to turn a 12-point deficit into a 31-all draw at Wembley.

As was the case throughout the year, Allister Coetzee's men deserved credit for the character they showed when behind.

SCORING SEQUENCE

Min	Action	Score
5	Nanai try, Du Preez missed conversion	B 5-0
12	Du Toit try, Lambie missed conversion	5-5
19	Ellis try, Du Preez conversion	B 12-5
23	Smit try, Lambie conversion	12-12
40	Naiyaravoro try, Du Preez missed conv.	B 17-12
44	Petersen try, Lambie conversion	SA 19-17
55	Morahan try, Mo'unga conversion	B 24-19
68	Morahan try, Mo'unga conversion	B 31-19
71	Venter try, Lambie conversion	B 31-26
77	Janse v Rensburg try, Lambie missed con.	31-31

However, in keeping with the general theme, the performance wasn't as good as one would expect. A particular worry was in defence where the Springboks were again surprisingly passive and allowed the Baabaas to get momentum through powerful backs such as left wing Teqele Naiyaravoro and fullback Melani Nanai.

In one such instance, Naiyaravoro knocked his opposite number, Sergeal Petersen, back in a Jonah Lomu-esque manner.

However, Petersen would have his revenge later in the second half when he dummied the big man and put on the afterburners on his way to the Barbarians' tryline.

Both teams deserve full marks for the spirit in which they played the game. It was played in the true tradition of festival rugby, with the Barbarians scoring some superb tries from turnover possession.

While aspects of the performance would have concerned Coetzee, he could also reflect positively on the contributions of newcomers such as Petersen, Toyota Free State Cheetahs centre Francois Venter, Vodacom Blue Bulls wing Jamba Ulengo and Bulls openside flank Roelof Smit. For many of the youngsters this was an eye-opener and it also served as a stepping stone to Test rugby for Ulengo, centres Rohan Janse van Rensburg and Venter, and substitute flank Jean-Luc du Preez.

England 37 South Africa 21
(Halftime 20-9)

Test # 462

Twickenham, London. Kick-off: 14:30. Attendance: 81 221. November 12, 2016

Referee: J Garcès *(France)*; Ass. Ref 1: GW Jackson *(New Zealand)*; Ass. Ref 2: A Brace *(Ireland)*; TMO: J Mason *(Wales)*.

ENGLAND

Tries: May, Lawes, Ford, Farrell. Conversions: Farrell (4). Penalty goals: Farrell (2), Daly.

MN Brown; MXG Yarde, EF Daly, OA Farrell, JJ May *(JBA Joseph, 63)**; GT Ford *(BJ Te'o, 71)****, BR Youngs *(DS Care, 68)*; VML Vunipola *(DMJ Attwood, 71)***, TA Wood *(NWJ Hughes, 54)*, CDC Robshaw, CL Lawes, JO Launchbury, DR Cole *(KNJS Sinckler, 72)*, DM Hartley *(C)* *(JE George, 56)*, MWIN Vunipola *(JWG Marler, 63)*.

*Joseph to outside centre, Daly to left wing. **Attwood to #5 lock, Lawes to #6 flank, Robshaw to #7 flank, Hughes to #8. ***Te'o to inside centre, Farrell to #10.

TEST DEBUTS: NWJ Hughes, BJ Te'o and KNJS Sinckler.

NOTE: This was England's 11th consecutive Test win and the 10th consecutive Test win under Coach Eddie Jones. Courtney Lawes played in his 50th Test match.

SOUTH AFRICA

Tries: Goosen, Le Roux. Conversion: Combrinck. Penalty goals: Lambie (2). Drop goal: Lambie.

WJ le Roux; RJ Combrinck, JF Venter, D de Allende, J-PR Pietersen *(LG Mapoe, 77)*; PJ Lambie *(JL Goosen, 54)*, R Paige *(F de Klerk, 63)*; WR Whiteley, PS du Toit, WS Alberts, L de Jager *(N Carr, 68)**, E Etzebeth *(F Mostert, 31)*, VP Koch *(LC Adriaanse, 56)*, JA Strauss *(C) (MT Mbonambi, 72)*, T Mtawarira *(S Kitshoff, 56)*.

*Carr to #7 flank, Du Toit to #5 lock. TEST DEBUT: JF Venter #877.

England end decade-long drought

SPRINGBOK coach Allister Coetzee cut a frustrated figure as he was left reflecting on "individual errors" following the first defeat to England in a decade.

Indeed, South Africa started brightly in their 37-21 defeat at Twickenham, but made mistakes that were ruthlessly exploited by the English, who had been transformed under the coaching prowess of Australian Eddie Jones.

It was all going according to plan as flyhalf Patrick Lambie struck an early penalty and, shortly after, the Springboks played him into position for a drop goal from in front of the posts. That made it 6-0 in just the seventh minute and it was game on for the Springboks to extend their unbeaten run against the English to 13 matches.

However, the continued defensive uncertainty in the Springboks' ranks allowed the England left wing, Jonny May, to round off after a sweet backline move. Until then the visitors had done most of the playing, but after 12 minutes the scoreboard read 7-6 to England.

Still, the tourists kept chipping away and were doing well in those little individual battles. Lambie missed a penalty that could almost immediately have restored the Springboks' lead, but made no mistake when the English scrum was penalised.

With a quarter of the game having passed, it was 9-7 to South Africa.

However, the defining moments of the game would follow as the first half drew to its close. First England restored their lead through inside centre Owen Farrell when the South African scrum collapsed in front of their posts.

Not long after that the Springboks' weakness under the high ball was exposed. The ball skidded here, there and everywhere on a wet Twickenham field before lock Courtney Lawes came out tops in the goal-line scramble.

Another cruel blow was to follow as centre Elliot Daly struck a long-distance penalty on the stroke of half-time. The Springboks, who had started so brightly, were suddenly down 20-9 at the break.

The second half is a period of play that South Africa's Player of the Year, Pieter-Steph du Toit, would rather forget. The towering lock had been an unexpected selection on the flank as coach Coetzee picked a big pack in the hope of achieving physical dominance and lineout supremacy over their hosts.

Du Toit, however, was twice dummied around the fringes by scrumhalf Ben Youngs, leading to tries for halfback partner George Ford and then Farrell.

Four mistakes, four tries to England.

A pleasing aspect to the Springboks' effort was that they crafted two impressive tries by keeping the ball in hand in the second half. Down 30-9 with half an hour left, one had an uneasy sense of the dam wall being ready to burst.

However, tries by substitute flyhalf Johan Goosen and fullback Willie le Roux brought some respectability to the scoreboard.

It might have been a different story had there been a little more mental discipline. Sadly, there was little cheer to be had other than some good early passages and the fighting spirit that avoided a far bigger defeat.

SCORING SEQUENCE

Min	Action	Score
4	Lambie penalty goal	SA 3-0
7	Lambie drop goal	SA 6-0
11	May try, Farrell conversion	E 7-6
14	Lambie missed penalty goal	E 7-6
21	Lambie penalty goal	SA 9-7
28	Ford missed drop goal	SA 9-7
34	Farrell penalty goal	E 10-9
36	Lawes try, Farrell conversion	E 17-9
41	Daly penalty goal	E 20-9
44	Ford try, Farrell conversion	E 27-9
49	Farrell penalty goal	E 30-9
59	Goosen try, Goosen missed conversion	E 30-14
63	Farrell missed penalty goal	E 30-14
67	Farrell try, Farrell conversion	E 37-14
79	Le Roux try, Combrinck conversion	E 37-21

Italy 20 South Africa 18
(Halftime 10-12)

Test # 463

Stadio Artemio Franchi, Florence. Kick-off: 15:00. Attendance: 21 169. November 19, 2016
Referee: GJ Clancy *(Ireland)*; Ass. Ref 1: N Owens *(Wales)*; Ass. Ref 2: D Wilkinson *(Ireland)*;
TMO: P Fitzgibbon *(Ireland)*.

ITALY

Tries: Van Schalkwyk, Venditti. Conversions: Canna (2). Penalty goals: Padovani, Canna.
E Padovani; G Bisegni, T Benvenuti, LJ McLean, G Venditti; C Canna *(T Allan, 71)*, G Bronzini
(E Gori, 71); SM Parisse *(C)*, S Favaro, F Minto *(A Steyn, 60)*, A van Schalkwyk *(GF Biagi, 28)*,
M Fuser*, L Cittadini *(S Ferrari, H/T)*, O Gega, SD Panico *(N Quaglio, H/T)*.
UNUSED SUBSTITUTES: T d'Apice & T Boni. *YELLOW CARD: 42 – M Fuser.
TEST DEBUTS: N Quaglio & S Ferrari.
NOTE: This was Italy's first ever win in 13 Test matches against South Africa since 1995

SOUTH AFRICA

Tries: Habana, De Allende. Conversion: Lambie. Penalty goals: Lambie, Jantjies.
WJ le Roux *(JL Goosen, 71)*; RJ Combrinck, JF Venter, D de Allende, BG Habana; PJ Lambie
(ET Jantjies, 53), R Paige *(F de Klerk, 53)*; WR Whiteley, WS Alberts *(TS Mohojé, 65)*, N Carr,
L de Jager *(FJ Mostert, 71)*, PS du Toit, VP Koch *(TN Nyakane, 53)*, JA Strauss *(C)*
(MT Mbonambi, 18-19, 77), T Mtawarira *(S Kitshoff, 53)*.
*NOTE: This was South Africa's seventh Test loss of the season, equaling the two previous records during the 1965
and 2006 seasons. Bryan Habana played in his 124th Test match, becoming the most capped Springbok against
Italy with seven appearances. He also scored his 67th Test try, now only 2 tries short of the World record. With this
try he became the joint record holder with Stefan Terblanche, for most career tries by a Springbok against Italy.*

Day to forget as Azzurri celebrate

SPRINGBOK coach Allister Coetzee described it as the "darkest moment" of his career after his team's historic, shock defeat to perennial Six Nations wooden-spoonists Italy in Florence.

The 20-18 loss was the first in South Africa's history against the Azzurri. To compound matters the Springboks were beaten by a largely young and inexperienced Italy team.

Notwithstanding their shortcomings, the Springboks enjoyed some bright moments in the first half. The catalyst was fullback Willie le Roux's incursions into the backline and neat touches that set up tries for left wing Bryan Habana and inside centre Damian de Allende.

Habana finished off after sustained Springbok pressure, while De Allende shrugged off veteran Italian skipper and No 8 Sergio Parisse on his way to the tryline.

De Allende's try featured the kind of daring and incisive play that South African fans had been craving. There was a calculated decision of attacking from their 22-metre area and good build-up play by flyhalf Patrick Lambie, right wing Ruan Combrinck and Le Roux.

Sandwiched in between those two tries was one from a lineout drive by Italy's journeyman South African lock Dries van Schalkwyk.

By contrast, the Springboks were struggling to set their mauls as a highly motivated Italian team got stuck in physically on defence.

In general this was a lacklustre display from a physical perspective by the Springboks and they endured another afternoon to forget at the breakdowns.

Italy reduced the deficit to two points with a penalty by fullback Edoardo Padovani after the Springboks' scrum had collapsed within kicking distance on the stroke of half-time.

But even then one didn't anticipate the drama that was to follow.

The Springboks were up against a resolute Italian defence, but were doing most of the playing. All that pressure would surely produce a result, right?

It certainly looked that way when Van Schalkwyk's lock partner Marco Fuser was yellow-carded for playing a man in the air at the lineout early in the second half. This offered the men in green and gold a perfect springboard to all but secure the match.

However, the neat touches that were a feature of the Springboks' tries in the first half somehow deserted them and they could not produce anything that significantly troubled Italy's solid defence, ironically masterminded by none other than former Springbok centre Brendan Venter.

South Africa could add no more than a penalty by Lambie during Fuser's 10-minute absence and, while down 15-10, the Italians drew energy from their outstanding defensive effort.

A sustained period of pressure culminated in a try for Italy's left wing Giovanbattista Venditti, who perfectly illustrated the home side's physical dominance by knocking over South Africa's substitute flyhalf Elton Jantjies before dotting down.

The Springboks momentarily reclaimed the lead with a penalty by Jantjies, but Italy's flyhalf, Carlo Canna, replied in kind to give his side the two-point lead that carried them over the line and into the history books.

There were 15 minutes left after Canna's strike – more than enough for the Springboks to regroup against a team that, at least on paper, was inferior.

However, Italy were a team in the true sense of the word and had nothing to lose.

By contrast the Springboks were a side low on confidence and clearly rattled in the home straight. Italy almost compounded the humiliation with a try from a lineout drive in the closing stages.

The television match official ruled against them, but substitute lock George Fabio Biagi got ahead of Pieter-Steph du Toit to pinch South Africa's resultant lineout and the ball was cleared into touch to seal a spectacular upset.

SCORING SEQUENCE

Min	Action	Score
9	Habana try, Lambie missed conversion	SA 5-0
12	Van Schalkwyk try, Canna conversion	It 7-5
17	De Allende try, Lambie conversion	SA 12-7
30	Padovani penalty goal	SA 12-10
46	Lambie penalty goal	SA 15-10
50	Venditty try, Canna conversion	It 17-15
61	Jantjies penalty goal	SA 18-17
65	Canna penalty goal	It 20-18

Wales 27 South Africa 13
(Halftime 12-6)

Test # 464

Principality Stadium, Cardiff. Kick-off: 17:30. Attendance: 55 122. November 26, 2016
Referee: R Poite *(France)*; Ass. Ref 1: GM Garner *(England)*; Ass. Ref 2: T Foley *(England)*;
TMO: G Hughes *(England)*.

WALES

Tries: Owens, Tipuric. Conversion: Halfpenny. Penalty goals: Halfpenny (5).

SL Halfpenny; GP North, JJV Davies, MS Williams *(JH Roberts, 79)*, LB Williams *(SC Davies, 59)***; DR Biggar, DG Davies; CR Moriarty, JC Tipuric, DJ Lydiate *(TT Faletau, H/T)**, A-W Jones, LC Charteris *(CL Hill, 79)*, TW Francis *(S Lee, 68)*, KJ Owens *(SJ Baldwin, 60)*, GD Jenkins (C) *(NP Smith, 67)*.

*Faletau to #8, Moriarty to #6 flank. **SC Davies to fullback, Halfpenny to left wing.

UNUSED SUBSTITUTE: LD Williams.

NOTE: This was only Wales' third win against South Africa in 32 Test matches since 1906.

SOUTH AFRICA

Try: Cassiem. Conversion: Lambie. Penalty goals: Jantjies (2).

JL Goosen; RJ Combrinck *(LG Mapoe, 68)*, JF Venter, R Janse van Rensburg, JI Ulengo; ET Jantjies *(PJ Lambie, 59)*, F de Klerk* *(PE van Zyl, 65)*; WR Whiteley, U Cassiem, N Carr *(J-L du Preez, 79)*, L de Jager, PS du Toit *(FJ Mostert, 68)*, LC Adriaanse *(TN Nyakane, 68)*, JA Strauss (C) *(MJ Marx, 71)*, T Mtawarira *(S Kitshoff, 59)*.

*YELLOW CARD: 42 - F de Klerk. TEST DEBUTS: U Cassiem #878, JI Ulengo #879, R Janse van Rensburg #880 and J-L du Preez #881. NOTE: This was the Springboks' eighth loss of the season – the most losses in a season ever. It was also the biggest loss against Wales since 1906. Adriaan Strauss played in his last Test match as he retired from Test rugby. Uzair Cassiem's try was the 1300th try in SA Rugby Test match history. South Africa dropped to #6 in the World Rugby rankings after this loss against Wales.

Dragons' fire douses Bok spirit

SOUTH Africa capped a season to forget with yet another battling performance in going down 27-13 to Wales at the Principality Stadium in Cardiff.

Springbok coach Allister Coetzee, shell-shocked after a defeat to Italy in Florence the previous weekend, gave his team an infusion of youthful enthusiasm in the hope it would have the desired effect against the Dragons.

In the backline there was a combined total of 40 caps in the Springboks' starting line-up, with fullback Johan Goosen the most experienced player with 12. And he, of course, was still adapting to playing fullback!

Of the four debutants, flank Uzair Cassiem gave an excellent account of himself, but robust inside centre Rohan Janse van Rensburg was trapped behind the advantage line by the Welsh defence and wing Jamba Ulengo didn't have any opportunities to leave his mark.

Flank Jean-Luc du Preez also made his debut off the substitutes' bench, but it was nothing more than a brief cameo in the closing stages after the horse had bolted.

It was apparent early on that the Springboks were keen to test the Welsh defence by keeping the ball in hand, but not much inroads were made.

In addition, the Springboks also continued with the tendency to, in the words of skipper Adriaan Strauss, play against themselves.

A lack of discipline was much to blame, with the tourists committing sins such as playing the man in the air at the lineouts, drifting offside unnecessarily and deliberately knocking the ball down in open play.

The latter resulted in a yellow card for scrumhalf Faf de Klerk early in the second half, when the Springboks were already battling a half-time deficit of six points.

Wales fullback Leigh Halfpenny added a fifth penalty and, not long thereafter, hooker Ken Owens rounded off a rolling maul. It was 20-6 to Wales and for Springbok supporters there was little reason to believe that the team had it in them to fight back.

Up until that point the Welsh had been giving the Springboks a lesson in how to play Test rugby, exerting pressure in the right areas of the field, converting their opportunities and defending resolutely.

The Springboks' cause was not helped by the off-form halfback pairing of De Klerk and flyhalf Elton Jantjies, whose forward passes disrupted the team's rhythm.

One positive is that the visitors didn't capitulate when one had a bad feeling in one's stomach that the end result might be humiliation.

In fact, they turned the screws on the Welsh and Cassiem was eventually driven over with 10 minutes left. Substitute flyhalf Patrick Lambie's conversion brought the Springboks to within seven points.

But the draw didn't remain in their sights for long. Wales landed the killer blow four minutes before the end with flank Justin Tipuric finishing delightfully after a patient build-up.

Halfpenny's conversion increased the deficit to 14 points, and with the Springboks unable to muster a reply in the closing stages, they were condemned to their heaviest defeat against Wales.

Coetzee summed it up succinctly afterwards: "In four actions early in the second half we conceded three penalties. The yellow card was really vital. We are way below the standards of what is expected of a Springbok team."

SCORING SEQUENCE

Min	Action	Score
7	Jantjies penalty goal	SA 3-0
12	Halfpenny penalty goal	3-3
18	Halfpenny penalty goal	W 6-3
22	Halfpenny penalty goal	W 9-3
24	Jantjies penalty goal	W 9-6
34	Halfpenny penalty goal	W 12-6
43	Halfpenny penalty goal	W 15-6
46	Owens try, Halfpenny missed conversion	W 20-6
57	Biggar missed drop goal	W 20-6
70	Cassiem try, Lambie conversion	W 20-13
76	Tipuric try, Halfpenny conversion	W 27-13

TOUR APPEARANCES & POINTS

PLAYER	Province/Club	Date of birth	Height	Weight	Barbarians	England	Italy	Wales	Test Apps	T	C	P	D6	Pts
JA Kriel (Jesse)	Blue Bulls	15/02/1994	1,86	96	15	-	-	-	0	0	0	0	0	0
SP Petersen	Free State	01/08/1994	1,75	80	14	-	-	-	0	1	0	0	0	5
JF Venter	Free State	19/04/1991	1,85	91	13	13	13	13	3	1	0	0	0	5
R Janse v Rensburg	Golden Lions	11/09/1994	1,86	100	12	-	-	12	1	1	0	0	0	5
JI Ulengo	Blue Bulls	07/01/1990	1,85	88	11	-	-	11	1	0	0	0	0	0
PJ Lambie	Kwazulu-Natal	17/10/1990	1,78	87	10	10	10	R	3	0	5	3	1	22
R Paige	Blue Bulls	02/08/1989	1,76	100	9	9	9	-	2	0	0	0	0	0
N Carr	Western Province	04/04/1991	1,84	93	8	R	6	6	3	0	0	0	0	0
TS Mohojé	Free State	03/08/1990	1,92	103	7	-	R	-	1	0	0	0	0	0
RA Smit	Blue Bulls	11/01/1993	1,90	90	6	-	-	-	0	1	0	0	0	5
PS du Toit	Western Province	20/08/1992	2,00	116	5	7	4	4	3	1	0	0	0	5
RG Snyman	Blue Bulls	29/01/1995	2,06	117	4	-	-	-	0	0	0	0	0	0
LC Adriaanse	Kwazulu-Natal	02/02/1988	1,80	115	3	R	-	3	2	0	0	0	0	0
MJ Marx	Golden Lions	13/07/1994	1,88	119	2	-	-	R	1	0	0	0	0	0
T Mtawarira	Kwazulu-Natal	01/08/1985	1,83	115	1	1	1	1	3	0	0	0	0	0
RJ Combrinck	Golden Lions	10/05/1990	1,83	97	R	14	14	14	3	0	1	0	0	2
MT Mbonambi	Western Province	07/01/1991	1,76	106	R	R	t+R	-	2	0	0	0	0	0
E Etzebeth	Western Province	29/10/1991	2,04	117	R	4	-	-	1	0	0	0	0	0
J-L du Preez	Kwazulu-Natal	05/08/1995	1,93	110	R	-	-	R	1	0	0	0	0	0
TN Nyakane	Blue Bulls	04/05/1989	1,78	123	R	-	R	R	2	0	0	0	0	0
L Gqoboka	Blue Bulls	24/03/1990	1,83	115	R	-	-	-	0	0	0	0	0	0
PE van Zyl	Blue Bulls	14/09/1989	1,74	81	R	-	-	R	1	0	0	0	0	0
CF Schoeman	Blue Bulls	23/09/1991	1,82	89	x	-	-	-	0	0	0	0	0	0
WJ le Roux	Kwazulu-Natal	18/08/1989	1,86	90	-	15	15	-	2	1	0	0	0	5
J-PR Pietersen	Kwazulu-Natal	12/07/1986	1,90	106	-	11	-	-	1	0	0	0	0	0
LG Mapoe	Golden Lions	13/07/1988	1,82	87	-	R	-	R	2	0	0	0	0	0
D de Allende	Western Province	25/11/1991	1,89	101	-	12	12	-	2	1	0	0	0	5
F de Klerk	Golden Lions	19/10/1991	1,72	80	-	R	R	9	3	0	0	0	0	0
L de Jager	Free State	17/12/1992	2,05	120	-	5	5	5	3	0	0	0	0	0
JA Strauss	Blue Bulls	18/11/1985	1,84	114	-	2*	2*	2*	3	0	0	0	0	0
WR Whiteley	Golden Lions	18/09/1987	1,92	97	-	8	8	8	3	0	0	0	0	0
FJ Mostert	Golden Lions	27/11/1990	1,98	103	-	R	R	R	3	0	0	0	0	0
S Kitshoff	Bordeaux-Bègles, France	10/02/1992	1,84	125	-	R	R	R	3	0	0	0	0	0
JL Goosen	Racing 92, France	27/07/1992	1,85	85	-	R	R	15	3	1	0	0	0	5
WS Alberts	Stade Français, France	11/05/1984	1,92	120	-	6	7	-	2	0	0	0	0	0
VP Koch	Saracens, England	13/03/1990	1,85	118	-	3	3	-	2	0	0	0	0	0
BG Habana	Toulon, France	12/06/1983	1,80	93	-	-	11	-	1	1	0	0	0	5
ET Jantjies	Golden Lions	01/08/1990	1,76	88	-	-	R	10	2	0	0	3	0	9
U Cassiem	Free State	07/03/1990	1,89	98	-	-	-	7	1	1	0	0	0	5
JA Kriel (Jaco)	Golden Lions	21/08/1989	1,84	97	-	-	-	-	0	0	0	0	0	0
TJ du Toit	Kwazulu-Natal	05/05/1995	1,89	130	-	-	-	-	0	0	0	0	0	0
C Kolbe	Western Province	28/10/1993	1,70	69	-	-	-	-	0	0	0	0	0	0
42 PLAYERS										10	6	6	1	83

Head Coach: Allister Coetzee
Assistant Coaches: Matthew Proudfoot, Johann van Graan, Franco Smith & Mzwandile Stick
Defence Coach: JP Ferreira **Kicking Coach:** Louis Koen
Team Manager: Ian Schwartz **Team Doctor:** Jerome Mampane
Strenghth & Conditioning Coach: Warren Adams **Physiotherapist:** Vivian Verwant
Physiotherapist: Tanu Pillay **Massage Therapist:** Daliah Hurwitz
Logistics Manager: JJ Fredericks **Public Relations Manager:** Annelee Murray
Media Manager: Rayaan Adriaanse **Technical Analyst:** Willie Maree

Allister Coetzee and Springbok captain Adriaan Strauss.

South Africa's Internationals
1891-2016

A complete list of all 881 players to have played Test rugby as well as other Springbok matches for South Africa, with Springbok number. For country abbreviations, please see page 8.

324 **Ackermann, DSP** (Dawie) b 03/06/1930 d 01/01/1970 - WP - 8 Tests (3 - 1T) 19 matches (27 - 9T) *1955: BI2, 3, 4. 1956: A1, 2, NZ1, 3. 1958: F2.*

632 **Ackermann, JN** (Johan) b 03/06/1970 - NTvl - 13 Tests (-) 15 matches (-) *1996: Fj, A1, NZ1, A2. 2001: F2(R), It1, NZ1(R), A1. 2006: I, E1, 2. 2007: Sm1, A2. 2007: Tour of UK – No Tests*

805 **Adams, HJ** (Heinie) b 29/05/1980 - BB - No Tests - 2 matches (-) *Toured F, It, I & E. 2009.*

853 **Adriaanse, LC** (Lourens) b 05/02/1988 - GW - 6 Tests (-) 7 matches (-) *2013: F(R). 2016: Arg2(R), A1, NZ1(R), E(R),W.*

658 **Aitken, AD** (Andrew) b 10/06/1968 - WP - 7 Tests (-) 9 matches (-) *1997: F2(R), E. 1998: I2(R), W1(R), NZ1, 2(R), A2(R).*

822 **Alberts, WS** (Willem) b 11/05/1984 - KZN - 43 Tests (35 - 7T) 45 matches (35 - 7T) *2010: W2(R), S(t+R), E(R). 2011: NZ2, [W(R), Fj(R), Nam, Sm(t+R), A3(t+R).]. 2012: E1, 2, Arg1, 2, A1, NZ1, A2, NZ2, I, S, E4. 2013: Sm, Arg1, 2, A1, NZ1, A2, NZ2, W, S2, F. 2014: W1, 2. 2015: Arg2, [S(R), US(R), W(R), NZ2(t+R), Arg3(R)]. 2016: NZ1(R), A2(R), NZ2(R), E, It.*

179 **Albertyn, PK** (Pierre) b 27/05/1897 d 07/03/1973 - SWD - 4 Tests (3 - 1T) 4 matches (3 - 1T) *1924:BI1*, 2*, 3*, 4*.*

673 **Alcock, CD** (Chad) b 09/01/1973 - EP - No Tests - 4 matches (5 - 1T) *Toured BI & I. 1998.*

13 **Alexander, FA** (Fred) b 30/12/1870 d 20/04/1937 - GW - 2 Tests (-) 2 matches (-) *1891: BI1, 2.*

594 **Allan, J** (John) b 25/11/1963 - Natal - 13 Tests (-) 25 matches (30 - 6T) *1993: A1(R), Arg1, 2(R). 1994: E1, 2, NZ1, 2, 3. 1996: Fj, A1, NZ1, A2, NZ2.*

355 **Allen, PB** (Peter) b 10/04/1930 d 22/01/1998 - EP - 1 Test (-) 1 match (-) *1960: S.*

121 **Allport, PH** (Percy) b 24/03/1885 d 01/01/1959 - WP - 2 Tests (3 - 1T) 2 matches (3 - 1T) *1910:BI2, 3.*

31 **Anderson, JH** (Biddy) b 26/04/1874 d 11/03/1926 - WP - 3 Tests (-) 3 matches (-) *1896:BI1, 3, 4.*

89 **Anderson, JW** (Joe) b 31/12/1881 d 02/11/1953 - WP - 1 Test (-) 1 match (-) *1903:BI3.*

47 **Andrew, JB** (Ben) b 15/05/1870 d 09/04/1911 - Tvl - 1 Test (-) 1 match (-) *1896:BI2.*

759 **Andrews, EP** (Eddie) b 18/03/1977 - WP - 23 Tests (-) 23 matches (-) *2004: I1, 2, W1(t+R), PI, NZ1, A1, NZ2, A2, W2, I3, E. 2005: F1, A2, NZ2(t), Arg(R), F3(R). 2006: S1, 2, F, A1(R), NZ1(t). 2007:A2(R), NZ2(R).*

574 **Andrews, KS** (Keith) b 03/05/1962 - WP - 9 Tests (-) 31 matches (-) *1992: E. 1993: F1, 2, A1(R), 2, 3, Arg1(R), 2. 1994: NZ3.*

602 **Andrews, MG** (Mark) b 21/02/1972 - Natal - 77 Tests (60 - 12T) 90 matches (60 - 12T) *1993: Tour of Arg - No Tests. 1994:E2, NZ1, 2, 3, Arg1, 2, S, W. 1995:WS1, [A, WS2, F, NZ], W, It, E. 1996:Fj, A1, NZ1, A2, NZ2, 3, 4, 5, Arg1, 2, F1, 2, W. 1997:T(R), BI1, 2, NZ1, A1, NZ2, A2, It, F1, 2, E, S. 1998:I1, 2, W1, E1, A1, NZ1, 2, A2, W2, S, I3, E2. 1999:NZ1, 2(R), A2(R), [S, U, E, A3, NZ3]. 2000:A2, NZ2, A3, Arg, I, W, E3. 2001:F1, 2, It1, NZ1, A1, 2, NZ2, F3, E.*

358 **Antelme, JGM** (Mike) b 23/04/1934 - Tvl - 5 Tests (-) 25 matches (45 - 15T) *1960:NZ1, 2, 3, 4. 1961:F.*

816 **Aplon, GG** (Gio) b 06/10/1982 - WP - 17 Tests (25 - 5T) 18 matches (25 - 5T) *2010: W1, F, It1, 2, NZ1(R), 2(R), A1, NZ3, A3(R), I, W2, S, E. 2011: A1, 2, [Nam]. 2012: E3. 2013: Tour of W, S & F - No Tests.*

243 **Apsey, JT** (John) b 16/04/1911 d 12/11/1987 - WP - 3 Tests (-) 3 matches (-) *1933:A4, 5. 1938:BI2.*

76 **Ashley, S** (Syd) b 23/02/1880 d 20/01/1959 - WP - 1 Test (-) 1 match (-) *1903:BI2.*

32 **Aston, FTD** (Ferdy) b 18/09/1871 d 15/10/1926 - Tvl - 4 Tests (-) 4 matches (-) *1896:BI1*, 2*, 3*, 4.*

576 **Atherton, S** (Steve) b 17/03/1965 - Natal - 8 Tests (-) 23 matches (5 - 1T) *1992: Tour of F & E – No Tests. 1993:Arg1, 2. 1994:E1, 2, NZ1, 2, 3. 1996:NZ2.*

178 **Aucamp, J** (Hans) b 27/10/1898 d 14/03/1970 - WTvl - 2 Tests (3 - 1T) 2 matches (3 - 1T) *1924:BI1, 2.*

376 **Baard, AP** (Attie) b 17/05/1933 d 01/05/2009 - WP - 1 Test (-) 13 matches (9 - 3T) *1960:I.*

246 **Babrow, L** (Louis) b 24/04/1915 d

26/01/2004 - WP - 5 Tests (9 - 3T) 16 matches (42 - 14T) *1937:A1, 2, NZ1, 2, 3.*

712 **Badenhorst, AJ** (Adri) b 18/07/1978 - WP - No Tests - 1 match (-) *Toured E. 2000.*

610 **Badenhorst, C** (Chris) b 12/12/1965 - OFS - 2 Tests (10 - 2T) 12 matches (45 - 9T) *1994: T Tours of NZ & W, S & I – No Tests. 1994: Arg2. 1995:WS1(R).*

745 **Bands, RE** (Richard) b 25/03/1974 - BB - 11 Tests (10 - 2T) 11 matches (10 - 2T) *2003: S1, 2, Arg(R), A1, NZ1, A2, NZ2, [U, E, Sm(R), NZ3(R)].*

538 **Barnard, AS** (Anton) b 07/04/1958 - EP - 4 Tests (-) 4 matches (-) *1984: S.Am&Sp1, 2. 1986: NZC1, 2.*

399 **Barnard, JH** (Jannie) b 29/01/1945 d 21/02/1985 - Tvl - 5 Tests (-) 18 matches (21 - 7T) *1965: S, A1, 2, NZ3, 4.*

442 **Barnard, RW** (Robbie) b 26/11/1941 d 20/10/2013 - Tvl - 1 Test (-) 10 matches (9 - 3T) *1969-70: Tour of UK – No Tests. 1970:NZ2(R). 1971: Tour of A – No Tests.*

285 **Barnard, WHM** (Willem) b 07/08/1923 d 13/06/2012 - NTvl - 2 Tests (-) 14 matches (3 - 1T) *1949:NZ4. 1951:W.*

690 **Barry, D** (De Wet) b 24/06/1978 - WP - 39 Tests (15 - 3T) 41 matches (20 - 4T) *2000: C, E1, 2, A1(R), NZ1, A2. 2001: F1, 2, US(R). 2002: W2, Arg, Sm, NZ1, A1, NZ2, A2. 2003: A1, NZ1, A2, [U, E, Sm, NZ3]. 2004: PI, NZ1, A1, NZ2, A2, W2, I3, E, Arg(t). 2005: F1, 2, A1, NZ2, W(R), F3(R). 2006: F.*

63 **Barry, J** (Joe) b 16/03/1876 d 29/03/1961 - WP - 3 Tests (3 - 1T) 3 matches (3 - 1T) *1903: BI1, 2, 3.*

545 **Bartmann, WJ** (Wahl) b 13/06/1963 - Tvl - 8 Tests (-) 15 matches (5 - 1T) *1986: NZC1, 2, 3, 4. 1992: NZ, A, F1, 2.*

817 **Basson, BA** (Bjorn) b 11/02/1987 - GW - 11 Tests (15 - 3T) 11 matches (15 - 3T) *2010: W1(R), It1(R), I, W2. 2011: A1, NZ1. 2013: It, S, Sm, Arg1,2.*

661 **Basson, WW** (Wium) b 23/10/1975 d 22/04/2001 - BB - No Tests - 2 matches (-) *Toured It, F, E & S. 1997.*

252 **Bastard, WE** (Ebbo) b 10/12/1912 d 14/02/1949 - Natal - 6 Tests (6 - 2T) 18 matches (15 - 5T) *1937: A1, NZ1, 2, 3. 1938: BI1, 3.*

438 **Bates, AJ** (Albie) b 18/04/1941 - WTvl - 4 Tests (-) 18 matches (3 - 1T). *1969: E. 1970: NZ1, 2. 1971: Tour of A – No Tests. 1972: E.*

468 **Bayvel, PCR** (Paul) b 28/03/1949 - Tvl - 10 Tests (-) 13 matches (-) *1974: BI2, 4, F1, 2. 1975: F1, 2. 1976: NZ1, 2, 3, 4.*

524 **Beck, JJ** (Colin) b 27/03/1959 - WP - 3 Tests (4 - 1T) 12 matches (35 - 5T, 3C, 2P, 1D)

1981: NZ2(R), 3(R), US.

387 **Bedford, TP** (Tommy) b 08/02/1942 - Natal - 25 Tests (3 - 1T) 48 matches (12 - 4T) *1963: A1, 2, 3, 4. 1964: W, F. 1965: I, A1, 2. 1968: BI1, 2, 3, 4, F1, 2. 1969: A1, 2*, 3*, 4, S*, E. 1970: I, W. 1971: F1, 2. 1971: Tour of A – No Tests.*

795 **Bekker, A** (Andries) b 05/12/1983 - WP - 29 Tests (5 - 1T) 31 matches (5 - 1T) *2008: W1, 2(R), It(R), NZ1(R), 2(t+R), A1(t+R), Arg(R), NZ3, A2, 3, W3(R), S(R), E(R). 2009: BI1(R), 2(R), NZ2(R), A1(R), 2(R), F(t+R), It, I. 2010: It2, NZ1(R), 2(R). 2012:Arg1, 2, NZ1(t+R), A2, NZ2.*

527 **Bekker, HJ** (Hennie) b 12/09/1952 - WP - 2 Tests (4 - 1T) 10 matches (16 - 4T) *1981: NZ1, 3.*

298 **Bekker, HPJ** (Jaap) b 11/02/1925 d 06/08/1999 - NTvl - 15 Tests (3 - 1T) 39 matches (12 - 4T) *1952: E, F. 1953: A1, 2, 3, 4. 1955: BI2, 3, 4. 1956: A1, 2, NZ1, 2, 3, 4.*

353 **Bekker, MJ** (Martiens) b 03/05/1930 d 10/11/1971 - NTvl - 1 Test (-) 1 match (-) *1960: S.*

308 **Bekker, RP** (Dolph) b 15/12/1926 d 17/06/2012 - NTvl - 2 Tests (3 - 1T) 2 matches (3 - 1T) *1953: A3, 4.*

639 **Bekker, S** (Schutte) b 21/10/1971 - NTvl - 1 Test (-) 3 matches (15 - 3T) *1996: Tour of Arg, F & W – No Tests. 1997: A2(t).*

640 **Bennett, RG** (Russell) b 27/11/1971 - Border - 6 Tests (10 - 2T) 10 matches (25 - 5T) *1996: Tour of Arg, F & W – No Tests. 1997: T(R), BI1(R), 3, NZ1, A1, NZ2.*

228 **Bergh, WF v R v O** (Ferdie) b 02/11/1906 d 28/05/1973 - SWD - 17 Tests (21 - 7T) 41 matches (42 - 14T) *1931: W, I. 1932: E, S. 1933: A1, 2, 3, 4, 5. 1937: A1, 2, NZ1, 2, 3. 1938: BI1, 2, 3.*

485 **Bestbier, A** (André) b 31/03/1946 - OFS - 1 Test (-) 5 matches (-) *1974: F2(R).*

186 **Bester, JJN** (Jack) b 02/03/1898 d 27/10/1943 - WP - 2 Tests (3 - 1T) 2 matches (3 - 1T) *1924: BI2, 4.*

247 **Bester, JLA** (Johnny) b 25/12/1917 d 14/05/1977 - WP - 2 Tests (6 - 2T) 14 matches (30 - 10T) *1937: Tour of A & NZ – No Tests. 1938: BI2, 3.*

49 **Beswick, AM** (Allan) b 30/06/1870 d 06/09/1908 - Border - 3 Tests (-) 3 matches (-) *1896: BI2, 3, 4.*

383 **Bezuidenhout, CE** (Chris) b 13/10/1937 d ??/??/2002 - NTvl - 3 Tests (-) 3 matches (-) *1962: BI2, 3, 4.*

751 **Bezuidenhout, CJ** (Christo) b 14/05/1970 - Mpu - 4 Tests (-) 4 matches (-) *2003: NZ2(R), [E, Sm, NZ3].*

457 **Bezuidenhout, NSE** (Niek) b 04/08/1950

- NTvl - 9 Tests (-) 13 matches (-) *1972: E. 1974: BI2, 3, 4, F1, 2. 1975: F1, 2. 1977: WT.*

225 **Bierman, JN** (Nic) b 13/02/1910 d 08/06/1977 - Tvl - 1 Test (-) 14 matches (18 - 6T) *1931: I.*

8 **Bisset, WM** (William) b 11/09/1867 d 23/02/1958 - WP - 2 Tests (-) 2 matches (-) *1891: BI1, 3.*

494 **Blair, R** (Robbie) b 03/06/1953 - WP - 1 Test (21 - 3C, 5P) 1 match (21 - 3C, 5P) *1977: WT.*

747 **Bobo, G** (Gcobani) b 12/09/1979 - GL - 6 Tests (-) 6 matches (-) *2003:S2(R), Arg, A1(R), NZ2. 2004: S(R). 2008:It.*

670 **Boome, CS** (Selborne) b 16/05/1975 - WP - 20 Tests (10 - 2T) 25 matches (15 - 3T) *1998: Tour of UK & I - No Tests. 1999: It1, 2, W, NZ1(R), A1, NZ2, A2. 2000: C, E1, 2. 2003: S1(R), 2(R), Arg(R), A1(R), NZ1(R), A2, NZ2(R), [U(R), Geo, NZ3(R)].*

467 **Bosch, GR** (Gerald) b 12/05/1949 - Tvl - 9 Tests (89 - 7C, 23P, 2D) 14 matches (132 - 15C, 31P, 3D) *1974: BI2, F1, 2. 1975: F1, 2. 1976: NZ1, 2, 3, 4.*

861 **Boshoff, ML** (Marnitz) b 11/01/1989 - GL - 1 Test (2 -1C) 1 match (2 - 1C) *2014: S(R).*

771 **Bosman, HM** (Meyer) b 19/04/1985 - FS - 3 Tests (7 - 2C, 1P) 6 matches (7 - 2C, 1P) *2005: W, F3. 2006: A1(R). 2009: Tour of F, It, I & E – No Tests.*

185 **Bosman, NJS** (Nico) b 06/10/1902 d 26/05/1967 - Tvl - 3 Tests (-) 3 matches (-) *1924: BI2, 3, 4.*

843 **Botha, AF** (ArNo) b 26/10/1991 - BB - 2 Tests (-) 2 matches (-) *2012: Toured I, S & E. - No Tests. 2013: It, S.*

778 **Botha, BJ** (BJ) b 04/01/1980 - KZN - 25 Tests (5 - 1T) 26 matches (5 - 1T). *2006: NZ2(R), 3, A3, I(R), E1, 2. 2007: E1, Sm1, A1, NZ1, Nam(R), S(t+R), [Sm(R), E3, T(R), US.]. 2008: W2. 2009: It(R), I. 2010: W1, F, It2(R), NZ1(R), 2(R), A1.*

522 **Botha, DS** (Darius) b 26/06/1955 - NTvl - 1 Test (-) 8 matches (12 - 3T). *1981: NZ1.*

770 **Botha, GvG** (Gary) b 12/10/1981 - BB - 12 Tests (-) 14 matches (-). *2005:A3(R), F3(R). 2006: Tour of I & E – No Tests. 2007: E1(R), 2(R), Sm1(R), A1(R), NZ1, A2, NZ2(R), Nam, S, [T.].*

502 **Botha, HE** (Naas) b 27/02/1958 - NTvl - 28 Tests (312 - 2T, 50C, 50P, 18D) 40 matches (485 - 6T, 91C, 66P, 27D) *1980: S.Am1, 2, BI1, 2, 3, 4, S.Am3, 4, F. 1981: I1, 2, NZ1, 2, 3, US. 1982: S.Am1, 2. 1986: NZC1*, 2*, 3*, 4*. 1989: WT1, 2. 1992: NZ*, A*, F1*, 2*, E*.*

90 **Botha, JA** (John) b 19/11/1879 d 08/12/1920 - Tvl - 1 Test (-) 1 match (-) *1903: BI3.*

733 **Botha, JP** (Bakkies) b 22/09/1979 - BB - 85 Tests (35 - 7T) 87 matches (45 - 9T) *2002: F. 2003: S1, 2, A1, NZ1, A2(R), [U, E, Geo, Sm, NZ3]. 2004: I1, PI, NZ1, A1, NZ2, A2, W2, I3, E, S, Arg. 2005: A1, 2, 3, NZ1, A4, NZ2, Arg, W, F3. 2007: E1, 2, A1, NZ1, Nam, S.[Sm, E3, T, US/Fj, Arg, E4.], W. 2008: W1, 2, It, NZ1, 2, A1, Arg, W3, S, E. 2009: BI1, 2, NZ1, 2, A1, 2, 3, NZ3, F, It. 2010: It1, 2, NZ1, I, W2, S, E. 2011: A2, NZ2, [Fj, Nam]. 2013: S2, F(R). 2014: W1, Arg1,2(R), A2(R), NZ2(R), I(R), E(R).*

374 **Botha, JPF** (Hannes) b 11/05/1937 d 30/08/2011 - NTvl - 3 Tests (-) 10 matches (9 - 3T) *1960–61: Tour of BI, I & F – No Tests. 1962: BI2, 3, 4.*

412 **Botha, PH** (Piet) b 13/09/1935 - Tvl - 2 Tests (-) 11 matches (3 - 1T) *1965: A1, 2.*

4 **Boyes, HC** (Harry) b 12/03/1868 d 26/10/1892 - GW - 2 Tests (-) 2 matches (-) *1891: BI1, 2.*

149 **Braine, JS** (Jack) b 01/05/1891 d 25/10/1940 - GW - No Tests - 11 matches (-) *Toured BI, I & F. 1912/13.*

204 **Brand, GH** (Gerry) b 08/10/1906 d 04/02/1996 - WP - 16 Tests (55 - 13 C, 7P, 2D) 46 matches (293 - 2T, 100C, 25P, 3D) *1928: NZ2, 3. 1931: W, I. 1932: E, S. 1933: A1, 2, 3, 4, 5. 1937: A1, 2, NZ2, 3. 1938: BI1.*

39 **Bredenkamp, MJ** (Mike) b 02/05/1873 d 22/12/1940 - GW - 2 Tests (-) 2 matches (-) *1896: BI1, 3.*

547 **Breedt, JC** (Jannie) b 04/06/1959 - Tvl - 8 Tests (-) 8 matches (-) *1986: NZC1, 2, 3, 4. 1989: WT1*, 2*. 1992: NZ, A.*

268 **Brewis, JD** (Hannes) b 15/06/1920 d 09/09/2007 - NTvl - 10 Tests (18 - 1T, 5D) 19 matches (36 - 6T, 6D) *1949: NZ1, 2, 3, 4. 1951: S, I, W. 1952: E, F. 1953: A1.*

313 **Briers, TPD** (Theuns) b 11/07/1929 - WP - 7 Tests (15 - 5T) 12 matches (27 - 9T) *1955: BI1, 2, 3, 4. 1956: NZ2, 3, 4.*

104 **Brink, DJ** (Koei) b 07/11/1882 d 29/10/1970 - WP - 3 Tests (-) 18 matches (9 - 3T) *1906: S, W, E.*

626 **Brink, RA** (Robby) b 21/07/1971 - WP - 2 Tests (-) 2 matches (-) *1995: [R, C].*

799 **Brits, SB** (Schalk) b 16/05/1981 - WP - 10 Tests (5 - 1T) 11 matches (5 - 1T) *2008: It(R), NZ2(R), A1. 2012: S(R), E4(R). 2014: W1(R),2(R). 2015: [Arg2(R), Sm(R), US(R)].*

760 **Britz, GJJ** (Gerrie) b 14/04/1978 - FS - 13 Tests (-) 14 matches (-) *2004: I1(R), 2(R), W1(R), PI, A1, NZ2, A2(R), I3(t), S(t+R), Arg(R). 2005: U. 2006: E2(R). 2007: NZ2(R).*

725 **Britz, WK** (Warren) b 07/11/1973 - Natal - 1 Test (-) 1 match (-) *2002: W1.*

244 **Broodryk, JA** (Tallie) b 11/04/1910 d

22/10/1993 - Tvl - No Tests - 6 matches (22 - 6T, 1D) *Toured A & NZ. 1937.*

100 **Brooks, D** (Cocky) b 22/09/1881 d 14/11/1962 - Border - 1 Test (-) 11 matches (3 - 1T) *1906: S.*

655 **Brosnihan, WG** (Warren) b 28/12/1971 - GL - 6 Tests (5 - 1T) 10 matches (10 - 2T) *1997: A2. 2000: NZ1(t+R), A2(t+R), NZ2(R), A3(R), E3(R).*

74 **Brown, CB** (Charlie) b 29/01/1878 d 18/06/1944 - WP - 3 Tests (-) 3 matches (-) *1903: BI1, 2, 3.*

801 **Brüssow, HW** (Heinrich) b 21/07/1986 - FS - 23 Tests (5 - 1T) 23 matches (5 - 1T) *2008: E(R). 2009: BI1, 2(R), 3, NZ1, 2, A1, 2, 3, NZ3, F, It, I. 2011: A2, NZ2, [W, Fj, Nam(R), Sm, A3]. 2015: NZ1, Arg1, 2.*

407 **Brynard, GS** (Gertjie) b 21/10/1938 - WP - 7 Tests (6 - 2T) 21 matches (42 - 14T) *1965: A1, NZ1, 2, 3, 4. 1968: BI3, 4.*

287 **Buchler, JU** (Johnny) b 07/04/1930 - Tvl - 10 Tests (8 - 1C, 1P, 1D) 26 matches (26 - 4C, 5P, 1D) *1951: S, I, W. 1952: E, F. 1953: A1, 2, 3, 4. 1956: A2.*

837 **Burden, CB** (Craig) b 13/05/1985 - KZN - No Tests - No matches *Rugby Championship Squad 2012*

108 **Burdett, AF** (Adam) b 20/08/1882 d 04/11/1918 - WP - 2 Tests (-) 11 matches (6 - 2T) *1906: S, I.*

552 **Burger, JM** (Kobus) b 31/03/1964 - WP - 2 Tests (-) 2 matches (-) *1989: WT1, 2.*

511 **Burger, MB** (Thys) b 10/11/1954 - NTvl - 3 Tests (8 - 2T) 13 matches (52 - 13 T) *1980: BI2(R), S.Am3. 1981: US(R).*

535 **Burger, SWP** (Schalk) b 06/10/1955 - WP - 6 Tests (-) 6 matches (-) *1984: E1, 2. 1986: NZC1, 2, 3, 4.*

754 **Burger, SWP** (Schalk) b 13/04/1983 - WP - 86 Tests (80 - 16T) 88 matches (80 - 16T) *2003: [Geo(R), Sm(R), NZ3(R)]. 2004: I1, 2, W1, PI, NZ1, A1, NZ2, A2, W2, I3, E. 2005: F1, 2, A1, 2(R), 3(R), NZ1, A4, NZ2, Arg(R), W, F3. 2006: S1, 2. 2007: E1, 2, A1, NZ1, Nam, S, [Sm, US, Fj, Arg, E4], W. 2008: It(R), NZ1, 2, A1, NZ3, A2,3, W3, S, E. 2009: BI2, A2(R),3(R), 2(R), NZ3, F, I. 2010: F, It2, NZ1, 2, A1, NZ3, A2,3. 2011: [W, Fj, Nam, Sm, A3.]. 2014: W1(R),2(R), A2(R), NZ(R), I(R), E. 2015: A1, NZ1*, Arg1,2 [J, Sm, S, US, W, NZ2, Arg3].*

99 **Burger, WAG** (Bingo) b 12/08/1883 d 08/08/1963 - Border - 4 Tests (-) 23 matches (3 - 1T) *1906: S, I, W. 1910: BI2.*

91 **Burmeister, ARD** (Arthur) b 01/05/1885 d 25/05/1952 - WP - No Tests - 10 matches (-) *Toured BI, I & F. 1906/07.*

395 **Carelse, G** (Gawie) b 21/07/1941 d 03/08/2002 - EP - 14 Tests (-) 30 matches (5 - 1T, 1C) *1964: W, F. 1965: I, S. 1967: F1, 2, 3. 1968: F1, 2. 1969: A1, 2, 3, 4, S.*

456 **Carlson, RA** (Ray) b 02/10/1948 - WP - 1 Test (-) 1 match (-) *1972: E.*

83 **Carolin, HW** (Paddy) b 10/04/1881 d 15/03/1967 - WP - 3 Tests (-) 18 matches (73 - 6T, 15C, 3P, 4D) *1903: BI3. 1906: S*, I.*

865 **Carr, N** (Nizaam) b 04/04/1991 - WP - 5 Tests (-) 6 matches (-) *2014: It(R), W3(R). 2016: E(R) ,It, W.*

734 **Carstens, PD** (Deon) b 03/06/1979 - Natal - 9 Tests (-) 10 matches (-) *2002: S, E. 2006: E1(t+R), 2(R). 2007: E1, 2(t+R), Sm1(R). 2009: BI1(R), 3(t).*

878 **Cassiem, U** (Uzair) b 07/03/1990 - FS - 1 Test (5 - 1T) 1 match (5 - 1T) *2016:W.*

9 **Castens, HH** (Herbert) b 23/11/1864 d 18/10/1929 - WP - 1 Test (-) 1 match (-) *1891: BI1*.*

768 **Chavhanga, T** (Tonderai) b 24/12/1983 - WP - 4 Tests (30 - 6T) 4 matches (30 - 6T) *2005: U. 2007: NZ2(R). 2008: W1, 2.*

28 **Chignell, TW** (Charlie) b 28/04/1866 d 17/10/1952 - WP - 1 Test (-) 1 match (-) *1891: BI3.*

384 **Cilliers, GD** (Gert) b 28/07/1940 d 26/01/1986 - OFS - 3 Tests (3 - 1T) 6 matches (3 - 1T) *1963: A1, 3, 4. 1965: Tour of I & S - No Tests.*

637 **Cilliers, NV** (Vlok) b 26/03/1968 - WP - 1 Test (-) 1 match (-) *1996: NZ3(t).*

835 **Cilliers, PM** (Pat) b 03/03/1987 - GL - 6 Tests (-) 6 matches (-) *2012: Arg1(t+R), 2(R), A1(t+R), 2(R), I(R), E4(R).*

319 **Claassen, JT** (Johan) b 23/09/1929 - WTvl - 28 Tests (10 - 2T, 2C) 56 matches (16 - 4T, 2C) *1955: BI1, 2, 3, 4. 1956: A1, 2, NZ1, 2, 3, 4. 1958: F1*, 2*. 1960: S, NZ1, 2, 3, W, I. 1961: E, S, F, I*, A1*, 2*. 1962: BI1*, 2*, 3*, 4*.*

519 **Claassen, W** (Wynand) b 16/01/1951 - Natal - 7 Tests (-) 13 matches (8 - 2T) *1981: I1*, 2*, NZ2*, 3*, US*. 1982: S.Am 1*, 2*.*

611 **Claassens, JP** (Jannie) b 30/06/1969 - NTvl - No Tests - 8 matches (15 - 3T). Toured *NZ 1994 and W, S & I 1994.*

765 **Claassens, M** (Michael) b 28/10/1982 - FS - 8 Tests (-) 8 matches (-) *2004: W2(R), S(R), Arg(R). 2005: Arg(R), W, F3. 2007: A2(R), NZ2(R).*

240 **Clark, WHG** (Ginger) b 22/09/1906 d 20/09/1999 - Tvl - 1 Test (-) 1 match (-) *1933: A3.*

157 **Clarkson, WA** (Wally) b 08/07/1896 - 03/06/1973 - Natal - 3 Tests (-) 11 matches (9 -

3T) *1921: NZ1, 2. 1924: BI1.*

61 **Cloete, HA** (Patats) b 15/06/1873 d 29/03/1959 - WP - 1 Test (-) 1 match (-) *1896: BI4.*

441 **Cockrell, CH** (Charlie) b 10/01/1939 d 04/10/2016 - WP - 3 Tests (-) 10 matches (-) *1969: S. 1970: I, W.*

486 **Cockrell, RJ** (Robert) b 04/04/1950 d 26/05/2000 - WP - 11 Tests (4 - 1T) 25 matches (8 - 2T) *1974: F1, 2. 1975: F1, 2. 1976: NZ1, 2. 1977: WT. 1980: Tour of S.Am – No Tests. 1981: NZ1, 2(R), 3, US.*

513 **Cocks, TMD** (Tim) b 29/09/1952 - Natal - No Tests - 3 matches (8 - 2T) *Toured S.Am. 1980.*

730 **Coetzee, D** (Danie) b 02/09/1977 - BB - 15 Tests (5 - 1T) 15 matches (5 - 1T). *2002: Sm. 2003: S1, 2, Arg, A1, NZ1, A2, NZ2, [U, E, Sm(R), NZ3(R)]. 2004: S(R), Arg(R). 2006: A1(R).*

463 **Coetzee, JHH** (Boland) b 20/01/1945 - WP - 6 Tests (-) 6 matches (-) *1974: BI1. 1975: F2(R). 1976: NZ1, 2, 3, 4.*

831 **Coetzee, MC** (Marcell) b 08/05/1991 - KZN - 28 Tests (30 - 6T) 29 matches (30 - 6T) *2012: E1, 2, 3, Arg1, 2, A1, NZ1(R), A2(R), NZ2(t+R), I(R), S(R), E4(R). 2013: It(t+R), S1,2(R). 2014: S, Arg1,2(R), A1, NZ1, A2, NZ2, I, E.It, W3. 2015: A, Arg1.*

X **Coetzee, RL** (Robbie) - Springbok Tour Squad Member - b 02/05/1989 - GL - No Tests (-) No matches (-) *Toured I,E,It & W 2014. Not considered a Springbok until such time as he appears in a Test, after which he will receive a Springbok number.*

871 **Combrinck, RJ** (Ruan) b 10/05/1990 - GL - 7 Tests (15 - 2T, 1C, 1P) 8 matches (15 - 2T, 1C, 1P) *2016: I2(R), 3, Arg1, 2, E, It,W.*

724 **Conradie, JHJ** (Bolla) b 24/02/1978 - WP - 18 Tests (13 - 2T, 1D) 18 matches (13 - 2T, 1D) *2002: W1, 2, Arg(R), Sm, NZ1, A1, NZ2(R), A2(R), S, E. 2004: W1(R), PI, NZ2, A2. 2005:Arg. 2008:W1, 2(R), NZ1(R).*

404 **Conradie, SC** (Faan) b 27/06/1942 d 21/10/1992 - WP - No Tests - No matches *Toured I & S. 1965.*

41 **Cope, DG** (Davie) b 14/08/1877 d 16/08/1898 - Tvl - 1 Test (2 - 1C) 1 match (2 - 1C) *1896: BI2.*

53 **Cotty, WAH** (Bill) b 24/02/1875 d 06/09/1928 - GW - 1 Test (-) 1 match (-) *1896: BI3.*

81 **Crampton, G** (George) b 30/03/1875 d 27/12/1946 - GW - 1 Test (-) 1 match (-) *1903:BI2.*

219 **Craven, DH** (Danie) b 11/10/1910 d 04/01/1993 - WP - 16 Tests (6 - 2T) 38 matches (24 - 8T) *1931: W, I. 1932: S. 1933: A1, 2, 3, 4, 5. 1937: A1, 2, NZ1*, 2, 3. 1938: BI1*, 2*, 3*.*

406 **Cronjé, CJC** (Kerneels) b 16/04/1940 d 13/05/2009 - ETvl - No Tests - No matches *Toured A & NZ. 1965.*

750 **Cronjé, G** (Geo) b 23/07/1980 - BB - 3 Tests (-) 3 matches (-) *2003: NZ. 2004: I2(R), W1(R).*

758 **Cronjé, J** (Jacques) b 04/08/1982 - BB - 32 Tests (20 - 4T) 33 matches (25 - 5T) *2004: I1, 2, W1, PI, NZ1, A1, NZ2(R), A2(t+R), S(t+R), Arg. 2005: U, F1, 2, A1, 3, NZ1(R), 2(t), Arg, W, F3. 2006: S2(R), F(R), A1(t+R), NZ1, A2, NZ2, A3(R), I(R), E1. 2007: A2(R), NZ2, Nam.*

447 **Cronjé, PA** (Peter) b 21/09/1949 - Tvl - 7 Tests (10 - 3T) 15 matches (16 - 5T) *1971: F1, 2, A1, 2, 3. 1974: BI3, 4.*

X **Cronjé, R** (Ross) - Springbok Tour Squad Member - b 26/07/1989 - GL - No Tests (-) No matches (-) *Toured I,E,It & W 2014. Not considered a Springbok until such time as he appears in a Test, after which he will receive a Springbok number.*

144 **Cronjé, SN** (Fanie) b 24/04/1886 d 20/09/1972 - Tvl - No Tests - 7 matches (3 - 1T) *Toured BI, I & F. 1912/13.*

51 **Crosby, JH** (Jim) b 03/07/1873 d 25/02/1960 - Tvl - 1 Test (-) 1 match (-). *1896: BI2.*

116 **Crosby, NJ** (Nic) b 21/08/1883 d 14/07/1938 - Tvl - 2 Tests (-) 2 matches (-) *1910: BI1, 3.*

78 **Currie, C** (Clem) b 21/10/1880 d 12/10/1937 - GW - 1 Test (-) 1 match (-) *1903: BI2.*

235 **D'Alton, G** (George) b 17/08/1908 d 22/11/1975 - WP - 1 Test (-) 1 match (-) *1933: A1.*

614 **Dalton, J** (James) b 16/08/1972 - Tvl - 43 Tests (25 - 5T) 58 matches (25 - 5T) *1994: Tour of NZ and of W,S,& I – No Tests. 1994: Arg1(R). 1995:[A, C], W, It, E. 1996: NZ2(R), 3, Arg1, 2, F1, 2, W. 1997: T(R), BI3, NZ2, A2, It, F1, 2, E, S. 1998: I1, 2, W1, E1, A1, NZ1, 2, A2, W2, S, I3, E2. 2002: W1, 2, Arg, NZ1, A1, NZ2, A2, F, E.*

197 **Daneel, GM** (George) b 29/08/1904 d 19/10/2004 - WP - 8 Tests (6 - 2T) 20 matches (9 - 3T) *1928: NZ1, 2, 3, 4. 1931: W, I. 1932:E, I.*

102 **Daneel, HJ** (Pinkie) b 04/05/1882 d 07/01/1947 - WP - 4 Tests (-) 15 matches (3 - 1T) *1906: S, I, W, E.*

823 **Daniel, KR** (Keegan) b 05/03/1985 - KZN - 5 Tests (-) 6 matches (-). *2010: I(R). 2012: E1(R), 2(R), Arg1, 2(R).*

302 **Dannhauser, G** (Gert) b 16/04/1918 d 07/10/1983 - Tvl - No Tests - 12 matches (-) *Toured BI, I & F. 1951/52.*

706 **Davids, Q** (Quinton) b 17/08/1975 - WP - 9 Tests (-) 13 matches (-) *2000: Tour to Arg & Arg,I,W&E – No Tests. 2002: W2, Arg(R), Sm(R). 2003: Arg. 2004:I1(R), 2, W1, PI(t+R), NZ1(R).*

700 **Davidson, CD** (Craig) b 23/02/1977 -

Natal - 5 Tests (10 - 2T) 8 matches (10 - 2T) *2000: Tour to Arg & Arg,I,W&E – No Tests. 2002: W2(R), Arg. 2003: Arg, NZ1(R), A2.*

119 **Davison, PM** (Max) b 05/06/1885 d 14/11/1931 - EP - 1 Test (-) 1 match (-) *1910: BI1.*

862 **De Allende, D** (Damian) b 25/11/1991 - WP - 22 Tests (15 - 3T) 23 matches (25 - 5T) *2014: Arg1,2, W3(R). 2015: A, NZ1, Arg1, 2, [Sm, S, US, W, NZ2, Arg3]. 2016: I1, 2, 3, Arg1, 2, NZ1(R), 2, E, It.*

653 **De Beer, JH** (Jannie) b 22/04/1971 - FS - 13 Tests (181 - 2T, 33C, 27P, 8D) 14 matches (188 - 3T, 34C, 27P, 8D). *1997: BI3, NZ1, A1, NZ2, A2, F2(R), S. 1999: A2, [S, Sp, U, E, A3].*

475 **De Bruyn, J** (Johan) b 12/10/1948 - OFS - 1 Test (-) 4 matches (-) *1974: BI3. 1974: Tour of F – No Tests.*

856 **De Jager, L** (Lood) b 17/12/1992 - FS - 28 Tests (20 - 4T) 28 matches (20 - 4T) *2014: W1(R),2(R), S, Arg1,2, A1(R), NZ1(R), It(R), W3(R). 2015: A(R), NZ1, Arg1, [J, Sm(R), S, US, W, NZ2, Arg3(R)]. 2016: I1, Arg1, 2, A1, 2(R), NZ2(R), E, It, W.*

205 **De Jongh, HPK** (Manus) b 10/10/1902 d 05/09/1974 - WP - 1 Test (3 - 1T) 1 match (3 - 1T) *1928:NZ3.*

806 **De Jongh, JL** (Juan) b 15/04/1988 - WP - 19 Tests (15 - 3T) 21 matches (20 - 4T) *2010: W1, F(R), It1(R), 2, A1(R), NZ3. 2011: A1, NZ1, [Fj(R), Nam(R).]. 2012: A2(R), NZ2(R), S, E4. 2016: Arg1(R), A1, NZ1, A2, NZ2.*

870 **De Klerk, F** (Faf) b19/10/1991 - GL - 11 Tests - (-) 11 matches (-) *2016: I1, 2, 3, Arg1, 2, A1, NZ1, 2, E(R), It(R),W.*

440 **De Klerk, IJ** (Sakkie) b 28/10/1938 - Tvl - 3 Tests (-) 9 matches (-) *1969: E. 1970: I, W.*

464 **De Klerk, KBH** (Kevin) b 06/06/1950 - Tvl - 13 Tests (-) 18 matches (4 - 1T) 1974: BI1, 2, 3(R). *1974: Tour of F – No Tests. 1975: F1, 2. 1976: NZ2(R), 3, 4. 1980: S.Am1, 2, BI2. 1981: I1, 2.*

16 **De Kock, AN** (Arthur) b 11/01/1866 d 06/07/1957 - GW - 1 Test (-) 1 match (-) *1891: BI2.*

722 **De Kock, D** (Deon) b 11/05/1975 - GF - 2 Tests (-) 2 matches (-) *2001: It2(R), US.*

160 **De Kock, JS** (Sas) b 17/08/1896 d 04/11/1972 - WP - 2 Tests (-) 7 matches (6 - 2T) *1921: NZ3. 1924: BI3.*

717 **De Kock, NA** (Neil) b 20/11/1978 - WP - 10 Tests (10 - 2T) 10 matches (10 - 2T) *2001: It1. 2002: Sm(R), NZ1(R), 2, A2, F. 2003: [U(R), Geo, Sm(R), NZ3(R)].*

75 **De Melker, SC** (Syd) b 31/03/1884 d 01/11/1953 - GW - 2 Tests (-) 14 matches (9 - 3T) *1903: BI2. 1906: E.*

334 **De Nysschen, CJ** (Chris) b 31/01/1936 - Natal - No Tests - 10 matches (3 - 1T) *Toured A & NZ. 1956.*

112 **De Villiers, DI** (Dirkie) b 20/07/1889 d 01/10/1958 - Tvl - 3 Tests (3 - 1T) 3 matches (3 - 1T) *1910: BI1, 2, 3.*

382 **De Villiers, DJ** (Dawie) b 10/07/1940 - WP - 25 Tests (9 - 3T) 53 matches (29 - 5T, 4C, 2P) *1962: BI2, 3. 1965: I, NZ1*, 3*, 4*. 1967: F1*, 2*, 3*, 4*. 1968: BI1*, 2*, 3*, 4*, F1*, 2*. 1969: A1*, 4*, E*. 1970: I*, W*, NZ1*, 2*, 3*, 4*.*

95 **De Villiers, HA** (Boy) b 05/01/1883 d 09/11/1944 - WP - 3 Tests (-) 18 matches (22 - 6T, 1D) *1906: S, W, E.*

418 **De Villiers, HO** (HO) b 10/03/1945 - WP - 14 Tests (26 - 7C, 4P) 29 matches (80 - 2T, 22C, 10P) *1967: F1, 2, 3, 4. 1968: F1, 2. 1969: A1, 2, 3, 4, S, E. 1970: I, W.*

151 **De Villiers, IB** (IB) b 10/03/1892 d 09/01/1966 - Tvl - No Tests - 10 matches (35 - 10C, 5P) *Toured A & NZ. 1921.*

735 **De Villiers, J** (Jean) b 24/02/1981 - WP - 109 Tests (135 - 27T) 110 matches (135 - 27T) *2002: F. 2004: PI, NZ1, A1, NZ2, A2, W2(R), E. 2005: U, F1, 2, A1, 2, 3, NZ1, A4, NZ2, Arg, W, F3. 2006: S1, NZ2, 3, A3, I, E1, 2. 2007: E1, 2, A1, NZ1, Nam, [Sm.]. 2008: W1, 2, It, NZ1, 2, A1, Arg, NZ3, A2, 3, W3, S, E. 2009: BI1, 2, NZ1, 2, A1, 2, 3, NZ3, I. 2010: F(t+R), It1, 2, NZ1, 2, 3, A2, 3, I, W2, S, E. 2011:A2, NZ2, [W, Sm(R), A3.]. 2012: E1*, 2*, 3*, Arg1*, 2*, A1*, NZ1*, A2*, NZ2*, I*, S*, E4*. 2013: It*, S*, Sm*, Arg1*,2*, A1*, NZ1*, A2*, NZ2*, W*, S*, F*. 2014: Arg1*,2*, A1*, NZ1*, A2*, NZ2*, I*, E*, It*, W3*. 2015: Arg1*, [J*, Sm*]*

195 **De Villiers, P du P** (Pierie) b 14/06/1905 d 14/11/1975 - WP - 8 Tests (-) 28 matches (6 - 2T) *1928: NZ1, 3, 4. 1932: E. 1933: A4. 1937: A1, 2, NZ1.*

400 **De Vos, DJJ** (Dirkie) b 08/04/1941 d 12/02/2011 - WP - 3 Tests (-) 18 matches (9 - 3T) *1965: S. 1969: A3, S. 1971: Tour of A – No Tests.*

423 **De Waal, AN** (Albie) b 04/02/1942 - WP - 4 Tests (-) 4 matches (-) *1967: F1, 2, 3, 4.*

60 **De Waal, PJ** (Paul) b 02/06/1875 d 18/05/1945 - WP - 1 Test (-) 1 match (-) *1896: BI4.*

429 **De Wet, AE** (André) b 01/08/1946 - WP - 3 Tests (-) 11 matches (-) *1969: A3, 4, E.*

261 **De Wet, PJ** (Piet) b 12/03/1917 d 18/10/1968 - WP - 3 Tests (-) 3 matches (-) *1938: BI1, 2, 3.*

335 **De Wilzem, CJ** (Chris) b 14/10/1932 d 02/03/2006 - OFS - No Tests - 16 matches (3 - 1T) *Toured A & NZ. 1956.*

145 **Delaney, ETA** (Ned) b 12/06/1892 d

18/10/1918 - GW - No Tests - 13 matches (-)
Toured BI, I & F. 1912/13.

662 **Delport, GM** (Thinus) b 02/02/1975 -
GL - 18 Tests (15 - 3T) 20 matches (15 - 3T)
*1997: Tour of It, F, E & S - No Tests. 2000: C(R),
E1(t+R), A1, NZ1, A2, NZ2, A3, Arg, I, W. 2001:
F2, It1. 2003: A1, NZ2, [U, E, Sm, NZ3].*

297 **Delport, WH** (Willa) b 05/11/1920 d
14/10/1984 - EP - 9 Tests (6 - 2T) 21 matches
(12 - 4T) *1951: S, I, W. 1952: E, F. 1953: A1, 2,
3, 4.*

50 **Devenish, CE** (Charles) b 13/01/1874 d
11/01/1922 - GW - 1 Test (-) 1 match (-)
1896: BI2.

10 **Devenish, GE** (Tiger) b 27/07/1870 d
23/03/1930 - Tvl - 1 Test (-) 1 match (-)
1891: BI1.

45 **Devenish, G St L** (Long George) b
11/05/1871 d 01/02/1943 - Tvl - 1 Test (-) 1
match (-) *1896: BI2.*

189 **Devine, D** (Dauncie) b 20/03/1904 d
22/09/1965 - Tvl - 2 Tests (-) 2 matches (-)
1924: BI3. 1928: NZ2.

814 **Deysel, JR** (Jean) b 05/03/1985 - KZN - 4
Tests (-) 6 matches (-) *2009: It(R). 2011:
A1(R), NZ1, A2(R).*

300 **Dinkelmann, EE** (Ernst) b 14/05/1927 d
22/10/2010 - NTvl - 6 Tests (6 - 2T) 21 matches
(9 - 3T) *1951:S, I. 1952: E, F. 1953: A1, 2.*

597 **Dirks, CA** (Chris) b 23/05/1967 - Tvl - No
Tests - 2 matches (10 - 2T). *Toured Arg. 1993.*

393 **Dirksen, CW** (Corra) b 22/01/1938 - NTvl
- 10 Tests (9 - 3T) 11 matches (9 - 3T) *1963: A4.
1964: W. 1965: I, S. 1967: F1, 2, 3, 4. 1968: BI1, 2.*

713 **Dixon, PJ** (Pieter) b 17/10/1977 - WP - No
Tests - 1 match (-) *Toured E. 2000.*

762 **Dlulane, VT** (Tim) b 05/06/1981 - Mpu - 1
Test (-) 1 match (-) *2004: W2(R).*

67 **Dobbin, FJ** (Uncle) b 10/10/1879 d
05/02/1950 - GW - 9 Tests (3 - 1T) 36 matches
(21 - 7T) *1903: BI1, 2. 1906: S, W, E. 1910: BI1.
1912: S*, I, W.*

202 **Dobie, JAR** (John) b 04/08/1905 d
12/08/1989 - Tvl - 1 Test (-) 1 match (-)
1928: NZ2.

230 **Dold, JB** (Jack) b 03/01/1902 d 17/09/1968
- EP - No Tests - 10 matches (3 - 1T) *Toured BI
& I. 1931/32.*

54 **Dormehl, PJ** (Pieter) b 04/11/1872 d
01/09/1958 - WP - 2 Tests (-) 2 matches (-)
1896: BI3, 4.

40 **Douglass, FW** (Frank) b 15/07/1875 d Post
1920 - EP - 1 Test (-) 1 match (-) *1896: BI1.*

X **Dreyer, RM** (Ruan) - Springbok Tour Squad
Member - b 16/09/1990 - GL - No Tests (-) No
matches (-) *Toured I,E,It & W 2014. Not consid-*

*ered a Springbok until such time as he appears in a
Test, after which he will receive a Springbok number.*

601 **Drotské, AE** (Naka) b 15/03/1971 - OFS
- 26 Tests (15 - 3T) 34 matches (20 - 4T) *1993:
Arg(2). 1995: [WS2(R)]. 1996: A1(R). 1997: T,
BI1, 2, 3(R), NZ1, A1, NZ2(R). 1998: I2(R),
W1(R), I3(R). 1999: It1, 2, W, NZ1, A1, NZ2, A2,
[S, Sp(R), U, E, A3, NZ3].*

321 **Dryburgh, RG** (Roy) b 01/11/1929 d
10/05/2000 - WP - 8 Tests (28 - 3T, 5C, 3P) 20
matches (116 - 15T, 13C, 15P) *1955: BI2, 3, 4.
1956: A2, NZ1, 4. 1960: NZ1*, 2*.*

787 **Du Plessis, BW** (Bismarck) b 22/05/1984
- KZN - 79 Tests (55 - 11T) 83 matches (65
- 13T) *2007: A2(t+R), NZ2, Nam(R), S(R),
[Sm(R), E3(R), US(R), Arg(R), E4(t).], W(R).
2008: W1(R), 2(R), It, NZ1(R), 2, Arg, NZ3,
A2, 3, W3, S. 2009: BI1, 2, 3(R), NZ1, 2, A1, 2,
3, NZ3, F, I(R). 2010: I, W2, S, E. 2011: A2(R),
NZ2, [W(R), Fj(R), Sm, A3(R).]. 2012: E1, 2, 3,
Arg1. 2013: S(R), Sm(R), Arg1(R),2(R), A1, NZ1,
A2(R), NZ2, W, S(R), F. 2014: W1,2, S, Arg1,2,
A1(R), NZ1(R), A2(R), NZ2, I, E(R), It(R), W3.
2015: A, NZ1, Arg1, [J, S, US, W, NZ2, Arg3]*

523 **Du Plessis, CJ** (Carel) b 24/06/1960 - WP
- 12 Tests (16 - 4T) 22 matches (40 - 10T) 1981:
Tour of NZ & US - No Tests. *1982: S.Am1, 2.
1984: E1, 2, S.Am&Sp1, 2. 1986: NZC1, 2, 3, 4.
1989: WT1, 2.*

496 **Du Plessis, DC** (Daan) b 09/08/1948 - NTvl
- 2 Tests (-) 2 matches (-) *1977: WT. 1980:
S.Am2.*

275 **Du Plessis, F** (Felix) b 24/11/1919 d
01/05/1978 - Tvl - 3 Tests (-) 3 matches (-)
1949: NZ1, 2*, 3*.*

788 **Du Plessis, JN** (Jannie) b 16/11/1982 - FS
- 70 Tests (5 - 1T) 74 matches (5 - 1T) *2007:
A2, NZ2, [Fj, Arg(t+R).], W. 2008:A3(R), E.
2009:NZ1(t), 2(R), A1(R), 2(R), NZ3(R). 2009:
Tour of F,It,I&E - No Tests. 2010: W1(R), F(R),
It1, 2, NZ1, 3, A2, 3, I, w, S, E. 2011: A2, NZ2,
[W, Fj, Sm, A3.]. 2012: E1, 2, 3, Arg1, 2, A1, NZ1,
A2, NZ2, I, S, E4. 2013: It, S, Sm, Arg1,2, A1,
NZ1, A2, NZ2. 2014: W1,2, S, Arg1,2, A1, NZ1,
A2, NZ2, I, E. 2015: A, NZ1, [J, Sm, S, W(R),
NZ2(R), Arg3(R)].*

455 **Du Plessis, M** (Morné) b 21/10/1949 -
WP - 22 Tests (12 - 3T) 32 matches (18 - 5T)
1971: A1, 2, 3. 1974:BI1, 2, F1, 2. 1975: F1, 2*.
1976:NZ1*, 2*, 3*, 4*. 1977: WT*. 1980: S.Am1*,
2*, BI1*, 2*, 3*, 4*, S.Am4*, F*.*

537 **Du Plessis, MJ** (Michael) b 04/11/1958 -
WP - 8 Tests (7 - 1T, 1D) 8 matches (7 - 1T, 1D)
*1984: S.Am&Sp1, 2. 1986: NZC1, 2, 3, 4. 1989:
WT1, 2.*

166 **Du Plessis, NJ** (Nic) b 04/12/1894 d

10/08/1949 - WTvl - 5 Tests (-) 20 matches (-) *1921:NZ2, 3. 1924:BI1, 2, 3.*

458 **Du Plessis, PG** (Piet) b 23/07/1947 - NTvl - 1 Test (-) 1 match (-) *1972: E.*

503 **Du Plessis, TD** (Tommy) b 29/06/1953 - NTvl - 2 Tests (4 - 1T) 5 matches (12 - 3T) *1980: S.Am1, 2. 1980: Tour of S.Am – No Tests.*

500 **Du Plessis, W** (Willie) b 04/09/1955 - WP - 14 Tests (12 - 3T) 20 matches (28 - 7T) *1980: S.Am1, 2, BI1, 2, 3, 4, S.Am3, 4, F. 1981: NZ1, 2, 3. 1982: S.Am1, 2.*

317 **Du Plooy, AJJ** (Amos) b 31/05/1921 d 17/05/1980 - EP - 1 Test (-) 1 match (-) *1955: BI1.*

375 **Du Preez, FCH** (Frik) b 28/11/1935 - NTvl - 38 Tests (11 - 1T, 1C, 2P) 87 matches (87 - 12T, 15C, 7P) *1961: E, S, A1, 2. 1962: BI1, 2, 3, 4. 1963: A1. 1964: W, F. 1965: Tour of I & S – No Tests. 1965: A1, 2, NZ1, 2, 3, 4. 1967: F4. 1968: BI1, 2, 3, 4, F1, 2. 1969: A1, 2, S. 1970: I, W, NZ1, 2, 3, 4. 1971: F1, 2, A1, 2, 3.*

701 **Du Preez, GJD** (Delarey) b 12/06/1975 - GL - 2 Tests (5 - 1T) 5 matches (10 - 2T) *2000: Tour of Arg & I, W&E – No Tests. 2002: Sm(R), A1(R).*

327 **Du Preez, JGH** (Jan) b 06/10/1930 - WP - 1 Test (-) 6 matches (15 - 5T) *1956: NZ1.*

881 **Du Preez, J-L** (Jean-Luc) b 05/08/1995 - KZN - 1 Test (-) 2 matches (-) *2016: W(R).*

757 **Du Preez, PF** (Fourie) b 24/03/1982 - BB - 76 Tests (80 - 16T) 77 matches (80 - 16T) *2004: I1, 2, W1, PI(R), NZ1, A1, NZ2(R), A2(R), W2, I3, E, S, Arg. 2005: U(R), F1, 2(R), A1(R)2(R), 3, NZ1(R), A4(R). 2006: S1, 2, F, A1(R), NZ1, A2, NZ2, 3, A3. 2007: Nam, S, [Sm, E3, US, Fj, Arg, E4]. 2008: Arg(R), NZ3, A2,3, W3. 2009: BI1, 2, 3, NZ1, 2, A1, 2, 3, NZ3, F, It, I. 2011: A2, NZ2, [W, Fj, Nam(R), Sm, A3.]. 2013: Arg1(R), A2, NZ2, W, S. 2014: W1,2, S. 2015: [J(R), Sm, S*, US*, W*, NZ2*]*

562 **Du Preez, RJ** (Robert) b 19/07/1963 - Natal - 7 Tests (-) 15 matches (45 - 9T) *1992: NZ, A. 1993: F1, 2, A1, 2, 3.*

792 **Du Preez, WH** (Wian) b 30/10/1982 - FS - 1 Test (-) 2 matches (-) *2007: Tour of W&E – No Tests. 2009:It.*

281 **Du Rand, JA** (Salty) b 16/01/1926 d 27/02/1979 - Rhodesia - 21 Tests (12 - 4T) 47 matches (27 - 9T) *1949: NZ2, 3. 1951: S, I, W. 1952: E, F. 1953: A1, 2, 3, 4. 1955: BI1, 2, 3, 4. 1956: A1, 2, NZ1*, 2, 3, 4.*

619 **Du Randt, JP** (Os) b 08/09/1972 - OFS - 80 Tests (25 - 5T) 85 matches (25 - 5T) *1994: Arg1, 2, S, W. 1995: WS1, [A, WS2, F, NZ]. 1996: Fj, A1, NZ1, A2, NZ2, 3, 4. 1997: T, BI1, 2, 3, NZ1, A1, NZ2, A2, It, F1, 2, E, S. 1999: NZ1, A1, NZ2,*

A2, [S, Sp(R), U, E, A3, NZ3]. 2004: I1, 2, W1, PI, NZ1, A1, NZ2, A2, W2, I3, E, S(R), Arg(R). 2005: U(R), F1, A1, NZ1, A4, NZ2, Arg, W(R), F3. 2006: S1, 2, F, A1, NZ1, A2, NZ2, 3, A3. 2007: Sm1, NZ1, Nam, S, [Sm, E3, US, Fj, Arg, E4.].*

208 **Du Toit, AF** (AF) b 12/05/1899 d 09/09/1988 - WP - 2 Tests (-) 2 matches (-) *1928: NZ3, 4.*

253 **Du Toit, BA** (Ben) b 10/11/1912 d 25/01/1989 - Tvl - 3 Tests (3 - 1T) 10 matches (9 - 3T) *1937: Tour of A & NZ - No Tests. 1938: BI1, 2, 3.*

667 **Du Toit, GS** (Gaffie) b 24/03/1976 - GW - 14 Tests (108 - 5T, 25C, 11P) 23 matches (153 - 10T, 29C, 15P) *1998: I1. 1999: It1, 2, W(R), NZ1, 2. 2004: I1, W1(R), A1(R), S(R), Arg. 2006: S1(R), 2(R), F(R).*

279 **Du Toit, PA** (Fonnie) b 13/03/1920 d 21/07/2001 - NTvl - 8 Tests (6 - 2T) 25 matches (9 - 3T) *1949: NZ2, 3, 4. 1951: S, I, W. 1952: E, F.*

516 **Du Toit, PG** (Hempies) b 23/08/1953 - WP - 5 Tests (-) 16 matches (8 - 2T) *1980: Tour of S.Am – No Tests. 1981: NZ1. 1982: S.Am1, 2. 1984: E1, 2.*

332 **Du Toit, PS** (Piet) b 09/10/1935 d 26/02/1997 - WP - 14 Tests (-) 49 matches (9 - 3T) *1956: Tour of A & NZ - No Tests. 1958: F1, 2. 1960: NZ1, 2, 3, 4, W, I. 1961: E, S, F, I, A1, 2.*

854 **Du Toit, PS** (Pieter-Steph) b 20/08/1992 - KZN - 20 Tests (15 - 3T) 21 matches (20 - 4T) *2013: W(R), F(R). 2015: Arg1, 2, [J, S(R), US(R), W(R)]. 2016: I1(R), 2, 3, Arg1(R), 2(R), A1(R), NZ1, A2, NZ2, E, It, W.*

220 **Du Toit, SR** (Schalk) b 08/08/1902 d 18/11/1965 - WP - No Tests - 12 matches (3 - 1T) *Toured BI & I. 1931/32.*

X **Du Toit, TJ** (Thomas) - Springbok Tour Squad Member - b 05/05/1995 - KZN - No Tests - No Matches. *Toured E, It & W. 2016. Not considered a Springbok until such time as he appears in a Test, after which he will receive a Springbok number.*

1 **Duff, BR** (Ben) b 16/10/1867 d 25/06/1943 - WP - 3 Tests (-) 3 matches (-) *1891: BI1, 2, 3.*

194 **Duffy, BAA** (Bernie) b 17/11/1905 d 16/03/1958 - Border - 1 Test (-) 1 match (-) *1928: NZ1.*

430 **Durand, PJ** (Paul) b 21/01/1946 d 01/09/1988 - WTvl - No Tests - 2 matches (-) *Toured BI & I. 1969/70.*

265 **Duvenage, FP** (Floors) b 06/11/1917 d 16/09/1999 - GW - 2 Tests (-) 2 matches (-) *1949: NZ1, 3.*

499 **Edwards, P** (Pierre) b 23/05/1953 - NTvl - 2 Tests (-) 2 matches (-) *1980: S.Am1, 2.*

415 **Ellis, JH** (Jan) b 05/01/1942 d 08/02/2013 - SWA - 38 Tests (21 - 7T) 74 matches (97 - 32T)

1965: NZ1, 2, 3, 4. 1967: F1, 2, 3, 4. 1968: BI1, 2, 3, 4, F1, 2. 1969: A1, 2, 3, 4, S. 1970: I, W, NZ1, 2, 3, 4. 1971: F1, 2, A1, 2, 3. 1972: E. 1974: BI1, 2, 3, 4, F1, 2. 1976: NZ1.

165 **Ellis, MC** (Mervyn) b 16/09/1892 d 24/03/1959 - Tvl - 6 Tests (-) 20 matches (3 - 1T) *1921: NZ2, 3. 1924: BI1, 2, 3, 4.*

656 **Els, WW** (Braam) b 01/11/1971 - FS - 1 Test (-) 3 matches (-) *1997: A2(R).*

836 **Engelbrecht, JJ** (JJ) b 22/02/1989 - BB - 12 Tests (20 - 4T) 12 matches (20 - 4T) *2012: Arg1(R). 2013: It, S, Sm, Arg1,2, A1, NZ1, A2, NZ2, W(R), S(R).*

347 **Engelbrecht, JP** (Jannie) b 10/11/1938 - WP - 33 Tests (24 - 8T) 67 matches (132 - 44T) *1960: S, W, I. 1961: E, S, F, A1, 2. 1962: BI2, 3, 4. 1963: A2, 3. 1964: W, F. 1965: I, S, A1, 2, NZ1, 2, 3, 4. 1967: F1, 2, 3, 4. 1968: BI1, 2, F1, 2. 1969: A1, 2.*

549 **Erasmus, FS** (Frans) b 19/06/1959 d 07/03/1998 - NTvl - 3 Tests (-) 3 matches (-) *1986: NZC3, 4. 1989: WT2.*

649 **Erasmus, J** (Rassie) b 05/11/1972 - FS - 36 Tests (35 - 7T) 39 matches (35 - 7T) *1996: Tour of Arg, F & W - No Tests. 1997: BI3, A2, It, F1, 2, S. 1998: I1, 2, W1, E1, A1, NZ2, A2, W2, S, I3, E2. 1999: It1, 2, W, A1*, NZ2, A2, [S, U, E, A3, NZ3]. 2000: C, E1, A1, NZ1, 2, A3. 2001: F1, 2.*

692 **Esterhuizen, G** (Grant) b 28/04/1976 - GL - 7 Tests (-) 7 matches (-) *2000: NZ1(R), 2, A3, Arg, I, W(R), E3(t).*

58 **Etlinger, TE** (Tommy) b 07/09/1872 d 23/02/1953 - WP - 1 Test (-) 1 match (-) *1896: BI4.*

833 **Etzebeth, E** (Eben) b 29/10/1991 - WP - 54 Tests (10 - 2T) 56 matches (15 - 3T) *2012: E1, 2, 3, Arg1, 2, A1, 2, NZ2, I, S, E4. 2013: It, S, Sm, Arg1,2, A1, NZ1, A2, NZ2, W, S(R), F. 2014: Arg1(R),2, A1, NZ1, A2, NZ2, I, E, It, W3. 2015: A, NZ1, Arg1,2, [J(R), Sm, S, US, W, NZ2, Arg3]. 2016: I1, 2, 3, Arg1, 2, A1, NZ1, A2, NZ2, E.*

543 **Ferreira, C** (Christo) b 28/08/1960 - OFS - 2 Tests (-) 2 matches (-) *1986: NZC1, 2.*

540 **Ferreira, PS** (Kulu) b 17/03/1959 - WP - 2 Tests (4 - 1T) 2 matches (4 - 1T) *1984: S.Am & Sp1, 2.*

84 **Ferris, HH** (Hugh) b 06/12/1877 d 17/07/1929 - Tvl - 1 Test (-) 1 match (-) *1903: BI3.*

674 **Fleck, RF** (Robbie) b 17/07/1975 - WP - 31 Tests (50 - 10T) 36 matches (65 - 13T) *1998: Tour of UK & I - No Tests. 1999: It1, 2, NZ1(R), A1, NZ2(R), A2, [S, U, E, A3, NZ3]. 2000: C, E1, 2, A1, NZ1, A2, NZ2, A3, Arg, I, W, E3. 2001: F1(R), 2, It1, NZ1, A1, 2. 2002: S, E.*

784 **Floors, L** (Kabamba) b 15/11/1980 - FS - 1

Test (-) 1 match (-) *2006: E2.*

42 **Forbes, HH** (Spanner) b 02/01/1873 d 17/09/1955 - Tvl - 1 Test (-) 1 match (-) *1896: BI2.*

229 **Forrest, HM** (Skaap) b 17/11/1907 d 26/01/1989 - Tvl - No Tests - 7 matches (-) *Toured BI & I. 1931/32.*

780 **Fortuin, BA** (Bevin) b 06/02/1979 - FS - 2 Tests (-) 3 matches (-) *2006: I. 2007: A2.*

481 **Fourie, C** (Tossie) b 01/08/1950 - d 05/05/1997 - EP - 4 Tests (10 - 1T, 2P) 9 matches (14 - 2T, 2P) *1974: F1, 2. 1975: F1, 2.*

752 **Fourie, J** (Jaque) b 04/03/1983 - GL - 72 Tests (160 - 32T) 74 matches (160 - 32T) *2003: [U, Geo, Sm(R), NZ3(R)]. 2004: I2, E(R), S, Arg. 2005: U(R), F2(R), A1(R), 2, 3, NZ1, A4, NZ2, Arg, W, F3. 2006: S1, A1, NZ1, A2, NZ2, 3, A3. 2007: Sm1(R), A1, NZ1, Nam, S, [Sm2, E3, US, Fj, Arg, E4.], W. 2008: Arg(R), W3(R), S(R), E(R). 2009: BI1(R), 2(R), 3, NZ1, 2, A1, 2, 3, NZ3, F, It, I. 2010: W1, F, It2, NZ1, 2, A1, 2, 3. 2011: A2, NZ2, [W, Fj, Nam, Sm, A3.]. 2013: W, S2, F.*

476 **Fourie, TT** (Polla) b 10/07/1945 - SETvl - 1 Test (-) 5 matches (12 - 3T) *1974: BI3. 1974: Tour of F - No Tests.*

339 **Fourie, WL** (Loftie) b 23/07/1936 d 23/07/2001 - SWA - 2 Tests (3 - 1T) 2 matches (3 - 1T) *1958: F1, 2.*

148 **Francis, JAJ** (Joe) b 24/01/1889 d 20/12/1924 - Tvl - 5 Tests (6 - 2T) 19 matches (9 - 3T) *1912: S, I, W. 1913: E, F.*

218 **Francis, MG** (Tiny) b 26/08/1907 d 02/08/1961 - OFS - No Tests - 8 matches (18 - 1T, 4C, 1P, 1D) *Toured BI & I. 1931/32.*

469 **Frederickson, CA** (Dave) b 17/08/1950 - Tvl - 3 Tests (-) 3 matches (-) *1974: BI2. 1980: S.Am1, 2.*

68 **Frew, A** (Alex) b 24/10/1877 d 29/04/1947 - Tvl - 1 Test (3 - 1T) 1 match (3 - 1T) *1903: BI1*.*

492 **Froneman, DC** (Dirk) b 14/04/1954 - OFS - 1 Test (-) 1 match (-) *1977: WT.*

234 **Froneman, IL** (Fronie) b 18/12/1907 d 11/08/1984 - Border - 1 Test (-) 1 match (-) *1933: A1.*

294 **Fry, DJ** (Dennis) b 25/02/1926 d 25/02/2003 - WP - No Tests - 17 matches (12 - 4T) *Toured BI, I & F. 1951/52.*

303 **Fry, SP** (Stephen) b 14/07/1924 d 29/06/2002 - WP - 13 Tests (-) 28 matches (9 - 3T) *1951: S, I, W. 1952: E, F. 1953: A1, 2, 3, 4. 1955: BI1*, 2*, 3*, 4*.*

567 **Fuls, HT** (Heinrich) b 08/03/1971 - Tvl - 8 Tests (-) 21 matches (5 - 1T) *1992: NZ(R). 1992: Tour of F & E - No Tests. 1993: F1, 2, A1, 2, 3, Arg1, 2.*

710 **Fynn, EE** (Etienne) b 14/12/1972 - Natal - 2 Tests (-) 4 matches (-) *2000: Tour of Arg,I,W&E – No Tests. 2001: F1, It1(R).*

638 **Fyvie, WS** (Wayne) b 28/03/1972 - Natal - 3 Tests (-) 8 matches (10 - 2T) *1996: NZ4(t), 5(R), Arg2(R).*

233 **Gage, JH** (Jack) b 02/04/1907 d 30/06/1989 - OFS - 1 Test (-) 1 match (-) *1933: A1.*

348 **Gainsford, JL** (John) b 04/08/1938 d 18/11/2015 - WP - 33 Tests (24 - 8T) 71 matches (93 - 31T) *1960: S, NZ1, 2, 3, 4, W, I. 1961: E, S, F, A1, 2. 1962: BI1, 2, 3, 4. 1963: A1, 2, 3, 4. 1964: W, F. 1965: I, S, A1, 2, NZ1, 2, 3, 4. 1967: F1, 2, 3.*

645 **Garvey, AC** (Adrian) b 25/06/1968 - Natal - 28 Tests (20 - 4T) 28 matches (20 - 4T) *1996: Arg1, 2, F1, 2, W. 1997: T, BI1, 2, 3(R), A1(t), It, F1, 2, E, S. 1998: I1, 2, W1, E1, A1, NZ1, 2, A2, W2, S, I3, E2. 1999: [Sp].*

282 **Geel, PJ** (Flip) b 07/02/1914 d 12/06/1971 - OFS - 1 Test (-) 1 match (-) *1949: NZ3.*

227 **Geere, V** (Manie) b 09/09/1905 d 25/10/1989 - Tvl - 5 Tests (-) 17 matches (-) *1931-32 Tour of BI & I – No Tests. 1933: A1, 2, 3, 4, 5.*

270 **Geffin, AO** (Okey) b 28/05/1921 d 16/10/2004 - Tvl - 7 Tests (48 - 9C, 10P) 17 matches (121 - 1T, 26C, 22P) *1949: NZ1, 2, 3, 4. 1951: S, I, W.*

564 **Geldenhuys, A** (Adri) b 11/07/1964 - EP - 4 Tests (-) 11 matches (-) *1992: NZ, A, F1, 2.*

528 **Geldenhuys, SB** (Burger) b 18/05/1956 - NTvl - 7 Tests (4 - 1T) 15 matches (20 - 5T) *1981: NZ2, 3, US. 1982: S.Am1, 2. 1989: WT1, 2.*

316 **Gentles, TA** (Tommy) b 31/05/1934 d 29/06/2011 - WP - 6 Tests (-) 18 matches (9 - 3T) *1955: BI1, 2, 4. 1956: NZ2, 3. 1958: F2.*

283 **Geraghty, EM** (Carrots) b 20/04/1927 d 03/11/2015 - Border - 1 Test (-) 1 match (-) *1949: NZ4.*

514 **Gerber, DM** (Danie) b 14/04/1958 - EP - 24 Tests (82 - 19T, 1C) 35 matches (120 - 28T, 1C) *1980: S.Am3, 4, F. 1981: I1, 2, NZ1, 2, 3, US. 1982: S.Am1, 2. 1984: E1, 2, S.Am&Sp1, 2. 1986: NZC1, 2, 3, 4. 1992: NZ, A, F1, 2, E.*

709 **Gerber, HJ** (Hendrik) b 12/04/1976 - WP - 2 Tests (-) 6 matches (-) *2000: Tour of Arg,I,W&E – No Tests. 2003: S1, 2.*

337 **Gerber, MC** (Mickey) b 12/10/1935 d 07/10/2005 - EP - 3 Tests (8 - 4C) 3 matches (8 - 4C) *1958: F1, 2. 1960: S.*

351 **Gericke, FW** (Mannetjies) b 08/06/1933 d 22/10/2010 - Tvl - 1 Test (3 - 1T) 1 match (3 - 1T) *1960: S.*

465 **Germishuys, JS** (Gerrie) b 29/10/1949 - OFS - 20 Tests (48 - 12T) 29 matches (76 - 19T)

1974: BI2. 1976: NZ1, 2, 3, 4. 1977: WT. 1980: S.Am1, 2, BI1, 2, 3, 4, S.Am3, 4, F. 1981: I1, 2, NZ2, 3, US.

77 **Gibbs, EAH** (Bertie) b 25/08/1878 d 29/12/1952 - GW - 1 Test (-) 1 match (-) *1903: BI2.*

641 **Gillingham, JW** (Joe) b 27/02/1974 - GL - No Tests - 7 matches (5 - 1T) *Toured Arg, F & W. 1996 and It, F, E & S. 1997.*

413 **Goosen, CP** (Piet) b 03/02/1937 - d 06/06/1991 - OFS - 1 Test (-) 13 matches (3 - 1T) *1965: NZ2.*

839 **Goosen, JL** (Johan) b 27/07/1992 - FS - 13 Tests (25 - 3T, 2C, 2P) 14 matches (34 - 4T, 4C, 2P) *2012: A1(R), NZ1(R), A2, NZ2. 2014: W1(R), It. 2016: Arg1, 2, A1, NZ1, E(R), It(R),W.*

37 **Gorton, HC** (Hubert) b 28/10/1871 d 11/01/1900 - Tvl - 1 Test (-) 1 match (-) *1896: BI1.*

424 **Gould, RL** (Rodney) b 10/08/1942 - Natal - 4 Tests (3 - 1D) 7 matches (3 - 1D) *1968: BI1, 2, 3, 4. 1968: Tour to F - No Tests.*

X **Gqoboka, LP** (Lizo) - Springbok Tour Squad Member - b 24/03/1990 - BB - No Tests - 1 match (-) *Toured E, It & W. 2016. Not considered a Springbok until such time as he appears in a Test, after which he will receive a Springbok number.*

789 **Grant, PJ** (Peter) b 15/08/1984 - WP - 5 Tests (-) 5 matches (-) *2007: A2(R), NZ2(R). 2008: W1(t+R), It(R), A1(R).*

215 **Gray, BG** (Geoff) b 28/07/1909 d 04/08/1989 - WP - 4 Tests (-) 13 matches (12 - 4T) *1931: W. 1932: E, S. 1933: A5.*

729 **Greeff, WW** (Werner) b 14/07/1977 - WP - 11 Tests (31 - 4T, 4C, 1D) 11 matches (31 - 4T, 4C, 1D) *2002: Arg(R), Sm, NZ1, A1, NZ2, A2, F, S, E. 2003: [U, Geo].*

379 **Greenwood, CM** (Colin) b 25/01/1936 d 03/10/1998 - WP - 1 Test (6 - 2T) 1 match (6 - 2T) *1961: I.*

829 **Greyling, MD** (Dean) b 01/01/1986 - BB - 3 Tests (-) 3 matches (-) *2011: A1, NZ1. 2012: NZ1(R).*

422 **Greyling, PJF** (Piet) b 16/05/1942 - OFS - 25 Tests (15 - 5T) 43 matches (18 - 6T) *1967: F1, 2, 3, 4. 1968: BI1, F1, 2. 1969: A1, 2, 3, 4, S, E. 1970: I, W, NZ1, 2, 3, 4. 1971: F1, 2, A1, 2, 3. 1972: E*.*

478 **Grobler, CJ** (Kleintjie) b 24/08/1944 d 29/09/1999 - OFS - 3 Tests (4 - 1T) 7 matches (12 - 3T) *1974: BI4. 1974: Tour of F - No Tests. 1975: F1, 2.*

431 **Grobler, RN** (Rysmier) b 14/11/1946 d 26/05/1971 - NTvl - No Tests - 10 matches (9 - 3T) *Toured BI & I. 1969/70.*

5 **Guthrie, FEH** (Frank) b 03/11/1869 d

19/06/1954 - WP - 3 Tests (-) 3 matches (-) *1891: BI1, 3. 1896: BI1.*

766 **Habana, BG** (Bryan) b 12/06/1983 - GL - 124 Tests (335 - 67T) 128 matches (340 - 68T) *2004: E(R), S, Arg. 2005: U, F1, 2, A1, 2, 3, NZ1, A4, NZ2, Arg, W, F3. 2006: S2, F, A1, NZ1, A2, NZ2, 3, I, E1, 2. 2007: E1, 2, S, [Sm, E3, T(R), US, Fj, Arg, E4.], W. 2008: W1, 2, It, NZ1, 2, A1, NZ3, W3, S, E. 2009: BI1, 2, NZ1, 2, A1, 2, 3, NZ3, F, It, I. 2010: F, It1, 2, NZ1, 2, A1, NZ3, A2, 3, I, W2. 2011:A2, NZ2, [W, Nam, Sm, A3.]. 2012: E1, 2, 3, Arg1, 2, A1, NZ1.A2, NZ2. 2013: It, S1, Sm, Arg1,2, A1, NZ1, A2, NZ2, W, S, F. 2014: W1,2, Arg1,2, A1, NZ1, A2, NZ2, I, E, It. 2015: A, NZ1, Arg1,2, [J, Sm, S, US, W, NZ2, Arg3]. 2016: Arg1, 2, A1, NZ1, A2, NZ2, It.*

113 **Hahn, CHL** (Cocky) b 07/01/1886 - d 27/09/1948 - Tvl - 3 Tests (3 - 1T) 3 matches (3 - 1T) *1910: BI1, 2, 3.*

714 **Hall, DB** (Dean) b 02/09/1977 - GL - 13 Tests (20 - 4T) 13 matches (20 - 4T) *2001: F1, 2, NZ1, A1, 2, NZ2, It2, E, US. 2002: Sm, NZ1, 2, A2.*

720 **Halstead, TM** (Trevor) b 17/06/1976 - Natal - 6 Tests (15 - 3T) 6 matches (15 - 3T) *2001: F3, It2, E, US(R). 2003: S1, 2.*

15 **Hamilton, GH** (George) b 30/04/1863 d 07/08/1901 - EP - 1 Test (-) 1 match (-) *1891: BI1.*

333 **Hanekom, M v d S** (Melt) b 27/07/1931 d 1997/1998 - Boland - No Tests - 9 matches (9 - 3T) *Toured A & NZ 1956.*

809 **Hargreaves, AJ** (Alistair) b 29/04/1986 - KZN - 4 Tests (-) 7 matches (-) *2009: Tour of F,It,I&E – No Tests. 2010: W1(R), It1(R). 2010: Tour of UK - No Tests. 2011: A1, NZ1.*

251 **Harris, TA** (Tony) b 27/08/1916 d 07/03/1993 - Tvl - 5 Tests (3 - 1T) 13 matches (16 - 4T, 1D) *1937: NZ2, 3. 1938: BI1, 2, 3.*

24 **Hartley, AJ** (Jack) b 18/08/1873 d 15/05/1923 - WP - 1 Test (-) 1 match (-) *1891: BI3.*

568 **Hattingh, H** (Drikus) b 21/02/1968 - NTvl - 5 Tests (-) 17 matches (20 - 4T) *1992: A(R), F2(R), E. 1994: Arg1, 2. 1994: Tour of W,S & I – No Tests.*

239 **Hattingh, LB** (Lappies) b 01/09/1903 d 16/10/1974 - OFS - 1 Test (-) 1 match (-) *1933: A2.*

623 **Hattingh, SJ** (Ian) b 31/10/1964 - Tvl - No Tests - 7 matches (10 - 2T) *Toured W, S & I. 1994.*

22 **Heatlie, BH** (Fairy) b 25/04/1872 d 19/08/1951 - WP - 6 Tests (6 - 3C) 6 matches (6 - 3C) *1891: BI2, 3. 1896: BI1, 4*. 1903: BI1, 3*.*

855 **Hendricks, C** (Cornal) b 18/04/1988 - FS - 12 Tests (25 - 5T) 13 matches (25 - 5T) *2014: W1,2, S, Arg1,2, A1, NZ1, A2, NZ2, I, W3. 2015:* NZ1.

657 **Hendricks, M** (McNeil) b 10/07/1973 - Boland - 2 Tests (5 - 1T) 4 matches (5 - 1T) *1997: Tour of It, F, E & S - No Tests. 1998: I2(R), W1(R).*

559 **Hendriks, P** (Pieter) b 13/04/1970 - Tvl - 14 Tests (10 - 2T) 23 matches (30 - 6T) *1992: NZ, A. 1992: Tour of F & E – No Tests. 1994: S, W. 1995: [A, R, C]. 1996: A1, NZ1, A2, NZ2, 3, 4, 5.*

57 **Hepburn, TB** (Tommy) b 14/02/1872 d 13/09/1933 - WP - 1 Test (2 - 1C) 1 match (2 - 1C) *1896: BI4.*

521 **Heunis, JW** (Johan) b 26/01/1958 - NTvl - 14 Tests (41 - 2T, 6C, 7P) 24 matches (72 - 3T, 9C, 14P) *1981: NZ3(R), US. 1982: S.Am1, 2. 1984: E1, 2, S.Am&Sp1, 2. 1986: NZC1, 2, 3, 4. 1989: WT1, 2.*

372 **Hill, RA** (Ronnie) b 20/12/1934 d 06/01/2011 - Rhodesia - 7 Tests (-) 21 matches (18 - 6T) *1960: W, I. 1961: I, A1, 2. 1962: BI4. 1963: A3.*

575 **Hills, WG** (Willie) b 26/01/1962 - NTvl - 6 Tests (-) 13 matches (-) *1992: F1, 2, E. 1993: F1, 2, A1.*

96 **Hirsch, JG** (Jack) b 20/02/1883 d 26/02/1958 - EP - 2 Tests (-) 18 matches (37 - 11T, 1D) *1906: I. 1910: BI1.*

86 **Hobson, TEC** (Tommy) b 26/03/1881 d 02/09/1937 - WP - 1 Test (-) 1 match (-) *1903: BI3.*

307 **Hoffman, RS** (Steve) b 02/12/1931 d 15/05/1986 - Boland - 1 Test (-) 1 match (-) *1953: A3.*

248 **Hofmeyr, SR** (Koffie) b 23/08/1912 d 06/01/1975 - WP - No Tests - 11 matches (17 - 3T, 2D) *Toured A & NZ. 1937.*

352 **Holton, DN** (Dougie) b 28/09/1932 d 12/04/1994 - EP - 1 Test (-) 4 matches (-) *1960: S. 1960-61: Tour of BI, I & F – No Tests.*

590 **Honiball, HW** (Henry) b 01/12/1965 - Natal - 35 Tests (156 - 1T, 38C, 25P) 45 matches (191 - 1T, 45C, 32P) *1993: A3(R), Arg2. 1995: WS1(R). 1996: Fj, A1, NZ5, Arg1, 2, F1, 2, W. 1997: T, BI1, 2, 3(R), NZ1(R), A1(R), NZ2, A2, It, F1, 2, E. 1998: W1(R), E1, A1, NZ1, 2, A2, W2, S, I3, E2. 1999: [A3(R), NZ3].*

356 **Hopwood, DJ** (Doug) b 03/06/1934 d 10/01/2002 - WP - 22 Tests (15 - 5T) 53 matches (45 - 15T) *1960: S, NZ3, 4, W. 1961: E, S, F, I, A1, 2. 1962: BI1, 2, 3, 4. 1963: A1, 2, 3. 1964: W, F. 1965: S, NZ3, 4.*

753 **Hougaard, DJ** (Derick) b 04/01/1983 - BB - 8 Tests (69 - 2T, 13C, 10P, 1D) 8 matches (69 - 2T, 13C, 10P, 1D) *2003: [U(R), E(R), Geo, Sm, NZ3]. 2007: Sm1, A2, NZ2.*

807 **Hougaard, F** (Francois) b 06/04/1988 - BB

- 39 Tests (25 - 5T) 42 matches (25 - 5T) *2009: It(R). 2010: A1(R), NZ3, A2, 3, W2(R), S, E(t). 2011: A2(t), NZ2(R), [W(R), Fj(R), Nam, Sm(R), A3(R).]. 2012: E1, 2, 3, Arg1, 2, A1, NZ1, A2, NZ2, I, S, E4. 2014: S(R), Arg2(R), NZ1(R), A2, NZ2, I, It(R), W3(R). 2016: A1, NZ1, A2, NZ2.*

330 **Howe, BF** (Pee-Wee) b 30/08/1932 d 22/04/2010 - Border - 2 Tests (3 - 1T) 18 matches (9 - 3T) *1956: NZ1, 4.*

118 **Howe-Browne, NRFG** (Noel) b 24/12/1884 d 03/04/1943 - WP - 3 Tests (-) 3 matches (-) *1910: BI1, 2, 3.*

555 **Hugo, DP** (Niel) b 11/11/1958 - WP - 2 Tests (-) 2 matches (-) *1989: WT1, 2.*

726 **Human, DCF** (Daan) b 03/04/1976 - WP - 4 Tests (-) 4 matches (-) *2002: W1, 2, Arg(R), Sm(R).*

627 **Hurter, MH** (Marius) b 08/10/1970 - NTvl - 13 Tests (-) 18 matches (5 - 1T) *1995: [R, C], W. 1996: Fj, A1, NZ1, 2, 3, 4, 5. 1997: NZ1, 2, A2.*

139 **Immelman, JH** (Jack) b 02/08/1888 d 21/07/1960 - WP - 1 Test (-) 13 matches (3 - 1T) *1913: F.*

97 **Jackson, DC** (Mary) b 21/04/1885 d 17/09/1976 - WP - 3 Tests (-) 17 matches (29 - 7T, 4C) *1906: I, W, E.*

80 **Jackson, JS** (Jack) b 01/10/1878 d 30/06/1954 - WP - 1 Test (-) 1 match (-) *1903: BI2.*

721 **Jacobs, AA** (Adrian) b 14/08/1980 - GF - 34 Tests (35 - 7T) 35 matches (35 - 7T) *2001: It2(R), US. 2002: W1(R), Arg, Sm(R), NZ1(t+R), A1(R), F, S, E(R). 2008: W1, 2, NZ1, 2, Arg, NZ3, A2, 3, W3, S, E. 2009: BI1, 2, NZ2(R), A1(R), 2(R), 3(R), NZ3(R), F, It. 2010: I(R), E(R). 2011: A1(R), NZ1.*

715 **James, AD** (Butch) b 08/01/1979 - Natal - 42 Tests (154 - 3T, 26C, 28P, 1D) 43 matches (159 - 3T, 27C, 29P, 1D) *2001: F1, 2, NZ1, A1, 2, NZ2. 2002: F(R), S, E. 2006: NZ1, A2, NZ2, 3(R), E1. 2007: E1, 2, A1, NZ1, Nam, S, [Sm, E3, US, Fj, Arg, E4.]. 2008: W1, 2, NZ1, 2, A1, Arg, NZ3, A2, 3. 2010: It1, 2(R), NZ1(R), A1(R), 2(R). 2011: A2, [W(R).].*

847 **Janse van Rensburg, JC** (JC) b 09/01/1986 - GL - No Tests - No matches. *Toured I, S & E. 2012.*

436 **Janse van Rensburg, MC** (Martin) b 29/12/1944 - Natal - No Tests - 6 matches (10 - 2C, 2P) *Toured BI & I. 1969/70.*

880 **Janse van Rensburg, R** (Rohan) b 11/09/1994 - GL - 1 Test (-) 2 matches (5 - 1T) *2016: W.*

518 **Jansen, E** (Eben) b 05/06/1954 - OFS - 1 Test (-) 11 matches (16 - 4T) *1980: Tour of S.Am - No Tests. 1981: NZ1.*

444 **Jansen, JS** (Joggie) b 05/02/1948 - OFS - 10 Tests (3 - 1T) 15 matches (18 - 6T) *1970: NZ1, 2, 3, 4. 1971: F1, 2, A1, 2, 3. 1972: E.*

414 **Janson, A** (Andrew) b 29/05/1935 d 2007 - WP - No Tests - 11 matches (24 - 8T) *Toured A & NZ. 1965.*

716 **Jantjes, CA** (Conrad) b 24/03/1980 - GL - 24 Tests (22 - 4T, 1C) 25 matches (22 - 4T, 1C) *2001: It1, A1, 2, NZ2, F3, It2, E, US. 2005: Arg, W. 2007: W(R). 2008: W1, 2, It, NZ1, 2(R), A1, Arg, NZ3(R), A2, 3, W3, S, E.*

819 **Jantjies, ET** (Elton) b 01/08/1990 - GL - 11 Tests (78 - 12C, 18P) 12 matches (83 - 13C, 19P) *2012: A2(R), NZ2(R). 2016: I1(R), 2, 3, Arg1, 2, A1, NZ1, It(R),W.*

769 **Januarie, ER** (Ricky) b 01/02/1982 - GL - 47 Tests (25 - 5T) 50 matches (25 - 5T) *2005: U, F2, A1, 2, 3(R), NZ1, A4, NZ2. 2006: S1(R), 2(R), F(R), A1, I, E1, 2. 2007: E1, 2, Sm1, Nam(R), [Sm(R), T.], W. 2008: W2, It, NZ1, 2, A1, Arg, NZ3(R), A2(R), 3(R), W3(R), S, E. 2009: BI1(R), NZ1(R), 2(R), A1(R), 2(R), NZ3(R). 2010: W1, F, It1, 2, NZ1, 2, 3(R).*

254 **Jennings, CB** (CB) b 16/08/1914 d 02/10/1989 - Border - 1 Test (-) 11 matches (9 - 3T) *1937: NZ1.*

439 **Jennings, MW** (Mike) b 21/12/1946 - Boland - No Tests - 10 matches (6 - 2T) *Toured BI & I. 1969/70.*

377 **Johns, RG** (Bobby) b 21/02/1934 d 01/07/1990 - WP - No Tests - 1 match (-) *Toured BI, I & F. 1960/61.*

810 **Johnson, AF** (Ashley) b 16/05/1986 - FS - 3 Tests (-) 5 matches (-) *2009: Tour of F,It,I&E – No Tests. 2011: A1, NZ1(R), 2(t+R).*

604 **Johnson, GK** (Gavin) b 17/10/1966 - Tvl - 7 Tests (86 - 5T, 14C, 11P) 17 matches (173 - 9T, 25C, 26P). *1993: Arg2. 1994: NZ3, Arg1. 1994: Tour of W, S & I – No Tests. 1995: WS1, [R, C, WS2].*

291 **Johnstone, PGA** (Paul) b 30/06/1930 d 22/04/1996 - WP - 9 Tests (11 - 2T, 1C, 1P) 35 matches (68 - 14T, 7C, 4P) *1951:S, I, W. 1952: E, F. 1956: A1, NZ1, 2, 4.*

62 **Jones, CH** (Charlie) b 24/03/1880 d 06/03/1908 - Tvl - 2 Tests (-) 2 matches (-) *1903: BI1, 2.*

30 **Jones, PST** (Percy) b 13/09/1876 d 08/03/1954 - WP - 3 Tests (3 - 1T) 3 matches (3 - 1T) *1896: BI1, 3, 4.*

742 **Jordaan, N** (Norman) b 03/04/1975 - BB - 1 Test (-) 1 match (-) *2002: E(R).*

271 **Jordaan, RP** (Jorrie) b 13/07/1920 d 22/09/1998 - NTvl - 4 Tests (-) 4 matches (-) *1949: NZ1, 2, 3, 4.*

557 **Joubert, AJ** (André) b 15/04/1964 - OFS - 34 Tests (115 - 10T, 7C, 17P) 49 matches (258

- 18T, 39C, 30P) *1989: WT1(R). 1993: A3, Arg1. 1994: E1, 2, NZ1, 2(R), 3, Arg2, S, W. 1995: [A, C, WS2, F, NZ], W, It, E. 1996: Fj, A1, NZ1, 3, 4, 5, Arg1, 2, F1, 2, W. 1997: T, BI1, 2, A2.*

711 **Joubert, MC** (Marius) b 10/07/1979 - Boland - 30 Tests (45 - 9T) 31 matches (45 - 9T) *2000: Tour of Arg,I,W&E – No Tests. 2001: NZ1. 2002: W1, 2, Arg(R), Sm, NZ1, A1, NZ2, A2, F(R). 2003: S2, Arg, A1. 2004: I1, 2, W1, PI, NZ1, A1, NZ2, A2, W2, I3, E, S, Arg. 2005: U, F1, 2, A1.*

110 **Joubert, SJ** (Steve) b 08/04/1887 - d 27/03/1939 - WP - 3 Tests (8 - 1T, 1C, 1P) 6 matches (20 - 1T, 4C, 2P, 1D) *1906: I, W, E.*

689 **Julies, W** (Wayne) b 23/10/1978 - Boland - 11 Tests (10 - 2T) 12 matches (10 - 2T) *1999: [Sp]. 2004: I1, 2, W1, S, Arg. 2005: A2(R), 3(t). 2005: Tour of Arg,W & F. – No Tests. 2006: F(R). 2007: Sm1, [T.]. 2007: Tour of W & E – No Tests.*

509 **Kahts, WJH** (Willie) b 20/02/1947 - NTvl - 11 Tests (4 - 1T) 15 matches (12 - 3T) *1980: BI1, 2, S.Am3, 4, F. 1981: I1, 2, NZ2. 1982: S.Am1, 2.*

344 **Kaminer, J** (Joe) b 25/01/1934 - Tvl - 1 Test (-) 1 match (-) *1958: F2.*

791 **Kankowski, R** (Ryan) b 14/10/1985 - KZN - 20 Tests (5 - 1T) 22 matches (5 - 1T) *2007: W. 2008: W2(R), It, A1(R), W3(R), S(R), E(R). 2009: BI3, NZ3(R), F, It. 2010: W1(R), It1(R), NZ2(R), A1, 3(R), S. 2011: A1(R), NZ1(R). 2012: E3(R).*

675 **Kayser, DJ** (Deon) b 03/07/1970 - EP - 13 Tests (25 - 5T) 21 matches (30 - 6T) *1998: Tour of BI & I – No Tests. 1999: It2(R), A1(R), NZ2, A2, [S, Sp(R), U, E, A3]. 2001: It1(R), NZ1(R), A2(R), NZ2(R).*

599 **Kebble, GR** (Guy) b 02/05/1966 - Natal - 4 Tests (-) 12 matches (5 - 1T) *1993: Arg1, 2. 1994: NZ1(R), 2.*

288 **Keevy, AC** (Jakkals) b 12/11/1917 d 09/02/1990 - ETvl - No Tests - 13 matches (10 - 2C, 2P) *Toured BI, I & F. 1951/52.*

55 **Kelly, EW** (Ted) b 23/10/1869 d 11/03/1949 - GW - 1 Test (-) 1 match (-) *1896: BI3.*

669 **Kempson, RB** (Robbie) b 23/02/1974 - Natal - 37 Tests (5 - 1T) 38 matches (5 - 1T) *1998: I2(R), W1, E1, A1, NZ1, 2, A2, W2, S, I3, E2. 1999: It1, 2, W. 2000: C, E1, 2, A1, NZ1, A2, 3, Arg, I, W, E3. 2001: F1, 2(R), NZ1, A1, 2, NZ2. 2003: S1(R), 2(R), Arg, A1(R), NZ1(R), A2.*

286 **Kenyon, BJ** (Basil) b 19/05/1918 d 09/05/1996 - Border - 1 Test (-) 6 matches (13 - 2T , 2C, 1P) *1949: NZ4*. 1951-52: Tour of BI, I & F – No Tests.*

226 **Kipling, HG** (Bert) b 24/12/1903 d 13/09/1981 - GW - 9 Tests (-) 24 matches (-) *1931: W, I. 1932: E, S. 1933: A1, 2, 3, 4, 5.*

804 **Kirchner, Z** (Zane) b 16/06/1984 - BB - 31 Tests (25 - 5T) 31 matches (25 - 5T) *2009: BI13, F, It, I. 2010: W1(R), F, It1, NZ1, 2, A1, I, W2(R), S, E. 2012: E1, Arg1, 2, A1, NZ1, A2, NZ2, I, S, E4. 2013: A1, NZ1, A2, NZ2. 2014: S(R). 2015: Arg2, [J].*

306 **Kirkpatrick, AI** (Ian) b 25/07/1930 d 18/11/2012 - GW - 13 Tests (-) 43 matches (18 - 6T) *1953: A2. 1956: NZ2. 1958: F1. 1960: S, NZ1, 2, 3, 4, W, I. 1961: E, S, F.*

X **Kirsten, FBC** (Frik) - Springbok Tour Squad Member - b 18/08/1988 - BB - No Tests (-) No matches (-) *Toured W, S & F. 2013. Not considered a Springbok until such time as he appears in a Test, after which he will receive a Springbok number.*

873 **Kitshoff, S** (Steven) b 10/02/1992 - Bordeaux-Bègles, France - 10 Tests (-) 10 matches (-) *2016: I3(R), Arg1(R), 2(R), A1(R), NZ1(R), A2(R), NZ2(R), E(R), It(R), W(R).*

143 **Knight, AS** (Saturday) b 16/12/1885 d 01/07/1946 - Tvl - 5 Tests (-) 18 matches (3 - 1T) *1912: S, I, W. 1913: E, F.*

553 **Knoetze, F** (Faffa) b 18/01/1963 - WP - 2 Tests (4 - 1T) 8 matches (14 - 3T) *1989: WT1, 2.*

280 **Koch, AC** (Chris) b 21/09/1927 d 21/03/1986 - Boland - 22 Tests (15 - 5T) 46 matches (33 - 11T) *1949: NZ2, 3, 4. 1951: S, I, W. 1952: E, F. 1953: A1, 2, 4. 1955: BI1, 2, 3, 4. 1956: A1, NZ2, 3. 1958: F1, 2. 1960: NZ1, 2.*

274 **Koch, HV** (Bubbles) b 13/06/1921 d 02/11/2003 - WP - 4 Tests (-) 4 matches (-) *1949: NZ1, 2, 3, 4.*

868 **Koch, VP** (Vincent) b 13/03/1990 - Mpu - 9 Tests (-) 10 matches (-) *2015: NZ1(R), Arg1. 2016: Arg1(R), 2, NZ1, A2, NZ2, E, It.*

693 **Koen, LJ** (Louis) b 07/07/1975 - GL - 15 Tests (145 - 23C, 31P, 2D) 15 matches (145 - 23C, 31P, 2D) *2000: A1. 2001: It2, E, US. 2003: S1, 2, Arg, A1, NZ1, A2, NZ2, [U, E, Sm(R), NZ3(R)].*

X **Kolbe, C** (Cheslin) - Springbok Tour Squad Member - b 28/10/1993 - WP - No Tests – No Matches. *Toured E, It & W. 2016. Not considered a Springbok until such time as he appears in a Test, after which he will receive a Springbok number.*

851 **Kolisi, S** (Siya) b 16/06/1991 - WP - 13 Tests (-) 13 matches (-) *2013: S(R), Sm(R), Arg1(R),2(R), A1(R), NZ1(R), A2(R), NZ2(R), W(R), F(R). 2015: Arg1(R), [J(R), Sm(R)].*

420 **Kotzé, GJM** (Gert) b 12/08/1940 - WP - 4 Tests (-) 4 matches (-) *1967: F1, 2, 3, 4.*

487 **Krantz, EFW** (Edrich) b 10/08/1954 - OFS - 2 Tests (4 - 1T) 11 matches (48 - 12T) *1976: NZ1. 1980: Tour of S.Am – No Tests. 1981: I1. 1981: Tour of NZ & US – No Tests.*

874 **Kriel, JA** (Jaco) b 21/08/1989 - GL - 7 Tests (-) 7 matches (-) *2016: I3(R), Arg1(R), 2(R),*

A1(R), NZ1(R), A2(R), NZ2(R).

867 **Kriel, JA** (Jesse) b 15/02/1994 - BB - 17 Tests (15 - 3T) 19 matches (15 - 3T) *2015: A, NZ1, Arg1, 2, [J, Sm, S, US, W, NZ2, Arg3]. 2016: I1(R), Arg1(R), 2(R), A1, NZ1, A2.*

676 **Krige, CPJ** (Corné) b 21/03/1975 - WP - 39 Tests (10 - 2T) 43 matches (15 - 3T) *1998: : Tour of BI & I – No Tests. 1999: It2*, W, NZ1. 2000: C(R), E1(R), 2, A1(R), NZ1, A2, NZ2, A3, Arg, I, W, E3. 2001: F1, 2, It1(R), A1(t+R), It2(R), E(R). 2002: W2, Arg*, Sm*, NZ1*, A1*, NZ2*, A2*, F*, S*, E*. 2003: Arg*, A1*, NZ1*, A2*, NZ2*.[E*, Sm*, NZ3*].*

64 **Krige, JD** (Japie) b 05/07/1879 d 14/01/1961 - WP - 5 Tests (3 - 1T) 13 matches (12 - 4T) *1903: BI1, 3. 1906: S, I, W.*

136 **Krige, WA** (Willie) b 02/12/1887 d 20/08/1961 - WP - No Tests - 9 matches (10 - 2T, 1D) *Toured BI, I & F. 1912/13.*

477 **Kritzinger, JL** (Klippies) b 01/03/1948 - Tvl - 7 Tests (4 - 1T) 12 matches (4 - 1T) *1974: BI3, 4, F1, 2. 1975: F1, 2. 1976: NZ4.*

318 **Kroon, CM** (Colin) b 22/02/1931 d 13/11/1981 - EP - 1 Test (-) 1 match (-) *1955: BI1.*

550 **Kruger, PE** (Piet) b 11/04/1958 - Tvl - 2 Tests (-) 2 matches (-) *1986: NZC3, 4.*

832 **Kruger, PJJ** (Juandré) b 06/09/1985 - BB - 17 Tests (-) 17 matches (-) *2012: E1, 2, 3, A1, NZ1, I, S, E4. 2013: It, S, Sm(R), Arg1,2, A1(R), NZ1(R), A2(R), NZ2 (R).*

596 **Kruger, RJ** (Ruben) b 30/03/1970 d 27/01/2010 - OFS - 36 Tests (35 - 7T) 56 matches (105 - 21T) *1993: Tour of A - No Tests. 1993: Arg1, 2. 1994: Tour of NZ – No Tests. 1994: S, W. 1995: WS1, [A, R, WS2, F, NZ], W, It, E. 1996: Fj, A1, NZ1, A2, NZ2, 3, 4, 5, Arg1, 2, F1, 2, W. 1997: T, BI1, 2, NZ1, A1, NZ2. 1999: NZ2, A2(R), [Sp, NZ3(R)].*

169 **Krüger, TL** (Theuns) b 17/06/1896 d 06/07/1957 - Tvl - 8 Tests (-) 21 matches (6 - 2T) *1921: NZ1, 2. 1924: BI1, 2, 3, 4. 1928: NZ1, 2.*

828 **Kruger, W** (Werner) b 23/01/1985 - BB - 4 Tests (-) 5 matches (-) *2010: Tour of BI & I – No Tests. 2011:A1, NZ1. 2012: E2(R), 3(R).*

364 **Kuhn, SP** (Fanie) b 12/06/1935 d 22/01/2014 - Tvl - 19 Tests (-) 37 matches (-) *1960: NZ3, 4, W, I. 1961: E, S, F, I, A1, 2. 1962: BI1, 2, 3, 4. 1963: A1, 2, 3. 1965: I, S.*

191 **La Grange, JB** (Paul) b 25/05/1897 d 23/05/1971 - WP - 2 Tests (-) 2 matches (-) *1924: BI3, 4.*

694 **Labuschagne, JJ** (Jannes) b 16/04/1976 - GL - 11 Tests (-) 11 matches (-) *2000: NZ1(R). 2002: W1, 2, Arg, NZ1, A1, NZ2, A2,*

F, S, E.

820 **Lambie, PJ** (Patrick) b 17/10/1990 -KZN - 56 Tests (153 - 2T, 25C, 27P, 4D) 59 matches (163 - 2T, 30C, 27P, 4D) *2010: I(R), W2(R), S(R), E(R). 2011: A1(R), NZ1, 2, [Fj, Nam, Sm, A3]. 2012: E1(R), 2, A1, NZ1(R), A2(R), NZ2(R), I, S, E4. 2013: It(R), S(R), Sm(R), Arg1(R),2(R), A1(R), NZ1(R), A2(R), NZ2(R), W, S, F(R). 2014: A1(R), NZ1(R), A2(R), NZ2(R), I(R), E, It, W3. 2015: A(R), NZ1(R), Arg1(R), 2, [J, Sm(R), S(R), W(R), NZ2(R), Arg3(R)]. 2016: I1, A2, NZ2, E, It,W(R).*

46 **Larard, A** (Alf) b 30/12/1870 d 15/08/1936 - Tvl - 2 Tests (3 - 1T) 2 matches (3 - 1T) *1896: BI2, 4.*

266 **Lategan, MT** (Tjol) b 29/09/1925 d 08/03/2015 - WP - 11 Tests (9 - 3T) 26 matches (15 - 5T) *1949: NZ1, 2, 3, 4. 1951: S, I, W. 1952: E, F. 1953: A1, 2.*

620 **Laubscher, TG** (Tommie) b 08/10/1963 d 26/05/2007 - WP - 6 Tests (-) 12 matches (-) *1994: Arg1, 2, S, W. 1995: It, E.*

396 **Lawless, MJ** (Mike) b 17/09/1941 - WP - 4 Tests (-) 15 matches (12 - 1T, 1P, 2D) *1964: F. 1969: E(R). 1970: I, W.*

245 **Lawton, AD** (Dandy) b 21/08/1911 d 06/05/1967 - WP - No Tests - 5 matches (24 - 8T) *Toured A & NZ. 1937.*

600 **Le Roux, A-H** (Ollie) b 10/05/1973 - OFS - 54 Tests (5 - 1T) 68 matches (25 - 5T) *1993: Tour of Arg – No Tests. 1994:E1. 1994: Tour of NZ – No Tests. 1998: I1, 2, W1(R), E1(R), A1(R), NZ1(R), 2(R), A2(R), W2(R), S(R), I3(R), E2(t+R). 1999: It1(R), 2(R), W(R), NZ1(R), A1(R), NZ2(R), A2(R), [S(R), Sp, U(t+R), E(R), A3(R), NZ3(R)]. 2000: E1(t+R), 2(R), A1(R), 2(R), NZ2, A3(R), Arg(R), I(t), W(R), E3(R). 2001: F1(R), 2, It1, NZ1(R), A1(R), 2(R), NZ2(R), F3, It2, E, US(R). 2002: W1(R), 2(R), Arg, NZ1(R), A1(R), NZ2(R), A2(R).*

572 **Le Roux, HP** (Hennie) b 10/07/1967 - Tvl - 27 Tests (34 - 4T, 1C, 4P) 51 matches (90 - 12T, 6C, 6P) *1992: Tour of F &E – No Tests. 1993: F1, 2. 1993: Tour of A & Arg – No Tests. 1994: E1, 2, NZ1, 2, 3, Arg2, S, W. 1995: WS1, [A, R, C(R), WS2, F, NZ], W, It, E. 1996: Fj, NZ2, Arg1, 2, F1, 2, W.*

608 **Le Roux, JHS** (Johan) b 15/11/1961 - Tvl - 3 Tests (-) 7 matches (-) *1994: E2, NZ1, 2.*

94 **Le Roux, JSR** (Japie) b 21/08/1882 d 04/03/1949 - WP - No Tests - 9 matches (30 - 10T) *Toured BI, I & F. 1906/07.*

510 **Le Roux, M** (Martiens) b 30/03/1951 d 14/10/2006 - OFS - 8 Tests (-) 12 matches (4 - 1T) *1980: BI1, 2, 3, 4, S.Am3, 4, F. 1981: I1.*

103 **Le Roux, PA** (Pietie) b 22/01/1885 d

11/07/1954 - WP - 3 Tests (-) 16 matches (11 - 3T, 1C) *1906: I, W, E.*

848 **Le Roux, WJ** (Willie) b 18/08/1989 - GW - 41 Tests (50 - 10T) 43 matches (70 - 14T) *2013: It, S, Sm, Arg1,2, A1, NZ1, A2, NZ2, W(R), S, F. 2014: W1,2, S, Arg1,2, A1, NZ1, A2, NZ2, I, E, It, W3. 2015: A, NZ1, Arg1, [Sm, S, US, W, NZ2, Arg3]. 2016: I1, 2, 3, A2(R), NZ2(R), E, It.*

146 **Ledger, SH** (Sep) b 29/04/1889 d 30/01/1918 - GW - 4 Tests (3 - 1T) 15 matches (3 - 1T) *1912: S, I. 1913:E, F.*

688 **Leonard, A** (Anton) b 31/05/1974 - SWD - 2 Tests (5 - 1T) 2 matches (5 - 1T) *1999: A1, [Sp].*

860 **Lewies, JST** (Stephan) b 27/01/1992 - KZN - 1 Test (-) 1 match (-) *2014: S(R)*

794 **Liebenberg, CR** (Tiaan) b 18/12/1981 - WP - 5 Tests (-) 6 matches (-) *2007: Tour of W & E – No Tests. 2012: Arg2(R), A1(R), NZ1(R), A2(R), NZ2(R).*

591 **Linee, M** (Tinus) b 23/08/1969 d 03/11/2014 - WP - No Tests - 9 matches (10 - 2T)   *Toured A. 1993 and W, S & I. 1994.*

12 **Little, EM** (Edward) b 01/11/1864 d ??/05/1945 - GW - 2 Tests (-) 2 matches (-) *1891: BI1, 3.*

781 **Lobberts, H** (Hilton) b 11/06/1986 - BB - 2 Tests (-) 4 matches (-) *2006: E1(R). 2007: NZ2(R).*

326 **Lochner, GP** (Butch) b 01/02/1931 d 27/08/2010 - WP - 9 Tests (6 - 2T) 22 matches (15 - 5T) *1955: BI3. 1956: A1, 2, NZ1, 2, 3, 4. 1958: F1, 2.*

249 **Lochner, GP** (Flappie) b 11/01/1914 d 30/01/1996 - EP - 3 Tests (3 - 1T) 12 matches (27 - 9T) *1937: NZ3. 1938: BI1, 2.*

360 **Lockyear, RJ** (Dick) b 26/06/1931 d 03/03/1988 - GW - 6 Tests (20 - 4C, 4P) 20 matches (97 - 32C, 11P) *1960: NZ1, 2, 3, 4, I. 1961: F.*

127 **Lombard, AC** (Antonie) b 06/12/1885 d 22/02/1960 - EP - 1 Test (-) 1 match (-) *1910: BI2.*

736 **Lombard, F** (Friedrich) b 04/03/1979 - FS - 2 Tests (-) 2 matches (-) *2002: S, E.*

588 **Lötter, D** (Deon) b 10/11/1957 - Tvl - 3 Tests (-) 7 matches (5 - 1T) *1993: F2, A1, 2.*

255 **Lotz, JW** (Jan) b 26/08/1910 d 13/08/1986 - Tvl - 8 Tests (3 - 1T) 26 matches (6 - 2T) *1937: A1, 2, NZ1, 2, 3. 1938: BI1, 2, 3.*

697 **Loubscher, RIP** (Ricardo) b 11/06/1974 - EP - 4 Tests (-) 7 matches (-) *2000: Tour of Arg,I,W&E – No Tests. 2002: W1. 2003: S1, [U(R), Geo].*

85 **Loubser, JA** (Bob) b 06/08/1884 d 07/12/1962 - WP - 7 Tests (9 - 3T) 23 matches

(66 - 22T) *1903: BI3. 1906: S, I, W, E. 1910: BI1, 3.*

425 **Lourens, MJ** (Thys) b 15/05/1943 - NTvl - 3 Tests (3 - 1T) 11 matches (12 - 4T) *1968: BI2, 3, 4. 1968: Tour to F – No Tests. 1971: Tour to A – No Tests.*

704 **Louw, FH** (Hottie) b 02/03/1976 - WP - 3 Tests (-) 7 matches (-) *2000: Tour of Arg,I,W&E – No Tests. 2002: W2(R), Arg, Sm.*

11 **Louw, JS** (Japie) b 30/08/1867 d 17/08/1936 - Tvl - 3 Tests (-) 3 matches (-) *1891: BI1, 2, 3.*

147 **Louw, LH** (Louis) b 23/06/1884 d 13/09/1968 - WP - No Tests - 12 matches (3 - 1T) *Toured BI, I & F. 1912/13.*

815 **Louw, L-FP** (Francois) b 15/06/1985 - WP - 52 Tests (40 - 8T) 54 matches (40 - 8T) *2010: W1, F, It1, 2, NZ1, 2, 3(R). 2011: [Fj(t), Nam(t+R), A3(R).]. 2012: A1(R), NZ1, A2, NZ2, I, S, E4. 2013: It, Sm, Arg1,2, A1, NZ1, A2, NZ2, W, S, F. 2014: W1,2, Arg1, Arg2, A1, NZ1. 2015: A, NZ1, [J, Sm, S, US, W, NZ2, Arg3]. 2016: I1, 2, 3, Arg1, 2, A1, NZ1, A2, NZ2.*

454 **Louw, MJ** (Martiens) b 20/04/1938 d 12/10/2013 - Tvl - 2 Tests (-) 9 matches (-) *1971: A2, 3.*

207 **Louw, MM** (Boy) b 21/02/1906 d 03/05/1988 - WP - 18 Tests (3 - 1T) 49 matches (18 - 6T) *1928: NZ3, 4. 1931: W, I. 1932: E, S. 1933: A1, 2, 3, 4, 5. 1937: A1, 2, NZ2, 3. 1938: BI1, 2, 3.*

505 **Louw, RJ** (Rob) b 26/03/1955 - WP - 19 Tests (20 - 5T) 28 matches (44 - 11T) *1980: S.Am1, 2, BI1, 2, 3, 4, S.Am3, 4, F. 1981: I1, 2, NZ1, 3. 1982: S.Am1, 2. 1984: E1, 2, S.Am&Sp1, 2.*

222 **Louw, SC** (Fanie) b 16/09/1909 d 13/07/1940 - WP - 12 Tests (6 - 2T) 30 matches (24 - 8T) *1931-32 Tour of BI & I – No Tests. 1933: A1, 2, 3, 4, 5. 1937: A1, NZ1, 2, 3. 1938: BI1, 2, 3.*

650 **Lubbe, JMF** (Edrich) b 29/07/1969 - GW - 2 Tests (17 - 7C, 1P) 2 matches (17 - 7C, 1P) *1997: T, BI1.*

114 **Luyt, FP** (Freddie) b 26/02/1888 d 06/06/1965 - WP - 7 Tests (8 - 2T, 1C) 21 matches (27 - 5T, 6C) *1910: BI1, 2, 3. 1912: S, I, W. 1913: E.*

150 **Luyt, JD** (John) b 06/12/1884 d 03/10/1964 - EP - 4 Tests (-) 19 matches (3 - 1T) *1912: S, W. 1913: E, F.*

122 **Luyt, RR** (Dick) b 16/04/1886 d 14/01/1967 - WP - 7 Tests (3 - 1T) 21 matches (28 - 8T, 1D) *1910: BI2, 3. 1912: S, I, W. 1913: E, F.*

29 **Lyons, DJ** (Dykie) b 03/08/1873 d 01/05/1921 - EP - 1 Test (-) 1 match (-) *1896: BI1.*

236 **Lyster, PJ** (Pat) b 31/05/1913 d 25/07/2002 -

Natal - 3 Tests (-) 11 matches (39 - 13T) *1933: A2, 5. 1937: NZ1.*

409 **MacDonald, AW** (Andy) b 27/08/1934 d 18/08/1987 - Rhodesia - 5 Tests (-) 17 matches (3 - 1T) *1965: A1, NZ1, 2, 3, 4.*

470 **MacDonald, DA** (Dugald) b 20/01/1950 - WP - 1 Test (-) 1 match (-) *1974: BI2.*

811 **Maku, BG** (Bandise) b 24/06/1986 - BB - 1 Test (-) 4 matches (5 - 1T) *2009: Tour of UK - No Tests. 2010:It1(R). 2010: Tour of UK - No Tests.*

361 **Malan, AS** (Avril) b 09/04/1937 - Tvl - 16 Tests (-) 36 matches (3 - 1T) *1960: NZ1, 2, 3*, 4*, W*, I*. 1961: E*, S*, F*. 1962: BI1. 1963: A1, 2, 3*. 1964: W. 1965: I*, S*.*

556 **Malan, AW** (Adolf) b 06/09/1961 - NTvl - 7 Tests (-) 11 matches (-). *1989:WT1, 2. 1992: NZ, A, F1, 2, E.*

512 **Malan, E** (Ewoud) b 04/07/1953 - NTvl - 2 Tests (-) 2 matches (-) *1980: BI3(R), 4.*

345 **Malan, GF** (Abie) b 18/11/1935 d 23/10/2014 - WP - 18 Tests (3 - 1T) 44 matches (9 - 3T) *1958: F2. 1960: NZ1, 3, 4. 1961: E, S, F. 1962: BI1, 2, 3. 1963: A1*, 2*, 4*. 1964: W*. 1965: A1, 2, NZ1, 2.*

284 **Malan, P** (Piet) b 13/02/1919 d 05/07/2015 - Tvl - 1 Test (-) 1 match (-) *1949: NZ4.*

841 **Malherbe, JF** (Frans) b 14/03/1991 - WP - 15 Tests (-) 15 matches (-) *2013: W, S2. 2014: Arg1(R), 2(R). 2015: A(t+R), Arg2(R), [Sm(R), S (R), US, W, NZ2, Arg3]. 2016: I1, 2, 3.*

541 **Mallett, NVH** (Nick) b 30/10/1956 - WP - 2 Tests (4 - 1T) 2 matches (4 - 1T) *1984: S.Am&Sp1, 2.*

687 **Malotana, K** (Kaya) b 30/01/1976 - Border - 1 Test (-) 1 match (-) *1999: [Sp].*

708 **Manana, TD** (Thando) b 16/10/1977 - GW - No Tests - 3 matches (-) *Toured Arg, I, W & E. 2000.*

398 **Mans, WJ** (Wynand) b 21/02/1942 - WP - 2 Tests (5 - 1T, 1C) 19 matches (123 - 14T, 30C, 6P, 1D) *1965: I, S. 1965: Tour of A & NZ - No Tests.*

844 **Mapoe, LG** (Lionel) b 13/07/1988 - GL - 11 Tests (-) 11 matches (-) *2015: NZ(R). 2016: I1, 2, 3, Arg1, 2, A1,2(R), NZ2(R), E(R), W(R).*

685 **Marais, CF** (Charl) b 02/09/1970 - WP - 12 Tests (5 - 1T) 15 matches (5 - 1T) *1999: It1(R), 2(R). 2000: C, E1, 2, A1, NZ1, A2, NZ2, A3, Arg(R), W(R).*

264 **Marais, FP** (Buks) b 13/12/1927 d 12/12/1996 - Boland - 5 Tests (10 - 1T, 2C, 1P) 18 matches (40 - 11T, 2C, 1P) *1949: NZ1, 2. 1951: S. 1953: A1, 2.*

390 **Marais, JFK** (Hannes) b 21/09/1941 - WP - 35 Tests (3 - 1T) 75 matches (38 - 12T) *1963: A3. 1964: W, F. 1965: I, S, A2. 1968: BI1, 2, 3, 4,*

F1, 2. 1969: S, E, A1, 2, 3, 4. 1970: I, W, NZ1, 2, 3, 4. 1971: F1, 2*, A1*, 2*, 3*. 1974: BI1*, 2*, 3*, 4*, F1*, 2*.*

529 **Marais, JH** (Johan) b 28/05/1959 - NTvl - No Tests - 5 matches (4 - 1T) *Toured NZ & US. 1981.*

98 **Maré, DS** (Dietlof) b 02/07/1885 d 14/01/1913 - Tvl - 1 Test (-) 11 matches (31 - 2T, 11C, 1P) *1906: S.*

677 **Markram, RL** (Robert) b 15/09/1975 d 06/07/2001 - GW - No Tests - 4 matches (-) *Toured BI & I. 1998.*

92 **Marsberg, AFW** (Artie) b 24/09/1883 d 15/01/1942 - GW - 3 Tests (-) 18 matches (15 - 5T) *1906: S, W, E.*

111 **Marsberg, PA** (Archie) b 01/10/1885 d 23/10/1962 - GW - 1 Test (-) 1 match (-) *1910: BI1.*

598 **Martens, HJ** (Hentie) b 29/10/1971 - OFS - No Tests - 3 matches (5 - 1T) *Toured Arg. 1993.*

82 **Martheze, WC** (Rajah) b 29/11/1877 d 16/02/1912 - GW - 3 Tests (-) 16 matches (18 - 6T) *1903: BI2. 1906: I, W.*

256 **Martin, HJ** (Kalfie) b 10/06/1910 d 20/10/2000 - Tvl - 1 Test (-) 16 matches (9 - 3T) *1937: A2.*

876 **Marx, MJ** (Malcolm) b 13/07/1994 - GL - 2 Tests (-) 3 matches (-) *2016: NZ1(R), W(R).*

705 **Matfield, V** (Victor) b 11/05/1977 - GW - 127 Tests (35 - 7T) 133 matches (35 - 7T) *2000: Tour of Arg,I,W&E – No Tests. 2001: It1(R), NZ1, A2, NZ2, F3, It2, E, US. 2002: W1, Sm, NZ1, A1, NZ2(R). 2003: S1, 2, Arg, A1, NZ1, A2, NZ2, [U, E, Sm, NZ3]. 2004: I1, 2, W1, NZ2, A2, W2, I3, E, S, Arg. 2005: F1, 2, A1, 2, 3, NZ1, A4, NZ2, Arg, W, F3. 2006: S1, 2, F, A1, NZ1, A2, NZ2, 3, A3. 2007: E1, 2, A1, NZ1*, Nam*, S*, [Sm, E3, T(R), US, Fj, Arg, E4.]. 2008: W1(R), 2, It*, NZ1, 2*, A1*, Arg*, NZ3*, A2*, 3*, W3, S, E. 2009: BI1, 2, 3, NZ1, 2, A1, 2, 3, NZ3, F, It(R), I. 2010: W1, F, It1*, NZ1, 2, A1, NZ3, A2, 3, I*, W2*, S*, E*. 2011: A2, NZ2*, [W, Sm*, A3.]. 2014: W1,2, S, A1, NZ1, A2, NZ2, I, E, It, W3. 2015: A*, Arg2*, [J, Sm, NZ2(R), Arg3*].*

875 **Mbonambi, MT** (Bongi) b 07/01/1991 - 5 Tests (-) 6 matches (-) *2016: I3(R), A1(R), NZ2(R), E(R), It(t+R).*

443 **McCallum, ID** (Ian) b 30/07/1944 - WP - 11 Tests (62 - 10C, 14P) 17 matches (134 - 2T, 28C, 24P) *1970: NZ1, 2, 3, 4. 1971: F1, 2, A1, 2, 3. 1974: BI1, 2.*

462 **McCallum, RJ** (Roy) b 12/04/1946 - WP - 1 Test (-) 5 matches (4 - 1T) *1974: BI1. 1974: Tour of F - No Tests.*

138 **McCulloch, JD** (John) b 11/04/1885 d 23/04/1953 - GW - 2 Tests (-) 11 matches (3 -

1T) *1913: E, F.*

565 **McDonald, I** (Ian) b 22/02/1968 - Tvl - 6 Tests (-) 18 matches (25 - 5T) *1992: NZ, A. 1992: Tour of F & E - No Tests. 1993: F1, A3. 1994: E2. 1995: WS1(R).*

223 **McDonald, JAJ** (André) b 17/02/1909 - d 13/07/1991 - WP - 4 Tests (-) 15 matches (15 - 5T) *1931: W, I. 1932: E, S.*

69 **McEwan, WMC** (Willie) b 24/10/1875 d 04/04/1934 - Tvl - 2 Tests (-) 2 matches (-) *1903: BI1, 3.*

134 **McHardy, EE** (Boetie) b 11/06/1890 d 13/12/1959 - OFS - 5 Tests (18 - 6T) 17 matches (60 - 20T) *1912: S, I, W. 1913: E, F.*

27 **McKendrick, JA** (Jim) b 27/07/1870 d 01/01/1895 - WP - 1 Test (-) 1 match (-) *1891: BI3.*

826 **McLeod, C** (Charl) b 05/08/1983 - KZN - 1 Test (-) 2 matches (-) *2010: Tour of BI&I – No Tests. 2011: NZ1(R).*

131 **Meintjes, JJ** (Cooper) b 05/05/1887 d 30/01/1970 - GW - No Tests - 4 matches (-) *Toured BI, I & F. 1912/13.*

612 **Meiring, FA** (FA) b 24/08/1967 - NTvl - No Tests - 7 matches (10 - 2T) *Toured NZ. 1994.*

48 **Mellet, TB** (Tom) b 29/08/1871 d 29/07/1943 - GW - 1 Test (-) 1 match (-) *1896: BI2.*

172 **Mellish, FW** (Frank) b 26/03/1897 d 21/08/1965 - WP - 6 Tests (-) 15 matches (-) *1921: NZ1, 3. 1924: BI1, 2, 3, 4.*

427 **Menter, MA** (Alan) b 03/10/1941 - NTvl - No Tests - 2 matches (-) *Toured F. 1968.*

756 **Mentz, H** (HenNo) b 25/09/1979 - Natal - 2 Tests (-) 2 matches (-) *2004: I1, W1(R).*

14 **Merry, GA** (George) b 03/03/1869 d 02/05/1917 - EP - 1 Test (-) 1 match (-) *1891: BI1.*

79 **Metcalf, HD** (Henry) b 20/04/1878 d 03/03/1966 - Border - 1 Test (-) 1 match (-) *1903: BI2.*

159 **Meyer, C du P** (Charlie) b 14/01/1897 d 31/05/1980 - WP - 3 Tests (-) 15 matches (27 - 9T) *1921: NZ1, 2, 3.*

38 **Meyer, PJ** (PJ) b ??/05/1873 d 27/07/1919 - GW - 1 Test (-) 1 match (-) *1896: BI1.*

663 **Meyer, W** (Willie) b 06/11/1967 - FS - 26 Tests (5 - 1T) 31 matches (10 - 2T) *1997: S(R). 1999: It2, NZ1(R), A1(R). 2000: C(R), E1, NZ1(R), 2(R), Arg, I, W, E3. 2001: F1(R), 2, It1, F3(R), It2, E, US(t+R). 2002: W1, 2, Arg, NZ1, 2, A2, F.*

168 **Michau, JM** (Baby) b 14/08/1890 d 20/06/1945 - Tvl - 1 Test (-) 10 matches (-) *1921: NZ1.*

162 **Michau, JP** (Mannetjies) b 06/10/1900 d 22/05/1960 - WP - 3 Tests (-) 16 matches (6 -

2T) *1921: NZ1, 2, 3.*

109 **Millar, WA** (Billy) b 06/11/1883 d 18/03/1949 - WP - 6 Tests (6 - 2T) 37 matches (15 - 5T) *1906: E. 1910: BI2*, 3*. 1912: I*, W*. 1913: F*.*

123 **Mills, WJ** (Wally) b 16/06/1891 d 23/02/1975 - WP - 1 Test (3 - 1T) 13 matches (30 - 10T) *1910: BI2. 1912-13 Tour of BI&F - No Tests.*

859 **Mohojé, TS** (Teboho) b 03/08/1990 - FS - 15 Tests (-) 17 matches (-) *2014: S(R), A2, NZ2, I, E(R), It, W3. 2015: A(R). 2016: Arg1, 2, A1, NZ1, A2, NZ2, It(R).*

125 **Moll, TM** (Toby) b 20/07/1890 d 14/07/1916 - Tvl - 1 Test (-) 1 match (-) *1910: BI2.*

651 **Montgomery, PC** (Percy) b 15/03/1974 - WP - 102 Tests (893 - 25T, 153C, 148P, 6D) 104 matches (906 - 26T, 157C, 148P, 6D) *1997: BI2, 3, NZ1, A1, NZ2, A2, F1, 2, E, S. 1998: I1, 2, W1, E1, A1, NZ1, 2, A2, W2, S, I3, E2. 1999: It1, 2, W, NZ1, A1, NZ2, A2, [S, U, E, A3, NZ3]. 2000: C, E1, 2, A1, NZ1, A2(R), Arg, I, W, E3. 2001: F1, 2(t), It1, NZ1, F3(R), It2(R). 2004: I2, W1, PI, NZ1, A1, NZ2, A2, W2, I3, E, S. 2005: U, F1, 2, A1, 2, 3, NZ1, A4, NZ2, Arg, W, F3. 2006: S1, 2, F, A1, NZ1, A2, NZ2. 2007: E1, 2, Sm1(R), A1, NZ1, Nam, S, [Sm2, E3, T(R), US, Fj, Arg, E4.]. 2008: W1(R), 2(R), NZ1(R), 2, Arg(R), NZ3, A2(R), 3(R).*

328 **Montini, PE** (Pat) b 15/06/1929 d 26/08/2008 - WP - 2 Tests (-) 11 matches (6 - 1T, 1D) *1956: A1, 2.*

498 **Moolman, LC** (Louis) b 21/01/1951 d 10/02/2006 - NTvl - 24 Tests (-) 31 matches (12 - 3T) *1977: WT. 1980: S.Am1, 2, BI1, 2, 3, 4, S.Am3, 4, F. 1981: I1, 2, NZ1, 2, 3, US. 1982: S.Am1, 2. 1984: S.Am&Sp1, 2. 1986: NZC1, 2, 3, 4.*

501 **Mordt, RH** (Ray) b 15/02/1957 - Zimbabwe - 18 Tests (48 - 12T) 25 matches (88 - 22T) *1980: S.Am1, 2, BI1, 2, 3, 4, S.Am3, 4, F. 1981: I2, NZ1, 2, 3, US. 1982: S.Am1, 2. 1984: S.Am&Sp1, 2.*

106 **Morkel, DFT** (Dougie) b 26/10/1885 d 20/02/1950 - Tvl - 9 Tests (38 - 3T, 7C, 5P) 40 matches (137 - 8T, 37C, 13P) *1906: I, E. 1910: BI1*, 3. 1912: S, I, W. 1913: E*, F.*

66 **Morkel, DJA** (Andrew) b 04/08/1882 d 14/06/1965 - Tvl - 1 Test (-) 2 matches (-) *1903: BI1. 1906-07: Tour of BI,I&F – No Tests.*

173 **Morkel, HJL** (Harry) b 08/12/1888 d 16/07/1956 - WP - 1 Test (-) 13 matches (6 - 2T) *1921: NZ1.*

155 **Morkel, HW** (Henry) b 14/07/1894 d

25/12/1969 - WP - 2 Tests (-) 9 matches (18 - 6T) *1921: NZ1, 2.*

171 **Morkel, JA** (Royal) b 30/04/1894 d 22/10/1926 - WP - 2 Tests (-) 13 matches (9 - 2T, 1D) *1921: NZ2, 3.*

137 **Morkel, JWH** (Jacky) b 13/11/1890 d 15/05/1916 - WP - 5 Tests (16 - 4T, 2C) 18 matches (34 - 6T, 4C, 2D) *1912: S, I, W. 1913: E, F.*

130 **Morkel, PG** (Gerhard) b 15/10/1888 d 05/09/1963 - WP - 8 Tests (16 - 6C, 1D) 33 matches (79 - 33C, 3P, 1D) *1912: S, I, W. 1913: E, F. 1921: NZ1, 2, 3.*

211 **Morkel, PK** (PK) b 01/07/1905 d 24/07/1993 - WP - 1 Test (-) 1 match (-) *1928: NZ4.*

128 **Morkel, WH** (Boy) b 02/01/1885 d 06/02/1955 - WP - 9 Tests (6 - 2T) 31 matches (21 - 7T) *1910: BI3. 1912: S, I, W. 1913:E, F. 1921: NZ1*, 2*, 3*.*

105 **Morkel, WS** (Sommie) b 26/09/1879 d 11/07/1921 - Tvl - 4 Tests (-) 16 matches (3 - 1T) *1906: S, I, W, E.*

267 **Moss, C** (Cecil) b 12/02/1925 - Natal - 4 Tests (-) 4 matches (-) *1949: NZ1, 2, 3, 4.*

872 **Mostert, FJ** (Franco) b 27/11/1990 - GL - 7 Tests (-) 7 matches (-) *2016: I2(R), 3(R), A1(R), NZ1(R), E(R), It(R), W(R).*

830 **Mostert, G** (Gerhard) b 04/10/1984 - KZN - 2 Tests (-) 2 matches (-) *2011: NZ1, A2(R).*

176 **Mostert, PJ** (Phil) b 30/10/1898 d 03/10/1972 - WP - 14 Tests (6 - 1T, 1D) 40 matches (18 - 5T, 1D) *1921: NZ1, 2, 3. 1924: BI1, 2, 4. 1928: NZ1*, 2*, 3*, 4*. 1931: W, I. 1932: E, S.*

682 **Moyle, BS** (Brent) b 31/03/1974 - GF - No Tests - 1 match (-) *Toured BI & I. 1998.*

797 **Mtawarira, T** (Tendai) b 01/08/1985 - KZN - 87 Tests (10 - 2T) 91 matches (10 - 2T) *2008: W2, It, A1(R), Arg, NZ3, A2, 3, W3, S, E. 2009: BI1, 2, 3, NZ1, 2, A1, 2, 3, NZ3, F, It(R), I. 2010: I, W2, S, E. 2011: A2, NZ2(R), [W, Fj(R), Nam(R), Sm.]. 2012: E1,2,3, Arg1,2, A1, NZ1, A2, NZ2. 2012: Tour of I, S&E – No Tests. 2013: It, S, Sam, Arg1, Arg2, A1, NZ1, A2, NZ2, W, S(R), F. 2014: W1(R),2, Arg1,2(R), A1, NZ1, A2, NZ2, I, E, W3. 2015: A, NZ1, Arg1, 2(R), [J, Sm, S, US, W, NZ2, Arg3]. 2016: I1, 2, 3, Arg1, 2, A1, NZ1, A2, NZ2, E, It, W.*

642 **Muir, DJ** (Dick) b 20/03/1965 - Natal - 5 Tests (10 - 2T) 10 matches (20 - 4T) *1996: Tour of Arg, F & W – No Tests. 1997: It, F1, 2, E, S.*

796 **Mujati, BV** (Brian) b 28/09/1984 - WP - 12 Tests (-) 12 matches (-) *2008: W1, It(R), NZ1(R), 2(t), A1(R), Arg(R), NZ3(R), A2(R), 3, W3(t), S(R), E(R).*

405 **Mulder, CG** (Boet) b 21/05/1939 - ETvl -

No Tests - 13 matches (20 - 7C, 2P) *Toured A & NZ. 1965.*

617 **Mulder, JC** (Japie) b 18/10/1969 - Tvl - 34 Tests (30 - 6T) 43 matches (45 - 9T) *1994: NZ2, 3, S, W. 1995: WS1, [A, WS2, F, NZ], W, It, E. 1996: Fj, A1, NZ1, A2, NZ2, S, Arg1, 2, F1, 2, W. 1997: T, BI1. 1999: It1(R), 2, W, NZ1. 2000: C(R), A1, E3. 2001: F1, It1.*

428 **Müller, GH** (Gert) b 10/05/1948 - WP - 14 Tests (12 - 4T) 20 matches (45 - 15T) *1969: A3, 4, S. 1970: W, NZ1, 2, 3, 4. 1971: F1, 2. 1971: Tour of A – No Tests. 1972: E. 1974: BI1, 3, 4.*

773 **Muller, GJ** (Johan) b 01/06/1980 - KZN - 24 Tests (-) 26 matches (-) *2006: S1(R), NZ1(R), A2, NZ2, 3, A3, I(R), E1, 2. 2007: E1(R), 2(R), Sm1(R), A1(R), NZ1(R), A2, NZ2*, Nam(R), [Sm(R), E3(R), Fj(t+R), Arg(t+R).], W. 2009: BI3. 2011: [W(R)].*

748 **Müller, GP** (Jorrie) b 03/01/1981 - GL - 6 Tests (5 - 1T) 6 matches (5 - 1T) *2003: A2, NZ2, [E, Geo(R), Sm, NZ3].*

551 **Müller, HL** (Helgard) b 01/06/1963 - OFS - 2 Tests (-) 5 matches (-) *1986: NZC4(R). 1989: WT1(R). 1994 Tour of W, S&I – No Tests.*

277 **Muller, HSV** (Hennie) b 26/03/1922 d 26/04/1977 - Tvl - 13 Tests (16 - 3T, 2C, 1P) 28 matches (28 - 4T, 5C, 2P) *1949: NZ1, 2, 3, 4. 1951: S*, I*, W*. 1952: E*, F*. 1953: A1*, 2*, 3*, 4*.*

563 **Müller, LJJ** (Lood) b 05/07/1959 - Natal - 2 Tests (-) 2 matches (-) *1992: NZ, A.*

560 **Müller, PG** (Pieter) b 05/05/1969 - Natal - 33 Tests (15 - 3T) 52 matches (50 - 10T) *1992: NZ, A, F1, 2, E. 1993: F1, 2, A1, 2, 3, Arg1, 2. 1994: E1, 2, NZ1, S, W. 1998: I1, 2, W1, E1, A1, NZ1, 2, A2. 1999: It1, W, NZ1, A1, [Sp, E, A3, NZ3].*

785 **Murray, WM** (Waylon) b 27/04/1986 - KZN - 3 Tests (-) 4 matches (-) *2007: Sm1, A2, NZ2.*

821 **Mvovo, LN** (Lwazi) b 03/06/1986 - KZN - 17 Tests (30 - 6T) 19 matches (30 - 6T) *2010: S, E. 2011: A1, NZ1. 2012: Arg1, 2, A1(R). 2014: W1(R), S, W3. 2015: A(R), Arg1(R), 2, [J, US]. 2016: I1, 2.*

305 **Myburgh, B** (Ben) b 17/06/1919 d 30/10/1984 - ETvl - No Tests - 17 matches (12 - 4T) *Toured BI, I & F. 1951/52.*

34 **Myburgh, FR** (Francis) b 20/07/1871 d 30/11/1929 - EP - 1 Test (-) 1 match (-) *1896: BI1.*

371 **Myburgh, JL** (Mof) b 24/08/1936 d 15/06/2012 - NTvl - 18 Tests (-) 57 matches (9 - 3T) *1960-61: Tour of BI, I & F – No Tests. 1962: BI1. 1963: A4. 1964: W, F. 1968: BI1, 2, 3, F1, 2. 1969: A1, 2, 3, 4, E. 1970: I, W, NZ3, 4.*

182 **Myburgh, WH** (Champion) b 10/10/1897 d 14/03/1979 - WTvl - 1 Test (-) 1 match (-)

1924: BI1.

394 **Naudé, JP** (Tiny) b 02/11/1936 d 28/12/2006 - WP - 14 Tests (47 - 2T, 4C, 11P) 28 matches (90 - 6T, 9C, 18P) *1963: A4. 1965: A1, 2, NZ1, 3, 4. 1967: F1, 2, 3, 4. 1968: BI1, 2, 3, 4. 1968: Tour of F – No Tests.*

774 **Ndungane, AZ** (Akona) b 20/02/1981 - BB - 11 Tests (5 - 1T) 13 matches (5 - 1T) *2006: A1, 2, NZ2, 3, A3, E1, 2. 2007: E2, Nam(R), [US], W(R).*

798 **Ndungane, OM** (Odwa) b 20/02/1981 - KZN - 9 Tests (10 - 2T) 12 matches (15 - 3T) *2008: It, NZ1, A3. 2008: Tour of W,S & E – No Tests. 2009: BI3, A3, NZ3. 2009: Tour of F, It, I & E – No Tests. 2010:W1. 2010: 2010: Tour of BI & I – No Tests. 2011: NZ1(R), [Fj.].*

401 **Neethling, JB** (Tiny) b 06/07/1939 d 03/04/2009 - WP - 8 Tests (-) 23 matches (3 - 1T) *1965: Tour of I & S – No Tests. 1967: F1, 2, 3, 4. 1968: BI4. 1968: Tour of F – No Tests. 1969: S. 1970: NZ1, 2.*

101 **Neill, WA** (William) b 30/12/1882 d 03/02/1947 - Border - No Tests - 4 matches (-) *Toured BI, I & F. 1906/07.*

362 **Nel, JA** (Lofty) b 11/08/1935 d 18/07/2016 - Tvl - 11 Tests (-) 24 matches (18 - 6T) *1960: NZ1, 2. 1963: A1, 2. 1965: A2, NZ1, 2, 3, 4. 1970: NZ3, 4.*

329 **Nel, JJ** (Jeremy) b 21/09/1934 - WP - 8 Tests (3 - 1T) 23 matches (32 - 9T, 1C, 1P) *1956: A1, 2, NZ1, 2, 3, 4. 1958: F1, 2.*

72 **Nel, PARO** (PO) b 17/04/1877 d 23/07/1928 - Tvl - 3 Tests (-) 3 matches (-) *1903: BI1, 2, 3.*

199 **Nel, PJ** (Flip) b 17/06/1902 d 12/02/1984 - Natal - 16 Tests (3 - 1T) 46 matches (6 - 2T) *1928:NZ1, 2, 3, 4. 1931: W, I. 1932: E, S. 1933: A1*, 3*, 4*, 5*. 1937: A1*, 2*, NZ2*, 3*.*

238 **Nijkamp, JL** (Joe) b 16/10/1904 d 03/04/1969 - Tvl - 1 Test (-) 1 match (-) *1933: A2.*

369 **Nimb, CF** (Charlie) b 06/09/1938 d 15/06/2004 - WP - 1 Test (9 - 3C, 1P) 6 matches (20 - 2T, 4C, 2P) *1960-61: Tour of BI & F – No Tests. 1961: I.*

679 **Nkumane, SO** (Owen) b 10/08/1975 - GL - No Tests - 4 matches (-) *Toured BI & I. 1998.*

767 **Nokwe, JL** (Jongi) b 30/12/1981 - Boland - 4 Tests (25 - 5T) 7 matches (40 - 8T) *2004: Tour of BI & Arg – No Tests. 2008: Arg, A2, 3. 2008: Tour of W, S,& E – No Tests. 2009: BI3. 2009: Tour of F, It, I & E – No Tests.*

408 **Nomis, SH** (Syd) b 15/11/1941 - Tvl - 25 Tests (18 - 6T) 54 matches (45 - 15T) *1965: Tour of A & NZ – No Tests. 1967: F4. 1968: BI1, 2, 3, 4, F1, 2. 1969: A1, 2, 3, 4, S, E. 1970: I, W, NZ1, 2, 3, 4. 1971: F1, 2, A1, 2, 3. 1972: E.*

X **Ntubeni, S** (Scarra) - Springbok Tour Squad Member - b 18/02/1991 - WP - No Tests (-) No matches (-) *Toured W, S & F. 2013. Toured I,E,It & W 2014. Not considered a Springbok until such time as he appears in a Test, after which he will receive a Springbok number.*

850 **Nyakane, TN** (Trevor) b 04/05/1989 - FS - 28 Tests (5 - 1T) 30 matches (5 - 1T) *2013: It(R), S(R), Sm(R). 2014: S(R), Arg1(R), A1(R), NZ1(R), A2(R), NZ2(R), I(R), E(R), It, W3. 2015: NZ1(R), Arg1(R),2, [J(R), Sm(R), S(R), US(R), W(R), NZ2(R), Arg3(R)]. 2016: I1(R), 2(R), A1(R), It(R), W(R).*

289 **Ochse, JK** (Chum) b 09/02/1925 d 13/07/1996 - WP - 7 Tests (9 - 3T) 22 matches (48 - 16T) *1951: I, W. 1952: E, F. 1953: A1, 2, 4.*

295 **Oelofse, JSA** (Hansie) b 16/12/1926 d 31/05/1978 - Tvl - 4 Tests (6 - 2T) 13 matches (12 - 4T) *1951-52: Tour of BI & F – No Tests. 1953: A1, 2, 3, 4.*

209 **Oliver, JF** (John) b 17/05/1897 d ??/??/1980 - Tvl - 2 Tests (-) 2 matches (-) *1928: NZ3, 4.*

417 **Olivier, E** (Eben) b 10/04/1944 - WP - 16 Tests (15 - 5T) 34 matches (30 - 10T) *1965: Tour of A & NZ – No Tests. 1967: F1, 2, 3, 4. 1968: BI1, 2, 3, 4, F1, 2. 1969:A1, 2, 3, 4, S, E.*

570 **Olivier, J** (Jacques) b 13/11/1968 - NTvl - 17 Tests (15 - 3T) 34 matches (65 - 13T) *1992: F1, 2, E. 1993: F1, 2, A1, 2, 3, Arg1. 1994: Tour of W, S & I – No Tests. 1995: W, It(R), E. 1996: Arg1, 2, F1, 2, W.*

174 **Olivier, JS** (Fien) b 27/05/1897 d 08/06/1980 - WP - No Tests - 13 matches (2 - 1C) *Toured A & NZ. 1921.*

772 **Olivier, W** (Wynand) b 11/06/1983 - BB - 38 Tests (5 - 1T) 42 matches (5 - 1T) *2006: S1(R), 2, F, A1, NZ1, A2, NZ2(R), 3, A3, I(R), E1, 2. 2007: E1,2, NZ1(R), A2, NZ2, [E3(R), T, Arg(R).], W(R). 2009: BI3, NZ1(R), 2(R), F(R), It(R), I. 2010: F, It2(R), NZ1, 2, A1. 2011:A1, NZ1(R). 2012: E1(t), 2(R), 3. 2014: S(R).*

33 **Olver, E** (Ernest) b 27/07/1874 d 12/06/1943 - EP - 1 Test (-) 1 match (-) *1896: BI1.*

824 **Oosthuizen, CV** (Coenie) b 22/03/1989 - FS - 23 Tests (15 - 3T) 25 matches (15 - 3T) *2010: Tour of BI & I – No Tests. 2012: E1(R), NZ2(R). 2013: It(R), S(R), Sm(R), Arg1(R),2(R), A1(R), NZ1(R), A2(R), NZ2(R), W(R), S(R), F. 2014: W1(R),2(R), S, I(R), E(R), It, W3. 2015: [J(R), US(R)].*

460 **Oosthuizen, JJ** (Johan) b 04/07/1951 - WP - 9 Tests (8 - 2T) 14 matches (23 - 5T, 1D) *1974: BI1, F1, 2. 1975: F1, 2. 1976: NZ1, 2, 3, 4.*

646 **Oosthuizen, LT** (Theo) b 24/02/1964 - GW - No Tests - 4 matches (15 - 3T) *Toured Arg, F & W. 1996.*

520 **Oosthuizen, OW** (Okkie) b 01/04/1955
- NTvl - 9 Tests (4 - 1T) 14 matches (12 - 3T)
*1981: I1(R), 2, NZ2, 3, US. 1982: S.Am1, 2. 1984:
E1, 2.*

571 **Oosthuysen, DE** (Deon) b 04/12/1963 -
NTvl - No Tests - 12 matches (20 - 4T) *Toured F
& E. 1992 and A. 1993.*

181 **Osler, BL** (Bennie) b 23/11/1901 d
24/04/1962 - WP - 17 Tests (46 - 2T, 6C, 4P,
4D) 30 matches (108 - 7T, 17C, 7P, 8D) *1924:
BI1, 2, 3, 4. 1928: NZ1, 2, 3, 4. 1931: W*, I*. 1932:
E*, S*. 1933: A1, 2*, 3, 4, 5.*

193 **Osler, SG** (Sharkey) b 31/01/1907 d
16/04/1980 - WP - 1 Test (-) 1 match (-)
1928: NZ1.

615 **Otto, K** (Krynauw) b 08/10/1971 - NTvl
- 38 Tests (5 - 1T) 51 matches (30 - 6T) *1994:
Tours of NZ and W, S & I – No Tests. 1995:[R,
C(R), WS2(R)]. 1996: Tours of A – No Tests. 1997:
BI3, NZ1, A1, NZ2, It, F1, 2, E, S. 1998: I1, 2,
W1, E1, A1, NZ1, 2, A2, W2, S, I3, E2. 1999: It1,
W, NZ1, A1, [S(R), Sp, U, E, A3, NZ3]. 2000: C,
E1, 2, A1.*

359 **Oxlee, K** (Keith) b 17/12/1934 d 31/08/1998
- Natal - 19 Tests (88 - 5T, 14C, 14P, 1D) 48
matches (201 - 11T, 45C, 23P, 3D) *1960: NZ1, 2,
3, 4, W, I. 1961: S, A1, 2. 1962: BI1, 2, 3, 4. 1963:
A1, 2, 4. 1964: W. 1965: Tour of I & S – No Tests.
1965: NZ1, 2.*

628 **Pagel, GL** (Garry) b 17/09/1966 - WP - 5
Tests (-) 8 matches (-) *1995: [A(R), R, C,
NZ(R)]. 1996: NZ5(R).*

869 **Paige, R** (Rudy) b 02/08/1989 - BB - 7 Tests
(-) 8 matches (-) *2015: [US(R), Arg3(R)]. 2016:
I1(R), Arg2(R), A2, E, It.*

411 **Parker, WH** (Hambly) b 13/04/1934 d
19/09/2014 - EP - 2 Tests (-) 14 matches (-)
1965: A1, 2.

73 **Partridge, JEC** (Birdie) b 13/06/1879 d
01/07/1965 - Tvl - 1 Test (-) 1 match (-) *1903:
BI1.*

698 **Passens, GA** (Gavin) b 18/05/1976 - Mpu -
No Tests - 3 matches (10 - 2T) *Toured Arg, I, W
& E. 2000.*

647 **Paulse, BJ** (Breyton) b 25/04/1976 - WP
- 64 Tests (130 - 26T) 74 matches (195 - 39T)
*1996: Tour of Arg, F & W – No Tests. 1999: It1, 2,
NZ1, A1, 2(R), [S(R), Sp, NZ3]. 2000: C, E1, 2,
A1, NZ1, A2, NZ2, A3, Arg, W, E3. 2001: F1, 2,
It1, NZ1, A1, 2, NZ2, F3, It2, E. 2002: W1, 2, Arg,
Sm(R), A1, NZ2, A2, F, S, E. 2003: [Geo]. 2004:
I1, 2, W1, PI, NZ1, A1, NZ2, A2, W2, I3, E. 2005:
A2, 3, NZ1, A4, F3. 2006: S1, 2, A1(R), NZ1,
3(R), A3(R). 2007: A2, NZ2.*

183 **Payn, C** (Bill) b 09/08/1893 d 31/10/1959 -
Natal - 2 Tests (-) 2 matches (-) *1924: BI1, 2.*

341 **Pelser, HJM** (Martin) b 23/03/1934 - Tvl -
11 Tests (6 - 2T) 26 matches (18 - 6T) *1958: F1.
1960: NZ1, 2, 3, 4, W, I. 1961: F, I, A1, 2.*

X **Petersen, SP** (Sergeal) - Springbok Tour Squad
Member - b 01/08/1994 - FS - No Tests - 1
match (5 - 1T) *Toured E, It & W. 2016. Not considered a Springbok until such time as he appears in a
Test, after which he will receive a Springbok number.*

331 **Pfaff, BD** (Brian) b 02/03/1930 d
08/05/1998 - WP - 1 Test (-) 5 matches (6 -
2T) *1956: A1.*

301 **Pickard, JAJ** (Jan) b 25/12/1927 d
30/05/1998 - WP - 4 Tests (-) 34 matches (19 -
5T, 2C) *1951-52: Tour of BI & F – No Tests. 1953:
A3, 4. 1956: NZ2. 1958: F2.*

584 **Pienaar, JF** (Francois) b 02/01/1967 - Tvl
- 29 Tests (15 - 3T) 40 matches (20 - 4T) *1993:
F1*, 2*, A1*, 2*, 3*, Arg1*, 2*. 1994: E1*, 2*, NZ2*,
3*, Arg1*, 2*, S*, W*. 1995: WS1*, [A*, C*, WS2*, F*,
NZ*], W*, It*, E*. 1996: Fj*, A1*, NZ1*, A2*, NZ2*.*

779 **Pienaar, R** (Ruan) b 10/03/1984 - KZN - 88
Tests (135 - 8T, 22C, 17P) 95 matches (158 -
8T, 23C, 24P) *2006: NZ2(R), 3(R), A3(R), I(t),
E1(R). 2007: E1(R), 2(R), Sm1(R), A1, NZ1,
A2, NZ2, Nam(R), S(R), [E3(t+R), T, US(R),
Arg(R).], W. 2008: W1(R), It(R), NZ2(R), A1(R),
3(R), W3, S, E. 2009: BI1, 2, 3(R), NZ1, A1(R),
2, 3, It(R), I(R). 2010: W1, F(R), It1(R), 2(R),
NZ1(R), 2(R), A1, I, W2, S(R), E. 2011: A1,
NZ1, [Fj(R), Nam(R)]. 2012: E1(R), 2(R), 3(R),
Arg1(R), 2(R), A1, NZ1, A2, NZ2, I, S, E4. 2013:
It(R), S, Sm, Arg1,2, A1, NZ1,2(R), W(R), S2(R),
F. 2014: W1(R),2(t), Arg1,2, A1, NZ1. 2015: A,
NZ1, Arg1, 2, [J, Sm(R), S(R), Arg3]*

164 **Pienaar, TB** (Theo) b 23/11/1888 d
14/11/1960 - WP - No Tests - 10 matches (-)
Toured A & NZ. 1921.

506 **Pienaar, ZMJ** (Gysie) b 21/12/1954 - OFS -
13 Tests (14 - 2T, 2P) 21 matches (59 - 6T, 10C,
4P, 1D) *1980: S.Am2(R), BI1, 2, 3, 4, S.Am3, 4, F.
1981: I1, 2, NZ1, 2, 3.*

793 **Pieterse, BH** (Barend) b 23/01/1979 - FS -
No Tests (-) 1 match (5 - 1T) *Toured I & E, 2007.*

775 **Pietersen, J-PR** (JP) b 12/07/1986 - KZN
- 70 Tests (120 - 24T) 74 matches (120 - 24T)
*2006: A3. 2006: Tour of I & E – No Tests. 2007:
Sm1, A1, NZ1, A2, NZ2, Nam, S, [Sm, E3, T,
US(R), Fj, Arg, E4.], W. 2008: NZ2, A1, Arg, NZ3,
A2, W3, S, E. 2009: BI1, 2, NZ1, 2, A1, 2, F, It,
I. 2010: NZ3, A2, 3. 2011: A2, NZ2, [W, Fj, Sm,
A3.]. 2012: E1, 2, 3, I, S, E4. 2013: W, S, F. 2014:
W1,2, S, A2(t+R), NZ2(R), I(R), E, It. 2015: A,
[J(R), Sm, S, US, W, NZ2, Arg3]. 2016: I1, 2, 3, E.*

421 **Pitzer, G** (Gys) b 08/07/1939 - NTvl - 12
Tests (-) 16 matches (-) *1967: F1, 2, 3, 4. 1968:
BI1, 2, 3, 4, F1, 2. 1969: A3, 4. 1969-70: Tour of BI*

& I – No Tests.

857 **Pollard, H** (Handré) b 11/03/1994 - BB -
20 Tests (188 - 2T, 29C, 37, 3D) 21 matches (195
- 2T, 31C, 38P, 3D) *2014: S, Arg1,2, NZ1, A2,
NZ2, I, It(R), W3(R). 2015: A, NZ1, Arg1,2(R),
[J(R), Sm, S, US, W, NZ2, Arg3].*

461 **Pope, CF** (Chris) b 30/09/1952 - WP - 9
Tests (4 - 1T) 13 matches (4 - 1T) *1974: BI1, 2,
3, 4. 1974: Tour of F – No Tests. 1975: F1, 2. 1976:
NZ2, 3, 4.*

812 **Potgieter, DJ** (Dewald) b 22/02/1987 - BB
- 6 Tests (5 - 1T) 8 matches (5 - 1T) *2009: I(t).
2010: W1, F(R), It1, 2(R), A1(R).*

200 **Potgieter, HJ** (Hennie) b 24/10/1903 d
11/11/1957 - OFS - 2 Tests (-) 2 matches (-)
1928: NZ1, 2.

493 **Potgieter, HL** (Hermanus) b 11/01/1953
- OFS - 1 Test (4 - 1T) 1 match (4 - 1T) *1977:
WT.*

435 **Potgieter, R** (Ronnie) b 18/11/1943 - NTvl -
No Tests - 6 matches (-) *Toured BI & I, 1969/70.*

834 **Potgieter, UJ** (Jacques) b 24/04/1986 - BB -
3 Tests (-) 3 matches (-) *2012: E3, Arg1(R), 2.*

531 **Povey, SA** (Shaun) b 09/08/1954 - WP - No
Tests - 2 matches (-) *Toured NZ & US, 1981.*

52 **Powell, AW** (Bertie) b 18/07/1873 d
11/09/1948 - GW - 1 Test (-) 1 match (-)
1896: BI3.

17 **Powell, JM** (Jackie) b 12/12/1871 d
19/12/1955 - GW - 4 Tests (-) 4 matches (-)
1891: BI2. 1896: BI3. 1903: BI1, 2.*

504 **Prentis, RB** (Richard) b 27/02/1947 - Tvl
- 11 Tests (-) 14 matches (-). *1980: S.Am1, 2,
BI1, 2, 3, 4, S.Am3, 4, F. 1981: I1, 2.*

723 **Pretorius, AS** (André) b 29/12/1978 - GL
- 31 Tests (171 - 2T, 31C, 25P, 8D) 33 matches
(174 - 2T, 31C, 26P, 8D) *2002: W1, 2, Arg, Sm,
NZ1, A1, NZ2, F, S(R), E. 2003: NZ1(R), A2.
2005: A2, 3, NZ1, A4, NZ2, Arg. 2006: NZ2(R),
3, A3, I, E1(t+R), 2. 2007: S(R), [Sm(R), E3(R), T,
US(R), Arg(R).], W.*

782 **Pretorius, JC** (Jaco) b 10/12/1979 - GL - 2
Tests (-) 3 matches (-) *2006: I. 2007: NZ2.*

198 **Pretorius, NF** (Nick) b 10/12/1904 d
19/02/1990 - Tvl - 4 Tests (-) 4 matches (-)
1928: NZ1, 2, 3, 4.

577 **Pretorius, PIL** (Piet) b 17/08/1964 - NTvl -
No Tests - 6 matches (-) *Toured F & E. 1992.*

392 **Prinsloo, J** (Poens) b 11/10/1935 - NTvl - 1
Test (-) 1 match (-) *1963: A3.*

338 **Prinsloo, JC** (Jan) b 28/01/1935 d
28/07/1966 - Tvl - 2 Tests (-) 2 matches (-)
1958: F1, 2.

192 **Prinsloo, JP** (Boet) b 14/10/1905 d
04/10/1968 - Tvl - 1 Test (-) 1 match (-) *1928:
NZ1.*

622 **Putt, KB** (Kevin) b 28/07/1965 - Natal - No
Tests - 11 matches (15 - 3T) *Toured W, S & I.
1994 and Arg, F & W. 1996.*

386 **Putter, DJ** (Dick) b 13/02/1937 d
31/10/2002 - WTvl - 3 Tests (-) 3 matches (-)
1963: A1, 2, 4.

71 **Raaff, JWE** (Klondyke) b 10/03/1879 d
13/07/1949 - GW - 6 Tests (3 - 1T) 20 matches
(12 - 4T) *1903: BI1, 2. 1906: S, W, E. 1910: BI1.*

776 **Ralepelle, MC** (Chiliboy) b 11/09/1986
- BB - 22 Tests (5 - 1T) 24 matches (5 - 1T)
*2006: NZ2(R), E2(R). 2008: E(t+R). 2009: BI3,
NZ1(R), 2(R), A2(R), NZ3(R). 2009: Tour of F,
It, I & E – No Tests. 2010: W1(R), F(R), It1, 2(R),
NZ1(R), 2(R), A1(R), 2(R), 3(R), W2(R). 2011:
A1(R), NZ1(R), [Nam(R)]. 2012: Tour of UK – No
Tests. 2013: It(R).*

488 **Ras, WJ de W** (De Wet) b 28/01/1954 -
OFS - 2 Tests (-) 5 matches (69 - 4T, 25C, 1P).
*1976: NZ1(R). 1980: S.Am2(R). 1980: Tour of
S.Am – No Tests.*

813 **Raubenheimer, D** (Davon) b 16/07/1984
- GW - No Tests - 2 matches (-) *Toured F, It, I
& E. 2009.*

728 **Rautenbach, SJ** (Faan) b 22/02/1976 -
WP - 14 Tests (5 - 1T) 14 matches (5 - 1T)
*2002: W1(R), 2(t+R), Arg(R), Sm, NZ1(R), A1,
NZ2(R), A2(R). 2003: [U(R), Geo, Sm, NZ3].
2004: W1, NZ1(R).*

866 **Redelinghuys, J** (Julian) b 11/09/1989 - GL
- 8 Tests (-) 8 matches (-) *2014: It(R), W3(R).
2016: I1(R), 2(R), 3(R), Arg1, A2(R), NZ2(R).*

569 **Reece-Edwards, HM** (Hugh) b 05/01/1961
- Natal - 3 Tests (-) 12 matches (103 - 3T, 23C,
14P) *1992: F1, 2. 1993: A2.*

87 **Reid, A** (Oupa) b 23/11/1878 d 18/05/1952 -
WP - 1 Test (3 - 1T) 1 match (3 - 1T) *1903: BI3.*

242 **Reid, BC** (Bunny) b 12/07/1910 d
11/09/1976 - Border - 1 Test (-) 1 match (-)
1933: A4.

107 **Reid, HG** (Bert) b 19/12/1881 - d
30/05/1944 - Tvl - No Tests - 14 matches (6 -
2T) *Toured BI, I & F. 1906/07.*

542 **Reinach, J** (Jaco) b 01/01/1962 d
21/01/1997 - OFS - 4 Tests (8 - 2T) 4 matches
(8 - 2T) *1986: NZC1, 2, 3, 4.*

864 **Reinach, JM** (Cobus) b 07/02/1990 - KZN
- 10 Tests (10 - 2T) 11 matches (15 - 3T) *2014:
A2(R), NZ2(R), I(R), E, It.W3. 2015: A(R),
NZ1(R), Arg1(R),2(R).*

310 **Rens, IJ** (Natie) b 19/07/1929 d 19/12/1989
- Tvl - 2 Tests (19 - 5C, 2P, 1D) 2 matches (19 -
5C, 2P, 1D) *1953: A3, 4.*

320 **Retief, DF** (Daan) b 28/06/1925 d
22/09/2010 - NTvl - 9 Tests (12 - 4T) 21
matches (36 - 12T) *1955: BI1, 2, 4. 1956: A1, 2,*

NZ1, 2, 3, 4.

129 **Reyneke, HJ** (Koot) b 19/01/1882 d 22/03/1970 - WP - 1 Test (3 - 1T) 1 match (3 - 1T) *1910: BI3.*

845 **Rhule, RK** (Raymond) b 06/11/1992 - FS - No Tests - No matches *Toured I, S & E. 2012.*

6 **Richards, AR** (Alf) b 14/12/1867 d 09/01/1904 - WP - 3 Tests (-) 3 matches (-) *1891: BI1, 2, 3*.*

580 **Richter, AJ** (Adriaan) b 10/05/1966 - NTvl - 10 Tests (20 - 4T) 29 matches (55 - 11T) *1992: F1, 2, E. 1993: Tour of A - No Tests. 1994: E2, NZ1, 2, 3. 1995: [R*, C, WS2(R)].*

388 **Riley, NM** (Norman) b 25/02/1939 - ETvl - 1 Test (-) 1 match (-) *1963: A3.*

117 **Riordan, CA** (Cliff) b 24/12/1885 d 07/02/1958 - Tvl - 2 Tests (-) 2 matches (-) *1910: BI1, 2.*

573 **Roberts, H** (Harry) b 03/12/1960 - Tvl - No Tests - 6 matches (5 - 1T) *Toured F & E. 1992.*

480 **Robertson, IW** (Ian) b 28/04/1950 d 24/08/2015 - Rhodesia - 5 Tests (3 - 1D) 10 matches (21 - 3T, 1P, 2D) *1974: F1, 2. 1976: NZ1, 2, 4.*

554 **Rodgers, PH** (Heinrich) b 23/06/1962 - NTvl - 5 Tests (-) 12 matches (-) *1989: WT1, 2. 1992: NZ, F1, 2.*

534 **Rogers, CD** (Chris) b 10/10/1956 - Tvl - 4 Tests (-) 4 matches (-) *1984: E1, 2, S.Am&Sp1, 2.*

126 **Roos, GD** (Gideon) b 20/07/1890 d 08/03/1920 - WP - 2 Tests (3 - 1T) 2 matches (3 - 1T) *1910: BI2, 3.*

88 **Roos, PJ** (Paul) b 30/10/1880 d 22/09/1948 - WP - 4 Tests (-) 22 matches (5 - 1T, 1C) *1903: BI3. 1906: I*, W*, E*.*

802 **Rose, EE** (Earl) b 12/01/1984 - GL - No Tests - 2 matches (-) *Toured BI, 2008 and E, F, It & I, 2009.*

322 **Rosenberg, W** (Wilf) b 18/06/1934 - Tvl - 5 Tests (6 - 2T) 9 matches (6 - 2T) *1955: BI2, 3, 4. 1956: NZ3. 1958: F1.*

699 **Rossouw, C** (Chris) b 14/11/1976 - WP - No Tests - 4 matches (-) *Toured Arg, I, W & E. 2000.*

624 **Rossouw, C le C** (Chris) b 14/09/1969 - Tvl - 9 Tests (10 - 2T) 10 matches (10 - 2T) *1995: WS1, [R, WS2, F, NZ]. 1999: NZ2(R), A2(R), [Sp, NZ3(R)].*

309 **Rossouw, DH** (Daantjie) b 05/09/1930 d 28/01/2010 - WP - 2 Tests (3 - 1T) 2 matches (3 - 1T) *1953: A3, 4.*

755 **Rossouw, DJ** (Danie) b 05/06/1978 - BB - 63 Tests (50 - 10T) 67 matches (55 - 11T) *2003: [U, Geo, Sm(R), NZ3]. 2004: E(R), S, Arg. 2005: U, F1, 2, A1, W(R), F3(R). 2006: S1, 2, F, A1, I,*

E1, 2. 2007: E1, Sm1, A1(R), NZ1, S, [Sm, E3, T, Fj, Arg, E4.]. 2008: W1(t+R), NZ3(R), A3(R), S(R), E. 2009: BI1(R), 2(R), NZ1(R), 2(R), A1(R), 3(R), NZ3(R), F(R), It, I. 2010: W1, F, NZ1(R), 2, A1, NZ3(t+R), A2(R), 3. 2011: A1, NZ1, A2, NZ2(t+R), [W, Fj, Nam, Sm, A3.].

578 **Rossouw, PB** (Botha) b 03/11/1969 - WTvl - No Tests - 2 matches (5 - 1T) *Toured F & E. 1992.*

652 **Rossouw, PWG** (Pieter) b 03/12/1971 - WP - 43 Tests (105 - 21T) 43 matches (105 - 21T) *1997: BI2, 3, NZ1, A1, NZ2(R), A2(R), It, F1, 2, E, S. 1998: I1, 2, W1, E1, A1, NZ1, 2, A2, W2, S, I3, E2. 1999: It1, W, NZ1, A1(R), NZ2, A2, [S, U, E, A3]. 2000: C, E1, 2, A2, Arg(R), I, W. 2001: F3, US. 2003: Arg.*

206 **Rousseau, WP** (Willie) b 11/08/1906 d 28/12/1996 - WP - 2 Tests (-) 2 matches (-) *1928: NZ3, 4.*

367 **Roux, F du T** (Mannetjies) b 12/04/1939 - WP - 27 Tests (18 - 6T) 56 matches (39 - 13T) *1960: W. 1961: A1, 2. 1962: BI1, 2, 3, 4. 1963: A2. 1965: A1, 2, NZ1, 2, 3, 4. 1968: BI3, 4, F1, 2. 1969: A1, 2, 3, 4. 1970: I, NZ1, 2, 3, 4.*

607 **Roux, JP** (Johan) b 25/02/1969 - Tvl - 12 Tests (10 - 2T) 17 matches (20 - 4T) *1994: E2, NZ1, 2, 3, Arg1. 1995: [R, C, F(R)]. 1996: A1(R), NZ1, A2, NZ3.*

426 **Roux, OA** (Tonie) b 22/02/1947 - NTvl - 7 Tests (-) 31 matches (15 - 4T, 1D) *1968: Tour of F - No Tests. 1969: S, E. 1970: I, W. 1971: Tour of A - No Tests. 1972: E. 1974: BI3, 4.*

737 **Roux, WG** (Wessel) b 01/10/1976 - Blue Bulls - 3 Tests (-) 3 matches (-) *2002: F(R), S, E.*

727 **Russell, RB** (Brent) b 05/03/1980 - Mpu - 23 Tests (40 - 8T) 23 matches (40 - 8T) *2002: W1(R), 2, Arg, A1(R), NZ2(R), A2, F, E(R). 2003: Arg(R), A1(R), NZ1, A2(R). 2004 :I2(t+R), W1, NZ1(R), W2(R), Arg(R). 2005: U(R), F2(R), A1(t), Arg(R), W(R). 2006: F.*

44 **Samuels, TA** (Theo) b 21/07/1873 d 16/11/1896 - GW - 3 Tests (6 - 2T) 3 matches (6 - 2T) *1896: BI2, 3, 4.*

666 **Santon, D** (Dale) b 18/08/1969 - Boland - 4 Tests (-) 5 matches (-) *1997: Tour of It, F, E & S - No Tests. 2003: A1(R), NZ1(R), A2(t), [Geo(R)].*

449 **Sauermann, JT** (Theo) b 16/11/1944 d 13/06/2014 - Tvl - 5 Tests (-) 11 matches (-) *1971: F1, 2, A1. 1972: E. 1974: BI1.*

290 **Saunders, MJ** (Cowboy) b 26/11/1927 d 17/05/2006 - Border - No Tests - 14 matches (33 - 11T) *Toured BI, I & F. 1951/52.*

472 **Schlebusch, JJJ** (Jan) b 05/05/1949 - OFS - 3 Tests (-) 3 matches (-) *1974: BI3, 4. 1975: F2.*

346 **Schmidt, LU** (Louis) b 06/02/1936 d 23/01/1999 - NTvl - 2 Tests (-) 2 matches (-) *1958: F2. 1962: BI2.*

544 **Schmidt, UL** (Uli) b 10/07/1961 - NTvl - 17 Tests (9 - 2T) 25 matches (29 - 6T) *1986: NZC1, 2, 3, 4. 1989: WT1, 2. 1992: NZ, A. 1993: F1, 2, A1, 2, 3. 1994: Arg1, 2, S, W.*

391 **Schoeman, J** (Haas) b 15/03/1940 d 01/01/2006 - WP - 7 Tests (-) 23 matches (15 - 5T) *1963: A3, 4. 1965: I, S, A1, NZ1, 2.*

X **Schoeman, CF** (Tian) - Springbok Tour Squad Member - b 23/09/1991 - BB - No Tests (-) No matches (-) *Toured E, It & W. 2016. Not considered a Springbok until such time as he appears in a Test, after which he will receive a Springbok number.*

618 **Scholtz, CP** (Christiaan) b 22/10/1970 - Tvl - 4 Tests (-) 4 matches (-) *1994: Arg1. 1995: [R, C, WS2].*

732 **Scholtz, H** (Hendro) b 22/03/1979 - FS - 5 Tests (5 - 1T) 5 matches (5 - 1T) *2002: A1(R), NZ2(R), A2(R). 2003: [U(R), Geo].*

177 **Scholtz, H** (Tokkie) b 29/08/1892 d 08/04/1959 - WP - 2 Tests (-) 15 matches (-) *1921: NZ1, 2.*

X **Schreuder, L** (Louis) - Springbok Tour Squad Member - b 25/04/1990 - WP - No Tests (-) No matches (-) *Toured W, S & F. 2013. Not considered a Springbok until such time as he appears in a Test, after which he will receive a Springbok number.*

582 **Schutte, PJW** (Phillip) b 07/10/1969 - NTvl - 2 Tests (-) 8 matches (-) *1992: Tour of F & E - No Tests. 1994: S, W.*

36 **Scott, PA** (Paul) b 26/10/1872 d (unkNown) - Tvl - 4 Tests (-) 4 matches (-) *1896: BI1, 2, 3, 4.*

X **Senatla, SM** (Seabelo) - Springbok Tour Squad Member - b 10/02/1993 - WP - No Tests (-) No matches (-). *Toured I,E,It & W 2014. Not considered a Springbok until such time as he appears in a Test, after which he will receive a Springbok number.*

156 **Sendin, WD** (Billy) b 04/10/1895 d 16/07/1977 - GW - 1 Test (3 - 1T) 9 matches (18 - 6T) *1921: NZ2.*

702 **Sephaka, LD** (Lawrence) b 08/08/1978 - GF - 24 Tests (-) 29 matches (-) *2000: Tour of Arg, I, W & E – No Tests. 2001: US. 2002: Sm, NZ1, A1, NZ2, A2, F. 2003: S1, 2, A1, NZ1, A2(t+R), NZ2, [U, E(t+R), Geo]. 2005: F2, A1, 2(R), W. 2006: S1(R), NZ3(t+R), A3(R), I.*

508 **Serfontein, DJ** (Divan) b 03/08/1954 - WP - 19 Tests (12 - 3T) 26 matches (16 - 4T) *1980: BI1, 2, 3, 4, S.Am3, 4, F. 1981: I1, 2, NZ1, 2, 3, US. 1982: S.Am1, 2. 1984: E1, 2, S.Am&Sp1*, 2*.*

849 **Serfontein, JL** (Jan) b 15/04/1992 - Blue Bulls - 26 Tests (10 - 2T) 26 matches (10 - 2T) *2013: It(R), S(R), Sm(R), Arg1(R),2(R), A1(R), NZ1(R), A2(R), NZ2(R). 2014: W1,2, S, A1, NZ1, A2, NZ2, I, E, It, W3. 2015: Arg2(R), [S(R), US(t+R), W(R), NZ2(R), Arg3(R)].*

19 **Shand, R** (Bob) b 27/08/1866 d 01/03/1934 - GW - 2 Tests (-) 2 matches (-) *1891: BI2, 3.*

613 **Sherrell, LR** (Lance) b 09/02/1966 - NTvl - No Tests - 6 matches (31 - 3T, 5C, 2P) *Toured NZ. 1994.*

257 **Sherriff, AR** (Roger) b 17/03/1913 d 04/12/1951 - Tvl - 3 Tests (-) 6 matches (3 - 1T) *1927: Tour of A & NZ - No Tests. 1938: BI1, 2, 3.*

761 **Shimange, MH** (Hanyani) b 17/04/1978 - FS - 9 Tests (-) 9 matches (-) *2004: W1(R), NZ2(R), A2(R), W2(R). 2005: U(R), A1(R), 2(R), Arg(R). 2006: S1(R).*

140 **Shum, EH** (Baby) b 17/08/1886 d 27/06/1952 - Tvl - 1 Test (-) 15 matches (6 - 2T) *1913: E.*

175 **Siedle, LB** (Jack) b 01/07/1891 d 07/11/1962 - Natal - No Tests - 1 match (-) *Toured A & NZ. 1921.*

292 **Sinclair, DJ** (Des) b 14/07/1927 d 29/04/1996 - Tvl - 4 Tests (-) 17 matches (15 - 5T) *1951-52: Tour of BI & F – No Tests. 1955: BI1, 2, 3, 4.*

70 **Sinclair, JH** (Jimmy) b 16/10/1876 d 23/02/1913 - Tvl - 1 Test (-) 1 match (-) *1903: BI1.*

343 **Skene, AL** (Alan) b 02/10/1932 d 13/08/2001 - WP - 1 Test (-) 1 match (-) *1958: F2.*

659 **Skinstad, RB** (Bob) b 03/07/1976 - WP - 42 Tests (55 - 11T) 47 matches (70 - 14T) *1997: E(t). 1998: W1(R), E1(t), NZ1(R), 2(R), A2(R), W2(R), S, I3, E2. 1999: [S, Sp(R), U, E, A3]. 2001: F1(R), 2(R), It1*, NZ1*, A1*, 2*, NZ2*, F3*, It2*, E*. 2002: W1*, 2*, Arg, Sm, NZ1, A1, NZ2, A2. 2003: Arg(R). 2007: E2(t+R), Sm1, NZ1, A2*, [E3(R), T*, US(R), Arg(R).].*

416 **Slabber, LJ** (Louis) b 05/03/1935 d 11/05/2003 - OFS - No Tests - 7 matches (9 - 3T) *Toured A & NZ. 1965.*

188 **Slater, JT** (Jack) b 16/04/1901 d 16/02/1986 - EP - 3 Tests (6 - 2T) 3 matches (6 - 2T) *1924:BI3, 4. 1928: NZ1.*

546 **Smal, GP** (Gert) b 27/12/1961 - WP - 6 Tests (4 - 1T) 6 matches (4 - 1T) *1986: NZC1, 2, 3, 4. 1989: WT1, 2.*

561 **Small, JT** (James) b 10/02/1969 - Tvl - 47 Tests (100 - 20T) 60 matches (135 - 27T) *1992: NZ, A, F1, 2, E. 1993: F1, 2, A1, 2, 3, Arg1, 2. 1994: E1, 2, NZ1, 2, 3(t), Arg1. 1995: WS1, [A, R, F, NZ], W, It, E(R). 1996: Fj, A1, NZ1, A2, NZ2, Arg1, 2, F1, 2, W. 1997: T, BI1, NZ1(R), A1(R),*

NZ2, A2, It, F1, 2, E, S.

583 Smit, FC (FC) b 13/08/1966 - WP - 1 Test (-) 4 matches (-) *1992: E.*

691 Smit, JW (John) b 03/04/1978 - Natal - 111 Tests (40 - 8T) 112 matches (40 - 8T) *2000: C(t), A1(R), NZ1(t+R), A2(R), NZ2(R), A3(R), Arg, I, W, E3. 2001: F1, 2, I1t, NZ1(R), A1(R), 2(R), NZ2(R), F3(R), It2, E, US(R). 2003: [U(R), E(t+R), Geo*, Sm, NZ3]. 2004: I1*, 2*, W1*, PI*, NZ1*, A1*, NZ2*, A2*, W2*, I3*, E*, S*, Arg*. 2005: U*, F1*, 2*, A1*, 2*, 3*, NZ1*, A4*, NZ2*, Arg*, W*, F3*. 2006: S1*, 2*, F*, A1*, NZ1*, A2*, NZ2*, 3*, A3*, I*, E1*, 2*. 2007: E1*, 2*, Sm1*, A1*, [Sm*, E3*, T(R), US*, Fj*, Arg*, E4*.], W*. 2008: W1*, 2*, NZ1*, W3*, S*, E*. 2009: BI1*, 2*, 3*, NZ1*, 2*, A1*, A2*, A3*, NZ3*, F*, It*, I*. 2010: W1*, F*, It2*, NZ1*, 2*, A1*, NZ3*, A2*, 3*. 2011: A1*, NZ1*, A2*, NZ2(R), [W*, Fj*, Nam*, Sm(R), A3*.].*

660 Smit, PL (Philip) b 27/07/1973 - GW - No Tests - 5 matches (-) *Toured It, F, E & S. 1997 and BI & I. 1998.*

X Smit, RA (Roelof) - Springbok Tour Squad Member - b 11/01/1993 - BB - No Tests - 1 match (5 - 1T) *Toured E, It & W. 2016. Not considered a Springbok until such time as he appears in a Test, after which he will receive a Springbok number.*

389 Smith, CM (Nelie) b 08/05/1934 d 01/05/2016 - OFS - 7 Tests (12 - 1T, 3P) 19 matches (21 - 4T, 3P) *1963: A3, 4. 1964: W, F*. 1965: A1*, 2*, NZ2*.*

23 Smith, CW (Toski) b 09/04/1871 d 28/02/1934 - GW - 3 Tests (-) 3 matches (-) *1891: BI2. 1896: BI2, 3.*

507 Smith, DJ (David) b 09/11/1957 - Zimbabwe - 4 Tests (-) 4 matches (-) *1980: BI1, 2, 3, 4.*

21 Smith, DW (Dan) b 08/04/1869 d 27/02/1926 - GW - 1 Test (-) 1 match (-) *1891: BI2.*

262 Smith, GAC (George) b 31/08/1916 d 23/03/1978 - EP - 1 Test (-) 1 match (-) *1938: BI3.*

746 Smith, JH (Juan) b 30/07/1981 - FS - 70 Tests (60 - 12T) 72 matches (60 - 12T) *2003: S1(R), 2(R), A1, NZ1, A2, NZ2, [U, E, Sm, NZ3]. 2004: W2. 2005: U(R), F2(R), A2, 3, NZ1, A4, NZ2, Arg, W, F3. 2006: S1, 2, F, A1, NZ1, A2, I, E2. 2007: E1, 2, A1, Nam, S, [Sm, E3, T(R), US, Fj, Arg, E4.], W. 2008: W1, 2, It, NZ1, 2, A1, Arg, NZ3, A2, 3, W3, S. 2009: BI1, 2, 3, NZ1, 2, A1, 2, 3. 2010: NZ3, A2, 3, I, W2, S, E. 2014: Arg2.*

643 Smith, PF (Franco) b 29/07/1972 - GW - 3 Tests (23 - 2T, 2C, 3P) 18 matches (85 - 5T, 21C, 6P) *1996: Tour of Arg, F & W - No Tests. 1997: S(R). 1998: I1(t), 2, W1, NZ1(R), 2(R), A2(R), W2. 1999: NZ2.*

241 Smollan, FC (Fred) b 20/08/1908 d 02/08/1998 - Tvl - 3 Tests (-) 3 matches (-) *1933: A3, 4, 5.*

18 Snedden, RCD (Bob) b 20/03/1867 d 03/04/1931 - GW - 1 Test (-) 1 match (-) *1891: BI2*.*

636 Snyman, AH (André) b 02/02/1974 - NTvl - 38 Tests (50 - 10T) 42 matches (60 - 12T) *1996: NZ3, 4, Arg2(R), W(R). 1997: T, BI1, 2, 3, NZ1, A1, NZ2, A2, It, F1, 2, E, S. 1998: I1, 2, W1, E1, A1, NZ1, 2, A2, W2, S, I3, E2. 1999: NZ2. 2001: NZ2, F3, US. 2002: W1. 2003: S1, NZ1. 2006: S1, 2.*

453 Snyman, DSL (Dawie) b 05/07/1949 - WP - 10 Tests (24 - 1T, 1C, 4P, 2D) 22 matches (86 - 7T, 13C, 8P, 4D) *1971: Tour of A - No Tests. 1972: E. 1974: BI1, 2(R), F1, 2. 1975: F1, 2. 1976: NZ2, 3. 1977: WT.*

466 Snyman, JCP (Jackie) b 14/04/1948 - OFS - 3 Tests (18 - 6P) 7 matches (29 - 4C, 6P, 1D) *1974: BI2, 3, 4. 1974: Tour of F - No Tests.*

X Snyman, RG (RG) - Springbok Tour Squad Member - b 29/01/1995 - BB - No Tests (-) - 1 match (-) *Toured E, It & W. 2016. Not considered a Springbok until such time as he appears in a Test, after which he will receive a Springbok number.*

473 Sonnekus, GHH (Gerrie) b 01/02/1953 - OFS - 3 Tests (4 - 1T) 3 matches (4 - 1T) *1974: BI3. 1984: E1, 2.*

731 Sowerby, RS (Shaun) b 01/07/1978 - Natal - 1 Test (-) 1 match (-) *2002: Sm(R).*

446 Spies, JJ (Johan) b 08/05/1945 - NTvl - 4 Tests (-) 11 matches (-) *1970: NZ1, 2, 3, 4. 1971: Tour of A - No Tests.*

777 Spies, PJ (Pierre) b 08/06/1985 - BB - 53 Tests (35 - 7T) 53 matches (35 - 7T) *2006: A1, NZ2, 3, A3, I, E1. 2007: E1(R), 2, A1. 2008: W1, 2, A1, Arg, NZ3, A2, 3, W3, S, E. 2009: BI1, 2, 3(R), NZ1, 2, A1, 2, 3, NZ3. 2010: F, It1, 2, NZ1, 2, A1, NZ3, A2, 3, I, W2, E. 2011: A2, NZ2, [W, Fj, Nam, Sm, A3.]. 2012: E1, 2, 3. 2013: It, S, Sm.*

479 Stander, JCJ (Rampie) b 25/12/1944 d 28/08/1980 - OFS - 5 Tests (-) 8 matches (4 - 1T) *1974: BI4(R). 1974: Tour of F - No Tests. 1976: NZ1, 2, 3, 4.*

482 Stapelberg, WP (Willem) b 29/01/1947 - NTvl - 2 Tests (8 - 2T) 6 matches (12 - 3T) *1974: F1, 2.*

336 Starke, JJ (James) b 16/05/1931 - WP - 1 Test (-) 8 matches (3 - 1T) *1956: NZ4.*

180 Starke, KT (Kenny) b 18/06/1900 d 03/01/1982 - WP - 4 Tests (13 - 3T, 1D) 4 matches (13 - 3T, 1D) *1924: BI1, 2, 3, 4.*

342 Steenekamp, J (Johan) b 02/09/1935 d 16/08/2007 - Tvl - 1 Test (-) 1 match (-) *1958: F1.*

764 **Steenkamp, GG** (Gurthrö) b 12/06/1981
- FS - 53 Tests (30 - 6T) 56 matches (30 - 6T)
*2004: S, Arg. 2005: U, F2(R), A2, 3, NZ1(R),
A4(R). 2007: E1(R), 2, A1, [T, Fj(R).]. 2008: W1,
2(R), NZ1, 2, A1, W3(R), S(R). 2009: BI1(R),
3(R). 2009: Tour of F, It, I & E – No Tests. 2010: F,
It1, 2, NZ1, 2, A1, NZ3, A2, 3. 2011: A2(R), NZ2,
[W(R), Fj, Nam, Sm(R), A3.]. 2012: S, E4. 2013:
Arg1(R),2(R), A1(R), NZ1(R), A2(R), NZ2(R),
W(R), S, F(R). 2014: W1,2(R), Arg2, It(R).*

93 **Stegmann, AC** (Anton) b 25/08/1883 d
23/01/1972 - WP - 2 Tests (3 - 1T) 16 matches
(54 - 18T) *1906: S, I.*

825 **Stegmann, GJ** (Deon) b 22/03/1986 - BB
- 6 Tests (-) 6 matches (-) *2010: I, W2, S, E.
2011: A1, NZ1.*

132 **Stegmann, JA** (Jan) b 21/06/1887 d
07/12/1984 - Tvl - 5 Tests (15 - 5T) 16 matches
(39 - 13T) *1912: S, I, W. 1913: E, F.*

350 **Stewart, DA** (Dave) b 14/07/1935 - WP -
11 Tests (9 - 1T, 2P) 30 matches (25 - 5T, 2C,
2P) *1960: S. 1961: E, S, F, I. 1963: A1, 3, 4. 1964:
W, F. 1965: I.*

678 **Stewart, JC** (Christian) b 17/10/1966 - WP
- 3 Tests (-) 5 matches (-) *1998: S, I3, E2.*

783 **Steyn, FPL** (Francois) b 14/05/1987 - KZN
- 53 Tests (132 - 10T, 5C, 21P, 3D) 56 matches
(141 - 10T, 8C, 22P, 3D) *2006: I, E1, 2. 2007:
E1(R), 2(R), Sm1, A1(R), NZ1(R), S, [Sm(R),
E3, T(R), US, Fj, Arg, E4.], W. 2008: W2(R), It,
NZ1(R), 2(R), A1, NZ3(R), A2(R), W3(R), S(R),
E(R). 2009: BI1, 2, 3(R), NZ1, 2, A1, 2(R), 3(R),
NZ3. 2010: W1, A2, 3, W2, S, E. 2011: A2, [W, Fj,
Nam, Sm]. 2012: E1, 2, Arg1, 2, A1, NZ1.*

803 **Steyn, M** (Morné) b 11/07/1984 - BB - 66
Tests (736 - 8T, 102C, 154P, 10D) 67 matches
(749 - 8T, 104C, 157P, 10D) *2009: BI1(t+R),
2(R), 3, NZ1(R), 2, A1, 2, 3, NZ3, F, It, I. 2010: F,
It1, 2, NZ1, 2, A1, NZ3, A2, 3, I, W2, S, E. 2011:
A1, NZ1, A2(R), NZ2, [W, Fj, Nam, Sm, A3.].
2012: E1, 2, 3, Arg1, A1, NZ1, S(R). 2013: It, S,
Sm, Arg1,2, A1, NZ1, A2, NZ2, W, S(R), F. 2014:
W1,2, Arg1(R),2(R), A1. 2015: [US(R)]. 2016:
I2(t), Arg2(R), A1(R), NZ1(R), A2, NZ2.*

489 **Stofberg, MTS** (Theuns) b 06/06/1955 -
OFS - 21 Tests (24 - 6T) 29 matches (36 - 9T)
*1976: NZ2, 3. 1977: WT. 1980: S.Am1, 2, BI1, 2,
3, 4, S.Am3*, 4, F. 1981: I1, 2, NZ1*, 2, US. 1982:
S.Am1, 2. 1984: E1*, 2*.*

224 **Strachan, LC** (Louis) b 12/09/1907 d
04/03/1985 - Tvl - 10 Tests (-) 38 matches (18
- 6T) *1932: E, S. 1937: A1, 2, NZ1, 2, 3. 1938:
BI1, 2, 3.*

616 **Straeuli, RAW** (Rudolf) b 20/08/1963 - Tvl
- 10 Tests (20 - 4T) 23 matches (45 - 9T) *1994:
NZ1, Arg1, 2, S, W. 1995: WS1, [A, WS2, NZ(R)],*

E(R).

592 **Stransky, JT** (Joel) b 16/07/1967 - Natal
- 22 Tests (240 - 6T, 30C, 47P, 3D) 36 matches
(329 - 9T, 55C, 55P, 3D) *1993: A1, 2, 3, Arg1.
1994: Arg1, 2. 1994: Tour of W, S & I – No Tests.
1995: WS1, [A, R(t), C, F, NZ], W, It, E. 1996:
Fj(R), NZ1, A2, NZ2, 3, 4, 5(R).*

827 **Strauss, AJ** (Andries) b 05/03/1984 - FS -
No Tests - 1 match (-) *Toured BI & I. 2010.*

579 **Strauss, CP** (Tiaan) b 28/06/1965 - WP - 15
Tests (20 - 4T) 37 matches (55 - 11T) *1992:
F1, 2, E. 1993: F1, 2, A1, 2, 3, Arg1, 2. 1994: E1,
NZ1*, 2, Arg1, 2. 1994: Tour of W, S & I – No Tests.*

539 **Strauss, JA** (Attie) b 02/09/1959 - WP - 2
Tests (-) 2 matches (-) *1984: S.Am&Sp1, 2.*

800 **Strauss, JA** (Adriaan) b 18/11/1985 - FS -
66 Tests (30 - 6T) 69 matches (30 - 6T) *2008:
A1(R), Arg(R), NZ3(R), A2(R), 3(R). 2009: F(R),
It. 2010: S(R), E(R). 2012: E1(R), 2(R), 3(R),
Arg1(R), 2, A1, NZ1, A2, NZ2, I, S, E4. 2013:
It, S, Sm, Arg1,2, A1(R), NZ1(R), A2, NZ2(R),
W(R), S, F(R). 2014: S(R), Arg1(R),2(R), A1,
NZ1, A2, NZ2(R), I(R), E, It, W3(R). 2015: A(R),
NZ1(R), Arg1(R), 2, [J(R), Sm, S(R), W(R),
NZ2(R), Arg3(R)]. 2016: I1*, 2*, 3*, Arg1*, 2*, A1*,
NZ1*, A2*, NZ2*, E*, It*, W*.*

490 **Strauss, JHP** (Johan) b 27/09/1951 - Tvl - 3
Tests (-) 3 matches (-) *1976: NZ3, 4. 1980:
S.Am1.*

158 **Strauss, SSF** (Sarel) b 24/11/1891 d
06/02/1946 - GW - 1 Test (-) 12 matches (23 -
5T, 2D) *1921: NZ3.*

325 **Strydom, CF** (Popeye) b 20/01/1932 d
31/03/2001 - OFS - 6 Tests (-) 17 matches (3 -
1T) *1955: BI3. 1956: A1, 2, NZ1, 4. 1958: F1.*

586 **Strydom, JJ** (Hannes) b 13/07/1965 - Tvl
- 21 Tests (5 - 1T) 31 matches (10 - 2T) *1993:
F2, A1, 2, 3, Arg1, 2. 1994: E. 1995: [A, C, F, NZ].
1996: A2(R), NZ2(R), 3, 4, W(R). 1997: T, BI1,
2, 3, A2.*

276 **Strydom, LJ** (Ou-Boet) b 27/10/1921 d
11/05/2003 - NTvl - 2 Tests (-) 2 matches (-)
1949: NZ1, 2.

566 **Styger, JJ** (Johan) b 31/01/1962 - OFS - 7
Tests (-) 18 matches (-) *1992: NZ(R), A, F1, 2,
E. 1993: F2(R), A3(R).*

403 **Suter, MR** (SNowy) b 14/12/1939 - Natal -
2 Tests (-) 4 matches (3 - 1T) *1965: I, S.*

654 **Swanepoel, W** (Werner) b 15/04/1973 -
FS - 20 Tests (25 - 5T) 25 matches (30 - 6T)
*1997: BI3(R), A2(R), F1(R), 2, E, S. 1998:
I2(R), W1(R), E2(R). 1999: It1, 2(R), W, A1, [Sp,
NZ3(t)]. 2000: A1, NZ1, A2, NZ2, A3.*

452 **Swanson, PS** (Peter) b 26/12/1946 d
26/10/2003 - Tvl - No Tests - 4 matches (5 - 1T,
1C) *Toured A. 1971.*

595 **Swart, IS de V** (Balie) b 18/05/1964 - Tvl -
16 Tests (-) 31 matches (-) *1993: A1, 2, 3, Arg1.
1994: E1, 2, NZ1, 3, Arg2(R). 1994: Tour of W, S
& I – No Tests. 1995: WS1, [A, WS2, F, NZ], W.
1996: A2.*

630 **Swart, J** (Justin) b 23/07/1972 - WP - 10
Tests (5 - 1T) 13 matches (15 - 3T) *1996: Fj,
NZ1(R), A2, NZ2, 3, 4, 5. 1997: BI3(R), It, S(R).*

312 **Swart, JJN** (Sias) b 29/07/1934 d 18/01/1993
- SWA - 1 Test (3 - 1T) 1 match (3 - 1T) *1955:
BI1.*

43 **Taberer, WS** (Bill) b 11/04/1872 d
10/02/1938 - GW - 1 Test (-) 1 match (-)
1896: BI2.

842 **Taute, JJ** (Jaco) b 21/03/1991 - GL - 3 Tests
(-) 3 matches (-) *2012: A2, NZ2, I.*

380 **Taylor, OB** (Ormy) b 05/06/1937 - Natal - 1
Test (-) 1 match (-) *1962:BI1.*

603 **Teichmann, GH** (Gary) b 09/01/1967 -
Natal - 42 Tests (30 - 6T) 52 matches (35 - 7T)
*1993: Tour of Arg – No Tests. 1995:W. 1996: Fj, A1,
NZ1, A2, NZ2, 3*, 4*, 5*, Arg1*, 2*, F1*, 2*, W*.
1997: T*, BI1*, 2*, 3*, NZ1*, A1*, NZ2*, A2*, It*,
F1*, 2*, E*, S*. 1998: I1*, 2*, W1*, E1*, A1*, NZ1*,
2*, A2*, W2*, S*, I3*, E2*. 1999: It1*, W*, NZ1*.*

668 **Terblanche, CS** (Stefan) b 02/07/1975 -
Boland - 37 Tests (95 - 19T) 41 matches (115
- 23T) *1998: I1, 2, W1, E1, A1, NZ1, 2, A2, W2,
S, I3, E2. 1999: It1(R), 2, W, A1, NZ2(R), [Sp,
E(t), A3(R), NZ3]. 2000: E3. 2002: W1, 2, Arg,
Sm, NZ1, A1, 2(R). 2003: S1, 2, Arg, A1, NZ1, A2,
NZ2, [Geo].*

633 **Theron, DF** (Dawie) b 15/09/1966 - GW
- 13 Tests (-) 15 matches (-) *1996: A2(R),
NZ2(R), 5, Arg1, 2, F1, 2, W. 1997: BI2(R), 3,
NZ1(R), A1, NZ2(R).*

749 **Theron, JT** (Gus) b 10/01/1975 - WP - No
Tests - No matches *Toured Aus & NZ. 2003.*

56 **Theunissen, DJ** (Danie) b 12/07/1869 d
19/03/1964 - GW - 1 Test (-) 1 match (-)
1896: BI3.

142 **Thompson, G** (Tommy) b 04/10/1886 d
20/06/1916 - WP - 3 Tests (-) 15 matches (-)
1912: S, I, W.

648 **Thomson, JRD** (Jeremy) b 24/06/1967 -
Natal - No Tests - 4 matches (5 - 1T) *Toured Arg,
F & W. 1996.*

161 **Tindall, JC** (Jackie) b 26/03/1900 d
03/05/1946 - WP - 5 Tests (-) 27 matches (3 -
1T) *1921: Tour of A & NZ – No Tests. 1924: BI1.
1928: NZ1, 2, 3, 4. 1931-32 Tour of UK – No Tests.*

515 **Tobias, EG** (Errol) b 18/03/1950 - Boland
- 6 Tests (22 - 1T, 3C, 4P) 15 matches (65 - 5T,
15C, 5P) *1980: Tour of S.Am – No Tests. 1981: I1,
2. 1981: Tour of NZ & USA – No Tests. 1984: E1,
2, S.Am&Sp1, 2.*

201 **Tod, NS** (Jacko) b 11/03/1904 d 01/05/1965
- Natal - 1 Test (-) 1 match (-) *1928: NZ2.*

163 **Townsend, WH** (Taffy) b 12/03/1896 d
27/01/1943 - Natal - 1 Test (-) 11 matches (3 -
1T) *1921: NZ1.*

20 **Trenery, WE** (Wilfred) b 21/09/1867 d
23/08/1905 - GW - 1 Test (-) 1 match (-)
1891: BI2.

635 **Tromp, H** (Henry) b 29/12/1966 - NTvl - 4
Tests (-) 8 matches (5 - 1T) *1996: NZ3, 4,
Arg2(R), F1(R).*

581 **Truscott, JA** (Andries) b 22/07/1968 - NTvl
- No Tests - 4 matches (-) *Toured F & E. 1992.*

187 **Truter, DR** (Pally) b 19/04/1897 d
21/11/1962 - WP - 2 Tests (-) 2 matches (-)
1924: BI2, 4.

385 **Truter, JT** (Trix) b 05/06/1939 - Natal - 3
Tests (3 - 1T) 16 matches (33 - 11T) *1963: A1.
1964: F. 1965: A2.*

680 **Trytsman, JW** (Johnny) b 29/07/1971 - WP
- No Tests - 4 matches (-) *Toured BI & I. 1998.*

232 **Turner, FG** (Freddy) b 18/03/1914 d
12/09/2003 - EP - 11 Tests (29 - 4T, 4C, 3P) 24
matches (131 - 18T, 26C, 7P, 1D) *1933: A1, 2, 3.
1937: A1, 2, NZ1, 2, 3. 1938: BI1, 2, 3.*

349 **Twigge, RJ** (Robert) b 24/07/1936 - NTvl -
1 Test (-) 1 match (-) *1960: S.*

763 **Tyibilika, S** (Solly) b 23/06/1979 d
13/11/2011 - KZN - 8 Tests (15 - 3T) 8 matches
(15 - 3T) *2004: S, Arg. 2005: U, A2, Arg. 2006:
NZ1, A2, NZ2.*

879 **Ulengu, JI** (Jamba) b 07/01/1990 - BB - 1
Test (-) 2 matches (-) *2016:W.*

315 **Ulyate, CA** (Clive) b 11/12/1933 - Tvl - 7
Tests (6 - 1T, 1D) 16 matches (12 - 2T, 2D)
1955: BI1, 2, 3, 4. 1956: NZ1, 2, 3.

370 **Uys, P de W** (Piet) b 10/12/1937 d
12/12/2009 - NTvl - 12 Tests (-) 29 matches
(12 - 4T) *1960: W. 1961: E, S, I, A1, 2. 1962: BI1,
4. 1963: A1, 2. 1968: Tour of F – No Tests. 1969:
A1(R), 2.*

738 **Uys, PJ** (Pierre) b 05/02/1976 - Mpu - 1 Test
(-) 1 match (-) *2002: S.*

525 **Van Aswegen, HJ** (Henning) b 11/02/1955
- WP - 2 Tests (-) 10 matches (-) *1981: NZ1.
1982: S.Am2(R).*

718 **Van Biljon, L** (Lukas) b 16/03/1976 - Natal
- 13 Tests (5 - 1T) 13 matches (5 - 1T) *2001:
It1(R), NZ1, A1, 2, NZ2, F3, It2(R), E(R), US.
2002: F(R), S, E(R). 2003: NZ2(R).*

59 **Van Broekhuizen, HD** (Broekie) b
17/06/1872 d 04/08/1953 - WP - 1 Test (-) 1
match (-) *1896: BI4.*

2 **Van Buuren, MCWE** (Mosey) b 12/08/1865
d 03/10/1951 - Tvl - 1 Test (-) 1 match (-)
1891: BI1.

250 **Van de Vyver, DF** (Vandie) b 14/12/1909 d 18/03/1977 - WP - 1 Test (-) 14 matches (12 - 4T) *1937: A2.*

484 **Van den Berg, DS** (Derek) b 02/01/1946 - Natal - 4 Tests (-) 7 matches (-) *1974: Tour of F - No Tests. 1975: F1, 2. 1976: NZ1, 2.*

258 **Van den Berg, MA** (Mauritz) b 09/05/1909 d 09/04/1948 - WP - 4 Tests (-) 18 matches (15 - 5T) *1937: A1, NZ1, 2, 3.*

684 **Van den Berg, PA** (Albert) b 26/01/1974 - GW - 51 Tests (20 - 4T) 55 matches (30 - 6T) *1999: It1(R), 2, NZ2, A2, [S, U(R), E(R), A3(R), NZ3(R)]. 2000: E1(t+R), A1, NZ1, A2, NZ2(R), A3(t+R), Arg, I, W, E3. 2001: F1(R), 2, A2(R), NZ2(R), US. 2004: NZ1. 2005: U, F1, 2, A1(R), 2(R), 3(R), 4(R), Arg(R), F3(R). 2006: S2(R), A1(R), NZ1, A2(R), NZ2(R), A3(R), I, E1(R), 2(R). 2007: Sm1, A2(R), NZ2, Nam(t+R), S(R), [T, US.], W(R).*

621 **Van den Bergh, E** (Elandré) b 09/12/1966 - EP - 1 Test (-) 8 matches (5 - 1T) *1994: Arg2(t+R).*

133 **Van der Hoff, AD** (Apie) b 24/09/1888 d 09/03/1970 - Tvl - No Tests - 9 matches (30 - 10T) *Toured BI, I & F. 1912/13.*

629 **Van der Linde, A** (Toks) b 30/12/1969 - WP - 7 Tests (-) 18 matches (10 - 2T) *1995: It, E. 1996: Arg1(R), 2(R), F1(R), W(R). 2001: F3(R).*

741 **Van der Linde, CJ** (CJ) b 27/08/1980 - FS - 75 Tests (20 - 4T) 80 matches (20 - 4T) *2002: S(R), E(R). 2004: I1(R), 2(R), PI(R), A1(R), NZ2(t+R), A2(R), W2(R), I3(R), E(t+R), S, Arg. 2005: U, F1(R), 2, A1(R), 3, NZ1, A4, NZ2, Arg, W, F3. 2006: S2(R), F(R), A1, NZ1, A2, NZ2, I, E1, 2. 2007: E1(R), 2, A1(R), NZ1(R), A2, NZ2, Nam, S, [Sm, E3(R), T, US(R), Arg, E4.], W. 2008: W1(t+R), It, NZ1, 2, A1, Arg, NZ3, A2. 2009: F(R), I(t). 2010: W1, It1(R), NZ2, A1(t+R), NZ3(R), A2(R), 3(R), I(R), W2(R), S(R), E(R). 2011: A1(t+R), NZ1(R), 2(R), [Nam]. 2012: I, S(R).*

323 **Van der Merwe, AJ** (Bertus) b 14/07/1929 d 23/11/1971 - Boland - 12 Tests (-) 26 matches (3 - 1T) *1955: BI2, 3, 4. 1956: A1, 2, NZ1, 2, 3, 4. 1958: F1. 1960: S, NZ2.*

221 **Van der Merwe, AV** (Alvi) b 14/09/1908 d 18/09/1986 - WP - 1 Test (-) 13 matches (6 - 2T) *1931: W.*

273 **Van der Merwe, BS** (Fiks) b 02/01/1917 d 11/07/2005 - NTvl - 1 Test (-) 1 match (-) *1949: NZ1.*

703 **Van der Merwe, CP** (Carel) b 05/10/1971 - Boland - No Tests - 4 matches (-) *Toured Arg, I, W & E. 2000.*

846 **Van der Merwe, F** (Franco) b 15/03/1983 - GL - 1 Test (-) 1 match (-) *2012 - Tour of I, S & E. - No Tests. 2013: NZ2(R)*

365 **Van der Merwe, HS** (Stompie) b 24/08/1936 d 04/06/1988 - NTvl - 5 Tests (-) 17 matches (6 - 2T) *1960: NZ4. 1960-61: Tour of BI & F – No Tests. 1963: A2, 3, 4. 1964: F.*

790 **Van der Merwe, HS** (Heinke) b 03/05/1985 - GL - 5 Tests (-) 8 matches (-). *2007: W(t+R). 2009: Tour of F, It, I & E – No Tests. 2012: I(R), S(R), E4(R). 2015: A(R).*

433 **Van der Merwe, JP** (JP) b 07/12/1947 - WP - 1 Test (-) 12 matches (9 - 3T) *1970: W.*

858 **Van der Merwe, M** (Marcel) b 24/10/1990 - BB - 7 Tests (-) 7 matches (-) *2014: S(R), A1(R), NZ1(R), A2(R), NZ2(R). 2015: Arg1(R), 2.*

526 **Van der Merwe, PR** (Flippie) b 08/07/1957 - SWD - 6 Tests (-) 12 matches (-) *1981: NZ2, 3, US. 1986: NZC1, 2. 1989: WT1.*

818 **Van der Merwe, PR** (Flip) b 03/06/1985 - BB - 37 Tests (5 - 1T) 39 matches (5 - 1T) *2010: F(R), It2(R), A1(R), NZ3, A2, 3(R), I(R), W2(R), S(R), E(R). 2011: A1. 2012: E1(R), 2(R), 3(R), Arg1(R), 2(R), A1(R), NZ1, A2(R), NZ2(R), I(R), S(R), E4(R). 2013: It(R), S(R), Sm, Arg1(R),2(R), A1, NZ1, A2, W, S, F. 2014: W2. 2015: NZ1(R), Arg2(R).*

299 **Van der Ryst, FE** (Franz) b 17/10/1920 d 21/02/1981 - Tvl - No Tests - 14 matches (-) *Toured BI, I & F. 1951/52.*

263 **Van der Schyff, JH** (Jack) b 11/06/1928 d 02/12/2001 - GW - 5 Tests (10 - 2C, 2P) 5 matches (10 - 2C, 2P) *1949: NZ1, 2, 3, 4. 1955: BI1.*

434 **Van der Schyff, PJ** (Johan) b 19/01/1942 - WTvl - No Tests - 2 matches (-) *Toured BI & I. 1969/70.*

432 **Van der Watt, AE** (Andy) b 10/10/1946 - WP - 3 Tests (-) 22 matches (42 - 14T) *1969: S(R), E. 1970: I. 1971: Tour of A - No Tests.*

203 **Van der Westhuizen, JC** (JC) b 22/11/1905 d 08/07/2003 - WP - 4 Tests (3 - 1T) 19 matches (25 - 7T, 1D) *1928: NZ2, 3, 4. 1931: I.*

609 **Van der Westhuizen, JF** (Cabous) b 11/01/1965 - Natal - No Tests - 11 matches (10 - 2T) *Toured NZ 1994 and W, S & I. 1994.*

593 **Van der Westhuizen, JH** (Joost) b 20/02/1971, d 06/02/2017 - NTvl - 89 Tests (190 - 38T) 111 matches (280 - 56T) *1993: Tour of A - No Tests. 1993: Arg1, 2. 1994: E1, 2(R) 1994: Tour of NZ - No Tests. 1994: Arg2, S, W. 1995: WS1, [A, C(R), WS2, F, NZ], W, It, E. 1996: Fj, A1, 2(R), NZ2, 3, (R), A, 5, Arg1, 2, F1, 2, W. 1997: T, BI1, 2, 3, NZ1, A1, NZ2, A2, It, F1. 1998: I1, 2, W1, E1, A1, NZ1, 2, A2, W2, S, I3, E2. 1999: NZ2*, A2*, [S*, Sp(R), U*, E*, A3*, NZ3*]. 2000: C, E1, 2, A1(R), NZ1(R), A2(R), Arg, I, W, E3. 2001: F1, 2, It1(R), NZ1, A1, 2, NZ2, F3, It2, E, US(R). 2003:*

S1*, S2*, A1, NZ1, A2(R), NZ2, [U*, E, Sm, NZ3].

213 Van der Westhuizen, JH (Ponie) b 04/11/1909 d 05/03/1995 - WP - 3 Tests (-) 16 matches (45 - 12T, 1C, 2D) *1931: I. 1932: E, S.*

696 Van der Westhuyzen, JNB (Jaco) b 06/04/1978 - Mpu - 32 Tests (51 - 5T, 7C, 1P, 3D) 32 matches (51 - 5T, 7C, 1P, 3D) *2000: NZ2(R). 2001: It1(R). 2003: S1(R), 2, Arg, A1, [E, Sm, NZ3]. 2004: I1, 2, W1, PI, NZ1, A1, NZ2, A2, W2, I3, E, S, Arg. 2005: U, F1, 2, A1, 4(R), NZ2(R). 2006: S1, 2, F, A1.*

437 Van Deventer, PI (Piet) b 06/06/1946 d 14/03/2013- GW - No Tests - 12 matches (12 - 4T) *Toured BI & I. 1969/70.*

184 Van Druten, NJV (Jack) b 12/06/1898 d 16/01/1989 - Tvl - 8 Tests (6 - 2T) 8 matches (6 - 2T) *1924: BI1, 2, 3, 4. 1928: NZ1, 2, 3, 4.*

152 Van Heerden, AJ (Attie) b 10/03/1898 d 14/10/1965 - Tvl - 2 Tests (3 - 1T) 17 matches (42 - 14T) *1921: NZ1, 3.*

606 Van Heerden, FJ (Fritz) b 29/06/1970 - WP - 14 Tests (5 - 1T) 26 matches (5 - 1T) *1994: E1, 2(R), NZ3. 1995: It, E. 1996: NZ5(R), Arg1(R), 2(R). 1997: T, BI2(t+R), 3(R), NZ1(R), 2(R). 1999: [Sp].*

474 Van Heerden, JL (Moaner) b 18/07/1951 - NTvl - 17 Tests (4 - 1T) 23 matches (4 - 1T) *1974: BI3, 4, F1, 2. 1975: F1, 2. 1976: NZ1, 2, 3, 4. 1977: WT. 1980: BI1, 3, 4, S.Am3, 4, F.*

744 Van Heerden, JL (Wikus) b 25/02/1979 - GL - 14 Tests (5 - 1T) 16 matches (10 - 2T). *2003: S1, 2, A1, NZ1, A2(t). 2005: Tour of Arg, W & F – No Tests. 2006: Tour of UK – No Tests. 2007: A2, NZ2, S(R), [Sm(R), E3, T, US, Fj(R), E4(R).].*

272 Van Jaarsveld, CJ (Hoppy) b 21/02/1917 d 08/12/1980 - Tvl - 1 Test (-) 1 match (-) *1949: NZ1.*

354 Van Jaarsveldt, DC (Des) b 31/03/1929 - Rhodesia - 1 Test (3 - 1T) 1 match (3 - 1T) *1960: S*.*

368 Van Niekerk, BB (Bennie) b 01/12/1937 d 21/08/2000 - OFS - No Tests - 5 matches (3 - 1T) *Toured BI, I & F. 1960/61.*

210 Van Niekerk, JA (Jock) b 01/06/1907 d 19/04/1983 - WP - 1 Test (-) 2 matches (-) *1928: NZ4. 1931-32 Tour of BI & I – No Tests.*

719 Van Niekerk, JC (Joe) b 14/05/1980 - GL - 52 Tests (50 - 10T) 52 matches (50 - 10T) *2001: NZ1(R), A1(R), NZ2(t+R), F3(R), It2, US. 2002: W1(R), 2(R), Arg(R), Sm, NZ1, A1, NZ2, A2, F, S, E. 2003: A2, NZ2, [U, E, Geo, Sm]. 2004: NZ1(R), A1(t), NZ2, A2, W2, I3, E, S, Arg(R). 2005: U(R), F2(R), A1(R), 2, 3, NZ1, A4, NZ2. 2006: S1, 2, F, A1, NZ1(R), A2(R). 2008: It(R), NZ1, 2, Arg(R), A2(R). 2010: W1.*

259 Van Reenen, GL (George) b 29/03/1914 d

12/11/1967 - WP - 2 Tests (6 - 2T) 11 matches (24 - 8T) *1937: A2, NZ1.*

26 Van Renen, CG (Charlie) b 23/08/1868 d 20/07/1942 - WP - 3 Tests (-) 3 matches (-) *1891: BI3. 1896: BI1, 4.*

65 Van Renen, WA (Willie) b 29/08/1880 d 17/02/1942 - WP - 2 Tests (-) 2 matches (-) *1903: BI1, 3.*

558 Van Rensburg, JTJ (Theo) b 26/05/1967 - Tvl - 7 Tests (40 - 2C, 12P) 22 matches (182 - 7T, 21C, 34P, 1D) *1992: NZ, A, E. 1993: F1, 2, A1. 1994: NZ2.*

167 Van Rooyen, GW (Tank) b 09/12/1892 d 21/09/1942 - Tvl - 2 Tests (-) 13 matches (3 - 1T) *1921: NZ2, 3.*

124 Van Ryneveld, RCB (Clive) b 07/07/1891 d 25/08/1969 - WP - 2 matches (-) *1910: BI2, 3.*

631 Van Schalkwyk, D (Danie) b 01/02/1975 - NTvl - 8 Tests (10 - 2T) 8 matches (10 - 2T) *1996: Fj(R), NZ1, 2, 3. 1997: BI2, 3, NZ1, A1.*

278 Van Schoor, RAM (Ryk) b 03/12/1921 d 22/03/2009 - Rhodesia - 12 Tests (6 - 2T) 23 matches (21 - 7T) *1949: NZ2, 3, 4. 1951: S, I, W. 1952: E, F. 1953: A1, 2, 3, 4.*

483 Van Staden, JA (André) b 15/12/1945 - NTvl - No Tests - 3 matches (-) *Toured F. 1974.*

671 Van Straaten, AJJ (Braam) b 28/09/1971 - GF - 21 Tests (221 - 2T, 23C, 55P) 27 matches (294 - 5T, 46C, 59P) *1998: Tour of BI & I – No Tests. 1999: It2(R), W, NZ1(R), A1. 2000: C, E1, 2, NZ1, A2, NZ2, A3, Arg(R), I(R), W, E3. 2001: A1, 2, NZ2, F3, It2, E.*

314 Van Vollenhoven, KT (Tom) b 29/04/1935 - NTvl - 7 Tests (15 - 4T, 1D) 23 matches (63 - 20T, 1D) *1955: BI1, 2, 3, 4. 1956: A1, 2, NZ3.*

141 Van Vuuren, TFJ (Tom) b 09/07/1889 d 07/07/1947 - EP - 5 Tests (-) 17 matches (6 - 2T) *1912: S, I, W. 1913: E, F.*

304 Van Wyk, CJ (Basie) b 05/11/1923 d 29/08/2002 - Tvl - 10 Tests (18 - 6T) 23 matches (24 - 8T) *1951: S, I, W. 1952: E, F. 1953: A1, 2, 3, 4. 1955: BI1. 1956: Tour of A & NZ – No Tests*

445 Van Wyk, JFB (Piston) b 21/12/1943 - NTvl - 15 Tests (-) 19 matches (-) *1970: NZ1, 2, 3, 4. 1971: F1, 2, A1, 2, 3. 1972: E. 1974: BI1, 3, 4. 1976: NZ3, 4.*

196 Van Wyk, SP (SP) b 12/01/1901 d 22/01/1978 - WP - 2 Tests (-) 2 matches (-) *1928: NZ1, 2.*

378 Van Zyl, BP (Ben-Piet) b 01/08/1935 d 10/03/1973 - WP - 1 Test (6 - 2T) 5 matches (12 - 4T) *1960-61: Tour of BI, I & F – No Tests. 1961: I.*

410 Van Zyl, CGP (Sakkie) b 01/07/1932 - OFS - 4 Tests (-) 16 matches (6 - 2T) *1965: NZ1,*

2, 3, 4.

665 Van Zyl, DJ (Dan) b 08/01/1971 - Mpu - 1 Test (-) 7 matches (10 - 2C, 2P) *1997: Tour of It, F, E & S - No Tests. 2000: E(R).*

340 Van Zyl, GH (Hugo) b 20/08/1932 d 08/05/2007 - WP - 17 Tests (12 - 4T) 35 matches (27 - 9T) *1958: F1. 1960: S, NZ1, 2, 3, 4, W, I. 1961: E, S, F, I, A1, 2. 1962: BI1, 3, 4.*

357 Van Zyl, HJ (Hennie) b 31/01/1936 - Tvl - 10 Tests (18 - 6T) 24 matches (54 - 18T) *1960: NZ1, 2, 3, 4, I. 1961: E, S, I, A1, 2.*

852 Van Zyl, PE (Piet) b 14/09/1989 - FS - 3 Tests (-) 4 matches (-). *2013: S(R), Sm(R). 2016: W(R).*

373 Van Zyl, PJ (Piet) b 23/07/1933 d 28/05/1988 - Bol - 1 Test (-) 17 matches (3 - 1T) *1960-61: Tour of BI, I & F – No Tests. 1961: I.*

190 Vanderplank, BE (BV) b 29/04/1894 d 22/12/1990 - Natal - 2 Tests (-) 2 matches (-) *1924: BI3, 4.*

497 Veldsman, PE (Piet) b 11/03/1952 - WP - 1 Test (-) 1 match (-) *1977: WT.*

634 Venter, AG (André) b 14/11/1970 - FS - 66 Tests (45 - 9T) 70 matches (50 - 10T) *1996: NZ3, 4, 5, Arg1, 2, F1, 2, W. 1997: T, BI1, 2, 3, NZ1, A1, NZ2, It, F1, 2, E, S. 1998: I1, 2, W1, E1, A1, NZ1, 2, A2, W2, S(R), I3(R), E2(R). 1999: It1, 2(R), W(R), NZ1, A1, NZ2, A2, [S, U, E, A3, NZ3]. 2000: C, E1, 2, A1, NZ1, A2, NZ2, A3, Arg, I, W, E3. 2001: F1, It1, NZ1, A1, 2, NZ2, F3(R), It2(R), E(t+R), US(R).*

695 Venter, AJ (AJ) b 29/07/1973 - Natal - 25 Tests (-) 28 matches (-) *2000: W(R), E3(R). 2001: F3, It2, E, US. 2002: W1, 2, Arg, NZ1(R), 2, A2, F, S(R), E. 2003: Arg. 2004: PI, NZ1, A1, NZ2(R), A2, I3, E. 2006: NZ3, A3.*

605 Venter, B (Brendan) b 29/12/1969 - OFS - 17 Tests (10 - 2T) 26 matches (30 - 6T) *1994: E1, 2, NZ1, 2, 3, Arg1, 2. 1994: Tour of W, S & I – No Tests. 1995: [R, C, WS2(R), NZ(R)]. 1996: A1, NZ1, A2. 1999: A2, [S, U].*

214 Venter, FD (Floors) b 13/04/1909 d ??/??/1992 - Tvl - 3 Tests (-) 14 matches (24 - 8T) *1931: W. 1932: S. 1933: A3.*

877 Venter, JF (Francois) b 19/04/1991 - FS - 3 Tests (-) 4 matches (5 - 1T) *2016:E,It,W.*

672 Venter, SL (Lourens) b 25/06/1976 - GW - No Tests - 4 matches (15 - 3T) *Toured BI & I. 1998.*

838 Vermaak, J (Jano) b 01/01/1985 - BB - 3 Tests (-) 3 matches (-) *2013: It, A1(R), NZ1(R). Tour of W, S & F - No Tests.*

840 Vermeulen, DJ (Duane) b 03/07/1986 - WP - 37 Tests (10 - 2T) 38 matches (10 - 2T) *2012: A1, NZ1, A2, NZ2, I, S, E4. 2013: Arg1,2, A1, NZ1, A2, NZ 2, W, S, F. 2014: W1,2, S, Arg1,2, A1, NZ1, A2, NZ2, I, E, It, W3. 2015: [Sm, S, US, W, NZ2, Arg3]. 2016: I1, 2.*

25 Versfeld, C (Hasie) b 24/09/1866 d 06/01/1942 - WP - 1 Test (-) 1 match (-) *1891: BI3.*

7 Versfeld, M (Oupa) b 15/05/1860 d 01/09/1931 - WP - 3 Tests (-) 3 matches (-) *1891: BI1, 2, 3.*

3 Vigne, JT (Chubb) b 23/12/1868 d 09/04/1955 - Tvl - 3 Tests (-) 3 matches (-) *1891: BI1, 2, 3.*

448 Viljoen, JF (Joggie) b 14/05/1945 - GW - 6 Tests (6 - 2T) 10 matches (12 - 4T) *1971: F1, 2, A1, 2, 3. 1972: E.*

451 Viljoen, JT (Hannes) b 21/04/1943 - Natal - 3 Tests (6 - 2T) 10 matches (48 - 16T) *1971: A1, 2, 3.*

644 Viljoen, R (Joggie) b 22/07/1976 - WP - No Tests - 3 matches (-) *Toured Arg, F & W. 1996.*

808 Viljoen, R (Riaan) b 04/01/1983 - GW - No Tests - 2 matches (-) *Toured F, It, I & E. 2009.*

532 Villet, JV (John) b 03/11/1954 - WP - 2 Tests (-) 2 matches (-) *1984: E1, 2.*

530 Visagie, GP (Gawie) b 31/03/1955 d 19/11/2014 - Natal - No Tests - 3 matches (8 - 2T) *Toured NZ & US. 1981.*

683 Visagie, IJ (Cobus) b 31/10/1973 - WP - 29 Tests (-) 29 matches (-) *1999: It1, W, NZ1, A1, NZ2, A2, [S, U, E, A3, NZ3]. 2000: C, E2, A1, NZ1, A2, NZ2, A3. 2001: NZ1, A1, 2, NZ2, F3, It2(R), E(t+R), US. 2003: S1(R), 2(R), Arg.*

419 Visagie, PJ (Piet) b 16/04/1943 - GW - 25 Tests (130 - 6T, 20C, 19P, 5D) 44 matches (240 - 8T, 36C, 40P, 8D) *1967: F1, 2, 3, 4. 1968: BI1, 2, 3, 4, F1, 2. 1969: A1, 2, 3, 4, S, E. 1970: NZ1, 2, 3, 4. 1971: F1, 2, A1, 2, 3.*

536 Visagie, RG (Rudi) b 27/06/1959 - OFS - 5 Tests (-) 9 matches (5 - 1T) *1984: E1, 2, S.Am&Sp1, 2. 1993: F1. 1993: Tour of A No Tests.*

517 Visser, J de V (De Villiers) b 26/11/1958 - WP - 2 Tests (-) 12 matches (16 - 4T) *1980: Tour of S.Am – No Tests. 1981: NZ2, US.*

625 Visser, M (Mornay) b 30/03/1969 - WP - 1 Test (-) 1 match (-) *1995: WS1(R).*

237 Visser, PJ (Paul) b 25/12/1903 d 25/04/1963 - Tvl - 1 Test (-) 1 match (-). *1933: A2.*

293 Vivier, SS (Basie) b 01/03/1927 d 18/10/2009 - OFS - 5 Tests (11 - 4C, 1P) 31 matches (165 - 5T, 45C, 17P, 3D) *1951-52: Tour of BI & F – No Tests. 1956: A1*, 2*, NZ2*, 3*, 4*.*

471 Vogel, ML (Leon) b 22/10/1949 - OFS - 1 Test (-) 1 match (-) *1984: BI2(R).*

686 Von Hoesslin, DJB (Dave) b 10/05/1975 - GW - 5 Tests (10 - 2T) 5 matches (10 - 2T) *1999: It1(R), 2, W(R), NZ1, A1(R).*

681 Vos, AN (André) b 09/01/1975 - GL - 33 Tests (25 - 5T) 38 matches (30 - 6T) *1998: Tour of BI & I – No Tests. 1999: It1(t+R), 2, NZ1(R), 2(R), A2, [S(R), Sp*, E(R), A3(R), NZ3]. 2000: C*, E1*, 2*, A1*, NZ1*, A2*, NZ2*, A3*, Arg*, I*, W*, E3*. 2001: F1*, 2*, It1, NZ1, A1, 2, NZ2, F3,*

It2, E, US*.

491 **Wagenaar, C** (Christo) b 11/03/1952 - NTvl - 1 Test (-) 1 match (-) *1977: WT.*

269 **Wahl, JJ** (Ballie) b 10/07/1920 d 25/06/1978 - WP - 1 Test (-) 1 match (-) *1949: NZ1.*

170 **Walker, AP** (Alf) b 08/05/1893 d 17/07/1971 - Natal - 6 Tests (-) 14 matches (-) *1921: NZ1, 3. 1924: BI1, 2, 3, 4.*

311 **Walker, HN** (Harry) b 01/07/1928 d 05/08/2008 - OFS - 4 Tests (-) 19 matches (-) *1953: A3. 1956: A2, NZ1, 4.*

115 **Walker, HW** (Henry) b 22/02/1884 d 21/08/1951 - Tvl - 3 Tests (-) 3 matches (-) *1910: BI1, 2, 3.*

397 **Walton, DC** (Don) b 05/04/1939 - Natal - 8 Tests (-) 31 matches (12 - 4T) *1964: F. 1965: I, S, NZ3, 4. 1968: Tour of F - No Tests. 1969: A1, 2, E.*

739 **Wannenburg, PJ** (Pedrie) b 02/01/1981 - BB - 20 Tests (15 - 3T) 20 matches (15 - 3T) *2002: F(R), E. 2003: S1, 2, Arg, A1(t+R), NZ1(R). 2004: I1, 2, W1, PI(R). 2006: S1(R), F, NZ2(R), 3, A3. 2007: Sm1(R), NZ1(R), A2, NZ2.*

216 **Waring, FW** (Franky) b 07/11/1908 d 24/01/2000 - WP - 7 Tests (6 - 2T) 19 matches (12 - 4T) *1931: I. 1932: E. 1933: A1, 2, 3, 4, 5.*

707 **Wasserman, JG** (Johan) b 29/07/1977 - SWD - No Tests - 4 matches (5 - 1T) *Toured Arg, I, W & E. 2000*

786 **Watson, LA** (Luke) b 26/10/1983 - WP - 10 Tests (-) 10 matches (-) *2007: Sm1. 2008: W1, 2, It, NZ1(R), 2(R), Arg, NZ3(R), A2(R), 3(t+R).*

260 **Watt, HH** (Howard) b 01/03/1911 d 18/08/2005 - WP - No Tests - 7 matches (9 - 3T) *Toured A & NZ. 1937.*

154 **Weepner, JS** (Jackie) b 16/01/1896 d 14/12/1965 - WP - No Tests - 9 matches (6 - 2T) *Toured A & NZ. 1921.*

587 **Wegner, GN** (Nico) b 03/12/1968 - WP - 4 Tests (-) 12 matches (-) *1993: F2, A1, 2, 3.*

366 **Wentzel, GJ** (Giepie) b 28/02/1938 d 01/07/1996 - EP - No Tests - 12 matches (37 - 2T, 14C, 1P) *Toured BI, I & F. 1960/61.*

740 **Wentzel, M v Z** (Marco) b 05/05/1979 - Mpu - 2 Tests (-) 2 matches (-) *2002: F(R), S.*

664 **Wessels, JC** (Boeta) b 30/06/1973 - GW - No Tests - 1 match (-) *Toured It, F, E & S. 1997.*

35 **Wessels, JJ** (Scraps) b 13/09/1874 d 06/04/1929 - WP - 3 Tests (-) 3 matches (-) *1896: BI1, 2, 3.*

402 **Wessels, JW** (John) b 14/05/1935 b 22/01/2006 - OFS - No Tests - 2 matches (-) *Toured I & S. 1965.*

296 **Wessels, PW** (Piet) b 11/02/1926 d 24/08/1997 - OFS - No Tests - 14 matches (-) *Toured BI, I & F. 1951/52.*

459 **Whipp, PJM** (Peter) b 22/09/1950 - WP - 8 Tests (4 - 1T) 10 matches (4 - 1T) *1974: BI1, 2. 1974: Tour of F - No Tests. 1975: F1. 1976: NZ1, 3, 4. 1980: S.Am1, 2.*

217 **White, J** (Jimmy) b 20/05/1911 d 03/07/1997 - Border - 10 Tests (10 - 2T, 1D) 26 matches (23 - 5T, 2D) *1931: W. 1933: A1, 2, 3, 4, 5. 1937: A1, 2, NZ1, 2.*

863 **Whiteley, WR** (Warren) b 18/09/1987 - GL - 15 Tests (15 - 3T) 16 matches (15 - 3T) *2014: A1(R), NZ1(R). 2015: NZ1(R). 2016: I1(R), 2(R), 3, Arg1, 2, A1, NZ1, A2, NZ2, E, It, W.*

585 **Wiese, JJ** (Kobus) b 16/05/1964 - Tvl - 18 Tests (5 - 1T) 32 matches (15 - 3T) *1993: Tour of A – No Tests. 1994: Tours of NZ, W, S & I – No Tests. 1993: F1. 1995: WS1, [R, C, WS2, F, NZ], W, It, E. 1996: NZ3(R), 4(R), 5, Arg1, 2, F1, 2, W.*

743 **Willemse, AK** (Ashwin) b 08/09/1981 - GL - 19 Tests (20 - 4T) 20 matches (25 - 5T) *2003: S1, 2, NZ1, A2, NZ2, [U, E, Sm, NZ3]. 2004: W2, I3. 2007: E1, 2(R), Sm1, A1, NZ1, Nam, S(R), [T].*

120 **Williams, AE** (Arthur) b 01/07/1879 d 21/07/1930 - GW - 1 Test (-) 1 match (-) *1910: BI1.*

533 **Williams, AP** (Avril) b 10/02/1961 - WP - 2 Tests (-) 2 matches (-) *1984: E1, 2.*

589 **Williams, CM** (Chester) b 08/08/1970 - WP - 27 Tests (70 - 14T) 47 matches (135 - 27T) *1993: Tour of A – No Tests. 1993: Arg2. 1994: E1, 2, NZ1, 2, 3, Arg1, 2, S, W. 1995: WS1, [WS2, F, NZ], It, E. 1998: A1(t), NZ1(t). 2000: C(R), E1(t), 2(R), A1(R), NZ2, A3, Arg, I, W(R).*

231 **Williams, DO** (Dai) b 16/06/1913 d 24/12/1975 - WP - 8 Tests (15 - 5T) 18 matches (51 - 17T) *1931-32 Tour of BI & I – No Tests. 1937: A1, 2, NZ1, 2, 3. 1938: BI1, 2, 3.*

450 **Williams, JG** (John) b 29/10/1946 - NTvl - 13 Tests (-) 24 matches (3 - 1T) *1971: F1, 2, A1, 2, 3. 1972: E. 1974: BI1, 2, 4, F1, 2. 1976: NZ1, 2.*

363 **Wilson, LG** (Lionel) b 25/05/1933 - WP - 27 Tests (6 - 2D) 58 matches (19 - 3T, 2C, 2D) *1960: NZ3, 4, W, I. 1961: E, F, I, A1, 2. 1962: BI1, 2, 3, 4. 1963: A1, 2, 3, 4. 1964: W, F. 1965: I, S, A1, 2, NZ1, 2, 3, 4.*

495 **Wolmarans, BJ** (Barry) b 22/02/1953 - OFS - 1 Test (4 - 1T) 7 matches (4 - 1T) *1977: WT. 1981: Tour of NZ & US – No Tests.*

135 **Wrentmore, GM** (Bai) b 20/02/1893 d 16/08/1953 - WP - No Tests - 9 matches (27 - 3T, 5C, 2D) *Toured BI, I & F. 1912/13.*

548 **Wright, GD** (Garth) b 09/09/1963 - EP - 7 Tests (4 - 1T) 12 matches (4 - 1T) *1986: NZC3, 4. 1989: WT1, 2. 1992: F1, 2, E.*

381 **Wyness, MRK** (Wang) b 23/01/1937 d 06/11/2011 - WP - 5 Tests (3 - 1T) 5 matches (3 - 1T) *1962: BI1, 2, 3, 4. 1963: A2.*

153 **Zeller, WC** (Bill) b 18/07/1894 d 27/07/1969 - Natal - 2 Tests (-) 14 matches (39 - 13T) *1921: NZ2, 3.*

212 **Zimerman, M** (Morris) b 08/06/1911 - d 09/01/1992 - WP - 4 Tests (3 - 1T) 18 matches (42 - 14T) *1931: W, I. 1932: E, S.*

PROVINCIAL REPRESENTATION

South Africa's 881 International Players have come from 15 unions as follows:

Western Province	262
Golden Lions (former Transvaal)	170
Blue Bulls (former Northern Transvaal)	112
Free State (former Orange Free State)	85
KwaZulu-Natal (former Natal)	79
Griqualand West	63
Eastern Province	34
Border	16
Boland	15
Falcons (former Eastern Transvaal)	10
Mpumalanga (former South Eastern Transvaal)	10
Leopards (former Western Transvaal)	9
Zimbabwe (former Rhodesia)	8
South Western Districts	5
Namibia (former South West Africa)	3
TOTAL	881

Western Province's latest Springbok, Bongi Mbonambi.

SOUTH AFRICA TEST RESULTS 1891 – 2016

OPPONENTS	PLAYED	WON	LOST	DRAWN	% WON	PF	PA	SOUTH AFRICA T	C	P	D	OPPONENTS T	C	P	D
Argentina	24	21	2	1	88%	857	472	100	78	65	2	42	35	60	4
Australia	83	46	36	1	55%	1607	1448	188	110	180	21	148	95	179	12
British Isles	46	23	17	6	50%	600	516	95	48	52	7	68	30	59	14
Canada	2	2	0	0	100%	71	18	10	6	3	0	2	1	2	0
England	38	23	13	2	61%	801	629	74	50	102	15	46	31	109	7
Fiji	3	3	0	0	100%	129	41	16	11	9	0	4	3	5	0
France	39	22	11	6	56%	783	578	89	60	93	7	51	28	81	19
Georgia	1	1	0	0	100%	46	19	7	4	1	0	1	1	4	0
Ireland	25	18	6	1	72%	503	342	69	39	42	5	31	21	50	4
Italy	13	12	1	0	92%	617	165	84	67	21	0	14	10	24	1
Japan	1	0	1	0	0%	32	34	4	3	2	0	3	2	5	0
Namibia	2	2	0	0	100%	192	13	27	24	2	0	3	1	2	0
New Zealand	93	35	55	3	38%	1458	1863	140	93	190	29	201	123	212	21
NZ Cavaliers	4	3	1	0	75%	96	62	7	7	15	3	5	3	11	1
Pacific Islands	1	1	0	0	100%	38	24	4	1	4	0	4	2	0	0
Romania	1	1	0	0	100%	21	8	2	1	3	0	1	0	1	0
Scotland	26	21	5	0	81%	686	286	86	60	54	6	28	21	37	3
South America	6	5	1	0	83%	156	86	22	16	6	6	7	5	13	3
S America & Spain	2	2	0	0	100%	54	28	9	3	6	0	3	2	4	2
Spain	1	1	0	0	100%	47	3	7	6	0	0	0	0	3	0
Tonga	2	2	0	0	100%	104	35	16	9	2	0	4	3	3	0
USA	4	4	0	0	100%	209	42	33	23	2	0	4	1	6	1
Uruguay	3	3	0	0	100%	245	12	38	23	3	0	0	0	4	0
Wales	32	28	3	1	88%	850	486	103	71	68	3	39	24	78	5
Western Samoa/Samoa	9	9	0	0	100%	431	99	59	38	19	1	12	6	9	0
World Teams (official Tests)	3	3	0	0	100%	87	59	11	5	10	0	9	7	3	0
	464	291	152	21	62,7%	10720	7368	1300	858	953	106	728	455	962	95

Records

COMPARATIVE WIN RATIO vs MAJOR RIVALS*

	Played	Won	Win%
New Zealand	552	426	77,2%
SOUTH AFRICA	464	291	62,7%
England	705	385	54,6%
France	732	399	54,5%
Argentina	418	223	53,3%
Wales	694	358	51,6%
Australia	604	309	51,2%
Ireland	666	289	43,4%
Scotland	663	282	42,5%
Italy	473	181	38,3%

Correct as at 31 December, 2016

TEST MATCHES BY DECADE

	Played	Won	Lost	Drawn	Win %	Prog. win %
1891-1900	7	1	6	0	14,3%	14,3%
1901-1910	10	5	2	3	50%	35,3%
1911-1920	5	5	0	0	100%	50%
1921-1930	11	6	3	2	54,5%	51,5%
1931-1940	17	13	4	0	76,5%	60,0%
1941-1950	4	4	0	0	100%	63,0%
1951-1960	28	18	8	2	64,3%	63,4%
1961-1970	46	26	14	6	56,5%	60,9%
1971-1980	28	20	6	2	71,4%	62,8%
1981-1990	18	14	4	0	77,8%	64,4%
1991-2000	94	60	32	2	63,8%	64,2%
2001-2010	127	78	47	2	61,4%	63,3%
2011-2020	69	41	26	2	59,4%	62,7%
	464	291	152	21		

WORLD RUGBY RANKINGS AS AT 5 DECEMBER, 2016

1	New Zealand	94,78	9	Argentina	79,91
2	England	90,46	10	Fiji	76,46
3	Australia	86,35	11	Japan	74,22
4	Ireland	84,62	12	Georgia	74,14
5	Wales	82,55	13	Italy	72,47
6	SOUTH AFRICA	81,79	14	Tonga	71,94
7	Scotland	80,67	15	Samoa	71,25
8	France	80,13			

SOUTH AFRICA'S TEST, OVERSEAS TOUR & OTHER SPRINGBOK MATCHES

Test No.	Tour Match	Date	Venue	Opponent	Captain	Result	PF	PA
1		30/07/1891	Port Elizabeth	BRITISH ISLES	HH Castens	Lost	0	4
2		29/08/1891	Kimberley	BRITISH ISLES	RCD Snedden	Lost	0	3
3		05/09/1891	Cape Town	BRITISH ISLES	AR Richards	Lost	0	4
4		30/07/1896	Port Elizabeth	BRITISH ISLES	FTD Aston	Lost	0	8
5		22/08/1896	Johannesburg	BRITISH ISLES	FTD Aston	Lost	8	17
6		29/08/1896	Kimberley	BRITISH ISLES	FTD Aston	Lost	3	9
7		05/09/1896	Cape Town	BRITISH ISLES	BH Heatlie	Won	5	0
8		26/08/1903	Johannesburg	BRITISH ISLES	A Frew	Drew	10	10
9		05/09/1903	Kimberley	BRITISH ISLES	JM Powell	Drew	0	0
10		12/09/1903	Cape Town	BRITISH ISLES	BH Heatlie	Won	8	0
	1	27/09/1906	Northampton	East Midlands	PJ Roos	Won	37	0
	2	29/09/1906	Leicester	Midland Counties	PJ Roos	Won	29	0
	3	03/10/1906	Blackheath	Kent	PJ Roos	Won	21	0
	4	06/10/1906	West Hartlepool	Durham	PJ Roos	Won	22	4
	5	10/10/1906	Newcastle	Northumberland	PJ Roos	Won	44	0
	6	13/10/1906	Leeds	Yorkshire	PJ Roos	Won	34	0
	7	17/10/1906	Plymouth	Devon	PJ Roos	Won	22	6
	8	20/10/1906	Taunton	Somerset	WAG Burger	Won	14	0
	9	24/10/1906	Richmond	Middlesex	PJ Roos	Won	9	0
	10	27/10/1906	Newport	Newport	PJ Roos	Won	8	0
	11	31/10/1906	Cardiff	Glamorgan	PJ Roos	Won	6	3
	12	03/11/1906	Gloucester	Gloucestershire	HW Carolin	Won	23	0
	13	07/11/1906	Oxford	Oxford University	PJ Roos	Won	24	3
	14	10/11/1906	Cambridge	Cambridge University	FJ Dobbin	Won	29	0
	15	13/11/1906	Hawick	South of Scotland	HW Carolin	Won	32	5
11		17/11/1906	Glasgow	SCOTLAND	HW Carolin	Lost	0	6
	16	20/11/1906	Aberdeen	North of Scotland	FJ Dobbin	Won	35	3
12		24/11/1906	Belfast	IRELAND	PJ Roos	Won	15	12
	17	27/11/1906	Dublin	Dublin University	HW Carolin	Won	28	3
13		01/12/1906	Swansea	WALES	PJ Roos	Won	11	0
14		08/12/1906	London	ENGLAND	PJ Roos	Drew	3	3
	18	12/12/1906	Manchester	Lancashire	PJ Roos	Won	11	8
	19	15/12/1906	Carlisle	Cumberland	PJ Roos	Won	21	0
	20	19/12/1906	Richmond	Surrey	PJ Roos	Won	33	0
	21	22/12/1906	Redruth	Cornwall	PJ Roos	Won	9	3
	22	26/12/1906	Newport	Monmouthshire	PJ Roos	Won	17	0
	23	29/12/1906	Llanelli	Llanelli	PJ Roos	Won	16	3
	24	01/01/1907	Cardiff	Cardiff	PJ Roos	Lost	0	17
15		06/08/1910	Johannesburg	BRITISH ISLES	DFT Morkel	Won	14	10
16		27/08/1910	Port Elizabeth	BRITISH ISLES	WA Millar	Lost	3	8
17		03/09/1910	Cape Town	BRITISH ISLES	WA Millar	Won	21	5
	25	03/10/1912	Bath	Somerset	WA Millar	Won	24	3
	26	05/10/1912	Exeter	Devon	WA Millar	Won	8	0
	27	10/10/1912	Redruth	Cornwall	DFT Morkel	Won	15	6
	28	12/10/1912	Newport	Monmouthshire	WA Millar	Won	16	0
	29	17/10/1912	Cardiff	Glamorgan	WA Millar	Won	35	3
	30	19/10/1912	Llanelli	Llanelli	FJ Dobbin	Won	8	7
	31	24/10/1912	Newport	Newport	WA Millar	Lost	3	9
	32	26/10/1912	Blackheath	London	WA Millar	Won	12	8

SPRINGBOKS

SOUTH AFRICA'S TESTS & OTHER SPRINGBOK MATCHES

Test No.	Tour Match	Date	Venue	Opponent	Captain	Result	PF	PA
	33	30/10/1912	Portsmouth	United Services	WA Millar	Won	18	16
	34	02/11/1912	Northampton	East Midlands	WA Millar	Won	14	5
	35	06/11/1912	Oxford	Oxford University	WA Millar	Won	6	0
	36	09/11/1912	Leicester	Midland Counties	WA Millar	Won	25	3
	37	14/11/1912	Cambridge	Cambridge University	DFT Morkel	Won	24	0
	38	16/11/1912	Twickenham	London	WA Millar	Lost	8	10
	39	20/11/1912	Newcastle	North of England	DFT Morkel	Won	17	0
18		23/11/1912	Edinburgh	SCOTLAND	FJ Dobbin	Won	16	0
	40	27/11/1912	Glasgow	West of Scotland	WA Millar	Won	38	3
19		30/11/1912	Dublin	IRELAND	WA Millar	Won	38	0
	41	04/12/1912	Belfast	Ulster	WA Millar	Won	19	0
	42	07/12/1912	Birkenhead	North of England	DFT Morkel	Won	21	8
20		14/12/1912	Cardiff	WALES	WA Millar	Won	3	0
	43	19/12/1912	Neath	Neath	WA Millar	Won	8	3
	44	21/12/1912	Cardiff	Cardiff	WA Millar	Won	7	6
	45	26/12/1912	Swansea	Swansea	WA Millar	Lost	0	3
	46	28/12/1912	Bristol	Gloucestershire	DFT Morkel	Won	11	0
21		04/01/1913	Twickenham	ENGLAND	DFT Morkel	Won	9	3
22		11/01/1913	Bordeaux	FRANCE	WA Millar	Won	38	5
	47	25/06/1921	Sydney	New South Wales	TB Pienaar	Won	25	10
	48	27/06/1921	Sydney	New South Wales	TB Pienaar	Won	16	11
	49	02/07/1921	Sydney	New South Wales	WH Morkel	Won	28	9
	50	06/07/1921	Sydney	Metropolitan	WH Morkel	Won	14	8
	51	13/07/1921	Wanganui	Wanganui	TB Pienaar	Won	11	6
	52	16/07/1921	New Plymouth	Taranaki	WH Morkel	Drew	0	0
	53	20/07/1921	Masterton	Wairarapa-Bush	TB Pienaar	Won	18	3
	54	23/07/1921	Wellington	Wellington	TB Pienaar	Won	8	3
	55	27/07/1921	Greymouth	West Coast - Buller	HJL Morkel	Won	33	3
	56	30/07/1921	Christchurch	Canterbury	TB Pienaar	Lost	4	6
	57	03/08/1921	Timaru	South Canterbury	WH Morkel	Won	34	3
	58	06/08/1921	Invercargill	Southland	TB Pienaar	Won	12	0
	59	10/08/1921	Dunedin	Otago	WH Morkel	Won	11	3
23		13/08/1921	Dunedin	NEW ZEALAND	WH Morkel	Lost	5	13
	60	17/08/1921	Palmerston N.	Manawatu-Horowhenua	TB Pienaar	Won	3	0
	61	20/08/1921	Auckland	Auckland - North Auckland	TL Krüger	Won	24	8
	62	24/08/1921	Rotorua	Bay of Plenty	TL Krüger	Won	17	9
24		27/08/1921	Auckland	NEW ZEALAND	WH Morkel	Won	9	5
	63	31/08/1921	Hamilton	Waikato	TB Pienaar	Won	6	0
	64	03/09/1921	Napier	Hawkes Bay - Poverty Bay	TB Pienaar	Won	14	8
	65	07/09/1921	Napier	New Zealand Maoris	WH Morkel	Won	9	8
	66	10/09/1921	Nelson	Nelson, Marlborough & Golden Bay - Motueka	JP Michau	Won	26	3
25		17/09/1921	Wellington	NEW ZEALAND	WH Morkel	Drew	0	0
26		16/08/1924	Durban	BRITISH ISLES	PK Albertyn	Won	7	3
27		23/08/1924	Johannesburg	BRITISH ISLES	PK Albertyn	Won	17	0
28		13/09/1924	Port Elizabeth	BRITISH ISLES	PK Albertyn	Drew	3	3
29		20/09/1924	Cape Town	BRITISH ISLES	PK Albertyn	Won	16	9
30		30/06/1928	Durban	NEW ZEALAND	PJ Mostert	Won	17	0
31		21/07/1928	Johannesburg	NEW ZEALAND	PJ Mostert	Lost	6	7

216

www.sarugby.co.za   SA RUGBY ANNUAL 2017

SOUTH AFRICA'S TESTS & OTHER SPRINGBOK MATCHES

Test No.	Tour Match	Date	Venue	Opponent	Captain	Result	PF	PA
32		18/08/1928	Port Elizabeth	NEW ZEALAND	PJ Mostert	Won	11	6
33		01/09/1928	Cape Town	NEW ZEALAND	PJ Mostert	Lost	5	13
	67	03/10/1931	Bristol	Gloucestershire & Somerset	BL Osler	Won	14	3
	68	08/10/1931	Newport	Newport	BL Osler	Won	15	3
	69	10/10/1931	Swansea	Swansea	JC van der Westhuizen	Won	10	3
	70	14/10/1931	Abertillery	Abertillery & Cross Keys	BL Osler	Won	10	9
	71	17/10/1931	Twickenham	London	BL Osler	Won	30	3
	72	21/10/1931	Birmingham	Midland Counties	PJ Mostert	Won	13	3
	73	24/10/1931	Sunderland	Durham & Northumberland	JC van der Westhuizen	Won	41	0
	74	28/10/1931	Glasgow	Glasgow	JC van der Westhuizen	Won	21	13
	75	31/10/1931	Melrose	South of Scotland	MM Louw	Drew	0	0
	76	04/11/1931	Cambridge	Cambridge University	BL Osler	Won	21	9
	77	07/11/1931	Twickenham	Combined Services	BL Osler	Won	23	0
	78	12/11/1931	Oxford	Oxford University	BL Osler	Won	24	3
	79	14/11/1931	Leicester	Midland Counties	JC van der Westhuizen	Lost	21	30
	80	18/11/1931	Devonport	Devon & Cornwall	BL Osler	Drew	3	3
	81	21/11/1931	Cardiff	Cardiff	BL Osler	Won	13	5
	82	24/11/1931	Llanelli	Llanelli	MM Louw	Won	9	0
	83	28/11/1931	Neath	Neath & Aberavon	BL Osler	Won	8	3
34		05/12/1931	Swansea	WALES	BL Osler	Won	8	3
	84	09/12/1931	Liverpool	Lancashire & Cheshire	BL Osler	Won	20	9
	85	12/12/1931	Belfast	Ulster	MM Louw	Won	30	3
35		19/12/1931	Dublin	IRELAND	BL Osler	Won	8	3
	86	26/12/1931	Twickenham	London	BL Osler	Won	16	8
36		02/01/1932	Twickenham	ENGLAND	BL Osler	Won	7	0
	87	06/01/1932	Workington	Yorkshire & Cumberland	BL Osler	Won	27	5
	88	09/01/1932	Aberdeen	North of Scotland	JC van der Westhuizen	Won	9	0
37		16/01/1932	Edinburgh	SCOTLAND	BL Osler	Won	6	3
38		08/07/1933	Cape Town	AUSTRALIA	PJ Nel	Won	17	3
39		22/07/1933	Durban	AUSTRALIA	BL Osler	Lost	6	21
40		12/08/1933	Johannesburg	AUSTRALIA	PJ Nel	Won	12	3
41		26/08/1933	Port Elizabeth	AUSTRALIA	PJ Nel	Won	11	0
42		02/09/1933	Bloemfontein	AUSTRALIA	PJ Nel	Lost	4	15
	89	12/06/1937	Melbourne	Victoria	PJ Nel	Won	45	11
	90	16/06/1937	Orange	Combined Western Districts	GH Brand	Won	63	0
	91	19/06/1937	Sydney	New South Wales	PJ Nel	Lost	6	17
43		26/06/1937	Sydney	AUSTRALIA	PJ Nel	Won	9	5
	92	30/06/1937	Newcastle	Newcastle	PJ Nel	Won	58	8
	93	03/07/1937	Brisbane	Australian XV	PJ Nel	Won	36	3
	94	07/07/1937	Toowoomba	Toowoomba	PJ Nel	Won	60	0
	95	10/07/1937	Brisbane	Queensland	PJ Nel	Won	39	4
44		17/07/1937	Sydney	AUSTRALIA	PJ Nel	Won	26	17
	96	24/07/1937	Auckland	Auckland	PJ Nel	Won	19	5
	97	28/07/1937	Hamilton	Waikato-King Country-Thames Valley	PJ Nel	Won	6	3
	98	31/07/1937	New Plymouth	Taranaki	PJ Nel	Won	17	3
	99	04/08/1937	Palmerston N.	Manawatu	PJ Nel	Won	39	3
	100	07/08/1937	Wellington	Wellington	GH Brand	Won	29	0

SOUTH AFRICA'S TESTS & OTHER SPRINGBOK MATCHES

Test No.	Tour Match	Date	Venue	Opponent	Captain	Result	PF	PA
45		14/08/1937	Wellington	NEW ZEALAND	DH Craven	Lost	7	13
	101	18/08/1937	Blenheim	Nelson-Golden Bay-Motueka-Marlborough	PJ Nel	Won	22	0
	102	21/08/1937	Christchurch	Canterbury	PJ Nel	Won	23	8
	103	25/08/1937	Greymouth	West Coast-Buller	PJ Nel	Won	31	6
	104	28/08/1937	Timaru	South Canterbury	PJ Nel	Won	43	6
46		04/09/1937	Christchurch	NEW ZEALAND	PJ Nel	Won	13	6
	105	08/09/1937	Invercargill	Southland	PJ Nel	Won	30	17
	106	11/09/1937	Dunedin	Otago	DH Craven	Won	47	7
	107	15/09/1937	Napier	Hawke's Bay	PJ Nel	Won	21	12
	108	18/09/1937	Gisborne	Poverty Bay-Bay of Plenty-East Coast	PJ Nel	Won	33	3
47		25/09/1937	Auckland	NEW ZEALAND	PJ Nel	Won	17	6
	109	29/09/1937	Whangarei	North Auckland	PJ Nel	Won	14	6
48		06/08/1938	Johannesburg	BRITISH ISLES	DH Craven	Won	26	12
49		03/09/1938	Port Elizabeth	BRITISH ISLES	DH Craven	Won	19	3
50		10/09/1938	Cape Town	BRITISH ISLES	DH Craven	Lost	16	21
51		16/07/1949	Cape Town	NEW ZEALAND	F du Plessis	Won	15	11
52		13/08/1949	Johannesburg	NEW ZEALAND	F du Plessis	Won	12	6
53		03/09/1949	Durban	NEW ZEALAND	F du Plessis	Won	9	3
54		17/09/1949	Port Elizabeth	NEW ZEALAND	BJ Kenyon	Won	11	8
	110	10/10/1951	Bournemouth	South Eastern Counties	BJ Kenyon	Won	31	6
	111	13/10/1951	Plymouth	South Western Counties	HSV Muller	Won	17	8
	112	18/10/1951	Pontypool	Pontypool & Newbridge	BJ Kenyon	Won	15	6
	113	20/10/1951	Cardiff	Cardiff	HSV Muller	Won	11	9
	114	23/10/1951	Llanelli	Llanelli	BJ Kenyon	Won	20	11
	115	27/10/1951	Liverpool	North Western Counties	BJ Kenyon	Won	16	9
	116	31/10/1951	Glasgow	Glasgow & Edinburgh	HSV Muller	Won	43	11
	117	03/11/1951	Newcastle	North Eastern Counties	BJ Kenyon	Won	19	8
	118	08/11/1951	Cambridge	Cambridge University	HSV Muller	Won	30	0
	119	10/11/1951	Twickenham	London Counties	HSV Muller	Lost	9	11
	120	15/11/1951	Oxford	Oxford University	HSV Muller	Won	24	3
	121	17/11/1951	Port Talbot	Neath & Aberavon	HSV Muller	Won	22	0
55		24/11/1951	Edinburgh	SCOTLAND	HSV Muller	Won	44	0
	122	28/11/1951	Aberdeen	North of Scotland	JA du Rand	Won	14	3
	123	01/12/1951	Belfast	Ulster	HSV Muller	Won	27	5
56		08/12/1951	Dublin	IRELAND	HSV Muller	Won	17	5
	124	11/12/1951	Limerick	Munster	PA du Toit	Won	11	6
	125	15/12/1951	Swansea	Swansea	HSV Muller	Won	11	3
57		22/12/1951	Cardiff	WALES	HSV Muller	Won	6	3
	126	26/12/1951	Twickenham	Combined Services	SP Fry	Won	24	8
	127	29/12/1951	Leicester	Midland Counties	B Myburgh	Won	3	0
58		05/01/1952	Twickenham	ENGLAND	HSV Muller	Won	8	3
	128	10/01/1952	Newport	Newport	HSV Muller	Won	12	6
	129	12/01/1952	Bristol	Western Counties	PA du Toit	Won	16	5
	130	16/01/1952	Coventry	Midland Counties	PA du Toit	Won	19	8
	131	19/01/1952	Hawick	South of Scotland	HSV Muller	Won	13	3
	132	26/01/1952	Cardiff	Barbarians	HSV Muller	Won	17	3
	133	02/02/1952	Lyon	South Eastern France	HSV Muller	Won	9	3

SOUTH AFRICA'S TESTS & OTHER SPRINGBOK MATCHES

Test No.	Tour Match	Date	Venue	Opponent	Captain	Result	PF	PA
	134	07/02/1952	Bordeaux	South Western France	SP Fry	Won	20	12
	135	09/02/1952	Toulouse	France 'B'	HSV Muller	Won	9	6
59		16/02/1952	Paris	FRANCE	HSV Muller	Won	25	3
60		22/08/1953	Johannesburg	AUSTRALIA	HSV Muller	Won	25	3
61		05/09/1953	Cape Town	AUSTRALIA	HSV Muller	Lost	14	18
62		19/09/1953	Durban	AUSTRALIA	HSV Muller	Won	18	8
63		26/09/1953	Port Elizabeth	AUSTRALIA	HSV Muller	Won	22	9
64		06/08/1955	Johannesburg	BRITISH ISLES	SP Fry	Lost	22	23
65		20/08/1955	Cape Town	BRITISH ISLES	SP Fry	Won	25	9
66		03/09/1955	Pretoria	BRITISH ISLES	SP Fry	Lost	6	9
67		24/09/1955	Port Elizabeth	BRITISH ISLES	SP Fry	Won	22	8
	136	15/05/1956	Canberra	Australian Capital Territories	SS Vivier	Won	41	6
	137	19/05/1956	Sydney	New South Wales	SS Vivier	Won	29	9
	138	22/05/1956	Tamworth	New South Wales Country	JAJ Pickard	Won	15	8
68		26/05/1956	Sydney	AUSTRALIA	SS Vivier	Won	9	0
	139	29/05/1956	Brisbane	Queensland	SS Vivier	Won	47	3
69		02/06/1956	Brisbane	AUSTRALIA	SS Vivier	Won	9	0
	140	09/06/1956	Hamilton	Waikato	JAJ Pickard	Lost	10	14
	141	13/06/1956	Whangarei	North Auckland	SS Vivier	Won	3	0
	142	16/06/1956	Auckland	Auckland	SS Vivier	Won	6	3
	143	20/06/1956	Palmerston N.	Manawatu-Horowhenua	AC Koch	Won	14	3
	144	23/06/1956	Wellington	Wellington	JA du Rand	Won	8	6
	145	27/06/1956	Gisborne	Poverty Bay-East Coast	JA du Rand	Won	22	0
	146	30/06/1956	Napier	Hawke's Bay	JA du Rand	Won	20	8
	147	04/07/1956	Nelson	Nelson, Marlborough & Golden Bay - Motueka	JA du Rand	Won	41	3
	148	07/07/1956	Dunedin	Otago	JA du Rand	Won	14	9
70		14/07/1956	Dunedin	NEW ZEALAND	JA du Rand	Lost	6	10
	149	18/07/1956	Timaru	S Canterbury, Mid Canterbury & North Otago	JAJ Pickard	Won	20	8
	150	21/07/1956	Christchurch	Canterbury	JA du Rand	Lost	6	9
	151	25/07/1956	Westport	West Coast-Buller	SS Vivier	Won	27	6
	152	28/07/1956	Invercargill	Southland	JA du Rand	Won	23	12
	153	31/07/1956	Masterton	Wairarapa-Bush	SS Vivier	Won	19	8
71		04/08/1956	Wellington	NEW ZEALAND	SS Vivier	Won	8	3
	154	08/08/1956	Wanganui	Wanganui-King Country	SS Vivier	Won	36	16
	155	11/08/1956	New Plymouth	Taranaki	SS Vivier	Drew	3	3
72		18/08/1956	Christchurch	NEW ZEALAND	SS Vivier	Lost	10	17
	156	22/08/1956	Wellington	New Zealand Universities	SS Vivier	Lost	15	22
	157	25/08/1956	Auckland	New Zealand Maoris	SS Vivier	Won	37	0
	158	28/08/1956	Rotorua	Bay of Plenty-Thames Valley-Counties	SS Vivier	Won	17	6
73		01/09/1956	Auckland	NEW ZEALAND	SS Vivier	Lost	5	11
74		26/07/1958	Cape Town	FRANCE	JT Claasen	Drew	3	3
75		16/08/1958	Johannesburg	FRANCE	JT Claasen	Lost	5	9
76		30/04/1960	Port Elizabeth	SCOTLAND	DC van Jaarsveld	Won	18	10
77		25/06/1960	Johannesburg	NEW ZEALAND	RG Dryburgh	Won	13	0
78		23/07/1960	Cape Town	NEW ZEALAND	RG Dryburgh	Lost	3	11
79		13/08/1960	Bloemfontein	NEW ZEALAND	AS Malan	Drew	11	11

SOUTH AFRICA'S TESTS & OTHER SPRINGBOK MATCHES

Test No.	Tour Match	Date	Venue	Opponent	Captain	Result	PF	PA
80		27/08/1960	Port Elizabeth	NEW ZEALAND	AS Malan	Won	8	3
	159	22/10/1960	Hove	Southern Counties	AS Malan	Won	29	9
	160	26/10/1960	Oxford	Oxford University	RJ Lockyear	Won	24	5
	161	29/10/1960	Cardiff	Cardiff	AS Malan	Won	13	0
	162	02/11/1960	Pontypool	Pontypool & Cross Keys	JT Claasen	Won	30	3
	163	05/11/1960	Leicester	Midland Counties	RJ Lockyear	Drew	3	3
	164	09/11/1960	Cambridge	Cambridge University	AS Malan	Won	12	0
	165	12/11/1960	Twickenham	London Counties	AS Malan	Won	20	3
	166	16/11/1960	Glasgow	Glasgow & Edinburgh	JT Claasen	Won	16	11
	167	19/11/1960	Hawick	South of Scotland	AS Malan	Won	19	3
	168	23/11/1960	Manchester	North Western Counties	JT Claasen	Won	11	0
	169	26/11/1960	Swansea	Swansea	RJ Lockyear	Won	19	3
	170	29/11/1960	Ebbw Vale	Ebbw Vale & Abertillery	AS Malan	Won	3	0
81		03/12/1960	Cardiff	WALES	AS Malan	Won	3	0
	171	07/12/1960	Camborne	South Western Counties	AS Malan	Won	21	9
	172	10/12/1960	Gloucester	Western Counties	AS Malan	Won	42	0
	173	13/12/1960	Llanelli	Llanelli	AS Malan	Won	21	0
82		17/12/1960	Dublin	IRELAND	AS Malan	Won	8	3
	174	21/12/1960	Cork	Munster	JT Claasen	Won	9	3
	175	26/12/1960	Twickenham	Combined Services	AS Malan	Won	14	5
	176	28/12/1960	Birmingham	Midland Couties	AS Malan	Won	16	5
	177	31/12/1960	Gosforth	North Eastern Counties	JT Claasen	Won	21	9
	178	03/01/1961	Bournemouth	South Eastern Counties	AS Malan	Won	24	0
83		07/01/1961	Twickenham	ENGLAND	AS Malan	Won	5	0
	179	11/01/1961	Newport	Newport	AS Malan	Won	3	0
	180	14/01/1961	Neath	Neath & Aberavon	AS Malan	Won	25	5
84		21/01/1961	Edinburgh	SCOTLAND	AS Malan	Won	12	5
	181	25/01/1961	Aberdeen	North of Scotland	AS Malan	Won	22	9
	182	28/01/1961	Belfast	Ulster	JT Claasen	Won	19	6
	183	01/02/1961	Dublin	Leinster	AS Malan	Won	12	5
	184	04/02/1961	Cardiff	Barbarians	AS Malan	Lost	0	6
	185	08/02/1961	Bordeaux	South Western France	RJ Lockyear	Won	29	3
	186	11/02/1961	Toulouse	France 'B'	RJ Lockyear	Won	26	10
	187	14/02/1961	Bayonne	Coast of Basque	AS Malan	Won	36	9
85		18/02/1961	Paris	FRANCE	AS Malan	Drew	0	0
86		13/05/1961	Cape Town	IRELAND	JT Claasen	Won	24	8
87		05/08/1961	Johannesburg	AUSTRALIA	JT Claasen	Won	28	3
88		12/08/1961	Port Elizabeth	AUSTRALIA	JT Claasen	Won	23	11
89		23/06/1962	Johannesburg	BRITISH ISLES	JT Claasen	Drew	3	3
90		21/07/1962	Durban	BRITISH ISLES	JT Claasen	Won	3	0
91		04/08/1962	Cape Town	BRITISH ISLES	JT Claasen	Won	8	3
92		25/08/1962	Bloemfontein	BRITISH ISLES	JT Claasen	Won	34	14
93		13/07/1963	Pretoria	AUSTRALIA	GF Malan	Won	14	3
94		10/08/1963	Cape Town	AUSTRALIA	GF Malan	Lost	5	9
95		24/08/1963	Johannesburg	AUSTRALIA	AS Malan	Lost	9	11
96		07/09/1963	Port Elizabeth	AUSTRALIA	GF Malan	Won	22	6
97		23/05/1964	Durban	WALES	GF Malan	Won	24	3
98		25/07/1964	Springs	FRANCE	CM Smith	Lost	6	8
	188	03/04/1965	Belfast	Combined Provinces (Ireland)	AS Malan	Drew	8	8

SOUTH AFRICA'S TESTS & OTHER SPRINGBOK MATCHES

Test No.	Tour Match	Date	Venue	Opponent	Captain	Result	PF	PA
	189	06/04/1965	Limerick	Combined Universities, Past & Present	AS Malan	Lost	10	12
99		10/04/1965	Dublin	IRELAND	AS Malan	Lost	6	9
	190	13/04/1965	Hawick	Scottish Districts XV	DJ de Villiers	Lost	8	16
100		17/04/1965	Edinburgh	SCOTLAND	AS Malan	Lost	5	8
	191	10/06/1965	Perth	Western Australia	DJ de Villiers	Won	60	0
	192	12/06/1965	Melbourne	Victoria	CM Smith	Won	52	6
	193	14/06/1965	Sydney	New South Wales	DJ de Villiers	Lost	3	12
101		19/06/1965	Sydney	AUSTRALIA	CM Smith	Lost	11	18
	194	22/06/1965	Brisbane	Queensland	CM Smith	Won	50	5
102		26/06/1965	Brisbane	AUSTRALIA	CM Smith	Lost	8	12
	195	30/06/1965	Gisborne	Poverty Bay - East Coast	CM Smith	Won	32	3
	196	03/07/1965	Wellington	Wellington	CM Smith	Lost	6	23
	197	07/07/1965	Palmerston N.	Manawatu-Horowhenua	DJ de Villiers	Won	30	8
	198	10/07/1965	Dunedin	Otago	DJ de Villiers	Won	8	6
	199	14/07/1965	Christchurch	New Zealand Juniors	CM Smith	Won	23	3
	200	17/07/1965	New Plymouth	Taranaki	DJ de Villiers	Won	11	3
	201	21/07/1965	Invercargill	Southland	CM Smith	Won	19	6
	202	24/07/1965	Christchurch	Canterbury	DJ de Villiers	Won	6	5
	203	27/07/1965	Greymouth	West Coast-Buller	CM Smith	Won	11	0
103		31/07/1965	Wellington	NEW ZEALAND	DJ de Villiers	Lost	3	6
	204	04/08/1965	Wanganui	Wanganui-King Country	DJ de Villiers	Won	24	19
	205	07/08/1965	Hamilton	Waikato	CM Smith	Won	26	13
	206	11/08/1965	Whangarei	North Auckland	CM Smith	Won	14	11
	207	14/08/1965	Auckland	Auckland	DJ de Villiers	Lost	14	15
	208	17/08/1965	Blenheim	Marlborough, Nelson & Golden Bay- Motueka	CM Smith	Won	45	6
104		21/08/1965	Dunedin	NEW ZEALAND	CM Smith	Lost	0	13
	209	25/08/1965	Timaru	S Canterbury, Mid Canterbury & North Otago	DJ de Villiers	Won	28	13
	210	28/08/1965	Wellington	New Zealand Maoris	DJ de Villiers	Won	9	3
	211	31/08/1965	Masterton	Wairarapa-Bush	CM Smith	Won	36	0
105		04/09/1965	Christchurch	NEW ZEALAND	DJ de Villiers	Won	19	16
	212	08/09/1965	Auckland	New Zealand Universities	CM Smith	Won	55	11
	213	11/09/1965	Napier	Hawke's Bay	DJ de Villiers	Won	30	12
	214	14/09/1965	Rotorua	Bay of Plenty-Counties- Thames Valley	DJ de Villiers	Won	33	17
106		18/09/1965	Auckland	NEW ZEALAND	DJ de Villiers	Lost	3	20
107		15/07/1967	Durban	FRANCE	DJ de Villiers	Won	26	3
108		22/07/1967	Bloemfontein	FRANCE	DJ de Villiers	Won	16	3
109		29/07/1967	Johannesburg	FRANCE	DJ de Villiers	Lost	14	19
110		12/08/1967	Cape Town	FRANCE	DJ de Villiers	Drew	6	6
111		08/06/1968	Pretoria	BRITISH ISLES	DJ de Villiers	Won	25	20
112		22/06/1968	Port Elizabeth	BRITISH ISLES	DJ de Villiers	Drew	6	6
113		13/07/1968	Cape Town	BRITISH ISLES	DJ de Villiers	Won	11	6
114		27/07/1968	Johannesburg	BRITISH ISLES	DJ de Villiers	Won	19	6
	215	29/10/1968	Toulon	Littoral-Provence	DJ de Villiers	Won	24	3
	216	02/11/1968	Lyon	South Eastern France	TP Bedford	Won	3	0
	217	05/11/1968	Clermont-Ferrand	Auvergne-Limousin	DJ de Villiers	Won	26	9

SOUTH AFRICA'S TESTS & OTHER SPRINGBOK MATCHES

Test No.	Tour Match	Date	Venue	Opponent	Captain	Result	PF	PA
115		09/11/1968	Bordeaux	FRANCE	DJ de Villiers	Won	12	9
	218	11/11/1968	Toulouse	South Western France	TP Bedford	Lost	3	11
116		16/11/1968	Paris	FRANCE	DJ de Villiers	Won	16	11
117		02/08/1969	Johannesburg	AUSTRALIA	DJ de Villiers	Won	30	11
118		16/08/1969	Durban	AUSTRALIA	TP Bedford	Won	16	9
119		06/09/1969	Cape Town	AUSTRALIA	TP Bedford	Won	11	3
120		20/09/1969	Bloemfontein	AUSTRALIA	DJ de Villiers	Won	19	8
	219	05/11/1969	Twickenham	Oxford University	DJ de Villiers	Lost	3	6
	220	08/11/1969	Leicester	Midland Counties (E)	TP Bedford	Won	11	9
	221	12/11/1969	Newport	Newport	DJ de Villiers	Lost	6	11
	222	15/11/1969	Swansea	Swansea	DJ de Villiers	Won	12	0
	223	19/11/1969	Ebbw Vale	Gwent	JFK Marais	Lost	8	14
	224	22/11/1969	Twickenham	London Counties	DJ de Villiers	Won	22	6
	225	26/11/1969	Manchester	North Western Counties	DJ de Villiers	Won	12	9
	226	02/12/1969	Aberdeen	North & Midlands of Scotland	DJ de Villiers	Won	37	3
121		06/12/1969	Edinburgh	SCOTLAND	TP Bedford	Lost	3	6
	227	10/12/1969	Aberavon	Aberavon & Neath	TP Bedford	Won	27	0
	228	13/12/1969	Cardiff	Cardiff	DJ de Villiers	Won	17	3
	229	16/12/1969	Aldershot	Combined Services	JFK Marais	Won	14	6
122		20/12/1969	Twickenham	ENGLAND	DJ de Villiers	Lost	8	11
	230	27/12/1969	Exeter	South Western Counties	DJ de Villiers	Won	9	6
	231	31/12/1969	Bristol	Western Counties	TP Bedford	Drew	3	3
	232	03/01/1970	Gosforth	North Eastern Counties	DJ de Villiers	Won	24	11
	233	06/01/1970	Coventry	Midland Counties (W)	TP Bedford	Won	21	6
123		10/01/1970	Dublin	IRELAND	DJ de Villiers	Drew	8	8
	234	14/01/1970	Limerick	Munster	DJ de Villiers	Won	25	9
	235	17/01/1970	Galashiels	South of Scotland	TP Bedford	Drew	3	3
	236	20/01/1970	Llanelli	Llanelli	DJ de Villiers	Won	10	9
124		24/01/1970	Cardiff	WALES	DJ de Villiers	Drew	6	6
	237	28/01/1970	Gloucester	Southern Counties	TP Bedford	Won	13	0
	238	31/01/1970	Twickenham	Barbarians	DJ de Villiers	Won	21	12
125		25/07/1970	Pretoria	NEW ZEALAND	DJ de Villiers	Won	17	6
126		08/08/1970	Cape Town	NEW ZEALAND	DJ de Villiers	Lost	8	9
127		29/08/1970	Port Elizabeth	NEW ZEALAND	DJ de Villiers	Won	14	3
128		12/09/1970	Johannesburg	NEW ZEALAND	DJ de Villiers	Won	20	17
129		12/06/1971	Bloemfontein	FRANCE	JFK Marais	Won	22	9
130		19/06/1971	Durban	FRANCE	JFK Marais	Drew	8	8
	239	26/06/1971	Perth	Western Australia	JFK Marais	Won	44	18
	240	30/06/1971	Adelaide	South Australia	TP Bedford	Won	43	0
	241	03/07/1971	Melbourne	Victoria	JFK Marais	Won	50	0
	242	06/07/1971	Sydney	Sydney	JFK Marais	Won	21	12
	243	10/07/1971	Sydney	New South Wales	JFK Marais	Won	25	3
	244	13/07/1971	Orange	New South Wales Country	PJF Greyling	Won	19	3
131		17/07/1971	Sydney	AUSTRALIA	JFK Marais	Won	19	11
	245	21/07/1971	Canberra	Australian Capital Territories	JFK Marais	Won	34	3
	246	24/07/1971	Brisbane	Queensland	JFK Marais	Won	33	14
	247	27/07/1971	Brisbane	Junior Wallabies	JFK Marais	Won	31	12
132		31/07/1971	Brisbane	AUSTRALIA	JFK Marais	Won	14	6

SOUTH AFRICA'S TESTS & OTHER SPRINGBOK MATCHES

Test No.	Tour Match	Date	Venue	Opponent	Captain	Result	PF	PA
	248	03/08/1971	Toowoomba	Queensland Country	PJF Greyling	Won	45	14
133		07/08/1971	Sydney	AUSTRALIA	JFK Marais	Won	18	6
134		03/06/1972	Johannesburg	ENGLAND	PJF Greyling	Lost	9	18
135		08/06/1974	Cape Town	BRITISH ISLES	JFK Marais	Lost	3	12
136		22/06/1974	Pretoria	BRITISH ISLES	JFK Marais	Lost	9	28
137		13/07/1974	Port Elizabeth	BRITISH ISLES	JFK Marais	Lost	9	26
138		27/07/1974	Johannesburg	BRITISH ISLES	JFK Marais	Drew	13	13
	249	06/11/1974	Nice	South Eastern France	JFK Marais	Won	10	7
	250	09/11/1974	Lyon	North Eastern France	DSL Snyman	Won	25	12
	251	13/11/1974	Agen	South Western France	JFK Marais	Won	16	3
	252	16/11/1974	Tarbes	Second Division Clubs	JFK Marais	Won	36	4
	253	20/11/1974	Clermont-Ferrand	Central France	DSL Snyman	Won	29	10
139		23/11/1974	Toulouse	FRANCE	JFK Marais	Won	13	4
	254	27/11/1974	Angoulême	Western France	JCP Snyman	Lost	4	7
140		30/11/1974	Paris	FRANCE	JFK Marais	Won	10	8
	255	04/12/1974	Reims	Northern France	JFK Marais	Won	27	19
141		21/06/1975	Bloemfontein	FRANCE	M du Plessis	Won	38	25
142		28/06/1975	Pretoria	FRANCE	M du Plessis	Won	33	18
143		24/07/1976	Durban	NEW ZEALAND	M du Plessis	Won	16	7
144		14/08/1976	Bloemfontein	NEW ZEALAND	M du Plessis	Lost	9	15
145		04/09/1976	Cape Town	NEW ZEALAND	M du Plessis	Won	15	10
146		18/09/1976	Johannesburg	NEW ZEALAND	M du Plessis	Won	15	14
147		27/08/1977	Pretoria	WORLD TEAM	M du Plessis	Won	45	24
148		26/04/1980	Johannesburg	SOUTH AMERICA	M du Plessis	Won	24	9
149		03/05/1980	Durban	SOUTH AMERICA	M du Plessis	Won	18	9
150		31/05/1980	Cape Town	BRITISH ISLES	M du Plessis	Won	26	22
151		14/06/1980	Bloemfontein	BRITISH ISLES	M du Plessis	Won	26	19
152		28/06/1980	Port Elizabeth	BRITISH ISLES	M du Plessis	Won	12	10
153		12/07/1980	Pretoria	BRITISH ISLES	M du Plessis	Lost	13	17
	256	09/10/1980	Asunción	Paraguay Invitation XV	RB Prentiss	Won	84	6
	257	11/10/1980	Asunción	South America Invitation XV	MTS Stofberg	Won	79	18
	258	14/10/1980	Montevideo	British Schools Old Boys	MTS Stofberg	Won	83	13
154		18/10/1980	Montevideo	SOUTH AMERICA	MTS Stofberg	Won	22	13
	259	21/10/1980	Santiago	Chile Invitation XV	M du Plessis	Won	78	12
155		25/10/1980	Santiago	SOUTH AMERICA	M du Plessis	Won	30	16
156		08/11/1980	Pretoria	FRANCE	M du Plessis	Won	37	15
157		30/05/1981	Cape Town	IRELAND	W Claassen	Won	23	15
158		06/06/1981	Durban	IRELAND	W Claassen	Won	12	10
	260	22/07/1981	Gisborne	Poverty Bay	E Jansen	Won	24	6
	261	29/07/1981	New Plymouth	Taranaki	W Claassen	Won	34	9
	262	01/08/1981	Palmerston N.	Manawatu	MTS Stofberg	Won	31	19
	263	05/08/1981	Wanganui	Wanganui	W Claassen	Won	45	9
	264	08/08/1981	Invercargill	Southland	MTS Stofberg	Won	22	6
	265	11/08/1981	Dunedin	Otago	W Claassen	Won	17	13
159		15/08/1981	Christchurch	NEW ZEALAND	MTS Stofberg	Lost	9	14
	266	22/08/1981	Nelson	Nelson Bays	W Claassen	Won	83	0
	267	25/08/1981	Napier	New Zealand Maoris	DJ Serfontein	Drew	12	12
160		29/08/1981	Wellington	NEW ZEALAND	W Claassen	Won	24	12
	268	02/09/1981	Rotorua	Bay of Plenty	MTS Stofberg	Won	29	24

SOUTH AFRICA'S TESTS & OTHER SPRINGBOK MATCHES

Test No.	Tour Match	Date	Venue	Opponent	Captain	Result	PF	PA
	269	05/09/1981	Auckland	Auckland	W Claassen	Won	39	12
	270	08/09/1981	Whangarei	North Auckland	E Jansen	Won	19	10
161		12/09/1981	Auckland	NEW ZEALAND	W Claassen	Lost	22	25
	271	19/09/1981	Wisconsin	Midwest	MTS Stofberg	Won	46	12
	272	22/09/1981	New York	Eastern	W Claassen	Won	41	0
162		25/09/1981	New York	USA	W Claassen	Won	38	7
163		27/03/1982	Pretoria	SOUTH AMERICA	W Claassen	Won	50	18
164		03/04/1982	Bloemfontein	SOUTH AMERICA	W Claassen	Lost	12	21
165		02/06/1984	Port Elizabeth	ENGLAND	MTS Stofberg	Won	33	15
166		09/06/1984	Johannesburg	ENGLAND	MTS Stofberg	Won	35	9
167		20/10/1984	Pretoria	S AMERICA & SPAIN	DJ Serfontein	Won	32	15
168		27/10/1984	Cape Town	S AMERICA & SPAIN	DJ Serfontein	Won	22	13
169		10/05/1986	Cape Town	NZ CAVALIERS	HE Botha	Won	21	15
170		17/05/1986	Durban	NZ CAVALIERS	HE Botha	Lost	18	19
171		24/05/1986	Pretoria	NZ CAVALIERS	HE Botha	Won	33	18
172		31/05/1986	Johannesburg	NZ CAVALIERS	HE Botha	Won	24	10
173		26/08/1989	Cape Town	WORLD TEAM	JC Breedt	Won	20	19
174		02/09/1989	Johannesburg	WORLD TEAM	JC Breedt	Won	22	16
175		15/08/1992	Johannesburg	NEW ZEALAND	HE Botha	Lost	24	27
176		22/08/1992	Cape Town	AUSTRALIA	HE Botha	Lost	3	26
	273	03/10/1992	Bordeaux	French Selection	HE Botha	Lost	17	24
	274	07/10/1992	Pau	Aquitaine XV	WJ Bartmann	Won	29	22
	275	10/10/1992	Toulouse	Midi-Pyrenées XV	HE Botha	Won	18	15
	276	13/10/1992	Marseilles	Provence-Côte D'Azur XV	RJ du Preez	Won	41	12
177		17/10/1992	Lyon	FRANCE	HE Botha	Won	20	15
	277	20/10/1992	Béziers	Languedoc XV	RJ du Preez	Won	36	15
178		24/10/1992	Paris	FRANCE	HE Botha	Lost	16	29
	278	28/10/1992	Tours	French Universities	RJ du Preez	Lost	13	18
	279	31/10/1992	Lille	French Barbarians	HE Botha	Lost	20	25
	280	04/11/1992	Leicester	Midland Division	HE Botha	Won	32	9
	281	07/11/1992	Bristol	England 'B'	HE Botha	Won	20	16
	282	10/11/1992	Leeds	Northern Division	RJ du Preez	Won	19	3
179		14/11/1992	Twickenham	ENGLAND	HE Botha	Lost	16	33
180		26/06/1993	Durban	FRANCE	JF Pienaar	Drew	20	20
181		03/07/1993	Johannesburg	FRANCE	JF Pienaar	Lost	17	18
	283	14/07/1993	Perth	Western Australia	JF Pienaar	Won	71	8
	284	17/07/1993	Adelaide	South Australian Invitation XV	CP Strauss	Won	90	3
	285	21/07/1993	Melbourne	Victoria	AH Richter	Won	78	3
	286	24/07/1993	Sydney	New South Wales	JF Pienaar	Lost	28	29
	287	27/07/1993	Orange	New South Wales Country	AH Richter	Won	41	7
182		31/07/1993	Sydney	AUSTRALIA	JF Pienaar	Won	19	12
	288	04/08/1993	Canberra	Australian Capital Territories	AH Richter	Won	57	10
	289	08/08/1993	Brisbane	Queensland	JF Pienaar	Won	17	3
	290	11/08/1993	Mackay	Queensland Country	AH Richter	Won	63	5
183		14/08/1993	Brisbane	AUSTRALIA	JF Pienaar	Lost	20	28
	291	18/08/1993	Sydney	Sydney	AH Richter	Won	31	20
184		21/08/1993	Sydney	AUSTRALIA	JF Pienaar	Lost	12	19
	292	27/10/1993	Cordoba	Provincial XV	CP Strauss	Won	55	37
	293	30/10/1993	Buenos Aires	Buenos Aires XV	WJ Bartmann	Lost	27	28

SOUTH AFRICA'S TESTS & OTHER SPRINGBOK MATCHES

Test No.	Tour Match	Date	Venue	Opponent	Captain	Result	PF	PA
	294	03/11/1993	Tucumán	Tucumán	CP Strauss	Won	40	12
185		06/11/1993	**Buenos Aires**	**ARGENTINA**	**JF Pienaar**	**Won**	**29**	**26**
	295	09/11/1993	Rosario	Provincial XV	WJ Bartmann	Won	40	26
186		13/11/1993	**Buenos Aires**	**ARGENTINA**	**JF Pienaar**	**Won**	**52**	**23**
187		04/06/1994	**Pretoria**	**ENGLAND**	**JF Pienaar**	**Lost**	**15**	**32**
188		11/06/1994	**Cape Town**	**ENGLAND**	**JF Pienaar**	**Won**	**27**	**9**
	296	23/06/1994	Taupo	King Country	JF Pienaar	Won	46	10
	297	25/06/1994	Pukekohe	Counties	WJ Bartmann	Won	37	26
	298	28/06/1994	Wellington	Wellington	JF Pienaar	Won	36	26
	299	02/07/1994	Invercargill	Southland	AH Richter	Won	51	15
	300	05/07/1994	Timaru	Hanan Shield Districts	CP Strauss	Won	67	19
189		09/07/1994	**Dunedin**	**NEW ZEALAND**	**CP Strauss**	**Lost**	**14**	**22**
	301	13/07/1994	New Plymouth	Taranaki	RAW Straeuli	Won	16	12
	302	16/07/1994	Hamilton	Waikato	CP Strauss	Won	38	17
	303	19/07/1994	Palmerston N.	Manawatu	JF Pienaar	Won	47	21
190		23/07/1994	**Wellington**	**NEW ZEALAND**	**JF Pienaar**	**Lost**	**9**	**13**
	304	27/07/1994	Dunedin	Otago	CP Strauss	Lost	12	19
	305	30/07/1994	Christchurch	Canterbury	JF Pienaar	Won	21	11
	306	02/08/1994	Rotorua	Bay of Plenty	CP Strauss	Won	33	12
191		06/08/1994	**Auckland**	**NEW ZEALAND**	**JF Pienaar**	**Drew**	**18**	**18**
192		08/10/1994	**Port Elizabeth**	**ARGENTINA**	**JF Pienaar**	**Won**	**42**	**22**
193		15/10/1994	**Johannesburg**	**ARGENTINA**	**JF Pienaar**	**Won**	**46**	**26**
	307	22/10/1994	Cardiff	Cardiff	RAW Straeuli	Won	11	6
	308	26/10/1994	Newport	Wales 'A'	RAW Straeuli	Won	25	13
	309	29/10/1994	Llanelli	Llanelli	JF Pienaar	Won	30	12
	310	02/11/1994	Neath	Neath	CP Strauss	Won	16	13
	311	05/11/1994	Swansea	Swansea	JF Pienaar	Won	78	7
	312	09/11/1994	Melrose	Scotland 'A'	CP Strauss	Lost	15	17
	313	12/11/1994	Glasgow	Scottish Combined Districts	JF Pienaar	Won	33	6
	314	15/11/1994	Aberdeen	Scottish Select	CP Strauss	Won	35	10
194		19/11/1994	**Edinburgh**	**SCOTLAND**	**JF Pienaar**	**Won**	**34**	**10**
	315	22/11/1994	Pontypridd	Pontypridd	CP Strauss	Won	9	3
195		26/11/1994	**Cardiff**	**WALES**	**JF Pienaar**	**Won**	**20**	**12**
	316	29/11/1994	Belfast	Combined Provinces	RAW Straeuli	Won	54	19
	317	03/12/1994	Dublin	Barbarians	JF Pienaar	Lost	15	23
196		13/04/1995	**Johannesburg**	**WESTERN SAMOA**	**JF Pienaar**	**Won**	**60**	**8**
197		25/05/1995	**Cape Town**	**AUSTRALIA**	**JF Pienaar**	**Won**	**27**	**18**
198		30/05/1995	**Cape Town**	**ROMANIA**	**AJ Richter**	**Won**	**21**	**8**
199		03/06/1995	**Port Elizabeth**	**CANADA**	**JF Pienaar**	**Won**	**20**	**0**
200		10/06/1995	**Johannesburg**	**WESTERN SAMOA**	**JF Pienaar**	**Won**	**42**	**14**
201		17/06/1995	**Durban**	**FRANCE**	**JF Pienaar**	**Won**	**19**	**15**
202		24/06/1995	**Johannesburg**	**NEW ZEALAND**	**JF Pienaar**	**Won**	**15**	**12**
203		02/09/1995	**Johannesburg**	**WALES**	**JF Pienaar**	**Won**	**40**	**11**
204		12/11/1995	**Rome**	**ITALY**	**JF Pienaar**	**Won**	**40**	**21**
205		18/11/1995	**Twickenham**	**ENGLAND**	**JF Pienaar**	**Won**	**24**	**14**
206		02/07/1996	**Pretoria**	**FIJI**	**JF Pienaar**	**Won**	**43**	**18**
207		13/07/1996	**Sydney**	**AUSTRALIA**	**JF Pienaar**	**Lost**	**16**	**21**
208		20/07/1996	**Christchurch**	**NEW ZEALAND**	**JF Pienaar**	**Lost**	**11**	**15**
209		03/08/1996	**Bloemfontein**	**AUSTRALIA**	**JF Pienaar**	**Won**	**25**	**19**

SOUTH AFRICA'S TESTS & OTHER SPRINGBOK MATCHES

Test No.	Tour Match	Date	Venue	Opponent	Captain	Result	PF	PA
210		10/08/1996	Cape Town	NEW ZEALAND	JF Pienaar	Lost	18	29
211		17/08/1996	Durban	NEW ZEALAND	GH Teichmann	Lost	19	23
212		24/08/1996	Pretoria	NEW ZEALAND	GH Teichmann	Lost	26	33
213		31/08/1996	Johannesburg	NEW ZEALAND	GH Teichmann	Won	32	22
	318	05/11/1996	Rosario	Rosario	WS Fyvie	Won	45	36
214		09/11/1996	Buenos Aires	ARGENTINA	GH Teichmann	Won	46	15
	319	12/11/1996	Mendoza	Mendoza	WS Fyvie	Won	89	19
215		16/11/1996	Buenos Aires	ARGENTINA	GH Teichmann	Won	44	21
	320	23/11/1996	Brive	French Barbarians	WS Fyvie	Lost	22	30
	321	26/11/1996	Lyon	South East Selection	WS Fyvie	Won	36	20
216		30/11/1996	Bordeaux	FRANCE	GH Teichmann	Won	22	12
	322	03/12/1996	Lille	French Universities	WS Fyvie	Lost	13	20
217		07/12/1996	Paris	FRANCE	GH Teichmann	Won	13	12
218		15/12/1996	Cardiff	WALES	GH Teichmann	Won	37	20
219		10/06/1997	Cape Town	TONGA	GH Teichmann	Won	74	10
220		21/06/1997	Cape Town	BRITISH ISLES	GH Teichmann	Lost	16	25
221		28/06/1997	Durban	BRITISH ISLES	GH Teichmann	Lost	15	18
222		05/07/1997	Johannesburg	BRITISH ISLES	GH Teichmann	Won	35	16
223		19/07/1997	Johannesburg	NEW ZEALAND	GH Teichmann	Lost	32	35
224		02/08/1997	Brisbane	AUSTRALIA	GH Teichmann	Lost	20	32
225		09/08/1997	Auckland	NEW ZEALAND	GH Teichmann	Lost	35	55
226		23/08/1997	Pretoria	AUSTRALIA	GH Teichmann	Won	61	22
227		08/11/1997	Bologna	ITALY	GH Teichmann	Won	62	31
	323	11/11/1997	Biarritz	French Barbarians	AD Aitken	Lost	22	40
228		15/11/1997	Lyon	FRANCE	GH Teichmann	Won	36	32
	324	18/11/1997	Toulon	France 'A'	AD Aitken	Lost	7	21
229		22/11/1997	Paris	FRANCE	GH Teichmann	Won	52	10
230		29/11/1997	Twickenham	ENGLAND	GH Teichmann	Won	29	11
231		06/12/1997	Edinburgh	SCOTLAND	GH Teichmann	Won	68	10
232		13/06/1998	Bloemfontein	IRELAND	GH Teichmann	Won	37	13
233		20/06/1998	Pretoria	IRELAND	GH Teichmann	Won	33	0
234		27/06/1998	Pretoria	WALES	GH Teichmann	Won	96	13
235		04/07/1998	Cape Town	ENGLAND	GH Teichmann	Won	18	0
236		18/07/1998	Perth	AUSTRALIA	GH Teichmann	Won	14	13
237		25/07/1998	Wellington	NEW ZEALAND	GH Teichmann	Won	13	3
238		15/08/1998	Durban	NEW ZEALAND	GH Teichmann	Won	24	23
239		22/08/1998	Johannesburg	AUSTRALIA	GH Teichmann	Won	29	15
	325	10/11/1998	Firhill	Glasgow Caledonians	RB Skinstad	Won	62	9
240		14/11/1998	London	WALES	GH Teichmann	Won	28	20
	326	17/11/1998	Edinburgh	Edinburgh Reivers	RB Skinstad	Won	49	3
241		21/11/1998	Edinburgh	SCOTLAND	GH Teichmann	Won	35	10
	327	24/11/1998	Cork	Combined Provinces	AN Vos	Won	32	5
242		28/11/1998	Dublin	IRELAND	GH Teichmann	Won	27	13
	328	01/12/1998	Belfast	Ireland 'A'	AN Vos	Won	50	19
243		05/12/1998	Twickenham	ENGLAND	GH Teichmann	Lost	7	13
244		12/06/1999	Port Elizabeth	ITALY	GH Teichmann	Won	74	3
245		19/06/1999	Durban	ITALY	CPJ Krige	Won	101	0
246		26/06/1999	Cardiff	WALES	GH Teichmann	Lost	19	29
247		10/07/1999	Dunedin	NEW ZEALAND	GH Teichmann	Lost	0	28

SOUTH AFRICA'S TESTS & OTHER SPRINGBOK MATCHES

Test No.	Tour Match	Date	Venue	Opponent	Captain	Result	PF	PA
248		17/07/1999	Brisbane	AUSTRALIA	J Erasmus	Lost	6	32
249		07/08/1999	Pretoria	NEW ZEALAND	JH van der Westhuizen	Lost	18	34
250		14/08/1999	Cape Town	AUSTRALIA	JH van der Westhuizen	Won	10	9
251		03/10/1999	Edinburgh	SCOTLAND	JH van der Westhuizen	Won	46	29
252		10/10/1999	Edinburgh	SPAIN	AN Vos	Won	47	3
253		15/10/1999	Glasgow	URUGUAY	JH van der Westhuizen	Won	39	3
254		24/10/1999	Paris	ENGLAND	JH van der Westhuizen	Won	44	21
255		30/10/1999	London	AUSTRALIA	JH van der Westhuizen	Lost	21	27
256		04/11/1999	Cardiff	NEW ZEALAND	JH van der Westhuizen	Won	22	18
257		10/06/2000	East London	CANADA	AN Vos	Won	51	18
258		17/06/2000	Pretoria	ENGLAND	AN Vos	Won	18	13
259		24/06/2000	Bloemfontein	ENGLAND	AN Vos	Lost	22	27
260		08/07/2000	Melbourne	AUSTRALIA	AN Vos	Lost	23	44
261		22/07/2000	Christchurch	NEW ZEALAND	AN Vos	Lost	12	25
262		29/07/2000	Sydney	AUSTRALIA	AN Vos	Lost	6	26
263		19/08/2000	Johannesburg	NEW ZEALAND	AN Vos	Won	46	40
264		26/08/2000	Durban	AUSTRALIA	AN Vos	Lost	18	19
	329	08/11/2000	Tucumán	Argentina 'A'	DJ van Zyl	Won	32	21
265		12/11/2000	Buenos Aires	ARGENTINA	AN Vos	Won	37	33
	330	15/11/2000	Limerick	Ireland 'A'	A-H le Roux	Lost	11	28
266		19/11/2000	Dublin	IRELAND	AN Vos	Won	28	18
	331	22/11/2000	Cardiff	Wales 'A'	DJ van Zyl	Won	34	15
267		26/11/2000	Cardiff	WALES	AN Vos	Won	23	13
	332	28/11/2000	Worcester	England National Divisions XV	V Matfield	Lost	30	35
268		02/12/2000	Twickenham	ENGLAND	AN Vos	Lost	17	25
	333	09/12/2000	Cardiff	Barbarians	AN Vos	Won	41	31
269		16/06/2001	Johannesburg	FRANCE	AN Vos	Lost	23	32
270		23/06/2001	Durban	FRANCE	AN Vos	Won	20	15
271		30/06/2001	Port Elizabeth	ITALY	RB Skinstad	Won	60	14
272		21/07/2001	Cape Town	NEW ZEALAND	RB Skinstad	Lost	3	12
273		28/07/2001	Pretoria	AUSTRALIA	RB Skinstad	Won	20	15
274		18/08/2001	Perth	AUSTRALIA	RB Skinstad	Drew	14	14
275		25/08/2001	Auckland	NEW ZEALAND	RB Skinstad	Lost	15	26
276		10/11/2001	Paris	FRANCE	RB Skinstad	Lost	10	20
277		17/11/2001	Genoa	ITALY	RB Skinstad	Won	54	26
278		24/11/2001	London	ENGLAND	RB Skinstad	Lost	9	29
279		01/12/2001	Houston	USA	AN Vos	Won	43	20
280		08/06/2002	Bloemfontein	WALES	RB Skinstad	Won	34	19
281		15/06/2002	Cape Town	WALES	RB Skinstad	Won	19	8
282		29/06/2002	Springs	ARGENTINA	CPJ Krige	Won	49	29
283		06/07/2002	Pretoria	SAMOA	CPJ Krige	Won	60	18
284		20/07/2002	Wellington	NEW ZEALAND	CPJ Krige	Lost	20	41
285		27/07/2002	Brisbane	AUSTRALIA	CPJ Krige	Lost	27	38
286		10/08/2002	Durban	NEW ZEALAND	CPJ Krige	Lost	23	30
287		17/08/2002	Johannesburg	AUSTRALIA	CPJ Krige	Won	33	31
288		09/11/2002	Marseilles	FRANCE	CPJ Krige	Lost	10	30
289		16/11/2002	Edinburgh	SCOTLAND	CPJ Krige	Lost	6	21
290		23/11/2002	London	ENGLAND	CPJ Krige	Lost	3	53
291		07/06/2003	Durban	SCOTLAND	JH van der Westhuizen	Won	29	25

SOUTH AFRICA'S TESTS & OTHER SPRINGBOK MATCHES

Test No.	Tour Match	Date	Venue	Opponent	Captain	Result	PF	PA
292		14/06/2003	Johannesburg	SCOTLAND	JH van der Westhuizen	Won	28	19
293		28/06/2003	Port Elizabeth	ARGENTINA	CPJ Krige	Won	26	25
294		12/07/2003	Cape Town	AUSTRALIA	CPJ Krige	Won	26	22
295		19/07/2003	Pretoria	NEW ZEALAND	CPJ Krige	Lost	16	52
296		02/08/2003	Brisbane	AUSTRALIA	CPJ Krige	Lost	9	29
297		09/08/2003	Dunedin	NEW ZEALAND	CPJ Krige	Lost	11	19
298		11/10/2003	Perth	URUGUAY	JH van der Westhuizen	Won	72	6
299		18/10/2003	Perth	ENGLAND	CPJ Krige	Lost	6	25
300		24/10/2003	Sydney	GEORGIA	JW Smit	Won	46	19
301		01/11/2003	Brisbane	SAMOA	CPJ Krige	Won	60	10
302		08/11/2003	Melbourne	NEW ZEALAND	CPJ Krige	Lost	9	29
303		12/06/2004	Bloemfontein	IRELAND	JW Smit	Won	31	17
304		19/06/2004	Cape Town	IRELAND	JW Smit	Won	26	17
305		26/06/2004	Pretoria	WALES	JW Smit	Won	53	18
306		17/07/2004	Gosford	PACIFIC ISLANDS	JW Smit	Won	38	24
307		24/07/2004	Christchurch	NEW ZEALAND	JW Smit	Lost	21	23
308		31/07/2004	Perth	AUSTRALIA	JW Smit	Lost	26	30
309		14/08/2004	Johannesburg	NEW ZEALAND	JW Smit	Won	40	26
310		21/08/2004	Durban	AUSTRALIA	JW Smit	Won	23	19
311		06/11/2004	Cardiff	WALES	JW Smit	Won	38	36
312		13/11/2004	Dublin	IRELAND	JW Smit	Lost	12	17
313		20/11/2004	London	ENGLAND	JW Smit	Lost	16	32
314		27/11/2004	Edinburgh	SCOTLAND	JW Smit	Won	45	10
315		04/12/2004	Buenos Aires	ARGENTINA	JW Smit	Won	39	7
316		11/06/2005	East London	URUGUAY	JW Smit	Won	134	3
317		18/06/2005	Durban	FRANCE	JW Smit	Drew	30	30
318		25/06/2005	Port Elizabeth	FRANCE	JW Smit	Won	27	13
319		09/07/2005	Sydney	AUSTRALIA	JW Smit	Lost	12	30
320		23/07/2005	Johannesburg	AUSTRALIA	JW Smit	Won	33	20
321		30/07/2005	Pretoria	AUSTRALIA	JW Smit	Won	22	16
322		06/08/2005	Cape Town	NEW ZEALAND	JW Smit	Won	22	16
323		20/08/2005	Perth	AUSTRALIA	JW Smit	Won	22	19
324		27/08/2005	Dunedin	NEW ZEALAND	JW Smit	Lost	27	31
325		05/11/2005	Buenos Aires	ARGENTINA	JW Smit	Won	34	23
326		19/11/2005	Cardiff	WALES	JW Smit	Won	33	16
327		26/11/2005	Paris	FRANCE	JW Smit	Lost	20	26
328		10/06/2006	Durban	SCOTLAND	JW Smit	Won	36	16
329		17/06/2006	Port Elizabeth	SCOTLAND	JW Smit	Won	29	15
330		24/06/2006	Cape Town	FRANCE	JW Smit	Lost	26	36
331		15/07/2006	Brisbane	AUSTRALIA	JW Smit	Lost	0	49
332		22/07/2006	Wellington	NEW ZEALAND	JW Smit	Lost	17	35
333		05/08/2006	Sydney	AUSTRALIA	JW Smit	Lost	18	20
334		26/08/2006	Pretoria	NEW ZEALAND	JW Smit	Lost	26	45
335		02/09/2006	Rustenburg	NEW ZEALAND	JW Smit	Won	21	20
336		09/09/2006	Johannesburg	AUSTRALIA	JW Smit	Won	24	16
337		11/11/2006	Dublin	IRELAND	JW Smit	Lost	15	32
338		18/11/2006	London	ENGLAND	JW Smit	Lost	21	23
339		25/11/2006	London	ENGLAND	JW Smit	Won	25	14
	334	03/12/2006	Leicester	World XV	GvG Botha	Won	32	7

SPRINGBOKS

SOUTH AFRICA'S TESTS & OTHER SPRINGBOK MATCHES

Test No.	Tour Match	Date	Venue	Opponent	Captain	Result	PF	PA
340		26/05/2007	Bloemfontein	ENGLAND	JW Smit	Won	58	10
341		02/06/2007	Pretoria	ENGLAND	JW Smit	Won	55	22
342		09/06/2007	Johannesburg	SAMOA	JW Smit	Won	35	8
343		16/06/2007	Cape Town	AUSTRALIA	JW Smit	Won	22	19
344		23/06/2007	Durban	NEW ZEALAND	V Matfield	Lost	21	26
345		07/07/2007	Sydney	AUSTRALIA	RB Skinstad	Lost	17	25
346		14/07/2007	Christchurch	NEW ZEALAND	GJ Muller	Lost	6	33
347		15/08/2007	Cape Town	NAMIBIA	V Matfield	Won	105	13
	335	21/08/2007	Galway	Connacht	RB Skinstad	Won	18	3
348		25/08/2007	Edinburgh	SCOTLAND	V Matfield	Won	27	3
349		09/09/2007	Paris	SAMOA	JW Smit	Won	59	7
350		14/09/2007	St Denis	ENGLAND	JW Smit	Won	36	0
351		22/09/2007	Lens	TONGA	RB Skinstad	Won	30	25
352		30/09/2007	Montpellier	USA	JW Smit	Won	64	15
353		07/10/2007	Marseilles	FIJI	JW Smit	Won	37	20
354		14/10/2007	St Denis	ARGENTINA	JW Smit	Won	37	13
355		20/10/2007	St Denis	ENGLAND	JW Smit	Won	15	6
356		24/11/2007	Cardiff	WALES	JW Smit	Won	34	12
	336	01/12/2007	London	Barbarians	GJ Muller	Lost	5	22
357		07/06/2008	Bloemfontein	WALES	JW Smit	Won	43	17
358		14/06/2008	Pretoria	WALES	JW Smit	Won	37	21
359		21/06/2008	Cape Town	ITALY	V Matfield	Won	26	0
360		05/07/2008	Wellington	NEW ZEALAND	JW Smit	Lost	8	19
361		12/07/2008	Dunedin	NEW ZEALAND	V Matfield	Won	30	28
362		19/07/2008	Perth	AUSTRALIA	V Matfield	Lost	9	16
363		09/08/2008	Johannesburg	ARGENTINA	V Matfield	Won	63	9
364		16/08/2008	Cape Town	NEW ZEALAND	V Matfield	Lost	0	19
365		23/08/2008	Durban	AUSTRALIA	V Matfield	Lost	15	27
366		30/08/2008	Johannesburg	AUSTRALIA	V Matfield	Won	53	8
367		08/11/2008	Cardiff	WALES	JW Smit	Won	20	15
368		15/11/2008	Edinburgh	SCOTLAND	JW Smit	Won	14	10
369		22/11/2008	London	ENGLAND	JW Smit	Won	42	6
370		20/06/2009	Durban	BRITISH ISLES	JW Smit	Won	26	21
371		27/06/2009	Pretoria	BRITISH ISLES	JW Smit	Won	28	25
372		04/07/2009	Johannesburg	BRITISH ISLES	JW Smit	Lost	9	28
373		25/07/2009	Bloemfontein	NEW ZEALAND	JW Smit	Won	28	19
374		01/08/2009	Durban	NEW ZEALAND	JW Smit	Won	31	19
375		08/08/2009	Cape Town	AUSTRALIA	JW Smit	Won	29	17
376		29/08/2009	Perth	AUSTRALIA	JW Smit	Won	32	25
377		05/09/2009	Brisbane	AUSTRALIA	JW Smit	Lost	6	21
378		12/09/2009	Hamilton	NEW ZEALAND	JW Smit	Won	32	29
	337	06/11/2009	Leicester	Leicester Tigers	MC Ralepelle	Lost	17	22
379		13/11/2009	Toulouse	FRANCE	JW Smit	Lost	13	20
	338	17/11/2009	London	Saracens	DJ Potgieter	Lost	23	24
380		21/11/2009	Florence	ITALY	JW Smit	Won	32	10
381		28/11/2009	Dublin	IRELAND	JW Smit	Lost	10	15
382		05/06/2010	Cardiff	WALES	JW Smit	Won	34	31
383		12/06/2010	Cape Town	FRANCE	JW Smit	Won	42	17
384		19/06/2010	Witbank	ITALY	V Matfield	Won	29	13

SOUTH AFRICA'S TESTS & OTHER SPRINGBOK MATCHES

Test No.	Tour Match	Date	Venue	Opponent	Captain	Result	PF	PA
385		26/06/2010	East London	ITALY	JW Smit	Won	55	11
386		10/07/2010	Auckland	NEW ZEALAND	JW Smit	Lost	12	32
387		17/07/2010	Wellington	NEW ZEALAND	JW Smit	Lost	17	31
388		24/07/2010	Brisbane	AUSTRALIA	JW Smit	Lost	13	30
389		21/08/2010	Johannesburg	NEW ZEALAND	JW Smit	Lost	22	29
390		28/08/2010	Pretoria	AUSTRALIA	JW Smit	Won	44	31
391		04/09/2010	Bloemfontein	AUSTRALIA	JW Smit	Lost	39	41
392		06/11/2010	Dublin	IRELAND	V Matfield	Won	23	21
393		13/11/2010	Cardiff	WALES	V Matfield	Won	29	25
394		20/11/2010	Edinburgh	SCOTLAND	V Matfield	Lost	17	21
395		27/11/2010	London	ENGLAND	V Matfield	Won	21	11
	339	04/12/2010	London	Barbarians	JH Smith	Lost	20	26
396		23/07/2011	Sydney	AUSTRALIA	JW Smit	Lost	20	39
397		30/07/2011	Wellington	NEW ZEALAND	JW Smit	Lost	7	40
398		13/08/2011	Durban	AUSTRALIA	JW Smit	Lost	9	14
399		20/08/2011	Port Elizabeth	NEW ZEALAND	V Matfield	Won	18	5
400		11/09/2011	Wellington	WALES	JW Smit	Won	17	16
401		17/09/2011	Wellington	FIJI	JW Smit	Won	49	3
402		22/09/2011	Albany	NAMIBIA	JW Smit	Won	87	0
403		30/09/2011	Albany	SAMOA	V Matfield	Won	13	5
404		09/10/2011	Wellington	AUSTRALIA	JW Smit	Lost	9	11
405		09/06/2012	Durban	ENGLAND	J de Villiers	Won	22	17
406		16/06/2012	Johannesburg	ENGLAND	J de Villiers	Won	36	27
407		23/06/2012	Port Elizabeth	ENGLAND	J de Villiers	Drawn	14	14
408		18/08/2012	Cape Town	ARGENTINA	J de Villiers	Won	27	6
409		25/08/2012	Mendoza	ARGENTINA	J de Villiers	Drawn	16	16
410		08/09/2012	Perth	AUSTRALIA	J de Villiers	Lost	19	26
411		15/09/2012	Dunedin	NEW ZEALAND	J de Villiers	Lost	11	21
412		29/09/2012	Pretoria	AUSTRALIA	J de Villiers	Won	31	8
413		06/10/2012	Johannesburg	NEW ZEALAND	J de Villiers	Lost	16	32
414		10/11/2012	Dublin	IRELAND	J de Villiers	Won	16	12
415		17/11/2012	Edinburgh	SCOTLAND	J de Villiers	Won	21	10
416		24/11/2012	London	ENGLAND	J de Villiers	Won	16	15
417		08/06/2013	Durban	ITALY	J de Villiers	Won	44	10
418		15/06/2013	Nelspruit	SCOTLAND	J de Villiers	Won	30	17
419		22/06/2013	Pretoria	SAMOA	J de Villiers	Won	56	23
420		17/08/2013	Johannesburg	ARGENTINA	J de Villiers	Won	73	13
421		24/08/2013	Mendoza	ARGENTINA	J de Villiers	Won	22	17
422		07/09/2013	Brisbane	AUSTRALIA	J de Villiers	Won	38	12
423		14/09/2013	Auckland	NEW ZEALAND	J de Villiers	Lost	15	29
424		28/09/2013	Cape Town	AUSTRALIA	J de Villiers	Won	28	8
425		05/10/2013	Johannesburg	NEW ZEALAND	J de Villiers	Lost	27	38
426		09/11/2013	Cardiff	WALES	J de Villiers	Won	24	15
427		17/11/2013	Edinburgh	SCOTLAND	J de Villiers	Won	28	0
428		23/11/2013	Paris	FRANCE	J de Villiers	Won	19	10
	340	07/06/2014	Cape Town	World XV (non-Test)	V Matfield	Won	47	13
429		14/06/2014	Durban	WALES	V Matfield	Won	38	16
430		21/06/2014	Nelspruit	WALES	V Matfield	Won	31	30
431		28/06/2014	Port Elizabeth	SCOTLAND	V Matfield	Won	55	6

SOUTH AFRICA'S TESTS & OTHER SPRINGBOK MATCHES

Test No.	Tour Match	Date	Venue	Opponent	Captain	Result	PF	PA
432		16/08/2014	Pretoria	ARGENTINA	J de Villiers	Won	13	6
433		23/08/2014	Salta	ARGENTINA	J de Villiers	Won	33	31
434		06/09/2014	Perth	AUSTRALIA	J de Villiers	Lost	23	24
435		13/09/2014	Wellington	NEW ZEALAND	J de Villiers	Lost	10	14
436		27/09/2014	Cape Town	AUSTRALIA	J de Villiers	Won	28	10
437		04/10/2014	Johannesburg	NEW ZEALAND	J de Villiers	Won	27	25
438		08/11/2014	Dublin	IRELAND	J de Villiers	Lost	15	29
439		15/11/2014	London	ENGLAND	J de Villiers	Won	31	28
440		22/11/2014	Padova	ITALY	J de Villiers	Won	22	6
441		29/11/2014	Cardiff	WALES	J de Villiers	Lost	6	12
	341	11/07/2015	Cape Town	World XV (non-Test)	V Matfield	Won	46	10
442		18/07/2015	Brisbane	AUSTRALIA	V Matfield	Lost	20	24
443		25/07/2015	Johannesburg	NEW ZEALAND	SWP Burger	Lost	20	27
444		08/08/2015	Durban	ARGENTINA	J de Villiers	Lost	25	37
445		15/08/2015	Buenos Aires	ARGENTINA	V Matfield	Won	26	12
446		19/09/2015	Brighton	JAPAN	J de Villiers	Lost	32	34
447		26/09/2015	Birmingham	SAMOA	J de Villiers	Won	46	6
448		03/10/2015	Newcastle	SCOTLAND	PF du Preez	Won	34	16
449		07/10/2015	London	USA	PF du Preez	Won	64	0
450		17/10/2015	London	WALES	PF du Preez	Won	23	19
451		24/10/2015	London	NEW ZEALAND	PF du Preez	Lost	18	20
452		30/10/2015	London	ARGENTINA	V Matfield	Won	24	13
453		11/06/2016	Cape Town	Ireland	JA Strauss	Lost	20	26
454		18/06/2016	Johannesburg	Ireland	JA Strauss	Won	32	26
455		25/06/2016	Port Elizabeth	Ireland	JA Strauss	Won	19	13
456		20/08/2016	Nelspruit	Argentina	JA Strauss	Won	30	23
457		27/08/2016	Salta	Argentina	JA Strauss	Lost	24	26
458		10/09/2016	Brisbane	Australia	JA Strauss	Lost	17	23
459		17/09/2016	Christchurch	New Zealand	JA Strauss	Lost	13	41
460		01/10/2016	Pretoria	Australia	JA Strauss	Won	18	10
461		08/10/2016	Durban	New Zealand	JA Strauss	Lost	15	57
	342	05/11/2016	London	Barbarians	PJ Lambie	Drawn	31	31
462		12/11/2016	London	England	JA Strauss	Lost	21	37
463		19/11/2016	Florence	Italy	JA Strauss	Lost	18	20
464		26/11/2016	Cardiff	Wales	JA Strauss	Lost	13	27
						TESTS	10720	7368
						OTHER	8392	2812

TEST RESULTS BY OPPONENT

ARGENTINA

Played 24 - Won 21 - Lost 2 - Drawn 1
PF - 857 - PA 472

Year	Winner	Score	Venue
1993	South Africa	29-26	Buenos Aires
1993	South Africa	52-23	Buenos Aires
1994	South Africa	42-22	Port Elizabeth
1994	South Africa	46-26	Johannesburg
1996	South Africa	46-15	Buenos Aires
1996	South Africa	44-21	Buenos Aires
2000	South Africa	37-33	Buenos Aires
2002	South Africa	49-29	Springs
2003	South Africa	26-25	Port Elizabeth
2004	South Africa	39-7	Buenos Aires
2005	South Africa	34-23	Buenos Aires
2007	South Africa	37-13	Paris
2008	South Africa	63-9	Johannesburg
2012	South Africa	27-6	Cape Town
2012	Drawn	16-16	Mendoza
2013	South Africa	73-13	Johannesburg
2013	South Africa	22-17	Mendoza
2014	South Africa	13-6	Pretoria
2014	South Africa	33-31	Salta
2015	Argentina	37-25	Durban
2015	South Africa	26-12	Buenos Aires
2015	South Africa	24-13	London
2016	South Africa	30-23	Nelspruit
2016	Argentina	26-24	Salta

AUSTRALIA

Played 83 - Won 46 - Lost 36 - Drawn 1
PF - 1 607 - PA 1 448

Year	Winner	Score	Venue
1933	South Africa	17-3	Cape Town
1933	Australia	6-21	Durban
1933	South Africa	12-3	Johannesburg
1933	South Africa	11-0	Port Elizabeth
1933	Australia	4-15	Bloemfontein
1937	South Africa	9-5	Sydney
1937	South Africa	26-17	Sydney
1953	South Africa	25-3	Johannesburg
1953	Australia	14-18	Cape Town
1953	South Africa	18-8	Durban
1953	South Africa	22-9	Port Elizabeth
1956	South Africa	9-0	Sydney
1956	South Africa	9-0	Brisbane
1961	South Africa	28-3	Johannesburg
1961	South Africa	23-11	Port Elizabeth
1963	South Africa	14-3	Pretoria
1963	Australia	5-9	Cape Town
1963	Australia	9-11	Johannesburg
1963	South Africa	22-6	Port Elizabeth
1965	Australia	11-18	Sydney
1965	Australia	8-12	Brisbane
1969	South Africa	30-11	Johannesburg
1969	South Africa	16-9	Durban
1969	South Africa	11-3	Cape Town
1969	South Africa	19-8	Bloemfontein
1971	South Africa	19-11	Sydney
1971	South Africa	14-6	Brisbane
1971	South Africa	18-6	Sydney
1992	Australia	3-26	Cape Town
1993	South Africa	19-12	Sydney
1993	Australia	20-28	Brisbane
1993	Australia	12-19	Sydney
1995	South Africa	27-18	Cape Town
1996	Australia	16-21	Sydney
1996	South Africa	25-19	Bloemfontein
1997	Australia	20-32	Brisbane
1997	South Africa	61-22	Pretoria
1998	South Africa	14-13	Perth
1998	South Africa	29-15	Johannesburg
1999	Australia	6-32	Brisbane
1999	South Africa	10-9	Cape Town
1999	Australia	21-27	London
2000	Australia	23-44	Melbourne
2000	Australia	6-26	Sydney
2000	Australia	18-19	Durban
2001	South Africa	20-15	Pretoria
2001	Drawn	14-14	Perth
2002	Australia	27-38	Brisbane
2002	South Africa	33-31	Johannesburg
2003	South Africa	26-22	Cape Town
2003	Australia	9-29	Brisbane
2004	Australia	26-30	Perth
2004	South Africa	23-19	Durban
2005	Australia	12-30	Sydney
2005	South Africa	33-20	Johannesburg
2005	South Africa	22-16	Pretoria
2005	South Africa	22-19	Perth
2006	Australia	0-49	Brisbane
2006	Australia	18-20	Sydney
2006	South Africa	24-16	Johannesburg
2007	South Africa	22-19	Cape Town
2007	Australia	17-25	Sydney
2008	Australia	9-16	Perth
2008	Australia	15-27	Durban
2008	South Africa	53-8	Johannesburg
2009	South Africa	29-17	Cape Town
2009	South Africa	32-25	Perth
2009	Australia	6-21	Brisbane
2010	Australia	13-30	Brisbane

TEST RESULTS BY OPPONENT

Year		Score	Venue	Year		Score	Venue
2010	South Africa	44-31	Pretoria	1974	British Isles	3-12	Cape Town
2010	Australia	39-41	Bloemfontein	1974	British Isles	9-28	Pretoria
2011	Australia	20-39	Sydney	1974	British Isles	9-26	Port Elizabeth
2011	Australia	9-14	Durban	1974	Drawn	13-13	Johannesburg
2011	Australia	9-11	Wellington	1980	South Africa	26-22	Cape Town
2012	Australia	19-26	Perth	1980	South Africa	26-19	Bloemfontein
2012	South Africa	31-8	Pretoria	1980	South Africa	12-10	Port Elizabeth
2013	South Africa	38-12	Brisbane	1980	British Isles	13-17	Pretoria
2013	South Africa	28-8	Cape Town	1997	British Isles	16-25	Cape Town
2014	Australia	24-23	Perth	1997	British Isles	15-18	Durban
2014	South Africa	28-10	Cape Town	1997	South Africa	35-16	Johannesburg
2015	Australia	24-20	Brisbane	2009	South Africa	26-21	Durban
2016	Australia	17-23	Brisbane	2009	South Africa	28-25	Pretoria
2016	South Africa	18-10	Pretoria	2009	British Isles	9-28	Johannesburg

BRITISH ISLES

Played 46 – Won 23 – Lost 17 – Drawn 6
PF 600 – PA 516

Year	Winner	Score	Venue
1891	British Isles	0-4	Port Elizabeth
1891	British Isles	0-3	Kimberley
1891	British Isles	0-4	Cape Town
1896	British Isles	0-8	Port Elizabeth
1896	British Isles	8-17	Johannesburg
1896	British Isles	3-9	Kimberley
1896	South Africa	5-0	Cape Town
1903	Drawn	10-10	Johannesburg
1903	Drawn	0-0	Kimberley
1903	South Africa	8-0	Cape Town
1910	South Africa	14-10	Johannesburg
1910	British Isles	3-8	Port Elizabeth
1910	South Africa	21-5	Cape Town
1924	South Africa	7-3	Durban
1924	South Africa	17-0	Johannesburg
1924	Drawn	3-3	Port Elizabeth
1924	South Africa	16-9	Cape Town
1938	South Africa	26-12	Johannesburg
1938	South Africa	19-3	Port Elizabeth
1938	British Isles	16-21	Cape Town
1955	British Isles	22-23	Johannesburg
1955	South Africa	25-9	Cape Town
1955	British Isles	6-9	Pretoria
1955	South Africa	22-8	Port Elizabeth
1962	Drawn	3-3	Johannesburg
1962	South Africa	3-0	Durban
1962	South Africa	8-3	Cape Town
1962	South Africa	34-14	Bloemfontein
1968	South Africa	25-20	Pretoria
1968	Drawn	6-6	Port Elizabeth
1968	South Africa	11-6	Cape Town
1968	South Africa	19-6	Johannesburg

CANADA

Played 2 – Won 2 – Lost 0 – Drawn 0
PF 71 – PA 18

Year	Winner	Score	Venue
1995	South Africa	20-0	Port Elizabeth
2000	South Africa	51-18	East London

ENGLAND

Played 38 – Won 23 – Lost 13 – Drawn 2
PF – 801 – PA 629

Year	Winner	Score	Venue
1906	Drawn	3-3	Crystal Palace
1913	South Africa	9-3	Twickenham
1932	South Africa	7-0	Twickenham
1952	South Africa	8-3	Twickenham
1961	South Africa	5-0	Twickenham
1969	England	8-11	Twickenham
1972	England	9-18	Johannesburg
1984	South Africa	33-15	Port Elizabeth
1984	South Africa	35-9	Johannesburg
1992	England	16-33	Twickenham
1994	England	15-32	Pretoria
1994	South Africa	27-9	Cape Town
1995	South Africa	24-14	Twickenham
1997	South Africa	29-11	Twickenham
1998	South Africa	18-0	Cape Town
1998	England	7-13	Twickenham
1999	South Africa	44-21	Paris
2000	South Africa	18-13	Pretoria
2000	England	22-27	Bloemfontein
2000	England	17-25	Twickenham
2001	England	9-29	Twickenham
2002	England	3-53	Twickenham
2003	England	6-25	Perth
2004	England	16-32	Twickenham
2006	England	21-23	Twickenham

TEST RESULTS BY OPPONENT

2006	South Africa	25-14	Twickenham		1996	South Africa	13-12	Paris
2007	South Africa	58-10	Bloemfontein		1997	South Africa	36-32	Lyon
2007	South Africa	55-22	Pretoria		1997	South Africa	52-10	Paris
2007	South Africa	36-0	Paris		2001	France	23-32	Johannesburg
2007	South Africa	15-6	Paris		2001	South Africa	20-15	Durban
2008	South Africa	42-6	Twickenham		2001	France	10-20	Paris
2010	South Africa	21-11	Twickenham		2002	France	10-30	Marseilles
2012	South Africa	22-17	Durban		2005	Drawn	30-30	Durban
2012	South Africa	36-27	Johannesburg		2005	South Africa	27-13	Port Elizabeth
2012	Drawn	14-14	Port Elizabeth		2005	France	20-26	Paris
2012	South Africa	16-15	Twickenham		2006	France	26-36	Cape Town
2014	South Africa	31-28	London		2009	France	13-20	Toulouse
2016	England	21-37	London		2010	South Africa	42-17	Cape Town
					2013	South Africa	19-10	Paris

FIJI

Played 3 – Won 3 – Lost 0 – Drawn 0
PF 129 – PA 41

Year	Winner	Score	Venue
1996	South Africa	43-18	Pretoria
2007	South Africa	37-20	Marseille
2011	South Africa	49-3	Wellington

FRANCE

Played 39 – Won 22 – Lost 11 – Drawn 6
PF 783 – PA 578

Year	Winner	Score	Venue
1913	South Africa	38-5	Bordeaux
1952	South Africa	25-3	Paris
1958	Drawn	3-3	Cape Town
1958	France	5-9	Johannesburg
1961	Drawn	0-0	Paris
1964	France	6-8	Springs
1967	South Africa	26-3	Durban
1967	South Africa	16-3	Bloemfontein
1967	France	14-19	Johannesburg
1967	Drawn	6-6	Cape Town
1968	South Africa	12-9	Bordeaux
1968	South Africa	16-11	Paris
1971	South Africa	22-9	Bloemfontein
1971	Drawn	8-8	Durban
1974	South Africa	13-4	Toulouse
1974	South Africa	10-8	Paris
1975	South Africa	38-25	Bloemfontein
1975	South Africa	33-18	Pretoria
1980	South Africa	37-15	Pretoria
1992	South Africa	20-15	Lyon
1992	France	16-29	Paris
1993	Drawn	20-20	Durban
1993	France	17-18	Johannesburg
1995	South Africa	19-15	Durban
1996	South Africa	22-12	Bordeaux

GEORGIA

Played 1 – Won 1 – Lost 0 – Drawn 0
PF 46 – PA 19

Year	Winner	Score	Venue
2003	South Africa	46-19	Sydney

IRELAND

Played 25 – Won 18 – Lost 6 – Drawn 1
PF – 503 – PA 342

Year	Winner	Score	Venue
1906	South Africa	15-12	Belfast
1912	South Africa	38-0	Dublin
1931	South Africa	8-3	Dublin
1951	South Africa	17-5	Dublin
1960	South Africa	8-3	Dublin
1961	South Africa	24-8	Cape Town
1965	Ireland	6-9	Dublin
1970	Drawn	8-8	Dublin
1981	South Africa	23-15	Cape Town
1981	South Africa	12-10	Durban
1998	South Africa	37-13	Bloemfontein
1998	South Africa	33-0	Pretoria
1998	South Africa	27-13	Dublin
2000	South Africa	28-18	Dublin
2004	South Africa	31-17	Bloemfontein
2004	South Africa	26-17	Cape Town
2004	Ireland	12-17	Dublin
2006	Ireland	15-32	Dublin
2009	Ireland	10-15	Dublin
2010	South Africa	23-21	Dublin
2012	South Africa	16-12	Dublin
2014	Ireland	29-15	Dublin
2016	Ireland	20-26	Cape Town
2016	South Africa	32-26	Johannesburg
2016	South Africa	19-13	Port Elizabeth

TEST RESULTS BY OPPONENT

ITALY

Played 13 - Won 12 - Lost 1 - Drawn 0
PF - 617 - PA 165

Year	Winner	Score	Venue
1995	South Africa	40-21	Rome
1997	South Africa	62-31	Bologna
1999	South Africa	74-3	Port Elizabeth
1999	South Africa	101-0	Durban
2001	South Africa	60-14	Port Elizabeth
2001	South Africa	54-26	Genoa
2008	South Africa	26-0	Cape Town
2009	South Africa	32-10	Udine
2010	South Africa	29-13	Witbank
2010	South Africa	55-11	East London
2013	South Africa	44-10	Durban
2014	South Africa	22-6	Padova
2016	Italy	18-20	Florence

JAPAN

Played 1 - Won 0 - Lost 1 - Drawn 0
PF 32 - PA 34

Year	Winner	Score	Venue
2015	Japan	34-32	Brighton

NAMIBIA

Played 2 - Won 2 - Lost 0 - Drawn 0
PF 192 - PA 13

Year	Winner	Score	Venue
2007	South Africa	105-13	Cape Town
2011	South Africa	87-0	Albany

NEW ZEALAND

Played 93 - Won 35 - Lost 55 - Drawn 3
PF - 1 458 - PA 1 863

Year	Winner	Score	Venue
1921	New Zealand	5-13	Dunedin
1921	South Africa	9-5	Auckland
1921	Drawn	0-0	Wellington
1928	South Africa	17-0	Durban
1928	New Zealand	6-7	Johannesburg
1928	South Africa	11-6	Port Elizabeth
1928	New Zealand	5-13	Cape Town
1937	New Zealand	7-13	Wellington
1937	South Africa	13-6	Christchurch
1937	South Africa	17-6	Auckland
1949	South Africa	15-11	Cape Town
1949	South Africa	12-6	Johannesburg
1949	South Africa	9-3	Durban
1949	South Africa	11-8	Port Elizabeth
1956	New Zealand	6-10	Dunedin
1956	South Africa	8-3	Wellington
1956	New Zealand	10-17	Christchurch
1956	New Zealand	5-11	Auckland
1960	South Africa	13-0	Johannesburg
1960	New Zealand	3-11	Cape Town
1960	Drawn	11-11	Bloemfontein
1960	South Africa	8-3	Port Elizabeth
1965	New Zealand	3-6	Wellington
1965	New Zealand	0-13	Dunedin
1965	South Africa	19-16	Christchurch
1965	New Zealand	3-20	Auckland
1970	South Africa	17-6	Pretoria
1970	New Zealand	8-9	Cape Town
1970	South Africa	14-3	Port Elizabeth
1970	South Africa	20-17	Johannesburg
1976	South Africa	16-7	Durban
1976	New Zealand	9-15	Bloemfontein
1976	South Africa	15-10	Cape Town
1976	South Africa	15-14	Johannesburg
1981	New Zealand	9-14	Christchurch
1981	South Africa	24-12	Wellington
1981	New Zealand	22-25	Auckland
1992	New Zealand	24-27	Johannesburg
1994	New Zealand	14-22	Dunedin
1994	New Zealand	9-13	Wellington
1994	Drawn	18-18	Auckland
1995	South Africa	15-12	Johannesburg
1996	New Zealand	11-15	Christchurch
1996	New Zealand	18-29	Cape Town
1996	New Zealand	19-23	Durban
1996	New Zealand	26-33	Pretoria
1996	South Africa	32-22	Johannesburg
1997	New Zealand	32-35	Johannesburg
1997	New Zealand	35-55	Auckland
1998	South Africa	13-3	Wellington
1998	South Africa	24-23	Durban
1999	New Zealand	0-28	Dunedin
1999	New Zealand	18-34	Pretoria
1999	South Africa	22-18	Cardiff
2000	New Zealand	12-25	Christchurch
2000	South Africa	46-40	Johannesburg
2001	New Zealand	3-12	Cape Town
2001	New Zealand	15-26	Auckland
2002	New Zealand	20-41	Wellington
2002	New Zealand	23-30	Durban
2003	New Zealand	16-52	Pretoria
2003	New Zealand	11-19	Dunedin
2003	New Zealand	9-29	Melbourne
2004	New Zealand	21-23	Christchurch
2004	South Africa	40-26	Johannesburg
2005	South Africa	22-16	Cape Town
2005	New Zealand	27-31	Dunedin

TEST RESULTS BY OPPONENT

2006	New Zealand	17-35	Wellington
2006	New Zealand	26-45	Pretoria
2006	South Africa	21-20	Rustenburg
2007	New Zealand	21-26	Durban
2007	New Zealand	6-33	Christchurch
2008	New Zealand	8-19	Wellington
2008	South Africa	30-28	Dunedin
2008	New Zealand	0-19	Cape Town
2009	South Africa	28-19	Bloemfontein
2009	South Africa	31-19	Durban
2009	South Africa	32-29	Hamilton
2010	New Zealand	12-32	Auckland
2010	New Zealand	17-31	Wellington
2010	New Zealand	22-29	Johannesburg
2011	New Zealand	7-40	Wellington
2011	South Africa	18-5	Port Elizabeth
2012	New Zealand	11-21	Dunedin
2012	New Zealand	16-32	Johannesburg
2013	New Zealand	15-29	Auckland
2013	New Zealand	27-38	Johannesburg
2014	New Zealand	14-10	Wellington
2014	South Africa	27-25	Johannesburg
2015	New Zealand	27-20	Johannesburg
2015	New Zealand	20-18	London
2016	New Zealand	13-41	Christchurch
2016	New Zealand	15-57	Durban

NEW ZEALAND CAVALIERS

Played 4 – Won 3 – Lost 1 – Drawn 0
PF 96 – PA 62

Year	Winner	Score	Venue
1986	South Africa	21-15	Cape Town
1986	NZ Cavaliers	18-19	Durban
1986	South Africa	33-18	Pretoria
1986	South Africa	24-10	Johannesburg

PACIFIC ISLANDS

Played 1 – Won 1 – Lost 0 – Drawn 0
PF 38 – PA 24

Year	Winner	Score	Venue
2004	South Africa	38-24	Gosford

ROMANIA

Played 1 – Won 1 – Lost 0 – Drawn 0
PF 21 – PA 8

Year	Winner	Score	Venue
1995	South Africa	21-8	Cape Town

SAMOA

Played 9 – Won 9 – Lost 0 – Drawn 0
PF 431 – PA 99

Year	Winner	Score	Venue
1995	South Africa	60-8	Johannesburg
1995	South Africa	42-14	Johannesburg
2002	South Africa	60-18	Pretoria
2003	South Africa	60-10	Brisbane
2007	South Africa	35-8	Johannesburg
2007	South Africa	59-7	Paris
2011	South Africa	13-5	Albany
2013	South Africa	56-23	Pretoria
2015	South Africa	46-6	Birmingham

SCOTLAND

Played 26 – Won 21 – Lost 5 – Drawn 0
PF 686 – PA 286

Year	Winner	Score	Venue
1906	Scotland	0-6	Glasgow
1912	South Africa	16-0	Edinburgh
1932	South Africa	6-3	Edinburgh
1951	South Africa	44-0	Edinburgh
1960	South Africa	18-10	Port Elizabeth
1961	South Africa	12-5	Edinburgh
1965	Scotland	5-8	Edinburgh
1969	Scotland	3-6	Edinburgh
1994	South Africa	34-10	Edinburgh
1997	South Africa	68-10	Edinburgh
1998	South Africa	35-10	Edinburgh
1999	South Africa	46-29	Edinburgh
2002	Scotland	6-21	Edinburgh
2003	South Africa	29-25	Durban
2003	South Africa	28-19	Johannesburg
2004	South Africa	45-10	Edinburgh
2006	South Africa	36-16	Durban
2006	South Africa	29-15	Port Elizabeth
2007	South Africa	27-3	Edinburgh
2008	South Africa	14-10	Edinburgh
2010	Scotland	17-21	Edinburgh
2012	South Africa	21-10	Edinburgh
2013	South Africa	30-17	Nelspruit
2013	South Africa	28-0	Edinburgh
2014	South Africa	55-6	Port Elizabeth
2015	South Africa	34-16	Newcastle

TEST RESULTS BY OPPONENT

SOUTH AMERICA
(*indicates includes Spain)
Played 8 – Won 7 – Lost 1 – Drawn 0
PF 210 – PA 114

Year	Winner	Score	Venue
1980	South Africa	24-9	Johannesburg
1980	South Africa	18-9	Durban
1980	South Africa	22-13	Montevideo
1980	South Africa	30-16	Santiago
1982	South Africa	50-18	Pretoria
1982	South America	12-21	Bloemfontein
1984*	South Africa	32-15	Pretoria
1984*	South Africa	22-13	Cape Town

SPAIN
Played 1 – Won 1 – Lost 0 – Drawn 0
PF 47 – PA 3

Year	Winner	Score	Venue
1999	South Africa	47-3	Edinburgh

TONGA
Played 2 – Won 2 – Lost 0 – Drawn 0
PF 104 – PA 35

Year	Winner	Score	Venue
1997	South Africa	74-10	Cape Town
2007	South Africa	30-25	Lens

UNITED STATES OF AMERICA
Played 4 – Won 4 – Lost 0 – Drawn 0
PF 209 – PA 42

Year	Winner	Score	Venue
1981	South Africa	38-7	Glenville
2001	South Africa	43-20	Houston
2007	South Africa	64-15	Montpellier
2015	South Africa	64-0	London

URUGUAY
Played 3 – Won 3 – Lost 0 – Drawn 0
PF 245 – PA 12

Year	Winner	Score	Venue
1999	South Africa	39-3	Glasgow
2003	South Africa	72-6	Perth
2005	South Africa	134-3	East London

WALES
Played 32 – Won 28 – Lost 3 – Drawn 1
PF – 850 – PA 486

Year	Winner	Score	Venue
1906	South Africa	11-0	Swansea
1912	South Africa	3-0	Cardiff
1931	South Africa	8-3	Swansea
1951	South Africa	6-3	Cardiff
1960	South Africa	3-0	Cardiff
1964	South Africa	24-3	Durban
1970	Drawn	6-6	Cardiff
1994	South Africa	20-12	Cardiff
1995	South Africa	40-11	Johannesburg
1996	South Africa	37-20	Cardiff
1998	South Africa	96-13	Pretoria
1998	South Africa	28-20	Wembley
1999	Wales	19-29	Cardiff
2000	South Africa	23-13	Cardiff
2002	South Africa	34-19	Bloemfontein
2002	South Africa	19-8	Cape Town
2004	South Africa	53-18	Pretoria
2004	South Africa	38-36	Cardiff
2005	South Africa	33-16	Cardiff
2007	South Africa	34-12	Cardiff
2008	South Africa	43-17	Bloemfontein
2008	South Africa	37-21	Pretoria
2008	South Africa	20-15	Cardiff
2010	South Africa	34-31	Cardiff
2010	South Africa	29-25	Cardiff
2011	South Africa	17-16	Wellington, NZ
2013	South Africa	24-15	Cardiff
2014	South Africa	38-16	Durban
2014	South Africa	31-30	Nelspruit
2014	Wales	12-6	Cardiff
2015	South Africa	23-19	London
2016	Wales	13-27	Cardiff

WORLD TEAMS*
Played 3 – Won 3 – Lost 0 – Drawn 0
PF 87 – PA 59

Year	Winner	Score	Venue
1977	South Africa	45-24	Pretoria
1989	South Africa	20-19	Cape Town
1989	South Africa	22-16	Johannesburg

South Africa also played two further matches against World XVs in 2014 and 2015, but these did not enjoy Test status and players did not receive caps.

South African Test Records

MATCH RECORDS AT HOME (TEAM)

Highest score	134-3	v Uruguay	East London	11/06/2005
Biggest winning margin	131	v Uruguay	East London	11/06/2005
Most tries	21	v Uruguay	East London	11/06/2005
Most conversions	13	v Italy	Durban	19/06/1999
	13	v Uruguay	East London	11/06/2005
Most penalty goals	8	v Scotland	Port Elizabeth	17/06/2006
	8	v New Zealand	Durban	01/08/2009
Most drop goals	3	v South America	Durban	03/05/1980
	3	v Ireland	Durban	06/06/1981
Biggest defeat	42 (15-57)	v New Zealand	Durban	08/10/2016
Most points conceded	57	v New Zealand	Durban	08/10/2016
Most tries conceded	9	v New Zealand	Durban	08/10/2016
Most conversions by opposition	6	v New Zealand	Durban	08/10/2016
Most penalty goals by opposition	8	v England	Bloemfontein	24/06/2000
Most drop goals by opposition	2	On 7 occasions		

MATCH RECORDS AWAY FROM HOME (TEAM)

Highest score	87-0	v Namibia	Albany	22/09/2011
Biggest winning margin	87	v Namibia	Albany	22/09/2011
Most tries	12	v Uruguay	Perth	11/10/2003
	12	v Namibia	Albany	22/09/2011
Most conversions	12	v Namibia	Albany	22/09/2011
Most penalty goals	6	v Australia	London	30/10/1999
	6	v Australia	Perth	06/09/2014
	6	v New Zealand	London	24/10/2015
Most drop goals	5	v England	Paris	24/10/1999
Biggest defeat	50 (3-53)	v England	London	23/11/2002
Most points conceded	55	v New Zealand	Auckland	09/08/1997
Most tries conceded	7	v New Zealand	Auckland	09/08/1997
	7	v England	London	23/11/2002
Most conversions by opposition	6	v England	London	23/11/2002
Most penalty goals by opposition	8	v Australia	London	30/10/1999
Most drop goals by opposition	2	v France	Paris	16/11/1968
	2	v England	Perth	18/10/2003

MATCH RECORDS AT HOME (PLAYER)

Most points	35	PC Montgomery	v Namibia	Cape Town	15/08/2007
Most tries	6	T Chavhanga	v Uruguay	East London	11/06/2005
Most conversions	12	PC Montgomery	v Namibia	Cape Town	15/08/2007
Most penalty goals	8	M Steyn	v New Zealand	Durban	01/08/2009
Most drop goals	3	HE Botha	v South America	Durban	03/05/1980
	3	HE Botha	v Ireland	Durban	06/06/1981

All points	31	M Steyn	v New Zealand	Durban	01/08/2009
Scored all four ways	22	JT Stransky *(t, c, 4p, d)*	v Australia	Cape Town	25/05/1995

MATCH RECORDS AWAY FROM HOME (PLAYER)

Most points	34	JH de Beer	v England	Paris	24/10/1999
Most tries	4	PWG Rossouw	v France	Paris	22/11/1997
	4	BG Habana	v Samoa	Paris	09/09/2007
Most conversions	8	PC Montgomery	v Scotland	Edinburgh	06/12/1997
Most penalty goals	6	JH de Beer	v Australia	London	30/10/1999
	6	M Steyn	v Australia	Perth	06/09/2014
Most drop goals	5	JH de Beer	v England	Paris	24/10/1999
All points	21	JH de Beer	v Australia	London	30/10/1999
Scored all four ways	21	DJ Hougaard *(t, 5c, p, d)*	v Samoa	Brisbane	01/11/2003

MATCH RECORDS BY AN OPPONENT AT HOME (PLAYER)

Most points	27	CR Andrew (England)	Pretoria	04/06/1994
	27	JP Wilkinson (England)	Bloemfontein	24/06/2000
	27	G Merceron (France)	Johannesburg	16/06/2001
Most tries	3	JJ Imhoff (Argentina)	Durban	08/08/2015
Most conversions	4	A Cameron (British Isles)	Johannesburg	06/08/1955
	4	PE McLean (World Team)	Pretoria	27/08/1977
	4	AP Mehrtens (New Zealand)	Johannesburg	19/08/2000
	4	CJ Spencer (New Zealand)	Pretoria	19/07/2003
	4	DW Carter (New Zealand)	Pretoria	26/08/2006
	4	MJ Giteau (Australia)	Pretoria	28/08/2010
	4	MJ Giteau (Australia)	Bloemfontein	04/09/2010
	4	J-M Hernández (Argentina)	Durban	08/08/2015
Most penalty goals	8	JP Wilkinson (England)	Bloemfontein	24/06/2000
Most drop goals	2	G Camberabero (France)	Johannesburg	29/07/1967
	2	P Bennett (British Isles)	Port Elizabeth	13/07/1974
	2	DR Biggar (Wales)	Durban	14/06/2014

MATCH RECORDS BY AN OPPONENT AWAY FROM HOME (PLAYER)

Most points	29	SA Mortlock (Australia)	Melbourne	08/07/2000
Most tries	2	23 times by 20 players		
Most conversions	5	SA Mortlock (Australia)	Brisbane	15/07/2006
Most penalty goals	8	MC Burke (Australia)	London	30/10/1999
Most drop goals	2	JP Wilkinson (England)	Perth	18/10/2003

SEASON RECORDS (TEAM)

Most points	658	17 Tests	38.7 per game	2007
Most tries	81	17 Tests	4.8 per game	2007
Most conversions	62	17 Tests	3.6 per game	2007
Most penalty goals	46	14 Tests	3.3 per game	2010
Most drop goals	8	13 Tests		1999

SEASON RECORDS (PLAYER)

Most points	219	PC Montgomery (14 Tests)	2007
Most tries	13	BG Habana (11 Tests)	2007
Most conversions	52	PC Montgomery (14 Tests)	2007
Most penalty goals	40	M Steyn (13 Tests)	2010
Most drop goals	6	HE Botha (9 Tests)	1980
	6	JH de Beer (6 Tests)	1999

Percy Montgomery in 2007.

MOST CONSECUTIVES

		Start date	Opposition	Ground	End date	Opposition	Ground
Most consecutive wins	17	23/08/1997	Australia	Pretoria	28/11/1998	Ireland	Dublin
Most consecutive wins at home	13	11/06/1994	England	Cape Town	03/08/1996	Australia	Bloemfontein
Most consecutive wins away from home	10	08/11/1997	Italy	Bologna	28/11/1998	Ireland	Dublin
Most consecutive defeats	7	25/07/1964	France	Springs	21/08/1965	New Zealand	Dunedin
Most consecutive defeats at home	6	30/07/1891	British Isles	Port Elizabeth	29/08/1896	British Isles	Kimberley
Most consecutive defeats away from home	7	20/07/2002	New Zealand	Wellington	09/08/2003	New Zealand	Dunedin
Most consecutive matches without a try	4	30/07/1891	British Isles	Port Elizabeth	30/07/1896	British Isles	Port Elizabeth
Most consecutive matches without defeat	16	03/06/1972	England	Johannesburg	13/07/1974	British Isles	Port Elizabeth
Most consecutive wins against an opponent	16	26/11/2000	Wales	Cardiff	21/06/2014	Wales	Nelspruit
Most consecutive matches without defeat against an opponent	19	06/11/1993	Argentina	Buenos Aires	23/08/2014	Argentina	Salta
Most consecutive matches scoring >four tries	10	09/08/1997	New Zealand	Auckland	27/06/1998	Wales	Pretoria
Most consecutive matches without conceding a try	5	10/10/1999	Spain	Edinburgh	04/11/1999	New Zealand	Cardiff
Most consecutive matches without scoring	4	30/07/1891	British Isles	Port Elizabeth	30/07/1896	British Isles	Port Elizabeth
Most consecutive matches without conceding a point	3	23/11/1912	v Scotland	Inverleith	14/12/1912	Wales	Cardiff

MOST CONSECUTIVE WINS AWAY FROM HOME

10

08/11/1997 – Italy (Bologna)

28/11/1998 – Ireland (Dublin)

CAREER RECORDS

Most Test match appearances	127	V Matfield	2001-2015
Most appearances in all Springbok matches	133	V Matfield	2001-2015
Most points in Test matches	893	PC Montgomery *(102 Tests)*	1997-2008
Most points in all Springbok matches	906	PC Montgomery *(104 matches)*	1997-2008
Most tries in Test matches	67	BG Habana *(124 Tests)*	2004-2016
Most tries in all Springbok matches	68	BG Habana *(128 matches)*	2004-2016
Most conversions in Test matches	153	PC Montgomery *(102 Tests)*	1997-2008
Most conversions in all Springbok matches	157	PC Montgomery *(104 matches)*	1997-2008
Most penalty goals in Test matches	154	M Steyn *(66 Tests)*	2009-2016
Most penalty goals in all Springbok matches	157	M Steyn *(67 matches)*	2009-2016
Most drop goals in Test matches	18	HE Botha *(28 Tests)*	1980-1992
Most drop goals in all Springbok matches	27	HE Botha *(40 matches)*	1980-1992

CAREER RECORDS BY OPPONENTS

Most Test match appearances against SA	30	GM Gregan *(Australia)*	1994-2007
Most points in Test matches against SA	255	DW Carter *(New Zealand) (19 tests)*	2003-2015
Most tries in Test matches against SA	10	CM Cullen *(New Zealand) (15 tests)*	1996-2002
Most conversions in Test matches against SA	33	DW Carter *(New Zealand) (19 tests)*	2003-2015
Most penalty goals in Test matches against SA	55	DW Carter *(New Zealand) (19 tests)*	2003-2015
Most drop goals in Test matches against SA	4	AP Mehrtens *(New Zealand) (16 tests)*	1995-2004

MISCELLANEOUS RECORDS

Most test match appearances in each position

Fullback	PC Montgomery [1]	87
Wing	BG Habana [2]	123
Centre	J de Villiers [3]	94
Flyhalf	M Steyn [4]	64
Scrumhalf	JH van der Westhuizen [5]	87
Prop	T Mtawarira	87
Hooker	JW Smit [6]	96
Lock	V Matfield	127
Flank	SWP Burger [7]	79
Eighthman	PJ Spies [8]	48
Captain	JW Smit	83

[1] Also made nine appearances as a centre, five as flyhalf and one as wing.

[2] Also made one appearance as a centre.

[3] also made fifteen appearance as a wing.

[4] Also made one appearance as a fullback and one as a replacement flank.

[5] Also made two appearances as a replacement wing.

[6] Also made two appearances as a replacement prop and thirteen as a prop in the starting 15.

[7] Also made seven appearances as No 8.

[8] Also made four appearances as a flank and one as wing.

Most consecutive test match appearances by position

Fullback	PC Montgomery *(1997-1999)*	24
Wing	PWG Rossouw *(1997-1999)*	24
Centre	J de Villiers *(2011-2013)*	25
Flyhalf	BL Osler *(1924-1933)*	17
	HE Botha *(1980-1982)*	17
	JNB van der Westhuyzen *(2004-2005)*	17
Scrumhalf	PF du Preez *(2004-2006)*	21
Prop	A-H le Roux *(1998-1999)*	25
Hooker	JW Smit *(2003-2007)*	46
Lock	E Etzebeth *(2014-2016)*	31
Flank	RJ Kruger *(1995-1997)*	22
Eighthman	GH Teichmann *(1996-1999)*	39
Captain	JW Smit *(2004-2007)*	43

Most consecutive test match appearances

46	JW Smit *(hooker)*	2003-2007
39	GH Teichmann *(eighthman)*	1996-1999
31	E Etzebeth *(lock)*	2014-2016
29	M Steyn *(Flyhalf/fullback)*	2010-2012
28	V Matfield *(lock)*	2008-2010
28	WJ le Roux *(fullback/wing)*	2013-2015
27	BW du Plessis *(hooker)*	2013-2015
26	AH Snyman *(centre/wing)*	1996-1998
26	AN Vos *(eighthman/flank)*	1999-2001
26	J de Villiers *(centre)*	2011-2013

Most test match tries in each position

Fullback	18	PC Montgomery	*87 tests
Wing	67	BG Habana	*123 tests
Centre	28	J Fourie	*61 tests
Flyhalf	8	M Steyn	*64 tests
Scrumhalf	38	JH van der Westhuizen	*87 tests
Prop	6	GG Steenkamp	53 tests
Hooker	11	BW du Plessis	*78 tests
Lock	12	MG Andrews	*75 tests
Flank	14	SWP Burger	*79 tests
Eighthman	7	PJ Spies	*48 tests

Excludes tests played in other positions

Most test match tries as a forward

Burger, SWP	16	86 Tests
Andrews, MG	12	77 Tests
Smith, JH	12	70 Tests

Longest international career

15 seasons	V Matfield *(2001-2015)*	14 years, 122 days
14 seasons	JP du Randt *(1994-2007)*	13 years, 12 days
14 seasons	J de Villiers *(2002-2015)*	12 years, 321 days
13 seasons	HE Botha *(1980-1992)*	12 years, 202 days
13 seasons	DM Gerber *(1980-1992)*	12 years, 27 days
13 seasons	BH Heatlie *(1891-1903)*	12 years, 14 days
13 seasons	JM Powell *(1891-1903)*	12 years, 7 days
13 seasons	JP Botha *(2002-2014)*	12 years, 6 days

Most test matches as a substitute

		Total tests
43	A-H le Roux	54
43	R Pienaar	88

Most test matches as an unused substitute

		Total tests
22	W Swanepoel	20

Oldest living Springboks*

C Moss	91y, 10m, 19d
DC van Jaarsveld	87y, 9m
TPD Briers	87y, 5m, 20d
JT Claassen	87y, 3m, 8d
JU Buchler	86y, 8m, 24d
JGH du Preez	86y, 2m, 25d
JJ Starke	85y, 7d, 15m

Age as at 31/12/2016

Most appearances as a test match combination

Fullback/wings	PC Montgomery, CS Terblanche & PWG Rossouw *(1998-1999)*	13
Wing pairing	BG Habana & J-PR Pietersen *(2007-2015)*	44*
Centre pairing	J de Villiers & J Fourie *(2005-2013)*	29
Halfbacks	JH van der Westhuizen & HW Honiball *(1993-1999)*	24
Loose forwards	WS Alberts, L-FP Louw & DJ Vermeulen *(2012-2014)*	17
Flank pairing	SWP Burger & JH Smith *(2004-2009)*	30
Locks	V Matfield & JP Botha *(2003-2014)*	63*
Front row	JN du Plessis, T Mtawarira & BW du Plessis *(2010-2015)*	20
Prop pairing	JN du Plessis & T Mtawarira *(2010-2015)*	37

World record

Springboks sent off in Tests (8)

Player	Opponent	Referee	Venue	Date
JT Small	v Australia	EF Morrison *(England)*	Brisbane	1993
J Dalton	v Canada	DTM McHugh *(Ireland)*	Port Elizabeth	1995
AG Venter	v New Zealand	WD Bevan *(Wales)*	Auckland	1997
B Venter	v Uruguay	PL Marshall *(Australia)*	Glasgow	1999
MC Joubert	v Australia	PD O'Brien *(New Zealand)*	Johannesburg	2002
JJ Labuschagne	v England	PD O'Brien *(New Zealand)*	Twickenham	2002
PC Montgomery*	v Wales	SJ Dickinson *(Australia)*	Cardiff	2005

Montgomery's first yellow card was subsequently dismissed by a disciplinary commission and his red card rescinded.

BW du Plessis*	v New Zealand	R Poite *(France)*	Auckland	2013

* Du Plessis' first yellow card was subsequently dismissed by a disciplinary commission and his red card recinded.

Players sent off in Tests against South Africa (6)

Player	Team	Referee	Venue	Date
R Snow	Canada	DTM McHugh *(Ireland)*	Port Elizabeth	1995
GL Rees	Canada	DTM McHugh *(Ireland)*	Port Elizabeth	1995
GR Jenkins	Wales	J Dumé *(France)*	Johannesburg	1995
PB Williams	Samoa	N Owens *(Wales)*	Albany	2011
AT Tuilagi	Samoa	P Gauzère *(France)*	Pretoria	2013
CJ Stander	Ireland	M Raynal *(France)*	Cape Town	2016

Most yellow cards by the Springboks

7	BG Habana
6	SWP Burger
5	V Matfield
4	JP Botha
4	PR van der Merwe
3	BJ Paulse
3	D Barry
3	RB Kempson

Most yellow cards issued by referees to the Springboks

10	SR Walsh *(New Zealand / Australia)*
9	N Owens *(Wales)*
7	AC Rolland *(Ireland)*
7	W Barnes *(England)*
6	PD O'Brien *(New Zealand)*
6	GJ Clancy *(Ireland)*
6	J Garcès *(France)*

International referees in South African Test matches

Tests	Referee	Country	SA Won	SA Lost	Drawn	% Wins
18	SR Walsh	NZ/Australia	14	1	3	78%
17	AC Rolland	Ireland	10	7	-	59%
14	N Owens	Wales	8	6	-	57%
13	W Barnes	England	10	3	-	83%
12	PD O'Brien	New Zealand	7	5	-	58%
11	SJ Dickinson	Australia	3	8	-	27%
10	CJ Hawke	New Zealand	7	3	-	70%
10	GJ Clancy	Ireland	6	4	-	60%
10	J Garcès	France	3	7	-	30%

Highest winning percentage as a Springbok (20 or more Tests)

	Played	Won	Lost	Drawn	% Wins
AC Garvey	28	24	4	0	86%
M du Plessis	22	18	4	0	82%
J Dalton	43	35	8	0	81%
MTS Stofberg	21	17	4	0	81%
JS Germishuys	20	16	4	0	80%

Lowest winning percentage as a Springbok (20 or more Tests)

	Played	Won	Lost	Drawn	% Wins
AJJ van Straaten	21	9	11	1	43%
D Barry	39	18	20	1	46%
CPJ Krige	39	18	21	0	46%
L de Jager	28	13	15	0	46%
EP Andrews	23	11	11	1	48%
IJ Visagie	29	14	14	1	48%

SPRINGBOK CAPTAINS

	Captain	Test as Captain (Total tests)	Debut as captain	Debut match
1	**HH Castens** - Prop, Western Province	1 (1)	1891	British Isles 1st test
2	**RCD Snedden** - Prop, Griqualand West	1 (1)	1891	British Isles 2nd test
3	**AR Richards** - Flyhalf, Western Province	1 (3)	1891	British Isles 3rd test
4	**FTD Aston** - Centre & wing, Transvaal	3 (4)	1896	British Isles 1st test
5	**BH Heatlie** - Prop & lock, Western Province	2 (6)	1896	British Isles 4th test
6	**A Frew** - Prop, Transvaal	1 (1)	1903	British Isles 1st test
7	**JM Powell** - Flyhalf, Griqualand West	1 (4)	1903	British Isles 2nd test
8	**HW Carolin** - Flyhalf, Western Province	1 (3)	1906	Scotland
9	**PJ Roos** - Prop, Western Province	3 (4)	1906	Ireland
10	**DFT Morkel** - Prop, Transvaal	2 (9)	1910	British Isles 1st test
11	**WA Millar** - No. 8 & flank, Western Province	5 (6)	1910	British Isles 2nd test
12	**FJ Dobbin** - Scrumhalf, Griqualand West	1 (9)	1912	Scotland
13	**TB Pienaar** - Prop, Western Province	0 (0)	1921	Did not play in tests
14	**WH Morkel** - No. 8, Transvaal	3 (9)	1921	New Zealand 1st test
15	**PK Albertyn** - Centre, South Western Districts	4 (4)	1924	British Isles 1st test
16	**PJ Mostert** - Prop & hooker, Western Province	4 (14)	1928	New Zealand 1st test
17	**BL Osler** - Flyhalf, Western Province	5 (17)	1931	Wales
18	**PJ Nel** - Lock & prop, Natal	8 (16)	1933	Australia 1st test
19	**DH Craven** - Flyhalf & scrumhalf, Eastern Province	4 (16)	1937	New Zealand 1st test
20	**F du Plessis** - Lock, Transvaal	3 (3)	1949	New Zealand 1st test
21	**BJ Kenyon** - Flank, Border	1 (1)	1949	New Zealand 4th test
22	**HSV Muller** - No. 8, Transvaal	9 (13)	1951	Scotland
23	**SP Fry** - Flank, Western Province	4 (13)	1955	British Isles 1st test
24	**SS Viviers** - Fullback & flyhalf	5 (5)	1956	Australia 1st test
25	**JA du Rand** - Lock, Northern Transvaal	1 (21)	1956	New Zealand 1st test
26	**JT Claassen** - Lock, Western Transvaal	9 (28)	1958	France 1st test
27	**DC van Jaarsveldt** - Flank, Rhodesia	1 (1)	1960	Scotland

SOUTH AFRICAN TEST RECORDS

SPRINGBOK CAPTAINS

	Captain	Test as Captain (Total tests)	Debut as captain	Debut match
28	**RG Dryburgh** - Fullback, Natal	2 (8)	1960	New Zealand 1st test
29	**AS Malan** - Lock, Transvaal	10 (16)	1960	New Zealand 3rd test
30	**GF Malan** - Hooker, Transvaal	4 (18)	1963	Australia 1st test
31	**CM Smith** - Scrumhalf, Orange Free State	4 (7)	1964	France
32	**DJ de Villiers** - Scrumhalf, Western Province	22 (25)	1965	New Zealand 1st test
33	**TP Bedford** - No. 8, Natal	3 (25)	1969	Australia 2nd test
34	**JFK Marais** - Prop, Eastern Province	11 (35)	1971	France 1st test
36	**M du Plessis** - No. 8, Western Province	15 (22)	1975	France 1st test
37	**MTS Stofberg** - Flank, Northern Transvaal	4 (21)	1980	South America 1st test
38	**W Claassen** - No. 8, Natal	7 (7)	1981	Ireland 1st test
39	**DJ Serfontein** - Scrumhalf, Western Province	2 (19)	1984	South America & Sp. 1st test
40	**HE Botha** - Flyhalf, Northern Transvaal	9 (28)	1986	NZ Cavaliers 1st test
41	**JC Breedt** - No. 8, Transvaal	2 (8)	1989	World Team 1st test
42	**JF Pienaar** - Flank & No. 8, Transvaal	29 (29)	1993	France 1st test
43	**CP Strauss** - Flank, Western Province	1 (15)	1994	New Zealand 1st test
44	**AJ Richter** - No. 8, Northern Transvaal	1 (10)	1995	Romania
45	**GH Teichmann** - No. 8, Natal	36 (42)	1996	New Zealand 1st test
46	**CPJ Krige** - Flank, Western Province	18 (39)	1999	Italy 2nd test
47	**J Erasmus** - Flank, Golden Lions	1 (36)	1999	Australia 1st test
48	**JH van der Westhuizen** - Scrumhalf, Blue Bulls	10 (89)	1999	New Zealand 2nd test
49	**AN Vos** - No. 8, Golden Lions	16 (33)	1999	Spain
50	**RB Skinstad** - No. 8, Western Province	12 (42)	2001	Italy
51	**JW Smit** - Hooker, Natal	83 (111)	2003	Georgia
52	**V Matfield** - Lock, Blue Bulls	23 (127)	2007	New Zealand 1st test
53	**GJ Muller** - Lock, Natal	1 (24)	2007	New Zealand 2nd test
54	**J de Villiers** - Centre, Western Province	37 (109)	2012	England 1st test
55	**SWP Burger** - No. 8, Western Province	1 (86)	2015	New Zealand 1st test
56	**PF du Preez** - Scrumhalf, Suntory Sungoliath (Japan)	4 (76)	2015	Scotland
57	**JA Strauss** - Hooker, Blue Bulls	12 (66)	2016	Ireland 1st test

WINNING PERCENTAGES OF SPRINGBOK CAPTAINS (10 OR MORE TESTS)

	Player	M	W	D	L	PF	PA
86,67%	M du Plessis	15	13	0	2	357	230
80,00%	JH van der Westhuizen	10	8	0	2	329	191
72,22%	GH Teichmann	36	26	0	10	1228	661
69,57%	V Matfield	23	16	0	7	693	351
65,52%	JF Pienaar	29	19	2	8	780	503
65,06%	JW Smit	83	54	1	28	2436	1668
64,86%	J de Villiers	37	24	2	11	960	658
59,09%	DJ de Villiers	22	13	4	5	306	210
56,25%	AN Vos	16	9	0	7	434	371
54,55%	JFK Marais	11	6	2	3	138	131
50,00%	AS Malan	10	5	2	3	67	50
50,00%	RB Skinstad	12	6	1	5	285	233
38,89%	CPJ Krige	18	7	0	11	495	502
33,33%	JA Strauss	12	4	0	8	240	329

Percentage of Springbok points scored during a Test career

	Player	Player points	Springbok points
50,73%	HE Botha	312	615
42,08%	M Steyn	736	1749
42,02%	AJJ van Straaten	221	526

Percentage of Springbok tries scored during a Test career

	Player	Tries	Springbok tries
26,76%	DM Gerber	19	71
18,51%	BG Habana	67	362

Springbok relationships

Father & son	Thirteen sets	Last RJ du Preez & J-L du Preez	1992-1993 & 2016
Three brothers	Three sets	Last W, CJ & MJ du Plessis	1980-1982, 1981-1989 & 1984-1989
Two brothers	Thirty two sets	Last AK & OM Ndungane	2008

Brothers in Tests (since World War II)

Twice	HPJ & RP Bekker	1953
Once	ID & RJ McCallum	1974
Once	DSL & JCP Snyman	1974
Once	HE & DS Botha	1981
Twice	CJ & W du Plessis	1982
Eight times	CJ & MJ du Plessis	1984-1989
Twice	G & J Cronjé	2004
Fifty times	JN & BW du Plessis	2007-2015

Tallest, shortest, heaviest, lightest

Tallest	A Bekker	2.08m
Shortest	TA Gentles	1.60m
Heaviest	RG Visagie	138kg
Lightest	WD Sendin	60kg

Youngest Springboks on Test debut

18 Years, 18 days	AJ Hartley	British Isles *(3rd test)*	1891
19 Years, 8 days	DG Cope	British Isles *(2nd test)*	1896
19 Years, 37 days	JA Loubser	British Isles *(3rd test)*	1903
19 Years, 51 days	RCB van Ryneveld	British Isles *(2nd test)*	1910
19 Years, 72 days	WJ Mills	British Isles *(2nd test)*	1910
19 Years, 112 days	FG Turner	Australia *(1st test)*	1933
19 Years, 126 days	BH Heatlie	British Isles *(2nd test)*	1891
19 Years, 158 days	SC de Melker	British Isles *(2nd test)*	1903

Oldest Springboks in final Test

38 Years, 172 days	V Matfield	Argentina *(3rd test)*	2015
37 Years, 34 days	JN Ackermann	Australia *(2nd test)*	2007
36 Years, 258 days	WH Morkel	New Zealand *(3rd test)*	1921
35 Years, 277 days	D Lötter	Australia *(2nd test)*	1993
35 Years, 252 days	FCH du Preez	Australia *(3rd test)*	1971
35 Years, 208 days	PJ Geel	New Zealand *(3rd test)*	1949
35 Years, 130 days	LC Moolman	NZ Cavaliers *(4th test)*	1986

Least and most experienced Springbok starting XVs since 1992

40 Caps - vs. France, Durban, 1993: JTJ van Rensburg *(3)*; JT Small *(5)*, PG Müller *(5)*, HT Fuls *(1)*, J Olivier *(3)*; HP le Roux *(0)*, RJ du Preez *(2)*; CP Strauss *(3)*, I McDonald *(2)*, JF Pienaar *(0)*, RG Visagie *(4)*, JJ Wiese *(0)*, KS Andrews *(1)*, UL Schmidt *(8)*, WG Hills *(3)*.

891 Caps - vs. Samoa, Birmingham, 2015: WJ le Roux *(28)*; J-PR Pietersen *(61)*, J de Villiers *(108)*, D de Allende *(7)*, BG Habana *(111)*; H Pollard *(14)*; PF du Preez *(71)*; DJ Vermeulen *(29)*, SWP Burger *(80)*, L-FP Louw *(37)*, V Matfield *(124)*, E Etzebeth *(38)*, JN du Plessis *(65)*, JA Strauss *(49)*, T Mtawarira *(69)*.

(This is the most experienced Springbok side of all time)

SPRINGBOK COACHES SINCE 1992											
	Date of Birth	P	W	L	D	PF	PA	Diff	TF	TA	Win %
GHH Sonnekus	01/02/1953	-	-	-	-	-	-	-	-	-	-
Did not take up appointment											
GM Christie	31/01/1940	14	14	0	0	450	191	259	54	16	100,00%
October 94 - November 95											
NVH Mallett	30/10/1956	38	27	11	0	1251	678	573	152	49	71,05%
November 97 - August 00											
JA White	19/03/1963	54	36	17	1	1740	1097	643	194	110	66,67%
June 04 - December 07											
H Meyer	06/10/1967	48	32	14	2	1313	841	472	143	72	66,67%
June 12 - October 15											
P de Villiers	03/06/1957	48	30	18	0	1262	921	341	126	87	62,50%
June 08 - October 11											
AT Markgraaff	23/12/1956	13	8	5	0	352	260	92	38	21	61,54%
July 96 - December 96											
HJ Viljoen	16/07/1959	15	8	6	1	376	312	64	38	18	53,33%
November 00 - December 01											
RAW Straeuli	20/08/1963	23	12	11	0	622	598	24	71	61	52,17%
June 02 - November 03											
CJ du Plessis	24/06/1960	8	3	5	0	288	213	75	39	22	37,50%
June 97 - August 97											
IB McIntosh	24/09/1938	12	4	6	2	252	240	12	25	14	33,33%
June 93 - August 94											
A Coetzee	23/05/1963	12	4	8	0	240	329	-89	20	35	33,33%
June 16 -											
JG Williams	29/10/1946	5	1	4	0	79	130	-51	7	14	20,00%
August 92 - November 92											

SPRINGBOKS BY STADIUM - HOME

		P	W	L	D	PF	PA	TF	TA	Avg. score	%Win
East London	Border Rugby Stadium	3	3	0	0	240	32	36	3	80-11	100%
Johannesburg	Wanderers (New)	1	1	0	0	24	9	3	1	24-9	100%
Nelspruit	Mbombela Stadium	3	3	0	0	91	70	10	7	31-23	100%
Rustenburg	Royal Bafokeng Sports Palace	1	1	0	0	21	20	2	2	21-20	100%
Witbank	Puma Stadium	1	1	0	0	29	13	4	1	29-13	100%
Port Elizabeth	EPRFU Stadium	16	14	1	1	423	182	49	17	26-11	88%
Durban	Kingsmead	5	4	1	0	57	35	7	7	11-7	80%
Pretoria	Loftus Versfeld	34	26	8	0	1103	666	131	66	32-20	76%
Port Elizabeth	Nelson Mandela Bay Stadium	4	3	0	1	106	38	10	3	27-10	75%
Bloemfontein	Vodacom Stadium	18	13	4	1	504	307	57	28	28-17	72%
Johannesburg	Ellis Park	48	33	13	2	1263	797	157	74	26-17	69%
Cape Town	Newlands	52	35	15	2	1014	637	131	67	20-12	67%
Port Elizabeth	Crusader Ground	10	6	3	1	102	57	18	15	10-6	60%
Durban	Growthpoint Kings Park	32	19	10	3	764	565	77	54	24-18	59%
Johannesburg	Wanderers (Old)	4	2	1	1	49	37	12	7	12-9	50%
Springs	PAM Brink Stadium	2	1	1	0	55	37	7	3	28-19	50%
Johannesburg	FNB Stadium	3	1	2	0	111	74	11	8	37-25	33%
Bloemfontein	Springbok Park	1	0	1	0	4	15	0	3	4-15	0%
Kimberley	Eclectic Ground	1	0	1	0	0	3	0	0	0-3	0%
Kimberley	KAC Ground	2	0	1	1	3	9	1	1	2-5	0%
		241	166	62	13	5963	3603	723	367		69%

SPRINGBOKS BY STADIUM - AWAY

		P	W	L	D	PF	PA	TF	TA	Avg. score	% Win
Belfast	Balmoral Ground	1	1	0	0	15	12	4	3	15-12	100%
Bologna	Stadio Dall 'Ara	1	1	0	0	62	31	9	3	62-31	100%
Bordeaux	Route de Médoc, Le Bouscat	1	1	0	0	38	5	9	1	38-5	100%
Bordeaux	Municipal Stadium	1	1	0	0	12	9	0	3	12-9	100%
Bordeaux	Parc Lescure	1	1	0	0	22	12	2	0	22-12	100%
Brisbane	Exhibition Ground	2	2	0	0	23	6	5	0	12-3	100%
Buenos Aires	Ferro Carril Oeste Stadium	4	4	0	0	171	85	24	8	43-22	100%
Buenos Aires	River Plate Stadium	1	1	0	0	37	33	5	3	37-33	100%
Buenos Aires	Velez Sarsfield Stadium	3	3	0	0	99	42	10	4	33-14	100%
Edinburgh	Inverleith	1	1	0	0	16	0	4	0	16-0	100%
Genoa	Luigi Ferraris Stadium	1	1	0	0	54	26	8	2	54-26	100%
Glenville, New York	Owl Creek Polo Field	1	1	0	0	38	7	8	1	38-7	100%
Hamilton	Waikato Stadium	1	1	0	0	32	29	2	2	32-29	100%
Houston, Texas	Robertson Stadium	1	1	0	0	43	20	6	1	43-20	100%
Lyon	Stade Gerland	2	2	0	0	56	47	7	5	28-24	100%
Montevideo	Wanderers Club	1	1	0	0	22	13	3	2	22-13	100%
Padova, Italy	Stadio Euganio	1	1	0	0	22	6	3	0	22-6	100%
Rome	Olympic Stadium	1	1	0	0	40	21	4	2	40-21	100%
Santiago	Prince of Wales Country Club	1	1	0	0	30	16	6	2	30-16	100%
Swansea	St Helen's	2	2	0	0	19	3	5	1	10-2	100%
Udine	Stadio Friuli	1	1	0	0	32	10	4	1	32-10	100%

SPRINGBOKS BY STADIUM - AWAY

		P	W	L	D	PF	PA	TF	TA	Avg. score	% Win
Sydney	Sydney Cricket Ground	6	5	1	0	92	57	18	8	15-10	83%
Cardiff[1]	Millennium Stadium	17	13	3	1	348	272	38	20	20-16	76%
Paris	Parc des Princes	4	3	1	0	91	59	10	5	30-13	75%
Edinburgh	Murrayfield	16	12	4	0	411	156	56	14	27-9	75%
Paris	Colombes Stadium	3	2	0	1	41	14	9	1	14-5	67%
Dublin	Lansdowne Road/Aviva Stadium	13	8	4	1	221	170	33	15	17-13	62%
London	Twickenham	20	11	9	0	335	361	32	33	17-19	55%
Salta	Estadio Padre Ernesto Martearena	2	1	1	0	57	57	5	5	29-29	50%
Mendoza	Malvinas Argentinas Stadium	2	1	0	1	38	33	2	3	19-16	50%
Toulouse	Municipal Stadium	2	1	1	0	26	24	2	2	13-12	50%
Wellington	Athletic Park	7	3	3	1	64	50	5	6	9-7	43%
Perth	Subiaco Oval	8	3	4	1	159	167	13	17	24-19	38%
Paris	Stade de France	3	1	2	0	49	56	4	5	26-14	33%
Sydney	Aussie Stadium	3	1	2	0	47	52	6	3	23-18	33%
Christchurch	Jade Stadium	8	2	6	0	101	149	13	17	13-19	25%
Auckland	Eden Park	10	2	7	1	151	227	19	26	15-23	20%
Dunedin	Carisbrook	8	1	7	0	93	164	9	18	12-21	13%
Brisbane[2]	Suncorp Stadium	10	1	9	0	137	264	15	25	18-25	10%
Glasgow	Hampden Park	1	0	1	0	0	6	0	2	20-5	0%
Marseille	Stade Velodrome	1	0	1	0	10	30	1	2	24-25	0%
Wellington	Wellington Regional Stadium	6	0	6	0	79	180	9	19	19-26	0%
Florence	Stadio Artemio Franchi	1	0	1	0	18	20	2	2	18-20	0%
Brisbane	Ballymore	1	0	1	0	20	28	2	3	20-28	0%
Brisbane	The Gabba	1	0	1	0	27	38	4	4	27-38	0%
Dublin	Croke Park	1	0	1	0	10	15	1	0	10-15	0%
Dunedin	Forsyth Barr Stadium	1	0	1	0	11	21	1	2	11-21	0%
London	Crystal Palace	1	0	0	1	3	3	1	1	3-3	0%
Melbourne	Telstra Dome	1	0	1	0	23	44	3	5	16-37	0%
Sydney	Telstra Stadium	5	0	5	0	73	140	6	17	15-28	0%
Christchurch	AMI Stadium	1	0	1	0	13	41	1	6	13-41	0%
		192	100	84	8	3631	3331	448	330		52%

1 Includes records of the original Cardiff Arms Park on the Millennium Stadium site.
2 Includes one match at Lang Park on which site the Suncorp Stadium was developed.

SPRINGBOKS BY STADIUM - AWAY (NEUTRAL VENUES)

		P	W	L	D	PF	PA	TF	TA	Avg. score	% Win
Albany	North Harbour Stadium (Nm, Sm)	2	2	0	0	100	5	13	1	50-3	100%
Birmingham	Villa Park (Sm)	1	1	0	0	46	6	6	0	46-6	100%
Gosford, Australia	Advocate Express (PI)	1	1	0	0	38	24	4	4	38-24	100%
Lens	Stade Felix Bollaert (T)	1	1	0	0	30	25	4	3	30-25	100%
London	Wembley Stadium (W)	1	1	0	0	28	20	3	1	28-20	100%
Montpellier	Stade de la Mosson (US)	1	1	0	0	64	15	9	2	64-15	100%
Newcastle	St James Park	1	1	0	0	34	16	3	1	34-16	100%
London	Olympic Stadium (US, Arg)	2	2	0	0	88	13	12	1	44-7	100%
Cardiff	Millennium Stadium (NZ)	1	1	0	0	22	18	1	0	22-18	100%
Edinburgh	Murrayfield (Sp)	1	1	0	0	47	3	7	0	47-3	100%
Paris	Stade de France (E, E, Arg, E)	4	4	0	0	132	40	9	1	33-10	100%
Glasgow	Hampden Park (Ur)	1	1	0	0	39	3	5	0	39-3	100%
Marseille	Stade Velodrome (Fj)	1	1	0	0	37	20	5	2	37-20	100%
Sydney	Aussie Stadium (Geo)	1	1	0	0	46	19	7	1	46-19	100%
Brisbane	Suncorp Stadium (Sm)	1	1	0	0	60	10	8	1	60-10	100%
Paris	Parc des Princes (Sm)	1	1	0	0	59	7	8	1	59-7	100%
Wellington	Wellington Regional Stadium (W, Fj, A)	3	2	1	0	75	30	8	2	25-10	67%
Perth	Subiaco Oval (Ur, E)	2	1	1	0	78	31	12	1	39-16	50%
London	Twickenham (W, A, NZ)	3	1	2	0	62	66	1	3	21-22	33%
Brighton	Brighton Community Stadium (J)	1	0	1	0	32	34	4	3	32-34	0%
Melbourne	Telstra Dome	1	0	1	0	9	29	0	3	9-29	0%
		31	25	6	0	1126	434	129	31		

Bryan Habana during the 2011 Rugby World Cup match against Samoa in Albany, New Zealand.

Springbok coach Allister Coetzee faces the media.

SECTION 5:
OTHER NATIONAL TEAMS

www.sarugby.co.za SA RUGBY ANNUAL 2017

SOUTH AFRICA 'A'

Saxons lesson for Springbok hopefuls

By Vata Ngobeni

THIRTEEN long years since the South African 'A' side had played their last match (against Argentina in Wellington), the Springbok second-stringers were resuscitated back to rugby life with a two-match series against the England Saxons.

They were drawn together hastily and given little time to prepare for the ambush by the Saxons, but the Springbok hopefuls nevertheless gave a good account of themselves despite both matches.

Winning the series would have been memorable for Johan Ackermann and his group of Springboks-in-the-making but it was more important that most of the country's fringe international players were given enough exposure and experience at this level of the game.

And it was at the start of the series, at the Toyota Stadium in Bloemfontein, that most of the team got a taste of what international rugby is all about.

For the first 40 minutes of their opening encounter the hosts were chasing shadows in the cold air that had engulfed the Free State capital and were taught a valuable lesson of how small the margin for error is at international level.

Trailing 22-3 at half-time, the South Africans fought back and, given a timely injection by their replacements, came agonisingly close to clinching a miraculous come-from-behind win.

The Saxons emerged 32-24 victors but not without a handful of players enhancing their names and knocking on the door of the Springbok team.

Stormers loose forward Sikhumbuzo Notshe continues to grow in stature and was undoubtedly the South Africans standout player of the first game.

Notshe, along with Scarra Ntubeni, Garth April and Nic Groom, had joined the team in time for just two training sessions and it was

Notshe who proved that it is only a matter of time before he becomes capped as a Springbok.

There were other notable contributions made by Francois Venter, RG Snyman, Lizo Gqoboka, Coenie Oosthuizen and Malcolm Marx, which would have given Ackermann plenty of hope ahead of the second match at Outeniqua Park in George.

It was that very hope, as well as a growing understanding within the team, that energised them in George as they led 12-8 at half-time and looked set to grab a morale-boosting victory.

However, experience combined with the fresh belief sweeping through all levels of English rugby since former Wallabies coach Eddie Jones had taken over the national team's coaching reins, saw the Saxons burgle a 29-26 win.

Again there were players who lifted up their hands as they seek recognition for higher honours. Toyota Cheetahs speedster Sergeal Petersen scored a brace of tries to underline his talent as a deadly finisher and a player with a great feel for the game.

Southern Kings utility back Lukhanyo Am was another who made a good case for himself and his future could lie at centre instead of on the wing where he has been playing at Vodacom Super Rugby level.

SA 'A' captain Teboho 'Oupa' Mohoje reveled in the added responsibility of leadership and he too would have done enough to convince the powers that be of his potential as a future Springbok captain.

As good an exercise as it was for the players, the Saxons tour was equally beneficial for Ackermann's aspirations as a future Springbok coach, while it would also have been a worthwhile experience for assistant coaches Chumani Booi and Abe Davids.

Having led the SA 'A' side will certainly be a feather in Ackermann's cap considering that

Teboho Mohojé and Francois Venter both performed superbly for South Africa A.

he had little say in the composition of the team until the second match.

One wonders what the future holds for this team, especially if given time and more formidable opposition coming more often to South African shores. Perhaps the South Africans could be allowed to embark on overseas tours as well?

For Ackermann, having had a taste for international rugby from the coach's box, it re-affirmed his belief in the talent that is available in South Africa and he believes with more exposure, the Springboks and South African rugby in general can rule the world again.

"Results-wise it was disappointing but there were good things that came out of the series," he said. "These games have helped a lot for the Springbok coach to be able to give exposure to many of our talented players who did not make it into the Springbok squad but are guys to watch for the future.

"For a team that was put together in a short space of time, we did well and there are some players who showed they are ready to make the step up to international rugby. There is talent in this country and more opportunities like these need to be made available to the players," he added.

SOUTH AFRICA A VS ENGLAND SAXONS RESULTS AND SCORERS IN 2016

Played	*Won*	*Lost*	*Drawn*	*Points for*	*Points against*	*Tries for*	*Tries against*
2	0	2	0	50	61	7	8

Date	Venue	Opponent	Result	Score	Referees	Scorers
June 10	Toyota Stadium, Bloemfontein	England Saxons	Lost	24-32	R Rasivhenge	T: Brummer, Van Zyl, Notshe. C: Brummer (3). P: April.
June 17	Outeniqua Park, George	England Saxons	Lost	26-29	J van Heerden	T: Petersen (2), Venter, Du Preez. C: Brummer (2), Zas.

SOUTH AFRICA A APPEARANCES AND POINTS IN 2016

	Date of Birth	Height	Weight	Province	England Saxons 1	England Saxons 2	Apps	T	C	P	DG	PTS
LL (Leolin) Zas	20/10/1995	1,84	87	Western Province	15	15	2	–	1	–	–	2
TK (Travis) Ismaiel	02/06/1992	1,90	95	Blue Bulls	14	11R	2	–	–	–	–	0
JF (Francois) Venter	19/04/1991	1,85	94	Free State	13	13	2	1	–	–	–	5
XH (Howard) Mnisi	13/07/1989	1,86	100	Golden Lions	12	12R	2	–	–	–	–	0
CD (Courtnall) Skosan	24/07/1991	1,84	90	Golden Lions	11	11	2	–	–	–	–	0
GG (Garth) April	16/07/1991	1,76	80	Sharks	10	–	1	–	–	1	–	3
NJ (Nic) Groom	21/02/1990	1,73	83	Western Province	9	–	1	–	–	–	–	0
N (Nizaam) Carr	04/04/1991	1,84	103	Western Province	8	7R	2	–	–	–	–	0
TS (Oupa) Mohojé	03/08/1990	1,93	108	Free State	7c	7c	2	–	–	–	–	0
S (Sikhumbuzo) Notshe	28/05/1993	1,90	100	Western Province	6	–	1	1	–	–	–	5
JST (Stephan) Lewies	27/01/1992	2,00	114	Sharks	5	–	1	–	–	–	–	0
JD (JD) Schickerling	09/05/1995	2,02	109	Western Province	4	5R	2	–	–	–	–	0
VP (Vincent) Koch	13/03/1990	1,85	118	Pumas	3	–	1	–	–	–	–	0
S (Scarra) Ntubeni	18/02/1991	1,74	102	Western Province	2	–	1	–	–	–	–	0
TJ (Thomas) du Toit	05/05/1995	1,90	132	Sharks	1	1	2	–	–	–	–	0
MJ (Malcolm) Marx	13/07/1994	1,89	115	Golden Lions	2R	2	2	–	–	–	–	0
LP (Lizo) Gqoboka	24/03/1990	1,83	115	Blue Bulls	1R	1R	2	–	–	–	–	0
CV (Coenie) Oosthuizen	22/03/1989	1,81	127	Sharks	3R	3R	2	–	–	–	–	0
RG (RG) Snyman	29/01/1995	2,06	117	Blue Bulls	5R	5	2	–	–	–	–	0
J-L (Jean-Luc) du Preez	05/08/1995	1,94	113	Sharks	8R	6	2	1	–	–	–	5
PE (Piet) van Zyl	14/09/1989	1,74	85	Blue Bulls	9R	9	2	1	–	–	–	5
F (Francois) Brummer	17/05/1989	1,83	92	Blue Bulls	10R	10	2	1	5	–	–	15
L (Lukhanyo) Am	28/11/1993	1,86	96	Border Bulldogs	12R	12	2	–	–	–	–	0
SP (Sergeal) Petersen	01/08/1994	1,71	82	Free State	–	14	1	2	–	–	–	10
NL (Ntando) Kebe	19/08/1988	1,79	80	Border Bulldogs	–	9	1	–	–	–	–	0
AF (Arno) Botha	26/10/1991	1,90	103	Blue Bulls	–	8	1	–	–	–	–	0
J (Jason) Jenkins	02/12/1995	2,01	121	Blue Bulls	–	4	1	–	–	–	–	0
M (Marcel) van der Merwe	24/10/1990	1,88	128	Blue Bulls	–	3	1	–	–	–	–	0
E (Edgar) Marutlulle	20/12/1987	1,74	100	EP Kings	–	2R	1	–	–	–	–	0
29 players							46	7	6	1	0	50

ENGLAND SAXONS APPEARANCES AND POINTS IN SOUTRH AFRICA IN 2016

	Date of Birth	Height	Weight	Club	South Africa 'A'1	South Africa 'A'2	Apps	T	C	P	DG	PTS
MPJ (Mike) Haley	28/06/1994	1,88	91	Sale Sharks	15	15	2	–	–	–	–	0
S (Semesa) Rokoduguni	28/08/1987	1,83	98	Bath Rugby	14	14	2	1	–	–	–	5
NA (Nick) Tompkins	16/02/1995	1,83	94	Saracens	13	13	2	–	–	–	–	0
OJ (Ollie) Devoto	22/09/1993	1,88	103	Bath Rugby	12	12	2	1	–	–	–	5
A (Alex) Lewington	20/09/1991	1,85	95	London Irish	11	–	1	–	–	–	–	0
DJ (Danny) Cipriani	02/11/1987	1,85	91	Sale Sharks	10	10	2	–	6	3	–	21
DJ (Dan) Robson	14/03/1992	1,70	77	Wasps	9	9	2	1	–	–	–	5
SF (Sam) Jones	15/12/1991	1,88	113	Wasps	8	8R	2	–	–	–	–	0
MB (Matthew) Kvesic	14/04/1992	1,86	105	Gloucester	7	7	2	1	–	–	–	5
DW (Don) Armand	23/09/1988	1,91	110	Exeter Chiefs	6	8	2	–	–	–	–	0
CJ (Charlie) Ewels	29/06/1995	1,99	112	Bath Rugby	5	5	2	–	–	–	–	0
DMJ (Dave) Attwoodd	05/04/1987	2,01	119	Bath Rugby	4c	4c	2	–	–	–	–	0
K (Kieran) Brookes	29/08/1990	1,88	125	Northampton Saints	3	3	2	–	–	–	–	0
TWJ (Tommy) Taylor	11/11/1991	1,88	104	Sale Sharks	2	2	2	2	–	–	–	10
AW (Alec) Hepburn	30/03/1993	1,83	108	Exeter Chiefs	1	1	2	1	–	–	–	5
GP (George) McGuigan	30/03/1990	1,82	120	Newcastle Falcons	2R	2R	2	–	–	–	–	0
RA (Ross) Harrison	03/09/1992	1,85	118	Sale Sharks	1R	x	1	–	–	–	–	0
J (Jake) Cooper-Woolley	18/11/1989	1,90	124	Wasps	3R	3R	2	–	–	–	–	0
MR (Mitch) Lees	12/10/1988	1,96	122	Exeter Chiefs	4R	5R	2	–	–	–	–	0
DP (Dave) Ewers	03/11/1990	1,93	115	Exeter Chiefs	8R	6	2	–	–	–	–	0
MLR (Michael) Young	31/12/1988	1,73	82	Newcastle Falcons	9R	9R	2	–	–	–	–	0
SG (Sam) James	03/07/1994	1,93	94	Sale Sharks	11R	15R	2	–	–	–	–	0
C (Christian) Wade	15/05/1991	1,73	85	Wasps	14R	11	2	1	–	–	–	5
SAC (Sam) Hill	04/04/1993	1,84	98	Exeter Chiefs	–	14R	1	–	–	–	–	0
JR (James) Craig	08/11/1988	2,01	113	Northampton Saints	–	–	–	–	–	–	–	0
JR (James) Chisholm	11/08/1995	1,91	107	Harlequins	–	–	–	–	–	–	–	0
26 players							45	8	6	3	0	61

SOUTH AFRICA 'A' MANAGEMENT TEAM

Head Coach: Johan Ackermann **Assistant Coach:** Chumani Booi
Assistant Coach: Abe Davids **Conditioning Coach:** Thulani Nteta
Team Doctor: Dr Rob Collins **Physiotherapist:** Karabo Morokane
Team Manager: Willem Oliphant

ENGLAND SAXONS MANAGEMENT TEAM

Head Coach: Ali Hepher *(Exeter Chiefs)* **Assistant Coach:** Andy Titterell *(Wasps)*
Assistant Coach: Alan Dickens *(Northampton Saints)* **Team Manager:** Richard Hill *(Saracens)*

Curwin Bosch.

Fourth for Junior Springboks

By Zeena van Tonder

IT was a disappointing 2016 season for the Junior Springboks as the team finished the World Rugby U20 Championship in fourth place in Manchester, England, following two defeats against Argentina in the tournament.

Coach Dawie Theron's team kicked off their campaign with an encouraging 59-19 victory against Japan at the Academy Stadium after outscoring their opponents eight tries to three, despite trailing 19-14 at the break.

They stumbled in their second outing against the determined Argentineans at the AJ Bell Stadium, with the team going down 19-13 in a tightly-contested encounter. The South Africans trailed 13-6 at the break after leaking a try on the stroke of half-time, and tried hard to bounce back, but errors and poor discipline at crucial times cost them dearly.

Theron's team, however, managed to qualify for the Quarter-final by defeating France 40-31 in their final pool match as they scored five tries to four by France, while flyhalf Curwin Bosch slotted over three penalty goals and three conversions to keep the scoreboard ticking.

The SA U20's met the toughest team in the competition and eventual champions, England, in the Quarter-final, and to their disappointment they were unable to make their presence felt as England dominated proceedings and did well to convert their try-scoring chances into points. After trailing 31-3 at the break, the SA U20's stepped up their attack and defence, and managed to limit England to scoring only eight points in the second half. But the damage inflicted in the first half proved too much for the team to recover from and they were forced to settle for a 39-17 defeat.

The Junior Springboks had one last shot to finish the tournament on a high note in the bronze playoff against Argentina, and they started the match strongly and built up a 19-7 lead thanks to their strong set pieces and enterprising attack. This lead, however, was short-lived as Argentina staged a dramatic comeback to score a total of six tries to only three by the SA U20's, which saw them go down 49-19.

This match brought down the curtain on Theron's six-year term as the Junior Springbok coach, as he opted to take up a contract in Japan.

On a positive note for the team, however, Bosch was one of five players nominated for the World Rugby U20 Championship Player of the Tournament award.

LOG

Pool A	P	W	D	L	PF	PA	PD	TF	TA	BP	PTS
Ireland	3	3	0	0	94	56	38	10	9	1	13
New Zealand	3	2	0	1	97	50	47	15	4	2	10
Wales	3	1	0	2	52	53	-1	6	5	3	7
Georgia	3	0	0	3	16	100	-84	1	14	1	1
Pool B											
England	3	3	0	0	109	23	86	12	2	2	14
Scotland	3	2	0	1	42	73	-31	6	9	1	9
Australia	3	1	0	2	61	42	19	7	4	3	7
Italy	3	0	0	3	39	113	-74	5	15	0	0
Pool C											
Argentina	3	3	0	0	82	48	34	8	6	1	13
South Africa	3	2	0	1	112	69	43	14	8	3	11
France	3	1	0	2	92	78	14	13	9	2	6
Japan	3	0	0	3	53	144	-91	8	20	0	0

Note: BP = Bonus point

FINAL POSITIONS

1 England **2** Ireland **3** Argentina **4** South Africa **5** New Zealand **6** Australia
7 Wales **8** Scotland **9** France **10** Georgia **11** Italy **12** Japan

---

MATCH DETAILS

South Africa 59, Japan 19
(halftime 14-19)
June 7. Manchester City Academy Stadium. Referee: Elia Rizzo *(Italy)*

SOUTH AFRICA
T: Ward (2), Davids (2), Jackson, Libbok, Mafuma, Sadie. C: Bosch (8). P: Bosch.
Bosch, Nkosi, Ward *(c)*, Jackson *(Naude, 54)*, Mafuma, Libbok *(Vers, 77)*, Hall *(Papier, 72)*, Pokomela, Van Rhyn, Davids, Snyman *(De Villiers, 56)*, Wiese, Holtzhausen *(Sadie 56)*, Balekile *(Campher, 77)*, Blose *(Van den Berg, H/T)*.
UNUSED SUB: Hill.

JAPAN
T: Moeakiola (3). C: Kanai (2).

South Africa 13, Argentina 19
(halftime 6-13)
June 11. AJ Bell Stadium, Salford. Referee: Craig Evans *(Wales)*

SOUTH AFRICA
T: Van den Berg. C: Bosch. P: Bosch (2).
Libbok, Nkosi, Ward *(c)*, Naude *(Jackson, 76)*, Mafuma *(Van der Merwe, 59)*, Bosch, Hall *(Jansen Van Vuren, 70)*, Pokomela, Van Rhyn, Davids, Snyman *(Wiese, 56)*, Zandberg *(De Villiers, 46)*, Sadie *(Oosthuizen, 69)*, Balekile *(Campher, H/T)*, Van den Berg.
UNUSED SUB: Holtzhausen.

ARGENTINA
T: Malanos. C: Miotti. P: Miotti (4).

South Africa 40, France 31

(halftime 18-24)

June 15. Manchester City Academy Stadium. Referee: Craig Maxwell-Keys *(England)*

SOUTH AFRICA

T: Bosch, Van der Merwe, Papier, Libbok, Davids. C: Bosch (3). P: Bosch (3).

Bosch, Nkosi, Ward *(c) (Naude, 72)*, Jackson, Van der Merwe, Libbok, Papier *(Hall, 58)*, Pokomela, Wiese, Davids, Snyman *(Van Rhyn, 57)*, De Villiers, Sadie *(Holtzhausen, 71)*, Campher *(Balekile, 49)*, Van den Berg *(Oosthuizen, 57)*.

UNUSED SUBS: Hill, Vers.

FRANCE

T: Ngandbe, Tanguy, Simutoga, Buros. C: Belleau (4). P: Belleau.

South Africa 17, England 39

(halftime 3-31)

June 20. Manchester City Academy Stadium. Referee: Paul Williams *(New Zealand)*

SOUTH AFRICA

T: Bosch, Van der Merwe. C: Bosch (2). P: Bosch.

Bosch, Mafuma *(Naude, 68)*, Ward *(c)*, Jackson, Van der Merwe, Libbok, Van Vuren *(Hall, 61)*, Pokomela, Van Rhyn *(Wiese, H/T)*, Davids, Snyman, De Villiers, Holtzhausen *(Sadie, H/T)*, Balekile *(Campher, 76)*, Oosthuizen *(Van den Berg, H/T)*.

UNUSED SUB: Vers.

ENGLAND

T: Taylor, Williams, Green, Malins, Wright, Aspland-Robinson. C: Mallinder (3). P: Mallinder.

South Africa 19, Argentina 49

(halftime 19-17)

June 25. AJ Bell Stadium, Salford. Referee: Andrew Brace *(Ireland)*

SOUTH AFRICA

T: Campher, Van der Merwe, Libbok. C: Bosch (2).

Bosch, Gans, Naude, Jackson *(Vers,78)*, Van der Merwe, Libbok *(Janse van Rensburg,61)*, Van Vuren *(Hall, 47)*, Pokomela *(c) (Hill, 68)*, Wiese, Davids, Snyman, De Villiers *(Zandberg, H/T)*, Sadie, Campher *(Balekile, 47)*, Van den Berg *(Blose, 56)*.

UNUSED SUB: Oosthuizen.

ARGENTINA

T: Mallia (3), Dominguez, Romanini, Baldunciel. C: Miotti (5). P: Miotti (3).

RESULTS

June 07

South Africa	59	Japan	19
France	15	Argentina	24
Wales	25	Ireland	26
Australia	10	Scotland	15
England	48	Italy	10
New Zealand	55	Georgia	0

June 11

Australia	38	Italy	10
New Zealand	24	Ireland	33
Wales	10	Georgia	9
France	46	Japan	14
South Africa	13	Argentina	19
England	44	Scotland	0

June 15

Argentina	39	Japan	20
Scotland	27	Italy	19
Ireland	35	Georgia	7
New Zealand	18	Wales	17
South Africa	40	France	31
England	17	Australia	13

June 20

9th place Semi Final

Georgia	18	Italy	17
France	41	Japan	27

5th place Semi Final

New Zealand	71	Wales	12
Scotland	19	Australia	35

Semi Finals

Ireland	37	Argentina	7
England	39	South Africa	17

June 25

11th Place Play-Off

Italy	41	Japan	17

9th Place Play-Off

Georgia	24	France	27

7th Place Play-Off

Scotland	19	Wales	42

5th Place Play-Off

Australia	24	New Zealand	55

3rd Place Play-Off

Argentina	49	South Africa	19

Final

England	45	Ireland	21

Zain Davids about to tackle Johnny Williams of England.

LEADING SCORERS

POINTS			TRIES		
Harry Mallinder	England	68	Ataata Moekiola	Japan	6
Curwin Bosch	South Africa	63	Antoine Dupont	France	5
Domingo Miotti	Argentina	52	Caleb Makene	New Zealand	5
Jordie Barrett	New Zealand	52	Shaun Stevenson	New Zealand	5
Johnny McPhillips	Ireland	45	Jacob Stockdale	Ireland	4
Mack Mason	Australia	41	Joe Marchant	England	4
Ataata Moekiola	Japan	39	Juan Cruz Mallia	Argentina	4
Antoine Dupont	France	36	Tevita Tatafu	Japan	4
Anthony Belleau	France	35			
Leonardo Mantelli	Italy	32			

Mosolwa Mashudu Mafuma.

SOUTH AFRICA AT THE JUNIOR WORLD CHAMPIONSHIPS *

Year	Host	Place		
2008	New Zealand in Wales	3rd	Gerrit-Jan van Velze	Eric Sauls
2009	New Zealand in Japan	3rd	Robert Ebersohn	Eric Sauls
2010	New Zealand in Argentina	3rd	CJ Stander	Eric Sauls
2011	New Zealand in Italy	5th	Arno Botha	Dawie Theron
2012	South Africa in South Africa	1st	Wian Liebenberg	Dawie Theron
2013	England in France	3rd	Ruan Steenkamp	Dawie Theron
2014	England in New Zealand	2nd	Handré Pollard	Dawie Theron
2015	New Zealand in Italy	3rd	Hanro Liebenberg **	Dawie Theron
2016	England in England	4th	Jeremy Ward	Dawie Theron

* This tournament replaced the separate Under 19 & Under 21 IRB Junior World Championships.
** Wian and Hanro Liebenberg are brothers.

WORLD JUNIOR PLAYERS OF THE YEAR

2008	Luke Braid (New Zealand)	2013	Sam Davies (Wales)
2009	Aaron Cruden (New Zealand)	2014	Handré Pollard (South Africa)
2010	Julian Savea (New Zealand)	2015	No award given
2011	George Ford (England)	2016	Max Deegan (Ireland)
2012	Jan Serfontein (South Africa)		

SQUAD

	Position	Date of Birth	Height (m)	Weight	Union
BACKS					
CD (Curwin) Bosch	Fullback/Flyhalf	25/06/1997	1,80	80	Sharks
KA (Keanu) Vers	Fullback	04/02/1996	1,75	80	Eastern Province
SR (S'busiso) Nkosi	Wing	21/01/1996	1,81	97	Sharks
MM (Mosolwa) Mafuma	Wing	13/02/1996	1,83	89	Free State
EC (Edwill) van der Merwe	Wing	12/04/1996	1,80	82	Western Province
S-GR (Stedman) Gans	Centre	19/03/1997	1,80	85	Blue Bulls
JT (JT) Jackson	Centre	10/07/1996	1,91	100	Blue Bulls
FJ (Franco) Naudé	Centre	28/03/1996	1,88	101	Blue Bulls
JC (Jeremy) Ward (capt)	Centre	10/01/1996	1,87	86	Eastern Province
BJ (Benhard) Janse van Rensburg	Flyhalf	14/01/1997	1,86	86	Leopards
I (Manie) Libbok	Flyhalf/Fullback	15/07/1997	1,82	80	Blue Bulls
JR (James) Hall	Scrumhalf	02/01/1996	1,73	82	Eastern Province
EC (Embrose) Papier	Scrumhalf	25/04/1997	1,76	80	Blue Bulls
M (Marco) Jansen Van Vuren	Scrumhalf	14/06/1996	1,86	90	Golden Lions
FORWARDS					
DF (Denzel) Hill	No. 8	17/01/1996	1,90	99	Blue Bulls
JS (Junior) Pokomela	No. 8	10/12/1996	1,87	100	Eastern Province
MZ (Zain) Davids	Flanker	04/05/1997	1,81	104	Western Province
JH (Cobus) Wiese	Lock/Flanker	02/06/1997	1,97	103	Western Province
E (Ernst) van Rhyn	Flanker	19/09/1997	1,91	104	Western Province
E le R (Eduard) Zandberg	Lock	14/02/1996	2,01	121	Western Province
EC (Eli) Snyman	Lock	25/01/1996	2,01	111	Blue Bulls
RC (Ruben) de Villiers	Lock	22/03/1997	1,97	103	Western Province
F (Franco) van den Berg	Prop	31/10/1996	1,82	100	Blue Bulls
CJ (Carlu) Sadie	Prop	07/05/1997	1,80	124	Western Province
NJ (Nicolaas) Oosthuizen	Prop	19/11/1996	1,85	119	Eastern Province
JJ (Jaco) Holtzhausen	Prop	12/01/1996	1,81	117	Blue Bulls
KN (Kwenzo) Blose	Prop	12/05/1997	1,86	108	Free State
J-H (Jan-Henning) Campher	Hooker	10/12/1996	1,86	103	Blue Bulls
T (Tango) Balekile	Hooker	07/03/1996	1,81	100	Eastern Province

Head Coach: Dawie Theron **Assistant coach:** Nazeem Adams
Defence Coach: Joey Mongalo **Physiotherapist:** Aneurin Robyn
Video Analyst: Chris Venter **Team Manager:** Trevor Barnes
Strength & Conditioning: André Smith **Media Manager:** Zeena Isaacs

APPEARANCES & POINTS

	Japan	Argentina	France	England	Argentina	Apps	T	C	P	DG	PTS
Curwin Bosch	15	10	15	15	15	5	2	16	7	–	63
S'busiso Nkosi	14	14	14	–	–	3	–	–	–	–	0
Jeremy Ward	13c	13c	13c	13c	–	4	2	–	–	–	10
JT Jackson	12	12R	12	12	12	5	1	–	–	–	5
Mosolwa Mafuma	11	11	–	14	–	3	1	–	–	–	5
Manie Libbok	10	15	10	10	10	5	3	–	–	–	15
James Hall	9	9	9R	9R	9R	5	–	–	–	–	0
Junior Pokomela	8	8	8	8	8c	5	–	–	–	–	0
Ernst van Rhyn	7	7	5R	7	–	4	–	–	–	–	0
Zain Davids	6	6	6	6	6	5	3	–	–	–	15
Eli Snyman	5	5	5	5	5	5	–	–	–	–	0
Cobus Wiese	4	5R	7	7R	7	5	–	–	–	–	0
Jaco Holtzhausen	3	x	3R	3	–	3	–	–	–	–	0
Tango Balekile	2	2	2R	2	2R	5	–	–	–	–	0
Kwenzo Blose	1	–	–	–	1R	2	–	–	–	–	0
Jan-Henning Campher	2R	2R	2	2R	2	5	1	–	–	–	5
Franco van den Berg	1R	1	1	1R	1	5	1	–	–	–	5
Carlu Sadie	3R	3	3	3R	3	5	1	–	–	–	5
Ruben de Villiers	5R	4R	4	4	4	5	–	–	–	–	0
Denzel Hill	x	–	x	–	8R	1	–	–	–	–	0
Embrose Papier	9R	–	9	–	–	2	1	–	–	–	5
Franco Naudé	12R	12	12R	14R	13	5	–	–	–	–	0
Keanu Vers	10R	–	x	x	12R	2	–	–	–	–	0
Eduard Zandberg	–	4	–	4R	4R	3	–	–	–	–	0
Edwill van der Merwe	–	11R	11	11	11	4	3	–	–	–	15
Nicolaas Oosthuizen	–	3R	1R	1	x	3	–	–	–	–	0
Marco Jansen van Vuren	–	9R	–	9	9	3	–	–	–	–	0
Stedman Gans	–	–	–	–	14	1	–	–	–	–	0
Benhard Janse van Rensburg	–	–	–	–	10R	1	–	–	–	–	0
29 players						109	19	16	7	0	148

SA Under-20 2008-2016

† Indicates became a Springbok

Adendorff, S (Shaun) - BB - 2012
Andrews, HD (Hyron) - KZN - 2015
Afrika, CS (Cecil) - Grif - 2008
Badenhorst, WHB (Brummer) - WP - 2010
Balekile, T (Tango) - EP - 2016
Bali, M (Mlungisi) - BB - 2010
Bantjes, HJ (Henri) - BB - 2008
Barry, C (Craig) - WP - 2011
Beerwinkel, A (Andrew) - BB - 2013
Beyers, U (Ulrich) - BB - 2011
Blommetjies, C (Clayton) - BB - 2009
Blose, KN (Kwenzo) - FS - 2016
Booysen, FCF (Fabian) - GL - 2012
Bosch, CD (Curwin) - KZN - 2016
† Botha, AF (Arno) - BB - 2011
Botha, R (Ruan) - GL - 2012
Botha, ZW (Zane) - BB - 2009
Bothma, PL (Rikus) - WP - 2015
Brink, CJ (Cyle) - GL - 2014
Brummer, F (Francois) - BB - 2008, 2009
Bullbring, DJ (David) - GL - 2009
Campher, J-H (Jan-Henning) - BB - 2016
† Carr, N (Nizaam) - WP - 2011
Chikukwa, TA (Tendayi) - BB - 2009
Coetzee, M (Marne) - BB - 2013
Cook, JG (Jean) - FS - 2011
Cooper, KL (Kyle) - KZN - 2009
Cronjé, L (Lionel) - FS - 2009
Cronjé, R (Ross) - KZN - 2009
Davids, MZ (Zain) - WP - 2016
Davis, A (Aidon) - EP - 2013, 2014
De Beer, MH (Tinus) - BB - 2015
De Bruin, L (Luan) - FS - 2013
De Chaves, SJ (Sebastian) - GL - 2010
De Villiers, RC (Ruben) - WP - 2016
Dell, AME (Allan) - KZN - 2012
Dippenaar, SC (Stephan) - BB - 2008
Dreyer, RM (Ruan) - GL - 2010
Du Rand, CW (Wessel) - GL - 2010
Du Toit, F (Francois) - GL - 2010
Du Toit, OJJ (Jacques) - FS - 2013
† Du Toit, PS (Pieter-Steph) - KZN - 2012
Du Toit, TJ (Thomas) - KZN - 2014, 2015
Duvenage, DO (Dewaldt) - Bol - 2008
Du Plessis, DM (Daniel) - WP - 2015
Du Plessis, J-L (Jean-Luc) - KZN - 2014
Du Plessis, WHJ (Jacques) - BB - 2013
Du Preez, BBN (Branco) - BB - 2010
Du Preez, CG (Cornell) - Leop - 2011
Du Preez, D (Daniel) - KZN - 2015
† Du Preez, J-L (Jean-Luc) - KZN - 2014, 2015

Du Preez, RJ (Rob) - KZN - 2013
Dweba, J (Joseph) - FS - 2014
Ebersohn, JM (Sias) - FS - 2008, 2009
Ebersohn, RT (Robert) - FS - 2008, 2009
Els, CW (Corniel) - BB - 2014
Elstadt, R (Rynhardt) - WP - 2009
Esterhuizen, AP (André) - KZN - 2014
† Etzebeth, E (Eben) - WP - 2011
Fourie, C (Corné) - BB - 2008
Gans, S-GR (Stedman) - BB - 2016
Geduld, JG (Justin) - WP - 2013
Gelant, WW (Warrick) - BB - 2014, 2015
† Goosen, JL (Johan) - FS - 2011
Greeff, LD (Lloyd) - Leop - 2014
Griesel, AJ (Abrie) - BB - 2012
Gumede, N (Njabula) - BB - 2015
Hadebe, MS (Monde) - KZN - 2010
Hall, JR (James) - EP - 2016
Hammond, D (Dean) - WP - 2012
Hanekom, NJ (Nicolaas) - WP - 2009
Hartzenberg, Y (Yaasir) - WP - 2009
Howard, PB (Patrick) - WP - 2012
Herbst, IP (Irne) - BB - 2013
Herbst, WJ (Wiehan) - Leop - 2008
Hermanus, GH (Grant) - WP - 2015
Hess, CN (Cornell) - BB - 2008
Hill, DF (Denzel) - BB - 2016
Holtzhausen, JJ (Jaco) - BB - 2016
† Hougaard, F (Francois) - BB - 2008
Ismaiel, TK (Travis) - BB - 2012
Jaer, MAE (Malcolm) - EP - 2015
Jackson, JT (JT) - BB - 2015, 2016
Jacobs, AJ (Adri) - BB - 2010
Jacobs, WJ (Lohan) - BB - 2010, 2011
Janse van Rensburg, BJ (Benhard) - Leop - 2016
Janse van Rensburg, Nico - BB - 2014
† Janse van Rensburg, Rohan - BB - 2013, 2014
Jansen van Vuren, M (Marco) GL - 2015, 2016
Jantjies, A (Tony) - BB - 2012
† Jantjies, ET (Elton) - GL - 2010
Jenkins, JH (Jason) - BB - 2015
Jenkinson, JR (John-Roy) - Leop - 2011
Jordaan, PA (Paul) - KZN - 2011, 2012
Kebble, Q (Oliver) - WP - 2012
Kirsten, FBC (Frik) - BB - 2008
Kirsten, JC (Jannes) - BB - 2013
† Kitshoff, S (Steven) - WP - 2012

Kleinhans, F (Francois) - KZN - 2011
Kolbe, C (Cheslin) - WP - 2013
† Kolisi, S (Siya) - WP - 2010, 2011
Koster, RN (Nick) - WP - 2008
Kotze, SC (Stephan) - FS - 2011
Kriel, DD (Dan) - BB - 2014
† Kriel, JA (Jesse) - BB - 2013, 2014
† Lambie, PJ (Patrick) - KZN - 2010
Leyds, DY (Dillyn) - WP - 2012
Libbok, I (Manie) - BB - 2016
Liebenberg, H (Hanro) - BB - 2015
Liebenberg, WA (Wian) - BB - 2012
Louw, WM (Wilco) - BB - 2014
Lusaseni, L (Luyvuyiso) - KZN - 2008
Mabuza, ST (Thabo) - GL - 2014
Mafuma, MM (Mosolwa) - FS - 2016
Majola, K (Khaya) - KZN - 2012
Majola, M (Mzamo) - KZN - 2015
† Mapoe, LG (Lionel) - FS - 2008
Marais, FS (Franco) - KZN - 2012
Marais, JA (Jandré) - KZN - 2009
Marais, PC (Peet) - KZN - 2010
Marole, T (Thiliphatu) - KZN - 2008
Martinus, DR (Devon) - GL - 2013
Marx, MJ (Malcolm) - GL - 2014
Mastriet, S (Sampie) - BB - 2009, 2010
Mbovane, T (Tshotso) - WP - 2011, 2012
† Mbonambi, MT (Bongi) - BB - 2011
Mellett, MM (Morné) BB - 2009
Mjekevu, WG (Wandile) - GL - 2010, 2011
Mkhabela, MC (Mthokozi) - FS - 2014
Moolman, BJ (Bradley) - BB - 2011
Mtembu, LS (Lubabalo) - KZN - 2010
Muller, FJ (Freddie) - WP - 2010
Muller, MD (Martin) - WP - 2008
Mxoli, NM (Mox) - BB - 2014
Naudé, FJ (Franco) - BB - 2016
Nche, R (Ox) - FS - 2015
Ngcukana, KT (Khanyo) - WP - 2015
Nhlapo, S (Sabelo) - KZN - 2008
Nkosi, SR (S'busiso) - KZN - 2016
Nonkontwana, A (Abongile) - BB - 2014, 2015
Obi, LBS (Luther) - Leopards - 2013
Okafor, K (Kene) - KZN - 2009, 2010
Oosthuizen, CR (Caylib) - GL - 2009
† Oosthuizen, CV (Coenie) - FS - 2009
Oosthuizen, NJ (Nico) - EP - 2016
Orie, M (Marvin) - BB - 2012
† Paige, R (Rudy) - GL - 2009
Papier, EC (Embrose) - BB - 2016

Petersen, S (Sergeal) - EP - 2014
Pietersen, WJ (Wilton) - FS 2008
Pokomela, JS (Junior) - EP - 2016
† Pollard, H (Handré) - WP, BB - 2012, 13, 14
Pretorius, M (Mark) - GL - 2012
Rademan, PJ (Pieter) - FS - 2011
† Redelinghuys, J (Julian) - KZN - 2009
Rossouw, JJ (Jean-Jacques) - WP - 2008
† Ruhle, RK (Raymond) - FS - 2012
Sadie, CJ (Carlu) - WP - 2016
Sadie, J (Johann) - WP - 2009
Scheepers, JN (Nico) - FS - 2010
Schickerling, JD (JD) - WP - 2014
Schmidt, D (Marais) - GL - 2012
Schoeman, JL (Juan) - BB - 2011
Schoeman, M (Marnus) - BB - 2009
Schoeman, P (Pierre) - BB - 2014
Schonert, NP (Nic) - KZN - 2011
Schreuder, L (Louis) - WP - 2010
Seabela OT (Omphile) - BB - 2008, 2009
Sekekete, VK (Victor) - GL - 2014
Senatla, Seabelo - FS - 2013
† Serfontein, JL (Jan) - BB - 2012
Sithole, SMS (Sithembiso) - KZN - 2013
Sithole, ST (Sibusiso) - KZN - 2010

Skosan, CD (Courtnall) - BB - 2011
Small-Smith, WT (William) - BB - 2012
Smit, RA (Roelof) - BB - 2013
Smith, AS (Kwagga) - GL - 2013
Smith, J-P (Juan-Pierre) - BB - 2014
Snyman, EC (Eli) - BB - 2016
Snyman, RG (RG) - BB - 2015
Stander, CJ (CJ) - BB - 2009, 2010
Stander, JH (Jannie) - GL - 2013
Steenkamp, R (Ruan) - BB - 2013
Steyn, AJ (Braam) - KZN - 2012
Swanepoel, AE (Dries) - BB - 2013
† Taute, JJ (Jaco) - GL - 2010, 2011
Thomas, JN (Jason) - BB - 2012
Thomson, BT (Brandon) - WP - 2015
Ungerer, S (Stefan) - KZN - 2013
Van den Heever, GJ (Gerhard) - BB - 2009
Van der Merwe, D (Duhan) - BB - 2014
Van der Merwe, EC (Edwill) - WP - 2016
Van der Merwe, J (Jan) - BB - 2015
† Van der Merwe, M (Marcel) - FS - 2010
Van der Walt, HS (Fanie) - FS - 2010
Van der Watt, V (Vian) - GL - 2012
Van der Westhuizen, DL (Dayan) - BB - 2014
Van Deventer, JC (Johan) - GL - 2008
Van Dyk, NJJ (Nico) - KZN - 2012

Van Rhyn, E (Ernst) - WP - 2016
Van Velze, G-J (Gerrit-Jan) - BB - 2008
Van Vuuren, MT (Michael) - FS - 2011
Van Vuuren, P-W (PW) - FS - 2008
Van Wyk, A (Arno) - BB - 2014
Van Wyk, FRP (Frans) - WP - 2015
Van Wyk, JP (Kobus) - WP - 2012
Van Zyl, I (Ivan) - BB - 2015
Vermeulen, JF (Jacques) - WP - 2014, 2015
Venter, HC (Hanco) - KZN - 2013
Venter, JF (Francois) - BB - 2010, 2011
Venter, RC (Ruan) - GL - 2011
Vers, KA (Keanu) - EP - 2016
Viljoen, EW (EW) - WP - 2015
Visser, D (Dennis) - BB - 2013
Ward, JC (Jeremy) - EP - 2016
Watermeyer, S (Stefan) - BB - 2008
Wegner, C (Carl) - FS - 2011
Welthagen. JJ (Johnny) - Leop - 2011
Wiese, JH (Cobus) - WP - 2016
Willemse, ME (Michael) - BB - 2013
Wiillemse, P (Paul) - GL - 2012
Williams, K (Percy) - GL - 2013
Willis, VS (Vainon) - BB - 2008
Zandberg, E le R (Eduard) - WP - 2016
Zas, LL (Leolin) - WP - 2015

Jeremy Ward on the charge against Japan.

**SPRINGBOK
SEVENS**

Podium finish for Springbok Sevens

By JJ Harmse

AN Olympic bronze and a second-place finish in the HSBC World Rugby Sevens Series highlighted another stellar season for the Springbok Sevens team in 2016. The team travelled to Rio de Janeiro in August as a top three contender for the gold medal in Rugby Sevens and won bronze, the first ever rugby medal won by Team South Africa at the Olympic Games.

Fiji, who also won the World Series at the end of May 2016, won gold, while Team Great Britain won silver after edging out the South Africans 7-5 in their semifinal match.

With huge anticipation about the first ever participation at the Olympics for Rugby Sevens, much of the 2015/16 HSBC World Rugby Sevens Series saw teams experimenting with squads and a number of stars in the fifteens game trying their hand at sevens with the hope of getting to Rio and possible Olympic glory.

Springbok Sevens coach Neil Powell also entertained the idea and the likes of Bryan Habana, Francois Hougaard, Juan de Jongh and Ryan Kankowski were amongst the celebrated Springboks who tried to adapt to the shorter version of the game.

Hougaard and De Jongh were part of the squad for the opening two tournaments and quickly learned the difference between winning and losing. The Blitzboks lost in the quarterfinals in Dubai in the first week of December, but bounced back brilliantly a week later to win the inaugural HSBC Cape Town Sevens in the Cape Town Stadium. The South Africa leg of the World Series moved from Port Elizabeth, where the home side won consecutive tourna-

ments and made it three in a row at home with a solid win over Argentina.

The next two tournaments, in Australasia, again delivered good results. Philip Snyman took over the captaincy from Kyle Brown for the first time as coach Neil Powell broadened his captaincy options with the Olympic in mind, while Sandile Ngcobo made his debut.

The South Africans made the final in Wellington, but lost out to New Zealand after the final hooter, in a match where the officials came under fire from journalist for their calls. A week later, South Africa again played some solid rugby, but lost in the semifinals and finished fourth in the inaugural Sydney Sevens.

This became the norm for the team, who made the remaining six quarterfinals.

Leading the World Series log going to North America, Bryan Habana was a popular inclusion, while Tim Agaba, a debutant on the previous trip, was also making good strides. The Blitzboks finished third in Las Vegas, where they won the year before and again showed good composure. A week later, Vancouver hosted their first ever stop on the World Series. The Blitzboks again went to the final, but again New Zealand proved too strong and South Africa finished runners-up.

The Blitzboks never won in Hong Kong and that remained the case on the next stop. Siviwe Soyizwapi debuted at this popular venue, where a win by Fiji edged them away from South Africa on the log. The South Africans finished third.

A week later, in Singapore, it was third place again for South Africa, with Kenya the surprise winners of the tournament, back on the circuit after a number of years.

The final legs saw a return to Paris after ten years, but unfortunately for the South Africans, they slipped up in the quarters where they lost to Samoa. They fact that the Samoans then continued winning and beating Fiji in the final did not ease the pain, nor did it close the gap on Fiji.

Yet, with the last tournament of the series, in London, remaining, South Africa still have an outside chance to win the overall title. Fiji had to lose in the pool stages though and not make the Cup quarters, while the Springbok Sevens needed to win.

Fiji made the last eight and won the series, but a solid win over them gave the South Africans some satisfaction. They met Scotland in the final and looked to cruise towards a win with a minute left. Two tries by the Scots in 60 seconds edged them past the stunned Blitzboks and handed them a first ever title.

Fiji finished on 181 points, with South Africa on 171 and New Zealand a distant third on 158. The fact that the Blitzboks had the best points difference after ten tournaments counted little, but did reflect just how much a couple of soft defeats hurt.

Team South Africa started their quest for gold well in Rio, winning their opening two matches, but then fell to Australia in the final pool match. This resulted in them facing Australia again in the quarterfinals, but this time Kyle Brown's men won on a canter. The 7-5 defeat to the combined team of England, Wales and Scotland in the semis was a bitter pill to swallow, but the team rebounded well, beating Japan with a big score to secure a first ever bronze medal.

Seabelo Senatla was named World Rugby's Sevens Player of the Year at the end of the series, taking the crown from Werner Kok. Senatla and Kwagga Smith also made the Dream Team for the series.

• *At time of going to print, in February 2017, the Springbok Sevens team had won their third tournament out of four and were leading the 2016/17 HSBC World Rugby Sevens Series log.*

SA SEVENS REPORT 2015-16
TOURNAMENT 1: Dubai, 4-5 December 2015

SA results: *bt Samoa 33-7, bt Russia 45-0, bt Scotland 26-12, lost USA 19-21 (QF Cup), bt Argentina 26-5 (SF Plate), bt Australia 19-14 (Plate Final).*

TOURNAMENT 2: Cape Town, South Africa, 12-13 December 2015

SA results: *bt Zimbabwe 26-5, lost Kenya 12-14, bt England 10-0, bt Australia 25-5 (QF Cup), bt France 21-12 (SF Cup), bt Argentina 29-14 (Cup final).*

TOURNAMENT 3: Wellington, New Zealand, 30-31 January 2016

SA results: *bt Scotland 28-5, bt Russia 54-0, lost New Zealand 14-19, bt Australia 26-14 (QF Cup), bt Fiji 31-0 (SF Cup), lost New Zealand 21-24 (Cup final).*

TOURNAMENT 4: Sydney, Australia, 6-7 February 2016

SA results: *bt Scotland 33-7, bt Russia 40-0, bt Kenya 26-19, bt Argentina 26-0 (QF Cup), lost Australia 7-12 (SF Cup), lost Fiji 12-26 (Bronze final).*

TOURNAMENT 5: Las Vegas, USA, 6-7 February 2016

SA results: *bt Canada 33-7, bt Wales 36-7, bt USA 29-0, bt New Zealand 14-7 (QF Cup), lost Australia (SF Cup), bt USA 21-10 (Bronze final).*

TOURNAMENT 6: Vancouver, Canada, 12-13 March 2016

SA results: *bt Scotland 43-0, bt Brazil 26-7, bt Argentina 27-0, bt Wales 31-0 (QF Cup), bt Fiji 31-19 (SF Cup), lost New Zealand 14-19 (Cup final).*

TOURNAMENT 7: Hong Kong, China, 8-10 April 2016

SA results: *lost England 14-21, bt Russia 50-0, bt Scotland 31-0, bt USA 28-0 (QF Cup), lost New Zealand 7-12 (SF Cup), bt Australia 14-12 (Bronze final).*

TOURNAMENT 8: Singapore, 16-17 April 2016

SA results: *bt Scotland 33-0, bt Russia 21-10, bt Kenya 14-0, bt New Zealand 12-7 (QF Cup), lost Fiji (SF Cup), bt Argentina 28-0 (3rd place play-off).*

TOURNAMENT 9: Paris, France, 13-15 May 2016
SA results: *bt England 24-5, bt Brazil 30-7, bt Australia 31-0, lost Samoa 10-21 (QF Cup), bt New Zealand 29-19 (Plate SF), bt Australia 17-7 (Plate final).*
TOURNAMENT 10: London, England, 21-22 May 2016
SA results: bt Canada 21-7, bt USA 14-10, bt Samoa 22-0, bt Argentina 21-19 (QF Cup), bt Fiji 26-21 (SF Cup), lost Scotland 26-27 (Cup final).
OLYMPIC GAMES, Rio de Janeiro, Brazil , 9-11 August 2016
(part of SASCOC Team SA)
SA results: bt Spain 24-0, bt France 26-0, lost Australia 5-12, bt Australia 22-5(QF), lost Great Britain 5-7 (SF), bt Japan 54-14 (Bronze medal).

IRB SEVENS WORLD SERIES 2015-16
(Only top 15 countries listed)

Team	UAE	SA	NZ	AUS	USA	CAN	CHI	SIN	FR	ENG	Pts
Fiji	22	13	17	17	22	15	22	19	19	15	181
South Africa	13	22	19	15	17	19	17	17	13	19	171
New Zealand	15	10	22	22	13	22	19	12	10	13	158
Australia	12	10	13	19	19	17	15	10	12	7	134
Argentina	10	19	12	13	10	5	8	15	15	12	119
USA	17	12	10	10	15	12	12	7	5	17	117
Kenya	5	15	10	12	10	1	10	22	10	3	98
England	19	7	15	10	1	5	13	5	7	10	92
Samoa	10	3	8	7	3	13	5	13	22	5	89
Scotland	7	8	7	5	5	10	7	8	8	22	87
France	8	17	3	1	7	7	5	10	17	10	85
Wales	5	5	1	3	8	10	10	2	2	8	54
Canada	3	5	5	8	2	8	2	1	1	5	40
Russia	1	2	2	2	5	3	3	3	5	2	28
Japan	2	-	5	1	12	-	-	1	-	-	21

World Rugby Sevens Player of the Year: Seabelo Senatla.

SA SEVENS PLAYERS 2015-16

Player	Union	UAE	SA	NZ	AUS	USA	CAN	CHI	SIN	FR	ENG	OG
Dry, CA (Chris)	SARU contracted	X	X	x	X	X	X	-	X	-	X	-
Snyman, P (Philip)	SARU contracted	X	X	X(c)	X(c)	-	-	X	-	X(c)	X(c)	X
Hougaard, F (Francois)*	SARU contracted	X	X	X	X	-	-	-	-	X	X	X(r)
Smith, A S (Kwagga)	SARU contracted	X	X	X	X	X	X	X	X	X	-	X
Kok, W (Werner)	SARU contracted	X	-	-	-	-	-	-	-	-	-	X
Brown, K G (Kyle)	SARU contracted	X(c)	X(c)	-	-	X(c)	X(c)	X(c)	X(c)	X	X	X(c)
Kolbe, C (Cheslin)	DHL WP	X	X	X	X	-	-	-	-	-	-	X
Benjamin, R (Ryno)	Toyota Free State Cheetahs	X	X	X	-	-	-	-	-	-	-	-
Geduld, JG (Justin)	SARU contracted	X	X	X	-	X	X	X	X	-	-	X
Afrika, C (Cecil)	SARU contracted	X	-	-	-	X	X	X	X	X	X	X
Senatla, SM (Seabelo)	SARU contracted	X	X	X	X	X	X	X	X	X	X	X
De Jongh, J (Juan)	DHL WP	X	X	X	-	-	-	-	-	-	-	X
Sage D M (Dylan)*	SARU contracted	-	X	-	X	X	X	-	-	X	X	X
Specman, R (Rosco)	SARU contracted	-	X	X	X	X	X	-	-	X	X	X
Du Preez, C (Carel)	SARU contracted	-	-	-	X	X	-	-	-	-	-	-
Ngcobo, S C (Sandile)*	SARU contracted	-	-	X	X	-	-	-	-	-	-	-
Agaba, TE (Tim)*	SARU contracted	-	-	-	X	X	X	X	X	X	X	X
Habana, B G (Bryan)	Toulon	-	-	-	-	X	X	-	-	-	-	-
Du Preez, B (Branco)	SARU contracted	-	-	-	-	X	X	X	X	-	-	-
Nel, A R (Ruhan)	SARU contracted	-	-	-	-	X	X	X	X	X	-	-
Kankowski, R (Ryan)	SARU contracted	-	-	-	-	-	X	X	X	X	-	-
Soyizwapi, S (Sviwe)*	SARU contracted	-	-	-	-	-	X	X	-	X	-	-
Dippenaar, S (Stephan)	SARU contracted	-	-	-	-	-	X	X	X	X	-	-

New caps

Country, Tournament and Provincial Team Abbreviations

COUNTRY & TOURNAMENT ABBREVIATIONS:

A - Australia, Arg - Argentina, C - Canada, CG - Commonwealth Games, Ch - Chile, Chi - China, Dub - Dubai, E - England, F - France, Fj - Fiji, HK - Hong Kong, J - Japan, Mal - Malaysia, NZ - New Zealand, OG - Olympic Games, RWC - Rugby World Cup, S - Scotland, SA - South Africa, Sin - Singapore, Ur - Uruguay, US - United States of America, W - Wales, WG - World Games

PROVINCIAL TEAMS ABBREVIATIONS:

BB - Blue Bulls, Bol - Boland, Bor - Border, EP - Eastern Province, Fal - Falcons, FS - Free State, GL - Golden Lions, Gri - Griquas, GW - Griqualand West, KZN - Kwazulu Natal, Leo - Leopards, NTvl - Northern Transvaal, NW - North West, SWD - South Western Districts, Tvl - Transvaal, WP - Western Province

SA Sevens Internationals 1993-2016

An asterisk in this list indicates the captain in that particular tournament while
15 a side Springboks are indicated with †

Adams, BI (Bennie) - WP) - 6) - 2004: HK, Sin, F, E, Dub, SA.

Adendorff, S (Shaun)) - BB) - 2) - 2014: S, E.

Africa, CS (Cecil)) - SARU - 49) - 2009: WG, Dub, SA. 2010: NZ, US, A, HK, E, S, CG, Dub, SA. 2011: US, HK, A, E, S, A, SA. 2012: NZ, US, HK, A, SA. 2013: J, E, RWC, A, Dub, SA. 2014: US, NZ, HK, CG, A, SA. 2015: NZ, US, HK, J, S, Dub. 2016: US, C, HK, Sin, F, E, OG.

Agaba, TE (Tim)) - SARU) - 8) - 2016: A, US, C, HK, Sin, F, E, OG.

Alberts, N (Nico) - WP) - 1) - 2001: NZ.

†Aplon, GG (Gio)) - WP) - 15) - 2006: NZ, US, F, E. 2007: E, S. 2008: E, S, Dub, SA. 2009: NZ, US, E, S, RWC.

April, C (Chelton) - WP) - 1) - 1996: HK.

Arnold, P (Peet)) - NTvl) - 4) - 1996: Dub. 1998: Arg, Ur, Ch.

†Badenhorst, C (Chris)) - FS) - 3) - 1993: HK, RWC. 1996: Ur.

Basson, S (Stefan)) - WP) - 22 - 2004: HK, Sin, F, E. 2005: Sin, E, F, RWC, WG, Dub, SA. 2006: NZ, US, E, F, CG, Dub, SA. 2007: HK, A. 2008: E, S.

Benjamin, RS (Ryno)) - Bol) - 37) - 2005: Sin, E, F, WG. 2006: F, E, Dub, SA. 2007: US, HK, A. 2008: Dub, SA. 2009: NZ, US, HK, A, E, S, RWC, WG, Dub. 2010: NZ, US, A, HK, E, S, CG. 2013: RWC. 2014: Dub, SA. 2015: NZ, US, Dub, SA. 2016: NZ.

Blom, J (Jandré) - FS - 6 - 2005: Dub, SA. 2006: HK, Sin. 2007: NZ, US.

Blommetjies, C (Clayton) - SARU - 2 - 2012: S, E.

†Bobo, G (Gcobami) - Lions - 10 - 1999: SA. 2001: E, W, J. 2007: NZ, US, HK, A, E*, S*.

Bock, AG (Alshaun) - Bol - 1 - 2003: HK.

†Boome, CS (Selborne) - WP - 3 - 1998: Arg, Ur, Ch.

Botha, B (Bernardo) - GL - 16 - 2010: CG, Dub, SA. 2011: NZ, US, HK, A, Dub, SA, NZ, US, HK, J, SA. 2013: E, WG.

Bouwer, G (Graeme) - NTvl - 5 - 1996: Dub. 1997: RW. 1998: HK. 1999: Fj, HK.

Bowles, J (Jovan) - Sharks - 4 - 2006: Dub, SA. 2007: E, S.

Brand, J (Janneman) - WP - 2 - 1996: Ur, HK.

Breytenbach, C (Conrad) - NTvl - 1 - 1996: HK.

Brink, HM (Helgard) - FS - 28 - 1999: F, Dub, SA. 2000: NZ, Fj, A, HK, J, F, SA, Dub. 2001: RWC, HK, Ch, Mal, J, E, W, J, Dub, SA. 2002: Ch, Arg, A, NZ, Sin, Mal, A.

Brink, S (Stephen) - FS - 7 - 1996: Ur, HK, Dub*. 1997: RWC. 1998: Arg*, Ur*, Ch*

†Britz, GJJ (Gerrie) - FS - 4 - 2001: Dub, SA, Ch, Arg.

†Britz, WK (Warren) - Sharks - 14 - 1999: F, Dub, SA. 2000: Ur, Arg, NZ, Fj, A, HK, J, F, SA, Dub. 2001: RWC.

Brown, KG (Kyle) - WP - 62 - 2008: Dub, SA. 2009: NZ, US, HK, A, E, S, RWC, WG, Dub, SA. 2010: NZ, US, A*, HK*, Dub*, SA*. 2011: NZ*, US*, HK*, A*, E*, S*, A*, Dub*, SA*. 2012: NZ*, US*, HK*, J*, S*, E*, A*, SA*. 2013: RWC*, WG*, A*, Dub*, SA*. 2014: US*, NZ*, J*, HK*, J*, S*, E*. 2015: NZ*, US*, HK*, J*, S*, E*, Dub*, SA*. 2016: US*, C*, HK*, Sin*, F, E, OG*.

†Brüssow, HW (Heinrich) - FS - 2 - 2006: HK, Sin.

Burger, PB (Phillip) - FS - 9 - 2006: NZ, US, F, E, CG, Dub, SA, 2012: S, E.

Calitz, JP (Johan) - Leo - 18 - 1999: Arg, Ch, Fj, HK, J, F. 2000: HK, J, SA, Dub. 2001: NZ, HK, Ch, Mal, J, E, W, J.

†Chavhanga, T (Tonderai) - FS - 2 - 2003: Dub, SA.

†Cilliers, NV (Vlok) - WP - 4 - 1993: HK. 1994: HK. 1996: Dub. 1998: HK.

†Claassens, JP (Jannie) - NTvl - 4 - 1993: HK, RWC. 1996: HK, Dub.

Coeries, DB (Darryl) - SWD - 5 - 2002: Dub, SA. 2003: A, NZ, HK.

Coetzee, F (Fielies) - Fal - 2 - 1999: Arg, Ch.

Coetzee, R (Rudi) - Lions - 4 - 2002: Dub, SA. 2003: W, E.

†Conradie, JHJ (Bolla) - WP - 5 - 1999: Dub, SA. 2000: NZ, Fj, A.

Dames, A (Archer) - Pumas - 1 - 1999: F.

Damons, O (Ossie) - Gri - 2 - 2005: E, F.

Dazel, RL (Renfred) - Bol - 37 - 2005: WG, Dub, SA. 2006: NZ, US, HK, Sin, CG, SA. 2007: NZ, US, Dub, SA. 2008: NZ, US, HK, A, Dub, SA. 2009: NZ, US, HK, A, E, S, RWC, WG. 2010: E, S, CG, Dub. 2011: NZ, US, A, Dub. 2012: US, J.

†De Jongh, JL (Juan) - WP - 6 - 2008: NZ. 2015: Dub, SA. 2016: NZ, A, OG.

Delport, PS (Paul) - WP - 33 - 2003: Dub. 2004: NZ, US. 2006: F, E. 2008: Dub, SA. 2009: NZ, US, S, RWC, WG, Dub*, SA*, CG*. 2010: SA. 2011: NZ, HK, A, E, S, A, Dub, SA. 2012: NZ, HK, A, Dub, SA. 2013: NZ, US, HK, S.

De Marigny, MRD (Marc) - Sharks - 14 - 2003: A, NZ, HK, W, E, Dub*, SA*. 2004: NZ, US, HK*, Sin*, F*, E*, Dub.

Demas, D (Danwel) - WP - 23 - 2003: Dub, SA. 2004: NZ, US, HK, Sin, F, E. 2005: Sin, E, F, RWC, WG, Dub, SA. 2006: F, CG, Dub, SA. 2007: Dub, SA. 2008: E, S.

†De Villiers, J (Jean) - WP - 11 - 2002: Ch, Arg, A, NZ, Chi, HK, Sin, Mal, E, W, CG.

Dippenaar, D (Dirk) - SARU - 1 - 2012: J.

Dippenaar, S (Stephan) - SARU - 30 - 2012: NZ, US, HK, J, S, A, Dub, SA. 2013: NZ, US, HK, J, S, E, RWC, WG, A, Dub. 2014: US, NZ, J, HK, A. 2015: HK, S, E. 2016: HK, Sin, F, E.

†Dirks, CA (Chris) - Tvl - 1 - 1994: HK.

Dry, CA (Chris) - SARU - 53 - 2010: A, HK, E, S. 2011: NZ, US, HK, A, E, S, A, Dub, SA. 2012: NZ, US, HK, J, S, E, A, Dub, SA. 2013: NZ, US, HK, J, S, RWC, A, Dub, SA. 2014: US, NZ, J, HK, S, E, CG, A. 2015: NZ, US, HK, J, S, E, Dub, SA. 2016: NZ, A, US, C, Sin, E.

Du Plessis, M (Malan) - Bol - 1 - 2003: HK.

Du Plooy, JP (JP) - Lions - 3 - 1998: Arg, Ur, Ch.

Du Preez, B (Branco) - BB - 48 - 2010: NZ, US, A, HK, Dub, SA. 2011: NZ, US, HK, A, E, S, Dub, SA. 2012: NZ, US, HK, J, S, E, A. 2013: US, HK, J, RWC, Dub, SA. 2014: US, NZ, J, HK, S, E, CG, A, Dub, SA. 2015: NZ, US, HK, J, S, E. 2016: A US, C, HK, Sin.

Du Preez, C (Carel) - SARU - 5 - 2015: J, S, E. 2016: NZ, A.

†Du Toit, GS (Gaffie) - GW - 2 - 1998: CG. 2002: CG.

Ebersohn, RT (Robert) - FS - 12 - 2008: HK, A, Dub, SA. 2009: NZ, US, HK, A, E, RWC. 2011: A, Dub.

Engelbrecht, G (Gerrie) - GW - 8 - 2000: Ur, Arg, NZ, Fj, A, HK, J. 2001: NZ.

Engelbrecht, J (Jacques) - SARU - 1 - 2010: SA.

Engelbrecht, P (Pieter) - SARU - 13 - 2010: Dub, SA. 2011: NZ, US, A. 2012: HK, J, S, E. 2013: NZ, US, S, E.

†Esterhuizen, G (Grant) - Lions - 1 - 2003: NZ.

Eyre, NJ (Nicolas) - Lions - 3 - 2003: NZ. 2004: F, E.

Fihlani, IZ (Ian) - Bulldogs - 12 - 2001:

NZ. 2002: Chi, HK, Sin, Mal, E, W, Dub, SA. 2003: HK, W, E.

†Floors, L (Lucas) - SWD - 11 - 2003: Dub, SA. 2004: HK, Sin, F. 2005: Dub. 2006: Dub*, SA. 2007: SA. 2008: E, S.

Foote, KW (Kevin) - Natal - 8 - 2002: Dub. 2003: A, NZ, HK, W, E. 2004: NZ*, US*

Fourie, AJ (Andries) - EP - 24 - 1999: Arg, Ch, Fj, HK, F*, Dub, SA. 2000: Ur, Arg, NZ*, Fj*, A*, HK*, J*, F*, SA, Dub. 2001: NZ, HK, Chi, Mal, J, E, W.

Fourie, DA (Deon) - WP - 2 - 2007: E, S.

Fowles, JJ (Josh) - Bulldogs - 2 - 2002: Sin, Mal.

Francis, E (Eugene) - WP - 17 - 2002: A, NZ, Chi, HK, Sin, Mal, E, W. 2003: A, NZ, HK, W, E, Dub, SA. 2004: NZ, US.

Fredericks, ER (Eddie) - NW - 11 - 1999: F. 2000: NZ, Fj, A. 2004: Dub, SA. 2005: NZ, US, E, F, RWC.

Frolick, S (Shandré) - WP - 3 - 2005: NZ, US. 2006: Dub.

Geduld, JG (Justin) - SARU - 27 - 2013: NZ, HK, J, S, A, Dub, SA. 2014: US, NZ, J, HK, S, E, CG, A. 2015: NZ, HK, J, E, Dub, SA. 2016: NZ, US, C, HK, Sin, OG.

Gelant, WW (Warrick) - BB - 4 - 2014: Dub, SA. 2015: NZ, US.

†Gerber, HJ (Hendrik) - WP - 3 - 1998: Arg, Ur, Ch.

†Gillingham, JW (Joe) - Lions - 4 - 1998: Arg, Ur, Ch, CG.

Grobler, D (Daniel) - BB - 2 - 1999: Fj, HK.

†Habana, BG (Bryan) - Lions - 4 - 2004: NZ, US. 2016: US, C.

Haupt, PJ (Hanru) - FS - 2 - 2003: A, NZ.

Heidtmann, DM (Dale) - Bulldogs - 23 - 2001: NZ, Dub, SA. 2002: Ch, Arg, A, NZ, Chi, HK, Sin, Mal, E, W, CG. 2003: Dub, SA. 2014: NZ, US, HK, Sin, F, E, SA.

Helberg, D (Deon) - BB - 2 - 2009: Dub, SA.

†Hendricks, C (Cornal) - SARU - 19 - 2011: SA. 2012: NZ, US, HK, J, S, E, A, Dub, SA. 2013: NZ, US, HK, J, S, E, RWC, A. 2014: CG.

†Honiball, HW (Henry) - Natal - 1 - 1994: HK.

Horne, FH (Frankie) - SARU - 71 - 2007: Dub, SA. 2008: NZ, US, HK, A, E, S, Dub, SA. 2009: NZ, US, HK, A, E, S, RWC, WG, Dub, SA. 2010: NZ, US, A, HK, E, S, Dub, SA. 2011: NZ, US, HK, A, E, S, A, Dub, SA. 2012: NZ, US, HK, J, S, E, A, Dub, SA*. 2013: NZ*, US*, HK*, J*, S*, E*, A, Dub, SA. 2014: US, NZ, J, HK, S*, E*, CG, A*, Dub, SA. 2015: NZ, US, HK, J, S, E.

†Hougaard, F (Francois) - SARU - 7 - 2015: Dub, SA. 2016: NZ, A, F, E, OG.

Houtshamer, J (Juan) - Fal - 2 - 2000: HK, J.

Hulme, A (Alten) - BB - 1 - 2003: HK.

Human, WA (Wylie) - FS - 3 - 2000: HK, J, F.

Hunt, S (Steven) - WP - 24 - 2010: NZ, US, A, SA. 2011: NZ, US, E, S, A, SA. 2012: NZ, US, S, E, A, Dub. 2013: HK, J, S, WG, A, SA. 2014: J, A.

Isbell, R (Ruwellyn) - SARU - 4 - 2012: A, Dub, SA. 2013: WG.

Jackson, KL (Lesley) - Bol - 6 - 2004: Dub, SA, RWC. 2005: SA. 2006: HK, Sin.

†Jacobs, AA (Adi) - Fal - 2 - 2000: HK, J.

Jacobsz, SPE (Barry) - SWD - 1 - 2001: J.

†Jantjes, CA (Conrad) - Lions - 16 - 1999: Dub, SA. 2000: Ur, Arg, NZ, Fj, A, HK, J. F. 2001: Hk, Chi. 2002: CG, Dub. 2003: W, E.

Johannes, R (Reuben) - SARU - 2 - 2012: A. 2013: WG.

Joka, W (Wonga) - EP - 3 - 2000: NZ, Fj, A.

Jonker, J (Jacques) - FS - 1 - 1995: HK.

Jonker, JW (JW) - SARU - 4 - 2009: Dub, SA. 2010: A, HK.

Jordaan, P (Paul) - SARU - 3 - 2011: NZ, US, HK.

†Joubert, AJ (André) - Natal - 3 - 1993: HK*, RWC*. 1994: HK*.

Juries, FM (Fabian) - EP - 50 - 2000: SA, Dub. 2001: NZ, HK, Chi, Mal, J, E, W, J, Dub, SA. 2002: Ch, Arg, A, NZ, CG. 2003: W, E, Dub, SA. 2004: NZ, US, HK, Sin, F, E. 2005: NZ, US, Sin, E, F, RWC, WG, SA. 2006: NZ*, US*, HK, Sin, CG. 2007: Dub, SA. 2008: NZ, US, HK, A, E, S. 2010: E, S.

†Kankowski, R (Ryan) - KZN - 9 - 2006: NZ, US, HK, Sin, CG. 2016: HK, Sin, F, E.

†Kayser, DJ (Deon) - EP - 2 - 1998: HK, CG.

Kok, W (Werner) - SARU - 22 - 2013: E, WG, Dub, SA. 2014: US, NZ, J, HK, S, E, CG, A, Dub, SA. 2015: NZ, US, HK, J, S, E, Dub. 2016: OG.

Kolbe, C (Cheslin) - SARU - 11 - 2012: E, SA. 2013: NZ, US. 2014: Dub, SA. 2015: Dub, SA. 2016: NZ, A, OG.

Krause, GE (Gareth) - GW - 5 - 2004: Dub, SA. 2005: NZ, US, RWC.

Kriese, D (Dieter) - Natal - 3 - 1993: HK, RWC. 1995: HK.

Kruger, CR (Chris) - FS - 2 - 1998: Arg. 1999: Ch.

†Kruger, RJ (Ruben) - FS - 3 - 1993: HK, RWC. 1994: HK.

Kruger, HJ (Jorrie) - FS - 4 - 1996: Dub. 1998: Arg, Ur, Ch.

Kruger, O (Okkie) - BB - 1 - 2010: CG.

Kuün, GWF (Derick) - BB - 2 - 2005: NZ, US.

†Loubscher, RIP (Ricardo) - EP - 4 - 1999: Arg, Ch. 2000: F. 2001: RWC.

Luiters, K (Kevin) - FS - 1 - 2012: Dub.

†Mapoe, LG (Lionel) - FS - 4 - 2009: US, HK, A, RWC.

Maritz, H (Hoffman) - FS - 6 - 2010: NZ, US, A, HK, E, S.

Markow, A (Tony) - EP - 1 - 1995: HK.

Masina, M (Mac) - Lions - 7 - 1999: Dub.

2000: Ur, Arg, SA, Dub. 2002: A, NZ,

Mastriet, S (Sampie) - BB - 8 - 2010: A, HK. 2013: RWC, A, Dub, SA. 2014: US, NZ.

Mbiyozo, MM (Mpho) - WP - 33 - 2006: Dub. 2007: NZ, US, HK, A, E, S, Dub, SA. 2008: NZ, US, HK, A, E, S, Dub, SA. 2009: NZ, US*, HK, A, E, S, RWC*, WG, Dub, SA. 2010: NZ, US, A, HK, E, S.

Mbovane, T (Tshotsho) - SARU - 10 - 2011: HK, AS. 2012: A, Dub, SA. 2013: NZ, US, HK, J, E.

McBean, BJH (Baldwin) - GW - 3 - 2007: NZ, Dub, SA.

Mdaka, TLP (Thobela) - Bor - 31 - 2000: NZ, Fj, A, HK, J, F, SA, Dub. 2001: NZ, Dub. 2005: NZ, US, Sin, E, F, RWC, WG, Dub. 2006: NZ, US, HK, Sin, F, E, CG, Dub, SA. 2007: HK, A. 2008: NZ, US.

Mentz, MJ (MJ) - GW - 18 - 2007: E, S, Dub, SA. 2008: NZ, US, HK, A, E, S. 2009: Dub, SA. 2010: HK, E, S, CG, Dub. 2011: A.

Minnaar, C (Chase) - SARU - 16 - 2009: HK, A, E, WG, Dub, SA. 2010: NZ, US, A, HK, E, S, CG. 2011: A, Dub, SA.

Mofu, Z (Zolani) - Border - 6 - 2005: WG, Dub, SA. 2006: NZ, US, CG.

Mokuena, J (Jonathan) - Leopards - 24 - 2005: E, F, WG, Dub, SA. 2006: NZ, US, HK, Sin, F, E, CG, Dub*, SA*. 2007: NZ*, US*, HK*, A*, Dub. 2008: NZ, US, HK, A, S.

Mostert, H (Herman) - WP - 18 - 1999: Fj, HK, F. 2000: NZ, Fj, A, HK, J, F, SA, Dub. 2001: NZ, HK, Chi, Mal, J, E, W.

Mtembu, L (Lubabalo) - Sharks - 4 - 2010: CG, Dub. 2011: NZ, US.

†Müller, GP (Jorrie) - Lions - 14 - 2001: HK, Chi, Mal, J, Dub, SA. 2002: Ch, Arg, A, NZ, E, W, CG, SA.

Munn, W (Wayne) - SWD - 2 - 1999: Fj, HK.

†Muir, DJ (Dick) - Natal - 2 - 1993: RWC. 1995: HK.

†Ndungane, AZ (Akona) - Border - 4 - 2004: HK, Sin, F, E.

Ngcobo, SC (Sandile) - SARU - 2 - 2016: NZ, A.

Nel, R (Ryan) - SARU - 1 - 2012: S.

Nelson, NT (Norman) - SARU - 2 - 2008: E, S.

Noble, DC (Dusty) - Sharks - 6 - 2006: Dub, SA. 2007: HK, A, E, S.

Noble, HG (Howard) - Sharks - 7 - 2007: NZ, US, HK, A. 2009: NZ, US, A.

†Nokwe, JL (Jongi) - Bol - 2 - 2004: SA. 2005: Sin.

Nqoro, M (Milo) - Sharks - 1 - 2008: SA.

O'Cuinneagain, D (Dion) - WP - 5 - 1993: HK, RWC. 1995: HK*. 1996: Ur*, HK*.

†Olivier, J (Jacques) - NTvl - 17 - 1993: HK,

RWC. 1997: RWC. 1999: Arg*, Ch*, Dub*. 2000: Ur*, Arg*, SA, Dub. 2001: HK, Chi, Mal, J, E, W, J.

†**Oosthuysen, DE** (Deon) - Lions - 1 - 1999: Ch.

†**Paulse, BJ** (Breyton) - WP - 6 - 1996: Ur, HK. 1998: Arg, Ur, Ch. 2001: RWC.

Payne, L (Shaun) - Natal - 4 - 1995: HK. 1997: RWC. 1998: Ur, Ch.

Penrose, N (Neil) - WP - 1 - 1998: HK.

Petersen, PB (Patrick) - WP - 1 - 2000: F.

Philander, D (Daniel) - WP - 1 - 2001: J.

Pietersen, JC (Johan) - WP - 2 - 2004: Dub, SA.

Pietersen, WJ (Wilton) - WP - 2 - 2008: HK, A.

Pitout, AC (Anton) - FS - 14 - 2001: Dub, SA. 2002: Ch, Arg, A, NZ, Chi, HK, Sin, Mal, E, W, CG. 2004: Dub.

Plumtree, J (John) - Natal - 2 - 1994: HK. 1995: HK.

Potgieter, R (Riaan) - EP - 1 - 1995: HK.

Potgieter, SP (Sarel) - WP - 4 - 2006: HK, Sin, F, E.

Powell, JD (Neil) - FS - 33 - 2001: SA. 2002: Ch, Arg, Chi, HK, E, W, CG, Dub, SA. 2007: Dub*, SA*. 2008: NZ*, US*, HK*, A*, E*, S*. 2009: HK, A, E, S, RWC, WG, Dub. 2010: E, S, CG. 2011: HK, A, E, S. 2012: E.

Pretorius, A (Abrie) - GW - 1 - 1996: Ur.

†**Pretorius, AS** (André) - Lions - 8 - 2000: SA, Dub. 2001: RWC, NZ, Mal, J, E, W.

†**Pretorius, JC** (Jaco) - Lions - 22 - 2002: Dub, SA. 2003: A*, NZ*, HK*, W, E. 2004: Dub, SA*. 2005: NZ*, US*, Sin*, E*, F*, RWC*, Dub*, SA*. 2006: HK*. Sin*, F*, E*, CG*.

Prinsloo, JGP (Boom) - FS - 15 - 2010: CG, Dub, SA. 2011: NZ, HK, A, E, S, A, Dub, SA. 2012: NZ, US, HK, J.

†**Putt, KB** (Kevin) - Natal - 1 - 1995: HK.

Raats, W (Werner) - WP - 2 - 1998: HK, CG.

Rafferty, AC (Ashwell) - FS - 1 - 1999: F.

Rees, G (Grant) - Sharks - 2 - 2007: NZ, US.

Richards, M (Mark) - SARU - 14 - 2010: Dub, SA. 2011: E, S, A, Dub, SA. 2012: NZ, US. 2013: WG, A. 2014: S, E, CG.

†**Richter, AJ** (Adriaan) - NTvl - 1 - 1994: HK.

†**Rose, EE** (Earl) - WP - 8 - 2003: A, NZ, W, E, Dub, SA. 2004: NZ, US.

†**Rossouw, PWG** (Pieter) - WP - 3 - 1996: Dub. 1997: RWC. 1998: CG.

†**Russell, RB** (Brent) - Pumas - 11 - 2001: SA. 2002: Ch, Arg, A, NZ, Chi, HK, Sin, Mal, SA. 2003: SA.

Saayman, JIA (Izak) - Eagles - 1 - 2005: SA.

Sage, DM (Dylan) - SARU - 7 - 2015: SA. 2016: A, US, C, F, E, OG.

Schoeman, MW (Marius) - Pumas - 47 - 2001: HK, Chi, Mal, J, E, W, J. 2002: Chi, HK, Sin, Mal,

E, W, CG, Dub, SA. 2003: A, NZ, HK, W, E, Dub, SA. 2004: NZ, US, E. 2005: Sin, E, F, RWC, WG*. 2006: SA. 2007: NZ, US, HK, A, E, S, SA. 2008: NZ, US, Dub. 2009: S, WG, SA. 2010: NZ, US.

Seconds, ER (Egon) - WP - 10 - 2001: Dub, SA. 2002: Chi, HK, Sin, Mal, E, W, CG. 2005: Dub.

Senatla, SM (Seabelo) - SARU - 33 - 2013: NZ, US, HK, J, S, RWC, WG. 2014: US, J, HK, S, E, CG, A, Dub, SA. 2015: NZ, US, HK, J, S, E, Dub, SA. 2016: NZ, A, US, C, HK, Sin, F, E, OG.

Sithole, S (Sibusiso) - Sharks - 8 - 2010: CG, Dub, SA. 2011: HK, A, E, S. 2013: RWC.

Siwundla, O (Oginga) - GL - 2 - 2004: Dub, SA.

†**Skinstad, RB** (Bob) - WP - 4 - 1996: Dub. 1997: RWC. 1998: CG. 2001: RWC.

Small-Smith, W (William) - SARU - 5 - 2011: E, S, Dub. 2012: US, J.

Smith, AS (Kwagga) - SARU - 26 - 2013: SA. 2014: NZ, J, HK, S, E, CG, A, Dub, SA. 2015: NZ, US, HK, J, S, E, Dub, SA. 2016: NZ, A, US, C, HK, Sin, F, OG.

Smith, LA (Luke) - Natal - 1 - 1995: HK.

†**Smit, PL** (Philip) - GW - 2 - 1998: Ur, Ch.

Smith, RF (Rodger) - GW - 14 - 1998: HK. 1999: Arg, Ch, Fj*, HK*, Dub, SA. 2000: Ur, Arg, F. 2001: RWC. 2002: Dub, SA. 2003: A.

†**Snyman, AH** (André) - NTvl - 1 - 1997: RWC.

Snyman, PAB (Phillip) - FS - 40 - 2008: Dub, SA. 2009: NZ, US, HK, E, S, RWC, WG. 2012: Dub, SA. 2013: NZ, US, HK, J, S, E, RWC, A, Dub, SA. 2014: US, NZ, J, HK, S, E, A, Dub. 2015: NZ, US, HK, Dub, SA. 2016: NZ*, A*, HK, F*, E*, OG.

Soyizwapi, S (Siviwe) - SARU - 3 - 2016: HK, Sin, E.

Specman, R (Rosko) - Pumas - 14 - 2014: US. 2015: US, HK, J, S, E, SA. 2016: NZ, A, US, C, F, E, OG.

Stevens, J (Jeffrey) - Bol - 19 - 1996: Dub. 1997: RWC. 1998: CG. 1999: Arg, Ch, Fj, HK, J, F, Dub, SA. 2000: Ur, Arg, NZ, Fj, A, HK, J, F.

Stick, M (Mzwandile) - EP - 41 - 2004: HK, Sin, F, E, Dub. 2005: NZ, US, Sin, RWC, WG, Dub, SA. 2006: NZ, US, HK, Sin, CG. 2007: NZ, US, HK, A, E, S, Dub. 2008: US, HK, A, Dub*, SA*. 2009: NZ*, HK*, A*, E*, S*, WG*, Dub, SA. 2010: NZ*, US*, E*, S*.

†**Strauss, AJ** (Andries) - Sharks - 2 - 2007: E, S.

Strydom, DH (Dirkie) - NTvl - 16 - 1996: Dub. 1998: HK. 1999: Arg, Ch, Fj, J, Dub, SA. 2000: Ur, Arg, NZ, Fj, A, F, SA, Dub.

Strydom, WJ (Willem-Johannes) - SARU - 4 - 2013: S, E, WG. 2014: E.

Treu, PM (Paul) - SWD - 32 - 1999: Fj, HK, Dub, SA. 2000: Ur, Arg, SA, Dub. 2001: RWC, NZ, HK, Chi, Mal, J, E, W, J, Dub, SA. 2002: Ch, Arg, A, NZ,

Chi, HK, Sin, Mal, E, W, CG, Dub*, SA*.

Truter, HJ (Hendrik) - FS - 1 - 1994: HK.

†**Ulengo, J** (Jamba) - SARU - 14 - 2012: S, E. 2013: HK, J, S, E, WG, A, Dub. 2014: NZ, J, HK, S, E.

Van den Heever, LM (Leon) - Bol - 4 - 2002: Dub, SA. 2003: A, NZ.

Van der Merwe, SM (Schalk) - GL - 30 - 2005: NZ, US, Sin, E, F, RWC, WG, Dub, SA. 2006: NZ, US, F, E, CG, Dub, SA. 2007: NZ, US, HK, A, E, S, Dub, SA. 2008: NZ, US, HK, A, E, S.

Van der Walt, P (Phillip) - FS - 2 - 2010: NZ, US.

†**Van der Westhuizen, JH** (Joost) - NTvl - 4 - 1993: HK, RWC. 1994: HK. 1997: RWC*.

Van Heerden, W (Wayne) - EP - 25 - 2001: RWC, NZ, HK, Chi, Mal, J, E, W, Dub, SA. 2002: E, W, CG. 2003: Dub, SA. 2004: NZ, US, HK, Sin, F, E, Dub, SA. 2005: NZ, US.

†**Van Niekerk, JC** (Joe) - Lions - 6 - 2001: HK, Chi, Mal, J, E, W.

Van Rensburg, JM (José) - GW - 22 - 2002: Dub, SA. 2003: A, NZ, HK, W, E, Dub, SA. 2004: NZ, US, HK, Sin, F, E, Dub, SA. 2005: NZ, US, Sin, E, F.

Van Schalkwyk, J (Jaco) - FS - 8 - 2003: HK, W, E, SA. 2004: HK, Sin, Dub, SA.

Van Wyk, J-H (Jan-Harm) - FS - 10 - 1998: Arg, Ur, Ch. 2001: Dub. 2002: Ch, Arg, A, NZ, Chi, HK.

Van Zyl, R (Riaan) - WP - 2 - 1996: Ur, HK.

†**Venter, AG** (André) - FS - 4 - 1996: Ur, HK. 1997: RWC. 1998: CG.

†**Venter, AJ** (AJ) - FS - 3 - 1998: Arg, Ur, Ch.

Venter, J (Hannes) - BB - 6 - 1999: Arg, Ch, Dub, SA. 2000: Ur, Arg.

Venter, N (Nico) - Border - 1 - 1998: HK.

Venter, S (Shaun) - SARU - 1 - 2009: SA.

Verhoeven, AG (Antonius) - Bol - 13 - 2002: Ch, Arg, A, NZ. 2006: NZ, US, HK, Sin, F, E, CG. 2007: NZ, US.

†**Vermaak, J** (Jano) - GL - 3 - 2005: NZ, US, RWC.

Verster, E (Eben) - WP - 1 - 1999: F.

†**Watson, LA** (Luke) - EP - 1 - 2002: CG.

†**Whiteley, WR** (Warren) - GL - 5 - 2012: Dub, SA. 2013: NZ, US. 2014: CG.

†**Willemse, AK** (Ashwin) - Bol - 2 - 2001: Dub, SA.

†**Williams, CM** (Chester) - WP - 11 - 1993: RWC. 1994: HK. 1998: Arg, Ur, Ch, HK*, CG*. 1999: SA. 2000: Ur, Arg. 2001: RWC.

Winter, RG (Russell) - Lions - 2 - 1998: HK, CG.

Witbooi, N (Nigel) - WP - 2 - 1996: Ur, HK.

Zangqa, V (Vuyo) - Border - 21 - 2007: HK, A, E, S, Dub, SA. 2008: NZ, US, HK, A, E, S, Dub, SA. 2009: NZ, US, HK, A, E, S, RWC.

SA SCHOOLS

Whitewash for SA Schools team

By Zeena van Tonder

The 2016 season proved to be another rewarding year for the SA Schools team as they showed immense character to secure a whitewash in the Under-19 International Series in Cape Town against Wales, France and England respectively.

The SA Schools A team, meanwhile, won only one of their three matches in what proved to be a disappointing tournament for them.

The SA Schools team kicked off the series with a morale-boosting 23-17 victory against Wales at the City Park Stadium in Crawford, and then thumped France 42-3 at Bishops before closing off their campaign with a last-gasp 13-12 victory against England at Paarl Boys' High.

SA Schools fullback Gianni Lombard opened the scoring against Wales with two penalty goals, which the team backed up with three tries compliments of hooker PJ Botha, winger Wandisile Simelane and centre Rikus Pretorius respectively to take control of the match.

Wales, however, showed their fighting spirit in the closing stages as they broke through the defence to score two converted tries to add to an earlier penalty to reduce the gap on the scoreboard to 23-17 with minutes to play. But these efforts were too little too late, as the SA Schools team held on for the victory.

The clash between the SA Schools team and France at Bishops was equally thrilling as the hosts showed innovation on attack and did well to convert their chances into points, which they supported with a solid defensive effort.

This impressive attacking performance saw captain and lock Salmaan Moerat and winger Muller Du Plessis each cross the tryline twice, while flyhalf Damian Willemse and winger Mike Mavovana also added their name to the try-scorers' list. Lombard slotted over five of the six conversions, while Ruan de Swardt added a penalty goal for the team's 42 points.

The SA Schools team lined up against their toughest opponents, England, in their final match of the tournament, and the clash met expectations, as a last-gasp try by Moerat and successful conversion by Lombard steered the team to a 13-12 victory.

Lombard slotted over two penalty goals in the first 54 minutes, while England scored two tries, one of which was converted, to take a 12-6 lead. However, a try by Moerat on the stroke of full-time, successfully converted, handed the team a rewarding victory and ensured that they completed the series unbeaten.

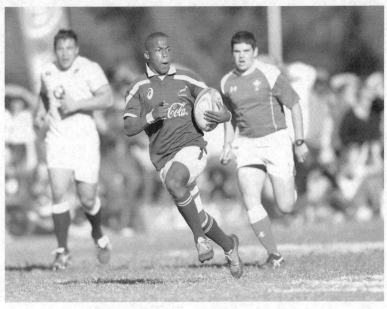

Mike Mavovana.

SA SCHOOLS - RESULTS & SCORERS

Date	Venue	Opponent	Result	Score	Referee	Scorers
Aug 12	City Park Stadium, Cape Town	Wales	WON	23-17	Matthew O'Grady	T: Botha, Pretorius, Simelane. C: Lombard. P: Lombard (2).
Aug 16	Bishops Diocesan College, CT	France	WON	42-03	Matthew O'Grady	T: Du Plessis (2), Moerat (2), Willemse, Mavovana. C: Lombard (5), De Swardt.
Aug 20	Paarl Boys High, Paarl	England	WON	13-12	Adam Jones	T: Moerat. C: Lombard. P: Lombard (2).

SA Schools A

Date	Venue	Opponent	Result	Score	Referee	Scorers
Aug 12	City Park Stadium, Cape Town	Italy	LOST	20-23	Adam Jones	T: Van Reenen, Hufkie, Nohamba. C: Van Reenen. P: Dobela.
Aug 16	Bishops Diocesan College, CT	England	WON	53-14	Quinton Immelman	T: Pieterse (2), Erasmus (2), Davids, Oliphant, Van Heyningen, Mujawo. C: Green (2), Davids (2), Van Reenen. P: Van Reenen.
Aug 20	Paarl Boys High, Paarl	Wales	LOST	17-18	Matthew O'Grady	T: Horn, Snyman, Green. C: Davids.

Aug 12	City Park Stadium, Cape Town	France 23, England 18
Aug 16	Bishops Diocesan College, CT	Wales 41, Italy 15
Aug 20	Paarl Boys' High, Paarl	France 21, Italy 30

SA SCHOOLS – APPEARANCES & POINTS

PLAYER	School	Union	Wales	France	England	Apps	T	C	P	DG	Pts
GD (Giani) Lombard	Paarl Boys High, Paarl	Western Province	15	15	15	3	–	7	4	–	26
M-JZ (Mike) Mavovana	Rondebosch Boys High, CT	Western Province	14	14	14	3	1	–	–	–	5
W (Wandisile) Simelane	Jeppe High, Johannesburg	Golden Lions	13	–	13R	2	1	–	–	–	5
R (Rikus) Pretorius	Grey College, Bloemfontein	Free State	12	12	12	3	1	–	–	–	5
S (Sihle) Njezula	Grey High, Port Elizabeth	Eastern Province	11	15R	–	2	–	–	–	–	0
D (Damian) Willemse	Paul Roos Gymnasium	Western Province	10	10	10	3	1	–	–	–	5
R (Rewan) Kruger	Grey College, Bloemfontein	Free State	9	–	–	1	–	–	–	–	0
NK (Khanya) Ncusane	Paarl Boys High, Paarl	Western Province	8	–	8R	2	–	–	–	–	0
M (Muller) Uys	Paarl Gymnasium, Paarl	Western Province	7	7	7	3	–	–	–	–	0
C (Charl) Serdyn	Paarl Boys High, Paarl	Western Province	6	6	6R	3	–	–	–	–	0
P-J (PJ) Steenkamp	Garsfontein, Pretoria	Blue Bulls	5	5R	5R	3	–	–	–	–	0
S (Salmaan) Moerat	Paarl Boys High, Paarl	Western Province	4c	4c	4c	3	3	–	–	–	15
S (Sazi) Sandi	St Andrews, Grahamstown	EP CD	3	3	3	3	–	–	–	–	0
P (Pieter) Botha	Monument, Krugersdorp	Golden Lions	2	2R	2R	3	1	–	–	–	5
N (Nathan) McBeth	Monument, Krugersdorp	Golden Lions	1	1	1R	3	–	–	–	–	0
D (Daniel) Jooste	Paarl Boys High, Paarl	Western Province	2R	2	2	3	–	–	–	–	0
R (Reece) Bezuidenhout	Paarl Boys High, Paarl	Western Province	1R	1R	1	3	–	–	–	–	0
J (Johan) Neethling	Paarl Boys High, Paarl	Western Province	3R	3R	3R	3	–	–	–	–	0
B-J (Ben-Jason) Dixon	Paul Roos Gymnasium	Western Province	5R	5	5	3	–	–	–	–	0
KJ (Kkwezi) Mafu	Grey High, Port Elizabeth	Eastern Province	7R	8	8	3	–	–	–	–	0
JC (JC) Pretorius	Middelburg THS	Pumas	6R	6R	6	3	–	–	–	–	0
MJ (Manuel) Ras	Paarl Boys High, Paarl	Western Province	13R	13	13	3	–	–	–	–	0
HM (Muller) du Plessis	Paarl Gymnasium, Paarl	Western Province	11R	11	11	3	2	–	–	–	10
RM (Richman) Gora	Welkom Gymnasium	Griffons	–	9	9	2	–	–	–	–	0
EJ (Emilio) Adonis	Garsfontein, Pretoria	Blue Bulls	–	14R	–	1	–	–	–	–	0
R (Ruan) de Swardt	Affies, Pretoria	Blue Bulls	–	10R	12R	2	–	1	–	–	2
26 PLAYERS						69	10	8	4	0	78

Coach: Lance Sendin (Boland)

SA SCHOOLS A - APPEARANCES & POINTS

PLAYER	School	Union	Italy	England	Wales	Apps	T	C	P	DG	Pts
AM (Abner) van Reenen	Garsfontein, Pretoria	Blue Bulls	15	15	–	2	1	2	1	–	12
AM (Austin) Davids	Garsfontein, Pretoria	Blue Bulls	14	14	15	3	1	3	–	–	11
LK (Louritz) van der Schyff	Affies, Pretoria	Blue Bulls	13c	12c	12c	3	–	–	–	–	0
S (Sicelo) Tole	Muir College	Eastern Province	12	–	12R	2	–	–	–	–	0
C (Cameron) Hufkie	Northern Cape, Kimberley	Griquas	11	–	11R	2	1	–	–	–	5
L (Lubabalo) Dobela	Grey High, Port Elizabeth	Eastern Province	10	10R	–	2	–	–	1	–	3
S (Sanele) Nohamba	Durban High School	Sharks	9	9R	9R	3	–	–	–	–	0
J (Jessie) Johnson	Paul Roos, Stellenbosch	Western Province	8	–	–	1	1	–	–	–	5
MD (Mark) Snyman	Helpmekaar College	Golden Lions	7	6R	6R	3	1	–	–	–	5
A (Athi) Magwala	Boland Agricultural	Western Province	6	6	6	3	–	–	–	–	0
C (Christopher) Havenga	Monument, Krugersdorp	Golden Lions	5	–	–	1	–	–	–	–	0
J (Jaco) van Tonder	Grey College, Bloemfontein	Free State	4	–	–	1	–	–	–	–	0
MJJ (Mornay) Smith	Eldoraigne HS, Centurion	Blue Bulls	3	3R	3R	3	–	–	–	–	0
DN (Dylan) Richardson	Kearsney College	Sharks	2	2R	2R	3	–	–	–	–	0
GZG (Gugu) Nelani	Northwood	Sharks	1	1R	1R	3	–	–	–	–	0
SWH (Schalk) Erasmus	Affies, Pretoria	Blue Bulls	2R	2	2	3	2	–	–	–	10
JJ (Cabous) Eloff	Affies, Pretoria	Blue Bulls	1R	1	1	3	–	–	–	–	0
K (Keegan) Glade	KES, Johannesburg	Golden Lions	3R	3	3	3	–	–	–	–	0
JJ (Juan) van der Mescht	Glenwood HS, Durban	Sharks	4R	5	5	3	–	–	–	–	0
DA (Dian) Schoonees	Grey College, Bloemfontein	Free State	6R	8	8	3	–	–	–	–	0
ZG (Zinedene) Booysen	Oakdale Agricultural	SWD	9R	9	9	3	–	–	–	–	0
T (Tyrone) Green	Jeppe Boys High	Golden Lions	10R	10	10	3	1	2	–	–	9
J (Janco) van Heyningen	Grey College, Bloemfontein	Free State	–	13	13	2	1	–	–	–	5
T (Tatenda) Mujawo	St Benedicts	Golden Lions	–	11	14	2	1	–	–	–	5
F (Francke) Horn	Paarl Boys High	Western Province	–	7	7	2	1	–	–	–	5
R (Ryno) Pieterse	Garsfontein, Pretoria	Blue Bulls	–	4	4	2	2	–	–	–	10
RS (Ruan) Vermaak	Monument, Krugersdorp	Golden Lions	–	5R	5R	2	–	–	–	–	0
A (Aya) Oliphant	Grey High, Port Elizabeth	Eastern Province	–	15R	11	2	1	–	–	–	5
28 PLAYERS						68	14	7	2	0	90

Coach: Sean Erasmus (WP)

SA Schools Players 1974-2016

Compiled by Heinrich Schulze
† Indicates became senior Springbok (15-man code).
* Indicates SA Schools captain (in second year if played for two years)

Adams, Ashwyn – (Rondebosch) – WP – 2015
Adams, Tythan – (Paul Roos Gym) – WP – 2008
Adonis, Emilio – (Garsfontein) – BB – 2016
Afrika, Cecil – (Harmony Sport) – Griffons – 2006
Alberts, Nicolaas – (AHS, Pretoria) – BB – 1996
†Alcock, Chad – (Alexander Road) – EP – 1991
Alexander, Enwill – (Stellenberg) – WP – 2002
Anderson, Severin – (Westering) – EP – 1978
April, Garth – (Bergrivier) – Boland – 2008
April, Randall – (Bergrivier) – Boland – 2004
Arends, Neil – (McCarthy Uitenhage) – EP – 1999
Arendse, Riaan – (Brandwag Uitenhage) – (EP) – 2007
Arlow, Wium – (Nelspruit) – Mpu – 2002
Baard, Le Roux – (Outeniqua) – SWD – 2014
Bakkes, Luther – (Diamantveld) – GW – 1989
Bali, Mlungisi – (St Albans) – BB – 2008
Bannink, Wimpie (Hans Strijdom) – Far North – 1992
Barker, Michael (DHS) – Natal – 1978
Barnard, Jan-Hendrik – (Menlopark) – BB – 1988
Barnard, Kierie – (Volkskool Potch.) – Leopards – 1981
Barnard, Lee – (King Edward VII) – GL – 1974-75
Barnies, Francois – (Parow HS) – WP – 2000
Baronet, Dennis – (Glenwood) – Natal – 1985
Barrett, Brett – (Kingswood Coll) – EP – 1991
¹Barritt, Bradley – (Kearsney Coll) – Natal – 2004
Barry, Craig – (Paul Roos Gimnasium – WP) – 2010
Bartle, Grant – (Middelburg THS) – Mpu – 1995
†Bartmann, Wahl – (Florida) – GL – 1981
Bartmann, Leon – (Florida) – GL – 1978
Basson, JP – (Boland Agric) – WP – 1994-95
Basson, Stefan – (Boland Agric) – WP – 2000
Beerwinkel, Andrew – (Porterville) – Boland – 2011
Bennett, Richard – (Dale Coll) – Border – 1992
Beukes, Chris – (DHS) – Natal – 1990

Bezuidenhout, Heino – (Daniel Pienaar) – EP – 2015
Bezuidenhout, Reece – (Paarl BH) – WP 2016
Bezuidenhout, Riaan – (Framesby) – EP – 1984
Bitterhout, Leroy – (Klein Nederb) – Boland – 2010
Bitzi, Anrich – (Grey Coll) – FS – 2010
Blignaut, Robert – (Muir Coll) – EP – 1978
†Bobo, Gcobani – (Dale Coll) – Border – 1996
Böhmer, Manfred – (Ermelo) – Mpu – 1998
Bolofo, Moeka – (Louis Botha) – Free State – 2007
Bolus, Robert – (Bishops) – WP – 1974-75
Bonthuys, John – (Abbots Coll) – WP – 1974-75
Bosch, Curwin – (Grey HS) – EP – 2014-15
Bosch, Jan – (Helpmekaar) – GL – 1991
†Boshoff, Marnitz – (Nelspruit) – Mpu – 2007
†Botha, Bakkies – (Vereeniging THS) – Valke – 1998
Botha, Pieter – (Monument) – GL – 2016
Bothma,* Rikus – (Paarl Gym) – WP – 2013
Botes, Bennie – (AHS, Pretoria) – BB – 1991
Botha, Calla – (DF Malan) – GL – 1979
Botha, Ettienne – (John Vorster, Nigel) – Valke – 1997
†Botha, Gary – (Overkruin) – BB – 1998-99
Botha, Justin – (Monument) – GL – 2006
Botha, Leon – (Grey Coll) – FS – 1981
Botha, Ruan – (Jeugland) – Valke – 2010
Botha, Wimpie – (Queens Coll) – Border – 1998
Breedt, Johan – (Wonderboom) – BB – 1993
Breedt, Nico – (Kearsney Coll) – Natal – 1998
Brink, Stephen – (Sentraal) – FS – 1991-92
Brits, David – (Selbourne Coll) – Border – 2015
†Brits, Schalk – (Paul Roos Gym.) – WP – 1999
Britz, Conraad – (Oakdale Agric) – SWD – 2005
Britz, Riaan – (Grey Coll) – FS – 2009
Bronkhorst, Stephan – (Randburg) – GL – 1992
Brown, Dick – (Pearson) – EP – 1986
Brown, John – (Hentie Cilliers) – NFS – 1999
†Brüssow, Heinrich – (Grey Coll) – FS – 2004
Buckle, Albertus – (Boland Agric) – Boland

– 2001
†Burger, Kobus – (Paarl Gym.) – WP – 1980-81
Burger, Altus – (Ermelo) – Mpu – 1982-83
Burton-Moore, Mark – (Bishops) – WP – 1978
Bushney, Marais – (Roodepoort) – GL – 1989
Caldo, Kobus – (Oakdale Agric) – SWD – 1998-99
Campbell-McGeachy, Walter – (Pietersburg) – Far North – 1994-95
Campher, Connie – (Potchefstroom THS) – Leopards – 1985
Campher, Fanie – (Wolmaransstad THS) – Stellaland – 1974-75
Campher, Jan-Henning – (Garsfontein) – BB – 2014
†Carr, Nizaam – (Bishops) – WP – 2009
†Carstens, Deon – (Boland Agric) – WP – 1997
Carswell, Michael – (Grey HS) – EP – 1984
Carty, Shane – (King Edward VII) – GL – 1974-75
Cattrell,* Brenton – (Maritzburg Coll) – Natal – 1987
Cawood, Mark – (Wynberg BH) – WP – 1974-75
Celliers,* Norman – (Ermelo) – Mpu – 1991
Chadwick, Dale – (Westville) – KwaZulu Natal – 2007
Chidoma, Ngonidzashe (Northwood) – KZN – 2014
Claassen, Andrew – (Andrew Rabie) – EP – 1988
Clancy, Sean – (Selborne Coll) – Border – 1995
Cloete, Chris – (Selbourne Coll) – Border – 2009
Cloete, Hannes – (Jim Fouché) – FS – 1995
Cloete, Jan – (Waterkloof) – BB – 1996
Coetzee, Deon – (Helpmekaar) – GL – 1979
Coetzee, Eduard – (AHS, Pretoria) – BB – 1997
Coetzee, Jaco – (Ellisras) – Far North – 1988
Coetzee,* Jaco – (Glenwood) – KZN – 2014
Coetzee, Jannie – (Bloemfontein THS) – FS – 1982
Coetzee, Marne – (Waterkloof) – BB – 2011
Coetzer, Jacques – (Middelburg THS) – Mpu – 1996
†Conradie, Bolla – (Kasselsvlei) – WP – 1996-97
Cook, Jean – (Grey Coll) – FS – 2009
Cooper, Barney – (Paarl Gym) – WP – 1986
Cooper, John – (Soa Bras Mosselbaai) – SWD – 1998

SA SCHOOLS

Coyle-Meybery,* Craig – (Dale Coll) – Border – 1983-84
Craven, Jean – (Grey Coll) – FS – 1990
Cronjé, Frans – (Grey Coll) – FS – 1985
†Cronjé, Jacques – (John Vorster THS) – BB – 2000
Croy, Ricardo – (Paarl Gym.) – WP – 2004
Daffue, Hendrik – (Grey Coll) – FS – 1980
Daffue, Willem – (Grey Coll) – FS – 1977
Damens, Leneve – (Grey Coll) – FS – 2011
Dames, Arno – (Framesby) – EP – 1990
Dames, Rudi – (Vereeniging THS) – Valke – 1999
Daniller, Hennie – (Paarl Gym) – WP – 2002
Danquah, Jerry – (Queens Coll) – Border – 2014
Davel, Chris – (Ermelo) – Mpu – 1985
Davids, Zain – (Rondebosch) – WP – 2015
Davis, Aidon – (Daniel Pienaar) – EP – 2012
Dayimani, Hacjivah – (Jeppe BH) – GL – 2015
De Beer,* Conrad – (Grey Coll) – FS – 1981
De Beer, Tinus – (Waterkloof) – BB – 2014
De Bruin, Michael – (Nelspruit) – Mpu – 2001
De Bruyn, Corné – (Worcester) – Boland – 1994
De Coning,* Basil – (Kingswood Coll) – EP – 1990
De Haas, Pieter – (Grey Coll) – FS – 1986
De Jager, Bruce – (Bishops) – WP – 1994
De Jager, Wilhelm – (Ermelo) – Mpu – 2002
De Kock, Jason – (Hugenote HS) – Valke – 1996
De Kock, Zander – (Vereeniging THS) – Valke – 2005
De Nobrega, Paul – (Worcester) – Boland – 1984
De Ru, Ian – (Marais Viljoen THS) – GL – 1989
De Swardt, Ruan – (AHS Pretoria) – BB – 2016
†De Villiers, Jean – (Paarl Gym) – WP Acad. – 1999
De Villiers, Ruben – (Paarl BH) – WP – 2015
De Waal, Adriaan – (Paarl BH) – WP Acad. – 1995
Dell, Allan – (Queens Coll) – Border – 2010
Delport,* Paul – (SACS) – WP – 2001-02
Delport, Marius – (Zwartkop) – BB – 2003
Derksen, Chris – (Grey Coll) – FS – 1993
Diedericks, Ernest – (Scottsville) – WP – 1994
Dixon, Ben-Jason – (Paul Roos) – WP – 2016
†Dixon,* Pieter – (Maritzburg Coll) – Natal – 1995
Dreyer, Hano – (Winterberg Agric) – NEC – 1995
†Drotské, Naka – (Grey Coll) – FS – 1989
†Du Plessis, Carel – (Paarl BH) – WP – 1978
†Du Plessis, Bismarck – (Grey Coll) – FS – 2001-02
Du Plessis, Charl – (Kroonstad Agric) –

NFS – 1978
Du Plessis, Daniel – (Paul Roos Gym) – WP – 2013
Du Plessis, Jacques – (Ermelo) – Mpu – 2011
Du Plessis, Johan – (Sand du Plessis) – FS – 1985
Du Plessis, JP – (Paul Roos Gym) – WP – 2009
Du Plessis, Morné – (Waterkloof) – BB – 2011
Du Plessis, Muller – (Paarl Gym) – WP – 2016
Du Plessis, Neil – (Selborne Coll) – Border – 1984
Du Plessis, Pierre – (Port Natal) – Natal – 1987
†Du Preez, Delarey – (Hangklip) – Border – 1994
Du Preez, André – (Oudtshoorn THS) – SWD – 1974
Du Preez, Daniel – (Kearsney) – KZN – 2012-13
Du Preez, Fransie – (EG Jansen) – GL – 1985
Du Preez, Jean–Luc – (Kearsney) – KZN – 2012-13
Du Preez, Philip – (Monument) – GL – 2011
†Du Preez, Wian – (Grey Coll) – FS – 1999-00
†Du Randt, Os – (Piet Retief) – NEC – 1990
Du Toit, Dawie – (Vereeniging THS) – GL – 1974-75
Du Toit, Dawie – (Monument) – GL – 1992-93
Du Toit, Franna – (Grey Coll) – FS – 2008
Du Toit, Jaco – (Paarl Gym) – WP – 1999
Du Toit, Thomas – (Paarl BH) – WP – 2013
Duvenhage, Braam – (HSS Hugenote) – Valke – 1982
Duvenhage, Stoffel – (Middelburg THS) – Mpu – 2004
Dweba, Joseph – (Florida) – GL – 2013
Ebersöhn, Robert – (Grey Coll) – Free State – 2007
Edgar, David – (Michaelhouse) – Natal – 2001
Ehrentraut,* Michael – (Bishops) – WP – 1989
Eksteen, Ryno – (AHS, Pretoria) – BB – 2012
Ellerd, Rialoo – (Jacobsdal) – Griquas – 2005
Eloff, Cabous – (AHS, Pretoria) – BB – 2015
†Els, Braam – (AHS, Kroonstad) – NFS – 1990
Els,* Anton – (DHS du Plessis) – EP – 1975
Engelbrecht, Andries – (Volkskool) – Leopards – 1981
Engelbrecht,* Fanus – (R Ferreira Witrivier) – Mpu – 1983
Engelbrecht,* Frankel – (Paarl Gym) – WP – 1986
Engelbrecht, Johan – (Paul Roos Gym) – WP – 1986
Engelbrecht, Morné – (Rustenburg) –

Leopards – 1994
Erasmus, Greyling – (Ermelo) – Mpu – 2000
Erasmus, Kerneels – (Frikkie Meyer) – Far North – 1982
Erlank, Karel – (Klerksdorp) – Leopards – 1979
Erwee,* Jurie – (Grey Coll) – FS – 1980
Espag,* Jaco – (Witbank THS) – Mpu – 1984-85
Esterhuizen, Francois – (Overberg) – Boland – 2012
Faas, Chuma – (Grey HS) – EP – 2008
Faku, Zolani – (Grey HS) – SA Acad (EP) – 2009
Farmer, Steven – (Kasselsvlei) – WP – 2001
Fenwick, Alex – (Grey Coll) – FS – 1990-91
Fenwick, Kobie – (Grey Coll) – FS – 1975
Ferreira, Andries – (AHS, Pretoria) – BB – 2008
†Ferreira, Christo – (Welkom Gym) – NFS – 1978
Ferreira, Freddie – (Brandwag) – EP – 1980
Ferreira, Marthinus – (Florida) – GL – 2000
Ferreira, Schalk – (Paul Roos Gym) – WP – 2002
Feurer, Lee – (Bishops) – WP – 1988
Fisher, Tyler – (Westville) – KZN – 2011
Fitchet, Christo – (Kirkwood) – EP – 1975
Flanagan, Sean – (Westville) – Natal – 1999
Forslara, Vuyani – (Grens HS) – Border – 1999
Fortuin, Aston (Southdowns Coll) – BB – 2014
Fortuin, Sean – (Bellville South HS) – WP – 1999
Fouche, Neethling – Grey Coll) – FS – 2010
Fourie, Andries – (Framesby) – EP – 1990
Fourie, Dawie – (Kroonstad Agric) – NFS – 1978-79
Fourie, Kenneth – (Port Shepstone) – Natal – 1994
Fourie, Nel – (Ermelo) – Mpu – 2000
Fourie, Stompie – (Grey Coll) – FS – 1984
Frolick, Shandré – (Worcester Gym.) – Boland – 2004
Froneman, Stephan – (Montana) – BB – 1995
Fullard, Neil – (Paarl BH) – WP – 2000
†Fynn, Etienne – (St Charles) – Natal – 1990
Gage, Shaun – (DHS) – Natal – 1985
Galant, Warrick – (Outeniqua) – SWD – 2012-13
Gans, Stedman – (Waterkloof) – BB – 2015
Geldenhuys, Jan – (Grey Coll) – FS – 1974-75
Genis, James – (DF Malan) – WP – 1977
Gerber, Arnold (Menlo Park) – BB – 2014
†Gerber,* Danie – (Despatch) – EP – 1975-77
†Gerber, Hendrik – (Nico Malan) – EP – 1993-94
Gericke, Jaco – (Port Elizabeth THS) – EP – 1988
Gericke, Neethling – (Oakdale Agric) –

SWD – 2008
Gibbs, Herchelle – (Bishops) – WP – 1992
Giezing, Kalf – (Grey Coll) – FS – 1983
†**Gillingham, Joe** – (Alberton) – GL – 1992
Glover, Shaun – (Maritzburg Coll) – Natal – 1985
Goedeke, Frank – (Carter) – Natal – 1990
Goedeke, Udo – (Maritzburg Coll) – Natal – 1987
Goosen, Gregory – (Kearsney Coll) – Natal – 2001
†**Goosen, Johan** – (Grey Coll) – FS – 2010
Goosen, Niel – (Waterkloof) – BB – 1997
Gora, Richman – (Welkom Gym) – Griffons – 2016
Gouws, Scheepers – (Grey Coll) – FS – 1981
Gqoba, Andisa – (Hudson Park) – Border – 2003
†**Grant, Peter** – (Maritzburg Coll) – Natal – 2002
Greyling, Gert – (Sand du Plessis) – FS – 2003
Griesel, Jannie – (Verwoerdburg) – BB – 1987
Gronum, Antonie – (Oakdale Agric) – SWD – 2003
Grobbelaar, Johan – (Paarl Gym.) – WP – 2015
Grobler, Gerbrand – (Grey Coll) – FS – 1981
Grobler, Jacques – (FH Odendaal) – BB – 1990
Grobler, Lukas – (Hugenote HS) – Valke – 1981
Gwavu, Vincent – (Daniël Pienaar – Uitenhage) – EP – 2005
‡**Hall, Stephen** – (Dale Coll) – Border – 1991
Hammer, Ernst – (Fakkel) – GL – 1993
Hancke, Wim – (Linden) – GL – 1974-75
Hankinson, Rob – (Michaelhouse) – Natal – 1974-75
†**Hargreaves,* Alistair** – (Durban HS) – Natal – 2004
Hartzenberg, Vaasir – (Paarl BHS) – WP – 2006
Hearne, Ashlyn – (Hottentots Holland) – WP – 2000
†**Hendriks, Pieter** – (Standerton) – Mpu – 1988
Hendriks, Braam – (Sandveld) – NFS – 1993
Herbst, Irne – (Waterkloof) – BB – 2011
Hermanus, Grant – (Paarl Gym) – WP – 2013
Hess, Cornel – (AHS Pretoria) – BB – 2006-07
Heuer, Merrick – (Queens Coll) – Border – 1988
Heunis, Nico – (Dirkie Uys) – Boland – 1994
Heydenrich,* Johan – (Standerton) – Mpu – 1982
Hickson, André – (Bosmansdam) – WP – 1985
Hill, Jaydon – (Glenwood) – Natal – 2002
Hlongwane, Nhlanhla – (Louis Botha) – FS (2011)

Hollenbach, Alwyn – (Grey Coll) – FS – 2003
Hopkins, Clifford – (Kearsney Coll) – Natal – 1979
Hopp, Dean – (Kairos SS) – SWD – 2000
†**Hougaard, Derick** – (Boland Agric) – Boland – 2001
Hough, André – (Framesby) – EP – 1988
Hugo, Jan-Harm – (Ermelo) – Mpu – 1997
Hugo, Werner – (Paarl BH) – WP – 1993
Hulme,* Altenstädt – (Voortrekker, CT) – WP – 1999
Human, Dewald – (Outeniqua) – SWD – 2013
Human, Gerhard – (Despatch) – EP – 1977
Ingles, Warren – (Alexander Road) – EP – 1987
Isbell, Ruwellyn (Grey College) – FS – 2011
†**Jacobs, Adrian** – (Scottsville) – WP – 1998
Jacobs, Divan – (Ermelo) – Mpu – 2001
Jacobs, Jaco – (Grey Coll) – FS – 1987
Jackson JT (Oakdale) – SWD – 2014
Jaer, Malcolm – (Brandwag) – EP – 2013
Jamieson, Craig – (Maritzburg Coll) – Natal – 1979
Jankowitz, Anton – (Hilton Coll) – Natal – 1989
Janse van Rensburg, Nicholaas – (AHS, Pretoria) – BB – 2012
Janse van Rensburg, Rohan – (Waterkloof) – BB – 2012
Janse van Vuuren, Marco – (Transvalia) – Valke – 2013-14
†**Jantjies, Conrad** – (CBS Boksburg) – Valke – 1997
†**Jantjies, Elton** – (Florida) – GL – 2008
Jantjies, Tony – (Menlo Park) – BB – 2009
Januarie, Enrico – (Weston HS) – Boland – 2000
Jho, Andile (Dale Coll) – Border – 2009-10
Job, Izak – (Pres. Steyn Bloemfontein) – FS – 1998
†**Johnson, Ashley** – (Paarl Gym.) – WP – 2004
Johnson, Nicolas – (Selborne Coll) – Border – 1998
Johnston, Gordon – (Paarl BH) – WP – 1999
Jooste, Daniel – (Paarl BH) – WP – 2016
Jooste, Morné – (The Settlers) – WP – 2005
Jordaan, Hennie – (Menlopark) – BB – 1980
Jordaan, Paul – (Grey Coll) – FS – 2010
Joubert, Jan–Hendrik – (Oakdale Agric) – SWD – 2001
Joubert, Morné (Glenwood) – KZN – 2014
Joubert, Riaan – (Grey Coll) – FS – 1978
Joubert, Wilhelm – (Overkruin) – BB – 1982
Juries, Christopher – (Kingswood Coll) – EP – 2005
Kalonji, Kadima – (Pretoria THS) – BB – 1998
Kankowski, Tino – (PJ Olivier) – EP – 1977
Kaplan, Kevin – (Kimberley THS) – GW – 1980
Kapp, Divan – (Middelburg THS) – Mpu

– 2005
Kapp, Neil – (Outeniqua) – SWD – 2008
Karemaker, Leon – (Bellville) – WP – 2003
Kasselman, Chris – (Sandveld) – NFS – 1979-80
Kelly, Richard – (Maritzburg Coll) – Natal – 1996
Kemp,* Scott – (Hudson Park) – Border – 1991-92
†**Kempson, Robert** – (Queens Coll) – Border – 1992
Keyter, Eduan (AHS, Pretoria) – BB – 2014
Khubeka, Sandile – (Kearsney) – KZN – 2012
King, Kelvano – (Alexandria) – Eastern Province – 2007
Kirsten, Frik – (AHS Pretoria) – BB – 2006
†**Kitshoff, Steven** – (Paul Roos) – WP – 2010
Kleinenberg, Mark – (Selborne Coll) – Border – 1974-75
Klopper, Chris – (Die Burger) – GL – 1978
Knoetze, Frederick – (Framesby) – EP – 1982
Kobese, Bangihlonbe – (Dale Coll) – Border –– 2009
Koch, Agie – (Paul Roos Gym) – WP – 1974-75
Koch, Hendrik – (Rustenburg) – Leopards – 1978
Koegelenberg, Gideon – (Hugenote) – Boland – 2012
†**Koen, Louis** – (Paarl Gym) – WP – 1993-94
Koen, Barabas – (Ermelo) – Mpu – 1991
†**Kolisi, Siyamthanda** – (Grey HS) – EP – 2008-09
Köster, Nick – (Bishops) – WP – 2006-07
Kotze, Christo – (Dirkie Uys) – Boland – 1977-78
Kotze, Divan – (Waterkloof) – BB – 2006
Kotze, Stephanus – (Grey Coll) – FS – 2009
Koyana, Ncedo – (Selbourne Coll) – Border – 2003
Kramer, Ruan – (Grey Coll) – FS – 2013
Krause, Piet – (Sasolburg THS) – Vaal Triangle – 1991
†**Kriel, Jesse** – (Maritzburg Coll) – KZN – 2012
†**Krige,* Corné** – (Paarl BH) – WP – 1993
†**Kruger,* Ruben** – (Grey Coll) – FS – 1987-88
Kruger, Bertus – (Die Burger) – GL – 1989
Kruger, Ernst – (Jeugland) – GL – 1974-75
Kruger, Kobus – (Middelburg THS) – Mpu – 1996
Kruger, Morné – (Monument) – GL – 2001
Kruger, Rewan – (Grey Coll) – FS – 2016
Kruger, Warren – (SACS) – WP – 1974-75
Kuttel, Peter – (Bishops) – WP – 1983
Kumbirai, Michael (St Alban's Coll) – BB – 2014
Kuün, Derick – (AHS, Pretoria) – BB – 2002
†**Lambie, Patrick** (Michaelhouse) – Natal – 2007-08
Lanning, Andrew – (Bishops) – WP – 1989
Laubscher, Michael – (Tygerberg) – WP

– 1974-75

Laufs, Gerhard – (Alberton) – GL – 1992

Le Grange, Anton – (Despatch) – EP – 1975

Le Maitre, Eugene – (Marais Viljoen) – GL – 2011

Le Marque,* Derek – (Glenwood) – Natal – 1979

†Le Roux, Ollie – (Grey Coll) – FS – 1991

Le Roux,* Chris – (Waterkloof) – BB – 1996-97

Le Roux, Kobus – (Boland Agric) – WP – 1995

Le Roux, Stephan – (Brits/Waterkloof) – BB – 1993-94

Lehmann, Helmut – (Paarl Gym) – WP – 2008

Leonard, Nico – (Paul Roos) – WP – 2015

Lewis, Marlon – (Bertram) – EP – 2004-05

Lewis, Jean-Paul – (Paul Roos) – WP – 2010-11

Libbok, Manie – (Outeniqua) – SWD – 2015

Liebenberg, Christo – (Roodepoort) – GL – 1986

Liebenberg, Wiaan – (Drostdy THS) – Boland – 2010

Lightfoot, Wessel – (Diamantveld) – GW – 1981

Linde, Jurie – (AHS, Pretoria) – BB – 2012-13

Linde, Nico – (Grey Coll) – FS – 1990

Linde, Rob – (Maritzburg Coll) – Natal – 1997

Lindeque, Piet – (Grey Coll) – FS – 2009

Lindsay, Paul – (Maritzburg Coll) – Natal – 1975-77

†Lobberts, Hilton – (N. Orleans Paarl) – Boland – 2004

Loest, Gary – (Queens Coll) – Border – 1985-86

†Lombard, Friedrich – (Wilgerivier) – NFS – 1997

Lombard, Gianni – (Paarl BH) – WP – 2016

Loubser, Andell – (Menlo Park) – BB – 2014-15

Loubser, Pieter – (Paarl BH/Bishops) – WP – 1975-76

Louw, Coenie – (Dirkie Uys) – Boland – 1995

†Louw, Hottie – (Boland Agric) – WP – 1994

Louw,* Pieter – (Paarl BH) – WP – 2003

Louw, Wilco – (Drostdy) – Boland – 2012

Luiters, Kevin – (Grey Coll) – FS – 2010

Lusaseni, Luvuyo – (Selbourne Coll) – Border – 2006

Mabuza, Thabo – (Centurion) – Blue Bulls – 2011-12

Mafu, Kwezi – (Grey HS) – EP – 2015-16

Maherry, Chet – (Grey Coll) – FS – 1985-86

Mahlangu, Daniel – (Oosterland Secunda) – Mpu – 1999

Majola, Khaya – (Westville) – KZN – 2010

Malan, Remu – (Outeniqua) – SWD – 2013

Malgas, Warren – (PW Botha) – SWD – 2003

†Malherbe, Frans – (Paarl BH) – WP – 2009

†Mallett, Nick – (St Andrews) – EP – 1974-75

Malton, Shaun – (Glenwood) – KZN – 2008

Manuel, David – (Waterkloof) – BB – 1997-98

Manuel, Rodrique – (Ben. Heigths) – WP – 1996

Marais, Abrie – (Grey Coll) – FS – 1977

Marais, Gert – (Grey Coll) – FS – 1983

Maritz, Dewald – (Nelspruit) – Mpu – 2015

Marothodi, Ompile – (Pretoria BHS) – BB – 2007

Martyn, Angus – (Michaelhouse) – Natal – 1998

Maruping, Victor (Louis Botha THS) – FS – 2014

Marutlulle, Edgar – (Potch, BHS) – Leopards – 2004-05

†Marx, Malcolm – (King Edward VII) – GL – 2012

Maseko, Sizo – (Ermelo) – Mpu – 2009

Mashele, Ntokozo – (Nelspruit) – Mpu – 2006

Masina, Sibi – (Standerton) – Mpu – 2007

Masuga, Tshepo – (Monument) – GL – 2006

Matthysen, John – (Sand du Plessis) – FS – 1974-75

Mavovana, Mike – (Rondebosch BH) – WP – 2016

†Mbonambi, Bongi – (St Alban's) – BB – 2009

Mbovane, Tshotso – (Paul Roos) – WP – 2010

McAlister, Daniel – (Selborne Coll) – Border – 1991

McBeth, Nathan – (Monument) – GL – 2016

McCann, Warren – (Jeppe BH) – GL – 1985

²McDonald, Aubrey – (Winterberg HS – Fort Beaufort) – EP – 2005

⁵McDonald, Aubrey – (Waterkloof HS) – BB – 2006

⁶McDonald, Barry – (Adelaide Gym) – NEC – 1996

⁶McDonald, Barry – (Waterkloof) – BB – 1997

McIntyre, Mark – (Grey Coll) – FS – 1989

†Meiring, FA – (Gill Coll) – NEC – 1986

Mentz, Kosie – (Paarl Gym) – WP – 1988

Mentz, MJ – (Ermelo) – Mpu – 2000

Meyer, Altus – (Vredenburg HS) – Boland – 1997

Meyer, Clinton – (Maritzburg Coll) – Natal – 1989

Meyer, Pieter – (Waterkloof) – BB – 2005

Meyer, Renier – (Wessel Maree) – NFS – 1998

Mguca, Lupumlo – (Daniel Pienaar) – EP – 2014

Mhlobiso, Luvuyo – (Daniel Pienaar) – EP – 2004

Michaels, Devan – (Kasselsvlei) – WP – 2001

Micklewood, Christopher (Westville) – Natal – 2005

Miller, Greg – (Grey Coll) – EP – 1991

Mills, David – (Maritzburg Coll) – Natal – 1978

Milton, Cliff – (AHS, Pretoria) – BB – 2001-02

Mjekevu, Wandile – (King Edward VII) – GL – 2008

Mkize, Njabula – (Westville) – KZN – 2008

Mkokeli, Tembani – (Msobomvu) – Border – 2001-02

Moerat,* Salmaan – (Paarl BH) – WP – 2015-16

Molapo, Matjikinyane – (Ben Vorster) – Limpopo BB – 2012

Moller, JD – (Paarl BH) – WP – 2000

†Montgomery, Percy – (SACS) – WP – 1992-93

Moolman, Hansie – (Ermelo) – Mpu – 2005

Mostert, Juan–Pierre – (Brits) – Leopards – 2006

Mthula, Petros – (Glenwood) – Natal – 2001

Moyle-Meyberry,* Craig – (Dale) – Border– 1984

Mtimka, Lonwaba – (Dale Coll) – Border – 1999

Mtsi, Thabani – (Selbourne Coll) – Border – 2013

†Müller, Helgard – (Grey Coll) – FS – 1981-82

†Müller, Pieter – (Grey Coll) – FS – 1987-88

†Müller, Jorrie – (Monument) – GL – 1999

Muller, Lourens – (Hartbeespoort) – BB – 1993

Muller, Rudi – (Potch. Gym) – Leopards – 1993

Munn, Wayne – (Maritzburg Coll) – Natal – 1994

Mxoli, Sangoni – (Durban OB) – Natal – 2003

Myburgh, Jaco – (Paarl BH) – WP – 1996

Myburgh, Pieter – (Paul Roos Gym.) – WP – 2004

Myburgh, Stefaan – (Paul Roos Gym) – WP – 1996

Naudé, Dawie – (David Ross) – NEC – 1986

Nche, Ox – (Louis Botha THS) – FS – 2012-13

Ncusane, Khanya – (Paarl BH) – WP – 2016

Neethling, Johan – (Paarl BH) – WP – 2016

Neethling, Sydwhill – (Worcester Gym) – Boland – 2000

Nel, Boeta – (Bloemfontein THS) – FS – 1979-80

Nel, Johan – (Wolmaranstad) – Stellaland – 1987

Nel, Leon – (Nelspruit) – Mpu – 1982

Nel, Pieter – (Patriot, Witbank) – Mpu – 1983

Nell, Jacques – (Grey Coll) – FS – 1977

Ngoro, Mlindazwe – (St Johns) – Border CD – 2006

Nieuwenhuys, Jacques – (Monument) – GL – 1984

Ngonyoza, Mtobeli – (Oscar Mpetha) – WP – 2003

Njezula, Sihle – (Grey HS) – EP – 2016

Nkala, Nazo (Welkom Gym) – Griffons – 2014

Nkosi, Malungisa (Giant) – (St Stithians) – GL – 2005

Nonkontwana, Abongile – (St Albans) – BB– 2012-13

North, Andrew – (Bishops) – WP – 1989

Nortjé, Danie – (Jan Viljoen) – GL – 1976

Notshe, Sikhumbuzo (Wynberg BH) – WP – 2010-11

Ntubeni, Siyabonga – (King Edward VII) – GL – 2009

Ntunja,* Kaunda – (Dale Coll) – Border – 1999-2000

Nyoka, Sinovuyo – (Dale Coll) – Border – 2008

²O'Cuinneagain, Dion – (Rondebosch BH) – WP – 1989-90

O'Neill, Pieter – (Despatch) – EP – 1988-89

Oberholster, Johan – (Vereeniging THS) – Valke – 1998

Oberholzer, Johan – (Jan Viljoen) – Golden Lions – 2007

Oberholzer, Lourens – (Linden) – GL – 1982

Ockafor, Kene – (Kearsney Coll) – Natal – 2007

Oelschig, Noël – (Grey Coll) – FS – 1997

Olckers, Riaan – (AHS, Pretoria) – BB – 1995

Olivier, HJ – (Kroonstad) – NFS – 1995

†Oosthuizen, Coenie – (Grey Coll) – FS – 2007

Oosthuizen. Josephus – (Grey Coll) – FS – 2005

Oosthuizen, JR – (Grey Coll) – FS – 1992

Oosthuizen,* Willie – (Helpmekaar) – GL – 1976

†Paige, Rudy,* – (Bastion) – Golden Lions – 2007

Palmer, Shaun – (Middelburg THS) – Mpu – 1986

Papier, Embrose – (Garsfontein) – BB – 2014-15

Penzhorn, Adrian – (Maritzburg Coll) – Natal – 2002

Petersen, Patrick – (Florida) – WP – 1995

Petersen, Sergeal – (Grey HS) – EP – 2012

Peyper, Nico von B – (EG Jansen) – Valke – 2015

Phillips, Justin – (Waterkloof) – BB – 2012-13

Pienaar, Andries – (Paarl BH) – WP – 1975

Pienaar,* Bernard – (Paarl Gym) – WP – 1974-75

†Pienaar, Francois – (Patriot Witbank) – Mpu – 1985

Pienaar, Pieter – (Paarl BH) – Boland – 2001

Pienaar, Roelof – (Grey Coll) – Free State – 2007

†Pienaar, Ruan – (Grey Coll) – FS – 2002

Pieterse, Koen – (Grey Coll) – FS – 1980

Pietersen, Ricardo – (Groot Brak) – SWD – 1999

Plaatjies, Jeremy – (Outeniqua) – SWD – 2001

Plaatjies,* Sean – (Brandwag Uitenhage) – EP – 1996

Pokomela, Junior – (Grey HS) – EP – 2014

†Pollard, Handré – (Paarl Gym) – WP – 2012

Poni, Onke – (Selbourne) – Border – 2002

†Potgieter,* Dewald (Daniël Pienaar – Uitenhage) – EP – 2005

Pretorius, Christo – (Paarl Gym) – WP – 1996

Pretorius, Herman – (Grey Coll) – FS – 2004

Pretorius, Flippie – (De Wet Nel THS) – NFS – 1979

Pretorius, JC – (Middelburg THS) – Mpu – 2016

Pretorius, Johannes – (Hentie Cilliers) – NFS – 1984

Pretorius, Riaan – (Ben Viljoen, Groblersdal) – Mpu – 1994

Pretorius, Rikus – (Grey Coll) – FS – 2016

Pretorius, Wynand – (Sand du Plessis) – FS – 1975-76

Prinsloo, Carlo – (Paarl Gym.) – WP – 2004

Prinsloo, Ig (Grey Coll) – FS – 2014

Prinsloo, Jamie – (John Vorster THS) – BB – 1975

Prinsloo, Michael – (Ficksburg THS) – EFS – 1977

Radebe, Colin – (Secunda HS) – Mpu – 2000

Rademan, Pieter* – (Grey Coll) – FS – 2009

†Ralepelle, Chiliboy – (Pretoria BHS) – BB – 2002-03

Rampeta, Refuoe (Louis Botha THS) – FS – 2013

Ras, Manuel – (Paarl BH) – WP – 2015-16

³Rathbone, Clyde – (Kingsway High) – Natal – 1999

†Rautenbach, Faan – (Kroonstad Agric) – NFS – 1993-94

Rautenbach, George – (Paul Roos Gym) – WP – 1974-75

†Redelinghuys, Julian – (Monument) – GL – 2006-07

Reid, Grant – (Maritzburg Coll) – Natal – 1987

†Reinach, Jaco – (Grey Coll) – FS – 1979-80

Reingold, Jeremy – (Constantia) – WP – 1985

Rheeder, Edmund – (Klerksdorp) – Leopards – 2014

Rich, Rockey – (Kearsney Coll) – Natal – 1975

Richardson, Craig – (Despatch) – EP – 1986

Richardson, Michael – (Despatch) – EP – 1989

Richter, Jan – (Grey Coll) – FS – 1977

Richter, Toppie – (Grey Coll) – FS – 1977

Ries, Alfred – (Monument) – GL – 2006

Roberts, Steph – (Grey Coll) – FS – 2003

Robinson, Sean – (Waterkloof) – BB – 2011

Roodt, Hendrik – (Lichtenburg HS) – Leopards – 2005

†Rose, Earl – (Strand) – WP – 2002

Rose, Jody – (Paul Roos Gym) – WP – 2003

†Rossouw, Chris – (Hugenote HS) – Valke – 1987

Rossouw, Francois – (HTS Middelburg) – Mpu – 1986

Rossouw,* Jean–Jacques – (Paarl Gym) – WP – 2006

Rossouw, Johan – (Durbanville) – WP – 1977

Roux, Daan – (Lichtenburg) – Stellaland – 1974-75

Roux, Paul – (Paul Roos Gym) – WP – 2000

Ruiters, Marlin – (Greyn Coll) – EP – 2006

Saaiman, Willem – (Menlopark) – BB – 1991

Saayman, Daniel – (Daniel Pienaar THS) – EP – 1992

Sadie, Carlu – (Bellville) – WP – 2015

Sadie, Ian – (Grey Coll) – FS – 1979

Sandi, Sazi – (St Andrews) EP CD – 2016

Scheepers, Eben – (Grey Coll) – FS – 1983

Schnetler, Fredrick – (Glenwood) – KZN – 2009

Schickerling, Adriaan – (Boland Agric) – Boland – 1984

Schickerling, JD – (Paarl Gym) – WP – 2012

Schoeman, Barry – (Verwoerdburg) – BB – 1975

Schoeman, Marnus – (Waterkloof) – BB – 2006-07

Schoeman,* Pierre – (AHS, Pretoria) – BB – 2011-12

†Scholtz, Hendro – (Voortrekker, Bethlehem) – NFS – 1997

Schurmann, Deon – (Eldoraigne) – BB – 1984

Schwartz, Lean – (Waterkloof) – BB – 2009

Scott, Ashwin – (Parkdene) – SWD – 2003

Scriba, Hans – (Outeniqua) – SWD – 1983

Searson, Paul – (Bishops) – WP – 1989

Senekal, Dawie – (Abbots Coll) – WP – 1988

Serdyn, Charl – (Paarl BH) – WP – 2016

⁵Serfontein,* Jan – (Otto du Plessis) – EP – 1976-78

⁶†Serfontein, Jan – (Grey Coll) – FS – 2011

Siegelaar, Alastair – (Paul Roos Gym.) – WP – 2004

Sihunu, Akhona – (Dale Coll) – Border – 2012

Simelane, Wandise – (Jeppe BH) – GL – 2015-16

Sitole, Martin – (Embalenthele) – Mpu – 2001-02

Sithole, Sibusiso – (Queens Coll) – Border – 2008

Skeate, Ross – (SACS) – WP – 2000

†Skinstad, Bob – (Hilton Coll) – Natal – 1994

Skosana, Brian – (St Andrews) – EP CD – 2009

Slabbert, Henk – (Potch. Gym) – Leopards – 1980

†Small, James – (Greenside) – GL – 1987

Small-Smith,* William – (Grey Coll) – FS – 2010

Smit,* Barend – (Middelburg THS) –

Mpu – 2014
Smit, Chris – (Grey Coll) – FS – 1979
†**Smit, John** – (Pretoria BHS) – BB – 1996
Smith, André – (Paarl Gym.) – WP – 2005
†**Smith, David** – (Hamilton, Rhodesia) – Rhodesia – 1975-76
Smith, Hadley – (Grey Coll) – FS – 2007
Smith, Philip – (Hangklip) – Border – 1975
Smith, Ruan – (Paarl Gym) – WP – 2008
Smith, Sarel–Marco – (Eldoraigne) – BB – 2014
Snyman, Earl – (Outeniqua) – SWD – 2007
Snyman, Johan – (Outeniqua) – SWD – 2004
Snyman, RG – (AHS, Pretoria) – BB – 2013
Snyman, Tiaan – (AHS, Pretoria) – BB – 1997-98
Sofoko, Jerry – (Pretoria THS) – BB – 2002
Sogidashe, Luvo – (Kama) – Border – 2002
Solomon, Chad – (Paul Roos Gym) – WP – 2012
Sonnekus, Pieter – (Bloemfontein THS) – FS – 1980
†**Sowerby, Shaun** – (HTS Sasolburg) – Vaal Triangle – 1996
Spamer, Pieter – (Pietersburg) – Limpopo BB – 2003
Sparks, Bradley – (Selborne Coll) – Border – 1998
Squires, Brandon – (Maritzburg Coll) – Natal – 2002
Stampu, Yondela – (St Albans) – BB – 2007
Stander,* CJ – (Oakdale Agric) – SWD – 2008
Stassen, Hendre – (EG Jansen) – GL – 2015
Steenkamp, Buks – (Grey Coll) – FS – 1985-86
Steenkamp, Corrie – (Vereeniging THS) – Valke – 1997
Steenkamp, Wilhelm – (Paarl BH) – WP – 2003
Steenkamp, Pieta – (Grey Coll) – FS – 1990
Steenkamp, PJ – (Garsfontein) – BB – 2016
Steenkamp,* Ruan – (Monument) – GL – 2011
Steenkamp, Virgulle – (Excelsior Belhar) – WP – 1997
Steenkamp, Willie – (Grey Coll) – FS – 2000
†**Stegmann, Deon** – (Grey Coll) – FS – 2004
Stevens, Jeffrey – (Breërivier) – Boland – 1995-96
Stevens, Kees – (Grey Coll) – FS – 1983
Stevenson, Jacques – (Ermelo) – Mpu –1989
Stewart, Clayton – (Strand HS) – WP – 2006
Stewart, Errol – (Westville) – Natal – 1987
Steyn, Christo – (Bloemfontein THS) – FS – 1976
Steyn, Francois – (AHS, Pretoria) – BB – 2013
Steyn, Jacques – (Andrew Rabie) – EP – 1995
Stoop, Ockert – (John Vorster, Nigel) – Valke – 1974-75
†**Stransky, Joel** – (Maritzburg Coll) – Natal

– 1984
†**Strauss, Adriaan** – (Grey Coll) – FS – 2003
Strauss, Johan – (Kearsney Coll) – Natal – 2004
°**Strauss, Richardt** – (Grey Coll) – FS – 2003
Strydom, Emil–Jan – (Grey Coll) – FS – 1986
Swanepoel, Dries – (Grey Coll) – FS – 2011
Swanepoel, Jaco – (Grey Coll) – FS - 1986
†**Swanepoel, Werner** – (Grey Coll) – FS – 1991
†**Swart, Justin** – (Paul Roos Gym) – WP – 1991
Swart, Hakkies – (Drostdy THS) – Boland – 1988
Swart, Johan – (Paarl Gym) – WP – 1982
†**Swart, Balie** – (Paarl Gym) – WP – 1983
Swartbooi, Dewey – (Worcester Gym) – Boland – 2000
Swiegers, Gielie – (Monument) – GL – 1984
Swiel, Timothy – (Bishops) – WP – 2011
Taute, Jaco – (Klerksdorp) – Leopards – 1989
Temple, Stephan – (Pretoria Boys High) – BB – 1993
Theron, Danie – (Kimberley THS) – GW – 1980
Theron, Gerrie – (Rustenburg) – Leopards – 1994-95
Theron, Jannie – (Sand du Plessis) – FS – 1987
Theron, Pieter – (Grey Coll) – FS – 1975
Thomas, Gray – (Volkskool) – Leopards – 1984
Thomas, Jason – (Muir Coll) – EP – 2010
Thomson, Brandon – (Ermelo) – Mpu – 2013
†**Thompson, Jeremy** – (Maritzburg Coll) – Natal – 1986
Thompson, Malcolm – (Maritzburg Coll) – Natal – 1974-75
Tile, Mandilakhe – (Dale Coll) – Border – 2005
Toerien, PJ – (Garsfontein) – BB – 2013
Tom, Siyabonga – (Glenwood) – KZN – 2011
Topkin, Gareth – (Rondebosch) – WP – 2008
†**Truscott, Andries** – (Grey Coll) – FS – 1986
Uys, Muller – (Paarl Gym) – WP – 2016
Uys, Petrus – (Monument) – GL – 2008
Van Buuren, Albertus – (Hoopstad) – NFS – 1992
Van Coller, Stephan – (Volkskool) – Leopards – 1981
†**Van der Linde, CJ** – (Grey Coll) – FS – 1998
Van der Linden, Lallie – (Pretoria–Noord) – BB – 1974-75
Van der Merwe, Bennie – (Paarl BH) – WP – 1979-80
Van der Merwe, Danie – (Mariental) – SWA – 1980
Van der Merwe, Duhan – (Outeniqua) – SWD – 2012-13
Van der Merwe, Gert – (DF Malan) –

WP – 1976
Van der Merwe, Jaco – (Bishops) – WP – 1983
Van der Merwe, Joepie – (Grey Coll) – FS – 1979-80
Van der Merwe, Marinus – (Standerton) – Pumas – 2010
†**Van der Merwe, Flip** – (Grey Coll) – FS – 2003
Van der Merwe, Pikkie – (Helpmekaar) – GL – 1978
Van der Mescht, JP – (Daniel Pienaar) – EP – 1993
Van der Schyff, Jonathan – (Monument) – GL – 2001
Van der Walt, CP – (Piet Potgieter) – Far North – 1981
Van der Walt, Danie – (Ermelo) – Mpu – 1989
Van der Walt, James – (Ermelo) – Mpu – 1997
Van der Walt, Jaco – (Monument) – GL – 2011
Van der Walt, Kobus – (AHS, Pretoria) – BB – 1999
Van der Walt, Nardus – (AHS, Pretoria) – BB – 2010
Van der Walt, Nicky – (Ermelo) – Mpu – 1993
Vd Westhuizen, Chrisjan – (Menlopark) – BB – 1995
Vd Westhuizen, Dayan – (Centurion) – BB – 2012
Vd Westhuizen, Richard – (Vryburger) – GL – 1976
Vd Westhuizen, Roedolf – (AHS, Pretoria) – BB – 2000
†**Vd Westhuyzen, Jaco** – (Ben Viljoen) – Mpu – 1996
Van Genderen, Jan – (Monument) – GL – 1978
Van Genderen, Kolie – (Monument) – GL – 1980
Van Heerden, Frans – (Langenhoven) – BB – 1975
Van Heerden, Ruben – (AHS, Pretoria) – BB – 2015
Van Heerden, Schalk – (AHS, Pretoria) – BB – 2010
Van Heerden, Wayne – (Brandwag, Uit.) – EP – 1997-98
Van Heerden, Wickus – (Voortrekkerhoogte) – BB – 1982
Van Niekerk, Ernst – (Paarl Gym) – WP – 1986
†**Van Niekerk, Joe** – (King Edward VII) – GL – 1997-98
Van Niekerk, Kenneth – (Glenwood) – KZN – 2014
Van Niekerk, Niekie – (De Wet Nel THS) – NFS – 1985
Van Rensburg, Charl – (Queens Coll) – Border – 1992
Van Rensburg, Robbie – (AHS, Pretoria) – BB – 1998
Van Rhyn,* Ernst – (Paarl Gym) – WP – 2015

Van Rooyen, Leon – (Estcourt) – Natal – 1987

Van Rooyen, Nico – (Rustenburg) – Leopards – 1981

Van Rooyen, Rudi – (AHS, Pretoria) – BB – 2010

Van Vuuren, Coenraad – (Nelspruit) – Mpu – 2013

Van Vuuren, Kosie – (AHS, Kroonstad) – NFS – 1994

Van Rooyen, Marchand – (Jan Viljoen) – Golden Lions – 2007

Van Vuuren, Pieter-Willem – (Grey Coll) – FS – 2006

Van Vuuren, Rodney – (AHS, Kroonstad) – NFS – 1983

Van Westing, Carl – (Marais Viljoen) – GL – 1992

Van Wyk, Cobus – (Schoonspruit) – Leopards – 1976

Van Wyk, William – (Paarl Gym) – WP – 2009

Van Zyl, Jaco – (JG Meiring) – WP – 1994

Van Zyl, Willem-Petrus – (Paarl BH) – WP – 1997

Venske, Herman – (Vanderbijlpark) – GL – 1979

†Venter, Brendan – (Monument) – GL – 1987

⁷Venter, André – (Grey Coll) – FS – 1990-91

⁷Venter, André – (Monument) – GL – 1989

Venter, Deon – (AHS, Pretoria) – BB – 2001

Venter, Francois – (Grey Coll) – FS – 2008

Venter, Hugo – (Grey Coll) – FS – 1991

Venter, Jano – (Middelburg THS) – Mpu – 2012

Venter, Ruan – (Monument) – GL – 2010

Verhoeven, Antonius – (Charlie Hofmeyer) – Boland – 1995

†Vermaak, Jano – (Vereeniging THS) – Valke – 2003

Vermeulen, Gielie – (Paul Roos Gym) – WP – 1983

Vermeulen, Jacques – (Paarl Gym) – WP – 2013

Vermeulen, PJ – (Noordkaap HS) – Griquas – 2005

Vermeulen, Riaan – (Grey Coll) – FS – 2002

Vers, Keanu (Grey HS) – EP – 2014

Viljoen, EW – (Grey Coll) – FS – 2013

Viljoen, Gert – (De Wet Nel THS) – NFS – 1980

Viljoen, Harry – (Florida) – GL – 1976-77

†Viljoen, Roelof – (Joggie) – (Framesby) – EP – 1993-94

Visagie, Johan – (Potchefstroom THS) – Leopards – 1974

Visagie, Ronnie – (Rob Ferreira, Witrivier) – Mpu – 1983-84

†Visser, De Villiers – (Voortrekker, CT) – WP – 1976

Visser, Jacques – (Paarl Gym) – WP – 1982

Visser, Johan – (Paarl Gym) – WP – 2015

†Visser, Mornay – (Paarl Gym) – WP – 1988

Volschenk, Johan – (Oakdale Agric.) – SWD – 2004

†Von Hoesslin, David – (Bishops) – WP – 1993

Vundla, Tshipiso – (St Albans) – BB – 2000

Wagenstroom, Frank – (Tygerberg) – WP – 2003

Wait, Clayton – (Pearson) – EP – 1989

Walker, Robert – (St Johns) – GL – 1981

Walters, Clint – (Woodridge) – EP – 1993

Walters, Rowan – (Upington HS) – Griquas – 2005

Wannenburg, Callie – (Oakdale Agric) – SWD – 2001

†Wannenburg, Pedrie – (Oakdale Agric) – SWD – 1999

Watermeyer, Stefan – (Waterkloof) – BB – 2005-06

†Watson,* Luke – (Grey Coll) – EP – 2001

Weideman, Greyling – (Drostdy THS) – Boland – 1996

Weitz, Gerhard – (Grey Coll) – FS – 1974-75

Wenger, Charl – (Grey Coll) – FS – 2009

White, Bruce – (Maritzburg Coll) – Natal – 1974-75

Whitfield, Brendon – (Selborne Coll) – Border – 1994

Wiese, Cornel – (Paarl Gym) – WP League – 1988

Wiese, Cobus – (Upington) – Griquas CD – 2014-15

Wiggins, Deon – (Hugenote) – Boland – 1988

Willemse, Coenie – (Hendrik Verwoerd) – BB – 1982

Willemse, Damian – (Paul Roos Gym) – WP – 2015-16

Willemse, Jaco – (Paarl Gym) – WP – 2014

Willemse, Martin – (Sandveld) – NFS – 1993

Williams, Jerome – (Middelande Sec.) – EP – 2004

Williams, Jondre – (Boland Agric) – Boland – 2015

Williams, Percey – (Oudtshoorn) – SWD – 2011

Willis, Vainon – (Waterkloof) – BB – 2006

Wilson, Warren – (Maritzburg Coll) – Natal – 1987

Wolmarans, Jan – (Wonderboom) – BB – 1982

Zaltsman, Neil – (Northlands) – Natal – 1985

Zandberg,* Eduan (Outeniqua) – SWD – 2014

Zass, Leolin – (Hermanus) – Boland – 2013

---

1 *Appeared for England at full international level* 2 *Appeared for Ireland at full international level.* 3 *Appeared for Australia at full international level.* 4 *Appeared for France at full international level.* 5, 6 & 7 *Earned SA Schools caps from two different provinces.* 8 *Jan (snr) and Jan (jnr) Serfontein are the first father–son combination to have represented the SA Schools team.* 9 *Appeared for Ireland at full international level.*

Five SA Schools players gained senior national colours in other sports than rugby: Warren McCann, Jaco Reinach, Herman Venske (athletics); and Errol Stewart and Herschelle Gibbs (cricket).

Two SA School players later coached the Springbok team: Harry Viljoen and Nick Mallett

PROVINCIAL REPRESENTATION

Western Province	146	Griquas	7
Free State	107	Far North/Limpopo BB	7
Blue Bulls	94	North Eastern Cape/EP CD	7
Golden Lions	66	Stellaland	3
KwaZulu–Natal	66	Vaal Triangle	2
Eastern Province	60	WP Academy	2
Mpumalanga Pumas	49	Griquas CD	2
Border Bulldogs	33	WP League	1
Boland Cavaliers	30	Border CD	1
South Western Districts Eagles	28	Zimbabwe (Rhodesia)	1
Northern Free State Griffons	22	Namibia (South West Africa)	1
North West Leopards	18	SA Academy (EP)	1
Valke	17		

SECTION 6:
FIRST-CLASS RUGBY

CURRIE CUP

South African First-Class Records

MATCH RECORDS

Highest score by a team

163	Lowveld vs Transkei *(163-10)*		1994

Biggest win by a team

158 Golden Lions v Limpopo BB *(161-3)* 2013

Most tries by a team

26	Lowveld vs Transkei *(163-10)*		1994

Most tries by a player

9 AA Volmink, Golden Lions vs Lim BB
2013

Most conversions by a player

20 WJ de W Ras, Free State vs EOFS 1977

Most penalty goals by a player

9	JH Kruger, N-Transvaal vs WP	1996
9	E Herbert, NFS vs Valke	1997
9	E Herbert, Griffons vs Pumas	2001
9	DJ Hougaard, Blue Bulls vs WP	2002
9	PC Montgomery, SA XV vs World XV	
		2006
9	ET Jantjies, Lions vs Cheetahs	2012

Most drop goals by a player

5	HE Botha, N-Transvaal vs Natal	1992
5	JH de Beer, SA vs England	1999

SEASON RECORDS

Most points by a team

1434	Free State	1996

Most tries by a team

191	Free State	1996

Most points by a player

528	NB Scholtz, WP	1988

Most tries by a player

35	P Hendriks, Transvaal	1992

CAREER RECORDS

Most points by a player

3781	HE Botha *(N-Tvl, SA)*	1977-1995

Most tries by a player

173	C Badenhorst *(FS, SA)*	1986-1999

Most conversions by a player

669	HE Botha *(N-Tvl, SA)*	1977-1995

Most penalties by a player

710	E Herbert *(NFS, FS)*	1986-2001

Most drop goals by a player

210	HE Botha *(N-Tvl, SA)*	1977-1995

Most appearances in a single position

159	HM Reece Edwards *(KZN)*	Fullback
221	C Badenhorst *(Free State)*	Wing
225	HL Müller *(Free State)*	Centre
205	E Herbert *(NFS)*	Flyhalf
162	E Hare *(W-Tvl)*	Scrumhalf
154	AWA van Wyk	No. 8
183	SB Geldenhuys *(N-Tvl)*	Flank
191	WH Lessing *(Leo)*	Lock
177	CJ Botha *(SWD)*	Prop

157	T van der Walt	Hooker

Most matches as a provincial captain

129	E Hare *(W-Tvl)*	1989-1996

Fastest to 100 games

3 years, 240 days CJ Kapp *(SWD)* 1997-2000

Youngest player to 100 games

24 years, 339 days P Hendriks *(Transvaal)*
18/03/1995

Played for seven provinces

J-P Joubert   NFS, SWD, Bol, GW, BB, FS, GL
R Geldenhuys Bor, Pum, GL, Bol, Griff, FS, EP

More than 300 first-class matches *

389	V Matfield *(BB, GW, Cats, Bulls, SA)*
344	CS Terblanche *(Bol, KZN, Sharks, SA)*
343	A-H le Roux *(FS, KZN, Cheetahs, SA)*
338	PA van den Berg *(Vaal Triangle, GW, KZN, SA)*
328	JW Smit *(KZN, Sharks, SA)*
327	JN du Plessis *(Free State, Sharks, SA)*
310	OM Ndungane *(Border, Blue Bulls, Sharks, SA)*

* for South African teams only

Odwa Ndungane – a Sharks legend.

Blue Bulls Records

MATCH RECORDS

Biggest win	147-8	vs South Western Districts (CC) (Currie Cup Record)	Polokwane	1996
Heaviest defeat	13-57	vs Transvaal (CC)	Johannesburg	1994
Highest score	147	vs South Western Districts (147-8, CC)	Polokwane	1996
Most points conceded	64	vs Wellington Hurricanes (32-64)	New Plymouth	1997
Most tries	23	vs SWD (147-8, CC) (Currie Cup Record)		
			Polokwane	1996
Most points by a player	40	CP Steyn vs SWD Eagles (CC)	Pretoria	2000
Most tries by a player	7	J Olivier vs SWD (CC) (Currie Cup Record)	Polokwane	1996
Most conversions by a player	15	W du Plessis vs Limpopo (VC)	Lephalele	2013
	14	LR Sherrell vs SWD (CC) (Currie Cup Record)	Polokwane	1996
Most penalties by a player	9	JH Kruger vs Western Province (CC) (SA Record)	Pretoria	1996
	9	DJ Hougaard vs Western Province (CC) (SA Record)	Pretoria	2002
Most drop goals by a player	5	HE Botha vs Natal (CC Record)	Pretoria	1992

SEASON RECORDS

Most team points	1193	28 matches	1996
Most team points in Currie Cup	783	13 matches	1997
Most points by a player	361	CP Steyn	1999
Most Currie Cup points	268	JW Heunis (Currie Cup Record)	1989
Most team tries	142	28 matches	2004
Most tries by a player	25	PJ Spies	1975
Most Currie Cup tries by a player	18	E Botha	2004

CAREER RECORDS

Most appearances	184	SB Geldenhuys	1977-1989
Most points	2511	HE Botha (179 matches)	1977-1992
Most tries	85	DE Oosthuysen (140 matches)	1986-1994

HONOURS

Currie Cup	1946, 1956, 1968, 1969, 1971 (shared), 1973, 1974, 1975, 1977, 1978, 1979 (shared), 1980, 1981, 1987, 1988, 1989 (shared), 1991, 1998, 2002, 2003, 2004, 2006 (shared), 2009.
Lion Cup	1985, 1990, 1991
Bankfin Cup	2000
Vodacom Cup	2001, 2008, 2009

Boland Records

MATCH RECORDS

Biggest win	96-5	vs Zimbabwe	1996
Biggest win (Currie Cup)	65-5	vs Mpumalanga	2007
Heaviest defeat	8-96	vs Western Province	1993
	3-91	vs Free State Cheetahs (Currie Cup)	2007
Highest score	96	vs Zimbabwe (96-5)	1996
Highest score (Currie Cup)	79	vs Valke (79-26)	2012
Moist points conceded	96	vs Western Province (8-96)	1993
Moist points conceded (Currie Cup)	91	vs Free State Cheetahs	2007
Most tries	15	vs Zimbabwe	1996
Most tries (Currie Cup)	12	vs Valke	2012
Most points by a player	34	F Horn vs South Western Districts	1996
Most points by a player (Currie Cup)	25	P O'Neill vs Northern Free State	1997
Most tries by a player (Currie Cup)	6	FP Marais vs North Eastern Districts	1952

SEASON RECORDS

Most team points	956	24 matches	2001
Most team points (Currie Cup)	566	12 matches	2011
Most points by a player	355	F Horn	1996
Most points by a player (Currie Cup)	197	EG Watts	2011
Most team tries	137	24 matches	2001
Most team tries (Currie Cup)	75	12 matches	2011
Most tries by a player	20	CS Terblanche	1997
Most tries by a player (Currie Cup)	16	RS Benjamin	2006

CAREER RECORDS

Most appearances	154	N Papier	2001-2012
Most points	524	P O'Neill	1996-2002
Most tries	82	JI Daniels	1998-2008

HONOURS

First Division	2001, 2003, 2004, 2006, 2011
Vodacom Shield	2004

Eastern Province Records

MATCH RECORDS

Biggest win	110-17	vs Welwitschias (Namibia)	2001
Biggest Currie Cup win	63-7	vs Griffons	2013
Heaviest defeat	12-80	vs Griqualand West	1998
Heaviest Currie Cup defeat	7-71	vs Golden Lions	2016
Highest score	110	vs Welwitschias (Namibia) (110-17)	2001
Most points conceded	80	vs Griqualand West (12-80)	1998
Most tries	16	vs Welwitschias (Namibia) (110-17)	2001
Most Currie Cup tries	11	vs Griffons (67-26)	2011
Most points by a player	38	HP le Roux vs Eastern Transvaal	1991
Most Currie Cup points by a player	29	AP Kruger vs North West	1996
Most tries by a player	5	FW Knoetze vs Stellaland	1991
	5	FG Crous vs Western Transvaal	1994
	5	N Nelson vs Valke (Currie Cup, First Div.)	2010

SEASON RECORDS

Most team points	875	27 matches	2012
Most Currie Cup points by team	611	18 matches	2012
Most points by a player	282	AP Kruger	1996
Most Currie Cup points by a player	153	B Hennessey	2002
Most team tries	103	24 matches	2003
	103	27 matches	2012
Most Currie Cup tries by team	76	18 matches	2012
Most tries by a player	14	M Van Vuuren	1994
	14	H Pedro	1998
	14	FM Juries	2003
Most Currie Cup tries by a player	13	H Pedro	1998
	13	L Watson	2012

CAREER RECORDS

Most appearances	173	BC Pinnock	1993-2002
Most points	1126	GC van Zyl	1981-1988
Most Currie Cup points	755	GC van Zyl	1981-1988
Most tries	56	NT Nelson	2006-2013

HONOURS

Vodacom Shield	2002
First Division	2010, 2012

Free State Records

MATCH RECORDS

Biggest win	132-3	vs Eastern Orange Free State	1977
Biggest Currie Cup win	106-0	vs Northern Free State	1997
Heaviest defeat	0-50	vs Eastern Province (Currie Cup)	1993
Highest score	132	vs Eastern Orange Free State (132-3)	1977
Highest Currie Cup score	113	vs South Western Districts (113-11)	1996
Most points conceded	73	vs Golden Lions (31-73)	2015
Most tries	23	vs Eastern Orange Free State (132-3)	1977
Most Currie Cup tries	17	vs South Western Districts (113-11)	1996
Most points by a player	48	WJ de W Ras vs Eastern Orange Free State	1977
Most Currie Cup points by player	46	JH de Beer vs Northern Free State	1977
Most tries by a player	6	HL Potgieter vs Eastern Orange Free State	1977
Most Currie Cup tries by a player	4	On seven occasions	
Most conversions by a player	20	WJ de W Ras vs Eastern Orange Free State (SA Record)	1977
Most Currie Cup conversions	14	JH de Beer vs Northern Free State	1977
Most penalties by a player	8	AF Fourie vs Griqualand West (Currie Cup)	1997

SEASON RECORDS

Most team points	1434	31 matches (SA Record)	1996
Most Currie Cup points by team	703	15 matches	1997
Most points by a player	460	MJ Smith	1996
Most Currie Cup points by player	230	K Tsimba	2003
Most team tries	191	31 matches (SA Record)	1996
Most Currie Cup tries by team	91	15 matches	1997
Most tries by a player	24	J-H van Wyk	1996
Most Currie Cup tries by a player	16	J-H van Wyk	1997

CAREER RECORDS

Most appearances	245	HL Müller (SA Record)	1983-1998
Most Currie Cup appearances	142	HL Müller	1983-1998
Most points	1707	WJ de W Ras	1974-1986
Most Currie Cup points	1101	WJ de W Ras	1974-1986
Most tries	136	C Badenhorst	1986-1999
Most Currie Cup tries	65	C Badenhorst	1986-1999

HONOURS

Currie Cup	1976, 2005, 2006 (shared), 2007, 2016
Lion Cup	1983
Bankfin Nite Series	1996
Vodacom Cup	2000

Golden Lions Records

MATCH RECORDS

Biggest win	116-10	vs South Eastern Transvaal	1993
Biggest Currie Cup win	99-9	vs Far North	1973
	104-14	vs SWD	2003
Heaviest defeat	10-74	vs British Lions	2009
Heaviest Currie Cup defeat	5-59	vs Free State	2006
Highest score	116	vs South Eastern Transvaal (116-10)	1993
Most points conceded	74	vs British Lions (10-74)	2009
Most tries	18	vs Madrid XV (96-6)	1979
Most Currie Cup tries	16	vs Far North (99-9)	1973
Most points by a player	40	L Barnard vs North East Cape	1979
Most CC points by a player	36	GR Bosch vs Far North	1973
Most tries by a player	6	SA Smit vs Orange Free State	1941
Most Currie Cup tries by a player	4	On seven occasions (most recently by GM Delport vs Griffons 1997)	
Most conversions by a player	16	L Barnard vs North East Cape	1979
Most Currie Cup conversions	13	GR Bosch vs Far North	1973
Most penalties by a player	7	On five occasions in Currie Cup	
Most drop goals by a player	3	GR Bosch vs Eastern Transvaal (CC, 1972) & vs WP (CC, 1974)	
	3	JC Robbie vs Eastern Province (1987)	1987
	3	AS Pretorius vs Griquas (CC)	2005

SEASON RECORDS

Most team points	1390	33 matches	1999
Most team points in Currie Cup	580	14 matches	1997
Most points by a player	414	J Engelbrecht	1999
Most CC points by a player	263	GE Lawless	1996
Most team tries	181	33 matches	1999
Most team tries in Currie Cup	74	14 matches	1997
Most tries by a player	23	P Hendriks	1994
Most Currie Cup tries by a player	14	JA van der Walt	1996

CAREER RECORDS

Most appearances	153	HP le Roux	1992-2000
Most Currie Cup appearances	108	PJJ Grobbelaar	2003-2012
Most points	896	GR Bosch	1972-1978
Most Currie Cup points	521	GR Bosch	1972-1978
Most tries	89	P Hendriks	1990-1997
Most Currie Cup tries	38	P Hendriks	1990-1997

HONOURS

Currie Cup	1922, 1939, 1950, 1952, 1971 (shared), 1972, 1993, 1994, 1999, 2011, 2015
Lion Cup	1986, 1987, 1992, 1993, 1994
Super 10	1993
Vodacom Cup	1999, 2002, 2003, 2004, 2013

Griqualand West Records

MATCH RECORDS

Biggest win	94-0	vs South Western Districts Federation	1978
Biggest win (Currie Cup)	87-14	vs Border	1998
	80-7	vs Cavaliers	2009
Heaviest defeat	3-75	vs Western Province	1985
Heaviest defeat (Currie Cup)	7-78	vs Natal Sharks	2002
Highest score	94	vs South Western Districts Federation (94-0)	1978
Highest score (Currie Cup)	87	vs Border (87-14)	1998
Most points conceded	75	vs Western Province	1985
Most points conceded (CC)	78	vs Natal Sharks (7-78)	2002
	78	vs Western Province (31-78)	2004
Most tries	18	vs South Western Districts Federation	1978
Most tries (Currie Cup)	14	vs Griffons (84-12)	2002
Most points by a player	42	IP Olivier vs Griffons	2009
Most points by a player (CC)	33	PJ Visagie vs Rhodesia	1968
Most tries by a player	7	J Jonker vs Namibia	1996
Most tries by a player (CC)	4	D Prins vs Eastern Province	1978
	4	J Nicholas vs North West	1998
	4	BA Basson vs Sharks	2010
Most conversions by a player (CC)	11	JC Wessels vs Border	1998

SEASON RECORDS

Most team points	1428	32 matches	1998
Most team points (Currie Cup)	489	14 matches	1998
Most points by a player	361	GS du Toit	1998
Most points by a player (CC)	173	IP Olivier	2010
Most team tries	210	32 matches	1998
Most team tries (Currie Cup)	86	21 matches	2003
Most tries by a player	29	BA Basson	2010
Most tries by a player (CC)	21	BA Basson	2010
Most conversions by a player	98	GS du Toit	1998
Most drop goals by a player	7	GS du Toit	1998

CAREER RECORDS

Most appearances	165	WAS Roberts	2007-2016
Most appearances (Currie Cup)	88	WAS Roberts	2007-2016
Most consecutive games	97	P Smith	1963-1973
Most matches as captain	66	AWA van Wyk	1989-1994
Most points	719	JMF Lubbe	1995-2001
Most points (Currie Cup)	440	CS Erasmus	1977-1985
Most tries	61	J Nicholas	1998-2002
Most tries (Currie Cup)	37	D Prins	1979-1987
Most conversions by a player	133	JMF Lubbe	1995-2001
Most penalties by a player	91	JMF Lubbe	1995-2001
Most drop goals by a player	15	PJ Visagie	1964-1974
Most drop goals by a player (CC)	8	PJ Visagie	1964-1974

HONOURS

Currie Cup	1899, 1911, 1970
Vodacom Cup	1998, 2005, 2007, 2009

KwaZulu-Natal Records

MATCH RECORDS

Biggest win	90-9	vs South Eastern Transvaal (Currie Cup)	1996
Heaviest defeat	6-62	vs Northern Transvaal	1991
Heaviest Currie Cup defeat	0-52	vs Western Province	1932
Highest score	90	vs South Eastern Transvaal (Currie Cup) (90-9)	1996
Most points conceded	62	vs Northern Transvaal (6-62)	1991
Most tries	15	vs Northern Natal (78-0)	1990
Most Currie Cup tries	13	vs South Eastern Transvaal (90-9)	1996
Most points by a player	50	GK Lawless vs Otago Highlanders	1997
Most Currie Cup points by a player	38	HW Honiball vs Boland	1996
Most tries by a player	4	By 11 players - most recently by JP Pietersen vs Leopards	2005
Most conversions by a player	11	HW Honiball vs South Eastern Transvaal (Currie Cup)	1996
Most penalties by a player	8	GS du Toit vs Western Province (Currie Cup)	2001
Most drop goals by a player	4	WJ de W Ras vs Western Province (Currie Cup)	1979

SEASON RECORDS

Most team points	1348	30 matches	1996
Most Currie Cup points by team	792	15 matches	1996
Most points by a player	304	JT Stransky	1990
Most Currie Cup points by a player	205	P Lambie	2010
Most team tries	184	30 matches	1996
Most Currie Cup tries by team	112	15 matches	1996
Most tries by a player	28	JF van der Westhuizen	1993
Most Currie Cup tries by a player	13	JF van der Westhuizen	1996
	13	J Joubert	1996
	13	H Mentz	2005

CAREER RECORDS

Most appearances	165	HM Reece-Edwards	1982-1995
	165	S Atherton	1988-2000
Most points	1114	HM Reece-Edwards	1982-1995
Most tries	90	JF van der Westhuizen	1992-1998

HONOURS

Currie Cup	1990, 1992, 1995, 1996, 2008, 2010, 2013

Mpumalanga Records

MATCH RECORDS

Biggest win	154-0	vs Limpopo Blue Bulls	2013
Biggest Currie Cup win	111-14	vs Vodacom Eagles	2001
Heaviest defeat	10-116	vs Transvaal	1993
Heaviest Currie Cup defeat	9-90	vs Natal	1996
Highest score	154	vs Limpopo Blue Bulls (154-0)	2013
Most points conceded	116	vs Transvaal (10-116)	1993
Most tries	22	vs Limpopo Blue Bulls	2013
Most Currie Cup tries	16	vs Vodacom Eagles (111-14)	2001
Most points by a player	37	J Benade vs Lowveld	1995
	37	CP Steyn vs Vodacom Cheetahs (Currie Cup)	2003
Most tries by a player	5	D Pretorius vs South Western Districts Federation	1978
Most Currie Cup tries by a player	4	A Fourie vs North West	1998

SEASON RECORDS

Most team points	1283	28 matches	2013
Most Currie Cup points by team	758	18 matches	2013
Most points by a player	353	C Bezuidenhout	2013
Most Currie Cup points by a player	225	C Bezuidenhout	2013
Most team tries	163	28 matches	2013
Most Currie Cup tries by team	92	18 matches	2013
Most tries by a player	24	A Kettledas	2009
Most Currie Cup tries by a player	18	A Kettledas	2009

CAREER RECORDS

Most appearances	183	FJ Rossouw	1991-2000
Most points	869	JH Muller	1973-1985
Most tries	57	K Grobler	1979-1990

HONOURS

First Division	2005, 2009, 2013
Vodacom Cup	2015
Paul Roos Trophy	1972 (shared)

W.P. RUGBY

Western Province Records

MATCH RECORDS

Biggest win	151-3	vs Eastern Transvaal	1995
Biggest win (Currie Cup)	107-23	vs South Western Districts	1996
Heaviest defeat	18-58	vs Pumas	2002
Heaviest defeat (Currie Cup)	13-50	vs Lions	2002
Highest score	151	vs Eastern Transvaal (151-3)	1995
Highest score (Currie Cup)	107	vs South Western Districts (107-23)	1996
Moist points conceded	62	vs Griqualand West (26-62)	1998
Moist points conceded (Currie Cup)	66	vs Transvaal	1992
Most tries	23	vs Eastern Transvaal (151-3)	1995
Most tries (Currie Cup)	17	vs South Western Districts (107-23)	1996
Most points by a player	46	JT Stransky vs Eastern Transvaal	1995
Most points by a player (Currie Cup)	33	C Rossouw vs Blue Bulls	2003
Most tries by a player	6	S Berridge vs Eastern Transvaal	1995
Most tries by a player (Currie Cup)	5	J Swart vs Northern Free State	1996
	5	BJ Paulse vs Falcons	1997
	5	ER Seconds vs Griquas	2004
	5	A Bekker vs Valke	2008
Most conversions by a player	18	JT Stransky vs Eastern Transvaal	1995
Most conversions by a player (Currie Cup)	11	LJ Koen vs South Western Districts	1996
Most penalties by a player (Currie Cup)	7	LR Sherrell vs Northern Transvaal	1991
	7	NV Cilliers vs Transvaal	1993
	7	C Rossouw vs Falcons	2001
	7	AJJ van Straaten vs Cheetahs	2001
Most drop goals by a player (Currie Cup)	4	L Rodriguez vs Griqualand West	1950

SEASON RECORDS

Most team points	1357	31 matches	1997
Most team points (Currie Cup)	619	15 matches	1997
Most points by a player	391	NB Scholtz	1988
Most points by a player (Currie Cup)	227	NB Scholtz	1988
Most team tries	182	31 matches	1997
Most team tries (Currie Cup)	84	15 matches	1997
Most tries by a player	25	CJ du Plessis	1989
	25	J Swart	1997
Most tries by a player (Currie Cup)	19	CJ du Plessis	1989
Most conversions by a player	80	NB Scholtz	1989
Most penalties by a player	73	LR Sherrell	1991
Most drop goals by a player	5	NV Cilliers	1997

CAREER RECORDS

Most appearances	156	CP Strauss	1986-1995
Most points	1570	NB Scholtz (116 matches)	1982-1989
Most points (Currie Cup)	992	NB Scholtz	1982-1989
Most tries	95	NJ Burger	1982-1991
Most tries (Currie Cup)	70	BJ Paulse	1996-2007
Most conversions by a player	293	NB Scholtz	1982-1989
Most penalties by a player	256	NB Scholtz	1982-1989
Most drop goals by a player	12	NB Scholtz	1982-1989

HONOURS

Currie Cup
1889, 1892, 1894, 1895, 1897, 1898, 1904, 1906, 1908, 1914, 1920, 1925, 1927, 1929, 1932, (shared), 1934 (shared), 1936, 1947, 1954, 1959, 1964, 1966, 1979 (shared), 1982, 1983, 1984, 1985, 1986, 1989 (shared), 1997, 2000, 2001, 2012, 2014

Vodacom Cup
2012

Lion Cup
1984, 1988, 1989

Bankfin Nite Series
1997

Border Records

MATCH RECORDS

Biggest win	85-3	vs Zimbabwe	1996
Biggest Currie Cup win	61-7	vs Welwitchias	2016
Heaviest defeat	15-103	vs Leopards (Currie Cup)	2014
	9-84	vs Griqualand West (Vodacom Cup)	2011
Highest score	85	vs Zimbabwe (85-3)	1996
Most points conceded	103	vs Leopards (15-103)	2014
Most tries	15	vs Zimbabwe (85-3)	1996
Most Currie Cup tries	9	vs Welwitchias (61-7)	2016
Most points by a player	31	L Basson vs Valke	2010
Most Currie Cup points by player	31	L Basson vs Valke	2010
Most tries by a player	4	A Stephenson vs Far North	1976
	4	RG Bennett vs Zimbabwe	1996
	4	M Mapimpi vs Sharks XV and Welwitchias	2016

SEASON RECORDS

Most team points	778	27 matches	1996
Most Currie Cup points by team	332	12 matches	2004
Most points by a player	299	M Flutey	1995
Most Currie Cup points by player	125	R Gerber	2004
Most team tries	101	27 matches	1996
Most Currie Cup tries by team	42	14 matches	2012
Most tries by a player	20	RG Bennett	1996
Most Currie Cup tries by a player	10	A Ndungane	2004

CAREER RECORDS

Most appearances	183	W Weyer	1988-2000
Most points	672	GK Miller	1996-2001
Most tries	44	A Alexander	

HONOURS

Currie Cup	1932 (shared), 1934 (shared)
Vodacom Shield	2003

GRIFFONS
RUGBY

Griffons Records

MATCH RECORDS

Biggest win	101	vs Welwitschias (101-0)	2016
Biggest win (Currie Cup)	68	vs Eastern Orange Free State (74-6)	1988
Heaviest defeat	83	vs Free State (8-91)	1995
Heaviest defeat (Currie Cup)	106	vs Free State Cheetahs (0-106)	1997
Highest score	101	vs Welwitschias (101-0)	2016
Highest score (Currie Cup)	84	vs Welwitschias (84-25)	2016
Moist points conceded	91	vs Free State (8-91)	1995
Moist points conceded (Currie Cup)	106	vs Free State Cheetahs (0-106)	1997
Most tries	15	vs Welwitschias (101-0)	2016
Most tries (Currie Cup)	12	vs Eastern Orange Free State (74-6)	1988
	12	vs Welwitschias (84-25)	2016
Most points by a player	36	E Herbert vs Stellaland	1992
Most points by a player (Currie Cup)	36	E Herbert vs Falcons	1997
Most tries by a player (Currie Cup)	5	P Maritz vs SE Tvl	1982
Most conversions by a player	13	GA Whitehead vs Welwitschias	2016
Most conversions by a player (Currie Cup)	12	GA Whitehead vs Welwitschias	2016
Most penalties by a player	9	E Herbert vs Pumas	2001
Most penalties by a player (Currie Cup)	9	E Herbert vs Falcons	1997
Most drop goals by a player (Currie Cup)	3	E Herbert vs FS Cheetahs	2000

SEASON RECORDS

Most team points	812	21 matches	2016
Most team points (Currie Cup)	506	15 matches	2012
Most points by a player	291	GA Whitehead	2016
Most points by a player (Currie Cup)	195	E Herbert	1988
Most team tries	104	21 matches	2016
Most team tries (Currie Cup)	68	15 matches	2012
Most tries by a player	19	S Davids	2016
Most tries by a player (Currie Cup)	8	GA Passens	1999
	8	MP Goosen	2005
	8	CS Afrika	2008
	8	J Nel	2013
Most conversions by a player	82	GA Whitehead	2016
Most penalties by a player	56	E Herbert	2001
Most drop goals by a player	10	E Herbert	1988

CAREER RECORDS

Most appearances	205	E Herbert	1986-2001
Most consecutive games	102	A Gerber	1979-1985
Most matches as captain	95	JJ Jerling	1989-1997
Most points	2608	E Herbert	1986-2001
Most tries	56	NPJ Steyn	2008-2015
Most conversions by a player	331	E Herbert	1986-2001
Most penalties by a player	544	E Herbert	1986-2001
Most drop goals by a player	66	E Herbert	1986-2001

HONOURS

Paul Roos Trophy	1970
Vodacom Shield	2001
Bankfin Cup	2008, 2014, 2016

Leopards Records

MATCH RECORDS

Biggest win	80-3	vs Niteroi, Brasilia	1993
Biggest win (Currie Cup)	103-9	vs Eastern Orange Free State	1988
Heaviest defeat	12-98	vs Transvaal	1996
Heaviest defeat (Currie Cup)	21-92	vs Blue Bulls	2011
Highest score	83	vs Uruguay (83-10)	1994
Highest score (Currie Cup)	103	vs Eastern Orange Free State (103-9)	1988
Moist points conceded	98	vs Transvaal (12-98)	1996
Moist points conceded (Currie Cup)	92	vs Blue Bulls (21-92)	2011
Most tries (Currie Cup)	18	vs Eastern Orange Free State	1988
Most points by a player	41	D Basson vs Namibia	1994
Most points by a player (Currie Cup)	31	T Marais vs Eastern Orange Free State	1988
	31	IP Olivier vs Pumas	2005
Most tries by a player	5	T van Niekerk vs Eastern Transvaal	1965
Most tries by a player (Currie Cup)	5	A Kettledas vs SWD Eagles	2012

SEASON RECORDS

Most points by a player	368	D Basson	1994
Most points by a player (Currie Cup)	204	C Durand	2008
Most tries by a player	25	CR Lloyd	2006
Most tries by a player (Currie Cup)	19	CR Lloyd	2006

CAREER RECORDS

Most appearances	191	WH (Werner) Lessing	1998-2007
Most matches as captain	129	E Hare	1989-1996
Most points	1183	D Basson	1991-1998
Most points (Currie Cup)	703	T Marais	1980-1988
Most tries	48	CR (Colin) Lloyd	2004-2011

HONOURS

First Division	2015

SWD Records

MATCH RECORDS

Biggest win	102-0	vs Transkei	1995
Biggest win (Currie Cup)	102-0	vs Griffons	1999
Heaviest defeat	0-97	vs British Lions	1974
Heaviest defeat (Currie Cup)	8-147	vs Northern Transvaal	1996
Highest score	105	vs Transkei (105-8)	1994
Highest score (Currie Cup)	102	vs Griffons (102-0)	1999
Most points conceded	97	vs British Lions (0-97)	1974
Most points conceded (Currie Cup)	147	vs Northern Transvaal (8-147)	1996
Most tries	16	vs Transkei (102-0)	1995
Most tries (Currie Cup)	16	vs Griffons (102-0)	1999
Most points by a player	28	AJJ Van Straaten	1997
Most points by a player (Currie Cup)	29	CR van As vs Leopards	2002
Most tries by a player	4	G Cilliers vs North Eastern Districts	1965
	4	F Amsterdam vs Northern Natal	1992
Most tries by a player (Currie Cup)	4	MG Joubert vs Valke	2009

SEASON RECORDS

Most team points	943	29 matches	1998
Most team points (Currie Cup)	493	15 matches	2013
Most points by a player	252	AJJ Van Straaten	1997
Most points by a player (Currie Cup)	173	CR van As	2002
Most team tries	132	29 matches	1998
Most team tries (Currie Cup)	79	21 matches	2003
Most tries by a player	20	AG Bock	2013
Most tries by a player (Currie Cup)	17	AG Bock	2013

CAREER RECORDS

Most appearances	191	C Botha	1993-2011
Most points	638	CR van As	2000-2004
Most points (Currie Cup)	480	CR van As	2000-2004
Most tries	55	AG Bock	2012-2015
Most conversions by a player	134	CR van As	2000-2004
Most penalties by a player	105	CR van As	2000-2004

HONOURS

Bankfin Cup	2002
First Division	2007

Falcons Records

MATCH RECORDS

Biggest win	109-0	vs Vagabonds	1998
Biggest Currie Cup win	66-12	vs Boland Cavaliers	2015
Heaviest defeat	3-151	vs Western Province	1995
Heaviest Currie Cup defeat	14-95	vs Pumas	2009
Highest score	109	vs Vagabonds (109-0)	1998
Most points conceded	151	vs Western Province (3-151)	1995
Most points conceded (CC)	95	vs Pumas (14-95)	2009
Most tries	17	vs Vagabonds	1998
Most Currie Cup tries	11	vs Griquas	2001
	11	vs Griffons	2003
Most points by a player	33	A de Kock vs Eastern Orange Free State	1994
	33	A de Kock vs Namibia	1995
Most Currie Cup points by a player	27	G Peens vs Border	1997
Most tries by a player	4	C van Zyl vs North West Cape	1980
	4	P Hiten vs Curda	1986
	4	D Nortjé vs Eastern Orange Free State	1989
	4	W Geyer vs Northern Free State	1998
	4	W Geyer vs Blue Bulls	1998
	4	J Houtsamer vs Mighty Elephants	2001
	4	LD Lubbe vs Griffons	2003
	4	G Mbangeni vs Leopards	2004
	4	JP Mostert vs Limpopo	2013
	4	K Hendricks vs Griquas	2015

SEASON RECORDS

Most team points	884	35 matches	1998
Most Currie Cup points by team	393	14 matches	2012
Most points by a player	277	J Viljoen	1996
Most Currie Cup points by a player	158	Louis Strydom	2005
Most team tries	118	35 matches	1998
Most Currie Cup tries by team	56	14 matches	2012
Most tries by a player	22	W Geyer	1998
Most Currie Cup tries by a player	10	LD Lubbe	1989
	10	E Botha	2001

CAREER RECORDS

Most appearances	158	E Rossouw	1997-2004
Most points	732	H Labuschagne	
Most tries	55	LD Lubbe	

HONOURS

Vodacom Cup	2006

Lions fall short but win hearts

Wellington bridge too far but season achievements remarkable

By John Bishop

THE Emirates Lions' rag-to-riches Vodacom Super Rugby story, and the style in which it was written, captured the imagination of the South African rugby public and it was only a masterclass in wet-weather rugby by the Hurricanes in Wellington that denied them their fairytale ending.

While the other five South African franchises were largely bit-players during the season – only occasionally grabbing the spotlight – the Lions held centre-stage from start to finish. They made history in week two with their first win (36-32) over the Chiefs in Hamilton in nine attempts and their popular, expansive approach carried them all the way to the final showdown in faraway Wellington.

The Lions' group of unheralded players, who had won promotion to Super Rugby by beating the Southern Kings three years earlier, married an ambitious attacking approach with solid forward play. They scored the most tries of any team in the season and only sacrificed top spot on the combined log in the final round of pool games when coach Johan Ackermann opted to send a second-string team to Buenos Aires to play the Jaguares, in order to rest his 15 regulars for the play-offs.

The plan worked, at least initially, as they eliminated first the Crusaders and then the Highlanders. Ultimately, however, it resulted in them having to travel to New Zealand where they lost the final 20-3 as the Hurricanes flourished in the demanding but familiar conditions – and the Lions did not.

Home-ground advantage is obviously important in any sporting contest but at certain venues such as the Westpac Stadium in Wellington, where the wind blows a gale and the rain falls in sheets, it is critical.

While the elements were busy negating the strengths of the Lions, they were tailor-made for the Hurricanes as the hosts tapped into fly-half Beauden Barrett's sublime tactical kicking game and pressured the Lions with their rush defence. The Lions attempted to play too much rugby deep in their own territory and when the mistakes came – and they were inevitable in the slippery conditions – the Hurricanes pounced to score their two tries.

But the Lions, their coaching staff and their growing band of supporters around South Africa and further afield, had much to celebrate in showing South Africa that pretty rugby can still be winning rugby. They started the Super Rugby campaign without a single World Cup Springbok but by the time it ended they had nine players in Allister Coetzee's Rugby Championship squad.

Their worst moments came when the Hurricanes caught them cold at Ellis Park and racked up 50 points; the most satisfying were the play-off wins over two leading New Zealand teams.

The Lions' success was built on an enthusiastic team effort but captain Warren Whiteley, flanker Jaco Kriel, workaholic lock Franco Mostert, hooker Malcolm Marx, halfbacks Faf de Klerk and Elton Jantjies, young centre Rohan Janse van Rensburg and wing Ruan Combrinck made massive contributions.

The Lions and the DHL Stormers topped the two African conferences and hosted quarter-finals while the Cell C Sharks pipped the Vodacom Bulls to claim the wildcard quarter-final berth and the dubious honour of a midweek trek to Wellington for a 41-0 thumping by the Hurricanes.

The convoluted pool system both helped and hindered the Stormers. They were comfortable winners in their conference with 10 victories in 15 pool games to finish nine points clear of the Bulls, but they had the most accommodating draw, which pitted them against Australian rather than New Zealand opposition. It was only in the quarter-final that they encountered Kiwis for the first time and they were exposed by the Chiefs' pace and intensity in going down 60-21 in front of a stunned Newlands crowd.

The Stormers, with Springboks Eben Etzebeth and Pieter-Steph du Toit locking the scrum, had the best defensive lineout in the competition and their defence was also impressive as they leaked only 28 tries in 15 pool games.

Springbok back-rower Schalk Burger called time on his distinguished Newlands career after the quarter-final loss and he and Test prop Vincent Koch joined European champions Saracens for the 2016/17 season.

The Bulls, who also did not play against any of the New Zealand teams in the pool stages, started strongly with six wins and a draw from their first eight matches. But they then lost four of their next five games and were overhauled by the Sharks in the race for the final play-off spot.

The Bulls were without injured Springbok flyhalf Handré Pollard for the year and coach Nollis Marais turned to youth to replace a host of senior players who had left Loftus. He said that collecting only four bonus points had cost them a place in the play-offs.

The final impression is in many cases the lasting one and the Sharks' campaign will be remembered by many for their 41-0 loss to a slick Hurricanes outfit in the wet of Wellington. But the young Sharks, with the odds stacked heavily against them from the start, in many ways exceeded expectations and at least overcame the toughest of draws and unrealistic travel demands to reach the quarter-finals.

Head coach Gary Gold said he would have taken the Sharks' nine wins from 15 games, and the quarter-final spot, if offered it back in February – "considering the tour from hell (three games in 15 days on three different continents),

being in the New Zealand pool and starting with major injuries (to Marcell Coetzee, Pat Lambie and Cobus Reinach)."

The Sharks were at their most impressive against New Zealand opposition. They beat the Highlanders (15-14) on their tour and lost narrowly to the Blues (23-18) and the Chiefs (24-22) before flying back to Durban and stunning the Hurricanes 32-15.

They faded badly after the June internationals, conceding 20 tries in 12 games before the break and 16 in four games after they returned.

The Cheetahs, forever young and in a constant state of rebuilding, had one of their familiar seasons as they fluctuated between good and bad, between enterprising attack and porous defence. They picked up four wins, none against any of the more fancied teams, beating the Southern Kings, Rebels and Sunwolves (twice).

They largely marked time on the combined log, finishing 14th out of 18 teams.

The drain of talented players remains a perennial problem for the Cheetahs and they suffered a major blow after the season when Springbok lock Lood de Jager, the-then South African player of the year, signed for the Bulls.

They did show some enterprise on attack with captain and centre Francois Venter – whose form eventually resulted in a Test cap by the end of the year – wing Sergeal Petersen and fullback Clayton Blommetjies prominent but Franco Smith's team, hit by injuries, lacked depth and the necessary consistency.

The Southern Kings, back in Super Rugby after three years, were on a hiding to nothing in Port Elizabeth and, unsurprisingly, they ended together with the Sunwolves at the foot of the combined log.

Their two home wins in 15 outings came against the Sunwolves (33-28) and then a laboured effort against the Jaguares (29-22) who played the whole second half with 13 men. The season ended with many of their more talented players heading for the exit and the chances of the Kings continuing to play Super Rugby are, at best, gloomy.

But the Lions provided the indelible memories of the season. Ackermann and his players, both in style and attitude, opened the door to a bright future and it remains to be seen whether the other franchises will follow their lead.

Still, Lions supporters will be left with that nagging feeling of what might have been. The decision to travel to Buenos Aires with a B team gave the Lions the best possible chance of making history in reaching the Super Rugby final for the first time – but not in winning it.

LOG

Team	Pos.	P	W	L	D	PF	PA	PD	TF	TA	B4	B7	BP	Pts
Hurricanes (NZC1)	1	15	11	4	0	458	314	144	61	37	7	2	9	53
Lions (AF2)	2	15	11	4	0	535	349	186	71	42	7	1	8	52
Stormers (AF1)	3	15	10	4	1	440	274	166	49	28	5	4	9	51
Brumbies (AC 1)	4	15	10	5	0	425	326	99	56	40	3	0	3	43
Highlanders (WC)	5	15	11	4	0	422	273	149	50	28	4	4	8	52
Chiefs (WC)	6	15	11	4	0	491	341	150	68	39	6	1	7	51
Crusaders (WC)	7	15	11	4	0	487	317	170	65	40	5	1	6	50
Sharks (WC)	8	15	9	5	1	360	269	91	40	30	2	3	5	43
Bulls	9	15	9	5	1	399	339	60	47	37	4	0	4	42
Waratahs	10	15	8	7	0	413	317	96	55	37	4	4	8	40
Blues	11	15	8	6	1	374	380	-6	45	47	2	3	5	39
Rebels	12	15	7	8	0	365	486	-121	46	65	2	1	3	31
Jaguares	13	15	4	11	0	376	427	-51	44	51	1	5	6	22
Cheetahs	14	15	4	11	0	377	425	-48	47	48	1	4	5	21
Reds	15	15	3	11	1	290	458	-168	33	57	0	3	3	17
Force	16	15	2	13	0	260	441	-181	25	60	0	5	5	13
Kings	17	15	2	13	0	282	684	-402	34	95	1	0	1	9
Sunwolves	18	15	1	13	1	293	627	-334	33	88	0	3	3	9

Note: NZC1 = NZ Conference winner, AC1 = Australian Conference winner, AF1 = African Conference 1 winner, AF2 = African Conference 2 winner, WC = Wild card. B7 = Losing Bonus, B4 = Try Bonus

LEADING SCORERS

60 POINTS OR MORE

	TEAM	T	C	P	DG	Pts
Beauden Barrett	Hurricanes	9	50	25	1	223
Damian McKenzie	Chiefs	10	43	21	0	199
Elton Jantjies	Lions	3	44	27	2	190
Lima Sopoaga	Highlanders	5	34	29	2	186
Richard Mo'unga	Crusaders	5	41	24	0	179
Christian Leali'ifano	Brumbies	3	41	22	0	163
Nicolás Sánchez	Jaguares	2	24	27	1	142
Ihaia West	Blues	4	19	24	0	130
Jean-Luc du Plessis	Stormers	2	26	22	0	128
Jack Debreczeni	Rebels	2	25	20	0	120
Bernard Foley	Waratahs	1	35	15	0	120
Francois Brummer	Bulls	1	22	19	1	109
Tusi Pisi	Sunwolves	2	16	21	0	105
Jake McIntyre	Reds	2	15	14	1	85
Louis Fouché	Kings	1	17	14	0	81
Fred Zeilinga	Cheetahs	0	17	15	0	79
Joe Pietersen	Sharks	1	11	15	0	72
Niel Marais	Cheetahs	2	17	9	0	71
Garth April	Sharks	2	11	11	0	65
Reece Hodge	Rebels	9	3	4	0	63
Tian Schoeman	Bulls	0	12	11	1	60

6 TRIES OR MORE

Israel Folau	Waratahs	11	Stephen Moore	Brumbies	7
Damian McKenzie	Chiefs	10	TJ Perenara	Hurricanes	7
Courtnall Skosan	Lions	10	Nemani Nadolo	Crusaders	6
Matt Faddes	Highlanders	10	Adriaan Strauss	Bulls	6
Rohan Janse van Rensburg	Lions	10	Augustín Creevy	Jaguares	6
Beauden Barrett	Hurricanes	9	Cory Jane	Hurricanes	6
Reece Hodge	Rebels	9	Jaco Kriel	Lions	6
Akihito Yamada	Sunwolves	9	Jerome Kaino	Blues	6
Lionel Mapoe	Lions	9	Jone Macilai	Crusaders	6
Sergeal Petersen	Cheetahs	9	Joe Tomane	Brumbies	6
Seta Tamanivalu	Chiefs	9	Julian Savea	Hurricanes	6
Ruan Combrinck	Lions	8	Martín Landajo	Jaguares	6
Leolin Zas	Stormers	8	Sefanaia Naivalu	Rebels	6
Waisake Naholo	Highlanders	8	Travis Ismaiel	Bulls	6
James Lowe	Chiefs	7	Uzair Cassiem	Cheetahs	6
Johnny McNicholl	Crusaders	7	Vincent Koch	Stormers	6
Ryan Crotty	Crusaders	7			

PLAY-OFF RESULTS

QUARTER-FINAL: Brumbies 9 Highlanders 15 (halftime 6-10)

GIO Stadium, Canberra, Friday July 22.

Referee: Angus Gardner (Aus)

Brumbies - *Penalties: Leali'ifano (3).*

Highlanders - *Tries: Squire, Naholo. Conversion: Sopoaga. Penalty: Sopoaga.*

QUARTER-FINAL: Hurricanes 41 Sharks 0 (halftime 13-0)

Westpac Stadium, Wellington, Saturday July 23

Referee: Glen Jackson (NZ)

Hurricanes - *Tries: Shields, Woodward, Ubila, Perenara, Fifita, Marshall. Conversions: Barrett (3), Woodward. Penalty: Barrett.*

Sharks - *None.*

QUARTER-FINAL: Stormers 21 Chiefs 60 (halftime 14-34)

DHL Newlands Stadium, Cape Town, Saturday July 23.

Referee: Jaco Peyper (SA)

Stormers - *Tries: Koch (2). Conversions: Du Preez (2), Thomson.*

Chiefs - *Tries: Weber, McKenzie, Elliott, Lowe, McNicholl, Kerr-Barlow, Koloamatangi, Sanders. Conversions: McKenzie (7). Penalties: McKenzie (2).*

QUARTER-FINAL: Lions 42 Crusaders 25 (halftime 22-10)

Emirates Airline Park, Johannesburg, Saturday, July 23.

Referee: Craig Joubert (SA)

Lions - *Tries: Skosan, Marx, Janse van Rensburg, Cronjé, Combrinck. Conversions: Jantjies (4). Penalties: Jantjies (2). DG: Jantjies.*

Crusaders - *Tries: Drummond, Crotty, Volavola. Conversions: Mo'unga (2). Penalties: Mo'unga (2).*

SEMI-FINAL: Hurricanes 25 Chiefs 9 (halftime 15-6)
Westpac Stadium, Wellington, Saturday July 30.
Referee: Angus Gardner (Aus)
Hurricanes - *Tries: Barrett, Vito, Halaholo. Conversions: Barrett (2). Penalties: Barrett (2).*
Chiefs - *Penalties: McKenzie (3).*

SEMI-FINAL: Lions 42 Highlanders 30 (halftime 17-6)
Emirates Airline Park, Johannesburg, Saturday, July 30.
Referee: Jaco Peyper (SA)
Lions - *Tries: Skosan, Jantjies, Kriel, Erasmus, Janse van Rensburg. Conversions: Jantjies (4).*
Penalties: Jantjies (3).
Highlanders - *Tries: Wheeler, Sopoaga, Faddes, Naholo. Conversions: Sopoaga (2). Penalties: Sopoaga (2).*

FINAL: Hurricanes 20 Lions 3 (halftime 10-3)
Westpac Stadium, Wellington, Saturday August 6.
Referee: Glen Jackson (NZ)
Hurricanes - *Tries: Jane, Barrett. Conversions: Barrett (2). Penalties: Barrett (2).*
James Marshall, Cory Jane, Matt Proctor, Willis Halaholo *(Vince Aso, 50),* Jason Woodward
(Julian Savea, 70), Beauden Barrett, TJ Perenara *(Jamison Gibson-Park, 77),* Victor Vito, Ardie Savea,
Brad Shields *(Callum Gibbins, 74),* Michael Fatialofa *(Mark Abbott, 74),* Vaea Fifita,
Ben May *(Chris Eves, 52),* Dane Coles (c) *(Ricky Riccitelli, 43),* Loni Uhila *(Michael Kainga, 76),*
Lions - *Penalty: Jantjies.*
Andries Coetzee *(Jaco van der Walt, 70),* Ruan Combrinck, Lionel Mapoe, Rohan Janse van
Rensburg *(Howard Mnisi, 57-65, 74),* Courtnall Skosan, Elton Jantjies, Faf de Klerk
(Ross Cronjé, 68), Warren Whiteley (c) *(Ruan Ackermann, 70),* Warwick Tecklenburg, Jaco Kriel,
Franco Mostert, Andries Ferreira *(Lourens Erasmus, 74),* Julian Redelinghuys *(Jacques van Rooyen,*
74), Malcolm Marx *(Akker van der Merwe, 70),* Dylan Smith *(Corné Fourie, 70).*

Ruan Ackermann congratulates Rohan Janse van Rensburg after scoring against the Highlanders in the semi-final. Van Rensburg won the South African Super Rugby Player of the year award.

POSITIONS LOG

	1996	1997	1998	1999	2000	2001	2002	2003	2004	2005	2006	2007
Crusaders	12th	6th	**2nd**	**4th**	2nd	10th	**1st**	2nd	2nd	**1st**	**1st**	3rd
ACT Brumbies	5th	2nd	10th	5th	1st	**1st**	3rd	4th	**1st**	5th	6th	5th
NSW Waratahs	7th	9th	6th	8th	9th	8th	2nd	5th	8th	2nd	3rd	13th
Sharks/Natal	4th	4th	3rd	7th	12th	2nd	10th	11th	7th	12th	5th	1st
Bulls/NTransvaal	3rd	8th	11th	12th	11th	12th	12th	6th	6th	3rd	4th	**2nd**
Chiefs	6th	11th	7th	6th	10th	6th	8th	10th	4th	6th	7th	6th
Stormers/WP	11th	-	9th	2nd	5th	7th	7th	9th	3rd	9th	11th	10th
Blues	**2nd**	**1st**	1st	9th	6th	11th	6th	**1st**	5th	7th	8th	4th
Hurricanes	9th	3rd	8th	10th	8th	9th	9th	3rd	11th	4th	2nd	8th
Queensland Reds	1st	10th	5th	1st	7th	4th	5th	8th	10th	10th	12th	14th
Highlanders	8th	12th	4th	3rd	3rd	5th	4th	7th	9th	8th	9th	9th
Free State/Cheetahs	-	7th	-	-	-	-	-	-	-	-	10th	11th
Lions/Cats	10th	5th	12th	11th	4th	3rd	11th	12th	12th	11th	13th	12th
Western Force	-	-	-	-	-	-	-	-	-	-	14th	7th
Melbourne Rebels	-	-	-	-	-	-	-	-	-	-	-	-
Southern Kings	-	-	-	-	-	-	-	-	-	-	-	-
Jaguares	-	-	-	-	-	-	-	-	-	-	-	-
Sunwolves	-	-	-	-	-	-	-	-	-	-	-	-

Bold type indicates champion

WIN PERCENTAGE LOG

Team	P	W	L	D	PF	PA
Crusaders	300	200	94	6	8913	6511
ACT Brumbies	289	169	115	5	7696	6330
NSW Waratahs	281	153	124	4	7193	6147
Hurricanes	281	152	124	5	7358	6865
Blues	281	150	126	5	7508	6810
Stormers	267	140	120	7	6156	6032
Chiefs	281	147	127	7	7275	6975
Sharks	286	147	131	8	7009	6716
Bulls	281	139	133	9	7293	7358
Highlanders	281	135	144	2	6837	7001
Queensland Reds	277	127	144	6	6195	6980
Cheetahs	172	55	114	3	3949	4949
Melbourne Rebels	95	30	65	0	2012	2901
Lions	259	81	172	6	5906	7736
Western Force	160	50	103	7	3086	4022
Jaguares	15	4	11	0	376	427
Southern Kings	31	5	25	1	580	1248
Sunwolves	15	1	13	1	293	627
	3852	1885	1885	82	95635	95635

POSITIONS LOG

2008	2009	2010	2011	2012	2013	2014	2015	2016	Play-offs	Quarter-finals	Semi-finals	Finals	Total	Champions	Avg. Pos
1st	4th	4th	3rd	4th	4th	2nd	7th	7th	3	1	16	11	31	7	3,90
9th	7th	6th	13th	7th	3rd	4th	6th	4th	3	1	9	5	16	2	5,09
2nd	5th	3rd	5th	11th	9th	1st	2nd	10th	1	-	7	3	10	1	6,14
3rd	6th	9th	6th	6th	8th	3rd	11th	8th	3	1	8	4	16	-	6,57
10th	1st	1st	7th	5th	2nd	9th	9th	9th	2	-	7	3	12	3	6,62
7th	2nd	11th	10th	2nd	1st	5th	5th	6th	2	1	5	3	10	2	6,48
5th	10th	2nd	2nd	1st	7th	11th	3rd	3rd	1	1	5	1	7	-	6,40
6th	9th	7th	4th	12th	10th	10th	14th	11th	1	-	6	4	11	3	6,86
4th	3rd	8th	9th	8th	11th	7th	1st	1st	-	1	8	3	10	1	6,43
12th	13th	5th	1st	3rd	5th	13th	13th	15th	2	-	4	1	7	1	7,90
11th	11th	12th	8th	9th	14th	6th	4th	5th	2	1	6	2	8	1	7,66
13th	14th	10th	11th	10th	6th	14th	12th	14th	1	-	-	-	1	-	11,00
14th	12th	14th	14th	15th	-	12th	8th	2nd	-	1	3	1	5	-	10,35
8th	8th	13th	12th	14th	13th	8th	15th	16th	-	-	-	-	0	-	12,63
-	-	-	15th	13th	12th	15th	10th	12th	-	-	-	-	0	-	12,83
-	-	-	-	-	15th	-	-	17th	-	-	-	-	0	-	16,00
-	-	-	-	-	-	-	-	13th	-	-	-	-	-	-	13,00
-	-	-	-	-	-	-	-	18th	-	-	-	-	-	-	18,00

WIN PERCENTAGE LOG

PD	TF	TA	B7	B4	Pts	Win rate
2402	986	701	38	101	847	66,67%
1366	912	651	48	96	760	58,48%
1046	820	657	56	89	732	54,45%
493	854	747	42	87	715	54,09%
698	891	743	54	101	725	53,38%
124	627	629	49	53	651	52,43%
300	824	762	59	77	692	52,31%
293	762	718	56	74	694	51,40%
-65	763	823	47	69	640	49,47%
-164	740	795	58	61	658	48,04%
-785	675	780	50	64	598	45,85%
-1000	431	563	35	31	280	31,98%
-889	221	354	23	14	152	31,58%
-1830	625	903	57	47	452	31,27%
-936	317	457	34	25	273	31,25%
-51	44	51	1	5	22	26,67%
-668	61	164	1	2	11	16,13%
-334	33	88	0	3	9	6,67%
0	10586	10586	708	999	8911	48,94%

Records

CHAMPIONS

1996	Blues	2003	Blues	2010	Bulls
1997	Blues	2004	Brumbies	2011	Reds
1998	Crusaders	2005	Crusaders	2012	Chiefs
1999	Crusaders	2006	Crusaders	2013	Chiefs
2000	Crusaders	2007	Bulls	2014	Waratahs
2001	Brumbies	2008	Crusaders	2015	Highlanders
2002	Crusaders	2009	Bulls	2016	Hurricanes

RESULTS OF FINALS

1996	Blues	45	Sharks	21	Auckland
1997	Blues	23	Brumbies	7	Auckland
1998	Blues	13	Crusaders	20	Auckland
1999	Highlanders	19	Crusaders	24	Dunedin
2000	Brumbies	19	Crusaders	20	Canberra
2001	Brumbies	36	Sharks	6	Canberra
2002	Crusaders	31	Brumbies	13	Christchurch
2003	Blues	21	Crusaders	17	Auckland
2004	Brumbies	47	Crusaders	38	Canberra
2005	Crusaders	35	Waratahs	25	Christchurch
2006	Crusaders	19	Hurricanes	12	Christchurch
2007	Sharks	19	Bulls	20	Durban
2008	Crusaders	20	Waratahs	12	Christchurch
2009	Bulls	61	Chiefs	17	Pretoria
2010	Bulls	25	Stormers	17	Soweto
2011	Reds	18	Crusaders	13	Brisbane
2012	Chiefs	37	Sharks	6	Hamilton
2013	Chiefs	27	Brumbies	33	Hamilton
2014	Waratahs	33	Crusaders	32	Sydney
2015	Hurricanes	14	Highlanders	21	Wellington
2016	Hurricanes	20	Lions	3	Wellington

MATCH RECORDS

Most points scored by a team - ALL TEAMS

96-19	Crusaders vs New South Wales	Christchurch	2002

Most points scored by a South African team

92-3	Bulls vs Queensland	Pretoria	2007
92-17	Toyota Cheetahs vs Sunwolves	Bloemfontein	2016

Biggest winning margin by a team - ALL TEAMS

89	Bulls vs Queensland (92-3)	Pretoria	2007

Most tries scored by a team - ALL TEAMS

14	Crusaders vs New South Wales (96-19)	Christchurch	2002

Most tries scored by a South African team

13	Bulls vs Queensland (92-3)	Pretoria	2007

Most points scored by a player - ALL TEAMS

50	GE Lawless (4t, 9c, 4p) Natal vs Highlanders	1997

Most tries scored by a player - ALL TEAMS

4	JWC Roff, Brumbies vs Natal	1996
4	GE Lawless, Natal vs Highlanders	1997
4	CS Terblanche, Sharks vs Chiefs	1998
4	J Vidiri, Blues vs Bulls	2000
4	DC Howlett, Blues vs Hurricanes	2002
4	M Muliaina, Blues vs Bulls	2002
4	CS Ralph, Crusaders vs NSW Waratahs	2002
4	SW Sivivatu, Chiefs vs Blues	2009
4	DA Mitchell, Waratahs vs Lions	2010
4	SD Maitland, Crusaders vs Brumbies	2011
4	AT Tikoroituma, Chiefs vs Blues	2012
4	CJ Ngatai, Chiefs vs Force	2016
4	HRF Jones, Stormers vs Kings	2016

Most conversions by a player - ALL TEAMS

13	AP Mehrtens, Crusaders vs Waratahs	2002

Most conversions by a South African player

11	DJ Hougaard, Bulls vs Queensland Reds	2007

Most penalties by a player - ALL TEAMS

9	ET Jantjies, Lions vs Cheetahs	2012

Most drop drop goals by a player - ALL TEAMS

4	M Steyn, Bulls vs Crusaders	2009

SEASON RECORDS

Most points scored by a player - ALL TEAMS

		Team	Season	T	C	P	DG
263	M Steyn	Bulls	2010	5	38	51	3
258	BT Foley	NSW	2014	6	45	46	0
251	AW Cruden	Chiefs	2012	3	43	50	0
248	M Steyn	Bulls	2013	2	32	57	1
228	QS Cooper	Reds	2011	5	31	43	4
223	BJ Barrett	Hurricanes	2016	9	50	25	1
221	DW Carter	Crusaders	2006	5	38	37	3
216	M Steyn	Bulls	2011	0	33	46	4
209	BJ Barrett	Hurricanes	2014	5	32	40	0
206	AP Mehrtens	Crusaders	1998	5	23	41	4
201	DW Carter	Crusaders	2004	6	27	39	0

Most tries by a player - ALL TEAMS

15	JWC Roff	Brumbies	1997
15	RL Gear	Crusaders	2005
13	JT Small	Natal	1996
13	AM Walker	Brumbies	2000
13	WR Naholo	Highlanders	2015
12	AJ Joubert	Natal	1996
12	JF Umaga	Hurricanes	1997
12	RQ Randle	Chiefs	2002
12	DC Howlett	Blues	2003
12	J-PR Pietersen	Sharks	2007
12	I Folau	NSW	2014
12	N Nadolo	Crusaders	2014

Most conversions by a player - ALL TEAMS

51	JWC Roff	ACT Brumbies	2004
50	BJ Barrett	Hurricanes	2016
45	BT Foley	NSW	2014
44	ET Jantjies	Lions	2016
43	AW Cruden	Chiefs	2012
43	DS McKenzie	Chiefs	2016
41	R Mo'unga	Crusaders	2016
41	CP Leali'ifano	Brumbies	2016
39	SA Mortlock	ACT Brumbies	2000
38	DW Carter	Crusaders	2006
38	M Steyn	Bulls	2010, 2012
38	LZ Sopoaga	Highlanders	2015
37	DW Carter	Crusaders	2005
36	SR Donald	Crusaders	2009
35	JWC Roff	ACT Brumbies	2003

Most penalties by a player - ALL TEAMS

58	CP Leali'ifano	Brumbies	2013
57	M Steyn	Bulls	2013
51	M Steyn	Bulls	2010
50	AW Cruden	Chiefs	2012
47	JD O'Connor	Western Force	2011
46	M Steyn	Bulls	2011
46	CR Slade	Crusaders	2014
46	BT Foley	NSW	2014
44	JC Pietersen	Stormers	2013

Most drop goals by a player - ALL TEAMS

11	M Steyn	Bulls	2009
8	ML Boshoff	Lions	2014
7	LJ Koen	Bulls	2003
6	AS Pretorius	Lions	2009

TEAM RECORDS

Most points in a log season - ALL TEAMS

535	Lions	2016

Most points in a log season - SA TEAMS

622	Lions *(18 matches)*	2016

Most points in all matches - ALL TEAMS

541	Crusaders *(13 matches)*	2005

Most points conceded - ALL TEAMS

684	Southern Kings	2016

Most log points - ALL TEAMS

66	Reds	2011
66	Stormers	2012
66	Chiefs	2013
66	Hurricanes	2015

Fewest log points - ALL TEAMS

4	Bulls	2002

Fewest log points to reach semi-finals - ALL

30	Sharks	1997
31	Brumbies	2003

Most tries in a log season - ALL TEAMS

71	Lions	2016

Most tries in all matches - ALL TEAMS

81	Lions	2016

Fewest tries scored - ALL TEAMS

13	Lions	2007
15	Blues	1999
15	Queensland Reds	2007

Most tries conceded - ALL

95	Southern Kings	2016

Most wins in a log season - ALL TEAMS

14	Stormers	2013
14	Hurricanes	2015
13	Reds	2011

Fewest wins in a season - ALL TEAMS

0	Lions	2010
0	Bulls	2002

South Africa celebrate victory at the inaugural Cape Town Sevens at Cape Town Stadium, which formed part of the 2015/16 HSBC World Series.

Rosko Specman of South Africa in action during the 2016 Sydney Sevens match between South Africa and Fiji at Allianz Stadium.

Pukke celebrate winning the 2016 Varsity Cup Final against Maties at Danie Craven Stadium in Stellenbosch.

Fundiswa Plaatjie of SA Select evades a tackle against France at Stade Jean Bouin.

Howard Mnisi on the charge for SA 'A' against England Saxons at Toyota Stadium, Bloemfontein.

Embrose Papier scores for the Junior Springboks against France at the World Rugby Under-20 Championship in Manchester, England.

Francois Venter surges ahead for South Africa 'A' against England Saxons at Outeniqua Park, George.

Eben Etzebeth carries the ball for South Africa during the second Test against Ireland in Johannesburg.

Curwin Bosch runs in for a try against England at the World Rugby Under-20 Championship semi-final in Manchester, England.

Francois Louw, Siya Kolisi and Warren Whiteley sing the national anthem ahead of the third Test against Ireland in Port Elizabeth.

JP Pietersen fields a cross-field kick during the series-deciding third Test against Ireland in Port Elizabeth.

Jordan Mbuyamba of the Golden Lions wins possession against the Sharks during the Under-18 Academy Week at Kearsney College.

Sam McNicol of the Chiefs shrugs off the tackle of Schalk Burger during their Vodacom Super Rugby quarter-final against the DHL Stormers at Newlands.

Rohan Janse van Rensburg of the Emirates Lions sprints for the line against the Highlanders in Johannesburg.

Seabelo Senatla evades Tom Cusack of Australia to score a try during the match between South Africa and Australia at the Olympic Games in Rio de Janeiro.

Louritz van der Schyff of SA Schools A makes a break during the Under-19 International Series against England Under-18 at Bishops, Cape Town.

SA Schools and England Under-18 clash at Paarl Boys' High.

Mustageem Jappie of DirectAxis False Bay during the Gold Cup match against SA Home Loans Durban Collegians.

Samu Kerevi of the Wallabies is tackled by Tebobo Moboje during the Rugby Championship match in Brisbane.

Francois Hougaard fends against Ryan Crotty of New Zealand during the Rugby Championship match in Christchurch.

The Women's Interprovincial Section A final between Border and Western Province took place in East London.

Great defence by Francois Louw on Stephen Moore of the Wallabies during the the Rugby Championship match at Loftus Versfeld, Pretoria.

Pieter-Steph du Toit and Sam Whitelock of New Zealand compete for the ball during the Rugby Championship match between South Africa and New Zealand in Durban.

Pieter Botha of Pretoria Police scores during the Gold Cup quarter-final against DirectAxis False Bay at Loftus Versfeld, Pretoria.

Riaan O'Neill of DirectAxis False Bay during the Gold Cup semi-final against defending champions Durbanville–Bellville in Cape Town.

Steak Pienaar of the Xerox Golden Lions during the Under-19 provincial championship final against Western Province.

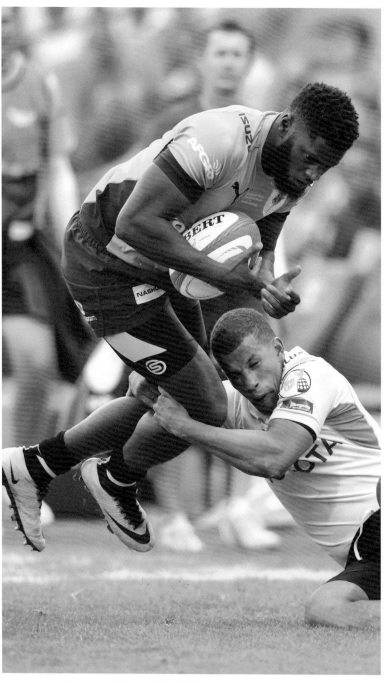

Jamba Ulengo of the Vodacom Blue Bulls during the Currie Cup final against the Toyota Free State Cheetahs in Bloemfontein.

Uzair Cassiem of the Cheetahs during the Currie Cup final.

The Toyota Free State Cheetahs celebrate winning the Currie Cup final.

The Toyota Free State Cheetahs hoist the Currie Cup.

Robbie Rawlins of Rustenburg Impala during the Gold Cup Final against DirectAxis False Bay in Rustenburg.

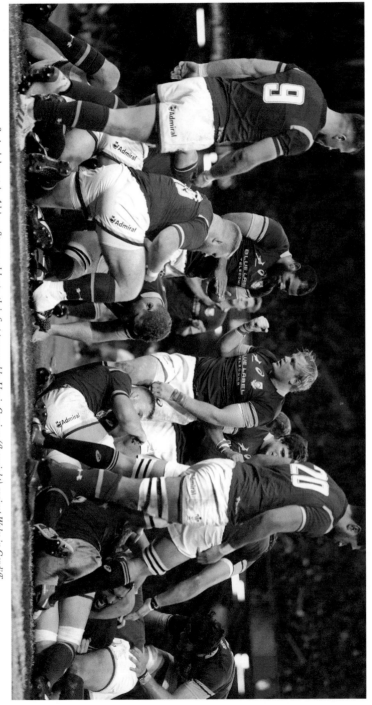

Springbok captain Adriaan Strauss celebrates their first try scored by Uzair Cassiem (floor right) against Wales in Cardiff.

CAREER RECORDS
Most points by a player - ALL TEAMS

	Player	Team	Matches	Tries	Cons	Pens	DG
1708	DW Carter	Crusaders	141	36	287	307	11
1449	M Steyn	Bulls	123	13	242	275	25
1037	SA Mortlock	ACT Brumbies	138	55	162	146	0
990	AP Mehrtens	Crusaders	87	13	134	202	17
959	MC Burke	NSW Waratahs	79	24	160	173	0
942	TE Brown	Highl/Sharks/Stormers	107	5	148	199	8
924	PJ Grant	Stormers/Force	116	10	134	202	0
882	BJ Barrett	Hurricanes	82	21	135	168	1
859	SR Donald	Chiefs	90	19	151	153	1
751	MJ Giteau	Brumbies/Force	104	33	113	117	3
770	QS Cooper	Reds	105	24	112	135	7
700	DE Holwell	Hurricanes/Blues	82	8	123	138	–

Most tries by a player - ALL TEAMS

59	DC Howlett	Hurricanes/Highlanders/Blues	104 matches
58	CS Ralph	Chiefs/Crusaders	135 matches
57	JWC Roff	Brumbies	83 matches
56	CM Cullen	Hurricanes	85 matches
56	BG Habana	Bulls/Stormers	118 matches
55	SA Mortlock	Brumbies	138 matches
53	MA Nonu	Hurricanes/Blues/Highlanders	160 matches
48	JF Umaga	Hurricanes/Chiefs	129 matches
43	J Vidiri	Blues	61 matches
42	LR MacDonald	Crusaders	127 matches
42	SW Sivivatu	Chiefs	89 matches

Most conversions by a player - ALL TEAMS

287	DW Carter	Crusaders	141 matches
242	M Steyn	Bulls	123 matches
162	SA Mortlock	ACT Brumbies/Rebels	138 matches
160	MC Burke	NSW Waratahs	79 matches
151	SR Donald	Chiefs	90 matches
148	TE Brown	Highlanders/Sharks/Stormers	107 matches
134	AP Mehrtens	Crusaders	87 matches
134	PJ Grant	Stormers/Force	116 matches
123	DE Holwell	Hurricanes/Blues	82 matches
121	CS Spencer	Blues/Lions	108 matches

Most penalties by a player - ALL TEAMS

307	DW Carter	Crusaders	141 matches
275	M Steyn	Bulls	123 matches
202	AP Mehrtens	Crusaders	87 matches
202	PJ Grant	Stormers/Force	116 matches
199	TE Brown	Highl./Sharks/Stormers	107 matches
179	MC Burke	NSW Waratahs	71 matches
168	BJ Barrett	Hurricanes	82 matches
153	SR Donald	Chiefs	90 matches
150	AW Cruden	Chiefs	82 matches
146	SA Mortlock	ACT Brumbies	138 matches
144	PJ Lambie	Sharks	63 matches
138	DE Holwell	Hurricanes/Blues	82 matches
130	EJ Flatley	Reds	87 matches

Most drop goals by a player - ALL TEAMS

25	M Steyn	Bulls	123 matches
17	AP Mehrtens	Crusaders	87 matches
13	AS Pretorius	Cats/Lions	72 matches
11	LJ Koen	Bulls	51 matches
11	DW Carter	Crusaders	141 matches
10	DJ Hougaard	Bulls	51 matches
9	BS Barnes	Reds/Waratahs	59 matches
8	TE Brown	Highlanders/Sharks	107 matches
8	ML Boshoff	Lions	28 matches
6	AJD Mauger	Crusaders	89 matches

100 appearances by a player - ALL TEAMS

175	KF Mealamu	Blues/Chiefs	125	JW Smit	Sharks
170	WWV Crockett	Crusaders	124	PAT Weepu	Blues/Hurricanes
164	ST Moore	Brumbies/Reds	124	KJ Beale	Waratahs/Rebels
162	NC Sharpe	Reds/Force	123	SP Hardman	Reds
160	MA Nonu	Highl/Hurr/Blues	123	M Steyn	Bulls
153	AM Ellis	Crusaders	123	OT Franks	Crusaders
150	CR Flynn	Crusaders	123	SWP Burger	Stormers
149	TD Woodcock	Blues/Highlanders	122	CC King	Crusaders, Highlanders
148	V Matfield	Cats/Bulls	122	CS Terblanche	Sharks
148	BJ Robinson	Waratahs	122	QJ Cowan	Highlanders
144	LJ Messam	Chiefs	121	AKE Baxter	NSW Waratahs
145	JN du Plessis	Sharks/Cheetahs	120	W Kruger	Bulls
145	RH McCaw	Crusaders	120	BR Smith	Highlanders
144	GS Holmes	Reds	119	PJ Spies	Bulls
142	GB Smith	ACT Brumbies	119	J Kaino	Blues
141	AK Hore	Highl/Hurr/Crus	118	BG Habana	Bulls/Stormers
141	DW Carter	Crusaders	118	NJ Henderson	Rebels/Force/ACT
141	OM Ndungane	Bulls/Sharks	118	TD Latimer	Chiefs/Blues
141	SUT Polota-Nau	Waratahs	117	AJ Williams	Blues/Crusaders
139	AP Ashley-Cooper	Waratahs/Brumbies	117	CP Leali'ifano	Brumbies
138	SA Mortlock	ACT Brumbies/Rebels	117	PJM Cowan	Force
137	J-PR Pietersen	Sharks	117	KR Daniel	Sharks
136	CS Ralph	Chiefs/Crusaders/Reds	116	SJ Larkham	ACT Brumbies
136	GM Gregan	ACT Brumbies	116	DJ Rossouw	Bulls
134	WL Palu	Waratahs	116	JE Horwill	Reds
133	KJ Read	Crusaders	104	PJ Grant	Stormers/Force
132	PR Waugh	NSW Waratahs	115	LJ Botes	Sharks
132	JA Strauss	Cheetahs/Bulls	115	KJ Beale	Waratahs/Rebels
131	GM Somerville	Crusaders/Rebels	115	SW Genia	Reds
131	BW du Plessis	Sharks	115	HTP Elliott	Chiefs
131	MJ Hodgson	Force	113	JA Paul	ACT Brumbies
131	AS Mathewson	Force/Blues	113	PJ Wannenburg	Bulls
130	SUT Polota-Nau	Waratahs	113	AA Jacobs	Cats/Bulls/Sharks
130	BE Alexander	Brumbies	113	TE Ellison	Highlanders/Rebels
129	RD Thorne	Crusaders	112	PF du Preez	Bulls
128	JF Umaga	Hirricanes/Chiefs	111	MJ Dunning	NSW Waratahs/Force
128	BJ Franks	Hurricanes/Crusaders	111	A Mitchell	Reds/Force/NSW
127	AD Oliver	Highlanders	111	BC Thorn	Highlanders/Crusaders
127	LR MacDonald	Crusaders/Chiefs	111	CS Jane	Hurricanes
126	CG Smith	Hurricanes	110	CR Jack	Crusaders
126	SM Fainga'a	Reds/Brumbies	110	W Olivier	Bulls
126	T Mtawarira	Sharks	110	WS Alberts	Sharks/Lions
125	AJ Venter	Cats/Sharks/Stormers	110	S Higginbotham	Reds/Rebels
			110	JI Thrush	Hurricanes

110	JJG Bekhuis	Blues
109	CE Latham	Waratahs/Reds
109	AZ Ndungane	Bulls
109	DJ Vermeulen	Cheetahs/Stormers
109	SR Sykes	Sharks/Cheetahs/Kings
108	HM Bosman	Cheetahs/Sharks
108	A-H le Roux	Sharks/Cheetahs
108	CJ Spencer	Blues/Lions
108	HE Gear	Highlanders/Hurr/Chiefs
108	SA Hoiles	Brumbies/Waratahs
108	J Vermaak	Bulls/Lions/Cats/Stormers
107	CJ Whitaker	NSW Waratahs
107	TE Brown	Highl./Stormers/Sharks
107	MA Gerrard	Rebels/Brum/NSW
107	RS Crotty	Crusaders
107	DA Dennis	Waratahs
106	BJ Cannon	Waratahs/Force
106	AKE Baxter	NSW Waratahs
106	SNG Staniforth	Waratahs/Force
105	JW Marshall	Crusaders
105	J de Villiers	Stormers
105	QS Cooper	Reds
104	DC Howlett	Highlanders/Blues
104	MJ Giteau	Brumbies/Force

104	JM Muliaina	Chiefs/Blues
104	A Bekker	Stormers
104	AL Freier	Rebels/Brum/NSW
104	J Vermaak	Bulls/Lions/Cats
103	JA Collins	Blues/Chiefs
103	MD Chisholm	ACT Brumbies
103	R Kankowski	Sharks
102	PA van den Berg	Cats/Sharks
102	MJ Chapman	Reds/Brumbies/NSW
102	RG Horne	Waratahs
101	R So'oialo	Hurricanes
101	IF Afoa	Blues
101	NS Tialata	Hurricanes
101	SL Whitelock	Crusaders
101	RA Simmons	Reds
100	DJ Lyons	Waratahs
100	WK Young	ACT Brumbies
100	JP Botha	Bulls
100	VVJ Vito	Hurricanes

Tallest player ever

2.09m	J-P du Preez	Lions

JP du Preez, the tallest player in Super Rugby, stands at 2.09m.

Vodacom Bulls

Ground: Loftus Versfeld **Capacity:** 50 000 **Address:** Kirkness Street, Sunnyside, Pretoria, 0132
Telephone number: 012-420 0700 **Website:** www.vodacombulls.co.za
Colours: Navy fading from chest to hem. Herringbone design under arm and sides.
Navy collar with faded sleeves. Navy shorts with herringbone insert.
Coach: Nollis Marais **Captain:** Adriaan Strauss **CEO:** Barend van Graan
Chairman: John Newbury **President:** Gert Wessels

Head Coach: Nollis Marais **Assistant Coach (Backline):** David Manuel
Assistant Coach (Forwards): Anton Leonard **Assistant Coach (Defence):** Pine Pienaar
Assistant Coach (Scrum): Gary Botha **Team Manager:** Tim Dlulane
Strength and Conditioning: Neil du Plessis **Team Doctor:** Dr Herman Roussouw
Physiotherapist: Pieter du Plessis & Wernich Smit **Kit Manager:** Elias Bennett
Masseuse: Elzanne van Coller **Analyst:** John-William Meyer & Divan Roussouw
Mental Life Coach: Dr Jannie Botha

1996*	1997*	1998	1999	2000	2001	2002	2003	2004	2005	2006
3rd	8th	11th	12th	11th	12th	12th	6th	6th	3rd	4th

2007	2008	2009	2010	2011	2012	2013	2014	2015	2016
2nd	10th	1st	1st	7th	5th	2nd	9th	9th	9th

Played	Won	Lost	Drawn	Points for	Points against	Tries for	Tries against
15	9	5	1	399	339	37	37

Date	Venue	Opponent	Result	Score	Referee	Scorers
Febr 27	Cape Town	Stormers	LOST	09-33	C Joubert	P: Brummer (3).
Mrch 05	Pretoria	Rebels	WON	45-25	B O'Keeffe	T: Basson (3), De Jager, Kirsten, Ismaiel. C: Brummer (6). P: Brummer.
Mrch 18	Pretoria	Sharks	DREW	16-16	G Jackson	T: Gelant. C: Brummer. P: Brummer, Schoeman. DG: Brummer.
Mrch 26	Singapore	Sunwolves	WON	30-27	W Houston	T: Strauss, Ulengo, Smit. C: Schoeman (3). P: Schoeman (3).
April 02	Pretoria	Cheetahs	WON	23-18	C Joubert	T: Snyman, Jenkins, Ulengo. C: Schoeman. P: Schoeman (2).
April 09	Port Elizabeth	Kings	WON	38-06	S Kubo	T: Ulengo (2), Marais (2), Serfontein, Snyman. C: Schoeman (3), Brummer.
April 16	Pretoria	Reds	WON	41-22	A Gardner	T: Strauss, Van der Merwe, P van Zyl, Labuschagne Ismaiel. C: Brummer (5). P: Brummer (2).
April 29	Perth	Force	WON	42-20	J van Heerden	T: Serfontein (2), Strauss (2), Liebenberg. C: Brummer (4). P: Brummer (3).
May 06	Canberra	Brumbies	LOST	06-23	B O'Keeffe	P: Brummer (2).
May 14	Sydney	Waratahs	LOST	08-31	G Jackson	T: Swanepoel. P: Schoeman.
May 21	Pretoria	Stormers	WON	17-13	B O'Keeffe	T: Van Zyl. P: Brummer (3). DG: Schoeman.
May 28	Pretoria	Lions	LOST	20-56	C Joubert	T: Strauss, Stegmann, Kriel. C: Schoeman. P: Brummer
July 02	Buenos Aires	Jaguares	LOST	11-29	C Joubert	T: Van Zyl. P: Brummer (2).
July 09	Pretoria	Sunwolves	WON	50-03	Q Immelman	T: Ismaiel (2), Strauss, Swanepoel, Brummer, Kirsten, Labuschagne. C: Brummer (4), Schoeman (2). P: Brummer.
July16	Bloemfontein	Cheetahs	WON	43-17	C Joubert	T: Ismaiel (2), Bothma, Ulengo. C: Schoeman (2), Brummer. P: Schoeman (4)

Note: ■ = *Champion,* * *Played as Northern Transvaal*

2016 SQUAD

PLAYER	Union	Debut	BULLS CAREER						Debut	SUPER RUGBY CAREER					
			M	T	C	P	DG	Pts		M	T	C	P	DG	Pts
BA (Bjorn) Basson	BB	2011	86	29	–	–	–	145	2009	95	35	–	–	–	175
AF (Arno) Botha	BB	2012	46	1	–	–	–	5	2012	46	1	–	–	–	5
R (Renaldo) Bothma	PUM	2016	3	2	–	–	–	10	2015	18	3	–	–	–	15
F (Francois) Brummer	PUM	2010	15	1	23	19	1	111	2010	19	1	27	22	1	128
NJK (Nic) de Jager	BB	2016	5	1	–	–	–	5	2016	5	1	–	–	–	5
WW (Warrick) Gelant	BB	2016	4	1	–	–	–	5	2016	4	1	–	–	–	5
LP (Lizo) Gqoboka	BB	2016	12	–	–	–	–	0	2016	12	–	–	–	–	0
GN (Grant) Hattingh	BB	2013	46	1	–	–	–	5	2012	55	2	–	–	–	10
TK (Travis) Ismaiel	BB	2015	17	6	–	–	–	30	2015	17	6	–	–	–	30
NJ (Nico) Janse van Rensburg	BB	2014	5	–	–	–	–	0	2014	5	–	–	–	–	0
JH (Jason) Jenkins	BB	2016	13	1	–	–	–	5	2016	13	1	–	–	–	5
JC (Jannes) Kirsten	BB	2016	15	2	–	–	–	10	2016	15	2	–	–	–	10
DD (Dan) Kriel	BB	2016	3	–	–	–	–	0	2016	3	–	–	–	–	0
JA (Jesse) Kriel	BB	2014	31	2	–	–	–	10	2014	31	2	–	–	–	10
W (Werner) Kruger	BB	2008	120	8	–	–	–	40	2008	120	8	–	–	–	40
PHC (Pieter) Labuschagne	BB	2015	23	5	–	–	–	25	2012	51	7	–	–	–	35
H (Hanro) Liebenberg	BB	2015	8	–	–	–	–	0	2015	8	–	–	–	–	0
SP (SP) Marais	BB	2016	11	2	–	–	–	10	2013	46	3	–	1	–	18
BG (Bandise) Maku	BB	2008	28	–	–	–	–	0	2008	58	–	–	–	–	0
NM (Nqobo) Mxoli	BB	2016	2	–	–	–	–	0	2016	2	–	–	–	–	0
TN (Trevor) Nyakane	BB	2015	28	–	–	–	–	0	2012	70	3	–	–	–	15
MB (Burger) Odendaal	BB	2015	18	2	–	–	–	10	2015	18	2	–	–	–	10
M (Marvin) Orie	BB	2014	10	–	–	–	–	0	2014	10	–	–	–	–	0
R (Rudy) Paige	BB	2013	34	–	–	–	–	0	2013	34	–	–	–	–	0
CF (Tian) Schoeman	BB	2015	22	–	17	12	1	73	2015	22	–	17	12	1	73
P (Pierre) Schoeman	BB	2016	9	–	–	–	–	0	2016	9	–	–	–	–	0
JL (Jan) Serfontein	BB	2013	48	13	–	–	–	65	2013	48	13	–	–	–	65
RA (Roelof) Smit	BB	2014	13	1	–	–	–	5	2014	13	1	–	–	–	5
RG (RG) Snyman	BB	2016	12	2	–	–	–	10	2016	12	2	–	–	–	10
GJ (Deon) Stegmann	BB	2008	95	9	–	–	–	45	2008	95	9	–	–	–	45
JA (Adriaan) Strauss	BB	2006	35	6	–	–	–	30	2006	132	14	–	–	–	70
AE (Dries) Swanepoel	BB	2016	7	2	–	–	–	10	2016	7	2	–	–	–	10
JI (Jamba) Ulengo	BB	2016	10	5	–	–	–	25	2016	10	5	–	–	–	25
M (Marcel) van der Merwe	BB	2014	45	5	–	–	–	25	2012	48	5	–	–	–	25
HJ (Hencus) van Wyk	BB	2013	2	–	–	–	–	–	2013	2	–	–	–	–	0
I (Ivan) van Zyl	BB	2016	2	–	–	–	–	0	2016	2	–	–	–	–	0
PE (Piet) van Zyl	BB	2014	36	6	–	–	–	30	2012	68	11	–	–	–	55
GJ (Jaco) Visagie	BB	2015	8	–	–	–	–	0	2015	8	–	–	–	–	0
TOTALS				113	40	31	2	744			140	44	35	2	899

Note: BB = Blue Bulls, PUM = Pumas

APPEARANCES & POINTS

PLAYER	Stormers	Rebels	Sharks	Sunwolves	Cheetahs	Kings	Reds	Force	Brumbies	Waratahs	Stormers	Lions	Jaguares	Sunwolves	Cheetahs	Apps	T	C	P	DG	Pts
Gelant	15	15	15	15	–	–	–	–	–	–	–	–	–	–	–	4	1	–	–	–	5
Ismaiel	14	14	–	–	14	14	14	14	14	–	14	–	14	14	14	11	6	–	–	–	30
Kriel, J	13	–	13R	13	15	13	13	13	13	13	13	13	13	15	15	14	1	–	–	–	5
Serfontein	12	13	13	15R	13	12	12	12	12	12	12	12	–	–	–	12	3	–	–	–	15
Basson	11	11	11	11	–	–	11	11	11	11	–	11	–	–	–	9	3	–	–	–	15
Brummer	10	10	10	10R	10R	10R	10	10	10	x	10	10	10	10	10R	14	1	22	19	1	109
Paige	9	9	9	9	9	–	9	9R	9R	9	x	9R	9	9R	9R	13	–	–	–	–	0
Botha	8	8	8	8	–	8	8	7	7	–	8	8	8	7R	6R	13	–	–	–	–	0
Kirsten	7	7	7	7	7	7	7	8R	7R	7	7	7	8R	7	7	15	2	–	–	–	10
De Jager	6	6	7R	8R	8	–	–	–	–	–	–	–	–	–	–	5	1	–	–	–	5
Hattingh	5	5	5	–	–	–	–	–	–	4R	4R	–	5R	5R	–	7	–	–	–	–	0
Snyman	4	4	4	5	5	5	5	4	4	5	5	5	–	–	–	12	2	–	–	–	10
Van der Merwe	3	3	3	3	3	3	3	3	3	3	3	3	3	3R	3	15	1	–	–	–	5
Strauss	2c	2c	2c	2c	2c	2c	2c	2c	2c	2c	2c	2c	–	2c	2c	14	6	–	–	–	30
Nyakane	1	1	1	1R	1R	1	1	1	1	3R	1R	1R	–	–	–	12	–	–	–	–	0
Visagie, J	2R	x	–	–	–	–	2R	–	–	2R	x	–	2R	2R	–	5	–	–	–	–	0
Gqoboka	1R	3R	3R	1	1	–	3R	1R	1R	1	1	1	1	–	–	12	–	–	–	–	0
Van Wyk	3R	x	x	–	–	–	–	–	–	–	–	–	–	–	–	1	–	–	–	–	0
Jenkins	4R	4R	4R	4	4	4	4	–	–	4	4	4	4	4	4	13	1	–	–	–	5
Smit	6R	8R	7	6	6	7R	–	7R	8R	8R	–	–	6	–	–	10	1	–	–	–	5
Van Zyl, P	9R	9R	9R	9R	–	9	9R	9	9	9R	9	9	9R	9	9	14	3	–	–	–	15
Schoeman, T	10R	10R	10R	10	10	10	10R	10R	10R	10	10R	10R	10R	10R	10	15	–	12	11	1	60
Odendaal	13R	12	12	12	–	–	–	–	–	–	–	12	12	12	–	8	–	–	–	–	0
Swanepoel	–	12R	–	–	–	–	12R	–	15R	x	13R	12R	13	13	–	7	2	–	–	–	10
Ulengo	–	–	14	14	11	11	–	–	–	14	11	14	11	11	11	10	5	–	–	–	25
Maku	–	–	x	x	2R	2R	–	2R	2R	–	–	2R	2	–	2R	7	–	–	–	–	0
Janse van Rensburg	–	–	–	4R	4R	–	–	–	–	–	–	–	–	–	–	2	–	–	–	–	0
Schoeman, P	–	–	–	3R	3R	1R	–	–	1R	3R	3R	1R	1	1	–	9	–	–	–	–	0
Labuschagne	–	–	–	–	6R	6	6	6	6	6	6	7c	6	6	–	11	2	–	–	–	10
Marais	–	–	–	–	12R	15	15	15	15	15	15	15	15	15R	15R	11	2	–	–	–	10
Van Zyl, I	–	–	–	–	9R	9R	–	–	–	–	–	–	–	–	–	2	–	–	–	–	0
Orie	–	–	–	–	–	4R	5R	5	5	4R	–	5	5	5	5	8	–	–	–	–	0
Kriel, D	–	–	–	–	–	13R	13R	–	12R	–	–	–	–	–	–	3	–	–	–	–	0
Kruger	–	–	–	–	–	8R	1R	3R	3R	–	–	3R	3	3R	–	7	–	–	–	–	0
Stegmann	–	–	–	–	–	–	8R	–	–	8R	8R	–	–	–	–	3	1	–	–	–	5
Liebenberg	–	–	–	–	–	–	–	8	8	8	–	–	–	–	–	3	1	–	–	–	5
Bothma	–	–	–	–	–	–	–	–	–	–	6R	8	8	–	–	3	2	–	–	–	10
Mxoli	–	–	–	–	–	–	–	–	–	–	–	1R	1R	–	–	2	–	–	–	–	0
38 PLAYERS																	47	34	30	2	399

Records

CHAMPIONS: 2007, 2009, 2010

MATCH RECORDS

Biggest winning margin	89	vs Queensland Reds (92-3)	Pretoria	2007
Heaviest defeat	64	vs ACT Brumbies (9-73)	Canberra	1999
Highest score	92	vs Queensland Reds (92-3)	Pretoria	2007
Most points conceded	75	vs Crusaders (25-75)	Christchurch	2000
Most tries	13	vs Queensland Reds (92-3)	Pretoria	2007
Most tries conceded	11	vs Crusaders (25-75)	Christchurch	2000
Most points by a player	39	JH Kruger (1t 5c 8p) vs H'landers	Pretoria	1996
Most tries by a player	3	AJ Richter vs Blues	Pretoria	1997
	3	PF du Preez vs Cats	Pretoria	2004
	3	W Olivier vs Rebels	Pretoria	2011
	3	BA Basson vs Rebels	Pretoria	2016
Most conversions by a player	11	DJ Hougaard vs Queensland Reds	Pretoria	2007
Most penalties by a player	8	JH Kruger vs Highlanders	Pretoria	1996
	8	DJ Hougaard vs Crusaders	Pretoria	2007
Most drop goals by a player	4	M Steyn vs Crusaders	Pretoria	2009

SEASON RECORDS

Most team points	500	from 15 matches	2010
Most points by a player	263	M Steyn	2010
Most team tries	52	from 17 matches	2012
Most tries by a player	10	BA Basson	2012
Most conversions by a player	38	M Steyn	2010
	38	M Steyn	2012
Most penalties by a player	57	M Steyn	2013
Most drop goals by a player	11	M Steyn	2009

CAREER RECORDS

Most appearances	140	V Matfield	2001-2015
Most points	1449	M Steyn	2005-2013
Most tries	37	BG Habana	2005-2009
Most conversions	242	M Steyn	2005-2013
Most penalties	275	M Steyn	2005-2013
Most drop goals	25	M Steyn	2005-2013

Jamba Ulengo, who capped off a stellar season with a Springbok Test cap.

Toyota Cheetahs

Ground: Free State Stadium **Capacity:** 46 000 **Address:** Att Horak Ave, Bloemfontein
Telephone: 051-407 1700 **Colours:** White jersey with an orange collar and russet orange and
Biscay bay detail. White shorts, russet orange socks **Website:** www.fscheetahs.co.za
Coach: Franco Smith **Captain:** Francois Venter
Manager: Ashwell Rafferty **CEO:** Harold Verster **Chairman:** Randal September

Head Coach: Franco Smith **Forwards Coach:** Corniel van Zyl
Scrum Coach: Daan Human **Strength & Conditioning:** Quintin Kruger
Video Analyst & Defence Coach: Charl Strydom **Team Manager:** Ashwell Rafferty
Doctor: Dr Rudi de Wet **Physiotherapist:** JP du Toit
Kit Manager: Sakkie Wessels **Media officer:** Ronel Pienaar

1996*	1997* 7th	1998	1999	2000	2001	2002	2003	2004	2005	2006 10th
2007 11th	2008 13th	2009 14th	2010 10th	2011 11th	2012 10th	2013 6th	2014 14th	2015 12th	2016 14th	

Played	Won	Lost	Drawn	Points for	Points against	Tries for	Tries against
15	4	11	0	377	435	47	48

Date	Venue	Opponent	Result	Score	Referee	Scorers
Febr 26	Bloemfontein	Jaguares	LOST	33-44	S Berry	T: F Venter, Small-smith, Van Jaarsveld, Penalty try. C: Zeilinga (2). P: Zeilinga (2), N Marais
Mrch 05	Bloemfontein	Stormers	LOST	10-20	C Joubert	T: F Venter. C: Zeilinga. P: Zeilinga.
Mrch 12	Singapore	Sunwolves	WON	32-31	Q Immelman	T: N Marais (2), Cassiem, Prinsloo. C: N Marais (3). P: N Marais (2).
Mrch 19	Johannesburg	Lions	LOST	22-39	S Berry	T: Petersen, Meyer, Du Toit. C: N Marais (2). P: N Marais.
Mrch 26	Bloemfontein	Brumbies	LOST	18-25	G Jackson	T: Cassiem, Petersen. C: N Marais. P: N Marais (2).
April 02	Pretoria	Bulls	LOST	18-23	C Joubert	T: Petersen, Van Jaarsveld. C: N Marais. P: N Marais (2).
April 15	Bloemfontein	Sunwolves	WON	92-17	N Berry	T: Petersen (3), Schoeman (3), Van Jaarsveld, F Venter, Cassiem, Rhule, S Venter, Blommetjies, Lobberts, Du Toit. C: N Marais (8), Zeilinga (3).
April 22	Melbourne	Rebels	LOST	14-36	G Jackson	T: Van Jaarsveld, Blommetjies. C: N Marais.
April 30	Brisbane	Reds	LOST	17-30	B O'Keeffe	T: Cassiem, Rhule. C: zeilinga (2). P: Zeilinga.
May 07	Sydney	Waratahs	LOST	06-21	N Berry	P: Zeilinga (2).
May 14	Bloemfontein	Kings	WON	34-20	F Anselmi	T: Van der Spuy, Rhule, Petersen, Cassiem. C: Zeilinga (4). P: Zeilinga (2).
May 28	Cape Town	Stormers	LOST	24-31	G Jackson	T: Schoeman, Petersen. C: Zeilinga. P: Zeilinga (3), N Marais
July 02	Bloemfontein	Force	WON	30-29	S Kubo	T: Blommetjies, Scxhoeman, Petersen, Cassiem. C: Zeilinga (2). P: Zeilinga (2).
July 09	Durban	Sharks	LOST	10-26	S Berry	T: Rhule. C: Zeilinga. P: Zeilinga.
July 16	Bloemfontein	Bulls	LOST	17-43	C Joubert	T: Blommetjies, Wegner. C: Zeilinga, Whitehead. P: Zeilinga.

2016 SQUAD

PLAYER	Union	Debut	CHEETAHS CAREER M	T	C	P	DG	Pts	Debut	SUPER RUGBY CAREER M	T	C	P	DG	Pts
RS (Rayno) Benjamin	FS	2011	54	14	–	–	–	70	2006	77	18	–	–	–	90
CA (Clayton) Blommetjies	FS	2015	24	6	–	–	–	30	2015	24	6	–	–	–	30
WS (Willie) Britz	FS	2015	12	–	–	–	–	0	2014	25	–	–	–	–	0
U (Uzair) Cassiem	FS	2015	15	6	–	–	–	30	2015	15	6	–	–	–	30
JV (Aranos) Coetzee	FS	2015	8	–	–	–	–	0	2016	8	–	–	–	–	0
L (Luan) de Bruin	FS	2016	8	–	–	–	–	0	2016	8	–	–	–	–	0
L (Lodewyk) de Jager	FS	2013	40	1	–	–	–	5	2013	40	1	–	–	–	5
OJJ (Jacques) du Toit	FS	2016	8	2	–	–	–	10	2016	8	2	–	–	–	10
J (Joseph) Dewba	FS	2016	3	–	–	–	–	0	2016	3	–	–	–	–	0
JM (Sias) Ebersohn	FS	2010	31	2	36	44	2	220	2010	74	4	62	91	5	432
GJ (Joubert) Engelbrecht	FS	2016	1	–	–	–	–	0	2016	1	–	–	–	–	0
E (Elandre) Huggett	FS	2015	3	–	–	–	–	0	2015	3	–	–	–	–	0
DP (Reniel) Hugo	FS	2016	4	–	–	–	–	0	2016	4	–	–	–	–	0
DN (Niell) Jordaan	FS	2015	5	1	–	–	–	5	2015	5	1	–	–	–	5
A (Armandt) Koster	FS	2016	3	–	–	–	–	0	2016	3	–	–	–	–	0
NJ (Nico) Lee	FS	2016	7	–	–	–	–	0	2016	7	–	–	–	–	0
H (Hilton) Lobberts	FS	2014	7	1	–	–	–	5	2007	19	1	–	–	–	5
CM (Charles) Marais	FS	2016	14	–	–	–	–	0	2016	14	–	–	–	–	0
DR (Niel) Marais	FS	2015	13	2	24	9	–	85	2015	13	2	24	9	–	85
TC (Tian) Meyer	FS	2014	29	1	–	–	–	5	2012	40	3	–	–	–	15
DJ (Danie) Mienie	FS	2015	17	–	–	–	–	0	2013	18	–	–	–	–	0
TS (Oupa) Mohoje	FS	2014	25	1	–	–	–	5	2014	25	1	–	–	–	5
R (Ox) Nche	FS	2016	12	–	–	–	–	0	2016	12	–	–	–	–	0
SP (Sergeal) Petersen	FS	2015	20	9	–	–	–	45	2013	28	13	–	–	–	65
JGP (Boom) Prinsloo	FS	2012	49	14	–	–	–	70	2012	49	14	–	–	–	70
RK (Raymond) Rhule	FS	2013	52	13	–	–	–	65	2013	52	13	–	–	–	65
PA (Paul) Schoeman	FS	2016	14	5	–	–	–	25	2016	14	5	–	–	–	25
WT (William) Small-Smith	FS	2016	7	1	–	–	–	5	2014	14	2	–	–	–	10
FJ (Francois) Uys	FS	2009	77	1	–	–	–	5	2009	77	1	–	–	–	5
MG (Michael) van der Spuy	FS	2015	17	2	–	–	–	10	2014	21	2	–	–	–	10
NJJ (Maks) van Dyk	FS	2014	39	–	–	–	–	0	2014	39	–	–	–	–	0
TG (Torsten) van Jaarsveld	FS	2014	36	5	–	–	–	25	2014	36	5	–	–	–	25
JF (Francois) Venter	FS	2014	34	11	–	–	–	55	2012	45	11	–	–	–	55
HP (Henco) Venter	FS	2014	18	1	–	–	–	5	2014	18	1	–	–	–	5
SH (Shaun) Venter	FS	2014	35	1	–	–	–	5	2013	51	3	–	–	–	15
CA (Carl) Wegner	FS	2014	30	3	–	–	–	15	2014	30	3	–	–	–	15
GA (George) Whitehead	Grif	2016	3	–	1	–	–	2	2016	3	–	1	–	–	2
FJ (Fred) Zeilinga	FS	2016	15	–	17	15	–	79	2013	26	1	27	25	–	134
TOTALS			668	77	60	53	2	881		949	119	86	100	5	1213

Note: FS = Free State, Grif = Griffons

APPEARANCES & POINTS

PLAYER	Jaguares	Stormers	Sunwolves	Lions	Brumbies	Bulls	Sunwolves	Rebels	Reds	Waratahs	Kings	Stormers	Force	Sharks	Bulls	Apps	T	C	P	DG	Pts
Blommetjies	15	15	–	15	15	15	15	15	15	15	15	15	15	15	15	14	4	–	–	–	20
Petersen	14	14	14	14	14	14	14	14	14	14	14	14	14	14	14	15	9	–	–	–	45
Venter, F	13c	13c	13c	13c	13c	13c	12c	12c	–	12c	13c	13c	13c	13c	13c	13	3	–	–	–	15
Small-Smith	12	12	12	12	–	–	–	–	–	–	–	–	13R	12R	13	7	1	–	–	–	5
Rhule	11	11	11	11	11	11	11	11	11	11	11	11	11	11	11	15	4	–	–	–	20
Zeilinga	10	10	15R	12R	12R	13R	12R	15R	10	10	10	10	10	10	10	15	–	17	15	–	79
Venter, S	9	9	9	9	9	9	9	9	9	6R	9	9R	9R	9	9	15	1	–	–	–	5
Jordaan	8	8	–	–	–	–	–	–	–	–	8R	–	–	–	–	3	–	–	–	–	0
Cassiem	7	7	7	7	7	7	7	7	7	7R	6	6	6	6	6	15	6	–	–	–	30
Prinsloo	6	6R	6R	7R	6	6	–	–	–	–	–	–	–	–	–	6	1	–	–	–	5
De Jager	5	5	–	5	4	4	4	4	5c	4R	4	4	–	–	–	11	–	–	–	–	0
Wegner	4	4	4	4	4R	4R	4R	5R	4	4	–	–	4	4	4R	13	1	–	–	–	5
Van Dyk	3	3	3R	3	3R	3R	3	3	3	3R	3	3	3	3	3	15	–	–	–	–	0
Van Jaarsveld	2	2	2R	2	2	2	2	2	2	2R	2	2	2	2	2	15	4	–	–	–	20
Marais, C	1	1	1R	1	1R	1R	1	1	1	1R	1	1	–	1R	1	14	–	–	–	–	0
Du Toit	2R	2R	2	2R	x	x	2R	2R	2R	–	2R	x	–	–	–	8	2	–	–	–	10
Nche	3R	1R	1	1	1	1	–	–	1	1R	1R	1	1	1R	–	12	–	–	–	–	0
De Bruin	1R	3R	–	–	–	–	3R	1R	3	3R	3R	3R	–	–	–	8	–	–	–	–	0
Hugo	7R	–	4R	–	–	–	–	–	–	–	–	4R	4R	x	–	4	–	–	–	–	0
Venter, H	8R	8R	8	8	6R	6R	6R	7R	8	8	7R	–	7R	7R	–	13	–	–	–	–	0
Schoeman	6R	6	6	6	8	8	8	8	6	–	8	8	8	8	8	14	5	–	–	–	25
Meyer	14R	12R	13R	9R	9R	9R	15R	x	9R	9	9R	9	9	9R	9R	14	1	–	–	–	5
Marais, N	10R	15R	10	10	10	10	10	10	x	14R	13R	10R	–	–	–	11	2	17	9	–	71
Uys, F	–	7R	5R	5	5	5	5	4R	5	5	5	5	5	5	5	14	–	–	–	–	0
Coetzee	–	–	3	3R	3	3	3R	–	3R	–	–	x	3R	3R	–	8	–	–	–	–	0
Ebersohn	–	–	15	–	–	–	–	–	–	–	–	–	–	–	–	1	–	–	–	–	0
Lobberts	–	–	5R	8R	7R	7R	6	6	–	–	–	–	–	–	–	6	1	–	–	–	5
Engelbrecht	–	–	–	12	–	–	–	–	–	–	–	–	–	–	–	1	–	–	–	–	0
Lee	–	–	–	–	12	13	13	13	13	14R	12R	–	–	–	–	7	–	–	–	–	0
Mienie	–	–	–	–	1R	1R	–	–	–	–	–	–	–	–	–	2	–	–	–	–	0
Mohoje	–	–	–	–	7R	6R	7R	7	7	7	7	7	7c	–	–	9	–	–	–	–	0
Van der Spuy	–	–	–	–	–	–	12	15R	12	12	12	12	12	–	–	7	1	–	–	–	5
Britz	–	–	–	–	–	–	8R	6	–	–	–	–	–	–	–	2	–	–	–	–	0
Huggett	–	–	–	–	–	–	–	2	–	–	–	–	–	–	–	1	–	–	–	–	0
Koster	–	–	–	–	–	–	–	–	–	4R	4R	–	–	4	–	3	–	–	–	–	0
Dweba	–	–	–	–	–	–	–	–	–	–	–	2R	2R	2R	–	3	–	–	–	–	0
Whitehead	–	–	–	–	–	–	–	–	–	–	–	12R	15R	10R	–	3	–	1	–	–	2
Benjamin	–	–	–	–	–	–	–	–	–	–	–	–	–	12R	–	1	–	–	–	–	0
Penalty try	–	–	–	–	–	–	–	–	–	–	–	–	–	–	–	0	1	–	–	–	5
38 PLAYERS																338	47	35	24	0	377

Records

MATCH RECORDS

Biggest win	75	vs. Sunwolves (92-17)	Bloemfontein	2016
Heaviest defeat	46	vs Brumbies (15-61)	Canberra	2010
Highest score	92	vs. Sunwolves (92-17)	Bloemfontein	2016
Most points conceded	61	vs Brumbies (15-61)	Canberra	2010
Most tries	14	vs. Sunwolves (92-17)	Bloemfontein	2016
Most tries conceded	9	vs Brumbies (15-61)	Canberra	2010
Most points by a player	26	HM Bosman vs Stormers	Cape Town	2006
Most tries by a player	3	SJ Pretorius vs Hurricanes	Bloemfontein	2011
	3	R Viljoen vs Lions	Johannesburg	2011
	3	RS Benjamin vs Stormers	Bloemfontein	2011
	3	SP Petersen vs Sunwolves	Bloemfontein	2016
	3	P Schoeman vs Sunwolves	Bloemfontein	2016
Most conversions by a player	8	DR Marais vs Sunwolves	Bloemfontein	2016
Most penalties by a player	8	HM Bosman vs Stormers	Cape Town	2006
Most drop goals by a player	2	JM Ebersohn vs Hurricanes	Bloemfontein	2011
	2	R Viljoen vs Brumbies	Bloemfontein	2011

SEASON RECORDS

Most team points	435	in 16 games	2011
Most points by a player	179	JM Ebersohn	2011
Most team tries	47	in 15 games	2016
Most tries by a player	9	SJ Pretorius	2011
	9	SP Petersen	2016
Most conversions by a player	32	JM Ebersohn	2011
Most penalties by a player	33	JM Ebersohn	2011
Most drop goals by a player	2	IP Olivier	2010
	2	JM Ebersohn	2011
	2	R Viljoen	2011
	2	JC Pietersen	2015

CAREER RECORDS

Most appearances	97	JA Strauss	2007-2014
Most points	331	JL Goosen	2012-2014
Most tries	24	SJ Pretorius	2009-2015
Most conversions	46	JL Goosen	2012-2014
Most penalties	70	JL Goosen	2012-2014
Most drop goals	2	IP Olivier	2009-2010
	2	JM Ebersohn	2010-2011
	2	R Viljoen	2010-2011

2015 South African Rugby Player of the Year, Cheetahs lock Lood de Jager.

Emirates Lions

Ground: Emirates Airline Park (previously Ellis Park) **Capacity:** 62 300
Address: South Office Block, Johannesburg Stadium, 124 Van Beek Street, Doornfontein 2094
Telephone number: 011-402 2960 **Colours:** White and red trim jersey, black shorts and black socks
Website: www.lionsrugby.co.za **Captain:** Warren Whiteley **Coach:** Johan Ackermann
CEO: Rudolf Straeuli **President:** Kevin de Klerk

Head Coach: Johan Ackermann **Assistant Coach:** Swys de Bruin
Forward coach: Johan Ackermann **Team Manager:** Mustapha Boomgaard
Performance Analyst: JP Ferreira **Strength & Conditioning:** Ivan van Rooyen
Doctor: Dr Rob Collins **Physiotherapist:** David van Wyk
Assistant Team Manager: Johane Singwane **Media Officer:** Annemie Bester

1996[1]	1997[2]	1998	1999	2000	2001	2002	2003	2004	2005	2006
10th	5th	12th	11th	4th	3rd	11th	12th	12th	11th	13th

2007	2008	2009	2010	2011	2012	2013	2014	2015	2016
12th	14th	12th	13th	14th	15th		12th	8th	2nd

Played	Won	Lost	Drawn	Points for	Points against	Tries for	Tries against
18	13	5	0	622	404	81	51

Date	Venue	Opponent	Result	Score	Referee	Scorers
Febr 27	Tokyo	Sunwolves	WON	26-13	B O'Keefe	T: Skosan, R Coetzee, Kriel, Mapoe. C: Jantjies (3).
Mrch 05	Hamilton	Chiefs	WON	36-32	A Lees	T: Skosan, Marx, Combrinck, Whiteley. C: Jantjies (2). P: Jantjies (4).
Mrch 12	Dunedin	Highlanders	LOST	15-34	C Pollock	T: Janse van Rensburg, Ackermann. C: Jantjies. P: Jantjies.
Mrch 19	Johannesburg	Cheetahs	WON	39-22	S Berry	T: Jantjies, De Klerk, Mnisi, Ackermann, Fourie. C: Jantjies (3), Combrinck. P: Jantjies (2).
April 01	Johannesburg	Crusaders	LOST	37-43	S Berry	T: Van der Merwe (2), Mapoe, Jantjies. C: Jantjies (4). P: Jantjies (3).
April 09	Durban	Sharks	WON	24-09	A Gardner	T: Ferreira, Mapoe. C: Jantjies. P: Jantjies (4).
April 16	Johannesburg	Stormers	WON	29-22	S Berry	T: Combrinck, De Klerk. C: Jantjies (2). P: Jantjies (4). DG: Jantjies.
April 23	Port Elizabeth	Kings	WON	45-10	R Rasivhenge	T: Combrinck (2), Van der Merwe, Fourie, Skosan. Janse van Rensburg, Whiteley. C: Jantjies (5)
April 30	Johannesburg	Hurricanes	LOST	17-30	M v/d westhuizen	T: Van der Merwe, Kriel, Mapoe. C: Jantjies.
May 14	Johannesburg	Blues	WON	43-05	J van Heerden	T: Mapoe (3), Skosan, Janse van Rensburg, Whiteley, Tecklenburg. C: Jantjies (4).
May 21	Johannesburg	Jaguares	WON	52-24	S Berry	T: Combrinck (2), Skosan (2), Brink, Kriel, Mapoe, Erasmus. C: Jantjies (2), Combrinck. P: Combrinck (2).
May 28	Pretoria	Bulls	WON	56-20	C Joubert	T: Janse van Rensburg (2), Skosan, De Klerk, Kriel, Redelinghuys, Mapoe. C: Boshoff (6). P: Boshoff (3)
July 02	Johannesburg	Sharks	WON	37-10	J Peyper	T: Kriel, Marx, Janse van Rensburg, Ackermann, Combrinck. C: Jantjies (3). P: Jantjies (2).
July 08	Johannesburg	Kings	WON	57-21	J van Heerden	T: Janse van Rensburg (2), Coetzee, Skosan, De Klerk, Mostert, Marx, Mahuza. C: Jantjies (5), Combrinck (2). P: Jantjies.
July 16	Buenos Aires	Jaguares	LOST	22-34	R Hoffmann	T: Volmink (2), Mahuza. C: Van der Walt (2). P: Van der Walt.

QUARTER-FINAL

Date	Venue	Opponent	Result	Score	Referee	Scorers
July 23	Johannesburg	Crusaders	WON	42-25	C Joubert	T: Skosan, Marx, Janse van Rensburg, Cronje, Combrinck. C: Jantjies (4). P: Jantjies (2). DG: Jantjies

SEMI-FINAL

Date	Venue	Opponent	Result	Score	Referee	Scorers
July 30	Johannesburg	Highlanders	WON	42-30	J Peyper	T: Jantjies, Skosan, Kriel, Janse van Rensburg, Erasmus. C: Jantjies (4). P: Jantjies (3).

FINAL

Date	Venue	Opponent	Result	Score	Referee	Scorers
Aug 06	Wellington	Hurricanes	LOST	03-20	G Jackson	P: Jantjies

Note: 1 = As Transvaal, 2 = As Golden Lions.

2016 SQUAD

PLAYER	Union	Debut	M	T	C	P	DG	Pts	Debut	M	T	C	P	DG	Pts
			LIONS CAREER							SUPER RUGBY CAREER					
R (Ruan) Ackermann	GL	2016	16	3	–	–	–	15	2016	16	3	–	–	–	15
JW (JW) Bell	GL	2016	2	–	–	–	–	0	2016	2	–	–	–	–	0
FCF (Fabian) Booysen	GL	2016	2	–	–	–	–	0	2016	2	–	–	–	–	0
ML (Marnitz) Boshoff	GL	2014	29	1	25	52	8	235	2014	29	1	25	52	8	235
CJ (Cyle) Brink	GL	2016	13	1	–	–	–	5	2016	13	1	–	–	–	5
A (Andries) Coetzee	GL	2012	43	3	–	–	1	18	2012	43	3	–	–	1	18
RL (Robbie) Coetzee	GL	2014	28	2	–	–	–	10	2014	28	2	–	–	–	10
RJ (Ruan) Combrinck	GL	2012	45	13	4	4	–	85	2012	45	13	4	4	–	85
R (Ross) Cronjé	GL	2012	48	2	–	–	–	10	2009	49	2	–	–	–	10
A (Ashlon) Davids	GL	2016	1	–	–	–	–	0	2016	1	–	–	–	–	0
F (Faf) de Klerk	GL	2014	49	12	–	–	–	60	2014	49	12	–	–	–	60
AS (Steph) de Witt	GL	2016	2	–	–	–	–	0	2016	2	–	–	–	–	0
RM (Ruan) Dreyer	GL	2012	43	1	–	–	–	5	2012	43	1	–	–	–	5
LJ (Lourens) Erasmus	GL	2016	8	2	–	–	–	10	2016	8	2	–	–	–	10
AS (Andries) Ferreira	GL	2015	22	1	–	–	–	5	2013	42	2	–	–	–	10
C (Corné) Fourie	Mpu	2014	40	3	–	–	–	15	2014	40	3	–	–	–	15
NJ (Stokkies) Hanekom	GL	2014	6	–	–	–	–	0	2014	6	–	–	–	–	0
R (Rohan) Janse van Rensburg	GL	2016	17	10	–	–	–	50	2016	17	10	–	–	–	50
ET (Elton) Jantjies	GL	2011	70	4	109	117	3	598	2011	83	4	110	120	3	609
JA (Jaco) Kriel	GL	2011	55	13	–	–	–	65	2011	55	13	–	–	–	65
RA (Robert) Kruger	GL	2015	28	–	–	–	–	0	2015	28	–	–	–	–	0
RS (Ruaan) Lerm	GL	2015	3	–	–	–	–	0	2015	3	–	–	–	–	0
S (Sylvian) Mahuza	GL	2016	6	2	–	–	–	10	2016	6	2	–	–	–	10
LG (Lionel) Mapoe	GL	2011	62	20	–	–	–	100	2010	79	23	–	–	–	115
KP (Koch) Marx	GL	2016	1	–	–	–	–	0	2016	1	–	–	–	–	0
MJ (Malcolm) Marx	GL	2014	20	5	–	–	–	25	2014	20	5	–	–	–	25
XH (Howard) Mnisi	GL	2014	32	2	–	–	–	10	2014	35	2	–	–	–	10
FJ (Franco) Mostert	GL	2014	47	1	–	–	–	5	2014	47	1	–	–	–	5
MD (Martin) Muller	GL	2014	16	–	–	–	–	0	2009	30	–	–	–	–	0
JJ (Jacques) Nel	GL	2016	2	–	–	–	–	0	2016	2	–	–	–	–	0
J (Julian) Redelinghuys	GL	2014	45	1	–	–	–	5	2014	45	1	–	–	–	5
RC (Ramone) Samuels	GL	2016	3	–	–	–	–	0	2016	3	–	–	–	–	0
PE (Pieter) Scholtz	GL	2016	2	–	–	–	–	0	2016	2	–	–	–	–	0
CD (Courtnall) Skosan	GL	2014	36	16	–	–	–	80	2014	36	16	–	–	–	80
D (Dillon) Smit	GL	2015	6	–	–	–	–	0	2015	6	–	–	–	–	0
DT (Dylan) Smith	GL	2016	16	–	–	–	–	0	2016	16	–	–	–	–	0
WJ (Warwick) Tecklenburg	GL	2014	45	6	–	–	–	30	2014	45	6	–	–	–	30
C (Clinton) Theron	GL	2016	1	–	–	–	–	0	2016	1	–	–	–	–	0
AHP (Armand) van der Merwe	GL	2014	39	6	–	–	–	30	2014	39	6	–	–	–	30
J (Jako) van der Walt	GL	2015	18	–	3	1	–	9	2015	18	–	3	1	–	9
J (Jacques) van Rooyen	GL	2014	31	1	–	–	–	5	2014	31	1	–	–	–	5
AA (Anthony) Volmink	GL	2012	12	3	–	–	–	15	2012	12	3	–	–	–	15
HW (Harold) Vorster	GL	2015	17	4	–	–	–	20	2015	17	4	–	–	–	20
WR (Warren) Whiteley	GL	2011	66	8	–	–	–	40	2011	66	8	–	–	–	40
TOTALS			1093	146	141	174	12	1570		1161	150	142	177	12	1601

Note: GL = Golden Lions, Mpu = Mpumalanga

APPEARANCES & POINTS

PLAYER	Sunwolves	Chiefs	Highlanders	Cheetahs	Crusaders	Sharks	Stormers	Kings	Hurricanes	Blues	Jaguares	Bulls	Sharks	Kings	Jaguares	Crusaders	Highlanders	Hurricanes	Apps	T	C	P	DG	Pts
Coetzee, A	15	15	x	15	15	15R	15R	–	–	–	–	–	15	15	–	15	15	15	11	1	–	–	–	5
Combrinck	14	14	14	14	14	14	14	14	14	14	14	14	14	–	14	14	14	14	17	8	4	2	–	54
Mapoe	13	13	–	13	13	13	13	13	13	13	13	13	13	13	–	13	13	13	16	9	–	–	–	45
Mnisi	12	12R	12	12	12	12R	12R	12	12	12R	12	13R	12R	13R	12	12R	12R	12R	18	1	–	–	–	5
Skosan	11	11	11	11	11	11	11	11	11	11	11	11	11	11	–	11	11	11	17	10	–	–	–	50
Jantjies	10	10	10	10	10	10	10	10	10	10	10	–	10	10	–	10	10	10	16	3	44	27	2	190
De Klerk	9	9	9	9	9	9R	9R	9	9	9R	9	9	9	9	–	9	9	9	17	4	–	–	–	20
Whiteley	8c	8c	8c	8c	8c	8c	8c	8c	8c	8c	8c	8c	–	–	–	8c	–	8c	14	3	–	–	–	15
Tecklenburg	7	7	7	–	7	7	7	7	7	7	6R	7	7	7	–	7	7	7	16	1	–	–	–	5
Kriel	6	6	6	6	6	6	6	8R	6	6	6	6	6c	6c	–	6	6c	6	17	6	–	–	–	30
Mostert	5	5	5	5	5	5	5	5	5	5	5	5	5	5	–	5	5	5	17	1	–	–	–	5
Ferreira	4	4	4	4	4	4	4	4	–	–	4	4	4	–	4	4	4	4	15	1	–	–	–	5
Redelinghuys	3	3	3R	3	3	3	3	–	–	3	3	3	3	3	–	3	3	3	15	1	–	–	–	5
Coetzee, R	2	–	2	–	–	–	–	–	–	–	–	–	–	–	–	–	–	–	2	1	–	–	–	5
Dreyer	1	3R	3	3R	3R	3R	3R	3	–	–	–	–	–	–	–	–	–	–	8	–	–	–	–	0
Marx, M	2R	2	–	2	2	2	2	–	–	2	2R	2	2	2	–	2	2	2	14	4	–	–	–	20
Smith	1R	1	–	1	1	1	1	1R	1	1	1R	1	1	1	–	1	1	1	16	–	–	–	–	0
Van Rooyen	3R	–	1	–	–	–	–	3R	3R	3R	3R	3R	3R	3	3R	3R	3R	–	13	–	–	–	–	0
Kruger	4R	4R	4R	–	–	–	–	–	4R	–	–	–	–	7	–	–	–	–	5	–	–	–	–	0
Ackermann	7R	–	6R	7	6R	7R	4R	7R	4R	4	4R	6R	8	8	–	8R	8	8R	16	3	–	–	–	15
Van der Walt	9R	x	15	15R	15R	15	15	15	15	15	15	–	–	–	10	10R	15R	15R	14	–	2	1	–	7
Vorster	12R	12	–	–	–	–	–	–	–	–	–	–	–	–	–	–	–	–	2	–	–	–	–	0
Janse van Rensburg	13R	13R	13	12R	12R	12	12	13R	12R	12	13R	12	12	–	12	12	12	–	17	10	–	–	–	50
Van der Merwe	–	2R	2R	2R	2R	2R	2	2	2R	2	2R	2R	2R	2	2R	2R	2R	–	17	4	–	–	–	20
Fourie	–	1R	1R	1R	1R	1R	1R	1	1R	1R	1	1R	1R	1	1R	1R	1R	–	17	2	–	–	–	0
Booysen	–	7R	–	–	–	–	–	–	–	–	–	–	20R	–	–	–	–	–	2	–	–	–	–	0
Smit	–	–	9R	9R	9R	–	–	–	–	–	–	–	9R	–	–	–	–	–	4	–	–	–	–	0
Nel	–	13R	–	–	–	–	–	–	–	–	–	–	13R	–	–	–	–	–	2	–	–	–	–	0
Brink	–	–	6R	4R	6R	7R	6	7R	6R	7	7R	8R	7R	8	7R	–	–	–	13	1	–	–	–	5
Erasmus	–	–	4R	–	–	–	–	4	4R	4R	4R	5	–	4R	4R	–	–	–	8	2	–	–	–	10
Cronje	–	–	–	9	9	9R	9R	9	9R	9R	9R	9R	9c	–	9R	9R	9R	–	13	1	–	–	–	5
Bell	–	–	–	–	15R	10R	–	–	–	–	–	–	–	–	–	–	–	–	2	–	–	–	–	0
Samuels	–	–	–	–	2R	2R	–	–	–	–	–	2R	–	–	–	–	–	–	3	–	–	–	–	0
Scholtz	–	–	–	–	3	–	–	–	–	–	–	3R	–	–	–	–	–	–	2	–	–	–	–	0
Mahuza	–	–	–	–	–	–	10R	15R	15	15R	10R	15	–	–	–	–	–	–	6	2	–	–	–	10
Boshoff	–	–	–	–	–	–	–	10	–	–	–	–	–	–	–	–	–	–	1	–	6	3	–	21
Volmink	–	–	–	–	–	–	–	–	–	–	–	11	–	–	–	–	–	–	1	2	–	–	–	10
Marx, K	–	–	–	–	–	–	–	–	–	–	–	14	–	–	–	–	–	–	1	–	–	–	–	0
Hanekom	–	–	–	–	–	–	–	–	–	–	–	13	–	–	–	–	–	–	1	–	–	–	–	0
De Witt	–	–	–	–	–	–	–	–	–	–	–	6	–	6R	–	–	–	–	2	–	–	–	–	0
Muller	–	–	–	–	–	–	–	–	–	–	–	4	–	–	–	–	–	–	1	–	–	–	–	0
Lerm	–	–	–	–	–	–	–	–	–	–	–	7R	–	–	–	–	–	–	1	–	–	–	–	0
Davids	–	–	–	–	–	–	–	–	–	–	–	10R	–	–	–	–	–	–	1	–	–	–	–	0
Theron	–	–	–	–	–	–	–	–	–	–	–	1R	–	–	–	–	–	–	1	–	–	–	–	0
44 PLAYERS																			412	81	56	33	2	622

Records

MATCH RECORDS

Biggest winning margin	50	vs Chiefs (53-3)	Bloemfontein	2000
Heaviest defeat	64	vs ACT Brumbies (0-64)	Canberra	2000
Highest score	65	vs Chiefs (65-72)	Johannesburg	2010
Most points conceded	72	vs Chiefs (65-72)	Johannesburg	2010
Most tries	9	vs Chiefs (65-72)	Johannesburg	2010
Most tries conceded	10	vs ACT Brumbies (16-64)	Canberra	2002
Most points by a player	32	GK Johnson vs Highlanders	Johannesburg	1997
Most tries by a player	3	JA van der Walt vs Bulls	Pretoria	1998
	3	JA van der Walt vs Stormers	Johannesburg	1998
	3	C Stoltz vs Crusaders	Nelson	1999
	3	G Bobo vs Bulls	Pretoria	2002
	3	GJJ Britz vs Bulls	Pretoria	2004
	3	J Fourie vs Blues	Johannesburg	2006
	3	H Mentz vs Reds	Brisbane	2009
	3	WG Mjekevu vs Chiefs	Johannesburg	2010
	3	LG Mapoe	Johannesburg	2016
Most conversions by a player	7	CJN Fourie vs Bulls	Pretoria	2004
Most penalties by a player	9	ET Jantjies vs Cheetahs	Johannesburg	2012
Most drop goals by a player	2	GS du Toit vs Stormers	Cape Town	1999
	2	AS Pretorius vs Waratahs	Johannesburg	2009

SEASON RECORDS

Most team points	622	in 18 matches	2016
Most points by a player	190	ET Jantjies	2016
Most team tries	81	in 18 matches	2016
Most tries by a player	10	R Janse van Rensburg	2016
	10	CD Skosan	2016
Most conversions by a player	44	ET Jantjies	2016
Most penalties by a player	36	LJ Koen	2001
Most drop goals by a player	6	AS Pretorius	2009

CAREER RECORDS

Most appearances	94	PJJ Grobbelaar	2004-2012
Most points	661	AS Pretorius	2002-2011
Most tries	24	J Fourie	2003-2009
Most conversions	102	AS Pretorius	2002-2011
Most penalties	121	AS Pretorius	2002-2011
Most drop goals	11	AS Pretorius	2002-2009

Courtnall Skosan had a season to remember for the Lions.

Cell C Sharks

Ground: Growthpoint Kings Park **Capacity:** 52 000 **Address:** Isaiah Ntshangane Road, Durban
Telephone Number: 031-308 8400 **Colours:** Grey jersey with black and white trim,
blacks shorts and socks **Website:** www.sharksrugby.co.za
Head Coach: Gary Gold **Captain:** Patrick Lambie **CEO:** John Smit
Chairman: Stephen Saad **President:** Graham McKenzie

Head Coach: Gary Gold **Forwards Coach:** Ryan Strudwick
Skills Coach: Sean Everitt **Attack Coach:** Robert du Preez **Defence Coach:** Omar Mouneimne
Manager: Trevor Barnes **Doctor:** Dr Alan Kourie **Physiotherapist:** Deane Macquet
Strength & Conditioning: Johan Pretorius **Biokineticist:** Jimmy Wright
Media Officer: Novashni Chetty

1996	1997	1998	1999	2000	2001	2002	2003	2004	2005	2006
4th	4th	3rd	7th	12th	2nd	10th	11th	7th	12th	5th

2007	2008	2009	2010	2011	2012	2013	2014	2015	2016
1st	3rd	6th	9th	6th	6th	8th	3rd	11th	8th

Played	Won	Lost	Drawn	Points for	Points against	Tries for	Tries against
16	9	6	1	360	310	40	36

Date	Venue	Opponent	Result	Score	Referee	Scorers
Febr 27	Port Elizabeth	Kings	WON	43-08	J van Heerden	T: Ndungane (2), J-L du Preez, Mvovo, Jordaan, Le Roux. C: Pietersen (5). P: Pietersen.
Mrch 05	Durban	Jaguares	WON	19-15	J Peyper	T: Coetzee. C: Pietersen. P: Pietersen (4).
Mrch 12	Cape Town	Stormers	WON	18-13	M Fraser	T: Pietersen, Penalty try. C: Pietersen. P: Pietersen (2).
Mrch 18	Pretoria	Bulls	DREW	16-16	G Jackson	T: Le Roux. C: Pietersen. P: Pietersen (3).
Mrch 26	Durban	Crusaders	LOST	14-19	J Peyper	T: Mvovo (2). C: Pietersen (2).
April 09	Durban	Lions	LOST	09-24	A Gardner	P: Pietersen (3).
April 16	Auckland	Blues	LOST	18-23	J Peyper	T: Mtawarira, Jordaan. C: Pietersen. P: Pietersen.
April 22	Dunedin	Highlanders	WON	15-14	B O'Keeffe	P: April (5)
April 29	New Plymouth	Chiefs	LOST	22-24	C Pollock	T: Cooper, April, Ralepelle. C: April (2). P: April.
May 07	Durban	Hurricanes	WON	32-15	M v/d Westhuizen	T: JP Pietersen (2), D du Preez, Claassens. C: April (2), Lambie. P: April, Lambie.
May14	Buenos Aires	Jaguares	WON	25-22	M v/d Westhuizen	T: D du Preez. C: Lambie. P: Lambie (6).
May 21	Durban	Kings	WON	53-00	Q Immelman	T: Lambie (2), Jordaan (2), Esterhuizen, Le Roux, JP Pietersen, Du Toit. C: Lambie (5). P: Lambie.
July 02	Johannesburg	Lions	LOST	10-37	J Peyper	T: Mvovo, Ralepelle.
July 09	Durban	Cheetahs	WON	26-10	S Berry	T: Pietersen, Ungerer. C: April (2). P: April (4).
July 15	Durban	Sunwolves	WON	40-29	R Rasivhenge	T: Esterhuizen, C Oosthuizen, Bosch, April, Pietersen, Mvovo. C: April (5).

QUARTER-FINAL

Date	Venue	Opponent	Result	Score	Referee	Scorers
July 23	Wellington	Hurricanes	LOST	00-41	G Jackson	

2016 SQUAD

PLAYER	Union	Debut	M	T	C	P	DG	Pts	Debut	M	T	C	P	DG	Pts
			SHARKS CAREER						**SUPER RUGBY CAREER**						
LC (Lourens) Adriaanse	KZN	2014	46	–	–	–	–	0	2011	76	–	–	–	–	0
HD (Hyron) Andrews	KZN	2016	9	–	–	–	–	0	2016	9	–	–	–	–	0
GG (Garth) April	KZN	2016	12	2	11	11	–	65	2016	12	2	11	11	–	65
CD (Curwin) Bosch	KZN	2016	3	1	–	–	–	5	2016	3	1	–	–	–	5
R (Ruan) Botha	KZN	2016	3	–	–	–	–	0	2012	29	1	–	–	–	5
DM (Dale) Chadwick	KZN	2012	44	1	–	–	–	5	2012	44	1	–	–	–	5
M (Michael) Claassens	KZN	2016	15	1	–	–	–	5	2005	44	1	–	–	–	5
MC (Marcell) Coetzee	KZN	2011	74	14	–	–	–	70	2011	74	14	–	–	–	70
KL (Kyle) Cooper	KZN	2012	48	3	–	–	–	15	2012	48	3	–	–	–	15
KR (Keegan) Daniel	KZN	2007	117	16	–	–	–	80	2007	117	16	–	–	–	80
JR (Jean) Deysel	KZN	2008	78	1	–	–	–	5	2008	78	1	–	–	–	5
D (Daniel) du Preez	KZN	2015	13	2	–	–	–	10	2015	13	2	–	–	–	10
J-L (Jean-Luc) du Preez	KZN	2016	13	1	–	–	–	5	2016	13	1	–	–	–	5
TJ (Thomas) du Toit	KZN	2014	20	2	–	–	–	10	2014	20	2	–	–	–	10
AP (André) Esterhuizen	KZN	2014	29	2	–	–	–	10	2014	29	2	–	–	–	10
PA (Paul) Jordaan	KZN	2012	43	9	–	–	–	45	2012	43	9	–	–	–	45
PJ (Patrick) Lambie	KZN	2010	66	13	86	158	1	714	2010	66	13	86	158	1	714
WJ (Willie) le Roux	KZN	2016	13	3	–	–	–	15	2012	71	21	–	–	–	105
JST (Joseph) Lewies	KZN	2014	35	–	–	–	–	0	2014	35	–	–	–	–	0
FS (Franco) Marais	KZN	2014	21	–	–	–	–	0	2014	21	–	–	–	–	0
D (David) McDuling	KZN	2016	1	–	–	–	–	0	2012	13	–	–	–	–	0
T (Tendai) Mtawarira	KZN	2007	126	4	–	–	–	20	2007	126	4	–	–	–	20
LS (Lubabalo) Mtembu	KZN	2012	24	1	–	–	–	5	2012	24	1	–	–	–	5
L (Lubabalo) Mtyanda	MPU	2015	13	–	–	–	–	0	2015	13	–	–	–	–	0
LN (Lwazi) Mvovo	KZN	2010	99	29	–	–	–	145	2010	99	29	–	–	–	145
OM (Odwa) Ndungane	KZN	2005	131	33	–	–	–	165	2004	141	36	–	–	–	180
CV (Coenie) Oosthuizen	KZN	2016	14	1	–	–	–	5	2010	88	9	–	–	–	45
E (Etienne) Oosthuizen	KZN	2014	39	–	–	–	–	0	2012	45	–	–	–	–	0
JC (Joe) Pietersen	KZN	2016	9	1	11	15	–	72	2006	70	10	65	117	2	537
J-P R (JP) Pietersen	KZN	2006	137	39	–	–	–	195	2006	137	39	–	–	–	195
MC (Chiliboy) Ralepelle	KZN	2016	9	2	–	–	–	10	2006	78	6	–	–	–	30
JM (Cobus) Reinach	KZN	2012	44	9	–	–	–	45	2012	44	9	–	–	–	45
JL (Juan) Schoeman	KZN	2016	5	–	–	–	–	–	2016	5	–	–	–	–	0
SCT (S'bura) Sithole	KZN	2013	33	4	–	–	–	20	2013	33	4	–	–	–	20
RC (Rhyno) Smith	Leo	2016	3	–	–	–	–	0	2016	3	–	–	–	–	0
S (Stefan) Ungerer	KZN	2014	17	5	–	–	–	25	2014	17	5	–	–	–	25
CP (Philip) van der Walt	KZN	2016	11	–	–	–	–	0	2011	60	5	–	–	–	25
H (Heimar) Williams	KZN	2014	16	1	–	–	–	5	2014	16	1	–	–	–	5
TOTALS			**1433**	**200**	**108**	**184**	**1**	**1771**		**1857**	**248**	**162**	**286**	**3**	**2431**

Note: KZN = KwaZulu-Natal, Mpu = Mpumalanga, Leo = Leopards

APPEARANCES & POINTS

PLAYER	Kings	Jaguares	Stormers	Bulls	Crusaders	Lions	Blues	Highlanders	Chiefs	Hurricanes	Jaguares	Kings	Lions	Cheetahs	Sunwolves	Hurricanes	Apps	T	C	P	DG	Pts
Le Roux	15	15	15	15	15	15	15	15	15	15	15	15	–	–	–	15	13	3	–	–	–	15
Ndungane	14	14	14	14R	11R	x	14R	14	14R	13R	14	15R	15	–	14	11R	14	2	–	–	–	10
Jordaan	13	13	13	13	13	13	13	–	13	13	13	13	12	–	–	13	13	4	–	–	–	20
Esterhuizen	12	12	12	12	12	12	12	12	12	12	12	12	–	12	12	12	15	2	–	–	–	10
Mvovo	11	–	–	11	11	11	11	11	11	11	–	11	11	11	11	11	13	5	–	–	–	25
Pietersen, Joe	10	10	10	10	10	10	10	15R	x	–	9R	–	–	–	–	–	9	1	11	15	–	72
Reinach	9	9	9	9R	9	9	9	9	9	–	–	–	–	–	–	–	8	–	–	–	–	0
Du Preez, D	8	8	8	7	8R	8	8	–	8	8	8	8	–	–	–	–	11	2	–	–	–	10
Du Preez, J-L	7	7	7	–	7	7	7	7	7	7	7	–	7	7	7	7	13	1	–	–	–	5
Coetzee	6	6	6	6	6	6	–	–	–	–	–	–	–	–	–	–	6	1	–	–	–	5
Andrews	5	5R	5R	5R	20R	5	8R	x	x	4R	–	–	–	–	–	4R	9	–	–	–	–	0
Oosthuizen, E	4	4	4	4	4	4	4	4	4	4	4R	4	4	4	4	4	16	–	–	–	–	0
Oosthuizen, C	3	3	3	3R	3	3	3R	3	3R	–	3	–	3R	3	3	3	14	1	–	–	–	5
Marais	2	2	2	2R	2	2	2	2	–	2	2	–	2	2	–	2	13	–	–	–	–	0
Mtawarira	1c	1c	1c	1c	1c	1c	1c	1c	–	1c	1	–	1c	1c	–	1c	13	1	–	–	–	5
Cooper	2R	2R	2R	2	2R	2R	2R	–	2	–	–	2R	–	–	2R	–	10	1	–	–	–	5
Schoeman	1R	x	1R	1R	x	1R	–	–	–	–	–	1R	–	–	–	–	5	–	–	–	–	0
Adriaanse	3R	3R	3R	3	3R	3R	3	3R	3	3	3R	3	3	3R	3R	–	15	–	–	–	–	0
McDuling	5R	–	–	–	–	–	–	–	–	–	–	–	–	–	–	–	1	–	–	–	–	0
Van der Walt	8R	8R	8R	8	8	–	6	8	–	–	–	–	8	8	8	8	11	–	–	–	–	0
Claassens	9R	9R	9R	9	9R	9R	9R	9R	9	9	–	9	9	9	9R	9	15	1	–	–	–	5
April	15R	x	x	15R	10R	10R	x	10	10	10	x	12R	10	10	10	10	12	2	11	11	–	65
Sithole	11R	14R	x	–	–	–	–	14R	–	–	14R	–	14	14	–	–	6	–	–	–	–	0
Pietersen, JP	–	11	11	14	14	14	14	13	14	14	11	14	13	13c	14		15	5	–	–	–	25
Lewies	–	5	5	5	5	–	5	5	5	5	5	5	5	5	4R	5	14	–	–	–	–	0
Daniel	–	–	–	7R	–	6R	6R	6	6c	6	6	6	6	6	6	6	12	–	–	–	–	0
Mtyanda	–	–	–	–	–	4R	–	–	–	4	5R	–	–	–	–	–	3	–	–	–	–	0
Du Toit	–	–	–	–	–	1R	1R	1R	1R	–	3R	1R	1R	1	3R		9	1	–	–	–	5
Deysel	–	–	–	–	–	–	8R	7R	7R	7	–	–	–	8R	–		5	–	–	–	–	0
Ralepelle	–	–	–	–	–	–	2R	2R	2R	2R	2	2	2R	2	2R		9	2	–	–	–	10
Chadwick	–	–	–	–	–	–	1	1R	1R	1	–	–	1R	1R			6	–	–	–	–	0
Ungerer	–	–	–	–	–	–	x	9R	9	9R	9R	9R	9	9R			7	1	–	–	–	5
Lambie	–	–	–	–	–	–	10R	10c	10c	–	–	–	–	–			3	2	7	8	–	48
Mtembu	–	–	–	–	–	–	7R	8R	6R	7R	7	8R					6	–	–	–	–	0
Williams	–	–	–	–	–	–	–	–	12R	12R	x	–					2	–	–	–	–	0
Smith	–	–	–	–	–	–	–	–	15R	15	15	–					3	–	–	–	–	0
Botha	–	–	–	–	–	–	–	–	4R	4R	5	–					3	–	–	–	–	0
Bosch	–	–	–	–	–	–	–	–	15R	15R	10R						3	1	–	–	–	5
Penalty try	–	–	–	–	–	–	–	–	–	–	–	–						1	–	–	–	5
38 PLAYERS																	355	40	29	34	0	360

Records

MATCH RECORDS

Biggest winning margin	57	vs Rebels (64-7)	Durban	2013
Heaviest defeat	43	vs Crusaders (34-77)	Christchurch	2005
Highest score	75	vs Highlanders (75-43)	Durban	1997
Most points conceded	77	vs Crusaders (34-77)	Christchurch	2005
Most tries	10	vs Rebels (64-7)	Durban	2013
Most tries conceded	11	vs Crusaders (34-77)	Christchurch	2005
Most points by a player (Natal)	50	GE Lawless (4t, 9c, 4p) vs Highlanders	Durban	1997
Most points by a player (Sharks)	28	PJ Lambie (1t, 1c, 7p) vs Highlanders	Durban	2012
Most tries by a player (Natal)	4	GE Lawless vs Highlanders	Durban	1997
Most tries by a player (Sharks)	4	CS Terblanche vs Chiefs	Port Elizabeth	1998
Most conversions by a player	9	GE Lawless vs Highlanders	Durban	1997
Most penalties by a player	7	GE Lawless vs NSW Waratahs	Durban	1997
	7	PJ Lambie vs Highlanders	Durban	2012
	7	PJ Lambie vs Crusaders	Durban	2013
Most drop goals by a player	2	FPL Steyn vs Blues	Albany	2007
	2	F Michalak vs Stormers	Cape Town	2012

SEASON RECORDS

Most team points	498	in 19 matches	2012
Most points by a player	193	PJ Lambie	2011
Most team tries	56	in 13 matches	1996
Most tries by a player (Natal)	13	JT Small	1996
Most tries by a player (Sharks)	12	J-PR Pietersen	2007
Most conversions by a player	28	PJ Lambie	2011
Most penalties by a player	43	PJ Lambie	2013
Most drop goals by a player	4	FPL Steyn	2007

CAREER RECORDS

Most appearances	131	BW du Plessis	2005-2015
	131	OM Ndungane	2005-2016
Most points	714	PJ Lambie	2010-2016
Most tries	39	J-PR Pietersen	2006-2016
Most conversions	86	PJ Lambie	2010-2016
Most penalties	158	PJ Lambie	2010-2016
Most drop goals	8	FPL Steyn	2007-2014

Jean-Luc du Preez ended the 2016 season as a Test Springbok.

Southern Kings

Ground: Nelson Mandela Bay Stadium, Port Elizabeth **Capacity:** 46 000
Address: 70 Prince Alfred Road, Sydenham, PE **Telephone number:** + 27 41 408 8902
Colours: Black jersey with Team Charcoal/Ebony inserts and white piping. Black shorts and socks
Website: www.skings.co.za **Coach:** Deon Davids **Captain:** Steven Sykes
Charmain: Cheeky Watson **CEO:** Charl Crous

Head Coach: Deon Davids **Forwards Coach:** Barend Pieterse
Backs Coach: Mzwandile Stick **Physiotherapist:** Kim Naidoo **Doctor:** Dr Conrad van Hagen
Team Manager: Zingi Hela **Logistics Manager:** Sydney Goba
Analyst: Lindsay Weyer **Media Manager:** Derrick Spies

1996	1997	1998	1999	2000	2001	2002	2003	2004	2005	2006

2007	2008	2009	2010	2011	2012	2013 15th	2014	2015	2016 17th

Played	Won	Lost	Drawn	Points for	Points against	Tries for	Tries against
15	2	13	0	282	684	34	95

Date	Venue	Opponent	Result	Score	Referee	Scorers
Febr 27	Port Elizabeth	Sharks	LOST	08-43	J van Heerden	T: Cloete. P: Watts.
Mrch 12	Port Elizabeth	Chiefs	LOST	24-58	J van Heerden	T: Marutlulle (2). C: Fouche. P: Fouche (4).
Mrch 19	Christchurch	Crusaders	LOST	24-57	W Houston	T: Cloete, Marutlulle, Vulindlu. C: Fouche (3). P: Fouche.
Mrch 25	Wellington	Hurricanes	LOST	20-42	B Pickerill	T: Sykes, Fouche. C: Fouche (2). P: Fouche (2).
April 02	Port Elizabeth	Sunwolves	WON	33-28	R Rasivhenge	T: Jaer, Gates, Sykes, Watts. C: Fouche (2). P: Fouche (3).
April 09	Port Elizabeth	Bulls	LOST	06-38	S Kubo	P: Fouche (2).
April 23	Port Elizabeth	Lions	LOST	10-45	R Rasivhenge	T: Cloete, Vulindlu.
April 30	Buenos Aires	Jaguares	LOST	27-73	S Berry	T: Cloete, Watermeyer, Sykes, Bholi. C: Watts (2). P: Watts.
May 07	Port Elizabeth	Blues	LOST	18-34	F Anselmi	T: Marutlulle, Hall. C: Watts. P: Watts, Visser.
May 14	Bloemfontein	Cheetahs	LOST	20-34	F Anselmi	T: Du Plessis, Am. C: Fouche (2). P: Watts (2).
May 21	Durban	Sharks	LOST	00-53	Q Immelman	
May 27	Port Elizabeth	Jaguares	WON	29-22	N Briant	T: Human, Ferreira, Mjekevu, Penalty try. C: Fouche (3). P: Fouche.
July 02	Port Elizabeth	Highlanders	LOST	18-48	M v/d westhuizen	T: Sykes, Mjekevu. C: Fouche. P: Watts, Fouche.
July 08	Johannesburg	Lions	LOST	21-57	J van Heerden	T: Watermeyer, Ferreira, Hall. C: Fouche (3).
July 16	Cape Town	Stormers	LOST	24-52	J Peyper	T: Jaer, Watermeyer, Mjekevu. C: Watts, Human, Watermeyer. P: Human.

2016 SQUAD

PLAYER	Union	Debut	SOUTHERN KINGS CAREER						Debut	SUPER RUGBY CAREER					
			M	T	C	P	DG	Pts		M	T	C	P	DG	Pts
J (Justin) Ackerman	Lio	2016	8	–	–	–	–	0	2016	8	–	–	–	–	0
JP (Jacobie) Adriaanse	EP	2016	12	–	–	–	–	0	2011	26	–	–	–	–	0
LE (Louis) Albertse	EP	2016	2	–	–	–	–	0	2016	2	–	–	–	–	0
L (Lukhanyo) Am	KZN	2016	10	1	–	–	–	5	2016	10	1	–	–	–	5
JC (JC) Astle	EP	2016	15	–	–	–	–	0	2016	15	–	–	–	–	0
MJ (Martin) Bezuidenhout	EP	2016	8	–	–	–	–	0	2011	40	3	–	–	–	15
T (Thembelani) Bholi	EP	2016	9	1	–	–	–	5	2016	9	1	–	–	–	5
T (Tom) Botha	EP	2016	15	–	–	–	–	0	2016	15	–	–	–	–	0
CA (Chris) Cloete	EP	2016	9	4	–	–	–	20	2016	9	4	–	–	–	20
A (Aidon) Davis	EP	2013	10	–	–	–	–	0	2013	10	–	–	–	–	0
PJS (JP) du Plessis	EP	2016	8	1	–	–	–	5	2011	11	1	–	–	–	5
L (Leighton) Eksteen	SWD	2016	5	–	–	–	–	0	2016	5	–	–	–	–	0
JJ (Jacques) Engelbrecht	EP	2013	25	1	–	–	–	5	2013	25	1	–	–	–	5
M (Martin) Ferreira	EP	2016	9	–	–	–	–	0	2016	9	–	–	–	–	0
SJP (Schalk) Ferreira	EP	2013	27	3	–	–	–	15	2007	43	3	–	–	–	15
LD van Z (Louis) Fouché	EP	2016	14	1	17	14	–	81	2012	37	3	22	22	1	128
SE (Shane) Gates	EP	2013	19	1	–	–	–	5	2013	19	1	–	–	–	5
S (Siyanda) Grey	EP	2013	5	–	–	–	–	0	2013	5	–	–	–	–	0
JR (James) Hall	EP	2016	7	2	–	–	–	10	2016	7	2	–	–	–	10
LC (Liam) Hendricks	EP	2016	1	–	–	–	–	0	2016	1	–	–	–	–	0
CN (Cornell) Hess	EP	2016	1	–	–	–	–	0	2016	1	–	–	–	–	0
DD (Dewald) Human	BB	2016	3	1	1	1	–	10	2016	3	1	1	1	–	10
MAE (Malcolm) Jaer	EP	2016	10	2	–	–	–	10	2016	10	2	–	–	–	10
JP (JP) Jonck	EP	2016	1	–	–	–	–	0	2016	1	–	–	–	–	0
NL (Ntando) Kebe	Bor	2016	13	–	–	–	–	0	2016	13	–	–	–	–	0
K (Kevin) Luiters	EP	2016	8	–	–	–	–	0	2016	8	–	–	–	–	0
S (Sintu) Manjezi	EP	2016	2	–	–	–	–	0	2016	2	–	–	–	–	0
E (Edgar) Marutlulle	Leo	2013	17	4	–	–	–	20	2011	25	4	–	–	–	20
WG (Wandile) Mjekevu	KZN	2016	4	3	–	–	–	15	2010	14	7	–	–	–	35
A (Andisa) Ntsila	EP	2016	2	–	–	–	–	0	2016	2	–	–	–	–	0
SW (Schalk) Oelofse	EP	2016	13	–	–	–	–	0	2016	13	–	–	–	–	0
CR (Carlo) Radebe	SWD	2016	1	–	–	–	–	0	2016	1	–	–	–	–	0
SMS (Sti) Sithole	EP	2016	10	–	–	–	–	0	2016	10	–	–	–	–	0
SR (Steven) Sykes	EP	2013	26	5	–	–	–	25	2007	109	14	–	–	–	70
J (Jaco) van Tonder	EP	2016	5	–	–	–	–	0	2013	8	–	–	–	–	0
C-J (CJ) Velleman	EP	2016	10	–	–	–	–	0	2016	10	–	–	–	–	0
PJ (Jurgens) Visser	EP	2016	10	–	–	1	–	3	2013	41	2	0	2	–	16
L (Luzuko) Vulindlu	SWD	2016	11	2	–	–	–	10	2016	11	2	–	–	–	10
JC (Jeremy) Ward	EP	2016	2	–	–	–	–	0	2016	2	–	–	–	–	0
S (Stefan) Watermeyer	EP	2016	12	3	1	–	–	17	2010	26	5	1	–	–	27
EG (Elgar) Watts	EP	2016	11	1	4	6	–	31	2013	30	2	21	22	–	117
S (Stefan) Willemse	EP	2016	11	–	–	–	–	0	2016	11	–	–	–	–	0
TOTALS			401	36	23	22	0	292		657	59	45	47	1	528

Note: EP = Eastern Province Kings, KZN = KwaZulu-Natal, SWD = South Western Disctricts,
Leo = Leopards, Lio = Golden Lions, Bor = Border Bulldogs

APPEARANCES & POINTS

PLAYER	Sharks	Chiefs	Crusaders	Hurricanes	Sunwolves	Bulls	Lions	Jaguares	Blues	Cheetahs	Sharks	Jaguares	Highlanders	Lions	Stormers	Apps	T	C	P	DG	Pts
Visser	15	15	15	15	15	15	–	–	15	15	15	15	–	–	–	10	–	–	1	–	3
Vulindlu	14	14	14	14	–	14	14	11	11	11	11	–	13R	–	–	11	2	–	–	–	10
Du Plessis	13	–	15R	14R	–	14R	11	–	–	13	13	13R	–	–	–	8	1	–	–	–	5
Gates	12	12	12	12	12	–	12	12	12	12c	12	12	12	12	12	14	1	–	–	–	5
Jaer	11	11	11	11	11	11	15	–	–	–	15	15	15	–	–	10	2	–	–	–	10
Watts	10	12R	10R	23R	14R	–	–	10	10	10	13R	–	10	–	10R	11	1	4	6	–	31
Kebe	9	9	9R	9	9	9R	9R	9	9R	9R	9	9	9	–	–	13	–	–	–	–	0
Engelbrecht	8	8	8	8	–	7R	–	–	–	6R	6R	6R	8R	8	–	10	–	–	–	–	0
Bholi	7	7	7	–	–	–	7	7	7	7	7	6	–	–	–	9	1	–	–	–	5
Cloete	6	6	6	8R	8R	6	6	6	6	–	–	–	–	–	–	9	4	–	–	–	20
Astle	5	5	5	5	5	5	5R	5	5	5	4R	5	5	5	5	15	–	–	–	–	0
Sykes	4c	4c	4c	4c	4c	4c	4c	4c	4c	–	4c	4c	4c	–	4c	13	4	–	–	–	20
Botha	3	3R	3R	3R	3R	3	3R	3	3	3	3R	3R	3	3R	3R	15	–	–	–	–	0
Ferreira, M	2	–	2	–	2R	2R	2	2R	2R	2R	2	–	–	–	–	9	–	–	–	–	0
Ferreira, S	1	1	1	–	1R	1R	1	1	–	–	1	1	1	1R	1R	12	2	–	–	–	10
Marutlulle	2R	2	2R	2	2	2	–	2	2	2	–	2	2	2c	2	13	4	–	–	–	20
Sithole	1R	1R	1R	1	1	1	–	–	1	–	–	1R	1	1	–	10	–	–	–	–	0
Albertse	3R	–	–	–	–	–	1R	–	–	–	–	–	–	–	–	2	–	–	–	–	0
Oelofse	4R	5R	5R	4R	5R	4R	5	–	4R	4	5	7R	4R	4	–	13	–	–	–	–	0
Velleman	6R	8R	6R	6	6	7R	8	8	8	–	–	6	–	–	–	10	–	–	–	–	0
Eksteen	9R	–	–	–	–	10R	15R	15R	12R	–	–	–	–	–	–	5	–	–	–	–	0
Fouche	10R	10	10	10	10	10	10	10R	10R	10R	10	10	10R	10	–	14	1	17	14	–	81
Radebe	13R	–	–	–	–	–	–	–	–	–	–	–	–	–	–	1	–	–	–	–	0
Watermeyer	–	13	13	13	13	12	11R	13	13	–	–	13	13	13	13	12	3	1	–	–	17
Adriaanse	–	3	3	3	3	–	3	3R	3R	3R	3	3	–	3	3	12	–	–	–	–	0
Van Tonder	–	15R	–	–	12R	15R	–	15	–	–	11R	–	–	–	–	5	–	–	–	–	0
Luiters	–	9R	9	9R	9R	–	–	–	–	9R	x	9R	9R	9R	–	8	–	–	–	–	0
Bezuidenhout	–	2R	–	2R	–	2R	–	–	–	2R	2R	7R	6R	2R	–	8	–	–	–	–	0
Willemse	–	–	–	7	7	7	–	5R	7R	6R	6	7	7	7	7	11	–	–	–	–	0
Ackerman	–	–	–	1R	–	3R	1R	1R	1R	–	–	1R	1R	3R	–	8	–	–	–	–	0
Grey	–	–	–	14	–	–	–	–	–	–	–	–	–	–	–	1	–	–	–	–	0
Davis	–	–	–	8	8	–	6R	–	8	8	8	8	8	7R	–	9	–	–	–	–	0
Am	–	–	–	–	13	13	14	14	14	14	14	14	14	14	–	10	1	–	–	–	5
Hall	–	–	–	–	9	9	9R	9	9	–	–	–	9	9	–	7	2	–	–	–	10
Hendricks	–	–	–	–	–	–	–	–	–	1	–	–	–	–	–	1	–	–	–	–	0
Jonck	–	–	–	–	–	–	–	–	6	–	–	–	–	–	–	1	–	–	–	–	0
Hess	–	–	–	–	–	–	–	–	5R	–	–	–	–	–	–	1	–	–	–	–	0
Mjekevu	–	–	–	–	–	–	–	–	–	–	11	11	11	11	–	4	3	–	–	–	15
Human	–	–	–	–	–	–	–	–	–	–	15R	–	15R	10	–	3	1	1	1	–	10
Ntsila	–	–	–	–	–	–	–	–	–	–	–	–	6	6	–	2	–	–	–	–	0
Manjezi	–	–	–	–	–	–	–	–	–	–	–	–	4R	5R	–	2	–	–	–	–	0
Ward	–	–	–	–	–	–	–	–	–	–	–	–	13R	15R	–	2	–	–	–	–	0
Penalty try	–	–	–	–	–	–	–	–	–	–	–	–	–	–	–	0	1	–	–	–	5
42 PLAYERS																**344**	**34**	**23**	**22**	**0**	**282**

Records

MATCH RECORDS

Biggest win	12	vs Western Force (22-10)	Port Elizabeth	2013
Heaviest defeat	62	vs Waratahs (10-72)	Port Elizabeth	2013
Highest score	34	vs Highlanders (34-27)	Port Elizabeth	2013
Most points conceded	73	vs Jaguares (27-73)	Buenos Aires	2016
Most tries	4	vs Brumbies (28-28)	Canberra	2013
	4	vs Highlanders (34-27)	Port Elizabeth	2013
	4	vs Sunwolves (33-28)	Port Elizabeth	2016
	4	vs Jaguares (27-73)	Buenos Aires	2016
	4	vs Jaguares (29-22)	Port Elizabeth	2016
Most tries conceded	11	vs Waratahs (10-72)	Port Elizabeth	2013
	11	vs Jaguares (27-73)	Buenos Aires	2016
Most points by a player	15	D Catrakilis vs Rebels (3c, 2p, 1dg)	Melbourne	2013
	15	D Catrakilis vs Cheetahs (5p)	Port Elizabeth	2013
Most tries by a player	2	S Petersen vs Force	Port Elizabeth	2013
	2	CG du Preez vs Brumbies	Canberra	2013
	2	LA Watson vs Highlanders	Port Elizabeth	2013
	2	PW van der Walt vs Bulls	Pretoria	2013
	2	E Maratlulle vs Chiefs	Port Elizabeth	2016
Most conversions by a player	4	D Catrakilis vs Highlanders	Port Elizabeth	2013
Most penalties by a player	5	D Catrakilis vs Cheetahs	Port Elizabeth	2013
Most drop goals by a player	1	D Catrakilis vs Rebels	Melbourne	2013

SEASON RECORDS

Most team points	298	from 16 matches	2013
Most points by a player	142	D Catrakilis	2013
Most team tries	34	from 15 matches	2016
Most tries by a player	6	PW van der Walt	2013
Most conversions by a player	14	D Catrakilis	2013
Most penalties by a player	37	D Catrakilis	2013
Most drop goals by a player	1	D Catrakilis	2013

CAREER RECORDS

Most appearances	27	SJP Ferreira	2013-2016
Most points	142	D Catrakilis	2013
Most tries	6	PW van der Walt	2013
Most conversions	14	D Catrakilis	2013
Most penalties	37	D Catrakilis	2013
Most drop goals	1	D Catrakilis	2013

Edgar Marutlulle fought hard throughout a challenging 2016 season for the Kings.

DHL Stormers

Ground: Newlands **Capacity:** 49 000
Address: 11 Boundary Road, Newlands, Cape Town **Telephone Number:** 021-659 4500
Colours: Navy blue jersey, shorts and socks **Website:** www.iamastormer.com
Coach: Robbie Fleck **Captain:** Juan de Jongh
CEO: Gavin Lewis **Chairman:** Sam Dube **President:** Thelo Wakefield

---

Head Coach: Robbie Fleck **Forwards Coach:** Russel Winter
Backline Coach: Paul Treu **Defence Coach:** Jacques Nienaber
Doctor: Dr Jason Suter **Strenght & Conditioning:** Stephan du Toit
Kicking Coach: Vlok Cilliers **Physiotherapist:** Wayne Hector
Masseur: Greg Daniels **Media Officer:** Howard Kahn
Video Analyst: Human Kriek **Manager:** Chippie Solomon
Mental Skills Coach: Henning Gericke

1996	1997	1998	1999	2000	2001	2002	2003	2004	2005	2006
11th		9th	2nd	5th	7th	7th	9th	3rd	9th	11th

2007	2008	2009	2010	2011	2012	2013	2014	2015	2016
10th	5th	10th	2nd	2nd	1st	7th	11th	3rd	3rd

Played	Won	Lost	Drawn	Points for	Points against	Tries for	Tries against
16	10	5	1	461	337	52	36

Date	Venue	Opponent	Result	Score	Referee	Scorers
Febr 27	Cape Town	Bulls	WON	33-09	C Joubert	T: Du Preez, Etzebeth, Ntubeni. C: Du Preez (3). P: Du Preez (4).
Mrch 05	Bloemfontein	Cheetahs	WON	20-10	C Joubert	T: Zas, Notshe. C: du Preez, Coleman. P: Coleman (2).
Mrch 12	Cape Town	Sharks	LOST	13-18	M Fraser	T: Zas. C: Coleman. P: Coleman (2).
Mrch 19	Cape Town	Brumbies	WON	31-11	J Peyper	T: Kolisi, Leyds, Koch. C: Coleman, Du Plessis. P: Coleman (4).
Mrch 26	Buenos Aires	Jaguares	WON	13-08	C Pollock	T: Kolbe. C: Coleman. P: Coleman (2).
April 08	Cape Town	Sunwolves	WON	46-19	N Berry	T: Notshe (2), Kolbe, Van Wyk, Schreuder, Ntubeni, Du Plessis. C: Du Plessis (4). P: Du Plessis.
April 16	Johannesburg	Lions	LOST	22-29	S Berry	T: Kolisi. C: Du Plessis. P: Du Plessis (5).
April 23	Cape Town	Reds	WON	40-22	M v/d Westhuizen	T: Van Wyk, Zas, Groom, Koch. C: Du Plessis (3), Thomson. P: Thomson (3), Du Plessis.
April 30	Cape Town	Waratahs	LOST	30-32	M Fraser	T: Du Toit (2), Burger. C: Du Plessis (3). P: Du Plessis (3)
May 14	Singapore	Sunwolves	DREW	17-17	P Williams	T: Du Toit, Koch. C: Du Plessis, Thomson. P: Du Plessis.
May 21	Pretoria	Bulls	LOST	13-17	B O'Keeffe	T: De Allende. C: Du Plessis. P: Du Plessis (2).
May 28	Cape Town	Cheetahs	WON	31-27	G Jackson	T: D du Plessis, Van Wyk, Zas. C: Du Plessis (2). P: Du Plessis (4).
July 02	Melbourne	Rebels	WON	57-31	A Gardner	T: De Allende, Etzebeth, J-L du Plessis, Zas, Groom, Ntubeni, Koch. C: Du Plessis (5). P: Du Plessis (4)
July 09	Perth	Force	WON	22-03	M Fraser	T: Van Wyk (2), Kolisi. C: Du Plessis (2). P: Du Plessis.
July 16	Cape Town	Kings	WON	52-24	J Peyper	T: Jones (4), Zas (3), Thomson. C: Du Plessis (3), Thomson (3).

QUARTER-FINAL

Date	Venue	Opponent	Result	Score	Referee	Scorers
July 23	Cape Town	Cheetahs	LOST	21-60	J Peyper	T: Koch (2), Carr. C: Du Preez (2), Thomson

2016 SQUAD

PLAYER	Union	Debut	STORMERS CAREER						Debut	SUPER RUGBY CAREER					
			M	T	C	P	DG	Pts		M	T	C	P	DG	Pts
SWP (Schalk) Burger	WP	2004	123	9	–	–	–	45	2004	123	9	–	–	–	45
N (Nizaam) Carr	WP	2012	67	6	–	–	–	30	2012	67	6	–	–	–	30
KK (Kurt) Coleman	WP	2011	35	2	25	38	1	177	2011	35	2	25	38	1	177
D (Damian) de Allende	WP	2013	55	10	–	–	–	50	2013	55	10	–	–	–	50
JL (Juan) de Jongh	WP	2010	93	15	–	–	–	75	2010	93	15	–	–	–	75
JC (Jan) de Klerk	WP	2015	2	–	–	–	–	0	2015	2	–	–	–	–	0
D (Daniel) du Plessis	WP	2016	3	1	–	–	–	5	2016	3	1	–	–	–	5
J-L (Jean-Luc) du Plessis	WP	2016	12	2	26	22	–	128	2016	12	2	26	22	–	128
RJ (Robert) du Preez	WP	2015	4	1	6	4	–	29	2015	4	1	6	4	–	29
PS (Pieter-Steph) du Toit	WP	2016	14	3	–	–	–	15	2012	41	3	–	–	–	15
R (Rynhardt) Elstadt	WP	2011	52	–	–	–	–	0	2011	52	–	–	–	–	0
E (Eben) Etzebeth	WP	2012	42	4	–	–	–	20	2012	42	4	–	–	–	20
NJ (Nick) Groom	WP	2011	57	5	–	–	–	25	2011	57	5	–	–	–	25
JC (JC) Janse van Rensburg	WP	2016	11	–	–	–	–	0	2008	64	1	–	–	–	5
HRF (Huw) Jones	WP	2015	23	5	–	–	–	25	2015	23	5	–	–	–	25
OR (Oliver) Kebble	WP	2014	34	1	–	–	–	5	2014	34	1	–	–	–	5
J (Jean) Kleyn	WP	2014	18	–	–	–	–	0	2014	18	–	–	–	–	0
VP (Vincent) Koch	Mpu	2015	33	7	–	–	–	35	2015	33	6	–	–	–	35
C (Cheslin) Kolbe	WP	2014	35	3	–	–	–	15	2014	35	3	–	–	–	15
S (Siya) Kolisi	WP	2012	76	8	–	–	–	40	2012	76	8	–	–	–	40
J-B (Johnny) Kotze	WP	2015	19	1	–	–	–	5	2015	19	1	–	–	–	5
DY (Dillyn) Leyds	WP	2015	19	7	–	–	–	35	2014	22	7	–	–	–	35
WM (Wilco) Louw	WP	2015	3	–	–	–	–	0	2015	3	–	–	–	–	0
JF (Frans) Malherbe	WP	2011	66	2	–	–	–	10	2011	66	2	–	–	–	10
GHD (Godlen) Masimla	WP	2015	2	–	–	–	–	0	2015	2	–	–	–	–	0
MT (Bongi) Mbonambi	WP	2015	30	–	–	–	–	0	2012	45	–	–	–	–	0
S (Sikhumbuzo) Notshe	WP	2014	23	5	–	–	–	25	2014	23	5	–	–	–	25
S (Scarra) Ntubeni	WP	2011	45	4	–	–	–	20	2011	45	4	–	–	–	20
JD (JD) Schickerling	WP	2016	13	–	–	–	–	–	2016	13	–	–	–	–	–
L (Louis) Schreuder	WP	2011	66	2	–	–	–	10	2011	66	2	–	–	–	10
JP (JP) Smith	WP	2016	3	–	–	–	–	–	2010	27	–	–	–	–	0
JJ (Jaco) Taute	WP	2013	23	1	–	–	1	8	2010	54	10	–	2	1	59
BT (Brendon) Thomson	WP	2016	6	1	6	3	–	26	2016	6	1	6	3	–	26
SA (Scott) van Breda	WP	2016	3	–	–	–	–	0	2016	3	–	–	–	–	0
JJ (Kobus) van Dyk	WP	2016	1	–	–	–	–	–	2016	1	–	–	–	–	0
JP (Kobus) van Wyk	WP	2014	30	9	–	–	–	45	2014	30	9	–	–	–	45
CM (Chris) van Zyl	WP	2016	1	–	–	–	–	0	2016	1	–	–	–	–	0
AF (Allistair) Vermaak	WP	2014	21	–	–	–	–	0	2014	21	–	–	–	–	0
J (Jano) Vermaak	WP	2016	4	–	–	–	–	0	2006	108	17	3	4	–	103
ME (Michael) Willemse	WP	2014	4	–	–	–	–	0	2014	4	–	–	–	–	0
LL (Leolin) Zas	WP	2016	15	8	–	–	–	40	2016	15	8	–	–	–	40
TOTALS			1186	114	63	67	2	943		1443	140	66	73	2	1102

Note: WP = Western Province, Mpu = Mpumalanga

APPEARANCES & POINTS

PLAYER	Bulls	Cheetahs	Sharks	Brumbies	Jaguares	Sunwolves	Lions	Reds	Waratahs	Sunwolves	Bulls	Cheetahs	Rebels	Force	Kings	Chiefs	Apps	T	C	P	DG	Pts
Kolbe	15	15	15	15	15	15	15	15	15	15	15	15	–	–	–	–	12	1	–	–	–	5
Van Wyk	14	–	–	14	14	14	14	14	14	14	14	14	14	14	14	14	14	5	–	–	–	25
Kotze	13	13	13	13	13	13	13	13	–	14	13	x	–	–	–	–	10	–	–	–	–	0
De Jongh	12c	12c	12c	12c	12c	12c	12c	–	13c	13c	–	–	–	–	–	–	9	1	–	–	–	5
Leyds	11	14	14	11	–	–	–	–	–	–	–	–	–	–	–	–	4	1	–	–	–	5
Du Preez	10	10	–	–	–	–	–	–	–	–	–	–	–	–	–	10	3	1	6	4	–	29
Vermaak, J	9	9	9	–	–	–	–	–	–	–	–	–	–	–	9R	–	4	–	–	–	–	0
Carr	8	8	6	6	8	8R	6	8	6	8	6	6	6	–	–	20R	14	1	–	–	–	5
Burger	7	7	8	8	7R	8	8	6R	8	4R	8	–	8c	8c	8c	8c	15	1	–	–	–	5
Notshe	6	6	7R	7R	6	6	7	6	7	8R	6R	8	6R	6	6	6	16	3	–	–	–	15
Du Toit	5	5	5	5	–	5	5	5	5	5	5	5	5	5	–	5	14	3	–	–	–	15
Etzebeth	4	4	4	4	4	–	–	–	–	4	4	4	4	–	4	–	10	2	–	–	–	10
Koch	3	3	3R	3R	3R	3	3	3	3R	3R	3R	3R	3	3	3	3	16	6	–	–	–	30
Mbonambi	2	2	2	2	2R	2R	2	2	2	2R	2	2	2	2	2R	2	16	–	–	–	–	0
Kebble	1	1	1R	1R	1R	1	1R	1	1R	1R	1	1	1	–	–	1R	14	–	–	–	–	0
Ntubeni	2R	2R	2R	2R	2	2	–	–	2R	2	2R	2R	2R	2R	2	2R	14	3	–	–	–	15
Janse van Rensburg	1R	1R	1	1	1	1R	1	1R	1	1	–	–	–	–	1R	–	11	–	–	–	–	0
Malherbe	3R	3R	3	3	3	3R	3R	–	3	3	3c	3c	–	–	–	3R	12	–	–	–	–	0
Schickerling	5R	5R	5R	4R	5	4	4	4R	4R	4	–	x	5R	5R	–	5R	13	–	–	–	–	0
Kolisi	6R	8R	7	7	7	7	8R	7	8R	7	7	7	7	7	6R	7	16	3	–	–	–	15
Groom	9R	9R	9R	9	9	–	9	9	9	9R	9	9	9	9	–	9	14	2	–	–	–	10
Coleman	12R	10R	10	10	10	–	–	–	–	–	–	–	–	–	–	–	5	–	4	10	–	38
Zas	14R	11	11	13R	11	11	11	11	11	–	11	11	11	11	11	11	15	8	–	–	–	40
Jones	–	13R	13R	–	11R	15R	x	14R	x	x	13R	–	13R	13	13	–	9	4	–	–	–	20
Du Plessis, J-L	–	–	x	10R	10R	10	10	10	10	10	10	10	10	10	10	–	12	2	26	22	–	128
Schreuder	–	–	–	9R	9R	9	9R	9R	9R	9	x	15R	9R	9R	9	9R	12	1	–	–	–	5
De Klerk	–	–	–	–	5R	–	–	–	–	–	–	–	–	–	–	–	1	–	–	–	–	0
Elstadt	–	–	–	–	4R	4R	4	4	6	4R	8R	7R	7R	7	–	7R	11	–	–	–	–	0
De Allende	–	–	–	–	13R	13R	12c	12	12	12	12	12	12	12	12	12	11	2	–	–	–	10
Masimla	–	–	–	–	9R	–	–	–	–	–	–	–	–	–	–	–	1	–	–	–	–	0
Willemse	–	–	–	–	2R	2R	–	–	–	–	–	–	–	–	–	–	2	–	–	–	–	0
Thomson	–	–	–	–	–	10R	10R	10R	x	11R	–	–	–	–	10R	10R	6	1	6	3	–	26
Smith	–	–	–	–	–	x	–	–	–	–	3R	3R	3R	–	–	–	3	–	–	–	–	0
Vermaak, A	–	–	–	–	–	–	–	–	1R	1R	1R	1	1	1	–	–	6	–	–	–	–	0
Du Plessis, D	–	–	–	–	–	–	–	–	–	–	13	13	13	–	–	–	3	1	–	–	–	5
Taute	–	–	–	–	–	–	–	–	–	–	–	–	15	15	15	15	4	–	–	–	–	0
Van Breda	–	–	–	–	–	–	–	–	–	–	–	13R	15R	14R	–	–	3	–	–	–	–	0
Louw	–	–	–	–	–	–	–	–	–	–	–	–	3R	–	–	–	1	–	–	–	–	0
Van Zyl	–	–	–	–	–	–	–	–	–	–	–	–	–	5	–	–	1	–	–	–	–	0
Kleyn	–	–	–	–	–	–	–	–	–	–	–	–	–	4	–	–	1	–	–	–	–	0
Van Dyk	–	–	–	–	–	–	–	–	–	–	–	–	–	7R	–	–	1	–	–	–	–	0
41 players																	359	52	42	39	0	461

Records

MATCH RECORDS

Biggest winning margin	38	vs Lions (56-18)	Cape Town	2009
Heaviest defeat	61	vs Bulls (14-75)	Pretoria	2005
Highest score	56	vs Lions (56-18)	Cape Town	2009
Most points conceded	75	vs Bulls (14-75)	Pretoria	2005
Most tries	8	vs Blues (51-23)	Auckland	2004
	8	vs Lions (56-18)	Cape Town	2009
Most tries conceded	11	vs Blues (28-74)	Auckland	1998
Most points by a player	28	AJJ van Straaten (1t 4c 5p) vs Hurricanes	Cape Town	2000
Most tries by a player	4	HRF Jones vs Kings	Cape Town	2016
Most conversions by a player	6	PJ Grant vs W Force	Cape Town	2011
Most penalties by a player	7	JT Stransky vs Transvaal (for WP)	Johannesburg	1996
	7	AJJ van Straaten vs Bulls	Pretoria	1999
	7	PJ Grant vs Crusaders	Cape Town	2010
	7	PJ Grant vs Cheetahs	Cape Town	2011
Most drop goals by a player	2	PC Montgomery vs Cats	Johannesburg	2000

SEASON RECORDS

Most team points	461	in 16 matches	2016
Most points by a player	170	JC Pietersen	2013
	170	D Catrakilis	2015
Most team tries	52	in 16 matches	2016
Most tries by a player	11	PWG Rossouw	2002
Most conversions by a player	26	J-L du Preez	2016
Most penalties by a player	44	JC Pietersen	2013
Most drop goals by a player	2	PC Montgomery	2000

CAREER RECORDS

Most appearances	123	SWP Burger	2004-2016
Most points	866	PJ Grant	2006-2014
Most tries	35	BJ Paulse	1998-2007
Most conversions	126	PJ Grant	2006-2014
Most penalties	188	PJ Grant	2006-2014
Most drop goals	2	PC Montgomery	1996-2002

Sikhumbuzo Notshe represented SA A in 2016 on the back of a solid season with the Stormers.

Blues

Ground: Eden Park **Capacity:** 46 500 **Address:** Walters Road, Mount Eden, Auckland
Telephone number: +64 9 815 4850 **Colours:** Blue with navy sleeves and white piping,
blue shorts and socks **Website:** www.theblues.co.nz
Captain: James Parsons **CEO:** Michael Redman **Chairman:** Tony Carter
Coach: Tana Umaga

Head Coach: Tana Umaga **Assistant Coaches:** Alastair Rogers, Paul Feeney & Glenn Moore
Mental Skills: Kylie Wilson **Scrum Coach:** Nick White
Strength & Conditioning: Jason Price **Doctor:** Dr Stephen Kara
Physiotherapist: Mark Plummer **Analyst:** Troy Webber
Manager: Richard Fry **Media Officer:** Ian Heppenstall

1996	1997	1998	1999	2000	2001	2002	2003	2004	2005	2006
2nd	1st	1st	9th	6th	11th	6th	1st	5th	7th	8th

2007	2008	2009	2010	2011	2012	2013	2014	2015	2016
4th	6th	9th	7th	4th	12th	10th	10th	14th	11th

Played	Won	Lost	Drawn	Points for	Points against	Tries for	Tries against
15	8	6	1	374	380	45	47

Date	Venue	Opponent	Result	Score	Referee	Scorers
Febr 26	Auckland	Highlanders	WON	33-31	G Jackson	T: Gibson, Nanai, Tuipoluto. C: West (3). P: West (4).
Mrch 04	Christchurch	Crusaders	LOST	13-28	P Williams	T: Li. C: West. P: McGahan, West.
Mrch 11	Auckland	Hurricanes	LOST	19-23	N Briant	T: Ranger, Moala. P: West (3)
Mrch 19	Brisbane	Reds	DREW	25-25	A Lees	T: Hall, West, Guyton. C: West (2). P: West (2).
April 02	Albany	Jaguares	WON	24-16	M Fraser	T: Luatua, West. C: West. P: West (4).
April 08	Hamilton	Chiefs	LOST	23-29	J Nutbrown	T: Nanai, R Ioane. C:West (2). P: West (3).
April 16	Auckland	Sharks	WON	23-18	J Peyper	T: Moala, R Ioane. C: West (2). P: West (3).
April 30	Auckland	Rebels	WON	36-30	C Joubert	T: Faumuina, West, Parsons, Kaino, Visinia, Li. C: West (2), Francis.
May 07	Port Elizabeth	Kings	WON	34-18	F Anselmi	T: Nanai (2), Parsons, Li, Guyton. C: West (3). P: West.
May 14	Johannesburg	Lions	LOST	05-43	J van Heerden	T: Pryor.
May 21	Perth	Force	WON	17-13	J Nutbrown	T: Kaino, Li. C: West (2). P: West.
May 28	Auckland	Crusaders	LOST	21-26	A Gardner	T: West, Moala. C: West. P: West (2), Francis.
July 02	Wellington	Hurricanes	LOST	27-37	C Pollock	T: Kaino, Pryor. C: Francis. P: Francis.
July 08	Auckland	Brumbies	WON	40-15	B O'Keeffe	T: Kaino (2), Duffie (2), Prattley, Parsons. C: Francis (5).
July 15	Auckland	Waratahs	WON	34-28	M Fraser	T: Moala, Nanai, Tuipolutou, Francis, Penalty try. C: Francis (3). P: Francis.

Note: ■ = *Champion*

2016 SQUAD

PLAYER	Date of Birth	Height	Weight	M	T	C	P	DG	Pts
J.J.G. (Josh) Bekhuis	26/04/86	2,00	115	110	2	–	–	–	10
G (Gerard) Cowley-Tuitoti	16/06/92	1,96	110	1	–	–	–	–	0
M (Matt) Duffie	16/08/90	1,92	90	7	2	–	–	–	10
JR (Joe) Edwards	21/09/93	1,94	108	8	–	–	–	–	0
CC (Charlie) Faumuina	24/12/86	1,86	125	86	5	–	–	–	25
PG (Piers) Francis	20/06/90	1,88	92	11	1	12	4	–	41
BT (Blake) Gibson	19/04/95	1,86	102	13	1	–	–	–	5
B-JA (Billy) Guyton	17/03/90	1,87	91	16	2	–	–	–	10
BD (Bryn) Hall	03/02/92	1,83	89	32	4	–	–	–	20
AL (Akira) Ioane	15/06/95	1,94	111	17	1	–	–	–	5
R (Rieko) Ioane	18/03/97	1,88	103	5	2	–	–	–	10
J (Jerome) Kaino	06/04/83	1,96	110	119	14	–	–	–	70
TD (Tanerau) Latimer	06/05/86	1,86	111	118	10	–	–	–	50
T (Tevita) Li	23/03/95	1,82	95	30	7	–	–	–	35
DS (Steven) Luatua	29/04/91	1,96	115	63	7	–	–	–	35
QJRWJ (Quentin) MacDonald	25/09/88	1,81	102	56	1	–	–	–	5
M (Matt) McGahan	21/04/93	1,85	91	12	1	–	1	–	8
S (Sione) Mafileo	14/04/93	1,78	120	9	–	–	–	–	0
H (Hoani) Matenga	13/04/87	1,95	106	9	–	–	–	–	0
NJ (Nick) Mayhew	28/11/88	1,8	112	11	–	–	–	–	0
G (George) Moala	05/11/90	1,88	99	53	17	–	–	–	85
MG (Matt) Moulds	15/05/91	1,88	107	4	–	–	–	–	0
MH (Melani) Nanai-Vai	03/08/93	1,94	90	24	8	–	–	–	40
SJ (Sam) Nock	18/06/96	1,78	85	1	–	–	–	–	0
JN (James) Parsons	27/11/86	1,85	110	64	5	–	–	–	25
SMJ (Sam) Prattley	16/01/90	1,96	116	33	1	–	–	–	5
K (Kara) Pryor	02/04/91	1,89	104	13	2	–	–	–	10
JD (Jack) Ram	14/01/87	1,83	100	2	–	–	–	–	0
RMN (Rene) Ranger	30/09/86	1,82	96	72	26	–	–	–	130
M (Male) Sa'u	13/10/87	1,82	100	18	–	–	–	–	0
SN (Scott) Scrafton	18/04/93	2,00	114	1	–	–	–	–	0
P (Patrick) Tuipulotu	23/01/93	1,98	120	34	5	–	–	–	25
AOHM (Ofa) Tu'ungafasi	19/04/92	1,95	120	43	–	–	–	–	0
MD (Matt) Vaega	07/09/94	1,78	89	5	1	–	–	–	5
L (Lolagi) Visina	17/01/93	1,92	103	33	8	1	–	–	42
NT (Namatahi) Waa	24/09/90	1,88	130	3	–	–	–	–	0
IT (Ihaia) West	16/01/92	1,75	84	37	7	45	53	–	286
					140	58	58	0	992

APPEARANCES & POINTS

PLAYER	Highlanders	Crusaders	Hurricanes	Reds	Jaguares	Chiefs	Sharks	Rebels	Kings	Lions	Force	Crusaders	Hurricanes	Brumbies	Waratahs	Apps	T	C	P	DG	Pts
Visinia	15	–	15	15	15	–	15	15	15	15	14R	14R	–	11R	11R	12	1	–	–	–	5
Nanai	14	14	14R	–	–	15	–	–	14	14	15	15	15	15	15	11	5	–	–	–	25
Sa'u	13	13R	13	13	–	–	–	–	12R	13R	13R	13R	13	13	13	11	–	–	–	–	0
Moala	12	12	12	12	12R	12R	13R	13	13	13	13	13	–	–	13R	13	4	–	–	–	20
Li	11	11	11	11	11	11	11	11	11	11	11	11	11	11	11	15	4	–	–	–	20
West	10	10R	10	10	10	10	10	10	10	10	10	10	10	10	10	15	4	19	24	–	130
Hall	9	9R	9	9	9	9	9	9	9	9	9	9R	9R	9	9	15	1	–	–	–	5
Luatua	8	8	4	8	8	8	8	8	8	8	8	8	8	8	8	15	1	–	–	–	5
Gibson	7	7	7	7	7	7	–	–	–	–	–	8R	7R	7R		9	1	–	–	–	5
Edwards	6	–	–	6R	6	–	–	–	6R	–	–	–	–	–		4	–	–	–	–	0
Bekhuis	5	5	5	5	5	5	5	5	5	–	4	5	5	5	5	14	–	–	–	–	0
Tuipulotu	4	4	8R	4	4	–	–	4	4	5	5	4	4	4	4	13	2	–	–	–	10
Mafileo	3	3	x	3R	–	–	–	–	–	–	3R	1R	3R	3R	–	7	–	–	–	–	0
Parsons	2c	2R	2	2	2	2c	2c	2c	2c	2c	2c	2c	2c	2c	2c	15	3	–	–	–	15
Tu'ungafasi	1	1	1	1	3R	3R	3R	3R	3	3R	1	3R	3	3	3	15	–	–	–	–	0
MacDonald	2R	2	2R	2R	2R	2R	2R	2R	–	2R	2R	2R	2R	–		13	–	–	–	–	0
Waa	x	–	–	–	1R	1R	–	–	–	–	1R	–	–			3	–	–	–	–	0
Faumuina	3R	3R	3	3	3	3	3	3	3R	3	3	–	–	3R		13	1	–	–	–	5
Ioane, A	6R	4R	8	8	8R	6R	4R	6R	–	–	–	–	–	–		8	–	–	–	–	0
Pryor	8R	8R	7R	–	–	4R	7R	7R	7R	7R	7R	7	7	7	7	13	2	–	–	–	10
Guyton	9R	9	–	9R	9R	9R	9R	9R	9R	9R	9	9	9R	9R	9R	14	2	–	–	–	10
McGahan	15R	10	11R	12R	x	13R	11R	10R	10R	15R	–	–	12R	–	–	10	–	–	1	–	3
Ranger	13R	13	14	–	13	13	13	–	–	–	–	–	–	–	–	6	1	–	–	–	5
Duffie	–	15	–	–	–	–	15R	–	–	14	14	14	14	14		7	2	–	–	–	10
Kaino	–	6c	6c	6c	–	6	6	6	6	6	6	6	6	6	6	13	6	–	–	–	30
Prattley	–	x	–	1R	1	1	1	1	1	–	1	1	1			10	1	–	–	–	5
Nock	–	–	9R	–	–	–	–	–	–	–	–	–	–			1	–	–	–	–	0
Mayhew	–	–	x	1R	1	–	–	1R	1R	1R	1R	–	1R	1R		8	–	–	–	–	0
Ioane, R	–	–	–	14	14	14	14	14	–	–	–	–	–	–		5	2	–	–	–	10
Matenga	–	–	–	4R	4R	4	4	–	5R	4	4R	4R	5R	–	–	9	–	–	–	–	0
Francis	–	–	–	12	12	12	12	12	12	12	12	12	12	12	12	11	1	12	4	–	41
Latimer	–	–	–	–	–	7	7	7	7	7	–	–	–	–		5	–	–	–	–	0
Moulds	–	–	–	–	–	–	2R	–	–	–	–	–	–	2R		2	–	–	–	–	0
Ram	–	–	–	–	–	–	–	–	7R	–	–	–	–			1	–	–	–	–	0
Vaega	–	–	–	–	–	–	–	–	–	13R	12R	–	–			2	–	–	–	–	0
Cowley-Tuitoti	–	–	–	–	–	–	–	–	–	–	4R	–	–			1	–	–	–	–	0
Scrafton	–	–	–	–	–	–	–	–	–	–	4R	–				1	–	–	–	–	0
Penalty try	–	–	–	–	–	–	–	–	–	–	–	–	–	–		–	1	–	–	–	5
37 PLAYERS																340	45	31	29	0	374

Records

CHAMPIONS: 1996, 1997, 2003

MATCH RECORDS

Biggest winning margin	53	vs Hurricanes (60-7)	Wellington	2002
Heaviest defeat	47	vs Crusaders (12-59)	Christchurch	2012
Highest score	74	vs Stormers (74-28)	Auckland	1998
Most points conceded	63	vs Chiefs (34-63)	Hamilton	2009
Most tries	11	vs Stormers (74-28)	Auckland	1998
Most tries conceded	9	vs Chiefs (34-63)	Hamilton	2009
Most points by a player	29	GW Anscombe (2t, 2c, 5p) vs Bulls	Pretoria	2012
Most tries by a player	4	J Vidiri vs Bulls	Auckland	2000
	4	DC Howlett vs Hurricanes	Wellington	2002
	4	JM Muliaina vs Bulls	Auckland	2002
Most conversions by a player	7	AR Cashmore vs Stormers	Auckland	1998
	7	AR Cashmore vs Bulls	Auckland	2000
	7	CJ Spencer vs Bulls	Auckland	2002
Most penalties by a player	6	AR Cashmore vs Chiefs	Auckland	1998
	6	AR Cashmore vs Hurricanes	Auckland	1999
	6	JA Arlidge vs Bulls	Auckland	2001
	6	SA Brett vs Bulls	Auckland	2010
	6	C Noakes vs Stormers	Albany	2013
	6	I West vs Chiefs	Albany	2015
Most drop goals by a player	1	on eleven occasions		

SEASON RECORDS

Most team points	513	in 13 matches	1997
Most points by a player	180	AR Cashmore	1998
Most team tries	70	in 13 matches	1996
Most tries by a player	12	DC Howlett	2003
Most conversions by a player	34	AR Cashmore	1998
Most penalties by a player	34	AR Cashmore	1999
Most drop goals by a player	2	O Ai'i	2000
	2	SA Brett	2010

CAREER RECORDS

Most appearances	164	KF Mealamu	2000-2014
Most points	619	AR Cashmore	1996-2000
Most tries	55	DC Howlett	1999-2007
Most conversions	120	CJ Spencer	1996-2005
Most penalties	114	AR Cashmore	1996-2000
Most drop goals	3	CJ Spencer	1996-2005

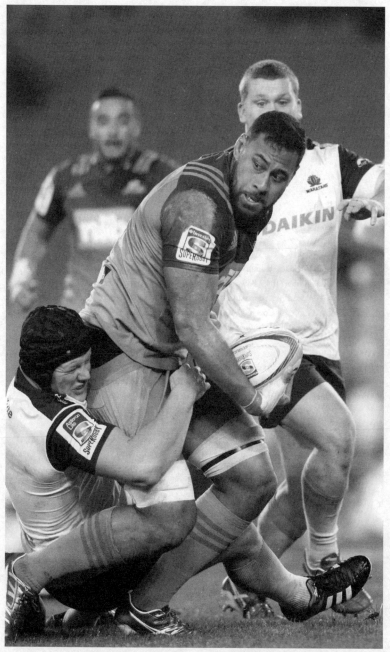

Patrick Tuipulotu was a regular member of the All Black squad by the end of 2016.

Chiefs

Ground: Waikato Stadium **Capacity:** 25 000 **Address:** Seddon Road, Hamilton
Telephone number: +64 7 839 5675 **Colours:** Black jersey with red and yellow panels.
Black shorts and socks **Website:** www.chiefs.co.nz
Coach: Dave Rennie **Captain:** Sam Cane
CEO: Andrew Flexman **Chairman:** Dallas Fisher

Head Coach: Dave Rennie **Assistant Coaches:** Neil Barnes, Kieran Keane & Andrew Strawbridge
Strength & Conditioning Coach: Phil Healey **Video Analyst:** Regan Hall
Doctor: Dr Kevin Bell **Physiotherapist:** Kevin McQuoid & Mike Lovell
Manager: Stewart Williams **Media Officer:** Kylie Sousa

1996	1997	1998	1999	2000	2001	2002	2003	2004	2005	2006
6th	11th	7th	6th	10th	6th	8th	10th	4th	6th	7th

2007	2008	2009	2010	2011	2012	2013	2014	2015	2016
6th	7th	2nd	11th	10th	2nd	1st	5th	5th	6th

Played	Won	Lost	Drawn	Points for	Points against	Tries for	Tries against
17	12	5	0	560	387	76	45

Date	Venue	Opponent	Result	Score	Referee	Scorers
Febr 27	Christchurch	Crusaders	WON	27-21	C Pollock	T: Cane, Tamanivalu, Stevenson, McKenzie. C: McKenzie (2). P: McKenzie .
Mrch 05	Hamilton	Lions	LOST	32-36	A Lees	T: McKenzie, Lowe, Sanders, Weber. C: McKenzie (3). P: McKenzie (2).
Mrch 12	Port Elizabeth	Kings	WON	58-24	J van Heerden	T: Cane (2), Cruden, Ngatai, McKenzie, Fisiiahi, Seu. C: McKenzie (7). P: McKenzie (3).
Mrch 19	Buenos Aires	Jaguares	WON	30-26	C Pollock	T: Weber, McKenzie, Lowe, McNichol. C: McKenzie (2). P: Cruden, McKenzie.
Mrch 26	Hamilton	Force	WON	53-10	M Fraser	T: Ngatai (4), McKenzie (2), Lowe, Leitch, Pulu. C: McKenzie (3), Donald.
April 02	Canberra	Brumbies	WON	48-23	A Gardner	T: Lowe (2), Pulu, Weber, Sanders, McKenzie. C: McKenzie (3). P: Mckenzie (3).
April 08	Hamilton	Blues	WON	29-23	J Nutbrown	T: Cruden, Retallick, Graham, Tamanivalu, Stevenson. C: Mckenzie (2).
April 23	Wellington	Hurricanes	WON	28-27	C Joubert	T: Tamanivalu (2), Leitch, Seu. C: McKenzie (4).
April 29	New Plymouth	Sharks	WON	24-22	C Pollock	T: Tamanivalu, Leitch. C: Cruden. P: Cruden (4).
May 07	Hamilton	Highlanders	LOST	13-26	A Gardner	T: Cruden, Vaka. P: Cruden.
May 21	Hamilton	Rebels	WON	36-15	A Gardner	T: Tamanivalu, Pulu, Harris, Cruden, Horrell. C: Cruden (3), McKenzie. P: Cruden.
May 27	Sydney	Waratahs	LOST	25-45	J Peyper	T: Cruden, Harris, Tamanivalu, Pulu. C: McKenzie. P: McKenzie.
July 01	Suva	Crusaders	WON	23-13	A Lees	T: Lowe, Weber. C: McKenzie (2). P: McKenzie (3).
July 08	Brisbane	Reds	WON	50-05	N Briant	T: McKenzie (2), Tamanivalu (2), Moli, Harris, Cane, Penalty try. C: McKenzie (5).
July 16	Dunedin	Highlanders	LOST	15-25	G Jackson	T: Boshier, Pulu. C: McKenzie. P: McKenzie.

QUARTER-FINAL

Date	Venue	Opponent	Result	Score	Referee	Scorers
July 23	Cape Town	Chiefs	WON	60-21	J Peyper	T: Weber, McKenzie, Elliott, Lowe, McNichol, Kerr-Barlow, Koloamatangi, Sanders. C: McKenzie (7). P: McKenzie (2)

SEMI-FINAL

Date	Venue	Opponent	Result	Score	Referee	Scorers
July 30	Wellington	Hurricanes	LOST	09-25	A Gardner	P: McKenzie (3)

Note: ■ = Champion

2016 SQUAD

PLAYER	Province	Date of Birth	Height	Weight	M	T	C	P	DG	Pts
MG (Michael) Allardice		19/10/91	2,00	112	17	–	–	–	–	0
JM (Johan) Bardoul		16/06/87	1,92	112	11	–	–	–	–	0
DJ (Dominic) Bird		09/04/91	2,06	119	41	–	–	–	–	0
LS (Lachlan) Boshier		16/11/94	1,90	102	7	1	–	–	–	5
M (Mitchell) Brown		15/08/93	1,93	110	2	–	–	–	–	0
SJ (Sam) Cane		13/01/92	1,89	104	82	11	–	–	–	55
AW (Aaron) Cruden		08/01/89	1,78	82	96	16	110	150	–	750
SR (Stephen) Donald		03/12/83	1,90	98	90	19	151	153	1	859
HTP (Hika) Elliot		22/12/86	1,86	115	115	8	–	–	–	40
GV (Glen) Fisi'iahi		02/12/90	1,84	92	3	1	–	–	–	5
S (Siegfried) Fisi'ihoi		08/06/89	1,85	122	10	1	–	–	–	5
MB (Mitchell) Graham		30/01/91	1,87	122	25	1	–	–	–	5
KS (Kane) Hames		28/08/88	1,84	120	29	1	–	–	–	5
KW (Kayne) Hammington		24/09/90	1,70	75	5	–	–	–	–	0
NP (Nathan) Harris		08/03/92	1,86	110	23	3	–	–	–	15
ST (Sam) Henwood		28/03/91	1,86	104	2	–	–	–	–	0
AA (Andrew) Horrell		18/07/86	1,82	93	54	4	8	6	–	54
TNJ (Tawera) Kerr-Barlow		15/08/90	1,87	90	67	7	–	–	–	35
TMPM (Tevita) Koloamatangi		07/09/88	1,89	105	9	2	–	–	–	10
MG (Michael) Leitch		07/10/88	1,88	105	23	6	–	–	–	30
AR (Anton) Lienert-Brown		15/04/95	1,85	96	23	–	–	–	–	0
JFR (James) Lowe		08/07/92	1,87	101	36	14	–	–	–	70
DS (Damian) McKenzie		20/04/95	1,75	81	33	10	50	30	–	240
SJ (Sam) McNichol		06/10/95	1,85	94	11	2	–	–	–	10
P (Pauliasi) Manu		23/12/87	1,84	115	54	1	–	–	–	5
RJJ (Rhys) Marshall		12/10/92	1,84	104	30	1	–	–	–	5
LJ (Liam) Messam		25/03/84	1,90	108	146	30	–	–	–	150
A (Atunaisa) Moli		12/06/95	1,89	125	10	1	–	–	–	5
CJ (Charlie) Ngatai		17/08/90	1,86	100	51	17	–	–	–	85
TN (Toni) Pulu		28/11/89	1,85	95	12	5	–	–	–	25
BA(Brodie) Retallick		31/05/91	2,04	121	71	5	–	–	–	25
TB (Tom) Sanders		05/02/94	1,91	109	13	3	–	–	–	15
TJA (Taleni) Seu		26/12/93	1,98	110	17	2	–	–	–	10
ST (Shaun) Stevenson		14/11/96	1,94	88	6	2	–	–	–	10
S (Seta) Tamanivalu		23/06/92	1,89	104	22	9	–	–	–	45
SF (Siate) Tokolahi		16/03/92	1,84	116	28	–	–	–	–	0
JF (James) Tucker		08/08/94	1,97	112	4	–	–	–	–	0
LM (Latu) Vaeno		05/01/95	1,92	98	2	–	–	–	–	0
S (Sam) Vaka		26/10/92	1,87	97	3	1	–	–	–	5
M (Ma'ama) Vaipulu		21/07/89	1,9	112	18	–	–	–	–	0
BM (Brad) Weber		17/01/91	1,72	75	41	6	–	–	–	30
H (Hiroshi) Yamashita		01/01/86	1,82	120	8	–	–	–	–	0
					1350	190	319	339	1	2608

APPEARANCES & POINTS

PLAYER	Crusaders	Lions	Kings	Jaguares	Force	Brumbies	Blues	Hurricanes	Sharks	Highlanders	Rebels	Waratahs	Crusaders	Reds	Highlanders	Stormers	Hurricanes	Apps	T	C	P	DG	Pts
McKenzie	15	15	15	15	15	15	15	15	15	15	15	15	15	15	15	15	15	17	10	43	21	–	199
Stevenson	14	–	–	–	14R	14	–	11R	–	–	–	–	–	–	–	10R	14R	6	2	–	–	–	10
Tamanivalu	13	13	13	12R	13	12R	13	13	13	13	13	13	13	13	–	–	13	16	9	–	–	–	45
Ngatai	12	12	12	12	12	12	12	–	–	12	–	–	–	–	–	–	–	8	5	–	–	–	25
Lowe	11	11	11	11	11	11	11	–	–	11	11	11	11	11	11	11	11	15	7	–	–	–	35
Cruden	10	10	10	10	10	10	10	10	10	10	10R	10	10	10	10	10	10	17	5	4	7	–	54
Kerr-Barlow	9	9	9R	9	–	–	20R	9R	–	–	–	–	9R	9	9	9R	9	11	1	–	–	–	5
Sanders	8	6	–	6	6	6	–	6	–	–	8R	8	8	6	8	8		13	3	–	–	–	15
Cane	7c	7c	7c	7c	7c	7c	7c	7c	7c	7c	7c	7c	7c	8c	7c	7c	7c	17	4	–	–	–	20
Seu	6	5R	6	5R	5	5	4R	20R	6	6	6	6	6	5R	6	6		17	2	–	–	–	10
Retallick	5	5	–	–	–	–	5	5	5	5	5	5	–	5	5	5		12	1	–	–	–	5
Allardice	4	4	4	4	4	4	–	4	–	4R	4R	4R	–	–	–	–		10	–	–	–	–	0
Yamashita	3	3	–	3	–	–	–	3	3	3	3	3	–	x	–	–		8	–	–	–	–	0
Marshall	2	2	2	2R	2R	2R	2R	2	–	–	–	–	–	–	–	–		8	–	–	–	–	0
Manu	1	1	1R	1R	–	–	–	–	–	–	–	–	–	–	–	–		4	–	–	–	–	0
Harris	2R	2R	–	–	–	–	–	2R	2R	2	2	2R	2	2	2	2		11	3	–	–	–	15
Graham	1R	1R	1	1	1	1	1	1	1	1	1	1	–	–	1R	3R		14	1	–	–	–	5
Tokolahi	3R	3R	3	3R	3	3	3R	3R	3R	3R	–	–	3R	–	–	–		11	–	–	–	–	0
Vaipulu	6R	8	7R	6R	–	6R	6	6R	–	8R	–	–	–	–	–	–		8	–	–	–	–	0
Bardoul	8R	–	5	5	–	–	–	–	–	–	–	–	–	–	–	–		3	–	–	–	–	0
Weber	9R	9R	9	9R	9	9	9	9	9	9	9	9	9	9R	9R	9	9R	17	5	–	–	–	25
Lienert-Brown	13R	13R	12R	13	–	13	–	–	12	13R	12	12	12	12	12	13	12	14	–	–	–	–	0
Vaeno	14R	14	–	–	–	–	–	–	–	–	–	–	–	–	–	–		2	–	–	–	–	0
Fisi'iahi	–	14R	14	14R	–	–	–	x	–	–	–	–	–	–	–	–		3	1	–	–	–	5
Leitch	–	8R	8	8	8	8	8	8	8	8	8	8	–	–	–	–		10	3	–	–	–	15
Elliott	–	–	2R	2	2	2	2	2R	2	2	2R	2	2	2R	2R	2R	2R	15	1	–	–	–	5
McNichol	–	–	10R	14	14	–	14R	11	11	–	–	–	14R	13R	14R	14	14	11	2	–	–	–	10
Moli	–	–	3R	–	3R	3R	3	3	–	–	–	3R	3	3	3	3		10	1	–	–	–	5
Tucker	–	–	4R	–	5R	4R	–	–	4R	–	–	–	–	–	–	–		4	–	–	–	–	0
Pulu	–	–	–	14R	14	–	14	14	14	14	14	14	14	14	13R	13R		12	5	–	–	–	25
Fisi'ihoi	–	–	–	1R	1R	1R	x	–	–	3R	3R	1R	1R	1R	3R	1R		10	–	–	–	–	0
Henwood	–	–	–	7R	–	6R	–	–	–	–	–	–	–	–	–	–		2	–	–	–	–	0
Hammington	–	–	–	9R	9R	–	–	x	9R	9R	9R	–	–	–	–	–		5	–	–	–	–	0
Donald	–	–	–	10R	–	12R	x	–	–	–	–	10	–	13R	12	–		5	1	–	–	–	2
Bird	–	–	–	–	4	–	4	4	4	4	4	4	4	4	4	–		10	–	–	–	–	0
Horrell	–	–	–	–	12	13R	–	13R	13R	–	12R	–	–	–	–	–		5	1	–	–	–	5
Hames	–	–	–	–	–	1R	1R	1R	1R	1	1	1	1	1	–	–		9	–	–	–	–	0
Boshier	–	–	–	–	–	–	6R	–	–	6R	6R	7	8R	7R	8R	–		7	1	–	–	–	5
Vaka	–	–	–	–	–	–	–	–	14R	10R	11R	–	–	–	–	–		3	1	–	–	–	5
Brown	–	–	–	–	–	–	–	–	–	–	–	–	8R	5R	–	–		2	–	–	–	–	0
Messam	–	–	–	–	–	–	–	–	–	–	–	–	8R	8	–	–		2	–	–	–	–	0
Koloamatangi	–	–	–	–	–	–	–	–	–	–	–	–	–	–	6R	6R		2	1	–	–	–	5
Penalty tries	–	–	–	–	–	–	–	–	–	–	–	–	–	–	–	–	–		1	–	–	–	5
42 PLAYERS																		**386**	**76**	**48**	**28**	**0**	**560**

Records

CHAMPIONS: 2012, 2013

MATCH RECORDS

Biggest winning margin	42	vs Cheetahs (45-3)	Hamilton	2013
Heaviest defeat	50	vs Cats (3-53)	Bloemfontein	2000
Highest score	72	vs Lions (72-65)	Johannesburg	2010
Most points conceded	65	vs Lions (72-65)	Johannesburg	2010
Most tries	9	vs Western Force (64-36)	Hamilton	2007
	9	vs Blues (63-34)	Hamilton	2009
	9	vs Lions (72-65)	Johannesburg	2010
	9	vs Force (53-10)	Hamilton	2016
Most tries conceded	9	vs Lions (72-65)	Johannesburg	2010
Most points by a player	32	SR Donald (1t, 9c, 3p) vs Lions	Johannesburg	2010
Most tries by a player	4	SW Sivivatu vs Blues	Hamilton	2009
	4	AT Tikoirotuma vs Blues	Albany	2012
	4	CJ Ngatai vs Force	Hamilton	2016
Most conversions by a player	9	SR Donald vs Lions	Johannesburg	2010
Most penalties by a player	6	GW Jackson vs Queensland Reds	Rotorua	2001
	6	SR Donald vs Crusaders	Christchurch	2007
Most drop goals by a player	1	on eight occasions		

SEASON RECORDS

Most team points	560	in 17 matches	2016
Most points by a player	251	AW Cruden	2012
Most team tries	53	in 18 matches	2012
Most tries by a player	12	RQ Randle	2002
Most conversions by a player	43	AW Cruden	2012
	43	DS McKenzie	2016
Most penalties by a player	50	AW Cruden	2012
Most drop goals by a player	2	ID Foster	1996

CAREER RECORDS

Most appearances	146	LJ Messam	2006-2016
Most points	859	SR Donald	2005-2016
Most tries	42	SW Sivivatu	2003-2011
Most conversions	150	SR Donald	2005-2011
Most penalties	153	SR Donald	2005-2011
Most drop goals	2	ID Foster	1996-1998
	2	GW Jackson	1999-2004

Damian McKenzie was a constant threat from fullback for the Chiefs.

Crusaders

Ground: AMI Stadium **Capacity:** 39 000 **Address:** 30 Stevens Street, Christchurch
Telephone: + 64 3 379 8300 **Colours:** Red jersey with black side panels.
Black shorts and black socks **Website:** www.crusaders.co.nz
Coach: Todd Blackadder **Captain:** Kieran Read **CEO:** Hamish Riach
Chairman: Grant Jarrod

Head Coach: Todd Blackadder **Assistant Coaches:** Dave Hewett, Brad Mooar & Tabai Matson
Media Manager: Juliet Calder **Analyst:** Jon Gardner
Logistics: John Miles **Doctor:** Deb Robinson
Physiotherapist: John Roche **Manager:** Angus Gardiner
Strength & Conditioning: Mark Drury

1996	1997	1998	1999	2000	2001	2002	2003	2004	2005	2006
12th	6th	2nd	4th	2nd	10th	1st	2nd	2nd	1st	1st

2007	2008	2009	2010	2011	2012	2013	2014	2015	2016
3rd	1st	4th	4th	3rd	4th	4th	2nd	7th	6th

Played	Won	Lost	Drawn	Points for	Points against	Tries for	Tries against
16	11	5	0	512	359	68	45

Date	Venue	Opponent	Result	Score	Referee	Scorers
Febr 27	Christchurch	Chiefs	LOST	21-27	C Pollock	T: Havili, Mo'unga. C: Mo'unga. P: Mo'unga (3).
Mrch 05	Christchurch	Blues	WON	28-13	P Williams	T: Penalty try, Read, Mo'unga. C: Mo'unga (2). P: Mo'unga (3).
Mrch 19	Christchurch	Kings	WON	57-24	W Houston	T: Nadolo (2), Funnell, McNicholl, Macilai, Drummond, Samu, Mo'unga. C: Mo'unga (4), Volavola (3).
Mrch 26	Durban	Sharks	WON	19-14	J Peyper	T: Nadolo, Read, Havili. C: Mo'unga, Nadolo.
April 01	Johannesburg	Lions	WON	43-37	S Berry	T: Crotty (3), McNicholl, Drummond, Crockett. C: Mo'unga (5). P: Mo'unga.
April 08	Perth	Force	WON	20-19	B O'Keeffe	T: McNicholl, Drummond, Taufua. C: Mo'unga. P: Mo'unga.
April 15	Christchurch	Jaguares	WON	32-15	C Joubert	T: Dagg (2), Ellis, Mo'unga, Read. C: Mo'unga (2). P: Mo'unga.
April 24	Canberra	Brumbies	WON	40-14	J Peyper	T: Taylor (2), Nadolo, Dagg, Macilai, McKenzie. C: Mo'unga (4), McKenzie.
May 06	Christchurch	Reds	WON	38-05	B Pickerill	T: Macilai (3), Taylor, Taufua, Barrett. C: Mo'unga (3), McKenzie.
May 13	Dunedin	Highlanders	LOST	26-34	C Pollock	T: Taufua, Dagg. C: Mo'unga (2). P: Mo'unga (4).
May 20	Christchurch	Waratahs	WON	29-10	J Peyper	T: McNicholl, Dagg, Mo'unga, Taufua. C: Mo'unga (3). P: Mo'unga.
May 28	Auckland	Blues	WON	26-21	A Gardner	T: Nadolo, Ellis. C: Mo'unga (2). P: Mo'unga (4).
July 01	Suva	Chiefs	LOST	13-23	N Briant	T: Macilai. C: Mo'unga. P: Mo'unga (2).
July 09	Christchurch	Rebels	WON	85-26	G Jackson	T: McNicholl (3), Crotty (2), Taylor (2), Whitelock, Barrett, Hodgman, Nadolo, Todd, Samu. C: Mo'unga (7), Nadolo (3).
July 16	Christchurch	Hurricanes	LOST	10-35	B O'Keeffe	T: Crotty. C: Mo'unga. P: Mo'unga.
QUARTER-FINAL						
July 23	Johannesburg	Lions	LOST	25-42	C Joubert	T: Drummond, Crotty, Volavola. C: Mo'unga (2). P: Mo'unga (2).

Note: ■ = *Champion*

2016 SQUAD

PLAYER	Date of Birth	Height	Weight	M	T	C	P	DG	Pts
MS (Michael) Alaatoa	28/08/91	1,89	135	16	–	–	–	–	0
SK (Scott) Barrett	20/11/93	1,97	112	21	3	–	–	–	15
TP (Tim) Boys	19/02/84	1,88	99	55	1	–	–	–	5
WWV (Wyatt) Crockett	24/01/83	1,93	118	170	14	–	–	–	70
RS (Ryan) Crotty	23/09/88	1,81	91	107	20	–	–	–	100
IJA (Israel) Dagg	06/06/88	1,86	96	99	32	19	21	–	258
MD (Mitchell) Drummond	15/12/94	1,8	84	29	6	–	–	–	30
AM (Andy) Ellis	21/02/84	1,82	89	153	27	–	–	3	144
KT (Kieron) Fonotia	02/02/88	1,86	108	39	4	–	–	–	20
OT (Owen) Franks	23/12/87	1,85	118	123	2	–	–	–	10
L (Leon) Fukofua	08/08/94	1,85	91	4	–	–	–	–	0
BCJ (Ben) Funnell	06/06/90	1,80	105	58	2	–	–	–	10
DK (David) Havili	23/01/94	1,84	88	25	4	–	–	–	20
ATOA (Alex) Hodgman	16/07/93	1,90	115	9	1	–	–	–	5
MJ (Mitchell) Hunt	19/06/95	1,74	80	2	–	–	–	–	0
J (Jone) Macilai	27/08/90	1,77	87	14	7	–	–	–	35
M (Marty) McKenzie	14/08/92	1,83	87	14	1	6	5	–	32
JZ (Johnny) McNicholl	24/09/90	1,85	96	39	15	–	–	–	75
JPT (Joe) Moody	18/09/88	1,88	112	46	1	–	–	–	5
R (Richie) Mo'unga	25/05/94	1,79	86	16	5	41	24	–	179
N (Nemani) Nadolo	06/01/91	1,94	125	39	27	4	–	–	143
RJ (Reed) Prinsep	17/02/93	1,92	108	1	–	–	–	–	0
KJ (Kieran) Read	26/10/85	1,93	110	133	22	–	–	–	110
G (Ged) Robinson	20/06/83	1,78	104	70	8	–	–	–	40
L (Luke) Romano	16/02/86	1,99	118	80	6	–	–	–	30
P (Pete) Samu	17/12/91	1,85	101	4	3	–	–	–	15
J (Jordan) Taufua	29/01/92	1,82	100	50	9	–	–	–	45
CJ (Codie) Taylor	31/03/91	1,83	106	35	6	–	–	–	30
MB (Matt) Todd	24/03/88	1,85	104	94	20	–	–	–	100
J (Jimmy) Tupou	08/08/92	1,96	109	37	–	–	–	–	0
B (Ben) Volavola	13/01/91	1,91	89	15	1	5	2	–	21
ST (Seaun) Wainui	23/10/95	1,91	102	7	–	–	–	–	0
SL (Sam) Whitelock	12/10/88	2,02	116	101	5	–	–	–	25

APPEARANCES & POINTS

PLAYER	Chiefs	Blues	Kings	Sharks	Lions	Force	Jaguares	Brumbies	Reds	Highlanders	Waratahs	Blues	Chiefs	Rebels	Hurricanes	Lions	Apps	T	C	P	DG	Pts
Havili	15	15	12	15	15	–	–	12	12	12	13R	14R	12	12	12	12	14	2	–	–	–	10
Macilai	14	14	10R	–	–	15R	–	14	11	11	11	–	14	–	–	11	10	6	–	–	–	30
Wainui	13	13	–	–	12R	13	14R	12R	–	–	–	12R	–	–	–	–	7	–	–	–	–	0
Fonotia	12	12	13	13	13	13R	13	13	13	13	13	13	13	12R	11R	13R	16	–	–	–	–	0
Nadolo	11	11	11	11	11	11	11	11	11	–	11	11	11	11	11	–	12	6	4	–	–	38
Mo'unga	10	10	10	10	10	10	10	10	10	10	10	10	10	10	10	10	16	5	41	24	–	179
Ellis	9	9	–	9	9	9R	9	9	9R	9	9	9R	9	9	–	9	14	2	–	–	–	10
Read	8	8	–	8c	8c	8c	8c	8c	8c	8c	8c	8c	8c	–	8c	8c	14	3	–	–	–	15
Boys	7	7	7R	7R	–	–	6R	8R	8R	6R	5R	6R	–	–	–	–	10	–	–	–	–	0
Taufua	6	6	6	6	6R	6	6	6	6	6	6	6	6	6	x	6	15	4	–	–	–	20
Whitelock, S	5c	5c	5c	5	5R	5	–	5R	5	5	5	–	5	5c	–	5	13	1	–	–	–	5
Barrett	4	4	–	4	5	5R	5	5	4	5R	4R	5	4	4	5	5R	15	2	–	–	–	10
Franks	3	3	3	3	3	3	3	3	3R	3	3	3	3	3	3	3	16	–	–	–	–	0
Taylor	2	2	–	2	2	2	2	2	2	2	2	2	2	2	2	2	15	5	–	–	–	25
Moody	1	1	–	1	1R	1R	1	1	1R	1R	1	1	1R	–	–	–	12	–	–	–	–	0
Funnell	2R	2R	2	2R	2R	–	–	2R	–	–	–	x	2R	2R	2R	–	9	–	–	–	–	5
Crockett	1R	1R	1	1R	1	1	1R	1R	1	1	1R	1R	1	1R	1	1	16	1	–	–	–	5
Alaalatoa	x	3R	3R	3R	3R	3R	3R	3R	3	3R	3R	3R	3R	3R	3R	3R	15	–	–	–	–	0
Tupou	4R	4R	8	6R	6	6R	4R	–	–	–	–	4R	6R	8	6	6R	12	–	–	–	–	0
Prinsep	7R	–	–	–	–	–	–	–	–	–	–	–	–	–	–	–	1	–	–	–	–	0
Fukofua	20R	9R	9R	–	–	–	–	–	–	–	–	–	–	9R	–	–	4	–	–	–	–	0
Volavola	15R	13R	15	x	15R	15	15R	–	–	–	–	–	–	–	12R	–	7	1	3	–	–	11
McNicholl	14R	15R	14	14	14	14	–	14	14	14	14	–	14	14	14	14	14	7	–	–	–	35
Samu	–	7R	6R	–	–	–	–	–	–	–	–	6R	6R	–	–	–	4	2	–	–	–	10
Drummond	–	–	9	x	9R	9	9R	9R	9	9R	9	9R	9	9	9	9R	13	4	–	–	–	20
Todd	–	–	7	7	7	7	7	7	7	7	7	7	7	7	7	7	14	1	–	–	–	5
Romano	–	–	4	4R	4	4	4	4	5R	4	4	4	–	4R	4	4	13	–	–	–	–	0
Hodgman	–	–	1R	–	–	–	–	–	–	–	–	–	1	1R	1R	–	4	1	–	–	–	5
Robinson	–	–	2R	–	–	x	2R	2R	–	x	2R	x	–	–	–	–	4	–	–	–	–	0
Crotty	–	12R	12	12	12	12	–	14R	13R	12	12	–	13	13	13	–	12	7	–	–	–	35
Dagg	–	–	–	–	–	15	15	15	15	15	15	15	15	15	15	–	10	5	–	–	–	25
McKenzie	–	–	–	–	–	–	10R	10R	x	15R	13R	–	–	–	–	–	4	1	2	–	–	9
Brown	–	–	–	–	–	–	–	–	–	–	x	–	–	–	–	–	0	–	–	–	–	0
Hunt	–	–	–	–	–	–	–	–	–	–	–	x	10R	14R	–	–	2	–	–	–	–	0
Penalty try	–	–	–	–	–	–	–	–	–	–	–	–	–	–	–	–	–	1	–	–	–	5
34 PLAYERS																	357	68	50	24	0	512

Records

CHAMPIONS: 1998, 1999, 2000, 2002, 2005, 2006, 2008

MATCH RECORDS

Biggest winning margin	77	vs NSW Waratahs (96-19)	Christchurch	2002
Heaviest defeat	36	vs Queensland Reds (16-52)	Brisbane	1996
Highest score	96	vs NSW Waratahs (96-19)	Christchurch	2002
Most points conceded	58	vs Natal (26-58)	Durban	1996
Most tries	14	vs NSW Waratahs (96-19)	Christchurch	2002
Most tries conceded	8	vs Natal (26-58)	Durban	1996
Most points by a player	31	TJ Taylor (1t, 1c, 8p) vs Stormers	Christchurch	2012
Most tries by a player	4	CS Ralph vs NSW Waratahs	Christchurch	2002
	4	SD Maitland vs Brumbies	Nelson	2011
Most conversions by a player	13	AP Mehrtens vs NSW Waratahs	Christchurch	2002
Most penalties by a player	8	TJ Taylor vs Stormers	Christchurch	2012
Most drop goals by a player	3	AP Mehrtens vs Highlanders	Christchurch	1998

SEASON RECORDS

Most team points	541	from 13 matches	2005
Most points by a player	221	DW Carter	2006
Most team tries	71	from 13 matches	2005
Most tries by a player	15	RL Gear	2005
Most conversions by a player	37	DW Carter	2005
Most penalties by a player	43	AP Mehrtens	1999
Most drop goals by a player	4	AP Mehrtens	1998, 1999, 2000

CAREER RECORDS

Most appearances	170	WWV Crockett	2006-2016
Most points	1708	DW Carter	2003-2015
Most tries	52	CS Ralph	1999-2008
Most conversions	287	DW Carter	2003-2015
Most penalties	307	DW Carter	2003-2015
Most drop goals	17	AP Mehrtens	1996-2005

Mitchell Drummond.

www.sarugby.co.za

Highlanders

Ground: Forsyth Barr Stadium **Capacity:** 29 000 **Address:** Anzac Ave, Dunedin
Telephone number: +64 3 446 4010 **Colours:** Blue jersey with gold stripes. Blue shorts and socks
Website: www.thehighlanders.co.nz **Captains:** Ben Smith & Shane Christie
General Manager: Roger Clark **Chairman:** Doug Harvie

Head Coach: Jamie Joseph **Assistant Coaches:** Scott McLeod & Tony Brown
Scrum Coach: Clarke Dermody **Conditioning Coach:** Andrew Beardmore
Physiotherapist: Adam Letts **Video Analyst:** Andy Watts
Doctor: Dr Greg MacLeod **Manager:** Paul McLaughlan
Media officer: Greg O'Brien **Nutrionist:** Fiona Simpson
Mind skills Coach: Natalie van Leeuwen **High Performance Coach:** Jon Preston

1996	1997	1998	1999	2000	2001	2002	2003	2004	2005	2006
8th	12th	4th	3rd	3rd	5th	4th	7th	9th	8th	9th

2007	2008	2009	2010	2011	2012	2013	2014	2015	2016
9th	11th	11th	12th	8th	9th	14th	6th	4th	5th

VODACOM SUPER RUGBY

Played	Won	Lost	Drawn	Points for	Points against	Tries for	Tries against
17	12	5	0	467	324	56	33

Date	Venue	Opponent	Result	Score	Referee	Scorers
Febr 26	Auckland	Blues	LOST	31-33	G Jackson	T: B Smith (2), Walden, Naholo. C: Sopoaga (3), Parker. P: Sopoaga.
Mrch 05	Dunedin	Hurricanes	WON	17-16	G Jackson	T: Fekitoa. P: Sopoaga (3), Parker.
Mrch 12	Dunedin	Lions	WON	34-15	C Pollock	T: Faddes (2), B Smith, Fekitoa. C: Sopoaga (4). P: Sopoaga. DG: Sopoaga.
Mrch 18	Sydney	Waratahs	WON	30-26	N Briant	T: E Dixon (2), Squire, Tongia. C: Sopoaga (2). P: Sopoaga. DG: Sopoaga.
Mrch 26	Melbourne	Rebels	WON	27-03	A Lees	T: Wilson, Osborne, Thompson. C: Sopoaga (3). P: Sopoaga (3).
April 01	Dunedin	Force	WON	32-20	B Pickerill	T: Osborne, Pryor, Faddes, Emery. C: Parker (2), Banks. P: Parker (2).
April 09	Brisbane	Reds	LOST	27-28	G Jackson	T: A Smith, Sopoaga, Fekitoa. C: Sopoaga (2), Parker. P: Sopoaga (2).
April 22	Dunedin	Sharks	LOST	14-15	B O'Keeffe	T: Faddes. P: Sopoaga (3).
April 30	Invercargill	Brumbies	WON	23-10	N Briant	T: B Smith, Sopoaga. C: Sopoaga (2). P: Sopoaga (3).
May 07	Hamilton	Chiefs	WON	26-13	A Gardner	T: Naholo (2), Lienert-Brown. C: Banks. P: Sopoaga (3).
May 13	Dunedin	Crusaders	WON	34-26	C Pollock	T: Faddes (2), Naholo (2), Squire. C: Sopoaga (3). P: Sopoaga.
May 27	Wellington	Hurricanes	LOST	20-27	M Fraser	T: Sopoaga, Lienert-Brown. C: Sopoaga (2). P: Sopoaga, Banks.
July 02	Port Elizabeth	Kings	WON	48-18	M v/d Westhuizen	T: Faddes (3), Seiuli, Pryor, Wilson, Osborne. C: Sopoaga (4), Smith. P: Sopoaga.
July 09	Buenos Aires	Jaguares	WON	34-08	A Gardner	T: E Dixon (2), Thompson, B Smith. C: Sopoaga (4). P: Sopoaga (2).
July 16	Dunedin	Chiefs	WON	25-15	G Jackson	T: Pryor, Sopoaga, Naholo. C: Sopoaga (2). P: Sopoaga (2).

QUARTER-FINAL

| July 22 | Canberra | Brumbies | WON | 15-09 | A Gardner | T: Naholo, Squire. C: Sopoaga. P: Sopoaga. |

SEMI-FINAL
July 30

| Johannesburg | Lions | LOST | 30-42 | J Peyper | T: Sopoaga, Faddes, Naholo, Wheeler. C: Sopoaga (2). P:Sopoaga (2). |

Note: ■ = *Champion*

2016 SQUAD

PLAYER	Date of Birth	Height	Weight	M	T	C	P	DG	Pts
AN (Alex) Ainley	16/07/81	1,97	109	19	–	–	–	–	0
M (Marty) Banks	19/09/89	1,90	91	22	1	5	9	–	45
JP (Jamie) Booth	13/01/94	1,71	82	1	–	–	–	–	0
S (Shane) Christie	23/07/85	1,84	107	29	2	–	–	–	10
LJ (Liam) Coltman	25/01/90	1,85	109	56	–	–	–	–	0
AL (Ash) Dixon	01/09/88	1,82	102	51	1	–	–	–	5
EC (Elliot) Dixon	04/09/89	1,95	110	65	9	–	–	–	45
BM (Brendon) Edmonds	28/11/90	1,83	119	25	1	–	–	–	5
JWC (Jason) Emery	21/09/93	1,73	88	35	2	–	–	–	10
GO (Gareth) Evans	05/08/91	1,90	105	29	5	–	–	–	25
MA (Matt) Faddes	06/11/91	1,85	95	16	10	–	–	–	50
M (Malakai) Fekitoa	10/05/92	1,87	99	49	14	–	–	–	70
TSG (Tom) Franklin	11/08/90	2,00	114	38	1	–	–	–	5
R (Ross) Geldenhuys	19/04/83	1,88	122	39	–	–	–	–	0
S (Siosiua) Halanukonuka	09/08/86	1,81	117	14	–	–	–	–	0
JW (Josh) Hohneck	06/01/86	1,90	118	51	2	–	–	–	10
JAR (James) Lentjes	16/01/91	1,87	101	10	–	–	–	–	0
D (Daniel) Lienert-Brown	09/02/93	1,84	101	30	2	–	–	–	10
CW (Craig) Millar	29/10/90	1,85	110	8	–	–	–	–	0
WR (Waisake) Naholo	08/05/91	1,86	96	28	22	–	–	–	110
PJJ (Patrick) Osborne	14/06/87	1,89	105	54	19	–	–	–	95
HJ (Hayden) Parker	19/11/90	1,75	80	30	1	13	22	2	103
GW (Greg) Pleasants-Tate	12/05/91	1,82	110	8	–	–	–	–	0
DJ (Dan) Pryor	14/04/88	1,90	103	32	6	–	–	–	30
MJ (Mark) Reddish	03/03/85	1,96	112	53	1	–	–	–	5
JD (Josh) Renton	25/04/94	1,74	80	4	–	–	–	–	0
AJ (Aki) Seiuli	22/12/92	1,84	116	7	1	–	–	–	5
AL (Aaron) Smith	21/11/88	1,71	83	94	19	–	–	–	95
BR (Ben) Smith	01/06/86	1,90	92	120	31	–	–	1	158
FH (Fletcher) Smith	01/03/95	1,81	88	2	–	1	–	–	2
LZ (Lima) Sopoaga	03/02/91	1,75	91	65	10	110	117	6	639
L (Liam) Squire	20/03/91	1,95	113	28	7	–	–	–	35
F (Fumiaki) Tanaka	03/01/85	1,63	75	46	2	–	–	–	10
R (Rob) Thompson	29/08/91	1,84	103	11	2	–	–	–	10
TTLMA (Te Aihe) Toma	15/03/93	1,73	88	3	–	–	–	–	0
RP (Ryan) Tongia	31/05/90	1,78	87	4	4	–	–	–	20
TT (Teihorangi) Walden	25/05/93	1,82	94	6	1	–	–	–	5
JT (Joe) Wheeler	20/10/87	2,00	111	52	1	–	–	–	5
LC (Luke) Whitelock	29/01/91	1,94	108	62	3	–	–	–	15
J (Jack) Wilson	11/12/92	1,75	82	10	3	–	–	–	15
				1306	177	129	148	9	1647

APPEARANCES & POINTS

PLAYER	Blues	Hurricanes	Lions	Waratahs	Rebels	Force	Reds	Sharks	Brumbies	Chiefs	Crusaders	Hurricanes	Kings	Jaguares	Chiefs	Brumbies	Lions	Apps	T	C	P	DG	Pts
Smith, B	15c	15c	15c	15c	15c	15c	–	15c	15c	15c	15c	–	15c	15c	15c	15c	15c	15	5	–	–	–	25
Naholo	14	–	–	–	–	–	–	–	14	14	14	–	14	14	14	14	–	8	8	–	–	–	40
Fekitoa	13	13	13	13	13	13	13	13	13	12	12	12	–	13	12	12	12	16	3	–	–	–	15
Walden	12	12	–	–	–	–	–	12R	13R	14R	13R	–	–	–	–	–	–	6	1	–	–	–	5
Osborne	11	11	11	–	11	11	14R	11	11	11	11	11R	11	11	11	11	11	16	3	–	–	–	15
Sopoaga	10	10	10	10	10	–	10	10	10	10	10	10	10	10	10	10	10	16	5	34	29	2	186
Smith, A	9	9	9	9	9	9	9	9	9	9	9	9	9	–	9	9	9	16	1	–	–	–	5
Squire	8	8R	–	8	8	8	8	8	8	–	7R	7R	8R	–	5R	8	x	14	3	–	–	–	15
Christie	7	7	8R	7	7	7R	7c	7	7	–	–	–	7c	–	7	–	–	11	–	–	–	–	0
Dixon, E	6	6	6	6	6R	6	–	6	6	6	6	6	–	6	6	6	6	15	4	–	–	–	20
Wheeler	5	5	5	–	5	5R	5	5	8R	5	–	–	5	–	–	–	x	11	1	–	–	–	5
Franklin	4	4	–	5	–	5	4R	4	5	5	5R	5	5	4	4	4	5	15	–	–	–	–	0
Hohneck	3	3	–	–	3R	3R	3R	3	3	3	1	3	3	1	3R	3	3	15	–	–	–	–	0
Coltman	2	2	2	2	2R	2	2	2R	–	–	–	–	–	2R	2R	–	–	10	–	–	–	–	0
Lienert-Brown	1	1R	1R	1R	–	1R	1	1	1	1	–	1	1	–	1	1	1	14	2	–	–	–	10
Dixon, A	2R	2R	2R	2R	2	2R	2R	2	2	2	2	2	2	2	2	2	2	17	–	–	–	–	0
Edmonds	1R	1	1	1	1	1	–	–	–	–	–	–	–	–	–	–	–	6	–	–	–	–	0
Geldenhuys	3R	–	3R	3R	–	–	1R	3R	–	–	3R	–	–	3R	–	x	–	8	–	–	–	–	0
Ainley	4R	–	4	4	–	4	–	4R	4	4	4	4	–	–	5	–	4	11	–	–	–	–	0
Pryor	8R	7R	7	–	8R	7	6R	7R	7R	7	7	7	7R	7R	7R	7R	x	16	3	–	–	–	15
Renton	9R	x	9R	x	9R	–	–	–	–	–	–	–	–	–	–	–	–	3	–	–	–	–	0
Parker	10R	10R	10R	10R	10R	10	12R	8R	–	–	–	–	–	–	–	–	–	8	–	4	3	–	17
Faddes	12R	14	14	14	–	14	15	14	15R	13	13	13	15	12R	13	13	13	16	10	–	–	–	50
Whitelock	–	8	8	–	6	–	6	–	8	8	8	8	8	8	5	8	–	12	–	–	–	–	0
Emery	–	12R	11R	11R	13R	15R	14R	12	–	–	–	13	–	–	–	–	–	8	1	–	–	–	5
Halanukonuka	–	3R	3	3	3	3	3	–	3R	3R	3	3R	3R	3	3	–	3R	14	–	–	–	–	0
Thompson	–	–	12	12	12	12	12	–	12	–	–	12	12	–	13R	–	–	9	2	–	–	–	10
Evans	–	–	5R	6R	–	–	–	–	5R	–	6	–	–	–	–	–	–	4	–	–	–	–	0
Tongia	–	–	–	11	–	–	–	–	–	–	–	11	–	–	–	–	–	2	1	–	–	–	5
Reddish	–	–	5R	4	–	4	–	–	–	–	4R	4	4R	4R	4R	–	–	8	–	–	–	–	0
Wilson	–	–	–	14	–	14	11	14	–	–	–	14	–	–	–	–	–	5	2	–	–	–	10
Millar	–	–	–	1R	–	–	1R	1R	–	1R	–	–	–	–	–	–	–	4	–	–	–	–	0
Banks	–	–	–	–	10R	–	–	–	10R	10R	10R	–	–	–	–	x	–	5	–	2	1	–	7
Tanaka	–	–	–	–	–	x	9R	x	9R	9R	9R	9R	–	–	–	–	–	5	–	–	–	–	0
Pleasants-Tate	–	–	–	–	–	–	–	–	2R	2R	2R	2R	2R	2R	–	–	x	7	–	–	–	–	0
Lentjes	–	–	–	–	–	–	–	7R	–	–	–	7	7	–	–	7	–	4	–	–	–	–	0
Seiuli	–	–	–	–	–	–	–	1R	–	1R	1R	1R	1R	1R	–	x	–	7	1	–	–	–	5
Smith, F	–	–	–	–	–	–	–	–	–	13R	10R	x	x	–	–	–	–	2	–	1	–	–	2
Toma	–	–	–	–	–	–	–	–	–	–	–	–	9	9R	x	x	x	3	–	–	–	–	0
Booth	–	–	–	–	–	–	–	–	–	–	–	9R	–	–	–	–	–	1	–	–	–	–	0
Penalty try	–	–	–	–	–	–	–	–	–	–	–	–	–	–	–	–	–						0
40 PLAYERS																		383	56	41	33	2	467

Records

CHAMPIONS: 2015

MATCH RECORDS

Biggest winning margin	42	vs Bulls (65-23)	Invercargill	1999
Heaviest defeat	44	vs ACT Brumbies (26-70)	Canberra	1996
Highest score	65	vs Bulls (65-23)	Invercargill	1999
Most points conceded	75	vs Sharks (43-75)	Durban	1997
Most tries	9	vs Bulls (65-23)	Invercargill	1999
Most tries conceded	9	vs ACT Brumbies (26-70)	Canberra	1996
Most points by a player	28	BA Blair vs Sharks	Durban	2005
Most tries by a player	3	TM Vaega vs Western Province	Cape Town	1996
	3	DC Howlett vs Chiefs	Hamilton	1997
	3	JW Wilson vs Stormers	Cape Town	1998
	3	JC Stanley vs Stormers	Cape Town	1998
	3	TR Nicholas vs Bulls	Pretoria	2002
	3	BA Blair vs Sharks	Durban	2005
	3	IJA Dagg vs Bulls	Pretoria	2010
	3	AJ Thomson vs Rebels	Invercargill	2012
	3	KI Poki vs Cheetahs	Invercargill	2013
	3	MA Faddes vs Kings	Port Elizabeth	2016
Most conversions by a player	7	TE Brown vs Bulls	Invercargill	1999
Most penalties by a player	8	WC Walker vs Chiefs	Hamilton	2003
Most drop goals by a player	1	on 27 occasions		

SEASON RECORDS

Most team points	530	from 19 matches	2015
Most points by a player	191	LZ Sopoaga	2015
Most team tries	63	from 19 matches	2015
Most tries by a player	13	WR Naholo	2015
Most conversions by a player	38	LZ Sopoaga	2015
Most penalties by a player	38	LZ Sopoaga	2014
Most drop goals by a player	2	SD Culhane	1996
	2	BJ Laney	1999
	2	NJ Evans	2005
	2	HJ Parker	2014

CAREER RECORDS

Most appearances	127	AD Oliver	1996-2007
Most points	857	TE Brown	1996-2011
Most tries	35	JW Wilson	1996-2002
Most conversions	137	TE Brown	1996-2011
Most penalties	180	TE Brown	1996-2011
Most drop goals	5	TE Brown	1996-2011

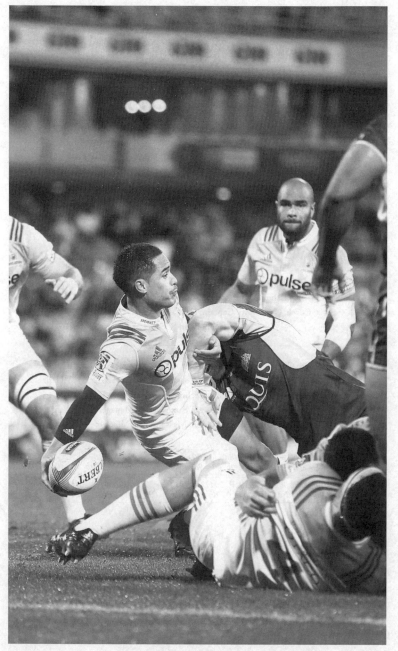

Aaron Smith remains a hugely influential figure for the Highlanders and New Zealand from scrumhalf.

Hurricanes

Ground: Westpac Stadium **Capacity:** 34 500 **Address:** Waterloo Quay, Wellington
Telephone number: + 64 4 389 0020 **Colours:** Yellow jersey with black piping,
black shorts and socks **Website:** www.hurricanes.co.nz
Coach: Chris Boyd **Captain:** Dane Coles **CEO:** Avan Lee
Chairman: Brian Roche

Head Coach: Chris Boyd **Assistant Coaches:** John Plumtree & Jason Holland
Scrum Coach: Dan Cron **Conditioning Coaches:** David Gray & David Wildash
Doctor: Dr Theo Dorfling **Technical Advisor:** Jason Ross
Physiotherapists: Cam Shaw & Lee van Santos **Team Manager:** Tony Ward
Media Officer: Toby Robson **Masseur:** Paul Minehan

1996	1997	1998	1999	2000	2001	2002	2003	2004	2005	2006
9th	3rd	8th	10th	8th	9th	9th	3rd	11th	4th	2nd

2007	2008	2009	2010	2011	2012	2013	2014	2015	2016
8th	4th	3rd	8th	9th	8th	11th	7th	1st	1st

Played	Won	Lost	Drawn	Points for	Points against	Tries for	Tries against
18	14	4	0	544	326	72	37

Date	Venue	Opponent	Result	Score	Referee	Scorers
Febr 26	Canberra	Brumbies	LOST	10-52	A Lees	T: Laumape. C: Barrett. P: Barrett.
Mrch 05	Dunedin	Highlanders	LOST	16-17	G Jackson	T: Perenara. C: Barrett. P: Barrett (3).
Mrch 11	Auckland	Blues	WON	23-19	N Briant	T: Perenara (2). Vito. C: Barrett. P: Barrett (2).
Mrch 18	Palmerston North	Force	WON	41-06	P Williams	T: A Savea, Thomson, Coles, Marshall, Laumape, Perenara. C: Barrett (4). P: Barrett.
Mrch 25	Wellington	Kings	WON	42-20	B Pickerill	T: A Savea, Barrett, Thomson, Laumape, Aso. C: Barrett (4). P: Barrett (3).
April 09	Wellington	Jaguares	WON	40-22	N Briant	T: J Savea (3), May, Coles, Barrett. C: Barrett (5).
April 15	Melbourne	Rebels	WON	38-13	R Hoffmann	T: Barrett (2), Jane, Woodward, Vito, A Savea. C: Barrett (4).
April 23	Wellington	Chiefs	LOST	27-28	C Joubert	T: Barrett, Jane, Coles, Perenara. C: Barrett, Woodward. DG: Barrett.
April 30	Johannesburg	Lions	WON	50-17	M v/d Westhuizen	T: Jane (2), J Savea (2), Proctor, Goodes, Aso. C: Barrett (6). P: Barrett.
May 07	Durban	Sharks	LOST`	15-32	M v/d Westhuizen	T: Goodes, Marshall. C: Woodward. P: Barrett.
May 14	Wellington	Reds	WON	29-14	B Pickerill	T: Woodward (2), Goosen, Coles, Laumape. C: Barrett (2).
May 27	Wellington	Highlanders	WON	27-20	M Fraser	T: A Savea (2), Shields. C: Barrett (3). P: Barrett (2)
July 02	Wellington	Blues	WON	37-27	C Pollock	T: Fifita (2), Coles, Goodes. C: Barrett (4). P: Barrett (3).
July 09	Sydney	Waratahs	WON	28-17	C Pollock	T: Barrett, Jane, J Savea. C: Barrett (2). P: Barrett (3).
July 16	Christchurch	Crusaders	WON	35-10	B O'Keeffe	T: Barrett, Gibbins, Woodward, Perenara, Halaholo. C: Barrett (5).

QUARTER-FINAL

Date	Venue	Opponent	Result	Score	Referee	Scorers
July 23	Wellington	Sharks	WON	41-00	G Jackson	T: Shields, Marshall, Woodward, Uhila, Perenara, Fifita. C: Barrett (3), Woodward. P: Barrett.

SEMI-FINAL

Date	Venue	Opponent	Result	Score	Referee	Scorers
July 30	Wellington	Chiefs	WON	25-09	A Gardner	T: Halaholo, Barrett, Vito. C: Barrett (2). P: Barrett (2)

FINAL

Date	Venue	Opponent	Result	Score	Referee	Scorers
Aug 06	Wellington	Lions	WON	20-03	G Jackson	T: Jane, Barrett. C: Barrett (2). P: Barrett (2).

Note: ■ = *Champion*

2016 SQUAD

PLAYER	Date of Birth	Height	Weight	M	T	C	P	DG	Pts
MH (Mark) Abbott	20/02/90	1,98	112	31	1	–	–	–	5
LCA (Leni) Apisai	08/03/96	1,81	108	5	–	–	–	–	0
VT (Vince) Aso	05/01/95	1,86	98	16	2	–	–	–	10
BJ (Beauden) Barrett	27/05/91	1,87	92	82	21	135	168	1	938
OW (Otere) Black	04/05/95	1,84	87	7	–	4	3	–	17
DS (Dane) Coles	10/12/86	1,84	108	94	14	–	–	–	70
G (Geoffrey) Cridge	06/02/95	2,00	114	1	–	–	–	–	0
CI (Chris) Eves	11/12/87	1,87	123	45	1	–	–	–	5
MJ (Michael) Fatialofa	14/09/92	1,98	113	15	–	–	–	–	0
VTL (Vaea) Fifita	17/06/92	1,96	107	20	3	–	–	–	15
CJ (Callum) Gibbins	14/09/88	1,86	102	26	3	–	–	–	15
(Jamison) Gibson-Park	23/02/92	1,76	80	42	2	–	–	–	10
R (Reggie) Goodes	04/04/92	1,84	112	60	7	–	–	–	35
WT (Wes) Goosen	20/10/95	1,79	92	2	1	–	–	–	5
SAU (Willis) Halaholo	06/07/90	1,88	102	18	2	–	–	–	10
CS (Cory) Jane	08/02/83	1,83	89	111	30	–	–	–	150
MZH (Michael) Kainga	28/01/91	1,87	117	6	–	–	–	–	0
TA (Tony) Lamborn	31/07/91	1,87	107	4	–	–	–	–	0
KH (Ngani) Laumape	24/04/93	1,69	107	11	4	–	–	–	20
JR (James) Marshall	07/12/88	1,83	90	44	7	17	6	–	87
MD (Motu) Matu'u	30/04/87	1,84	108	47	2	–	–	–	10
B (Ben) May	13/10/82	1,94	119	83	1	–	–	–	5
NR (Nehe) Milner-Skudder	15/12/90	1,80	90	17	4	–	–	–	20
TTR (TJ) Perenara	23/01/93	1,84	94	79	37	–	–	–	185
M (Matt) Proctor	26/10/92	1,80	90	36	6	–	–	–	30
JR (Ricky) Riccitelli	03/02/95	1,75	110	9	–	–	–	–	0
AS (Ardie) Savea	14/10/93	1,88	95	49	10	–	–	–	50
SJ (Julian) Savea	07/08/90	1,92	103	88	39	–	–	–	195
BDF (Brad) Shields	02/04/91	1,93	111	69	8	–	–	–	40
HJT (Te Toirioa) Tahuriorangi	31/03/95	1,73	82	1	–	–	–	–	0
BN (Blade) Thomson	04/12/90	1,98	106	37	7	–	–	–	35
J (Jeffery) To'omaga-Allen	19/11/90	1,92	125	69	3	–	–	–	15
L (Loni) Uhila	07/04/89	1,81	125	15	1	–	–	–	5
VVJ (Victor) Vito	27/03/87	1,93	109	100	12	–	–	–	60
JC (Jason) Woodward	17/05/90	1,88	99	44	11	34	43	–	252
				1383	239	190	220	1	2294

APPEARANCES & POINTS

PLAYER	Brumbies	Highlanders	Blues	Force	Kings	Jaguares	Rebels	Chiefs	Lions	Sharks	Reds	Highlanders	Blues	Waratahs	Crusaders	Sharks	Chiefs	Lions	Apps	T	C	P	DG	Pts
Milner-Skudder	15	–	14	–	–	–	–	–	–	–	–	–	–	–	–	–	–	–	2	–	–	–	–	0
Jane	14	14	14R	14	14	15	14	14	14	14	–	14	14	14	14	14	14	14	17	6	–	–	–	30
Aso	13	13	13	13	14R	12R	12	12	12	13	12	12	12	–	10R	12R	12R		16	2	–	–	–	10
Laumape	12	12	12	12	12	15R	–	–	12	12R	12R	–	13R	–	–	–	–	–	11	4	–	–	–	20
Savea, J	11	11	11	11	–	11	11	11	11	11	–	11	11	11	14R	14R	11R		17	6	–	–	–	30
Barrett	10	10	10	10	10	10	10	10	10	10	10	10	10	10	10	10	10	10	18	9	49	25	1	223
Perenara	9c	9c	9c	9	9	9	9	9	9	9	9	9	9	9	9	9	9	9	18	7	–	–	–	35
Vito	8	8	8	8	–	8	8	8	8	8	–	8	8	8	8	8	8	8	16	3	–	–	–	15
Savea, A	7	7	7	7	7	7	7	7	7	7	–	7	7	7	7	7	7	7	17	5	–	–	–	25
Shields	6	6	6	–	6	6	6	6	6	6	6	6	6	6	6	6	6	6	16	2	–	–	–	10
Abbott	5	5	5	5	5	–	6R	–	–	5R	5R	–	5R	5R	5R	8R	5R	5R	14	–	–	–	–	0
Thomson	4	4	4	4	8	4	–	4	4R	4R	8	4	–	–	–	–	–	–	11	2	–	–	–	10
Toomaga-Allen	3	3	3	3	3	3	3	3	3	3	3	3	3	–	–	–	–	–	13	–	–	–	–	0
Apisai	2	2	2	–	–	–	2R	–	–	–	–	–	–	–	–	2R	–		4	–	–	–	–	0
Goodes	1	1	1	–	–	1	1	1	1	1	1	1	1	1	1	–	–	–	13	3	–	–	–	15
Riccitelli	2R	2R	2R	2R	x	–	–	–	–	–	–	x	2R	2R	2R	2	2R		9	–	–	–	–	0
Eves	3R	3R	18R	1	1	1R	1R	3R	3R	1R	–	1R	3R	3	3	3R	3R	3R	17	–	–	–	–	0
Uhila	1R	1R	1R	1R	1R	–	–	1R	1R	–	1R	3R	1R	1R	1R	1	1	1	15	1	–	–	–	5
Fifita	5R	6R	6R	6	6	8R	4	6R	4	4	4	4R	4	4	4	4	4	4	18	3	–	–	–	15
Gibbins	7R	x	4R	8R	4R	5R	–	4R	6R	–	7	6R	–	6R	8R	7R	–	6R	13	1	–	–	–	5
Gibson-Park	9R	x	x	9R	–	9R	9R	–	9R	9R	–	9R	9R	9R	9R	9R	9R	9R	13	–	–	–	–	0
Black	10R	–	–	–	15R	10R	x	–	–	–	–	–	–	x	–	–	–		3	–	–	–	–	0
Halaholo	12R	15R	11R	13R	13	13	–	12R	13R	13R	x	–	12R	12	12	12	12	12	15	2	–	–	–	10
Marshall	–	15	15	15	15	–	–	–	15R	15	15	15	15	15	15	15	15	15	14	3	–	–	–	15
Woodward	–	14R	–	11R	11	–	15	15	10R	14	11R	11R	11R	13	11	11	11	11	15	5	3	–	–	31
Coles	–	–	–	2c	2c	2c	2c	2c	2c	2c	2c	2c	2c	2c	2c	2c	–	2c	14	5	–	–	–	25
May	–	–	–	3R	3R	3R	3R	–	3R	3R	–	3R	3R	3	3	3	–		11	1	–	–	–	5
Fatialofa	–	–	–	5R	4	5	5	5	5	5	5	5	5	5	5	5	5	5	15	–	–	–	–	0
Proctor	–	–	–	–	15R	14	13	13	13	–	13	13	13	13	–	13	13	13	12	1	–	–	–	5
Tahuriorangi	–	–	–	–	9R	–	–	x	–	–	x	–	–	–	–	–	–	–	1	–	–	–	–	0
Cridge	–	–	–	–	4R	–	–	–	–	–	–	–	–	–	–	–	–	–	1	–	–	–	–	0
Matu'u	–	–	–	–	–	x	–	x	2R	2R	2R	x	–	–	–	–	–	–	3	–	–	–	–	0
Lamborn	–	–	–	–	–	–	19R	–	–	–	4R	–	4R	–	–	–	7R	–	4	–	–	–	–	0
Goosen	–	–	–	–	–	–	–	–	11	–	–	–	11R	–	–	–	–		2	1	–	–	–	5
Kainga	–	–	–	–	–	–	–	–	–	–	–	–	–	–	1R	1R	1R		3	–	–	–	–	0
Penalty try	–	–	–	–	–	–	–	–	–	–	–	–	–	–	–	–	–	–						0
35 players																			**401**	**72**	**52**	**25**	**1**	**544**

Records

CHAMPIONS: 2016

MATCH RECORDS

Biggest winning margin	49	vs Brumbies (56-7)	Wellington	2009
Heaviest defeat	53	vs Blues (7-60)	Wellington	2002
Highest score	64	vs Northern Transvaal (64-32)	New Plymouth	1997
	66	vs Melbourne Rebels (66-24)	Wellington	2012
Most points conceded	60	vs Blues (7-60)	Wellington	2002
Most tries	9	vs Highlanders (60-34)	Wellington	1997
	9	vs Melbourne Rebels (66-24)	Wellington	2012
	9	vs Cheetahs (60-27)	Wellington	2014
Most tries conceded	8	vs Blues (7-60)	Wellington	2002
Most points by a player	30	DE Holwell (1t, 2c, 7p) vs Highlanders	Napier	2001
Most tries by a player	3	JF Umaga vs Northern Transvaal	New Plymouth	1997
	3	JF Umaga vs Highlanders	Wellington	1997
	3	CM Cullen vs Free State	Wellington	1997
	3	JD O'Halloran vs Blues	Wellington	1998
	3	JF Umaga vs Queensland Reds	New Plymouth	2000
	3	MA Nonu vs ACT Brumbies	Wellington	2005
	3	AK Hore vs Chiefs	Wellington	2006
	3	HE Gear vs Reds	Wellington	2010
	3	TJ Perenara vs Force	Perth	2012
	3	SJ Savea vs Melbourne Rebels	Wellington	2012
	3	CS Jane vs Reds	Wellington	2014
	3	SJ Savea vs Jaguares	Wellington	2016
Most conversions by a player	9	BJ Barrett vs Melbourne Rebels	Wellington	2012
Most penalties by a player	7	JB Cameron vs Blues	Palmerston North	1996
	7	DE Holwell vs Highlanders	Napier	2001
Most drop goals by a player	1	By five players		

SEASON RECORDS

Most team points	544	from 18 matches	2016
Most points by a player	223	BJ Barrett	2016
Most team tries	72	from 18 matches	2016
Most tries by a player	12	JF Umaga	1997
Most conversions by a player	50	BJ Barrett	2016
Most penalties by a player	40	BJ Barrett	2013
Most drop goals by a player	1	By five players	

CAREER RECORDS

Most appearances	126	MA Nonu	2003-2015
	126	CG Smith	2004-2015
Most points	938	BJ Barrett	2011-2016
Most tries	56	CM Cullen	1996-2003
Most conversions	163	BJ Barrett	2011-2016
Most penalties	172	BJ Barrett	2011-2016
Most drop goals	1	By five players	

The victorious Hurricanes squad celebrate their long-awaited maiden Super Rugby title.

ACT Brumbies

Ground: Canberra Stadium **Capacity:** 27 000 **Address:** Battye St, Bruce, ACT
Telephone number: +61 2 6260 8588 **Colours:** Navy blue jersey with gold trim and white sides,
navy shorts and socks **Website:** www.brumbies.com.au **Director of Rugby:** Laurie Fisher
Head Coach: Stephen Larkham **Captain:** Stephen Moore **CEO:** Michael Jones
Chairman: Sean Hammond **President:** Geoff Larkham

Head Coach: Stephen Larkham **Scrum Coach:** Dan Palmer
Contact Coach: Peter Ryan **Forwards Coach:** Dan McKellar **Kicking Coach:** Damien Hill
Team Manager: Ben Gathercole **Assistant Manager:** Sam Rolfe
Strength & Conditioning: Christos Argus **Strength & Conditioning Coach:** Ben Serpell
Performance Analyst: Trent Hopkinson **Doctor:** Dr Steve Freeman
Physiotherapist: Dan Fasch & Byron Field **Media Manager:** Paul Glover

1996	1997	1998	1999	2000	2001	2002	2003	2004	2005	2006
5th	2nd	10th	5th	1st	1st	3rd	4th	1st	5th	6th

2007	2008	2009	2010	2011	2012	2013	2014	2015	2016
5th	9th	7th	6th	13th	7th	3rd	4th	6th	4th

Played	Won	Lost	Drawn	Points for	Points against	Tries for	Tries against
16	10	6	0	434	341	56	42

Date	Venue	Opponent	Result	Score	Referee	Scorers
Febr 26	Canberra	Hurricanes	WON	52-10	A Lees	T: Pocock, Carter, Fardy, Moore, Kuridrani, Cubelli, Mann-Rea. C: Leali'ifano (7). P: Leali'ifano .
Mrch 04	Canberra	Waratahs	WON	32-15	M v/d westhuizen	T: Leali'ifano , Tomane, Ah Wong, Penalty try. C: Leali'ifano (2), Toomua. P: Leali'ifano (2).
Mrch 11	Perth	Force	WON	31-14	A Lees	T: Toomua, Moore, Tomane, Mann-Rea. C: Leali'ifano (4). P: Leali'ifano .
Mrch 19	Cape Town	Stormers	LOST	11-31	J Peyper	T: Speight. P: Leali'ifano (2).
Mrch 26	Bloemfontein	Cheetahs	WON	25-18	G Jackson	T: Alexander, Vaea, Toua. C: Leali'ifano , Toomua. P: Leali'ifano (2).
April 02	Canberra	Chiefs	LOST	23-48	A Gardner	T: Fardy, Sio. C: Leali'ifano (2). P: Leali'ifano (3).
April 16	Sydney	Waratahs	WON	26-20	N Briant	T: Tomane (3), Moore. C: Leali'ifano (3).
April 24	Canberra	Crusaders	LOST	14-40	J Peyper	T: Coleman, Tomane. C: Leali'ifano (2).
April 30	Invercargill	Highlanders	LOST	10-23	N Briant	T: Mann-Rea. C: Leali'ifano . P: Leali'ifano
May 06	Canberra	Bulls	WON	23-06	B O'Keeffe	T: Ah Wong, Cubelli. C: Leali'ifano (2). P: Leali'ifano (3).
May 14	Melbourne	Rebels	WON	30-22	R Hoffmann	T: Pocock, Ah Wong, Arnold, , Leali'ifano , Fardy. C: Leali'ifano . P: Leali'ifano
May 28	Canberra	Sunwolves	WON	66-05	J van Heerden	T: Moore (2), Ah Wong (2), Fardy, Dowsett, Toua, Jackson-Hope, Dargaville, Taliauli. C: Leali'ifano (8)
July 01	Canberra	Reds	WON	43-24	A Lees	T: Moore (2), Alexander, Leali'ifano , Taliauli, Cubelli. C: Leali'ifano (5). P: Leali'ifano .
July 08	Auckland	Blues	LOST	15-40	B O'Keeffe	T: Toomua, Penalty try. C: Leali'ifano . P: Leali'ifano .
July 16	Canberra	Force	WON	24-10	P Williams	T: Toomua, Kuridrani, Penalty try. C: Leali'ifano (2), Toomua. P: Leali'ifano

QUARTER-FINAL

Date	Venue	Opponent	Result	Score	Referee	Scorers
July 22	Canberra	Highlanders	LOST	09-15	A Gardner	P: Leali'ifano (3).

Note: ■ = *Champion*

2016 SQUAD

PLAYER	Date of Birth	Height	Weight	M	T	C	P	DG	Pts
R (Robbie) Abel	04/07/89	1,83	108	2	–	–	–	–	0
NF (Nigel) Ah Wong	30/05/90	1,93	102	22	5	–	–	–	25
AEA (Allan) Ala'alatoa	28/01/94	1,82	120	29	1	–	–	–	5
BE (Ben) Alexander	13/11/84	1,89	120	130	21	–	–	–	105
RW (Rory) Arnold	01/07/90	2,08	120	29	2	–	–	–	10
JM (Jarrad) Butler	20/07/91	1,86	106	61	4	–	–	–	20
STG (Sam) Carter	10/09/89	2,00	110	79	5	–	–	–	25
R (Robbie) Coleman	03/08/90	1,79	83	80	17	–	–	–	85
T (Tomás) Cubelli	12/06/89	1,77	81	15	3	–	–	–	15
J (James) Dargaville	25/04/92	1,87	90	22	2	–	–	–	10
MD (Michael) Dowsett	23/03/92	1,82	85	22	–	–	–	–	0
BT (Blake) Enever	12/10/91	2,00	115	18	1	–	–	–	5
SM (Scott) Fardy	05/07/84	1,98	113	82	9	–	–	–	45
J (Jordan) Jackson-Hope	04/05/96	1,75	80	2	1	–	–	–	5
C (Cameron) Hyne	07/03/94	1,93	105	1	–	–	–	–	0
RTRN (Tevita) Kuridrani	31/03/91	1,96	102	74	14	–	–	–	70
CP (Christian) Leali'ifano	24/09/87	1,79	95	117	19	125	148	2	798
L (Leslie) Leulua'iali'i-Makin	02/01/92	1,74	112	10	–	–	–	–	0
JW (Josh) Mann-Rea	19/02/81	1,81	105	44	3	–	–	–	15
ST (Stephen) Moore	20/01/83	1,86	112	164	17	–	–	–	85
DW (David) Pocock	23/04/88	1,84	104	99	18	–	–	–	90
JP (Joe) Powell	11/04/94	1,77	83	11	–	–	–	–	0
ST (Scott) Sio	16/10/91	1,87	116	65	4	–	–	–	20
JLMR (Jordan) Smiler	19/06/85	1,93	107	45	1	–	–	–	5
A (Andrew) Smith	10/01/85	1,94	104	57	6	–	–	–	30
R-H (Ruan) Smith	24/01/90	1,88	121	53	–	–	–	–	0
HV (Henry) Speight	24/03/88	1,86	97	78	27	–	–	–	135
T (Tom) Staniforth	13/08/94	1,98	113	13	–	–	–	–	0
LO (Lousi'i) Taliauli	08/06/93	1,93	101	15	3	–	–	–	15
JM (Joseph) Tomane	02/02/90	1,90	102	68	25	–	–	–	125
MP (Matt) To'omua	02/01/90	1,82	91	89	17	7	–	1	108
A (Aiden) Toua	19/01/90	1,83	89	26	3	–	–	–	15
IT (Ita) Vaea	09/02/89	1,87	119	48	5	–	–	–	25
M (Michael) Wells	03/05/93	1,90	103	7	–	–	–	–	0

APPEARANCES & POINTS

PLAYER	Hurricanes	Waratahs	Force	Stormers	Cheetahs	Chiefs	Waratahs	Crusaders	Highlanders	Bulls	Rebels	Sunwolves	Reds	Blues	Force	Highlanders	Apps	T	C	P	DG	Pts
Toua	15	15	15	15	15	15	15	15	15	15	15	15	15	15	15	15	16	2	–	–	–	10
Speight	14	14	14	14	–	–	–	–	–	–	–	–	–	–	–	–	4	1	–	–	–	5
Kuridrani	13	13	13	13	13	13	13	13	13	13	13	13	13	13	13	13	16	2	–	–	–	10
To'omua	12	12	12	12	12	12	12	12	12	–	–	–	12	12	12	12	13	3	3	–	–	21
Tomane	11	11	11	11	11	14	14	14	14	–	–	–	–	–	–	–	8	6	–	–	–	30
Leali'ifano	10	10	10	10	10	10	10	10	10	10	10	10	10	10	10	10	16	3	41	22	–	163
Cubelli	9	9	9	9	9	9	9	9	9	9	9	–	9R	9	9	9	15	3	–	–	–	15
Vaea	8	8	–	–	8	8	–	–	–	–	–	–	–	–	–	–	4	1	–	–	–	5
Pocock	7	7	7	7	7	7	–	–	7	7	7	7	–	–	–	7	11	2	–	–	–	10
Fardy	6	6	6	6	6	6	6	6	6	6	6	6	6	6	6	6	16	4	–	–	–	20
Carter	5	5	5	5	5	5	5	5	5	5	5	5	5	5	5	5	16	1	–	–	–	5
Arnold	4	–	4	4	4	4	4	4R	4	4	4	4	4	4	4	–	14	1	–	–	–	5
Alexander	3	3	3	3	3	3	3	–	3	3	–	3	3	3R	–		13	2	–	–	–	10
Moore	2c	2c	2c	2c	2c	2c	2c	2c	–	2c	2c	2c	2c	2c	2c	2c	15	7	–	–	–	35
Ala'alatoa	1	1R	1R	1R	1R	1R	1R	1R	1	1	1R	1R	1R	1R	1R	1R	16	–	–	–	–	0
Mann-Rea	2R	2R	2R	2R	–	2R	2R	2R	2	2R	2R	2R	2R	2R	2R		15	3	–	–	–	15
Sio	1R	1	1	1	1	1	1	1	1R	1	1	1	1	1	1	1	16	1	–	–	–	5
Leulua'iali'i-Makin	3R	3R	3R	3R	–	3R	3R	3R	3R	–	–	3R	–	–	–	3R	10	–	–	–	–	0
Smiler	4R	4R	6R	8	8R	8R	8	8	8R	8R	8R	6R	–	–	–	–	12	–	–	–	–	0
Butler	8R	8R	8	–	–	–	7	7	8	8	8	8	7	7	7	8	13	–	–	–	–	0
Dowsett	9R	9R	9R	9R	9R	–	–	9R	–	–	–	9	–	–	–	–	7	1	–	–	–	5
Smith, A	14R	x	–	–	–	–	–	–	–	–	–	14R	13R	13R	11R		5	–	–	–	–	0
Ah Wong	11R	19R	11R	14R	14R	11R	x	15R	14	14	14	14	14	14	14	14	15	5	–	–	–	25
Enever	–	4	–	–	–	–	–	–	5R	5R	–	4R	4R	4R	4		7	–	–	–	–	0
Staniforth	–	–	4R	4R	4R	4R	4R	4	4R	4R	4R	–	6R	5R	4R		13	–	–	–	–	0
Coleman	–	–	12R	15R	11	11	11	11	11	11	12	–	12	–	–	11	10	1	–	–	–	5
Wells	–	–	–	8R	–	–	8R	14R	–	–	–	8R	8	8	8R		7	–	–	–	–	0
Smith, R	–	–	–	–	3R	–	–	–	3	3R	3R	3	3R	3R	3	3	9	–	–	–	–	0
Abel	–	–	–	–	2R	–	–	–	2R	–	–	–	–	–	–		2	–	–	–	–	0
Dargaville	–	–	–	11R	5R	x	12R	14R	11	12	11	11	11	11	11	–	10	1	–	–	–	5
Powell	–	–	–	–	9R	x	–	9R	9R	9R	9R	9	9R	9R	x		8	–	–	–	–	0
Taliauli	–	–	–	–	–	–	12R	14R	11	7R	11R	11R	10R	14R			8	2	–	–	–	10
Jackson-Hope	–	–	–	–	–	–	–	11R	12R	–	–	–	–				2	1	–	–	–	5
Hyne	–	–	–	–	–	–	–	–	–	–	8	–	–	–	–		1	–	–	–	–	0
Penalty tries	–	–	–	–	–	–	–	–	–	–	–	–	–	–	–	–	–	3	–	–	–	15
34 PLAYERS																	363	56	44	22	0	434

Records

CHAMPIONS: 2001, 2004

MATCH RECORDS

Biggest winning margin	64	vs Bulls (73-9)	Canberra	1999
	64	vs Cats (64-0)	Canberra	2000
Heaviest defeat	49	vs Hurricanes (7-56)	Wellington	2009
Highest score	73	vs Bulls (73-9)	Canberra	1999
Most points conceded	56	vs Hurricanes (7-56)	Wellington	2009
Most tries	10	vs Bulls (73-9)	Canberra	1999
	10	vs Cats (64-16)	Canberra	2002
	10	vs Cats (68-28)	Canberra	2004
	10	vs Sunwolves (66-5)	Canberra	2016
Most tries conceded	8	vs Hurricanes (7-56)	Wellington	2009
Most points by a player	25	SA Mortlock (1t, 4c, 4p) vs Stormers	Canberra	2001
	25	JWC Roff (1t, 7c, 2p) vs Chiefs	Canberra	2003
Most tries by a player	4	JWC Roff vs Sharks	Manuka	1996
Most conversions by a player	9	JWC Roff vs Cats	Canberra	2004
Most penalties by a player	6	JL Huxley vs Highlanders	Canberra	2002
Most drop goals by a player	1	on 21 occasions		

SEASON RECORDS

Most team points	487	in 13 matches	2004
Most points by a player	233	CP Leali'ifano	2013
Most team tries	67	in 13 matches	2004
Most tries by a player	15	JWC Roff	1997
Most conversions by a player	51	JWC Roff	2004
Most penalties by a player	57	CP Leali'ifano	2013
Most drop goals by a player	2	GM Gregan	2001
	2	SJ Larkham	2001 & 2002
	2	CP Leali'ifano	2009

CAREER RECORDS

Most appearances	142	GB Smith	2000-2013
Most points	1019	SA Mortlock	1998-2010
Most tries	57	JWC Roff	1996-2004
Most conversions	161	SA Mortlock	1998-2010
Most penalties	148	CP Leali'ifano	1998-2016
Most drop goals	5	SJ Larkham	1996-2007

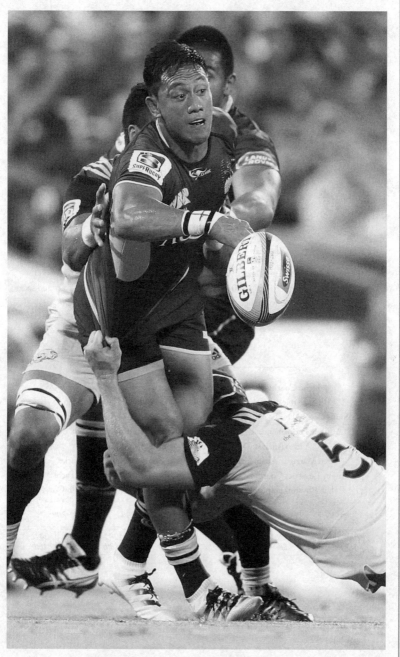

Christian Leali'ifano – dependable for the Brumbies and Wallabies.

Western Force

Ground: NIB Stadium **Capacity:** 20526 **Address:** 310 Pier Street, Perth, WA 6000
Telephone number: + 61 8 9387 0700 **Colours:** Ocean blue jersey with black shorts and socks
Website: www.rugbywa.com.au **Head Coach:** Michael Foley
Captain: Matt Hodgson **CEO:** Mark Sinderberry **Chairman:** Dr Russel Perry
President: David Redpath

Head Coach: Michael Foley **Snr Assistant Coach:** David Wessels
Backs/Attack Coach: Kevin Foote **Linout Consultant:** Elwee Prinsloo
Skills Coach: Dwayne Nestor **Strength & Conditioning Coach:** Will Markwick
Head Of Athletic Performance: Charlie Higgins **Assistant Conditioning Coach:** Ben Brugman
Video Analyst: Damian Pacecca **Doctor:** Dr Mike Cadogan
Tean Manager: Adam Crane **Rugby Support Coordinator:** Adrian Blacker
Rugby Logistics Coordinator: Tobias Hoskins **Physiotherapist:** Emidio Pacceca
Rehab Physiotherapist: Ben Mather **Player Development Manager:** Sam Cox

1996	1997	1998	1999	2000	2001	2002	2003	2004	2005	2006 14th

2007 7th	2008 8th	2009 8th	2010 13th	2011 12th	2012 14th	2013 13th	2014 8th	2015 15th	2016 16th

Played	Won	Lost	Drawn	Points for	Points against	Tries for	Tries against
15	2	13	0	260	441	25	60

Date	Venue	Opponent	Result	Score	Referee	Scorers
Febr 27	Perth	Rebels	LOST	19-25	M v/d Westhuizen	T: Lance. C: Lance. P: Lance (4).
Mrch 05	Brisbane	Reds	WON	22-06	A Gardner	T: Morahan. C: Prior. P: Lance.
Mrch 11	Perth	Brumbies	LOST	14-31	A Lees	T: Morahan, Tapuai. C: Lance, Grant.
Mrch 18	Palmerston North	Hurricanes	LOST	06-41	P Williams	P: Grant (2).
Mrch 26	Hamilton	Chiefs	LOST	10-53	M Fraser	T: Tapuai. C: Grant. P: Grant.
April 01	Dunedin	Highlanders	LOST	20-32	B Pickerill	T: D Haylett-Petty, McCalman. C: Grant (2). P: Grant (2).
April 08	Perth	Crusaders	LOST	19-20	B O'Keeffe	T: Louwrens. C: Grant. P: Grant (4).
April 23	Perth	Waratahs	LOST	13-49	R Hoffmann	T: Scoble. C: Tapuai. P: Grant (2).
April 29	Perth	Bulls	LOST	20-42	J van Heerden	T: Hodgson, Godwin. C: Prior (2). P: Prior (2).
May 07	Tokyo	Sunwolves	WON	40-22	M Fraser	T: Brache (3), Stander, McCalman, Cottrell. C: Prior (4), Grant
May 21	Perth	Blues	LOST	13-17	J Nutbrown	T: Hodgson. C: Tapuai. P: Prior, Tapuai.
May 29	Melbourne	Rebels	LOST	22-27	C Pollock	T: Morahan (2), Scoble. C: Grant (2). P: Grant.
July 02	Bloemfontein	Cheetahs	LOST	29-30	S Kubo	T: D Haylett-Petty (2), Godwin. C: Prior. P: Prior (2). P: Grant (2).
July 09	Perth	Stormers	LOST	03-22	M Fraser	P: Lance.
July 16	Canberra	Brumbies	LOST	10-24	P Williams	T: Tapuai. C: Prior. P: Prior.

2016 SQUAD

PLAYER	Date of Birth	Height	Weight	M	T	C	P	DG	Pts
J (Jermaine) Ainsley	08/08/95	1,80	111	9	–	–	–	–	0
CG (Chris) Alcock	26/06/88	1,82	103	55	3	–	–	–	15
MG (Marcel) Brache	15/10/87	1,90	92	38	3	–	–	–	15
LC (Luke) Burton	17/02/94	1,80	92	19	–	10	9	–	47
NL (Nathan) Charles	09/01/89	1,83	106	83	4	–	–	–	20
AP (Adam) Coleman	07/10/91	2,04	122	38	1	–	–	–	5
AJ (Angus) Cottrell	20/11/89	1,91	105	57	4	–	–	–	20
PJM (Pek) Cowan	02/06/86	1,85	115	117	5	–	–	–	25
TJ (Tetera) Faulkner	26/07/88	1,78	117	55	2	–	–	–	10
KW (Kyle) Godwin	30/07/92	1,87	93	52	7	3	2	–	47
PJ (Peter) Grant	15/08/94	1,90	100	116	10	134	202	–	924
DS (Dane) Haylett-Petty	18/06/89	1,89	95	46	6	–	–	–	30
RB (Ross) Haylett-Petty	10/01/94	1,97	110	15	–	–	–	–	0
R (Richard) Hardwick	31/05/94	1,83	102	4	–	–	–	–	0
C (Chris) Heiberg	01/06/85	1,83	115	23	–	–	–	–	0
MJ (Matt) Hodgson	25/06/81	1,84	100	131	18	–	–	–	90
KS (Kane) Koteka	01/01/94	1,82	94	11	–	–	–	–	0
J (Jono) Lance	27/06/90	1,83	92	40	3	2	10	1	52
R (Ryan) Louwrens	12/03/91	1,79	93	18	3	–	–	–	15
S (Semisi) Masirewa	09/06/91	1,84	95	15	–	–	–	–	0
A (Ammon) Matuauto	29/01/86	1,79	96	1	–	–	–	–	0
BJ (Ben) McCalman	18/03/88	1,92	106	91	11	–	–	–	55
S (Steve) Mafi	09/12/89	1,98	112	26	1	–	–	–	5
AS (Alby) Mathewson	13/12/85	1,73	93	131	20	–	–	–	100
GP (Guy) Millar	23/04/92	1,86	117	14	–	–	–	–	0
LJ (Luke) Morahan	13/04/90	1,89	95	80	22	–	–	–	110
A (Albert) Nikoro	07/08/92	1,74	98	8	–	–	1	–	3
M (Matt) Philip	07/03/94	1,96	95	3	–	–	–	–	0
IG (Ian) Prior	21/08/90	1,79	83	66	3	9	6	–	51
A (Anaru) Rangi	19/10/88	1,80	117	5	–	–	–	–	0
S (Junior) Rasolea	29/04/91	1,84	102	39	2	–	–	–	10
H (Harry) Scoble	12/11/94	1,78	101	8	2	–	–	–	10
B (Brynard) Stander	27/04/90	1,90	97	33	2	–	–	–	10
BNL (Ben) Tapuai	19/01/89	1,80	95	78	11	2	1	–	62
HR (Heath) Tessmann	03/03/84	1,82	105	63	1	–	–	–	5
FD (Francois) van Wyk	30/07/91	1,89	114	12	1	–	–	–	5
RM (Rory) Walton	11/04/89	1,95	111	15	–	–	–	–	0
				1615	145	160	231	1	1741

APPEARANCES & POINTS

PLAYER	Rebels	Reds	Brumbies	Hurricanes	Chiefs	Highlanders	Crusaders	Waratahs	Bulls	Sunwolves	Blues	Rebels	Cheetahs	Stormers	Brumbies	Apps	T	C	P	DG	Pts
Haylett-Petty, D	15	15	15	15	15	15	15	15	15	15	15	15	15	15	15	15	3	–	–	–	15
Morahan	14	14	14	–	–	14	14	–	11	11	11	11	11	11c	11c	12	4	–	–	–	20
Tapuai	13	13	13	13	13	13	13	13	–	–	13	13	–	13	13	12	3	2	1	–	22
Godwin	12	–	–	–	–	x	10R	13R	12	12	12	12	12	12	12	9	2	–	–	–	10
Brache	11	11R	11R	14	14	–	–	14	14	14	14	14	14	14	14	13	3	–	–	–	15
Lance	10	10	10	–	–	–	–	–	–	–	–	10	10	10		6	1	2	10	–	39
Mathewson	9	9	9R	9	9	9	–		9	9	9	9	9	–		11	–	–	–	–	0
Cottrell	8	8	6R	6	8	6	6	6	6	6R	6R	6R	8	8	–	14	1	–	–	–	5
Hodgson	7c	7c	7c	7c	7c	7c	7c	7c	7c	7c	7c	–				11	2	–	–	–	10
Stander	6	6	6	8R	6	–	–	7R	6R	6	6	6	6	8R	6	13	1	–	–	–	5
Coleman	5	5	5	5	5	5	5	5	5	5	5	5	–	–		12	–	–	–	–	0
Mafi	4	4	5R	5R	4R	4R	4	4	4	4R	–	–	–	–		10	–	–	–	–	0
Millar	3	3	3	–	–	–	–		3R	3	3	3	3R	3	3	10	–	–	–	–	0
Charles	2	2	2R	2	2R	6R	2R	–	–							7	–	–	–	–	0
Cowan	1	1	1	1	1	1	1	–	–	1R	1c	1c	1	1		12	–	–	–	–	0
Tessman	2R	2R	2	2R	2	2	2	2	–	–	2R	–	–			9	–	–	–	–	0
Heiberg	1R	1R	8R	1R	1R	1R	–	1R	1R	1R	–	–	–			9	–	–	–	–	0
Ainsley	3R	3R	3	3R	3R	3R	x	3R	–	–			3R	1R		9	–	–	–	–	0
Haylett-Petty, R	4R	4R	4	4	4	4	–	–	4R	4	4	4	4	4	4	13	–	–	–	–	0
Alcock	7R	–	–	–	–	–	–			7	7	7	7			5	–	–	–	–	0
Prior	9R	9R	9	10R	10R	10R	9	–	10	10	10	–	9	9R	9	13	–	9	6	–	36
Grant	12R	x	10R	10	10	10	10	10	–	10R	–	10	10R	10R	10R	12	–	8	14	–	58
Masirewa	19R	11	11	11	11	11	11	11	12R	13R	14R	13R	13R	11R	14R	15	–	–	–	–	0
Rasolea	–	12	12	12	12	12	12	12	12	13	–	12R	13	–		11	–	–	–	–	0
McCalman	–	6R	8	8	8R	8	8	8	8	8	8	8	–	–		11	2	–	–	–	10
Faulkner	–	–	–	3	3	3	3	3	3R	3R	3R	3	–	–		10	–	–	–	–	0
Louwrens	–	–	–	9R	9R	9R	9R	9R	9R	9R	9R	x	9	9R		11	1	–	–	–	5
Nikoro	–	–	11R	14R	x	x	11R	–	–							3	–	–	–	–	0
Hardwick	–	–	–	–	2R	x	–	–			6R	6	8			4	–	–	–	–	0
Van Wyk	–	–	–	–	–	1R	1	1	1	1	1R	1R	1R	x		8	–	–	–	–	0
Walton	–	–	–	–	–	x	4R	–	–	7R	4R	5	5	5		6	–	–	–	–	0
Scoble	–	–	–	–	–	–	16R	2	2	2	2	2	2	2		8	2	–	–	–	10
Matuauto	–	–	–	–	–	–	–	13	–	–						1	–	–	–	–	0
Rangi	–	–	–	–	–	–	2R	2R	x	–	2R	2R	2R			5	–	–	–	–	0
Burton	–	–	–	–	–	–	–	–	10R	–	–	–				1	–	–	–	–	0
Philip	–	–	–	–	–	–	–	–			5R	5R	5R			3	–	–	–	–	0
Koteka	–	–	–	–	–	–	–	–					6R			1	–	–	–	–	0
37 PLAYERS																335	25	21	31	0	260

Records

MATCH RECORDS

Biggest winning margin	41	vs Lions (55-14)	Perth	2009
Heaviest defeat	53	vs Crusaders (0-53)	Christchurch	2007
Highest score	55	vs Lions (55-14)	Perth	2009
Most points conceded	53	vs Crusaders (0-53)	Christchurch	2007
Most tries	8	vs Lions (55-14)	Perth	2009
Most tries conceded	8	vs Crusaders (0-53)	Christchurch	2007
Most points by a player	25	CB Shepherd vs Bulls (2t, 3c, 3p)	Pretoria	2007
Most tries by a player	3	SNG Staniforth vs Cats	Johannesburg	2006
	3	CB Shepherd vs Brumbies	Canberra	2009
	3	NM Cummins vs Waratahs	Perth	2014
	3	MG Brache vs Sunwolves	Tokyo	2016
Most conversions by a player	6	MJ Giteau vs Lions	Perth	2009
Most penalties by a player	6	JD O'Connor vs Bulls	Perth	2011
Most drop goals by a player	2	JM Ebersohn vs Bulls	Pretoria	2013

SEASON RECORDS

Most team points	343	from 16 matches	2014
Most points by a player	170	JD O'Connor	2011
Most team tries	42	from 13 matches	2009
Most tries by a player	9	SNG Staniforth	2006
Most conversions by a player	28	MJ Giteau	2009
Most penalties by a player	47	JD O'Connor	2011
Most drop goals by a player	2	JM Ebersohn	2013

CAREER RECORDS

Most appearances	131	MJ Hodgson	2006-2016
Most points	372	CB Shepherd	2006-2012
Most tries	30	CB Shepherd	2006-2012
Most conversions	55	MJ Giteau	2007-2009
Most penalties	70	JD O'Connor	2009-2011
Most drop goals	3	JM Ebersohn	2013-2015

Dane Haylett-Petty.

Melbourne Rebels

Ground: AAMI Park, Melbourne **Capacity:** 30 050 **Address:** Gate 3, Royal Parade,
Carlton North, VIC, 3054 **Telephone number:** + 61 3 9221 0700
Colours: Dark blue jersey with white and red trim. Dark blue shorts with white trim.
Dark blue socks with white band. **Website:** www.melbournerebels.com.au
Head Coach: Tony McGahan **Captain:** Scott Higginbotham **CEO:** Peter Leahy
Chairman: Jonathan Ling **President:** Gary Grey **Managing Director:** Andrew Cox

---

Head Coach: Tony Mcgahan **Asstistant Coaches:** Zane Hilton & Leo Crowley
Head Conditioning Coach: Shane Lehane **Assistant Conditioning Coach:** Brendan Whelan
Head Performance Analyst: Eion Toolan **Assistant Performance Analyst:** John Batina
Doctor: Dr Asheer Singh **Rehabilitation Coordinator:** Nick Court
Media Officer: Chris Gottaas **Team Manager:** Mark Rowe
Assistant Team Manager: Chris Thomson **Dietician:** Alison Paterson
Player Development Manager: Cameron Yorke

1996	1997	1998	1999	2000	2001	2002	2003	2004	2005	2006

2007	2008	2009	2010	2011 15th	2012 13th	2013 12th	2014 15th	2015 10th	2016 12th

Played	Won	Lost	Drawn	Points for	Points against	Tries for	Tries against
15	7	8	0	365	486	46	65

Date	Venue	Opponent	Result	Score	Referee	Scorers
Febr 27	Perth	Force	WON	25-19	M v/d Westhuizen	T: Hodge (2), Thomson. C: Hodge (2). P: Hodge (2).
Mrch 05	Pretoria	Bulls	LOST	25-45	B O'Keeffe	T: Meehan (2), Hanson, Placid. C: Debreczeni. P: Debreczeni.
Mrch 12	Melbourne	Reds	WON	25-23	P Williams	T: Placid. C: Debreczeni. P: Debreczeni (6).
Mrch 19	Tokyo	Sunwolves	WON	35-09	M Fraser	T: Reid, McMahon, Mehan, English. C: Debreczeni (2), Hawkins. P: Debreczeni.
Mrch 26	Melbourne	Highlanders	LOST	03-27	A Lees	P: Debreczeni.
April 03	Sydney	Waratahs	WON	21-17	A Lees	T: Smith, Debreczeni. C: Debreczeni. P: Debreczeni (3).
April 15	Melbourne	Hurricanes	LOST	13-38	R Hoffman	T: Crawford, Shipperley. P: Hodge.
April 22	Melbourne	Cheetahs	WON	36-14	G Jackson	T: Hodge (2), Placid, Timani, Ellison. C: Debreczeni (4). P: Debreczeni.
April 30	Auckland	Blues	LOST	30-36	C Joubert	T: Reid, Hodge, Naivalu, Fainga'a. C: Debreczeni (2). P: Debeczeni (2).
May 14	Melbourne	Brumbies	LOST	22-30	R Hoffman	T: Crawford, Hodge, Naivalu. C: Debreczeni (2). P: Debreczeni.
May 21	Hamilton	Chiefs	LOST	15-36	A Gardner	T: Harris, Hodge. C: Harris. P: Harris.
May 29	Melbourne	Force	WON	27-22	C Pollock	T: Naivalu (2), Hodge, Timani. C: Debreczeni, Hodge. P: Hodge.
July 02	Melbourne	Stormers	LOST	31-57	A Gardner	T: Meehan, Placid, Debreczeni, Naivalu. C: Debreczeni (4). P: Debreczeni.
July 09	Christchurch	Crusaders	LOST	26-85	G Jackson	T: Retallick, Stirzaker, Hodge, Naivalu. C: Debreczeni (3).
July 15	Brisbane	Reds	WON	31-28	W Houston	T: McMahon (2), Stirzaker, English. C: Debreczeni (4). P: Debreczeni.

2016 SQUAD

PLAYER	Date of Birth	Height	Weight	M	T	C	P	DG	Pts
CD (Cruze) Ah-Nau	10/08/90	1,81	117	38	–	–	–	–	0
P (Paul) Asquith	12/08/93	1,83	94	3	–	–	–	–	0
JC (Cam) Crawford	14/01/88	1,93	98	22	10	–	–	–	50
SB (Steve) Cummins	29/03/92	2,02	117	5	–	–	–	–	0
JM (Jack) Debreczeni	06/06/93	1,92	100	33	5	32	27	–	170
TE (Tamati) Ellison	01/04/83	1,84	95	113	15	–	–	–	75
TAJ (Tom) English	08/03/91	1,87	96	47	10	–	–	–	50
CG (Colby) Fainga'a	31/03/91	1,83	100	75	4	–	–	–	20
SA (Scott) Fuglistaller	16/04/87	1,83	101	52	3	–	–	–	15
J (Jamie) Hagan	15/04/87	1,90	125	11	–	–	–	–	0
JE (James) Hanson	15/09/88	1,83	104	97	8	–	–	–	40
MJ (Mike) Harris	08/07/88	1,86	96	65	8	62	78	1	401
D (Dan) Hawkins	20/04/91	1,80	84	4	–	1	–	–	2
R (Reece) Hodge	21/02/94	1,91	94	12	9	3	4	–	63
MBW (Mitch) Inman	24/10/88	1,91	105	88	6	–	–	–	30
SK (Sam) Jeffries	20/05/92	2,00	114	17	–	–	–	–	0
LM (Luke) Jones	02/04/91	1,97	110	75	1	–	–	–	5
PJ (Pat) Leafa	16/03/91	1,81	108	47	1	–	–	–	5
R (Rob) Leota	03/03/97	1,92	116	1	–	–	–	–	0
K (Kotaro) Matsushima	26/03/93	1,78	87	5	–	–	–	–	0
SP (Sean) McMahon	18/06/94	1,85	91	42	4	–	–	–	20
BIP (Ben) Meehan	21/01/93	1,78	85	23	4	–	–	–	20
TP (Tim) Metcher	10/05/91	1,80	119	6	–	–	–	–	0
T (Tom) Moloney	04/03/94	1,89	118	3	–	–	–	–	0
S (Sef) Naivalu	07/01/92	1,86	94	23	10	–	–	–	50
JR (Jonah) Placid	14/05/95	1,83	96	14	5	–	–	–	25
JT (Jordy) Reid	03/10/91	1,83	107	37	2	–	–	–	10
CJ (Culum) Retallick	08/05/85	1,98	116	53	1	–	–	–	5
DP (Dom) Shipperley	04/01/91	1,86	94	64	18	–	–	–	90
S (Siliva) Siliva	11/12/91	1,77	118	1	–	–	–	–	0
TJ (Toby) Smith	10/10/88	1,90	112	79	5	–	–	–	25
M (Mick) Snowden	18/12/87	1,85	93	8	–	–	–	–	0
NR (Nic) Stirzaker	08/03/91	1,79	82	49	5	–	–	–	25
AJ (Adam) Thomson	13/03/82	1,96	112	95	22	–	–	–	110
L (Lopeti) Timani	28/9/90	1,93	116	48	6	–	–	–	30
S (Sione) Tuipolotu	12/02/97	1,79	101	4	–	–	–	–	0
LS (Laurie) Weeks	05/04/86	1,80	115	95	1	–	–	–	5
				1454	163	98	109	1	1341

APPEARANCES & POINTS

PLAYER	Force	Bulls	Reds	Sunwolves	Highlanders	Waratahs	Hurricanes	Cheetahs	Blues	Brumbies	Chiefs	Force	Stormers	Crusaders	Reds	Apps	T	C	P	DG	Pts
Hodge	15	–	–	–	11R	15	15	13	13	12	12	12	15	12	12	12	9	3	4	–	63
Shipperley	14	14	14	14	14	14	14	–	–	–	–	–	–	–	–	7	1	–	–	–	5
Ellison	13	13	13	13	13	13	12	12	12	13	–	–	–	–	–	10	1	–	–	–	5
Inman	12	12	12	12	12	12	–	–	–	13	13	12	–	13	–	10	–	–	–	–	0
English	11	11	11	11	11	–	–	–	15R	11	11	11	11	11	–	11	2	–	–	–	10
Harris	10	–	–	–	–	–	15	15	10	–	15	–	–	–	–	5	1	1	1	–	10
Meehan	9	9	9	9	9	9R	9R	9R	9R	9R	9R	9R	9	9R	9R	15	4	–	–	–	20
Thomson	8	6	8	8	8	8	8	8	8	8	8	8R	–	8	–	13	1	–	–	–	5
McMahon	7c	7c	7c	7c	7c	7	7	7	7	6	6	6	6c	–	6	14	3	–	–	–	15
Reid	6	8R	6	6	6	6	6	6	6	6R	8R	7	7	6	7	15	2	–	–	–	10
Timani	5	8	5	5	5	5	5	5	–	5	5	5	5	–	–	12	2	–	–	–	10
Jones	4	4	4	4	4	4	4	4	4	–	4	4	4	–	4	13	–	–	–	–	0
Weeks	3	3	3	3	3	3	3	3	–	–	–	1R	3	3	–	11	–	–	–	–	0
Hanson	2	2	2	2R	2	2	2	2	2	2	2	2	2	2	2	15	1	–	–	–	5
Smith	1	1	1	1	1	1	–	1	1	1	1	3	3	1	1	14	1	–	–	–	5
Leafa	2R	2R	2R	2	2R	2R	2R	2R	2R	2R	–	2R	2R	2R	2R	14	–	–	–	–	0
Ah-Nau	1R	3R	x	1R	1R	1R	1	1R	1R	1R	1R	1	1	1R	1R	14	–	–	–	–	0
Hagan	3R	–	–	3R	3R	3R	3R	3R	3	3	3	–	–	3R	3R	11	–	–	–	–	0
Cummins	5R	5	x	–	–	–	–	–	–	–	–	4R	–	–	–	3	–	–	–	–	0
Faingaa	6R	–	–	–	–	–	6R	6R	7	7	8	8	7	8	–	9	1	–	–	–	5
Snowden	9R	9R	x	–	–	–	–	–	–	–	–	9R	–	–	–	3	–	–	–	–	0
Placid	10R	15	15	15	15	–	14R	15	15	–	10R	10R	14	15R	–	12	4	–	–	–	20
Hawkins	13R	10R	x	10R	–	x	15R	–	–	–	–	–	–	–	–	4	–	1	–	–	2
Debreczeni	–	10	10	10	10	10	10	10	10	10	10	15	10	10	10	14	2	25	20	–	120
Jeffries	–	5R	5R	5R	5R	5R	4R	5	5R	4	–	–	4	5R	–	12	–	–	–	–	0
Matsushima	–	14R	x	–	–	–	14R	13R	11R	11R	–	–	–	–	–	5	–	–	–	–	0
Moloney	–	1R	–	–	–	1R	–	–	–	–	x	3R	–	–	–	3	–	–	–	–	0
Cocker	–	–	x	–	–	–	–	–	–	–	–	–	–	–	–	0	–	–	–	–	0
Fuglistaller	–	–	–	6R	13R	6R	6R	–	–	–	7R	4R	–	–	–	6	–	–	–	–	0
Stirzaker	–	–	–	9R	9R	9c	9c	9c	9c	9c	9c	–	9c	9c	–	11	2	–	–	–	10
Tuipulotu	–	–	–	13R	–	–	13R	x	–	–	13R	13	x	–	–	4	–	–	–	–	0
Crawford	–	–	–	15R	11	11	11	11	11	–	–	–	–	–	–	6	2	–	–	–	10
Naivalu	–	–	–	–	12R	13	14	14	14	14	14	13	14	14	–	10	6	–	–	–	30
Metcher	–	–	–	–	–	–	3R	3R	3R	1R	–	–	–	–	–	4	–	–	–	–	0
Retallick	–	–	–	–	–	5R	–	4R	4R	5R	5	5	–	–	–	6	1	–	–	–	5
Siliva	–	–	–	–	–	–	–	2R	–	–	–	–	–	–	–	1	–	–	–	–	0
Asquith	–	–	–	–	–	–	–	–	–	–	–	14R	23R	15	–	3	–	–	–	–	0
Leota	–	–	–	–	–	–	–	–	–	–	–	–	12R	x	–	1	–	–	–	–	0
Maddocks	–	–	–	–	–	–	–	–	–	–	–	–	–	x	–	0	–	–	–	–	0
39 PLAYERS																333	46	30	25	0	365

Records

MATCH RECORDS

Biggest winning margin	21	vs Cheetahs (35-14)	Melbourne	2014
Heaviest defeat	57	vs Sharks (7-64)	Durban	2013
Highest score	42	vs Hurricanes (42-25)	Melbourne	2011
Most points conceded	66	vs Hurricanes (24-66)	Wellington	2012
Most tries	6	vs Hurricanes (42-25)	Melbourne	2011
Most tries conceded	10	vs Sharks (7-64)	Durban	2013
Most points by a player	27	JC Woodward vs Brumbies	Melbourne	2014
Most tries by a player	2	AM Campbell vs Hurricanes	Melbourne	2011
	2	KC Vuna vs Bulls	Melbourne	2012
	2	NJ Phipps vs Crusaders	Melbourne	2012
	2	C Neville vs Western Force	Perth	2012
	2	KC Vuna vs Hurricanes	Wellington	2012
	2	HW Pyle vs Lions	Johannesburg	2012
	2	J Woodward vs Force	Perth	2013
	2	HW Pyle vs Chiefs	Melbourne	2013
	2	M Inman vs Blues	Auckland	2013
	2	T English vs Waratahs	Melbourne	2013
	2	B Hegarty vs Highlanders	Melbourne	2013
	2	KC Vuna vs Highlanders	Melbourne	2013
	2	T English vs Highlanders	Melbourne	2013
	2	S Naivalu vs Reds	Brisbane	2015
	2	S Higginbotham vs Sharks	Durban	2015
	2	R Hodge vs Force	Perth	2016
	2	BIP Meehan vs Bulls	Pretoria	2016
	2	R Hodge vs Chetahs	Melbourne	2016
	2	S Naivalu vs Force	Melbourne	2016
	2	SP McMahon vs Reds	Brisbane	2016
Most conversions by a player	5	KJ Beale vs Bulls	Melbourne	2012
Most penalties by a player	6	DJ Cipriani vs Brumbies	Melbourne	2011
	6	JC Woodward vs Brumbies	Melbourne	2014
	6	JM Debreczeni vs Reds	Melbourne	2016
Most drop goals by a player	1	AT Roberts vs Cheetahs	Melbourne	2014

SEASON RECORDS

Most team points	382	from 16 matches	2013
Most points by a player	120	JM Debreczeni	2016
Most team tries	46	from 15 matches	2016
Most tries by a player	9	R Hodge	2016
Most conversions by a player	25	JM Debreczeni	2016
Most penalties by a player	33	JC Woodward	2014
Most drop goals by a player	1	AT Roberts	201

CAREER RECORDS

Most appearances	75	LM Jones	2011-2016
Most tries	13	KC Vuna	2011-2013
Most conversions	32	JM Debreczeni	2014-2016
Most penalties	44	JD O'Connor	2012-2013
Most drop goals	1	AT Roberts	2014

Tamati Ellison.

Queensland Reds

Ground: Suncorp Stadium **Address:** Castlemaine Street, Milton, Brisbane
Telephone: + 61 7 3354 9333 **Capacity:** 52 500 **Colours:** Cardinal red jersey, socks and shorts
Website: www.redsrugby.com.au **Coach:** Richard Graham
Captain: James Slipper **CEO:** Jim Carmichael **Chairman:** Rod McCall
President: Tony Shaw

Head Coach: Richard Graham *(Fired after week 2)*
Assistant Coaches: Nick Stiles & Matt O'Connor *(Took over as Co-Coach)*
Doctor: Dr Chris Thomas **Physiotherapist:** Cameron Lillicrap & Gina Nelson
Manager: Thomas Barker **Media Officer:** Tom Kennedy
Video Analyst: Michael Todd **Dietician:** Gary Slater

1996	1997	1998	1999	2000	2001	2002	2003	2004	2005	2006
1st	10th	5th	1st	7th	4th	5th	8th	10th	10th	12th

2007	2008	2009	2010	2011	2012	2013	2014	2015	2016
14th	12th	13th	5th	1st	3rd	5th	13th	13th	15th

Played	Won	Lost	Drawn	Points for	Points against	Tries for	Tries against
15	3	11	1	290	458	33	57

Date	Venue	Opponent	Result	Score	Referee	Scorers
Febr 27	Sydney	Waratahs	LOST	10-30	A Gardner	T: McIntyre. C: Goromaru. P: Goromaru.
Mrch 05	Brisbane	Force	LOST	06-22	A Gardner	P: Goromaru (2).
Mrch 12	Melbourne	Rebels	LOST	23-25	P Williams	T: Frisby, Ready. C: McIntyre (2). P: McIntyre (3).
Mrch 19	Brisbane	Blues	DREW	25-25	A Lees	T: Feauai-Sautia, McIntyre, Kerewi. C: McIntyre (2). P: McIntyre (2).
Mrch 27	Brisbane	Waratahs	LOST	13-15	B O'Keeffe	T: Penalty try. C: McIntyre. P: McIntyre (2).
April 09	Brisbane	Highlanders	WON	28-27	G Jackson	T: Gill, Frisby, Kerevi. C: McIntyre (2). P: McIntyre (2). DG: McIntyre.
April 16	Pretoria	Bulls	LOST	22-41	A Gardner	T: Kerevi (2), Feauai-Sautia. C: McIntyre (2). DG: Gill.
April 23	Cape Town	Stormers	LOST	22-40	M v/d Westhuizen	T: Ntabuli, Hunt, Gill. C: McIntyre (2). P: McIntyre.
April 30	Brisbane	Cheetahs	WON	30-17	B O'Keeffe	T: Frisby (2), Browning. C: McIntyre (3). P: McIntyre (3).
May 06	Christchurch	Crusaders	LOST	05-38	B Pickerill	T: Magnay.
May 14	Wellington	Hurricanes	LOST	14-29	B Pickerill	T: Feauai-Sautia. P: Goromaru (3).
May 21	Brisbane	Sunwolves	WON	35-25	W Houston	T: Browning (2), Slipper, Neville. C: Goromaru (2), McIntyre. P: Goromaru (2), McIntyre.
July 01	Canberra	Brumbies	LOST	24-43	A Lees	T: Ready, Paia'aua, Tupou. C: Taefu (3). P: Taefu.
July 08	Brisbane	Chiefs	LOST	05-50	N Briant	T: Kuridrani.
July 15	Brisbane	Rebels	LOST	28-31	W Houston	T: Gill (2), Frisby, Kerevi. C: Frisby (3), Taefu.

Note: ■ = *Champion*

2016 SQUAD

PLAYER	Date of Birth	Height	Weight	M	T	C	P	DG	Pts
TW (Thomas) Banks	18/06/94	1,86	93	2	–	–	–	–	0
CS (Curtis) Browning	30/10/93	1,90	108	35	4	–	–	–	20
BP (Ben) Daley	27/06/88	1,84	112	80	2	–	–	–	10
KP (Kane) Douglas	01/06/89	2,02	123	79	2	–	–	–	10
SK (Sef) Fa'agase	03/05/91	1,85	117	23	–	–	–	–	0
AS (Anthony) Fainga'a	020/2/87	1,82	92	92	5	–	–	–	25
SM (Saia) Fainga'a	02/02/87	1,87	106	126	8	–	–	–	40
C (Chris) Feauai-Sautia	17/11/93	1,81	88	47	11	–	–	–	55
NH (Nick) Frisby	29/10/92	1,83	84	54	11	3	–	1	64
ST (Scott) Gale	24/10/94	1,85	86	5	–	–	–	–	0
A (Alex) Gibbon	07/09/92	1,81	91	2	–	–	–	–	0
LB (Liam) Gill	08/06/92	1,83	96	76	11	–	–	–	55
A (Ayumu) Goromaru	01/03/86	1,85	90	8	–	3	8	–	30
SJ (Sam) Greene	16/08/94	1,78	88	6	–	–	–	–	0
MA (Michael) Gunn	16/06/95	1,89	96	8	–	–	–	–	0
GS (Greg) Holmes	11/06/83	1,85	114	144	7	–	–	–	35
LD (Leroy) Houston	10/11/86	1,88	114	48	2	–	–	–	10
KNM (Karmichael) Hunt	17/11/86	1,86	93	19	1	–	1	–	8
SV (Samu) Kerevi	27/09/93	1,86	108	31	12	–	–	–	60
CJ (Chris) Kuridrani	12/12/91	1,89	99	14	2	–	–	–	10
J (Junior) Laloifi	25/09/94	1,75	76	6	–	–	–	–	0
M (Matt) Mafi	26/05/91	1,78	118	4	–	–	–	–	0
JA (Jake) McIntyre	28/04/94	1,76	82	16	3	15	14	1	90
CK (Campbell) Magnay	10/11/96	1,95	98	12	1	–	–	–	5
B (Ben) Matwijow	14/02/90	1,97	117	11	–	–	–	–	0
E (Eto) Nabuli	24/08/88	1,97	108	15	1	–	–	–	5
C (Cadeyrn) Neville	09/11/88	2,02	123	63	4	–	–	–	20
DS (Duncan) Paia'au	20/01/95	1,80	91	8	1	–	–	–	5
PL (Pettowa) Paraka	16/11/93	1,79	118	7	–	–	–	–	0
AJ (Andrew) Ready	11/07/93	1,80	103	19	2	–	–	–	10
JW (Jake) Schatz	25/07/90	1,92	109	20	7	–	–	–	35
RA (Rob) Simmons	19/04/89	2,00	115	101	4	–	–	–	20
J A (James) Slipper	06/06/89	1,85	114	91	5	–	–	–	25
L (Lagi) Setu	25/02/88	1,87	104	3	–	–	–	–	0
H (Henry) Taefu	02/04/93	1,83	100	4	–	4	1	–	11
ST (Sam) Talakai	09/04/91	1,83	122	27	–	–	–	–	0
T (Taniela) Tupou	10/05/96	1,75	135	3	1	–	–	–	5
HF (Hendrik) Tui	13/12/87	1,89	110	16	–	–	–	–	0
L (Lukhan) Tui	19/09/96	1,98	121	4	–	–	–	–	0
J (Jack) Tuttle	02/02/95	1,86	92	2	–	–	–	–	0
J (James) Tuttle	13/05/96	1,76	84	5	–	–	–	–	0

APPEARANCES & POINTS

PLAYER	Waratahs	Force	Rebels	Blues	Waratahs	Highlanders	Bulls	Stormers	Cheetahs	Crusaders	Hurricanes	Sunwolves	Brumbies	Chiefs	Rebels	Apps	T	C	P	DG	Pts
Hunt	15	12	15	15	15	15	15	15	15	15	–	–	–	–	–	10	1	–	–	–	5
Feauai-Sautia	14	14	14	14	–	14	14	–	–	14	14	14	–	–	–	9	3	–	–	–	15
Kerevi	13	13	13	13	13	13	13	13	13	–	–	13	13	13	13	13	5	–	–	–	25
Taefu	12	–	–	–	–	–	–	–	–	–	–	–	12	12	12	4	–	4	1	–	11
Nabuli	11	11	11	11	11	11	11	11	11	11	11	11	11	–	11	15	1	–	–	–	5
McIntyre	10	10	10	10	10	10	10	10	10	10	10	10	10	–	11	13	2	15	14	1	85
Frisby	9	9	9	9	9	9	9	9	9	9	9	9	9	9	9	15	5	3	–	–	31
Schatz	8	8	8	8	8	8	8	–	–	–	–	–	–	–	–	7	–	–	–	–	0
Browning	7	7	7R	7R	7R	7R	8R	8	8	8	8	8	8	8	8	15	3	–	–	–	15
Tui, H	6	6	6	6	6	6	6	6	6	6	6	6	6	6	6	15	–	–	–	–	0
Simmons	5c	5c	5c	5c	5c	5	–	5	5	5	5	5	–	–	–	11	–	–	–	–	0
Neville	4	4	4	4	4	4	4	4R	6R	4R	4R	4	4	4	4	15	1	–	–	–	5
Holmes	3	3	3	3	3	3	3	3	3	3	3	3	3	–	3	14	–	–	–	–	0
Fainga'a, S	2	2	–	–	2R	2R	2R	2R	2R	2R	–	–	–	–	2R	9	–	–	–	–	0
Daley	1	1	1R	–	–	–	–	–	–	–	–	–	–	–	1R	4	–	–	–	–	0
Ready	2R	2R	2	2	2	2	2	2	2	2	2	2	2	2	2	15	2	–	–	–	10
Fa'agase	1R	1R	1	1	1	1R	1R	1R	1R	1R	1R	1R	1R	1R	1	15	–	–	–	–	0
Talakai	3R	3R	3R	3R	3R	3R	3R	3R	3R	3R	3R	3R	–	3	–	13	–	–	–	–	0
Matwijow	4R	6R	x	8R	4R	4R	5	4	4	4	4	4R	–	–	–	11	–	–	–	–	0
Gunn	7R	–	–	–	–	–	8R	8R	6R	6R	8R	–	–	–	6R	7	–	–	–	–	0
Gale	9R	9R	x	x	x	x	–	–	–	–	–	–	–	–	–	2	–	–	–	–	0
Greene	10R	x	x	10R	x	10R	10R	–	–	10R	–	–	–	–	–	5	–	–	–	–	0
Goromaru	12R	15	x	x	14R	15R	14R	15R	x	–	15	15	–	–	–	8	–	3	8	–	30
Setu	–	7R	7	7	–	–	–	–	–	–	–	–	–	–	–	3	–	–	–	–	0
Laloifi	–	11R	–	14	–	–	14	14	15R	14R	–	–	–	–	–	6	–	–	–	–	0
Fainga'a, A	–	–	12	12	12	12	12	12	12	12	12	12	–	–	–	10	–	–	–	–	0
Mafi	–	–	2R	2R	–	–	–	–	–	2R	x	x	2R	–	–	4	–	–	–	–	0
Paraka	–	–	–	1R	–	–	–	–	–	–	–	–	–	–	–	1	–	–	–	–	0
Gill	–	–	–	7	7	7	7	7	7	7	7	7	7	7c	–	11	4	–	–	1	23
Slipper	–	–	–	1R	1c	1c	1c	1c	1c	1c	1c	1c	–	–	–	10	1	–	–	–	5
Tuttle, James	–	–	–	–	9R	x	x	12R	9R	x	x	9R	10R	–	–	5	–	–	–	–	0
Tui, L	–	–	–	–	4R	–	–	–	–	–	5	5R	5R	–	–	4	–	–	–	–	0
Paia'aua	–	–	–	–	–	–	12R	13R	–	12R	15R	10R	10	10	–	7	1	–	–	–	5
Magnay	–	–	–	–	–	–	–	13	13	11R	14R	12R	12R	–	–	6	1	–	–	–	5
Kuridrani	–	–	–	–	–	–	–	–	–	–	14	14	14	–	–	3	1	–	–	–	5
Tuttle, Jack	–	–	–	–	–	–	–	–	–	–	15	15	–	–	–	2	–	–	–	–	0
Tupou	–	–	–	–	–	–	–	–	–	–	3R	3R	3R	–	–	3	1	–	–	–	5
Douglas	–	–	–	–	–	–	–	–	–	–	5R	5	5	–	–	3	–	–	–	–	0
Houston	–	–	–	–	–	–	–	–	–	–	8R	7R	–	–	–	2	–	–	–	–	0
Gibbon	–	–	–	–	–	–	–	–	–	–	–	15R	11R	–	–	2	–	–	–	–	0
Banks	–	–	–	–	–	–	–	–	–	–	–	–	–	–	15	1	–	–	–	–	0
Penalty try																–	1	–	–	–	5
41 PLAYERS																328	33	25	23	2	290

Records

CHAMPIONS: 2011

MATCH RECORDS

Biggest winning margin	50	vs Rebels (53-3)	Brisbane	2011
Heaviest defeat	89	vs Bulls (3-92)	Pretoria	2007
Highest score	53	vs Rebels (53-3)	Brisbane	2011
Most points conceded	92	vs Bulls (3-92)	Pretoria	2007
Most tries	7	vs Blues (51-13)	Brisbane	1996
	7	vs Bulls (48-12)	Brisbane	2002
	7	vs Force (50-10)	Brisbane	2010
	7	vs Rebels (53-3)	Brisbane	2011
Most tries conceded	13	vs Bulls (3-92)	Pretoria	2007
Most points by a player	31	QS Cooper (2t, 3c, 5p) vs Crusaders	Brisbane	2010
Most tries by a player	3	RW Davies vs Blues	Brisbane	2011
Most conversions by a player	5	JA Eales on four occasions		
	5	EJ Flatley vs Stormers	Brisbane	2002
	5	QS Cooper vs Force	Brisbane	2010
	5	QS Cooper vs Rebels	Brisbane	2011
	5	JD O'Connor vs Rebels	Brisbane	2015
Most penalties by a player	7	QS Cooper vs Brumbies	Canberra	2011
	7	MJ Harris vs Force	Brisbane	2012
Most drop goals by a player	2	BS Barnes vs Brumbies	Canberra	2008

SEASON RECORDS

Most team points	477	from 18 matches	2011
Most points by a player	228	QS Cooper	2011
Most team tries	51	from 18 matches	2011
Most tries by a player	10	CE Latham	2002
Most conversions by a player	31	QS Cooper	2010
	31	QS Cooper	2011
Most penalties by a player	43	QS Cooper	2011
Most drop goals by a player	4	BS Barnes	2008
	4	QS Cooper	2011

CAREER RECORDS

Most appearances	144	GS Holmes	2005-2016
Most points	770	QS Cooper	2007-2016
Most tries	41	CE Latham	1997-2008
Most conversions	112	QS Cooper	2007-2015
Most penalties	135	QS Cooper	2007-2015
Most drop goals	7	QS Cooper	2007-2015

Samu Kerevi.

Waratahs

Ground: Allianz Stadium **Capacity:** 44 000 **Address:** Driver Avenue, Moore Park
Telephone number: + 61 2 8354 3300 **Colours:** Sky blue jersey with navy collar,
navy shorts and sky blue socks **Website:** www.waratahs.com.au
Coach: Daryl Gibson **Captain:** Michael Hooper **CEO:** Andrew Hore
Chairman: Roger Davis

Head Coach: Daryl Gibson **Assistant Coaches:** Nathan Grey, Chris Malone & Cam Blades
High Performance Analyst: Anthony Wakeling **Doctor:** Dr Sharron Flahive
Physiotherapist: David Garrick **Strength & Conditioning:** Jordan Troester
Team Manager: Sam Cashman **Media officer:** Lauren DeGiola

1996	1997	1998	1999	2000	2001	2002	2003	2004	2005	2006
7th	9th	6th	8th	9th	8th	2nd	5th	8th	2nd	3rd

2007	2008	2009	2010	2011	2012	2013	2014	2015	2016
13th	2nd	5th	3rd	5th	11th	9th	1st	2nd	10th

Played	Won	Lost	Drawn	Points for	Points against	Tries for	Tries against
15	8	7	0	413	317	55	37

Date	Venue	Opponent	Result	Score	Referee	Scorers
Febr 27	Sydney	Rebels	WON	30-10	A Gardner	T: Horwitz, Carraro, Hooper, Phipps. C: Beale (2). P: Beale, Hegarty
Mrch 04	Canberra	Brumbies	LOST	15-32	M v/d Westhuizen	T: Folau, Phipps. C: Beale. P: Beale.
Mrch 18	Sydney	Highlanders	LOST	26-30	N Briant	T: Holloway (3), Robertson. C: Beale (3).
Mrch 27	Brisbane	Reds	WON	15-13	B O'Keeffe	T: Folau (2). C: Foley. P: Foley.
April 03	Sydney	Rebels	LOST	17-21	A Lees	T: Dempsey, Carraro. C: Foley (2). P: Foley.
April 16	Sydney	Brumbies	LOST	20-26	N Briant	T: Folau, Robinson. C: Foley (2). P: Foley (2).
April 23	Perth	Force	WON	49-13	R Hoffmann	T: Horne, Robinson, Phipps, Holloway, Folau, Ta'avao. C: Foley (5). P: Foley (3).
April 30	Cape Town	Stormers	WON	32-30	M Fraser	T: Beale, Folau, Hooper, Horne. C: Foley (2). P: Foley (2).
May 07	Sydney	Cheetahs	WON	21-06	N Berry	T: Foley, Robinson. C: Foley. P: Foley (3).
May 14	Sydney	Bulls	WON	31-08	G Jackson	T: Phipps (2), Mumm, Ta'avao. C: Foley (4). P: Foley.
May 20	Christchurch	Crusaders	LOST	10-29	J Peyper	T: Horne, Guildford.
May 27	Sydney	Chiefs	WON	45-25	J Peyper	T: Folau (2), Hooper (2). Kellaway. C: Foley (6). P: Foley.
July 02	Tokyo	Sunwolves	WON	57-12	B Pickerill	T: Lucas (2), Robinson (2), Kellaway, Folau, Dempsey, Carraro, Naiyaravoro. C: Foley (5), Horwitz.
July 09	Sydney	Hurricanes	LOST	17-28	C Pollock	T: Folau, Naiyaravoro. C: Foley (2). P: Foley.
July 15	Auckland	Blues	LOST	28-34	M Fraser	T: Ta'avao, Folau, Penalty try. C: Foley (4).

Note: ■ = *Champion*

2016 SQUAD

PLAYER	Date of Birth	Height	Weight	M	T	C	P	DG	Pts
KJ (Kurtley) Beale	06/01/89	1,84	90	124	26	80	71	3	512
MJ (Matt) Carraro	04/08/84	1,85	93	55	7	–	–	–	35
JJ (Jack) Dempsey	04/12/94	1,91	92	13	3	–	–	–	15
DA(Dave) Dennis	10/01/86	1,92	110	107	10	–	–	–	50
I(Israel) Folau	03/04/89	1,93	103	60	36	–	–	–	180
BT (Bernard) Foley	08/09/89	1,80	90	77	20	117	95	–	625
Z (Zac) Guildford	08/02/89	1,82	96	86	31	–	–	–	155
N (Ned) Hanigan	11/04/95	1,94	110	3	–	–	–	–	0
B (Bryce) Hegarty	28/08/92	1,84	90	35	7	4	–	1	52
J (James) Hilterbrand	21/05/89	1,88	114	3	–	–	–	–	0
J (Jed) Holloway	02/11/92	1,95	116	9	4	–	–	–	20
MK (Michael) Hooper	29/10/91	1,82	101	96	16	–	–	–	80
RG (Rob) Horne	15/08/89	1,86	92	102	26	–	–	–	130
D (David) Horwitz	30/09/94	1,83	94	13	1	1	–	–	7
A (Andrew) Kellaway	12/10/95	1,83	93	11	2	–	–	–	10
S (Tolo) Latu	23/02/93	1,78	110	32	1	–	–	–	5
ST (Sam) Lousi	20/07/91	1,98	121	18	–	–	–	–	0
M (Matt) Lucas	29/01/92	1,74	80	15	2	–	–	–	10
DW (Dean) Mumm	05/03/84	1,96	109	101	11	–	–	–	55
TT (Taqule) Naiyaravoro	07/12/91	1,94	123	22	11	–	–	–	55
WL(Wycliff) Palu	27/07/82	1,94	116	134	13	–	–	–	65
NJ (Nick) Phipps	09/01/89	1,80	87	97	16	–	–	–	80
SUT (Tatafu) Polota-Nau	26/07/85	1,81	115	141	12	–	–	–	60
HE (Hugh) Roach	11/09/92	1,78	105	21	–	–	–	–	0
T (Tom) Robertson	28/08/94	1,80	111	13	1	–	–	–	5
BA (Benn) Robinson	19/07/84	1,83	113	148	7	–	–	–	35
R (Reece) Robinson	13/06/87	1,80	90	13	5	–	–	–	25
PJ (Paddy) Ryan	09/08/88	1,89	117	77	2	–	–	–	10
WRJ (Will) Skelton	03/05/92	2,03	135	53	1	–	–	–	5
J (Jim) Stewart	05/01/94	1,80	90	1	–	–	–	–	0
A (Angus) Ta'avao	22/03/90	1,94	120	63	5	–	–	–	25
JD (Jeremy) Tilse	02/06/86	1,90	118	60	–	–	–	–	0
				1803	276	202	166	4	2306

APPEARANCES & POINTS

PLAYER	Reds	Brumbies	Highlanders	Reds	Rebels	Brumbies	Force	Stormers	Cheetahs	Bulls	Crusaders	Chiefs	Sunwolves	Hurricanes	Blues	Apps	T	C	P	DG	Pts
Folau	15	15	15	15	15	13	13	13	13	13	13	13	13	13	13	15	11	–	–	–	55
Carraro	14	14	14	14R	13	11	11R	15R	14R	14R	12R	11	13R	11	11	15	3	–	–	–	15
Horne	13	13	13	13	–	11	11	11	11	11	11	12	12	12	12	13	3	–	–	–	15
Horwitz	12	12	12	13R	12	11R	12R	x	x	12R	12	12R	10R	12R	11R	13	1	1	–	–	7
Guildford	11	11	11	11	11	–	–	–	–	14R	14	–	–	–	–	7	1	–	–	–	5
Beale	10	10	10	12	–	12	12	12	12	12	–	–	–	–	–	9	1	6	2	–	23
Phipps	9	9	9	9	9	9	9	9	9	9	9	9	9	9	9	15	5	–	–	–	25
Holloway	8	8	8R	8	8	8	8	8	–	–	8	–	–	–	–	9	4	–	–	–	20
Hooper	7c	7c	7c	7c	7c	7c	7c	7c	7c	7c	7c	7c	7c	7c	7c	15	4	–	–	–	20
Dennis	6	6	6	5	5	5R	4	4	4	4	4	4	8	4	8	15	–	–	–	–	0
Skelton	5	5	5	–	6R	5	5	5	5	5	5	5	5	5	5	14	–	–	–	–	0
Mumm	4	4	4	4	4	4	6R	6	6	6	6	6	4	6	4	15	1	–	–	–	5
Ta'avao	3	3	3	3	3	3R	3R	3R	3R	3R	3R	3R	3R	3R	3R	15	3	–	–	–	15
Polata-Nau	2	2	–	–	–	2R	2R	2	2	2	2	2	2	2	2	11	–	–	–	–	0
Ryan	1	1	1	1	1R	1R	1	1	1	1	1	1	1	1	1	15	–	–	–	–	0
Latu	2R	2R	2	2	–	–	–	–	–	–	–	–	–	–	–	4	–	–	–	–	0
Robinson, B	1R	–	–	1R	1	1	–	–	–	–	–	–	–	–	–	4	–	–	–	–	0
Tilse	17R	3R	1R	–	–	–	1R	1R	1R	1R	1R	1R	1R	1R	1R	12	–	–	–	–	0
Lousi	5R	5R	5R	5R	8R	6R	–	5R	5R	8R	5R	8R	7R	5R	5R	14	–	–	–	–	0
Dempsey	6R	6R	6R	6	6	6	6	–	–	–	5R	6	8R	6	–	11	3	–	–	–	15
Lucas	9R	23R	9R	9R	9R	9R	9R	9R	9R	9R	9R	9R	9	9R	9R	15	2	–	–	–	10
Hegarty	10R	13R	–	–	–	–	–	–	–	–	–	–	–	–	–	2	–	–	1	–	3
Robinson, R	x	–	14R	14	14	14	14	14	14	14	15R	14	15R	14	–	13	5	–	–	–	25
Sandell	–	x	–	–	–	–	–	–	–	–	–	–	–	–	–	0	–	–	–	–	0
Palu	–	8R	8	8R	5R	8R	5R	4R	8	8	8R	8	–	8	8R	13	–	–	–	–	0
Roach	–	–	2R	2R	2	2	2	2	2R	2R	2R	2R	2R	2R	2R	13	–	–	–	–	0
Robertson	–	–	3R	3R	3R	3	3	3	3	3	3	3	3	3	3	13	1	–	–	–	5
Foley	–	–	–	10	10	10	10	10	10	10	10	10	10	10	10	12	1	35	15	–	120
Kellaway	–	–	–	–	11R	15	15	15	15	15	15	15	15	15	15	11	2	–	–	–	10
Hilterbrand	–	–	–	–	2R	x	–	–	–	–	–	–	–	–	–	1	–	–	–	–	0
Hanigan	–	–	–	–	–	–	–	8R	5R	–	4R	–	–	–	–	3	–	–	–	–	0
Naiyaravoro	–	–	–	–	–	–	–	–	–	–	–	11	14	–	–	2	2	–	–	–	10
Stewart	–	–	–	–	–	–	–	–	–	–	–	–	–	14R	–	1	–	–	–	–	
Penalty tries	–	–	–	–	–	–	–	–	–	–	–	–	–	–	–	0	2	–	–	–	10
33 PLAYERS																340	55	42	18	0	413

Records

CHAMPIONS: 2014

MATCH RECORDS

Biggest winning margin	62	vs Kings (72-10)	Port Elizabeth	2013
Heaviest defeat	77	vs Crusaders (19-96)	Christchurch	2002
Highest score	73	vs Lions (73-12)	Sydney	2010
Most points conceded	96	vs Crusaders (19-96)	Christchurch	2002
Most tries	11	vs Lions (73-12)	Sydney	2010
	11	vs Kings (72-10)	Port Elizabeth	2013
Most tries conceded	14	vs Crusaders (19-96)	Christchurch	2002
Most points by a player	34	P Hewat (3t, 2c, 5p) vs Bulls	Sydney	2005
Most tries by a player	4	DA Mitchell vs Lions	Sydney	2010
	3	A Murdoch vs Hurricanes	Sydney	1996
	3	MC Burke vs Northern Transvaal	Sydney	1997
	3	S Taupeaafe vs Sharks	Sydney	1998
	3	SNG Staniforth vs Chiefs	Rotorua	2002
	3	P Hewat vs Bulls	Sydney	2005
	3	JC Crawford vs Kings	Port Elizabeth	2013
	3	J Holloway vs Highlanders	Sydney	2016
Most conversions by a player	9	BS Barnes	Sydney	2010
Most penalties by a player	7	MC Burke vs Blues	Sydney	2001
Most drop goals by a player	1	on eight occasions		

SEASON RECORDS

Most team points	540	from 18 matches	2014
Most points by a player	252	BT Foley	2014
Most team tries	60	from 18 matches	2014
Most tries by a player	12	I Folau	2014
Most conversions by a player	45	BT Foley	2014
Most penalties by a player	44	BT Foley	2014
Most drop goals by a player	3	BS Barnes	2010

CAREER RECORDS

Most appearances	148	BA Robinson	2006-2016
Most points	959	MC Burke	1996-2004
Most tries	36	I Folau	2013-2016
Most conversions	160	MC Burke	1996-2004
Most penalties	173	MC Burke	1996-2004
Most drop goals	3	KJ Beale	2007-2014
	3	BS Barnes	2010-2013

Giant Will Skelton – a truly enormous presence in the second-row for the Waratahs and Australia.

Jaguares

Ground: Vélez Sarsfield **Capacity:** 49 540 **Address:** 9200 Juan B. Justo Avenue, Buenos Aires
Telephone: 54 (11) 4898 8500 **Colours:** Black jersey. Black shorts and black socks
Website: www.jaguares.com.ar **Coach:** Raúl Pérez **Captain:** Augustín Creevy
Manager: Rafael Laria **General Manager:** Greg Peters

Head Coach: Raúl Pérez **Assistant coaches:** Jose Pellicena, Martin Gaitán & Felipe Contepomi
Physical Conditioning: Gonzalo Santos, Ignacio Saint Bonnet & Lelio de Crocce
Team Manager: Rafael Laria **Doctor:** Conrado López Alonso & Franco Dellavedova
Physiotherapist: Sergio Carossio & Maximiliano Marticorena, Juan Ignacio Otero &
Pero Escalante **Video Analyst:** Rodrigo Martinez **Media officer:** Joaquín Galán
Baggage Master: Facundo Goya **Nutrition:** Romina Garavaglia

1996	1997	1998	1999	2000	2001	2002	2003	2004	2005	2006
2007	2008	2009	2010	2011	2012	2013	2014	2015	2016 13th	

Played	Won	Lost	Drawn	Points for	Points against	Tries for	Tries against
15	4	11	0	376	427	44	51

Date	Venue	Opponent	Result	Score	Referee	Scorers
Febr 26	Bloemfontein	Cheetahs	WON	34-33	S Berry	T: Landajo (2), Creevy, Baez. C: Sánchez (4). P: Sánchez. DG: Sánchez.
Mrch 05	Durban	Sharks	LOST	15-19	J Peyper	T: Bofelli, Cordero. C: Sánchez. P: Sánchez.
Mrch 19	Buenos Aires	Chiefs	LOST	26-30	C Pollock	T: Creevy, Landajo, Moroni. C: Sánchez. P: Sánchez (3).
Mrch 26	Buenos Aires	Stormers	LOST	08-13	C Pollock	T: De la Fuente. P: Sánchez.
April 02	Albany	Blues	LOST	16-24	M Fraser	T: Bertranou. C: Sánchez. P: Gonzales Iglesias (3).
April 09	Wellington	Hurricanes	LOST	22-40	N Briant	T: Senatore, Landajo, Moroni. C: Sánchez (2). P: Sánchez.
April 15	Christchurch	Crusaders	LOST	15-32	C Joubert	T: Isa, González Iglesias. C: Hernández. P: Hernández.
April 23	Tokyo	Sunwolves	LOST	28-36	J Nutbrown	T: Crevy, Bofelli, Isa, González Amorosino. C: Hernández. P: Hernández (2).
April 30	Buenos Aires	Kings	WON	73-27	S Berry	T: Senatore (3), Creevy, Bofelli, Hernández, Montero, Landajo, Alemanno, Sánchez, Cordero. C: Sánchez (9)
May 14	Buenos Aires	Sharks	LOST	22-25	M v/d Westhuizen	T: Landajo, Lavanini, Garcia Botta. C: Sánchez (2). P: Sánchez.
May 21	Johannesburg	Lions	LOST	24-52	S Berry	T: Sánchez, Bertranou. C: González Iglesias. P: Sánchez (4).
May 27	Port Elizabeth	Kings	LOST	22-29	N Briant	T: Isa. C: Sánchez. P: Sánchez (5).
July 02	Buenos Aires	Bulls	WON	29-11	C Joubert	T: Creevy (2), Matera. C: Sánchez. P: Sánchez (4).
July 09	Buenos Aires	Highlanders	LOST	08-34	A Gardner	T: Hernández. P: Sánchez.
July 16	Buenos Aires	Lions	WON	34-22	R Hoffmann	T: Isa, Alemanno, Penalty try. C: Sánchez (2). P: Sánchez (5).

2016 SQUAD

PLAYER	Date of Birth	Height	Weight	M	T	C	P	DG	Pts
M (Matías) Alemanno	05/12/91	1,99	117	11	2	–	–	–	10
F (Felipe) Arregui	09/06/94	1,87	113	5	–	–	–	–	0
R (Rodrigo) Baez	08/02/89	1,91	101	6	1	–	–	–	5
G (Gonzalo) Bertranou	31/12/93	1,75	72	11	2	–	–	–	10
E (Emiliano) Bofelli	16/01/95	1.91	91	11	3	–	–	–	15
F (Facundo) Bosch	08/08/91	1,80	100	6	–	–	–	–	0
S (Santiago) Cordero	06/12/93	1.77	83	8	2	–	–	–	10
A (Agustin) Creevy	15/03/85	1,81	110	11	6	–	–	–	30
J (Jeronimo) de la Fuente	24/02/91	1.84	94	11	1	–	–	–	5
F (Felipe) Ezcurra	15/04/93	1,78	89	5	–	–	–	–	0
S (Santiago) Garcia Botta	19/06/92	1,82	115	14	1	–	–	–	5
F (Facundo) Gigena	15/09/94	1,80	111	5	–	–	–	–	0
LP (Lucas) González Amorosino	02/11/85	1,85	93	9	1	–	–	–	5
S (Santiago) González Iglesias	16/06/88	1,79	92	12	1	1	3	–	16
JC (Juan Cruz) Guillemaín	21/08/92	1,98	110	4	–	–	–	–	0
JM (Juan Martin) Hernández	07/08/82	1,87	92	9	2	2	3	–	23
R (Ramiro) Herrera	14/02/89	1,88	125	11	–	–	–	–	0
F (Facundo) Isa	21/09/93	1,88	106	13	4	–	–	–	20
M (Marcos) Kremer	30/07/97	1,96	115	2	–	–	–	–	0
M (Martin) Landajo	14/06/88	1,75	83	13	6	–	–	–	30
I (Ignacio) Larrague	25/10/95	2,01	118	2	–	–	–	–	0
TS (Tomás) Lavanini	22/01/93	2,00	125	12	1	–	–	–	5
JM (Juan Manuel) Leguizamón	06/06/83	1,90	105	9	–	–	–	–	0
T (Tomás) Lezana	16/02/94	1,89	105	4	–	–	–	–	0
PN (Pablo) Matera	18/07/93	1,93	100	11	1	–	–	–	5
M (Manuel) Montero	20/11/91	1,94	100	6	1	–	–	–	5
JS (Julian) Montoya	29/10/93	1,84	110	13	–	–	–	–	0
M (Matías) Moroni	20/03/91	1.85	87	8	2	–	–	–	10
R (Ramiro) Moyano	28/05/90	1,80	85	5	–	–	–	–	0
L (Lucas) Noguera Paz	05/10/93	1,79	110	1	–	–	–	–	0
M (Matías) Orlando	14/11/91	1,84	90	12	–	–	–	–	0
J (Javier) Ortega Desio	14/06/90	1,93	106	8	–	–	–	–	0
J (Joaquín) Paz	20/10/93	1,80	91	5	–	–	–	–	0
G (Guido) Petti Pagadizaval	17/11/94	1,94	108	13	–	–	–	–	0
E (Enrique) Pieretto	15/12/94	1,85	122	8	–	–	–	–	0
FN (Nicolás) Sánchez	26/10/88	1.76	83	13	2	24	27	1	142
LV (Leonardo) Senatore	13/05/84	1,91	102	8	4	–	–	–	20
R (Roberto) Tejerizo	15/04/88	1,78	95	4	–	–	–	–	0
FN (Nahuel) Tetaz Chaparo	11/06/89	1,90	120	12	–	–	–	–	0
J (Joaquín) Tuculet	08/08/89	1.80	87	11	–	–	–	–	0
S (Segundo) Tuculet	05/02/94	1,80	86	1	–	–	–	–	0
TOTALS				343	44	27	33	1	376

APPEARANCES & POINTS

PLAYER	Cheetahs	Sharks	Chiefs	Stormers	Blues	Hurricanes	Crusaders	Sunwolves	Kings	Sharks	Lions	Kings	Bulls	Highlanders	Lions	Apps	T	C	P	DG	Pts
Tuculet, J	15	–	15	15	–	15	15	–	15	15	15	15	15	15	15	11	–	–	–	–	0
Cordero	14	15	14	14R	–	–	–	–	14	–	–	–	14	14	14	8	2	–	–	–	10
Moroni	13	13	11R	13	13	13	–	–	13	–	–	–	13	–	–	8	2	–	–	–	10
De la Fuente	12	–	13	12	12	12R	13	13	13R	–	–	–	12	13	13	11	1	–	–	–	5
Bofelli	11	11	11	–	14	11	11	15R	15	14	14	11	–	–	–	11	3	–	–	–	15
Sánchez	10	10	10	10	15R	10	–	–	10	10	10	10	10	10	10	13	2	24	27	1	142
Landajo	9	9	9	9c	9c	–	–	9	9	9c	9	9	9	9c	–	13	6	–	–	–	30
Senatore	8	8	8	8	8	8	–	8	8	–	–	–	–	–	–	8	4	–	–	–	20
Baez	7	7	–	–	7	7	6	7R	–	–	–	–	–	–	–	6	1	–	–	–	5
Matera	6	6	6	6	6	6	7R	6	–	6	–	–	6	6	–	11	1	–	–	–	5
Lavanini	5	–	5	5	5	5	–	–	5	5	5	5	5	5	5	12	1	–	–	–	5
Petti Pagadizaval	4	4	4	5R	4	4	4	–	4R	4R	4R	4	4	–	4	13	–	–	–	–	0
Herrera	3	3	–	–	3	3	–	–	3	3	3	3	3	3	3	11	–	–	–	–	0
Creevy	2c	2c	2c	2c	–	–	2c	2c	2c	–	2c	2c	2c	–	–	11	6	–	–	–	30
Noguera Paz	1	–	–	–	–	–	–	–	–	–	–	–	–	–	–	1	–	–	–	–	0
Montoya	2R	2R	2R	2R	2	2	–	–	2R	2R	2	2R	2R	2R	2	13	–	–	–	–	0
Garcia Botta	1R	1	1	1	1R	1	1	–	1	1	1	1	1R	1R	1R	14	1	–	–	–	5
Tetaz Chaparo	3R	3R	3	–	–	–	3	3	3R	3R	3R	7R	1	1	1	12	–	–	–	–	0
Alemanno	4R	5	5R	4	–	–	5	5	4	4	4	4R	–	–	4R	11	2	–	–	–	10
Isa	7R	8R	7R	6R	–	–	8	8	6R	7R	8	8	8	8	8	13	4	–	–	–	20
Bertranou	9R	9R	–	9R	9R	x	9	9	9R	9R	9R	–	9R	–	9R	11	2	–	–	–	10
González Iglesias	13R	12	12R	10R	10	12	12	12	–	10R	12R	12R	–	–	13R	12	1	1	3	–	16
Orlando	15R	14	–	14	–	14	14	14R	–	13	13	14	14R	12R	11R	12	–	–	–	–	0
Gonzales Amorosino	–	14R	–	11	–	–	14R	11	14R	11R	11	–	13R	11R	–	9	1	–	–	–	5
Ortega Desio	–	7R	–	–	–	–	7	7	6	13R	6R	4	6	–	–	8	–	–	–	–	0
Arregui	–	1R	3R	3	x	–	1R	1	–	–	–	–	–	–	–	5	–	–	–	–	0
Paz	–	12R	–	–	10R	15R	10R	12R	–	–	–	–	–	–	–	5	–	–	–	–	0
Leguizamón	–	–	7	–	8R	7	7	–	–	7R	7	7	7	7	–	9	–	–	–	–	0
Ezcurra	–	–	9R	–	–	9R	9R	–	–	9R	–	9R	–	–	–	5	–	–	–	–	0
Tejeziro	–	–	1R	1R	1	1R	–	–	–	–	–	–	–	–	–	4	–	–	–	–	0
Hernández	–	–	12	–	–	10	10	12	12	12	12	–	12	12	–	9	2	2	3	–	23
Lezana	–	–	7	–	–	–	6	–	7	6	–	–	–	–	–	4	–	–	–	–	0
Pieretto	–	–	3R	3R	3R	3R	3R	–	–	–	3R	3R	3R	–	–	8	–	–	–	–	0
Moyano	–	–	–	15	15	–	14	–	–	11R	11R	–	–	–	–	5	–	–	–	–	0
Montero	–	–	–	11	–	–	11	11	–	–	11	11	11	–	–	6	1	–	–	–	5
Bosch	–	–	–	2R	2R	2R	2R	–	–	2R	–	–	–	2R	–	6	–	–	–	–	0
Guillemaín	–	–	–	4R	5R	4R	4	–	–	–	–	–	–	–	–	4	–	–	–	–	0
Gigena	–	–	–	–	1R	1R	1R	1R	1R	–	–	–	–	–	–	5	–	–	–	–	0
Tuculet, S	–	–	–	–	–	–	–	–	–	13	–	–	–	–	–	1	–	–	–	–	0
Larrague	–	–	–	–	–	–	–	–	–	–	5R	6R	–	–	–	2	–	–	–	–	0
Kremer	–	–	–	–	–	–	–	–	–	–	7R	8R	–	–	–	2	–	–	–	–	0
Penalty try	–	–	–	–	–	–	–	–	–	–	–	–	–	–	–	–	1	–	–	–	5
41 PLAYERS																343	44	27	33	1	376

Records

MATCH RECORDS

Biggest win	46	vs Southern Kings (73-27)	Buenos Aires	2016
Heaviest defeat	28	vs Lions (24-52)	Johannesburg	2016
Highest score	73	vs Southern Kings (73-27)	Buenos Aires	2016
Most points conceded	52	vs Lions (24-52)	Johannesburg	2016
Most tries	11	vs Southern Kings (73-27)	Buenos Aires	2016
Most tries conceded	8	vs Lions (24-52)	Johannesburg	2016
Most points by a player	23	FN Sánchez vs Southern Kings	Buenos Aires	2016
Most tries by a player	3	LV Senatore vs Southern Kings	Buenos Aires	2016
Most conversions by a player	9	FN Sánchez vs Southern Kings	Buenos Aires	2016
Most penalties by a player	5	FN Sánchez vs Southern Kings	Port Elizabeth	2016
	5	FN Sánchez vs Lions	Buenos Aires	2016
Most drop goals by a player	1	FN Sánchez vs Cheetahs	Bloemfontein	2016

SEASON RECORDS

Most team points	376	in 15 games	2016
Most points by a player	142	FN Sánchez	2016
Most team tries	44	in 15 games	2016
Most tries by a player	6	M Landajo	2016
	6	A Creevy	2016
Most conversions by a player	24	FN Sánchez	2016
Most penalties by a player	27	FN Sánchez	2016
Most drop goals by a player	1	FN Sánchez	2016

CAREER RECORDS

Most appearances	14	S Garcia Botta	2016
Most points	142	FN Sánchez	2016
Most tries	6	M Landajo	2016
	6	A Creevy	2016
Most conversions	24	FN Sánchez	2016
Most penalties	27	FN Sánchez	2016
Most drop goals	1	FN Sánchez	2016

Augustín Creevy led from the front for the Jaguares and Argentina in 2016.

Sunwolves

Ground: Prince Chichibu Memorial Stadium, Tokyo **Capacity:** 27 188
Address: 2-8-35 Kataaoyama, Minato Tokyo, Japan **Telephone:** 81 3 5771 1101
Colours: Orange shirt, black shorts and orange socks **Website:** www.superjapanrugby.com
Coach: Mark Hammett **Captain:** Shota Horie **Manager:** Shintaro Tanida
CEO: Yuichi Ueno **Chairman:** Yoshitaka Tashiro

Head Coach: Mark Hammett **Assistant Coaches:** Filo Tiatia, Nathan Mauger & Atushi Tanabe
Technical Coach: Chris Milsted **Strength & Conditioning:** Wayne Taylor
Team Manager: Shintaro Tanida **Assistant Team Manager:** Nayoki Toyoda
Doctor: Hidetaka Murakami, Masato Tanaka & Masataka Sakane
Operations Manager: Gen Fukushima **Pr Manager:** Daichi Noda
Media Officer: Nao Ishikawa

1996	1997	1998	1999	2000	2001	2002	2003	2004	2005	2006
2007	2008	2009	2010	2011	2012	2013	2014	2015	2016 18th	

Played	Won	Lost	Drawn	Points for	Points against	Tries for	Tries against
15	1	13	1	293	627	33	88

Date	Venue	Opponent	Result	Score	Referee	Scorers
Febr 27	Tokyo	Lions	LOST	13-26	B O'Keeffe	T: Horie. C: Pisi. P: Pisi (2).
Mrch 12	Singapore	Cheetahs	LOST	31-32	Q Immelman	T: Yamada (3), Horie. C: Pisi (4). P: Pisi.
Mrch 19	Tokyo	Rebels	LOST	09-35	M Fraser	P: Pisi (3).
Mrch 26	Singapore	Bulls	LOST	27-30	W Houston	T: Yamada, Durutalo, Yatomi. C: Pisi (3). P: Pisi (2).
April 02	Port Elizabeth	Kings	LOST	28-33	R Rasivhenge	T: Yamada, Horie, Bond, Pisi. C: Pisi. P: Pisi (2).
April 08	Cape Town	Stormers	LOST	19-46	N Berry	T: Viljoen (2), Yatomi. C: Tamura (2)
April 15	Bloemfontein	Cheetahs	LOST	17-92	N Berry	T: Carpenter, Paea. C: Pisi (2). P: Pisi
April 23	Tokyo	Jaguares	WON	36-28	J Nutbrown	T: Sasakura, Tatekawa, Carpenter. C: Pisi (3). P: Pisi (4), Viljoen
May 07	Tokyo	Force	LOST	22-40	M Fraser	T: Yamada (2), Pisi, Carpenter. C: Tamura.
May 14	Singapore	Stormers	DREW	17-17	P Williams	T: Yamada. P: Pisi (4).
May 21	Brisbane	Reds	LOST	25-35	W Houston	T: Carpenter (2), Moli. C: Pisi (2). P: Pisi (2).
May 28	Canberra	Brumbies	LOST	05-66	J van Heerden	T: Yamada.
July 02	Tokyo	Waratahs	LOST	12-57	B Pickerill	P: Tamura (3), Viljoen.
July 09	Pretoria	Bulls	LOST	03-50	Q Immelman	P: Tamura.
July 15	Durban	Sharks	LOST	29-40	R Rasivhenge	T: Paea (2), Lemalu, Shigeno. C: Tamura (3). P: Tamura.

2016 SQUAD

PLAYER	Date of Birth	Height	Weight	M	T	C	P	DG	Pts
T (Taiyo) Ando	22/08/87	1,81	96	7	–	–	–	–	0
T (Takuma) Asahara	07/09/87	1,78	113	14	–	–	–	–	0
(Timothy) Bond	25/10/89	1,93	113	7	1	–	–	–	5
D (Derek) Carpenter	26/07/88	1,83	94	12	5	–	–	–	25
A (Andrew) Durutalo	25/10/87	1,87	102	12	1	–	–	–	5
Z (Ziun) Gu	20/07/94	1,84	122	4	–	–	–	–	0
A (Atsushi) Hiwasa	22/05/87	1,66	72	8	–	–	–	–	0
S (Shota) Horie	21/01/86	1,80	104	12	3	–	–	–	15
Y (Yoshiya) Hosoda	05/08/87	1,92	100	13	–	–	–	–	0
K (Keita) Inagaki	02/06/90	1,86	116	10	–	–	–	–	0
D (Daisuke) Inoue	16/11/89	1,73	81	1	–	–	–	–	0
S (Shinnosuke) Kakinaga	19/12/91	1,80	115	15	–	–	–	–	0
S (Shokei) Kin	03/10/91	1,78	95	2	–	–	–	–	0
T (Takeshi) Kizu	15/07/88	1,83	115	12	–	–	–	–	0
K (Kentaro) Kodama	28/01/92	1,83	85	1	–	–	–	–	0
N (Naohiro) Kotaki	13/06/92	1,93	110	3	–	–	–	–	0
F (Faatiga) Lemalu	17/04/89	2,01	115	9	1	–	–	–	5
TC (Tomás) Leonardi	01/07/87	1,90	108	5	–	–	–	–	0
V (Viliami) Lolohea	04/07/93	1,80	93	5	–	–	–	–	0
S (Shinya) Makabe	26/03/87	1,92	119	6	–	–	–	–	0
M (Masataka) Mikami	04/06/88	1,78	115	14	–	–	–	–	0
L (Liaki) Moli	04/01/90	1,98	118	14	1	–	–	–	5
F (Futoshi) Mori	25/04/88	1,75	103	4	–	–	–	–	0
H (Hitoshi) Ono	06/05/78	1,92	105	12	–	–	–	–	0
M (Mifiposeti) Paea	06/07/87	1,78	108	13	3	–	–	–	15
T (Tusi) Pisi	18/06/82	1.83	91	11	2	16	21	–	105
EC (Ed) Quirk	28/08/91	1,91	108	15	–	–	–	–	0
Y (Yasutaka) Sasakura	04/08/88	1.86	92	9	1	–	–	–	5
K (Kaito) Shigeno	21/11/90	1,70	75	11	1	–	–	–	5
J (John) Stewart	17/02/88	1,70	80	3	–	–	–	–	0
Y (Yu) Tamura	09/01/89	1.81	92	15	–	6	5	–	27
H (Harumichi) Tatekawa	02/12/89	1.80	95	13	1	–	–	–	5
R (Riaan) Viljoen	01/04/83	1.85	90	15	2	–	2	–	16
A (Akihito) Yamada	26/07/85	1.82	88	10	9	–	–	–	45
K (Koki) Yamamoto	29/10/90	1,80	118	1	–	–	–	–	0
R (Ryohei) Yamanaka	22/06/88	1,88	95	2	–	–	–	–	0
H (Hajime) Yamashita	14/06/92	1,80	85	3	–	–	–	–	0
Y (Yuki) Yatomi	16/02/85	1,76	82	10	2	–	–	–	10
TOTALS				333	33	22	28	0	293

APPEARANCES & POINTS

PLAYER	Lions	Cheetahs	Rebels	Bulls	Kings	Stormers	Cheetahs	Jaguares	Force	Stormers	Reds	Brumbies	Waratahs	Bulls	Sharks	Apps	T	C	P	DG	Pts
Viljoen	15	15	15	15	15	15	15	15	15	15	15	15R	15	15	15	15	2	–	2	–	16
Yamada	14	14	14	11	11	11	–	–	14	14	14	14	–	–	–	10	9	–	–	–	45
Tatekawa	13	13	13	13	13	x	13	12	12	12c	12c	12	12c	12c	–	13	1	–	–	–	5
Tamura	12	12	12	12	12	10	13R	10R	10R	15R	10R	10	10	10	10c	15	–	6	5	–	27
Sasakura	11	11	x	x	–	11R	11R	14R	–	–	–	15	11	11	11	9	1	–	–	–	5
Pisi	10	10	10	10	10	–	10	10	10	10	10	10R	–	–	–	11	2	16	21	–	105
Hiwasa	9	9	9	–	–	9R	–	9	9R	9	9	–	–	–	–	8	–	–	–	–	0
Quirk	8	8	8	8R	8	7	8	8	8	8	8	8	8	8	8	15	–	–	–	–	0
Durutalo	7	7	7	7	7	8R	7	7	7	7	7	7	–	–	–	12	1	–	–	–	5
Moli	6	6	–	5	6	6	5	5	6	6	6	6	6	6	6	14	1	–	–	–	5
Ono	5	5	4	4	4	–	4	4	4	–	4R	4	–	4	4	12	–	–	–	–	0
Bond	4	4	5	–	5	5	–	–	–	4	4	–	–	–	–	7	1	–	–	–	5
Kakinaga	3	3	3R	3R	3	3R	3R	3	3	3	3	3R	3	3	3	15	–	–	–	–	0
Horie	2c	2c	2c	2c	2c	2c	2c	2c	2c	2R	2R	2c	–	–	–	12	3	–	–	–	15
Inagaki	1	1	1	1	1	–	–	–	–	1R	1	1R	1	2	–	10	–	–	–	–	0
Mikami	1R	1R	1R	1R	1R	1	1	1	1	1	1	–	1	1R	1R	14	–	–	–	–	0
Kizu	2R	2R	2R	–	–	2R	2R	x	2R	2	2	1R	2	2	2	12	–	–	–	–	0
Yamamoto	3R	–	–	–	–	–	–	–	–	–	–	–	–	–	–	1	–	–	–	–	0
Makabe	4R	5R	5R	16R	4R	4	–	–	–	–	–	–	–	–	–	6	–	–	–	–	0
Hosoda	5R	4R	6	6	5R	4R	6R	6	4R	x	–	4R	4R	5R	7R	13	–	–	–	–	0
Shigeno	9R	9R	9R	9	9	–	9R	9R	9	–	–	9	9R	9	–	11	1	–	–	–	5
Carpenter	x	10R	13R	–	–	12	12	13	13	13	13	13	13	13	13	12	5	–	–	–	25
Yamashita	x	–	–	–	–	–	–	–	–	–	–	11R	14	14	–	3	–	–	–	–	0
Asahara	–	3R	3	3	3R	3	3	3R	3R	3R	3R	3	3R	3R	3R	14	–	–	–	–	0
Paea	–	14R	11	x	11R	13	11	11	13R	11R	11R	11	14	23R	12	13	3	–	–	–	15
Leonardi	–	–	6R	8	7R	8	6	–	–	–	–	–	–	–	–	5	–	–	–	–	0
Lolohea	–	–	–	14	14	14	14	–	–	–	–	–	–	–	–	5	–	–	–	–	0
Yatomi	–	–	–	9R	9R	9	9	–	–	9R	9R	9	9R	9	9R	10	2	–	–	–	10
Mori	–	–	–	19R	x	–	–	–	–	–	–	–	2R	2R	2R	4	–	–	–	–	0
Gu	–	–	–	–	1R	1R	x	1R	x	–	1R	–	–	–	–	4	–	–	–	–	0
Lemalu	–	–	–	–	–	4R	6R	5	5	5	5	4	4R	5	–	9	1	–	–	–	5
Ando	–	–	–	–	–	4R	8R	7R	x	7R	7	7	7	7	–	7	–	–	–	–	0
Stewart	–	–	–	–	–	–	11	11	11	–	–	–	–	–	–	3	–	–	–	–	0
Inoue	–	–	–	–	–	–	–	9R	–	–	–	–	–	–	–	1	–	–	–	–	0
Kotaki	–	–	–	–	–	–	–	–	–	5	5	4R	–	–	–	3	–	–	–	–	0
Yamanaka	–	–	–	–	–	–	–	–	–	–	12R	–	7R	–	–	2	–	–	–	–	0
Kin	–	–	–	–	–	–	–	–	–	–	7R	7R	–	–	–	2	–	–	–	–	0
Kodama	–	–	–	–	–	–	–	–	–	–	–	11R	–	–	–	1	–	–	–	–	0
38 PLAYERS																333	33	22	28	0	293

Records

MATCH RECORDS

Biggest win	8	vs Jaguares (36-28)	Tokyo	2016
Heaviest defeat	75	vs Cheetahs (17-92)	Bloemfontein	2016
Highest score	36	vs Jaguares (36-28)	Tokyo	2016
Most points conceded	92	vs Cheetahs (17-92)	Bloemfontein	2016
Most tries	4	vs Cheetahs	Singapore	2016
	4	vs Force	Tokyo	2016
	4	vs Sharks	Durban	2016
Most tries conceded	14	vs Cheetahs	Bloemfontein	2016
Most points by a player	18	T Pisi vs Jaguares	Tokyo	2016
Most tries by a player	3	A Yamada vs Cheetahs	Singapore	2016
Most conversions by a player	4	T Pisi vs Cheetahs	Singapore	2016
Most penalties by a player	4	T Pisi vs Jaguares	Tokyo	2016
	4	T Pisi vs Stormers	Singapore	2016
Most drop goals by a player	0			

SEASON RECORDS

Most team points	293	in 15 Games	2016
Most points by a player	105	T Pisi	2016
Most team tries	33	in 15 games	2016
Most tries by a player	9	A Yamada	2016
Most conversions by a player	16	T Pisi	2016
Most penalties by a player	21	T Pisi	2016
Most drop goals by a player	0		

CAREER RECORDS

Most appearances	15	Y Tamura	2016
	15	E Quirk	2016
	15	S Kakinaga	2016
Most points	105	T Pisi	2016
Most tries	9	A Yamada	2016
Most conversions	16	T Pisi	2016
Most penalties	21	T Pisi	2016
Most drop goals	0		

Akihito Yamada.

Perfect 10 for Cheetahs

Franco Smith's young Turks sweep all before them

By Craig Ray

For the second time in two years the eventual Currie Cup champions went through the tournament with a 100 percent winning record, with the Toyota Free State Cheetahs dominating from start to finish in 2016.

Under their coach, Franco Smith, the Cheetahs emulated the 2015 feat by the Emirates Golden Lions to beat all opposition throughout the 10-match campaign and, in so doing, brought the famous trophy to Bloemfontein for the first time since 2007.

Smith, only 44, was enjoying his first full season at the helm of the union after starting his work during the Vodacom Super Rugby tournament where the Cheetahs learned some valuable lessons.

By the time the Currie Cup started, the Cheetahs were a honed and battle-hardened team that had continuity. They breezed through the pool phase even though they lost influential skipper Francois Venter to a knee injury for the bulk of the season. Venter only returned in time for the play-off stages.

In their eight pool matches the Cheetahs scored 366 points and 49 tries, which included seven try-scoring bonus points, while conceding only 18. Only the Golden Lions could match – they did so exactly – Free State in terms of try-scoring.

But the defending champions were not the same fluid unit of 2015, nor the flamboyant team that progressed to the 2016 Vodacom Super Rugby final. This success, inevitably, had led to international call-ups for key players.

The Golden Lions went through the entire Currie Cup without skipper and No 8 Warren Whiteley, halfbacks Faf de Klerk and Elton Jantjies, centre Lionel Mapoe and wing Ruan Combrinck. Coach Johan Ackermann did well to fill the gaps and the Lions duly made the semi-finals, but shorn of so much depth they were completely outplayed by Free State in the semi-final, losing 55-17 in Bloemfontein.

That performance marked the high point of the Cheetahs' campaign. Wing Sergeal Petersen, who scored a hat-trick on his return from injury, would later be included in the Springbok touring squad to Europe while flyhalf Niel Marais scored 21 points in the match from five penalties and three conversions.

At the other end of the table the Eastern Province Kings failed to win a match and the Steval Pumas registered only one win (over EP). The Boland Cavaliers were competitive despite earning only two wins while Griquas were always tricky opposition, winning four of their eight fixtures.

But those three teams were never realistically in the play-off hunt. The Vodacom Blue Bulls, DHL Western Province and the Cell C Sharks were the other sides in semi-final contention throughout the season and eventually it was the Durban-based side that missed out on the last four in what is effectively always a five-horse race. (WP, the Sharks and the Golden

Lions each lost three of their eight games in the tournament but the Sharks scored fewer bonus points and missed out.)

Their final pool match was an away fixture against the Lions and effectively a quarter-final. The hosts won a tight battle 28-16 to claim the fourth semi-final berth.

WP limped into the semis with a late 30-28 win over Boland at Newlands in the final week of pool play. WP needed a 78th-minute penalty from flyhalf Robert du Preez to see off the spirited Cavaliers' challenge and despite their progression to the play-offs, it was a season of struggle for the Cape side.

The Blue Bulls were too strong for WP at Loftus in their semi-final, winning an entertaining tussle 36-30 to set up a final against the Cheetahs in Bloemfontein. A late try from replacement scrumhalf Ivan van Zyl saw the Bulls through.

Flyhalf Tian Schoeman scored 21 points in that match and by the end of the season was the tournament's leading point-scorer on 146.

But the final was a bridge too far for the Blue Bulls, who were ill-disciplined, conceding 13 penalties and a yellow card for wing Jamba Ulengo. It was too much for the visitors who could never gain a foothold in the match, slumping to a 36-16 loss.

Cheetahs flyhalf Marais contributed 21 points in the final with seven penalties to set the home team on their way while two late tries underlined their dominance in the final quarter.

Fullback Clayton Blommetjies scored his team's first try in the 63rd minute, which ended the game as a contest with the home team taking an unassailable 28-9 lead.

Victory was built on the ability to continually look to crack open the Bulls' defence with ball in hand. The visitors simply couldn't manage the intensity the Cheetahs brought to the contest and spent most of the afternoon trapped deep in their own territory. Petersen's late try put gloss on the win and sent the capacity 45,000-strong crowd into raptures.

Cheetahs players such as Marais, centre Nico Lee, prop Ox Nche, flank Uzair Cassiem, scrumhalf Shaun Venter and Petersen, put in numerous eye-catching performances throughout the campaign. By the end of the season Petersen, Cassiem and Venter had joined the Springboks on the November tour to Britain and Italy, with the latter two players earning Test caps.

"We had continuity from Super Rugby and I believe that over time, if you work smart and hard enough, you can build a strong team," coach Smith said after the tournament. "We improved our defensive organisation under Charl Strydom, who did a great job. I also brought in some ideas I had from my time in Italy where I focused on huge line speed.

"It's taken the best part of 18 months to change the way we want to play and we're still a work in progress, but we have come a long way. We also took the conscious decision to have depth in every position and there was also an understanding by 45 players of what our game-plan and systems are so that we could manage injuries.

"Francois Venter is our main defensive organiser but when he was injured the value of being able to get our strategy across to everybody showed. If we had built everything around Francois our campaign would've fallen apart when he was injured. Nico Lee stepped in and controlled the defence while Francois was out."

Success for the Toyota Free State Cheetahs in 2016 was a triumph over big names for a team without stars.

LOG

Team	P	W	L	D	PF	PA	PD	TF	TA	LB	TB	Pts
Free State Cheetahs	8	8	0	0	366	181	185	49	18	0	7	39
Blue Bulls	8	6	2	0	310	207	103	39	26	1	5	30
Western Province	8	5	3	0	266	250	16	35	29	1	6	27
Golden Lions	8	5	3	0	355	191	164	49	23	1	5	26
Sharks	8	5	3	0	272	173	99	32	21	1	4	25
Griquas	8	4	4	0	265	323	-58	33	41	0	5	21
Boland	8	2	6	0	177	301	-124	24	41	1	3	12
Pumas	8	1	7	0	178	321	-143	24	43	2	4	10
EP Kings	8	0	8	0	137	379	-242	16	59	0	1	1

LEADING SCORERS

50 POINTS OR MORE

		T	C	P	DG	Pts
Tian Schoeman	Blue Bulls	2	35	22	0	146
Curwin Bosch	Sharks	1	19	20	1	106
Niel Marais	Free State	2	20	14	0	92
Fred Zeilinga	Free State	0	24	14	0	90
Clinton Swart	Griquas	1	23	12	0	87
Robert du Preez	WP	0	22	14	0	86
Jako van der Walt	Golden Lions	1	21	7	0	68

5 TRIES OR MORE

Frank Herne	Pumas	7	Ryno Benjamin	Free State	6
Howard Mnisi	Golden Lions	7	Anthony Volmink	Golden Lions	5
Huw Jones	WP	7	Rudi van Rooyen	Griquas	5
Jamba Ulengo	Blue Bulls	7	Sergeal Petersen	Free State	5
Kwagga Smith	Golden Lions	7	Shaun Venter	Free State	5
Leolin Zas	WP	6	Sylvian Mahuza	Golden Lions	5

PLAY-OFF RESULTS

Semi-finals: Free State Cheetahs beat the Golden Lions 55-17 *(Bloemfontein).*
Blue Bulls beat Western Province 36-30 *(Pretoria)*

2016 CURRIE CUP FINAL

Toyota Stadium, Bloemfontein, Saturday 22 October 2016. Referee: Jaco Peyper. Crowd: 43 400

Free State Cheetahs 36 (18)

(Tries: Blommetjies, Petersen. Conversion: Zeilinga. Penalties: N Marais 7, Zeilinga)

Blue Bulls 16 (9) *(Try: Van Zyl. Conversion: Stander. Penalties: Schoeman 3)*

FS Cheetahs: Clayton Blommetjies, Sergeal Petersen, Francois Venter *(Capt)*, Nico Lee *(Ryno Benjamin, 62)*, Raymond Rhule, Niel Marais *(Fred Zeilinga, 62)*, Shaun Venter *(Tian Meyer, 70)*, Niell Jordaan *(Henco Venter, 70)*, Uzair Cassiem, Paul Schoeman, Reniel Hugo, Justin Basson *(Armandt Koster, 56)*, Johan Coetzee *(Conraad van Vuuren, 56)*, Torsten van Jaarsveld *(Jacques du Toit, 73)*, Charles Marais *(Ox Nche, 56)*.

Blue Bulls: Ulrich Beyers, Travis Ismaiel, Dries Swanepoel, Burger Odendaal, Jamba Ulengo *(Bjorn Basson, 59)*, Tian Schoeman *(Joshua Stander, 72)*, Rudy Paige *(Piet van Zyl, 45)*, Arno Botha *(Capt, Hanro Liebenberg, 47)*, Jannes Kirsten, Roelof Smit, Marvin Orie *(Nic de Jager, 59)*, Jason Jenkins, Jacobie Adriaanse *(Martin Dreyer, 45)*, Jaco Visagie *(Bandise Maku, 59)*, Lizo Gqoboka *(Pierre Schoeman, 45)*.

Records

CHAMPIONS

1892	Western Province	1957-59	Western Province	1990	Natal
1894	Western Province	1964	Western Province	1991	Northern Transvaal
1895	Western Province	1966	Western Province	1992	Natal
1897	Western Province	1968	Northern Transvaal	1993	Transvaal
1898	Western Province	1969	Northern Transvaal	1994	Transvaal
1899	Griqualand West	1970	Griqualand West	1995	Natal
1904	Western Province	1971	Northern Transvaal	1996	Natal
1906	Western Province		& Transvaal	1997	Western Province
1908	Western Province	1972	Transvaal	1998	Blue Bulls
1911	Griqualand West	1973	Northern Transvaal	1999	Golden Lions
1914	Western Province	1974	Northern Transvaal	2000	Western Province
1920	Western Province	1975	Northern Transvaal	2001	Western Province
1922	Transvaal	1976	Orange Free State	2002	Blue Bulls
1925	Western Province	1977	Northern Transvaal	2003	Blue Bulls
1927	Western Province	1978	Northern Transvaal	2004	Blue Bulls
1929	Western Province	1979	Northern Transvaal	2005	Free State
1932	Western Province		& Western Province	2006	Free State & Blue Bulls
	& Border	1980	Northern Transvaal	2007	Free State
1934	Western Province	1981	Northern Transvaal	2008	Sharks
	& Border	1982	Western Province	2009	Blue Bulls
1936	Western Province	1983	Western Province	2010	Sharks
1939	Transvaal	1984	Western Province	2011	Golden Lions
1946	Northern Transvaal	1985	Western Province	2012	Western Province
1947	Western Province	1986	Western Province	2013	Sharks
1950	Transvaal	1987	Northern Transvaal	2014	Western Province
1952	Transvaal	1988	Northern Transvaal	2015	Golden Lions
1954	Western Province	1989	Northern Transvaal	2016	Free State
1956	Northern Transvaal		& Western Province		

Note: Western Province won the SA Rugby Board Trophy at the tournament in Kimberley in 1889

MOST TITLES

33	Western Province (four times shared)	last 2014
23	N Tvl/Blue Bulls (four times shared)	last 2009
11	Transvaal/Golden Lions (once shared)	last 2015
7	Natal/Sharks	last 2013
5	Free State (once shared)	last 2016
3	Griqualand West	last 1970
2	Border (twice shared)	last 1934

FINAL RECORDS

Most points by a team

56 (56-33) Transvaal vs Free State (1994)

Most tries by a team

7 Transvaal vs Free State (1994)

Most points by a player

26 Derick Hougaard, Blue Bulls vs Lions, 2002 (1try, 5 penalties, 2 drop goals)

Most conversions by a player

6 Gavin Johnson, Transvaal vs Free State, 1994

Most penalty goals by a player

6 Thierry Lacroix, Natal vs WP, 1995

6 Patrick Lambie, Sharks vs WP, 2012

Most drop goals by a player

4 Naas Botha, Northern Transvaal vs Transvaal, 1987

> # MOST 11 N Botha
> ## APPEARANCES IN FINALS
> ### Northern Transvaal
> #### 1977-1991

Most appearances in finals

11	Burger Geldenhuys	Northern Transvaal	1977-1989
11	Naas Botha	Northern Transvaal	1977-1991

Most points by a player in finals

138	Naas Botha	1t, 10c, 20p, 18dg	1977-1991

Most tries by a player in finals

4	Ettienne Botha	Blue Bulls	2003-2004

Oldest and youngest winning captains

35 years 138 days	Thys Lourens	Northern Transvaal	1978
22 years 217 days	Naas Botha	Northern Transvaal	1980

Most wins as Coach

11 *	Buurman van Zyl	Northern Transvaal	1968-1981

* including two draws

Most finals as a referee

7 André Watson (Valke/SARU)

Youngest winning coach

32 years 351 days Johan 'Rassie' Erasmus (FS Cheetahs in 2005)

MATCH RECORDS

Most points by a team

147	Blue Bulls vs SWD (147-8)		1996

Biggest winning margin

139	Blue Bulls vs SWD (147-8)		1996

wMost tries by a team

23	Blue Bulls vs SWD (147-8)		1996

Most points by a player

46	Jannie de Beer (3t, 14c, 1p)	Free State vs N Free State	1997

Most tries by a player

7	Jacques Olivier	Blue Bulls vs SWD (147-8)	1996

Most conversions by a player

14	Tjaart Marais	W-Tvl vs Eastern Free State	1988
14	MJ Smith	Free State vs SWD	1996
14	Lance Sherrell	Blue Bulls vs SWD	1996
14	Jannie de Beer	Free State vs N Free State	1997
14	Nel Fourie	Pumas vs SWD	2001

Most penalty goals by a player

9	Eric Herbert	Northern Free State vs Valke
9	Derick Hougaard	Blue Bulls vs Western Province

Most drop goals by a player

5	Naas Botha	Northern Transvaal vs Natal	1992

SEASON RECORDS

Most points by a team

792	Natal	15 matches	1996

Most tries by a team

112	Natal	15 matches	1996

Most points by a player

268	Johan Heunis	N Transvaal	1989

Most tries by a player

21	Bjorn Basson	Griquas	2010

Most conversions by a player

62	Louis Koen	WP	1997

Most penalties by a player

50	Willem de Waal	WP	2010

Most drop goals by a player

20	Naas Botha	N Transvaal	1985

CAREER RECORDS

Most matches

156	Jacques Botes	Pumas & Sharks	2002-2014

Most points

1699	Naas Botha	N Transvaal	1977-1992

Most tries

77	John Daniels	Boland & Lions	1998-2008

Most drop goals

135	Naas Botha	Northern Transvaal	1977-1992

Jacques Botes has played in more Currie Cup matches than any other player in history.

THE CURRIE CUP

CURRIE CUP FINAL PLAYERS 1939 - 2016

	PLAYER	Province	First & last final	Matches	Won	Lost	Drawn	Winning %
1	Ackermann D.S.P.(Dawie)	Western Province	1954	1	1	0	0	100%
2	Adams H.J.(Heini)	Blue Bulls	2006	1	0	0	1	0%
3	Adriaanse J.P.(Jacobie)	Blue Bulls	2016	1	0	1	0	0%
4	Aitken A.D.(Andréw)	Natal/WP	1990, 97	2	2	0	0	100%
5	Alberts F.N.F.(Frannie)	Northern Transvaal	1969-70	2	1	1	0	50%
6	Alberts W.S.(Willem)	Natal	2010-13	4	2	2	0	50%
7	Allan J.(John)	Natal	1992-93, 95	3	2	1	0	67%
8	Anderson W.	Western Province	1939	1	0	1	0	0%
9	Andréws K.S.(Keith)	Western Province	1986, 88, 97	3	2	1	0	67%
10	Andréws M.G.(Mark)	Natal	1993, 95-96, 00	4	2	2	0	50%
11	Aplon G.G.(Gio)	Western Province	2010, 12-13	3	1	2	0	33%
12	Armand D.(Don)	Western Province	2012	1	1	0	0	100%
13	Arnold P.(Peet)	Western Province	1997	1	1	0	0	100%
14	Atherton S.(Steve)	Natal	1990, 92-93, 96, 99	5	3	2	0	60%
15	Aucamp C.(Cobus)	Natal	1984	1	0	1	0	0%
16	Aucamp J.J.(Floors)	Northern Transvaal	1973	1	1	0	0	100%
17	Badenhorst A.J.(Adri)	Western Province	2000	1	1	0	0	100%
18	Badenhorst C.(Chris)	Orange Free State	1994, 97	2	0	2	0	0%
19	Badenhorst C.J.	Transvaal	1939	1	1	0	0	100%
20	Badenhorst D.S.(Daan)	Transvaal	1986-87	2	0	2	0	0%
21	Bands R.E.(Richard)	Blue Bulls	2002, 04	2	2	0	0	100%
22	Barnard J.H.(Jannie)	WP/Transvaal	1968-69, 71	3	0	2	1	0%
23	Barnard R.W.(Robbie)	Transvaal	1968, 71	2	0	1	1	0%
24	Barrit B.M.(Bradley)	Natal	2008	1	1	0	0	100%
25	Barry D.(De Wet)	Western Province	2000-01	2	2	0	0	100%
26	Bartmann W.J.(Wahl)	Transvaal/Natal	1986-87, 90, 92-93	5	2	3	0	40%
27	Basson B.A.(Bjorn)	Blue Bulls	2016	1	0	1	0	0%
28	Basson J.J.(Justin)	Free State	2016	1	1	0	0	100%
29	Basson S.(Stefan)	Blue Bulls	2006	1	0	0	1	0%
30	Basson W.W.(Wium)	Blue Bulls	1998	1	1	0	0	100%
31	Bates A.J.(Albie)	Northern Transvaal	1973-74	2	2	0	0	100%
32	Bayvel P.C.R.(Paul)	Transvaal	1972, 74	2	1	1	0	50%
33	Beck J.J.(Colin)	Western Province	1980, 82	2	1	1	0	50%
34	Bekker H.(Manie)	Western Province	1947	1	1	0	0	100%
35	Bekker H.J.(Hennie)	Free State/WP	1977-80, 82-85	8	4	3	1	50%
36	Bekker H.P.J.(Jaap)	Northern Transvaal	1954	1	0	1	0	0%
37	Bekker M.J.(Martiens)	Northern Transvaal	1954, 56	2	1	1	0	50%
38	Bekker R.P.(Dolf)	Northern Transvaal	1956	1	1	0	0	100%
39	Bekker S.(Schutte)	Blue Bulls	1998	1	1	0	0	100%
40	Benade J.J.	Transvaal	1939	1	1	0	0	100%
41	Beneke J.I.(Izak)	Northern Transvaal	1983	1	0	1	0	0%
42	Benjamin R.S.(Ryno)	Golden Lions/FS	2007, 2016	2	1	1	0	50%
43	Bennet R.G.(Russell)	Natal	1999	1	0	1	0	0%
44	Bestbier A.(André)	Orange Free State	1973	1	0	1	0	0%
45	Bester F.	Boland	1952	1	0	1	0	0%

CURRIE CUP FINAL PLAYERS 1939 - 2016

	PLAYER	Province	First & last final	Matches	Won	Lost	Drawn	Winning %
46	Bester J.	Western Province	1939	1	0	1	0	0%
47	Beukes J.H.T.(Joe)	Orange Free State	1994	1	0	1	0	0%
48	Beyers N.(Nellis)	Western Province	1946	1	0	1	0	0%
49	Beyers U.(Ulrich)	Blue Bulls	2016	1	0	1	0	0%
50	Bezuidenhoudt N.S.E.(Nic)	Northern Transvaal	1975, 77	2	2	0	0	100%
51	Bezuidenhout M.J.(Martin)	Transvaal	2011	1	1	0	0	100%
52	Bierman P.(Peet)	Eastern Transvaal	1972	1	0	1	0	0%
53	Blair R.(Robbie)	Western Province	1979-80	2	0	1	1	0%
54	Blakeway A.D.(Andréw)	Natal	1992-93	2	1	1	0	50%
55	Blom L.F.(Louis)	Western Province	1995, 97	2	1	1	0	50%
56	Blommetjies C.A.(Clayton)	Free State	2016	1	1	0	0	100%
57	Boer P.(Piet)	Blue Bulls	1998	1	1	0	0	100%
58	Bolton W.J.C.(Willie)	Orange Free State	1981	1	0	1	0	0%
59	Bolus R.V.M.(Rob)	Western Province	1980	1	0	1	0	0%
60	Bondesio M.(Michael)	Transvaal	2011	1	1	0	0	100%
61	Boome C.S.(Selborne)	Western Province	1998	1	0	1	0	0%
62	Booyens V.(Vic)	Northern Transvaal	1973	1	1	0	0	100%
63	Booysen F.C.F.(Fabian)	Golden Lions	2015	1	1	0	0	100%
64	Booysen J.(Jaco)	Golden Lions	2002	1	0	1	0	0%
65	Bosch G.R.(Gerald)	Transvaal	1972, 74	2	1	1	0	50%
66	Bosch P.W.(Paul)	Western Province	2010	1	0	1	0	0%
67	Bosch R.G.	Transvaal	1947	1	0	1	0	0%
68	Boshoff J.H.(Jannie)	Golden Lions	2007	1	0	1	0	0%
69	Boshoff L.(Leon)	Golden Lions	1999	1	1	0	0	100%
70	Boshoff M.L.(Marnitz)	Golden Lions	2014-15	2	1	1	0	50%
71	Bosman H.M.(Meyer)	Free State/Natal	2005-07, 09, 12	5	2	2	1	40%
72	Bosman P.(Piet)	Transvaal	1968, 72	2	1	1	0	50%
73	Botes L.J.(Jacques)	Natal	2008, 10, 13	3	3	0	0	100%
74	Botes P.J.(Paul)	Northern Transvaal	1985	1	0	1	0	0%
75	Botha A.(Attie)	Northern Transvaal	1946	1	1	0	0	100%
76	Botha A.A.(André)	Natal	1984, 90	2	1	1	0	50%
77	Botha A.F.(Arno)	Blue Bulls	2016	1	0	1	0	0%
78	Botha B.J.	Natal	2003	1	0	1	0	0%
79	Botha D.S.(Darius)	Northern Transvaal	1978-82	5	3	1	1	60%
80	Botha E.(Ettienne)	Blue Bulls	2003-04	2	2	0	0	100%
81	Botha G.v G.(Gary)	Blue Bulls	2002-06	5	3	1	1	60%
82	Botha H.E.(Naas)	Northern Transvaal	1977-81, 85, 87-91	11	7	2	2	64%
83	Botha J.F.(Jan)	Northern Transvaal	1946	1	1	0	0	100%
84	Botha J.F.(Johan)	Orange Free State	1973	1	0	1	0	0%
85	Botha J.J.(Koos)	Transvaal	1952	1	1	0	0	100%
86	Botha J.P.(Bakkies)	Blue Bulls	2002, 04-05, 09	4	3	1	0	75%
87	Botha R.(Ruan)	Western Province	2015	1	0	1	0	0%
88	Bothma A.(Arnold)	Transvaal	1974	1	0	1	0	0%
89	Boyes R.E.	Western Province	1950	1	0	1	0	0%
90	Brand C.P.(Piet)	Northern Transvaal	1969-70	2	1	1	0	50%

CURRIE CUP FINAL PLAYERS 1939 - 2016

	PLAYER	Province	First & last final	Matches	Won	Lost	Drawn	Winning %
91	Breedt J.C.(Jannie)	N Transvaal/TVL	1981-83, 86-87, 91-92	7	1	6	0	14%
92	Breedt N.(Nico)	Free State	2009	1	0	1	0	0%
93	Bresler A.(Anton)	Natal	2010, 12	2	1	1	0	50%
94	Brewis J.D.(Hansie)	Northern Transvaal	1946, 54	2	1	1	0	50%
95	Breytenbach C.L.(Conrad)	Blue Bulls	1998	1	1	0	0	100%
96	Brink R.A.(Rob)	Western Province	1995, 00	2	1	1	0	50%
97	Brink S.(Stephen)	Natal	2000	1	0	1	0	0%
98	Brits J.(Johan)	Eastern Transvaal	1972	1	0	1	0	0%
99	Britz G.J.J.(Gerrie)	Free State	2004	1	0	1	0	0%
100	Britz S.(Stefan)	Blue Bulls	1998	1	1	0	0	100%
101	Britz W.K.(Warren)	Natal	1999, 01	2	0	2	0	0%
102	Britz W.S.(Willie)	Golden Lions	2014	1	0	1	0	0%
103	Broderick F.(Frans)	Transvaal	1952	1	1	0	0	100%
104	Brooks J.Z.(Jannie)	Blue Bulls	1998	1	1	0	0	100%
105	Brosnihan W.G.(Warren)	Natal/Blue Bulls	2000-01, 04	3	1	2	0	33%
106	Brown C.G.(Cliffie)	Northern Transvaal	1982	1	0	1	0	0%
107	Brunow H.L.(Harry)	Western Province	1939	1	0	1	0	0%
108	Brüssow H.W.(Heinrich)	Free State	2006-07, 09	3	1	1	1	33%
109	Buchler J.U.(Johnny)	Transvaal	1950	1	1	0	0	100%
110	Burden C.B.(Craig)	Natal	2010-12	3	1	2	0	33%
111	Burger J.(Hannes)	Northern Transvaal	1956	1	1	0	0	100%
112	Burger J.(Jan)	Boland	1952	1	0	1	0	0%
113	Burger J.M.(Kobus)	Western Province	1985, 88-89	3	1	1	1	33%
114	Burger M.B.(Thys)	Northern Transvaal	1978-81	4	3	0	1	75%
115	Burger N.J.(Niel)	Western Province	1982, 84-85	3	3	0	0	100%
116	Burger P.B.(Philip)	Free State	2005-06	2	1	0	1	50%
117	Burger S.W.(Schalk)	Western Province	1985, 88	2	1	1	0	50%
118	Burger S.W.P.(Schalk) jnr.	Western Province	2010, 13	2	0	2	0	0%
119	Burger S.W.P.(Schalk) snr.	Western Province	1984-86	3	3	0	0	100%
120	Butler B.L.(Basil)	Western Province	1946	1	0	1	0	0%
121	Cabannes L.(Laurent)	Western Province	1995	1	0	1	0	0%
122	Calldo J.G.(Cobus)	Free State	2007	1	1	0	0	100%
123	Carey F.(Fraser)	Transvaal	1947	1	0	1	0	0%
124	Carizza M.(Manuel)	Western Province	2014	1	1	0	0	100%
125	Carr N.(Nizaam)	Western Province	2014-15	2	1	1	0	50%
126	Carstens P-D.(Deon)	Natal/WP	2001, 03, 08, 12	4	2	2	0	50%
127	Carstens W.(Cassie)	Western Province	1998	1	0	1	0	0%
128	Cassiem U.(Uzair)	Free State	2016	1	1	0	0	100%
129	Catrakilis D.(Demetri)	Western Province	2012-14	3	2	1	0	67%
130	Cilliers P.M.(Pat)	Golden Lions/WP	2011, 13-14	3	2	1	0	67%
131	Claassen K.(Koos)	Transvaal	1968	1	0	1	0	0%
132	Claassen W.(Wynand)	N Transvaal/Natal	1975, 77, 79, 84	4	2	1	1	50%
133	Claassens J.H.(Jacques)	Free State	2004	1	0	1	0	0%
134	Claassens J.P.(Jannie)	Northern Transvaal	1990-91	2	1	1	0	50%
135	Claassens M.(Michael)	Free State	2004-06	3	1	1	1	33%

CURRIE CUP FINAL PLAYERS 1939 - 2016

	PLAYER	Province	First & last final	Matches	Won	Lost	Drawn	Winning %
136	Clarke T.A.(Bossie)	Western Province	1976, 79-80	3	0	2	1	0%
137	Cloete A.(Abe)	Northern Transvaal	1954	1	0	1	0	0%
138	Cockrell C.H.(Charlie)	Western Province	1969	1	0	1	0	0%
139	Cockrell R.J.(Robert)	Western Province	1976, 80	2	0	2	0	0%
140	Cockrell W.J.(William)	Western Province	1986	1	1	0	0	100%
141	Coetzee A.(Andries)	Golden Lions	2015	1	1	0	0	100%
142	Coetzee A.(Johan)	Free State	2016	1	1	0	0	100%
143	Coetzee D.(Danie)	Blue Bulls	2002, 04-05	3	2	1	0	67%
144	Coetzee D.A.(Deon)	Northern Transvaal	1982	1	0	1	0	0%
145	Coetzee E.L.(Eduard)	Natal	2003	1	0	1	0	0%
146	Coetzee J.(Johan)	Eastern Transvaal	1972	1	0	1	0	0%
147	Coetzee J.H.(Johan)	Orange Free State	1981	1	0	1	0	0%
148	Coetzee J.H.H.(Jan-Boland)	Western Province	1969, 76, 79	3	0	2	1	0%
149	Coetzee J.J.(Jaco)	Orange Free State	1994	1	0	1	0	0%
150	Coetzee J.L.(Koot)	Northern Transvaal	1978	1	1	0	0	100%
151	Coetzee M.C.(Marcell)	Natal	2011-13	3	1	2	0	33%
152	Coetzee R.L.(Robbie)	Golden Lions	2014-15	2	1	1	0	50%
153	Coetzer J.H.(Joe)	Transvaal	1974	1	0	1	0	0%
154	Coleman K.K.(Kurt)	Western Province	2013-15	3	1	2	0	33%
155	Combrinck G.J.(Gerhard)	Transvaal	1994	1	1	0	0	100%
156	Combrinck J.(James)	Griquas	1970	1	1	0	0	100%
157	Combrinck R.J.(Ruan)	Golden Lions	2014	1	0	1	0	0%
158	Conradie J.H.J.(Bolla)	Western Province	2001	1	1	0	0	100%
159	Cooper K.L.(Kyle)	Natal	2012-13	2	1	1	0	50%
160	Craig B.K.(Pat)	Transvaal	1947	1	0	1	0	0%
161	Cronjé G.(Geo)	Blue Bulls	2002-03	2	2	0	0	100%
162	Cronjé J.(Jacques)	Blue Bulls/ GL	2003-05, 07	4	2	2	0	50%
163	Cronjé L.(Lionel)	Western Province	2010	1	0	1	0	0%
164	Cronjé P.A.(Peter)	Transvaal	1971-72	2	1	0	1	50%
165	Cronjé R.(Ross)	Natal/GL	2011, 14-15	3	1	2	0	33%
166	Cupido W.(Wilfred)	Western Province	1983	1	1	0	0	100%
167	Dalton J.(James)	Transvaal	1996	1	0	1	0	0%
168	Daniel K.R.(Keegan)	Natal	2008, 10-13	5	3	2	0	60%
169	Daniels J.I.(John)	Golden Lions	2002	1	0	1	0	0%
170	Daniller H.J.(Hennie)	Free State	2009	1	0	1	0	0%
171	Dannhauser G.(Gert)	Transvaal	1947, 50	2	1	1	0	50%
172	Dannhauser T.(Toy)	Transvaal	1968	1	0	1	0	0%
173	Davids Q.(Quinton)	Western Province	2000-01	2	2	0	0	100%
174	Davidson C.D.(Craig)	Natal	1999-03	4	0	4	0	0%
175	Dawson M.(Murray)	Natal	1984	1	0	1	0	0%
176	De Allende D.(Damian)	Western Province	2012-13	2	1	1	0	50%
177	De Beer J.H.(Jannie)	Free State	1997	1	0	1	0	0%
178	De Beer M.C.	Northern Transvaal	1954	1	0	1	0	0%
179	De Beer R.C.(Ski-Hi)	Northern Transvaal	1954, 56	2	1	1	0	50%
180	De Bruyn M.J.(Tewis)	Free State	2007, 09	2	1	1	0	50%

CURRIE CUP FINAL PLAYERS 1939 - 2016

	PLAYER	Province	First & last final	Matches	Won	Lost	Drawn	Winning %
181	De Jager N.J.K.(Nic)	Blue Bulls	2016	1	0	1	0	0%
182	De Jager S.H.F.(Frans)	Northern Transvaal	1956	1	1	0	0	100%
183	De Jongh J.L.(Juan)	Western Province	2010, 12-15	5	2	3	0	40%
184	De Klerk I.J.(Sakkie)	Transvaal	1968	1	0	1	0	0%
185	De Klerk K.B.H.(Kevin)	Transvaal	1971-72, 74	3	1	1	1	33%
186	De Klerk P.R.(Rossouw)	Blue Bulls	2009	1	1	0	0	100%
187	De Klerk W.P.(Moffie)	Northern Transvaal	1973	1	1	0	0	100%
188	De Kock C.(Con)	Western Province	1946	1	0	1	0	0%
189	De Kock D.(Deon)	Golden Lions	2002	1	0	1	0	0%
190	De Kock N.A.(Neil)	Western Province	2001	1	1	0	0	100%
191	De Meyer O.A.(Oeloff)	Northern Transvaal	1969, 75	2	2	0	0	100%
192	De Villers A.P.(Apie)	Western Province	1939	1	0	1	0	0%
193	De Villers D.J.(David)	Free State	2009	1	0	1	0	0%
194	De Villiers H.(Dirkie)	Western Province	1947	1	1	0	0	100%
195	De Villiers H.O.	Western Province	1969	1	1	0	0	100%
196	De Villiers J.(Hannes)	Northern Transvaal	1946	1	1	0	0	100%
197	De Villiers J.(Jean)	Western Province	2010, 13	2	0	2	0	0%
198	De Vos D.J.J.(Dirk)	Tvl/N Transvaaal	1968, 73-74	3	2	1	0	67%
199	De Waal W.(Willem)	Free State/WP	2004-07, 10	5	2	2	1	40%
200	De Wet A.(Bertie)	Western Province	1983-84	2	2	0	0	100%
201	De Wet D.J.(Daan)	Orange Free State	1973	1	0	1	0	0%
202	De Wet P.	Western Province	1939	1	0	1	0	0%
203	De Wet P.J.(Piet)	Western Province	1939	1	0	1	0	0%
204	De Wit A.S.(Stephan)	Golden Lions	2015	1	1	0	0	100%
205	Delaporte C.(Dollie)	Transvaal	1939	1	1	0	0	100%
206	Delport G.M.(Thinus)	Golden Lions	1999	1	1	0	0	100%
207	Delport M.(Marius)	Blue Bulls	2006, 08	2	0	1	1	0%
208	Demas D.(Danwel)	Free State	2009	1	0	1	0	0%
209	Dercksen B.(Bennie)	Eastern Transvaal	1972	1	0	1	0	0%
210	Des Dountain D.(Dylan)	Transvaal	2011	1	1	0	0	100%
211	Deuchar B.(Butch)	Western Province	1976	1	0	1	0	0%
212	Deysel J.R.(Jean)	Natal	2008, 11-12	3	1	2	0	33%
213	Dirks C.A.(Chris)	Transvaal	1993	1	1	0	0	100%
214	Dixon P.J.(Peter)	Western Province	2000-01	2	2	0	0	100%
215	Dorrington I.(Ivor)	Western Province	1954	1	1	0	0	100%
216	Downes G.(Graham)	Natal	1984	1	0	1	0	0%
217	Dreyer J.N.(Jannie)	Northern Transvaal	1983	1	0	1	0	0%
218	Dreyer K.L.(Kon)	Transvaal	1972	1	1	0	0	100%
219	Dreyer M.C.(Martin)	Blue Bulls	2016	1	0	1	0	0%
220	Dreyer R.M.(Ruan)	Golden Lions	2014-15	2	1	1	0	50%
221	Drotské A.E.(Naka)	Orange Free State	1994-97, 04-05	4	1	3	0	25%
222	Dryburgh R.G.(Roy)	WP/Natal	1950, 54, 56	3	1	2	0	33%
223	Du Plessis A.J.(Tiny)	Orange Free State	1976	1	1	0	0	100%
224	Du Plessis B.W.(Bismarck)	Natal	2008, 10-11, 13	4	3	1	0	75%
225	Du Plessis C.J.(Carel)	Western Province/Tvl	1982-84, 86-89	7	4	2	1	57%

CURRIE CUP FINAL PLAYERS 1939 - 2016

	PLAYER	Province	First & last final	Matches	Won	Lost	Drawn	Winning %
226	Du Plessis D.C.(Daan)	Northern Transvaal	1973-75, 77-79	6	5	0	1	83%
227	Du Plessis D.F.(Francois)	Northern Transvaal	1991	1	1	0	0	100%
228	Du Plessis F.(Felix)	Transvaal	1947	1	0	1	0	0%
229	Du Plessis F.(Francois)	Northern Transvaal	1982-83	2	0	2	0	0%
230	Du Plessis J.N.(Jannie)	Free State/Natal	2005-08, 10-13	8	5	2	1	63%
231	Du Plessis M.(Morné)	Western Province	1976, 79	2	0	1	1	0%
232	Du Plessis M.(Thys)	Western Province	1950	1	0	1	0	0%
233	Du Plessis M.J.(Michael)	Western Province/Tvl	1982, 84-85, 87-89	6	3	2	1	50%
234	Du Plessis P.G.(Piet)	Northern Transvaal	1971	1	0	1	0	0%
235	Du Plessis T.D.(Tommy)	Northern Transvaal	1975, 77-82, 85	8	5	2	1	63%
236	Du Plessis W.(Willie)	Western Province	1979-80, 82	3	1	1	1	33%
237	Du Plooy T.J.(Boela)	Free State	2004	1	0	1	0	0%
238	Du Preez F.C.H.(Frik)	Northern Transvaal	1968-71	4	2	1	1	50%
239	Du Preez G.J.D.(Delarey)	Golden Lions	2002	1	0	1	0	0%
240	Du Preez P.F.(Fourie) jnr.	Blue Bulls	2003-05, 08-09	5	3	2	0	60%
241	Du Preez P.F.(Fourie) snr.	Northern Transvaal	1968-70	3	2	1	0	67%
242	Du Preez R.J.(Robert) jnr.	Western Province	2015	1	0	1	0	0%
243	Du Preez R.J.(Robert) snr.	N Transvaal/Natal	1988-92	5	3	1	1	60%
244	Du Preez W.H.(Wian)	Free State	2005-07, 09	4	2	1	1	50%
245	Du Rand D.(Salty)	Transvaal	1974	1	0	1	0	0%
246	Du Rand H.G.J.(Hennie)	Northern Transvaal	1968, 75	2	2	0	0	100%
247	Du Rand J.A.(Salty)	WP/N Transvaal	1947, 54	2	1	1	0	50%
248	Du Randt J.P.(Os)	Orange Free State	1994, 97, 04-05	4	1	3	0	25%
249	Du Toit F.P.(Pikkie)	Orange Free State	1973, 75	2	0	2	0	0%
250	Du Toit G.S.(Gaffie)	Natal/Free State	2000-01, 06	3	0	2	1	0%
251	Du Toit J.(John)	Western Province	1954	1	1	0	0	100%
252	Du Toit J.C.(Jan)	Orange Free State	1981	1	0	1	0	0%
253	Du Toit O.J.J.(Jacques)	Free State	2016	1	1	0	0	100%
254	Du Toit P.A.(Fonnie)	Northern Transvaal	1946, 54	2	1	1	0	50%
255	Du Toit P.G.(Hempies)	Western Province	1979-80, 83, 85	4	2	1	1	50%
256	Du Toit P.S.(Pieter-Steph)	Natal	2013	1	1	0	0	100%
257	Du Toit T.(Tobias)	Transvaal	1968, 71	2	0	1	1	0%
258	Duffett D.	Western Province	1950	1	0	1	0	0%
259	Duffy G.(Gavin)	Natal	1956	1	0	1	0	0%
260	Dukas D.	Western Province	1950	1	0	1	0	0%
261	Duncan R.(Rory)	Free State	2006-07	2	1	0	1	50%
262	Durr J.(Johan)	Western Province	1983	1	1	0	0	100%
263	Duvenhage D.O.(Dewaldt)	Western Province	2010	1	0	1	0	0%
264	Duvenhage F.P.(Floris)	Transvaal	1939	1	1	0	0	100%
265	East M.(Mike)	Western Province	1954	1	1	0	0	100%
266	Edmunds P.(Peter)	Natal	1984	1	0	1	0	0%
267	Edwards P.(Pierre)	Northern Transvaal	1977-83	7	4	2	1	57%
268	Ellis C.E.(Clark)	Western Province	1986	1	1	0	0	100%
269	Eloff M.C.(Giel)	Northern Transvaal	1973	1	1	0	0	100%
270	Els W.W.(Braam)	Orange Free State	1994, 97	2	0	2	0	0%

CURRIE CUP FINAL PLAYERS 1939 - 2016

	PLAYER	Province	First & last final	Matches	Won	Lost	Drawn	Winning %
271	Elstadt R.(Rynhardt)	Western Province	2014-15	2	1	1	0	50%
272	Engelbrecht G.(Giel)	Boland	1952	1	0	1	0	0%
273	Engelbrecht K.(Kobus)	Golden Lions	1999	1	1	0	0	100%
274	Engels J.(Jaco)	Blue Bulls	2006	1	0	0	1	0%
275	Erasmus J.(Johan)	Free State	1997, 04	2	0	2	0	0%
276	Erasmus L.J.(Lourens)	Golden Lions	2015	1	1	0	0	100%
277	Esterhuizen G.(Grant)	Golden Lions	2002	1	0	1	0	0%
278	Esterhuizen J.(Johan)	Transvaal	1972	1	1	0	0	100%
279	Esterhuizen W.C.(Willa)	Northern Transvaal	1956	1	1	0	0	100%
280	Etzebeth E.(Eben)	Western Province	2012-13	2	1	1	0	50%
281	Faure C.L.(Chris)	Natal	1984	1	0	1	0	0%
282	Ferreira A.P.(Fief)	Northern Transvaal	1971	1	0	0	1	0%
283	Ferreira F.C.(Freddie)	Western Province	1985-86, 88-89	4	2	1	1	50%
284	Ferreira P.S.(Kulu)	Western Province	1984	1	1	0	0	100%
285	Fitchet C.(Christo)	Orange Free State	1981	1	0	1	0	0%
286	Fleck R.F.(Robbie)	Western Province	1998, 00	2	1	1	0	50%
287	Flemix J.F.(Jan)	Northern Transvaal	1968	1	1	0	0	100%
288	Floors L.(Kabamba)	Free State	2005-07, 09	4	2	1	1	50%
289	Fondse A.R.(Adriaan)	Western Province	2010	1	0	1	0	0%
290	Fortuin B.A.(Bevin)	Free State	2005-06	2	1	0	1	50%
291	Fourie A.(Braam)	Griquas	1970	1	1	0	0	100%
292	Fourie A.J.(Stompie)	Transvaal	1991	1	0	1	0	0%
293	Fourie B.G.(Bernard)	Transvaal	1993-94	2	2	0	0	100%
294	Fourie D.A.(Deon)	Western Province	2010, 12-13	3	1	2	0	33%
295	Fourie J.(Jaque)	Golden Lions	2002	1	0	1	0	0%
296	Fourie M.J.(Pote)	Northern Transvaal	1987-91	5	3	1	1	60%
297	Fourie S.A.(Andries)	Transvaal	1986	1	0	1	0	0%
298	Fourie T.T.(Polla)	Northern Transvaal	1968, 70	2	1	1	0	50%
299	Fredericks E.R.(Eddie)	Free State	2004-05, 07	3	2	1	0	67%
300	Fredericks K.P.(Keegan)	Blue Bulls	2004	1	1	0	0	100%
301	Frederickson C.A.(Dave)	Transvaal	1974	1	0	1	0	0%
302	Froneman D.C.(Dirk)	Orange Free State	1976, 78	2	1	1	0	50%
303	Fry D.J.(Dennis)	Western Province	1946-47, 50	3	1	2	0	33%
304	Fry S.P.(Stephen)	Western Province	1946-47, 50	3	1	2	0	33%
305	Fuls H.T.(Heinrich)	Transvaal	1992	1	0	1	0	0%
306	Fynn E.E.(Etienne)	Natal	1999-01	3	0	3	0	0%
307	Fyvie W.S.(Wayne)	Natal	1995-96, 99	3	2	1	0	67%
308	Garvey A.C.(Adrian)	Natal	1995-96	2	2	0	0	100%
309	Geel P.J.(Flip)	Northern Transvaal	1946	1	1	0	0	100%
310	Geffin A.O.(Okey)	Transvaal	1947, 50	2	1	1	0	50%
311	Geldenhuys A.(Adri)	Northern Transvaal	1987, 89	2	1	0	1	50%
312	Geldenhuys J.(Jan)	Western Province	1980	1	0	1	0	0%
313	Geldenhuys S.B.(Burger)	Northern Transvaal	1977-83, 85, 87-89	11	6	3	2	55%
314	Gerber H.J.(Hendrik)	Western Province	2000-01	2	2	0	0	100%
315	Gerber L.J.(Len)	Northern Transvaal	1974-75	2	2	0	0	100%

CURRIE CUP FINAL PLAYERS 1939 - 2016

	PLAYER	Province	First & last final	Matches	Won	Lost	Drawn	Winning %
316	Gerber R.(Rayno)	Free State/Blue Bulls	2004, 06, 08	3	0	2	1	0%
317	Germishuys J.S.(Gerrie)	Orange Free State	1973, 75-77	4	1	3	0	25%
318	Geyer C.(Chris)	Northern Transvaal	1954	1	0	1	0	0%
319	Gibson B.	Boland	1952	1	0	1	0	0%
320	Gie W.	Western Province	1939	1	0	1	0	0%
321	Gillingham J.W.(Joe)	Transvaal/Natal	1996, 99	2	0	2	0	0%
322	Gioia L.(Lieb)	Northern Transvaal	1956	1	1	0	0	100%
323	Goodes B.(Barry)	Free State	2005	1	1	0	0	100%
324	Gous R.(Riaan)	Western Province	1989	1	0	0	1	0%
325	Gouws J.J.(Koos)	Northern Transvaal	1989	1	0	0	1	0%
326	Gqoboka L.P.(Lizo)	Blue Bulls	2016	1	0	1	0	0%
327	Grace R.(Bobby)	Transvaal	1968	1	0	1	0	0%
328	Gradwell D.V.(Dudley)	Northern Transvaal	1971	1	0	0	1	0%
329	Greeff W.W.(Werner)	Western Province	2001	1	1	0	0	100%
330	Greyling P.J.F.(Piet)	Transvaal	1971-72	2	1	0	1	50%
331	Griffiths W.(Billy)	Western Province	1946	1	0	1	0	0%
332	Grobbelaar D.J.E.(Derrick)	Blue Bulls	1998	1	1	0	0	100%
333	Grobbelaar P.J.J.(Cobus)	Golden Lions	2007, 11	2	1	1	0	50%
334	Grobler C.J.(Kleintjie)	Orange Free State	1973, 75	2	0	2	0	0%
335	Grobler G.(Gerbrand)	N Transvaal/Tvl	1987-91, 94	6	4	1	1	67%
336	Grobler G.(Gerbrandt)	Western Province	2014	1	1	0	0	100%
337	Grobler R.N.(Renier)	Northern Transvaal	1969	1	1	0	0	100%
338	Groom N.J.(Nick)	Western Province	2012-15	4	2	2	0	50%
339	Grundlingh H.E.W.(Henk)	Northern Transvaal	1971	1	0	0	1	0%
340	Haarhoff R.A.(Ronnie)	Natal	1984	1	0	1	0	0%
341	Habana B.G.(Bryan)	Blue Bulls/WP	2005, 08-10, 12	5	2	3	0	40%
342	Hall D.B.(Dean)	Golden Lions	1999	1	1	0	0	100%
343	Halstead T.M.(Trevor)	Natal	1999-01	3	0	3	0	0%
344	Hamilton G.(Greg)	Natal	1984	1	0	1	0	0%
345	Hanekom N.J.(Stokkies)	Golden Lions	2015	1	1	0	0	100%
346	Hankinson R.G.(Rob)	Natal	1984	1	0	1	0	0%
347	Harding G.(Gerard)	Natal	1990, 92	2	2	0	0	100%
348	Hargreaves A.J.(Alistair)	Natal	2010-11	2	1	1	0	50%
349	Harris J.(Brok)	Western Province	2010, 12-14	4	2	2	0	50%
350	Harris T.A.(Tony)	Transvaal	1939	1	1	0	0	100%
351	Hattingh S.J.(Ian)	Transvaal	1994, 96	2	1	1	0	50%
352	Henderson S.(Skip)	Eastern Transvaal	1972	1	0	1	0	0%
353	Hendriks P.(Pieter)	Transvaal	1991-94	4	2	2	0	50%
354	Herbert E.(Eric)	Orange Free State	1994	1	0	1	0	0%
355	Herbst C.(Freddie)	Transvaal	1952	1	1	0	0	100%
356	Herbst W.J.(Wiehann)	Natal	2012-13	2	1	1	0	50%
357	Heunis J.W.(Johan)	Northern Transvaal	1981, 83, 87, 89	4	2	1	1	50%
358	Heymans J.H.(Dougie)	Orange Free State	1994	1	0	1	0	0%
359	Heynecke J.(Johnny)	Northern Transvaal	1954	1	0	1	0	0%
360	Hinrichsen W.	Western Province	1939	1	0	1	0	0%

CURRIE CUP FINAL PLAYERS 1939 - 2016

	PLAYER	Province	First & last final	Matches	Won	Lost	Drawn	Winning %
361	Hirst H.(Dummy)	Transvaal	1939	1	1	0	0	100%
362	Hoffman D.(Dirk)	Northern Transvaal	1981-82	2	1	1	0	50%
363	Hoffman R.S.(Steve)	Boland	1952	1	0	1	0	0%
364	Hoffman T.(Teddy)	Western Province	1969	1	0	1	0	0%
365	Hoffmann C.F.(Carel)	Natal	2011	1	0	1	0	0%
366	Hollenbach A.W.C.J.(Alwyn)	Free State/GL	2005, 07, 11	3	3	0	0	100%
367	Holtzhausen C.(Christo)	Eastern Transvaal	1972	1	0	1	0	0%
368	Honiball H.W.(Henry)	Natal	1992, 95-96	3	3	0	0	100%
369	Horn H.(Hendrik)	Eastern Transvaal	1972	1	0	1	0	0%
370	Hougaard D.J.(Derick)	Blue Bulls	2002, 04-06	4	2	1	1	50%
371	Hougaard F.(Francois)	Blue Bulls	2009	1	1	0	0	100%
372	Hugo D.P.(Niel)	Western Province	1986, 88-89	3	1	1	1	33%
373	Hugo D.P.(Reniel)	Free State	2016	1	1	0	0	100%
374	Hugo W.J.(Wouter)	Orange Free State	1975-78	4	1	3	0	25%
375	Human A.W.J.(Andries)	Blue Bulls	2003, 05	2	1	1	0	50%
376	Human P.R.(Flip)	Transvaal	1950, 52	2	2	0	0	100%
377	Human W.A.(Wylie)	Blue Bulls/GL	2002, 07	2	1	1	0	50%
378	Hurter M.H.(Marius)	Western Province	1998	1	0	1	0	0%
379	Immelman K.(Kobus)	Western Province	1976	1	0	1	0	0%
380	Irvine B.(Brian)	Natal	1956	1	0	1	0	0%
381	Ismaiel T.K.(Travis)	Blue Bulls	2016	1	0	1	0	0%
382	Jacklin B.(Brian)	Natal	1956	1	0	1	0	0%
383	Jacobs A.A.(Adrian)	Natal	2008, 11	2	1	1	0	50%
384	James A.D.(Butch)	Natal/GL	2000, 03, 11	3	1	2	0	33%
385	Jamieson C.M.(Craig)	Natal	1984, 90	2	1	1	0	50%
386	Janse van Rensburg R.(Rohan)	Golden Lions	2015	1	1	0	0	100%
387	Jansen E.(Eben)	Orange Free State	1976-77	2	1	1	0	50%
388	Jansen J.S.(Joggie)	Orange Free State	1976, 78	2	1	1	0	50%
389	Jantjes C.A.(Conrad)	Western Province	2010	1	0	1	0	0%
390	Jantjies E.T.(Elton)	Transvaal	2011	1	1	0	0	100%
391	Januarie E.R.(Enrico)	Western Province	2010	1	0	1	0	0%
392	Jenkins J.H.(Jason)	Blue Bulls	2016	1	0	1	0	0%
393	Johnson A.F.(Ashley)	Free State	2009	1	0	1	0	0%
394	Johnson G.K.(Gavin)	Transvaal	1993-94, 96	3	2	1	0	67%
395	Johnstone B.(Brett)	Golden Lions	1999	1	1	0	0	100%
396	Jones H.R.F.(Huw)	Western Province	2015	1	0	1	0	0%
397	Jonker J.W.	Free State	2006	1	0	0	1	0%
398	Jordaan D.N.(Niell)	Free State	2016	1	1	0	0	100%
399	Jordaan G.J.(Gert)	Orange Free State	1981	1	0	1	0	0%
400	Jordaan N.(Norman)	Blue Bulls	2002-03	2	2	0	0	100%
401	Jordaan P.A.(Paul)	Natal	2012	1	0	1	0	0%
402	Jordaan R.P.(Jorrie)	Northern Transvaal	1946	1	1	0	0	100%
403	Joubert A.J.(André)	Natal	1993, 95-96, 99	4	2	2	0	50%
404	Joubert C.H.B.(Tiaan)	Blue Bulls	2002	1	1	0	0	100%
405	Joubert E.(Ernst)	Golden Lions	2007	1	0	1	0	0%

CURRIE CUP FINAL PLAYERS 1939 - 2016

	PLAYER	Province	First & last final	Matches	Won	Lost	Drawn	Winning %
406	Joubert J.(Joos)	Natal	1995-96	2	2	0	0	100%
407	Joubert J-P.(J.P.)	Free State	2009	1	0	1	0	0%
408	Joubert M.C.(Marius)	Free State/Natal	2007, 11	2	1	1	0	50%
409	Juries F.M.(Fabian)	Free State	2009	1	0	1	0	0%
410	Kahts W.J.H.(Willie)	Northern Transvaal	1974-75, 77-80, 82	7	5	1	1	71%
411	Kamana J.(James)	Transvaal	2011	1	1	0	0	100%
412	Kankowski R.(Ryan)	Natal	2008, 10-11	3	2	1	0	67%
413	Kayser D.J.(Deon)	Natal	2000-01, 03	3	0	3	0	0%
414	Kebble G.R.(Guy)	Western Province/Natal	1988-90, 93	4	1	2	1	25%
415	Kebble O.R.(Oliver)	Western Province	2015	1	0	1	0	0%
416	Kempson R.B.(Rob)	Natal/WP	1995-96, 00-01	4	4	0	0	100%
417	Killian M.(Michael)	Transvaal	2011	1	1	0	0	100%
418	Kirchner Z.(Zane)	Blue Bulls	2008-09	2	1	1	0	50%
419	Kirkham T.A.(Tobie)	Orange Free State	1994	1	0	1	0	0%
420	Kirkham W.H.(Liaan)	Transvaal	1986-87	2	0	2	0	0%
421	Kirsten J.C.(Jannes)	Blue Bulls	2016	1	0	1	0	0%
422	Kirsten J.J.N.(Kobus)	Western Province	1989	1	0	0	1	0%
423	Kirsten J.M.(Michael)	Western Province	1995	1	0	1	0	0%
424	Kitshoff S.(Steven)	Western Province	2012-13, 15	3	1	2	0	33%
425	Kleyn J.(Jean)	Western Province	2014-15	2	1	1	0	50%
426	Klopper C.(Chris)	Natal	1956	1	0	1	0	0%
427	Klopper J.	Transvaal	1939	1	1	0	0	100%
428	Knoetze F.(Faffa)	Western Province	1985-86, 88-89	4	2	1	1	50%
429	Knoetze M.J.(Martin)	Transvaal	1991	1	0	1	0	0%
430	Knoetze N.J.(Kallie)	Northern Transvaal	1974	1	1	0	0	100%
431	Knox J.(John)	Northern Transvaal	1973-74, 77-79	5	4	0	1	80%
432	Koch A.C.(Chris)	Boland	1952	1	0	1	0	0%
433	Koch B.(Agie)	Western Province	1980	1	0	1	0	0%
434	Koch H.V.(Bubbles)	Western Province/Boland	1946-52	2	0	2	0	0%
435	Koch W.(Willem)	Boland	1952	1	0	1	0	0%
436	Koch W.J.(Wilhelm)	Golden Lions	2007	1	0	1	0	0%
437	Kockott R.M.(Rory)	Natal	2008, 10	2	2	0	0	100%
438	Koen L.J.(Louis)	Western Province	1997	1	1	0	0	100%
439	Kokoali T.C.(Tsepo)	Free State	2004	1	0	1	0	0%
440	Kolbe C.(Cheslin)	Western Province	2013-15	3	1	2	0	33%
441	Kolisi S.(Siya)	Western Province	2013	1	0	1	0	0%
442	Koster A.(Armandt)	Free State	2016	1	1	0	0	100%
443	Kotze G.J.M.(Gert)	Western Province	1969	1	0	1	0	0%
444	Kotze J.J.(Jimmy)	Transvaal	1947, 50	2	1	1	0	50%
445	Kotze J-B.(Johnny)	Western Province	2015	1	0	1	0	0%
446	Krantz E.F.W.(Edrich)	Free State/N Tvl	1976-78, 80	4	2	2	0	50%
447	Krause J.(Jackie)	Transvaal	1991	1	0	1	0	0%
448	Krause P.(Piet)	Blue Bulls	2003	1	1	0	0	100%
449	Kriel J.A.(Jaco)	Golden Lions	2014-15	2	1	1	0	50%
450	Kriel P.B.(Piet)	Boland	1952	1	0	1	0	0%

CURRIE CUP FINAL PLAYERS 1939 - 2016

	PLAYER	Province	First & last final	Matches	Won	Lost	Drawn	Winning %
451	**Kriel P.C.**(Piet)	Western Province	1939, 46, 50	3	0	3	0	0%
452	**Krige C.P.J.**(Corné)	Western Province	1997-98, 00-01	4	3	1	0	75%
453	**Kritzinger J.C.**	Western Province	2010	1	0	1	0	0%
454	**Kritzinger J.L.**(Klippies)	Transvaal/Free State	1974-76	3	1	2	0	33%
455	**Kruger C.R.**(Chris)	Free State	2004-05	2	1	1	0	50%
456	**Kruger G.H.J.**(Gert)	Transvaal	1950, 52	2	2	0	0	100%
457	**Kruger H.C.**(Herkie)	Natal	2001	1	0	1	0	0%
458	**Kruger H.E.**(Hendrik)	Northern Transvaal	1985, 87, 90	3	1	2	0	33%
459	**Kruger P.E.**(Piet)	N Transvaal/Tvl	1982-83, 86-87	4	0	4	0	0%
460	**Kruger T.**(Tjaart)	Eastern Transvaal	1972	1	0	1	0	0%
461	**Kruger W.**(Werner)	Blue Bulls	2008-09	2	1	1	0	50%
462	**Kuün G.W.F.**(Derick)	Blue Bulls	2006, 08-09	3	1	1	1	33%
463	**La Grange G.**(Doppies)	Transvaal	2011	1	1	0	0	100%
464	**La Marque D.**(Derek)	Natal	1984	1	0	1	0	0%
465	**Labuschagne C.**(Cas)	Natal	1956	1	0	1	0	0%
466	**Labuschagne J.J.**(Jannes)	Golden Lions	1999, 02	2	1	1	0	50%
467	**Labuschagne L.**(Lappies)	Natal	1956	1	0	1	0	0%
468	**Labuschagne W.A.**(Lappies)	Transvaal	1986, 91-92	3	0	3	0	0%
469	**Lacroix T.**(Thierry)	Natal	1995	1	1	0	0	100%
470	**Laing B.**(Balfour)	Natal	1956	1	0	1	0	0%
471	**Lambie P.J.**(Patrick)	Natal	2010-13	4	2	2	0	50%
472	**Lamprecht J.C.**(Johann)	Northern Transvaal	1985, 87-90	5	2	2	1	40%
473	**Lategan M.T.**(Tjol)	Western Province	1947	1	1	0	0	100%
474	**Laubscher T.G.**(Tommie)	Western Province	1995, 97	2	1	1	0	50%
475	**Lawless G.E.**(Gavin)	Transvaal	1996	1	0	1	0	0%
476	**Lawless M.J.**(Mike)	Western Province	1969	1	0	1	0	0%
477	**Lawton T.A.**(Tom)	Natal	1990	1	1	0	0	100%
478	**Le Roux A-H.**(Ollie)	Free State/Natal	1994-95, 00-01, 03, 05-06	7	2	4	1	29%
479	**Le Roux H.P.**(Hennie)	Transvaal	1992-94, 96, 99	5	3	2	0	60%
480	**Le Roux J.H.S.**(Johan)	Transvaal	1991	1	0	1	0	0%
481	**Le Roux M.**(Martiens)	Orange Free State	1973, 75-78, 81	6	1	5	0	17%
482	**Lee N.J.**(Nicolaas)	Free State	2016	1	1	0	0	100%
483	**Lensing G.**(Kees)	Blue Bulls	2004-05	2	1	1	0	50%
484	**Leonard A.**(Anton)	Blue Bulls	2002-05	4	3	1	0	75%
485	**Lewies J.S.T.**(Stephan)	Natal	2013	1	1	0	0	100%
486	**Leyds D.Y.**(Dillyn)	Western Province	2015	1	0	1	0	0%
487	**Liebenberg H.**(Hanro)	Blue Bulls	2016	1	0	1	0	0%
488	**Lightfoot W.**(Wessel)	Western Province	1988	1	0	1	0	0%
489	**Linee M.**(Tinus)	Western Province	1995	1	0	1	0	0%
490	**Lobberts H.**(Hilton)	Blue Bulls	2006	1	0	0	1	0%
491	**Lochner G.P.**(Flappie)	Western Province	1939	1	0	1	0	0%
492	**Lock J.L.**(Jan)	Northern Transvaal	1985, 87-88, 90	4	2	2	0	50%
493	**Lockyear R.J.**(Dick)	Western Province	1954	1	1	0	0	100%
494	**Lombaard P.**(Piet)	Western Province	1950	1	0	1	0	0%
495	**Lötter D.**(Deon)	WP/Tvl	1986, 91, 93	3	2	1	0	67%

CURRIE CUP FINAL PLAYERS 1939 - 2016

PLAYER	Province	First & last final	Matches	Won	Lost	Drawn	Winning %
496 Lotz J.W.(Jan)	Transvaal	1939, 47	2	1	1	0	50%
497 Loubscher H.(Hennie)	Western Province	1954	1	1	0	0	100%
498 Loubser J.(Kootjie)	Boland	1952	1	0	1	0	0%
499 Lourens J.P.(Johnnie)	Northern Transvaal	1946	1	1	0	0	100%
500 Lourens M.J.(Thys)	Northern Transvaal	1968-69, 71, 73-75, 77-78	8	7	0	1	88%
501 Louw F.H.(Hottie)	WP/BB	1998, 00-01, 06	4	2	1	1	50%
502 Louw L-F.P.(Francois)	Western Province	2010	1	0	1	0	0%
503 Louw M.J.(Martiens)	Transvaal	1971	1	0	0	1	0%
504 Louw P.(Pierre)	Western Province	1939	1	0	1	0	0%
505 Louw R.J.(Rob)	Western Province	1979-80, 82-85	6	4	1	1	67%
506 Louw S.C.(Fanie)	Transvaal	1939	1	1	0	0	100%
507 Louw W.M.(Wilco)	Western Province	2015	1	0	1	0	0%
508 Luck A.(Aubrey)	Western Province	1969	1	0	1	0	0%
509 Ludik L.(Louis)	Golden Lions/Natal	2007, 10, 12-13	4	2	2	0	50%
510 Lurie M.(Max)	Transvaal	1947	1	0	1	0	0%
511 Luther C.F.(Chris)	Northern Transvaal	1970-71, 74	3	1	1	1	33%
512 Maartens C.(Chris)	Transvaal	1968	1	0	1	0	0%
513 Macdonald I.(Ian)	Transvaal	1991-93, 96	4	1	3	0	25%
514 Maku B.G.(Bandise)	Blue Bulls/GL	2009, 11, 16	3	2	1	0	67%
515 Malan A.W.(Adolf)	Northern Transvaal	1983, 85, 87-91	7	3	3	1	43%
516 Malan P.(Piet)	Transvaal	1947, 50	2	1	1	0	50%
517 Malherbe J.F.(Frans)	Western Province	2012-13	2	1	1	0	50%
518 Mallet N.V.H.(Nick)	Western Province	1982-84	3	3	0	0	100%
519 Mametsa S.J.(John)	Blue Bulls	2003, 08	2	1	1	0	50%
520 Mapoe L.G.(Lionel)	Free State/GL	2009, 14	2	0	2	0	0%
521 Marais C.(Charlie)	Western Province	1980, 89	2	0	1	1	0%
522 Marais C.F.(Charl)	Western Province	1998, 00-01	3	2	1	0	67%
523 Marais C.N.(Charles)	Free State	2016	1	1	0	0	100%
524 Marais D.D.(Dawie)	Northern Transvaal	1983	1	0	1	0	0%
525 Marais D.R.(Niel)	Free State	2016	1	1	0	0	100%
526 Marais F.P.(Buks)	Boland	1952	1	0	1	0	0%
527 Marais J.A.(Jandré)	Natal	2012	1	0	1	0	0%
528 Marais J.H.(Johan)	Northern Transvaal	1981-82, 85	3	1	2	0	33%
529 Marais L.(Toetie)	Orange Free State	1981	1	0	1	0	0%
530 Marais P.C.(Peet)	Natal	2013	1	1	0	0	100%
531 Marais S.P.	Natal	2013	1	1	0	0	100%
532 Marchant A.R.(Reg)	Northern Transvaal	1983	1	0	1	0	0%
533 Marinos A.W.N.(Andy)	Western Province	1998	1	0	1	0	0%
534 Maritz A.(Dries)	Transvaal	1986	1	0	1	0	0%
535 Markgraaff A.T.(André)	Western Province	1983	1	1	0	0	100%
536 Marshall F.(Frank)	Natal	1956	1	0	1	0	0%
537 Martens H.J.(Hentie)	Free State/Natal	1994-99	2	0	2	0	0%
538 Marx M.J.(Malcolm)	Golden Lions	2015	1	1	0	0	0%
539 Masina M.(Mac)	Golden Lions	1999	1	1	0	0	100%
540 Matfield V.(Victor)	Blue Bulls	2002, 04-05, 08-09	5	3	2	0	60%

CURRIE CUP FINAL PLAYERS 1939 - 2016

	PLAYER	Province	First & last final	Matches	Won	Lost	Drawn	Winning %
541	Mather D.(Doug)	Western Province	1976	1	0	1	0	0%
542	Mbonambi, MT (Bongi)	Western Province	2015	1	0	1	0	0%
543	McCallum R.J.(Roy)	Western Province	1979	1	0	0	1	0%
544	McKechnie R.(Richard)	Eastern Transvaal	1972	1	0	1	0	0%
545	McLean D.A.(Des)	Natal	1984	1	0	1	0	0%
546	McLeod C.(Charl)	Natal	2010, 12-13	3	2	1	0	67%
547	McLeod-Henderson B.M.(Brad)	Natal	2003	1	0	1	0	0%
548	Meiring F.A.	Northern Transvaal	1991	1	1	0	0	100%
549	Meiring J.(Koos)	Northern Transvaal	1968	1	1	0	0	100%
550	Mellish F.C.B.(Francis)	Western Province	1946-47	2	1	1	0	50%
551	Mellish H.T.	Western Province	1939	1	0	1	0	0%
552	Méndez, FE (Federico)	Natal	1996	1	1	0	0	100%
553	Menter M.A.(Alan)	Northern Transvaal	1968	1	1	0	0	100%
554	Mentz H.(Henno)	Natal	2003	1	0	1	0	0%
555	Meyer H.P.(Hendrik)	Free State	2006-07	2	1	0	1	50%
556	Meyer T.C.(Tian)	Free State	2016	1	1	0	0	100%
557	Meyer W.(Willie)	Free State/GL	1997, 99, 02	3	1	2	0	33%
558	Meyer W.(Wim)	Blue Bulls	1998	1	1	0	0	100%
559	Michalak F.(Frederic)	Natal	2008, 11	2	1	1	0	50%
560	Mills P.M.G.(Pat)	Northern Transvaal	1956	1	1	0	0	100%
561	Minnaar W.(Walter)	Golden Lions	1999	1	1	0	0	100%
562	Minnie D.J.(Derrick)	Golden Lions	2011, 14	2	1	1	0	50%
563	Mnisi X.H.(Howard)	Golden Lions	2014-15	2	1	1	0	50%
564	Möller J.D.	Western Province	2010	1	0	1	0	0%
565	Monkley D.(Duane)	Western Province	1998	1	0	1	0	0%
566	Montgomery P.C.(Percy)	Western Province	1997-98, 00-01	4	3	1	0	75%
567	Moolman L.C.(Louis)	Northern Transvaal	1975, 77-83, 85	9	5	3	1	56%
568	Moore N.(Nick)	Golden Lions	1999	1	1	0	0	100%
569	Mordt R.H.(Ray)	Northern Transvaal	1983, 85	2	0	2	0	0%
570	Morkel C.T.(Charlie)	Western Province	1954	1	1	0	0	100%
571	Morkel J.(Hannes)	Western Province	1939, 46-47, 50	4	1	3	0	25%
572	Mostert F.J.(Franco)	Golden Lions	2014-15	2	1	1	0	50%
573	Mostert M.(Marius)	Golden Lions	1999	1	1	0	0	100%
574	Moyle B.S.(Brent)	Natal	1999-00	2	0	2	0	0%
575	Mtawarira T.(Tendai)	Natal	2008, 10-13	5	3	2	0	60%
576	Muir D.J.(Dick)	Natal/WP	1990, 92-93, 96-97	5	4	1	0	80%
577	Mulder J.C.(Japie)	Transvaal	1991, 93-94, 96	4	2	2	0	50%
578	Mulder K.(Koos)	Eastern Transvaal	1972	1	0	1	0	0%
579	Müller G.H.(Gert)	Western Province/Tvl	1969, 72, 74	3	1	2	0	33%
580	Muller G.J.(George)	Transvaal	1950	1	1	0	0	100%
581	Muller G.J.(Johann)	Natal	2008	1	1	0	0	100%
582	Müller G.P.(Jorrie)	Golden Lions	2002	1	0	1	0	0%
583	Müller H.L.(Helgard)	Orange Free State	1994, 97	2	0	2	0	0%
584	Muller H.S.V.(Hennie)	Transvaal	1947, 50	2	1	1	0	50%
585	Müller L.F.(Louis)	Northern Transvaal	1969-70, 75	3	2	1	0	67%

CURRIE CUP FINAL PLAYERS 1939 - 2016

	PLAYER	Province	First & last final	Matches	Won	Lost	Drawn	Winning %
586	Müller L.J.J.(Lood)	Natal	1992-93	2	1	1	0	50%
587	Müller M.D.(Martin)	Golden Lions	2014	1	0	1	0	0%
588	Müller P.G.(Pieter)	Natal	1992-93	2	1	1	0	50%
589	Murray W.M.(Waylon)	Natal	2008	1	1	0	0	100%
590	Mvovo L.N.(Lwazi)	Natal	2010-13	4	2	2	0	50%
591	Myburgh J.L.(Mof)	Northern Transvaal	1968-71	4	2	1	1	50%
592	Myburgh K.(Kat)	Griquas	1970	1	1	0	0	100%
593	Naudé F.S.(Frikkie)	Free State/WP	1973, 79	2	0	1	1	0%
594	Naudé J.(Johan)	Boland	1952	1	0	1	0	0%
595	Naudé S.W.(Schalk)	Transvaal	1986-87	2	0	2	0	0%
596	Nche R (Ox)	Free State	2016	1	1	0	0	100%
597	Ndungane A.Z.(Akona)	Blue Bulls	2005-06	2	0	1	1	0%
598	Ndungane O.M.(Odwa)	Natal	2008, 10-13	5	3	2	0	60%
599	Neethling J.B.(Tiny)	Western Province	1969	1	0	1	0	0%
600	Nel C.(Christo)	Western Province	1976	1	0	1	0	0%
601	Nel G.P.(Giepie)	Northern Transvaal	1982, 85, 87, 89	4	1	2	1	25%
602	Nel H.J.(Hennie)	Northern Transvaal	1956	1	1	0	0	100%
603	Nel J.(Johan)	Northern Transvaal	1991	1	1	0	0	100%
604	Nel J.P.	Blue Bulls	2002-06	5	3	1	1	60%
605	Nel J.T.	Western Province	1939	1	0	1	0	0%
606	Nel P.J.L.(Pieter)	Northern Transvaal	1987-88	2	2	0	0	100%
607	Nel S.(Soon)	Griquas	1970	1	1	0	0	100%
608	Nel W.P.	Free State	2009	1	0	1	0	0%
609	Nell D.P.(Darron)	Free State	2006-07	2	1	0	1	50%
610	Nell H.(Hekkie)	Transvaal	1968	1	0	1	0	0%
611	Neuhoff C.M.(Mauritz)	Northern Transvaal	1968	1	1	0	0	100%
612	Newham C.(Charlie)	Transvaal	1947	1	0	1	0	0%
613	Nieuwoudt G.(Bill)	Western Province	1984, 86	2	2	0	0	100%
614	Noble C.D.(Christie)	Natal	1990	1	1	0	0	100%
615	Nomis S.H.(Syd)	Transvaal	1968	1	0	1	0	0%
616	Nortjé B.D.(Bennie)	Golden Lions	2002	1	0	1	0	0%
617	Norwood S.T.(Simon)	Transvaal	1971-72	2	1	0	1	50%
618	Notshe S.(Sikhumbuzo)	Western Province	2014-15	2	1	1	0	50%
619	Ntubeni S.(Siyabonga)	Western Province	2012-14	3	2	1	0	67%
620	Oberholzer A.F.(Anton)	Transvaal	1971-72, 74	3	1	1	1	33%
621	Oberholzer J.H.(Jan)	Northern Transvaal	1978-82	5	3	1	1	60%
622	Ochse J.K.(Chum)	Western Province	1950, 54	2	1	1	0	50%
623	Odendaal M.B.(Burger)	Blue Bulls	2016	1	0	1	0	0%
624	Oelofse J.S.A.(Hansie)	Transvaal	1952	1	1	0	0	100%
625	Oelschig N.H.(Noël)	Free State	2004-07	4	2	1	1	50%
626	Olivier E.(Eben)	Western Province	1969	1	0	1	0	0%
627	Olivier J.(Jacques)	Northern Transvaal	1991, 98	2	2	0	0	100%
628	Olivier W.(Wynand)	Blue Bulls	2005, 08-09	3	1	2	0	33%
629	Oosthuizen C.V.(Coenie)	Free State	2009	1	0	1	0	0%
630	Oosthuizen J.J.(Johan)	Western Province	1976	1	0	1	0	0%

CURRIE CUP FINAL PLAYERS 1939 - 2016

	PLAYER	Province	First & last final	Matches	Won	Lost	Drawn	Winning %
631	Oosthuizen J.P. de V.(Jan)	Northern Transvaal	1971	1	0	0	1	0%
632	Oosthuizen O.W.(Okkie)	Northern Transvaal	1980-81	2	2	0	0	100%
633	Oosthuizen P.(Pierre)	Western Province	1979	1	0	0	1	0%
634	Oosthuizen S.(Schalk)	Orange Free State	1981	1	0	1	0	0%
635	Oosthuysen D.E.(Deon)	Northern Transvaal	1988-91	4	2	1	1	50%
636	Opperman R.J.(Ryno)	Orange Free State	1994, 97	2	0	2	0	0%
637	Orie M.(Marvin)	Blue Bulls	2016	1	0	1	0	0%
638	Otto K.(Krynauw)	Blue Bulls	1998	1	1	0	0	100%
639	Oxlee K.(Keith)	Natal	1956	1	0	1	0	0%
640	Paige R.(Rudy)	Blue Bulls	2016	1	0	1	0	0%
641	Passens G.A.(Gavin)	Blue Bulls/Free State	2002-04, 06-07	5	4	0	1	80%
642	Patterson A.C.(Andréw)	Western Province	1989	1	0	1	0	0%
643	Paulse B.J.(Breyton)	Western Province	1998, 00-01	3	2	1	0	67%
644	Pawson A.L.(André)	Orange Free State	1994	1	0	1	0	0%
645	Payne S.(Shaun)	Natal	1999	1	0	1	0	0%
646	Peens P.W.S.(Pierre)	Northern Transvaal	1980	1	1	0	0	100%
647	Pelser E.(Eugene)	Northern Transvaal	1983	1	0	1	0	0%
648	Pelser P.A.(Piet)	Transvaal	1952	1	1	0	0	100%
649	Perry M.(Floris)	Northern Transvaal	1946	1	1	0	0	100%
650	Piater H.W.(Hein)	Northern Transvaal	1977	1	1	0	0	100%
651	Pickard J.A.J.(Jan)	Western Province	1954	1	1	0	0	100%
652	Pienaar J.A.(Japie)	Orange Free State	1973	1	0	1	0	0%
653	Pienaar J.F.(Francois)	Transvaal	1991-94, 96	5	2	3	0	40%
654	Pienaar R.(Ruan)	Natal	2008	1	1	0	0	100%
655	Pienaar Z.M.J.(Gysie)	Orange Free State	1976-78	3	1	2	0	33%
656	Pieterse B.H.(Barend)	Free State	2004-07	4	2	1	1	50%
657	Pieterse C.(Charles)	Transvaal	1987	1	0	1	0	0%
658	Pietersen J.(Joe)	Western Province	2012	1	1	0	0	100%
659	Pietersen J-P.R.(J.P.)	Natal	2008, 11-12	3	1	2	0	33%
660	Pietersen S.P.(Sergeal)	Free State	2016	1	1	0	0	100%
661	Pitout C.A.(Anton)	Free State	2004	1	0	1	0	0%
662	Pitzer G.(Gys)	Northern Transvaal	1968-70	3	2	1	0	67%
663	Platford S.(Shaun)	Natal	1992	1	1	0	0	100%
664	Plumtree J.(John)	Natal	1990, 96	2	2	0	0	100%
665	Pope C.F.(Chris)	Western Province	1976	1	0	1	0	0%
666	Potgieter D.J.(Dewald)	Blue Bulls	2008-09	2	1	1	0	50%
667	Potgieter H.L.(Hermanus)	Orange Free State	1975, 77-78	3	0	3	0	0%
668	Potgieter J-L.(Jacques-Louis)	Free State	2009	1	0	1	0	0%
669	Potgieter R.(Ronnie)	Northern Transvaal	1968-71	4	2	1	1	50%
670	Potgieter W.C.(Wilhelm)	Orange Free State	1975	1	0	1	0	0%
671	Povey S.A.(Shaun)	Western Province	1979, 82-86	6	5	0	1	83%
672	Powell J.D.(Neil)	Blue Bulls	2006	1	0	0	1	0%
673	Pretorius A.S.(André)	Golden Lions/Natal	2002, 10	2	1	1	0	50%
674	Pretorius J.C.(Jaco)	Golden Lions/Blue Bulls	2002, 07, 09	3	1	2	0	33%
675	Pretorius J.J.D.(Jannie)	Transvaal	1987	1	0	1	0	0%

CURRIE CUP FINAL PLAYERS 1939 - 2016

	PLAYER	Province	First & last final	Matches	Won	Lost	Drawn	Winning %
676	Pretorius P.I.L.(Piet)	Northern Transvaal	1991	1	1	0	0	100%
677	Pretorius W.J.J.(Fatty)	Transvaal	1939	1	1	0	0	100%
678	Putt K.B.(Kevin)	Natal	1993, 95-96	3	2	1	0	67%
679	Pypers C.G.(Corrie)	Transvaal	1974	1	0	1	0	0%
680	Rademeyer H.N.(Hempas)	Transvaal	1986-87	2	0	2	0	0%
681	Rahn J.A.(Jackie)	Transvaal	1952	1	1	0	0	100%
682	Ralepelle M.C.(Chiliboy)	Blue Bulls	2008	1	0	1	0	0%
683	Ras A.(Abel)	Northern Transvaal	1954	1	0	1	0	0%
684	Ras W.J. de W.(De Wet)	Orange Free State	1975-78, 81	5	1	4	0	20%
685	Rautenbach N.(Neil)	Western Province	2014	1	1	0	0	100%
686	Rautenbach S.J.(Faan)	Western Province	2000	1	1	0	0	100%
687	Redelinghuys J.(Julian)	Golden Lions	2014-15	2	1	1	0	50%
688	Reece-Edwards H.M.(Hugh)	Natal	1984, 90, 92	3	2	1	0	67%
689	Reinach J.M.(Cobus)	Natal	2012-13	2	1	1	0	50%
690	Rens I.J.(Natie)	Transvaal	1952	1	1	0	0	100%
691	Retief D.F.(Daan)	Northern Transvaal	1946, 54	2	1	1	0	50%
692	Reynecke E.(Ethienne)	Golden Lions	2007	1	0	1	0	0%
693	Rheeder G.(Gert)	Western Province	1954	1	1	0	0	100%
694	Rhodes M.K.(Michael)	Golden Lions/WP	2011, 13-14	3	2	1	0	67%
695	Rhule R.K.(Raymond)	Free State	2016	1	1	0	0	100%
696	Ribbens P.J.(Pierre)	Blue Bulls	1998	1	1	0	0	100%
697	Richards M.(Mark)	Golden Lions	2014	1	0	1	0	0%
698	Richter A.H.(Adriaan)	Northern Transvaal	1991	1	1	0	0	100%
699	Robbie J.C.(John)	Transvaal	1986-87	2	0	2	0	0%
700	Roberts H.(Harry)	Transvaal	1991-92	2	0	2	0	0%
701	Robertson P.(Preston)	Western Province	1969	1	0	1	0	0%
702	Robinson J.(Johnny)	Transvaal	1950	1	1	0	0	100%
703	Rodgers P.H.(Heinrich)	N Transvaal/Tvl	1985, 87-90, 92-93	7	3	3	1	43%
704	Rodriguez L.(Len)	Western Province	1954	1	1	0	0	100%
705	Roets J.(Johan)	Blue Bulls	2003-06	4	2	1	1	50%
706	Rogers C.D.(Chris)	Transvaal	1986-87	2	0	2	0	0%
707	Roos G.J.	Transvaal	1939	1	1	0	0	100%
708	Rose E.E.(Earl)	Golden Lions	2007	1	0	1	0	0%
709	Rossouw C. le C.(Chris)	Transvaal/Natal	1996, 00	2	0	2	0	0%
710	Rossouw C.(Charles)	Transvaal	1994	1	1	0	0	100%
711	Rossouw C.(Chris)	Western Province	2000-01	2	2	0	0	100%
712	Rossouw D.J.(Danie)	Blue Bulls	2004-06, 08-09	5	2	2	1	40%
713	Rossouw P.W.G.(Pieter)	Western Province	1995, 97-98, 00-01	5	3	2	0	60%
714	Roumat O.(Olivier)	Natal	1995	1	1	0	0	100%
715	Roux C.(Chean)	Western Province	1998	1	0	1	0	0%
716	Roux F. du T.(Mannetjies)	Griquas	1970	1	1	0	0	100%
717	Roux F.(Francois)	Northern Transvaal	1954	1	0	1	0	0%
718	Roux J.P.(Johan)	N Transvaal/Tvl	1991, 93-94, 96	4	3	1	0	75%
719	Roux O.A.(Tonie)	Northern Transvaal	1970-71	2	0	1	1	0%
720	Roux W.G.(Wessel)	Blue Bulls	2002-05	4	3	1	0	75%

CURRIE CUP FINAL PLAYERS 1939 - 2016

	PLAYER	Province	First & last final	Matches	Won	Lost	Drawn	Winning %
721	**Russell R.B.**(Brent)	Natal	2003	1	0	1	0	0%
722	**Sauerman A.**(Archie)	Boland	1952	1	0	1	0	0%
723	**Sauermann J.T.**(Theo)	Transvaal	1971-72, 74	3	1	1	1	33%
724	**Scheepers G.**(Gert)	Griquas	1970	1	1	0	0	100%
725	**Schlebusch J.J.J.**(Jan)	Orange Free State	1973, 75, 77, 78	4	0	4	0	0%
726	**Schmidt B.O.**(Barry)	Transvaal	1950, 52	2	2	0	0	100%
727	**Schmidt U.L.**(Uli)	N Transvaal/Tvl	1985, 87-91, 93-94	8	5	2	1	63%
728	**Schoeman B.J.**(Barry)	Orange Free State	1981	1	0	1	0	0%
729	**Schoeman C.F.**(Tian)	Blue Bulls	2016	1	0	1	0	0%
730	**Schoeman P.**(Pierre)	Blue Bulls	2016	1	0	1	0	0%
731	**Schoeman P.A.**(Paul)	Free State	2016	1	1	0	0	100%
732	**Scholtz A.W.**(Dries)	Blue Bulls	2002, 06	2	1	0	1	50%
733	**Scholtz C.P.**(Christiaan)	Transvaal	1994	1	1	0	0	100%
734	**Scholtz H.**(Hendro)	Free State	2004-05, 07	3	2	1	0	67%
735	**Scholtz N.B.**(Calla)	Western Province	1983-86, 88	5	4	1	0	80%
736	**Schreuder L.**(Louis)	Western Province	2012-13	2	1	1	0	50%
737	**Schutte G.A.**(Gert)	Transvaal	1971	1	0	0	1	0%
738	**Schutte P.J.W.**(Phillip)	N Transvaal/Tvl	1990-91, 94	3	2	1	0	67%
739	**Scriba H.M.**(Hans)	Western Province	1985, 89	2	1	0	1	50%
740	**Scrooby C.W.**(Chris)	Transvaal	1939	1	1	0	0	100%
741	**Senatla S.M.**(Seabelo)	Western Province	2014-15	2	1	1	0	50%
742	**Sephaka L.D.**(Lawrence)	Golden Lions	2002, 07	2	0	2	0	0%
743	**Serfontein D.J.**(Divan)	Western Province	1976, 79-80, 82-84	6	3	2	1	50%
744	**Sherrell R.**(Reg)	Natal	1956	1	0	1	0	0%
745	**Simpson B.**(Barry)	Natal	1956	1	0	1	0	0%
746	**Sinclair D.J.**(Des)	Transvaal	1950	1	1	0	0	100%
747	**Sinclair J.**(Jebb)	Western Province	2012	1	1	0	0	100%
748	**Skeate R.C.**(Ross)	Natal	2011	1	0	1	0	0%
749	**Skene A.L.**(Alan)	Western Province	1954	1	1	0	0	100%
750	**Skinner A.**(André)	N Transvaal/Tvl	1981-82, 87, 88, 90	5	2	3	0	40%
751	**Skinstad R.B.**(Bob)	Western Province	1997-98, 01	3	2	1	0	67%
752	**Skosan C.D.**(Courtnall)	Golden Lions	2014-15	2	1	1	0	50%
753	**Slade J.**(John)	Natal	1999	1	0	1	0	0%
754	**Smal G.P.**(Gert)	Western Province	1985-86, 88-89	4	2	1	1	50%
755	**Small J.T.**(James)	Tvl/Natal/WP	1991-93, 95-97	6	3	3	0	50%
756	**Smit B.C.**(Chris)	Western Province	1986	1	1	0	0	100%
757	**Smit F.C.**	Western Province	1995	1	0	1	0	0%
758	**Smit G.A.**(Gert)	Northern Transvaal	1956	1	1	0	0	100%
759	**Smit J.W.**(John)	Natal	1999-01, 08	4	1	3	0	25%
760	**Smit P.L.**(Phillip)	Natal	2001, 03	2	0	2	0	0%
761	**Smit R.A.**(Roelof)	Blue Bulls	2016	1	0	1	0	0%
762	**Smit W.J.**	Transvaal	1939	1	1	0	0	100%
763	**Smith A.S.**(Kwagga)	Golden Lions	2014-15	2	1	1	0	50%
764	**Smith J.**	Eastern Transvaal	1972	1	0	1	0	0%
765	**Smith J.H.**(Juan)	Free State	2004-05	2	1	1	0	50%

CURRIE CUP FINAL PLAYERS 1939 - 2016

	PLAYER	Province	First & last final	Matches	Won	Lost	Drawn	Winning %
766	Smith K.(Kat)	Western Province	1969	1	0	1	0	0%
767	Smith M.J.	Free State	1997	1	0	1	0	0%
768	Smith P.(Peet)	Griquas	1970	1	1	0	0	100%
769	Smith P.F.(Franco)	Free State/Blue Bulls	1994, 98	2	1	1	0	50%
770	Smith R.F.(Rodger)	Natal	2000-01	2	0	2	0	0%
771	Smith T.(Tos)	Griquas	1970	1	1	0	0	100%
772	Snyman A.H.(André)	Blue Bulls/Natal	1998, 01, 03	3	1	2	0	33%
773	Snyman D.S.L.(Dawie)	Western Province	1976	1	0	1	0	0%
774	Snyman J.C.P.(Jackie)	Orange Free State	1973	1	0	1	0	0%
775	Sonnekus G.H.H.(Gerrie)	Orange Free State	1975-78, 81	5	1	4	0	20%
776	Sonnekus P.J.(Pieter)	Northern Transvaal	1983	1	0	1	0	0%
777	Sowerby R.S.(Shaun)	Natal	2000-01, 03	3	0	3	0	0%
778	Spangenberg J.C.(Christo)	Northern Transvaal	1987-89	3	2	0	1	67%
779	Spies J.J.(Johan)	Northern Transvaal	1968-71	4	2	1	1	50%
780	Spies P.J.(Pierre) jnr.	Blue Bulls	2006, 08-09	3	1	1	1	33%
781	Spies P.J.(Pierre) snr.	Northern Transvaal	1975, 77	2	2	0	0	100%
782	Stander B.(Ben)	Eastern Transvaal	1972	1	0	1	0	0%
783	Stander J.C.J.(Rampie)	Orange Free State	1973, 76, 78	3	1	2	0	33%
784	Stander J.T.(Joshua)	Blue Bulls	2016	1	0	1	0	0%
785	Stapelberg W.P.(Willem)	Northern Transvaal	1968, 73-74	3	3	0	0	100%
786	Steenkamp G.G.(Gurthrö)	Free State/Blue Bulls	2004, 08-09	3	1	2	0	33%
787	Steenkamp M.D.(De Kock)	Western Province	2010, 12-13	3	1	2	0	33%
788	Stegmann G.J.(Deon)	Blue Bulls	2008-09	2	1	1	0	50%
789	Steinhobel J.(Tiny)	Transvaal	1947	1	0	1	0	0%
790	Stewart J.C.(Christian)	Western Province	1988, 95, 98	3	0	3	0	0%
791	Steyn F.P.L.(Francois)	Natal	2008, 13	2	2	0	0	100%
792	Steyn M.(Morné)	Blue Bulls	2005-06, 08-09	4	1	2	1	25%
793	Stofberg M.T.S.(Theuns)	Free State/N Tvl/WP	1976-80, 82-83	7	4	2	1	57%
794	Stoltz W.(Willem)	Golden Lions	2002	1	0	1	0	0%
795	Stolz T.(Thys)	Western Province	2000-01	2	2	0	0	100%
796	Straeuli R.A.W.(Rudolf)	N Transvaal/Tvl	1990, 93, 96	3	1	2	0	33%
797	Stransky J.T.(Joel)	Natal	1990, 93, 95	3	1	2	0	33%
798	Strauss A.J.(Andries)	Natal	2010	1	1	0	0	100%
799	Strauss C.P.(Tiaan)	Western Province	1986, 88-89, 95	4	1	2	1	25%
800	Strauss C.R.(Richardt)	Free State	2006-07, 09	3	1	1	1	33%
801	Strauss J.A.(Adriaan)	Blue Bulls/Free State	2006, 09	2	0	1	1	0%
802	Strauss J.A.(Attie)	Western Province	1984	1	1	0	0	100%
803	Strauss J.C.	Northern Transvaal	1981, 83	2	1	1	0	50%
804	Strauss J.H.P.(Johan)	Transvaal	1974	1	0	1	0	0%
805	Strauss J.Z.(Joshua)	Transvaal	2011	1	1	0	0	100%
806	Strydom A.(Andries)	Eastern Transvaal	1972	1	0	1	0	0%
807	Strydom A.(Basie)	Transvaal	1968	1	0	1	0	0%
808	Strydom G.J.(Gert)	Transvaal	1972, 74	2	1	1	0	50%
809	Strydom J.J.(Hannes)	Transvaal	1993, 96, 99	3	2	1	0	67%
810	Strydom L.I.(Louis)	Blue Bulls/GL	2003, 07	2	1	1	0	50%

THE CURRIE CUP

CURRIE CUP FINAL PLAYERS 1939 - 2016

	PLAYER	Province	First & last final	Matches	Won	Lost	Drawn	Winning %
811	Strydom L.J.(Louis)	Northern Transvaal	1946	1	1	0	0	100%
812	Strydom P.A.(Piet)	Orange Free State	1975	1	0	1	0	0%
813	Strydom W.T.(Willie)	Orange Free State	1973	1	0	1	0	0%
814	Swanepoel A.E.(Dries)	Blue Bulls	2016	1	0	1	0	0%
815	Swanepoel R.(Riaan)	Natal	2010	1	1	0	0	100%
816	Swanepoel W.(Werner)	Free State	1997	1	0	1	0	0%
817	Swart F.J.(Francois)	Blue Bulls	2003	1	1	0	0	100%
818	Swart I.S. de V.(Balie)	Western Province/Tvl	1989, 92-94	4	2	1	1	50%
819	Swart J.C.(Jakes)	Orange Free State	1973	1	0	1	0	0%
820	Swart J.S.(Justin)	Western Province/Natal	1995, 97, 99, 01, 03	5	1	4	0	20%
821	Swartz B.(Buddy)	Griquas	1970	1	1	0	0	100%
822	Swartz E.(Enrico)	Natal	2003	1	0	1	0	0%
823	Sykes S.R.(Steven)	Natal	2008, 10, 12	3	2	1	0	67%
824	Symington A.(George)	Northern Transvaal	1946	1	1	0	0	100%
825	Symons T.A.W.(Tommy)	Transvaal	1971-72, 74	3	1	1	1	33%
826	Taute J.J.(Jaco)	Golden Lions/WP	2011, 14	2	2	0	0	100%
827	Taylor P.(Peter)	Natal	1956	1	0	1	0	0%
828	Taylor T.(Tich)	Natal	1956	1	0	1	0	0%
829	Tecklenburg W.J.(Warwick)	Golden Lions	2014	1	0	1	0	0%
830	Teichmann G.H.(Gary)	Natal	1992-93, 95-96, 99	5	3	2	0	60%
831	Terblanche C.S.(Stefan)	Natal	2000-01, 08, 10-11	5	2	3	0	40%
832	Thiart D.(Danie)	Blue Bulls	2006	1	0	0	1	0%
833	Thomson J.R.D.(Jeremy)	Natal/Tvl	1990, 92, 95-96	4	3	1	0	75%
834	Thoresson K.R.(Keith)	Northern Transvaal	1975	1	1	0	0	100%
835	Thorne B.(Bruce)	Golden Lions	1999	1	1	0	0	100%
836	Thorne G.S.(Grahame)	Northern Transvaal	1971	1	0	0	1	0%
837	Tiedt J.A.(Jannie)	Transvaal	1986	1	0	1	0	0%
838	Townsend A.(Ashton)	Transvaal/Natal	1952, 56	2	1	1	0	50%
839	Tromp J.A.(Kleinjan)	Golden Lions	2002	1	0	1	0	0%
840	Truscott J.A.(Andries)	Blue Bulls	1998	1	1	0	0	100%
841	Truter H.J.(Hendrik)	Transvaal/Free State	1991, 94	2	0	2	0	0%
842	Trytsman J.W.(Johnny)	Western Province	1998	1	0	1	0	0%
843	Turner F.G.(Freddie)	Western Province	1939	1	0	1	0	0%
844	Tyibilika S.(Solly)	Natal	2003	1	0	1	0	0%
845	Ulengo J.I.(Jamba)	Blue Bulls	2016	1	0	1	0	0%
846	Uys C.J.(Corné)	Free State	2009	1	0	1	0	0%
847	Uys P. de W.(Piet)	Northern Transvaal	1968-70	3	2	1	0	67%
848	Van As H.P.(Hugo)	Transvaal	1986-87	2	0	2	0	0%
849	Van Aswegen H.J.(Henning)	Free State/WP	1977, 79-80, 82-83, 85	6	3	2	1	50%
850	Van Aswegen J.(Jannie)	Griquas	1970-71	2	1	0	1	50%
851	Van Biljon L.(Lukas)	Natal	2001, 03	2	0	2	0	0%
852	Van Blerk J.A.R.	Western Province	1947	1	1	0	0	100%
853	Van Blommenstein J.(Johan)	Northern Transvaal	1969-70	2	1	1	0	50%
854	Van den Berg D.S.(Derek)	Western Province	1969, 76	2	0	2	0	0%
855	Van den Berg P.A.(Albert)	Natal	2000-01, 08	3	1	2	0	33%

CURRIE CUP FINAL PLAYERS 1939 - 2016

	PLAYER	Province	First & last final	Matches	Won	Lost	Drawn	Winning %
856	Van den Heever D.J.(Daantjie)	Northern Transvaal	1956	1	1	0	0	100%
857	Van den Heever G.J.(Gerhard)	Blue Bulls/WP	2009, 12-13	3	2	1	0	67%
858	Van der Berg C.R.(Riaan)	Blue Bulls	2005	1	0	1	0	0%
859	Van der Linde A.(Toks)	Western Province	1995, 97-98, 00-01	5	3	2	0	60%
860	Van der Linde C.J.	Free State/GL	2004-05, 11	3	2	1	0	67%
861	Van der Merwe A.H.P.(Akker)	Golden Lions	2014	1	0	1	0	0%
862	Van der Merwe A.J.(Bertus)	Boland	1952	1	0	1	0	0%
863	Van der Merwe B.S.(Fiks)	Northern Transvaal	1946	1	1	0	0	100%
864	Van der Merwe C.E.(Erik)	Golden Lions	1999	1	1	0	0	100%
865	Van der Merwe F.(Franco)	Golden Lions	2007, 11	2	1	1	0	50%
866	Van der Merwe G.(Tjokkie)	Northern Transvaal	1978-80	3	2	0	1	67%
867	Van der Merwe H.S.(Heinke)	Golden Lions	2007	1	0	1	0	0%
868	Van der Merwe P.(Piet)	Western Province	1954	1	1	0	0	100%
869	Van der Merwe R.C.(Ryno)	Free State	2005-06	2	1	0	1	50%
870	Van der Merwe S.(Schalk)	Golden Lions	2014	1	0	1	0	0%
871	Van der Ryst F.E.(Franz)	Transvaal	1950, 52	2	2	0	0	100%
872	Van der Schyff P.J.(Johan)	Transvaal	1968	1	0	1	0	0%
873	Van der Spuy S.J.(Fanie)	Transvaal	1939	1	1	0	0	100%
874	Van der Walt J.(Jaco)	Golden Lions	2014	1	0	1	0	0%
875	Van der Walt J.A.(Jannie)	Transvaal	1996, 99	2	1	1	0	50%
876	Van der Walt J.J.	Northern Transvaal	1988-89	2	1	0	1	50%
877	Van der Walt J.N.(Nicky)	Blue Bulls	1998	1	1	0	0	100%
878	Van der Walt K.(Kobus)	Blue Bulls	2003	1	1	0	0	100%
879	Van der Walt L.(Louis)	Northern Transvaal	1974	1	1	0	0	100%
880	Van der Watt A.E.(Andy)	Western Province	1969	1	0	1	0	0%
881	Van der Westhuizen J.F.(Cabous)	Natal	1992-93, 95	3	2	1	0	67%
882	Van der Westhuizen J.H.(Joost)	Blue Bulls	1998, 02	2	2	0	0	100%
883	Van der Westhuyzen J.N.B.(Jaco)	Blue Bulls	2002	1	1	0	0	100%
884	Van Deventer J.(Jannie)	Transvaal	1968, 71-72	3	1	1	1	33%
885	Van Deventer J.D.(Doerie)	Northern Transvaal	1946	1	1	0	0	100%
886	Van Deventer P.I.(Piet)	Griquas	1970	1	1	0	0	100%
887	Van Dyk S.(Stompie)	Western Province	1946	1	0	1	0	0%
888	Van Dyk S.W.A.(Schalk)	Northern Transvaal	1956	1	1	0	0	100%
889	Van Greuning K.(Kapstok)	Transvaal	1996	1	0	1	0	0%
890	Van Heerden F.J.(Fritz)	Western Province	1995-97	2	1	1	0	50%
891	Van Heerden H.J.N.(Herman)	Orange Free State	1978, 81	2	0	2	0	0%
892	Van Heerden J.J.(Goggie)	Western Province	1984, 86	2	2	0	0	100%
893	Van Heerden J.L.(Moaner)	Northern Transvaal	1973-74, 77, 80, 82	5	4	1	0	80%
894	Van Heerden J.L.(Wikus)	Golden Lions/Blue Bulls	2002, 08, 11	3	1	2	0	33%
895	Van Heerden N.(Nols)	Western Province	1947	1	1	0	0	100%
896	Van Heerden P.J.L.(Wickus)	Natal	1995-96	2	2	0	0	100%
897	Van Jaarsveld C.J.(Hoppy)	Transvaal	1947, 52	2	1	1	0	50%
898	Van Jaarsveld T.G.(Torsten)	Free State	2016	1	1	0	0	100%
899	Van Niekerk J.C.(Joe)	Golden Lions	2002	1	0	1	0	0%
900	Van Niekerk O.(Otto)	Transvaal/WP	1939, 46-47	3	2	1	0	67%

CURRIE CUP FINAL PLAYERS 1939 - 2016

	PLAYER	Province	First & last final	Matches	Won	Lost	Drawn	Winning %
901	Van Niekerk P.(Pietman)	Golden Lions	2002	1	0	1	0	0%
902	Van Niekerk W.(Willouw)	Western Province	1982	1	1	0	0	100%
903	Van Reenen A.	Boland	1952	1	0	1	0	0%
904	Van Reenen J.N.R.(Ross)	Orange Free State	1975-78	4	1	3	0	25%
905	Van Renen G.L.(George)	Western Province	1946-47	2	1	1	0	50%
906	Van Rensburg A.G.(Deon)	Transvaal	2011	1	1	0	0	100%
907	Van Rensburg C.(Clinton)	Natal	1999	1	0	1	0	0%
908	Van Rensburg C.Q.(Charl)	Natal	1999-01, 03	4	0	4	0	0%
909	Van Rensburg D.(Deon)	Eastern Transvaal	1972	1	0	1	0	0%
910	Van Rensburg J.C.J.(J.C.)	Golden Lions	2007, 11	2	1	1	0	50%
911	Van Rensburg J.T.J.(Theo)	N Transvaal/Tvl	1990, 92	2	0	2	0	0%
912	Van Rensburg P.J.(Vuile)	Northern Transvaal	1946	1	1	0	0	100%
913	Van Rooyen J.(Jacques)	Golden Lions	2015	1	1	0	0	100%
914	Van Schalkwyk D.(Danie)	Blue Bulls	1998	1	1	0	0	100%
915	Van Schalkwyk H.J.(Jaco)	Free State	2004	1	0	1	0	0%
916	Van Schouwenburg F.J.(Francois)	Blue Bulls	2006	1	0	0	1	0%
917	Van Staden E.(Eugene)	Natal	2010-11	2	1	1	0	50%
918	Van Staden F.(Fred)	Northern Transvaal	1971	1	0	0	1	0%
919	Van Staden H.J.(Fancy)	Transvaal	1950	1	1	0	0	100%
920	Van Staden J.A.(André)	Northern Transvaal	1969-71, 73-74	5	3	1	1	60%
921	Van Straaten A.J.J.(Braam)	Western Province	2000-01	2	2	0	0	100%
922	Van Vollenhoven K.T.(Tom)	Northern Transvaal	1954	1	0	1	0	0%
923	Van Vuuren B.J.J.(Koos)	Northern Transvaal	1956	1	1	0	0	100%
924	Van Vuuren J.C.(Conraad)	Free State	2016	1	1	0	0	100%
925	Van Vuuren J.G.(Jurie)	Western Province	2015	1	0	1	0	0%
926	Van Wyk C.J.(Basie)	Transvaal	1950, 52	2	2	0	0	100%
927	Van Wyk J.(Johan)	Western Province	1997-98	2	1	1	0	50%
928	Van Wyk J.P.(Kobus)	Western Province	2014	1	1	0	0	100%
929	Van Wyk J-H.(Jan-Harm)	Free State	1997	1	0	1	0	0%
930	Van Wyngaardt J.J.M.(Johan)	Transvaal	1971, 74	2	0	1	1	0%
931	Van Zyl A.(Anton)	Golden Lions/WP	2007, 10	2	0	2	0	0%
932	Van Zyl C.C.(Corniel)	Free State	2005, 07	2	2	0	0	100%
933	Van Zyl C.M.(Chris)	Western Province	2015	1	0	1	0	0%
934	Van Zyl D.J.(Dan)	Western Province	1998, 00	2	1	1	0	50%
935	Van Zyl J.F.F.(Freddie)	Golden Lions	2007	1	0	1	0	0%
936	Van Zyl M.C.(Thys)	Northern Transvaal	1956	1	1	0	0	100%
937	Van Zyl P.(Pierre)	Northern Transvaal	1973, 79	2	1	0	1	50%
938	Van Zyl P.A.(Piet)	Orange Free State	1973	1	0	1	0	0%
939	Van Zyl P.J.J.(Piet)	Blue Bulls	2016	1	0	1	0	0%
940	Venter A.G.(André)	Orange Free State	1994, 97	2	0	2	0	0%
941	Venter A.J.	Free State/GL/Natal	1997, 99-01, 03	5	1	4	0	20%
942	Venter B.(Brendan)	Orange Free State	1994, 97	2	0	2	0	0%
943	Venter H.P.(Henco)	Free State	2016	1	1	0	0	100%
944	Venter J.(Hannes)	Blue Bulls	1998	1	1	0	0	100%
945	Venter J.A.(Barabas)	Transvaal	1986-87, 91	3	0	3	0	0%

CURRIE CUP FINAL PLAYERS 1939 - 2016

	PLAYER	Province	First & last final	Matches	Won	Lost	Drawn	Winning %
946	Venter J.F.(Francois)	Free State	2016	1	1	0	0	100%
947	Venter S.H.(Shaun)	Free State	2016	1	1	0	0	100%
948	Venter W.(Walter)	Golden Lions	2007	1	0	1	0	0%
949	Venter W.(Wickus)	Golden Lions	1999	1	1	0	0	100%
950	Vermaak A.(Alistair)	Western Province	2014	1	1	0	0	100%
951	Vermaak B.S.(Bian)	Free State	2006	1	0	0	1	0%
952	Vermaak J.(Jano)	Golden Lions/WP	2007, 15	2	0	2	0	0%
953	Vermeulen D.J.(Duane)	Free State/WP	2007, 10, 12-13	4	2	2	0	50%
954	Vermeulen R.(Ruan)	Blue Bulls	2002-03	2	2	0	0	100%
955	Verster J.J.P.(Basie)	Orange Free State	1975	1	0	1	0	0%
956	Victor D.P.(Dennis)	Northern Transvaal	1956	1	1	0	0	100%
957	Vijoen E.J.(Ernest)	Orange Free State	1981	1	0	1	0	0%
958	Viljoen F.J.N.(Frans)	Free State	2009	1	0	1	0	0%
959	Viljoen J.F.(Joggie)	Griquas	1970	1	1	0	0	100%
960	Viljoen L.(Lucas)	Northern Transvaal	1973	1	1	0	0	100%
961	Viljoen R.(Joggie)	Western Province	1997	1	1	0	0	100%
962	Villet J.V.(John)	Western Province	1982-83	2	2	0	0	100%
963	Vintcent A.N.(Nellis)	Western Province	1947	1	1	0	0	100%
964	Visagie G.J.(Jaco)	Blue Bulls	2016	1	0	1	0	0%
965	Visagie G.P.(Gawie)	Natal	1984	1	0	1	0	0%
966	Visagie I.J.(Cobus)	Western Province	1998, 01	2	1	1	0	50%
967	Visagie J.C.	Transvaal	1952	1	1	0	0	100%
968	Visagie P.J.(Piet)	Griquas	1970	1	1	0	0	100%
969	Visagie R.G.(Vleis)	Free State/Natal	1981, 90	2	1	1	0	50%
970	Visser B.(Broekies)	Western Province	1954	1	1	0	0	100%
971	Visser J. de V.(De Villiers)	Western Province	1979-80, 82, 88-89	5	1	2	2	20%
972	Visser J.(Jan)	Western Province	1950	1	0	1	0	0%
973	Visser J.G.	Western Province	1950	1	0	1	0	0%
974	Visser M.(Mornay)	Western Province/Natal	1995, 99	2	0	2	0	0%
975	Volmink A.A.(Anthony)	Golden Lions	2015	1	1	0	0	100%
976	Von Hoeslin D.J.B.(Dave)	Natal	2001, 03	2	0	2	0	0%
977	Von Wezel S.A.(Syd)	Transvaal	1947	1	0	1	0	0%
978	Vorster D.(Denys)	Griquas	1970	1	1	0	0	100%
979	Vorster H.W.(Harold)	Golden Lions	2014	1	0	1	0	0%
980	Vos A.N.(André)	Golden Lions	2002	1	0	1	0	0%
981	Vos J.J.(Jack)	Western Province	1946-47	2	1	1	0	50%
982	Wagenaar C.(Christo)	Northern Transvaal	1975, 77-79, 81	5	4	0	1	80%
983	Wagner I.J.(Sias)	Blue Bulls	2002-03	2	2	0	0	100%
984	Wahl J.J.(Ballie)	Western Province	1946-47, 50	3	1	2	0	33%
985	Waldeck J.(John)	Griquas	1970	1	1	0	0	100%
986	Wannenburg P.J.(Pedrie)	Blue Bulls	2002-06, 09	6	4	1	1	67%
987	Wasserman J.G.(Johan)	Blue Bulls	2002-03, 05	3	2	1	0	67%
988	Watson A.C.(Tony)	Natal	1990, 92	2	2	0	0	100%
989	Watson K.(Ken)	Western Province	1950	1	0	1	0	0%
990	Watson L.A.(Luke)	Natal	2003	1	0	1	0	0%

CURRIE CUP FINAL PLAYERS 1939 - 2016

	PLAYER	Province	First & last final	Matches	Won	Lost	Drawn	Winning %
991	**Weber J.J.**(Hans)	Northern Transvaal	1974	1	1	0	0	100%
992	**Wegner C.A.**(Callie)	Orange Free State	1981	1	0	1	0	0%
993	**Wegner G.N.**(Nico)	Natal	1999	1	0	1	0	0%
994	**Welsh B.F.**(Frikkie)	Blue Bulls	2003-04	2	2	0	0	100%
995	**Wepener F.W.**(Willie)	Golden Lions	2007	1	0	1	0	0%
996	**Wessels F.H.**(Frans)	Northern Transvaal	1985	1	0	1	0	0%
997	**Wessels H.J.**(Japie)	Orange Free State	1978	1	0	1	0	0%
998	**Whipp P.J.M.**(Peter)	Western Province	1976, 79	2	0	1	1	0%
999	**Whitehead T.**(Tim)	Natal	2012	1	0	1	0	0%
1000	**Whiteley W.R.**(Warren)	Golden Lions	2011, 14-15	3	2	1	0	67%
1001	**Wiese J.J.**(Kobus)	Transvaal	1991-94, 96	5	2	3	0	40%
1002	**Wilkens V.**(Vic)	Northern Transvaal	1954	1	0	1	0	0%
1003	**Wilkenson B.**(Boesman)	Eastern Transvaal	1972	1	0	1	0	0%
1004	**Willemse M.E.**(Michael)	Western Province	2015	1	0	1	0	0%
1005	**Williams C.M.**(Chester)	Western Province/GL	1995, 98, 99	3	1	2	0	33%
1006	**Williams H.**(Heimar)	Natal	2013	1	1	0	0	100%
1007	**Williams J.G.**(John)	Northern Transvaal	1973-75	3	3	0	0	100%
1008	**Williamson A.**(Andréw)	Northern Transvaal	1987	1	1	0	0	100%
1009	**Winter R.G.**(Russell)	Golden Lions	1999, 02	2	1	1	0	50%
1010	**Wolmarans B.J.**(Barry)	Orange Free State	1975-78	4	1	3	0	25%
1011	**Wright G.D.**(Garth)	Transvaal	1992	1	0	1	0	0%
1012	**Zeeman W.**(Willie)	Western Province	1976	1	0	1	0	0%
1013	**Zeilinga F.J.**(Fred)	Free State	2016	1	1	0	0	100%
1014	**Zietsman D.W.**(Dave)	Western Province	1976	1	0	1	0	0%

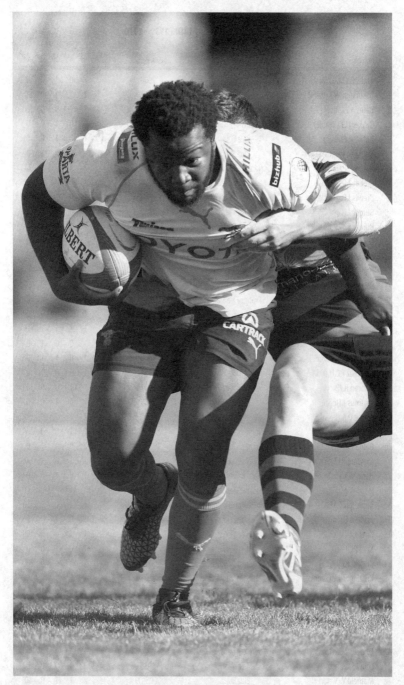

Ox Nche starred for the Free State Cheetahs in 2016.

CURRIE CUP FINAL CAPTAINS 1939 - 2016

	PLAYER	Province	First & last final	Matches	Won	Lost	Drawn	Winning %
1	Andréws M.G.(Mark)	Natal	2000	1	0	1	0	0
2	Bartmann W.J.(Wahl)	Natal	1992-93	2	1	1	0	50
3	Bates A.J.(Albie)	Northern Transvaal	1973	1	1	0	0	100
4	Bekker H.J.(Hennie)	Western Province	1980	1	0	1	0	0
5	Botha A.F.(Arno)	Blue Bulls	2016	1	0	1	0	0
6	Botha G. v G.(Gary)	Blue Bulls	2006	1	0	0	1	0
7	Botha H.E.(Naas)	Northern Transvaal	1980-91	7	5	2	0	71
8	Breedt J.C.(Jannie)	Transvaal	1986-92	4	0	4	0	0
9	Brewis J.D.(Hansie)	Northern Transvaal	1954	1	0	1	0	0
10	Burger J.(Jan)	Boland	1952	1	0	1	0	0
11	Burger S.W.P.(Schalk)	Western Province	2010	1	0	1	0	0
12	Claassen W.(Wynand)	Natal	1984	1	0	1	0	0
13	Daniel K.R.(Keegan)	Natal	2011-13	3	1	2	0	33
14	Dannhauser T.(Toy)	Transvaal	1968	1	0	1	0	0
15	De Jongh J.L.(Juan)	Western Province	2014-15	2	1	1	0	50
16	De Wet D.J.(Daan)	Orange Free State	1973	1	0	1	0	0
17	Drotské A.E.(Naka)	Orange Free State	2005	1	1	0	0	100
18	Du Plessis C.J.(Carel)	Western Province	1986-89	3	1	1	1	33
19	Du Plessis D.C.(Daan)	Northern Transvaal	1979	1	0	0	1	0
20	Du Plessis M.(Morné)	Western Province	1976-79	2	0	1	1	0
21	Du Preez F.C.H.(Frik)	Northern Transvaal	1971	1	0	0	1	0
22	Duncan R.(Rory)	Free State	2007	1	1	0	0	100
23	Erasmus J.(Johan)	Free State	2004	1	0	1	0	0
24	Fourie D.A.(Deon)	Western Province	2012-13	2	1	1	0	50
25	Geel P.J.(Flip)	Northern Transvaal	1946	1	1	0	0	100
26	Geldenhuys S.B.(Burger)	Northern Transvaal	1983-89	2	0	1	1	0
27	Greyling P.J.F.(Piet)	Transvaal	1971-72	2	1	0	1	50
28	Henderson S.(Skip)	Eastern Transvaal	1972	1	0	1	0	0
29	Hugo W.J.(Wouter)	Orange Free State	1976-78	3	1	2	0	33
30	Jamieson C.M.(Craig)	Natal	1990	1	1	0	0	100
31	Joubert E.(Ernst)	Golden Lions	2007	1	0	1	0	0
32	Kriel J.A.(Jaco)	Golden Lions	2015	1	1	0	0	100
33	Kriel P.C.(Piet)	Western Province	1946	1	0	1	0	0
34	Krige C.P.J.(Corné)	Western Province	2000-01	2	2	0	0	100
35	Kritzinger J.L.(Klippies)	Orange Free State	1975	1	0	1	0	0
36	Le Roux A-H.(Ollie)	Orange Free State	2006	1	0	0	1	0
37	Le Roux M.(Martiens)	Orange Free State	1981	1	0	1	0	0
38	Leonard A.(Anton)	Blue Bulls	2003-05	3	2	1	0	67
39	Lotz J.W.(Jan)	Transvaal	1947	1	0	1	0	0
40	Lourens M.J.(Thys)	Northern Transvaal	1974-78	4	4	0	0	100
41	Louw S.C.(Fanie)	Transvaal	1939	1	1	0	0	100
42	Matfield V.(Victor)	Blue Bulls	2008-09	2	1	1	0	50

CURRIE CUP FINAL CAPTAINS 1939 - 2016

	PLAYER	Province	First & last final	Matches	Won	Lost	Drawn	Winning %
43	**Morkel J.**(Hannes)	Western Province	1950	1	0	1	0	0
44	**Muir D.J.**(Dick)	Western Province	1997	1	1	0	0	100
45	**Muller G.J.**(Johann)	Natal	2008	1	1	0	0	100
46	**Müller H.L.**(Helgard)	Orange Free State	1994-97	2	0	2	0	0
47	**Muller H.S.V.**(Hennie)	Transvaal	1950	1	1	0	0	100
48	**Neethling J.B.**(Tiny)	Western Province	1969	1	0	1	0	0
49	**Nel H.J.**(Hennie)	Northern Transvaal	1956	1	1	0	0	100
50	**Oberholzer A.F.**(Anton)	Transvaal	1974	1	0	1	0	0
51	**Oberholzer J.H.**(Jan)	Northern Transvaal	1982	1	0	1	0	0
52	**Pickard J.A.J.**(Jan)	Western Province	1954	1	1	0	0	100
53	**Pienaar J.F.**(Francois)	Transvaal	1993-96	3	2	1	0	67
54	**Roux F. du T.**(Mannetjies)	Griquas	1970	1	1	0	0	100
55	**Serfontein D.J.**(Divan)	Western Province	1982-84	3	3	0	0	100
56	**Skinstad R.B.**(Bob)	Western Province	1998	1	0	1	0	0
57	**Smit J.W.**(John)	Natal	2001	1	0	1	0	0
58	**Sowerby R.S.**(Shaun)	Natal	2003	1	0	1	0	0
59	**Strauss C.P.**(Tiaan)	Western Province	1995	1	0	1	0	0
60	**Strauss J.A.**(Adriaan)	Free State	2009	1	0	1	0	0
61	**Strauss J.Z.**(Joshua)	Golden Lions	2011	1	1	0	0	100
62	**Strydom J.J.**(Hannes)	Transvaal	1999	1	1	0	0	100
63	**Taylor P.**(Peter)	Natal	1956	1	0	1	0	0
64	**Teichmann G.H.**(Gary)	Natal	1995-99	3	2	1	0	67
65	**Terblanche C.S.**(Stefan)	Natal	2010	1	1	0	0	100
66	**Turner F.G.**(Freddie)	Western Province	1939	1	0	1	0	0
67	**Uys P. de W.**(Piet)	Northern Transvaal	1968-70	3	2	1	0	67
68	**Van Aswegen H.J.**(Henning)	Western Province	1985	1	1	0	0	100
69	**Van der Westhuizen J.H.**(Joost)	Blue Bulls	1998-02	2	2	0	0	100
70	**Van Renen G.L.**(George)	Western Province	1947	1	1	0	0	100
71	**Van Wyk C.J.**(Basie)	Transvaal	1952	1	1	0	0	100
72	**Venter J.F.**(Francois)	Free State	2016	1	1	0	0	100
73	**Vos A.N.**(André)	Golden Lions	2002	1	0	1	0	0
74	**Whiteley W.R.**(Warren)	Golden Lions	2014	1	0	1	0	0

Blue Bulls Rugby Union

Founded: 1938 (as Northern Transvaal) **Ground:** Loftus Versfeld
Capacity: 50,000 **Address:** Kirkness Street, Sunnyside, Pretoria,
0002 **Postal address:** PO Box 27856, Sunnyside, Pretoria, 0132
Telephone Number: 012-420 0700 **Website:** www.thebulls.co.za
Colours: Sky blue jersey and socks, navy shorts
Head Coach: Nollis Marais **Currie Cup Coach:** Nollis Marais
Captains: Arno Botha, Hanro Liebenberg
President: Gerrit Wessels **Company CEO:** Barend van Graan
Union CEO: Dr Eugene Hare

'96* 2nd	'97* 5th	'98* 2nd	'99 5th	'00 10th	'01 7th
'02 4th	'03 1st	'04 1st	'05 1st	'06 2nd	'07 4th
'08 2nd	'09 3rd	'10 4th	'11 5th	'12 4th	'13 5th
		'14 4th	'15 2nd	'16 2nd	

Played	Won	Lost	Drawn	Points for	Points against	Tries for	Tries against
10	7	3	0	362	273	44	31

Date	Venue	Opponent	Result	Score	Referee	Scorers
Aug 05	Pretoria	WP	WON	45-26	S Berry	T: Basson, Stighling, Ulengo, P van Zyl, Orie, Jenkins. C: Schoeman (6). P: Schoeman.
Aug 13	Bloemfontein	Free State	LOST	20-43	L Legoete	T: Kirsten, Steenkamp. C: Schoeman, Stander. P: Schoeman (2).
Aug 19	Pretoria	EP Kings	WON	49-35	F Rasivhenge	T: Ulengo (2), Odendaal, Basson, Schoeman, Kirsten, Stander. C: Schoeman (7).
Aug 27	Durban	Sharks	LOST	19-26	M vd Westhuizen	T: Ulengo. C: Schoeman. P: Schoeman (4).
Sep 02	Pretoria	Golden Lions	WON	31-17	C Joubert	T: Ismaiel, Orie, Stander. C: Schoeman (2). P: Schoeman (4).
Sep 10	Nelspruit	Pumas	WON	41-14	S Berry	T: Ulengo (2), Beyers, Ismaiel, Liebenberg, De Jager. C: Schoeman (3), Stander. P: Schoeman.
Sep 16	Pretoria	Griquas	WON	57-20	Q Immelman	T: P van Zyl (2), Beyers, Ulengo, De Jager, Snyman, Basson, Penalty try. C: Schoeman (7). P: Schoeman.
Sep 23	Wellington	Boland	WON	48-26	S Kubo	T: Liebenberg (2), Beyers, Basson, Schoeman, Smit, Gqoboka. C: Schoeman (5). P: Schoeman.
SEMI-FINAL						
Oct 15	Pretoria	WP	WON	36-30	M vd Westhuizen	T: Ismaiel, Jenkins, I van Zyl. C: Schoeman (3). P: Schoeman (5).
FINAL						
Oct 22	Bloemfontein	Free State	LOST	16-36	J Peyper	T: P van Zyl. C: Stander. P: Schoeman (3).

Note: ■ = *Champion,* * *Played as Northern Transvaal*

APPEARANCES & POINTS

PLAYER	WP	Free State	EP Kings	Sharks	Golden Lions	Pumas	Griquas	Boland	WP	Free State	Apps	T	C	P	DG	Pts
Bjorn Basson	15	11	11	–	–	12R	11	15R	11R		7	4	–	–	–	20
Jade Stighling	14	–	–	–	–	–	–	–	–	–	1	1	–	–	–	5
Dries Swanepoel	13	–	–	13	13	13	13	13	13	13	8	–	–	–	–	0
Burger Odendaal	12	12	12	12	12	12	12	12	12	12	10	1	–	–	–	5
Jamba Ulengo	11	14	14	11	11	11	11	14	11	11	10	7	–	–	–	35
Tian Schoeman	10	10	10	10	10	10	10	10	10	10	10	2	35	22	–	146
Piet van Zyl	9	9	9	9	9	9	9	9	–	9R	9	4	–	–	–	20
Arno Botha	8c	8c	8c	8c	7c	–	–	–	8c	8c	7	–	–	–	–	0
Jannes Kirsten	7	7	7	7	–	–	7R	7R	7	7	8	2	–	–	–	10
Ruan Steenkamp	6	6	6	6	6	6	–	–	–	–	6	1	–	–	–	5
Marvin Orie	5	5	5	5	5	5	5	5	5	5	10	2	–	–	–	10
Jason Jenkins	4	4	–	–	–	5R	5R	5R	4		6	2	–	–	–	10
Entienne Swanepoel	3	3	3	–	–	–	–	–	–	–	3	–	–	–	–	0
Jaco Visagie	2	2	2	2	2	7R	2	2R	2	2	10	–	–	–	–	0
Pierre Schoeman	1	1	1R	–	1	–	1	–	1R	1R	7	–	–	–	–	0
Bandise Maku	2R	–	–	2R	x	2	2R	2	2R	2R	7	–	–	–	–	0
Mox Mxoli	3R	–	–	–	–	–	–	–	–	–	1	–	–	–	–	0
Eli Snyman	4R	–	–	–	–	–	–	–	–	–	1	–	–	–	–	0
Hanro Liebenberg	6R	4R	7R	7R	8	8c	8c	8c	8R	8R	10	3	–	–	–	15
André Warner	9R	9R	9R	9R	9R	9R	9R	–	–	–	7	–	–	–	–	0
Tony Jantjies	14R	–	–	–	–	–	–	–	–	–	1	–	–	–	–	0
Dan Kriel	13R	13	13	–	–	–	–	–	–	–	3	–	–	–	–	0
Ulrich Beyers	–	15	–	15R	15R	15	15	15	15	15	8	3	–	–	–	15
Edgar Marutlulle	–	2R	2R	–	–	–	–	–	–	–	2	–	–	–	–	0
Martin Dreyer	–	3R	–	3R	3R	3R	3	3R	3R	3R	8	–	–	–	–	0
RG Snyman	–	5R	4	4	4	4	4	4	4	–	8	1	–	–	–	5
Joshua Stander	–	10R	10R	10R	12R	10R	14R	12R	x	10R	8	2	3	–	–	16
Duncan Matthews	–	13R	15	15	15	–	–	–	–	–	4	–	–	–	–	0
Lizo Gqoboko	–	–	1	1	–	1	–	1	1	1	6	1	–	–	–	5
Jacobie Adriaanse	–	–	3R	3	3	3	–	3	3	3	7	–	–	–	–	0
Irné Herbst	–	–	5R	–	–	5R	–	–	–	–	2	–	–	–	–	0
Travis Ismaiel	–	–	–	14	14	14	14	–	14	14	6	3	–	–	–	15
Nic de Jager	–	–	–	6R	7R	7	7	7	–	5R	6	2	–	–	–	10
Roelof Smit	–	–	–	–	6R	6R	6	6	6	6	6	1	–	–	–	5
Divan Rossouw	–	–	–	–	–	15R	–	11R	–	–	2	–	–	–	–	0
John-Roy Jenkinson	–	–	–	–	–	3R	–	–	–	–	1	–	–	–	–	0
Rudy Paige	–	–	–	–	–	–	–	9R	9	9	3	–	–	–	–	0
Ivan van Zyl	–	–	–	–	–	–	–	–	9R	–	1	1	–	–	–	5
Penalty try	–	–	–	–	–	–	–	–	–	–	0	1	–	–	–	5
38 PLAYERS											220	44	38	22	0	362

CURRIE CUP SQUAD – CAREER CURRIE CUP APPEARANCES

PLAYER	BLUE BULLS						OTHER UNIONS						TOTAL					
	A	T	C	P	DG	Pts	A	T	C	P	DG	Pts	A	T	C	P	DG	Pts
JP (Jacobie) Adriaanse	7	0	0	0	0	0	60	4	0	0	0	20	67	4	0	0	0	20
BA (Bjorn) Basson	26	21	0	0	0	105	37	33	0	0	0	165	63	54	0	0	0	270
U (Ulrich) Beyers	28	4	0	0	0	20	0	0	0	0	0	0	28	4	0	0	0	20
AF (Arno) Botha	31	5	0	0	0	25	0	0	0	0	0	0	31	5	0	0	0	25
NJK (Nick) de Jager	7	2	0	0	0	10	0	0	0	0	0	0	7	2	0	0	0	10
MC (Martin) Dreyer	8	0	0	0	0	0	20	2	0	0	0	10	28	2	0	0	0	10
LP (Lizo) Gqoboko	6	1	0	0	0	5	31	2	0	0	0	10	37	3	0	0	0	15
IP (Irné) Herbst	2	0	0	0	0	0	0	0	0	0	0	0	2	0	0	0	0	0
TK (Travis) Ismaiel	20	8	0	0	0	40	0	0	0	0	0	0	20	8	0	0	0	40
A (Tony) Jantjies	8	0	6	9	0	39	0	0	0	0	0	0	8	0	6	9	0	39
JH (Jason) Jenkins	8	2	0	0	0	10	0	0	0	0	0	0	8	2	0	0	0	10
J-R (John-Roy) Jenkinson	1	0	0	0	0	0	33	3	0	0	0	15	34	3	0	0	0	15
JG (Jannes) Kirsten	11	2	0	0	0	10	0	0	0	0	0	0	11	2	0	0	0	10
DD (Dan) Kriel	5	0	0	0	0	0	0	0	0	0	0	0	5	0	0	0	0	0
H (Hanro) Liebenberg	13	3	0	0	0	15	0	0	0	0	0	0	13	3	0	0	0	15
BG (Bandise) Maku	59	2	0	0	0	10	23	1	0	0	0	5	82	3	0	0	0	15
E (Edgar) Marutlullu	2	0	0	0	0	0	42	7	0	0	0	35	44	7	0	0	0	35
DV (Duncan) Matthews	4	0	0	0	0	0	0	0	0	0	0	0	4	0	0	0	0	0
NM (Mox) Mxoli	2	0	0	0	0	0	0	0	0	0	0	0	2	0	0	0	0	0
MB (Burger) Odendaal	31	4	0	0	0	20	0	0	0	0	0	0	31	4	0	0	0	20
M (Marvin) Orie	21	2	0	0	0	10	0	0	0	0	0	0	21	2	0	0	0	10
R (Rudy) Paige	28	2	0	0	0	10	1	0	0	0	0	0	29	2	0	0	0	10
D (Divan) Rossouw	2	0	0	0	0	0	0	0	0	0	0	0	2	0	0	0	0	0
CF (Tian) Schoeman	23	3	61	50	0	287	0	0	0	0	0	0	23	3	61	50	0	287
P (Pierre) Schoeman	13	0	0	0	0	0	0	0	0	0	0	0	13	0	0	0	0	0
RA (Roelof) Smit	12	1	0	0	0	5	0	0	0	0	0	0	12	1	0	0	0	5
EC (Eli) Snyman	1	0	0	0	0	0	0	0	0	0	0	0	1	0	0	0	0	0
RG (RG) Snyman	19	1	0	0	0	5	0	0	0	0	0	0	19	1	0	0	0	5
JT (Joshua) Stander	9	2	4	0	0	18	0	0	0	0	0	0	9	2	4	0	0	18
R (Ruan) Steenkamp	9	2	0	0	0	10	0	0	0	0	0	0	9	2	0	0	0	10
JK (Jade) Stighling	1	1	0	0	0	5	0	0	0	0	0	0	1	1	0	0	0	5
AE (Dries) Swanepoel	19	4	0	0	0	20	0	0	0	0	0	0	19	4	0	0	0	20
JCE (Entienne) Swanepoel	3	0	0	0	0	0	0	0	0	0	0	0	3	0	0	0	0	0
JI (Jamba) Ulengo	22	18	0	0	0	90	0	0	0	0	0	0	22	18	0	0	0	90
I (Ivan) van Zyl	11	1	0	0	0	5	0	0	0	0	0	0	11	1	0	0	0	5
PE (Piet) van Zyl	20	5	0	0	0	25	22	4	0	0	0	20	42	9	0	0	0	45
GJ (Jaco) Visagie	18	0	0	0	0	0	0	0	0	0	0	0	18	0	0	0	0	0
AR (André) Warner	8	0	0	0	0	0	0	0	0	0	0	0	8	0	0	0	0	0
38 PLAYERS	518	96	71	59	0	799	269	56	0	0	0	280	787	152	71	59	0	1079

FIRST-CLASS APPEARANCES FOR BLUE BULLS IN 2016 – ALL MATCHES

PLAYER	CURRIE CUP QUALIFIER						CURRIE CUP						2016 TOTAL						CAREER MATCHES					
	A	T	C	P	DG	Pts	A	T	C	P	DG	Pts	A	T	C	P	DG	Pts	A	T	C	P	DG	Pts
JP (Jacobie) Adriaanse	0	0	0	0	0	0	7	0	0	0	0	0	7	0	0	0	0	0	7	0	0	0	0	0
BA (Bjorn) Basson	1	0	0	0	0	0	7	4	0	0	0	20	8	4	0	0	0	20	27	21	0	0	0	105
A (Andréw) Beerwinkel	6	0	0	0	0	0	0	0	0	0	0	0	6	0	0	0	0	0	10	0	0	0	0	0
U (Ulrich) Beyers	0	0	0	0	0	0	8	3	0	0	0	15	8	3	0	0	0	15	42	7	1	0	1	40
AF (Arno) Botha	0	0	0	0	0	0	7	0	0	0	0	0	7	0	0	0	0	0	34	6	0	0	0	30
R (Renaldo) Bothma	3	2	0	0	0	10	0	0	0	0	0	0	3	2	0	0	0	10	3	2	0	0	0	10
J-H (Henning) Campher	4	0	0	0	0	0	0	0	0	0	0	0	4	0	0	0	0	0	4	0	0	0	0	0
CE (Clyde) Davids	2	0	0	0	0	0	0	0	0	0	0	0	2	0	0	0	0	0	17	2	0	0	0	10
MH (Tinus) de Beer	2	0	1	0	0	2	0	0	0	0	0	0	2	0	1	0	0	2	4	0	4	1	0	11
NJK (Nick) de Jager	7	0	0	0	0	0	6	2	0	0	0	10	13	2	0	0	0	10	14	2	0	0	0	10
MC (Martin) Dreyer	2	0	0	0	0	0	8	0	0	0	0	0	10	0	0	0	0	0	10	0	0	0	0	0
CW (Corniel) Els	7	2	0	0	0	10	0	0	0	0	0	0	7	2	0	0	0	10	17	4	0	0	0	20
AB (Aston) Fortuin	9	0	0	0	0	0	0	0	0	0	0	0	9	0	0	0	0	0	9	0	0	0	0	0
J (Justin) Forwood	1	0	0	0	0	0	0	0	0	0	0	0	1	0	0	0	0	0	2	0	0	0	0	0
JN (Neethling) Fouché	2	0	0	0	0	0	0	0	0	0	0	0	2	0	0	0	0	0	3	0	0	0	0	0
WW (Warrick) Gelant	1	0	0	0	0	0	0	0	0	0	0	0	1	0	0	0	0	0	16	3	0	0	0	15
LP (Lizo) Gqoboka	0	0	0	0	0	0	6	1	0	0	0	5	6	1	0	0	0	5	6	1	0	0	0	5
MD (Dean) Greyling	1	1	0	0	0	5	0	0	0	0	0	0	1	1	0	0	0	5	85	10	0	0	0	50
N (Njabulo) Gumede	6	0	0	0	0	0	0	0	0	0	0	0	6	0	0	0	0	0	6	0	0	0	0	0
IP (Irné) Herbst	1	0	0	0	0	0	2	0	0	0	0	0	3	0	0	0	0	0	3	0	0	0	0	0
AM (Alcino) Isaacs	11	3	0	0	0	15	0	0	0	0	0	0	11	3	0	0	0	15	11	3	0	0	0	15
TK (Travis) Ismaiel	0	0	0	0	0	0	6	3	0	0	0	15	6	3	0	0	0	15	37	18	0	0	0	90
JT (JT) Jackson	3	0	0	0	0	0	0	0	0	0	0	0	3	0	0	0	0	0	3	0	0	0	0	0
NJ (Nico) Janse van Rensburg	5	0	0	0	0	0	0	0	0	0	0	0	5	0	0	0	0	0	26	0	0	0	0	0
A (Tony) Jantjies	8	3	16	6	0	65	1	0	0	0	0	0	9	3	16	6	0	65	29	6	52	37	0	245
JH (Jason) Jenkins	0	0	0	0	0	0	6	2	0	0	0	10	6	2	0	0	0	10	8	2	0	0	0	10
J-R (John-Roy) Jenkinson	0	0	0	0	0	0	1	0	0	0	0	0	1	0	0	0	0	0	1	0	0	0	0	0
JC (Jannes) Kirsten	0	0	0	0	0	0	8	2	0	0	0	10	8	2	0	0	0	10	12	2	0	0	0	10
DD (Dan) Kriel	5	1	0	0	0	5	3	0	0	0	0	0	8	1	0	0	0	5	15	1	0	0	0	5
W (Werner) Kruger	1	0	0	0	0	0	0	0	0	0	0	0	1	0	0	0	0	0	134	7	0	0	0	35
I (Manie) Libbok	4	1	0	1	0	8	0	0	0	0	0	0	4	1	0	1	0	8	4	1	0	1	0	8
H (Hanro) Liebenberg	8	3	0	0	0	15	10	3	0	0	0	15	18	6	0	0	0	30	22	6	0	0	0	30
A (Adrian) Maebane	2	0	0	0	0	0	0	0	0	0	0	0	2	0	0	0	0	0	2	0	0	0	0	0
KS (Kefentse) Mahlo	11	5	0	0	0	25	0	0	0	0	0	0	11	5	0	0	0	25	23	12	0	0	0	60
BG (Bandise) Maku	1	0	0	0	0	0	7	0	0	0	0	0	8	0	0	0	0	0	93	3	0	0	0	15
TD (Theo) Maree	3	1	0	0	0	5	0	0	0	0	0	0	3	1	0	0	0	5	3	1	0	0	0	5
E (Edgar) Marutlulle	0	0	0	0	0	0	2	0	0	0	0	0	2	0	0	0	0	0	2	0	0	0	0	0
DV (Duncan) Matthews	3	1	0	0	0	5	4	0	0	0	0	0	7	1	0	0	0	5	7	1	0	0	0	5
G (Ganfried) May	1	0	0	0	0	0	0	0	0	0	0	0	1	0	0	0	0	0	3	1	0	0	0	5
NM (Mox) Mxoli	10	2	0	0	0	10	1	0	0	0	0	0	11	2	0	0	0	10	14	3	0	0	0	15
DD (Dewald) Naudé	2	0	0	0	0	0	0	0	0	0	0	0	2	0	0	0	0	0	2	0	0	0	0	0
FJ (Franco) Naudé	4	1	0	0	0	5	0	0	0	0	0	0	4	1	0	0	0	5	4	1	0	0	0	5
TFN (Freddy) Ngoza	8	1	0	0	0	5	0	0	0	0	0	0	8	1	0	0	0	5	8	1	0	0	0	5
A (Abongile) Nonkontwana	12	1	0	0	0	5	0	0	0	0	0	0	12	1	0	0	0	5	12	1	0	0	0	5
LBS (Luther) Obi	2	0	0	0	0	0	0	0	0	0	0	0	2	0	0	0	0	0	2	0	0	0	0	0

FIRST-CLASS APPEARANCES FOR BLUE BULLS IN 2016 – ALL MATCHES

PLAYER	CURRIE CUP QUALIFIER						CURRIE CUP						2016 TOTAL						CAREER MATCHES					
	A	T	C	P	DG	Pts	A	T	C	P	DG	Pts	A	T	C	P	DG	Pts	A	T	C	P	DG	Pts
MB (Burger) Odendaal	0	0	0	0	0	0	10	1	0	0	0	5	10	1	0	0	0	5	38	8	0	0	0	40
M (Marvin) Orie	5	0	0	0	0	0	10	2	0	0	0	10	15	2	0	0	0	10	40	3	0	0	0	15
R (Rudy) Paige	0	0	0	0	0	0	3	0	0	0	0	0	3	0	0	0	0	0	36	2	0	0	0	10
L (Le Roux) Roets	1	0	0	0	0	0	0	0	0	0	0	0	1	0	0	0	0	0	1	0	0	0	0	0
D (Divan) Rossouw	10	3	1	0	0	17	2	0	0	0	0	0	12	3	1	0	0	17	12	3	1	0	0	17
P (Pierre) Schoeman	0	0	0	0	0	0	7	0	0	0	0	0	7	0	0	0	0	0	15	0	0	0	0	0
CF (Tian) Schoeman	0	0	0	0	0	0	10	2	35	22	0	146	10	2	35	22	0	146	29	5	82	60	0	369
MV (Marquit) September	9	8	0	0	0	40	0	0	0	0	0	0	9	8	0	0	0	40	18	12	0	0	0	60
RA (Roelof) Smit	5	5	0	0	0	25	6	1	0	0	0	5	11	6	0	0	0	30	32	14	0	0	0	70
EC (Eli) Snyman	1	0	0	0	0	0	1	0	0	0	0	0	2	0	0	0	0	0	2	0	0	0	0	0
RG (RG) Snyman	0	0	0	0	0	0	8	1	0	0	0	5	8	1	0	0	0	5	22	1	0	0	0	5
JT (Joshua) Stander	11	3	25	4	0	77	8	2	3	0	0	16	19	5	28	4	0	93	26	6	39	4	0	120
R (Ruan) Steenkamp	11	0	0	0	0	0	6	1	0	0	0	5	17	1	0	0	0	5	20	2	0	0	0	10
GJ (Deon) Stegmann	2	0	0	0	0	0	0	0	0	0	0	0	2	0	0	0	0	0	76	17	0	0	0	85
JK (Jade) Stighling	13	5	0	0	0	25	1	1	0	0	0	5	14	6	0	0	0	30	22	7	0	0	0	35
AE (Dries) Swanepoel	1	0	0	0	0	0	8	0	0	0	0	0	9	0	0	0	0	0	26	10	0	0	0	50
JCE (Entienne) Swanepoel	3	0	0	0	0	0	10	0	0	0	0	0	13	0	0	0	0	0	13	0	0	0	0	0
J (Jsuanre) Swanepoel	1	0	0	0	0	0	0	0	0	0	0	0	1	0	0	0	0	0	1	0	0	0	0	0
T (Tapiwa) Tsomondo	8	5	0	0	0	25	0	0	0	0	0	0	8	5	0	0	0	25	8	5	0	0	0	25
JI (Jamba) Ulengo	0	0	0	0	0	0	10	7	0	0	0	35	10	7	0	0	0	35	31	23	0	0	0	115
D (Duhan) van der Merwe	2	0	0	0	0	0	0	0	0	0	0	0	2	0	0	0	0	0	2	0	0	0	0	0
J (Jan) van der Merwe	7	0	0	0	0	0	0	0	0	0	0	0	7	0	0	0	0	0	8	0	0	0	0	0
DL (Dayan) van der Westhuizen	3	0	0	0	0	0	0	0	0	0	0	0	3	0	0	0	0	0	11	1	0	0	0	5
R (Ruben) van Heerden	9	1	0	0	0	5	0	0	0	0	0	0	9	1	0	0	0	5	9	1	0	0	0	5
A (AlAndré) van Rooyen	6	1	0	0	0	5	0	0	0	0	0	0	6	1	0	0	0	5	6	1	0	0	0	5
HJ (Hencus) van Wyk	1	0	0	0	0	0	0	0	0	0	0	0	1	0	0	0	0	0	22	4	0	0	0	20
I (Ivan) van Zyl	11	1	0	0	0	5	1	1	0	0	0	5	12	2	0	0	0	10	26	2	0	0	0	10
PE (Piet) van Zyl	0	0	0	0	0	0	9	4	0	0	0	20	9	4	0	0	0	20	20	5	0	0	0	25
C-T (Callie) Visagie	2	1	0	0	0	5	0	0	0	0	0	0	2	1	0	0	0	5	15	2	0	0	0	10
GJ (Jaco) Visagie	1	0	0	0	0	0	10	0	0	0	0	0	11	0	0	0	0	0	26	0	0	0	0	0
AR (André) Warner	14	3	0	0	0	15	7	0	0	0	0	0	21	3	0	0	0	15	25	3	0	0	0	15
KE (Kurt) Webster	4	1	6	1	0	20	0	0	0	0	0	0	4	1	6	1	0	20	7	1	6	1	0	20

77 PLAYERS

Boland Cavaliers

Boland Rugby Union

Founded: 1939 **Ground:** Boland Stadium **Capacity:** 11,000
Address: 50 Fontein Street, Wellington **Postal Address:** PO Box
127, Wellington, 7654 **Telephone Number:** 021-873 2317
Website: www.bolandrugby.com
Colours: Pink, black and white jersey, black shorts
Currie Cup Coach: Brent Janse van Rensburg
Captain: Ryan Nell **President:** Ivan Pekeur

'96	'97	'98	'99	'00	'01
8th	7th	10th	12th	5th	9th

'02	'03	'04	'05	'06	'07
12th	10th	9th	6th	10th	7th

'08	'09	'10	'11	'12	'13
7th	8th	11th	9th	12th	11th

'14	'15	'16
13th	13th	7th

Played	Won	Lost	Drawn	Points for	Points against	Tries for	Tries against
8	2	6	0	177	301	24	41

Date	Venue	Opponent	Result	Score	Referee	Scorers
Aug 06	Wellington	Free State	LOST	16-44	R Boneparte	T: Demas. C: Scheepers. P: Scheepers (3).
Aug 12	Port Elizabeth	EP Kings	WON	28-10	R Boneparte	T: Bosch, Cronjé, Torrens, Jordaan. C: Scheepers (4).
Aug 19	Wellington	Sharks	LOST	20-41	M v/d Westhuizen	T: Demas, Nell, Torrens. C: Kotze. P: Scheepers.
Aug 26	Johannesburg	Golden Lions	LOST	12-60	R Rasivhenge	T: Horn, Wilschut. C: Kotze.
Sep 02	Wellington	Pumas	WON	25-22	M v/d Westhuizen	T: Carelse, Adendorff, Louw. C: Kotze (2). P: Kotze. DG: Kotze.
Sep 08	Kimberley	Griquas	LOST	22-46	J van Heerden	T: Carelse, Lewis, Pheiffer. C: Kotze, Carelse. P: Kotze.
Sep 23	Wellington	Blue Bulls	LOST	26-48	S Kubo	T: Kotze (2), Demas, Z Jordaan. C: Kotze (3)
Sep 30	Cape Town	WP	LOST	28-30	AJ Jacobs	T: Hanekom, Engelbrecht, Adendorff, Carelse. C: Kotze (4).

APPEARANCES & POINTS

PLAYER	Free State	EP Kings	Sharks	Golden Lions	Pumas	Griquas	Blue Bulls	WP	Apps	T	C	P	DG	Pts
Nico Scheepers	15	15	15	–	–	–	–	–	3	–	5	4	–	22
Sergio Torrens	14	14	14	14	–	14	–	12R	6	2	–	–	–	10
Ryan Nell	13c	13c	12c	12c	12c	–	–	–	5	1	–	–	–	5
Christopher Bosch	12	12	13	13	13	12	12	–	7	1	–	–	–	5
Danwel Demas	11	11	11	11	11	11	11	14	8	3	–	–	–	15
Adriaan Carelse	10	10	10	15	15	10	15	15	8	3	1	–	–	17
Marnus Hugo	9	9	9	9R	9	9	9	9	8	–	–	–	–	0
Zandré Jordaan	8	8	8	–	–	4R	8	8	6	2	–	–	–	10
Jacques Engelbrecht	7	7	7	–	8	8	7	7	7	1	–	–	–	5
Kenan Cronjé	6	6	6R	4R	6R	–	6	–	6	1	–	–	–	5
Hanno Kitshoff	5	5	5	4	4	4	4R	5	8	–	–	–	–	0
Shaun McDonald	4	4	4	7	7	7	4	4	8	–	–	–	–	0
Basil Short	3	3	3	3	–	1R	3	1	7	–	–	–	–	0
Clemen Lewis	2	–	2R	2R	2	2c	2c	2c	7	1	–	–	–	5
SP Wessels	1	1	1	1R	1R	1	1	–	7	–	–	–	–	0
Chadley Wenn	2R	2	–	–	–	–	–	–	2	–	–	–	–	0
Francois Hanekom	3R	1R	1R	1	–	–	1R	3	6	1	–	–	–	5
Joubert Horn	5R	5R	5R	5	5	5	5	5R	8	1	–	–	–	5
Chaney Willemse	7R	6R	–	–	–	–	–	–	2	–	–	–	–	0
Jovelian de Koker	9R	12R	9R	–	–	–	–	–	3	–	–	–	–	0
William van Wyk	x	10R	–	–	–	–	–	–	1	–	–	–	–	0
Craig Pheiffer	x	14R	–	–	14R	–	–	–	2	1	–	–	–	5
Francois Esterhuyzen	–	2R	2	2	x	13R	2R	2R	6	–	–	–	–	0
Shaun Adendorff	–	–	6	6	6	6	–	6	5	2	–	–	–	10
Theuns Kotze	–	–	15R	10	10	15	10	10	6	2	12	2	1	43
Abongile Mnyaka	–	–	3R	3R	3	3	3R	1R	6	–	–	–	–	0
Gerhard Jordaan	–	–	–	9	14R	9R	9R	x	4	–	–	–	–	0
Wayne Wilschut	–	–	–	8	4R	8R	7R	x	4	1	–	–	–	5
Gerrit van Wyk	–	–	–	13R	14	–	13	13	4	–	–	–	–	0
Ockie van Zyl	–	–	–	5R	x	–	–	–	1	–	–	–	–	0
Linda Thwala	–	–	–	–	1	–	–	3R	2	–	–	–	–	0
Robbie Louw	–	–	–	–	12R	13	12R	–	3	1	–	–	–	5
Logan Basson	–	–	–	–	–	15R	14	11	3	–	–	–	–	0
PJ Vermeulen	–	–	–	–	–	–	–	12	1	–	–	–	–	0
34 players									170	24	18	6	1	177

CURRIE CUP SQUAD – CAREER CURRIE CUP APPEARANCES

PLAYER	BOLAND						OTHER UNIONS						TOTAL					
	A	T	C	P	DG	Pts	A	T	C	P	DG	Pts	A	T	C	P	DG	Pts
S (Shaun) Adendorff	5	2	–	–	–	10	–	–	–	–	–	0	5	2	–	–	–	10
LA (Logan) Basson	3	–	–	–	–	0	26	5	16	26	–	135	29	5	16	26	–	135
C (Christopher) Bosch	12	1	–	–	–	5	8	1	–	–	–	5	20	2	–	–	–	10
AJ (Adriaan) Carelse	17	4	1	1	1	28	–	–	–	–	–	0	17	4	1	1	1	28
K (Kenan) Cronjé	11	3	–	–	–	15	–	–	–	–	–	0	11	3	–	–	–	15
J (Jovelian) de Koker	19	1	–	–	–	5	–	–	–	–	–	0	19	1	–	–	–	5
D (Danwel) Demas	42	34	–	–	–	170	30	11	–	–	–	55	72	45	–	–	–	225
JJ (Jacques) Engelbrecht	7	1	–	–	–	5	67	5	–	–	–	25	74	6	–	–	–	30
F (Francois) Esterhuyzen	6	–	–	–	–	0	–	–	–	–	–	0	6	–	–	–	–	0
PF (Francois) Hanekom	26	1	–	–	–	5	–	–	–	–	–	0	26	1	–	–	–	5
APM (Marnus) Hugo	53	4	–	–	–	20	37	–	–	–	–	0	90	4	–	–	–	20
JP (Joubert) Horn	8	1	–	–	–	5	–	–	–	–	–	0	8	1	–	–	–	5
GJ (Gerhard) Jordaan	4	–	–	–	–	0	–	–	–	–	–	0	4	–	–	–	–	0
Z (Zandré) Jordaan	43	13	–	–	–	65	7	1	–	–	–	5	50	14	–	–	–	70
JJ (Hanno) Kitshoff	32	2	–	–	–	10	–	–	–	–	–	0	32	2	–	–	–	10
TAW (Theuns) Kotze	6	2	12	2	1	43	7	1	10	4	–	37	13	3	22	6	1	80
C (Clemen) Lewis	101	7	–	–	–	35	–	–	–	–	–	0	101	7	–	–	–	35
RMM (Robbie) Louw	3	1	–	–	–	5	–	–	–	–	–	0	3	1	–	–	–	5
S (Shaun) McDonald	8	–	–	–	–	0	–	–	–	–	–	0	8	–	–	–	–	0
AE (Abongile) Mnyaka	6	–	–	–	–	0	–	–	–	–	–	0	6	–	–	–	–	0
RD (Ryan) Nell	5	1	–	–	–	5	4	–	–	–	–	0	9	1	–	–	–	5
CL (Craig) Pheiffer	2	1	–	–	–	5	–	–	–	–	–	0	2	1	–	–	–	5
JN (Nico) Scheepers	3	–	5	4	–	22	35	8	45	54	–	292	38	8	50	58	–	314
BG (Basil) Short	7	–	–	–	–	0	5	–	–	–	–	0	12	–	–	–	–	0
L (Linda) Thwala	2	–	–	–	–	0	–	–	–	–	–	0	2	–	–	–	–	0
SL (Sergio) Torrens	6	2	–	–	–	10	11	2	–	–	–	10	17	4	–	–	–	20
GJ (Gerrit) van Wyk	7	–	–	–	–	0	–	–	–	–	–	0	7	–	–	–	–	0
WA (William) van Wyk	1	–	–	–	–	0	–	–	–	–	–	0	1	–	–	–	–	0
OP (Ockie) van Zyl	1	–	–	–	–	0	5	–	–	–	–	0	6	–	–	–	–	0
PJ (PJ) Vermeulen	31	5	–	–	–	25	19	5	–	–	–	25	50	10	–	–	–	50
C (Chadley) Wenn	8	–	–	–	–	0	–	–	–	–	–	0	8	–	–	–	–	0
SP (SP) Wessels	16	–	–	–	–	0	–	–	–	–	–	0	16	–	–	–	–	0
C (Chaney) Willemse	15	3	–	–	–	15	–	–	–	–	–	0	15	3	–	–	–	15
WP (Wayne) Wilschut	15	1	–	–	–	5	–	–	–	–	–	0	15	1	–	–	–	5
34 PLAYERS	531	90	18	7	2	513	261	39	71	84	0	589	792	129	89	91	2	1102

FIRST-CLASS APPEARANCES FOR BOLAND IN 2016 – ALL MATCHES

PLAYER	CURRIE CUP QUALIFIER						CURRIE CUP						2016 TOTAL						CAREER MATCHES					
	A	T	C	P	DG	Pts	A	T	C	P	DG	Pts	A	T	C	P	DG	Pts	A	T	C	P	DG	Pts
S (Shaun) Adendorff	12	3	0	0	0	15	5	2	0	0	0	10	17	5	0	0	0	25	17	5	0	0	0	25
YMT (Yves) Bashiya	2	0	0	0	0	0	0	0	0	0	0	0	2	0	0	0	0	0	25	1	0	0	0	5
LA (Logan) Basson	0	0	0	0	0	0	3	0	0	0	0	0	3	0	0	0	0	0	3	0	0	0	0	0
C (Christopher) Bosch	14	10	0	0	0	50	7	1	0	0	0	5	21	11	0	0	0	55	31	11	0	0	0	55
AJ (Adriaan) Carelse	14	1	5	0	0	15	8	3	1	0	0	17	22	4	6	0	0	32	31	5	6	1	1	43
K (Kenan) Cronjé	8	1	0	0	0	5	6	1	0	0	0	5	14	2	0	0	0	10	19	4	0	0	0	20
J (Jovelian) de Koker	6	0	0	0	0	0	3	0	0	0	0	0	9	0	0	0	0	0	34	1	0	0	0	5
D (Danwel) Demas	14	7	0	0	0	35	8	3	0	0	0	15	22	10	0	0	0	50	60	43	0	0	0	215
JJ (Jacques) Engelbrecht	0	0	0	0	0	0	7	1	0	0	0	5	7	1	0	0	0	5	7	1	0	0	0	5
F (Francois) Esterhuyzen	4	0	0	0	0	0	6	0	0	0	0	0	10	0	0	0	0	0	10	0	0	0	0	0
JC (JC) Genade	5	1	0	0	0	5	0	0	0	0	0	0	5	1	0	0	0	5	8	1	0	0	0	5
PF (Francois) Hanekom	14	1	0	0	0	5	6	1	0	0	0	5	20	2	0	0	0	10	65	2	0	0	0	10
G (Gavin) Hauptfleisch	1	0	0	0	0	0	0	0	0	0	0	0	1	0	0	0	0	0	1	0	0	0	0	0
JF (Ferdie) Horn	10	0	0	0	0	0	0	0	0	0	0	0	10	0	0	0	0	0	10	0	0	0	0	0
JP (Joubert) Horn	0	0	0	0	0	0	8	1	0	0	0	5	8	1	0	0	0	5	8	1	0	0	0	5
APM (Marnus) Hugo	13	1	0	0	0	5	8	0	0	0	0	0	21	1	0	0	0	5	76	5	0	0	0	25
GJ (Gerhard) Jordaan	8	0	0	0	0	0	4	0	0	0	0	0	12	0	0	0	0	0	12	0	0	0	0	0
Z (Zandré) Jordaan	14	3	0	0	0	15	6	2	0	0	0	10	20	5	0	0	0	25	94	28	0	0	0	140
JJ (Hanno) Kitshoff	14	2	0	0	0	10	8	0	0	0	0	0	22	2	0	0	0	10	62	4	0	0	0	20
TAW (Theuns) Kotze	8	1	12	6	0	47	6	2	12	2	1	43	14	3	24	8	1	90	14	3	24	8	1	90
C (Clemen) Lewis	3	0	0	0	0	0	7	1	0	0	0	5	10	1	0	0	0	5	144	11	0	0	0	55
RMM (Robbie) Louw	1	1	0	0	0	5	3	1	0	0	0	5	4	2	0	0	0	10	4	2	0	0	0	10
S (Shaun) McDonald	14	2	0	0	0	10	8	0	0	0	0	0	22	2	0	0	0	10	22	2	0	0	0	10
AE (Abongile) Mnyaka	0	0	0	0	0	0	6	0	0	0	0	0	6	0	0	0	0	0	6	0	0	0	0	0
RD (Ryan) Nell	13	12	0	0	0	60	5	1	0	0	0	5	18	13	0	0	0	65	18	13	0	0	0	65
N (Niel) Oelofse	3	0	0	0	0	0	0	0	0	0	0	0	3	0	0	0	0	0	3	0	0	0	0	0
CL (Craig) Pheiffer	2	0	0	0	0	0	2	1	0	0	0	5	4	1	0	0	0	5	4	1	0	0	0	5
E (Edwin) Sass	7	2	0	0	0	10	0	0	0	0	0	0	7	2	0	0	0	10	31	5	0	0	0	25
JN (Nico) Scheepers	12	5	41	13	0	140	3	0	5	4	0	22	15	5	46	17	0	162	15	5	46	17	0	162
BG (Basil) Short	12	1	0	0	0	5	7	0	0	0	0	0	19	1	0	0	0	5	19	1	0	0	0	5
L (Linda) Thwala	4	0	0	0	0	0	2	0	0	0	0	0	6	0	0	0	0	0	6	0	0	0	0	0
SL (Sergio) Torrens	13	7	0	0	0	35	6	2	0	0	0	10	19	9	0	0	0	45	19	9	0	0	0	45
GJ (Gerrit) van Wyk	5	0	0	0	0	0	4	0	0	0	0	0	9	0	0	0	0	0	13	0	0	0	0	0
WA (William) van Wyk	6	2	0	0	0	10	1	0	0	0	0	0	7	2	0	0	0	10	7	2	0	0	0	10
OP (Ockie) van Zyl	12	1	0	0	0	5	1	0	0	0	0	0	13	1	0	0	0	5	13	1	0	0	0	5
PJ (PJ) Vermeulen	0	0	0	0	0	0	1	0	0	0	0	0	1	0	0	0	0	0	40	6	0	0	0	30
C (Chadley) Wenn	14	3	0	0	0	15	2	0	0	0	0	0	16	3	0	0	0	15	22	3	0	0	0	15
SP (SP) Wessels	6	0	0	0	0	0	7	0	0	0	0	0	13	0	0	0	0	0	30	0	0	0	0	0
C (Chaney) Willemse	1	0	0	0	0	0	2	0	0	0	0	0	3	0	0	0	0	0	22	3	0	0	0	15
WP (Wayne) Wilschut	13	0	0	0	0	0	4	1	0	0	0	5	17	1	0	0	0	5	35	1	0	0	0	5

40 PLAYERS

Clemen Lewis.

Eastern Province Rugby Union

Founded: 1888 **Ground:** Nelson Mandela Bay Stadium
Capacity: 45,000 **Address:** 70 Prince Alfred Road, North End,
Port Elizabeth, 6001 **Postal address:** PO Box 13111,
Humewood, 6013 **Telephone Number:** 041-408 8902
Email: info@eprugby.co.za **Colours:** Red and black hooped jersey,
black shorts, red and black socks
Currie Cup Coach: Barend Pieterse **Captain:** Ricky Schroeder
President: Cheeky Watson **Company CEO:** Anele Pamba
CEO: Vacant

'96	'97	'98	'99	'00	'01
9th	14th	9th	7th	9th	11th

'02	'03	'04	'05	'06	'07
11th	11th	13th	12th	12th	10th

'08	'09	'10	'11	'12	'13
14th	12th	10th	10th	7th	8th

'14	'15	'16
14th	7th	9th

Played	Won	Lost	Drawn	Points for	Points against	Tries for	Tries against
8	0	8	0	137	379	16	59

Date	Venue	Opponent	Result	Score	Referee	Scorers
Aug 12	Port Elizabeth	Boland	LOST	10-28	R Boneparte	T: Tromp. C: Gosa. P: Marais.
Aug 19	Pretoria	Blue Bulls	LOST	35-49	F Rasivhenge	T: Tromp, Klaasen, Soyizwapi, Willemse, Bezuidenhout. C: Marais (2). P: Marais (2).
Aug 27	Port Elizabeth	WP	LOST	06-36	L Legoete	P: Marais (2).
Aug 31	Kimberley	Griquas	LOST	24-47	AJ Jacobs	T: Isaacs (2), Collopy. C: Gosa (2), De Wet. P: Gosa.
Sept 03	Bloemfontein	Free State	LOST	25-57	J van Heerden	T: Greyling, Klaasen, Jobo. C: De Wet, Marais. P: De Wet. D: De Wet.
Sept 17	Durban	Sharks	LOST	00-53	C Jadezweni	
Sept 24	Port Elizabeth	Golden Lions	LOST	07-71	C Jadezweni	T: Mastriet. C: De Wet.
Sept 30	Port Elizabeth	Pumas	LOST	30-38	Q Immelman	T: Tromp, Schroeder, Brown. C: De Wet (3). P: De Wet (3).

THE CURRIE CUP – PREMIER DIVISION

APPEARANCES & POINTS

PLAYER	Boland	Blue Bulls	WP	Griquas	Free State	Sharks	Golden Lions	Pumas	Apps	T	C	P	DG	Pts
Siwiwe Soyizwapi	15	14	14	12R	14	14	–	14	7	1	–	–	–	5
Alcino Izaacs	14	–	–	11	–	21R	14	–	4	2	–	–	–	10
Johan Tromp	13	15	15	–	15	–	15	15	6	3	–	–	–	15
Waylon Murray	12	12	–	–	–	12	12	12	5	–	–	–	–	0
Sampie Mastriet	11	11	11	–	11	11	11	11	7	1	–	–	–	5
Kobus Marais	10	10	10	–	10R	–	–	–	4	–	3	5	–	21
Ricky Schroeder	9	9c	9c	–	9c	9c	9c	9c	7	1	–	–	–	5
Christiaan de Bruin	8	8	8	–	8	8	8	8	7	–	–	–	–	0
Sebastian Ferreira	7	7	5	–	5	5	5	7	7	–	–	–	–	0
Vince Jobo	6	6	6	–	6	6	6R	–	6	1	–	–	–	5
David Antonites	5	5	–	–	–	–	4	–	3	–	–	–	–	0
Tazz Fuzani	4	4	4	–	–	–	–	4	4	–	–	–	–	0
Vukile Sofisa	3	3	3	–	3	1R	3R	3	7	–	–	–	–	0
Mike Willemse	2	2	2	–	2	–	–	–	4	1	–	–	–	5
Schalk Ferreira	1c	–	–	–	–	–	–	–	1	–	–	–	–	0
Martin Bezuidenhout	2R	2R	2R	2c	2R	2	2	2	8	1	–	–	–	5
Justin Forwood	1R	1	1	–	1	3	1	–	6	–	–	–	–	0
Dirk Grobbelaar	4R	–	–	8	–	–	–	–	2	–	–	–	–	0
Henry Brown	8R	–	8R	7	7R	7	7	6	7	1	–	–	–	5
Jacques Fick	9R	x	–	9	–	–	–	–	2	–	–	–	–	0
Berton Klaasen	12R	13	12	–	12	13	13	13	7	2	–	–	–	10
Lungelo Gosa	10R	10R	10R	10	–	15	15R	11R	7	–	3	1	–	9
Barend Potgieter	–	3R	3R	1	3R	1	–	1	6	–	–	–	–	0
Ettienne Oosthuizen	–	5R	7	8R	7	7R	4R	5R	7	–	–	–	–	0
Luke van der Smit	–	6R	6R	6	–	6R	6	6R	6	–	–	–	–	0
Minenthle Mthethwa	–	13R	–	14	–	14R	–	–	3	–	–	–	–	0
JC Greyling	–	–	13	12	13	–	12R	–	4	1	–	–	–	5
Dylan Pieterse	–	–	5R	5	4	4	–	5	5	–	–	–	–	0
Ganfried May	–	–	11R	15	13R	–	–	–	3	–	–	–	–	0
Hannes Huisamen	–	–	–	4	4R	–	–	–	2	–	–	–	–	0
Pieter Stemmet	–	–	–	3	–	–	3	3R	3	–	–	–	–	0
Warrick Venter	–	–	–	2R	–	2R	–	x	2	–	–	–	–	0
Caylib Oosthuizen	–	–	–	3R	–	–	–	–	1	–	–	–	–	0
Cullen Collopy	–	–	–	6R	–	–	2R	x	2	1	–	–	–	5
Vian van der Watt	–	–	–	9R	9R	9R	9R	9R	5	–	–	–	–	0
Pieter-Steyn de Wet	–	–	–	10R	10	10	10	10	5	–	6	4	1	27
Sipho Msutwana	–	–	–	13	–	–	–	–	1	–	–	–	–	0
37 PLAYERS									173	16	12	10	1	137

CURRIE CUP SQUAD – CAREER CURRIE CUP APPEARANCES

PLAYER	EP KINGS						OTHER UNIONS						TOTAL					
	A	T	C	P	DG	Pts	A	T	C	P	DG	Pts	A	T	C	P	DG	Pts
DA (David) Antonites	3	0	0	0	0	0	0	0	0	0	0	0	3	0	0	0	0	0
MJ (Martin) Bezuidenhout	8	1	0	0	0	5	55	4	0	0	0	20	63	5	0	0	0	25
HB (Brandon) Brown	7	1	0	0	0	5	0	0	0	0	0	0	7	1	0	0	0	5
CT (Cullen) Collopy	2	1	0	0	0	5	0	0	0	0	0	0	2	1	0	0	0	5
CP (Christiaan) de Bruin	7	0	0	0	0	0	3	0	0	0	0	0	10	0	0	0	0	0
P-S (Pieter-Steyn) de Wet	5	0	6	4	1	27	8	0	13	3	0	35	13	0	19	7	1	62
SJP (Schalk) Ferreira	21	1	0	0	0	5	31	1	0	0	0	5	52	2	0	0	0	10
SR (Sebastian) Ferreira	7	0	0	0	0	0	0	0	0	0	0	0	7	0	0	0	0	0
J (Jacques) Fick	2	0	0	0	0	0	0	0	0	0	0	0	2	0	0	0	0	0
J (Justin) Forwood	6	0	0	0	0	0	0	0	0	0	0	0	6	0	0	0	0	0
MG (Tazz) Fuzani	5	0	0	0	0	0	3	0	0	0	0	0	8	0	0	0	0	0
L (Lungelo) Gosa	7	0	3	1	0	9	0	0	0	0	0	0	7	0	3	1	0	9
JC (JC) Greyling	4	1	0	0	0	5	0	0	0	0	0	0	4	1	0	0	0	5
H (Dirk) Grobbelaar	2	0	0	0	0	0	3	0	0	0	0	0	5	0	0	0	0	0
JF (Hannes) Huisamen	2	0	0	0	0	0	0	0	0	0	0	0	2	0	0	0	0	0
AM (Alcino) Izaacs	4	2	0	0	0	10	0	0	0	0	0	0	4	2	0	0	0	10
VT (Vincent) Jobo	6	1	0	0	0	5	0	0	0	0	0	0	6	1	0	0	0	5
BW (Berton) Klaasen	7	2	0	0	0	10	7	0	0	0	0	0	14	2	0	0	0	10
JJ (Kobus) Marais	4	0	3	5	0	21	0	0	0	0	0	0	4	0	3	5	0	21
S (Sampie) Mastriet	7	1	0	0	0	5	24	6	0	0	0	30	31	7	0	0	0	35
G (Ganfried) May	3	0	0	0	0	0	0	0	0	0	0	0	3	0	0	0	0	0
SNP (Sipho) Msutwana	1	0	0	0	0	0	0	0	0	0	0	0	1	0	0	0	0	0
ML (Minenthie) Mthethwa	3	0	0	0	0	0	0	0	0	0	0	0	3	0	0	0	0	0
WM (Waylon) Murray	5	0	0	0	0	0	78	23	0	0	0	115	83	23	0	0	0	115
CR (Caylib) Oosthuizen	1	0	0	0	0	0	15	0	0	0	0	0	16	0	0	0	0	0
JE (Ettienne) Oosthuizen	7	0	0	0	0	0	0	0	0	0	0	0	7	0	0	0	0	0
DJ (Dylan) Pieterse	5	0	0	0	0	0	0	0	0	0	0	0	5	0	0	0	0	0
BJ (Barend) Potgieter	6	0	0	0	0	0	0	0	0	0	0	0	6	0	0	0	0	0
RD (Ricky) Schroeder	7	1	0	0	0	5	16	0	0	0	0	0	23	1	0	0	0	5
MG (Vukile) Sofisa	7	0	0	0	0	0	0	0	0	0	0	0	7	0	0	0	0	0
SS (Siviwe) Soyizwapi	23	5	0	0	0	25	0	0	0	0	0	0	23	5	0	0	0	25
PF (Pieter) Stemmet	4	0	0	0	0	0	9	1	0	0	0	5	13	1	0	0	0	5
JA (Johan) Tromp	6	3	0	0	0	15	0	0	0	0	0	0	6	3	0	0	0	15
L-K (Luke) van der Smit	6	0	0	0	0	0	0	0	0	0	0	0	6	0	0	0	0	0
V (Vian) van der Watt	5	0	0	0	0	0	6	0	0	0	0	0	11	0	0	0	0	0
W (Warrick) Venter	2	0	0	0	0	0	0	0	0	0	0	0	2	0	0	0	0	0
ME (Mike) Willemse	4	1	0	0	0	5	5	0	0	0	0	0	9	1	0	0	0	5
37 PLAYERS	211	21	12	10	1	162	263	35	13	3	0	210	474	56	25	13	1	372

FIRST-CLASS APPEARANCES FOR EP KINGS IN 2016 – ALL MATCHES

PLAYER	CURRIE CUP QUALIFIER						CURRIE CUP						2016 TOTAL						CAREER MATCHES					
	A	T	C	P	DG	Pts	A	T	C	P	DG	Pts	A	T	C	P	DG	Pts	A	T	C	P	DG	Pts
LE (Louis) Albertse	9	0	0	0	0	0	0	0	0	0	0	0	9	0	0	0	0	0	9	0	0	0	0	0
DA (David) Antonites	0	0	0	0	0	0	3	0	0	0	0	0	3	0	0	0	0	0	3	0	0	0	0	0
L (Lusanda) Badiyana	9	2	0	0	0	10	0	0	0	0	0	0	9	2	0	0	0	10	9	2	0	0	0	10
T (Tango) Balekile	3	0	0	0	0	0	0	0	0	0	0	0	3	0	0	0	0	0	3	0	0	0	0	0
MJ (Martin) Bezuidenhout	3	0	0	0	0	0	8	1	0	0	0	5	11	1	0	0	0	5	11	1	0	0	0	5
SN (Simon) Bolze	7	1	9	1	0	26	0	0	0	0	0	0	7	1	9	1	0	26	7	1	9	1	0	26
MM (Michael) Brink	7	0	4	2	0	14	0	0	0	0	0	0	7	0	4	2	0	14	7	0	4	2	0	14
HB (Brandon) Brown	1	0	0	0	0	0	7	1	0	0	0	5	8	1	0	0	0	5	8	1	0	0	0	5
DA (Davron) Cameron	3	0	0	0	0	0	0	0	0	0	0	0	3	0	0	0	0	0	3	0	0	0	0	0
W (Wihan) Coetzer	1	0	0	0	0	0	0	0	0	0	0	0	1	0	0	0	0	0	1	0	0	0	0	0
CT (Cullen) Collopy	0	0	0	0	0	0	2	1	0	0	0	5	2	1	0	0	0	5	2	1	0	0	0	5
CP (Christiaan) de Bruin	0	0	0	0	0	0	7	0	0	0	0	0	7	0	0	0	0	0	7	0	0	0	0	0
P-S (Pieter-Steyn) de Wet	0	0	0	0	0	0	5	0	6	4	1	27	5	0	6	4	1	27	5	0	6	4	1	27
S (Stephan) Deyzel	2	0	0	0	0	0	0	0	0	0	0	0	2	0	0	0	0	0	2	0	0	0	0	0
PJS (JP) du Plessis	5	0	0	0	0	0	0	0	0	0	0	0	5	0	0	0	0	0	15	1	0	0	0	5
I-J (Ivan-John) du Preez	2	0	0	0	0	0	0	0	0	0	0	0	2	0	0	0	0	0	7	2	0	0	0	10
P (Philip) du Preez	6	0	0	0	0	0	0	0	0	0	0	0	6	0	0	0	0	0	6	0	0	0	0	0
JJ (Jacques) Engelbrecht	4	0	0	0	0	0	0	0	0	0	0	0	4	0	0	0	0	0	35	5	0	0	0	25
RE (Riaan) Esterhuizen	4	0	0	0	0	0	0	0	0	0	0	0	4	0	0	0	0	0	4	0	0	0	0	0
CSK (Chuma) Faas	4	0	0	0	0	0	0	0	0	0	0	0	4	0	0	0	0	0	4	0	0	0	0	0
SJP (Schalk) Ferreira	0	0	0	0	0	0	1	0	0	0	0	0	1	0	0	0	0	0	22	1	0	0	0	5
SR (Sebastian) Ferreira	0	0	0	0	0	0	7	0	0	0	0	0	7	0	0	0	0	0	7	0	0	0	0	0
J (Jacques) Fick	0	0	0	0	0	0	2	0	0	0	0	0	2	0	0	0	0	0	2	0	0	0	0	0
J (Justin) Forwood	0	0	0	0	0	0	6	0	0	0	0	0	6	0	0	0	0	0	6	0	0	0	0	0
MG (Tazz) Fuzani	11	1	0	0	0	5	4	0	0	0	0	0	15	1	0	0	0	5	21	1	0	0	0	5
L (Lungelo) Gosa	0	0	0	0	0	0	7	0	3	1	0	9	7	0	3	1	0	9	7	0	3	2	0	9
W (Wynand) Grassmann	2	0	0	0	0	0	0	0	0	0	0	0	2	0	0	0	0	0	2	0	0	0	0	0
JC (JC) Greyling	0	0	0	0	0	0	4	1	0	0	0	5	4	1	0	0	0	5	4	1	0	0	0	5
H (Dirk) Grobbelaar	0	0	0	0	0	0	2	0	0	0	0	0	2	0	0	0	0	0	2	0	0	0	0	0
LC (Liam) Hendricks	8	1	0	0	0	5	0	0	0	0	0	0	8	1	0	0	0	5	8	1	0	0	0	5
CN (Cornéll) Hess	11	0	0	0	0	0	0	0	0	0	0	0	11	0	0	0	0	0	23	0	0	0	0	0
JW (Justin) Hollis	1	0	0	0	0	0	0	0	0	0	0	0	1	0	0	0	0	0	1	0	0	0	0	0
G (Gerrit) Huisamen	4	0	0	0	0	0	0	0	0	0	0	0	4	0	0	0	0	0	4	0	0	0	0	0
JF (Hannes) Huisamen	0	0	0	0	0	0	2	0	0	0	0	0	2	0	0	0	0	0	2	0	0	0	0	0
AM (Alcino) Izaacs	0	0	0	0	0	0	4	2	0	0	0	10	4	2	0	0	0	10	4	2	0	0	0	10
GAS (Gregory) Jackson	2	1	0	0	0	5	0	0	0	0	0	0	2	1	0	0	0	5	2	1	0	0	0	5
JP (JP) Jamieson	11	1	0	0	0	5	0	0	0	0	0	0	11	1	0	0	0	5	11	1	0	0	0	5
A (Andile) Jho	1	1	0	0	0	5	0	0	0	0	0	0	1	1	0	0	0	5	11	1	0	0	0	5
S (Somila) Jho	13	5	0	0	0	25	0	0	0	0	0	0	13	5	0	0	0	25	13	5	0	0	0	25
VT (Vincent) Jobo	0	0	0	0	0	0	6	1	0	0	0	5	6	1	0	0	0	5	6	1	0	0	0	5
JP (JP) Jonck	9	2	0	0	0	10	0	0	0	0	0	0	9	2	0	0	0	10	9	2	0	0	0	10
BW (Berton) Klaasen	0	0	0	0	0	0	7	2	0	0	0	10	7	2	0	0	0	10	7	2	0	0	0	10
J (Jordan) Koekemoer	3	0	0	0	0	0	0	0	0	0	0	0	3	0	0	0	0	0	3	0	0	0	0	0
RJ (Robert) Lyons	4	0	0	0	0	0	0	0	0	0	0	0	4	0	0	0	0	0	4	0	0	0	0	0
S (Sintu) Manjezi	11	0	0	0	0	0	0	0	0	0	0	0	11	0	0	0	0	0	11	0	0	0	0	0
JJ (Kobus) Marais	0	0	0	0	0	0	4	0	3	5	0	21	4	0	3	5	0	21	4	0	3	5	0	21

FIRST-CLASS APPEARANCES FOR EP KINGS IN 2016 – ALL MATCHES

PLAYER	CURRIE CUP QUALIFIER						CURRIE CUP						2016 TOTAL						CAREER MATCHES					
	A	T	C	P	DG	Pts	A	T	C	P	DG	Pts	A	T	C	P	DG	Pts	A	T	C	P	DG	Pts
S (Sampie) Mastriet	0	0	0	0	0	0	7	1	0	0	0	5	7	1	0	0	0	5	7	1	0	0	0	5
GF (Garrick) Mattheus	8	2	10	12	0	66	0	0	0	0	0	0	8	2	10	12	0	66	8	2	10	12	0	66
G (Ganfried) May	0	0	0	0	0	0	3	0	0	0	0	0	3	0	0	0	0	0	3	0	0	0	0	0
A (Athenkosi) Mayinje	10	2	2	0	0	14	0	0	0	0	0	0	10	2	2	0	0	14	10	2	2	0	0	14
MJN (Jixie) Molapo	3	0	0	0	0	0	0	0	0	0	0	0	3	0	0	0	0	0	3	0	0	0	0	0
SNP (Siphu) Msutwana	12	1	0	0	0	5	1	0	0	0	0	0	13	1	0	0	0	5	19	1	0	0	0	5
ML (Minenthie) Mthethwa	0	0	0	0	0	0	3	0	0	0	0	0	3	0	0	0	0	0	3	0	0	0	0	0
DG (David) Murray	8	1	0	0	0	5	0	0	0	0	0	0	8	1	0	0	0	5	8	1	0	0	0	5
WM (Waylon) Murray	0	0	0	0	0	0	5	0	0	0	0	0	5	0	0	0	0	0	6	0	0	0	0	0
R (Rouche) Nel	5	0	0	0	0	0	0	0	0	0	0	0	5	0	0	0	0	0	5	0	0	0	0	0
S (Sibusiso) Ngcokowane	6	0	0	0	0	0	0	0	0	0	0	0	6	0	0	0	0	0	6	0	0	0	0	0
SF (Stephanus) Nieuwoudt	9	1	0	0	0	5	0	0	0	0	0	0	9	1	0	0	0	5	9	1	0	0	0	5
CR (Caylib) Oosthuizen	0	0	0	0	0	0	1	0	0	0	0	0	1	0	0	0	0	0	1	0	0	0	0	0
NJ (Nicolaas) Oosthuizen	3	0	0	0	0	0	0	0	0	0	0	0	3	0	0	0	0	0	3	0	0	0	0	0
JE (Ettienne) Oosthuizen	0	0	0	0	0	0	7	0	0	0	0	0	7	0	0	0	0	0	7	0	0	0	0	0
YO (Yaw) Penxe	3	1	0	0	0	5	0	0	0	0	0	0	3	1	0	0	0	5	3	1	0	0	0	5
M (Mabhutana) Peter	3	0	0	0	0	0	0	0	0	0	0	0	3	0	0	0	0	0	3	0	0	0	0	0
DJ (Dylan) Pieterse	0	0	0	0	0	0	5	0	0	0	0	0	5	0	0	0	0	0	5	0	0	0	0	0
JS (Junior) Pokomela	3	0	0	0	0	0	0	0	0	0	0	0	3	0	0	0	0	0	3	0	0	0	0	0
BJ (Barend) Potgieter	0	0	0	0	0	0	6	0	0	0	0	0	6	0	0	0	0	0	6	0	0	0	0	0
JC (Jason) Reinecke	2	0	0	0	0	0	0	0	0	0	0	0	2	0	0	0	0	0	2	0	0	0	0	0
RD (Ricky) Schroeder	0	0	0	0	0	0	7	1	0	0	0	5	7	1	0	0	0	5	7	1	0	0	0	5
MG (Vukile) Sofisa	9	0	0	0	0	0	7	0	0	0	0	0	16	0	0	0	0	0	21	0	0	0	0	0
SS (Siviwe) Soyizwapi	0	0	0	0	0	0	7	1	0	0	0	5	7	1	0	0	0	5	35	9	0	0	0	45
PF (Pieter) Stemmet	0	0	0	0	0	0	3	0	0	0	0	0	3	0	0	0	0	0	8	1	0	0	0	5
JA (Johan) Tromp	0	0	0	0	0	0	6	3	0	0	0	15	6	3	0	0	0	15	6	3	0	0	0	15
FJ (Franswa) Ueckermann	8	2	0	0	0	10	0	0	0	0	0	0	8	2	0	0	0	10	8	2	0	0	0	10
L-K (Luke) van der Smit	0	0	0	0	0	0	6	0	0	0	0	0	6	0	0	0	0	0	6	0	0	0	0	0
V (Vian) van der Watt	0	0	0	0	0	0	5	0	0	0	0	0	5	0	0	0	0	0	5	0	0	0	0	0
J (Jaco) van Tonder	2	0	0	0	0	0	0	0	0	0	0	0	2	0	0	0	0	0	2	0	0	0	0	0
RC (Roche) van Zyl	2	0	0	0	0	0	0	0	0	0	0	0	2	0	0	0	0	0	2	0	0	0	0	0
W (Warrick) Venter	10	0	0	0	0	0	2	0	0	0	0	0	12	0	0	0	0	0	12	0	0	0	0	0
KA (Keanu) Vers	4	1	0	0	0	5	0	0	0	0	0	0	4	1	0	0	0	5	4	1	0	0	0	5
JC (Jeremy) Ward	4	1	0	0	0	5	0	0	0	0	0	0	4	1	0	0	0	5	4	1	0	0	0	5
ME (Mike) Willemse	0	0	0	0	0	0	4	1	0	0	0	5	4	1	0	0	0	5	4	1	0	0	0	5
CK (Courtney) Winnaar	5	4	1	2	0	28	0	0	0	0	0	0	5	4	1	2	0	28	5	4	1	2	0	28
S (Stephan) Zaayman	7	0	0	0	0	0	0	0	0	0	0	0	7	0	0	0	0	0	12	0	0	0	0	0
LS (Lindelwe) Zungu	13	1	0	0	0	5	0	0	0	0	0	0	13	1	0	0	0	5	13	1	0	0	0	5

84 PLAYERS

Free State Rugby Union

Founded: 1895 (as Orange Free State) **Ground:** Free State Stadium
Capacity: 46 000 **Address:** Att Horak St, Bloemfontein, 9300
Postal address: PO Box 15, Bloemfontein, 9300
Telephone Number: 051-407 1700 **Website:** www.fscheetahs.co.za
Colours: White jersey with orange stripes, black shorts
Currie Cup Coach: Franco Smith **Captain:** Francois Venter
President: Lindsay Mould **Company CEO:** Harold Verster
Union CEO: Lindsay Mould

'96	'97	'98	'99	'00	'01
3rd	3rd	5th	3rd	4th	4th

'02	'03	'04	'05	'06	'07
2nd	5th	3rd	4th	1st	1st

'08	'09	'10	'11	'12	'13
3rd	4th	3rd	3rd	6th	3rd

'14	'15	'16
5th	5th	1st

Played	Won	Lost	Drawn	Points for	Points against	Tries for	Tries against
10	10	0	0	457	214	57	22

Date	Venue	Opponent	Result	Score	Referee	Scorers
Aug 06	Wellington	Boland	WON	44-16	R Boneparte	T: F Venter, Rhule, Petersen, S Venter, Small-Smith. C: Zeilinga (5). P: Zeilinga (3).
Aug 13	Bloemfontein	Blue Bulls	WON	43-20	L Legoete	T: Blommetjies, F Venter, Nche, Benjamin, Cassiem. Small-Smith. C: Zeilinga (4), N Marais. P: Zeilinga
Aug 19	Cape Town	WP	WON	32-25	C Joubert	T: Lee, Meyer. C: Zeilinga (2). P: Zeilinga (6).
Sep 03	Bloemfontein	EP Kings	WON	57-25	J van Heerden	T: Lee (2), Schoeman (2), C Marais (2), Nche, Botha, N Marais. C: N Marais (2), Zeilinga. P: Zeilinga (2).
Sep 10	Durban	Sharks	WON	38-30	R Rasivhenge	T: Van der Spuy, S Venter, Meyer, Cassiem, Penalty try. C: Zeilinga (5). P: Zeilinga.
Sep 15	Bloemfontein	Golden Lions	WON	37-29	J van Heerden	T: Rhule, Hugo, Benjamin, S Venter, Meyer. C: N Marais (3). P: N Marais.
Sep 23	Nelspruit	Pumas	WON	52-10	L Legoete	T: Benjamin (3), Schoeman (2), Cassiem, F Venter, Huggett. C: N Marais (5), Zeilinga.
Oct 01	Bloemfontein	Griquas	WON	63-26	C Jadezweni	T: S Venter (2), H Venter, Lee, Rhule, Van Jaarsveld, Cassiem, N Marais, Pen try. C: N Marais (6), Zeilinga (3)
Semi Final						
Oct 15	Bloemfontein	Golden Lions	WON	55-17	R Rasivhenge	T: Petersen (3), Blommetjies, Jordaan, Benjamin. C: N Marais (3), Zeilinga (2). P: Marais (5).
Final						
Oct 22	Bloemfontein	Blue Bulls	WON	36-16	J Peyper	T: Blommetjies, Petersen. C: Zeilinga. P: N Marais (7), Zeilinga.

APPEARANCES & POINTS

PLAYER	Boland	Blue Bulls	WP	EP Kings	Sharks	Golden Lions	Pumas	Griquas	Golden Lions	Blue Bulls	Apps	T	C	P	DG	Pts
Clayton Blommetjies	15	15	15	15	15	15	15	15	15	15	10	3	–	–	–	15
Sergeal Petersen	14	–	–	–	–	14	–	14	14		4	5	–	–	–	25
Francois Venter	13c	13c	–	–	–	13c	13c	13c	13c		6	3	–	–	–	15
William Small-Smith	12	12	12	12	–	12	13R	12R	–	–	7	2	–	–	–	10
Raymond Rhule	11	11	11	11	11	11	–	11	11	11	9	3	–	–	–	15
Fred Zeilinga	10	10	10	10	10	x	10R	10R	10R	10R	9	–	24	14	–	90
Shaun Venter	9	9R	9R	9R	9R	9	9	9	9	9	10	5	–	–	–	25
Niell Jordaan	8	8	8	8	8R	8	8	8	8	8	10	1	–	–	–	5
Uzair Cassiem	7	7	7	7	7	7	7	7	7	7	10	4	–	–	–	20
Paul Schoeman	6	6	6	6	6	6	6	–	6	6	9	4	–	–	–	20
Reniel Hugo	5	5	5	5	5	5	5	5	5	5	10	1	–	–	–	5
Carl Wegner	4	4	4	4	–	–	–	–	–	–	4	–	–	–	–	0
Tom Botha	3	3	3R	3	3	3	–	–	–	–	6	1	–	–	–	5
Joseph Dweba	2	–	–	–	–	–	–	–	–	–	1	–	–	–	–	0
Ox Nche	1	1	1R	1	1	1	1R	1	1	1R	10	2	–	–	–	10
Jacques du Toit	2R	2R	2	2R	2R	1R	2	2	2R	2R	10	–	–	–	–	0
Charles Marais	3R	3R	1	3R	3R	3R	1	3R	1R	1	10	2	–	–	–	10
Justin Basson	4R	4R	x	5R	4	4	4	4	4	4	9	–	–	–	–	0
Henco Venter	8R	8R	8R	8R	8	–	–	6	8R	8R	8	1	–	–	–	5
Tian Meyer	9R	9	9c	9c	9c	9R	–	–	9R	9R	8	3	–	–	–	15
Sias Ebersohn	15R	–	–	–	–	–	–	–	–	–	1	–	–	–	–	0
Ryno Benjamin	14R	14	14	14	14	14	11	14	12R	12R	10	6	–	–	–	30
Torsten van Jaarsveld	–	2	2R	2	2	2	–	5R	2	2	8	1	–	–	–	5
Maphutha Dolo	–	13R	–	–	–	–	–	–	–	–	1	–	–	–	–	0
Niel Marais	–	10R	x	10R	12R	10	10	10	10	10	8	2	20	14	–	92
Nico Lee	–	–	13	13	13	13	12	12	12	12	8	4	–	–	–	20
Johan Coetzee	–	–	3	–	–	–	3	3	3	3	5	–	–	–	–	0
Michael van der Spuy	–	–	–	12R	12	12R	–	–	–	–	3	1	–	–	–	5
Armandt Koster	–	–	–	4R	4R	5R	–	4R	4R		5	–	–	–	–	0
Tienie Burger	–	–	–	x	7R	6R	7R	–	–		3	–	–	–	–	0
Elandré Huggett	–	–	–	–	–	7R	–	–	–		1	1	–	–	–	5
Zee Mkhabela	–	–	–	–	–	9R	9R	–	–		2	–	–	–	–	0
Willem Serfontein	–	–	–	–	–	–	4R	–	–		1	–	–	–	–	0
Conraad van Vuuren	–	–	–	–	–	–	–	3R	3R		2	–	–	–	–	0
Penalty tries	–	–	–	–	–	–	–	–	–	–	–	2	–	–	–	10
34 PLAYERS											218	57	44	28	0	457

www.sarugby.co.za

CURRIE CUP SQUAD – CAREER CURRIE CUP APPEARANCES

PLAYER	FREE STATE						OTHER UNIONS						TOTAL					
	A	T	C	P	DG	Pts	A	T	C	P	DG	Pts	A	T	C	P	DG	Pts
JJ (Justin) Basson	9	–	–	–	–	0	–	–	–	–	–	0	9	–	–	–	–	0
RS (Rayno) Benjamin	47	17	–	–	–	85	60	46	–	–	–	230	108	63	–	–	–	315
C (Clayton) Blommetjies	28	7	1	–	–	37	14	1	–	–	–	5	42	8	1	–	–	42
T (Tom) Botha	6	1	–	–	–	5	14	–	–	–	–	0	20	1	–	–	–	5
MA (Tienie) Burger	3	–	–	–	–	0	–	–	–	–	–	0	16	–	–	–	–	0
JV (Johan) Coetzee	5	–	–	–	–	0	–	–	–	–	–	0	5	–	–	–	–	0
U (Uzair) Cassiem	10	4	–	–	–	20	35	3	–	–	–	15	45	7	–	–	–	35
MS (Maphutha) Dolo	3	–	–	–	–	0	–	–	–	–	–	0	3	–	–	–	–	0
OJJ (Jacques) du Toit	19	–	–	–	–	0	–	–	–	–	–	0	19	–	–	–	–	0
J (Joseph) Dweba	1	–	–	–	–	0	–	–	–	–	–	0	1	–	–	–	–	0
JM (Sias) Ebersohn	11	2	7	4	–	36	–	–	–	–	–	0	51	5	46	22	3	192
E (Elandré) Huggett	7	2	–	–	–	10	15	2	–	–	–	10	22	4	–	–	–	20
DP (Reniel) Hugo	21	–	–	–	–	0	–	–	–	–	–	0	21	–	–	–	–	0
DN (Niell) Jordaan	19	2	–	–	–	10	–	–	–	–	–	0	19	2	–	–	–	10
A (Armandt) Koster	21	–	–	–	–	0	14	3	–	–	–	15	35	3	–	–	–	15
NJ (Nico) Lee	8	4	–	–	–	20	–	–	–	–	–	0	8	4	–	–	–	20
CM (Charles) Marais	11	2	–	–	–	10	4	–	–	–	–	0	15	2	–	–	–	10
DR (Niel) Marais	12	3	24	17	–	114	1	–	–	–	–	0	13	3	24	17	–	114
TC (Tian) Meyer	8	3	–	–	–	15	53	11	–	–	–	55	61	14	–	–	–	70
MC (Mthokozisi) Mkhabela	5	1	–	–	–	5	–	–	–	–	–	0	5	1	–	–	–	5
R (Ox) Nche	10	2	–	–	–	10	–	–	–	–	–	0	10	2	–	–	–	10
SP (Sergeal) Petersen	13	10	–	–	–	50	3	–	–	–	–	0	16	10	–	–	–	50
RK (Raymond) Rhule	55	22	–	–	–	110	–	–	–	–	–	0	55	22	–	–	–	110
PA (Paul) Schoeman	9	4	–	–	–	20	16	7	–	–	–	35	24	11	–	–	–	55
WJ (Willem) Serfontein	4	–	–	–	–	0	37	1	–	–	–	5	41	1	–	–	–	5
WT (William) Small-Smith	7	2	–	–	–	10	15	3	–	–	–	15	22	5	–	–	–	25
MG (Michael) van der Spuy	3	1	–	–	–	5	13	2	–	–	–	10	16	3	–	–	–	15
TG (Torsten) van Jaarsveld	19	1	–	–	–	5	38	4	–	–	–	20	57	5	–	–	–	25
JC (Conraad) van Vuuren	2	–	–	–	–	0	–	–	–	–	–	0	2	–	–	–	–	0
HP (Henco) Venter	25	1	–	–	–	5	–	–	–	–	–	0	25	1	–	–	–	5
JF (Francois) Venter	20	5	–	–	–	25	31	9	–	–	–	45	51	14	–	–	–	70
SH (Shaun) Venter	29	9	–	–	–	45	61	16	–	–	–	80	90	25	–	–	–	125
CA (Carl) Wegner	12	–	–	–	–	0	–	–	–	–	–	0	12	–	–	–	–	0
FJ (Fred) Zeilinga	17	1	40	22	–	151	18	2	19	41	3	180	35	3	59	63	–	322

34 PLAYERS

FIRST-CLASS APPEARANCES FOR FREE STATE IN 2016 – ALL MATCHES

PLAYER	2016 CURRIE CUP						CAREER MATCHES					
	A	T	C	P	DG	Pts	A	T	C	P	DG	Pts
JJ (Justin) Basson	9	–	–	–	–	0	9	–	–	–	–	0
RS (Rayno) Benjamin	10	6	–	–	–	30	47	17	–	–	–	85
C (Clayton) Blommetjies	10	3	–	–	–	15	28	7	1	–	–	37
T (Tom) Botha	6	1	–	–	–	5	6	1	–	–	–	5
MA (Tienie) Burger	3	–	–	–	–	0	16	2	–	–	–	10
U (Uzair) Cassiem	10	4	–	–	–	20	10	4	–	–	–	20
JV (Johan) Coetzee	5	–	–	–	–	0	5	–	–	–	–	0
MS (Maphutha) Dolo	1	–	–	–	–	0	3	–	–	–	–	0
OJJ (Jacques) du Toit	10	–	–	–	–	0	19	–	–	–	–	0
J (Joseph) Dweba	1	–	–	–	–	0	1	–	–	–	–	0
JM (Sias) Ebersohn	1	–	–	–	–	0	67	6	56	26	5	235
E (Elandré) Huggett	1	1	–	–	–	5	8	1	–	–	–	5
DP (Reniel) Hugo	10	1	–	–	–	5	21	1	–	–	–	5
DN (Niell) Jordaan	10	1	–	–	–	5	19	2	–	–	–	10
A (Armandt) Koster	5	–	–	–	–	0	13	–	–	–	–	0
NJ (Nico) Lee	8	4	–	–	–	20	8	4	–	–	–	20
CM (Charles) Marais	10	2	–	–	–	10	17	2	–	–	–	10
DR (Niel) Marais	8	2	20	14	–	92	12	3	24	17	–	114
TC (Tian) Meyer	8	3	–	–	–	15	8	3	–	–	–	15
MC (Mthokozisi) Mkhabela	2	–	–	–	–	0	5	1	–	–	–	5
R (Ox) Nche	10	2	–	–	–	10	10	2	–	–	–	10
SP (Sergeal) Petersen	4	5	–	–	–	25	13	11	–	–	–	55
RK (Raymond) Rhule	9	3	–	–	–	15	49	22	–	–	–	110
PA (Paul) Schoeman	9	4	–	–	–	20	9	4	–	–	–	20
WJ (Willem) Serfontein	1	–	–	–	–	0	4	–	–	–	–	0
WT (William) Small-Smith	7	2	–	–	–	10	7	2	–	–	–	10
MG (Michael) van der Spuy	3	1	–	–	–	5	3	1	–	–	–	5
TG (Torsten) van Jaarsveld	8	1	–	–	–	5	19	1	–	–	–	5
JC (Conraad) van Vuuren	2	–	–	–	–	0	2	–	–	–	–	0
HP (Henco) Venter	8	1	–	–	–	5	25	1	–	–	–	5
JF (Francois) Venter	6	3	–	–	–	15	26	8	–	–	–	40
SH (Shaun) Venter	10	5	–	–	–	25	29	9	–	–	–	45
CA (Carl) Wegner	4	–	–	–	–	0	12	–	–	–	–	0
Fred Zeilinga	9	–	24	14	–	90	17	1	40	22	–	151

34 PLAYERS

* Free State's Currie Cup Qualifying matches were also first-class but they played as the 'Free State XV', which the FSRU considers a completely different team. This table shows first-class matches played by the 'Free State Cheetahs' only. See Currie Cup Qualifying section for the Free State XV info.

Uzair Cassiem – from Cheetahs hero to Tes Springbok.

LIONS

Golden Lions Rugby Union

Founded: 1889 **Ground:** Emirates Airline Park (previously Ellis Park) **Capacity:** 60 000 **Address:** c/o Staib and Curry Streets, Doornfontein, 2028 **Postal address:** PO Box 15724, Doornfontein, 2028 **Telephone Number:** 011-402 2960
Website: www.lionsrugby.co.za **Colours:** White and red trim jersey, black shorts and black socks
Currie Cup Coach: Johan Ackermann & Swys de Bruin
Captains: Ross Cronjé, Howard Mnisi & Kwagga Smith
President: Kevin de Klerk **Company CEO:** Rudolf Straeuli

'96	'97	'98	'99	'00	'01
4th	4th	8th	1st	3rd	3rd

'02	'03	'04	'05	'06	'07
3rd	4th	4th	2nd	5th	3rd

'08	'09	'10	'11	'12	'13
4th	6th	3rd	1st	3rd	4th

'14	'15	'16
2nd	1st	4th

Played	Won	Lost	Drawn	Points for	Points against	Tries for	Tries against
9	5	4	0	372	246	52	29

Date	Venue	Opponent	Result	Score	Referee	Scorers
Aug 13	Johannesburg	Pumas	WON	68-26	S Berry	T: Volmink (2), Mahuza, K Marx, Mnisi, Van der Walt, Brink, Erasmus, Van der Merwe, Boshoff. C: Van der Walt (6), Boshoff (3).
Aug 20	Kimberley	Griquas	LOST	24-30	Q Immelman	T: Mnisi, Brink, Van der Merwe, Fourie. C: Boshoff, Van der Walt.
Aug 26	Johannesburg	Cavaliers	WON	60-12	R Rasivhenge	T: Gavor (2), Nel, Mnisi, Volmink, Smit, Sekekete, D Smith, Bell. C: Boshoff (6). P: Boshoff.
Sept 02	Pretoria	Blue Bulls	LOST	17-31	C Joubert	T: K Smith, Mnisi. C: Boshoff (2). P: Boshoff.
Sept 09	Johannesburg	WP	WON	58-32	J Peyper	T: K Smith (2), A Coetzee, Nel, Janse van Rensburg, Volmink, Du Preez, R Coetzee. C: Van der Walt (6). P: Van der Walt (2).
Sept 15	Bloemfontein	Cheetahs	LOST	29-37	J van Heerden	T: Janse van Rensburg, R Coetzee. C: Van der Walt (2). P: Van der Walt (4), A Coetzee.
Sept 24	Port Elizabeth	EP Kings	WON	71-07	C Jadezweni	T: K Smith (3), Nel (2), Mnisi (2), Mahuza, K Marx, Volmink, Ackermann. C: Van der Walt (5), A Coetzee (3).
Sept 30	Johannesburg	Sharks	WON	28-16	C Joubert	T: Mnisi, K Smith, Mahuza. C: Van der Walt, A Coetzee. P: A Coetzee (2), Van der Walt.

SEMI-FINAL

Date	Venue	Opponent	Result	Score	Referee	Scorers
Oct 15	Bloemfontein	Cheetahs	LOST	17-55	R Rasivhenge	T: Mahuza (2), Lerm. C: A Coetzee.

APPEARANCES & POINTS

PLAYER	WP	Blue Bulls	Free State	Blue Bulls	WP	Pumas	Free State	EP Kings	Sharks	Golden Lions	Apps	T	C	P	DG	Pts
Sylvian Mahuza	15	15	–	–	–	–	15	13R	11R		5	5	–	–	–	25
Koch Marx	14	–	12R	–	–	–	14	–	14		4	2	–	–	–	10
Stokkies Hanekom	13	13	–	–	–	–	–	14R			3	–	–	–	–	0
Howard Mnisi	12	12c	12c	12	13R	12R	12	13	–		8	7	–	–	–	35
Anthony Volmink	11	11	11	11	11	11	11	11	11		9	5	–	–	–	25
Jaco van der Walt	10	10	–	10R	10	10	10	10	10		8	1	21	7	–	68
Ross Cronjé	9c	9	9R	9c	9c	9c	9R	9	9		9	–	–	–	–	0
Ruan Ackermann	8	8	4	8	7	7R	7	4	4		9	1	–	–	–	5
Cyle Brink	7	7	6R	7	7	7	8R	7	7		9	2	–	–	–	10
Steph de Wit	6	6	6	–	–	–	–	7R	–		4	–	–	–	–	0
Lourens Erasmus	5	5	–	5	5	5	–	–	7R		5	1	–	–	–	5
Martin Muller	4	–	5	4	–	5R	–	–	–		4	–	–	–	–	0
Jacques van Rooyen	3	3	–	3	3R	–	–	1R	1		6	–	–	–	–	0
Akker van der Merwe	2	2	–	2R	2R	2R	–	–	2R		6	2	–	–	–	10
Corné Fourie	1	1R	1	1R	–	–	–	–	18R		5	1	–	–	–	5
Ramone Samuels	2R	2R	2	–	–	–	–	–	–		3	–	–	–	–	0
Justin Ackerman	1R	–									1	–	–	–	–	0
MB Lusaseni	4R	4									2	–	–	–	–	0
Victor Sekekete	7R	–	7	7R	–	–	–	–			3	1	–	–	–	5
Dillon Smit	9R	9R	9	9R	–	–	9	11R	–		6	1	–	–	–	5
Marnitz Boshoff	10R	15R	10	10	–	–	–	–			4	1	12	2	–	35
Jacques Nel	13R	13R	13	14R	13	13	13	14	13		9	4	–	–	–	20
Courtnall Skosan	–	14	–	14	–	–	–	–			2	–	–	–	–	0
Dylan Smith	–	1	3R	1	1	1	1	–			7	1	–	–	–	5
Bobby de Wee	–	7R	5R	–	–	–	5	5	5		5	–	–	–	–	0
Ruaan Lerm	–	4R	8	–	8R	8R	8	8	8R		7	1	–	–	–	5
Andries Coetzee	–	–	15	15	15	15	10R	15	15		7	1	5	3	–	24
Selom Gavor	–	14	14	14	–	–	–				3	2	–	–	–	10
Pieter Scholtz	–	–	3	–	–	3R	–	–			2	–	–	–	–	0
Robbie Coetzee	–	–	2R	2	2	2	2R	2	–		6	2	–	–	–	10
JW Bell	–	–	15R	–	–	–	–				1	1	–	–	–	5
Rohan Janse van Rensburg	–	–	–	13	12	12	12R	12	12		6	2	–	–	–	10
Kwagga Smith	–	–	–	6	6	6	6c	6c	6c		7	7	–	–	–	35
Fabian Booysen	–	–	–	4R	8	8	7R	8R	8		6	–	–	–	–	0
JP du Preez	–	–	–	–	4	4	4	5R	–		4	1	–	–	–	5
Ruan Dreyer	–	–	–	–	3	3	3R	3	3R		5	–	–	–	–	0
Andries Ferreira	–	–	–	–	5R	5	–	–			2	–	–	–	–	0
Ashlon Davids	–	–	–	–	22R	x	–	–			1	–	–	–	–	0
Julian Redelinghuys	–	–	–	–	–	3	–	3			2	–	–	–	–	0
Malcolm Marx	–	–	–	–	–	2	2R	2			3	–	–	–	–	0
Faf de Klerk	–	–	–	–	–	–	–	9R			1	–	–	–	–	0
41 PLAYERS											198	52	38	12	0	372

CURRIE CUP SQUAD – CAREER CURRIE CUP APPEARANCES

PLAYER	GOLDEN LIONS						OTHER UNIONS						TOTAL					
	A	T	C	P	DG	Pts	A	T	C	P	DG	Pts	A	T	C	P	DG	Pts
J (Justin) Ackerman	1	0	0	0	0	0	1	0	0	0	0	0	2	0	0	0	0	0
R (Ruan) Ackermann	9	1	0	0	0	5	0	0	0	0	0	0	9	1	0	0	0	5
JW (JW) Bell	1	1	0	0	0	5	42	13	0	0	0	65	43	14	0	0	0	70
ML (Marnitz) Boshoff	32	4	91	57	4	385	13	0	2	2	0	10	45	4	93	59	4	395
F (Fabian) Booysen	16	0	0	0	0	0	0	0	0	0	0	0	16	0	0	0	0	0
CJ (Cyle) Brink	9	2	0	0	0	10	0	0	0	0	0	0	9	2	0	0	0	10
A (Andries) Coetzee	40	8	6	3	0	61	0	0	0	0	0	0	40	8	6	3	0	61
RL (Robbie) Coetzee	34	4	0	0	0	20	3	0	0	0	0	0	37	4	0	0	0	20
R (Ross) Cronjé	45	4	0	0	0	20	14	0	0	0	0	0	59	4	0	0	0	20
A (Ashlon) Davids	2	0	0	0	0	0	0	0	0	0	0	0	2	0	0	0	0	0
F (Faf) de Klerk	1	0	0	0	0	0	38	2	0	0	0	10	39	2	0	0	0	10
AR (Bobby) de Wee	6	0	0	0	0	0	0	0	0	0	0	0	6	0	0	0	0	0
AS (Steph) de Wit	16	2	0	0	0	10	0	0	0	0	0	0	16	2	0	0	0	10
RM (Ruan) Dreyer	41	4	0	0	0	20	0	0	0	0	0	0	41	4	0	0	0	20
JP (JP) du Preez	4	1	0	0	0	5	0	0	0	0	0	0	4	1	0	0	0	5
L (Lourens) Erasmus	11	4	0	0	0	20	0	0	0	0	0	0	11	4	0	0	0	20
AS (Andries) Ferreira	2	0	0	0	0	0	4	1	0	0	0	5	6	1	0	0	0	5
C (Corné) Fourie	5	1	0	0	0	5	43	2	0	0	0	10	48	3	0	0	0	15
S (Selom) Gavor	4	2	0	0	0	10	0	0	0	0	0	0	4	2	0	0	0	10
NJ (Nico) Hanekom	24	9	0	0	0	45	0	0	0	0	0	0	24	9	0	0	0	45
R (Rohan) Janse van Rensburg	13	3	0	0	0	15	0	0	0	0	0	0	13	3	0	0	0	15
RS (Ruan) Lerm	11	1	0	0	0	5	8	1	0	0	0	5	19	2	0	0	0	10
L (MB) Lusaseni	16	0	0	0	0	0	29	2	0	0	0	10	45	2	0	0	0	10
S (Sylvian) Mahuza	5	5	0	0	0	25	19	16	0	0	0	80	24	21	0	0	0	105
K (Koch) Marx	4	2	0	0	0	10	0	0	0	0	0	0	4	2	0	0	0	10
MJ (Malcolm) Marx	15	1	0	0	0	5	0	0	0	0	0	0	15	1	0	0	0	5
XH (Howard) Mnisi	31	13	0	0	0	65	17	3	0	0	0	15	48	16	0	0	0	80
MD (Martin) Muller	20	1	0	0	0	5	24	1	0	0	0	5	44	2	0	0	0	10
J (Jacques) Nel	11	6	0	0	0	30	0	0	0	0	0	0	11	6	0	0	0	30
J (Julian) Redelinghuys	22	0	0	0	0	0	8	0	0	0	0	0	30	0	0	0	0	0
RC (Ramone) Samuels	3	0	0	0	0	0	0	0	0	0	0	0	3	0	0	0	0	0
PE (Pieter) Scholtz	3	0	0	0	0	0	0	0	0	0	0	0	3	0	0	0	0	0
VK (Victor) Sekekete	3	1	0	0	0	5	0	0	0	0	0	0	3	1	0	0	0	5
CD (Courtnall) Skosan	21	8	0	0	0	40	0	0	0	0	0	0	21	8	0	0	0	40
D (Dillon) Smit	6	1	0	0	0	5	17	8	0	0	0	40	23	9	0	0	0	45
AS (Kwagga) Smith	28	19	0	0	0	95	0	0	0	0	0	0	28	19	0	0	0	95
D (Dylan) Smith	10	1	0	0	0	5	0	0	0	0	0	0	10	1	0	0	0	5
AHP (Akker) van der Merwe	18	5	0	0	0	25	11	0	0	0	0	0	29	5	0	0	0	25
J (Jaco) van der Walt	29	3	35	12	1	124	0	0	0	0	0	0	29	3	35	12	1	124
J (Jacques) van Rooyen	39	3	0	0	0	15	0	0	0	0	0	0	39	3	0	0	0	15
AA (Anthony) Volmink	33	18	0	0	0	90	0	0	0	0	0	0	33	18	0	0	0	90

41 PLAYERS

FIRST-CLASS APPEARANCES FOR GOLDEN LIONS IN 2016 – ALL MATCHES

PLAYER	2016 CURRIE CUP						CAREER MATCHES					
	A	T	C	P	DG	Pts	A	T	C	P	DG	Pts
J (Justin) Ackerman	1	0	0	0	0	0	1	0	0	0	0	0
R (Ruan) Ackermann	9	1	0	0	0	5	9	1	0	0	0	5
JW Bell	1	1	0	0	0	5	1	1	0	0	0	5
FCF (Fabian) Booysen	6	0	0	0	0	0	16	0	0	0	0	0
ML (Marnitz) Boshoff	4	1	12	2	0	35	32	4	91	57	4	385
CJ (Cyle) Brink	9	2	0	0	0	10	9	2	0	0	0	10
A (Andries) Coetzee	7	1	5	3	0	24	40	8	6	3	0	61
RL (Robbie) Coetzee	6	2	0	0	0	10	34	4	0	0	0	20
R (Ross) Cronjé	9	0	0	0	0	0	45	4	0	0	0	20
A (Ashlon) Davids	1	0	0	0	0	0	2	0	0	0	0	0
F (Faf) de Klerk	1	0	0	0	0	0	1	0	0	0	0	0
AR (Bobby) de Wee	5	0	0	0	0	0	6	0	0	0	0	0
AS (Stephan) de Wit	4	0	0	0	0	0	16	2	0	0	0	10
RM (Ruan) Dreyer	5	0	0	0	0	0	41	4	0	0	0	20
JP (JP) du Preez	4	1	0	0	0	5	4	1	0	0	0	5
LJ (Lourens) Erasmus	5	1	0	0	0	5	11	4	0	0	0	20
AS (Andries) Ferreira	2	0	0	0	0	0	2	0	0	0	0	0
C (Corné) Fourie	5	1	0	0	0	5	5	1	0	0	0	5
S (Selom) Gavor	3	2	0	0	0	10	4	2	0	0	0	10
NJ (Nico) Hanekom	3	0	0	0	0	0	24	9	0	0	0	45
R (Rohan) Janse van Rensburg	6	2	0	0	0	10	13	3	0	0	0	15
RS (Ruaan) Lerm	7	1	0	0	0	5	11	1	0	0	0	5
L (MB) Lusaseni	2	0	0	0	0	0	16	0	0	0	0	0
S (Sylvian) Mahuza	5	5	0	0	0	25	5	5	0	0	0	25
K (Koch) Marx	4	2	0	0	0	10	4	2	0	0	0	10
MJ (Malcolm) Marx	3	0	0	0	0	0	15	1	0	0	0	5
XH (Howard) Mnisi	8	7	0	0	0	35	31	13	0	0	0	65
MD (Martin) Muller	4	0	0	0	0	0	20	1	0	0	0	5
J (Jacques) Nel	9	4	0	0	0	20	11	6	0	0	0	30
J (Julian) Redelinghuys	2	0	0	0	0	0	22	0	0	0	0	0
RC (Ramone) Samuels	3	0	0	0	0	0	3	0	0	0	0	0
PE (Pieter) Scholtz	2	0	0	0	0	0	3	0	0	0	0	0
VK (Victor) Sekekete	3	1	0	0	0	5	3	1	0	0	0	5
CD (Courtnall) Skosan	2	0	0	0	0	0	21	8	0	0	0	40
D (Dillon) Smit	6	1	0	0	0	5	6	1	0	0	0	5
AS (Kwagga) Smith	6	7	0	0	0	35	28	19	0	0	0	95
DT (Dylan) Smith	7	1	0	0	0	5	10	1	0	0	0	5
AHP (Akker) van der Merwe	6	2	0	0	0	10	18	5	0	0	0	25
J (Jaco) van der Walt	8	1	21	7	0	68	29	3	35	12	1	124
J (Jacques) van Rooyen	6	0	0	0	0	0	39	3	0	0	0	15
AA (Anthony) Volmink	9	5	0	0	0	25	33	18	0	0	0	90

41 PLAYERS

Golden Lions Currie Cup Qualifying matches were also first-class but they played as the 'Golden Lions XV', which the GLRU considers a completely different team. This table shows first-class matches played by the 'Golden Lions' only. See Currie Cup Qualifying section for the Golden Lions XV info.

Anthony Volmink.

Griqualand West Rugby Union

Founded: 1886 **Ground:** Griqua Park, Kimberley
Capacity: 11,000 **Address:** Jacobus Smit Avenue, New Park, Kimberley **Postal address:** PO Box 110825, Hadison Park, Kimberley 8306 **Telephone Number:** 053-832 8773
Website: www.griquasrugby.co.za **Colours:** Peacock blue and white hooped jersey, black shorts **Currie Cup Coach:** Peter Engledow
Captain: AJ Coertzen **President:** Jannie Louw
CEO: Riaan Vorster

'96 6th	'97 6th	'98 1st	'99 6th	'00 8th	'01 8th
'02 7th	'03 7th	'04 6th	'05 7th	'06 6th	'07 6th
'08 6th	'09 5th	'10 6th	'11 6th	'12 5th	'13 6th
			'14 7th	'15 8th	'16 6th

Played	Won	Lost	Drawn	Points for	Points against	Tries for	Tries against
8	4	4	0	265	323	33	41

Date	Venue	Opponent	Result	Score	Referee	Scorers
Aug 12	Durban	Sharks	LOST	24-46	J van Heerden	T: Bock, Jonker, Van Rooyen. C: Swart (3). P: Swart.
Aug 20	Kimberley	Golden Lions	WON	30-24	Q Immelman	T: Coertzen, Van Rooyen, Kotze. C: Swart (3). P: Swart (2), Swarts.
Aug 26	Nelspruit	Pumas	WON	41-35	S Berry	T: Van Rooyen (2), Bock, Wehr. C: Swart (3). P: Swart (5).
Aug 31	Kimberley	EP Kings	WON	47-24	AJ Jacobs	T: Coertzen (2), Bock, Arendse, Zana, Janse van Rensburg, Putuma. C: Swart (5), Swarts.
Sep 08	Kimberley	Boland	WON	46-22	J van Heerden	T: Watts (2), Coertzen, Swart, Arendse, Wehr. C: Swart (5). P: Swart (2).
Sep 16	Pretoria	Blue Bulls	LOST	20-57	Q Immelman	T: Bock, Putuma. C: Swart (2). P: Swart (2).
Sep 23	Kimberley	WP	LOST	31-52	J Peyper	T: Jonker, Van Rooyen, Swarts, Adendorf. C: Swart (2), Swarts (2). P: Swarts.
Oct 01	Bloemfontein	Free State	LOST	26-63	C Jadezweni	T: Swarts, Fraser, Francke, Botha. C: Swarts (2), Zana.

APPEARANCES & POINTS

PLAYER	Sharks	Golden Lions	Pumas	EP Kings	Boland	Blue Bulls	WP	Free State	Apps	T	C	P	DG	Pts
AJ Coertzen	15	15	15c	15c	15c	15c	15c	15c	8	4	–	–	–	20
Ederies Arendse	14	–	–	14	14	14	11	14	6	2	–	–	–	10
JW Jonker	13	14	14	13	–	–	14	–	5	2	–	–	–	10
Jonathan Francke	12	13	13	–	13	13	13	13	7	1	–	–	–	5
Alshaun Bock	11	11	11	11	11	11	–	11	7	4	–	–	–	20
Clinton Swart	10	12	12	12	12	12	12	–	7	1	23	12	–	87
Rudi van Rooyen	9	9	9	9	9	9	9	–	7	5	–	–	–	25
Jason Fraser	8	8	8	8	8	8	4R	8	8	1	–	–	–	5
RJ Liebenberg	7c	–	–	–	–	–	–	–	1	–	–	–	–	0
Wendal Wehr	6	6	6	6	6	6	6	6	8	2	–	–	–	10
Jono Janse van Rensburg	5	5	5	5	5	5	8	7	8	1	–	–	–	5
Mzwanele Zito	4	4	4	–	4R	4	–	5	6	–	–	–	–	0
Stephan Kotze	3	3	3	3	–	3	3	–	6	1	–	–	–	5
Marius Fourie	2	2R	2R	3R	2R	2R	2R	2	8	–	–	–	–	0
Steph Roberts	1	1c	1	1	–	–	1	1	6	–	–	–	–	0
AJ le Roux	2R	2	2	2	2	2	2	–	7	–	–	–	–	0
Devon Martinus	3R	1R	–	1R	1	3R	3R	3R	7	–	–	–	–	0
Liam Hendricks	1R	–	1R	–	3R	1	–	3	5	–	–	–	–	0
Sias Koen	7R	7	7	7	7	7	7	–	7	–	–	–	–	0
Stephan Vermeulen	4R	4R	–	–	–	–	–	–	2	–	–	–	–	0
Renier Botha	9R	9R	9R	9R	9R	9R	9R	9	8	1	–	–	–	5
Elgar Watts	14R	10	10	10	10	10	10	10	8	2	–	–	–	10
Eric Zana	–	11R	13R	13R	15R	14R	14R	10R	7	1	1	–	–	7
André Swarts	–	10R	x	12R	10R	11R	12R	12	6	2	5	2	–	26
Thabo Mabuza	–	18R	–	6R	7R	–	–	5R	4	–	–	–	–	0
Hilton Lobberts	–	–	4R	–	–	–	4	–	2	–	–	–	–	0
Steven Meiring	–	–	18R	8R	–	–	–	4R	3	–	–	–	–	0
Wandile Putuma	–	–	–	4	4	4R	5	–	4	2	–	–	–	10
Chase Morison	–	–	–	–	3	–	–	–	1	–	–	–	–	0
Jonathan Adendorf	–	–	–	–	–	8R	5R	4	3	1	–	–	–	5
Ntabeni Dukisa	–	–	–	–	–	–	–	13R	1	–	–	–	–	0
Sidney Tobias	–	–	–	–	–	–	–	2R	1	–	–	–	–	0
Steven Moir	–	–	–	–	–	–	–	12R	1	–	–	–	–	0
33 PLAYERS									**175**	**33**	**29**	**14**	**0**	**265**

CURRIE CUP SQUAD – CAREER CURRIE CUP APPEARANCES

PLAYER	GRIQUAS						OTHER UNIONS						TOTAL					
	A	T	C	P	DG	Pts	A	T	C	P	DG	Pts	A	T	C	P	DG	Pts
JW (Jonathan) Adendorf	25	1	–	–	–	5	–	–	–	–	–	0	25	1	–	–	–	5
E (Ederies) Arendse	21	9	–	–	–	45	–	–	–	–	–	0	21	9	–	–	–	45
AG (Alshaun) Bock	19	9	–	–	–	45	48	35	–	–	–	175	67	44	–	–	–	220
R (Renier) Botha	8	1	–	–	–	5	–	–	–	–	–	0	8	1	–	–	–	5
AJ (AJ) Coertzen	8	4	–	–	–	20	–	–	–	–	–	0	–	–	–	–	–	0
N (Ntabeni) Dukisa	9	2	2	5	–	29	28	8	13	23	1	138	37	10	15	28	1	167
M (Marius) Fourie	8	–	–	–	–	0	10	–	–	–	–	0	18	–	–	–	–	0
JC (Jonathan) Francke	32	3	–	–	–	15	26	4	–	–	–	20	58	7	–	–	–	35
J-C (Jason) Fraser	8	1	–	–	–	5	18	1	–	–	–	5	26	1	–	–	–	5
LC (Liam) Hendricks	5	–	–	–	–	0	–	–	–	–	–	0	5	–	–	–	–	0
JB (Jono) Janse van Rensburg	13	2	–	–	–	10	–	–	–	–	–	0	13	2	–	–	–	10
JW (JW) Jonker	5	2	–	–	–	10	73	20	–	–	–	100	78	22	–	–	–	110
S (Sias) Koen	7	–	–	–	–	0	–	–	–	–	–	0	7	–	–	–	–	0
SC (Stephan) Kotze	15	1	–	–	–	5	–	–	–	–	–	0	15	1	–	–	–	5
AJ (AJ) le Roux	17	3	–	–	–	15	17	1	–	–	–	5	34	4	–	–	–	20
RJ (RJ) Liebenberg	30	–	–	–	–	0	–	–	–	–	–	0	30	–	–	–	–	0
H (Hilton) Lobberts	18	1	–	–	–	5	46	3	–	–	–	15	64	4	–	–	–	20
ST (Thabo) Mabuza	4	–	–	–	–	0	–	–	–	–	–	0	4	–	–	–	–	0
DR (Devon) Martinus	7	–	–	–	–	0	–	–	–	–	–	0	7	–	–	–	–	0
S (Steven) Meiring	3	–	–	–	–	0	–	–	–	–	–	0	3	–	–	–	–	0
SA (Steven) Moir	1	–	–	–	–	0	–	–	–	–	–	0	1	–	–	–	–	0
CW (Chase) Morison	1	–	–	–	–	0	–	–	–	–	–	0	1	–	–	–	–	0
W (Wandile) Putuma	4	2	–	–	–	10	–	–	–	–	–	0	4	2	–	–	–	10
WAS (Steph) Roberts	88	3	–	–	–	15	–	–	–	–	–	0	88	3	–	–	–	15
CR (Clinton) Swart	16	2	34	23	–	147	4	–	–	–	1	3	20	2	34	23	1	150
ASW (André) Swarts	6	2	5	2	–	26	–	–	–	–	–	0	6	2	5	2	–	26
SM (Sidney) Tobias	2	–	–	–	–	0	13	–	–	–	–	0	15	–	–	–	–	0
R (Rudi) van Rooyen	14	5	–	–	–	25	–	–	–	–	–	0	14	5	–	–	–	25
EG (Elgar) Watts	8	2	–	–	–	10	80	29	74	49	–	440	88	31	74	49	–	450
WP (Wendal) Wehr	14	2	–	–	–	10	15	2	–	–	–	10	29	4	–	–	–	20
ES (Eric) Zana	7	1	1	–	–	7	50	11	33	32	1	225	57	12	34	32	1	232
MR (Mzwanele) Zito	6	–	–	–	–	0	33	4	–	–	–	20	39	4	–	–	–	20

32 PLAYERS

FIRST-CLASS APPEARANCES FOR GRIQUAS IN 2016 – ALL MATCHES

PLAYER	CURRIE CUP QUALIFIER						CURRIE CUP						2016 TOTAL						CAREER MATCHES					
	A	T	C	P	DG	Pts	A	T	C	P	DG	Pts	A	T	C	P	DG	Pts	A	T	C	P	DG	Pts
JW (Jonathan) Adendorf	9	0	0	0	0	0	3	1	0	0	0	5	12	1	0	0	0	5	64	6	0	0	0	30
DA (David) Antonites	2	0	0	0	0	0	0	0	0	0	0	0	2	0	0	0	0	0	2	0	0	0	0	0
E (Ederies) Arendse	10	4	0	0	0	20	6	2	0	0	0	10	16	6	0	0	0	30	49	20	0	0	0	100
AG (Alshaun) Bock	11	6	0	0	0	30	7	4	0	0	0	20	18	10	0	0	0	50	40	23	0	0	0	115
R (Renier) Botha	1	0	0	0	0	0	8	1	0	0	0	5	9	1	0	0	0	5	9	1	0	0	0	5
AJ (AJ) Coertzen	12	11	0	0	0	55	8	4	0	0	0	20	20	15	0	0	0	75	26	18	0	0	0	90
N (Ntabeni) Dukisa	9	4	2	0	0	24	1	0	0	0	0	0	10	4	2	0	0	24	29	13	4	5	0	88
TA (Tiaan) Dorfling	12	4	0	0	0	20	0	0	0	0	0	0	12	4	0	0	0	20	12	4	0	0	0	20
M (Marius) Fourie	11	1	0	0	0	5	8	0	0	0	0	0	19	1	0	0	0	5	19	1	0	0	0	5
JC (Jonathan) Francke	10	5	0	0	0	25	7	1	0	0	0	5	17	6	0	0	0	30	62	13	0	0	0	65
J-C (Jason) Fraser	13	5	0	0	0	25	8	1	0	0	0	5	21	6	0	0	0	30	21	6	0	0	0	30
LC (Liam) Hendricks	0	0	0	0	0	0	5	0	0	0	0	0	5	0	0	0	0	0	5	0	0	0	0	0
JB (Jono) Janse van Rensburg	12	1	0	0	0	5	8	1	0	0	0	5	20	2	0	0	0	10	37	6	0	0	0	30
JW (JW) Jonker	11	2	0	0	0	10	5	2	0	0	0	10	16	4	0	0	0	20	19	6	0	0	0	30
S (Sias) Koen	11	1	0	0	0	5	7	0	0	0	0	0	18	1	0	0	0	5	18	1	0	0	0	5
SC (Stephan) Kotze	11	2	0	0	0	10	6	1	0	0	0	5	17	3	0	0	0	15	39	4	0	0	0	20
L (Luxolo) Koza	3	0	0	0	0	0	0	0	0	0	0	0	3	0	0	0	0	0	12	0	0	0	0	0
AJ (AJ) le Roux	11	2	0	0	0	10	7	0	0	0	0	0	18	2	0	0	0	10	42	6	0	0	0	30
RJ (RJ) Liebenberg	11	0	0	0	0	0	1	0	0	0	0	0	12	0	0	0	0	0	54	1	0	0	0	5
H (Hilton) Lobberts	0	0	0	0	0	0	2	0	0	0	0	0	2	0	0	0	0	0	27	2	0	0	0	10
K (Kyle) Lombard	5	0	0	0	0	0	0	0	0	0	0	0	5	0	0	0	0	0	5	0	0	0	0	0
ST (Thabo) Mabuza	3	1	0	0	0	5	4	0	0	0	0	0	7	1	0	0	0	5	7	1	0	0	0	5
DR (Devon) Martinus	12	1	0	0	0	5	7	0	0	0	0	0	19	1	0	0	0	5	19	1	0	0	0	5
CJP (Chris) Meyer	5	1	0	0	0	5	0	0	0	0	0	0	5	1	0	0	0	5	5	1	0	0	0	5
S (Steven) Meiring	10	0	0	0	0	0	3	0	0	0	0	0	13	0	0	0	0	0	13	0	0	0	0	0
SA (Steven) Moir	2	0	0	1	0	3	1	0	0	0	0	0	3	0	0	1	0	3	3	0	0	1	0	3
CW (Chase) Morison	0	0	0	0	0	0	1	0	0	0	0	0	1	0	0	0	0	0	1	0	0	0	0	0
J (Jaco) Nepgen	4	0	0	0	0	0	0	0	0	0	0	0	4	0	0	0	0	0	89	8	0	0	0	40
T (Teunis) Nieuwoudt	2	0	0	0	0	0	0	0	0	0	0	0	2	0	0	0	0	0	2	0	0	0	0	0
JG (Gouws) Prinsloo	6	0	8	1	0	19	0	0	0	0	0	0	6	0	8	1	0	19	51	4	87	59	0	377
W (Wandile) Putuma	0	0	0	0	0	0	4	2	0	0	0	10	4	2	0	0	0	10	4	2	0	0	0	10
WAS (Steph) Roberts	10	0	0	0	0	0	6	0	0	0	0	0	16	0	0	0	0	0	165	6	0	0	0	30
CR (Clinton) Swart	12	4	21	10	0	94	7	1	23	12	0	87	19	5	44	22	0	181	39	9	58	35	0	268
ASW (André) Swarts	9	2	16	12	0	78	6	2	5	2	0	26	15	4	21	14	0	104	15	4	21	14	0	104
SM (Sidney) Tobias	6	0	0	0	0	0	1	0	0	0	0	0	7	0	0	0	0	0	12	0	0	0	0	0
E (Ewald) van der Westhuizen	7	0	0	0	0	0	0	0	0	0	0	0	7	0	0	0	0	0	41	3	0	0	0	15
R (Rudi) van Rooyen	5	3	0	0	0	15	7	5	0	0	0	25	12	8	0	0	0	40	30	10	0	0	0	50
SA (Stephan) Vermeulen	1	0	0	0	0	0	2	0	0	0	0	0	3	0	0	0	0	0	3	0	0	0	0	0
EG (Elgar) Watts	0	0	0	0	0	0	8	2	0	0	0	10	8	2	0	0	0	10	8	2	0	0	0	10
WP (Wendal) Wehr	13	0	0	0	0	0	8	2	0	0	0	10	21	2	0	0	0	10	34	4	0	0	0	20
ES (Eric) Zana	14	0	1	0	0	2	7	1	1	0	0	7	21	1	2	0	0	9	21	1	2	0	0	9
MR (Mzwanele) Zito	11	2	0	0	0	10	6	0	0	0	0	0	17	2	0	0	0	10	17	2	0	0	0	10

42 PLAYERS

AJ Coertzen.

KwaZulu-Natal Rugby Union

Founded: 1890 (as Natal Rugby Union) **Ground:** Growthpoint Kings Park **Capacity:** 53,000 **Address:** Jacko Jackson Drive, Durban **Postal address:** PO Box 307, Durban, 4000 **Telephone Number:** 031-308 8400 **Website:** www.sharksrugby.co.za **Colours:** Black and white jersey and socks, white shorts **Director of Rugby:** Gary Gold **Currie Cup Coach:** Robert du Preez **Captain:** Keegan Daniel **President:** Francois Louis **Company CEO:** John Smit (replaced by Gary Teichmann) **Union CEO:** Pete Smith

'96 1st	'97 2nd	'98 3rd	'99 2nd	'00 1st	'01 2nd
'02 1st	'03 2nd	'04 5th	'05 5th	'06 4th	'07 2nd
'08 1st	'09 1st	'10 1st	'11 2nd	'12 1st	'13 2nd
		'14 3rd	'15 5th	'16 5th	

Played	Won	Lost	Drawn	Points for	Points against	Tries for	Tries against
8	5	3	0	272	173	33	21

Date	Venue	Opponent	Result	Score	Referee	Scorers
Aug 05	Nelspruit	Pumas	WON	33-10	L Legoete	T: Ndungane, Esterhuizen, Sithole, Marais, Botha. C: Bosch (4).
Aug 12	Durban	Griquas	WON	46-24	J van Heerden	T: Esterhuizen, Sithole, Ungerer, Mtembu, Oosthuizen, Deysel. C: Bosch (5). P: Bosch (2).
Aug 19	Wellington	Boland	WON	41-20	M vd Westhuizen	T: Ndungane, Esterhuizen, Radebe, Ralepelle, Marais, Venter. C: Bosch (3), April. P: Bosch.
Aug 27	Durban	Blue Bulls	WON	26-19	M vd Westhuizen	T: Bosch, Botha. C: Bosch (2). P: Bosch (3). D: Bosch.
Sept 03	Cape Town	WP	LOST	27-34	R Rasivhenge	T: J-L du Preez, Smith. C: Bosch. P: Bosch (5).
Sept 10	Durban	Free State	LOST	30-38	R Rasivhenge	T: Kleinhans, Du Toit. C: Bosch. P: Bosch (6).
Sept 17	Durban	EP Kings	WON	53-00	C Jadezweni	T: Esterhuizen, Mjekevu, Radebe, Claassens, Kleinhans, J-L du Preez, K Majola, Oosthuizen, Ralepelle. C: Bosch (2), Lambie (2).
Sept 30	Johannesburg	Golden Lions	LOST	16-28	C Joubert	T: Claassens. C: Bosch. P: Bosch (3).

Note: ■ = *Champion*

APPEARANCES & POINTS

PLAYER	Pumas	Griquas	Boland	Blue Bulls	WP	Free State	EP Kings	Golden Lions	Apps	T	C	P	DG	Pts
Odwa Ndungane	15	–	14	14	14	14	–	–	5	2	–	–	–	10
Neil Maritz	14	14	–	–	–	–	14R	11R	4	–	–	–	–	0
Lukhanyo Am	13	13	–	13	13	13	13	13	7	–	–	–	–	0
André Esterhuizen	12	12	12	12	12	12	12	12	8	4	–	–	–	20
S'bura Sithole	11	11	11	13R	11	11	–	–	6	2	–	–	–	10
Curwin Bosch	10	15	15	15	15	15	15	15	8	1	19	20	1	106
Michael Claassens	9	9R	–	–	9R	9R	9	9	6	2	–	–	–	10
Philip van der Walt	8	7	8	8	8	8c	–	–	6	–	–	–	–	0
Jean-Luc du Preez	7	–	–	7	7	7	7	7	6	2	–	–	–	10
Keegan Daniel	6c	6c	6c	6c	6c	–	–	8c	6	–	–	–	–	0
Stephan Lewies	5	5	–	–	–	–	–	5R	3	–	–	–	–	0
Etienne Oosthuizen	4	4	4	4	4	4	4	4	8	2	–	–	–	10
Lourens Adriaanse	3	–	–	–	–	–	–	3	2	–	–	–	–	0
Franco Marais	2	2	2R	2	2	2	2R	2R	8	2	–	–	–	10
Dale Chadwick	1	1	1	–	–	–	–	–	3	–	–	–	–	0
Chiliboy Ralepelle	2R	2R	2	2R	2R	2R	2c	2	8	2	–	–	–	10
Thomas du Toit	3R	3	3	3	3	3	1	1	8	1	–	–	–	5
Ruan Botha	4R	5R	5	5	5	5	5	5	8	2	–	–	–	10
Tera Mtembu	7R	8	7	–	–	–	–	–	3	1	–	–	–	5
Stefan Ungerer	9R	9	9	9	9	9	9R	9R	8	1	–	–	–	5
Inny Radebe	15R	10	10	10	10	10	10	10	8	2	–	–	–	10
Heimar Williams	11R	14R	13	–	13R	–	–	–	4	–	–	–	–	0
John Meyer	–	3R	3R	3R	3R	1R	3	1R	7	–	–	–	–	0
Jean Deysel	–	8R	7R	7R	4R	–	7R	–	5	1	–	–	–	5
Rhyno Smith	–	10R	–	10R	10R	10R	14	14	6	1	–	–	–	5
JC Astle	–	–	4R	4R	–	–	–	–	2	–	–	–	–	0
Hanco Venter	–	–	9R	9R	–	–	–	–	2	1	–	–	–	5
Wandile Mjekevu	–	–	12R	–	–	14R	11	11	4	1	–	–	–	5
Garth April	–	–	15R	–	–	–	–	10R	2	–	1	–	–	2
Lwazi Mvovo	–	–	–	11	–	–	–	–	1	–	–	–	–	0
Juan Schoeman	–	–	–	1	1	1	3R	–	4	–	–	–	–	0
Jean Droste	–	–	–	–	6R	x	4R	–	2	–	–	–	–	0
Francois Kleinhans	–	–	–	–	–	6	8	6	3	2	–	–	–	10
Khaya Majola	–	–	–	–	–	8R	6	6R	3	1	–	–	–	5
Patrick Lambie	–	–	–	–	–	–	10R	–	1	–	2	–	–	4
35 PLAYERS									**175**	**33**	**22**	**20**	**1**	**272**

CURRIE CUP SQUAD – CAREER CURRIE CUP APPEARANCES

PLAYER	KWAZULU-NATAL						OTHER UNIONS						TOTAL					
	A	T	C	P	DG	Pts	A	T	C	P	DG	Pts	A	T	C	P	DG	Pts
LC (Lourens) Adriaanse	14	3	0	0	0	15	31	3	0	0	0	15	45	6	0	0	0	30
L (Lukhanyo) Am	7	0	0	0	0	0	11	1	0	0	0	0	18	1	0	0	0	0
GG (Garth) April	9	2	1	0	0	12	0	0	0	0	0	0	9	2	1	0	0	12
J-C (JC) Astle	12	0	0	0	0	0	19	1	0	0	0	5	31	1	0	0	0	5
CD (Curwin) Bosch	8	1	19	20	1	106	0	0	0	0	0	0	8	1	19	20	1	106
R (Ruan) Botha	8	2	0	0	0	10	18	0	0	0	0	0	26	2	0	0	0	10
DM (Dale) Chadwick	51	2	0	0	0	10	0	0	0	0	0	0	51	2	0	0	0	10
M (Michael) Claassens	15	3	0	0	0	15	45	7	0	0	0	35	60	10	0	0	0	50
KR (Keegan) Daniel	110	33	0	0	0	165	0	0	0	0	0	0	110	33	0	0	0	165
JR (Jean) Deysel	69	8	0	0	0	40	5	0	0	0	0	0	74	8	0	0	0	40
J (Jean) Droste	2	0	0	0	0	0	0	0	0	0	0	0	2	0	0	0	0	0
J-L (Jean-Luc) du Preez	12	2	0	0	0	10	0	0	0	0	0	0	12	2	0	0	0	10
TJ (Thomas) du Toit	25	2	0	0	0	10	0	0	0	0	0	0	25	2	0	0	0	10
AP (André) Esterhuizen	24	10	0	0	0	50	0	0	0	0	0	0	24	10	0	0	0	50
F (Francois) Kleinhans	24	5	0	0	0	25	0	0	0	0	0	0	24	5	0	0	0	25
PJ (Patrick) Lambie	30	6	52	63	2	329	0	0	0	0	0	0	30	6	52	63	2	329
JS (Stephan) Lewies	17	1	0	0	0	5	0	0	0	0	0	0	17	1	0	0	0	5
K (Khaya) Majola	9	1	0	0	0	5	0	0	0	0	0	0	9	1	0	0	0	5
FS (Franco) Marais	21	2	0	0	0	10	0	0	0	0	0	0	21	2	0	0	0	10
NK (Neil) Maritz	4	0	0	0	0	0	0	0	0	0	0	0	4	0	0	0	0	0
J-H (John) Meyer	7	0	0	0	0	0	0	0	0	0	0	0	7	0	0	0	0	0
WG (Wandile) Mjekevu	13	3	0	0	0	15	0	0	0	0	0	0	13	3	0	0	0	15
LS (Tera) Mtembu	25	5	0	0	0	25	0	0	0	0	0	0	25	5	0	0	0	25
LN (Lwazi) Mvovo	62	28	0	0	0	140	0	0	0	0	0	0	62	28	0	0	0	140
OM (Odwa) Ndungane	97	33	1	0	0	167	36	18	0	0	0	90	133	51	1	0	0	257
E (Etienne) Oosthuizen	29	3	0	0	0	15	3	0	0	0	0	0	32	3	0	0	0	15
I-C (Inny) Radebe	8	2	0	0	0	10	0	0	0	0	0	0	8	2	0	0	0	10
MC (Chilliboy) Ralepelle	8	2	0	0	0	10	25	1	0	0	0	5	33	3	0	0	0	15
JL (Juan) Schoeman	6	0	0	0	0	0	0	0	0	0	0	0	6	0	0	0	0	0
SCT (Sibusiso) Sithole	45	11	0	0	0	55	0	0	0	0	0	0	45	11	0	0	0	55
RC (Rhyno) Smith	6	1	0	0	0	5	17	11	7	0	2	75	23	12	7	0	2	80
S (Stefan) Ungerer	12	1	0	0	0	5	0	0	0	0	0	0	12	1	0	0	0	5
CP (Philip) van der Walt	16	0	0	0	0	0	29	5	0	0	0	25	45	5	0	0	0	25
HC (Hanco) Venter	5	1	0	0	0	5	7	2	0	0	0	10	12	3	0	0	0	15
H (Heimar) Williams	23	5	0	0	0	25	0	0	0	0	0	0	23	5	0	0	0	25

35 PLAYERS

FIRST-CLASS APPEARANCES FOR SHARKS IN 2016 – ALL MATCHES

PLAYER	2016 TOTAL						CAREER MATCHES					
	A	T	C	P	DG	Pts	A	T	C	P	DG	Pts
LC (Lourens) Adriaanse	2	0	0	0	0	0	14	3	0	0	0	15
L (Lukhanyo) Am	7	0	0	0	0	0	7	0	0	0	0	0
GG (Garth) April	2	0	1	0	0	2	9	2	1	0	0	12
J-C (JC) Astle	2	0	0	0	0	0	12	0	0	0	0	0
CD (Curwin) Bosch	8	1	19	20	1	106	8	1	19	20	1	106
R (Ruan) Botha	8	2	0	0	0	10	8	2	0	0	0	10
DM (Dale) Chadwick	3	0	0	0	0	0	51	2	0	0	0	10
M (Michael) Claassens	6	2	0	0	0	10	15	3	0	0	0	15
KR (Keegan) Daniel	6	0	0	0	0	0	110	33	0	0	0	165
JR (Jean) Deysel	5	1	0	0	0	5	70	8	0	0	0	40
J (Jean) Droste	2	0	0	0	0	0	2	0	0	0	0	0
J-L (Jean-Luc) du Preez	6	2	0	0	0	10	12	2	0	0	0	10
TJ (Thomas) du Toit	8	1	0	0	0	5	25	2	0	0	0	10
AP (André) Esterhuizen	8	4	0	0	0	20	24	10	0	0	0	50
F (Francois) Kleinhans	3	2	0	0	0	10	24	5	0	0	0	25
PJ (Patrick) Lambie	1	0	2	0	0	4	30	6	52	63	2	329
JS (Stephan) Lewies	3	0	0	0	0	0	17	1	0	0	0	5
K (Khaya) Majola	3	1	0	0	0	5	9	1	0	0	0	5
FS (Franco) Marais	8	2	0	0	0	10	21	2	0	0	0	10
NK (Neil) Maritz	4	0	0	0	0	0	4	0	0	0	0	0
J-H (John) Meyer	7	0	0	0	0	0	7	0	0	0	0	0
WG (Wandile) Mjekevu	4	1	0	0	0	5	13	3	0	0	0	15
LS (Tera) Mtembu	3	1	0	0	0	5	25	5	0	0	0	25
LN (Lwazi) Mvovo	1	0	0	0	0	0	63	28	0	0	0	140
OM (Odwa) Ndungane	5	2	0	0	0	10	97	33	1	0	0	167
E (Etienne) Oosthuizen	8	2	0	0	0	10	29	3	0	0	0	15
I-C (Inny) Radebe	8	2	0	0	0	10	8	2	0	0	0	10
MC (Chiliboy) Ralepelle	8	2	0	0	0	10	8	2	0	0	0	10
JL (Juan) Schoeman	4	0	0	0	0	0	6	0	0	0	0	0
SCT (Sibusiso) Sithole	6	2	0	0	0	10	45	11	0	0	0	55
RC (Rhyno) Smith	6	1	0	0	0	5	6	1	0	0	0	5
S (Stefan) Ungerer	8	1	0	0	0	5	12	1	0	0	0	5
CP (Philip) van der Walt	6	0	0	0	0	0	16	0	0	0	0	0
HC (Hanco) Venter	2	1	0	0	0	5	5	1	0	0	0	5
H (Heimar) Williams	4	0	0	0	0	0	23	5	0	0	0	25

35 PLAYERS

* Sharks Currie Cup Qualifying matches were also first-class but they played as the 'Sharks XV', which the KZNRU considers a completely different team. This table shows first-class matches played by the 'Sharks' only. See Currie Cup Qualifying section for the Sharks XV info.

Inny Radebe.

Mpumalanga Rugby Union

Founded: 1969 (as South Eastern Transvaal) **Ground:** Mbombela Stadium **Capacity:** 43,500 **Address:** 1 Bafana Bafana Str, Mataffin Ext, Nelspruit **Postal address:** 1 Bafana Bafana Str, Mataffin Ext, Nelspruit **Telephone Number:** 013-757 4600 **Email:** pieter@pumas.co.za **Colours:** Dove grey, black and pink jersey, shorts and socks **Currie Cup Coach:** MJ Mentz **Captains:** Hugo Kloppers & Renaldo Bothma **President:** Hein Mentz **Company CEO:** Pieter Burger

'96 7th	'97 9th	'98 11th	'99 9th	'00 7th	'01 6th
'02 6th	'03 6th	'04 7th	'05 10th	'06 8th	'07 12th
'08 12th	'09 9th	'10 9th	'11 7th	'12 8th	'13 7th
'14 6th	'15 6th	'16 6th			

Played	Won	Lost	Drawn	Points for	Points against	Tries for	Tries against
8	1	7	0	178	321	24	41

Date	Venue	Opponent	Result	Score	Referee	Scorers
Aug 05	Nelspruit	Sharks	LOST	10-33	L Legoete	T: Herne. C: Brummer. P: Brummer.
Aug 13	Johannesburg	Golden Lions	LOST	26-68	S Berry	T: Van Staden, Mona, Van Niekerk, Williams. C: Brummer (3).
Aug 26	Nelspruit	Griquas	LOST	35-41	S Berry	T: Herne, Stander, Lewis, Schoeman. C: Brummer (3). P: Brummer (3).
Sep 02	Wellington	Boland	LOST	22-25	M v/d Westhuizen	T: Herne, Van Wyk, Bothma, Luiters. C: Brummer.
Sep 10	Nelspruit	Blue Bulls	LOST	14-41	S Berry	T: Isbell. P: Brummer (3).
Sep 17	Cape Town	WP	LOST	23-31	A Ruiz	T: Lewis, Bothma, Fisher. C: Williams. P: Brummer. DG: Brummer.
Sep 23	Nelspruit	Free State	LOST	10-52	L Legoete	T: Herne. C: Steyl. P: Brummer.
Sep 30	Port Elizabeth	EP Kings	WON	38-30	Q Immelman	T: Herne (3), Shabangu, Lewis, Luiters. C: Steyl (2), Williams.

APPEARANCES & POINTS

PLAYER	Sharks	Golden Lions	Griquas	Boland	Blue Bulls	WP	Free State	EP Kings	Apps	T	C	P	DG	Pts
Justin van Staden	15	15	–	–	–	–	–	–	2	1	–	–	–	5
JP Lewis	14	14	11	11	11	11	11	11	8	3	–	–	–	15
Hennie Skorbinski	13	13	13	–	13	12	12	–	6	–	–	–	–	0
Marlou van Niekerk	12	12	13R	12R	12	–	–	–	5	1	–	–	–	5
Marcello Sampson	11	11	–	–	–	–	–	–	2	–	–	–	–	0
Francois Brummer	10	10	10	10	10	10	10	–	7	–	8	9	1	46
Reynier van Rooyen	9	9	–	–	–	–	–	–	2	–	–	–	–	0
Carel Greeff	8	6R	6R	–	6R	6R	8R	7	7	–	–	–	–	0
Lambert Groenewald	7	–	7R	7	7	7	7	–	5	–	–	–	–	0
Marnus Schoeman	6	6	6	6	–	–	–	–	4	1	–	–	–	5
Hugo Kloppers	5c	5c	4R	5	–	4R	–	5R	6	–	–	–	–	0
Stephan Greeff	4	–	–	–	4R	4	4	–	4	–	–	–	–	0
DJ Terblanche	3	1R	1	1	1	1R	3R	1	8	–	–	–	–	0
Frank Herne	2	2R	2	2	2	2	2	2	8	7	–	–	–	35
Khwezi Mona	1	1	–	–	–	1	1	–	4	1	–	–	–	5
Francois du Toit	2R	2	–	–	–	–	–	–	2	–	–	–	–	0
Jacques Kotze	3R	–	3R	3R	–	–	–	–	3	–	–	–	–	0
Wiehan Hay	4R	4	4	5R	4	–	–	–	5	–	–	–	–	0
Dylan Peterson	7R	–	–	–	–	–	–	–	1	–	–	–	–	0
Emile Temperman	9R	9R	9	9	9	9	9R	9	8	–	–	–	–	0
Deon Helberg	12R	13R	–	–	–	–	–	10R	3	–	–	–	–	0
Devon Williams	15R	11R	15	15	15	15	10R	15	8	1	3	–	–	11
Renaldo Bothma	–	8	8c	8c	8c	8c	8c	8c	7	2	–	–	–	10
Nardus van der Walt	–	7	7	7	–	–	–	–	3	–	–	–	–	0
Louis Albertse	–	3	3	–	3R	3	3	3	6	–	–	–	–	0
Jannie Stander	–	4R	5	4	5	5	5	5	7	1	–	–	–	5
Bernado Botha	–	–	14	14	14	–	–	–	3	–	–	–	–	0
Leighton van Wyk	–	–	12	12	12R	–	–	12	4	1	–	–	–	5
Simon Westraadt	–	–	7R	1R	1R	3R	1R	1R	6	–	–	–	–	0
Tyler Fisher	–	–	11R	13	–	12R	12R	14	5	1	–	–	–	5
Kevin Luiters	–	–	9R	9R	9R	9R	9	9R	6	2	–	–	–	10
Marné Coetzee	–	–	–	3	3	–	–	3R	3	–	–	–	–	0
Ruwellyn Isbel	–	–	–	14R	14R	14	14	14R	5	1	–	–	–	5
Brian Shabangu	–	–	–	–	6	6	6	6	4	1	–	–	–	5
Hoffman Maritz	–	–	–	–	–	13	13	13	3	–	–	–	–	0
Heinrich Steyl	–	–	–	–	–	10R	15	10	3	–	3	–	–	6
Jeremy Jordaan	–	–	–	–	–	–	7R	4	2	–	–	–	–	0
Reuben Johannes	–	–	–	–	–	–	–	6R	1	–	–	–	–	0
38 PLAYERS									**176**	**24**	**14**	**9**	**1**	**178**

CURRIE CUP SQUAD – CAREER CURRIE CUP APPEARANCES

PLAYER	PUMAS						OTHER UNIONS						TOTAL					
	A	T	C	P	DG	Pts	A	T	C	P	DG	Pts	A	T	C	P	DG	Pts
LE (Louis) Albertse	6	–	–	–	–	0	–	–	–	–	–	0	6	–	–	–	–	0
BC (Bernardo) Botha	12	1	–	–	–	5	5	–	–	–	–	0	17	1	–	–	–	5
R (Renaldo) Bothma	27	9	–	–	–	45	8	2	–	–	–	10	35	11	–	–	–	55
F (Francois) Brummer	7	–	8	9	1	46	71	3	54	65	4	330	78	3	62	74	5	376
M (Marné) Coetzee	4	–	–	–	–	0	–	–	–	–	–	0	4	–	–	–	–	0
F (Francois) du Toit	30	1	–	–	–	5	3	–	–	–	–	0	33	1	–	–	–	5
TL (Tyler) Fisher	5	1	–	–	–	5	–	–	–	–	–	0	5	1	–	–	–	5
CFK (Carel) Greeff	7	–	–	–	–	0	35	17	–	–	–	85	42	17	–	–	–	85
S (Stephan) Greeff	4	–	–	–	–	0	11	–	–	–	–	0	15	–	–	–	–	0
LS (Lambert) Groenewald	7	–	–	–	–	0	–	–	–	–	–	0	7	–	–	–	–	0
W (Wiehan) Hay	5	–	–	–	–	0	–	–	–	–	–	0	5	–	–	–	–	0
GG (Deon) Helberg	5	–	–	–	–	0	10	2	–	–	–	10	15	2	–	–	–	10
F (Frank) Herne	42	11	–	–	–	55	9	2	–	–	–	10	51	13	–	–	–	65
RM (Ruwellyn) Isbel	5	1	–	–	–	5	–	–	–	–	–	0	5	1	–	–	–	5
RB (Reuben) Johannes	1	–	–	–	–	0	–	–	–	–	–	0	1	–	–	–	–	0
J (Jeremy) Jordaan	2	–	–	–	–	0	–	–	–	–	–	0	2	–	–	–	–	0
PH (Hugo) Kloppers	6	–	–	–	–	0	23	–	–	–	–	0	29	–	–	–	–	0
AJ (Jacques) Kotze	3	–	–	–	–	0	–	–	–	–	–	0	–	–	–	–	–	0
JP (JP) Lewis	8	3	–	–	–	15	–	–	–	–	–	0	8	3	–	–	–	15
K (Kevin) Luiters	6	2	–	–	–	10	12	2	–	–	–	10	18	4	–	–	–	20
H van H (Hoffman) Maritz	11	–	–	–	–	0	20	10	–	–	–	50	31	10	–	–	–	50
KJ (Khwezi) Mona	11	1	–	–	–	5	–	–	–	–	–	0	11	1	–	–	–	5
D (Dylan) Peterson	2	–	–	–	–	0	–	–	–	–	–	0	2	–	–	–	–	0
MED (Marcello) Sampson	2	–	–	–	–	0	–	–	–	–	–	0	2	–	–	–	–	0
M (Marnus) Schoeman	14	8	–	–	–	40	43	26	–	–	–	130	57	34	–	–	–	170
SB (Brian) Shabangu	4	1	–	–	–	5	–	–	–	–	–	0	4	–	–	–	–	0
AH (Hennie) Skorbinski	11	1	1	–	–	7	13	2	–	–	–	10	24	3	1	–	–	17
JH (Jannie) Stander	10	1	–	–	–	5	–	–	–	–	–	0	10	1	–	–	–	5
HD (Heinrich) Steyl	3	–	3	–	–	6	–	–	–	–	–	0	3	–	3	–	–	6
ENG (Emile) Temperman	8	–	–	–	–	0	–	–	–	–	–	0	8	–	–	–	–	0
DJ (De-Jay) Terblanche	85	5	–	–	–	25	–	–	–	–	–	0	85	5	–	–	–	25
HB (Nardus) van der Walt	3	–	–	–	–	0	1	–	–	–	–	0	4	–	–	–	–	0
MD (Marlou) van Niekerk	5	1	–	–	–	5	–	–	–	–	–	0	5	1	–	–	–	5
R (Reynier) van Rooyen	24	2	–	–	–	10	–	–	–	–	–	0	24	2	–	–	–	10
J (Justin) van Staden	21	4	23	30	–	156	12	1	24	25	2	134	33	5	47	55	2	290
L-RM (Leighton) van Wyk	4	1	–	–	–	5	–	–	–	–	–	0	4	1	–	–	–	5
S (Simon) Westraad	8	–	–	–	–	0	26	–	–	–	–	0	34	–	–	–	–	0
DF (Devon) Williams	8	1	3	–	–	11	–	–	–	–	–	0	0	–	–	–	–	0

FIRST-CLASS APPEARANCES FOR PUMAS IN 2016 – ALL MATCHES

PLAYER	CURRIE CUP QUALIFYING						CURRIE CUP						2016 TOTAL						CAREER MATCHES					
	A	T	C	P	DG	Pts	A	T	C	P	DG	Pts	A	T	C	P	DG	Pts	A	T	C	P	DG	Pts
LE (Louis) Albertse	0	0	0	0	0	0	6	0	0	0	0	0	6	0	0	0	0	0	6	0	0	0	0	0
BC (Bernado) Botha	12	1	0	0	0	5	3	0	0	0	0	0	15	1	0	0	0	5	39	8	1	0	0	42
R (Renaldo) Bothma	0	0	0	0	0	0	7	2	0	0	0	10	7	2	0	0	0	10	61	24	0	0	0	120
F (Francois) Brummer	0	0	0	0	0	0	7	0	8	9	1	46	7	0	8	9	1	46	7	0	8	9	1	46
M (Marné) Coetzee	7	0	0	0	0	0	3	0	0	0	0	0	10	0	0	0	0	0	11	0	0	0	0	0
F (Francois) du Toit	14	4	0	0	0	20	2	0	0	0	0	0	16	4	0	0	0	20	46	6	0	0	0	30
TL (Tyler) Fisher	10	5	0	0	0	25	5	1	0	0	0	5	15	6	0	0	0	30	15	6	0	0	0	30
CFK (Carel) Greeff	12	4	0	0	0	20	7	0	0	0	0	0	19	4	0	0	0	20	19	4	0	0	0	20
S (Stephan) Greeff	12	0	0	0	0	0	4	0	0	0	0	0	16	0	0	0	0	0	16	0	0	0	0	0
LS (Lambert) Groenewald	13	5	0	0	0	25	5	0	0	0	0	0	18	5	0	0	0	25	28	7	0	0	0	35
W (Wiehan) Hay	4	0	0	0	0	0	5	0	0	0	0	0	9	0	0	0	0	0	9	0	0	0	0	0
GG (Deon) Helberg	6	1	0	0	0	5	3	0	0	0	0	0	9	1	0	0	0	5	11	1	0	0	0	5
JD (Johan) Herbst	1	0	0	0	0	0	0	0	0	0	0	0	1	0	0	0	0	0	9	1	0	0	0	5
F (Frank) Herne	13	5	0	0	0	25	8	7	0	0	0	35	21	12	0	0	0	60	71	22	0	0	0	110
RM (Ruwellyn) Isbell	1	0	0	0	0	0	5	1	0	0	0	5	6	1	0	0	0	5	21	8	0	0	0	40
D (Damian) Jansen van Rensburg	4	1	0	0	0	5	0	0	0	0	0	0	4	1	0	0	0	5	4	1	0	0	0	5
EA (Rassie) Jansen van Vuuren	1	0	0	0	0	0	0	0	0	0	0	0	1	0	0	0	0	0	21	5	0	0	0	25
RB (Reuben) Johannes	4	1	0	0	0	5	1	0	0	0	0	0	5	1	0	0	0	5	5	1	0	0	0	5
J (Jeremy) Jordaan	0	0	0	0	0	0	2	0	0	0	0	0	2	0	0	0	0	0	2	0	0	0	0	0
PH (Hugo) Kloppers	12	0	0	0	0	0	6	0	0	0	0	0	18	0	0	0	0	0	18	0	0	0	0	0
AJ (Jacques) Kotze	9	2	0	0	0	10	3	0	0	0	0	0	12	2	0	0	0	10	12	2	0	0	0	10
JP (JP) Lewis	1	2	0	0	0	10	8	3	0	0	0	15	9	5	0	0	0	25	9	5	0	0	0	25
WD (Wilmaure) Louw	6	0	0	0	0	0	0	0	0	0	0	0	6	0	0	0	0	0	51	3	0	0	0	15
K (Kevin) Luiters	0	0	0	0	0	0	6	2	0	0	0	10	6	2	0	0	0	10	6	2	0	0	0	10
H van H (Hoffman) Maritz	9	3	0	0	0	15	3	0	0	0	0	0	12	3	0	0	0	15	20	3	0	0	0	15
KJ (Khwezi) Mona	9	0	0	0	0	0	4	1	0	0	0	5	13	1	0	0	0	5	30	2	0	0	0	10
L (Lubabalo) Mtyanda	1	0	0	0	0	0	0	0	0	0	0	0	1	0	0	0	0	0	47	4	0	0	0	20
S (Sabelo) Nhlapo	2	0	0	0	0	0	0	0	0	0	0	0	2	0	0	0	0	0	13	0	0	0	0	0
D (Dylan) Peterson	3	0	0	0	0	0	1	0	0	0	0	0	4	0	0	0	0	0	5	0	0	0	0	0
MED (Marcello) Sampson	12	4	0	0	0	20	2	0	0	0	0	0	14	4	0	0	0	20	23	7	0	0	0	35
M (Marnus) Schoeman	7	1	0	0	0	5	4	1	0	0	0	5	11	2	0	0	0	10	29	16	0	0	0	80
SB (Brian) Shabangu	7	2	0	0	0	10	4	1	0	0	0	5	11	3	0	0	0	15	25	6	0	0	0	30
AH (Hennie) Skorbinski	9	2	0	0	0	10	6	0	0	0	0	0	15	2	0	0	0	10	28	6	0	0	0	30
JH (Jannie) Stander	13	1	0	0	0	5	7	1	0	0	0	5	20	2	0	0	0	10	27	2	0	0	0	10
HD (Heinrich) Steyl	12	2	3	3	0	25	3	0	3	0	0	6	15	2	6	3	0	31	21	4	6	3	0	41
ENG (Emile) Temperman	13	0	0	0	0	0	8	0	0	0	0	0	21	0	0	0	0	0	21	0	0	0	0	0
DJ (De-Jay) Terblanche	11	3	0	0	0	15	8	0	0	0	0	0	19	3	0	0	0	15	157	11	0	0	0	55
HB (Nardus) van der Walt	11	1	0	0	0	5	3	0	0	0	0	0	14	1	0	0	0	5	14	1	0	0	0	5
MD (Marlou) van Niekerk	10	1	2	0	0	9	5	1	0	0	0	5	15	2	2	0	0	14	15	2	2	0	0	14
R (Reynier) van Rooyen	13	3	0	0	0	15	2	0	0	0	0	0	15	3	0	0	0	15	60	7	0	0	0	35
J (Justin) van Staden	13	0	30	19	0	117	2	1	0	0	0	5	15	1	30	19	0	122	49	4	68	55	0	321
L-RM (Leighton) van Wyk	4	1	2	0	0	9	4	1	0	0	0	5	8	2	2	0	0	14	8	2	2	0	0	14
S (Simon) Westraad	5	0	0	0	0	0	6	0	0	0	0	0	11	0	0	0	0	0	20	0	0	0	0	0
DF (Devon) Williams	1	0	1	0	0	2	8	1	3	0	0	11	9	1	4	0	0	13	9	1	4	0	0	13

Namibian international Renaldo Bothma.

W.P. RUGBY

Western Province RFU

Founded: 1883 **Ground:** Newlands **Capacity:** 49,000
Address: 11 Boundary Road, Newlands **Postal address:** PO Box
66, Newlands 7725 **Telephone Number:** 021-659 4500
Website: www.wprugby.com **Colours:** Royal blue & white hoops,
black shorts & socks **Currie Cup Coach:** John Dobson
Captain: Chris van Zyl **President:** Thelo Wakefield
Company CEO: Rob Wagner (retired) Paul Zacks
as from 1 May 2016

'96	'97	'98	'99	'00	'01
5th	1st	4th	11th	2nd	1st

'02	'03	'04	'05	'06	'07
5th	3rd	2nd	3rd	3rd	5th

'08	'09	'10	'11	'12	'13
5th	2nd	2nd	4th	3rd	1st

'14	'15	'16
1st	3rd	3rd

Played	Won	Lost	Drawn	Points for	Points against	Tries for	Tries against
9	5	4	0	296	286	38	32

Date	Venue	Opponent	Result	Score	Referee	Scorers
Aug 05	Pretoria	Blue Bulls	LOST	26-45	S Berry	T: Jones, Kotze, Zas, Van Breda. C: Thomson (3).
Aug 19	Cape Town	Free State	LOST	25-32	C Joubert	T: Jones, Van Wyk, Zas. C: Thomson, Du Preez. P: Thomson (2).
Aug 27	Port Elizabeth	EP Kings	WON	36-06	L Legoete	T: Jones (3), J Vermaak, Zas, Notshe. C: Thomson (3).
Sep 03	Cape Town	Sharks	WON	34-27	R Rasivhenge	T: Viljoen (2), Kotze, Van Dyk, Kok. C: Du Preez (3). P: Du Preez.
Sep 09	Johannesburg	Golden Lions	LOST	32-58	J Peyper	T: Vermeulen (2), Duvenage, Zas. C: Du Preez (3). P: Du Preez (2).
Sep 17	Cape Town	Pumas	WON	31-23	A Ruiz	T: Jones, De Klerk, Zas, Kok. C: Du Preez (4). P: Du Preez.
Sep 23	Kimberley	Griquas	WON	52-31	J Peyper	T: Jones, de Jongh, Zas, Mbonambi, Carr, Kok. C: Du Preez (5). P: Du Preez (4).
Sep 30	Cape Town	Boland	WON	30-28	AJ Jacobs	T: Van Dyk, Van Breda, Ribbans. C: Du Preez (3). P: Du Preez (3).
SEMI-FINAL						
Oct 15	Pretoria	Blue Bulls	LOST	30-36	M v/d Westhuizen	T: De Klerk, Carr, Kok. C: Du Preez (3). P: Du Preez (3).

Note: ■ = *Champion*

APPEARANCES & POINTS

PLAYER	Blue Bulls	Free State	EP Kings	Sharks	Golden Lions	Pumas	Griquas	Boland	Blue Bulls	Apps	T	C	P	DG	Pts
Scott van Breda	15	–	–	6R	11R	13R	12R	14	11R	7	2	–	–	–	10
Khanyo Ngcukana	14	–	–	–	–	–	–	–	–	1	–	–	–	–	0
Huw Jones	13	12	13	–	–	12	12	–	13	6	7	–	–	–	35
Daniel du Plessis	12	–	12	–	–	–	–	–	–	2	–	–	–	–	0
Leolin Zas	11	11	11	11	11	11	11	11	11	9	6	–	–	–	30
Robert du Preez	10	10R	12R	10	10	10	10	10	10	9	–	22	14	–	86
Jano Vermaak	9	9	9	9	9	–	9R	9	9R	8	1	–	–	–	5
Jacques Vermeulen	8	–	–	–	6R	7R	–	–	–	3	2	–	–	–	10
Jurie van Vuuren	7	6R	6	8R	7	8R	6R	6R	–	8	–	–	–	–	0
Rynhardt Elstadt	6	6	–	–	6	–	6	6	6	6	–	–	–	–	0
Chris van Zyl	5c	5c	5c	5c	5c	5c	5c	5c	5c	9	–	–	–	–	0
JD Schickerling	4	–	4	4	–	–	–	–	5R	4	–	–	–	–	0
Wilco Louw	3	3	3	3	3	3	3	3	3	9	–	–	–	–	0
Siyabonga Ntubeni	2	2	2	2	–	–	–	–	–	4	–	–	–	–	0
Alistair Vermaak	1	1	1R	1R	1R	1	1R	1	1	9	–	–	–	–	0
Chad Solomon	2R	–	–	–	–	–	–	–	–	1	–	–	–	–	0
Oliver Kebble	1R	–	3R	–	–	–	–	–	–	2	–	–	–	–	0
JP Smith	3R	3R	–	3R	3R	3R	3R	3R	3R	8	–	–	–	–	0
Kobus van Dyk	8R	7	7	7	8	6	7	7	7	9	2	–	–	–	10
Godlen Masimla	9R	9R	9R	–	–	9	–	–	–	4	–	–	–	–	0
Brandon Thomson	10R	10	10	–	–	–	–	–	–	3	–	7	2	–	20
Johnny Kotze	12R	13	–	12	12	–	–	13	14R	6	2	–	–	–	10
Jaco Taute	–	15	–	–	–	–	–	–	–	1	–	–	–	–	0
Kobus van Wyk	–	14	–	–	–	–	–	–	–	1	1	–	–	–	5
Sikhumbuszo Notshe	–	8	8	8	–	–	–	–	–	3	1	–	–	–	5
Jan de Klerk	–	4	4R	4R	4	4	4	4	4	8	2	–	–	–	10
Cheslin Kolbe	–	15R	15	15	15	15	15	15	15	8	–	–	–	–	0
JC Janse van Rensburg	–	1R	1	1	1	–	1	1R	1	7	–	–	–	–	0
Martin Ferreira	–	2R	–	–	–	–	–	–	–	1	–	–	–	–	0
Werner Kok	–	–	14	14	14	14	14	14R	14	7	4	–	–	–	20
Stefan Willemse	–	–	6R	6	–	7	–	–	7R	4	–	–	–	–	0
Neil Rautenbach	–	–	2R	2R	2R	2R	–	x	–	4	–	–	–	–	0
EW Viljoen	–	–	–	13	13	13	–	–	–	3	2	–	–	–	10
Dewaldt Duvenage	–	–	–	9R	9R	9R	9	–	9	5	1	–	–	–	5
Michael Willemse	–	–	–	–	2	2	2R	2	2R	5	–	–	–	–	0
Eital Bredenkamp	–	–	–	–	5R	–	–	–	–	1	–	–	–	–	0
Nizaam Carr	–	–	–	–	–	8	8	8	8	4	2	–	–	–	10
Sti Sithole	–	–	–	–	–	1R	–	–	–	1	–	–	–	–	0
Juan de Jongh	–	–	–	–	–	13	–	12	–	2	1	–	–	–	5
Bongi Mbonambi	–	–	–	–	–	2	–	2	–	2	1	–	–	–	5
David Ribbans	–	–	–	–	–	5R	5R	–	–	2	1	–	–	–	5
Damian de Allende	–	–	–	–	–	–	12	–	–	1	–	–	–	–	0
Justin Phillips	–	–	–	–	–	–	x	–	–	0	–	–	–	–	0
43 PLAYERS										197	38	29	16	0	296

CURRIE CUP SQUAD – CAREER CURRIE CUP APPEARANCES

PLAYER	WP						OTHER UNIONS						TOTAL					
	A	T	C	P	DG	Pts	A	T	C	P	DG	Pts	A	T	C	P	DG	Pts
E (Eital) Bredenkamp	1	–	–	–	–	0	1	–	–	–	–	0	2	–	–	–	–	0
N (Nizaam) Carr	42	14	–	–	–	70	–	–	–	–	–	0	42	14	–	–	–	70
D (Damian) de Allende	13	4	–	–	–	20	–	–	–	–	–	0	13	4	–	–	–	20
JL (Juan) de Jongh	56	22	–	–	–	110	–	–	–	–	–	0	56	22	–	–	–	110
JC (Jan) de Klerk	12	2	–	–	–	10	–	–	–	–	–	0	12	2	–	–	–	10
DM (Daniel) du Plessis	2	–	–	–	–	0	–	–	–	–	–	0	2	–	–	–	–	0
RJ (Robert) du Preez	18	4	41	28	–	186	–	–	–	–	–	0	18	4	41	28	–	186
DO (Dewaldt) Duvenage	32	4	–	–	–	20	–	–	–	–	–	0	32	4	–	–	–	20
R (Rynhardt) Elstad	36	4	–	–	–	20	–	–	–	–	–	0	36	4	–	–	–	20
M (Martin) Ferreira	1	–	–	–	–	0	36	6	–	–	–	30	37	6	–	–	–	30
JC (JC) Janse van Rensburg	7	–	–	–	–	0	31	3	–	–	–	15	38	3	–	–	–	15
HRF (Huw) Jones	14	8	–	–	–	40	–	–	–	–	–	0	14	8	–	–	–	40
OR (Oliver) Kebble	16	–	–	–	–	0	–	–	–	–	–	0	16	–	–	–	–	0
W (Werner) Kok	7	4	–	–	–	20	–	–	–	–	–	0	7	4	–	–	–	20
C (Cheslin) Kolbe	40	9	1	–	–	47	–	–	–	–	–	0	40	9	1	–	–	47
J-B (Johnny) Kotze	16	3	–	–	–	15	–	–	–	–	–	0	16	3	–	–	–	15
WM (Wilco) Louw	21	–	–	–	–	0	–	–	–	–	–	0	21	–	–	–	–	0
GHD (Godlen) Masimla	11	1	–	–	–	5	–	–	–	–	–	0	11	1	–	–	–	5
MT (Mbongeni) Mbonambi	14	2	–	–	–	10	22	1	–	–	–	5	34	3	–	–	–	15
KT (Khanyo) Ngcukana	1	–	–	–	–	0	–	–	–	–	–	0	1	–	–	–	–	0
S (Sikumbuzo) Notshe	22	8	–	–	–	40	–	–	–	–	–	0	22	8	–	–	–	40
S (Scarra) Ntubeni	40	2	–	–	–	10	–	–	–	–	–	0	40	2	–	–	–	10
N (Neil) Rautenbach	4	–	–	–	–	0	13	–	–	–	–	0	17	–	–	–	–	0
DG (David) Ribbans	2	1	–	–	–	5	–	–	–	–	–	0	2	1	–	–	–	5
JD (JD) Schickerling	4	–	–	–	–	0	–	–	–	–	–	0	4	–	–	–	–	0
SMS (Sti) Sithole	1	–	–	–	–	0	–	–	–	–	–	0	1	–	–	–	–	0
J-P (Jean-Pierre) Smith	10	–	–	–	–	0	–	–	–	–	–	0	10	–	–	–	–	0
C (Chad) Solomon	1	–	–	–	–	0	–	–	–	–	–	0	1	–	–	–	–	0
JJ (Jaco) Taute	17	3	–	–	–	15	31	13	–	1	–	68	48	16	–	1	–	83
BT (Brandon) Thomson	3	–	7	2	–	20	–	–	–	–	–	0	3	–	7	2	–	20
SA (Scott) van Breda	7	2	–	–	–	10	31	3	48	56	–	279	38	5	48	56	–	289
JJ (Kobus) van Dyk	9	2	–	–	–	10	–	–	–	–	–	0	9	2	–	–	–	10
JG (Jurie) van Vuuren	18	1	–	–	–	5	–	–	–	–	–	0	18	1	–	–	–	5
JP (Kobus) van Wyk	20	7	–	–	–	35	–	–	–	–	–	0	20	7	–	–	–	35
CM (Chris) van Zyl	18	–	–	–	–	0	8	–	–	–	–	0	26	–	–	–	–	0
AF (Alistair) Vermaak	25	1	–	–	–	5	–	–	–	–	–	0	25	1	–	–	–	5
J (Jano) Vermaak	16	4	–	–	–	20	89	24	3	4	–	138	105	28	3	4	–	158
JF (Jacques) Vermeulen	3	2	–	–	–	10	–	–	–	–	–	0	3	2	–	–	–	10
EW (EW) Viljoen	5	2	–	–	–	10	–	–	–	–	–	0	5	2	–	–	–	10
ME (Michael) Willemse	10	–	–	–	–	0	–	–	–	–	–	0	10	–	–	–	–	0
S (Stefan) Willemse	4	–	–	–	–	0	28	5	–	–	–	25	32	5	–	–	–	25
LL (Leolin) Zas	10	6	–	–	–	30	–	–	–	–	–	0	10	6	–	–	–	30
42 PLAYERS	609	122	49	30	0	798	290	55	51	61	0	560	897	177	100	91	0	1358

FIRST-CLASS APPEARANCES FOR WP IN 2016 – ALL MATCHES

PLAYER	CURRIE CUP QUALIFY						CURRIE CUP						2015 TOTAL						CAREER MATCHES					
	A	T	C	P	DG	Pts	A	T	C	P	DG	Pts	A	T	C	P	DG	Pts	A	T	C	P	DG	Pts
PL (Rikus) Bothma	2	0	0	0	0	0	0	0	0	0	0	0	2	0	0	0	0	0	2	0	0	0	0	0
A (Alvin) Brandt	1	0	0	0	0	0	0	0	0	0	0	0	1	0	0	0	0	0	1	0	0	0	0	0
E (Eital) Bredenkamp	12	3	0	0	0	15	1	0	0	0	0	0	13	3	0	0	0	15	19	3	0	0	0	15
N (Nizaam) Carr	0	0	0	0	0	0	4	2	0	0	0	10	4	2	0	0	0	10	43	11	0	0	0	55
W (Wesley) Chetty	2	0	0	0	0	0	0	0	0	0	0	0	2	0	0	0	0	0	2	0	0	0	0	0
CT (Cullen) Collopy	7	2	0	0	0	10	0	0	0	0	0	0	7	2	0	0	0	10	7	2	0	0	0	10
DC (Dennis) Cox	5	1	1	0	0	7	0	0	0	0	0	0	5	1	1	0	0	7	5	1	1	0	0	7
T (Tertius) Daniller	3	0	0	0	0	0	0	0	0	0	0	0	3	0	0	0	0	0	20	1	0	0	0	5
D (Damian) de Allende	0	0	0	0	0	0	1	0	0	0	0	0	1	0	0	0	0	0	25	6	0	0	0	30
JL (Juan) de Jongh	0	0	0	0	0	0	2	1	0	0	0	5	2	1	0	0	0	5	58	23	0	0	0	115
JC (Jan) de Klerk	0	0	0	0	0	0	8	2	0	0	0	10	8	2	0	0	0	10	25	3	0	0	0	15
BJ (Beyers) de Villiers	7	2	0	0	0	10	0	0	0	0	0	0	7	2	0	0	0	10	7	2	0	0	0	10
DM (Daniel) du Plessis	6	4	0	0	0	20	2	0	0	0	0	0	8	4	0	0	0	20	8	4	0	0	0	20
RJ (Robert) du Preez	5	2	19	3	0	57	9	0	22	14	0	86	14	2	41	17	0	143	34	9	69	34	0	285
DO (Dewaldt) Duvenage	0	0	0	0	0	0	5	1	0	0	0	5	5	1	0	0	0	5	56	6	2	1	0	37
R (Rynhardt) Elstad	0	0	0	0	0	0	6	0	0	0	0	0	6	0	0	0	0	0	46	4	0	0	0	20
M (Martin) Ferreira	0	0	0	0	0	0	1	0	0	0	0	0	1	0	0	0	0	0	1	0	0	0	0	0
GH (Grant) Hermanus	12	3	16	4	0	59	0	0	0	0	0	0	12	3	16	4	0	59	14	4	16	4	0	64
HJ (Herschel) Jantjies	1	0	0	0	0	0	0	0	0	0	0	0	1	0	0	0	0	0	1	0	0	0	0	0
JC (JC) Janse van Rensburg	1	0	0	0	0	0	7	0	0	0	0	0	8	0	0	0	0	0	7	0	0	0	0	0
HR (Huw) Jones	0	0	0	0	0	0	6	7	0	0	0	35	6	7	0	0	0	35	16	9	0	0	0	45
OR (Oliver) Kebble	0	0	0	0	0	0	2	0	0	0	0	0	2	0	0	0	0	0	18	0	0	0	0	0
BW (Berton) Klaassen	4	0	0	0	0	0	0	0	0	0	0	0	4	0	0	0	0	0	28	2	0	0	0	10
J (Jean) Kleyn	2	1	0	0	0	5	0	0	0	0	0	0	2	1	0	0	0	5	24	1	0	0	0	5
C (Cheslin) Kolbe	0	0	0	0	0	0	8	0	0	0	0	0	8	0	0	0	0	0	47	13	1	0	0	67
W (Werner) Kok	0	0	0	0	0	0	7	4	0	0	0	20	7	4	0	0	0	20	7	4	0	0	0	20
J-B (Johnny) Kotze	5	1	0	0	0	5	6	2	0	0	0	10	11	3	0	0	0	15	27	5	0	0	0	25
J-P (JP) Lewis	10	5	0	0	0	25	0	0	0	0	0	0	10	5	0	0	0	25	23	8	0	0	0	40
WM (Wilco) Louw	5	0	0	0	0	0	9	0	0	0	0	0	14	0	0	0	0	0	36	1	0	0	0	5
GHD (Godlen) Masimla	8	2	0	0	0	10	4	0	0	0	0	0	12	2	0	0	0	10	39	5	0	0	0	25
SN (Sibahle) Maxwane	8	2	0	0	0	10	0	0	0	0	0	0	8	2	0	0	0	10	8	2	0	0	0	10
MT (Bongi) Mbonambi	0	0	0	0	0	0	2	1	0	0	0	5	2	1	0	0	0	5	14	2	0	0	0	10
SP (Percy) Mngadi	1	0	0	0	0	0	0	0	0	0	0	0	1	0	0	0	0	0	1	0	0	0	0	0
FJ (Freddie) Muller	1	1	0	0	0	5	0	0	0	0	0	0	1	1	0	0	0	5	5	1	0	0	0	5
KT (Khanyo) Ngcukana	10	6	0	0	0	30	1	0	0	0	0	0	11	6	0	0	0	30	11	6	0	0	0	30
S (Sikumbuzo) Notshe	0	0	0	0	0	0	3	1	0	0	0	5	3	1	0	0	0	5	44	17	0	0	0	85
S (Scarra) Ntubeni	0	0	0	0	0	0	4	0	0	0	0	0	4	0	0	0	0	0	47	2	0	0	0	10
JD (Justin) Phillips	10	5	0	0	0	25	0	0	0	0	0	0	10	5	0	0	0	25	14	5	0	0	0	25
N (Neil) Rautenbach	0	0	0	0	0	0	4	0	0	0	0	0	4	0	0	0	0	0	19	0	0	0	0	0
DG (David) Ribbans	4	0	0	0	0	0	2	1	0	0	0	5	6	1	0	0	0	5	7	1	0	0	0	5
DB (Denzel) Riddles	2	0	0	0	0	0	0	0	0	0	0	0	2	0	0	0	0	0	8	0	0	0	0	0
JD (JD) Schickerling	1	0	0	0	0	0	4	0	0	0	0	0	5	0	0	0	0	0	6	0	0	0	0	0
SMS (Sti) Sithole	0	0	0	0	0	0	1	0	0	0	0	0	1	0	0	0	0	0	13	0	0	0	0	0
J-P (Jean-Pierre) Smith	7	0	0	0	0	0	8	0	0	0	0	0	15	0	0	0	0	0	22	0	0	0	0	0
C (Chad) Solomon	13	6	0	0	0	30	1	0	0	0	0	0	14	6	0	0	0	30	16	6	0	0	0	30

FIRST-CLASS APPEARANCES FOR WP IN 2016 – ALL MATCHES

PLAYER	CURRIE CUP QUALIFY						CURRIE CUP						2015 TOTAL						CAREER MATCHES					
	A	T	C	P	DG	Pts	A	T	C	P	DG	Pts	A	T	C	P	DG	Pts	A	T	C	P	DG	Pts
DL (Damian) Stevens	4	0	0	0	0	0	0	0	0	0	0	0	4	0	0	0	0	0	4	0	0	0	0	0
LJ (Luke) Stringer	13	3	0	0	0	15	0	0	0	0	0	0	13	3	0	0	0	15	13	3	0	0	0	15
M (Meyer) Swanepoel	5	1	0	0	0	5	0	0	0	0	0	0	5	1	0	0	0	5	5	1	0	0	0	5
JJ (Jaco) Taute	2	2	0	0	0	10	1	0	0	0	0	0	3	2	0	0	0	10	23	7	0	0	0	35
BT (Brandon) Thomson	2	0	3	3	0	15	3	0	7	2	0	20	5	0	10	5	0	35	5	0	10	5	0	35
SA (Scott) van Breda	8	3	17	7	0	70	7	2	0	0	0	10	15	5	17	7	0	80	15	5	17	7	0	80
C (Christo) van der Merwe	4	1	0	0	0	5	0	0	0	0	0	0	4	1	0	0	0	5	4	1	0	0	0	5
EC (Edwill) van der Merwe	3	2	0	0	0	10	0	0	0	0	0	0	3	2	0	0	0	10	3	2	0	0	0	10
JJ (Kobus) van Dyk	10	2	0	0	0	10	9	2	0	0	0	10	19	4	0	0	0	20	19	4	0	0	0	20
JG (Jurie) van Vuuren	12	1	0	0	0	5	8	0	0	0	0	0	20	1	0	0	0	5	35	2	0	0	0	10
CJ (Christo) van Wyk	2	0	0	0	0	0	0	0	0	0	0	0	2	0	0	0	0	0	6	1	0	0	0	5
FRP (Frans) van Wyk	5	1	0	0	0	5	0	0	0	0	0	0	5	1	0	0	0	5	7	1	0	0	0	5
JP (Kobus) van Wyk	0	0	0	0	0	0	1	1	0	0	0	5	1	1	0	0	0	5	25	10	0	0	0	50
CM (Chris) van Zyl	13	1	0	0	0	5	9	0	0	0	0	0	22	1	0	0	0	5	41	1	0	0	0	5
AF (Alistair) Vermaak	6	0	0	0	0	0	9	0	0	0	0	0	15	0	0	0	0	0	47	2	0	0	0	10
J (Jano) Vermaak	3	0	0	0	0	0	8	1	0	0	0	5	11	1	0	0	0	5	19	4	0	0	0	20
JS (Jacques) Vermeulen	5	0	0	0	0	0	3	2	0	0	0	10	8	2	0	0	0	10	12	2	0	0	0	10
J (Janco) Venter	4	1	0	0	0	5	0	0	0	0	0	0	4	1	0	0	0	5	4	1	0	0	0	5
EW (EW) Viljoen	8	5	0	0	0	25	3	2	0	0	0	10	11	7	0	0	0	35	20	10	0	0	0	50
AD (Ashley) Wells	1	0	0	0	0	0	0	0	0	0	0	0	1	0	0	0	0	0	11	0	0	0	0	0
TJ (Tim) Whitehead	10	3	0	0	0	15	0	0	0	0	0	0	10	3	0	0	0	15	33	6	0	0	0	30
KJ (Kyle) Whyte	9	0	0	0	0	0	0	0	0	0	0	0	9	0	0	0	0	0	9	0	0	0	0	0
ME (Michael) Willemse	7	3	0	0	0	15	5	0	0	0	0	0	12	3	0	0	0	15	36	4	0	0	0	20
S (Stefan) Willemse	0	0	0	0	0	0	4	0	0	0	0	0	4	0	0	0	0	0	4	0	0	0	0	0
DF (Devon) Williams	6	2	0	0	0	10	0	0	0	0	0	0	6	2	0	0	0	10	22	13	0	0	0	65
DT (Dale) Wilson	2	0	0	0	0	0	0	0	0	0	0	0	2	0	0	0	0	0	2	0	0	0	0	0
E le R (Eduard) Zandberg	3	0	0	0	0	0	0	0	0	0	0	0	3	0	0	0	0	0	3	0	0	0	0	0
LL (Leolin) Zas	0	0	0	0	0	0	9	6	0	0	0	30	9	6	0	0	0	30	10	6	0	0	0	30

74 PLAYERS

What a journey for Huw Jones – from Cape Town club player just a few years ago, to star with Scotland in 2016.

The Griffons celebrate their victory in the Currie Cup First Division final.

LOG

Team	P	W	L	D	PF	PA	PD	TF	TA	LB	TB	Pts
Leopards	5	5	0	0	214	149	65	31	23	0	5	25
Border	5	4	1	0	211	110	101	31	15	1	5	22
Griffons	5	3	2	0	224	163	61	29	23	0	3	15
Valke	5	2	3	0	159	198	-39	26	27	0	4	12
SWD	5	1	4	0	168	170	-2	23	22	3	3	10
Welwitschias	5	0	5	0	117	303	-186	15	45	0	2	2

Note: LB = Lost Bonus, TB = Try Bonus

LEADING SCORERS

30 POINTS OR MORE

		T	C	P	DG	Pts
George Whitehead	Griffons	2	32	17	0	125
Johan Deysel	Leopards	5	29	6	0	101
Masixole Banda	Border	6	26	5	0	97
Eugene Jantjies	Welwitschias	2	12	6	0	52
Gene Willemse	Leopards	8	0	0	0	40
Hansie Graaff	SWD	0	13	4	0	38
Karlo Aspeling	Valke	0	13	3	0	35
Henro-Pierre Swart	Leopards	6	0	0	0	30
Johan Pretorius	Valke	6	0	0	0	30

4 TRIES OR MORE

Gene Willemse	Leopards	8	Sipho Nofemele	Border	5
Masixole Banda	Border	6	Warren Williams	Griffons	5
Henro-Pierre Swart	Leopards	6	Bradley Moolman	Leopards	4
Johan Pretorius	Valke	6	Charles Mayeza	Valke	4
Johan Deysel	Leopards	5	Etienne Taljaard	Valke	4
Lesley Klim	Welwitschias	5			

PLAY-OFF RESULTS
SEMI-FINALS: Border lost to the Griffons 16-25 *(East London).*
Leopards bt Valke 40-30 *(Potchefstroom).*

2016 CURRIE CUP FIRST DIVISION FINAL
Profert Olen Park, Potchefstroom, Friday, 7 October 2016.
Referee: Quinton Immelman. Crowd: 1200
Leopards 25
(Tries: Hayward, Vermeulen, Deysel. Conversions: Deysel 2. Penalties: Deysel 2).
Griffons 44
(Tries: Kruger 2, Whitehead, Davids, Penalty try. Conversions: Whitehead 5. Penalties: Whitehead 3).

Leopards: Jaco Hayward, Dean Gordon, Adrian Vermeulen *(Sandile Kubeka, 38),* Johan Deysel, Bradley Moolman, Gene Willemse, Malherbe Swart *(Chriswill September, 54),* Jeandré Rudolph *(Capt),* HP Swart *(Marno Redelinghuys, 65),* Juan Language *(Jaco Jordaan, HT),* Walt Steenkamp, Sti Mhlongo *(Francois Robertse, 45),* Dewald Dekker, Dane van der Westhuyzen *(Louis van der Westhuizen, 54),* Roan Grobbelaar *(Kabelo Motloung, 61).*
Griffons: Selvyn Davids, Vuyo Mbotho *(Joubert Engelbrecht, 72),* Tertius Kruger, Japie Nel, Warren Williams *(Duan Pretorius, 32),* George Whitehead, Boela Abrahams *(Louis Venter, 66),* Martin Sithole *(Elandré Huggett, 61),* Boela Venter, Vincent Maruping *(Samora Fihlani, 10),* Dennis Visser *(Willem Serfontein, HT),* Gavin Annandale *(Capt),* Gerhard Engelbrecht *(Heinrich Roelfse, 66),* Khwezi Mkhafu, Danie van der Merwe.

Border Rugby Football Union

Founded: 1891 **Ground:** Buffalo Stadium (formerly the Basil Kenyon Stadium) **Capacity:** 15 000
Address: Recreation Road, East London, 5201 **Postal address:** PO Box 75, East London, 5200
Telephone Number: 043-743 5998 **Website:** www.borderbulldogs.co.za **Colours:** Brown jersey
with white, red and green stripes and white shorts with green stripes. Brown socks with
two white stripes. **Currie Cup Coach:** Elliot Fana **Captains:** Siya Mdaka & Blake Kyd
President: Phumlani Mkoto **CEO:** Vacant

1996	1997	1998	1999	2000	2001	2002	2003	2004	2005	2006
8th	7th	10th	12th	5th	9th	12th	10th	9th	6th	10th

2007	2008	2009	2010	2011	2012	2013	2014	2015	2016
7th	7th	8th	11th	9th	12th	11th	13th	13th	11th

Played	Won	Lost	Drawn	Points for	Points against	Tries for	Tries against
6	4	2	0	227	135	32	16

Date	Venue	Opponent	Result	Score	Referee	Scorers
Aug 12	East London	Leopards	LOST	24-26	AJ Jacobs	T: Nofemele, Banda, Manentsa, Makase. C: Banda (2).
Aug 26	East London	Welwitschias	WON	61-07	E Seconds	T: Mqalo (2), Nofemele (2), Mapimpi, Banda, Nyoka, Dubase, Zono. C: Banda (8).
Sept 02	East London	Griffons	WON	41-24	J Peyper	T: Zono (2), Banda, Nofemele, Dubase, Makase. C: Banda (4). P: Banda.
Sept 09	Kempton Park	Valke	WON	54-29	C Jadezweni	T: Banda (2), Nofemele, Dumezweni, Mapimpi, Gemashe, Welemu, Mqalo. C: Banda (7).
Sept 16	East London	SWD	WON	31-24	M Adamson	T: Banda, Dubase, Khethani, Kota. C: Banda (4). P: Banda.

SEMI FINAL:

Date	Venue	Opponent	Result	Score	Referee	Scorers
Sept 30	East London	Griffons	LOST	16-25	L Legoete	T: Mapimpi. C: Banda. P: Banda (3).

APPEARANCES & POINTS

PLAYER	Leopards	Welwitchias	Griffons	Valke	SWD	Griffons	Apps	T	C	P	DG	Pts
Sonwabiso Mqalo	15	15	–	10R	15	10R	5	3	–	–	–	15
Sipho Nofemele	14	14	14	14	14	14	6	5	–	–	–	25
Lundi Ralarala	13	13	13	13	13	13	6	–	–	–	–	0
Lunga Dumezweni	12	12	12	12	12R	12	6	1	–	–	–	5
Makazole Mapimpi	11	11	11	11	11	11	6	3	–	–	–	15
Masixole Banda	10	10	15	15	10	15	6	6	26	5	–	97
Sino Nyoka	9	9	9	9R	9R	9R	6	1	–	–	–	5
Athi Mamentsa	8	–	–	–	–	–	1	1	–	–	–	5
Siya Mdaka	7c	7c	7c	–	–	7c	4	–	–	–	–	0
Onke Dubase	6	6	6	6	6	6	6	3	–	–	–	15
Hendri Storm	5	5	5	5	5	5	6	–	–	–	–	0
Lindokuhle Welemu	4	4	4	4	–	4	5	1	–	–	–	5
Johannes Jonker	3	–	3	3	–	3	4	–	–	–	–	0
Mihlali Mpafi	2	2	2	2	2R	2	6	–	–	–	–	0
Blake Kyd	1	1	1	1c	3c	1	6	–	–	–	–	0
Mbeko Kota	2R	2R	x	2R	2	x	4	1	–	–	–	5
Siya Ngande	1R	1R	–	–	1	1R	4	–	–	–	–	0
Nkosi Nofuma	6R	–	–	–	–	–	1	–	–	–	–	0
Billy Dutton	8R	–	7R	–	7	5R	4	–	–	–	–	0
Bangi Kobese	9R	9R	9R	9	9	9	6	–	–	–	–	0
Oliver Zono	12R	15R	10	10	–	10	5	3	–	–	–	15
Michael Makase	14R	–	10R	–	14R	–	3	2	–	–	–	10
Johannes J van Rensburg	–	8	8	7	8	8	5	–	–	–	–	0
Phumlani Blaauw	–	3	–	–	17R	–	2	–	–	–	–	0
Yanga Xakalashe	–	3R	1R	3R	1R	–	4	–	–	–	–	0
Athi Khethani	–	5R	8R	5R	4	–	4	1	–	–	–	5
Soso Xakalashe	–	7R	–	–	–	–	1	–	–	–	–	0
Sethu Tom	–	–	13R	13R	12	13R	4	–	–	–	–	0
Ndzondelelo Gemashe	–	–	–	8	–	–	1	1	–	–	–	5
Lukhanyo Nomzanga	–	–	–	8R	7R	7R	3	–	–	–	–	0
30 PLAYERS							**130**	**32**	**26**	**5**	**0**	**227**

CURRIE CUP SQUAD – CAREER CURRIE CUP APPEARANCES

PLAYER	BORDER						OTHER UNIONS						TOTAL					
	A	T	C	P	DG	Pts	A	T	C	P	DG	Pts	A	T	C	P	DG	Pts
M (Masixole) Banda	26	11	48	25	0	226	0	0	0	0	0	0	26	11	48	25	0	226
P (Phumlani) Blaauw	2	0	0	0	0	0	0	0	0	0	0	0	2	0	0	0	0	0
OS (Onke) Dubase	31	5	0	0	0	25	0	0	0	0	0	0	31	5	0	0	0	25
L (Lunga) Dumezweni	6	1	0	0	0	5	0	0	0	0	0	0	6	1	0	0	0	5
B (Billy) Dutton	11	0	0	0	0	0	0	0	0	0	0	0	11	0	0	0	0	0
N (Ndzondelelo) Gemashe	1	1	0	0	0	5	0	0	0	0	0	0	1	1	0	0	0	5
JC (Johannes) Janse van Rensburg	5	0	0	0	0	0	0	0	0	0	0	0	5	0	0	0	0	0
JGA (Johann) Jonker	15	1	0	0	0	5	0	0	0	0	0	0	15	1	0	0	0	5
AE (Athi) Khethani	4	1	0	0	0	5	0	0	0	0	0	0	4	1	0	0	0	5
B (Bangi) Kobese	22	1	0	0	0	5	0	0	0	0	0	0	22	1	0	0	0	5
M (Mbeko) Kota	8	1	0	0	0	5	0	0	0	0	0	0	8	1	0	0	0	5
BJ (Blake) Kyd	34	1	0	0	0	5	0	0	0	0	0	0	34	1	0	0	0	5
M (Michael) Makase	20	6	0	0	0	30	0	0	0	0	0	0	20	6	0	0	0	30
A (Athenkosi) Manentsa	7	1	0	0	0	5	0	0	0	0	0	0	7	1	0	0	0	5
M (Makazole) Mapimpi	26	9	0	0	0	45	0	0	0	0	0	0	26	9	0	0	0	45
S (Siya) Mdaka	37	0	0	0	0	0	4	0	0	0	0	0	41	0	0	0	0	0
M (Mihlali) Mpafi	25	2	0	0	0	10	0	0	0	0	0	0	25	2	0	0	0	10
S (Sonwabiso) Mqalo	5	3	0	0	0	15	0	0	0	0	0	0	5	3	0	0	0	15
S (Siyamthanda) Ngande	9	0	0	0	0	0	0	0	0	0	0	0	9	0	0	0	0	0
S (Sipho) Nofemele	18	8	0	0	0	40	0	0	0	0	0	0	18	8	0	0	0	40
N (Nkosi) Nofuma	15	0	0	0	0	0	0	0	0	0	0	0	15	0	0	0	0	0
LW (Lukhanyo) Nomzanga	18	0	0	0	0	0	0	0	0	0	0	0	18	0	0	0	0	0
S (Sino) Nyoka	24	1	0	0	0	5	9	0	0	0	0	0	33	1	0	0	0	5
LS (Lundi) Ralarala	25	7	0	0	0	35	0	0	0	0	0	0	25	7	0	0	0	35
H (Hendri) Storm	6	0	0	0	0	0	0	0	0	0	0	0	6	0	0	0	0	0
S (Sethu) Tom	7	1	0	0	0	5	0	0	0	0	0	0	7	1	0	0	0	5
L (Lindokuhle) Welemu	22	1	0	0	0	5	0	0	0	0	0	0	22	1	0	0	0	5
S (Soso) Xakalashe	1	0	0	0	0	0	0	0	0	0	0	0	1	0	0	0	0	0
Y (Yanga) Xakalashe	25	1	0	0	0	5	0	0	0	0	0	0	25	1	0	0	0	5
O (Oliver) Zono	18	7	7	2	0	55	0	0	0	0	0	0	18	7	7	2	0	55
30 PLAYERS	473	70	55	27	0	541	13	0	0	0	0	0	486	70	55	27	0	541

FIRST-CLASS APPEARANCES FOR BORDER IN 2016 – ALL MATCHES

PLAYER	CURRIE CUP QUALIFYING						CURRIE CUP						2016 TOTAL						CAREER MATCHES					
	A	T	C	P	DG	Pts	A	T	C	P	DG	Pts	A	T	C	P	DG	Pts	A	T	C	P	DG	Pts
M (Masixole) Banda	14	4	15	12	0	86	6	6	26	5	0	97	20	10	41	17	0	183	46	15	65	46	0	343
LA (Logan) Basson	7	2	12	4	0	46	0	0	0	0	0	0	7	2	12	4	0	46	38	11	28	31	0	204
P (Phumlani) Blaauw	0	0	0	0	0	0	2	0	0	0	0	0	2	0	0	0	0	0	2	0	0	0	0	0
AL (Ludwe) Booi	13	1	0	0	0	5	0	0	0	0	0	0	13	1	0	0	0	5	35	2	0	0	0	10
OS (Onke) Dubase	2	0	0	0	0	0	6	3	0	0	0	15	8	3	0	0	0	15	50	7	0	0	0	35
L (Lunga) Dumezweni	9	2	0	0	0	10	6	1	0	0	0	5	15	3	0	0	0	15	17	3	0	0	0	15
B (Billy) Dutton	11	1	0	0	0	5	4	0	0	0	0	0	15	1	0	0	0	5	30	1	0	0	0	5
N (Ndzondelelo) Gemashe	0	0	0	0	0	0	1	1	0	0	0	5	1	1	0	0	0	5	1	1	0	0	0	5
JC (Johannes) J van Rensburg	4	0	0	0	0	0	5	0	0	0	0	0	9	0	0	0	0	0	9	0	0	0	0	0
JGA (Johann) Jonker	14	2	0	0	0	10	4	0	0	0	0	0	18	2	0	0	0	10	43	5	0	0	0	25
AE (Athi) Khetani	6	2	0	0	0	10	4	1	0	0	0	5	10	3	0	0	0	15	10	3	0	0	0	15
B (Bangi) Kobese	13	0	0	0	0	0	6	0	0	0	0	0	19	0	0	0	0	0	45	1	5	1	0	18
M (Mbeko) Kota	2	0	0	0	0	0	4	1	0	0	0	5	6	1	0	0	0	5	10	1	0	0	0	5
BJ (Blake) Kyd	14	0	0	0	0	0	6	0	0	0	0	0	20	0	0	0	0	0	86	2	0	0	0	10
M (Michael) Makase	12	4	0	0	0	20	3	2	0	0	0	10	15	6	0	0	0	30	45	11	0	0	0	55
A (Athenkosi) Manentsa	7	0	0	0	0	0	1	1	0	0	0	5	8	1	0	0	0	5	15	1	0	0	0	5
M (Makazole) Mapimpi	14	13	0	0	0	65	6	3	0	0	0	15	20	16	0	0	0	80	54	28	3	1	0	149
S (Siya) Mdaka	12	1	0	0	0	5	4	0	0	0	0	0	16	1	0	0	0	5	70	2	0	0	0	10
TM (Thembani) Mkokeli	3	0	0	0	0	0	0	0	0	0	0	0	3	0	0	0	0	0	120	18	0	1	0	93
M (Mihlali) Mpafi	13	1	0	0	0	5	6	0	0	0	0	0	19	1	0	0	0	5	50	3	0	0	0	15
S (Sonwabiso) Mqalo	9	3	0	0	0	15	5	3	0	0	0	15	14	6	0	0	0	30	14	6	0	0	0	30
S (Sibabalwe) Mtsulwana	1	0	0	0	0	0	0	0	0	0	0	0	1	0	0	0	0	0	1	0	0	0	0	0
B (Buhle) Mxunyelwa	3	0	0	0	0	0	0	0	0	0	0	0	3	0	0	0	0	0	43	2	0	0	0	10
S (Siyasonga) Ncanywa	2	0	0	0	0	0	0	0	0	0	0	0	2	0	0	0	0	0	2	0	0	0	0	0
N (Nkululuko) Ndlovu	6	1	0	0	0	5	0	0	0	0	0	0	6	1	0	0	0	5	6	1	0	0	0	5
S (Siyamthanda) Ngande	9	1	0	0	0	5	4	0	0	0	0	0	13	1	0	0	0	5	23	1	0	0	0	5
S (Sanelise) Ngoma	1	0	0	0	0	0	0	0	0	0	0	0	1	0	0	0	0	0	1	0	0	0	0	0
S (Sipho) Nofemele	8	1	0	0	0	5	6	5	0	0	0	25	14	6	0	0	0	30	38	14	0	0	0	70
N (Nkosi) Nofuma	11	2	0	0	0	10	1	0	0	0	0	0	12	2	0	0	0	10	40	2	0	0	0	10
LW (Lukhanyo) Nomzanga	11	0	0	0	0	0	3	0	0	0	0	0	14	0	0	0	0	0	35	0	0	0	0	0
S (Sino) Nyoka	3	0	0	0	0	0	6	1	0	0	0	5	9	1	0	0	0	5	58	3	0	0	0	15
W (Wandile) Putuma	14	2	0	0	0	10	0	0	0	0	0	0	14	2	0	0	0	10	48	4	0	0	0	20
LS (Lundi) Ralarala	6	0	0	0	0	0	6	0	0	0	0	0	12	0	0	0	0	0	39	9	0	0	0	45
H (Hendri) Storm	5	1	0	0	0	5	6	0	0	0	0	0	11	1	0	0	0	5	11	1	0	0	0	5
S (Sethu) Tom	9	2	0	0	0	10	4	0	0	0	0	0	13	2	0	0	0	10	16	3	0	0	0	15
Z (Zukisani) Tywaleni	7	0	0	0	0	0	0	0	0	0	0	0	7	0	0	0	0	0	8	0	0	0	0	0
L (Lindokuhle) Welemu	14	0	0	0	0	0	5	1	0	0	0	5	19	1	0	0	0	5	47	3	0	0	0	15
S (Soso) Xakalashe	0	0	0	0	0	0	1	0	0	0	0	0	1	0	0	0	0	0	1	0	0	0	0	0
Y (Yanga) Xakalashe	6	0	0	0	0	0	4	0	0	0	0	0	10	0	0	0	0	0	43	1	0	0	0	5
O (Oliver) Zono	9	2	4	3	0	27	5	3	0	0	0	15	14	5	4	3	0	42	36	9	14	6	0	91
Penalty try	0	1	0	0	0	5	0	0	0	0	0	0	0	1	0	0	0	5	0	0	0	0	0	0

40 PLAYERS

GRIFFONS

RUGBY

Griffons Rugby Union

Founded: 1968 (as Northern Free State) **Ground:** HT Pelatona Investment Stadium, Welkom
(previously North West Stadium) **Capacity:** 7,500 **Address:** Rugby Street, Welkom
Postal address: PO Box 631, Welkom 9460 **Telephone Number:** 057-352 6482
Email: rugbybond@icon.co.za **Colours:** Purple and yellow jersey, white shorts
Currie Cup Coach: Oersond Gorgonzola **Captains:** Gavin Annandale & Joubert Engelbrecht
President: Randall September **CEO:** Eugene van Wyk

1996	1997	1998	1999	2000	2001	2002	2003	2004	2005	2006
12th	12th	14th	13th	14th	13th	14th	14th	14th	11th	10th

2007	2008	2009	2010	2011	2012	2013	2014	2015	2016
11th	9th	11th	12th	12th	9th	12th	10th	10th	12th

Played	Won	Lost	Drawn	Points for	Points against	Tries for	Tries against
7	5	2	0	293	204	35	27

Date	Venue	Opponent	Result	Score	Referee	Scorers
Aug 12	Welkom	Valke	WON	50-27	Q Immelman	T: Mbotho (3), Davids (2), Huggett, Sithole, C: Whitehead (6). P: Whitehead.
Aug 19	George	SWD	WON	33-27	E Seconds	T: Abrahams, Erwee, Penalty try. C: Whitehead (3). P: Whitehead (3). DG: Abrahams.
Aug 26	Potchefstroom	Leopards	LOST	33-43	R Boneparte	T: B Venter, Whitehead, Nel, Sithole, Williams. C: Whitehead (4).
Sep 02	East London	Border	LOST	24-41	J Peyper	T: Annandale, Nel. C: Whitehead. P: Whitehead (4).
Sep 10	Welkom	Welwitschias	WON	84-25	Q Immelman	T: Williams (4), D Kruger (3), Visser (2), Van der Merwe, Erwee, B Venter. C: Whitehead (12).

SEMI-FINAL

Date	Venue	Opponent	Result	Score	Referee	Scorers
Sep 30	East London	Border	WON	25-16	L Legoete	T: Van der Merwe. C: Whitehead. P: Whitehead (6).

FINAL

Date	Venue	Opponent	Result	Score	Referee	Scorers
Oct 07	Potchefstroom	Leopards	WON	44-25	Q Immelman	T: T Kruger (2), Davids, Whitehead, Penalty try. C: Whitehead (5). P: Whitehead (3).

APPEARANCES & POINTS

PLAYER	Valke	SWD	Leopards	Border	Welwitchias	Border	Leopards	Apps	T	C	P	DG	Pts
Vuyo Mbotho	14	11	14	14	14	14	14	7	3	–	–	–	15
Tertius Kruger	13	13	13	13R	13R	13	13	7	2	–	–	–	10
Joubert Engelbrecht	12c	12c	12c	13c	13c	x	14R	6	–	–	–	–	0
Warren Williams	11	15R	11	11	11	11	11	7	5	–	–	–	25
George Whitehead	10	10	10	10	10	10	10	7	2	32	17	–	125
Boela Abrahams	9	9	9	9	9	9	9	7	1	–	–	1	8
De Wet Kruger	8	8	8	8	8	8	–	6	3	–	–	–	15
Vincent Maruping	7	7	6	6	6	6	6	7	–	–	–	–	0
Martin Sithole	6	6	8R	8R	6R	8R	8	7	2	–	–	–	10
Dennis Visser	5	–	5	5	5	5	5	6	2	–	–	–	10
Gavin Annandale	4	4	4	4	4	4c	4c	7	1	–	–	–	5
Gerhard Engelbrecht	3	3	3	3	3	3	3	7	–	–	–	–	0
Elandré Huggett	2	2	2	2	–	2R	8R	6	1	–	–	–	5
Daniel van der Merwe	1	1	1	1	1	1	1	7	2	–	–	–	10
Khwezi Mkhafu	6R	17R	12R	2R	2	2	2	7	–	–	–	–	0
PW Botha	1R	–	–	–	–	–	–	1	–	–	–	–	0
George Marich	3R	3R	–	–	1R	–	–	3	–	–	–	–	0
Willem Serfontein	4R	5	x	4R	4R	–	5R	5	–	–	–	–	0
Louis Venter	9R	x	9R	9R	9R	9R	9R	6	–	–	–	–	0
Tertius Maarman	11R	–	–	11R	–	–	–	2	–	–	–	–	0
Japie Nel	13R	13R	13R	12	12	12	12	7	2	–	–	–	10
Reinhardt Erwee	–	15	–	–	12R	–	–	2	2	–	–	–	10
Boela Venter	–	6R	7	7	7	7	7	6	2	–	–	–	10
Samora Fihlani	–	x	–	–	–	6R	6R	2	–	–	–	–	0
Duan Pretorius	–	–	14R	–	15	11R	11R	4	–	–	–	–	0
Rudi Britz	–	–	3R	3R	–	–	–	2	–	–	–	–	0
Hennie Venter	–	–	–	–	2R	–	–	1	–	–	–	–	0
Heinrich Roelfse	–	–	–	–	–	3R	3R	2	–	–	–	–	0
Penalty try	–	–	–	–	–	–	–	–	2	–	–	–	10
28 PLAYERS								150	35	32	17	1	293

CURRIE CUP SQUAD – CAREER CURRIE CUP APPEARANCES

PLAYER	GRIFFONS						OTHER UNIONS						TOTAL					
	A	T	C	P	DG	Pts	A	T	C	P	DG	Pts	A	T	C	P	DG	Pts
YW (Boela) Abrahams	31	8	–	–	2	46	5	–	–	–	–	0	36	8	–	–	2	46
GB (Gavin) Annandale	10	–	–	–	–	0	31	1	–	–	–	5	41	1	–	–	–	5
PW (PW) Botha	7	–	–	–	–	0	–	–	–	–	–	0	7	–	–	–	–	0
RM (Rudi) Britz	18	1	–	–	–	5	–	–	–	–	–	0	18	1	–	–	–	5
S (Selvyn) Davids	6	3	–	–	–	15	–	–	–	–	–	0	6	3	–	–	–	15
GP (Gerhard) Engelbrecht	7	–	–	–	–	0	12	–	–	–	–	0	19	–	–	–	–	0
GJ (Joubert) Engelbrecht	6	–	–	–	–	0	–	–	–	–	–	0	6	–	–	–	–	0
R (Reinardt) Erwee	2	2	–	–	–	10	–	–	–	–	–	0	2	2	–	–	–	10
LS (Samora) Fihlani	2	–	–	–	–	0	33	–	–	–	–	0	35	–	–	–	–	0
E (Elandré) Huggett	23	3	–	–	–	15	3	1	–	–	–	5	26	4	–	–	–	20
De W (De Wet) Kruger	6	3	–	–	–	15	–	–	–	–	–	0	6	3	–	–	–	15
T (Tertius) Kruger	7	2	–	–	–	10	–	–	–	–	–	0	7	2	–	–	–	10
T (Tertius) Maarman	59	20	2	–	–	104	–	–	–	–	–	0	59	20	2	–	–	104
G (George) Marich	3	–	–	–	–	0	0	–	–	–	–	0	3	–	–	–	–	0
MV (Vincent) Maruping	12	3	–	–	–	15	–	–	–	–	–	0	12	3	–	–	–	15
V (Vuyo) Mbotho	39	12	–	–	–	60	10	5	–	–	–	25	49	17	–	–	–	85
K (Khwezi) Mkhafu	17	1	–	–	–	5	41	4	–	–	–	20	58	5	–	–	–	25
J (Japie) Nel	66	29	–	–	–	145	16	4	–	–	–	20	92	33	–	–	–	165
DJ (Duan) Pretorius	2	–	–	–	–	0	–	–	–	–	–	0	–	–	–	–	–	0
HR (Heinrich) Roelfse	27	–	–	–	–	0	–	–	–	–	–	0	27	–	–	–	–	0
WJ (Willem) Serfontein	11	1	–	–	–	5	41	1	–	–	–	5	52	1	–	–	–	5
SM (Martin) Sithole	40	11	–	–	–	55	23	6	–	–	–	30	63	17	–	–	–	85
DJ (Daniel) van der Merwe	42	6	–	–	–	30	–	–	–	–	–	0	42	6	–	–	–	30
HOA (Hennie) Venter	1	–	–	–	–	0	–	–	–	–	–	0	1	–	–	–	–	0
JA (Boela) Venter	6	2	–	–	–	10	–	–	–	–	–	0	–	–	–	–	–	0
L (Louis) Venter	6	–	–	–	–	0	–	–	–	–	–	0	6	–	–	–	–	0
D (Dennis) Visser	6	2	–	–	–	10	–	–	–	–	–	0	6	2	–	–	–	10
GA (George) Whitehead	7	2	32	17	–	125	30	4	27	8	1	101	37	6	59	25	1	226
WP (Warren) Williams	7	5	–	–	–	25	–	–	–	–	–	0	7	5	–	–	–	25
29 PLAYERS	476	116	34	17	2	705	245	26	27	8	1	211	723	139	61	25	3	901

FIRST-CLASS APPEARANCES FOR GRIFFONS IN 2016 – ALL MATCHES

PLAYER	CURRIE CUP QUALIFYING						CURRIE CUP						2016 TOTAL						CAREER MATCHES					
	A	T	C	P	DG	Pts	A	T	C	P	DG	Pts	A	T	C	P	DG	Pts	A	T	C	P	DG	Pts
YW (Boela) Abrahams	11	0	0	0	0	0	7	1	0	0	1	8	18	1	0	0	1	8	51	8	0	0	2	46
GB (Gavin) Annandale	14	1	0	0	0	5	7	1	0	0	0	5	21	2	0	0	0	10	48	4	0	0	0	20
ZN (Zingisa) April	4	0	0	0	0	0	0	0	0	0	0	0	4	0	0	0	0	0	4	0	0	0	0	0
G (Gerard) Baard	7	0	0	0	0	0	0	0	0	0	0	0	7	0	0	0	0	0	23	0	0	0	0	0
PW (PW) Botha	3	0	0	0	0	0	1	0	0	0	0	0	4	0	0	0	0	0	19	0	0	0	0	0
RM (Rudi) Britz	0	0	0	0	0	0	2	0	0	0	0	0	2	0	0	0	0	0	52	3	0	0	0	15
S (Selvyn) Davids	14	16	0	0	0	80	6	3	0	0	0	15	20	19	0	0	0	95	20	19	0	0	0	95
P-S (Pieter-Steyn) de Wet	1	0	0	0	0	0	0	0	0	0	0	0	1	0	0	0	0	0	5	0	7	2	0	20
FC (Franna) du Toit	1	0	0	0	0	0	0	0	0	0	0	0	1	0	0	0	0	0	29	1	44	20	0	153
GP (Gerhard) Engelbrecht	0	0	0	0	0	0	7	0	0	0	0	0	7	0	0	0	0	0	7	0	0	0	0	0
GJ (Joubert) Engelbrecht	5	0	0	0	0	0	6	0	0	0	0	0	11	0	0	0	0	0	25	2	5	1	0	23
R (Reinhardt) Erwee	0	0	0	0	0	0	2	2	0	0	0	10	2	2	0	0	0	10	26	6	20	12	0	106
LS (Samora) Fihlani	12	0	0	0	0	0	2	0	0	0	0	0	14	0	0	0	0	0	21	0	0	0	0	0
H (Dirk) Grobbelaar	6	2	0	0	0	10	0	0	0	0	0	0	6	2	0	0	0	10	15	2	0	0	0	10
WR (Wilmar) Groenewald	4	0	0	0	0	0	0	0	0	0	0	0	4	0	0	0	0	0	37	5	0	0	0	25
C (Colin) Herbert	2	0	2	0	0	4	0	0	0	0	0	0	2	0	2	0	0	4	25	1	6	1	0	20
E (Elandré) Huggett	0	0	0	0	0	0	6	1	0	0	0	5	6	1	0	0	0	5	25	3	0	0	0	15
De W (De Wet) Kruger	12	5	0	0	0	25	6	3	0	0	0	15	18	8	0	0	0	40	18	8	0	0	0	40
T (Tertius) Kruger	0	0	0	0	0	0	7	2	0	0	0	10	7	2	0	0	0	10	7	2	0	0	0	10
L (Lohan) Lubbe	2	0	0	0	0	0	0	0	0	0	0	0	2	0	0	0	0	0	2	0	0	0	0	0
W (Wayne) Ludick	4	0	0	0	0	0	0	0	0	0	0	0	4	0	0	0	0	0	4	0	0	0	0	0
T (Tertius) Maarman	10	4	0	0	0	20	2	0	0	0	0	0	12	4	0	0	0	20	120	37	5	0	0	195
G (George) Marich	4	0	0	0	0	0	3	0	0	0	0	0	7	0	0	0	0	0	7	0	0	0	0	0
MV (Vincent) Maruping	12	0	0	0	0	0	7	0	0	0	0	0	19	0	0	0	0	0	24	3	0	0	0	15
TS (Siward) Mavundla	11	1	0	0	0	5	0	0	0	0	0	0	11	1	0	0	0	5	11	1	0	0	0	5
V (Vuyo) Mbotho	12	4	0	0	0	20	7	3	0	0	0	15	19	7	0	0	0	35	70	23	0	0	0	115
K (Khwezi) Mkhafu	12	0	0	0	0	0	7	0	0	0	0	0	19	0	0	0	0	0	36	1	0	0	0	5
J (Japie) Nel	9	5	0	0	0	25	7	2	0	0	0	10	16	7	0	0	0	35	126	47	0	0	0	235
NT (Norman) Nelson	6	1	0	0	0	5	0	0	0	0	0	0	6	1	0	0	0	5	42	18	0	0	0	90
O (Oshwill) Nortjie	3	1	0	0	0	5	0	0	0	0	0	0	3	1	0	0	0	5	51	8	0	0	0	40
DJ (Duan) Pretorius	12	3	5	3	0	34	4	0	0	0	0	0	16	3	5	3	0	34	16	3	5	3	0	34
N (Neil) Rautenbach	5	1	0	0	0	5	0	0	0	0	0	0	5	1	0	0	0	5	5	1	0	0	0	5
HR (Heinrich) Roelfse	14	3	0	0	0	15	2	0	0	0	0	0	16	3	0	0	0	15	63	3	0	0	0	15
WJ (Willem) Serfontein	0	0	0	0	0	0	5	0	0	0	0	0	5	0	0	0	0	0	11	1	0	0	0	5
FL (Frans) Sisita	3	0	0	0	0	0	0	0	0	0	0	0	3	0	0	0	0	0	21	2	0	0	0	10
SM (Martin) Sithole	11	1	0	0	0	5	7	2	0	0	0	10	18	3	0	0	0	15	89	32	0	0	0	160
SM (Sherwin) Slater	3	0	0	0	0	0	0	0	0	0	0	0	3	0	0	0	0	0	3	0	0	0	0	0
M-K (Malcolm) Till	5	0	0	0	0	0	0	0	0	0	0	0	5	0	0	0	0	0	7	0	0	0	0	0
DJ (Danie) van der Merwe	14	4	0	0	0	20	7	2	0	0	0	10	21	6	0	0	0	30	68	12	0	0	0	60
CG (Coenie) van Wyk	1	0	0	0	0	0	0	0	0	0	0	0	1	0	0	0	0	0	3	2	0	0	1	13
HOA (Hennie) Venter	8	0	0	0	0	0	1	0	0	0	0	0	9	0	0	0	0	0	10	0	0	0	0	0
JA (Boela) Venter	10	3	0	0	0	15	6	2	0	0	0	10	16	5	0	0	0	25	16	5	0	0	0	25
L (Louis) Venter	6	0	0	0	0	0	6	0	0	0	0	0	12	0	0	0	0	0	12	0	0	0	0	0
D (Dennis) Visser	0	0	0	0	0	0	6	2	0	0	0	10	6	2	0	0	0	10	6	2	0	0	0	10
GA (George) Whitehead	11	3	50	15	2	166	7	2	32	17	0	125	18	5	82	32	2	291	18	5	82	32	2	291
WP (Warren) Williams	11	10	0	0	0	50	7	5	0	0	0	25	18	15	0	0	0	75	18	15	0	0	0	75
Penalty try	0	1	0	0	0	5	0	2	0	0	0	10	0	3	0	0	0	15	0	0	0	0	0	0

Leopards Rugby Union

Founded: 1920 (as Western Transvaal) **Ground:** Olën Park
Capacity: 22 000 **Address:** Cnr James Moroka & Piet Bosman Streets
Postal address: PO Box 422, Potchefstroom 2520 **Telephone Number:** 018-297 5304/5
Email: karen@leopardsrugby.co.za **Colours:** Green & red jersey, white shorts
Currie Cup Coach: Robert du Preez **Captain:** Juandré Rudolph
President: Adv. André May **CEO:** Andries de Kock

1996	1997	1998	1999	2000	2001	2002	2003	2004	2005	2006
13th	13th	13th	14th	12th	10th	12th	9th	11th	8th	9th

2007	2008	2009	2010	2011	2012	2013	2014	2015	2016
13th	10th	7th	8th	8th	10th	9th	9th	9th	10th

Played	Won	Lost	Drawn	Points for	Points against	Tries for	Tries against
7	6	1	0	279	223	39	31

Date	Venue	Opponent	Result	Score	Referee	Scorers
Aug 12	Potchefstroom	Border	WON	26-24	AJ Jacobs	T: Le Roux (2), Willemse, HP Swart. C: M Swart (3).
Aug 20	Windhoek	Welwitschias	WON	54-42	AJ Jacobs	T: Willemse (3), Deysel (2), HP Swart, Morrison, Beukman. C: Deysel (7).
Aug 26	Potchefstroom	Griffons	WON	43-33	R Boneparte	T: HP Swart (3), Moolman, Robertse, Morrison. C: Deysel (5).
Sep 03	Kempton Park	Valke	WON	42-19	AJ Jacobs	T: Willemse (2), Vermeulen, Moolman, HP Swart, Deysel. C: Deysel (5), Welthagen.
Sep 10	Potchefstroom	SWD Eagles	WON	49-31	A Ruiz	T: Gordon (2), Vermeulen, Moolman, Willemse, Morrison, Penalty try. C: Deysel (7).

SEMI-FINAL

Date	Venue	Opponent	Result	Score	Referee	Scorers
Sep 30	Potchefstroom	Valke	WON	40-30	J van Heerden	T: Moolman, Gordon, Willemse, J Jordaan, Deysel.

FINAL

Date	Venue	Opponent	Result	Score	Referee	Scorers
Oct 07	Potchefstroom	Griffons	LOST	25-44	Q Immelman	T: Vermeulen, Hayward, Deysel. C: Deysel (2). P: Deysel (2).

APPEARANCES & POINTS

PLAYER	Border	Welwitchias	Griffons	Valke	SWD Eagles	Valke	Griffons	Apps	T	C	P	DG	Pts
Ryno Wepener	15	15	11R	15R	15R	–	–	5	–	–	–	–	0
Rowayne Beukman	14	14	14	–	–	–	–	3	1	–	–	–	5
Bradley Moolman	13	–	11	11	11	11	11	6	4	–	–	–	20
Johan Deysel	12	12c	12	12	12	12	12	7	5	29	6	–	101
Jaco Hayward	11	11	15	15	15	15	15	7	1	–	–	–	5
Gene Willemse	10	10	10	10	10	10	10	7	8	–	–	–	40
Malherbe Swart	9	9R	10R	9R	9	9R	9	7	–	3	–	–	6
Marno Redelinghuys	8	8	8R	–	7R	5R	7R	6	–	–	–	–	0
HP Swart	7	7	7	4R	–	7	7	6	6	–	–	–	30
Juan Language	6c	–	–	–	6	–	6	3	–	–	–	–	0
Walt Steenkamp	5	4R	5	5	–	5	5	6	–	–	–	–	0
Sthembiso Mhlongo	4	4	–	–	4	4	4	5	–	–	–	–	0
Nhlanhla Ngcamu	3	–	–	1R	–	–	–	2	–	–	–	–	0
Wilmar Arnoldi	2	x	–	–	2R	2R	–	3	–	–	–	–	0
Bart le Roux	1	3	3R	–	–	–	–	3	2	–	–	–	10
Dane van der Westhuyzen	2R	2	2	2	–	2	2	6	–	–	–	–	0
Roan Grobbelaar	3R	1	1	1	1	1	1	7	–	–	–	–	0
Loftus Morrison	8R	5	4	7	7	7R	–	6	3	–	–	–	15
Jaco Jordaan	6R	6	6	6	–	6	6R	6	1	–	–	–	5
Chriswill September	9R	9	9	9	9R	9	9R	7	–	–	–	–	0
Adrian Vermeulen	11R	13	13	13	13	13	13	7	3	–	–	–	15
Myburgh Briers	15R	15R	–	–	–	–	–	2	–	–	–	–	0
Dewald Dekker	–	3R	3	3	3	3	3	6	–	–	–	–	0
Sandile Kubeka	–	11R	14R	14	12R	x	13R	5	–	–	–	–	0
Francois Robertse	–	7R	7R	4	5	4R	4R	6	1	–	–	–	5
Jeandré Rudolph	–	–	8c	8c	8c	8c	8c	5	–	–	–	–	0
Louis van der Westhuizen	–	–	2R	2R	2	–	2R	4	–	–	–	–	0
Johnny Welthagen	–	–	12R	–	–	–		1	–	1	–	–	2
Danie Jordaan	–	–	–	8R	4R	–	–	2	–	–	–	–	0
Dean Gordon	–	–	–	14	14	14		3	3	–	–	–	15
Kabelo Motloung	–	–	–	1R	1R	1R		3	–	–	–	–	0
Penalty try	–	–	–	–	–	–			1	–	–	–	5
31 PLAYERS								152	39	33	6	0	279

CURRIE CUP SQUAD – CAREER CURRIE CUP APPEARANCES

PLAYER	LEOPARDS						OTHER UNIONS						TOTAL					
	A	T	C	P	DG	Pts	A	T	C	P	DG	Pts	A	T	C	P	DG	Pts
W (Wilmar) Arnoldi	10	1	–	–	–	5	–	–	–	–	–	0	10	1	–	–	–	5
RE (Rowayne) Beukman	13	1	–	–	–	5	–	–	–	–	–	0	13	1	–	–	–	5
JAM (Myburgh) Briers	2	–	–	–	–	0	–	–	–	–	–	0	2	–	–	–	–	0
D (Dewald) Dekker	6	–	–	–	–	0	–	–	–	–	–	0	6	–	–	–	–	0
J (Johan) Deysel	16	9	29	6	–	121	–	–	–	–	–	0	16	9	29	6	–	121
D (Dean) Gordon	3	3	–	–	–	15	–	–	–	–	–	0	3	3	–	–	–	15
R (Roan) Grobbelaar	7	–	–	–	–	0	–	–	–	–	–	0	7	–	–	–	–	0
J (Jaco) Hayward	9	1	–	–	–	5	–	–	–	–	–	0	9	1	–	–	–	5
SM (Sandile) Kubeka	5	–	–	–	–	0	–	–	–	–	–	0	5	–	–	–	–	0
JM (Juan) Language	24	13	–	–	–	65	–	–	–	–	–	0	24	13	–	–	–	65
BG (Bart) le Roux	9	4	–	–	–	20	–	–	–	–	–	0	9	4	–	–	–	20
S (Sthembiso) Mhlongo	22	1	–	–	–	5	9	1	–	–	–	5	31	2	–	–	–	10
BJ (Bradley) Moolman	6	4	–	–	–	20	–	–	–	–	–	0	6	4	–	–	–	20
NL (Loftus) Morrison	19	7	–	–	–	35	–	–	–	–	–	0	19	7	–	–	–	35
M (Marno) Redelinghuys	19	–	–	–	–	0	–	–	–	–	–	0	19	–	–	–	–	0
F (Francois) Robertse	23	7	–	–	–	35	–	–	–	–	–	0	23	7	–	–	–	35
J (Jeandré) Rudolph	6	–	–	–	–	0	–	–	–	–	–	0	6	–	–	–	–	0
CB (Chriswill) September	7	–	–	–	–	0	–	–	–	–	–	0	7	–	–	–	–	0
W (Walt) Steenkamp	11	–	–	–	–	0	–	–	–	–	–	0	11	–	–	–	–	0
HP (HP) Swart	28	9	–	–	–	45	–	–	–	–	–	0	28	9	–	–	–	45
M (Malherbe) Swart	16	1	3	–	–	11	–	–	–	–	–	0	16	1	3	–	–	11
L (Louis) van der Westhuizen	4	–	–	–	–	0	–	–	–	–	–	0	4	–	–	–	–	0
DR (Dane) van der Westhuyzen	17	2	–	–	–	10	–	–	–	–	–	0	17	2	–	–	–	10
A de W (Adrian) Vermeulen	20	8	–	–	–	40	–	–	–	–	–	0	20	8	–	–	–	40
JJ (Johnny) Welthagen	4	–	1	–	–	2	–	–	–	–	–	0	4	–	1	–	–	2
R (Ryno) Wepener	5	–	–	–	–	0	–	–	–	–	–	0	5	–	–	–	–	0
GG (Gene) Willemse	7	8	–	–	–	40	–	–	–	–	–	0	7	8	–	–	–	40
K (Percy) Williams	6	–	–	–	–	0	–	–	–	–	–	0	6	–	–	–	–	0
28 PLAYERS	324	79	33	6	0	479	9	1	0	0	0	5	333	80	33	6	0	484

FIRST-CLASS APPEARANCES FOR LEOPARDS IN 2016 – ALL MATCHES

PLAYER	CURRIE CUP QUALIFYING						CURRIE CUP						2016 TOTAL						CAREER MATCHES					
	A	T	C	P	DG	Pts	A	T	C	P	DG	Pts	A	T	C	P	DG	Pts	A	T	C	P	DG	Pts
W (Wilmar) Arnoldi	3	0	0	0	0	0	11	4	0	0	0	20	14	4	0	0	0	20	21	5	0	0	0	25
RE (Rowayne) Beukman	3	1	0	0	0	5	9	4	0	0	0	20	12	5	0	0	0	25	22	5	0	0	0	25
ME (Molotsi) Bouwer	0	0	0	0	0	0	7	0	0	0	0	0	7	0	0	0	0	0	13	0	0	0	0	0
JAM (Myburgh) Briers	2	0	0	0	0	0	1	0	0	0	0	0	3	0	0	0	0	0	3	0	0	0	0	0
LR (Lucien) Cupido	0	0	0	0	0	0	5	0	0	0	0	0	5	0	0	0	0	0	11	1	0	0	0	5
D (Dewald) Dekker	6	0	0	0	0	0	0	0	0	0	0	0	6	0	0	0	0	0	6	0	0	0	0	0
J (Johan) Deysel	7	5	29	6	0	101	6	5	0	0	0	25	13	10	29	6	0	126	22	14	29	6	0	146
C (Cecil) Dumond	0	0	0	0	0	0	2	0	0	0	0	0	2	0	0	0	0	0	28	2	18	29	2	139
LA (Leon) du Plessis	0	0	0	0	0	0	1	1	0	0	0	5	1	1	0	0	0	5	1	1	0	0	0	5
D (Dean) Gordon	3	3	0	0	0	15	0	0	0	0	0	0	3	3	0	0	0	15	3	3	0	0	0	15
R (Roan) Grobbelaar	7	0	0	0	0	0	9	1	0	0	0	5	16	1	0	0	0	5	16	1	0	0	0	5
J (Jaco) Hayward	7	1	0	0	0	5	8	5	0	0	0	25	15	6	0	0	0	30	17	6	0	0	0	30
SB (Schalk) Hugo	0	0	0	0	0	0	5	0	4	1	0	11	5	0	4	1	0	11	11	3	7	1	0	32
BJ (Benhard) Janse van Rensburg	0	0	0	0	0	0	10	2	8	2	0	32	10	2	8	2	0	32	10	2	8	2	0	32
DB (Danie) Jordaan	2	0	0	0	0	0	4	0	0	0	0	0	6	0	0	0	0	0	15	0	0	0	0	0
J (Jaco) Jordaan	6	1	0	0	0	5	9	1	0	0	0	5	15	2	0	0	0	10	22	2	0	0	0	10
SM (Sandile) Kubeka	5	0	0	0	0	0	0	0	0	0	0	0	5	0	0	0	0	0	5	0	0	0	0	0
JM (Juan) Language	3	0	0	0	0	0	5	2	0	0	0	10	8	2	0	0	0	10	29	15	0	0	0	75
BG (Bart) le Roux	3	2	0	0	0	10	10	1	0	0	0	5	13	3	0	0	0	15	19	5	0	0	0	25
CR (Tiaan) Liebenberg	0	0	0	0	0	0	2	1	0	0	0	5	2	1	0	0	0	5	2	1	0	0	0	5
MC (Mashudu) Mafela	0	0	0	0	0	0	10	0	0	0	0	0	10	0	0	0	0	0	10	0	0	0	0	0
HJ (Henko) Marais	0	0	0	0	0	0	9	4	0	0	0	20	9	4	0	0	0	20	9	4	0	0	0	20
S (Sthembiso) Mhlongo	5	0	0	0	0	0	9	0	0	0	0	0	14	0	0	0	0	0	26	1	0	0	0	5
BJ (Bradley) Moolman	6	4	0	0	0	20	14	3	0	0	0	15	20	7	0	0	0	35	20	7	0	0	0	35
NL (Loftus) Morrison	6	3	0	0	0	15	9	3	0	0	0	15	15	6	0	0	0	30	28	10	0	0	0	50
KM (Kabelo) Motloung	3	0	0	0	0	0	0	0	0	0	0	0	3	0	0	0	0	0	3	0	0	0	0	0
B (Bruce) Muller	0	0	0	0	0	0	1	1	0	0	0	5	1	1	0	0	0	5	1	1	0	0	0	5
N (Nhlanhla) Ngcamu	2	0	0	0	0	0	13	0	0	0	0	0	15	0	0	0	0	0	15	0	0	0	0	0
M (Marno) Redelinghuys	6	0	0	0	0	0	8	2	0	0	0	10	14	2	0	0	0	10	27	2	0	0	0	10
F (Francois) Robertse	6	1	0	0	0	5	7	0	0	0	0	0	13	1	0	0	0	5	30	7	0	0	0	35
J (Jeandré) Rudolph	5	0	0	0	0	0	11	3	0	0	0	15	16	3	0	0	0	15	17	3	0	0	0	15
CB (Chriswill) September	7	0	0	0	0	0	14	0	0	0	0	0	21	0	0	0	0	0	21	0	0	0	0	0
RC (Rhyno) Smith	0	0	0	0	0	0	10	5	33	17	2	148	10	5	33	17	2	148	27	16	40	17	2	223
W (Walt) Steenkamp	6	0	0	0	0	0	11	1	0	0	0	5	17	1	0	0	0	5	22	1	0	0	0	5
D (Dean) Stokes	0	0	0	0	0	0	5	0	0	0	0	0	5	0	0	0	0	0	5	0	0	0	0	0
HP (HP) Swart	6	6	0	0	0	30	7	0	0	0	0	0	13	6	0	0	0	30	39	10	0	0	0	50
M (Malherbe) Swart	7	0	3	0	0	6	13	1	1	0	0	7	20	1	4	0	0	13	29	2	4	0	0	18
L (Louis) van der Westhuizen	4	0	0	0	0	0	7	0	0	0	0	0	11	0	0	0	0	0	11	0	0	0	0	0
DR (Dane) van der Westhuyzen	6	0	0	0	0	0	9	1	0	0	0	5	15	1	0	0	0	5	26	3	0	0	0	15
RC (Ruan) Venter	0	0	0	0	0	0	7	0	0	0	0	0	7	0	0	0	0	0	7	0	0	0	0	0
A de W (Adrian) Vermeulen	7	3	0	0	0	15	8	2	0	0	0	10	15	5	0	0	0	25	28	10	0	0	0	50
JJ (Johnny) Welthagen	1	0	1	0	0	2	1	2	0	0	0	10	2	2	1	0	0	12	5	2	1	0	0	12
R (Ryno) Wepener	5	0	0	0	0	0	3	1	0	0	0	5	8	1	0	0	0	5	8	1	0	0	0	5
GG (Gene) Willemse	7	8	0	0	0	40	12	2	0	0	0	10	19	10	0	0	0	50	19	10	0	0	0	50
K (Percy) Williams	0	0	0	0	0	0	1	0	0	0	0	0	1	0	0	0	0	0	7	0	0	0	0	0
Penalty try	0	1	0	0	0	5	0	0	0	0	0	0	0	1	0	0	0	5	0	0	0	0	0	0

45 PLAYERS

South Western Districts Rugby Football Union

Founded: 1899 **Ground:** Outeniqua Park **Capacity:** 7,500
Address: CJ Langenhoven Road, George **Postal address:** PO Box 10471, George 6530
Telephone Number: 044-873 0137 **Email:** rugby@swdeagles.co.za
Colours: White & green jersey, white shorts and green socks **Currie Cup Coach:** Abe Davids
Captain: Davon Raubenheimer **President:** Hennie Baartman
Union CEO: Johan Prinsloo *(retired)* **Union CEO:** Vanessa Roelfse *(acting)*

1996	1997	1998	1999	2000	2001	2002	2003	2004	2005	2006
14th	8th	7th	4th	6th	14th	9th	8th	8th	13th	11th

2007	2008	2009	2010	2011	2012	2013	2014	2015	2016
9th	11th	10th	9th	11th	11th	10th	11th	12th	14th

Played	Won	Lost	Drawn	Points for	Points against	Tries for	Tries against
5	1	4	0	168	170	23	22

Date	Venue	Opponent	Result	Score	Referee	Scorers
Aug 12	George	Welwitschias	WON	54-23	S Ngcese	T: Pretorius (2), Ntsila, Snell, Steyn, Du Plessis, Halvorsen, Digue. C: Graaff (7).
Aug 19	George	Griffons	LOST	27-33	E Seconds	T: Du Plessis, Steyn, Pretorius. C: Graaff (3). P: Graaff (2).
Aug 27	Kempton Park	Valke	LOST	32-34	J van Heerden	T: Ntsila, Radebe, Pedro, Stander. C: Graaff (3). P: Graaff (2).
Sep 10	Potchefstroom	Leopards	LOST	31-49	A Ruiz	T: Du Toit (2), Haupt, Roberts, Du Plessis. C: Eksteen (3).
Sep 16	East London	Border	LOST	24-31	M Adamson	T: Haupt (2), Vulindlu. P: Kean (3).

APPEARANCES & POINTS

PLAYER	Welwitchias	Griffons	Valke	Leopards	Border	Apps	T	C	P	DG	Pts
Jaquin Jansen	15	–	–	–	–	1	–	–	–	–	0
Carlo Radebe	14	14	11	–	11	4	1	–	–	–	5
Kirsten Heyns	13	13	13	–	–	3	–	–	–	–	0
Luzuko Vulindlu	12	12	14	–	12	4	1	–	–	–	5
Hentzwill Pedro	11	11	13R	11	–	4	1	–	–	–	5
Hansie Graaff	10	10	10	13	13R	5	–	13	4	–	38
Johan Steyn	9	9	9	–	9	4	2	–	–	–	10
Christo du Plessis	8	8	8	4R	8	5	3	–	–	–	15
Thor Halvorsen	7c	7	7	6	7	5	1	–	–	–	5
Andisa Ntsila	6	6	8R	8	8R	5	2	–	–	–	10
Lodewyk Uys	5	5	5	5	5	5	–	–	–	–	0
Schalk Oelofse	4	4	–	–	–	2	–	–	–	–	0
Nemo Roelofse	3	3	3	3R	3R	5	–	–	–	–	0
Mark Pretorius	2	2c	2c	2c	–	4	3	–	–	–	15
Dean Hopp	1	3R	3R	3	3	5	–	–	–	–	0
Kurt Haupt	2R	x	2R	2R	2	4	3	–	–	–	15
Juamdré Dique	3R	–	–	–	–	1	1	–	–	–	5
Grant le Roux	5R	4R	4	–	4R	4	–	–	–	–	0
Buran Parks	6R	–	–	–	–	1	–	–	–	–	0
Dillin Snel	9R	9R	9R	9	–	4	1	–	–	–	5
Wilneth Engelbrecht	11R	11R	12	–	–	3	–	–	–	–	0
Daniel Roberts	15R	15	–	13R	13	4	1	–	–	–	5
Layle Delo	–	1	–	–	1R	2	–	–	–	–	0
Janneman Stander	–	6R	6	8R	6	4	1	–	–	–	5
Thomas Kean	–	15R	x	15	15	3	–	–	3	–	9
Leighton Eksteen	–	–	15	10	14	3	–	3	–	–	6
Teunis Nieuwoudt	–	–	1	1	1	3	–	–	–	–	0
Marco Kruger	–	–	4R	–	–	1	–	–	–	–	0
Martin du Toit	–	–	–	12	10	2	2	–	–	–	10
Clinton Wagman	–	–	–	14	–	1	–	–	–	–	0
Davon Raubenheimer	–	–	–	7	4c	2	–	–	–	–	0
Lyndon Hartnick	–	–	–	4	6R	2	–	–	–	–	0
Mzo Dyantyi	–	–	–	9R	9R	2	–	–	–	–	0
Riaan Arends	–	–	–	11R	–	1	–	–	–	–	0
34 PLAYERS						108	23	16	7	0	168

CURRIE CUP SQUAD – CAREER CURRIE CUP APPEARANCES

PLAYER	SWD						OTHER UNIONS						TOTAL					
	A	T	C	P	DG	Pts	A	T	C	P	DG	Pts	A	T	C	P	DG	Pts
RA (Riaan) Arends	1	–	–	–	–	0	–	–	–	–	–	0	1	–	–	–	–	0
LA (Layle) Delo	28	2	–	–	–	10	–	–	–	–	–	0	28	2	–	–	–	10
JC (Juamdré) Dique	11	1	–	–	–	5	–	–	–	–	–	0	11	1	–	–	–	5
CJ (Christo) du Plessis	42	10	–	–	–	50	–	–	–	–	–	0	42	10	–	–	–	50
OM (Martin) du Toit	33	8	1	–	–	42	–	–	–	–	–	0	33	8	1	–	–	42
M (Mzo) Dyantyi	24	2	–	–	–	10	2	–	–	–	–	0	26	2	–	–	–	10
L (Leighton) Eksteen	21	4	19	20	–	118	–	–	–	–	–	0	21	4	19	20	–	118
WR (Wilneth) Engelbrecht	3	–	–	–	–	0	7	1	–	–	–	5	10	1	–	–	–	5
JPJ (Hansie) Graaff	5	–	13	4	–	38	4	–	–	–	–	0	9	–	13	4	–	38
T (Thor) Halvorsen	5	1	–	–	–	5	18	2	–	–	–	10	23	3	–	–	–	15
LL (Lyndon) Hartnick	45	6	–	–	–	30	6	–	–	–	–	0	45	6	–	–	–	30
KS (Kurt) Haupt	27	8	–	–	–	40	–	–	–	–	–	0	27	8	–	–	–	40
KR (Kirsten) Heyns	12	–	–	–	–	0	–	–	–	–	–	0	12	–	–	–	–	0
DLJ (Dean) Hopp	41	–	–	–	–	0	19	1	–	–	–	5	60	1	–	–	–	5
J (Jaquin) Jansen	1	–	–	–	–	0	37	9	34	13	–	152	38	9	34	13	–	152
TM (Thomas) Kean	6	–	1	3	–	11	–	–	–	–	–	0	6	–	1	3	–	11
M (Marco) Kruger	1	–	–	–	–	0	–	–	–	–	–	0	1	–	–	–	–	0
G (Grant) le Roux	31	2	–	–	–	10	24	–	–	–	–	0	55	2	–	–	–	10
T (Teunis) Nieuwoudt	3	–	–	–	–	0	–	–	–	–	–	0	3	–	–	–	–	0
A (Andisa) Ntsila	12	3	–	–	–	15	–	–	–	–	–	0	12	3	–	–	–	15
SW (Schalk) Oelofse	30	2	–	–	–	10	–	–	–	–	–	0	30	2	–	–	–	10
BJ (Buran) Parks	27	2	–	–	–	10	–	–	–	–	–	0	27	2	–	–	–	10
HN (Hentzwill) Pedro	4	1	–	–	–	5	–	–	–	–	–	0	4	1	–	–	–	5
M (Mark) Pretorius	4	3	–	–	–	15	–	–	–	–	–	0	4	3	–	–	–	15
CR (Carlo) Radebe	13	5	–	–	–	25	–	–	–	–	–	0	13	5	–	–	–	25
DS (Davon) Raubenheimer	63	2	–	–	–	10	59	3	–	–	–	15	122	5	–	–	–	25
DC (Daniel) Roberts	33	4	–	–	–	20	–	–	–	–	–	0	33	4	–	–	–	20
NG (Nemo) Roelofse	5	–	–	–	–	0	–	–	–	–	–	0	5	–	–	–	–	0
D C-L (Dillin) Snel	13	2	–	–	–	10	–	–	–	–	–	0	13	2	–	–	–	10
JH (Janneman) Stander	9	2	–	–	–	10	–	–	–	–	–	0	9	2	–	–	–	10
JH (Johan) Steyn	15	3	–	–	–	15	–	–	–	–	–	0	15	3	–	–	–	15
JL (Lodewyk) Uys	5	–	–	–	–	0	–	–	–	–	–	0	5	–	–	–	–	0
L (Luzuko) Vulindlu	27	5	–	–	–	25	9	1	–	–	–	5	36	6	–	–	–	30
CA (Clinton) Wagman	30	7	–	–	–	35	–	–	–	–	–	0	30	7	–	–	–	35
34 PLAYERS	630	85	34	27	0	574	185	17	34	13	0	192	809	102	68	40	0	766

FIRST-CLASS APPEARANCES FOR SWD IN 2016 – ALL MATCHES

PLAYER	CURRIE CUP QUALIFYING						CURRIE CUP						2016 TOTAL						CAREER MATCHES					
	A	T	C	P	DG	Pts	A	T	C	P	DG	Pts	A	T	C	P	DG	Pts	A	T	C	P	DG	Pts
RA (Riaan) Arends	7	1	0	0	0	5	1	0	0	0	0	0	8	1	0	0	0	5	8	1	0	0	0	5
BJ (Brianton) Booysen	6	0	0	0	0	0	0	0	0	0	0	0	6	0	0	0	0	0	6	0	0	0	0	0
LA (Layle) Delo	12	2	0	0	0	10	2	0	0	0	0	0	14	2	0	0	0	10	64	4	0	0	0	20
JC (Juamdré) Dique	5	0	0	0	0	0	1	1	0	0	0	5	6	1	0	0	0	5	16	1	0	0	0	5
CJ (Christo) du Plessis	13	3	0	0	0	15	5	3	0	0	0	15	18	6	0	0	0	30	82	17	0	0	0	85
OM (Martin) du Toit	10	5	0	0	0	25	2	2	0	0	0	10	12	7	0	0	0	35	68	16	0	0	0	80
M (Mzo) Dyantyi	9	0	0	0	0	0	2	0	0	0	0	0	11	0	0	0	0	0	78	8	0	0	0	40
WR (Wilneth) Engelbrecht	10	1	0	0	0	5	3	0	0	0	0	0	13	1	0	0	0	5	13	1	0	0	0	5
L (Leighton) Eksteen	4	3	0	1	0	18	3	0	3	0	0	6	7	3	3	1	0	24	33	8	19	21	0	141
JPJ (Hansie) Graaff	11	0	15	12	0	66	5	0	13	4	0	38	16	0	28	16	0	104	16	0	28	16	0	104
T (Thor) Halvorsen	5	1	0	0	0	5	5	1	0	0	0	5	10	2	0	0	0	10	10	2	0	0	0	10
LL (Lyndon) Hartnick	9	1	0	0	0	5	2	0	0	0	0	0	11	1	0	0	0	5	88	10	0	0	0	50
KS (Kurt) Haupt	9	5	0	0	0	25	4	3	0	0	0	15	13	8	0	0	0	40	39	14	0	0	0	70
KR (Kirsten) Heyns	7	1	0	0	0	5	3	0	0	0	0	0	10	1	0	0	0	5	26	4	0	0	0	20
DLJ (Dean) Hopp	8	1	0	0	0	5	5	0	0	0	0	0	13	1	0	0	0	5	66	5	0	0	0	25
J (Jaquin) Jansen	11	1	11	2	0	33	1	0	0	0	0	0	12	1	11	2	0	33	12	1	11	2	0	33
TM (Thomas) Kean	11	0	14	18	0	52	3	0	0	3	0	9	14	0	14	21	0	61	17	0	15	21	0	63
M (Marco) Kruger	10	0	0	0	0	0	1	0	0	0	0	0	11	0	0	0	0	0	11	0	0	0	0	0
G (Grant) le Roux	6	0	0	0	0	0	4	0	0	0	0	0	10	0	0	0	0	0	68	4	0	0	0	20
LV (Leegan) Moos	1	0	0	0	0	0	0	0	0	0	0	0	1	0	0	0	0	0	1	0	0	0	0	0
GP (Gideon) Muller	4	0	0	0	0	0	0	0	0	0	0	0	4	0	0	0	0	0	5	0	0	0	0	0
T (Teunis) Nieuwoudt	0	0	0	0	0	0	3	0	0	0	0	0	3	0	0	0	0	0	3	0	0	0	0	0
L (Lenes) Nomdo	6	0	0	0	0	0	0	0	0	0	0	0	6	0	0	0	0	0	6	0	0	0	0	0
A (Andisa) Ntsila	11	1	0	0	0	5	5	2	0	0	0	10	16	3	0	0	0	15	28	4	0	0	0	20
SW (Schalk) Oelofse	0	0	0	0	0	0	2	0	0	0	0	0	2	0	0	0	0	0	40	2	0	0	0	10
BJ (Buran) Parks	10	1	0	0	0	5	1	0	0	0	0	0	11	1	0	0	0	5	52	3	0	0	0	15
HN (Hentzwill) Pedro	3	2	0	0	0	10	4	1	0	0	0	5	7	3	0	0	0	15	25	11	0	0	0	55
M (Mark) Pretorius	12	7	0	0	0	35	4	3	0	0	0	15	16	10	0	0	0	50	16	10	0	0	0	50
CR (Carlo) Radebe	8	1	0	0	0	5	4	1	0	0	0	5	12	2	0	0	0	10	21	7	0	0	0	35
DS (Davon) Raubenheimer	5	0	0	0	0	0	2	0	0	0	0	0	7	0	0	0	0	0	98	5	0	0	0	25
DC (Daniel) Roberts	14	7	0	0	0	35	4	1	0	0	0	5	18	8	0	0	0	40	77	14	0	0	0	70
NG (Nemo) Roelofse	13	0	0	0	0	0	5	0	0	0	0	0	18	0	0	0	0	0	20	1	0	0	0	5
DC-L (Dillen) Snell	5	0	0	0	0	0	4	1	0	0	0	5	9	1	0	0	0	5	21	2	0	0	0	10
JH (Janneman) Stander	10	2	0	0	0	10	4	1	0	0	0	5	14	3	0	0	0	15	32	7	0	0	0	35
PF (Pieter) Stemmet	1	0	0	0	0	0	0	0	0	0	0	0	1	0	0	0	0	0	18	1	0	0	0	5
JH (Johan) Steyn	14	2	0	0	0	10	4	2	0	0	0	10	18	4	0	0	0	20	31	5	0	0	0	25
JL (Lodewyk) Uys	9	2	0	0	0	10	5	0	0	0	0	0	14	2	0	0	0	10	14	2	0	0	0	10
AP (Peet) van der Walt	12	1	0	0	0	5	0	0	0	0	0	0	12	1	0	0	0	5	29	1	0	0	0	5
L (Luzuko) Vulindlu	1	0	0	0	0	0	4	1	0	0	0	5	5	1	0	0	0	5	34	5	0	0	0	25
CA (Clinton) Wagman	5	1	0	0	0	5	1	0	0	0	0	0	6	1	0	0	0	5	67	17	0	0	0	85

Valke Rugby Union

Founded: 1947 (as Eastern Transvaal) **Ground:** Barnard Stadium, Kempton Park
Capacity: 7,000 **Address:** CR Swart Avenue, Kempton Park
Postal address: PO Box 12703, Edleen 1625 **Telephone Number:** 011-975 2822/2487
Email: valke@global.co.za **Colours:** Red jersey, shorts and socks
Currie Cup Coach: Rudy Joubert **Captain:** JP Mostert
President: Vivian Lottering
CEO: Jurie Coetzee

1996	1997	1998	1999	2000	2001	2002	2003	2004	2005	2006
11th	*10th*	*6th*	*10h*	*11th*	*5th*	*8th*	*12th*	*12th*	*9th*	*7th*

2007	2008	2009	2010	2011	2012	2013	2014	2015	2016
8th	*8th*	*14th*	*12th*	*11th*	*12th*	*14th*	*12th*	*13th*	*13th*

Played	*Won*	*Lost*	*Drawn*	*Points for*	*Points against*	*Tries for*	*Tries against*
6	2	4	0	189	238	29	32

Date	Venue	Opponent	Result	Score	Referee	Scorers
Aug 12	Welkom	Griffons	LOST	27-50	Q Immelman	T: Taljaard (2), Mayeza, Williams. C: Aspeling (2). P: Aspeling.
Aug 27	Kempton Park	SWD	WON	34-32	J van Heerden	T: Olivier (2), C Cronjé, Pretorius, Enslin, Muller. C: Aspeling (2).
Sept 03	Kempton Park	Leopards	LOST	19-42	AJ Jacobs	T: Pretorius, Schutte, X Cronjé. C: Aspeling (2).
Sept 09	Kempton Park	Border	LOST	29-54	C Jadezweni	T: Engledoe, Mayeza, Van Wyk, Taljaard, Richter. C: Aspeling (2).
Sept 17	Windhoek	Welwitschias	WON	50-20	R Boneparte	T: Mayeza (2), Pretorius (2), Taljaard, Truter, Muller, Richter. C: Aspeling (3), Potgieter (2).

SEMI-FINAL

Date	Venue	Opponent	Result	Score	Referee	Scorers
Sept 30	Potchefstroom	Leopards	LOST	30-40	J van Heerden	T: Pretorius (2), Williams. C: Aspeling (2), Potgieter. P: Aspeling (2), Potgieter.

APPEARANCES & POINTS

PLAYER	Griffons	SWD	Leopards	Border	Welwitchias	Leopards	Apps	T	C	P	DG	Pts
Coert Cronjé	15	15	15	–	–	15	4	1	–	–	–	5
Charles Mayeza	14	14	14	14	14	14	6	4	–	–	–	20
Andries Truter	13	11	–	–	13	13	4	1	–	–	–	5
Andréw van Wyk	12	12	12	12	–	13R	5	1	–	–	–	5
Etienne Taljaard	11	–	11	11	11	11	5	4	–	–	–	20
Karlo Aspeling	10	10	10R	10	10	10	6	–	13	3	–	35
Johan Pretorius	9	9	9	9	9	9	6	6	–	–	–	30
Friedle Olivier	8	8	7	7	–	6R	5	2	–	–	–	10
Ernst Ladendorf	7	7	–	7R	7	7	5	–	–	–	–	0
JP Mostert	6c	6c	6c	6c	6R	6c	6	–	–	–	–	0
Isak Deetlefs	5	5R	5R	–	4	–	4	–	–	–	–	0
Shane Kirkwood	4	4	4	4	–	4	5	–	–	–	–	0
Andries Schutte	3	3	3	3	3	3	6	1	–	–	–	5
Henri Boshoff	2	–	1R	1R	1	–	4	–	–	–	–	0
Koos Strauss	1	1	1	1	–	1	5	–	–	–	–	0
Dwight Pansegrouw	2R	2R	2R	6R	2R	2R	6	–	–	–	–	0
Grant Watts	3R	–	–	1R	–		2	–	–	–	–	0
Marlyn Williams	5R	5	5	5	5	5	6	2	–	–	–	10
Reg Muller	7R	7R	8	8	8	8	6	2	–	–	–	10
Warren Potgieter	13R	9R	10	15R	10R	10R	6	–	3	1	–	9
Grant Janke	12R	13	13	13	12	12	6	–	–	–	–	0
Damian Engledoe	14R	–	15R	15	–	–	3	1	–	–	–	5
Jan Enslin	–	2	2	2	–	2	4	1	–	–	–	5
Heinrich Els	–	1R	–	–	–	–	1	–	–	–	–	0
Xander Cronjé	–	11R	12R	14R	12R	–	4	1	–	–	–	5
Christo Coetzee	–	x	–	–	–	–	–	–	–	–	–	0
Thabo Mamojele	–	–	7R	–	6c	–	2	–	–	–	–	0
Jacques Alberts	–	–	–	5R	4R	5R	3	–	–	–	–	0
Anrich Richter	–	–	–	9R	9R	11R	3	2	–	–	–	10
Kyle Hendricks	–	–	–	–	15	–	1	–	–	–	–	0
Gihard Visagie	–	–	–	–	2	1R	2	–	–	–	–	0
31 PLAYERS							**131**	**29**	**16**	**4**	**0**	**189**

CURRIE CUP SQUAD – CAREER CURRIE CUP APPEARANCES

PLAYER	VALKE						OTHER UNIONS						TOTAL					
	A	T	C	P	DG	Pts	A	T	C	P	DG	Pts	A	T	C	P	DG	Pts
GDJ (Jacques) Alberts	31	0	0	0	0	0	0	0	0	0	0	0	31	0	0	0	0	0
KG (Karlo) Aspeling	20	4	38	13	2	141	28	1	19	8	1	70	48	5	57	21	3	211
HB (Henri) Boshoff	4	0	0	0	0	0	0	0	0	0	0	0	4	0	0	0	0	0
CF (Coert) Cronjé	53	24	0	0	0	120	0	0	0	0	0	0	53	24	0	0	0	120
X (Xander) Cronjé	4	1	0	0	0	5	0	0	0	0	0	0	4	1	0	0	0	5
IP (Isak) Deetlefs	12	0	0	0	0	0	0	0	0	0	0	0	12	0	0	0	0	0
H (Heinrich) Els	1	0	0	0	0	0	0	0	0	0	0	0	1	0	0	0	0	0
DC (Damian) Engledoe	3	1	0	0	0	5	11	4	0	0	0	20	14	5	0	0	0	25
J-F (Jan) Enslin	4	1	0	0	0	5	0	0	0	0	0	0	4	1	0	0	0	5
K (Kyle) Hendricks	53	31	7	4	0	181	0	0	0	0	0	0	53	31	7	4	0	181
GD (Grant) Janke	19	4	0	0	0	20	1	0	0	0	0	0	20	4	0	0	0	20
SM (Shane) Kirkwood	39	6	0	0	0	30	0	0	0	0	0	0	39	6	0	0	0	30
EFE (Ernst) Ladendorf	22	1	0	0	0	5	0	0	0	0	0	0	22	1	0	0	0	5
T (Thabo) Mamojele	7	0	0	0	0	0	26	2	0	0	0	10	33	2	0	0	0	10
CN (Charles) Mayeza	6	4	0	0	0	20	0	0	0	0	0	0	6	4	0	0	0	20
J-PF (JP) Mostert	43	9	0	0	0	45	9	1	0	0	0	5	52	10	0	0	0	50
R-H (Reg) Muller	52	22	0	0	0	110	0	0	0	0	0	0	52	22	0	0	0	110
F (Friedle) Olivier	21	8	0	0	0	40	0	0	0	0	0	0	21	8	0	0	0	40
A-D (Dwight) Pansegrouw	6	0	0	0	0	0	0	0	0	0	0	0	6	0	0	0	0	0
WJ (Warren) Potgieter	6	0	3	1	0	9	0	0	0	0	0	0	6	0	3	1	0	9
JW (Johan) Pretorius	15	10	0	0	0	50	0	0	0	0	0	0	15	10	0	0	0	50
A (Anrich) Richter	44	17	6	0	1	100	0	0	0	0	0	0	44	17	6	0	1	100
AS (Andries) Schutte	23	2	0	0	0	10	0	0	0	0	0	0	23	2	0	0	0	10
JM (Koos) Strauss	5	0	0	0	0	0	0	0	0	0	0	0	5	0	0	0	0	0
E (Etienne) Taljaard	18	9	0	0	0	45	0	0	0	0	0	0	18	9	0	0	0	45
JA (Andries) Truter	7	2	0	0	0	10	0	0	0	0	0	0	7	2	0	0	0	10
AJD (Andréw) van Wyk	24	3	0	0	0	15	13	5	0	0	0	25	37	8	0	0	0	40
G (Gihard) Visagie	2	0	0	0	0	0	0	0	0	0	0	0	2	0	0	0	0	0
G (Grant) Watts	2	0	0	0	0	0	0	0	0	0	0	0	2	0	0	0	0	0
ME (Marlyn) Williams	23	4	0	0	0	20	0	0	0	0	0	0	23	4	0	0	0	20
30 PLAYERS	569	163	54	18	3	986	88	13	19	8	1	130	657	176	73	26	4	1116

FIRST-CLASS APPEARANCES FOR VALKE IN 2016 – ALL MATCHES

PLAYER	CURRIE CUP QUALIFYING						CURRIE CUP						2016 TOTAL						CAREER MATCHES					
	A	T	C	P	DG	Pts	A	T	C	P	DG	Pts	A	T	C	P	DG	Pts	A	T	C	P	DG	Pts
GDJ (Jacques) Alberts	1	0	0	0	0	0	3	0	0	0	0	0	4	0	0	0	0	0	67	2	0	0	0	10
R (Ruan) Allerston	4	0	0	0	0	0	0	0	0	0	0	0	4	0	0	0	0	0	4	0	0	0	0	0
KG (Karlo) Aspeling	11	2	25	10	0	90	6	0	13	3	0	35	17	2	38	13	0	125	31	6	63	23	2	231
HB (Henri) Boshoff	13	1	0	0	0	5	4	0	0	0	0	0	17	1	0	0	0	5	17	1	0	0	0	5
C (Christo) Coetzee	7	1	5	0	0	15	0	0	0	0	0	0	7	1	5	0	0	15	7	1	5	0	0	15
CF (Coert) Cronjé	10	1	0	0	0	5	4	1	0	0	0	5	14	2	0	0	0	10	99	36	0	0	0	180
X (Xander) Cronjé	1	0	0	0	0	0	4	1	0	0	0	5	5	1	0	0	0	5	5	1	0	0	0	5
IP (Isak) Deetlefs	8	0	0	0	0	0	4	0	0	0	0	0	12	0	0	0	0	0	20	0	0	0	0	0
J-P (JP) du Plessis	4	0	0	0	0	0	0	0	0	0	0	0	4	0	0	0	0	0	4	0	0	0	0	0
H (Heinrich) Els	0	0	0	0	0	0	1	0	0	0	0	0	1	0	0	0	0	0	1	0	0	0	0	0
DC (Damian) Engledoe	10	0	1	0	0	2	3	1	0	0	0	5	13	1	1	0	0	7	13	1	1	0	0	7
J-F (Jan) Enslin	0	0	0	0	0	0	4	1	0	0	0	5	4	1	0	0	0	5	4	1	0	0	0	5
K (Kyle) Hendricks	8	4	0	0	0	20	1	0	0	0	0	0	9	4	0	0	0	20	102	48	19	10	0	308
GD (Grant) Janke	12	5	0	0	0	25	6	0	0	0	0	0	18	5	0	0	0	25	43	11	0	0	0	55
VT (Vincent) Jobo	6	0	0	0	0	0	0	0	0	0	0	0	6	0	0	0	0	0	6	0	0	0	0	0
SM (Shane) Kirkwood	14	6	0	0	0	30	5	0	0	0	0	0	19	6	0	0	0	30	63	13	0	0	0	65
EFE (Ernst) Ladendorf	10	0	0	0	0	0	5	0	0	0	0	0	15	0	0	0	0	0	41	3	0	0	0	15
T (Thabo) Mamojele	10	2	0	0	0	10	2	0	0	0	0	0	12	2	0	0	0	10	17	2	0	0	0	10
CN (Charles) Mayeza	1	0	0	0	0	0	6	4	0	0	0	20	7	4	0	0	0	20	7	4	0	0	0	20
J-PF (JP) Mostert	13	0	0	0	0	0	6	0	0	0	0	0	19	0	0	0	0	0	75	13	0	0	0	65
D (Dean) Muir	14	3	0	0	0	15	0	0	0	0	0	0	14	3	0	0	0	15	39	4	0	0	0	20
R-H (Reg) Muller	10	4	0	0	0	20	6	2	0	0	0	10	16	6	0	0	0	30	94	33	0	0	0	165
S (Sino) Nyoka	4	1	0	0	0	5	0	0	0	0	0	0	4	1	0	0	0	5	5	1	0	0	0	5
F (Friedle) Olivier	6	0	0	0	0	0	5	2	0	0	0	10	11	2	0	0	0	10	44	12	0	0	0	60
A-D (Dwight) Pansegrouw	13	1	0	0	0	5	6	0	0	0	0	0	19	1	0	0	0	5	19	1	0	0	0	5
WJ (Warren) Potgieter	7	0	11	2	0	28	6	0	3	1	0	9	13	0	14	3	0	37	13	0	14	3	0	37
JW (Johan) Pretorius	9	2	0	0	0	10	6	6	0	0	0	30	15	8	0	0	0	40	31	13	0	0	0	65
A (Anrich) Richter	8	1	0	0	0	5	3	2	0	0	0	10	11	3	0	0	0	15	92	34	6	0	1	185
HC (Christian) Rust	4	3	0	0	0	15	0	0	0	0	0	0	4	3	0	0	0	15	4	3	0	0	0	15
AS (Andries) Schutte	13	1	0	0	0	5	6	1	0	0	0	5	19	2	0	0	0	10	43	3	0	0	0	15
BS (Barend) Steyn	11	1	0	0	0	5	0	0	0	0	0	0	11	1	0	0	0	5	13	1	0	0	0	5
JM (Koos) Strauss	5	0	0	0	0	0	5	0	0	0	0	0	10	0	0	0	0	0	10	0	0	0	0	0
E (Etienne) Taljaard	13	9	0	0	0	45	5	4	0	0	0	20	18	13	0	0	0	65	33	19	0	0	0	95
JA (Andries) Truter	10	4	1	0	0	22	4	1	0	0	0	5	14	5	1	0	0	27	17	6	1	0	0	32
AJD (Andréw) van Wyk	8	3	0	0	0	15	5	1	0	0	0	5	13	4	0	0	0	20	46	11	0	0	0	55
G (Gihard) Visagie	5	0	0	0	0	0	2	0	0	0	0	0	7	0	0	0	0	0	7	0	0	0	0	0
G (Grant) Watts	1	0	0	0	0	0	2	0	0	0	0	0	3	0	0	0	0	0	3	0	0	0	0	0
ME (Marlyn) Williams	13	2	0	0	0	10	6	2	0	0	0	10	19	4	0	0	0	20	50	6	0	0	0	30

38 PLAYERS

Welwitschias

1996	1997	1998	1999	2000	2001	2002	2003	2004	2005	2006

2007	2008	2009	2010	2011	2012	2013	2014	2015	2016 15th

Played	Won	Lost	Drawn	Points for	Points against	Tries for	Tries against
5	0	5	0	117	303	15	45

Date	Venue	Opponent	Result	Score	Referee	Scorers
Aug 12	George	Eagles	LOST	23-54	S Ngcese	T: Lotter, Klim. C: Jantjies (2). P: Jantjies (3).
Aug 20	Windhoek	Leopards	LOST	42-54	AJ Jacobs	T: Klim (2), Botha, Nashikaku, Wilson, Damens. C: Jantjies (6).
Aug 26	East London	Bulldogs	LOST	07-61	E Seconds	T: Klim. C: Jantjies.
Sept 10	Welkom	Griffons	LOST	25-84	Q Immelman	T: Klim, Blom, Kaizemi, Moore. C: Jantjies. P: Jantjies.
Sept 17	Windhoek	Valke	LOST	20-50	R Boneparte	T: Jantjies (2). C: Jantjies (2). P: Jantjies (2).

[1]King Zwelithini Stadium, Umlazi

[2]Ermelo High School

APPEARANCES & POINTS

PLAYER	SWD	Leopards	Border	Griffons	Valke	Apps	T	C	P	DG	Pts
Chrysander Botha	15	15	15	15	10	5	1	–	–	–	5
Philip Nashikaku	14	14	11R	11	11	5	1	–	–	–	5
Heinrich Smit	13	13	14	–	13	4	–	–	–	–	0
Darryl de la Harpe	12	12	12	12	–	4	–	–	–	–	0
Gino Wilson	11	11	–	14	–	3	1	–	–	–	5
Eugene Jantjies	10	10	10	9	9	5	2	12	6	–	52
Camerol Klassen	9	9	–	10R	–	3	–	–	–	–	0
Leneve Damens	8	8	4R	8	8	5	1	–	–	–	5
Morné Blom	7	6R	8	7	–	4	1	–	–	–	5
Zayne Groenewaldt	6	6	6	6	8R	5	–	–	–	–	0
Ruan Ludick	5	5	5	5	5	5	–	–	–	–	0
Munio Kasiringua	4	–	x	5R	7R	3	–	–	–	–	0
Abel de Klerk	3c	3c	3c	3c	3c	5	–	–	–	–	0
Gerhard Lotter	2	2	7	2	2	5	1	–	–	–	5
Casper Viviers	1	1	–	–	–	2	–	–	–	–	0
Shaun du Preez	3R	–	1	–	3R	3	–	–	–	–	0
Quintin Esterhuizen	1R	1R	–	–	–	2	–	–	–	–	0
Denzil van Wyk	4R	4	4	4	4	5	–	–	–	–	0
Johann Wohler	8R	–	–	6R	7	3	–	–	–	–	0
Nandi Konuonbe	11R	–	–	–	–	1	–	–	–	–	0
Lesley Klim	13R	11R	13	13	–	4	5	–	–	–	25
Mahco Prinsloo	9R	14R	9R	–	–	3	–	–	–	–	0
Rohan Kitshoff	–	7	–	–	6	2	–	–	–	–	0
Petri Burger	–	2R	2	3R	–	3	–	–	–	–	0
Alberto Engelbrecht	–	4R	–	–	–	1	–	–	–	–	0
JC Winkler	–	9R	9	–	14R	3	–	–	–	–	0
Russell van Wyk	–	–	11	–	–	1	–	–	–	–	0
Collen Smith	–	–	2R	1R	–	2	–	–	–	–	0
Thomas Khali	–	–	6R	–	–	1	–	–	–	–	0
Justin Nel	–	–	12R	10	15R	3	–	–	–	–	0
Hauta Veii	–	–	–	1	1	2	–	–	–	–	0
Shaun Kaizemi	–	–	–	12R	12	2	1	–	–	–	5
Malcolm Moore	–	–	–	14R	14	2	1	–	–	–	5
Riaan van Zyl	–	–	–	–	15	1	–	–	–	–	0
Nian Berg	–	–	–	–	1R	1	–	–	–	–	0
Francois Wiese	–	–	–	–	12R	1	–	–	–	–	0
36 PLAYERS						109	15	12	6	0	117

Blue Bulls

Played	Won	Lost	Drawn	Points for	Points against	Tries for	Tries against
14	7	7	0	459	376	65	45

Date	Venue	Opponent	Result	Score	Referee	Scorers
Apr 08	Cape Town	WP	LOST	16-30	AJ Jacobs	T: Mxoli. C: Jantjies. P: Jantjies (3).
Apr 16	Pretoria	Free State XV	WON	20-17	Q Immelman	T: Libbok, C Visagie, Tsomondo. C: Stander. P: Libbok.
Apr 23	Alberton	Golden Lions	LOST	17-38	L van der Merwe	T: Tsomondo, Els. C: Stander (2). P: Stander.
May 07	Port Elizabeth	EP Kings	LOST	14-19	R Rasivhenge	T: Stander, Greyling. C: Stander (2).
May 13	Pretoria	Pumas	LOST	13-25	J Peyper	T: September. C: Stander. P: Stander (2).
May 21	Kimberley	Griquas	LOST	38-39	L Legoete	T: Smit (3), Matthews, Bothma. C: Stander (5). P: Stander.
May 28	Pretoria	Leopards	LOST	26-51	A Sehlako	T: Stander, Liebenberg, Bothma, Webster. C: Stander (3).
Jun 04	Welkom[1]	Griffons	WON	57-28	J Peyper	T: Mahlo (2), Smit (2), Isaacs, September, Els, Maree. C: Webster (5), Rossouw, Stander. P: Webster.
Jun 10	Pretoria	Sharks XV	WON	22-18	E Seconds	T: Mahlo (2), September (2). C: Webster.
Jun 17	Pretoria	Valke	WON	42-15	AJ Jacobs	T: Jantjies (2), Kriel, Warner, Mxoli, Van Zyl. C: Jantjies (6).
Jun 24	George	SWD	WON	28-23	S Ngcese	T: Rossouw, Van Heerden, Van Rooyen. C: Jantjies, De Beer. P: Jantjies (3).
July 01	Pretoria	Boland	LOST	26-35	Q Immelman	T: Liebenberg (2), Rossouw, Warner. C: Stander (2), Jantjies.
July 09	East London	Border	WON	45-26	C Jadezweni	T: September (2), Tsomondo (2), Mahlo, Naudé, Stiglingh. C: Stander (5).
July 15	Pretoria	Welwitchias	WON	95-12	R Bonaparte	T: Stighlingh (4), September (2), Isaacs (2), Rossouw, Jantjies, Warner, Ngoza, Nonkontwana, Tsomondo, Stander. C: Jantjies (7), Stander (3).

[1]HT Pelatona Projects Stadium

APPEARANCES & POINTS IN 2016 CURRIE CUP QUALIFIERS

	WP	Free State XV	Lions XV	EP Kings	Pumas	Griquas	Leopards	Griffons	Sharks XV	Valke	SWD	Boland	Border	Welwitchias	Apps	T	C	P	DG	Pts
Manie Libbok	15	15	15	15R	–	–	–	–	–	–	–	–	–	–	4	1	0	1	0	8
Luther Obi	14	14	–	–	–	–	–	–	–	–	–	–	–	–	2	–	–	–	–	0
Jade Stighling	13	11	11	11	11	–	14	11	11	11	11	11	11	11	13	5	0	0	0	25
Franco Naudé	12	–	13	–	–	–	–	–	–	–	–	13	13	–	4	1	0	0	0	5
Kefentse Mahlo	11	14R	14	14	–	–	15R	14	14	14	14	14	14	–	11	5	0	0	0	25
Tony Jantjies	10	10	–	–	–	–	–	10R	10	10	10	10R	10	–	8	3	16	6	0	65
André Warner	9	9R	9R	9R	9	9R	9	9	9	9	9	9R	9R	9c	14	3	0	0	0	15
Hanro Liebenberg	8c	8c	–	–	–	–	8c	8c	8c	8c	8c	8c	–	–	8	3	0	0	0	15
Freddy Ngoza	7	6	7c	8R	7	6R	–	–	–	–	–	–	8R	8	8	1	0	0	0	5
Deon Stegmann	6	–	7R	–	–	–	–	–	–	–	–	–	–	–	2	–	–	–	–	0
Nicolaas Janse van Rensburg	5	5	5	5	5	–	–	–	–	–	–	–	–	–	5	–	–	–	–	0
Irné Herbst	4	–	–	–	–	–	–	–	–	–	–	–	–	–	1	–	–	–	–	0
Entienne Swanepoel	3	3	3	–	3	–	3R	3	3	3	3	–	3	–	10	–	–	–	–	0
Callie Visagie	2	2R	–	–	–	–	–	–	–	–	–	–	–	–	2	1	0	0	0	5
Mox Mxoli	1	1	1	1	1	1	1	1	–	1	1	–	–	–	10	2	0	0	0	10
Corniel Els	2R	–	2	2	2	2	2R	2	–	–	–	–	–	–	7	2	0	0	0	10
Njabulo Gumede	1R	–	–	1R	1R	–	–	–	–	1	1	1	–	–	6	–	–	–	–	0
Dayan van der Westhuizen	3R	–	3R	3	–	–	–	–	–	–	–	–	–	–	3	–	–	–	–	0
Le Roux Roets	4R	–	–	–	–	–	–	–	–	–	–	–	–	–	1	–	–	–	–	0
Tapiwa Tsomondo	6R	7R	6	–	6	–	–	–	–	6R	6R	7	6	–	8	5	0	0	0	25
Theo Maree	9R	–	–	–	–	–	9R	9R	–	–	–	–	–	–	3	1	0	0	0	5
Joshua Stander	10R	10R	10	10	10	10	10	10	–	–	10R	10	10R	–	11	3	25	4	0	77
Dries Swanepoel	–	13	–	–	–	–	–	–	–	–	–	–	–	–	1	–	–	–	–	0
JT Jackson	–	12	12	–	–	–	–	–	–	–	–	–	–	12	3	–	–	–	–	0
Ivan van Zyl	–	9	9	9c	9R	9	9	–	–	9R	9R	9	9	9R	11	1	0	0	0	5
Nic de Jager	–	7	–	7	–	–	–	7R	6R	7	7	8	–	–	7	–	–	–	–	0
Abongile Nonkontwana	–	4	4	4	4R	–	4R	4	4	4	5	5	5	7	12	1	0	0	0	5
Bandise Maku	–	2	–	–	–	–	–	–	–	–	–	–	–	–	1	–	–	–	–	0
Hencus van Wyk	–	3R	–	–	–	–	–	–	–	–	–	–	–	–	1	–	–	–	–	0
Ruben van Heerden	–	4R	–	–	4R	–	4R	4R	5R	4	4	4	4	–	9	1	0	0	0	5
Ruan Steenkamp	–	–	8	6	8c	8c	5R	7	7	7	6	6	6c	–	11	–	–	–	–	0
Henning Campher	–	2R	–	–	–	–	–	–	–	–	2R	2R	2R	–	4	–	–	–	–	0
Aston Fortuin	–	4R	4R	4	4	4	–	–	–	4R	4R	4R	5	–	9	–	–	–	–	0
Adrian Maebane	–	13R	12	–	–	–	–	–	–	–	–	–	–	–	2	–	–	–	–	0
Bjorn Basson	–	15R	–	–	–	–	–	–	–	–	–	–	–	–	1	–	–	–	–	0
Duncan Matthews	–	–	15	15	15	–	–	–	–	–	–	–	–	–	3	1	0	0	0	5
Alcino Isaacs	–	–	13	13	11	13	13	13R	11R	14R	13	13R	14	–	11	3	0	0	0	15
Renaldo Bothma	–	–	8	–	7	7	–	–	–	–	–	–	–	–	3	2	0	0	0	10
Jan van der Merwe	–	–	2R	2R	2R	–	2R	2	2	2	–	–	–	–	7	–	–	–	–	0
Dean Greyling	–	–	3R	–	–	–	–	–	–	–	–	–	–	–	1	1	0	0	0	5
Duhan van der Merwe	–	–	14R	14	–	–	–	–	–	–	–	–	–	–	2	–	–	–	–	0
Marquit September	–	–	–	12	13	–	12	12	12	12	12	12	13	–	9	8	0	0	0	40
Clyde Davids	–	–	–	7R	–	6R	–	–	–	–	–	–	–	–	2	–	–	–	–	0
Kurt Webster	–	–	–	12R	x	13R	10R	10	–	–	–	–	–	–	4	1	6	1	0	20
Divan Rossouw	–	–	–	14R	14	11	15	15	15	15	15	15	15	–	10	3	1	0	0	17
Dan Kriel	–	–	–	–	12	12	–	13	13	13	–	–	–	–	5	1	0	0	0	5
Roelof Smit	–	–	–	–	6	6	6	6	6	–	–	–	–	–	5	5	0	0	0	25
Marvin Orie	–	–	–	–	5	5	5	5	5	–	–	–	–	–	5	–	–	–	–	0
Andréw Beerwinkel	–	–	–	–	3	–	3R	1	1R	1R	3	–	–	–	6	–	–	–	–	0
Dewald Naudé	–	–	–	–	15R	–	11R	–	–	–	–	–	–	–	2	–	–	–	–	0
Warrick Gelant	–	–	–	–	15	–	–	–	–	–	–	–	–	–	1	–	–	–	–	0
Werner Kruger	–	–	–	–	3	–	–	–	–	–	–	–	–	–	1	–	–	–	–	0
Jaco Visagie	–	–	–	–	2	–	–	–	–	–	–	–	–	–	1	–	–	–	–	0
Elandré van Rooyen	–	–	–	–	–	–	2R	2R	2R	2	2	2	–	–	6	1	0	0	0	5
Neethling Fouché	–	–	–	–	–	–	3R	–	–	3R	–	–	–	–	2	–	–	–	–	0
Tinus de Beer	–	–	–	–	–	–	–	10R	10R	–	–	–	–	–	2	0	1	0	0	2
Martin Dreyer	–	–	–	–	–	–	–	–	–	–	3R	3	–	–	2	–	–	–	–	0
Justin Forwood	–	–	–	–	–	–	–	–	–	–	–	–	3R	–	1	–	–	–	–	0
Eli Snyman	–	–	–	–	–	–	–	–	–	–	–	–	–	4R	1	–	–	–	–	0
Juan-re Swanepoel	–	–	–	–	–	–	–	–	–	–	–	–	–	8R	1	–	–	–	–	0
Ganfried May	–	–	–	–	–	–	–	–	–	–	–	–	–	15R	1	–	–	–	–	0
61 PLAYERS															**307**	**65**	**49**	**12**	**0**	**459**

Boland Cavaliers

Played	Won	Lost	Drawn	Points for	Points against	Tries for	Tries against
14	11	3	0	502	289	67	38

Date	Venue	Opponent	Result	Score	Referee	Scorers
Apr 08	Durban[1]	Sharks XV	WON	37-24	R Bonaparte	T: Carelse, Demas, Nell, Adendorff, McDonald. C: Scheepers (3). P: Scheepers (2).
Apr 16	Wellington	EP Kings	WON	37-18	F Pretoruis	T: Demas (2), Wenn, Van Zyl, Jordaan. C: Scheepers (3). P: Scheepers (2).
Apr 23	Nelspruit	Pumas	LOST	10-12	S Geldenhuys	T: Scheepers. C: Scheepers. P: Scheepers.
Apr 29	Wellington	Griquas	LOST	14-30	C Jadezweni	T: Bosch, Van Wyk. C: Carelse (2).
May 07	Potchefstroom[2]	Leopards	WON	43-31	J van Heerden	T: Torrens (2), Bosch, Nell, Kotze, Sass. C: Kotze (5). P: Kotze
May 13	Wellington	Griffons	WON	56-17	L v/d Merwe	T: Nell, Z Jordaan, Scheepers, Demas, Hugo, Sass, Genade. C: Kotze (3), Carelse (3). P: Kotze (3).
May 20	Kempton Park	Valke	WON	24-22	AJ Jacobs	T: Nell (2), Jordaan. C: Scheepers (2), Kotze. P: Scheepers.
May 27	Wellington	SWD Eagles	WON	32-16	AJ Jacobs	T: Nell (2), Adendorff, Bosch. C: Kotze (3). P: Kotze (2).
Jun 16	East London	Border	WON	38-17	Q Immelman	T: Wenn (2), Nell, Hanekom, Adendorff. C: Scheepers (5). P: Scheepers.
Jun 25	Wellington	Welwitschias	WON	110-10	AJ Jacobs	T: Nell (4), Bosch (4), Scheepers (3), Torrens (2), Kitshoff, Cronjé, W van Wyk. C: Scheepers (15).
July 01	Pretoria	Blue Bulls	WON	35-26	Q Immelman	T: Torrens (2), Short, Demas. C: Scheepers (3). P: Scheepers (3).
July 09	Piketberg	Western Province	LOST	14-25	R Bonaparte	T: Bosch, Demas. C: Scheepers (2).
July 16	Bloemfontein	Free State XV	WON	24-17	AJ Jacobs	T: Bosch (2), Demas. C: Scheepers (3). P: Scheepers.
July 23	Grabouw	Golden Lions XV	WON	28-24	P Brousset	T: Kitshoff, Louw, Torrens, McDonald. C: Scheepers (4).

[1] Sugar Ray Xulu Stadium, Clermont

[2] Johann du Randt Stadium

APPEARANCES & POINTS IN 2016 CURRIE CUP QUALIFIERS

	Sharks XV	EP Kings	Pumas	Griquas	Leopards	Griffons	Valke	SWD	Border	Welwitchias	Blue Bulls	WP	Free State XV	Lions XV	Apps	T	C	P	DG	Pts
Nico Scheepers	15	15	15	–	–	15	15	15	15	15	15	15	15	15	12	5	41	13	–	146
Sergio Torrens	14	–	14	14	14	14	14	14	14	14	14	14	14	14	13	7	–	–	–	35
Ryan Nell	13c	13c	13c	13c	13c	13c	13c	13c	13c	13c	13c	13c	13c	–	13	12	–	–	–	60
Christopher Bosch	12	12	12	12R	12	12	12	12	12	12	12	12	12	12	14	10	–	–	–	50
Danwel Demas	11	14	14	11	11	11	11	11	11	11	11	11	11	11R	14	7	–	–	–	35
Adriaan Carelse	10	10	10R	15	15	10R	10	15R	10	10	10	10	10R	10	14	1	5	–	–	15
Marnus Hugo	9	9	9	9R	9	9	9	9	9	9	9	9	9R	–	13	1	–	–	–	5
Zandré Jordaan	8	8	8	8	8	8	8	8	8	8	8	8	8	8c	14	3	–	–	–	15
Shaun McDonald	7	7	7	4R	7	7	7	7	7	7	7	7	7R	7	14	2	–	–	–	10
Shaun Adendorff	6	6	6	6R	6	6	6	6	6	–	6	6	6	–	12	3	–	–	–	15
Ockie van Zyl	5	5	5	5	5	5	5	–	5R	8R	5R	4R	–	5	12	1	–	–	–	5
Hanno Kitshoff	4	4	4	4	4	4	4	4	4	4	4	4	4	4	14	2	–	–	–	10
Basil Short	3	3	3	1R	3	3	3	1	1	–	3	3	3	–	12	1	–	–	–	5
Chadley Wenn	2	2	2	2R	2R	2	2	2	2	2	2	2	2	2	14	3	–	–	–	15
Francois Hanekom	1	1	1R	3	1R	1R	1	3	3	3	1R	1	1R	3	14	1	–	–	–	5
JC Genade	2R	–	–	–	–	2R	x	2R	2R	–	–	2R	x	–	5	1	–	–	–	5
SP Wessels	1R	1R	1	1	1	1	–	–	–	–	–	–	–	–	6	–	–	–	–	0
Kenan Cronjé	4R	4R	4R	6	–	–	–	6R	–	6	–	–	5R	6	8	1	–	–	–	5
Wayne Wilschut	6R	8R	6R	7	5R	7R	4R	5R	6R	7R	4R	6R	7	–	13	–	–	–	–	0
Jovelian de Koker	12R	x	–	–	–	–	–	–	9R	9R	9R	9	9	–	6	–	–	–	–	0
Edwin Sass	14R	12R	12R	12	12R	13R	–	12R	–	–	–	–	–	–	7	2	–	–	–	10
Gavin Hauptfleisch	10R	–	–	–	–	–	–	–	–	–	–	–	–	–	1	–	–	–	–	0
Craig Pheiffer	–	11	–	–	–	–	–	–	–	–	–	–	–	11	2	–	–	–	–	0
Theuns Kotze	–	10R	10	10	10	10	10R	10	–	–	–	–	–	10R	8	1	12	6	–	47
Francois Esterhuizen	–	2R	2R	2	2	–	–	–	–	–	–	–	–	–	4	–	–	–	–	0
Gerhard Jordaan	–	–	9R	9	9R	9R	9R	9R	9R	–	–	–	–	9R	8	–	–	–	–	0
William van Wyk	–	–	–	10R	14R	–	–	10R	10R	x	10R	10	–	–	6	2	–	–	–	10
Ferdie Horn	–	–	–	–	4R	4R	4R	5	5	5	5	5	5	5R	10	–	–	–	–	0
Linda Thwala	–	–	–	–	–	–	1R	3R	–	1	–	x	–	1R	4	–	–	–	–	0
Gerrit van Wyk	–	–	–	–	–	–	x	–	14R	13R	12R	12R	13R	–	5	–	–	–	–	0
Yves Bashiya	–	–	–	–	–	–	–	–	1R	3R	–	–	–	–	2	–	–	–	–	0
Clemen Lewis	–	–	–	–	–	–	–	2R	2R	–	–	–	2R	–	3	–	–	–	–	0
Niel Oelofse	–	–	–	–	–	–	–	–	–	1	–	1	1	–	3	–	–	–	–	0
Robert Louw	–	–	–	–	–	–	–	–	–	–	–	–	13	–	1	1	–	–	–	5
Chaney Willemse	–	–	–	–	–	–	–	–	–	–	–	–	–	6R	1	–	–	–	–	0
35 PLAYERS															302	67	58	19	0	508

Border

Played 14	Won 5	Lost 9	Drawn 0	Points for 364	Points against 424	Tries for 49	Tries against 55

Date	Venue	Opponent	Result	Score	Referee	Scorers
Apr 08	Johannesburg	Golden Lions XV	WON	27-23	J van Heerden	T: Mapimpi, Thom, Putuma. C: Banda, Zono, Basson. P: Zono (2).
Apr 15	East London	Sharks XV	WON	37-32	L Legoete	T: Mapimpi (4), Zono (2). C: Banda (2). P: Banda.
Apr 23	Port Elizabeth	EP Kings	WON	26-14	AJ Jacobs	T: Makase, Zono, Booi, Ngande. C: Zono (4).
Apr 30	East London	Pumas	LOST	03-28	F Pretorius	P: Zono.
May 07	Kimberley	Griquas	LOST	12-21	L Legoete	T: Banda, Putuma. C: Banda.
May 13	East London	Leopards	LOST	22-34	L Legoete	T: Mapimpi, Jonker, Nofuma. C: Banda (2). P: Banda.
May 21	Welkom[1]	Griffons	LOST	23-34	J Kotze	T: Nofuma, Mdaka. C: Banda (2). P: Banda (3).
May 27	East London	Valke	WON	29-24	R Bonaparte	T: Banda (2), Dumezweni, Mapimpi. C: Banda (2), Basson. P: Banda.
Jun 10	George	SWD	LOST	22-39	M v/d Westhuizen	T: Banda, Makase, Mpafi, Basson. C: Banda.
Jun 16	East London	Boland	LOST	17-38	Q Immelman	T: Mapimpi, Dutton, Penalty try. C: Basson.
July 02	Windhoek	Welwitschias	WON	76-18	E Seconds	T: Mapimpi (4), Mqalo (2), Khetani (2), Basson, Makase, Jonker, Ndlovu. C: Basson (7), Banda.
July 09	East London	Blue Bulls	LOST	26-45	C Jadezweni	T: Nofemele, Makase. C: Basson (2). P: Basson (4).
July 16	Cape Town	WP	LOST	26-52	P Brousset	T: Mqalo, Dumezweni. C: Banda (2). P: Banda (4).
July 22	East London	Free State XV	LOST	18-22	L van der Merwe	T: Tom, Mapimpi. C: Banda. P: Banda (2).

[1]HT Pelatona Projects Stadium

APPEARANCES & POINTS IN 2016 CURRIE CUP QUALIFIERS

	Lions XV	Sharks XV	EP Kings	Pumas	Griquas	Leopards	Griffons	Valke	SWD	Boland	Welwitchias	Blue Bulls	WP	Free State XV	Apps	T	C	P	DG	Pts
Masixole Banda	15	15	15	15	15	15	15	15	15	15	10	10	10	10	14	4	15	12	0	86
Makazole Mapimpi	14	14	14	14	14	14	14	14R	13R	13	13	13	13	11	14	13	0	0	0	65
Lundi Ralarala	13	–	–	–	13R	11R	13	13	13	–	–	–	–	–	6	–	–	–	–	0
Sethu Tom	12	12	12	12	–	12	13R	–	–	–	14R	13R	13	–	9	2	0	0	0	10
Michael Makase	11	11	11	11	11	–	11	11	11	11	11	11	11	–	12	4	0	0	0	20
Oliver Zono	10	10	10	10	–	10	–	10	10	10	–	–	–	13R	9	2	4	3	0	27
Bangi Kobese	9	9	9	9	–	9	9	9	9	9	9R	9	9R	9R	13	–	–	–	–	0
Billy Dutton	8	8	8	8	8	8	–	7	6R	8	6	6	–	–	11	1	0	0	0	5
Siya Mdaka	7c	7c	7c	7c	7c	7c	7c	–	7c	7c	7c	7c	7c	–	12	1	0	0	0	5
Nkosikhana Nofuma	6	–	–	8R	7R	4R	8	8	8	–	8	8	5R	7	11	2	0	0	0	10
Wandile Putuma	5	5	5	5	5	5	5	5	5	5	5	5	5	4R	14	2	0	0	0	10
Lindokuhle Welemu	4	4	4	4	4	4	4	4	4	4	4	4	4	4	14	–	–	–	–	0
Johannes Jonker	3	3	3	3	3	3	3	3	3	3	3	3	3	3R	14	2	0	0	0	10
Mihlali Mpafi	2	2	2	2R	2R	2R	2	2R	2R	2R	2	–	2R	2R	13	1	0	0	0	5
Blake Kyd	1	1	1	1	1	1	1R	1c	1	1	1	1	1	3c	14	–	–	–	–	0
Ludwe Booi	2R	2R	2R	2	2	2R	2	2	2	–	2	2	2	2	13	1	0	0	0	5
Siya Ngande	3R	1R	1R	1R	1R	–	–	–	1R	3R	–	3R	1	–	9	1	0	0	0	5
Hendri Storm	4R	4R	4R	5R	–	–	–	–	–	–	–	–	–	5	5	1	0	0	0	5
Athenkosi Mamentsa	6R	6	6	–	–	8R	–	–	–	4R	–	8	8	–	7	–	–	–	–	0
Zukisani Tywaleni	x	x	9R	–	9	9R	9R	9R	x	9R	9	–	–	–	7	–	–	–	–	0
Nkululuko Ndlovu	13R	13R	14R	10R	–	–	–	–	–	10R	15R	–	–	–	6	1	0	0	0	5
Logan Basson	10R	x	–	–	10R	–	13R	10R	14R	15	15	–	–	–	7	2	12	4	0	46
Sonwabiso Mqalo	–	13	13	13	13	13	–	–	12R	14R	–	15	15	–	9	3	0	0	0	15
Lukhanyo Nomzanga	–	6R	6R	6	6	6	6	6	6	6	–	8R	6R	–	11	–	–	–	–	0
Buhle Mxunyelwa	–	–	3R	3R	3R	–	–	–	–	–	–	–	–	–	3	–	–	–	–	0
Siyasonga Ncanywa	–	–	–	19R	–	11	–	–	–	–	–	–	–	–	2	–	–	–	–	0
Lunga Dumezweni	–	–	–	–	12	–	12	12	12	12	12	12	12	12	9	2	0	0	0	10
Thembani Mkokeli	–	–	–	–	10	12R	10	–	–	–	–	–	–	–	3	–	–	–	–	0
Sibabalwe Msutwana	–	–	–	9R	–	–	–	–	–	–	–	–	–	–	1	–	–	–	–	0
Yanga Xakalashe	–	–	–	–	1R	1	1R	1R	–	–	1R	–	1R	–	6	–	–	–	–	0
Athi Khethani	–	–	–	–	–	4R	4R	8R	4R	5R	4R	–	–	–	6	2	0	0	0	10
Johannes Janse van Rensburg	–	–	–	–	5R	8R	–	6R	–	–	–	–	–	5R	4	–	–	–	–	0
Sipho Nofemele	–	–	–	–	11R	14	14	14	14	14	14	14	14	–	8	1	0	0	0	5
Mbeko Kota	–	–	–	–	–	–	–	–	2R	2R	–	–	–	–	2	–	–	–	–	0
Sino Nyoka	–	–	–	–	–	–	–	–	–	9R	9	9	–	–	3	–	–	–	–	0
Onke Dubase	–	–	–	–	–	–	–	–	–	–	6	6	–	–	2	–	–	–	–	0
Sanelise Ngoma	–	–	–	–	–	–	–	–	–	–	11R	–	–	–	1	–	–	–	–	0
Penalty try	–	–	–	–	–	–	–	–	–	–	–	–	–	–		1	0	0	0	5
37 PLAYERS															304	49	31	19	0	364

EP Kings

Played	Won	Lost	Drawn	Points for	Points against	Tries for	Tries against
14	2	11	1	278	513	35	72

Date	Venue	Opponent	Result	Score	Referee	Scorers
Apr 09	Port Elizabeth	SWD	LOST	14-37	C Joubert	T: Ward, Penalty try. C: Brink (2).
Apr 16	Wellington	Boland	LOST	18-37	F Pretorius	T: Winnaar, S Jho. C: Bolze. P: Winnaar (2).
Apr 23	Port Elizabeth	Border	LOST	14-26	AJ Jacobs	T: Winnaar, Bolze. C: Winnaar, Bolze.
Apr 30	Windhoek	Welwitschias	WON	31-18	P Legoete	T: Winnaar, Mayinje, S Jho, Nieuwoudt, Msutwana. C: Mayinje (2), Bolze.
May 07	Port Elizabeth	Blue Bulls	WON	19-14	R Rasivhenge	T: Hendricks. C: Mattheus. P: Mattheus (4).
May 14	Cape Town*	WP	LOST	10-50	S Geldenhuys	T: A Jho. C: Mattheus. P: Mattheus.
May 20	Port Elizabeth	Free State XV	LOST	15-35	R Bonaparte	T: Mayinje, S Jho. C: Brink. P: Brink.
May 28	Johannesburg[1]	Golden Lions XV	DREW	35-35	L van der Merwe	T: S Jho, Jonck, Jackson, Penalty try. C: Mattheus (3). P: Mattheus (3).
Jun 03	Port Elizabeth	Sharks XV	LOST	26-34	M v/d Westhuizen	T: Mattheus, Ueckermann. C: Mattheus (2). P: Mattheus (4).
Jun 24	Nelspruit	Pumas	LOST	20-53	L van der Merwe	T: Penxe, S Jho, Winnaar. C: Brink. P: Brink.
July 02	Port Elizabeth	Griquas	LOST	12-29	J van Heerden	T: Badiyana, Jamieson. C: Mattheus.
July 08	Potchefstroom	Leopards	LOST	14-54	J Sylvestre	T: Jonck, Fuzani. C: Mattheus, Bolze.
July 15	Port Elizabeth	Griffons	LOST	24-32	L Legoete	T: Zungu, Mattheus, Penalty try. C: Bolze (2), Mattheus. P: Bolze.
July 22	Kempton Park	Valke	LOST	26-59	M v/d Westhuizen	T: Vers, Ueckermann, Badiyana, Murray. C: Bolze (3).

* *City Park Stadium*
[1]*Pirates Rugby Club, Greenside*

APPEARANCES & POINTS IN 2016 CURRIE CUP QUALIFIERS

	SWD	Boland	Border	Welwitchias	Blue Bulls	WP	Free State XV	Lions XV	Sharks XV	Pumas	Griquas	Leopards	Griffons	Valke	Apps	T	C	P	DG	Pts
Keanu Vers	15	–	10R	–	–	–	–	–	–	–	–	–	14	14	4	1	0	0	0	5
Jixie Molapo	14	14	–	–	–	–	–	–	–	14	–	–	–	–	3	–	–	–	–	0
Somila Jho	13	13	13	13	x	13	13	13	13	13	13	13	11R	12R	13	5	0	0	0	25
Jeremy Ward	12c	–	12c	–	12c	–	–	–	–	–	–	–	–	12c	4	1	0	0	0	5
Athenkosi Mayinje	11	14R	14	14	14	14	11	14	14	–	–	14	–	–	10	2	2	0	0	14
Michael Brink	10	–	–	–	–	–	10	15	15	15	–	–	12	15	7	0	4	2	0	14
Chuma Faas	9	–	9R	9R	–	9R	–	–	–	–	–	–	–	–	4	–	–	–	–	0
Junior Pokomela	8	8	8	–	–	–	–	–	–	–	–	–	–	–	3	–	–	–	–	0
Sintu Manjezi	7	7c	7	7c	4	7c	7c	7c	7c	5c	7c	–	–	–	11	–	–	–	–	0
JP Jonck	6	6	6	–	6	–	–	6	6	6	6R	6	–	–	9	2	0	0	0	10
Tazz Fuzani	5	4	4	4	–	4	4	4	4	4	4	4	–	–	11	1	0	0	0	5
Philip du Preez	4	4R	7R	4R	7R	5	x	x	–	–	–	–	–	–	6	–	–	–	–	0
Louis Albertse	3	3	3	3	3	–	3	3	3	3	–	–	–	–	9	–	–	–	–	0
Warrick Venter	2	2	2	2	2R	–	2	–	2R	2	2	–	–	2	10	–	–	–	–	0
David Murray	1	1	–	–	1R	1	–	–	–	–	1	1	1	1	8	1	0	0	0	5
JP Jamieson	2R	2R	–	2R	–	5R	2R	2	–	2R	2R	2	2R	2R	11	1	0	0	0	5
Vukile Sofisa	1R	3R	–	1R	–	3R	3R	x	3R	3R	3	–	–	3	10	–	–	–	–	0
Stephan Zaayman	4R	–	–	7R	6R	6	8	–	6R	7	–	–	–	–	7	–	–	–	–	0
Cornéll Hess	5R	5	5	5	5	–	5	5	5	8R	5	5c	–	–	11	–	–	–	–	0
Stephanus Nieuwoudt	6R	6R	4R	6	7	–	–	8R	–	7R	6	7	–	–	9	1	0	0	0	5
Davron Cameron	9R	11R	–	9	–	–	–	–	–	–	–	–	–	–	3	–	–	–	–	0
Courtney Winnaar	15R	15	15	15	–	–	–	–	–	10	–	–	–	–	5	4	1	2	0	28
Siphu Msutwana	–	12	–	10R	11	11	14	12	15R	13R	14R	13R	13	13	12	1	0	0	0	5
Lindelwe Zungu	–	11	11	11	15	15	15	11	11	11	11	11	15	11	13	1	0	0	0	5
Simon Bolze	–	10	10	10	–	–	–	–	–	13R	10R	10	10		7	1	9	1	0	26
Franswa Ueckermann	–	9	9	–	9	–	9	9	9	–	–	–	9	9	8	2	0	0	0	10
Riaan Esterhuizen	–	12R	13R	–	–	–	12	–	12	–	–	–	–	–	4	–	–	–	–	0
Nicolaas Oosthuizen	–	–	1	–	–	–	–	–	–	–	–	–	3	3R	3	–	–	–	–	0
Tango Balekile	–	–	2R	–	–	–	–	–	–	–	2R	2	–	–	3	–	–	–	–	0
Gregory Jackson	–	–	3R	–	–	–	2R	–	–	–	–	–	–	–	2	1	0	0	0	5
JP du Plessis	–	–	–	12	13	–	–	–	–	12	12	12	–	–	5	–	–	–	–	0
Jacques Engelbrecht	–	–	–	8	8	8	–	–	8	–	–	–	–	–	4	–	–	–	–	0
Liam Hendricks	–	–	–	1	1	–	1	1	1	1	1R	3	–	–	8	1	0	0	0	5
Yaw Penxe	–	–	–	15R	–	10R	–	x	–	14	–	–	–	–	3	1	0	0	0	5
Garrick Mattheus	–	–	–	–	10	10	–	10	10	11R	10	10	10R	–	8	2	10	12	0	66
Martin Bezuidenhout	–	–	–	–	2	2	–	–	2	–	–	–	–	–	3	–	–	–	–	0
Sibusiso Ngcokowane	–	–	–	–	9R	9	x	–	–	9R	9R	9	–	9R	6	–	–	–	–	0
Jordan Koekemoer	–	–	–	–	15R	12R	10R	–	–	–	–	–	–	–	3	–	–	–	–	0
Andile Jho	–	–	–	–	12	–	–	–	–	–	–	–	–	–	1	1	0	0	0	5
Roche van Zyl	–	–	–	–	3	–	–	–	–	–	x	3R	–		2	–	–	–	–	0
Gerrit Huisamen	–	–	–	–	5R	5R	–	–	–	–	–	4	5	–	3	–	–	–	–	0
Lusanda Badiyana	–	–	–	–	6R	6	8	5R	8	8	8	8c	8		9	2	0	0	0	10
Mabhutana Peter	–	–	–	–	–	12R	–	–	–	–	–	11	15R		3	–	–	–	–	0
Rouche Nel	–	–	–	–	–	x	9R	9	9	9R	13R	–			5	–	–	–	–	0
Ivan-John du Preez	–	–	–	–	–	–	14R	14R	–	–	–	–	–	–	2	–	–	–	–	0
Jaco van Tonder	–	–	–	–	–	–	–	15	15	–	–	–	–		2	–	–	–	–	0
Robert Lyons	–	–	–	–	–	–	–	4R	5R	6	6	–			4	–	–	–	–	0
Wihan Coetzer	–	–	–	–	–	–	–	–	6R	–	–	–			1	–	–	–	–	0
Jayson Reinecke	–	–	–	–	–	–	–	–	–	7	7				2	–	–	–	–	0
Wynand Grassmann	–	–	–	–	–	–	–	–	–	5	4				2	–	–	–	–	0
Justin Hollis	–	–	–	–	–	–	–	–	–	6R	–				1	–	–	–	–	0
Stephan Deyzel	–	–	–	–	–	–	–	–	–	7R	7R				2	–	–	–	–	0
Henry Brown	–	–	–	–	–	–	–	–	–	6R					1	–	–	–	–	0
Penalty try	–	–	–	–	–	–	–	–	–	–	–	–	–	–	–	3	0	0	0	15
53 PLAYERS															301	35	26	17	0	278

Free State XV

Played	Won	Lost	Drawn	Points for	Points against	Tries for	Tries against
14	8	6	0	372	337	52	41

Date	Venue	Opponent	Result	Score	Referee	Scorers
Apr 09	Bloemfontein	Welwitschias	WON	32-17	Q Immelman	T: Erwee (2), Mohojé, Hugo, Dweba, Huggett. C: Van Rensburg.
Apr 16	Pretoria	Blue Bulls	LOST	17-20	Q Immelman	T: Vidima, Nche. C: De Wet (2). P: De Wet.
Apr 22	Bloemfontein[1]	WP	LOST	31-36	B Crouse	T: Mafuma (2), Smith, Dweba, Liebenberg. C: Ebersohn (3).
May 07	Randburg[2]	Golden Lions XV	WON	29-15	F Pretorius	T: Ebersohn, Wiese, Dolo, Dweba. C: Ebersohn (3). P: Ebersohn.
May 14	Bloemfontein	Sharks XV	WON	19-13	S Berry	T: JP Coetzee (2), Dolo. C: Ebersohn (2).
May 20	Port Elizabeth	EP Kings	WON	35-15	R Bonaparte	T: Dweba (2), Uys, Liebenberg, Van Rensburg. C: Ebersohn (5).
May 27	Bloemfontein	Pumas	LOST	26-29	M v/d Westhuizen	T: A Coetzee, Dweba, Gordon, Kruger. C: Ebersohn (3).
Jun 04	Kimberley	Griquas	LOST	31-44	R Rasivhenge	T: Wegner, Erwee, Hugo, Kruger. C: Marais (4). P: Marais.
Jun 17	Bloemfontein	Leopards	WON	23-14	R Bonaparte	T: Rampeta, Hugo. C: Marais (2). P: Marais (2), Smith.
Jun 25	Welkom	Griffons	LOST	33-49	L Legoete	T: Erwee (2), Du Toit, Rampeta, Kruger. C: Ebersohn (3), Baron.
July 02	Bloemfontein	Valke	WON	33-27	AJ Jacobs	T: Mgijima, JP Coetzee, Vidima, Erwee, Kruger. C: Ebersohn (4).
July 08	George	SWD	WON	24-16	L Legoete	T: Mafuma, Burger. C: Ebersohn. P: Ebersohn (4).
July 16	Bloemfontein	Boland	LOST	17-24	AJ Jacobs	T: CJ Coetzee, Gordon. C: Ebersohn (2). P: Ebersohn.
July 22	East London	Border	WON	22-18	L v/d Merwe	T: Erasmus, Rautenbach, Penalty try. C: Labuschagne (2). P: Van Rensburg.

[1] *CUT Stadium*
[2] *Diggers Rugby Club*

APPEARANCES & POINTS IN 2016 CURRIE CUP QUALIFIERS

	Welwitchias	Blue Bulls	WP	Lions XV	Sharks XV	EP Kings	Pumas	Griquas	Leopards	Griffons	Valke	SWD	Boland	Border	Apps	T	C	P	DG	Pts
Reinhardt Erwee	15	15	15	15	15	15	15	15	15	15	11R	15	15	–	13	6	–	–	–	30
Kholo Ramashala	14	–	–	–	–	x	–	–	–	–	–	–	–	–	1	–	–	–	–	0
Tertius Kruger	13	12	12	12	12	–	13	13	12	13	13	12	12	–	12	4	–	–	–	20
Michael van der Spuy	12	–	–	–	–	–	–	–	–	–	–	–	–	–	1	–	–	–	–	0
Maphutla Dolo	11	11	11	11	11	11	11	–	11	11	11	11	11	–	12	2	–	–	–	10
Darren Baron	10	x	–	10R	x	10R	10R	–	–	10R	22R	10R	10R	10	9	–	1	–	–	2
Ruan van Rensburg	9	–	–	9R	9	9	–	–	–	9R	9R	9R	10R	–	8	1	1	1	–	10
Tienie Burger	8	7	7	7	–	7	7	7	–	–	7	7	–	–	9	1	–	–	–	5
Oupa Mohojé	7	–	–	–	–	–	–	–	–	–	–	–	–	–	1	1	–	–	–	5
Ntokozo Vidima	6	6	6	7R	8R	6	–	–	8R	7	6	6	7	–	11	2	–	–	–	10
Reniel Hugo	5c	5c	5c	5c	5c	5c	5c	5c	5c	–	–	–	–	–	9	3	–	–	–	15
Armandt Koster	4	4	4	4	–	4	–	4R	–	–	5	–	–	–	7	–	–	–	–	0
Luan de Bruin	3	–	–	–	–	–	3	3	–	–	–	–	–	–	3	–	–	–	–	0
Joseph Dweba	2	2	2	2	2	2	2	2	2R	–	–	–	–	–	9	6	–	–	–	30
BG Uys	1	1R	1	1	1	1	1	1R	–	–	–	–	–	–	8	1	–	–	–	5
Elandré Huggett	2R	–	–	–	–	–	2R	–	–	2R	2R	2R	2R	–	6	1	–	–	–	5
Danie Mienie	1R	–	–	–	–	–	–	–	–	–	–	–	–	–	1	–	–	–	–	0
Gunther Janse van Vuuren	3R	3R	3	3	–	–	–	–	–	3	3	3R	–	–	7	–	–	–	–	0
Justin Basson	7R	4R	–	4R	4	–	–	–	–	4	4	4	4	–	8	–	–	–	–	0
Refuoe Rampeta	8R	6R	4R	6	6	–	6	6	6	6	–	6	–	–	10	2	–	–	–	10
JP Smith	12R	9	9	9	9	11R	14R	9	9	9	9	–	–	9R	12	1	–	1	–	8
Lorenzo Gordon	14R	14	–	x	14R	14	11	12R	x	14	–	12R	11	–	9	2	–	–	–	10
Carel-Jan Coetzee	–	13	13	13	13	13	–	13	–	–	–	13	13	–	8	1	–	–	–	5
Pieter-Steyn de Wet	–	10	–	–	–	–	–	–	–	–	–	–	–	–	1	–	2	1	–	7
Jasper Wiese	–	8	8	8	7	–	–	8	6R	8	8	–	6	–	9	1	–	–	–	5
Yosuke Takahashi	–	3	–	–	–	–	–	–	–	–	–	–	–	–	1	–	–	–	–	0
Ox Nche	–	1	1R	–	–	–	1	1	–	–	–	–	–	–	4	1	–	–	–	5
Tiaan Liebenberg	–	2R	2R	2R	2R	2R	–	–	–	–	–	–	–	–	5	2	–	–	–	10
Renier Botha	–	9R	9R	9R	–	–	9R	–	9R	–	–	–	–	–	5	–	–	–	–	0
Mosolwa Mafuma	–	–	14	14R	–	–	–	–	–	–	14	–	–	–	3	3	–	–	–	15
Sias Ebersohn	–	–	10	10	10	10	10	–	10c	10c	10c	10c	–	–	10	1	26	6	–	75
Willie Britz	–	–	8R	–	–	–	–	–	–	–	–	–	–	–	1	–	–	–	–	0
Jean-Pierre Coetzee	–	–	11R	14	14	14	–	14	14	14	15	14R	14	14	11	3	–	–	–	15
Chase Morrison	–	–	3R	3R	3R	3R	3R	3R	3R	–	–	–	–	3R	9	–	–	–	–	0
Niell Jordaan	–	–	–	8	8	–	8	–	–	–	–	–	–	–	3	–	–	–	–	0
Aranos Coetzee	–	–	–	3	3	3	–	3	–	–	–	–	–	–	4	1	–	–	–	5
Johan Grundlingh	–	–	–	4R	4R	8	–	1R	4	5	–	–	–	5R	7	–	–	–	–	0
Gerrie Labuschagne	–	–	–	–	12	–	–	–	–	–	–	–	15	–	2	2	–	–	–	4
Musa Mahlasela	–	–	–	–	6R	–	–	–	–	–	–	–	–	–	1	–	–	–	–	0
Ali Mgijima	–	–	–	–	–	12	10R	10R	12	12	–	–	–	12	6	1	–	–	–	5
Carl Wegner	–	–	–	–	–	4	4	4	–	–	–	–	–	–	3	1	–	–	–	5
Neil Claassen	–	–	–	–	4R	–	–	5	–	–	–	5	7c	–	4	–	–	–	–	0
Henco Venter	–	–	–	–	6R	–	7	8	–	–	–	–	–	–	3	–	–	–	–	0
Neil Marais	–	–	–	–	–	12	10	–	–	–	–	–	–	–	2	–	6	3	–	21
Jacques du Toit	–	–	–	–	–	2R	2	2	2	2	2	–	–	–	6	1	–	–	–	5
Victor Maruping	–	–	–	–	–	7R	–	x	–	–	–	–	–	–	1	–	–	–	–	0
Arrie Vosloo	–	–	–	–	–	–	x	–	–	–	–	–	–	–	0	–	–	–	–	0
Johan Kotze	–	–	–	–	–	–	–	–	1	1	–	1	1	–	4	–	–	–	–	0
Gopolang Molefe	–	–	–	–	–	–	x	7R	8R	7R	x	–	–	–	3	–	–	–	–	0
Erich de Jager	–	–	–	–	–	–	–	1R	1	3	3	–	–	–	4	–	–	–	–	0
Rayno Benjamin	–	–	–	–	–	–	–	–	–	–	13	–	–	–	1	–	–	–	–	0
Zee Mkhabela	–	–	–	–	–	–	–	–	9	9	9	–	–	–	3	–	–	–	–	0
Quintin Vorster	–	–	–	–	–	–	–	–	–	–	1R	–	–	–	1	–	–	–	–	0
Brendan Verster	–	–	–	–	–	–	–	–	–	–	4R	4R	–	–	2	–	–	–	–	0
Nardus Erasmus	–	–	–	–	–	–	–	–	–	–	–	8	8	–	2	1	–	–	–	5
Neil Rautenbach	–	–	–	–	–	–	–	–	–	–	–	–	2	–	1	1	–	–	–	5
Willem Serfontein	–	–	–	–	–	–	–	–	–	–	–	–	5	–	1	–	–	–	–	0
Arno van Staden	–	–	–	–	–	–	–	–	–	–	–	–	–	11R	1	–	–	–	–	0
Reinach Venter	–	–	–	–	–	–	–	–	–	–	–	–	–	2R	1	–	–	–	–	0
Penalty try	–	–	–	–	–	–	–	–	–	–	–	–	–	–	0	1	–	–	–	5
59 PLAYERS															**299**	**52**	**38**	**12**	**0**	**372**

Golden Lions XV

Played	Won	Lost	Drawn	Points for	Points against	Tries for	Tries against
14	8	5	1	594	353	83	45

Date	Venue	Opponent	Result	Score	Referee	Scorers
Apr 08	Johannesburg	Border	LOST	23-27	J van Heerden	T: Erasmus, Schroeder. C: Boshoff. P: Boshoff (3).
Apr 16	Windhoek	Welwitchias	WON	66-12	A Sehlako	T: Gavor (3), Lerm (2), Bell (2), Marx, Nel, Samuels. C: Boshoff (6), Reynolds (2).
Apr 23	Alberton[1]	Blue Bulls	WON	38-17	L v/d Merwe	T: Hanekom, Nel, Volmink, Lerm, Malherbe. C: Reynolds (4), Davids. P: Reynolds.
Apr 30	Cape Town	WP	LOST	24-27	R Rasivhenge	T: Mahuza (2), Reynolds. C: Reynolds (2), Boshoff. P: Boshoff.
May 07	Randburg[2]	Free State XV	LOST	15-29	F Pretorius	T: Marx, Davids. C: Reynolds. P: Reynolds.
May 20	Kwa-Mashu[3]	Sharks XV	WON	53-16	E Seconds	T: Bell, Marx, Hanekom, Sage, Lerm, Samuels, Minnie, Reynolds. C: Reynolds (3), Boshoff (2). P: Boshoff.
May 28	Johannesburg[4]	EP Kings	DREW	35-35	L v/d Merwe	T: Lerm, De Wee, Samuels, Schroeder. C: Reynolds (3). P: Reynolds (3).
Jun 04	KaNyamazane	Pumas	LOST	24-35	J van Heerden	T: Volmink, Lerm, Booysen, Reynolds. C: Davids (2).
Jun 11	Johannesburg[5]	Griquas	WON	52-37	Q Immelman	T: Hanekom (3), Bell (2), Reynolds, Erasmus. C: Boshoff (7). P: Boshoff.
Jun 24	Potchefstroom	Leopards	WON	64-28	S Berry	T: Erasmus (2), Sage, Volmink, Ackermann, Brink, Van Rooyen, Samuels, Janse van Rensburg, Mahuza. C: Boshoff (7).
July 02	Johannesburg	Griffons	WON	66-19	L Legoete	T: Hanekom (2), Lerm (2), Bell, Marx, Nel, De Wit, Theron, Sage. C: Boshoff (4), Davids (4).
July 09	Kempton Park	Valke	WON	75-14	B Crouse	T: Volmink (3), Gavor (2), Bell, Nel, Theron, Jansen, Lusaseni, Reynolds. C: Reynolds (6), Van der Walt (4).
July 16	Johannesburg	SWD	WON	35-29	C Jadezweni	T: Bell, Ramaboea, Venter, De Villiers. C: Masuku (3). P: Masuku (3).
July 23	Grabouw	Boland	LOST	24-28	P Brousset	T: De Wee (2), Nel. C: Reynolds (3). P: Reynolds.

[1] *Alberton Rugby Club*
[2] *Diggers Rugby Club*
[3] *Princess Magogo Stadium*
[4] *Pirates Rugby Club, Greenside*
[5] *Jhb Police RC, Marks Park*

APPEARANCES & POINTS IN 2016 CURRIE CUP QUALIFIERS

Player	Border	Welwitchias	Blue Bulls	WP	Free State XV	Sharks XV	EP Kings	Pumas	Griquas	Leopards	Griffons	Valke	SWD	Boland	Apps	T	C	P	DG	Pts
Anthony Volmink	15	14R	11	11	11	11	11	11	–	11	11	11	–	–	11	6	–	–	–	30
Koch Marx	14	14	–	–	14	14	–	14	14	–	14	12R	–	14	9	4	–	–	–	20
Jacques Nel	13	13	12	12	13	–	–	–	–	–	12	12	–	13	8	5	–	–	–	25
Jarryd Sage	12	12	13R	13R	12	12	12	12	12	12R	12R	–	12c	12	13	3	–	–	–	15
Selom Gavor	11	11	14	14	14R	–	14	14R	11	14	–	14	11	11	12	5	–	–	–	25
Marnitz Boshoff	10	10	–	10	–	10	–	–	10	10c	10	–	–	–	7	–	29	6	–	76
Dillon Smit	9	–	–	–	–	–	9	–	–	–	9	9	–	–	4	–	–	–	–	0
Ruaan Lerm	8c	8c	8c	8c	8c	8c	8c	8c	6c	–	8c	8c	–	–	11	8	–	–	–	40
Robert Kruger	7	–	7	7	–	4	–	–	7	7R	4	8R	–	–	8	–	–	–	–	0
Stephan de Wit	6	6	6R	6	6	6	6R	6	–	–	6	6	–	–	10	1	–	–	–	5
Martin Muller	5	5	5	5	–	–	5	5	5	6R	–	5	–	–	9	–	–	–	–	0
Lourens Erasmus	4	–	–	4	–	–	–	–	4	5	–	–	–	–	4	4	–	–	–	20
Jacques van Rooyen	3	3	–	–	–	–	–	–	3	3	–	–	–	–	4	1	–	–	–	5
Ramone Samuels	2	2	–	–	–	2	2	2	2	2	2	2	–	–	9	4	–	–	–	20
Clint Theron	1	–	1R	1R	1	1	1	–	–	–	1	1	–	3R	9	2	–	–	–	10
Pieter Jansen	x	2R	2	2	2	2R	2R	–	2R	2R	2R	2R	2	2	12	1	–	–	–	5
Pieter Scholtz	1R	1R	3	–	–	3	3	3	–	–	3	3	–	–	8	–	–	–	–	0
MB Lusaseni	5R	4	4	4R	5	5	–	4R	–	–	5R	5R	5	5c	11	1	–	–	–	5
Jano Venter	6R	–	–	–	–	–	–	–	–	–	–	–	–	–	1	–	–	–	–	0
Ricky Schroeder	9R	9	9	9	9	9	9R	9	9	–	9R	–	–	–	10	2	–	–	–	10
Shaun Reynolds	12R	10R	10	10R	10	10R	10	9R	15	–	–	10R	–	10	11	5	24	6	–	91
JW Bell	11R	15	–	–	–	15	15	15R	–	15	15	15	15	10	10	8	–	–	–	40
Derick Minnie	–	7	6	8R	7	6R	6	–	–	–	–	–	–	–	6	1	–	–	–	5
Justin Ackermann	–	1	–	–	–	–	–	1	–	1R	–	1R	–	3	5	–	–	–	–	0
Bobby de Wee	–	4R	4R	–	4	5R	4	–	–	–	5	4	–	7	8	3	–	–	–	15
Victor Sekekete	–	7R	–	–	4R	7R	5R	7R	–	–	7R	–	7	6	8	–	–	–	–	0
Ashlon Davids	–	9R	10R	9R	15	9R	–	10	13R	9R	10R	–	–	9R	10	1	7	–	–	19
Sylvian Mahuza	–	–	15	15	–	–	–	–	15R	–	–	–	–	–	3	3	–	–	–	15
Stokkies Hanekom	–	–	13	13	–	13	13	13	13	13	13	13	–	–	9	7	–	–	–	35
Arnout Malherbe	–	–	1	1	–	–	–	–	–	–	–	1	1	1	4	1	–	–	–	5
Jannes Snyman	–	–	2R	2R	2R	–	2R	–	–	–	–	–	–	2R	5	–	–	–	–	0
Nico du Plessis	–	–	3R	3	3	3R	1R	–	–	–	–	–	–	–	5	–	–	–	–	0
Henco Smit	–	–	–	1R	–	–	1R	–	–	1R	–	1R	–	–	4	–	–	–	–	0
Luvuyo Pupuma	–	–	–	3R	–	–	–	–	–	–	–	3R	–	–	2	–	–	–	–	0
Fabian Booysen	–	–	–	–	6R	7	7	7	8R	–	7	7	–	8	8	1	–	–	–	5
Cameron Rooi	–	–	–	13R	–	–	–	–	–	–	–	13	–	–	2	–	–	–	–	0
Curtis Jonas	–	–	–	–	–	x	–	–	–	–	–	9R	–	–	1	–	–	–	–	0
Lloyd Greeff	–	–	–	–	14R	–	–	–	–	–	–	–	–	–	1	–	–	–	–	0
JP du Preez	–	–	–	–	–	–	4	–	–	–	–	4	4	–	3	–	–	–	–	0
Barend Smit	–	–	–	–	–	15R	–	–	–	–	–	13R	–	–	2	–	–	–	–	0
Rohan Janse van Rensburg	–	–	–	–	–	–	–	12	12R	–	–	–	–	–	2	1	–	–	–	5
Ruan Ackermann	–	–	–	–	–	–	–	8	8	–	–	–	–	–	2	1	–	–	–	5
Cyle Brink	–	–	–	–	–	–	–	6	7	–	–	–	–	–	2	1	–	–	–	5
Corné Fourie	–	–	–	–	–	–	–	1	1	–	–	–	–	–	2	–	–	–	–	0
Dylan Smith	–	–	–	–	–	–	–	1R	–	–	–	–	–	–	1	–	–	–	–	0
Andries Coetzee	–	–	–	–	–	–	–	15	–	–	–	–	–	–	1	–	–	–	–	0
Ross Cronjé	–	–	–	–	–	–	–	9	–	–	–	–	–	–	1	–	–	–	–	0
Warwick Tecklenburg	–	–	–	–	–	–	–	6	–	–	–	–	–	–	1	–	–	–	–	0
Andries Ferreira	–	–	–	–	–	–	–	4	–	–	–	–	–	–	1	–	–	–	–	0
Jaco van der Walt	–	–	–	–	–	–	–	–	–	–	10	–	–	–	1	–	4	–	–	8
Marco Jansen van Vuuren	–	–	–	–	–	–	–	–	–	9R	9	9	–	–	3	–	–	–	–	0
Godfrey Ramaboea	–	–	–	–	–	–	–	–	–	–	14	–	–	–	1	1	–	–	–	5
Siya Masuku	–	–	–	–	–	–	–	–	–	–	10	10R	–	–	2	–	3	3	–	15
Jo-Hanco de Villiers	–	–	–	–	–	–	–	–	–	–	8	–	–	–	1	1	–	–	–	5
James Venter	–	–	–	–	–	–	–	–	–	–	6	–	–	–	1	1	–	–	–	5
Kyle Kruger	–	–	–	–	–	–	–	–	–	–	3	–	–	–	1	–	–	–	–	0
Le Roux Baard	–	–	–	–	–	–	–	–	–	–	2R	–	–	–	1	–	–	–	–	0
Driaan Bester	–	–	–	–	–	–	–	–	–	–	–	4R	4R	–	2	–	–	–	–	0
Wiehan Jacobs	–	–	–	–	–	–	–	–	–	–	–	8R	8R	–	2	–	–	–	–	0
Aphiwe Dyantyi	–	–	–	–	–	–	–	–	–	–	–	–	14R	–	1	–	–	–	–	0
60 Players															306	83	67	15	0	594

Griffons

Played	Won	Lost	Drawn	Points for	Points against	Tries for	Tries against
14	7	7	0	519	498	69	70

Date	Venue	Opponent	Result	Score	Referee	Scorers
Apr 07	Kimberley	Griquas	LOST	14-34	J Peyper	T: Sithole, Davids. C: Whitehead (2).
Apr 16	Welkom	Leopards	WON	76-26	L v/d Merwe	T: Whitehead (3), Davids (3), Mbotho (2), Kruger, Nelson, Maarman. C: Whitehead (8). P: Whitehead.
Apr 27	Kempton Park	Valke	WON	49-26	L v/d Merwe	T: Williams (3), Davids, Pretorius, Kruger, Maarman. C: Whitehead (4). P: Whitehead (2).
May 06	Welkom	SWD	WON	30-14	S Geldenhuys	T: Davids (2), Pretorius. C: Whitehead (3). P: Whitehead (3).
May 13	Wellington	Boland	LOST	17-56	L v/d Merwe	T: Davids, Roelfse. C: Whitehead (2). P: Whitehead.
May 21	Welkom	Border	WON	34-23	J Kotze	T: B Venter, Pretorius, Roelfse, Davids. C: Whitehead (4). P: Whitehead (2).
May 28	Windhoek	Welwitschias	WON	101-0	L Legoete	T: Williams (3), Davids (2), Maarman (2), Grobbelaar (2), B Venter (2), V/d Merwe, Kruger, Rautenbach, Nortjé. C: Whitehead (13)
Jun 04	Welkom	Blue Bulls	LOST	28-57	B Crouse	T: Van der Merwe (2), Roelfse, Mavundla. C: Whitehead (4).
Jun 18	Cape Town	WP	LOST	26-43	S Ngcese	T: Kruger, Van der Merwe. C: Whitehead (2). P: Whitehead (3). DG: Whitehead.
Jun 25	Welkom	Free State XV	WON	49-33	L Legoete	T: Nel (2), Williams (2), Mbotho, Penalty try. C: Whitehead (5), P: Whitehead (2). DG: Whitehead.
July 02	Johannesburg	Golden Lions XV	LOST	10-66	L Legoete	T: Davids (2), Mbotho. C: Herbert (2).
July 09	Welkom	Sharks XV	LOST	27-36	J Peyper	T: Nel (2), Annandale, Williams. C: Pretorius (2). P: Pretorius.
July 15	Port Elizabeth	EP Kings	WON	34-24	L Legoete	T: Davids (2), Nel, Williams. C: Pretorius (3). P: Pretorius (2).
July 23	Welkom	Pumas	LOST	17-60	R Bonaparte	T: Davids, Kruger. C: Whitehead (2). P: Whitehead.

APPEARANCES & POINTS IN 2016 CURRIE CUP QUALIFIERS

	Griquas	Leopards	Valke	SWD	Boland	Border	Welwitchias	Blue Bulls	WP	Free State XV	Lions XV	Sharks XV	EP Kings	Pumas	Apps	T	C	P	DG	Pts
Tertius Maarman	15	15	15	15	15	–	15	15	15	x	10	–	–	14	10	4	–	–	–	20
Selvyn Davids	14	14	14	14	14	15	14	14	14	15	15	15	15	15	14	16	–	–	–	80
Vuyo Mbotho	13	13	13	13	13	11	–	12R	15R	14	14	14	14	–	12	4	–	–	–	20
Duan Pretorius	12	12	12	12	12	13	13	13	13	–	–	10	10	12R	12	3	5	3	–	34
Norman Nelson	11	11	–	–	–	–	–	13R	x	11R	14R	14R	–	–	6	1	–	–	–	5
George Whitehead	10	10	10	10	10	10	10	10	10	10	–	–	–	10	11	3	50	15	2	166
Boela Abrahams	9	9	9	9	9	–	9	9	9	9	9	–	–	9R	11	–	–	–	–	0
Martin Sithole	8	6	6	7	8	8R	4R	–	4R	–	–	6	6	6	11	1	–	–	–	5
Frans Sisita	7	7	7	–	–	–	–	–	–	–	–	–	–	–	3	–	–	–	–	0
Siward Mavundla	6	8R	6R	6	6	6	6	6	6	6	6	–	–	–	11	1	–	–	–	5
Samora Fihlani	5	6R	4R	4R	4R	4	4	4	4	–	–	4	4	4	12	–	–	–	–	0
Gavin Annandale	4c	4c	5c	5c	5c	5c	5c	5c	5c	5	5	5	5	5	14	1	–	–	–	5
Heinrich Roelfse	3	3	3	3	1R	3	3	3	3	3	3	3	3	3	14	3	–	–	–	15
Khwezi Mkhafu	2	2	2	2	2	–	2	2	2	2	2	2	2	2	12	–	–	–	–	0
Danie vd Merwe	1	1	1	1	3	1	1	1	1	1	1	1	1	1	14	4	–	–	–	20
Neil Rautenbach	2R	2R	–	x	2R	2	2	–	–	–	–	–	–	–	5	1	–	–	–	5
PW Botha	3R	3R	–	–	–	–	–	–	–	–	–	–	–	3R	3	–	–	–	–	0
Wayne Ludick	5R	–	–	–	–	–	–	–	–	4	4	x	x	5R	4	–	–	–	–	0
De Wet Kruger	6R	8	8	8	–	–	8R	8	8	8	8	8	8	8	12	5	–	–	–	25
Vincent Maruping	7R	7R	6R	8R	7	6R	–	4R	x	4R	7R	7	7	7	12	–	–	–	–	0
Malcolm-Kerr Till	x	9R	9R	9R	9R	9	–	–	–	–	–	–	–	–	5	–	–	–	–	0
Coenie van Wyk	11R	–	–	–	–	–	–	–	–	–	–	–	–	–	1	–	–	–	–	0
Boela Venter	–	5	4	4	4	7	7	7	7	7	7	–	–	–	10	3	–	–	–	15
Franna du Toit	–	11R	–	–	–	–	–	–	–	–	–	–	–	–	1	–	–	–	–	0
Warren Williams	–	–	11	11	11	14	11	11	11	11	11	11	11	–	11	10	–	–	–	50
Hennie Venter	–	–	2R	–	–	2R	2R	2R	x	2R	2R	2R	x	22R	8	–	–	–	–	0
George Marich	–	–	3R	–	–	3R	3R	3R	–	–	–	–	–	–	4	–	–	–	–	0
Lohan Lubbe	–	–	11R	–	–	–	15R	–	–	–	–	–	–	–	2	–	–	–	–	0
Wilmar Goenewald	–	–	–	6R	6R	–	–	–	–	6R	4R	–	–	–	4	–	–	–	–	0
Gerard Baard	–	–	–	3R	1	–	–	–	3R	3R	1R	3R	3R	–	7	–	–	–	–	0
Sherwin Slater	–	–	–	x	11R	14R	–	–	–	–	–	–	–	11	3	–	–	–	–	0
Dirk Grobbelaar	–	–	–	–	7R	8	8	8R	–	–	–	8R	–	6R	6	2	–	–	–	10
Japie Nel	–	–	–	–	12	12	12	12	12	12	12	12	12	12	9	5	–	–	–	25
Louis Venter	–	–	–	–	9R	–	9R	x	9R	9R	9	9	–	–	6	–	–	–	–	0
Zingisa April	–	–	–	–	4R	6R	–	–	–	–	–	6R	4R	–	4	–	–	–	–	0
Ossie Nortjé	–	–	–	–	–	9R	–	–	–	–	x	9R	9	–	3	1	–	–	–	5
Pieter-Steyn de Wet	–	–	–	–	–	–	14R	–	–	–	–	–	–	–	1	–	–	–	–	0
Joubert Engelbrecht	–	–	–	–	–	–	–	–	–	13c	13c	13c	13c	13c	5	–	–	–	–	0
Colin Herbert	–	–	–	–	–	–	–	–	–	10R	x	13R	–	–	2	–	2	–	–	4
Penalty try	–	–	–	–	–	–	–	–	–	–	–	–	–	–		1	–	–	–	5
39 PLAYERS															295	69	57	18	2	519

Griquas

Played	Won	Lost	Drawn	Points for	Points against	Tries for	Tries against
14	11	3	0	483	333	63	47

Date	Venue	Opponent	Result	Score	Referee	Scorers
Apr 07	Kimberley	Griffons	WON	34-14	J Peyper	T: Zito, Francke, Coertzen, Swart. C: Swart. P: Swart (4).
Apr 15	Kempton Park	Valke	WON	56-29	S Geldenhuys	T: Fraser (2), Van Rooyen (2), Coertzen, Bock, Swart, Arendse. C: Swart (7), Prinsloo.
Apr 23	Kimberley	SWD	WON	27-17	L Legoete	T: Coertzen, Bock, Swart, Francke. C: Swart, Zana. P: Swart.
Apr 29	Wellington	Boland	WON	30-14	C Jadezweni	T: Coertzen, Bock, Fraser, Fourie. C: Swart, Dukisa. P: Swart (2).
May 07	Kimberley	Border	WON	21-12	L Legoete	T: Le Roux, Francke, Van Rooyen. C: Swart (2), Dukisa.
May 14	Windhoek	Welwitschias	WON	55-25	E Seconds	T: Dorfling (2), Coertzen (2), Swarts, Jonker, Kotze, Mabuza. C: Prinsloo (6). P: Prinsloo.
May 21	Kimberley	Blue Bulls	WON	39-38	L Legoete	T: Francke (2), Coertzen, Swart, Arendse. C: Swarts (2), Swart, Prinsloo. P: Swarts (2).
May 28	Cape Town	WP	LOST	23-24	Q Immelman	T: Janse van Rensburg, Dorfling. C: Swarts (2). P: Swarts (3).
Jun 04	Kimberley	Free State XV	WON	44-31	R Rasivhenge	T: Dorfling, Coertzen, Martinus, Arendse, Penalty try. C: Swarts (3), Swart. P: Swarts (3).
Jun 11	Johannesburg [1]	Golden Lions XV	LOST	37-52	Q Immelman	T: Bock (2), Coertzen, Kotze. C: Swarts (4). P: Swarts (3).
Jun 25	Upington	Sharks XV	WON	36-14	J van Heerden	T: Le Roux, Arendse, Jonker, Dukisa, Koen. C: Swart (4). P: Swart.
July 02	Port Elizabeth	EP Kings	WON	29-12	J van Heerden	T: Dukisa (2), Bock, Swarts. C: Swarts (3). P: Swarts.
July 07	Kimberley	Pumas	WON	37-14	R Rasivhenge	T: Coertzen (2), Meyer, Zito, Dukisa. C: Swart (3). P: Swart (2).
July 22	Potchefstroom	Leopards	LOST	17-37	E Seconds	T: Fraser (2). C: Swarts (2). P: Moir.

[1] Police Rugby Club

APPEARANCES & POINTS IN 2016 CURRIE CUP QUALIFIERS

	Griffons	Valke	SWD	Boland	Border	Welwitschias	Blue Bulls	WP	Free State XV	Lions XV	Sharks XV	EP Kings	EP Kings	Leopards	Apps	T	C	P	DG	Pts
Eric Zana	15	15	15	15	15	9R	15R	15	10R	14R	14R	15	14R	15	14	–	1	–	–	2
Alshaun Bock	14	14	11	11	11	11	–	11	11	11	–	11	11	–	11	6	–	–	–	30
AJ Coertzen	13	13	14	14	14	14c	14c	14	15	15	15	–	15c	–	12	11	–	–	–	55
Jonathan Francke	12	12	12	12	12	–	12	12	–	–	12	13	12	–	10	5	–	–	–	25
Ederies Arendse	11	11	–	10R	12R	–	11	–	14	14	14	10R	–	14	10	4	–	–	–	20
Clinton Swart	10	10	10	10	10	–	10R	12R	12	12	10	–	10	15R	12	4	21	10	–	92
Rudi van Rooyen	9	9	9	9	9R	–	–	–	–	–	–	–	–	–	5	3	–	–	–	15
Jason Fraser	8	8	8	8	8	8	8	8	8	–	8	8	8	8R	13	5	–	–	–	25
RJ Liebenberg	7c	7c	7c	7c	7c	–	–	7c	6c	7c	7c	7c	7R	–	11	–	–	–	–	0
Wendal Wehr	6	6	–	6	6	6	6	6	8R	6	6	6	6	6	13	–	–	–	–	0
Jaco Nepgen	5	5	7R	5	–	–	–	–	–	–	–	–	–	–	4	–	–	–	–	0
Mxwanele Zito	4	4	5	4	5	–	5	4	4	5	–	–	4	5	11	2	–	–	–	10
Stephan Kotze	3	–	3R	3	3R	3	3R	3	3	3	3	–	3	1R	11	2	–	–	–	10
AJ le Roux	2	2	–	2	2	–	2R	2R	2	–	2	2R	2	2R	11	2	–	–	–	10
Steph Roberts	1	1R	–	1R	–	1	1R	1R	1	1	1	–	1	–	10	–	–	–	–	0
Marius Fourie	2R	2R	2	2R	2R	2	2	2	2R	2	–	–	2R	–	11	1	–	–	–	5
Ewald v/d Westhuizen	3R	3	3	3	3	–	3	3R	–	–	–	–	–	–	7	–	–	–	–	0
Jonathan Adendorf	6R	4R	4	–	–	–	5R	8R	5	4	–	–	4R	4	9	–	–	–	–	0
Jono J van Rensburg	8R	6R	4R	5R	4	4	4	5	–	8R	5	5	5	–	12	1	–	–	–	5
Steven Meiring	7R	–	6	–	–	5R	6R	–	6R	7R	6R	7R	6R	8	10	–	–	–	–	0
Tiaan Dorfling	9R	9R	9R	9R	9	9	9	9	9	–	9	9	–	9	12	4	–	–	–	20
Ntabeni Dukisa	14R	–	13R	13R	10R	–	–	–	11R	–	11	14	14	11	9	4	2	–	–	24
Devon Martinus	–	1	1	1	1	3R	1	1	1R	1R	1R	3	1R	–	12	1	–	–	–	5
Kyle Lombard	–	12R	–	–	–	12	–	–	10R	–	12	–	12	–	5	–	–	–	–	0
Gouws Prinsloo	–	10R	10R	–	–	15	15	15R	–	12R	–	–	–	–	6	–	8	1	–	19
JW Jonker	–	–	13	13	13	13	13	13	13	13	13	x	13	13c	11	2	–	–	–	10
Sidney Tobias	–	–	2R	–	2R	–	–	–	2R	2R	2	–	2	–	6	–	–	–	–	0
Sias Koen	–	–	–	11R	8R	7	7	7R	7	8	4	4	7	7R	11	1	–	–	–	5
David Antonites	–	–	–	–	5R	5	–	–	–	–	–	–	–	–	2	–	–	–	–	0
André Swarts	–	–	–	–	–	10	10	10	10	10	11R	10	13R	10R	9	2	16	12	–	78
Thabo Mabuza	–	–	–	–	–	6R	–	–	–	–	7R	6R	–	–	3	1	–	–	–	5
Luxolo Koza	–	–	–	–	–	1R	–	–	–	–	–	1	–	1	3	–	–	–	–	0
Steven Moir	–	–	–	–	–	10R	–	–	–	–	–	–	–	10	2	–	–	1	–	3
Chris Meyer	–	–	–	–	–	–	–	9R	9	9R	9R	9	–	–	5	1	–	–	–	5
Teunis Nieuwoudt	–	–	–	–	–	–	–	–	–	–	3R	–	–	3	2	–	–	–	–	0
Stephan Vermeulen	–	–	–	–	–	–	–	–	–	–	–	–	–	7	1	–	–	–	–	0
Renier Botha	–	–	–	–	–	–	–	–	–	–	–	–	–	9R	1	–	–	–	–	0
Penalty try	–	–	–	–	–	–	–	–	–	–	–	–	–	–	0	1	–	–	–	5
37 PLAYERS															307	63	48	24	0	483

Leopards

Played	Won	Lost	Drawn	Points for	Points against	Tries for	Tries against
14	6	8	0	448	450	58	62

Date	Venue	Opponent	Result	Score	Referee	Scorers
Apr 16	Welkom	Griffons	LOST	26-76	L v/d Merwe	T: Vermeulen, Du Plessis, Grobbelaar, Liebenberg. C: Smith (3).
Apr 22	Potchefstroom	Valke	WON	26-24	C Jadezweni	T: Smith, Steenkamp. C: Smith (2). P: Smith (4).
Apr 27	George	SWD	LOST	21-26	R Bonaparte	T: Vermeulen, Arnoldi. C: Smith. P: Smith (3).
May 07	Potchefstroom[1]	Boland	LOST	31-43	J van Heerden	T: Rudolph (2), Deysel (2), Willemse. C: Janse van Rensburg (2) Hugo.
May 13	East London	Border	WON	34-22	L Legoete	T: Arnoldi, Smith, Morrison, Deysel. C: Smith (4). P: Smith. DG: Smith.
May 20	Potchefstroom	Welwitschias	WON	42-17	S Ngcese	T: Beukman (2), Moolman, Muller, Marais, Smith. C: Smith (6).
May 28	Pretoria	Blue Bulls	WON	51-26	A Sehlako	T: Marais (2), Rudolph, Deysel, Redelinghuys, Van der Westhuyzen. C: Smith (6). P: Smith (3).
Jun 04	Potchefstroom	WP	LOST	34-43	E Seconds	T: Smith (2), Redelinghuys, Hayward. C: Smith (4). P: Smith. DG: Smith.
Jun 18	Bloemfontein	Free State XV	LOST	14-23	R Bonaparte	T: Hayward. P: Smith (3).
Jun 24	Potchefstroom	Golden Lions XV	LOST	28-64	S Berry	T: Moolman, Hayward, Swart, Arnoldi. C: Smith (4).
July 01	Durban[2]	Sharks XV	LOST	23-26	R Bonaparte	T: Janse van Rensburg, J Jordaan, Beukman. C: Janse van Rensburg. P: Janse van Rensburg (2)
July 08	Potchefstroom	EP Kings	WON	54-14	J Sylvestre	T: Hayward (2), Language (2), J van Rensburg, Willemse, Beukman, Wepener. C: J van Rensburg (5), Hugo (2)
July 15	Nelspruit	Pumas	LOST	27-29	J van Heerden	T: Hayward (2), Morrison (2). C: Hugo, M Swart. P: Hugo.
July 22	Potchefstroom	Griquas	WON	37-17	E Seconds	T: Le Roux, Moolman, Marais, Deysel, Arnoldi. C: Smith (3). P: Smith (2).

[1] *Johann du Randt Stadium*

[2] *Crusaders Rugby Club*

APPEARANCES & POINTS IN 2016 CURRIE CUP QUALIFIERS

	Griffons	Valke	SWD	Boland	Border	Welwitchias	Blue Bulls	WP	Free State XV	Lions XV	Sharks XV	EP Kings	EP Kings	Leopards	Apps	T	C	P	DG	Pts
Myburgh Briers	15	–	–	–	–	–	–	–	–	–	–	–	–	–	1	–	–	–	–	0
Lucian Cupido	14	14	14	–	–	–	–	–	11	11	–	–	–	–	5	–	–	–	–	0
Bradley Moolman	13	13	13	11	11	11	11	11	14R	14	11	13	13	11	14	3	–	–	–	15
Adrian Vermeulen	12	12	12	12	–	–	–	13	13	13	13	–	–	–	8	2	–	–	–	10
Dean Stokes	11	11	11	14R	–	–	–	–	–	–	–	14R	–	–	5	–	–	–	–	0
Rhyno Smith	10	15	15	–	15	15c	15	15	15	15	–	–	–	15	10	5	33	17	2	148
Percy Williams	9	–	–	–	–	–	–	–	–	–	–	–	–	–	1	–	–	–	–	0
Jeandré Rudolph	8c	8c	8c	8c	8c	–	8c	8c	8c	8c	–	8c	8c	–	11	3				15
Tiaan Liebenberg	7	–	–	–	5R	–	–	–	–	–	–	–	–	–	2	1				5
Molotsi Bouwer	6	8R	6R	7R	8R	6	–	–	–	–	7R	–	–	–	7					0
Danie Jordaan	5	–	–	4R	5R	5	–	–	–	–	–	–	–	–	4					0
Sithembiso Mhlongo	4	4	4	–	–	–	–	–	4R	5R	4	4	4	4	9					0
Nhlanhla Ngcamu	3	3	3R	1R	3R	3R	3R	3R	3	1R	–	3	3	3	13					0
Dane van der Westhuyzen	2	x	–	–	2R	2R	–	2R	7R	2	2	2R	2R		9	1				5
Mashudu Mafela	1	1	1	1	1	–	1	1	1	1	–	1	1	–	10					0
Louis van der Westhuizen	2R	–	2R	2R	2R	2	2	2R	–	–	–	–	–	–	7					0
Roan Grobbelaar	3R	3R	1R	–	–	–	–	–	1R	1	3R	1R	1R	1R	9	1				5
Ruan Venter	5R	4R	4R	4	4	4	–	4R	–	–	–	–	–	–	7					0
Leon du Plessis	7R	–	–	–	–	–	–	–	–	–	–	–	–	–	1	1				5
Chriswill September	9R	9R	9R	9R	9R	9	9	9R	9R	9R	9R	9	9	9R	14					0
Johnny Welthagen	15R	–	–	–	–	–	–	–	–	–	–	–	–	–	1	2				10
Jaco Hayward	14R	–	–	–	–	–	14R	14	11R	14	11	11	14R		8	5	–	–	–	25
Benhard Janse van Rensburg	–	10	10	10R	10	10	10	10	10	–	10	10	–	–	10	2	8	2		32
Malherbe Swart	–	9	9	9	9	9R	9R	9	9	9	9	9R	9R	9	13	1	1			7
Loftus Morrison	–	7	7	7	7	7	7	–	–	–	8R	8R	4R		9	3				15
Jaco Jordaan	–	6	6	–	–	8R	6R	7R	6	6	6	–	–	6	9	1				5
Walt Steenkamp	–	5	5	5	5	–	5	5	5	5	4R	5R	x	5	11	1				5
Wilmar Arnoldi	–	2	2	2	2	–	–	2	2	2	2R	2R	2	2	11	4				20
Gene Willemse	–	x	14R	15	14R	12R	14R	11R	11R	10R	15	15	15	10	12	2				10
Wesley Cupido	–	x	–	–	–	–	–	–	–	–	–	–	–	–	0					0
Bart le Roux	–	–	3	3	3	3	3	–	3	3	–	1	1		10	1				5
Johan Deysel	–	–	–	13	13	13	13	–	12	–	–	–	13		6	5				25
Schalk Hugo	–	–	–	10	–	12R	–	10	x	10R	10	–			5		4	1		11
Rowayne Beukman	–	–	–	14	14	14	14	–	–	13R	14	14	14		9	4				20
Marno Redelinghuys	–	–	–	6	6	8	6	6	7	7	–	–	–	7R	8	2				10
Henko Marais	–	–	–	12	12	12	12	12	–	12	12	12	12		9	4				20
Cecil Dumond	–	–	–	10R	10R	–	–	–	–	–	–	–	–	–	2					0
Bruce Muller	–	–	–	–	1	–	–	–	–	–	–	–	–	–	1	1				5
Francois Robertse	–	–	–	–	4	4	4	4	5	5	5	–			7					0
HP Swart	–	–	–	–	7R	7	6R	–	7	7	7	7			7					0
Juan Language	–	–	–	–	–	–	–	8R	8c	6	6	8c			5	2				10
Ryno Wepener	–	–	–	–	–	–	–	–	–	14R	10R	8R			3	1				5
42 PLAYERS															**303**	**58**	**46**	**20**	**2**	**448**

Pumas

Played	Won	Lost	Drawn	Points for	Points against	Tries for	Tries against
14	10	4	0	417	261	55	34

Date	Venue	Opponent	Result	Score	Referee	Scorers
Apr 08	Nelspruit	Valke	LOST	09-12	C Jadezweni	P: Van Staden (3).
Apr 16	George	SWD Eagles	LOST	21-25	R Bonaparte	T: Schoeman, Sampson. C: Van Staden. P: Van Staden (3).
Apr 22	Nelspruit	Boland	WON	12-10	S Geldenhuys	P: Van Staden (4).
Apr 30	East London	Border	WON	28-03	C du Preez	T: Sampson, Skorbinski, Fisher. C: Van Staden (2). P: Van Staden (3).
May 07	Ermelo[1]	Welwitschias	WON	47-07	E Seconds	T: Du Toit (3), Groenewald (2), Terblanche, Skorbinski. C: Van Staden (5), Van Niekerk.
May 13	Pretoria	Blue Bulls	WON	25-13	J Peyper	T: Herne, Van Rooyen, Sampson, Maritz. C: Van Staden. P: Van Staden.
May 20	Nelspruit	WP	LOST	20-27	M v/d Westhuizen	T: C Greeff, Simpson. C: Van Staden (2). P: Van Staden (2).
May 28	Bloemfontein	Free State XV	WON	29-26	M v/d Westhuizen	T: Maritz, Stander, Shabangu, Fisher. C: Van Staden (3). P: Van Staden.
Jun 04	KaNyamazane	Golden Lions XV	WON	35-24	J van Heerden	T: Botha, Herne, Steyl, Van Rooyen. C: Steyl (3). P: Steyl (3).
Jun 18	Newcastle	Sharks XV	WON	35-13	E Seconds	T: Maritz, Kotze, Groenewald, Van der Walt, Van Rooyen. C: Van Staden (5).
Jun 25	Nelspruit	EP Kings	WON	53-20	L v/d Merwe	T: Groenewald (2), Herne (2), Shabangu, Helberg, Terblanche, Johannes. C: Van Staden (5). P: Van Staden.
Jul 07	Kimberley	Griquas	LOST	14-37	R Rasivhenge	T: C Greeff, Steyl. C: Van Staden (2).
Jul 15	Nelspruit	Leopards	WON	29-27	J van Heerden	T: C Geeff (2), Terblanche, Du Toit, Fisher. C: Williams, Van Staden.
Jul 23	Welkom	Griffons	WON	60-17	R Bonaparte	T: Lewis (2), Fisher (2), J van Rensburg, Herne, Kotze, Van Wyk, Van Niekerk. C: Van Staden (3), Van Wyk (2), Van Niekerk. P: Van Staden.

[1] Ermelo HS

APPEARANCES & POINTS IN 2016 CURRIE CUP QUALIFIERS

	Valke	SWD	Boland	Border	Welwitchias	Blue Bulls	WP	Free State XV	Lions XV	Sharks XV	EP Kings	Griquas	Leopards	Griffons	Apps	T	C	P	DG	Pts
Heinrich Steyl	15	15	15	15	15	15	15	15	15	15	15	15	–	–	12	2	3	3	–	25
Ruwellyn Isbell	14	–	–	–	–	–	–	–	–	–	–	–	–	–	1	–	–	–	–	0
Tyler Fisher	13	14	15R	14R	15R	–	13R	11R	11	–	–	–	14	14	10	5	–	–	–	25
Hennie Skorbinski	12	–	–	12R	12	12	12	12	12	12	12	–	–	–	9	2	–	–	–	10
Marcello Sampson	11	11	11	11	11	11	11	11	–	11	11	11	11	–	12	4	–	–	–	20
Justin van Staden	10	10	10	10	10	10	10	10	–	10	10	10	14R	15	13	–	30	19	–	117
Emile Temperman	9	9R	9R	9R	9	9R	9R	9	–	9R	9R	9R	9	9	13	–	–	–	–	0
Carel Greeff	8	8	8	8	7R	8	6R	8	8	–	–	6R	8	6	12	4	–	–	–	20
Lambert Groenewald	7	7	7	7	7	7	8	7	7	7	7	7	–	7	13	5	–	–	–	25
Marnus Schoeman	6	6	6R	6	–	6	6	–	–	–	–	7R	–	–	7	1	–	–	–	5
Hugo Kloppers	5c	5c	5c	5c	–	5c	5c	5c	5c	–	5c	5c	19R	5c	12	–	–	–	–	0
Stephan Greeff	4	4	4	4	5R	4	4	4	–	4	4	4	–	4R	12	–	–	–	–	0
Marné Coetzee	3	3	3	3	3	3	3	–	–	–	–	–	–	–	7	–	–	–	–	0
Frankie Herne	2	2	2	2	20R	2	2R	2R	2	2	2	2	–	2R	13	5	–	–	–	25
Khwezi Mona	1	1	–	3R	–	–	1	1	1	–	1	1	1	–	9	–	–	–	–	0
Francois du Toit	1R	2R	2R	2R	2	2R	2	2	2R	2R	2R	2R	2R	2	14	4	–	–	–	20
Simon Westraadt	3R	3R	1	1	–	1	–	–	–	–	–	–	–	–	5	–	–	–	–	0
Jannie Stander	4R	4R	4R	5R	5	5R	4R	4R	4	5	4R	4R	5	–	13	1	–	–	–	5
Reuben Johannes	6R	–	–	–	–	–	–	–	–	6R	8R	–	7R	–	4	1	–	–	–	5
Reynier van Rooyen	9R	9	9	–	9	9	9R	9	9	9	9	9	9R	9R	13	3	–	–	–	15
Leighton van Wyk	13R	x	–	–	–	–	–	11R	–	–	–	12	12	–	4	1	2	–	–	9
Bernado Botha	14R	11R	14	14	–	14	14	14	14	14	14	14	–	15R	12	1	–	–	–	5
Hoffman Maritz	–	13	13	13	13c	13	13	13	13	13c	–	–	–	–	9	3	–	–	–	15
Wilmaure Louw	–	12	12	12	–	–	–	12R	–	13	11R	–	–	–	6	–	–	–	–	0
Dylan Peterson	–	7R	–	–	8	–	–	–	–	–	–	–	–	8	3	–	–	–	–	0
Nardus van der Walt	–	–	6	8R	6	8R	7	6	6	8	8	8	7	–	11	1	–	–	–	5
DJ Terblanche	–	–	3R	3R	1	3R	1	3	3	3	1	3	3c	–	11	3	–	–	–	15
Deon Helberg	–	–	14R	–	14	–	–	–	–	14R	13	13	13	13	6	1	–	–	–	5
Wiehan Hay	–	–	–	–	4	–	–	–	4R	–	–	4	4	4	4	–	–	–	–	0
Marlou van Niekerk	–	–	–	10R	10R	12R	12R	10	12R	12R	12	10	10	–	10	1	2	–	–	9
Johan Herbst	–	–	–	9R	–	–	–	–	–	–	–	–	–	–	1	–	–	–	–	0
Jacques Kotze	–	–	–	–	1R	3R	3R	3R	1R	3	1R	3R	3	–	9	2	–	–	–	10
Brian Shabangu	–	–	–	–	–	–	6R	6R	6	6	6	6	7R	–	7	2	–	–	–	10
Lubabalo Mtyanda	–	–	–	–	–	–	–	4R	–	–	–	–	–	–	1	–	–	–	–	0
Damien Janse van Rensburg	–	–	–	–	–	–	–	14R	14R	–	–	11R	10R	–	4	1	–	–	–	5
Sabelo Nhlapo	–	–	–	–	–	–	–	–	–	3R	–	–	–	3R	2	–	–	–	–	0
Devon Williams	–	–	–	–	–	–	–	–	–	–	–	15	–	–	1	–	1	–	–	2
Rassie Jansen Van Vuuren	–	–	–	–	–	–	–	–	–	–	–	2	–	–	1	–	–	–	–	0
JP Lewis	–	–	–	–	–	–	–	–	–	–	–	–	–	11	1	2	–	–	–	10
39 PLAYERS															307	55	38	22	0	417

Sharks XV

Played	Won	Lost	Drawn	Points for	Points against	Tries for	Tries against
14	6	8	0	338	399	43	58

Date	Venue	Opponent	Result	Score	Referee	Scorers
Apr 08	Durban[1]	Boland	LOST	25-37	R Bonaparte	T: Sithole, Mjekevu, K Majola. C: Radebe (2). P: Radebe (2).
Apr 15	East London	Border	LOST	32-37	L Legoete	T: Mjekevu (2), Van Vuuren, Vosloo. C: Tedder (2), Radebe. P: Radebe, Tedder.
Apr 23	Durban[2]	Welwitchias	WON	48-18	R Bonaparte	T: Louw (3), Tedder, Coetzee, Bosch. C: Tedder (6). P: Tedder (2).
May 07	Durban	WP	WON	24-16	Q Immelman	T: Eksteen, Louw, Tedder. C: Tedder (3). P: Tedder.
May 13	Bloemfontein	Free State XV	LOST	13-19	S Berry	T: Marwana, Kubeka. P: Tedder.
May 20	Kwa-Mashu[3]	Golden Lions XV	LOST	16-53	E Seconds	T: Williams. C: Tedder. P: Tedder (3).
Jun 03	Port Elizabeth	EP Kings	WON	34-26	M v/d Westhuizen	T: Eksteen, Mjekevu, Williams, K Majola, Botha. C: M Coetzee (3). P: M Coetzee.
Jun 10	Pretoria	Blue Bulls	LOST	18-22	E Seconds	T: Joubert, Sithole. C: Campbell. P: Coetzee (2).
Jun 18	Newcastle	Pumas	LOST	13-35	E Seconds	T: Marwana. C: Tedder. P: Tedder (2).
Jun 25	Upington[4]	Griquas	LOST	14-36	J van Heerden	T: K Majola, Louw. C: Tedder, Joubert.
July 01	Durban[5]	Leopards	WON	26-23	R Bonaparte	T: Maritz, Marwana, Radebe, McDuling. C: Radebe (3).
July 09	Welkom	Griffons	WON	36-27	J Peyper	T: Cele (2), Joubert, Maritz, S Coetzee. C: Radebe (4). P: Campbell.
July 15	Durban	Valke	LOST	10-26	J Sylvestre	T: S Coetzee. C: Radebe. P: Radebe.
July 22	George	SWD	WON	29-24	S Ngcese	T: Venter (2), Du Toit, Engelbrecht. C: Radebe (3). P: Radebe.

[1] Sugar Ray Xulu Stadium, Clermont
[2] King Zwelithini Stadium, Umlazi
[3] Princess Magogo Stadium
[4] Mxolisi Dicky Jacobs Stadium
[5] Crusaders RC

APPEARANCES & POINTS IN 2016 CURRIE CUP QUALIFIERS

	Boland	Border	Welwitchias	WP	Free State XV	Lions XV	EP Kings	Blue Bulls	Pumas	Griquas	Leopards	Griffons	Valke	SWD	Apps	T	C	P	DG	Pts
Alrin Eksteen	15	15	15	15	15	15	15	15	15	–	–	15	14R	15	12	2	–	–	–	10
Neil Maritz	14	14	14	–	14	–	–	–	–	–	13	13	13	13	8	2	–	–	–	10
Wandile Mjekevu	13	13	–	–	–	–	14	–	–	–	–	–	–	–	3	4	–	–	–	20
Heimar Williams	12	12	12	12R	12	12	10	–	12	13	–	–	–	12c	10	2	–	–	–	10
S'bura Sithole	11	–	–	11	–	11	13	13	13	14	–	–	–	–	7	2	–	–	–	10
Innocent Radebe	10	10	–	–	–	–	–	–	–	–	10	10	10	10	6	1	14	5	–	48
Dylan Marcus	9	9	9	9	9	9	9R	9R	9R	9	9	–	–	–	11	–	–	–	–	0
Retief Marais	8	8	8	8	8	8	–	–	–	–	–	8	–	4R	8	–	–	–	–	0
Johan du Toit	7	–	7	7	7	7	–	–	–	–	–	–	–	7	6	1	–	–	–	5
Khaya Majola	6c	6c	6c	6c	6c	6c	6c	6c	6c	6c	–	8R	6	–	12	3	–	–	–	15
Tijiuee Uanivi	5	5	5	5	5R	–	–	–	–	–	–	–	–	–	5	–	–	–	–	0
Wian Vosloo	4	7R	4R	4	–	7R	4R	7R	7R	8R	7	7	7	4	13	1	–	–	–	5
Ruan Kramer	3	3R	3	3	–	3R	3R	3R	3R	3R	3R	3	–	3R	12	–	–	–	–	0
Andréw du Plessis	2	–	–	–	–	2R	–	–	–	–	–	–	–	–	2	–	–	–	–	0
Mzamo Majola	1	1	–	1	–	1	1R	1R	x	1R	1R	1	–	1R	10	–	–	–	–	0
Stephan Coetzee	2R	2	2R	2	2	2	2R	2R	2	2	2	2R	2	2	14	3	–	–	–	15
Dale Chadwick	1R	–	–	–	–	–	–	–	–	–	–	–	–	–	1	–	–	–	–	0
Thomas du Toit	3R	–	–	–	3	–	–	–	–	–	–	–	–	–	2	–	–	–	–	0
Dave McDuling	7R	4	4	–	4	4	–	5R	4R	4	4c	4c	4c	–	11	1	–	–	–	5
Matt Alborough	x	–	–	–	–	–	–	–	–	–	–	–	–	–	0	–	–	–	–	0
Tristan Tedder	12R	10R	10	10	10	10	–	–	10	10	–	–	–	–	8	2	14	10	–	68
Khulu Marwana	14R	11	11	13	13	13	12	12	11	11	11	12	14	–	13	3	–	–	–	15
Christiaan de Bruin	–	7	–	–	–	–	7	7	7	7	7R	–	–	8	7	–	–	–	–	0
Gerhard Engelbrecht	–	3	–	3R	3R	3	3	3	3	3	3	–	3	3	11	1	–	–	–	5
Kerrod van Vuuren	–	2R	2	2R	2R	–	–	–	–	2R	5R	2	2R	6R	9	1	–	–	–	5
Barend Potgieter	–	x	1R	–	–	–	–	–	–	–	1R	1R	–	–	3	–	–	–	–	0
Rowan Gouws	–	9R	–	–	–	–	–	–	–	–	–	–	–	–	1	–	–	–	–	0
Marius Louw	–	12R	13	12	–	–	–	–	–	12	12	–	12	–	6	5	–	–	–	25
Juan Schoeman	–	–	1	–	1	–	1	1	1	1	1	–	1	1	9	–	–	–	–	0
John Meyer	–	–	3R	–	1R	1R	–	–	–	–	–	3R	3R	–	5	–	–	–	–	0
Tristan Blewett	–	–	12R	–	–	14R	–	–	–	–	–	–	–	–	2	–	–	–	–	0
Curwin Bosch	–	–	15R	–	–	–	–	–	–	–	–	–	–	–	1	1	–	–	–	5
Sibusiso Nkosi	–	–	11R	14	–	–	–	–	–	–	–	–	–	–	2	–	–	–	–	0
Lubabalo Mthembu	–	–	–	6R	–	–	8	8	8	–	–	–	–	–	4	–	–	–	–	0
Ayron Schramm	–	–	–	8R	–	–	–	–	–	8	8	–	8	–	4	–	–	–	–	0
Hanco Venter	–	–	–	9R	9R	–	9	9	9	–	–	9	9	9	8	2	–	–	–	10
Sandile Kubeka	–	–	–	x	14R	–	–	–	–	–	–	13R	–	12R	3	1	–	–	–	5
Sipho Mkhize	–	–	–	–	11	14	–	–	–	–	–	–	–	–	2	–	–	–	–	0
Hyron Andréws	–	–	–	–	5	5	4	4	4	5	5	–	5	–	8	–	–	–	–	0
Francois Kleinhans	–	–	–	–	6R	–	7R	–	–	–	–	–	–	6	3	–	–	–	–	0
Ruan Botha	–	–	–	–	5R	5	5	5	–	–	–	–	–	–	4	1	–	–	–	5
Jaywin Juries	–	–	–	–	9R	–	–	–	x	x	9R	15R	9R	–	4	–	–	–	–	0
Marcel Coetzee	–	–	–	–	–	11	11	14	15R	x	–	–	–	–	4	–	3	3	–	15
Chiliboy Ralepelle	–	–	–	–	–	2	2	–	–	–	–	–	–	–	2	–	–	–	–	0
Kevin Elder	–	–	–	–	–	15R	15R	15R	15	–	–	–	–	–	4	–	–	–	–	0
Morné Joubert	–	–	–	–	–	–	14	–	10R	15	14	15	14	–	6	2	1	–	–	12
Duncan Campbell	–	–	–	–	–	–	10	–	x	10R	12R	x	–	–	3	–	1	1	–	5
Chris de Beer	–	–	–	–	–	–	–	8R	–	–	–	–	–	–	1	–	–	–	–	0
Malcolm Cele	–	–	–	–	–	–	–	–	–	14	11	11	11	–	4	2	–	–	–	10
Graham Geldenhuys	–	–	–	–	–	–	–	–	–	6	6	–	–	–	2	–	–	–	–	0
Jean Droste	–	–	–	–	–	–	–	–	–	–	5	4R	5	–	3	–	–	–	–	0
51 PLAYERS															**299**	**43**	**33**	**19**	**0**	**338**

SWD Eagles

Played	Won	Lost	Drawn	Points for	Points against	Tries for	Tries against
14	5	9	0	409	376	52	44

Date	Venue	Opponent	Result	Score	Referee	Scorers
Apr 09	Port Elizabeth	EP Kings	WON	37-14	C Joubert	T: Roberts, Eksteen, Du Toit, Arends. C: Graaff (3), Jansen.
Apr 15	George [1]	Pumas	WON	25-21	R Bonaparte	T: Pretorius (2), Du Toit, Du Plessis. C: Graaff. P: Graaff .
Apr 23	Kimberley	Griquas	LOST	17-27	L Legoete	T: Haupt, Pretorius. C: Graaff (2). P: Graaff.
Apr 27	George	Leopards	WON	26-32	R Bonaparte	T: Radbe, Steyn. C: Graaff (2). P: Graaff (4).
May 06	Welkom	Griffons	LOST	14-30	S Geldenhuys	T: Pretorius, Roberts. C: Graaff (2).
May 13	George	Valke	LOST	30-32	Q Immelman	T: Pedro (2), Roberts. C: Kean (3). P: Kean (3).
May 27	Wellington	Boland	LOST	16-32	AJ Jacobs	T: Eksteen (2). P: Eksteen, Kean.
Jun 10	George	Border	WON	39-22	M v/d Westhuizen	T: Du Plessis, Roberts, Stander, Pretorius, Van der Walt. C: Kean (4). P: Kean (2).
Jun 18	Windhoek	Welwitschias	WON	96-05	F Pretorius	T: Du Toit (3), Roberts (2), Ntsila, Du Plessis, Jansen, Stander, Haupt, Delo, Uys, Halvorsen, Engelbrecht. C: Jansen (7), Kean (4), Graaff (2).
Jun 24	George	Blue Bulls	LOST	23-28	S Ngcese	T: Haupt, Delo, Hartnick. C: Jansen. P: Jansen, Kean.
July 02	Cape Town [2]	Western Province	LOST	17-45	B Crouse	T: Roberts, Haupt. C: Jansen (2). P: Jansen.
July 08	George	Free State XV	LOST	16-24	L Legoete	T: Steyn. C: Graaff. P: Graaff (2), Kean.
July 16	Johannesburg	Golden Lions XV	LOST	29-35	C Jadezweni	T: Parks, Haupt, Heyns, Pretorius. C: Graaff (2), Kean. P: Graaff.
July 22	George	Sharks XV	LOST	24-29	S Ngcese	T: Wagman, Hopp, Uys, Pretorius. C: Kean (2).

[1] *NMMU Saasveld*

[2] *City Park Stadium*

APPEARANCES & POINTS IN 2016 CURRIE CUP QUALIFIERS

	EP Kings	Pumas	Griquas	Leopards	Griffons	Valke	Boland	Border	Welwitschias	Blue Bulls	WP	Free State XV	Lions XV	Sharks XV	Apps	T	C	P	DG	Pts
Jaquin Jansen	15	15	15	–	–	–	15R	15R	15	15	15	15	15	15	11	1	11	2	–	33
Leighton Eksteen	14	14	–	–	–	–	14	15	–	–	–	–	–	–	4	3	–	1	–	18
Daniel Roberts	13	13	13	15	15	13	13	11	11	11	11	11	13	10R	14	7	–	–	–	35
Martin du Toit	12	12	12	12	12	10	10	–	10c	10c	12c	–	–	–	10	5	–	–	–	25
Riaan Arends	11	11R	11	11	11	–	–	–	–	–	–	–	11R	11	7	1	–	–	–	5
Hansie Graaff	10	10	10	10	10	–	–	–	15R	15R	10	10	10	13	11	–	15	12	–	66
Mzo Dyantyi	9	9c	9	9R	9R	9	–	9R	9R	9R	–	–	–	–	9	–	–	–	–	0
Christo du Plessis	8	7	8	–	8R	8	7	7R	8R	4R	8	8	7	8	13	3	–	–	–	15
Davon Raubenheimer	7c	–	7c	7c	7c	7c	–	–	–	–	–	–	–	–	5	–	–	–	–	0
Buran Parks	6	6	–	6	6	6	8R	–	–	6R	6R	8R	6R		10	1	–	–	–	5
Grant le Roux	5	5	5	5	5	5	–	–	–	–	–	–	–	–	6	–	–	–	–	0
Peet van der Walt	4	4	4	4	4	4	4	4	4	–	4	4	4		12	1	–	–	–	5
Dean Hopp	3	–	–	–	3	3	3	3	3	–	1R	3			8	1	–	–	–	5
Mark Pretorius	2	2	2	2R	2	2	2c	2c	–	2R	2	–	2R	2R	12	7	–	–	–	35
Layle Delo	1	1	1	1R	1	1	1	1	1	1	–	1	–	3R	12	2	–	–	–	10
Brianton Booysen	2R	x	–	–	2R	7R	2R	–	2R	–	–	2R	–	–	6	–	–	–	–	0
Jeandré Digue	3R	–	–	1	–	–	–	–	–	1	1R	1			5	–	–	–	–	0
Marco Kruger	4R	7R	4R	–	4R	–	4R	–	–	4	4	4R	4R	4R	10	–	–	–	–	0
Andisa Ntsila	6R	8	6	8	8	6R	8	8R	4R	6R	8R	–	–		11	1	–	–	–	5
Johan Steyn	9R	9R	9R	9	9	9R	9	9	9	9	9R	9	9	9	14	2	–	–	–	10
Wilneth Engelbrecht	10R	13R	13R	13	13	12	12	12	12	12	–	–	–	–	10	1	–	–	–	5
Carlo Radebe	11R	11	14	14	14	–	–	–	–	14	–	14	14		8	1	–	–	–	5
Gideon Muller	–	3	3	3	3	–	–	–	–	–	–	–	–	–	4	–	–	–	–	0
Nemo Roelofse	–	3R	3R	3R	3R	3R	3R	3R	3R	3R	3	3	3	1	13	–	–	–	–	0
Lyndon Hartnick	–	6R	6R	5R	–	–	6R	7	7	7	–	8	7		9	1	–	–	–	5
Kurt Haupt	–	–	2R	2	–	–	2R	2	2	2R	2c	2c	2c		9	5	–	–	–	25
Clinton Wagman	–	–	11R	–	14	–	–	–	–	12R	14	–	11R		5	1	–	–	–	5
Thomas Kean	–	–	–	11R	12R	15	15	10	12R	14R	10R	10R	13R	10	11	–	14	8	–	52
Janneman Stander	–	–	–	8R	6R	–	6	6	6	6	6	6	6	6	10	2	–	–	–	10
Hentzwill Pedro	–	–	–	–	11	11	14	–	–	–	–	–	–		3	2	–	–	–	10
Lodewyk Uys	–	–	–	–	5R	5	5	5	5	5	5	5	5		9	2	–	–	–	10
Lenes Nomdo	–	–	–	–	14R	–	14R	14	14	–	14R	11	–		6	–	–	–	–	0
Leegan Moos	–	–	–	–	12R	–	–	–	–	–	–	–	–		1	–	–	–	–	0
Dillin Snell	–	–	–	–	–	9R	–	–	–	9	9R	9R	9R		5	–	–	–	–	0
Kirsten Heyns	–	–	–	–	–	–	13	13	13	13	13	12	12		7	1	–	–	–	5
Thor Halvorsen	–	–	–	–	–	–	8	8	8	7	7	–	–		5	1	–	–	–	5
Pieter Stemmet	–	–	–	–	–	–	–	–	–	1R	–	–			1	–	–	–	–	0
Luzuko Vulindlu	–	–	–	–	–	–	–	–	–	12	–	–			1	–	–	–	–	0
38 PLAYERS															307	52	40	23	0	409

Valke

Played	Won	Lost	Drawn	Points for	Points against	Tries for	Tries against
14	5	9	0	407	473	57	64

Date	Venue	Opponent	Result	Score	Referee	Scorers
Apr 08	Nelspruit	Pumas	WON	12-09	C Jadezweni	T: Van Wyk, Muir. C: Aspeling.
Apr 15	Kempton Park	Griquas	LOST	29-56	S Geldenhuys	T: Taljaard (3), Truter, Mamojele. C: Coetzee (2).
Apr 22	Potchefstroom	Leopards	LOST	24-26	C Jadezweni	T: Hendricks (2), Nyoka. C: Aspeling (3). P: Aspeling.
Apr 27	Kempton Park	Griffons	LOST	26-49	L van der Merwe	T: Janke, Taljaard, Muller, Kirkwood. C: Aspeling (2), Engledoe.
May 13	George	SWD	WON	32-30	Q Immelman	T: Hendricks, Kirkwood, Muir. C: Aspeling. P: Aspeling (5).
May 20	Kempton Park	Boland	LOST	22-24	AJ Jacobs	T: Richter, Kirkwood, Taljaard. C: Aspeling (2). P: Aspeling.
May 27	East London	Border	LOST	24-29	R Bonaparte	T: Kirkwood, Boshoff, Coetzee. C: Aspeling (2). P: Aspeling.
Jun 11	Kempton Park	Welwitchias	WON	66-05	R Bonaparte	T: Muller (3), Truter (2), Hendricks, Taljaard, Aspeling, Williams, Van Wyk. C: Aspeling (7), Truter.
Jun 17	Pretoria	Blue Bulls	LOST	15-42	AJ Jacobs	T: Cronjé, Van Wyk. C: Aspeling. P: Aspeling.
Jun 24	Kempton Park	WP	LOST	31-59	Q Immelman	T: Truter, Janke, Williams, Kirkwood. C: Aspeling (2), Coetzee (2). P: Aspeling.
July 02	Bloemfontein	Free State XV	LOST	27-33	AJ Jacobs	T: Janke, Taljaard, Pansegrouw. C: Potgieter (3). P: Potgieter (2).
July 09	Kempton Park	Golden Lions XV	LOST	14-75	B Crouse	T: Rust, Steyn. C: Potgieter, Coetzee.
July 15	Durban	Sharks XV	WON	26-10	J Sylvestre	T: Rust (2), Mamojele, Muir. C: Potgieter (3).
July 22	Kempton Park	EP Kings	WON	59-26	M v/d Westhuizen	T: Janke (2), Taljaard (2), Pretorius (2), Kirkwood, Schutte, Aspeling. C: Aspeling (4), Potgieter (3).

APPEARANCES & POINTS IN 2016 CURRIE CUP QUALIFIERS

	Pumas	Griquas	Leopards	Griffons	SWD	Boland	Border	Welwitschias	Blue Bulls	WP	Free State XV	Lions XV	Sharks XV	EP Kings	Apps	T	C	P	DG	Pts
Damien Engledoe	15	15	15	15	15	15	–	–	–	–	14R	15	15R	15	10	–	1	–	–	2
Kyle Hendricks	14	14	14	14	14	14	–	14	15	–	–	–	–	–	8	4	–	–	–	20
Andries Truter	13	13	13	13	13	–	13	12	13	13	–	–	13	–	10	4	1	–	–	22
Andréw van Wyk	12	14R	–	–	–	12	12	13R	12	–	13	–	–	12R	8	3	–	–	–	15
Coert Cronjé	11	–	–	10R	11	11	11	15R	14	14	–	–	14	14	10	1	–	–	–	5
Karlo Aspeling	10	10	10	10	10	10	10	10	10	10	–	–	–	10R	11	2	25	10	–	90
Anrich Richter	9	9	x	9R	9	9	–	10R	9	9	–	–	–	–	8	1	–	–	–	5
Reg Muller	8	8	8R	8	8	8	–	8	8	8R	–	8	–	–	10	4	–	–	–	20
Friedle Olivier	7	7	–	–	–	–	–	–	–	–	7R	5R	5R	8R	6	–	–	–	–	0
JP Mostert	6c	6c	6c	6c	6c	6c	6c	–	6c	7c	7c	7R	7c	6c	13	–	–	–	–	0
Marlyn Williams	5	5	–	5	5	5	5	5	5	5	5	5	5	5	13	2	–	–	–	10
Shane Kirkwood	4	4	4	4	4	4	4R	4	4	4	4	4	4	4	14	6	–	–	–	30
Andries Schutte	3	3	3	3	3	3	3	–	3	3R	3	3	3	3	13	1	–	–	–	5
Dean Muir	2	2	2	2	2	2	2	2R	2	2	2	2	2	2	14	3	–	–	–	15
Barend Steyn	1	1	1R	3R	3R	1R	–	3	1R	1R	3R	1R	–	–	11	1	–	–	–	5
Dwight Pansegrouw	4R	8R	7R	8R	7R	8R	7R	6	5R	6	6	6	6	–	13	1	–	–	–	5
Henri Boshoff	1R	–	1	1	1	1	1	1	1	1	1	1R	1R	1R	13	1	–	–	–	5
Isak Deetlefs	5R	5R	5	–	5R	5R	5R	4	–	–	–	–	–	5R	8	–	–	–	–	0
Thabo Mamojele	8R	7R	8	–	–	–	4R	7c	7	–	8R	7c	8	8	10	2	–	–	–	10
Johan Pretorius	x	–	9R	–	x	9R	9	9R	9R	9	9	9	9	9	9	2	–	–	–	10
Grant Janke	x	12	12	12	12	13	14R	–	11R	11	14	14	8R	13	12	5	–	–	–	25
Etienne Taljaard	14R	11	11	11	14R	15R	14	11	11	–	11	11	11	11	13	9	–	–	–	45
Koos Strauss	–	1R	–	1R	–	–	–	1	–	–	–	–	1	1	5	–	–	–	–	0
Sino Nyoka	–	9R	9	9	–	x	9	–	–	–	–	–	–	–	4	1	–	–	–	5
Christo Coetzee	–	10R	15R	–	–	–	15	15	15R	14R	–	11R	–	–	7	1	5	–	–	15
Ernst Ladendorf	–	–	7	7	7	7	7	–	7R	8	8	–	6R	7	10	–	–	–	–	0
Jacques Alberts	–	–	5R	–	–	–	–	–	–	–	–	–	–	–	1	–	–	–	–	0
Gihard Visagie	–	–	–	2R	–	–	–	2	–	2R	x	2R	x	2R	5	–	–	–	–	0
Vincent Jobo	–	–	–	5R	6R	7R	8	6R	8R	–	–	–	–	–	6	–	–	–	–	0
Warren Potgieter	–	–	–	10R	10R	10R	–	–	10	10	10	10	–	–	7	–	11	2	–	28
Themba Thabethe	–	–	–	–	x	–	–	–	–	–	–	–	–	–	0	–	–	–	–	0
Xander Cronjé	–	–	–	–	–	–	13	–	–	–	–	–	–	–	1	–	–	–	–	0
Christian Rust	–	–	–	–	–	–	–	–	15	15	13	15	–	–	4	3	–	–	–	15
Ruan Allerston	–	–	–	–	–	–	–	–	12	12	12	12	–	–	4	–	–	–	–	0
Grant Watts	–	–	–	–	–	–	–	–	–	3	–	–	–	–	1	–	–	–	–	0
JP du Plessis	–	–	–	–	–	–	–	–	10R	12R	10R	–	–	12	4	–	–	–	–	0
Etienne Storm	–	–	–	–	–	–	–	–	–	–	x	x	x	–	0	–	–	–	–	0
Charles Mayeza	–	–	–	–	–	–	–	–	–	–	–	–	–	15R	1	–	–	–	–	0
38 PLAYERS															297	57	43	12	0	407

WP

Played	Won	Lost	Drawn	Points for	Points against	Tries for	Tries against
14	13	1	0	548	303	77	34

Date	Venue	Opponent	Result	Score	Referee	Scorers
Apr 08	Cape Town	Blue Bulls	WON	30-16	AJ Jacobs	T: D du Plessis, Swanepoel, Whitehead. C: Thomson (3). P: Thomson (3).
Apr 22	Bloemfontein	Free State XV	WON	36-31	B Crouse	T: D du Plessis (2), Van Vuuren, Phillips, Stringer. C: Van Breda (4). P: Hermanus.
Apr 30	Cape Town	Golden Lions XV	WON	27-24	R Rasivhenge	T: Willemse (2), Ngcukana, Maxwane. C: Hermanus (2). P: Hermanus.
May 07	Durban	Sharks XV	LOST	16-24	Q Immelman	T: Masimla, Ngcukana. P: Hermanus 920.
May 14	Cape Town[1]	EP Kings	WON	50-10	S Geldenhuys	T: Van Breda (2), D du Plessis, Williams, Van Wyk, Phillips, Stringer, Willemse. C: Van Breda (4), Hermanus.
May 20	Nelspruit	Pumas	WON	27-20	M v/d Westhuizen	T: Lewis (2). C: Van Breda. P: Van Breda (5).
May 28	Cape Town	Griquas	WON	24-23	Q Immelman	T: Solomon, Venter, Ngcukana. C: Van Breda (3). P: Van Breda.
Jun 04	Potchefstroom	Leopards	WON	43-34	E Seconds	T: Hermanus (2), De Villiers, Muller, Kleyn, Ngcukana. C: Van Breda (5). P: Van Breda.
Jun 18	Cape Town[1]	Griffons	WON	43-26	S Ngcese	T: Viljoen (2), Taute (2), Bredenkamp, Phillips, Solomon. C: Du Preez (4).
Jun 24	Kempton Park	Valke	WON	59-31	Q Immelman	T: Lewis (3), Solomon, Collopy, Williams, Bredenkamp, Ngcukana, Du Preez. C: Du Preez (7).
July 02	Cape Town[1]	SWD	WON	45-17	B Crouse	T: Solomon, Van Zyl, Kotze, Stringer, Maxwane, Whitehead. C: Du Preez (6). P: Du Preez.
July 09	Piketberg	Boland	WON	25-14	R Bonaparte	T: Solomon, Viljoen, Du Preez. C: Du Preez (2). P: Du Preez (2).
July 16	Cape Town	Border	WON	52-26	P Brousset	T: Van der Merwe (2), Solomon, Collopy, Masimla, Hermanus, Phillips, Whitehead. C: Hermanus (5), Cox.
July 23	Windhoek	Welwitschias	WON	71-07	A Sehlako	T: Viljoen (2), Van Dyk (2), De Villiers, Van der Merwe, Cox, Bredenkamp, Phillips, Ngcukana, Van Breda. C: Hermanus (8).

[1] *City Park Stadium*

APPEARANCES & POINTS IN 2016 CURRIE CUP QUALIFIERS

	Blue Bulls	Free State XV	Lions XV	Sharks XV	EP Kings	Pumas	Griquas	Leopards	Griffons	Valke	SWD	Boland	Border	Welwitchias	Apps	T	C	P	DG	Pts
Grant Hermanus	15	15	15	15	15	–	15R	15	15	15	–	15	15	15	12	3	16	4	–	59
Sibahle Maxwane	14	11	11	11	15R	15R	–	–	11	–	11	–	–	–	8	2	–	–	–	10
Tim Whitehead	13	13	13	13	–	13	12	–	–	12	12	12	12c	–	10	3	–	–	–	15
Daniel du Plessis	12	12	12	12	12	12	–	–	–	–	–	–	–	–	6	4	–	–	–	20
JP Lewis	11	22R	11R	11R	14	11	11	11	11	13R	11	–	–	–	10	5	–	–	–	25
Brandon Thomson	10	–	–	–	–	–	–	–	–	11R	–	–	–	–	2	–	3	3	–	15
Justin Phillips	9	9R	9	9R	9	9	9	–	9R	–	–	–	9R	9	10	5	–	–	–	25
Jacques Vermeulen	8	7	–	–	–	–	–	–	–	–	7	8	5R	–	5	–	–	–	–	0
Luke Stringer	7	6	6	6	6	6	6	7	8R	6	7	6	7	–	13	3	–	–	–	15
Eital Bredenkamp	6	8R	8R	6R	8R	–	6R	–	6	7R	6R	7R	6	6R	12	3	–	–	–	15
Chris van Zyl	5c	5c	5c	5c	5c	5c	5c	5c	5c	5c	5c	5c	–	5c	13	1	–	–	–	5
Jurie van Vuuren	4	4	7	4	–	–	4	5R	7	4	8R	4R	4R	4	12	1	–	–	–	5
JP Smith	3	3	3	3	1	1	1	–	–	–	–	–	–	–	7	–	–	–	–	0
Michael Willemse	2	–	2	2	2R	2R	2R	–	–	–	–	–	–	2R	7	3	–	–	–	15
Alistair Vermaak	1	1	1	1	–	–	1	1	–	–	–	–	–	–	6	–	–	–	–	0
Chad Solomon	2R	2	2R	2R	2	2	2	–	2	2	2	2	2	2	13	6	–	–	–	30
Frans van Wyk	3R	–	–	3	3	3	3R	–	–	–	–	–	–	–	5	1	–	–	–	5
Meyer Swanepoel	4R	–	4R	7	4	4R	–	–	–	–	–	–	–	–	5	1	–	–	–	5
Tertius Daniller	7R	8	8	–	–	–	–	–	–	–	–	–	–	–	3	–	–	–	–	0
Damian Stevens	9R	–	x	–	9R	9R	9R	–	–	–	–	–	–	–	4	–	–	–	–	0
Berton Klaasen	13R	–	x	12R	12R	13R	–	–	–	–	–	–	–	–	4	–	–	–	–	0
Devon Williams	11R	–	–	11	15	15	15R	–	14R	–	–	–	–	–	6	2	–	–	–	10
Khanyo Ngcukana	–	14	14	14	–	14	14	14	14	–	–	14	14	–	10	6	–	–	–	30
Scott van Breda	–	10	10	10	10	10	10	10	–	–	–	–	–	12R	8	3	17	7	–	70
Godlen Masimla	–	9	–	9	–	–	–	9R	9	9	9	9	11R	–	8	2	–	–	–	10
EW Viljoen	–	11R	–	–	–	13	13	13	–	14	14	13	13	–	8	5	–	–	–	25
Eduard Zandberg	–	4R	4	–	–	–	–	–	–	–	–	4	–	–	3	–	–	–	–	0
Kyle Whyte	–	3R	x	3R	3R	x	3R	–	3R	1	3	3	1	–	9	–	–	–	–	0
Cullen Collopy	–	2R	–	–	–	–	2	2R	2R	2R	3R	2R	–	–	7	2	–	–	–	10
Kobus van Dyk	–	–	8	8	8	8	8	8	8	8	8	–	8	–	10	2	–	–	–	10
Christo van der Merwe	–	–	4R	7R	–	7R	–	–	–	–	–	–	7	–	4	1	–	–	–	5
Ryan Oosthuizen	–	–	–	13	–	13R	–	–	–	–	–	–	–	–	2	–	–	–	–	0
Janco Venter	–	–	–	7	7	7	–	7	–	–	–	–	–	–	4	1	–	–	–	5
JD Schickerling	–	–	–	–	4	–	–	–	–	–	–	–	–	–	1	–	–	–	–	0
Beyers de Villiers	–	–	–	–	6R	–	6	5R	–	6	6R	6R	8R	–	7	2	–	–	–	10
Dale Wilson	–	–	–	–	4R	–	–	7R	–	–	–	–	–	–	2	–	–	–	–	0
Jaco Taute	–	–	–	–	–	12	12	–	–	–	–	–	–	–	2	2	–	–	–	10
Herschel Jantjies	–	–	–	–	–	9	–	–	–	–	–	–	–	–	1	–	–	–	–	0
Jean Kleyn	–	–	–	–	–	4	4	–	–	–	–	–	–	–	2	–	–	–	–	0
Wilco Louw	–	–	–	–	–	3	3	3	–	–	3	3	–	–	5	–	–	–	–	0
Freddie Muller	–	–	–	–	–	9R	–	–	–	–	–	–	–	–	1	1	–	–	–	5
Robert du Preez	–	–	–	–	–	12R	10	10	10	10	–	–	–	–	5	2	19	3	–	57
Percy Mngadi	–	–	–	–	–	2R	–	–	–	–	–	–	–	–	1	–	–	–	–	0
Johnny Kotze	–	–	–	–	–	–	13	13	13	12R	12	–	–	–	5	1	–	–	–	5
Jano Vermaak	–	–	–	–	–	–	9R	9R	15R	–	–	–	–	–	3	–	–	–	–	0
Christo van Wyk	–	–	–	–	–	–	3R	1R	–	–	–	–	–	–	2	–	–	–	–	0
David Ribbans	–	–	–	–	–	–	8R	4	4	5	–	–	–	–	4	–	–	–	–	0
Dennis Cox	–	–	–	–	–	–	12	15	13R	10	10	–	–	–	5	1	1	–	–	7
Wesley Chetty	–	–	–	–	–	–	–	1	1	–	–	–	–	–	2	–	–	–	–	0
Alvin Brandt	–	–	–	–	–	–	–	9R	–	–	–	–	–	–	1	–	–	–	–	0
Edwill van der Merwe	–	–	–	–	–	–	–	–	–	–	11	11	11	–	3	2	–	–	–	10
Ashley Wells	–	–	–	–	–	–	–	–	–	–	1R	–	–	–	1	–	–	–	–	0
Denzel Riddles	–	–	–	–	–	–	–	–	–	–	–	1R	3R	–	2	–	–	–	–	0
Rikus Bothma	–	–	–	–	–	–	–	–	–	–	–	7R	6	–	2	–	–	–	–	0
JC Janse van Rensburg	–	–	–	–	–	–	–	–	–	–	–	–	–	1	1	–	–	–	–	0
55 PLAYERS															304	77	56	17	0	548

Welwitschias

Played	Won	Lost	Drawn	Points for	Points against	Tries for	Tries against
14	0	14	0	171	936	25	141

Date	Venue	Opponent	Result	Score	Referee	Scorers
Apr 09	Bloemfontein	Free State XV	LOST	17-32	Q Immelman	T: Tromp, Moore. C: Kaizemi (2). P: Tromp.
Apr 16	Windhoek	Golden Lions XV	LOST	12-66	A Sehlako	T: Van Zyl, De la Harpe. C: Kaizemi.
Apr 23	Durban[1]	Sharks XV	LOST	18-48	R Bonaparte	T: Van Zyl, R van Wyk, Kitshoff. P: Kaizemi.
Apr 30	Windhoek	EP Kings	LOST	18-31	P Legoete	T: Tromp (2). C: Kaizemi. P: Kaizemi (2).
May 07	Ermelo[2]	Pumas	LOST	07-47	E Seconds	T: R van Wyk. C: Nel.
May 14	Windhoek	Griquas	LOST	25-55	E Seconds	T: Wiese, Nashikaku, Winkler, Nel. C: Nel. P: Smit.
May 20	Potchefstroom	Leopards	LOST	17-42	S Ngcese	T: Wiese, D van Wyk. C: Kaizemi (2). P: Kaizemi.
May 28	Windhoek	Griffons	LOST	0-101	L Legoete	
Jun 11	Kempton Park	Valke	LOST	05-66	R Bonaparte	T: Klim.
Jun 18	Windhoek	SWD	LOST	05-96	F Pretorius	T: Klim.
Jun 25	Wellington	Boland	LOST	10-110	AJ Jacobs	T: Nashikaku, Moore.
July 02	Windhoek	Border	LOST	18-76	E Seconds	T: Nashikaku, Prinsloo. C: Van Zyl. P: Van Zyl (2)
July 15	Pretoria	Blue Bulls	LOST	12-95	R Bonaparte	T: Van Zyl, Wohler. C: Kaizemi.
July 23	Windhoek	WP	LOST	07-71	A Sehlako	T: Prinsloo. C: Nel.

[1] *King Zwelithini Stadium, Umlazi*

[2] *Ermelo High School*

APPEARANCES & POINTS IN 2016 CURRIE CUP QUALIFIERS

	Free State XV	Lions XV	Sharks XV	EP Kings	Pumas	Griquas	Leopards	Griffons	Valke	SWD	Boland	Border	Blue Bulls	WP	Apps	T	C	P	DG	Pts
Johann Tromp	15	14	14	14	15	15	15	–	–	–	–	–	–	–	7	3	–	1	–	18
Russell van Wyk	14	11	11	–	11	–	14	11	–	–	–	11	–	11	8	2	–	–	–	10
JC Greyling	13	13	13	13	–	–	13	–	–	–	–	–	–	–	5	–	–	–	–	0
Darryl de la Harpe	12	12	12	12	13	13	–	–	–	–	–	–	–	–	6	1	–	–	–	5
Malcolm Moore	11	–	–	–	–	14	–	–	–	–	11	15R	11	–	5	2	–	–	–	10
Mahco Prinsloo	10	–	–	–	–	–	–	–	12R	–	10	10	10	–	5	2	–	–	–	10
Arthur Bouwer	9	9	9	9R	9	9	–	9R	–	–	–	–	–	–	7	–	–	–	–	0
Roderique Victor	8	8	8	8	–	–	–	–	–	–	–	–	–	–	4	–	–	–	–	0
Leneve Damens	7	7	7	7	8	8	8	–	–	–	–	–	–	8c	8	–	–	–	–	0
Rohan Kitshoff	6c	6c	6c	6c	6c	6c	6c	6c	–	–	–	–	–	–	8	1	–	–	–	5
Ruan Ludick	5	5	5	5	5	–	4R	5	–	–	–	–	–	–	7	–	–	–	–	0
Munio Kasiringua	4	4	4R	4	4	4	4	4	4	4	–	–	–	4	11	–	–	–	–	0
Collen Smith	3	1R	3R	–	–	–	–	3	–	–	3R	–	–	3	6	–	–	–	–	0
Gerhard Lotter	2	2	2	2	–	2	2	2	–	–	–	–	–	–	7	–	–	–	–	0
Quintin Esterhuizen	1	1	1	1	1	3R	1R	–	1	1	1c	–	–	1	11	–	–	–	–	0
Joe Hermann	7R	8R	2R	8R	7	–	7	8	8	8	–	–	–	–	9	–	–	–	–	0
Haula Veii	1R	–	–	2R	2R	–	–	3	3	3	–	3	–	–	7	–	–	–	–	0
Shaun du Preez	3R	3	3	3	1R	1	3R	–	–	–	2	–	–	–	8	–	–	–	–	0
Denzil van Wyk	4R	4R	4	–	5R	5R	5	–	–	–	–	–	–	–	6	1	–	–	–	5
JC Winkler	9R	9R	9R	9	–	9R	9	–	9	9	9R	9R	9R	9	12	1	–	–	–	5
Shaun Kaizemi	10R	10	10	10	10	–	10	10	10R	–	12	13R	11R	13R	12	–	7	4	–	26
Riaan van Zyl	12R	15	15	15	–	15R	–	15	–	11R	10R	15	15	–	10	3	1	2	–	23
Egon Cloete	–	7R	–	–	–	–	–	–	–	–	8	–	–	–	2	–	–	–	–	0
MP Pretorius	–	10R	10R	–	–	–	–	–	–	–	–	–	10R	–	3	–	–	–	–	0
Tuma Amulenya	–	15R	–	–	–	–	–	–	–	–	–	–	–	–	1	–	–	–	–	0
Morné Blom	–	–	5R	–	–	–	–	7	7	8	–	7	7	–	6	–	–	–	–	0
Francois Wiese	–	–	13R	13R	12	12	12	12	12c	12c	–	12c	12c	–	10	2	–	–	–	10
Philip Nashikaku	–	–	–	11	–	11	11	14	14	14	14	14	14	14	10	3	–	–	–	15
Petri Burger	–	–	–	2R	–	–	–	2R	–	–	2R	3R	2	2	5	–	–	–	–	0
AJ de Klerk	–	–	–	3R	3	3	3	3R	–	–	–	–	–	–	5	–	–	–	–	0
Zayne Groenewaldt	–	–	–	5R	7R	7R	8R	7	6	6	6	6	6	–	10	–	–	–	–	0
Justin Nel	–	–	–	10R	10R	13R	13R	15R	15	15	15	–	13	15	10	1	3	–	–	11
Lesley Klim	–	–	–	14	–	–	–	13	13	13	13	–	–	11R	6	2	–	–	–	10
Callie Swanepoel	–	–	–	–	2	–	–	–	–	–	–	–	–	–	1	–	–	–	–	0
Camerol Klassen	–	–	–	–	9R	–	9R	9	9R	9R	9	9	9	9R	9	–	–	–	–	0
Heinrich Smit	–	–	–	–	12R	10	10R	–	–	–	–	–	–	12	4	–	–	1	–	3
Herman Krause	–	–	–	–	–	7	–	–	–	–	–	–	–	–	1	–	–	–	–	0
Tinus du Plessis	–	–	–	–	–	5	–	–	–	–	–	–	–	–	1	–	–	–	–	0
Casper Viviers	–	–	–	–	–	–	1	1	–	–	–	–	–	–	2	–	–	–	–	0
Aleck Botha	–	–	–	–	–	–	1R	–	–	–	–	–	–	–	1	–	–	–	–	0
Thomas Khali	–	–	–	–	–	–	10R	–	–	–	4	–	–	–	2	–	–	–	–	0
Aurelio Plato	–	–	–	–	–	–	12R	10	10	10	–	–	–	–	4	–	–	–	–	0
Sylvano Beukes	–	–	–	–	–	–	–	11	11	–	–	–	–	–	2	–	–	–	–	0
Wikus Davis	–	–	–	–	–	–	–	5	5	5	5	5	–	–	5	–	–	–	–	0
Dewald Coetzee	–	–	–	–	–	–	–	2	2	2	–	–	–	–	3	–	–	–	–	0
Johann Wohler	–	–	–	–	–	–	–	2R	8R	6R	–	8	6R	–	5	1	–	–	–	5
Tjino Tirare	–	–	–	–	–	–	–	3R	–	–	–	–	–	–	1	–	–	–	–	0
Grant Nash	–	–	–	–	–	–	–	4R	–	4R	4R	–	–	–	3	–	–	–	–	0
Max Katjijeko	–	–	–	–	–	–	–	6R	6R	7	–	4R	7R	–	5	–	–	–	–	0
Ricardo Swartz	–	–	–	–	–	–	–	22R	–	–	–	–	–	–	1	–	–	–	–	0
Alberto Engelbrecht	–	–	–	–	–	–	–	–	4R	4	–	4	–	–	3	–	–	–	–	0
Anton Tripodi	–	–	–	–	–	–	–	–	7R	–	3	1R	–	–	3	–	–	–	–	0
Guiliano Lawrence	–	–	–	–	–	–	–	–	–	11R	–	–	–	–	1	–	–	–	–	0
HAndré Bezuidenhout	–	–	–	–	–	–	–	–	–	–	13	–	–	13	2	–	–	–	–	0
Johan Luttig	–	–	–	–	–	–	–	–	–	–	7	8R	6	–	3	–	–	–	–	0
Arno von Wielligh	–	–	–	–	–	–	–	–	–	–	1	–	–	–	1	–	–	–	–	0
Daniel van Vuuren	–	–	–	–	–	–	–	–	–	–	8R	2R	17R	–	3	–	–	–	–	0
Schalk Bergh	–	–	–	–	–	–	–	–	–	–	1R	1	3R	–	3	–	–	–	–	0
58 PLAYERS															308	25	11	8	0	171

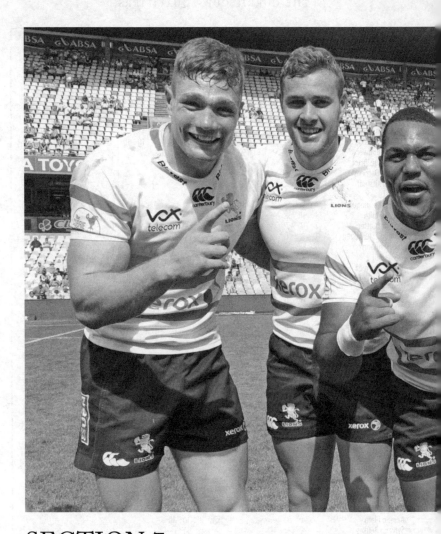

SECTION 7:
AGE-GROUP PROVINCIAL TOURNAMENTS

Golden Lions topple WP

THEIR senior team might not have defended their Currie Cup crown, but the Golden Lions age-group teams made sure that the Johannesburg-based union's trophy cabinet would remain well stocked going into the 2017 season when they won the Under-19 and Under-21 provincial championships, beating arch-rivals Western Province in both finals.

In a one-sided match, the Lions U19s overwhelmed their fancied Cape opponents 60-19, having already sewn up the match by half-time when they led 34-7. The U21 match was an altogether tighter affair, the Lions scraping home 38-34 against the defending champions in the main curtain-raiser to the Currie Cup final.

Having taken a slender lead into the final stages of the match, WP saw the title slip from their grasp thanks to a strong finish from their opponents.

It was just the second defeat of the season for WP, who had topped the log at the end of the league phase of the campaign. A see-saw match looked set to go into extra time when the Lions scored their third try with eight minutes remaining to tie the scores at 31 apiece.

But the Lions had the last laugh, captain Jarred Sage crossing the line for a last-gasp victory.

The Lions' U19s in turn scored eight tries en route to a rout of WP.

Wing Madosha Tambwe scored a hat-trick for the Lions, who quickly made life difficult for WP by speeding to a 27-0 lead inside the opening half hour through three converted tries and a couple of penalties – an early series of body blows from which the boys from the Cape could not recover.

SA Rugby U21 Champions: Xerox Golden Lions

UNDER-21 CUP
PLAY-OFF RESULT

SEMI-FINALS: Golden Lions bt Blue Bulls 37-15 *(Johannesburg)*;
Western Province bt Free State 26-23 *(Cape Town)*

FINAL

Toyota Stadium, Bloemfontein. Saturday, 22 October. Referee: AJ Jacobs.

WP 34

(Tries: Vermeulen, Phillips, Maxwane. Cons: Hermanus 2. Pens: Hermanus 5).

Golden Lions 38

(Tries: Jonas, Sage, Engelbrecht, Jansen van Vuren. Cons: Reynolds 3. Pens: Reynolds 4).

WP: Grant Hermanus, Sibahle Maxwane *(Leolin Zas, 56)*, Eduan Keyter, Ryan Oosthuizen, Edwill van der Merwe, Brandon Thomson, Justin Phillips Jacobus Coetzee *(Christo van der Merwe, 30)*, Jacques Vermeulen, Luke Stringer *(Capt)*, Eduard Zandberg, Jaco Willemse *(Nyasha Tarusenga, 73)*,   Frans van Wyk, Percy Mngadi *(Hanno Snyman, 38)*, Kyle White *(Michael Kumbirai, 67)*.
UNUSED SUBS: Herschel Jantjies, Dennis Cox.

Golden Lions: Kobus Engelbrecht, Ronald Brown *(Barend Smit, 73)*, Jarryd Sage *(Capt)*, Shaun Reynolds, Godfrey Ramaboea, Curtis Jonas *(Cameron Rooi, 69)*, Marco Jansen van Vuren, Jo-Hanco de Villiers *(Morney Moos, 65)*, Wiehan Jacobs, James Venter, Floris Pelser *(Estian Enslin, 15)*, Rhyno Herbst *(Driaan Bester, 56)*, Clinton Theron *(Kyle Kruger, 21)*, Pieter Jansen *(Le Roux Baard, 76)*, Arnout Malherbe.

U21 LOG

Section A	P	W	L	D	PF	PA	Diff	TF	TA	BP	BP7	PTS
Western Province	6	4	1	1	200	140	60	28	17	1	9	52
Golden Lions	6	5	1	0	198	144	54	22	21	2	9	45
Blue Bulls	6	3	2	1	185	171	14	26	22	1	6	37
Free State	6	3	3	0	177	184	-7	23	21	4	7	35
Eastern Province	6	3	3	0	164	155	9	19	18	1	7	34
Sharks	6	2	4	0	152	189	-37	20	25	0	5	13
Leopards	6	0	6	0	153	246	-93	22	36	0	1	5

Note: BP = Bonus point, BP7 = Less than 7

U21 LEADING SCORERS

40 POINTS OR MORE

PLAYER	PROVINCE	T	C	P	DG	Pts
Shaun Reynolds	Golden Lions	1	22	18	3	112
Grant Hermanus	Western Province	1	15	14	0	77
Garrick Mattheus	Eastern Province	1	15	11	0	68
Tinus de Beer	Blue Bulls	0	19	6	0	56
Gerrie Labuschagne	Free State	2	15	2	0	46

TRIES

Elden Schoeman	Leopards	6	Christo van der Merwe	Western Province	4
Tristan Blewett	Sharks	6	Dewald Naude	Blue Bulls	4
Jasper Wiese	Free State	5	Franco Naude	Blue Bulls	4
Sibahle Maxwane	Western Province	5	James Venter	Golden Lions	4
Malcolm Jaer	Eastern Province	4	Morne Joubert	Sharks	4

SA RUGBY UNDER-20 PROVINCIAL CUP
PLAY-OFF RESULT

Semi-finals: Boland bt SWD 41-27 *(Wellington)*;
Griffons bt Limpopo 53-29 *(Welkom)*

FINAL

Profert Olen Park, Potchefstroom. Friday, 7 October. Referee: Sindile Ngcese.

Griffons 22

(Try: Dlamini. Con: Christian. Pen: Christian 5).

Boland 16

(Try: April. Con: Fortune. Pen: Fortune 3).

Griffons: Domenic Smit *(Ezrick Alexander, 79)*, Nazo Nkala, Luciano Jones *(Lubabalo Mteyise, 70)*, Richman Gora, Jeandre Christian, Robbie Petzer, Shirwin Cupido, Francois Stemmet *(Capt)*, Gift Dlamini *(Boykie Herbert, 53)*, Cornelius Jacobs, Gideon van Eeden, Stephanus Malherbe *(Klaus-Andre Cellar, 70)*, Fanie Vermaak, Stephen Pelser *(Duke Jantjies, 66)*, JP Mans *(Neo Mohapi, 79)*. UNUSED SUBS: Riekert Botha.

Boland: Kurt-Lee Arendse, Andre Manuel *(Enzo Foutie, 76)*, Michaine Fick, Hendrik Carstens *(Keagan Fortune, 45)*, Barry Adonis, Jermaine Jansen, Caleb Louw *(Jaiden Baron, 53)*, Colin April, Willem Potgieter *(Benjamin Dwayi, 70)*, Ruhan Marais, Louis Conradie, Heinrich Basson, Robin Adams *(Clarence van Wyk, 73)*, Sachin Farmer *(Colwyn Manchest, 46)*, Cyle Davids. UNUSED SUB: Christo Cloete.

U20 LOG

	P	W	L	D	PF	PA	Diff	TF	TA	BP	BP7	PTS
Griffons	14	11	1	2	635	313	322	82	43	1	10	59
Boland	14	10	4	0	631	388	243	92	54	2	13	55
SWD	14	10	3	1	616	376	240	95	51	1	12	55
Limpopo	14	9	3	2	496	353	143	69	45	1	11	52
Pumas	14	7	7	0	479	427	52	72	60	0	10	38
Griquas	14	2	12	0	357	521	-164	52	78	3	7	18
Valke	14	2	10	2	301	736	-435	42	114	0	5	17
Border	14	1	12	1	177	578	-401	27	86	0	1	7

Note: BP = Bonus point, BP7 = Less than 7

U20 LEADING SCORERS

70 POINTS OR MORE

PLAYER	PROVINCE	T	C	P	DG	PTS
Jeandre Christians	Griffons	5	53	27	0	212
Hendrik Carstens	Boland	3	55	15	0	170
Robbie Petzer	Griffons	9	18	9	1	111
Shadward Fillies	SWD	20	1	0	0	102
Winrey Stoffels	SWD	4	33	5	0	101
Jan Kotze	Valke	6	18	9	0	93
Ruaan du Preez	Pumas	6	21	3	0	81
Andre Manuel	Boland	15	2	0	0	79
Theunis Sauer	Limpopo	4	19	6	0	76
Justin Bhana	SWD	14	0	0	0	70

JUNIOR PROVINCIAL CHAMPIONSHIPS

TRIES

Shadward Fillies	SWD	20	Robbie Petzer	Griffons	9
Andre Manuel	Boland	15	Colin April	Boland	9
Justin Bhana	SWD	14	Juvan Stimie	Limpop	9
Domenic Smit	Griffons	12	Lunathi Nxele	SWD	8
Danick Pheiffer	Pumas	12	Frans Botha	Limpop	8
Michaine Fick	Boland	12	Gerhard Holtzhausen	Griquas	8
Francois Venter	Griffons	11	Ian Truter	Pumas	8
Enzo Foutie	Boland	10	Riekert Botha	Griffons	8
Kurt-Lee Arendse	Boland	10	Clide Davids	SWD	7
Nazo Nkala	Griffons	10	Daniello Huyster	Griquas	7

SA Rugby U19 Champions: Xerox Golden Lions

UNDER-19 CUP
PLAY-OFF RESULTS
SEMI-FINALS: Western Province bt Free State 30-15 *(Cape Town).*
Blue Bulls lost to Golden Lions 24-34 *(Pretoria)*
FINAL
Toyota Stadium, Bloemfontein, Saturday, 22 October. Referee: Vusi Msibi.
Western Province 19
(Tries: Brits, van Rhyn, Augustus. Cons: Williams 2).
Golden Lions 60
(Tries: Tambwe 3, Jansen, Dayimani, Vermaak, Pienaar, February. Cons: Cilliers 7. Pens: Cilliers 2).

Western Province: Tristan Leyds, Nico Leonard *(Troy Payne, 62)*, David Brits, Cornel Smit, Ryan Muller, Damian Willemse *(Adriaan van der Bank, 21)*, Jondre Williams *(Brandon Salomo, 62)*, Juarno Augustus, Cobus Wiese, Zain Davids *(Johan Visser, 56)*, David Meihuzen *(Jacobus Swart, 41)*, Ernst van Rhyn *(Capt)*, Carlu Sadie *(Lee-Marvin Mazibuko, 41)*, Matt Wiseman *(Shane Farmer, 62)*, Ricky Nwagbara *(Roux Swart, 45)*.

Golden Lions: Jeanluc Cilliers, Tyreeq February *(Michael Tambwe, 51)*, Jan-Louis le Grange, Wayne van der Bank *(Xander Krause, 56)*, Stean Pienaar, Eddie Fouche, Bradley Thain *(Morne van den Berg, 56)*, Len Massyn, Hacjivah Dayimani, Edwin Jansen *(Patrick Wait 62)*, Reinhardt Nothnagel, Ruan Vermaak *(Thokozani Skhsona, 62)*, Chergin Fillies *(Rouxbann Baumann, 52)*, Hendrik van Schoor *(Capt, Justin Brandon, 54)*, Leo-Roubert Kruger *(Niell Bezuidenhout, 52)*.

U19 LOG

Section A	P	W	L	D	PF	PA	Diff	TF	TA	BP	BP7	PTS
Western Province	12	10	2	0	493	278	215	66	35	1	9	50
Blue Bulls	12	10	2	0	427	225	202	62	27	2	8	50
Golden Lions	12	9	3	0	537	236	301	73	30	2	8	46
Free State	12	6	6	0	366	308	58	49	39	1	5	30
Sharks	12	4	8	0	294	426	-132	44	61	2	6	24
Eastern Province	12	3	9	0	308	497	-189	39	73	3	5	20
Leopards	12	0	12	0	167	622	-455	22	90	2	1	3

Note: BP = Bonus point, BP7 = Less than 7

U19 LEADING SCORERS

80 POINTS OR MORE

PLAYER	PROVINCE	T	C	P	DG	PTS
Jeanluc Cilliers	Golden Lions	2	56	21	0	185
Jondre Williams	Western Province	4	35	15	0	135
Victor Foster	Eastern Province	6	20	13	0	109
Christiaan Schutte	Free State	2	20	13	0	89
Michael Tambwe	Golden Lions	16	0	0	0	80

TRIES

Michael Tambwe	Golden Lions	16	Erich Cronje	Blue Bulls	7
Stean Pienaar	Golden Lions	14	Jonathan Booysen	Eastern Province	7
Juarno Augustus	Western Province	12	Nico Leonard	Western Province	7
Yaw Penxe	Eastern Province	8	Stedman Gans	Blue Bulls	7
David Brits	Western Province	7			

WP dominate SA Rugby Youth Weeks

By Zeena van Tonder

WESTERN Province proved once again to be the force to be reckoned with at the SA Rugby Youth Weeks. The province won the final match in the Under-13 and Under-18 Coca-Cola Craven Weeks, as well as the Coca-Cola Academy Week, to reinforce their dominance.

WP's U13 Craven Week team beat the Sharks 12-5 in a tight clash at Paarl Gymnasium, while the U18 side edged the Golden Lions 27-20, and the Coca-Cola Academy Week team defeated the Blue Bulls 23-12 respectively at Kearsney College in Durban.

The victory for the U13s marked the fourth successive year that the union came out tops in the final match, while the U18 team took top honours for the second year running and the Academy Week side built on their success in the final match since the 2014 season.

The Blue Bulls, meanwhile, won the final game in the U16 Coca-Cola Grant Khomo Week thanks to a 23-20 victory against the Sharks, while Boland beat the Valke 30-14 in the grand finale of the Learners with Special Education Needs (LSEN) Week at Afrikaanse Hoër Seunskool (Affies) in Pretoria.

Boland's victory in the LSEN Week also marked a significant milestone as it was the third year in a row that the team emerged as the top side in the tournament.

The opening exchanges of the main game of the U18 Craven Week between WP and the Lions was tight as the teams exchanged penalty goals to force their way onto the scoreboard. Province scored the first try of the match in the 15th minute as they spread the ball wide, but this was later cancelled out by the Lions who won a turnover and touched down underneath the posts. The Cape side however scored down again before the break to take a 20-10 lead.

The Lions struck again with a try one minute into the second half, but this was cancelled out by Western Province two minutes later as they crossed the tryline for the third time. The Lions closed the gap on the scoreboard to 27-20 compliments of a penalty eight minutes before the final whistle. But that proved to be the

last points of the match, which allowed WP to emerge as the top team.

In the final match of the Coca-Cola Academy Week, the Blue Bulls ran hard at Western Province without reward. Penalties conceded in kickable positions, however, allowed the Pretoria side to slot over three first-half penalties for 9-0 lead. WP reduced the gap to 9-3 before the break.

Both teams gave everything in the second half, but WP scored two tries and two penalties to only one penalty by the Blue Bulls for a 23-12 victory.

In the closing match of the U13 Craven Week between Western Province and the Sharks, the Cape side dominated possession in the first half, and these efforts paid off with a well-worked try. The Sharks hit back five minutes later to score in the corner, which left the teams deadlocked at 5-5 going into the break.

WP struck again shortly after half-time with a strong upfield run and a handy kick-through to push them 12-5 ahead. The Sharks fought back with intent but they were denied by an effective defence.

In the grand finale of the U16 Grant Khomo Week, the Sharks dominated territory and possession early on and showed patience on attack, and this paid off as they scored the first points compliments of a converted try. The Blue Bulls levelled the scores three minutes later. But with neither team giving an inch on defence both sides opted for penalty goals to inflate their scores as the half progressed, with the Blue Bulls slotting over two penalties to only one by the Sharks for a 13-10 halftime lead.

The Bulls added their third penalty after the break and a second try following a series of phases to stretch their score to 23 points. But the Sharks showed composure on attack by taking a penalty before fighting back with a try in the corner minutes before full-time to reduce the deficit to 23-20. In a thrilling finish, the Sharks opted for a penalty goal on the stroke of full-time, but the attempt fell short, which sealed the win for the Pretoria side.

In the LSEN Week, meanwhile, Boland cruised to a 20-0 lead at the break against the

COCA-COLA UNDER-18 CRAVEN WEEK RESULTS

DAY ONE: July 11

GW CD (09) 09 - *P: Iwan Lombard (3).* **Zimbabwe (03) 16** - *T: Peter Davis. C: Matthew McNab (1). P: McNab (3).*

GW (03) 36 - *T: Cameron Huffke, Chadd Adams, De-Ann Ackermann, Gladwin Nieuwenhuizen, Jody Schmidt. C: Huffke (4). P: Huffke.* **Namibia (35) 54** - *T: Andre Rademeyer, Andre van der Berg, Chad Plato, Darius van Solms, Marco Beukes, Oderick Mouton, Rudi Pretorius. C: Palto (3), Denzo Bruwer (2). P: Plato (2), Bruwer.*

Griffons (12) 29 - *T: Gift Dlamini, Jason Roux, Kyle Els, Truimp Boloyi. C: Andrew Kota (3). P: Kota.* **Pumas (16) 31** - *T: Boet Heyl, JC Pretorius, Wandile Shabangu. C: Stephan van der Bank (2). P: Van der Bank (4).*

WP (21) 41 - *T: Gianni Lombard, Damian Willemse (2 each), Daniel Jooste, Khanya Ncusane. C: Lombard (4). P: Lombard.* **Boland (17) 20** - *T: Albert Liebenberg, Shandrey Pietersen. C: Anton du Toit (2). P: du Toit (2).*

KZN (18) 36 - *T: Dylan Richardson, Luke Crowshaw, Maartin Holtzhausen, Mayibongwe Maduna, Tonderai Ndudzo. C: Cameron Ritchie. P: Holtzhausen (3).* **EP (03) 24** - *T: Aya Oliphant, Keagan Tait, Sicelo Tole. C: Riaan van Rensburg (3). P: Van Rensburg.*

DAY TWO: July 12

Limpopo BB (19) 38 - *T: Danny Mokhoabane (2), Janne Jordaan, Nyiko Makamu, Stefan Nel, Tyrone Thompson. C: Masedi Manamela, Pieter Kruger (2 each). P: Pretorius.* **Border CD (03) 03** - *P: Litha Nkula.*

EP CD (12) 24 - *T: Athenkosi Halom, Keanen Murray, Matt More, Sazi Sandi. C: Izak Conradie, Vaughen Isaacs.* **Leopards (18) 26** - *T: Gerhard Fourie, Nathan Jordan, Zimosa Nokama. C: Fourie. P: Fourie (3).*

Free State (23) 68 - *T: Keaton Swart, Rikus Dreyer (2 each), David Kriel, Gomolemo Matlho, Janco van Heyningen, Jauan Venter, Kagiso Marumo, Rallston Dreyer, Thian du Randt. C: Mario Vieira (5). P: Pretorius.* **Valke (26) 26** - *T: Ruben Beytell (2), Ginter Smuts, Tumiso Linake. C: Smuts (3).*

SWD (12) 26 - *T: Andre Posthumus, Darren Adonis, Lance Lamprecht, Wilhelm van Heerden.*

C: Adonis (3). **Golden Lions (40) 59** - *T: Wandisile Simelane (3), Tyrone Green (2), Tinus Combrinck, Mark Snyman, Chuiner van Rooyen, Asenathi Ntlabakanye. C: Simelane (7).*

Blue Bulls (19) 48 - *T: Louis van der Schyff (2), Abner van Reenen, Lincoln Daniels, Phillip Krause, Ruan de Swardt, Ryno Pieterse. C: De Swardt (5). P: De Swardt.* **Border (03) 15** - *T: James Bruce, Libongo Yapi. C: Siphosethu Dlongodlongo. P: Dlongodlongo.*

DAY THREE: July 13

Griffons (24) 34 - *T: Gift Dlamini (2), Andrew Kota, Duke Jantjies, Lubabalo Mteyise, Michael Janse van Rensburg. C: Kola (2).* **GW CD (13) 32** - *T: Byron Coetzee, Daniel Oberholzer. C: Iwan Lombard (2). P: Lombard (6).*

GW (26) 78 - *T: Cameron Huffke (4), Ashwill Botha, De An Ackermann, Rian Kotze (2 each), Anton van Romburgh, Gladwin Nieuwenhuizen. C: Huffke (9).* **Zimbabwe (00) 05** - *T: Matthew McNab.*

Boland (07) 33 - *T: Michael Goodall (2), Caleb Dingaan, James Mao-Cheia, Wayne Wilschut. C: Anton du Toit (4).* **EP (30) 37** - *T: Sicelo Tole (2), Ayabonga Matroos, Le-Kleu Stokes, Lubabalo Dobela. C: Riaan van Rensburg (3). P: Van rensburg (2).*

Pumas (20) 51 - *T: Dewald Maritz, Jaco Joubert (2 each), JC Pretorius, Percy Mkhwanazi, Wandile Shabangu. C: Riekert Barnard (5). P: Barnard (2).* **Namibia (10) 15** - *T: Andre van der Berg, Chad Plato. C: Gerswin Mouton. P: Mouton.*

WP (43) 60 - *T: Liam Larkan, Muller du Plessis (2 each), Salmaan Moerat, Muller Uys, Deon Carstens, Manuel Rass, Mike Mavovana. C: Gianni Lombard (6). P: Lombard.* **KZN (00) 05** - *T: Maartin Holtzhausen.*

DAY FOUR: July 14

EP CD (26) 62 - *T: Chulu Chutu, Jonathan Crankshaw (2 each), Athenkosi Halom, Ewan Pieters, Lourens Oosthuizen, Lutho Nomoyi, Sibabalwe Mzanywa. C: Vaughen Isaacs (6), Crankshaw. P: Isaacs.* **Border CD (00) 05** - *T: Bonisile Mapongwane.*

Valke (17) 43 - *T: Ruben Beytell (2), Martin Steyn, Lee-Irwin Andries, Ginter Smuts, Donovan Stry-*

dom. C: Smuts (5). P: Smuts. Limpopo **BB (17) 24** - T: *Wernich Kachelhoffer, Tyrone Thompson, Stefan Engelbrecht, Noko Malatji. C: Kachelhoffer (2).*
Border (12) 19 - T: *David Coetzer, Hanru Sirgel, Hennie Otto. C: Coetzer (2).* **SWD (14) 21** - T: *Damian Bonaparte, Darren Adonis, Lithemba Mpoli. C: Zinedene Booysen (3).*
Free State (44) 86 - T: *David Kriel (3), Rikus Pretorius, Rewan Kruger (2 each), Aya Ntaba, Dian Schoonees, Gideon Beukes, Janco van Heyningen, Juan Venter, Mfez Moyo. C: Mario Vieira (9). P: Vieira.* **Leopards (00) 14** - T: *Andre Kock, Riaan van der Spuy. C: Gerhard Fourie (2).*
Blue Bulls (07) 14 - T: *Abner van Reenen, Marnus Potgieter. C: Ruan de Swardt (2).*
Golden Lions (20) 41 - T: *Wandisile Simelane (2), Tyrone Green, Mark Snyman, Chuiner van Rooyen. C: Simelane (5). P: Simelane (2).*

DAY FIVE: July 16
Zimbabwe (00) 03 - P: *Matthew McNab.*
Namibia (05) 34 - T: *Gerswin Mouton (3), Rudi Pretorius, Marco Beukes, Handre Klazinga. C: Mouton, Pretorius.*
Boland (19) 26 - T: *James Mao-Cheia, Igne Erasmus, Hannes van Zyl, Anton du Toit. C: Du Toit (2), Lloyd April.* **Border (26) 64** - T: *Sango Xamlashe (4), Mila Bomela (2), Libongo Yapi, Hanru Sirgel, David Coetzer, Aaron Brody. C: Coetzer (7).*
GW CD (14) 29 - T: *Zean Augustyn, Mpho Molaolwa, Johan Geldenhuys, Johannes Terblanche, Jacques Paige. C: Iwan Lombard (2).* **Border CD (03) 08** - T: *Khanya Sikrenya. P: Sikrenya.*
EP (12) 12 - T: *Riaan van Rensburg, Viaan Wolmarans. C: Van Rensburg.* **SWD (24) 64** - T: *Nicolus van Eeden (2), Zinedene Booysen, Wilhelm van Heerden, Sean Swart, Lance Lamprecht, Dian Bleuler, Damian Bonaparte, Bradley Kiewitz, Adriaan-Lee du Preez. C: Darren Adonis (5), Darryle Kameel (2).*
Limpopo BB (21) 35 - T: *Jan Coertze, Danny Mokhoabane (2 each), Stefan Engelbrecht. C: Wernich Kachelhoffer (5).* **EP (00) 05** - T: *Sazi Sandi.*
Blue Bulls (34) 74 - T: *Ruan de Swardt (3), Henk Pretorius, Emilio Adonis (2 each), Louis van der Schyff, Marnus Potgieter, Peter-John Steenkamp, Phillip Krause, Shaun Williams. C: De Swardt (7).* **Free State (08) 08** - T: *Mat-*

thew Wessels. P: Mario Vieira.
Griffons (05) 24 - T: *Marco Labuschagne, Jason Wagman, Hendrik van Staden, Dealin Jafta. C: Andrew Kota (2).* **Leopards (24) 36** - T: *Tiaan du Toit, Riaan van der Spuy, Marthinus de Villiers, Dane Booysen, Andre Fouche. C: Gerhard Fourie (4). P: Fourie.*
Pumas (13) 26 - T: *JC Pretorius, Jaco Joubert. C: Riekert Barnard (2). P: Barnard (4).* **KZN (12) 23** - T: *Gideon Lubbe (2), Angus Curtis. C: Sanele Nohamba. P: Maartin Holtzhausen (2).*
Valke (05) 12 - T: *Werner Fourie, Timothy van Dieman, Lee-Irwin Andries. C: Ginter Smuts, Andries.* **GW (21) 43** - T: *Willem du Plessis, Rian Schultz, Rian Kotze, Neil Coetzee, Dehan du Plessis, Cameron Huffke. C: Huffke (5). P: Huffke.*
WP (20) 27 - T: *Muller Uys, Manuel Rass, Khanya Ncusane. C: Gianni Lombard (3). P: Lombard (2).* **Golden Lions (10) 20** - T: *Tyrone Green, Tatenda Mujawo. C: Wandisile Simelane (2). P: Simelane (2).*

COCA-COLA UNDER-13 CRAVEN WEEK RESULTS

DAY ONE: July 04
Limpopo BB *(19)* 34. Border *(00)* 00.
Namibia *(07)* 19. KZN *(10)* 22.
GW *(17)* 25. Zimbabwe *(00)* 03.
Valke *(14)* 19. EP *(00)* 07.
Blue Bulls *(08)* 14. SWD *(00)* 12 .
Free State *(05)* 22. Golden Lions *(15)* 22.
Border CD *(00)* 00. Griffons *(28)* 45.
WP *(21)* 28. Pumas *(05)* 19.
Boalnd *(00)* 05. Leopards *(07)* 14.

DAY TWO: July 05
Zimbabwe *(07)* 12. Border CD *(03)* 06.
Namibia *(05)* 10. Border *(12)* 12.
EP *(15)* 27. Pumas *(07)* 12.
Griffons *(08)* 22. Boland *(08)* 29.
Leopards *(07)* 14. SWD *(18)* 21.
KZN *(05)* 10. GW *(00)* 05.
Blue Bulls *(05)* 05. Limpopo BB *(00)* 00.
WP *(00)* 05. Golden Lions *(03)* 03.
Valke *(13)* 16. Free State *(00)* 12.

DAY THREE: July 07

Border CD *(00)* 05. Namibia *(03)* 03.
GW *(18)* 35. Pumas *(12)* 36.
Border *(13)* 30. Zimbabwe *(00)* 07.
Griffons *(25)* 49. EP *(07)* 17.
Free State *(12)* 25. Leopards *(05)* 15.
Limpopo BB *(08)* 13. SWD *(12)* 17.
Golden Lions *(10)* 15. Boland *(10)* 10.
Valke *(07)* 14. KZN *(05)* 15.
WP *(08)* 11. Blue Bulls *(03)* 10.

DAY FOUR: July 08

EP *(24)* 48. Border CD *(00)* 00.
Namibia *(10)* 18. Zimbabwe *(07)* 14.
GW *(05)* 14. Border *(03)* 03.
Free State *(12)* 31. Griffons *(19)* 26.
Leopards *(07)* 07. Pumas *(14)* 14.
Valke *(05)* 20. Blue Bulls *(33)* 38.
Limpopo BB *(07)* 07. Boland *(07)* 07.
SWD *(05)* 23. Golden Lions *(14)* 14.
WP *(05)* 12. KZN *(05)* 05.

U16 GRANT KHOMO WEEK RESULTS

DAY ONE: July 04

Border CD *(00)* 00. Zimbabwe *(12)* 41.
WP XV *(05)* 13. Griffons *(06)* 12.
Valke *(05)* 24. Boland XV *(12)* 34.
Border *(06)* 11. Leopards *(19)* 38.
SWD *(08)* 20. Namibia *(00)* 00 .
EP *(03)* 10. GW *(10)* 13.
Golden Lions *(21)* 50. Free State *(10)* 15.
Blue Bulls *(33)* 62. Limpopo BB *(03)* 15.
KZN *(10)* 51. Pumas *(00)* 07.
WP *(05)* 12. Boland *(08)* 20.

DAY TWO: July 06

Border CD *(00)* 00. Limpopo BB *(15)* 46.
EP *(16)* 16. Griffons *(03)* 06.
Free State *(00)* 14. WP XV *(14)* 34.
Pumas *(22)* 32. Namibia *(00)* 07.
Valke *(10)* 20. Zimbabwe *(05)* 12.
WP *(15)* 29. GW *(00)* 07.
Leopards *(07)* 07. SWD *(17)* 39.
Boland XV *(00)* 00. Border *(18)* 42.
Golden Lions *(14)* 31. Blue Bulls *(25)* 35.
Boland *(00)* 05. KZN *(03)* 10.

DAY THREE: July 08

Namibia *(00)* 05. Zimbabwe *(05)* 15.
Griffons *(31)* 57. Border CD *(00)* 05.
Limpopo BB *(05)* 33. Valke *(17)* 17.
WP *(14)* 45. EP *(08)* 08.
Boland XV *(03)* 16. Free State *(12)* 26.
Pumas *(07)* 33. Leopards *(07)* 14.
Boland *(17)* 31. Border *(05)* 10.
Golden Lions *(19)* 34. SWD *(18)* 25.
WP XV *(10)* 25. GW *(05)* 19.
KZN *(10)* 20. Blue Bulls *(13)* 23.

U18 ACADEMY WEEK RESULTS

DAY ONE: July 11

Blue Valke *(00)* 08. SA LSEN *(00)* 15.
Griffons CD *(05)* 19. EP CD *(03)* 15.
Border *(14)* 28. GW CD *(06)* 13.
Golden Lions *(22)* 30. Pumas *(06)* 11.
KZN *(21)* 47. Griffons *(24)* 44 .
WP *(21)* 47. SWD *(00)* 00.

DAY TWO: July 12

Red Valke *(03)* 15. Namibia *(24)* 34.
KZN CD *(28)* 63. GW *(16)* 35.
Pumas CD *(10)* 46. Border CD *(07)* 07.
Limpopo BB *(17)* 31. Leopards *(18)* 53.
Blue Bulls *(31)* 57. EP *(05)* 15.
Free State *(00)* 14. Boland *(06)* 20.

DAY THREE: July 13

EP CD *(08)* 34. SWD *(00)* 30.
Blue Valke *(24)* 36. GW CD *(12)* 24.
Griffons *(05)* 17. Pumas *(19)* 41.
WP *(28)* 31. Golden Lions *(03)* 29.
KZN *(12)* 40. Border *(18)* 25.
Griffons CD *(00)* 26. SA LSEN *(21)* 38.

DAY FOUR: July 14

Limpopo BB *(14)* 21. Free State *(29)* 62.
Border CD *(03)* 43. GW *(19)* 43.
KZN CD *(20)* 32. Pumas CD *(10)* 27.
Blue Bulls *(41)* 77. Leopards *(07)* 07.
EP *(10)* 21. Red Valke *(07)* 21.
Boland *(16)* 37. Namibia *(17)* 28.

Christoff Brendel of Western Province receives the Man of the match award from former SA Rugby President Oregan Hoskins during day 5 of the 2016 U18 Coca-Cola Academy Week at Kearsney College in Durban.

DAY FIVE: July 16

Pumas *(00)* 17. SA LSEN *(08)* 15.
Border *(10)* 10. SWD *(07)* 24.
GW CD *(12)* 24. Border CD *(07)* 07.
Free State *(23)* 44. KZN CD *(10)* 10.
Griffons *(21)* 36. Leopards *(14)* 26.
Griffons CD *(00)*. Limpopo BB *(36)* 60.

Pumas *(03)* 03. Boland *(27)* 39.
Red Valke *(12)* 12. GW *(12)* 34.
Blue Valke *(03)* 13. EP CD *(00)* 18.
Golden Lions *(08)* 29. KZN *(17)* 22.
Namibia *(00)* 15. EP *(10)* 17.
WP *(03)* 23. Blue Bulls *(03)* 12.

BLUE BULLS U/18

No.	Name	School	Town	ID Number	Weight	Height (m)
1	Cabous Eloff	AHS	Pretoria	9807305209081	124	1.93
2	Schalk Erasmus	AHS	Pretoria	9804165138088	103	1.83
3	Mornay Smith	Southdowns College	Centurion	9801305049084	109	1.81
4	Peter Steenkamp	Eldoraigne HS	Centurion	9801035107087	100	1.95
5	Henk Pretorius	AHS	Pretoria	9805225030082	98	1.90
6	Regardt du Plessis	AHS	Pretoria	9802125015081	96	1.84
7	Phillip Krause	Garsfontein HS	Pretoria	9802195031083	101	1.87
8	Luke Fortuin	Garsfontein HS	Pretoria	9801175122086	101	1.90
9	Shawn Williams	Garsfontein HS	Pretoria	9804135025084	70	1.69
10	Ruan de Swart	AHS	Pretoria	9801215050081	76	1.79
11	Hluma Zondani	Southdowns College	Centurion	9806145201084	85	1.78
12	Louritz van der Schyff	AHS	Pretoria	9805205116083	94	1.88
13	Marnus Potgieter	AHS	Pretoria	9906205053084	86	1.87
14	Emilio Adonis	Garsfontein HS	Pretoria	9802045160082	76	1.79
15	Abner van Reenen	Centurion HS	Centurion	9807305017088	86	1.85
16	Carl Wijburg	Waterkloof HS	Pretoria	9811115084080	94	1.76
17	Wernich Barnard	AHS	Pretoria	9810265258080	118	1.88
18	Arno van Wyk	Garsfontein HS	Pretoria	9806085077080	104	1.80
19	Ryno Pieterse	Garsfontein HS	Pretoria	9808065055086	106	1.96
20	Asipesona Nonyukela	Garsfontein HS	Pretoria	9810125419088	98	1.86
21	Calderon Levens	Garsfontein HS	Pretoria	9803115014084	68	1.80
22	Lincoln Daniels	Garsfontein HS	Pretoria	9803035185089	86	1.81
23	Austin Davids	AHS	Pretoria	9806305131089	74	1.78
24	Thandolwethu Kambule	St Albans College	Pretoria	9808055236084	108	1.81
25	Barry Viljoen	Menlo Park HS	Pretoria	9909225099087	112	1.86
26	Xabiso Mtumtum	Pretoria THS	Pretoria	9808115226083	95	1.78

TEAM MANAGER: Ofentse Moeng **COACHES:** Piet van Wyk, Jan Mollentze, Andre Labuschagne.

BOLAND U/18

No.	Name	School	Town	ID Number	Weight	Height (m)
1	Kayden Kiewit	Hugenote HS	Wellington	9808045069082	116	1.88
2	Niel Burger	Swartland HS	Malmesbury	9801195153087	90	1.70
3	Cohen Kiewit	Hugenote HS	Wellington	9808045070080	118	1.91
4	Stiaan Basson	Vredendal HS	Vredendal	9808255202084	96	1.96
5	Albert Liebenberg	Drostdy THS	Worcester	9808045248082	100	1.98
6	Michael Goodall	Hugenote HS	Wellington	9903305130086	90	1.83
7	Charl Schoeman	Worcester Gymnasium	Worcester	9803185241088	88	1.89
8	Charlie Gerber	Swartland HS	Malmesbury	9812295118086	110	1.90
9	Rick Jordaan	Klein Nederburg SS	Paarl	9810235114082	73	1.69
10	Lloyd April	Hermanus HS	Hermanus	9906235264081	82	1.85
11	Caleb Dingaan	Weston SS	Vredenburg	9906295454085	79	1.89
12	Anton du Toit	Swartland HS	Malmesbury	9803135088084	97	1.95
13	Berto le Roux	Drostdy THS	Worcester	9902035124088	84	1.84
14	Bradley van Turha	Drostdy THS	Worcester	9906205255085	70	1.76
15	James Cheia	Hermanus HS	Hermanus	9801105189080	72	1.80
16	Henry Hagen	Vredendal HS	Vredendal	9806235107084	98	1.80
17	Igné Erasmus	Charlie Hofmeyr HS	Ceres	9807205048084	123	1.84
18	Gerrit Bester	Dirkie Uys HS	Moorreesburg	9805185294082	125	1.91
19	Jan-Ernst Terblanche	Swartland HS	Malmesbury	9805075094089	98	1.93
20	Bronlee Mouries	Drostdy THS	Worcester	9811205041081	102	1.89
21	Hanreco van Zyl	Stellenbosch HS	Stellenbosch		65	1.76
22	Keenan Williams	New Orleans SS	Paarl	9803065102087	69	1.69
23	Shandrey Pietersen	Bergrivier HS	Wellington	9808275172085	73	1.73
24	Jevan August	Weltevrede SS	Wellington	9905025206088	84	1.85
25	Wayne Wilschut			8606125128088		

TEAM MANAGER: Martin Dyason **COACH:** Athol Ontong, J.P. van Rhyn.

BORDER COUNTRY DISTRICTS U/18

No.	Name	School	Town	ID Number	Weight	Height (m)
1	Sixolile Mapoloba	Elliot HS	Ellioit	9910135474089	103	1.70
2	Sonwabise Batyi	Elliot HS	Ellioit	9811155676084	85	1.68
3	Liyasa Kauleza	Thomas Ntaba SSS	Elundini	9803165740083	98	1.78
4	Sinovuyo Bali	Indwe HS	Indwe	9812105213085	80	1.84
5	Mihlali Stamper	Steve Tshwete HS		9805075289085	105	1.92
6	Likhona Simoyi	Khanyisa HS	Mthatha	9903106355080	75	1.79
7	Pumezo Kanzi	Umtata HS	Mthatha	9809245098087	87	1.76
8	Siviwe Ngqono	Umtata HS	Mthatha	9804105132084	79	1.87
9	Willson Mapongwana	Thomas Ntaba SSS	Elundini	9806165516080	70	1.76
10	Yanga Mcaphukana	Thomas Ntaba SSS	Elundini	9904096013085	75	1.70
11	Kwaziwe Sigaqa	Umtata HS	Mthatha	9807175256089	83	1.76
12	Kwanele Lunika	St Johns College	Mthatha	9803135883088	85	1.80
13	Gacula Poswa	Aliwal North HS	Aliwal North	9912285024086	93	1.67
14	Siphosoxolo Dlongodlongo	Indwe HS	Indwe	9801265495087	70	1.75
15	Litha Nkula	Elliot HS	Ellioit	9806135584085	76	1.86
16	Sange Gulwa	St John's College	Mthatha	9901165610080	80	1.60
17	Ayabonga Mntonintshi	Umtata HS	Mthatha	9909156224084	116	1.94
18	Gerhard Pretorious	Ugie HS	Ugie	9808125088085	112	1.80
19	Sinethemba Stephen	Umtata HS	Mthatha	9902145564082	92	1.87
20	Athenkosi Mabandla	Umtata HS	Mthatha	9812045457081	90	1.83
21	Khanya Sikrenya	Khanyisa HS	Mthatha	9812175302081	72	1.80
22	Tabiso Stenge	Umtata HS	Mthatha	9804215705084	74	1.70
23	Luyolo Gwarube	St Christophers PS	King William's Town	9801295379087	75	1.75

TEAM MANAGERS: Matthews Nani **COACHES:** Sizwe Sodinga, Mpumzi Ndamase.

BORDER U/18

No.	Name	School	Town	ID Number	Weight	Height (m)
1	Leon Lyons	Selborne College	East London	9812025118083	105	1.87
2	Gareth Heidtmann	Queen's College	Queenstown	9810075331085	118	1.87
3	Alulutho Tshakweni	Hudson Park HS	East London	9809265053087	101	1.76
4	Aaron Brody	Queen's College	Queenstown	9812285175088	104	1.97
5	Tristan Waller	Queen's College	Queenstown	9801275048082	97	1.90
6	Cameron Cato	Queen's College	Queenstown	9803085074084	96	1.87
7	Libongo Yapi	Port Rex THS	East London	9802205504087	90	1.80
8	Hanru Sirgel	Grens HS	East London	9805085092081	94	1.88
9	James Bruce	Selborne College	East London	9808135091087	76	1.76
10	Siphosethu Dlongodlongo	Dale College	King William's Town	9801265493082	70	1.72
11	Nathan Church	Grens HS	East London	9803125141083	83	1.82
12	Saida Xamlashe (c)	Selborne College	East London	9810225916082	84	1.76
13	Sibulele Mbana	Dale College	King William's Town	9811095252087	73	1.86
14	Josh Amstrong	Selborne College	East London	9812305082082	86	1.84
15	Fassi Fassi	Dale College	King William's Town	9801235015080	73	1.89
16	Mila Bomela	Selborne College	East London	9803176333084	84	1.79
17	Sande Msengana	Selborne College	East London	9803025182088	110	1.80
18	Hennie Otto	Dale College	King William's Town	9802115247082	106	1.87
19	Darren Lemmer	Selborne College	East London	9801075213084	91	1.83
20	Siyamthanda Jwacu	Queen's College	Queenstown	9804065040087	98	1.88
21	Hlumelo Ndudula	Hudson Park HS	East London	9902106040080	73	1.73
22	David Coetzer	Selborne College	East London	9902055711087	78	1.74
23	Christopher Hollis	Queen's College	Queenstown	9806245506085	97	1.90

TEAM MANAGER: Mtobeli Kweliti. **COACHES:** Anton Jacobs, Mark Farnham. **PERMANENT REPRESENTATIVE:** Mtobeli Kweliti.

EASTERN PROVINCE COUNTRY DISTRICTS U/18

No.	Name	School	Town	ID Number	Weight	Height (m)
1	Thembinkosi Mangwana	Kingswood College	Kingswood	9805115389085	122	1.80
2	Johan Maartens	Burgersdorp HS	Burgersdorp	9801105160081	80	1.80
3	Sazi Sandi	St Andrews College	Grahamstown	9808115223080	115	1.81
4	Keanen Murray	Marlow AHS	Cradock	9811155177083	95	1.98
5	Stephanus Mentz	Marlow AHS	Cradock	9807185220083	94	1.94
6	Lourens Oosthuizen	Marlow AHS	Cradock	9810125255086	92	1.85
7	Johannes Odendaal	Aliwal North HS	Aliwal North	9804035278080	97	1.83
8	Olie Losaba	Kingswood College	Kingswood	9809295038082	92	1.87
9	J.C. Conradie	Volkskool HS	Graaff-Reinet	9805175215089	75	1.75
10	Vaughen Isaacs	Marlow AHS	Cradock	9903295327080	78	1.75
11	Tim Bloem	St Andrews College	Grahamstown	9801165014087	77	1.70
12	Matt More	St Andrews College	Grahamstown	9811255107089	80	1.72
13	Lutho Nomoyi	Kingswood College	Kingswood	9801215432081	71	1.67
14	Athi Halom	Kingswood College	Kingswood	9807205120081	78	1.71
15	Chulu Chutu	Union HS	Graaff-Reinet	9803315826089	75	1.70
16	Bonginkosi Ziya	Union HS	Graaff-Reinet	9802035527084	82	1.72
17	Francu Dreyer	Volkskool HS	Graaff-Reinet	9810205211082	123	1.83
18	Ewan Pieters	Kingswood College	Kingswood	9809075256086	120	1.84
19	Hentus Botha	Volkskool HS	Graaff-Reinet	9812155132086	90	1.84
20	Jay-Jay Human	Marlow AHS	Cradock	9904215511084	82	1.83
21	Jonathan Crankshaw	Union HS	Graaff-Reinet	9801015226089	82	1.85
22	Reynier Meyer	Burgersdorp HS	Burgersdorp	9807215022087	76	1.83
23	Sibabalwe Mzanywa	Kingswood College	Kingswood	9807225412088	86	1.74

TEAM MANAGER: Jonathan Plaatjies. **COACHES:** Damien Arends, Stegmann van Zyl, Cornelius Schreuder.

EASTERN PROVINCE U/18

No.	Name	School	Town	ID Number	Weight	Height (m)
1	Stefan van der Poel	Framesby HS	Port Elizabeth	9806085237080	100	1.80
2	Viaan Wolmarans	Framesby HS	Port Elizabeth	9908175056089	86	1.76
3	Etienne Janeke	Nico Malan HS	Humansdorp	9811175979088	118	1.95
4	Ruben le Roux	Framesby HS	Port Elizabeth	9803025224088	98	1.90
5	William Duckitt	Framesby HS	Port Elizabeth	9808125050085	88	1.86
6	Zane Barnard	Brandwag HS	Uitenhage	9904015158086	90	1.85
7	Tersius Groenewald	Grey HS	Port Elizabeth	9804075277083	86	1.87
8	Khwezi Mafu	Grey HS	Port Elizabeth	9803295260085	100	1.90
9	Louis Strydom	Framesby HS	Port Elizabeth	9806245142089	67	1.67
10	Keagan Tait	Framesby HS	Port Elizabeth	9809045046088	80	1.85
11	Ayabonga Matroos	Grey HS	Port Elizabeth	9908305594082	73	1.70
12	Sicelo Tole	Muir College	Uitenhage	9802095082087	90	1.80
13	Ayabonga Oliphant	Grey HS	Port Elizabeth	9803035265089	80	1.76
14	Sihle Njezula	Grey HS	Port Elizabeth	9806236089083	88	1.83
15	Riaan van Rensburg	Framesby HS	Port Elizabeth	9806225075085	83	1.88
16	Ruan Jonker	Grey HS	Port Elizabeth	9904062154087	96	1.74
17	Roelof Roodt	Framesby HS	Port Elizabeth	9804065097087	130	1.95
18	Le-Kleu Stokes	Brandwag HS	Uitenhage	9909165105084	118	1.88
19	Donavan Stevens	Brandwag HS	Uitenhage	9808095158082	108	1.98
20	Gregan Glover	Nico Malan HS	Humansdorp	9911195673081	72	1.83
21	Lubabalo Dobela	Grey HS	Port Elizabeth	9805025012082	80	1.74
22	Zukhanye Mafunda	Grey HS	Port Elizabeth	9805185205088	75	1.74
23	Waqar Solaan	Grey HS	Port Elizabeth	9902225557089	85	1.76

TEAM MANAGER: Gordon Noland. **COACHES:** Derik Olivier, Sebastian Hilpert, Jaco Janse van Rensburg.

FREE STATE U/18

No.	Name	School	Town	ID Number	Weight	Height (m)
1	Tristan Spies	Grey College	Bloemfontein	9801265015083	105	1.84
2	Matthew Wessels	Grey College	Bloemfontein	9802075022087	100	1.80
3	Gideon Beukes	Grey College	Bloemfontein	9809235022089	112	1.78
4	Jaco van Tonder	Grey College	Bloemfontein	9803036342085	112	1.96
5	Kagiso Marumo	Louis Botha THS	Bloemfontein	9801215656085	90	1.90
6	Teboho Rampai	Louis Botha THS	Bloemfontein	9910315235086	75	1.76
7	Juan Venter	Grey College	Bloemfontein	9808015164087	94	1.87
8	Dian Schoonees	Grey College	Bloemfontein	9804145375081	96	1.87
9	Rewan Kruger	Grey College	Bloemfontein	9803205134081	77	1.78
10	Mario Vieira	Grey College	Bloemfontein	9805095211085	81	1.75
11	Gomolemo Matlho	Louis Botha THS	Bloemfontein	9802195216080	78	1.80
12	Rikus Pretorius	Grey College	Bloemfontein	9901155043086	100	1.90
13	Janco van Heyningen	Grey College	Bloemfontein	9903315049086	78	1.79
14	Rallston Dreyer	Louis Botha THS	Bloemfontein	9803165287085	84	1.79
15	David Kriel	Grey College	Bloemfontein	9902155217084	84	1.92
16	Thian du Randt	Grey College	Bloemfontein	9801125226086	99	1.80
17	Edward Davids	Fichardt Park HS	Bloemfontein	9802045379088	101	1.75
18	Naude Naude	Grey College	Bloemfontein	9901015284086	94	1.75
19	Brentley Marais	Louis Botha THS	Bloemfontein	9803025207083	90	1.82
20	Ayabonga Ntaba	Louis Botha THS	Bloemfontein	9805045823088	90	1.80
21	Keaton Swart	Louis Botha THS	Bloemfontein	9902275181087	69	1.72
22	Mfezeko Moyo	Louis Botha THS	Bloemfontein	9808095689086	76	1.79
23	Kyle Kermis	Louis Botha THS	Bloemfontein	9804295153080	77	1.77
24	W.J. Kruger	Grey College	Bloemfontein	9804055021089	96	1.77
25	RuHann Greyling	Grey College	Bloemfontein	9905285666088	92	1.77
26	Willem Marais	Grey College	Bloemfontein	9901185168085	98	1.84

TEAM MANAGER: Jimmy Jimlongwe **COACHES:** Wessels du Plessis, Corné Erasmus.

GOLDEN LIONS U/18

No.	Name	School	Town	ID Number	Weight	Height (m)
1	Nathan McBeth	Monument HS	Krugersdorp	9806085021088	108	1.89
2	P.J. Botha (c)	Monument HS	Krugersdorp	9801205019088	100	1.82
3	Asenathi Ntlabakanye	St Stithians	Randburg	9904156103081	120	1.88
4	Toelie Havenga	Monument HS	Krugersdorp	9807055122088	98	1.96
5	Darrien landsberg	Northcliff HS	Johannesburg	9807266079085	97	1.98
6	Mark Snyman	Helpmekaar College	Johannesburg	9903125189080	88	1.79
7	Tiaan Scholtz	Helpmekaar College	Johannesburg	9805095074087	86	1.80
8	P.J. Jacobs	Monument HS	Krugersdorp	9910125077082	100	1.86
9	Tinus Combrinck	Monument HS	Krugersdorp	9902095058085	77	1.81
10	Tyrone Green	Jeppe BHS	Johannesburg	9803055064081	83	1.84
11	Maxwill van Louw	Florida HS	Florida	9903165157088	73	1.75
12	M.J. Pleser	Monument HS	Krugersdorp	9807285023080	100	1.84
13	Wandisile Simelane	Jeppe BHS	Johannesburg	9803215304088	87	1.78
14	David Cary	Helpmekaar College	Johannesburg	9909185045088	75	1.73
15	Chuiner vab Rooyen	Helpmekaar College	Johannesburg	9806025068082	81	1.78
16	Lehlogonolo Naka	Jeppe BHS	Johannesburg	9804265449088	100	1.80
17	Mpilo mabuza	King Edward VII	Johannesburg	9805205093084	100	1.80
18	Keagan Glade	King Edward VII	Johannesburg	9905125020082	109	1.83
19	Christen van Niekerk	Monument HS	Krugersdorp	9905275150085	98	1.90
20	Enrico Liut	Florida HS	Florida	9808125107083	92	1.88
21	Kalvin Mills	King Edward VII	Johannesburg	9807105147085	82	1.81
22	Tatenda Mujawo	St Benedict's College	Bedfordview		85	1.80
23	Kennedy Mepku	King Edward VII	Johannesburg	9902116309269	75	1.81
24	Kgosi-Etsile Mpete	St Benedict's College	Bedfordview	9806045159085	103	1.84
25	Dameon Venter	Helpmekaar College	Johannesburg	9912105159088	97	1.83

TEAM MANAGER: Adriaan van Blerk. **COACHES:** Carl Spilhaus, Stefan Lourens, Nkosi Mzwakue.

GRIFFONS U/18

No.	Name	School	Town	ID Number	Weight	Height (m)
1	Winrich Kennedy	Hentie Cilliers HS	Virginia	9805285146083	101	1.88
2	Reinard van der Vyver	Wessel Marree HS	Odendaalsrus	9807235109088	95	1.83
3	Francois Klopper	Voortrekker HS	Bethlehem	9909075120082	110	1.87
4	D.J. Hatting	Afrikaanse HS	Kroonstad	9909235027086	91	1.90
5	Pieter van der Westhuizen	Welkom Gymnasium	Welkom	9805305012083	91	1.94
6	Kyle Els	Welkom Gymnasium	Welkom	9809105059088	95	1.79
7	Jan Scheepers	Welkom Gymnasium	Welkom	9803205185083	95	1.95
8	Gift Dlamini	Welkom Gymnasium	Welkom	9809075349089	80	1.87
9	Richman Gora	Welkom Gymnasium	Welkom	9802175465087	75	1.63
10	Dealine Jafta	Hentie Cilliers HS	Virginia	9910195359089	70	1.70
11	Wian van Staden	Welkom Gymnasium	Welkom	9803255039081	75	1.76
12	Jason Wagman	Welkom Gymnasium	Welkom	9907195292088	73	1.60
13	Lubabalo Mtyise	Welkom Gymnasium	Welkom	9803125172088	78	1.79
14	Qamani Kota	Welkom Gymnasium	Welkom	9904205847084	76	1.70
15	Marco Labuschagne	Voortrekker HS	Bethlehem	9801305026082	90	1.86
16	Duke Jantjies	Welkom Gymnasium	Welkom	9810035171083	90	1.72
17	Ruben Breedt	Goudveld HS	Welkom	9806295026083	112	1.79
18	J.W. Meads	Witteberg HS	Bethlehem	9905255030083	115	1.88
19	Dian de Beer	Afrikaanse HS	Kroonstad	9810225130080	77	1.84
20	Michael Janse van Rensburg	Voortrekker HS	Bethlehem	9808095011083	90	1.85
21	Jason Roux	Witteberg HS	Bethlehem	9807155307084	80	1.74
22	Truimp Boloyi	Goudveld HS	Welkom	9901065239089	77	1.82
23	David Eyssen	Welkom Gymnasium	Welkom	9801055088084	70	1.78

TEAM MANAGER: D.C. Van Rheede. **COACHES:** Roean Bezuidenhout.

GRIQUAS COUNTRY DISTRICTS U/18

No.	Name	School	Town	ID Number	Weight	Height (m)
1	Zean Augustyn	Duineveld HS	Upington		100	1.83
2	Taliesen Dick	Concordia HS	Concordia	9806245066080	86	1.72
3	Gerhard Gregory	Kalahari HS	Kuruman	9805095011089	120	1.81
4	Jovan Oosthuizen	Duineveld HS	Upington	9903255192086	87	1.84
5	Daniël Oberholzer	Duineveld HS	Upington	9804276086085	96	1.90
6	Ruan Visser	Duineveld HS	Upington	9807315360080	80	1.80
7	Johannes Terblanche	Upington HS	Upington	9811255249089	77	1.77
8	Johan Geldenhuys	Duineveld HS	Upington	9803065060087	95	1.86
9	Etienne le Roux	Duineveld HS	Upington	9804135013080	76	1.75
10	Iwan Lombard	Upington HS	Upington	9901015179088	75	1.85
11	Oscar van Wyk	Kathu HS	Kathu	9804095129082	73	1.80
12	Delron Speelman	Danielskuil HS	Danielskuil	9904075473086	74	1.87
13	Jacques Page	Duineveld HS	Upington	9804025292083	75	1.77
14	Sabastian Jobb	Duineveld HS	Upington	9905206357080	72	1.80
15	Mpho Molaolwa	Kalahari HS	Kuruman	9807215427088	60	1.79
16	Waylen Cloete	Upington HS	Upington	9908025319083	88	1.70
17	Wilfred Saunderson	Saul Damon HS	Upington	9803205335084	91	1.74
18	Heinrich Fourie	Kalahari HS	Kuruman	9801085254086	107	1.80
19	Hanlu Kotze	Upington HS	Upington	9812095392089	83	1.92
20	Warren Vantura	Concordia HS	Concordia	9804145048084	65	1.80
21	Lourens de Jager	Upington HS	Upington	9909165011084	63	1.65
22	Harry Bowers	Namakawaland HS	Springbok	9807295030083	80	1.73
23	Byron Coetzee	Upington HS	Upington	9808235095087	70	1.79

TEAM MANAGER: Leonardo de Wet. **COACHES:** Fillip Venter, J-Ell Slabbert.

GRIQUALAND WEST U/18

No.	Name	School	Town	ID Number	Weight	Height (m)
1	Andre du Toit	Diamantveld HS	Kimberley	9802265326082	105	1.84
2	Anton van Romburgh	Diamantveld HS	Kimberley	9803065145086	78	1.70
3	Byron du Plooy	Weslaan HS	Douglas	9801255237085	85	1.60
4	Henrich Klopper	Hartswater HS	Hartswater	9801025140080	93	1.95
5	Bernard Jansen (c)	Diamantveld HS	Kimberley	9805095046085	108	2.00
6	Japheth Muzaza	Northern Cape HS	Kimberley	9908115246089	74	1.79
7	Rian Kotze	Northern Cape HS	Kimberley	9806305089089	94	1.89
8	Jacques Ackerman	Diamantveld HS	Kimberley	9803035095080	90	1.90
9	Chadd Adams	Northern Cape HS	Kimberley	9901085035087	58	1.67
10	Willem du Plessis	Vaalharts HS	Jan Kempdorp	9801235362086	80	1.85
11	Cameron Hufke	Northern Cape HS	Kimberley	9805055310083	67	1.85
12	Ruan Schultz	Northern Cape HS	Kimberley	9810025326086	102	1.90
13	Dean Ackermann	Diamantveld HS	Kimberley	9804215242088	83	1.89
14	Gladwin Nieuwenhuizen	Northern Cape HS	Kimberley	9805205013082	65	1.74
15	Ashwill Botha	Diamantveld HS	Kimberley	9811015666085	80	1.80
16	Justin Murphy	Northern Cape HS	Kimberley	9906225338085	100	1.75
17	Willem Coetzer	Diamantveld HS	Kimberley	9904165025085	96	1.83
18	Edwill Speelman	Diamantveld HS	Kimberley	9910205284087	95	1.60
19	Jody Schmidt	Diamantveld HS	Kimberley	9802015156086	99	1.87
20	Neil Cetzee	Hartswater HS	Hartswater	9809075261086	82	1.84
21	Dehan du Plessis	Diamantveld HS	Kimberley	9902115038083	85	1.78
22	Chadwin November	Northern Cape HS	Kimberley	9803055338089	75	1.75
23	Edmund Brand	Northern Cape HS	Kimberley	9909085454083	75	1.83

TEAM MANAGER: Adam Botha. **COACHES:** Derrick de Clerk, W.J. Smith, Jaco Dames.

KWAZULU-NATAL U/18

No.	Name	School	Town	ID Number	Weight	Height (m)
1	Gugu Nelani	Northwood	Durban	9810235269084	115	1.85
2	Dylan Richardson	Kearsney College		9901155139082	102	1.84
3	Barnard van Rooyen	Glenwood BHS	Durban	9805155155081	116	1.83
4	John van der Mescht	Glenwood BHS	Durban	9905045036085	120	2.00
5	Jared Meyer	Kearsney College	Botha's Hill	9811235103083	97	1.92
6	Luke Crowshaw	Kearsney College	Botha's Hill	9811065218084	84	1.80
7	Phendulani Buthelezi	Durban HS	Durban	9905305318082	92	1.87
8	James Miller	Kearsney College	Botha's Hill	9811065080088	97	1.86
9	Sanele Nohamba	Durban HS	Durban	9901195134085	63	1.64
10	Angus Curtis	Hilton College	Hilton		80	1.78
11	Gideon Lubbe	Glenwood BHS	Durban	9809205154086	82	1.78
12	Seun Maduna	Glenwood BHS	Durban	9804065722080	84	1.75
13	Marthinus Holtzhausen	Glenwood BHS	Durban	9808265143088	82	1.75
14	Tonderai Ndudzo	Durban HS	Durban		77	1.71
15	Cham Zondeki	Durban HS	Durban	9901015348089	72	1.74
16	Fezokuhle Mbatha	Maritzburg College	Pietermaritzburg	9908026086087	100	1.80
17	Quintin Vorster	Glenwood BHS	Durban	9809165206082	103	1.86
18	Calvin Zandamela	Clifton HS	Durban	9803116368083	115	1.85
19	Dylan Weideman	Glenwood BHS	Durban	9801065053086	105	1.90
20	Austin Brummer	Glenwood BHS	Durban	9801195061082	86	1.81
21	Sibonakaliso Dubazane	Glenwood BHS	Durban	9801085217083	72	1.70
22	Cameron Ritchie	Kearsney College	Botha's Hill	9801105085080	80	1.83
23	Onke Jiba	Durban HS	Durban	9912215710087	72	1.67
25	Conan le Fleur	Glenwood BHS	Durban	9912135295084	92	1.72

TEAM MANAGER: Dean Moodley. **COACHES:** Rudi Dames, Roland Norris, Mike Vowles.

LEOPARDS U/18

No.	Name	School	Town	ID Number	Weight	Height (m)
1	Simbonile Mnyazana	Vaal Reefs THS	Orkney	9903095682080	95	1.74
2	Rudolf Hattingh	Rustenburg HS	Rustenburg	9803055101081	99	1.82
3	Marthinus de Villiers	Rustenburg HS	Rustenburg	9803185022082	104	1.78
4	Nathan Jordan	Rustenburg HS	Rustenburg	9805255083084	112	1.93
5	Sosikela Khuselo	Vaal Reefs THS	Orkney	9801105654083	90	1.81
6	Zimasa Nokama	Vaal Reefs THS	Orkney	9909206162086	86	1.76
7	Christopher Kemm	Rustenburg HS	Rustenburg	9808205220087	91	1.88
8	Tiaan du Toit (c)	Rustenburg HS	Rustenburg	9806175017087	92	1.85
9	Ethan Ballot	Rustenburg HS	Rustenburg	9801225096082	70	1.65
10	Andre Kock	Vryburg HS	Vryburg	9806085369081	83	1.82
11	Lionel George	Rustenburg THS	Rustenburg	9807155330086	79	1.75
12	Yamkela Nyembe	Vaal Reefs THS	Orkney	9809226227085	78	1.74
13	Rassie Breedt	Rustenburg HS	Rustenburg	9801015093083	80	1.75
14	G.J. Jansen van Rensburg	Potchefstroom Gymnasium	Potchefstroom	9808285055080	83	1.84
15	Gerhard Fourie	Rustenburg HS	Rustenburg	9804105165084	85	1.78
16	Stefanus Mare	Klerksdorp HS	Klerksdorp	9805045068080	94	1.8
17	Pieter Carroll	Lichtenburg HS	Lichtenburg	9803055074080	92	1.83
18	Graivian Smith	Lichtenburg HS	Lichtenburg	9912155172080	100	1.75
19	Andries Fouche	Rustenburg HS	Rustenburg	9911035053080	95	1.85
20	Sonwabile Mangaliso	Vaal Reefs THS	Orkney	9808215991081	74	1.68
21	Pierre van der Spuy	Rustenburg HS	Rustenburg	9804235085087	75	1.72
22	Joaquim de Jenga	Potchefstroom BHS	Potchefstroom	9901255289084	79	1.72
23	Dane Booysen	Wesvalia HS	Klerksdorp	9810855116086	68	1.72
24	Bradley Wood	Potchefstroof Gymnasium	Potchefstroom	9801145193084	95	1.78

TEAM MANAGER: Marco van Wyk. **COACHES:** Hannes Esterhuizen, Gary Middleton, Boikanyo Nkolobe.

LIMPOPO BLUE BULLS U/18

No.	Name	School	Town	ID Number	Weight	Height (m)
1	Itumeleng Mononyane	Ben Vorster HS	Tzaneen	9909225135089	95	1.83
2	Bernard Vermaak	Ben Vorster HS	Tzaneen	9904265042089	94	1.82
3	Barend Lombard	Ben Vorster HS	Tzaneen	9902045349089	117	1.88
4	Matthew Sekele	Warmbad HS	Bela-Bela	9804305373082	85	1.88
5	Welmar Pieterse	Ben Vorster HS	Tzaneen	9802125220087	94	1.93
6	Ruben Koekemoer	Ben Vorster HS	Tzaneen	9805285116086	84	1.72
7	Stefan Engelbrecht	Ben Vorster HS	Tzaneen	9805245086080	92	1.85
8	Tyron Thomson	Pietersburg HS	Polokwane	9804215172087	85	1.88
9	Eduan Smit	Ben Vorster HS	Tzaneen	9807145079082	76	1.79
10	Pieter Kruger	Pietersburg HS	Polokwane	9803235067087	86	1.95
11	Chrizaan Strauss	Frikkie Meyer HS	Thabazimbi	9801275296087	80	1.70
12	Muzi Nyakane	Ben Vorster HS	Tzaneen	9905295293089	84	1.83
13	Jan Coertze	Pietersburg HS	Polokwane	9812015035081	98	1.80
14	Masedi Manamela	Merensky HS	Tzaneen	9811255816085	87	1.89
15	Danny Mokhoabane	Ben Vorster HS	Tzaneen	9812135095080	75	1.78
16	Nyiko Makamu	Capricorn HS	Polokwane	9809105654086	102	1.71
17	Tshepo Masakale	Tom Naude THS	Polokwane	9909085697087	108	1.80
18	Jannie Jordaan	Ben Vorster HS	Tzaneen	9803105012080	100	1.84
19	Clifford Sekgobela	Merensky HS	Tzaneen	9807095188081	87	1.84
20	Zander Human	Pietersburg HS	Polokwane	9804165242088	85	1.79
21	Wernich Kachelhoffer	Curru Heuwelkruin	Polokwane	9809045312084	76	1.78
22	Noko Malatji	Merensky HS	Tzaneen	9906135615085	78	1.75
23	Stefan Nel	Curru Heuwelkruin	Polokwane	9805105211083	95	1.86

TEAM MANAGERS: Gerald Marks. **COACHES:** André Hay, Pieter Stopforth.

MPUMALANGA U/18

No.	Name	School	Town	ID Number	Weight	Height (m)
1	Morgan Naude	Nelspruit HS	Nelspruit	9808115028083	108	1.79
2	Ruben Cross	Middelburg THS	Middelburg	9810125200082	100	1.85
3	Dewald Maritz (c)	Nelspruit HS	Nelspruit	9801095089084	117	1.81
4	Vusi Mkhonza	Ermelo HS	Ermelo	9801195012085	80	1.93
5	K.P Kruger	Nelspruit HS	Nelspruit	9803035076080	105	2.01
6	Johannes Pretorius	Middelburg THS	Middelburg	9801295069084	85	1.85
7	Whandile Shabangu	Middelburg HS	Middelburg	9808305188085	60	1.69
8	Junior Schmidt	Nelspruit HS	Nelspruit	9808205073080	85	1.84
9	Jaco Joubert	Nelspruit HS	Nelspruit	9807175049088	62	1.63
10	Stephan van der Bank	Nelspruit HS	Nelspruit	9901275025088	84	1.84
11	Percy Mkwanazi	Piet Retief HS	Piet Retief	9807206087081	68	1.60
12	Riaaz Adebayo	Nelspruit HS	Nelspruit	9802045288081	82	1.78
13	Boet Heyl	Middelburg THS	Middelburg	9803055149080	87	1.82
14	Prince kabinde	Hoogenhout HS	Bethal	9912115254085	87	1.88
15	Ryan Cloete	Middelburg THS	Middelburg	9804275024087	81	1.81
16	S.P. Muller	Nelspruit HS	Nelspruit	9905115930084	79	1.77
17	Nathi Mthethwa	Piet Retief HS	Piet Retief	9810265451081	95	1.80
18	Hloni Mphuthi	Standerton HS	Standerton	9808205538082	110	1.79
19	Sibusiso Madonsela	Piet Retief HS	Piet Retief	9904245652080	82	1.97
20	Brandon Magudulela	Volksrust HS	Volksrust	9803095141089	80	1.96
21	Thabiso Mkwabane	Ligbron THS	Ermelo	9904075398085	81	1.75
22	Riekert Barnard	Middelburg THS	Middelburg	9903275019087	80	1.80
23	Julian Claasen	General Hertzog HS	eMalahleni	9809045093080	69	1.68
25	Donell Griffiths	Volksrust HS	Volksrust	9808295502089	92	1.76

TEAM MANAGER: Pieter de Waal. **COACHES:** Cobus van Dyk, Coene Nolte.

NAMIBIA U/18

No.	Name	School	Town	ID Number	Weight	Height (m)
1	Andre Rademeyer	Windhoek Afrikaanse PS	Windhoek	1998-06-24	100	1.82
2	Darius van Solms	Windhoek Gymnasium	Windhoek	1998-05-12	95	1.86
3	Jano Rieckert	Windhoek Gymnasium	Windhoek	1998-02-08	106	1.84
4	Armand Kotze	Windhoek Gymnasium	Windhoek	1998-01-16	88	1.92
5	Loandro Erasmus	Windhoek HS	Windhoek	1998-06-15	98	1.90
6	Prince Gaoseb	Windhoek HS	Windhoek	1998-07-07	98	1.86
7	Peter Diergaardt	Windhoek Gymnasium	Windhoek	1998-08-18	92	1.85
8	Oderich Mouton	Windhoek HS	Windhoek	1998-01-24	91	1.85
9	Handre Klazinga	Windhoek HS	Windhoek	1998-07-30	72	1.84
10	Denna Bruwer	Windhoek Gymnasium	Windhoek	1999-11-22	75	1.78
11	Marco Beukes	Windhoek HS	Windhoek	1999-05-19	70	1.75
12	C.C. Olivier	Windhoek Gymnasium	Windhoek	1998-03-13	87	1.86
13	Raggies Plato	Walvis Bay Private HS	Walvis Bay	1998-04-21	76	1.78
14	Rudi Pretorius	Windhoek Gymnasium	Windhoek	1998-02-15	65	1.75
15	Andre van der Berg	Windhoek HS	Windhoek	1998-01-23	83	1.80
16	J.T. Basson	Windhoek HS	Windhoek	1998-05-23	98	1.80
17	Patrick Schickerling	Walvis Bay Private HS	Walvis Bay	1998-10-16	115	1.83
18	Dries Jacobs	Windoek HS	Windhoek	1998-02-10	111	1.82
19	Dylan Farmer	Windhoek Gymnasium	Windhoek	1998-05-11	89	1.85
20	Wynand Breytenbach	Walvis Bay Private HS	Walvis Bay	1999-01-18	96	1.88
21	Tertius Lambrechts	Windhoek Gymnasium	Windhoek	1998-12-01	72	1.80
22	Gerswin Mouton	Windhoek Afrikaanse PS	Windhoek	1999-12-16	77	1.80
23	Nico Horn	Windhoek Gymnasium	Windhoek	1999-01-28	74	1.78
24	Marius van Niekerk	Elnatan PS	Stampriet	1998-08-07	95	1.76

TEAM MANAGERS: Jo-Anne Krohne. **COACHES:** Henry Kemp, Vincent Dreyer.

SOUTH WESTERN DISTRICTS U/18

No.	Name	School	Town	ID Number	Weight	Height (m)
1	Dian Bleuler	Oakdale AHS	Riversdale	9908055100080	106	1.84
2	Sean Swar	Outeniqua HS	George	9805145012087	98	1.86
3	Andre Posthumus	Oakdale AHS	Riversdale	9808205197087	116	1.78
4	Xhantilomzi Nokoyo	Oudtshoorn HS	Oudtshoorn	9807175341089	86	1.88
5	Dawid Meiring	Outeniqua HS	George	9901255007080	103	1.95
6	Byron Booysen	Outeniqua HS	George	9805055167087	80	1.78
7	Willem van Heerden	Oakdale AHS	Riversdale	9802045265089	93	1.81
8	Lance Lamprecht	Outeniqua HS	George	9810165215081	98	1.85
9	Zinedine Booysen	Oakdale AHS	Riversdale	9812125190081	67	1.68
10	Xavier Swartbooi	Oakdale AHS	Riversdale	9811105197082	65	1.69
11	Darryle Kameel	Outeniqua HS	George	9802065157083	66	1.72
12	Jay Cee Nel	Oakdale AHS	Riversdale	9901075166082	90	1.9
13	Nicolus van Eeden	Oakdale AHS	Riversdale	9801205053087	78	1.78
14	Alexander Wallace	Oakdale AHS	Riversdale	9802275167088	91	1.86
15	Darren Adonis	Oakdale AHS	Riversdale	9809135045081	73	1.7
16	Adriaan-Lee du Preez	PW Botha College	George	9801255098081	91	1.72
17	Nicolai Weber	Oakdale AHS	Riversdale	9908025240081	93	1.82
18	Franco Boshoff	Outeniqua HS	George	9811025482085	107	1.77
19	Jaco Smit	Oakdale AHS	Riversdale	9803205223082	84	1.88
20	Daniel Victor	Oakdale AHS	Riversdale	9803165138080	93	1.82
21	Lithembia Mpoli	Wittedrift HS	Plettenberg Bay	9803025449081	88	1.76
22	Damian Bonaparte	Outeniqua HS	George	9809025295085	90	1.88
23	Bradley Kiewitz	Outeniqua HS	George	9806295186085	76	1.71

TEAM MANAGER: Rodney Thomas. **COACHES:** Robert Seconds, Jerome Jantjies.

VALKE U/18

No.	Name	School	Town	ID Number	Weight	Height (m)
1	Marcus Nyirenda	Parys HS	Parys	9901125246082	75	1.70
2	Werner Fourie	Dr EG Jansen HS	Boksburg	9807285132089	93	1.75
3	Andre van der Merwe	Dr EG Jansen HS	Boksburg	9811025160087	96	1.75
4	Reinhardt Venter	Dr EG Jansen HS	Boksburg	9904015102084	100	1.91
5	Francois du Preez	Dr EG Jansen HS	Boksburg	9802035126085	106	1.93
6	Ruben Roodt	Dr EG Jansen HS	Boksburg	9902085154084	80	1.75
7	Timothy van Diemann	Benoni HS	Benoni	9802015166085	89	1.80
8	Rynard Theron	Die Anker HS	Brakpan	9806095048089	82	1.85
9	Ginter Smuts	Dr EG Jansen HS	Boksburg	9809075086087	82	1.73
10	Ruben Beytell	Dr EG Jansen HS	Boksburg	9909035020083	75	1.74
11	Webster Swanepoel	Vereeniging Gymnasium	Vereeniging	9802125524082	71	1.70
12	Dwayne Fourie	Dr EG Jansen HS	Boksburg	9910265264086	78	1.78
13	Lee-Irwin Andries	Dr EG Jansen HS	Boksburg	9901285611083	75	1.80
14	Romano Jonkerman	Dr EG Jansen HS	Boksburg	9805065410089	72	1.78
15	Martin Steyn	Brandwag HS	Benoni	9802265521088	74	1.87
16	Donovan Strydom	Volkskool HS	Heidelberg	9803185044086	88	1.75
17	Kuhle Malao	Birchleigh HS	Kempton Park	9801135546085	106	1.70
18	Rehann Baumann	Dr EG Jansen HS	Boksburg	9811185125086	107	1.92
19	Jean-Jireh Yamwimbi	Rhodesfields HS	Kempton Park		78	1.85
20	Eshile Mbilini	Birchleigh HS	Kempton Park	9812256112086	94	1.97
21	J.J. Keyser	Die Anker HS	Brakpan	9804195047085	83	1.82
22	Erzath Boesak	Hugenote HS	Springs	9802265709089	70	1.79
23	Tumiso Lenake	Springs BHS	Springs	9905075620089	83	1.85

TEAM MANAGER: Allan Arnold. **COACHES:** Schalk van der Merwe, Kwagga Loubser.

WESTERN PROVINCE U/18

No.	Name	School	Town	ID Number	Weight	Height (m)
1	Andre Booysen	Paarl Gymnasium	Paarl	9807045089082	104	1.86
2	Daniel Jooste	Paarl BHS	Paarl	9802215410085	101	1.87
3	Adam Neethling	Paarl BHS	Paarl	9802165185083	120	1.84
4	Ben-Jason Dixon	Paul Roos Gymnasium	Stellenbosch	9804295179085	106	1.95
5	Salmaan Moerat	Paarl BHS	Paarl	9803065094086	115	2.00
6	Charl Serdyn	Paarl BHS	Paarl	9803285132088	87	1.80
7	Muller Uys	Paarl Gymnasium	Paarl	9809025315081	107	1.91
8	Ngwekazi Ncusane	Paarl BHS	Paarl	9806225129080	88	1.89
9	Vusile Dlepu	SACS	Newlands	9911075612084	70	1.72
10	Damian Willemse	Paul Roos Gymnasium	Stellenbosch	9805075285083	80	1.80
11	Hillegard du Plessis	Paarl Gymnasium	Paarl	9906255386087	80	1.82
12	Henlo Marais	Boland AHS	Paarl	9801305156087	95	1.84
13	Manuel Rass	Paarl BHS	Paarl	9804195177080	82	1.74
14	Mike Mavovana	Rondebosch BHS	Rondebosch	9803315188084	70	1.69
15	Gianni Lombard	Paarl BHS	Paarl	9801225031089	78	1.78
16	Liam Larkan	SACS	Newlands	9810295475084	98	1.79
17	Reece Bezuidenhout	Paarl BHS	Paarl	9803105070088	108	1.80
18	Tristan Leitch	Paul Roos Gymnasium	Stellenbosch	9901285256087	113	1.86
19	Jessie Johnson	Paul Roos Gymnasium	Stellenbosch	9807305041088	103	1.90
20	Athi Magwala	Boland AHS	Paarl	9808285781081	98	1.72
21	Deon Carstens	Boland AHS	Paarl	9801275155085	84	1.75
22	Lubelo Scott	Diocesan College	Rondebosch	9805266234080	85	1.80
23	Quan Eymann	Brackenfell HS	Brackenfell	9904065218087	77	1.79
24	Wian van Niekerk	Paarl Gymnasium	Paarl	9802275011088	95	1.85

TEAM MANAGER: Frikkie Coetzer **COACHES:** Elmo Wolfaardt, Faizel Adam.

ZIMBABWE U/18

No.	Name	School	Town	ID Number	Weight	Height (m)
1	Samuel Garnett	St John's College	Harare	1998-03-13	95	1.81
2	Tinashe Chaza	Prince Edward	Harare	1998-08-27	89	1.65
3	Cleopas Kundiona	Falcon College	Bulawayo	1998-12-15	114	1.83
4	Tonderai Chiwambutsa	Prince Edward	Harare	1999-05-26	88	1.94
5	Daniel Hutchings	Peterhouse	Mashonaland	1998-03-23	90	1.86
6	Stuart Marriott-Dodington	Falcon College	Bulawayo	1998-09-09	86	1.83
7	Tichaona Hwangwa	Churchill HS	Harare	1998-02-07	75	1.70
8	Tendekai Chigwendere	Kyle College	Masvingo	1998-05-05	90	1.84
9	Connor MacMillan	Peterhouse	Mashonaland	1998-10-22	70	1.69
10	Benjamin Meredith	Falcon College	Bulawayo	1998-05-31	81	1.76
11	Tapiwa Marimira	Prince Edward	Harare	1999-01-15	71	1.80
12	Matthew MacNab	Falcon College	Bulawayo	1998-06-08	88	1.86
13	Rodney Sachiti	Peterhouse	Mashonaland	1998-07-09	86	1.83
14	Rangarirai Mariwa	Kyle College	Masvingo	1999-10-15	69	1.75
15	Martin Mongongo	Peterhouse	Mashonaland	1998-06-09	71	1.70
16	Marcus Nichole	Peterhouse	Mashonaland	1999-02-26	87	1.78
17	Simbarashe Maringa	Falcon College	Bulawayo	1998-09-21	95	1.76
18	Desmond Annandale	St John's College	Harare	1999-01-21	92	1.79
19	Liam Burnett	St John's College	Harare	1998-10-25	87	1.85
20	Godfrey Magaramombe	Kyle College	Masvingo	1998-08-01	89	1.89
21	Jeremy Munyeza	St George's College	Harare	1999-04-02	61	1.67
22	Nqobisile Ncube	Falcon College	Bulawayo	1998-05-01	74	1.74
25	Peter Davis	Falcon College	Bulawayo	1998-04-06	79	1.84

TEAM MANAGERS: Tunga Mashungu. **COACHES:** Godwin Murambiwa, Graham Kaulback.

SECTION 8:
CLUB & AMATEUR PROVINCIAL RUGBY

Miners strike Gold again

RUSTENBURG Impala claimed their second Gold Cup title in three years in sweltering heat at the Impala Rugby Club in Rustenburg as they outplayed False Bay 48-24 in front of a 5,000-strong passionate home crowd.

The victory completed a dream season for Impala, who played in their third successive final, as they remained unbeaten and scored four tries or more in each of their matches.

They won the title in 2014, but stumbled against Durbanville-Bellville in a home final in 2015 which saw them go down 31-30.

While False Bay will be disappointed by their defeat, they will draw immense confidence from the season, as their participation in the Gold Cup marked their maiden national tournament after claiming their first WP Grand Challenge title in 44 years.

The teams took a few minutes to find their rhythm after kick-off as the temperature lingered close to 40 degrees Celsius in Rustenburg, but once they hit their straps it was a matter of time before Rustenburg Impala ran riot on attack.

False Bay showed their intent early on by running hard at the hosts, and their dominance on attack earned them three opportunities to slot over penalty goals in first 11 minutes. However all three attempts were unsuccessful.

Their determined efforts to open up their account, however, paid off in the 17th minute thanks to a well-worked try by left wing Mustaqeem Jappie who kicked the ball through from a turnover and gathered it to score, which handed the Capetonians a 7-0 lead.

Rustenburg Impala, however, hit back with a try two minutes later as winger Dumisani Matyeshana crossed the tryline after receiving the ball out wide, but the unsuccessful conversion left them trailing 7-5.

His team-mate, No 8 Leon du Plessis, added the team's second try 10 minutes later as he crashed through a bunch of defenders to dot down the ball, but False Bay reduced the deficit to two points with their first penalty goal by fullback Adriaan Osman.

Impala had the final say in the half as

Matyeshana rounded off another fantastic team try, which pushed them 17-10 ahead. They had an opportunity to score their fourth try on the stroke of halftime, but a knock-on denied them.

The hosts wasted no time adding to their score in the second half as flanker Justin Wheeler crossed the tryline two minutes after play resumed, which flyhalf Cecil Dumond backed up with two tries in three minutes.

The team built on this fine form which saw centre Justin St Jerry and Wheeler added two more tries to take their tally for the match to eight.

In turn, False Bay were only able to add two second-half tries compliments of Dylon Frylinck and Ashley Wells.

This secured a well-deserved 48-24 victory for Rustenburg Impala.

In a fitting end to the competition, meanwhile, the manager, coach, forward, back and club player of the year were named before the trophy handover.

Durbanville-Bellville's Peter Virgin was named the team manager of the year, Alrico Beukes of RSK Evergreens club coach of the year, Tythan Adams of College Rovers backline player of the year, Brakpan's Ian Oosthuizen forward of the year, and Leon du Plessis of Rustenburg Impala club player of the year. This was the second year in a row that Du Plessis wins the player of the year award.

All of the winners with the exception of Du Plessis would spend time at a top UK club as part of an international exchange programme sponsored by the British High Commission. Du Plessis spent six months overseas in 2015 after winning his award.

"The Gold Cup concept is quite simple," says SA Rugby CEO, Jurie Roux. "On the field it's all about courage, commitment and camaraderie. Off the field, it's all about community and crowds coming out to support their locals players, guys who might work in a factory or office all week long, only to transform into the town's heroes on a Saturday afternoon.

"For this year's opening match in Worcester, over 6,000 fans turned up to watch even though the game was televised on SuperSport, which drew a fantastic viewership of over 223,000. All these things are showing us that club rugby is fasting regaining its important place in South African rugby."

This year's Gold Cup also made history by including the champions of Namibia and Zimbabwe for the first time, thereby giving the tournament a regional footprint. "As SA Rugby we have a duty to assist our neighbours wherever we can and the inclusion of Namibia and Zimbabwe in the Gold Cup has already added tremendous value," says Roux. "This year, Gold Cup matches were played in three countries and some lifelong friendships were formed in the process, and that is what this tournament will be remembered for long after the scores have faded from memory."

The 2016 Gold Cup also signalled a huge leap forward in the quality of rugby played by the country's top non-university clubs – a consequence of much more competitive qualifying leagues in the 14 provincial unions. "Club rugby, even five years ago, was seen as a career cul-de-sac," says Roux. "Broadcasters weren't interested in showcasing it, sponsors weren't interested in coming on board, and there was a real danger that the club game would deteriorate to a point from which it could not recover.

"The Community Cup and now the Gold Cup has not solved all of club rugby's problems but we like to believe it has turned around the fortunes of the club game. This year's Gold Cup saw eight matches televised, and we are currently in talks with a number of potential sponsors, who have recognised the unique characteristics of the Gold Cup as an authentic, community tournament that is once again producing provincial quality players such as Garth April, who went from lifting the Gold Cup in 2015 to the Springbok training squad this year."

As Roux points out, the revival of club rugby remains a work-in-progress, but with the Gold Cup set to become a permanent addition to the rugby calendar, the future of the grassroots game seems brighter than ever.

LOG

Pool A	P	W	L	D	PF	PA	PD	TF	TA	LB	TB	Pts
Durbanville-Bellville	4	4	0	0	171	83	88	23	10	0	3	19
College Rovers	4	3	1	0	157	88	69	25	10	1	3	16
Old Selbornians	4	2	2	0	87	94	-7	11	13	1	1	10
Welkom Rovers	4	1	3	0	93	124	-31	11	18	1	1	6
Worcester Villagers	4	0	4	0	74	193	-119	10	29	0	1	1

Pool B												
Rustenburg Impala	4	4	0	0	194	99	95	30	14	0	4	20
Evergreens	4	3	1	0	116	122	-6	16	17	0	3	15
Pirates	4	2	2	0	141	142	-1	16	20	1	2	11
Wanderers Windhoek	4	1	3	0	152	154	-2	23	21	1	4	9
Rhinos	4	0	4	0	107	193	-86	15	28	1	2	3

Pool C												
Brakpan	4	4	0	0	129	80	49	17	9	0	3	19
False Bay	4	3	1	0	188	77	111	28	9	1	3	16
Old Georgians	4	2	2	0	99	107	-8	7	12	0	0	8
Durban Collegians	4	1	3	0	110	128	-18	16	17	1	2	7
White River	4	0	4	0	54	188	-134	5	26	1	0	1

Pool D												
Pretoria Police	4	4	0	0	195	70	125	29	10	0	4	20
PE Police	4	3	1	0	103	87	16	15	12	0	1	13
Sishen	4	2	2	0	128	103	25	19	16	1	2	11
East London Police	4	1	3	0	62	144	-82	11	21	1	1	6
Bloemfontein Police	4	0	4	0	71	155	-84	10	25	1	1	2

LEADING SCORERS

50 POINTS OR MORE

TEAM	T	C	P	DG	PTS
Cecil Dumond (Rustenburg Impala)	7	26	5	0	102
Andri Claassen (False Bay)	1	20	10	0	75
Lenience Tambwera (Old Georgians)	1	2	20	0	69
Gido Horn (Brakpan)	2	17	7	0	65
Leegan Moos (Evergreens)	2	9	9	0	55
Tiaan Radyn (Durbanville-Bellville)	0	9	2	0	54
Tythan Adams (College Rovers)	10	0	0	0	50

5 TRIES OR MORE

Tythan Adams (College Rovers)	10	Riaan O'Neill (False Bay)	6
Leon du Plessis (Rustenburg Impala)	8	Bruce Muller (Rustenburg Impala)	5
Cecil Dumond (Rustenburg Impala)	7	Dumisani Matyeshana (Rustenburg Impala)	5
Mustaqeem Jappie (False Bay)	7	Justin Wheeler (Rustenburg Impala)	5
Dan Roux (False Bay)	7	Nico Kruger (Rustenburg Impala)	5
Ian Oosthuizen (Brakpan)	6	Tinus Ueckermann (Brakpan)	5

PLAY-OFFS
QUARTER-FINALS:
Durbanville-Bellville beat Evergreens 27-19 *(Cape Town)*;
Brakpan beat PE Police 61-3 *(Brakpan)*;
Rustenburg Impala beat College Rovers 52-19 *(Rustenburg)*;
Pta Police lost to False Bay 12-40 *(Pretoria)*.

SEMI-FINALS:
Rustenburg Impala beat Brakpan 44-32 *(Rustenburg)*;
Durbanville-Bellville lost to False Bay 35-41 *(Cape Town)*.

FINAL:
Rustenburg Impala beat False Bay 48-24 *(Rustenburg)*.
Rustenburg Impala 48
(Tries: Dumond 2, Matyeshana 2, Wheeler 2, St Jerry, Du Plessis. Conversions: Dumond 3, Van Biljon).
False Bay 24
(Tries: Wells, Frylinck, Jappie. Conversions: Osman 2, Claassen. Penalty: Osman)

Rustenburg Impala: Xolani Nkosi, Dumisani Matyeshana, Justin St Jerry *(Mzi Duma, 61)*, Gysbert van Wyk, Maverick van der Merwe, Cecil Dumond *(David van Biljon, 65)*, Nico Kruger, *(Stefan Kruger, 74)*Leon du Plessis, Justin Wheeler *(Capt)*, Tiaan Prinsloo *(Johan Engelbrecht, 56)*, Tiaan Nel, Robbie Rawlins *(JP le Grange, 61)*, Zander de Kock *(Ivann Espag, 56)*, Bruce Muller *(Gavin Williamson, 65)*, Louis Hollamby.

False Bay: Adnaan Osman, Danie Roux, Byron Mohr *(Jason Pretorius, HT)*, Riaan O'Neill, Mustaqeem Jappie *(Roemark Smith, 43)*, Andri Claassen, Ridhaa Damon *(Dylon Frylinck, HT)*, Ryan Olivier *(Willie Coetzee, 53/Curtley Johnson, 55)*, Justin van Winkel, Aiden Monk, Brandon Wood, Graham Knoop *(Capt)*, Ashley Wells, Andre van Vuuren *(Dasch Barber, 52)*, Wesley Futter *(Royal Mwale, 44)*.

Durbanville-Bellville

Played	Won	Lost	Drawn	Points for	Points against	Tries for	Tries against
6	5	1	0	233	143	30	16

Date	Venue	Opponent	Result	Score	Referee	Scorers
10 Sept	Durbell RFC, Cape Town	Old Selbornians	WON	40-14	Nathan Barry	T: Constant, Esterhuizen, Roberts, Willemse, Moses. C: Radyn (3). P: Radyn (3).
17 Sept	Rovers RFC, Welkom	Welkom Rovers	WON	32-24	Griffon Cloby	T: Pretorius, Botes, Badenhorst, Moses. C: Radyn (3). P: Radyn (2).
01 Oct	Boland Park, Worcester	Worcester Villagers	WON	74-23	Blake Beattie	T: Badenhorst (2), Picoto, Cleopas, Brink, Esterhuizen, Pretorius, Botes, Swarts, Thiart, Vermaak, Penalty Try. C: Cleopas (4), Radyn (3).
08 Oct	Durbell RFC, Cape Town	College Rovers	WON	25-22	Darren Colby	T: Cleophas, Swarts. P: Radyn (5).
QUARTER-FINAL						
15 Oct	Durbell RFC, Cape Town	Evergreens	WON	27-19	Paul Mente	T: Picoto, Cleophas, Esterhuizen. C: Cleophas (2), Olivier. P: Cleophas, Olivier.
SEMI-FINAL						
23 Oct	Durbell RFC, Cape Town	False Bay	LOST	35-41	Rasta Rasivhenge	T: Swarts (2), Esterhuizen, Constant. C: Olivier (3). P: Radyn (2), Olivier.

2016 APPEARANCES & POINTS

	Old Selbornians	Welkom Rovers	Worcester Villagers	College Rovers	Evergreens	False Bay	Apps	T	C	P	DG	Pts
Angus Cleopas	15	15	15	11R	10	10R	6	3	6	1	–	30
Roderick Moses	14	14	14	14	14	14R	6	2	–	–	–	10
Etienne Swarts	13	13	13	13	10R	13	6	4	–	–	–	20
Jos Malherbe	12	12	–	13R	13	–	4	–	–	–	–	0
Cheslyn Roberts	11	11	11	–	14R	11	5	1	–	–	–	5
Tiaan Radyn	10	10	10	10	–	10	5	–	9	12	–	54
Denzel Willemse	9	9	22R	9R	9R	9	6	1	–	–	–	5
Conway Pretorius	8	8	8	8	6R	8	6	2	–	–	–	10
Karl Liebenberg	7	7	7	7	8	7	6	–	–	–	–	0
Andrew Picoto	6	6	6	6	6	8R	6	2	–	–	–	10
Daneel Botes	5	5	4	4	4	4	6	2	–	–	–	10
Daniel Krynauw	4	4	–	–	–	–	2	–	–	–	–	0
Aston Constant	3c	3c	3c	3c	3c	3c	6	2	–	–	–	10
Jacques Vermaak	2	2	2R	2	–	–	4	1	–	–	–	5
Thurlow Kohler	1	1	1	1	1	1	6	–	–	–	–	0
Steven-Floyd Robbeson	1R	–	1R	3R	–	–	3	–	–	–	–	0
Pieter Loubser	3R	7R	–	–	3R	3R	4	–	–	–	–	0
Michael Badenhorst	11R	4R	5	5	5	5	6	3	–	–	–	15
Brenden Esterhuizen	6R	6R	6R	6R	7	6	6	4	–	–	–	20
Gideon Thiart	15R	9R	9	9	9	7R	6	1	–	–	–	5
Janco Gunter	10R	12R	12	12	12	12	6	–	–	–	–	0
Frank Wagenstroom	14R	–	–	–	–	–	1	–	–	–	–	0
Jason Kriel	–	13R	11R	11	11	14	5	–	–	–	–	0
Arend Brink	–	2R	2	2R	2	2	5	1	–	–	–	5
Stephen Potgieter	–	–	4R	8R	x	5R	3	–	–	–	–	0
Raymond Olivier	–	–	10R	15	15	15	4	–	4	2	–	14
Jan-Ras van der Linde	–	–	–	–	2R	2R	2	–	–	–	–	0
Penalty Try	–	–	–	–	–	–	–	1	–	–	–	5
27 PLAYERS							**131**	**30**	**19**	**15**	**0**	**233**

College Rovers

Played	Won	Lost	Drawn	Points for	Points against	Tries for	Tries against
5	3	2	0	176	140	28	18

Date	Venue	Opponent	Result	Score	Referee	Scorers
17 Sept	KP 2, Kings Park, Durban	Worcester Villagers	WON	53-10	Johre Botha	T: Jacobs (3), Jordaan, Crouch, Phillips, Scheepers, Adams, Rheeder. C: Scott (2), Phillips (2).
24 Sept	Rovers RFC, Welkom	Welkom Rovers	WON	48-22	Darren Colby	T: Adams (4), Ngcungama, Jordaan, Viljoen, Rheeder. C: Scott (4).
01 Oct	KP 3, Kings Park, Durban	Old Selbornians	WON	34-31	Mike Adamson	T: Jordaan, Jacobs, Kankowski, Phillips, Adams. C: Phillips (3). P: Phillips.
08 Oct	Durbell RFC, Cape Town	Durbanville-Bellville	LOST	22-25	Darren Colby	T: Adams (2), Kemp. C: Scott, Phillips. P: Phillips.
QUARTER-FINAL						
15 Oct	Impala RFC, Rustenburg	Rustenburg Impala	LOST	19-52	Jaco Kotze	T: Adams (2), Phillips. C: Jordaan, Phillips.

2016 APPEARANCES & POINTS

	Worcester Villagers	Welkom Rovers	Old Selbornians	Durbanville-Bellville	Rustenburg Impala	Apps	T	C	P	DG	Pts
Brandon Bailing	15	–	12	12	12	4	–	–	–	–	0
Matt Phillips	14	R	13	13	13	5	3	7	2	–	35
Gareth Jenkinson	13	13	–	–	–	2	–	–	–	–	0
Michael Scheepers	12	12	–	–	–	2	1	–	–	–	5
Willem Rheeder	11	11	–	–	–	2	2	–	–	–	10
Chris Jordaan	10	10	10	–	10	4	3	1	–	–	17
Warren Randall	9	9R	9	9	9	5	–	–	–	–	0
Mesuli Mncwango	8	7R	–	7	8	4	–	–	–	–	0
Calvin Ngcungama	7	7	7	–	–	3	1	–	–	–	5
Jean Pretorius	6	6	–	6	6	4	–	–	–	–	0
Paul Bester	5	5	4R	5	4	5	–	–	–	–	0
Sanele Sibanda	4	–	4	4	5	4	–	–	–	–	0
Brian Habbick	3	1R	–	3R	–	3	–	–	–	–	0
Jandré Jacobs	2	2	2R	2	2	5	4	–	–	–	20
Jarrett Crouch	1	1	1R	1	1	5	1	–	–	–	5
Chris Kemp	8R	–	2	2R	2R	4	1	–	–	–	5
Njabulo Mkize	1R	–	1	–	3R	3	–	–	–	–	0
Witness Mandizha	4R	4	–	5R	4R	4	–	–	–	–	0
Le Roux Viljoen	6R	4R	5	–	7	4	1	–	–	–	5
Dumisani Dyonase	9R	9	9R	9R	9R	5	–	–	–	–	0
Gavin Scott	10R	15	15	10	15	5	–	7	–	–	14
Tythan Adams	14R	14	14	11	11	5	10	–	–	–	50
Kelvin Adam	–	8	8	8	–	3	–	–	–	–	0
Luciano Santos	–	3	3	3	3	4	–	–	–	–	0
Sheldon Norris	–	2R	–	–	–	1	–	–	–	–	0
Troy Chiocchetti	–	x	11	14	–	2	–	–	–	–	0
Jason Kankowski	–	–	6	8R	–	2	1	–	–	–	5
Nico Bezuidenhout	–	–	7R	–	7R	2	–	–	–	–	0
Kyle Wilkinson	–	–	11R	14R	15R	3	–	–	–	–	0
Gary Collins	–	–	12R	12R	12R	3	–	–	–	–	0
Mark Richards	–	–	–	15	14	2	–	–	–	–	0
31 PLAYERS						109	28	15	2	0	176

Old Selbornians

Played	Won	Lost	Drawn	Points for	Points against	Tries for	Tries against
4	2	2	0	87	94	11	13

Date	Venue	Opponent	Result	Score	Referee	Scorers
10 Sept	Durbell RFC, Cape Town	Durbanville-Bellville	LOST	14-40	Nathan Barry	T: Pieterse, Bassingthwaite. C: Mauer (2).
24 Sept	Mike Pendock Motors Park, East London	Worcester Villagers	WON	27-12	JP Clements	T: Birkholtz, Ntsebeza, Alberts, Bassingthwaite. C: Shone (2). P: Shone.
01 Oct	KP 3, Kings Park, Durban	College Rovers	LOST	31-34	Mike Adamson	T: Green, Bassingthwaite, Bursey. C: Gerber (2). P: Gerber (4).
08 Oct	Mike Pendock Motors Park, East London	Welkom Rovers	WON	15-08	Nathan Swartz	T: Ntsebeza, Alberts. C: Shone. P: Shone.

2016 APPEARANCES & POINTS

	Durbanville-Bell	Worcester Villagers	College Rovers	Welkom Rovers	Apps	T	C	P	DG	Pts
Andisa Gqobo	15	R	–	10	3	–	–	–	–	0
Joshua Bassingthwaite	14	12	12	12	4	3	–	–	–	15
Lonwabo Ntleki	13	13	13	–	3	–	–	–	–	0
Buhle Ntsebeza	12	14	15	15	4	2	–	–	–	10
Bradley Birkholtz	11	11	11	–	3	1	–	–	–	5
Leon Mauer	10	10	–	–	2	–	2	–	–	4
Yongama Mkaza	9	9	9	–	3	–	–	–	–	0
Roy Bursey	8	–	8	14	3	1	–	–	–	5
Craig Green	7	8	6	6	4	1	–	–	–	5
Shane Spring	6	6	14	8	4	–	–	–	–	0
Richard Osner	5	4	4	4	4	–	–	–	–	0
Neil Wood	4c	5c	5c	5c	4	–	–	–	–	0
Armon Fourie	3	–	–	3R	2	–	–	–	–	0
Dylan Pieterse	2	1	1	1	4	1	–	–	–	5
Sinethemba Tyokolwana	1	3	3	3	4	–	–	–	–	0
Sesethu Time	3R	2R	x	–	2	–	–	–	–	0
Ryan Pietersen	3R	2	2	2	4	–	–	–	–	0
Craig Gombert	8R	3R	4R	11R	4	–	–	–	–	0
Duran Alberts	4R	7	7	7	4	2	–	–	–	10
Antonio van Heerden	7R	7R	7R	–	3	–	–	–	–	0
Craig Shone	9R	15	–	9	3	–	3	2	–	7
Thabo Sisusa	10R	13R	11R	–	3	–	–	–	–	0
Lazzaar Volschenk	–	9R	x	10R	2	–	–	–	–	0
Akona Makalima	–	1R	3R	2R	3	–	–	–	–	0
Reinhardt Gerber	–	–	10	–	1	–	2	4	–	16
Andrew Klinkradt	–	–	6R	–	1	–	–	–	–	0
Phiwe Nomlomo	–	–	–	13	1	–	–	–	–	0
Bradley Hart	–	–	–	11	1	–	–	–	–	0
MJ le Marquand	–	–	–	13R	1	–	–	–	–	0
Marcel Swanepoel	–	–	–	4R	1	–	–	–	–	0
Gareth Catherine	–	–	–	x	0	–	–	–	–	0
31 PLAYERS					85	11	7	6	0	87

Welkom Rovers

Played	Won	Lost	Drawn	Points for	Points against	Tries for	Tries against
4	1	3	0	93	124	11	18

Date	Venue	Opponent	Result	Score	Referee	Scorers
10 Sept	Boland Park, Worcester	Worcester Villagers	WON	39-29	Divan Uys	T: Pretorius (3), Klopper. C: Van Wyk (2). P: Van Wyk (5).
17 Sept	Rovers RFC, Welkom	Durbanville-Bellville	LOST	24-32	Griffon Colby	T: Kleinhans (2), Du Preez. C: Van Wyk (3). P: Van Wyk.
24 Sept	Rovers RFC, Welkom	College Rovers	LOST	22-48	Darren Colby	T: Chabeli, Van Tonder, Olivier. C: Van Wyk (2). P: S Nieuwenhuyzen.
08 Oct	Mike Pendock Motors Park, East London	Old Selbornians	LOST	08-15	Nathan Swartz	T: Klopper. P: Van Wyk.

2016 APPEARANCES & POINTS

	Worcester Villagers	Durbanville-Bell	College Rovers	Old Selbornians	Apps	T	C	P	DG	Pts
Willem Botha	15	15	15	15	4	–	–	–	–	0
Freddie Wepener	14	14	14	14	4	–	–	–	–	0
Curtis Kleinhans	13	13	13	13	4	2	–	–	–	10
Shaun Nieuwenhuyzen	12	12	12	12R	4	–	–	–	–	0
Jovanian du Preez	11	11	9	11	4	1	–	–	–	5
Tiaan van Wyk	10	10	10	10	4	–	7	7	–	35
Jaco Pretorius	9	9	11R	9	4	3	–	–	–	15
Jackson Chabeli	8	8	8	6R	4	1	–	–	–	5
Ivan de Klerk	7c	7c	7c	7c	4	–	–	–	–	0
Willian Diesel	6	6	–	6	3	–	–	–	–	0
Donavan Nieuwenhuyzen	5	5	4R	5R	4	–	–	–	–	0
Clifford Cawood	4	4	4	4	4	–	–	–	–	0
Willie van Staden	3	3	3	3	4	–	–	–	–	0
Gerhard Klopper	2	2	2	2	4	2	–	–	–	10
Gert Luwes	1	1	1	1	4	–	–	–	–	0
Josias Blom	x	7R	7R	–	2	–	–	–	–	0
Tanki Sello	1R	1R	3R	1R	4	–	–	–	–	0
Ruan Olivier	4R	5R	5	5	4	1	–	–	–	5
Morné Mkwayi	8R	6R	16R	8	4	–	–	–	–	0
Floris du Plessis	6R	8R	7R	x	3	–	–	–	–	0
Jakobus Jordaan	13R	9R	–	x	2	–	–	–	–	0
Colin Odendaal	14R	10R	–	–	2	–	–	–	–	0
Jaco Jooste	–	–	11	x	1	–	–	–	–	0
LC van Tonder	–	–	6	–	1	1	–	–	–	5
Teboho Khampepe	–	–	13R	12	2	–	–	–	–	0
25 PLAYERS					84	11	7	7	0	90

Worcester Villagers

Played	Won	Lost	Drawn	Points for	Points against	Tries for	Tries against
4	0	4	0	74	193	10	29

Date	Venue	Opponent	Result	Score	Referee	Scorers
10 Sept	Boland Park, Worcester	Welkom Rovers	LOST	29-39	Divan Uys	T: Timm, Karriem, Eksteen, Van Sitters. C: Isaacs (2), Johnson. P: Isaacs.
17 Sept	KP 2, Kings Park, Durban	College Rovers	LOST	10-53	Johre Botha	T: Africa, Karriem.
24 Sept	Mike Pendock Motors Park, East London	Old Selbornians	LOST	12-27	JP Clements	T: Van Wyk, Eksteen. C: Isaacs.
01 Oct	Boland Park, Worcester	Durbanville-Bellville	LOST	23-74	Blake Beattie	T: Van Sitters (2). C: Isaacs (2). P: Isaacs (3).

2016 APPEARANCES & POINTS

	Welkom Rovers	College Rovers	Old Selbornians	Durbanville-Bell	Apps	T	C	P	DG	Pts
Kyle Jacobs	15	–	15R	11	3	–	–	–	–	0
Jacques Damons	14	14	14	11R	4	–	–	–	–	0
Shandro Issel	13	13	13	10	4	–	–	–	–	0
Jowayne van Wyk	12	12	12	12	4	1	–	–	–	5
Lincoln Eksteen	11	11	11	14R	4	2	–	–	–	10
Clayton Isaacs	10	–	15	15	3	–	5	4	–	22
Yazeed Johnson	9	15	–	–	2	–	1	–	–	2
Egan Uren	8	8	7R	6R	4	–	–	–	–	0
André du Toit	7	–	–	8	2	–	–	–	–	0
Kenan Cronjé	6	–	–	–	1	–	–	–	–	0
Morné Boshoff	5	5	5	5	4	–	–	–	–	0
Yrin Belelie	4c	R	4	4	4	–	–	–	–	0
Timothy Beukes	3	3	3	–	3	–	–	–	–	0
Franklin Kuhn	2	2	2	2R	4	–	–	–	–	0
Jasherie Karriem	1	1	1	1	4	2	–	–	–	10
Regarth Valla	2R	2R	–	3R	3	–	–	–	–	0
Sergeyodei Uys	3R	3R	3R	3	4	–	–	–	–	0
Ashley Dreyden	8R	7R	6	6	4	–	–	–	–	0
Curtley Timm	4R	4	7	7	4	1	–	–	–	5
Neshwille Simpson	13R	6	8	7R	4	–	–	–	–	0
Gurshwin Africa	10R	9	9	9	4	1	–	–	–	5
Nazeem van Sitters	15R	15R	10R	13	4	3	–	–	–	15
Cheslin Adams	–	10	10	–	2	–	–	–	–	0
Jason Basson	–	7	17R	–	2	–	–	–	–	0
Ricardo Jones	–	9R	9R	15R	3	–	–	–	–	0
Elton Valla	–	10R	–	–	1	–	–	–	–	0
Liano Lindoor	–	–	8R	2	2	–	–	–	–	0
Lorenzo Miggel	–	–	–	14	1	–	–	–	–	0
28 PLAYERS					88	10	6	4	0	74

Durbanville–Bellville and DirectAxis False Bay player take to the field in the historic televised Sunday semi-final.

Rustenburg Impala

Played	Won	Lost	Drawn	Points for	Points against	Tries for	Tries against
7	7	0	0	338	174	51	24

Date	Venue	Opponent	Result	Score	Referee	Scorers
10 Sept	Northam Platinum Rec Club, Setaria	Northam Rhinos	WON	46-19	Eduan Nel	T: McDonald, Müller, Matyeshana, Van Wyk, Wheeler, Du Plessis, Duma. C: Dumond (4). P: Dumond.
17 Sept	Pacaltsdorp Sports Ground, George	Evergreens	WON	29-10	Sinethemba Mrulwa	T: Dumons (2), McDonald, Müller, Du Plessis. C: Dumond (2).
01 Oct	Impala RFC, Rustenburg	Wanderers Windhoek	WON	62-39	Oregopotse Rametsi	T: Wheeler (2), Du Plessis (2), Kruger (2), Müller, Le Grange, Hollamby, Nel. C: Van Biljon (3), Dumond (2), Van Wyk.
08 Oct	Impala RFC, Rustenburg	Pirates	WON	57-31	Paul Mente	T: Kruger (2), Nkosi (2), McDonald, Matyeshana, Du Plessis, Van der Merwe. C: Dumond (5), van Biljon (2). P: Dumond.

QUARTER-FINAL

Date	Venue	Opponent	Result	Score	Referee	Scorers
15 Oct	Impala RFC, Rustenburg	College Rovers	WON	52-19	Jaco Kotze	T: Dumond (2), Du Plessis (2), McDonald, Müller, Le Grange, Penalty Try. C: Dumond (6).

SEMI-FINAL

Date	Venue	Opponent	Result	Score	Referee	Scorers
23 Oct	Impala RFC, Rustenburg	Brakpan	WON	44-32	Pro Legoete	T: Müller, Hollamby, Dumond, Kruger, Matyeshana. C: Dumond (4), Van Biljon. P: Dumond (3).

FINAL

Date	Venue	Opponent	Result	Score	Referee	Scorers
29 Oct	Impala RFC, Rustenburg	False Bay	WON	48-24	Jaco van Heerden	T: Dumond (2), Matyeshana (2), Wheeler (2), St.Jerry, Du Plessis. C: Dumond (3), Van Biljon.

2016 APPEARANCES & POINTS

	Northam Rhinos	Evergreens	Wanderers Windhoek	Pirates	College Rovers	Brakpan	False Bay	Apps	T	C	P	DG	Pts
Cecil Dumond	15	10	10	10	10	10	10	7	7	26	5	–	102
Dumisani Matyeshana	14	11	14	14R	14	14	14	7	5	–	–	–	25
Aubrey McDonald	13	14	11	11	11	11	–	6	4	–	–	–	20
Berto van Wyk	12	12	12	12	12	12	12	7	1	1	–	–	7
Maverick van der Merwe	11	–	–	14	–	13R	11	4	1	–	–	–	5
Justin St Jerry	10	13	13	13	13	13	13	7	1	–	–	–	5
Nico Kruger	9	9	9	9	9	9	9	7	5	–	–	–	25
Leon du Plessis	8	8	8	8	8	8	8	7	8	–	–	–	40
Justin Wheeler	7c	7c	7c	7c	7c	7c	7c	7	5	–	–	–	25
Joe Engelbrecht	6	6	–	4R	6	–	6R	5	–	–	–	–	0
Tiaan Nel	5	5	5	–	5	5	5	6	1	–	–	–	5
Robbie Rawlins	4	4	4R	5	4	4	4	7	–	–	–	–	0
Zander de Kock	3	3	3	3	3	3	3	7	–	–	–	–	0
Bruce Müller	2	2	2	2	2	2	2	7	5	–	–	–	25
Louis Hollamby	1	1	1	1	1	1	1	7	2	–	–	–	10
Gavin Williamson	2R	–	1R	3R	1R	1R	2R	6	–	–	–	–	0
Ivann Espag	3R	3R	3R	1R	3R	3R	3R	7	–	–	–	–	0
Marius Breytenbach	6R	–	–	–	–	–	–	1	–	–	–	–	0
JP le Grange	5R	5R	5R	6R	6R	6R	4R	7	2	–	–	–	10
Willie Kok	9R	9R	–	–	–	–	–	2	–	–	–	–	0
Mzivukile Duma	10R	13R	12R	–	12R	–	13R	5	1	–	–	–	5
Xolani Nkosi	11R	15R	15R	15	15	15	15	7	2	–	–	–	10
Stephan Kruger	–	15	15	13R	22R	9R	9R	6	–	–	–	–	0
Wian van Schalkwyk	–	1R	–	–	–	–	–	1	–	–	–	–	0
Tiaan Prinsloo	–	6R	6	6	–	6	6	5	–	–	–	–	0
Hendrik Huyser	–	–	4	4	4R	5R	–	4	–	–	–	–	0
Francois van Biljon	–	–	10R	10R	10R	10R	10R	5	–	7	–	–	14
Penalty Try	–	–	–	–	–	–	–	–	1	–	–	–	5
27 PLAYERS								154	51	34	5	0	338

Evergreens

Played	Won	Lost	Drawn	Points for	Points against	Tries for	Tries against
5	3	2	0	135	149	17	20

Date	Venue	Opponent	Result	Score	Referee	Scorers
17 Sept	Pacaltsdorp Sports Ground, George	Rustenburg Impala	LOST	10-29	Sinethemba Mrulwa	T: Africa. C: L Moos. P: L Moos.
24 Sept	Pacaltsdorp Sports Ground, George	Pirates	WON	35-31	Nathan Barry	T: L Moos (2), Smart (2), Parks. C: L Moos, Pojie. P: L Moos (2).
01 Oct	Northam Platinum Rec Club, Setaria	Northam Rhinos	WON	36-35	Johre Botha	T: Smart (2), Strydom, Africa, Lambrechts, Pojie. C: L Moos (3).
08 Oct	Wanderers Rugby Club, Windhoek	Wanderers Windhoek	WON	35-27	Danie Koen	T: Africa (2), Parks, Miller. C: L Moos (3). P: L Moos (3).
QUARTER-FINAL						
15 Oct	Durbell RFC, Cape Town	Durbanville-Bellville	LOST	19-27	Paul Mente	T: Strydom. C: L Moos. P: L Moos (3), C-T Moos.

2016 APPEARANCES & POINTS

	Rustenburg Impala	Pirates	Northam Rhinos	Wanderers Windhoek	Durbanville-Bellville	Apps	T	C	P	DG	Pts
Leegan Moos	15	15	15	15	15	5	2	9	9	–	55
Chadley Stride	14	–	–	–	10R	2	–	–	–	–	0
Divandré Strydom	13	13	13	13	13	5	2	–	–	–	10
Deon Stoffels	12	14R	12R	12	12	5	–	–	–	–	0
Duwayne Smart	11	14	14	14	14	5	4	–	–	–	20
C-Than Moos	10	13R	10R	10	10	5	–	–	1	–	3
Rudi Michaels	9	9R	9R	9	9	5	–	–	–	–	0
Gerschwin Muller	8	–	4R	8	8	4	–	–	–	–	0
Arden-Lee Wesso	7	4	4	4	4	5	–	–	–	–	0
Freginald Africa	6	8	8	6	6	5	4	–	–	–	20
Marvin November	5c	5c	5c	5c	5c	5	–	–	–	–	0
Darren April	4	–	–	–	–	1	–	–	–	–	0
Glenwynne Vaaltyn	3	3R	3R	3	3	5	–	–	–	–	0
Cheslin van Rayner	2	x	2R	2	–	3	–	–	–	–	0
Anvor Prins	1	3	3	1	1	5	–	–	–	–	0
Byron November	2R	2	2	–	3R	4	–	–	–	–	0
Anston Bernardo	3R	–	–	1R	8R	3	–	–	–	–	0
Isaac Treurnicht	4R	7	7	7R	7R	5	–	–	–	–	0
Buran Parks	8R	6	6	7	7	5	2	–	–	–	10
Alroy Louis	10R	9	9	x	–	3	–	–	–	–	0
Lee-Roy Pojie	9R	10	10	–	–	3	1	1	–	–	7
Gideon Lambrechts	12R	12	12	11R	12R	5	1	–	–	–	5
Clint Miller	–	11	11	11	11	4	1	–	–	–	5
Layle Delo	–	1	1	2R	2	4	–	–	–	–	0
Lluwellyn Treurnicht	–	5R	x	4R	6R	3	–	–	–	–	0
Grant November	–	4R	–	–	–	1	–	–	–	–	0
Alistair November	–	–	–	x	–	0	–	–	–	–	0
Mario Noordman	–	–	–	–	x	0	–	–	–	–	0
28 PLAYERS						**105**	**17**	**10**	**10**	**0**	**135**

Pirates

Played	Won	Lost	Drawn	Points for	Points against	Tries for	Tries against
4	2	2	0	141	142	16	20

Date	Venue	Opponent	Result	Score	Referee	Scorers
10 Sept	Pirates RFC, Greenside, Jhb	Wanderers Windhoek	WON	28-26	Johre Botha	T: Stead, Scheepers, Penalty Try. C: Visser (2). P: Visser (3).
17 Sept	Pirates RFC, Greenside, Jhb	Northam Rhinos	WON	51-24	JD de Meyer	T: Nicholson-Deh (2), Newman (2), Swart, Williamson. C: Deale (6). P: Deale (3).
24 Sept	Pacaltsdorp Sports Ground, George	Evergreens	LOST	31-35	Nathan Barry	T: Stead, Swart, Terblanché. C: Deale (2). P: Deale (4).
08 Oct	Impala RFC, Rustenburg	Rustenburg Impala	LOST	31-57	Paul Mente	T: Swart (2), Sekgobela, Williamson. C: Williams (4). P: Williams.

2016 APPEARANCES & POINTS

	Wanderers Windhoek	Northam Rhinos	Evergreens	Rustenburg Impala	Apps	T	C	P	DG	Pts
Sheldon Williamson	15	9R	9R	15	4	2	–	–	–	10
Bryce Nicholson-Deh	14	14	–	14	3	2	–	–	–	10
Estiaan Conradie	13	–	x	–	1	–	–	–	–	0
Christiaan Visser	12	13	–	13	3	–	2	3	–	13
Jacques Swart	11	11R	11	11	4	4	–	–	–	20
Chanley Williams	10	10	10	10	4	–	4	1	–	11
David Turnbull	9	9	9	9	4	–	–	–	–	0
Martin Scheepers	8c	8c	8c	8c	4	1	–	–	–	5
Dudley Stead	7	7	7	6R	4	2	–	–	–	10
Johannes Janse van Rensburg	6	–	7R	–	2	–	–	–	–	0
Rinus Bothma	5	5	5	5	4	–	–	–	–	0
Cole de Jager	4	–	–	–	1	–	–	–	–	0
Anthony Gallagher	3	1R	3R	3	4	–	–	–	–	0
Sheldon Terblanche	2	2	2	2	4	1	–	–	–	5
Jean-Pierre Olivier	1	–	1	1	3	–	–	–	–	0
Dylan Rigney	2R	2R	x	–	2	–	–	–	–	0
Johannes Zeeman	3R	3	3	–	3	–	–	–	–	0
Kiernan Rabie	1R	1	–	1R	3	–	–	–	–	0
Ernest van Niekerk	4R	4	4R	4	4	–	–	–	–	0
Johan Venter	13R	–	–	–	1	–	–	–	–	0
Zunaid Kock	11R	11	13	11R	4	–	–	–	–	0
Hanco Deale	x	15	15	15R	3	–	8	7	–	37
Duncan Delport	–	12	12	12	3	–	–	–	–	0
Chris Newman	–	6	6	6	3	2	–	–	–	10
Bradley van Niekerk	–	3R	1R	3R	3	–	–	–	–	0
Nqubeko Zulu	–	5R	4	4R	3	–	–	–	–	0
Jama Ntengo	–	14R	14	–	2	–	–	–	–	0
Ben Sekgobela	–	–	–	7	1	1	–	–	–	5
Steven du Plessis	–	–	–	9R	1	–	–	–	–	0
Penalty Try	–	–	–	–	–	1	–	–	–	5
29 PLAYERS					85	16	14	11	0	141

Wanderers Windhoek

Played	Won	Lost	Drawn	Points for	Points against	Tries for	Tries against
4	1	3	0	152	154	23	21

Date	Venue	Opponent	Result	Score	Referee	Scorers
10 Sept	Pirates RFC, Greenside, Jhb	Pirates	LOST	26-28	Johre Botha	T: Joseph, PrinsII, Prenn, Kritzinger. C: Prinsloo (3).
24 Sept	Wanderers Rugby Club, Windhoek	Northam Rhinos	WON	60-29	Jacky Husselman	T: Stoop (3), Engelbrech, D Wiese, F Wiese, Bergh, Botha, Coetzee. C: Prinsloo (6). P: Prinsloo.
01 Oct	Impala RFC, Rustenburg	Rustenburg Impala	LOST	39-62	Oregopotse Rametsi	T: Lotter (2), Engelbrecht, Moore, Van Zyl, Raubenheimer. C: Van Zyl (3). P: Van Zyl.
08 Oct	Wanderers Rugby Club, Windhoek	Evergreens	LOST	27-35	Danie Koen	T: Engelbrecht, Nell, Stoop, Raubenheimer. C: Prinsloo (2). P: Prinsloo.

2016 APPEARANCES & POINTS

	Pirates	Northam Rhinos	Rustenburg Impala	Evergreens	Apps	T	C	P	DG	Pts
Lean Stoop	15	15	15	15	4	4	–	–	–	20
Jamie Joseph	14	–	–	–	1	1	–	–	–	5
Heinrich Smit	13	13	10	–	3	–	–	–	–	0
Francois Wiese	12	12	12	12	4	1	–	–	–	5
De Selvano Beukes	11	11	–	11	3	–	–	–	–	0
Mahco Prinsloo	10	10	–	10	3	1	11	2	–	33
Nicolaas Kritzinger	9	9	–	–	2	1	–	–	–	5
Stephen Botha	8	8	7	7	4	1	–	–	–	5
Dirk de Meyer	7	5R	–	7R	3	–	–	–	–	0
Dian Wiese	6	6	–	4R	3	1	–	–	–	5
Alberto Engelbrecht	5c	4c	8c	8c	4	3	–	–	–	15
Willem van Zyl	4	–	5R	–	2	–	–	–	–	0
Nian Berg	3	1	–	–	2	–	–	–	–	0
Theo Coetzee	2	2R	–	–	2	1	–	–	–	5
Schalk Bergh	1	1R	1	1R	4	1	–	–	–	5
Shaun du Preez	7R	3R	1R	1	4	–	–	–	–	0
PG Louw	1R	–	–	3R	2	–	–	–	–	0
Morné Prenn	2R	–	4R	–	2	1	–	–	–	5
Mattheus Brand	4R	–	7R	–	2	–	–	–	–	0
Riaan van Zyl	12R	–	9	9	3	1	3	1	–	14
Heico Prinsloo	14R	9R	11R	11R	4	–	–	–	–	0
Terswin Raubenheimer	15R	–	13	13	3	2	–	–	–	10
Phillip Nashikaku	–	14	–	–	1	–	–	–	–	0
Rohan Kitshoff	–	7	6	6	3	–	–	–	–	0
Nico Esterhuyse	–	5	5	5	3	–	–	–	–	0
Abel de Klerk	–	3	3	3	3	–	–	–	–	0
Gerhard Lotter	–	2	2	2	3	2	–	–	–	10
Malcolm Moore	–	12R	14	14	3	1	–	–	–	5
Zaynor Platt	–	11R	10R	–	2	–	–	–	–	0
Ruan Ludick	–	–	4	4	2	–	–	–	–	0
Petri Burger	–	–	2R	–	1	–	–	–	–	0
Cody La Cock	–	–	13R	–	1	–	–	–	–	0
Eduardo Nell	–	–	–	9R	1	1	–	–	–	5
Gino Chiappini	–	–	–	14R	1	–	–	–	–	0
34 PLAYERS					88	23	14	3	0	152

Northam Rhinos

Played	Won	Lost	Drawn	Points for	Points against	Tries for	Tries against
4	0	4	0	107	193	15	28

Date	Venue	Opponent	Result	Score	Referee	Scorers
10 Sept	Northam Platinum Rec Club, Setaria	Rustenburg Impala	LOST	19-46	Eduan Nel	T: Loots, Harmzen, Fortuin. C: P Hattingh (2).
17 Sept	Pirates RFC, Greenside, Jhb	Pirates	LOST	24-51	JD de Meyer	T: Juries (2), Botha. C: P Hattingh (3). P: P Hattingh.
24 Sept	Wanderers Rugby Club, Windhoek	Wanderers Windhoek	LOST	29-60	Jacky Husselman	T: Loots (3), Marquardt. C: P Hattingh (3). P: P Hattingh.
01 Oct	Northam Platinum Rec Club, Setaria	Evergreens	LOST	35-36	Johre Botha	T: Majiedt (2), Juries, J Hattingh, P Hattingh. C: P Hattingh (5).

2016 APPEARANCES & POINTS

	Rustenburg Impala	Pirates	Wanderers Windhoek	Evergreens	Apps	T	C	P	DG	Pts
Hughwinn Majiedt	15	15	15	15	4	2	–	–	–	10
Whelan Fortuin	14	14	14	14	4	1	–	–	–	5
Christopher Juries	13	13	13	13	4	3	–	–	–	15
Juan-Pierre Jacobs	12	12	11	14R	4	–	–	–	–	0
Johannes Harmzen	11	11	11R	11R	4	1	–	–	–	5
Danie Loots	10	10	12	12	4	4	–	–	–	20
Patrick Hattingh	9	9	9	9	4	1	13	2	–	37
Dieter Marquardt	8	4	8	8	4	1	–	–	–	5
Adriaan Louw	7c	8c	4c	–	3	–	–	–	–	0
Paul Lindenberg	6	6	6	6	4	–	–	–	–	0
Willem Botha	5	5	5	5	4	1	–	–	–	5
Marthienus van den Berg	4	2	2	2	4	–	–	–	–	0
Tyson Mulamba	3	3	3	3	4	–	–	–	–	0
Adriaan Botha	2	1	1	–	3	–	–	–	–	0
Odwa Tinise	1	2R	1R	1	4	–	–	–	–	0
Sam Mcetywa	3R	1R	2R	3R	4	–	–	–	–	0
Jimmy Baloyi	8R	7	7	7	4	–	–	–	–	0
Nico Kriel	5R	20R	5R	4R	4	–	–	–	–	0
Jacques Hattingh	15R	–	15R	11	3	1	–	–	–	5
Amri Schlebush	14R	8R	–	–	2	–	–	–	–	0
Johan Harmse	12R	–	14R	10R	3	–	–	–	–	0
Stephan Jacobs	11R	11R	10	10	4	–	–	–	–	0
Moegamad Gasant	–	5R	–	4	2	–	–	–	–	0
Mark Humphries	–	12R	4R	–	2	–	–	–	–	0
J du Toit	–	–	–	x	0	–	–	–	–	0
Benhard van Heerden	–	–	–	7R	1	–	–	–	–	0
26 PLAYERS					87	15	13	2	0	107

Dumisani Matyeshana, one of Rustenburg Impala's stars.

Brakpan

Played	Won	Lost	Drawn	Points for	Points against	Tries for	Tries against
6	5	1	0	222	127	31	14

Date	Venue	Opponent	Result	Score	Referee	Scorers
17 Sept	Bosman Stadium, Brakpan	False Bay	WON	26-19	Eduan Nel	T: Robbertse, Mynhardt, Ueckermann. C: Horn. P: Horn (3).
24 Sept	KP 2, Kings Park, Durban	Durban Collegians	WON	36-33	Craig Joubert	T: Jordaan, Mumba, Oosthuizen, Becker, Ueckermann. C: Horn (4). P: Horn.
01 Oct	White River Rugby Club	White River	WON	38-12	Pieter Maritz	T: Oosthuizen (2), Lotter, Moller, Botha, Ndanda. C: Horn (4).
08 Oct	Bosman Stadium, Brakpan	Old Georgians	WON	29-16	Jaco Pretorius	T: Horn, Menezes, Becker, Ueckermann. C: Horn (2), Mumba. P: Horn.

QUARTER-FINAL

Date	Venue	Opponent	Result	Score	Referee	Scorers
15 Oct	Bosman Stadium, Brakpan	PE Police	WON	61-03	Pieter Maritz	T: Oosthuizen (3), Ueckermann (2), Gindan, Mumba, Walters, Roets. C: Mumba (5), Horn (3).

SEMI-FINAL

Date	Venue	Opponent	Result	Score	Referee	Scorers
23 Oct	Impala RFC, Rustenburg	Rustenburg Impala	LOST	32-44	Pro Legoete	T: Gindan (2), Lotter, Horn. C: Horn (3). P: Horn (2).

2016 APPEARANCES & POINTS

	Fake Bay	Durban Collegians	White River	Old Georgians	PE Police	Rustenburg Impala	Apps	T	C	P	DG	Pts
Hagen Mumba	15	11	11	15	15	11	6	2	6	–	–	22
Thinus Ueckermann	14	14	13	14	14	14	6	5	–	–	–	25
Franco Booysen	13	13	11R	13	–	–	4	–	–	–	–	0
Christo Joubert	12	12	–	12	12	12	5	–	–	–	–	0
Luzuko Ndanda	11	13R	R	–	14R	x	4	1	–	–	–	5
Gido Horn	10	15	10	11R	11R	10	6	2	17	7	–	65
Tiaan Ramat	9	–	–	–	–	–	1	–	–	–	–	0
Theo Mynhardt	8	8	3R	8	8	8	6	1	–	–	–	5
Francois Robbertse	7c	7c	–	–	7c	7c	4	1	–	–	–	5
Jaco Lotter	6	6	6R	7	6	6	6	2	–	–	–	10
Dwane Morrison	5	5	–	–	–	5	3	–	–	–	–	0
Theo Becker	4	4	4	4	4	4	6	2	–	–	–	10
Jason Arundel	3	1	–	3	3	3	5	–	–	–	–	0
Ian Oosthuizen	2	2	1	2	2	2	6	6	–	–	–	30
Pierre Foord	1	3	5R	–	1	1	5	–	–	–	–	0
Vernon du Preez	1R	–	–	1	–	–	2	–	–	–	–	0
Jacques Moller	3R	1R	2	–	3R	3R	5	1	–	–	–	5
Ricardo Menezes	5R	3R	8	8R	8R	7R	6	1	–	–	–	5
Wikus van der Berg	8R	–	6	6	R	8R	5	–	–	–	–	0
Shaun Botes	9R	9R	–	9	9R	13R	5	–	–	–	–	0
Tobie Strydom	12R	–	–	–	–	–	1	–	–	–	–	0
Zolile Mtshali	x	–	–	11	–	–	1	–	–	–	–	0
Raydall Walters	–	10	15	10	10	15	5	1	–	–	–	5
Clayton Gindan	–	9	9	9R	9	9	5	3	–	–	–	15
Jean-Pierre Snyman	–	x	7	5R	–	R	3	–	–	–	–	0
Armand Jordaan	–	6R	3	x	7R	–	3	1	–	–	–	5
Ronwin Roets	–	x	12	12R	13	13	4	1	–	–	–	5
Johannes Botha	–	–	14	–	–	–	1	1	–	–	–	5
Dean van der Merwe	–	–	5	5	5	5R	4	–	–	–	–	0
Garnett Parkin	–	–	1R	–	–	–	1	–	–	–	–	0
Daniel van der Walt	–	–	7R	–	–	–	1	–	–	–	–	0
Wihan Dippenaar	–	–	–	8R	–	–	1	–	–	–	–	0
Leon Potgieter	–	–	–	–	11	–	1	–	–	–	–	0
33 PLAYERS							127	31	23	7	0	222

DirectAxis False Bay

Played	Won	Lost	Drawn	Points for	Points against	Tries for	Tries against
7	5	2	0	293	172	40	23

Date	Venue	Opponent	Result	Score	Referee	Scorers
10 Sept	Phil Herbstein Field, Constantia	Durban Collegians	WON	37-19	Nathan Swartz	T: Olivier (2), Osman, Roux, Frylinck, Jappie, Smith. C: Claasen.
17 Sept	Bosman Stadium, Brakpan	Brakpan	LOST	19-26	Eduan Nel	T: Jappie, O'Neill. P: Osman (2), Claassen.
24 Sept	Morris Depot Police Grounds, Harare	Old Georgians	WON	38-25	Julian Mundawarara	T: Smith (2), Barber, Jappie, Chetty. C: Claassen (2). P: Claassen (3).
08 Oct	Phil Herbstein Field, Constantia	White River	WON	94-07	Rasta Rasivhenge	T: Roux (5), O'Neill (4), Jappie (2), Claassen, Wells, Chetty. C: Claassen (9), Osman (2), Jappie.

QUARTER-FINAL

Date	Venue	Opponent	Result	Score	Referee	Scorers
15 Oct	Loftus Versfeld Stadium, Pretoria	Pretoria Police	WON	40-12	Vusi Msibi	T: Barber, Frylinck, Pretorius, Jappie. C: Claassen (4). P: Claassen (4).

SEMI-FINAL

Date	Venue	Opponent	Result	Score	Referee	Scorers
23 Oct	Durbell RFC, Cape Town	Durbanville-Bellville	WON	41-35	Rasta Rasivhenge	T: Roux, O'Neill, Damon, Frylinck, Coetzee. C: Claassen (3), Osman, Damon. P: Claassen (2).

FINAL

Date	Venue	Opponent	Result	Score	Referee	Scorers
29 Oct	Impala RFC, Rustenburg	Rustenburg Impala	LOST	24-48	Jaco van Heerden	T: Jappie, Frylinck, Wells. C: Osman (2), Claassen. P: Osman.

2016 APPEARANCES & POINTS

	Durban Collegians	Brakpan	Old Georgians	White River	Pretoria Police	Durbanville-Bellville	Rustenburg Impala	Apps	T	C	P	DG	Pts
Adnaan Osman	15	15	14R	15	15	15	15	7	1	5	3	–	24
Danie Roux	14	14	–	14	14	14	14	6	7	–	–	–	35
Riaan O'Neill	13	13	–	12	12	12	12	6	6	–	–	–	30
Jason Pretorius	12	12	12	10R	13R	13R	13R	7	1	–	–	–	5
Mustaqeem Jappie	11	11	15	11R	11	11	11	7	7	1	–	–	37
Andri Claassen	10	10	10	10	10	10	10	7	1	20	10	–	75
Dylon Frylinck	9	9	9R	9R	9R	9R	9R	7	4	–	–	–	20
Ryan Olivier	8	8	8	2R	8	8	8	7	2	–	–	–	10
Justin van Winkel	7	7	7	4R	7	7	7	7	–	–	–	–	0
Brent Stevens	6	6	6	6	6	6	–	6	–	–	–	–	0
Brandon Wood	5	5	5	5	5	5	5	7	–	–	–	–	0
Graham Knoop	4c	4c	4c	4c	4c	4c	4c	7	–	–	–	–	0
Ashley Wells	3	3	3	3	3	3	3	7	2	–	–	–	10
André van Vuuren	2	2	–	2	2	2	2	6	–	–	–	–	0
Wesley Chetty	1	1	1	1	1	1	–	6	2	–	–	–	10
Dasch Barber	2R	2R	2	5R	2R	2R	2R	7	2	–	–	–	10
Royal Mwale	1R	1R	–	–	–	–	1R	3	–	–	–	–	0
Andrew Whitaker	6R	x	–	–	–	–	–	1	–	–	–	–	0
Willie Coetzee	7R	7R	7R	7	x	7R	8R	6	1	–	–	–	5
Ridhaa Damon	9R	9R	9	9	9	9	9	7	1	1	–	–	7
Byron Mohr	13R	x	13	13	13	13	13	6	–	–	–	–	0
Roemark Smith	R	10R	11	11	15R	x	11R	6	3	–	–	–	15
Joshua Pinn	–	–	14	–	–	–	–	1	–	–	–	–	0
André van Vuuren	–	–	x	–	–	–	–	0	–	–	–	–	0
Aiden Monk	–	–	6R	8	6R	x	6	4	–	–	–	–	0
Meryck Ward	–	–	12R	–	–	–	–	1	–	–	–	–	0
Wesley Futter	–	–	1R	1R	1R	1R	1	5	–	–	–	–	0
Curtley Johnson	–	–	–	–	–	–	18R	1	–	–	–	–	0
28 PLAYERS								148	37	24	12	0	269

Old Georgians

Played	Won	Lost	Drawn	Points for	Points against	Tries for	Tries against
4	2	2	0	99	107	7	12

Date	Venue	Opponent	Result	Score	Referee	Scorers
10 Sept	White River Rugby Club	White River	WON	20-18	JD de Meyer	T: Chipendu. P: Tambwera (5).
24 Sept	Morris Depot Police Grounds, Harare	False Bay	LOST	25-38	Julian Mundawarara	T: Sprake, Katsvere. P: Tambwera (5).
01 Oct	Old Georgians Sports Club, Harare	Durban Collegians	WON	38-22	Shemeah Mushiribindi	T: Lang, Tanbwera, Gunda. C: Tanbwera. P: Tambwera (7).
08 Oct	Bosman Stadium, Brakpan	Brakpan	LOST	16-29	Jaco Pretorius	T: De Beer. C: Tambwera. P: Tambwera (3).

2016 APPEARANCES & POINTS

	White River	False Bay	Durban Collegians	Brakpan	Apps	T	C	P	DG	Pts
Brandon Boshi	15	14	14	14	4	–	–	–	–	0
Sir Farai Jijita	14	11	x	–	2	–	–	–	–	0
David McWade	13	13	–	–	2	–	–	–	–	0
Boys Rouse	12	12	12	12	4	–	–	–	–	0
Stephan Hunduza	11	–	11	11	3	–	–	–	–	0
Lenience Tambwera	10	10	10	10	4	1	2	20	–	69
Graham Kaulback	9	9	9	9	4	–	–	–	–	0
Kingsley Lang	8	8	8	8	4	1	–	–	–	5
Jacques Leitao	7	7	7	7	4	–	–	–	–	0
Tendai Dzongodza	6	–	5R	5R	3	–	–	–	–	0
Fortunate Chipendu	5	6	6	6	4	1	–	–	–	5
Richard Wild	4	4	–	4R	3	–	–	–	–	0
David Makanda	3	3	3	3	4	–	–	–	–	0
Keith Murray	2	2	2	2	4	–	–	–	–	0
Wade Petzer	1	1	1	1	4	–	–	–	–	0
Kudzai Musorewa	x	5R	–	–	1	–	–	–	–	0
Graham Cochrane	x	2R	2R	2R	3	–	–	–	–	0
Kyle de Beer	x	5	4	4	3	1	–	–	–	5
Moses Gunda	4R	4R	5	5	4	1	–	–	–	5
Ryan Sprake	x	9R	9R	9R	3	1	–	–	–	5
Shingirai Katsvere	13R	15	13	13	4	1	–	–	–	5
Tafa Mukonyora	x	x	13R	15R	2	–	–	–	–	0
Derric Murangari	–	1R	x	–	1	–	–	–	–	0
Jakov Jakov	–	x	3R	–	1	–	–	–	–	0
Jonathan McWade	–	–	15	15	2	–	–	–	–	0
Gabriel Sipapate	–	–	–	1R	1	–	–	–	–	0
Chido Kapenzi	–	–	–	14R	1	–	–	–	–	0
27 PLAYERS					79	7	2	20	0	99

Durban Collegians

Played	Won	Lost	Drawn	Points for	Points against	Tries for	Tries against
4	1	3	0	110	128	16	17

Date	Venue	Opponent	Result	Score	Referee	Scorers
10 Sept	Phil Herbstein Field, Constantia	False Bay	LOST	19-37	Nathan Swartz	T: Ball (2), Mkhize. C: Beukes, Nanto.
17 Sept	Growthpoint Kings Park, Durban	White River	WON	36-17	Archie Sehlako	T: Zwane (2), Beukes, Harris, Nanto, Mkhize. C: Beukes (2), Nkosi.
24 Sept	KP 2, Kings Park, Durban	Brakpan	LOST	33-36	Craig Joubert	T: Genis (2), Holland, Elliott. C: Beukes (2). P: Beukes (3).
01 Oct	Old Georgians Sports Club, Harare	Old Georgians	LOST	22-38	Shemeah Mushiribindi	T: Marks, Genis, Seba. C: Beukes (2). P: Beukes.

2016 APPEARANCES & POINTS

	False Bay	White River	Brakpan	Old Georgians	Apps	T	C	P	DG	Pts
Shane Ball	15	–	14	15	3	2	–	–	–	10
Sipho Mkhize	14	14	14R	14	4	2	–	–	–	10
Andrew Holland	13c	13c	13c	13c	4	1	–	–	–	5
Bradley Ellse	12	12	12	12	4	–	–	–	–	0
Ngoni Chibuwe	11	11R	–	–	2	–	–	–	–	0
Mondi Nkosi	10	15	15	15R	4	–	1	–	–	2
Dylan Marcus	9	9R	9	–	3	–	–	–	–	0
Robert Izaks	8	–	–	7R	2	–	–	–	–	0
Wade Elliott	7	8	8	–	3	1	–	–	–	5
Sibulele Nanto	6	6	6	6	4	1	1	–	–	7
Chris van Leeuwen	5	5	5	–	3	–	–	–	–	0
Denham Fosteras	4	4	4R	5	4	–	–	–	–	0
Thobelani Mabaso	3	–	–	–	1	–	–	–	–	0
Mitchell Hildebrand	2	2	2	2	4	–	–	–	–	0
Robbie Harris	1	1	1	1	4	1	–	–	–	5
Jacobus Oosthuyzen	1R	1R	–	–	2	–	–	–	–	0
Francois van Zyl	3R	3	3	3	4	–	–	–	–	0
Carl Marks	x	–	6R	7	2	1	–	–	–	5
Fanelesibonge Zwane	R	7	7	8	4	2	–	–	–	10
Matthew Reece-Edwards	9R	9	9R	–	3	–	–	–	–	0
Ethan Beukes	14R	10	10	10	4	1	7	4	–	31
Liam Draycott	R	–	–	–	1	–	–	–	–	0
Jasper Genis	–	11	11	11	3	3	–	–	–	15
Matt Jones	–	3R	1R	3R	3	–	–	–	–	0
Jan Ferreira	–	4R	–	–	1	–	–	–	–	0
Jonathan Swiatek	–	8R	–	4R	2	–	–	–	–	0
Calvin Sacks	–	10R	12R	12R	3	–	–	–	–	0
Johannes Retief	–	–	4	4	2	–	–	–	–	0
Byron Johnstone	–	–	2R	2R	2	–	–	–	–	0
Matthew Seba	–	–	–	9	1	1	–	–	–	5
Justin Newman	–	–	–	14R	1	–	–	–	–	0
31 PLAYERS					87	16	9	4	0	110

White River

Played	Won	Lost	Drawn	Points for	Points against	Tries for	Tries against
4	0	4	0	54	188	5	26

Date	Venue	Opponent	Result	Score	Referee	Scorers
10 Sept	White River Rugby Club	Old Georgians	LOST	18-20	JD de Meyer	P: Huysamen (6).
17 Sept	Growthpoint Kings Park, Durban	Durban Collegians	LOST	17-36	Archie Sehlako	T: Labuschagne, Bekker. C: Huysamen, James. P: Huysamen.
01 Oct	White River Rugby Club	Brakpan	LOST	12-38	Pieter Maritz	T: Snyman, Marx. C: James.
08 Oct	Phil Herbstein Field, Constantia	False Bay	LOST	07-94	Rasta Rasivhenge	T: Janse van Rensburg. C: Huysamen.

2016 APPEARANCES & POINTS

	Old Georgians	Durban Collegians	Brakpan	False Bay	Apps	T	C	P	DG	Pts
Chris Brigi	15	15	15	15	4	–	–	–	–	0
Eldred James	14	14	14	14	4	–	2	–	–	4
Tiaan Marx	13	13	13	–	3	1	–	–	–	5
Dewald Pretorius	12	12	12	12	4	–	–	–	–	0
Johan Booysen	11	11	R	11	4	–	–	–	–	0
Andy Huysamen	10	10	10	10	4	–	2	7	–	25
Clive van Zyl	9	9	9	9	4	–	–	–	–	0
Ross O'Mahoney	8	8	8	8	4	–	–	–	–	0
Christiaan Labuschagné	7c	7c	7c	7c	4	1	–	–	–	5
Jaco Bouwer	6	–	–	–	1	–	–	–	–	0
Revive Mashego	5	5	4	4	4	–	–	–	–	0
Christo le Roux	4	–	–	–	1	–	–	–	–	0
Martin Mhlongo	3	–	1	1R	3	–	–	–	–	0
Willem Kotze	2	2	3	3	4	–	–	–	–	0
Jaco Marneweck	1	1	–	1	3	–	–	–	–	0
André Scholtz	3R	3	2R	2	4	–	–	–	–	0
Wilhelm Steenkamp	1R	–	x	–	1	–	–	–	–	0
Willem Janse van Rensburg	6R	6	6	6	4	1	–	–	–	5
Daniel Austin	4R	5R	–	6R	3	–	–	–	–	0
Johan Smit	11R	9R	14R	13	4	–	–	–	–	0
Denys Snyman	10R	11R	11	–	3	1	–	–	–	5
Conrad Botha	x	14R	x	13R	2	–	–	–	–	0
Johannes Jonker	–	4	5	5	3	–	–	–	–	0
Werner Bekker	–	3R	2	–	2	1	–	–	–	5
Hendrik Roos	–	1R	1R	3R	3	–	–	–	–	0
Ferdill Vilander	–	14R	–	14R	2	–	–	–	–	0
Henk van Tonder	–	–	R	–	1	–	–	–	–	0
Pule Sibiya	–	–	–	11R	1	–	–	–	–	0
Hendrik Botha	–	–	–	5R	1	–	–	–	–	0
29 PLAYERS					85	5	4	7	0	54

Theo Mynhardt of Siyaya Brakpan about to tackle Fortunate Chipendu of Old Georgians.

Pretoria Police

Played	Won	Lost	Drawn	Points for	Points against	Tries for	Tries against
5	4	1	0	207	110	31	14

Date	Venue	Opponent	Result	Score	Referee	Scorers
10 Sept	Sivos Stadium, Kathu	Sishen	WON	44-17	Darren Colby	T: Van der Nest (2), Venter (2), J Pieterse (2), Wasserman, Niemand. C: Laubscher, Van der Nest.
16 Sept	Loftus Versfeld, Pretoria	PE Police	WON	40-24	Morné Ferreira	T: Van der Nest, Van Deventer, Hoffman, Tshiovhe, Kruger. C: Laubscher (3). P: Laubscher (3).
24 Sept	Bobbies Park, Bloemfontein	Bloemfontein Police	WON	36-24	Griffon Colby	T: Botha (2), Laubscher, Tshiovhe, Odendaal. C: Laubscher (3), Hugo. P: Hugo.
08 Oct	Loftus B-Field, Pretoria	East London Police	WON	75-05	Stephan Geldenhuys	T: Van Deventer (3), J Pieterse, Hoffman, Strydom, Botha, Motsepe, Gwavu, Odendaal, Penalty Try. C: Hugo (10).

QUARTER-FINAL

Date	Venue	Opponent	Result	Score	Referee	Scorers
15 Oct	Loftus Versfeld Stadium, Pretoria	False Bay	LOST	12-40	Vusi Msibi	T: Botha, Van der Nest. C: Laubscher.

2016 APPEARANCES & POINTS

	Sishen	PE Police	Bloemfontein Police	East London Police	False Bay	Apps	T	C	P	DG	Pts
Phumudzo Tshiovhe	15	15	15	15	15	5	2	–	–	–	10
Theunis Kruger	14	13	–	–	–	2	1	–	–	–	5
Willie Odendaal	13	–	13	13	13	4	2	–	–	–	10
Pieter Strydom	12	12	12	12	12	5	1	–	–	–	5
Ivan Venter	11	11	11	11	11	5	2	–	–	–	10
Dillon Laubscher	10	10	10	–	10	4	1	8	3	–	30
Hendrik van der Nest	9	9	9	9	9	5	4	1	–	–	22
SJ Niemand	8	8	8	7R	7R	5	1	–	–	–	5
Vince Gwavu	7	7	7	7	7	5	1	–	–	–	5
Ian van Deventer	6	6	6	6	6	5	4	–	–	–	20
Divan Steenekamp	5	4R	5	5	5	5	–	–	–	–	0
Jerry Sefoko	4	4	4	4R	4	5	–	–	–	–	0
Rayno Wasserman	3c	3c	3c	3c	3c	5	1	–	–	–	5
Johan Pieterse	2	2	2	2	2	5	3	–	–	–	15
Rinus Moulder	1	1	–	–	–	2	–	–	–	–	0
Emwee Arlow	x	–	2R	–	–	1	–	–	–	–	0
Brendan Stelzer	7R	–	–	–	–	1	–	–	–	–	0
Imille Kayser	4R	5	4R	5R	4R	5	–	–	–	–	0
Louis van Biljon	7R	7R	–	8	8	4	–	–	–	–	0
Johannes le Grange	13R	–	–	–	–	1	–	–	–	–	0
Hendrik Pieterse	15R	15R	R	13R	–	4	–	–	–	–	0
Nhlalala Sithole	16R	–	–	–	–	1	–	–	–	–	0
Pieter Botha	–	14	14	14	14	4	4	–	–	–	20
Tinus Hoffman	–	2R	–	1R	1R	3	2	–	–	–	10
Hannes Ludik	–	1R	1	1	1	4	–	–	–	–	0
Michael Nienaber	–	11R	–	11R	10R	3	–	–	–	–	0
Tihabane Motsepe	–	5R	5R	4	5R	4	1	–	–	–	5
Pieter Matthews	–	–	7R	–	–	1	–	–	–	–	0
Morné Hugo	–	–	10R	10	15R	3	–	11	1	–	25
Boris van Jaarsveld	–	–	x	2R	x	1	–	–	–	–	0
Penalty Try	–	–	–	–	–		1	–	–	–	5
30 PLAYERS						107	31	20	4	0	207

PE Police

Played	Won	Lost	Drawn	Points for	Points against	Tries for	Tries against
5	3	2	0	106	148	15	21

Date	Venue	Opponent	Result	Score	Referee	Scorers
10 Sept	Kemsley Park, Port Elizabeth	Bloemfontein Police	WON	35-11	JP Clements	T: Loxsen (2), Vosloo, Huisamen, Scott, Deyzel. C: Allerston. P: Allerston.
16 Sept	Loftus Versfeld, Pretoria	Pretoria Police	LOST	24-40	Morné Ferreira	T: Jordaan, Scott, Moore. C: Allerston (3). P: Allerston.
24 Sept	Kemsley Park, Port Elizabeth	East London Police	WON	20-17	Sinethemba Mrulwa	T: Walters, Moore, Deyzel. C: Peach. P: Allerston.
01 Oct	Sivos Stadium, Kathu	Sishen	WON	24-19	Mpho Matsaung	T: Walters (2), Deyzel. C: Peach (2), Allerston. P: Allerston.

QUARTER-FINAL

Date	Venue	Opponent	Result	Score	Referee	Scorers
15 Oct	Bosman Stadium, Brakpan	Brakpan	LOST	03-61	Pieter Maritz	DG: Allerston.

2016 APPEARANCES & POINTS

	Bloemfontein Police	Pretoria Police	East London Police	Sishen	Brakpan	Apps	T	C	P	DG	Pts
Dwayne Kelly	15	15	15	9	–	4	–	–	–	–	0
Eben Barnard	14	–	14	14	14	4	–	–	–	–	0
Eckard Jacobs	13	13	13	13	13	5	–	–	–	–	0
Alwyn Jordaan	12c	12c	12c	12c	12c	5	1	–	–	–	5
Sebastian Loxsen	11	11	11	11	11	5	2	–	–	–	10
Ruan Allerston	10	10	10	10	15	5	–	5	4	1	25
Daniel Vosloo	9	9	9	R	9	5	1	–	–	–	5
Lyle Walters	8	8	8	8	8	5	3	–	–	–	15
Ferdi Gerber	7	7	7	7	6	5	–	–	–	–	0
Frans Gerber	6	6	6	6	7	5	–	–	–	–	0
Hannes Huisamen	5	5	–	–	5	3	1	–	–	–	5
Wayne van Heerden	4	4	5	5	4	5	–	–	–	–	0
Dwayne Kinghorn	3	3	1R	3	3	5	–	–	–	–	0
Stephen Deyzel	2	2	2	2	2	5	3	–	–	–	15
Lyle Lombard	1	1	1	1	1	5	–	–	–	–	0
Matthew Moore	3R	3R	3	–	1R	4	2	–	–	–	10
Bron-Lee Viviers	1R	x	–	x	–	1	–	–	–	–	0
Kaylor Timothy	4R	4R	–	–	–	2	–	–	–	–	0
Raynard Fourie	7R	–	–	–	–	1	–	–	–	–	0
Jaco Pretorius	11R	11R	x	14R	–	3	–	–	–	–	0
Kyle Scott	14R	14	11R	x	14R	4	2	–	–	–	10
Justin Peach	9R	–	9R	15	10	4	–	3	–	–	6
Ruben Fourie	–	6R	x	6R	–	2	–	–	–	–	0
Kevin Plaatjies	–	9R	–	–	R	2	–	–	–	–	0
Damien Moultre	–	x	–	–	10R	1	–	–	–	–	0
Ronald Scheckle	–	–	4	4	–	2	–	–	–	–	0
Dewald Meyer	–	–	x	7R	7R	2	–	–	–	–	0
Chris Zeelie	–	–	4R	4R	6R	3	–	–	–	–	0
Marius Olivier	–	–	–	–	5R	1	–	–	–	–	0
29 PLAYERS						103	15	8	4	1	106

P.E. SAP RUGBY CLUB

Sishen

Played	Won	Lost	Drawn	Points for	Points against	Tries for	Tries against
4	2	2	0	128	103	19	16

Date	Venue	Opponent	Result	Score	Referees	Scorers
10 Sept	Sivos Stadium, Kathu	Pretoria Police	LOST	17-44	Darren Colby	T: Van der Poll, Van der Linde. C: Coetzer, Olivier. P: Olivier.
17 Sept	Police Park, East London	East London Police	WON	30-18	Sindile Ngcese	T: Coetzer, McCarthy, Du Plessis, Strydom. C: Olivier (2). P: Olivier (2).
01 Oct	Sivos Stadium, Kathu	PE Police	LOST	19-24	Mpho Matsaung	T: Prinsloo (2), Dippenaar. C: Coetzer (2).
08 Oct	Bobbies Park, Bloemfontein	Bloemfontein Police	WON	62-17	Lourens v/d Merwe	T: Spence (3), Roux (2), Coetzer, Olivier, Le Roux, Van Rooyen, Du Plessis. C: Coetzer (6).

2016 APPEARANCES & POINTS

	Pretoria Police	East London Police	PE Police	Bloemfontein Police	Apps	T	C	P	DG	Pts
Brendon Coetzer	15	15	15	15	4	2	9	–	–	28
Prince Mofokeng	14	13	13	14	4	–	–	–	–	0
Thabang Molefe	13	12	–	–	2	–	–	–	–	0
Johan Peens	12	9R	12	12	4	–	–	–	–	0
Viljoen van der Linde	11	11	–	11R	3	1	–	–	–	5
Hendrik Olivier	10	10	10	10	4	1	3	3	–	20
Jandré du Plessis	9	9	9	9	4	1	–	–	–	5
Dawid Roux	8	2	8	8	4	2	–	–	–	10
John Spence	7	8	–	6R	3	3	–	–	–	15
Armand Martin	6	6	6	6	4	–	–	–	–	0
Tiaan Dippenaar	5	7R	2R	5	4	1	–	–	–	5
Henlo Boshoff	4	4	4	4	4	–	–	–	–	0
Jan Rossouw	3	–	3R	3	3	–	–	–	–	0
Augusto Chiula	2	x	2	2	3	–	–	–	–	0
Louwrens Strydom	1	3	3	3R	4	1	–	–	–	5
Nicolaas Steyn	3R	1	1	1	4	–	–	–	–	0
Petrus van der Linde	14R	–	–	–	1	–	–	–	–	0
Willie Vermeulen	2R	7	–	–	2	–	–	–	–	0
Cornelius Prinsloo	4R	5	5	7	4	2	–	–	–	10
Len le Roux	13R	14R	11	13	4	1	–	–	–	5
Hugo van der Poll	10R	x	x	10R	2	1	–	–	–	5
Charlton McCarthy	12R	14	14	–	3	1	–	–	–	5
BW van Dyk	–	1R	7	2R	3	–	–	–	–	0
Sarel du Plessis	–	12R	12R	9	3	1	–	–	–	5
Ivandré Knoetze	–	–	4R	4R	2	–	–	–	–	0
Mario van Rooyen	–	–	14R	11	2	1	–	–	–	5
Francois Swart	–	–	x	–	0	–	–	–	–	0
27 PLAYERS					84	19	12	3	0	128

East London Police

Played	Won	Lost	Drawn	Points for	Points against	Tries for	Tries against
4	1	3	0	62	144	11	21

Date	Venue	Opponent	Result	Score	Referees	Scorers
17 Sept	Police Park, East London	Sishen	LOST	18-30	Sindile Ngcese	T: Senoge, Kolanisi, Mateza. P: Mateza.
24 Sept	Kemsley Park, Port Elizabeth	PE Police	LOST	17-20	Sinethemba Mrulwa	T: Mntunjani, Coates, Kolanisi. C: Mateza.
01 Oct	Police Park, East London	Bloemfontein Police	WON	22-19	JP Clements	T: Williams, Ntlama, Rasmeni, Limani. C: Mateza.
08 Oct	Loftus B-Field, Pretoria	Pretoria Police	LOST	05-75	Stephan Geldenhuys	T: Maku.

2016 APPEARANCES & POINTS

	Sishen	PE Police	Bloemfontein Police	Pretoria Police	Apps	T	C	P	DG	Pts
Lonwabo Ntlama	15	11	11	11	4	1	–	–	–	5
Hlumelo Maku	14	R	11R	14	4	1	–	–	–	5
Eric Coates	13	13	13	13	4	1	–	–	–	5
Ayanda Davids	12	R	12R	12	4	–	–	–	–	0
Sabelo Kolanisi	11	14	14	12R	4	2	–	–	–	10
Odwa Rasmeni	10	15	15	15	4	1	–	–	–	5
Skhangele Mateza	9c	10c	10c	10c	4	1	2	1	–	12
Siya November	8	8	8	8	4	–	–	–	–	0
Bonga Mntunjani	7	7	4	4	4	1	–	–	–	5
Kuhle Thumani	6	6	6	6	4	–	–	–	–	0
Sokhana Mkhona	5	5	5	5	4	–	–	–	–	0
Mauel Senoge	4	4	–	–	2	1	–	–	–	5
Odwa Gxamza	3	1R	1R	1	4	–	–	–	–	0
Sikholisekile Sodlula	2	2	2	2R	4	–	–	–	–	0
Aden Williams	1	1	1	1R	4	1	–	–	–	5
Lutho Klaas	2R	2R	x	2	3	–	–	–	–	0
Paul Schonfeldt	3R	–	–	–	1	–	–	–	–	0
Sivuyile Kobokana	8R	4R	7R	–	3	–	–	–	–	0
Oscar Limani	6R	5R	7	7	4	1	–	–	–	5
Bayanda Siko	13R	9R	9	9R	4	–	–	–	–	0
Zwelivumile Tanana	14R	12	12	13R	4	–	–	–	–	0
Loyiso Ndaba	11R	9	9R	9	4	–	–	–	–	0
Xola Mapapu	–	3	3	3	3	–	–	–	–	0
Siseko Kepe	–	–	6R	7R	2	–	–	–	–	0
Mvuzo Mazibukwna	–	–	–	5R	1	–	–	–	–	0
25 PLAYERS					87	11	2	1	0	62

Bloemfontein Police

Played	Won	Lost	Drawn	Points for	Points against	Tries for	Tries against
4	0	4	0	71	155	10	25

Date	Venue	Opponent	Result	Score	Referees	Scorers
10 Sept	Kemsley Park, Port Elizabeth	PE Police	LOST	11-35	JP Clements	T: Visagie. P: Barnard (2).
24 Sept	Bobbies Park, Bloemfontein	Pretoria Police	LOST	24-36	Griffon Colby	T: Ferreira, Duvenhage, Swarts, Spies. C: Barnard (2).
01 Oct	Police Park, East London	East London Police	LOST	19-22	JP Clements	T: Visagie, Ball, Barnard. C: Barnard (2).
08 Oct	Bobbies Park, Bloemfontein	Sishen	LOST	17-62	Lourens v/d Merwe	T: Duvenhage, Cronje. C: Barnard (2). P: Barnard.

2016 APPEARANCES & POINTS

	PE Police	Pretoria Police	East London Police	Sishen	Apps	T	C	P	DG	Pts
Luzandré Swarts	15	11	14	–	3	1	–	–	–	5
Frank Ferreira	14	R	11	11	4	1	–	–	–	5
Rupert Cronjé	13	13	13	13	4	1	–	–	–	5
Johannes Duvenhage	12	12	12	12	4	2	–	–	–	10
Marco Matthee	11	–	–	–	1	–	–	–	–	0
Johannes Barnard	10	10	10	10	4	1	6	3	–	26
Marco Vermeulen	9	9	9	9R	4	–	–	–	–	0
Arno Visagie	8	8	8	–	3	2	–	–	–	10
Donavan Ball	7	4	7	8	4	1	–	–	–	5
Randall Nelson	6	6	5R	6	4	–	–	–	–	0
Lebohang Tsoeu	5	5	5	–	3	–	–	–	–	0
Michael Taylor	4	5R	4	–	3	–	–	–	–	0
Willem Steenkamp	3	3	3R	3	4	–	–	–	–	0
Renier Steyn	2	2	2	2	4	–	–	–	–	0
Johannes van der Vyver	1	1	–	–	2	–	–	–	–	0
Francois Bezuidenhout	2R	18R	1R	1	4	–	–	–	–	0
Joshua Saayman	1R	1R	1	–	3	–	–	–	–	0
Raymond Boshoff	4R	19R	6	7R	4	–	–	–	–	0
Johnny van der Merwe	6R	7	–	7	3	–	–	–	–	0
Clint Carson	21R	6R?	–	–	2	–	–	–	–	0
Eugene Erasmus	10R	–	–	x	1	–	–	–	–	0
Marco Marais	11R	–	–	–	1	–	–	–	–	0
Pieter Snyman	–	15	15	15	3	–	–	–	–	0
André Potgieter	–	14	–	14	2	–	–	–	–	0
Phillip Spies	–	4R	–	–	1	1	–	–	–	5
Frederick van Wyk	–	–	3	3R	2	–	–	–	–	0
Juan Jansen van Vuuren	–	–	4R	4	2	–	–	–	–	0
Riandré Muller	–	–	5R	–	1	–	–	–	–	0
Fourie Smuts	–	–	12R	9	2	–	–	–	–	0
Louis Koen	–	–	14R	x	1	–	–	–	–	0
Jandré Briedenhann	–	–	–	5	1	–	–	–	–	0
Izak Kruger	–	–	–	13R	1	–	–	–	–	0
Dirk Nel	–	–	–	4R	1	–	–	–	–	0
33 PLAYERS					86	10	6	3	0	71

Matthew Moore of Don's Pawn Shop PE Police tackles Hagen Mumba of Siyaya Brakpan.

Pukke win maiden crown at the death

POTCHEFSTROOM based Pukke won their maiden Varsity Cup title with a 7-6 win over Maties at the Danie Craven stadium.

In a closely fought encounter, both teams defended like trojans throughout the match, with the Pukke defence in particular keeping the Maties out from their line on a number of occasions in the first-half.

The teams went into the break deadlocked at 0-0.

In the second half, Maties took advantage of an early period of territorial advantage to finally put points on the board through two penalties by flyhalf Chris Smith, a late replacement in the team after regular pivot Theo Stapelberg picked up an injury during the warm-up.

Maties continued to have most of the territorial dominance as the half came to an end with Smith missing a crucial penalty attempt at goal.

With two minutes remaining however, Pukke thought they had stolen the match at the death after replacement winger Dean Stokes chased a kick and seemed to go over in the corner.

After numerous replays, the TMO ruled that he had knocked the ball on.

Pukke were awarded a penalty from the resulting defensive Maties scrum, electing to take another scrum with just a minute left in the game.

After a number of reset scrums and further penalties to Pukke, they eventually took the ball wide, receiving yet another penalty after a Maties player played the ball on the ground. He was sent to the sin-bin for his indiscretion.

The Maties then lost another player when scrumhalf Remu Malan was sent to the bin for a tackle from an offside position.

Pukke made the pressure eventually count when Manro Redelinghuys forced his way over from close in.

Ryno Smith converted from right in front to give the visitors an incredible victory.

Varsity Cup
PLAY-OFF RESULTS
SEMI-FINALS:
Pukke beat UJ 35-7 *(Johannesburg)*
Maties beat UP-Tuks 49-11 *(Stellenbosch)*

FINAL RESULTS
Danie Craven Stadium, Stellenbosch, Monday 11 April.
Referee: Lourens van der Merwe.
MATIES 6 *(0) (Penalties: Smith 2)*
NWU-PUKKE 7 *(0) (Try: Redelinghuys. Conversion: Smith)*

MATIES: Craig Barry, Duncan Saal, Paul Streicher, Barend Smit, Edwill van der Merwe, Chris Smith, Remu Malan, Kobus van Dyk, Janco Venter, Beyers de Villiers *(capt)*, Wilhelm van der Sluys *(Saud Abrahams, 73)*, Ian Groenewald *(Robey Labuschagne, 70)*, Jacobus van der Merwe, Freddie Kirsten *(Marko van Rensburg, 41)*, Niel Oelofse *(Wesley Adonis, 50/Johannes Kleinhans, 81)*.
SUB NOT USED: Bjorn Bernardo.
NWU-PUKKE: Rhyno Smith, Lucien Cupido, Johan Deysel, Henko Marais *(Sylvian Mahuza, 70)*, Barend Janse van Rensburg, Malherbe Swart, Jeandré Rudolph *(capt)*, Marno Redelinghuys, Jaco Jordaan, Walt Steenkamp *(Tiaan Liebenberg, 66)*, Loftus Morrison, Bart le Roux, Wilmar Arnoldi *(Louis van der Westhuizen, 64)*, Mashudu Mafela *(Joe Smith, 64)*.
UNUSED SUBS: Ruan Venter, Percy Williams, Akhona Nela

LOG

	P	W	L	D	PF	PA	PD	TF	TA	LB	TB	Pts
Maties	7	6	1	0	263	122	141	33	14	0	5	29
UJ	7	6	1	0	254	151	103	26	17	0	3	27
NWU-Pukke	7	5	2	0	232	166	66	28	18	1	5	26
UP-Tuks	7	4	3	0	333	195	138	38	23	1	5	22
Shimlas	7	4	3	0	210	235	-25	26	26	0	3	19
CUT	7	2	5	0	93	211	-118	11	26	1	1	8
NMMU	7	1	6	0	169	251	-82	21	31	2	1	7
UCT	7	0	7	0	103	326	-223	11	39	2	1	3

Note: LB = Losing bonus, TB = Try bonus

Note: CUT was docked 2 log points because they fielded an ineligible player against Maties on 8 February.

BACK OF THE TOURNAMENT: Craig Barry *(Maties)*
FORWARD OF THE TOURNAMENT: Beyers de Villiers *(Maties)*
OVERALL PLAYER OF THE TOURNAMENT: Mosolwa Mafuma *(UFS-Shimlas)*

FNB VARSITY CUP CHAMPIONS
2008 Maties, 2009 Maties, 2010 Maties, 2011 Ikeys, 2012 Tuks, 2013 Tuks, 2014 UCT
2015 Shimlas, 2016 NWU-Pukke

LEADING SCORERS

50 POINTS OR MORE

	TEAM	T	C	P	DG	Pts
Divan Nel	UJ	0	18	15	1	84
Ernst Stapelberg	Maties	2	24	8	0	82
Rhyno Smith	NWU-Pukke	0	20	10	1	73
Joshua Stander	UP-Tuks	0	29	4	0	70
Duhan van der Merwe	UP-Tuks	10	0	0	0	50

5 TRIES OR MORE

Duhan van der Merwe	UP-Tuks	10	Sylvian Mahuza	NWU-Pukke	6
Mosolwa Mafuma	UFS–Shimlas	7	Beyers de Villiers	Maties	5
Arthur Williams	UFS–Shimlas	6	Duncan Saal	Maties	5
Edwill van der Merwe	Maties	6	Riaan Britz	UP-Tuks	5

Mosolwa Mafuma.

Pukke

Played	Won	Lost	Drawn	Points for	Points against	Tries for	Tries against
9	8	1	0	274	179	31	19

Date	Venue	Opponent	Result	Score	Referees	Scorers
08 Feb	TuksRugby Stadium, Pretoria	UP-Tuks	WON	38-15	Stephan Geldenhuys	T: Janse van Rensburg (2), Mahuza, Steenkamp. C: R Smith (4). P: R Smith (2).
15 Feb	Fanie du Sports Grounds, Potch	UJ	WON	31-36	Lourens van der Merwe	T: Rudolph, Cupido, Mahuza, Arnoldi. C: R Smith (2). P: R Smith.
22 Feb	UCT Rugby Fields, CT	UCT	WON	24-06	Francois Pretorius	T: Le Roux, Steenkamp, Arnoldi. C: R Smith (2). P: R Smith.
14 Mar	FNB Stadium, Jhb.	NMMU	WON	46-18	Rodney Bonaparte	T: Mahuza (2), Janse van Rensburg, Jordaan, Van der Westhuizen, Penalty Try. C: R Smith (3).
21 Mar	FNB Stadium, Jhb.	Maties	Lost	12-56	Ben Crouse	T: Janse van Rensburg, Swart. C: R Smith.
24 Mar	Cape Town Stadium, CT	CUT	WON	44-14	Rasta Rasivhenge	T: Le Roux, Rudolph, Van der Westhuizen, Swart, Cupido. C: R Smith (4). P: R Smith.
28 Mar	Cape Town Stadium, CT	Shimlas	WON	37-21	AJ Jacobs	T: Rudolph (2), Cupido, Arnoldi. C: R Smith. P: Janse van Rensburg (2), R Smith.

SEMI-FINAL

Date	Venue	Opponent	Result	Score	Referees	Scorers
04 Apr	UJ Stadium, Jhb.	UJ	WON	35-07	Archie Sehlako	T: Mahuza (2). C: R Smith (2). P: R Smith (4). DG: R Smith.

FINAL

Date	Venue	Opponent	Result	Score	Referees	Scorers
11 Apr	Craven Stadium, Stellenbosch	Maties	WON	07-06	Lourens van der Merwe	T: Redelinghuys. C: R Smith.

2016 APPEARANCES & POINTS

PLAYER	UP-TUKS	UJ	UCT	NMMU	Maties	CUT	Shimlas	UJ (SF)	Maties (Final)	Apps	T	C	P	DG	Pts	Career Apps
Rhyno Smith	15	15	15	15	15	15	15	15	15	9	–	20	10	1	73	25
Lucian Cupido	14	14	14	–	–	11	14	14	14	7	3	–	–	–	15	11
Sylvian Mahuza	13	13	13	13	13	14	11	13	11	9	6	–	–	–	30	23
Henko Marais	12	12	12	–	–	12	12	12	12	7	–	–	–	–	0	7
Dean Stokes	11	11	11	11	11	–	13R	11	11R	8	–	–	–	–	0	15
Benhard Janse van Rensburg	10	10	10	10	10	10	10	10	10	9	4	0	2	–	26	9
Malherbe Swart	9	9	9	–	9	9	9	9	9	8	2	–	–	–	10	12
Marno Redelinghuys	8	8	8	8	8	8	7	7	7	9	1	–	–	–	5	18
Jeandré Rudolph	7c	7c	7c	7c	7c	6c	8c	8c	8c	9	4	–	–	–	20	17
Jaco Jordaan	6	6	6	6	6	6R	6	6	6	9	1	–	–	–	5	9
Walt Steenkamp	5	5	5	5	5	5	5	5	5	9	2	–	–	–	10	16
Loftus Morrison	4	4	4	4	4	7	4	4	4	9	–	–	–	–	0	18
Bart le Roux	3	3	3	3	3	3R	3	3	3	9	2	–	–	–	10	9
Wilmar Arnoldi	2	2	2	2	2	22R	2	2	2	9	3	–	–	–	15	13
Mashuda Mafela	1	1	1R	1R	x	1	1	1	1	8	–	–	–	–	0	26
Louis van der Westhuizen	2R	2R	2R	2R	2R	2	2R	2R	2R	9	2	–	–	–	10	9
Joe Smith	1R	1R	1	1	1	–	1R	1R	1R	8	–	–	–	–	0	25
Danie Jordaan	5R	x	5R	4R	–	–	–	–	–	3	–	–	–	–	0	24
Tiaan Liebenberg	4R	–	–	8R	5R	4	x	5R	5R	6	–	–	–	–	0	6
Percy Williams	9R	9R	9R	9	9R	–	–	–	x	5	–	–	–	–	0	6
AK Akhona Nela	12R	–	–	–	21R	14R	x	12R	x	4	–	–	–	–	0	5
Elden Schoeman	x	–	11R	14	14R	–	–	14R	–	4	–	–	–	–	0	4
Mogau Mabokela	3R	x	3R	3R	3R	1R	3R	3R	x	7	–	–	–	–	0	9
Gideon van der Merwe	–	6R	6R	–	6R	–	–	–	–	3	–	–	–	–	0	3
Schalk Hugo	–	10R	–	–	–	–	–	–	–	1	–	–	–	–	0	1
Eswyn Heyns	–	x	x	–	–	–	–	–	–	0	–	–	–	–	0	0
Johan Deysel	–	–	–	12	12	13	13	–	13	5	–	–	–	–	0	18
Chriswill September	–	–	–	9R	–	22R	x	9R	–	3	–	–	–	–	0	3
Nkululeko Mcuma	–	–	–	14R	14	–	–	–	–	2	–	–	–	–	0	2
Ryno Wepener	–	–	–	15R	–	11R	–	–	–	2	–	–	–	–	0	2
Dewald Dekker	–	–	–	–	–	3	–	–	–	1	–	–	–	–	0	1
Ruan Venter	–	–	–	–	4R	x	4R	x	–	2	–	–	–	–	0	4
Penalty Try	–	–	–	–	–	–	–	–	–	–	1	–	–	–	5	
32 Players										193	31	20	12	1	234	350

Note: ▇ = *Yellow Card*

Maties

Played	Won	Lost	Drawn	Points for	Points against	Tries for	Tries against
9	7	2	0	318	140	38	16

Date	Venue	Opponent	Result	Score	Referees	Scorers
08 Feb	Craven Stadium, Stellenbosch	CUT	WON	40-00	Francois Pretorius	T: Van Dyk (2), De Villiers, Stapelberg, E van der Merwe, Corbett. C: Stapelberg (4).
15 Feb	NMMU Madibaz Stadium, PE	NMMU	WON	27-25	Sindile Ngcese	T: De Villiers, Corbett, Streicher, Nell. C: Stapelberg (2). P: Stapelberg.
22 Feb	Craven Stadium, Stellenbosch	UP-Tuks	WON	29-16	Rodney Bonaparte	T: Saal (3), C: Stapelberg (2).
14 Mar	FNB Stadium, Jhb.	UCT	WON	60-13	Archie Sehlako	T: E van der Merwe (2), Jenkinson (2), Barry, Saal, Van Dyk. C: Stapelberg (4), Smith (2). P: Stapelberg.
21 Mar	FNB Stadium, Jhb.	PUK	WON	56-12	Ben Crouse	T: Barry (2), De Villiers, Saal, E van der Merwe, Streicher. C: Stapelberg (4). P: Stapelberg (2).
24 Mar	Cape Town Stadium, CT	Shimlas	WON	35-14	Cwengile Jadezweni	T: E van der Merwe, Stapelberg, Van Dyk, R Malan, Penalty Try. C: Stapelberg (3).
28 Mar	Cape Town Stadium, CT	UJ	Lost	16-42	Francois Pretorius	T: Asher-Wood, Nel.
SEMI-FINAL						
04 Apr	Craven Stadium, Stellenbosch	UP-Tuks	WON	49-11	AJ Jacobs	T: De Villiers (2), Asher-Wood, E van der Merwe, R Malan. C: Stapelberg (5). P: Stapelberg (4).
FINAL						
11 Apr	Craven Stadium, Stellenbosch	PUK	Lost	06-07	Lourens van der Merwe	P: C Smith (2).

2016 APPEARANCES & POINTS

PLAYER	CUT	NMMU	UP-Tuks	UCT	PUK	Shimlas	UJ	UP-Tuks (SF)	Maties (F)	Apps	T	C	P	DG	Pts	Career Apps
Craig Barry	15	15	15	15	15	15	–	15	15	8	3	–	–	–	15	32
Brandon Asher-Wood	14	14	–	–	11R	14R	14	14	14R	7	2	–	–	–	10	8
Paul Streicher	13	13	13	13	13	13	–	13	13	8	2	–	–	–	10	9
Braam Venter	12	12	12	12	12	12	–	–	–	6	–	–	–	–	0	6
Duncan Saal	11	11	14	14	14	14	–	–	14	7	5	–	–	–	25	7
Ernst Stapelberg	10	10	10	10	10	10	–	10	–	7	2	24	8	–	82	14
Remu Malan	9	9	9	9	9	9	–	9	9	8	2	–	–	–	10	11
Kobus van Dyk	8	8	8	8	8	8	–	8	8	8	4	–	–	–	20	14
Janco Venter	7	7	7	7	7	7	–	7	7	8	–	–	–	–	0	13
Beyers de Villiers	6c	6c	6c	6c	6c	–	–	6c	6c	7	5	–	–	–	25	24
Wilhelm van der Sluys	5	5	5	5	5	5c	–	5	5	8	–	–	–	–	0	29
Ian Martin Groenewald	4	4	4R	4	4	–	8	4	4	8	–	–	–	–	0	19
John-Roy Jenkinson	3	3	3	3	3	–	–	–	–	5	2	–	–	–	10	16
Craig Corbett	2	2	2R	2R	–	–	2R	–	–	5	2	–	–	–	10	10
Wesley Adonis	1	1	x	1R	1R	1R	1	1R	1R	8	–	–	–	–	0	19
Marko Janse van Rensburg	2R	2R	2	2	2R	2R	–	2R	2R	8	–	–	–	–	0	13
Niel Oelofse	1R	1R	1	1	1	1	–	1	1	8	–	–	–	–	0	13
Geor Malan	5R	x	5R	7R	–	–	6	–	–	4	–	–	–	–	0	4
Cornal Brown	7R	5R	7R	–	–	–	–	–	–	3	–	–	–	–	0	3
Brendon Nell	9R	9R	9R	–	–	–	11	–	–	4	1	–	–	–	5	4
Barend Smit	12R	12R	–	–	–	–	12	12	12	5	–	–	–	–	0	5
Chris Smith	–	–	12R	9R	13R	12R	10	12R	10	7	–	2	2	–	10	13
Edwill van der Merwe	14R	11R	11	11	11	11	–	11	11	8	6	–	–	–	30	8
JE van der Merwe	3R	3R	3R	3R	3R	3	–	3	3	8	–	–	–	–	0	13
Justin Moberly	–	–	4	–	–	4R	5	–	–	3	–	–	–	–	0	3
Johan Momsen	–	–	–	5R	5R	4	4	–	–	4	–	–	–	–	0	4
Saud Abrahams	–	–	–	6R	6R	6	x	6R	5R	5	–	–	–	–	0	5
Jason Worrall	–	–	13R	–	–	–	–	–	–	1	–	–	–	–	0	1
Freddie Kirsten	–	–	–	–	2	2	2c	2	2	5	–	–	–	–	0	13
Bjorn Bernardo	–	–	–	–	9R	9R	x	11R	x	3	–	–	–	–	0	10
Boeta Johannes Kleinhans	–	–	–	–	–	17R	1R	17R	17R	4	–	–	–	–	0	6
Robey Labuschagné	–	–	–	–	–	7R	7	8R	4R	4	–	–	–	–	0	14
Carlisle Nel	–	–	–	–	–	–	15	15R	–	2	1	–	–	–	5	2
Kyle Steyn	–	–	–	–	–	–	13	–	x	1	–	–	–	–	0	1
SP Ferreira	–	–	–	–	–	–	9	–	–	1	–	–	–	–	0	1
Marthinus Oosthuizen	–	–	–	–	–	–	3	–	–	1	–	–	–	–	0	1
Derick Marais	–	–	–	–	–	–	3R	–	–	1	–	–	–	–	0	1
Carlton Fortune	–	–	–	–	–	–	9R	–	–	1	–	–	–	–	0	1
Tyron Schultz	–	–	–	–	–	–	6R	–	–	1	–	–	–	–	0	1
Hadley Hendricks	–	–	–	–	–	–	x	–	–	0	–	–	–	–	0	0
Penalty Try	–	–	–	–	–	–	–	–	–	–	1	–	–	–	5	
40 Players										200	38	26	10	0	272	371

Note: ▓ = *Yellow Card*

UJ

Played	Won	Lost	Drawn	Points for	Points against	Tries for	Tries against
8	6	2	0	261	186	27	19

Date	Venue	Opponent	Result	Score	Referees	Scorers
08 Feb	UJ Stadium, Jhb	NMMU	WON	19-12	Rodney Bonaparte	T: Jordaan. C: Nel. P: Nel (4).
15 Feb	Fanie du Sports Grounds, Potch	PUK	WON	36-31	Lourens van der Merwe	T: Dyantyi (2), Penalty try. C: Nel (3). P: Nel (3).
22 Feb	UJ Stadium, Jhb	CUT	WON	14-00	Ben Crouse	T: Walters, Morowane. C: Nel (2).
14 Mar	FNB Stadium, Jhb	UP-Tuks	Lost	08-43	Cwengile Jadezweni	T: Snyman. P: Nel.
21 Mar	FNB Stadium, Jhb	Shimlas	WON	72-49	Rasta Rasivhenge	T: Brown (2), Moolman, Khoza, Antonites, De Bruyn, Conradie. C: Nel (6). P: Nel (3).
24 Mar	Cape Town Stadium, CT	UCT	WON	63-00	Jaco Kotze	T: Dyantyi (2), Snyman (2), Moolman, Antonites, Jordaan, De Bruyn. C: Nel (2), Brown (2). P: Nel.
28 Mar	Cape Town Stadium, CT	Maties	WON	42-16	Francois Pretorius	T: Khoza, Oosthuizen, Porter, Brown. C: Nel (3). P: Nel (3). DG: Nel.
SEMI-FINAL						
04 Apr	UJ Stadium, Jhb	PUK	Lost	07-35	Archie Sehlako	T: Mare. C: Nel.

2016 APPEARANCES & POINTS

PLAYER	NMMU	Pukke	CUT	UP-Tuks	Shimlas	UCT	Maties	Pukke (SF)	Apps	T	C	P	DG	Pts	Career Apps
Ronald Brown	15	15	15	15	15	15	15	15	8	3	2	–	–	19	13
Aphiwe Dyantyi	14	11	11	11	14	14	11	11	8	4	–	–	–	20	15
Bradley Moolman	13	13	13	13	13	13	13	13	8	2	–	–	–	10	23
Robert de Bruyn	12	12	12	12	12	12	12	12	8	2	–	–	–	10	16
Andries Oosthuizen	11	–	–	–	11R	–	–		2	–	–	–	–	0	9
Divan Nel	10	10	10	10	10	10	10	10	8	–	18	15	1	84	8
Hilton Mudariki	9	9	9R	9	9R	9R	9R	9R	8	–	–	–	–	0	13
Kobus Porter	8c	8c	8c	8c	8c	8c	8c	8c	8	1	–	–	–	5	29
Kyle van Dalen	7	7	4R	7	–	–	8R	7R	6	–	–	–	–	0	13
Wian Conradie	6	6	6	6	6	6	6	6	8	1	–	–	–	5	15
David Antonites	5	5	5	–	5	5	5	5	7	2	–	–	–	10	29
Jeremy Jordaan	4	4	4	4	4R	4R	5R	4R	8	2	–	–	–	10	9
Nico du Plessis	3	3	3	3	3	3	3	3	8	–	–	–	–	0	15
Jannes Snyman	2	2	2R	2	2	2	2	2	8	–	–	–	–	15	22
Siya Nzuzo	1	1	1	1	1	1	1	1	8	–	–	–	–	0	8
Emmanuel Morowane	x	x	2	2R	2R	2R	2R	2R	6	–	–	–	–	5	6
Kyle Kruger	1R	3R	1R	3R	1R	1R	3R	3R	8	–	–	–	–	0	8
Etienne Oosthuizen	7R	7R	7	7R	7	7	7	7	8	1	–	–	–	5	12
Phenyo Seriteng	x	x	6R	6R	–	–	–	–	2	–	–	–	–	0	2
Johan Esterhuizen	9R	9R	9	–	–	–	–	–	3	–	–	–	–	0	3
Kobus Engelbrecht	11R	x	10R	10R	–	–	–	–	3	–	–	–	–	0	3
PJ Walters	15R	14	14	14	14R	10R	14	14	8	1	–	–	–	5	15
Brandon Landsberg	x	–	–	–	–	–	–	–	0	–	–	–	–	0	5
Godfrey Ramaboea	–	11R	14R	13R	–	–	–	–	3	–	–	–	–	0	3
Waldo Weideman	–	x	3R	1R	3R	3R	1R	1R	6	–	–	–	–	0	6
FP Pelser	–	–	–	5	4	4	4	4	5	–	–	–	–	0	5
Devon Mare	–	–	–	9R	9	9	9	9	5	1	–	–	–	5	5
Caswell Khoza	–	–	–	–	11	11	15R	11R	4	2	–	–	–	10	4
Frederik Bezuidenhout	–	–	–	–	8R	8R	–	–	2	–	–	–	–	0	2
Dominic Kroezen	–	–	–	–	13R	–	12R	10R	3	–	–	–	–	0	8
Penalty Try	–	–	–	–	–	–	–	–	–	1	–	–	–	5	
30 Players									177	27	20	15	1	223	324

Note: ▢ = *Yellow Card*

UP-Tuks

Played	Won	Lost	Drawn	Points for	Points against	Tries for	Tries against
8	4	4	0	344	244	39	28

Date	Venue	Opponent	Result	Score	Referees	Scorers
08 Feb	TuksRugby Stadium, Pretoria	PUK	Lost	15-38	Stephan Geldenhuys	T: Beerwinkel, Van der Merwe. C: Stander. P: Stander.
15 Feb	TuksRugby Stadium, Pretoria	Shimlas	Lost	46-47	AJ Jacobs	T: Van der Merwe, Fouché, Britz, Steenkamp, Penalty try. C: Stander (4). P: Stander.
22 Feb	Craven Stadium, Stellenbosch	Maties	Lost	16-29	Rodney Bonaparte	T: Van Wyk, Els. C: Stander.
14 Mar	FNB Stadium, Jhb.	UJ	WON	43-08	Cwengile Jadezweni	T: Warner, Fortuin, Els, Matthews, Van Staden. C: Stander (4). P: Stander (2).
21 Mar	FNB Stadium, Jhb.	CUT	WON	68-25	AJ Jacobs	T: Britz (3), Van der Merwe (2), Warner, Matthews, Van der Smit. C: Stander (7).
24 Mar	Cape Town Stadium, CT	NMMU	WON	45-23	Jaco Kotze	T: Els, Swanepoel, Van der Smit, Britz, Penalty Try. C: Stander (5).
28 Mar	Cape Town Stadium, CT	UCT	WON	100-25	Cwengile Jadezweni	T: Van der Merwe (6), Enslin (2), Davids, Swanepoel, Steenkamp. C: Stander (6), De Beer (3). P: De Beer.

SEMI-FINAL

Date	Venue	Opponent	Result	Score	Referees	Scorers
04 Apr	Craven Stadium, Stellenbosch	Maties	Lost	11-49	AJ Jacobs	T: Swanepoel. C: Stander.

2016 APPEARANCES & POINTS

PLAYER	Pukke	Shimlas	Maties	UJ	CUT	NMMU	UCT	Maties (SF)	Apps	T	C	P	DG	Pts	Career Apps
Riaan Britz	15	15	15	15	14	14	14	14	8	5	–	–	–	25	27
Keanan van Wyk	14	14	14	14	15R	15R	15R	15R	8	1	–	–	–	5	8
Stedman Gans	13	13	13	–	–	–	–	–	3	–	–	–	–	0	3
Max Calitz	12	12R	13R	13R	–	–	–	–	4	–	–	–	–	0	4
Duhan van der Merwe	11	11	11	11	11	11	11	11	8	10	–	–	–	50	8
Joshua Stander	10	10	10	10	10	10	10	10	8	–	29	4	–	70	16
André Warner	9	9	9	9	9	9	9	9	8	2	–	–	–	10	16
Clyde Davids	8	8	8	8	8	8	8	8	8	1	–	–	–	5	16
Gerrit Engelbrecht	7	–	–	–	–	8R	–	–	2	–	–	–	–	0	2
Ruan Steenkamp	6c	6c	6c	6c	6c	6c	6c	6c	8	2	–	–	–	10	10
Eli Snyman	5	5	5	5	5	5	5	5	8	–	–	–	–	0	8
Pieter Jansen van Vuren	4	4R	5R	5R	4R	5R	5R	4R	8	–	–	–	–	0	12
Neethling Fouché	3	3	3	3	3	3	3	3	8	1	–	–	–	5	15
Corniel Els	2	2	2	2	2	2	2	2	8	3	–	–	–	15	14
Andrew Beerwinkel	1	1	1	1	1	1	1	1	8	1	–	–	–	5	25
Jan Enslin	2R	2R	2R	x	2R	2R	2R	–	6	2	–	–	–	10	12
Du Toit Genis	1R	1R	1R	1R	1R	1R	1R	1R	8	–	–	–	–	0	8
Aston Fortuin	4R	4	4	4	4	4	4	4	8	1	–	–	–	5	8
Marco van Staden	7R	7R	7R	7R	7	–	–	–	5	1	–	–	–	5	5
Carlo Engelbrecht	9R	9R	9R	x	9R	9R	9R	9R	7	1	–	–	–	5	14
Quaid Langeveldt	11R	14R	10R	x	–	–	–	–	3	–	–	–	–	0	3
Toko Adrian Maebane	12R	12	12	12	12	12	12	12	8	–	–	–	–	0	12
Justin Forwood	3R	3R	3R	3R	3R	3R	3R	3R	8	–	–	–	–	0	11
Frederik Eksteen	–	7	7	7	–	–	7	7	5	–	–	–	–	0	5
Duncan Matthews	–	–	–	13	15	15	15	15	5	2	–	–	–	10	12
Dries Swanepoel	–	–	–	–	13	13	13	13	4	3	–	–	–	15	4
Luke van der Smit	–	–	–	–	7R	7	8R	7R	4	2	–	–	–	10	4
Tinus de Beer	–	–	–	–	10R	10R	10R	13R	4	–	3	1	–	9	4
FJ Binneman	–	–	–	–	–	–	–	2R	1	–	–	–	–	0	1
Penalty Try	–	–	–	–	–	–	–	–	–	2	–	–	–	10	
29 Players									181	40	32	5	0	279	287

Note: ■ = *Yellow Card*

Shimlas

Played	Won	Lost	Drawn	Points for	Points against	Tries for	Tries against
7	4	3	0	210	235	26	26

Date	Venue	Opponent	Result	Score	Referees	Scorers
08 Feb	UCT Rugby Fields, CT	UCT	WON	23-17	Cwengile Jadezweni	T: Williams, Erasmus, Mafuma. C: Janse van Rensburg (2).
15 Feb	TuksRugby Stadium, Pretoria	UP-Tuks	WON	47-46	AJ Jacobs	T: Mafuma (2), Van Vuuren, Klopper, Immelman, Nieuwoudt. C: Mason (3), Janse van Rensburg. P: Janse van Rensburg.
22 Feb	Shimla Park, Bloem	NMMU	WON	46-19	Stephan Geldenhuys	T: Williams, Morison, Mason, Mafuma, Botha, Van Rensburg. C: Mason (4).
14 Mar	FNB Stadium, Jhb.	CUT	WON	10-09	Jaco Kotze	T: Mafuma.C: Mason. P: Mason.
21 Mar	FNB Stadium, Jhb.	UJ	Lost	49-72	Rasta Rasivhenge	T: Williams (2), Venter, Mafuma, Van Rensburg. C: De Wet (5).
24 Mar	Cape Town Stadium, CT	Maties	Lost	14-35	Cwengile Jadezweni	T: Williams, Mafuma. C: Mason (2).
28 Mar	Cape Town Stadium, CT	PUK	Lost	21-37	AJ Jacobs	T: Williams (2), Huggett. C: De Wet (2), Mason.

2015 APPEARANCES & POINTS

PLAYER	UCT	UP-Tuks	NMMU	CUT	UJ	Maties	PUK	Apps	T	C	P	DG	Pts	Career Apps
Sechaba Matsoele	15	–	–	–	–	–	–	1	–	–	–	–	0	1
Mosolwa Mashudu Mafuma	14	11	11	11	14	14	x	6	7	–	–	–	35	6
Stephan Janse van Rensburg	13	13	13	13	15R	13	13	7	2	3	1	–	19	10
Arthur Williams	12	12	12	12	12	12	12	7	6	–	–	–	30	9
Carel-Jan Coetzee	11	–	14	–	–	–	–	2	–	–	–	–	0	2
Pieter-Steyn de Wet	10	10	10	–	10	10	10	6	–	7	–	–	14	17
Zee Mkhabela	9	–	x	9	9	9	–	4	–	–	–	–	0	11
Nardus Erasmus	8	8	–	–	–	–	–	2	1	–	–	–	5	2
Neil Claassen	7c	7c	7c	7c	7c	7c	7c	7	–	–	–	–	0	20
Refuoe Rampeta	6	6	–	–	–	–	–	2	–	–	–	–	0	4
Dennis Visser	5	5	5	5	5	–	4	6	–	–	–	–	0	6
Nicolaas Immelman	4	4R	4R	4R	4R	4	–	6	1	–	–	–	5	11
Rudolph Botha	3	3	–	3	3	3R	3R	6	–	–	–	–	0	11
Reinach Venter	2	–	–	–	–	–	–	2	–	–	–	–	0	2
Teunis Nieuwoudt	1	1	1R	1R	1R	1	1R	7	1	–	–	–	5	14
Elandré Huggett	2R	2	2	2R	2R	2	2	7	1	–	–	–	5	23
Ox Nche	1R	1R	–	–	–	–	–	2	–	–	–	–	0	10
Boela Venter	4R	–	–	7R	5R	5	5	5	1	–	–	–	5	12
Ntokozo Vidima	x	4	4	4	4	7R	4R	6	–	–	–	–	0	6
Renier Botha	9R	9	9	10	9R	9R	9	7	1	–	–	–	5	17
Naldo Meyer	15R	x	x	x	15	14R	11	4	–	–	–	–	0	4
Daniel Maartens	6R	6R	6R	–	–	–	–	3	–	–	–	–	0	7
Jacobus van Vuuren	3R	3R	3R	–	–	–	–	3	1	–	–	–	5	11
Marco Mason	–	15	15	15	–	15	15	5	1	11	1	–	30	7
Apiwe Dinga	–	14	12R	–	–	x	x	2	–	–	–	–	0	2
Marco Klopper	–	2R	7R	–	2	2R	2R	5	1	–	–	–	5	8
Albertus Pretorius	–	14R	–	9R	–	–	15R	3	–	–	–	–	0	3
Musa Mahlasela	–	11R	6	6	x	6	6	5	–	–	–	–	0	5
Willandré Kotzenberg	–	–	8	8	8	6R	6R	5	–	–	–	–	0	5
Chase Morrison	–	–	3	3R	3R	3	3	5	1	–	–	–	5	12
Thabiso Khanye	–	–	1	1	1	–	1	4	–	–	–	–	0	4
Vuyani Maqina	–	–	–	14	11	11	14	4	1	–	–	–	5	13
Anrich Alberts	–	–	–	6R	6	–	–	2	–	–	–	–	0	2
Pieter Faber	–	–	–	–	13	–	–	1	–	–	–	–	0	1
Murray Bondesio	–	–	–	–	–	8	8	2	–	–	–	–	0	2
Gert Kotze	–	–	–	–	–	1R	–	1	–	–	–	–	0	1
36 Players								152	26	21	2	0	178	281

Note: ■ = *Yellow Card,* ■ = *Red Card*

CUT

Played	Won	Lost	Drawn	Points for	Points against	Tries for	Tries against
7	2	5	0	93	211	11	26

Date	Venue	Opponent	Result	Score	Referees	Scorers
08 Feb	Craven Stadium, Stellenbosch	Maties	Lost	00-40	Francois Pretorius	
15 Feb	CUT Rugby Stadium, Bloem	UCT	WON	10-09	Jaco Kotze	T: Toua. C: Baron. P: Baron.
22 Feb	UJ Stadium, Jhb.	UJ	Lost	00-14	Ben Crouse	
14 Mar	FNB Stadium, Jhb.	Shimlas	Lost	09-10	Jaco Kotze	P: Van Tonder (3).
21 Mar	FNB Stadium, Jhb.	UP-Tuks	Lost	25-68	AJ Jacobs	T: Baron, Wiese, Maruping. C: Baron (2).
24 Mar	Cape Town Stadium, CT	PUK	Lost	14-44	Rasta Rasivhenge	T: Grundlingh, Noort. C: Van Tonder (2).
28 Mar	Cape Town Stadium, CT	NMMU	WON	35-26	Lourens van der Merwe	T: Rossouw, Wiese, Noort, Bucuchane, Van Tonder. C: Van Tonder (3).

2016 APPEARANCES & POINTS

PLAYER	Maties	UCT	UJ	Shimlas	UP-Tuks	Pukke	NMMU	Apps	T	C	P	DG	Pts	Career Apps
Meyer van Tonder	15	15	15	15	15	15	15	7	1	5	3	–	24	7
Clinton Toua	14	14	–	–	–	–	–	2	1	–	–	–	5	2
Charles Hitchcock	13c	13c	13c	13c	13c	–	–	5	–	–	–	–	0	28
Johan Louis Nel	12	12	12	12	–	12	12	6	–	–	–	–	0	9
Henry Immelman	11	11	11	11	11	–	11	6	–	–	–	–	0	10
Darren Baron	10	10	10	10	10	10	10	7	1	3	1	–	14	7
Marius Grobler	9	9	9	9	9R	9	9	7	–	–	–	–	0	17
Jasper Wiese	8	8	8R	8	8	8c	8c	7	2	–	–	–	10	11
Vincent Maruping	7	7	8	7	7	7	7	7	1	–	–	–	5	22
Sylvester Makakole	6	6R	7R	7R	4R	7R	7R	7	–	–	–	–	0	7
Rayno Nel	5	5	5	5	5	6	5	7	–	–	–	–	0	13
Justin Basson	4	–	–	–	–	–	–	1	–	–	–	–	0	1
Gunther Janse van Vuuren	3	3	3	3	3R	3	3	7	–	–	–	–	0	7
Theunis Truter	2	2	2R	2	–	–	–	4	–	–	–	–	0	11
Gerard Baard	1	1R	1R	1R	1	1R	1R	7	–	–	–	–	0	22
Len Noort	2R	2R	2	2R	2	2R	2R	7	2	–	–	–	10	23
Jean Volkwyn	1R	1	1	1	x	1	1	6	–	–	–	–	0	6
Wikus Davis	5R	4	4	4	4	4	4	7	–	–	–	–	0	7
Junior Abraham Burger	6R	8R	7	6R	7R	6R	–	6	–	–	–	–	0	6
Dean Jacobs	x	x	9R	9R	9	–	–	3	–	–	–	–	0	7
Ali Mgijima	10R	12R	10R	12R	12	–	–	5	–	–	–	–	0	10
Lethole Mokoena	14R	14R	11R	x	13R	–	–	4	–	–	–	–	0	8
George Marich	3R	3R	3R	3R	–	3R	3R	6	–	–	–	–	0	6
Dean Rossouw	–	6	6	6	6	–	6	5	1	–	–	–	5	9
Ruan Wasserman	–	–	14	14	14	13	13	5	–	–	–	–	0	5
Neil Schoombee	–	–	–	–	3	–	–	1	–	–	–	–	0	6
Cameron van Heerden	–	–	–	–	2R	2	2	3	–	–	–	–	0	3
Johann Grundlingh	–	–	–	–	5R	5R	4R	3	1	–	–	–	5	11
Mauro Bucuchane	–	–	–	–	–	14	14	2	1	–	–	–	5	2
Masego Toolo	–	–	–	–	–	11	x	1	–	–	–	–	0	12
Sarel Roux	–	–	–	–	–	5	–	1	–	–	–	–	0	1
Olwethu Ndakisa	–	–	–	–	–	12R	12R	2	–	–	–	–	0	2
Tiisetso Madonsela	–	–	–	–	–	14R	x	1	–	–	–	–	0	1
33 Players								155	11	8	4	0	83	299

Note: ▓ = *Yellow Card*

NMMU

Played	Won	Lost	Drawn	Points for	Points against	Tries for	Tries against
7	1	6	0	169	251	21	31

Date	Venue	Opponent	Result	Score	Referees	Scorers
08 Feb	UJ Stadium, Jhb.	UJ	Lost	12-19	Rodney Bonaparte	T: Reinecke. C: Bolze. P: Bolze.
15 Feb	NMMU Madibaz Stadium, PE	Maties	Lost	25-27	Sindile Ngcese	T: Kaba, Maarman, Ngam. C: Bolze (2).
22 Feb	Shimla Park, Bloem	Shimlas	Lost	19-46	Stephan Geldenhuys	T: Ludick, Du Preez, Vers. C: Bolze.
14 Mar	FNB Stadium, Jhb.	PUK	Lost	18-46	Rodney Bonaparte	T: Brown, Swarts. C: Bolze, Kean.
21 Mar	FNB Stadium, Jhb.	UCT	WON	46-33	Stephan Geldenhuys	T: Du Preez (2), Brown, Pokomela, Nieuwoudt, Paul. C: Kean (3), Bolze.
24 Mar	Cape Town Stadium, CT	UP-Tuks	Lost	23-45	Jaco Kotze	T: Du Preez, Zungu, Paul. C: Kean (2).
28 Mar	Cape Town Stadium, CT	CUT	Lost	26-35	Lourens van der Merwe	T: Oosthuizen, Esterhuizen, Paul. C: Bolze (2). P: Kean.

2016 APPEARANCES & POINTS

PLAYER	UJ	Maties	Shimlas	Pukke	UCT	UP-Tuks	CUT	Apps	T	C	P	DG	Pts	Career Apps
Lindelwe Zungu	15	15	13R	–	15	15	–	5	1	–	–	–	5	5
Keanu Vers	14	14	15	15	13	13	15	7	1	–	–	–	5	7
Jeremy Ward	13	13	13	13	12c	12c	–	6	–	–	–	–	0	6
Andile Jho	12	12	–	–	15R	x	12	4	–	–	–	–	0	18
Yamkela Ngam	11	11	11	11	–	–	–	4	1	–	–	–	5	15
Simon Bolze	10	10	10R	10	10	x	10	6	–	6	3	–	21	6
Ivan Ludick	9c	9c	9c	9c	–	–	–	4	1	–	–	–	5	14
Kevin Kaba	8	8	8	7	4	–	–	5	1	–	–	–	5	5
Andisa Ntsila	7	6R	7	–	–	7	7R	5	–	–	–	–	0	11
Henry Brown	6	7	6	6	6	7R	7	7	2	–	–	–	10	7
Gerrit Huisamen	5	5	5	5	5	5	5	7	–	–	–	–	0	7
Elandré van der Merwe	4	4	7R	4R	–	5R	5R	6	–	–	–	–	0	8
Nemo Roelofse	3	3	1R	3R	3	1R	3R	7	–	–	–	–	0	7
JP Jamieson	2	2R	–	2R	2	–	–	4	–	–	–	–	0	4
Marzuq Maarman	1	3R	1	1R	3R	1	1	7	1	–	–	–	5	12
Jedwyn Harty	2R	–	–	–	2R	2R	–	3	–	–	–	–	0	3
Nico Oosthuizen	3R	1	3	3	1	3	3	7	1	–	–	–	5	7
Wynand Grassmann	x	4R	–	–	–	–	–	1	–	–	–	–	0	4
Jayson Reinecke	6R	6	–	–	4R	–	6R	4	1	–	–	–	5	4
Sibusiso Ngcokovane	9R	9R	9R	9R	9	9	–	6	–	–	–	–	0	6
Courtney Winnaar	x	–	–	–	–	–	–	0	–	–	–	–	0	0
Khaya Malotana	15R	5R	–	–	11	11	11	5	–	–	–	–	0	8
James Beyl	1R	x	3R	1	–	x	17R	4	–	–	–	–	0	4
Tango Balekile	–	2	2R	–	–	–	2R	3	–	–	–	–	0	3
Thomas Kean	–	10R	10	10R	10R	10	10R	6	–	6	1	–	15	6
Ivan-John du Preez	–	–	14	14	14	14	14	5	4	–	–	–	20	11
Riaan Esterhuizen	–	–	12	12	–	–	13	3	1	–	–	–	5	3
Tyler Paul	–	–	4	4	7	4	4	5	3	–	–	–	15	10
Warrick Venter	–	–	2	2	–	2	2	4	–	–	–	–	0	9
Hayden Tharratt	–	–	6R	–	–	–	–	1	–	–	–	–	0	1
Junior Pokomela	–	–	–	8	8	8	8	4	1	–	–	–	5	4
Warren Swarts	–	–	–	11R	–	–	–	1	1	–	–	–	5	1
Stephanus Nieuwoudt	–	–	–	x	5R	6	6	3	1	–	–	–	5	3
Luvo Claassen	–	–	–	–	9R	x	9	2	–	–	–	–	0	2
Zandre Vos	–	–	–	–	x	–	–	0	–	–	–	–	0	0
Luan Nieuwoudt	–	–	–	–	–	–	9R	1	–	–	–	–	0	1
36 Players								152	21	12	4	0	141	222

Note: ▓ = *Yellow Card*

UCT

Played	Won	Lost	Drawn	Points for	Points against	Tries for	Tries against
7	0	7	0	103	326	11	39

Date	Venue	Opponent	Result	Score	Referees	Scorers
08 Feb	UCT Rugby Fields, CT	Shimlas	Lost	17-23	Cwengile Jadezweni	T: Ngcukana, Nel. C: De Abreu. P: De Abreu.
15 Feb	CUT Rugby Stadium, Bloem	CUT	Lost	09-10	Jaco Kotze	T: Lategan. C: Anderson.
22 Feb	UCT Rugby Fields, CT	PUK	Lost	06-24	Francois Pretorius	P: Anderson (2).
14 Mar	FNB Stadium, Jhb.	Maties	Lost	13-60	Archie Sehlako	T: Stringer. C: Anderson. P: Bednall (2).
21 Mar	FNB Stadium, Jhb.	NMMU	Lost	33-46	Stephan Geldenhuys	T: Xoli (2), Van Rensburg, Porter. C: Bednall (2). P: Bednall.
24 Mar	Cape Town Stadium, CT	UJ	Lost	00-63	Jaco Kotze	
28 Mar	Cape Town Stadium, CT	UP-Tuks	Lost	25-100	Cwengile Jadezweni	T: Anderson (2), Alexander.

2016 APPEARANCES & POINTS

PLAYER	Shimlas	CUT	Pukke	Maties	NMMU	UJ	UP-Tuks	Apps	T	C	P	DG	Pts	Career Apps
Khanyo Ngcukana	15	–	15	–	–	–	–	2	1	–	–	–	5	10
Sebastian Roodt	14	–	–	–	–	–	14	2	–	–	–	–	0	2
Lihleli Xoli	13	13	–	13	12	12	–	5	2	–	–	–	10	29
Hennie Lategan	12	12	13	12	–	–	–	4	1	–	–	–	5	4
Suwi Chibale	11	11	11	11	10R	12R	12	7	–	–	–	–	0	9
Rob Anderson	10	10	10R	12R	15R	10R	10	7	2	2	2	–	20	7
Dylan-Lee Tidbury	9	9	9	9	9R	9R	9	7	–	–	–	–	0	7
Guy Alexander	8c	8c	–	8c	–	8c	8c	5	1	–	–	–	5	21
Luke Stringer	7	7	7	7	7	7	–	6	1	–	–	–	5	12
Jason Klaasen	6	6	6	6	–	–	–	4	–	–	–	–	0	28
Gary Porter	5	5	5	5	5	–	–	5	1	–	–	–	5	5
Mark Prior	4	4	–	6R	6	4	5	6	–	–	–	–	0	14
Michael Kumbirai	3	3	3	–	–	–	–	3	–	–	–	–	0	3
Brenton Greaves	2	2	2R	2	2	–	–	5	–	–	–	–	0	5
Joel Carew	1	1	1	1	1	1	1	7	–	–	–	–	0	24
Sean Paterson	2R	–	8R	2R	8	–	2R	5	–	–	–	–	0	5
Msizi Zondi	1R	x	1R	1R	1R	1R	1R	6	–	–	–	–	0	11
Olwethu Hans	4R	6R	5R	–	8R	6	6	6	–	–	–	–	0	6
Nyasha Tarusenga	6R	8R	8	–	–	5R	4	5	–	–	–	–	0	5
Steve Wallace	9R	9R	9R	9R	9	9	12R	7	–	–	–	–	0	9
Hilio De Abreu	10R	10R	10	–	–	–	–	3	–	1	1	–	5	3
Nate Nel	14R	14	14	14	11	11	15	7	1	–	–	–	5	21
Sam Theron	x	3R	–	3R	3R	3R	3	5	–	–	–	–	0	5
Joel Smith	–	15	12R	15	15	–	–	4	–	–	–	–	0	4
Gerard Pieterse	–	15R	–	–	–	15	–	2	–	–	–	–	0	2
Keagan Timm	–	x	2	–	2R	2	2	4	–	–	–	–	0	4
Kofi Appiah	–	–	12	10R	–	–	15R	3	–	–	–	–	0	3
Jade Kriel	–	–	4c	4	4c	–	–	3	–	–	–	–	0	10
David Maasch	–	–	3R	3	3	3	–	4	–	–	–	–	0	13
Thomas Bednall	–	–	–	10	10	10	–	3	–	2	3	–	13	5
Duncan Saffy	–	–	–	5R	5R	5	–	3	–	–	–	–	0	3
Bradley Janse van Rensburg	–	–	–	–	14	14	11	3	1	–	–	–	5	3
Justin Heunis	–	–	–	–	13	13	13	3	–	–	–	–	0	3
Struan Murray	–	–	–	–	–	2R	–	1	–	–	–	–	0	1
Alva Senderayi	–	–	–	–	–	4R	7	2	–	–	–	–	0	2
Rayno Mapoe	–	–	–	–	–	–	13R	1	–	–	–	–	0	1
Jason Landman	–	–	–	–	–	–	3R	1	–	–	–	–	0	1
Stuart Stopforth	–	–	–	–	–	–	7R	1	–	–	–	–	0	1
Brendon Clements	–	–	–	–	–	–	8R	1	–	–	–	–	0	1
39 Players								158	11	5	6	0	83	302

Note: ▨ = *Yellow Card*

FNB Varsity Shield

LOG

Team	P	W	L	D	PF	PA	PD	TF	TA	LB	TB	Pts
Wits	8	6	2	0	342	96	246	50	12	2	6	32
UWC	8	5	3	0	179	186	-7	28	25	0	3	24
UKZN	8	7	1	0	382	144	238	51	19	0	4	20
TUT	8	1	7	0	136	355	-219	17	50	2	2	8
UFH	8	1	7	0	102	360	-258	14	54	2	1	5

Note: LB = Losing bonus, TB = Try bonus
Note: UFH was docked 2 log points for fielding an ineligible player against UWC on the 1st of February. UWC were awarded 5 log points for the game.
Note: UKZN was docked 12 log points for fielding an ineligible player throughout the season.

LEADING SCORERS

40 POINTS OR MORE

	TEAM	T	C	P	DG	Pts
Tristan Tedder	UKZN	2	34	1	0	114
Warren Gilbert	Wits	1	29	0	2	96
Aidynn Cupido	UWC	4	7	3	1	49
Thobekani Buthelezi	UKZN	9	0	0	0	45
Cecil Conradie	Wits	8	0	0	0	40

5 TRIES OR MORE

Thobekani Buthelezi	UKZN	9	Kwanele Ngema	Wits	5
Cecil Conradie	Wits	8	Luvuyo Pupuma	Wits	5
Tristan Blewett	UKZN	7	Kerron van Vuuren	UKZN	5
Constant Beckerling	Wits	6	Shayne Makhombe	UKZN	5
Joshua Jarvis	Wits	5			

Varsity Shield
FINAL RESULT

Wits Rugby Stadium, Johannesburg. Monday 8 April. Referee: Cwengile Jadezweni

Wits 39 (23) (*Tries: Beckerling, Conradie, Logan, Weseman, Cloete. Conversions: Gilbert 4.*
Drop goal: Gilbert)

UWC 2 (2) (*Penalty A Cupido*)

Wits: Luxolo Ntsepe *(Adriaan van Blerk, 66)*, Keanele Ngema, Joshua Jarvis *(Wian Coetzee, 72)*, Kyle Weseman, Sicelo Champion *(Thato Marobels, 75)*, Warren Gilbert *(capt)*, Ruan Cloete, Constant Beckerling *(Ayabulela Mdudi, 72)*, Conor Brockschmidt, Ruan McDonald, Mitchell Fraser, Graham Logan *(Richard Crossman, 61)*, Luvuyo Pupuma *(Brandon Palmer, 66)*, Cecil Conradie *(Craig Hume, 72)*, Tidje Visser *(Ameer Williams, 75)*.

UWC: Jacquin Moses, Octaven van Stade, Courtney Cupido, Lubabalo Faleni *(Monre Lingeveldt, 49)*, Minenhle Mthethwa *(Melik Wana, 52)*, Aidynn Cupido, Clayton Daniels *(Matt Nortje, 67 / Byron Burgess, 75)*, Matthew Faught, Jeremy Papier, Verno Treu *(Sabelo Dlamini, 68)*, Matthew le Roux, Brandon Valentyn, Tahriq Allen *(Robin Paulse, 75)*, Peter Wanijiru *(Keenan Douw, 75)*, Kelvin de Bruyn *(capt)* *(Wayrin Losper, 56)*.

FNB VARSITY SHIELD CHAMPIONS
2011 CUT, 2012 Wits, 2013 CUT, 2014 CUT, 2015 UKZN, 2016 WITS

Rewarding year for Women's Sevens

By Zeena van Tonder

THE 2016 season will be remembered as a rewarding one for the Springbok Women's Sevens as they won the Hong Kong Women's Sevens Invitational, Roma Sevens and Rugby Africa Women's Sevens titles respectively.

The team kicked off the season on an encouraging note as they advanced to the Plate Final of the Las Vegas Invitational, before making history by winning the Hong Kong Women's Sevens Invitational Cup for the first time.

This tour was followed by an international invitational tournament in France where they defeated Brazil three times, but went down twice to France A and once to France B.

The team returned to their winning ways in Italy where they defeated France twice on the final day of the tournament to clinch the Roma Sevens title.

To the delight of Springbok Women's Sevens coach Renfred Dazel, they managed to secure back-to-back tournament wins by emerging victorious in the Rugby Africa Women's Sevens in Zimbabwe where the team held their nerve in a tightly-contested final against Kenya to win 22-17.

They backed this up with a third-place finish in the Hokkaido Invitational Sevens in Japan and then recorded an eighth-place finish in the Dubai HSBC Women's Sevens World Series for which they secured an invite from World Rugby.

On the provincial front, Border and Free State successfully defended their titles in a thrilling finale to the SA Rugby Women's Interprovincial competition at the BCM Stadium in East London.

Border defeated Western Province 29-16 to win the A Section of the competition and Free State beat the Golden Lions 19-5 to win the B Section.

The victory for Border also served as a special milestone for the team as it marked their fourth successive Women's Interprovincial title.

Border's U16 and U18 girls teams also had a successful season, as they were crowned the champions at the National Girls' U16 Week at the HT Pelatona Projects Stadium in Welkom and the National Girls' U18 Week at the Northern Cape High School in Kimberley respectively, where they both overcame archrivals Western Province.

The Border Rugby Union also earned the bragging rights for winning the U16 final in the South Section of the Women's Day Youth Training Centre (YTC) competition at PW Botha High School in George, while Western Province won the U18 section.

The Limpopo Blue Bulls U18s and Blue Bulls U16s, meanwhile, won the North Section of the tournaments respectively at the Eersterust Rugby Club in Pretoria.

The 2016 season also marked the return of women's 15-a-side rugby with a three-day testing at a training camp in Cape Town, which allowed SA Rugby to take stock of the women's talent on offer in the country.

RESULTS AND LOGS

Inter Provincial Women A

Jul 09	Eeastern Province 32, Western Province 17	*Zwide Stadium, P.E.*
Jul 09	South Western Districts 03, Border 72	*Bridgton Sports Grounds, Oudtshoorn*
Jul 09	KwaZulu-Natal 14, Blue Bulls 10	*KP2, Kings Park, Durban*
Jul 23	Western Province 51, South Western Districts 03	*City Park Stadium, Cape Town*
Jul 23	Blue Bulls 38, Eastern Province 17	*Loftus B, Pretoria*
Jul 23	Border 27, KwaZulu-Natal 03	*BCM Stadium, East London*
Aug 06	South Western Districts 03, Blue Bulls 37	*Outeniqua Park, George*
Aug 06	KwaZulu-Natal 26, Eastern Province 10	*KP2, Kings Park, Durban*
Aug 06	Border 05, Western Province 07	*BCM Stadium, East London*
Aug 20	Eastern Province 39, South Western Districts 07	*NMMU Missionvale Campus, P.E.*
Aug 20	Blue Bulls 00, Border 19	*Loftus B, Pretoria*
Aug 20	Western Province 12, KwaZulu-Natal 11	*City Park Stadium, Cape Town*

Sep 03	Western Province 12, Blue Bulls 07	*DHL Newlands Rugby Stadium, Cape Town*
Sep 03	KwaZulu-Natal 86, South Western Districts 00	*KP2, Kings Park, Durban*
Sep 03	Border 47, Eastern Province 10	*BCM Stadium, East London*

FINAL

| Sep 17 | Border 29, Western Province 16 | *BCM Stadium, East London* |

LOG

Section A	P	W	L	D	PF	PA	PD	TF	TA	BP	PTS
Border	5	4	1	0	170	23	147	30	3	4	20
Western Province	5	4	1	0	99	58	41	14	3	1	17
KwaZulu-Natal	5	3	2	0	140	59	81	22	11	3	15
Blue Bulls	5	2	3	0	92	65	27	14	10	4	12
Eastern Province	5	2	3	0	108	135	-27	14	18	1	9
South Western Districts	5	0	5	0	16	285	-269	1	50	0	0

RESULTS AND LOGS
Inter Provincial Women B

Jul 09	Limpopo Blue Bulls 19, Golden Lions 51	*HTS Tom Naudé, Polokwane*
Jul 09	Mpumalanga 50, Valke 20	*Witbank Stadium*
Jul 23	Valke 15, Limpopo Blue Bulls 19	*NWU Vaal RC Vanderbijlpark*
Jul 23	Leopards 53, Mpumalanga 10	*Profert Olën Park, Potchefstroom*
Aug 06	Limpopo Blue Bulls 29, Leopards 29	*Old Peter Mokaba Stadium, Polokwane*
Aug 06	Golden Lions 34, Valke 17	*Alberton Rugby Club, Alberton*
Aug 06	Griquas 58, Griffons 17	*Concordia, Namaqualand*
Aug 06	Boland 12, Free State 62	*Boland Stadium, Wellington*
Aug 19	Mpumalanga 05, Limpopo Blue Bulls 31	*Secunda Sasol Rugby Club*
Aug 20	Griffons 10, Boland 36	*Bronville Stadium*
Aug 20	Griquas 05, Free State 61	*Concordia, Namaqualand*
Aug 20	Leopards 05, Golden Lions 15	*Profert Olën Park, Potchefstroom*
Sep 03	Golden Lions 24, Mpumalanga 10	*University of Johannesburg, Johannesburg*
Sep 03	Valke 20, Leopards 34	*Barnard Stadium, Kempton Park*
Sep 03	Boland 22, Griquas 20	*Boland Stadium, Wellington*
Sep 03	Free State 110, Griffons 14	*Old Greys Rugby Club, Bloemfontein*

FINAL

| Sep 17 | Golden Lions 05, Free State 19 | *BCM Stadium, East London* |

LOG

Section A	P	W	L	D	PF	PA	PD	TF	TA	BP	PTS
Free State	3	3	0	0	233	31	202	38	5	3	15
Boland	3	2	1	0	70	92	-22	11	15	1	9
Griquas	3	1	2	0	83	100	-17	13	15	2	6
Griffons	3	0	3	0	41	204	-163	7	34	0	0

Section B	P	W	L	D	PF	PA	PD	TF	TA	BP	PTS
Golden Lions	4	4	0	0	124	51	73	22	9	3	19
Leopards	4	2	1	1	121	74	47	20	14	3	13
Limpopo Blue Bulls	4	2	1	1	98	100	-2	16	18	2	12
Mpumalanga	4	1	3	0	75	128	-53	13	22	1	5
Valke	4	0	4	0	72	137	-65	14	22	2	2

Border celebrate winning the 2016 Women's Interprovincial Section A.

AMATEUR RUGBY

Lions, Sharks, WP take APC honours

THE Golden Lions, Sharks Club XV and Western Province took top honours in the SA Rugby Northern, Central and Southern Amateur Provincial Competitions (APC) respectively following deserving victories in their respective Cup Finals.

All three teams advanced through their competitions unbeaten following three rounds of matches.

The Golden Lions defeated their Gauteng rivals, the Blue Bulls, 26-19 in the Northern APC final at the Alberton Rugby Club in Johannesburg.

The Valke finished third in the competition following their 36-14 victory against the Golden Lions XV, while Pumas Highveld overpowered the Limpopo Blue Bulls 34-17 to win the Plate Final and the Leopards took seventh place with their 31-21 victory against Pumas Lowveld.

In the Central APC, the Sharks Club XV outplayed Griquas Central 43-24 at Griqua Park in Kimberley to win their competition.

Also in Kimberly, the KwaZulu-Natal Wildebeest Rural capped off a good run for the Durban-based union as they worked their way to a 37-20 victory against Free State Rural to win the Plate Final, while Free State Central finished in third place as they edged Griffons Central 28-24, and Griquas Rural won the seventh-and-eighth place play-off thanks to a 30-25 victory against Griffons Rural.

Top honours in the Southern APC went to Western Province, who held their nerve against SWD to win the final 38-31 at Outeniqua Park in George.

Eastern Province finished the Southern tournament in third place after beating Boland 45-32, while their Eastern Province Rural counterparts completed a rewarding day for the union as they held off Border for a 29-25 victory in the Plate Final. Border Rural registered a 33-23 victory against the SWD XV to take seventh place.

Obituaries

By Paul Dobson

VAL ASHWORTH

VAL Ashworth was an eager sportsman whose name was biggest in South African basketball. He played first-league rugby, cricket, hockey and basketball. He played for South Africa at basketball and for Natal at rugby. In his day Natal had the great Springbok cricketer Roy McLean, Geoff Tasker and then the great Springbok, Keith Oxlee, as the flyhalves, and Ashworth got only one match for Natal.

Ashworth was very much a man of Pietermaritzburg. He grew up there from the age of eight, went to school at Boys' Model School and then Maritzburg College where he matriculated as the top mathematics pupil. He was awarded a scholarship to attend Natal University in Pietermaritzburg where he studied engineering – and played rugby.

He had not played for Maritzburg College 1st XV but he played for the university side and was chosen for Central Universities (Rhodes, Free State and Natal) for their tour to Northern Rhodesia, as Zambia then was. In 1951 he played for Natal Universities when they beat the Oxford & Cambridge touring team 8-5. And after university he played for Wasp Wanderers in Pietermaritzburg.

Val was his nickname, given to him as a baby because he was born on Valentine's Day. His real name was Ronald Edward Ashworth, born in Vryheid, northern Natal, on 14 February 1931. After university he joined the Natal Roads Department as materials manager, his life's career. His wife Joan died in 2005 and he died on 1 February 2016 in Pietermaritzburg, survived by his four sons, Mark, Dean, Paul and Lang, and five grandchildren.

BASIL BEY

BASIL Bey was one of South Africa's best and best-known schoolboy coaches. But he was much more.

Basil had a vast knowledge and understanding of rugby, was a player of great character and a brilliant coach. Alan Douglas remembers Bey, a new man at UCT, standing up at the rugby club's annual general meeting and introducing himself with the words: "My name is Basil Bey. I am a rugby fanatic."

Basil had come from Salisbury, Rhodesia (now Harare, Zimbabwe) where he had been the head prefect and captain of rugby at Prince Edward School. At UCT he changed from lock to prop and became the charismatic cap-

tain of UCT, loudly urging his team to PLAY. After a long spell at UCT, Basil went off to teach at Simon's Town High and played for False Bay, taking others with him. He captained False Bay.

From Simon's Town, Bey went to Plumstead High, where he, the principal Dieter Pakendorf and some boys built the three fields the school still has. Plumstead's rugby was brilliant at the time, as they ran sides, including Bishops, ragged. In 1971 he went to Bishops and in 1972 became the first team coach, where he stayed till 1998, 27 great seasons for the school. They did not always win, not at all, but they played the most adventurous, exciting brand of rugby, known as Bishops rugby.

He also found time to coach the first teams at UCT and False Bay. He was the False Bay coach in 1972 when the club won the Grand Challenge for the first time. The second time they won it was in 2016.

He was also a Western Province senior selector and coached the Western Province Craven Week team. After leaving Bishops Basil coached up in Welkom and at Stellenbosch.

With him, a vast store of rugby knowledge and wisdom has gone. Apart from a coaching column on an online platform, Basil, despite many urgings, did not put his philosophies and techniques on paper.

He was, of course, much more than a rugby man: a sensitive teacher of English, loving poetry in particular, and at Bishops he was the Housemaster of School House for the full term.

He was a man with a great understanding of and sympathy for other people.

Basil Bey was born in Harare on 6 April 1936. His father was an Athenian Greek who found English difficult and his mother a Van Wyk from Hammanskraal, who found English difficult. They had three sons - Nick, Basil and tennis player Adrian. Basil's wife, Zita (Robertson) predeceased him. After a painful battle with cancer, he died on 10 November 2016, survived by their children Martin and Michelle and grandchildren. His funeral service in the Memorial Chapel at Bishops was packed.

BABA BOTHA

THERE probably has not been a man in South African rugby so identified with his province as Baba Botha, a scrumhalf in his playing days. He played for the province, his son Riaan played for the province, his daughters married men who played for the province. If you wanted to know anything about the province, you asked Baba Botha. If Doc Craven wanted anything done in the province, he asked Baba Botha, whose province no longer exists.

The province was named North Eastern Districts when first founded in 1903. Towns in the province were Cradock, Graaff-Reinet, Aliwal North, Burgersdorp, De Aar, Murraysburg, Fort Beaufort, Jansenville and Maclear. Its name was changed to Northern Eastern Cape in 1967 and then ceased to exist with the restructuring of provincial rugby in South Africa at the end of 1995. This was decided at a meeting under president Louis Luyt at Ellis Park and when it was decided, Botha, the president of North Eastern Cape, walked out in a rage. The province was then divided into three: part to Griquas, part to Border and part to Eastern Province.

Botha played, mostly at scrumhalf but also at flyhalf and fullback, for North Eastern Cape from 1967 to 1976, and was its captain in 1972. He was then a selector, the coach, the manager of the union and its last president.

In 1970 he played his toughest match. The All Blacks had just lost the third Test in Port Elizabeth and thereby their chance of winning the series. Their next match was against North Eastern Cape in Burgersdorp. The All Blacks scored 17 tries and their fullback Gerald Kember kicked 34 points in an 85-0 victory.

Botha's wife Gussie was much involved in the Vukusebenze Shelter in Cradock where Gussie and her helpers fed between 30 and 90 people on a weekday while Baba taught young people skills such as carpentry and gardening.

Adolf Botha was born in Uitenhage on 8 July 1946 and was a clerk on the railways and played his club rugby for Noupoort. He died on 5 November 2016, survived by Gussie, his son and two daughters. Gussie, who was a year younger than her husband, died 18 days after him.

TOOL BOTHA
THE strange nickname came from his occupation, really. Tool Botha was born and grew up in Brits and matriculated from HTS Middelburg, a man set on a technical career. Leaving school he got a job as an apprentice at Thabazimbi, an iron-mining town, where he became a boilermaker and then advanced to a foreman and then in charge of maintenance, retiring in 1994 at the age of 55.

He played rugby at flyhalf for the Thabazimbi town team. Then in 1968 the Far North Rugby Union was established from Northern Transvaal and he played flyhalf for the new union for the first three years of its struggling existence. In their first years they were the weakest province in South Africa, but in 1971 they fared better and drew 6-6 with the Argentinian Pumas in an unseemly match.

After his playing days he remained involved in the Thabazimbi club.

JP Botha was born on 24 October 1939.

He was married twice – for 32 years to Tienie van Emmenis till 1993 and then from 1996 to Sarie Venter. He died in the Kloof Medi-Clinic in Pretoria, after a lengthy illness, on 16 January 2016, survived by Sarie, his three sons, Cobus, Fanie and Arno, his three stepdaughters, six grandchildren and three great grandchildren.

HENKIE BURGER
HENKIE Burger played his club rugby for Park in the northern part of Port Elizabeth. He was also the Eastern Province scrumhalf from 1953 to 1957, playing 30 matches in all.

In 1953 Burger played for Eastern Province when they lost 16-11 to Australia's Wallabies. Burger's brothers, Coetzee and Hannes, also played provincial rugby.

Hendrik Burger was born on 18 February 1934. He died on 25 January 2016 in Port Elizabeth.

CHARLIE COCKRELL
CHARLIE Cockrell, a great rugby man and a fine gentleman, died of a heart attack on the evening of 4 October 2016.

Three hookers named Cockrell played for Western Province from 1963 to 1982. Charlie played from 1963 to 1971 and was a Springbok. Robert played from 1972 to 1982 and was a Springbok. William played in 1981.

The three brothers, sons of Fred and Eileen Cockrell in a family of 10 children, were from the near northern suburbs of Cape Town. They went to school there and played their club rugby there. Charlie went to Parow High, and played his club rugby for Northerns and then for Paarl. In all Charlie played 67 times for Western Province, a huge number in those days of far fewer matches than is now the case. His younger brother Robert, who died in 2000 at the age of 50, played 102 times for Western Province.

Charlie, a bustling, energetic hooker, became a Springbok in 1969 at the age of 30. That was on the demo tour of the UK and Ireland. He played in 10 matches on the tour including the Tests against Scotland, Wales and Ireland. He went as a replacement for Gys Pitzer who was injured early in the tour and then when Don Walton was injured Charlie became the No 1 hooker.

Walton was back for the England Tests but then was again injured and replaced by Robbie Barnard. Charlie played in the last match of the tour, the Springboks' best performance when they beat the Barbarians 21-12.

After his playing days Charlie turned his hand to coaching – first Paarl, then from 1975 to 1978 Griquas and then as the assistant coach to Dawie Snyman of the legendary Western Province sides of the 1980s. Snyman greatly admired his understanding of forward play and the way he could get on with his job with no fuss.

Charles Herbert Cockrell was born in Cape

Town on 10 January 1939. He was a telephone technician who became a transmission manager at Telkom. He married Estelle Gouws and they had two children – Ian and Colleen. He died suddenly at home when he and Estelle were preparing to go out for the evening.

Charlie Cockrell died on 4 October 2016, survived by Estelle, their children, two grandsons and two granddaughters.

JANNIE COETZEE

JANNIE Coetzee who played his club rugby for Nigel played scrumhalf for Eastern Transvaal, now the Valke, for six seasons and 24 matches, ending in 1977. That means that he played in Eastern Transvaal's best year, 1972.

In that year, the Currie Cup was divided into two sections. At the end of the sectional matches there were six teams left in contention, which made for six play-off matches. Eastern Transvaal had beaten Northern Transvaal – something that should be said again in case it did not sink in the first time – Boland and Natal but they lost to Rhodesia and Eastern Province. In the play-offs Eastern Transvaal again beat Boland and this time beat Eastern Province, which saw them into the final against Transvaal who had beaten Free State in their only play-off.

The final was played at the Pam Brink Stadium in Springs. At half-time Transvaal led 18-3. Skip Henderson, Eastern Transvaal's captain, rallied his forwards but the Red Devils, who had extra devil because none of their players had been invited to the Springbok trials earlier in the year, were not quite good enough, going down 25-19. Coetzee was the scrumhalf for Eastern Transvaal.

The next year Coetzee played when Eastern Transvaal lost to San Isidro of Buenos Aires and Brive of France, but missed out on the 1974 Lions and the 1976 All Blacks.

Johan Coetzee, who was also a Junior Springbok gymnast, died in February 2016. He was 67.

BRANDY COETZEE

BRANDY Coetzee was long involved with rugby in Northern Transvaal (now the Blue Bulls) as a player and then as an administrator.

First he played for his local club in Louis Trichardt up near the border with Zimbabwe. Louis Trichardt was in the Northern Transvaal Sub-union, formed when the Northern Transvaal Rugby Union was formed in 1938. In 1968 the Sub-union became an independent union, called Far North. This lasted till 1995 when it became just a big part of the Blue Bulls though its still functions for some competitions as the Limpopo Blue Bulls. Big, strong Coetzee played for the Sub-union.

Then he went to Pretoria and joined Harlequins, leaving them in 1963 to play for Oostelikes who won Pretoria's tough Carlton League. After his playing days, which ended

in 1969, Coetzee coached at the club and then got into administration, holding several offices on the executive, including chairman and president. He was for years the club's representative on the mother union. He served on the union's liaison committee from 1979 and on the executive, elected as one of Fritz Eloff's vice-presidents from 1985-88.

In 1993 he threw in his lot with the Centurion RFC and represented them on the Union. After the death of his wife Miekie, Leon Coetzee moved to his daughter Karin in Cape Town and after a battle with his health died there in September 2016.

FRED CORIN

FRED Corin, in his day one of South Africa's very best referees, died in the Strand at the age of 92.

Corin had a long career as a referee, officiating in his first match with an overseas team in 1955 and the last in 1970, which was not the end of his career. He loved all sport and had a promising playing career cut short by a painful injury.

At Rondebosch Boys' High, which he loved and where his sons and grandsons were schooled, he played hooker for the 1st XV whom he captained and cricket (a wicket keeper) for the 1st XI. His family were living in Claremont at the time and after he left school he played for Villagers. He was hooking as an 18-year-old for the Under-20s on Newlands C Field (now the Kelvin Grove Field) with his older brother Arthur propping next to him when the scrum collapsed and he broke his leg with a sound like a pistol shot. He was taken off in an ambulance, pins were put into his leg and he could not play again, but he could referee.

Corin was an outstanding member of the Western Province Referees' Society – unfailingly cheerful with a catching laugh, helpful and reliable. He was on the Western Province panel for many years in the days when local referees refereed provincial matches. The visitors were given a panel of three to choose from. When this system was abandoned in 1973, Corin got his first away provincial match – Natal vs Transvaal at Kingsmead. Those were days before Kings Park existed.

In 1955, the exciting British & Irish Lions toured South Africa and Corin refereed their match with Western Province Universities at Newlands, a match they won 20-17 with a late try. His other match with a touring team was New Zealand vs Orange Free State in 1970, a match the All Blacks won 20-12.

Corin was an uncomplicated, uncompromising referee. The laws were the laws and his job was to apply them fairly. There was nothing showy about his refereeing but players had great respect for him that has remained beyond his career. The great HO de Villiers would phone him for every birthday up to 92 in September 2016 and called him Mr Corin.

If he wagged a finger for a player to go to him, the player knew he was in trouble and his anxiety grew with each step. In a Grand Challenge match out at Paarl, a Paarl lock lost his rag and punched an opponent. He did not wait for the summoning finger but turned and walked off to the dressing room, knowing that Corin justice would be visited upon him. In later years he recalled the incident: "Nee wat, nadat ek die man geslaan het, en onthou het dat Freddie Corin die skeidsregter is, toe stuur ek maar myself van die veld af, om hom die moeite te spaar".

Those were days when referees had a set of three gestures - scrum, penalty and try - and did not speak or explain. When he penalised Transvaal at Newlands, the Transvaal captain asked the reason for the penalty and Corin said: "I'm sorry, but I am not here to teach you the laws of the game. I am here to ensure you abide by them. Please, leave me to do so."

When Corin was living in Milnerton, he and fellow referee Harry Minnaar founded the Milnerton Rugby club. They later combined with Union to form UniMil and are playing in the Western Province Super League in 2017.

Frederick Joseph Corin was born in Parow, Cape Town, on 29 September 1924, the youngest of six children – four boys and two girls. His brothers, Clifford, Arthur and Edward, joined up and served in World War II. They survived and settled in Johannesburg after the war. He matriculated in 1942 and studied accountancy at night school. Most of his working life was as a bookkeeper for Caltex and after his retirement he continued to do bookkeeping for various clients.

Corin slowed up considerably in the last two years of his life and needed care. He suffered a stroke and was in the Busamed Paardevallei Hospital in the Strand when he died on the morning of 19 November 2016, survived by Joan Lötter, his partner for 36 years, his sons Reid and Anthony, their wives and his six grandchildren.

DAWIE CROWTHER

SCHOOLS in the Northern Free State all knew about Dawie Crowther. A rugby week, started in 2008, was named after him, there was a Dawie Crowther Golf Day a month before he died and there is a Dawie Crowther Sports Room at Hoërskool Kroonstad, the Blouskool, where he taught for many years.

Crowther was much involved in Craven Weeks and was for 13 years a South African Schools Selector. At the age of 76 Crowther was a still a departmental head at Blouskool.

David William Crowther, BA BEd, was born on 21 May 1937 and was educated at Ladybrand Secondary School. He died in the Bloemfontein Mediclinic on 19 October 2016. He was buried from the NG Kerk Kroonheuwelnoord. His wife Freda survived him.

POPEYE DE BRUIN

FLIP de Bruin was a man of Postmasburg, a small town about 190km northwest of Kimberley in the dry, dusty Northern Cape, best known for its manganese mine at nearby Beeshoek. He was born there, went to school there, and worked there.

De Bruin was not a big man for a tighthead prop (he weighed only about 85 kg) but a powerful man in his heyday and a popular one, known as Popeye or Oom Popeye or Oom Pops. The famous rugby man of Postmasburg, Colonel Jumbo Harris, gave Flip de Bruin his nickname, which stuck.

In the days when students, farmers, miners and a policeman typically made the South African side, Kimberley, made by mining, relied mostly on miners. In 1970 the mine providing most rugby players was the rich manganese mine of Postmasburg in an area where iron and diamonds are also mined, with keen Jumbo Harris ensuring that there were good rugby players, some of them national stars like his son-in-law Piet Visagie. De Bruin worked on the mine and played for its rugby club Ammosal, starting in the third team, the Tiekies, till Harris saw him and pulled him up to the first team.

He also played for Griqualand West twice in the good year of 1969 and the great year of 1970, the latter one of the very best for South Africa's second oldest rugby province. In 1969 Griquas beat the touring Wallabies 21-13, Eastern Province, and Natal in their seven wins out of 11 matches. In 1970 Griquas played nine matches, losing just one and that was to the All Blacks who won all their provincial matches on their tour. Amongst the teams that Griquas beat were Natal, Western Province, Eastern Transvaal and Free State. There were two sections to the Currie Cup that year and Griquas ended top of their section, thus qualifying for the Currie Cup Final, which would be against Northern Transvaal in Kimberley, a match which Griquas won 11-9. De Bruin did not play. In fact at the time he was in Postmasburg with his wife who was having complications in giving birth to their daughter.

Phillippus Jerimia Roedolph de Bruin was born in Postmasburg on 26 December 1943. In his old age he suffered greatly from emphysema, a not unknown problem for ex-miners, but eventually it was too much for the lively, good-humored old man and he died on 29 October 2016 in the Japie Kritzinger Home in Bloemhof, some 300 km northeast of Postmasburg.

De Bruin was married twice – first to Cathy with whom he had three children and then to Elsa with whom he had a son and acquired six stepchildren. Cathy lives but Elsa died on 15 April 2016. He is survived by 19 grandchildren and three great-grandchildren.

VIC DE KLERK

VIC de Klerk, brother of uncompromising Springbok lock Kevin, was a tough hooker in his day for Diggers and Transvaal. He played nine times for Transvaal, as the Golden Lions then were, from 1977 to 1980. Diggers were a powerful club at the time, winning the Pirates Grand Challenge in 1975, 1977 and 1978.

When his playing days were over he stayed involved in rugby, this time with the Edenvale Panthers. He coached them and was their chairman, a popular man.

Victor de Klerk was born in Johannesburg on 24 January 1951 and died in Johannesburg on 2 November 2016, survived by his children Kelly, Vicky, Whitney and Dershay.

His death at a young age is a surprise as he was a remarkably fit man, involved in the fitness industry all his life, the owner of a gym and often a fitness trainer.

THEUNS DE LA REY

IN 1971 Theuns de la Rey, a keen sportsman, started refereeing and joined the Northern Transvaal (now Blue Bulls) Referees' Society.

Refereeing in the Northern Transvaal has always been competitive and a young referee's target was always to officiate in the Carlton League, the union's top club competition. De la Rey worked hard and achieved Carlton League status, of which he was proud.

In a match between Adelaars and Police he sent off the South African heavyweight boxing champion Kallie Knoetze on his birthday. The two, referee and boxer, later became firm friends and worked together at the Adelaars Academy, which De la Rey had a hand in starting for school pupils.

De la Rey was for several years the referees' representative on the union's disciplinary committee. He became a life member of the Referees' Society. A keen cyclist, he won Northern Transvaal colours in the 1960s. Wrestling was his other interest. He was the manager of the Springbok wrestling team in the late 1980s.

He was educated at the Hoërskool Michael Brink, which is now Hoërskool Hendrik Verwoerd. He became a lithographer in a printing concern and was instrumental in the printing of the Loftus programmes and annual reports, including those for the Referees' Society.

Theunis Jan Horn de la Rey was born in Pretoria on 30 April 1938 and, suffering from brain atrophy, he died on 7 August 2016 in Pretoria, survived by his wife Issie, sons Theunis and Martin, and daughter Karin, four grandchildren and two great-grandchildren.

GERT DELPORT

GERT Delport became South Africa's appleseed king after he had finished his rugby career. And it all started in Bethal, a farming town east of Johannesburg, once in the Transvaal, now in Mpumalanga. The town, which takes its name from bits of the names of the founders' wives - Elizabeth du Plooy and Alida Naudé - used to hold a national potato festival each year, discontinued since 2007.

Delport grew up in Bethal and went to Hoërskool Hoogenhout. (The school was named after its first principal.) After school Delport played rugby for the Bethal club and at the age of 26 became involved in the potato industry. In 1974 he started his own seed potato business - Gert Delport Bemarking BK, which eventually had its head office in Pretoria.

Delport, a hooker, played for the town club and in 1965 he hooked for the Eastern Transvaal Country Districts in Ermelo against the Argentinian tourists, the first team to be called the Pumas, a match which the Pumas won 22-9. Bethal then played its rugby in the Eastern Transvaal and Delport played for Eastern Transvaal in 1967 and 1968, the year in which South Eastern Transvaal was formed out of Eastern Transvaal and Bethal became part of the new union. Delport hooked for South Eastern Transvaal and in 1971 he captained the province.

Gert Delport was born in Bethal on 30 September 1941. He was assaulted and traumatised during a car hijacking early in 2016 and suffered ill health after it. He died in Pretoria on 24 September 2016. He was never married.

FRANCOIS DE VOS

FRANCOIS de Vos played centre and wing for Orange Free State from 1968 to 1970 and then once for Northern Transvaal in 1971. They were not great years for Free State rugby.

De Vos scored a try in his first match for Free State. It was against South West Africa at Free State Stadium, a match that SWA won 16-14. De Vos's centre partner was the great Joggie Jansen. In 1969 he scored two tries when Free State beat Eastern Province but he was not chosen against the Wallabies that year, or against the All Blacks the following year. He played his club rugby for the Teachers' Training College and when he moved to Northern Transvaal he played for Oostelikes.

Francois de Vos's twin bother Japie also played for Free State, also at centre but only in 1967, which meant that the brothers did not get to play together but both played for Bloemfontein Teachers' Training College. Those were years when the College dominated Free State club rugby, winning the Town Cup in 1968 and 1970.

Francois de Vos's health became a problem in September and he died in hospital in George on 13 November 2016 at the age of 71 with his family gathered around his bed.

EDDIE ESTERHUIZEN

EDDIE Esterhuizen was a flank who played for Pretoria Police and between 1958 and 1960 he played four times for Northern Transvaal. His older brother, Willie, also played for Northern Transvaal - 11 times at centre in the late 1940s when he was playing for Pretoria club.

Esterhuizen died in Pretoria in February 2016.

HANNES ESTERHUIZEN

THERE were two short-lived Boer republics up in what is now North West Province - Stellaland and Goshen. They were founded in 1882 west of Potchefstroom and adjacent to each other. A year later they amalgamated to form the United States of Stellaland with its capital at Vryburg. That lasted till the British invaded and disbanded the US of Stellaland, incorporating it into Bechuanaland Protectorate, now Botswana. But the name did not entirely vanish for it was resurrected when a new rugby province was created around Lichtenburg in 1975 and called Stellaland. It lasted till 1995 and its area is now incorporated into the Leopards, whose main area used to be called Western Transvaal. In its first year Stellaland was ranked 20th out of 22 teams but not again as low as that, reaching 14th at one stage. The union's biggest win was 110-0 over North Western Cape.

Hannes Esterhuizen was a loose forward for Stellaland in 31 matches from 1991 until its last year in 1994.

JC Esterhuizen died of a heart attack on 26 September 2016 at the age of 46.

JANNIE FOURIE

JANNIE Fourie was just 14 when he died a horrible death in attempt to help his neighbour.

The Fouries live on the farm Dwaalhoek in the Caledon District where there were huge fires just before Christmas. When the fire reached the neighbour's farm, Jannie persuaded his father to go to help in fighting the fire. When they reached the fire Jannie fell off the back of the bakkie into the fire and was burnt by the fire. He was rushed to the Tygerberg Hospital in an ambulance and died there on Christmas Eve. A memorial service was held in Caledon on 30 December in the NG Kerk Caledon-West Church, which was jam-packed.

Though quiet and modest, Jannie was a prominent pupil at Paarl Boys' High and there were informal gatherings in various places at the same time as the memorial service in places like Hermanus, Hartenbos, Vleesbaai, Stilbaai, Struisbaai and Langebaan.

When Jannie was at Overberg Primary, he was the head boy and captained the Boland team at the Under-13 Craven Week and in June 2015 was named SuperSport's Let's Play player of the month. In his first year Jannie captained the Paarl Boys' High Under-14 team.

Jannie Pieter de Villiers Fourie died in Tygerberg Hospital on 24 December 2016, survived by his parents, Jannie and Christelle, and his brothers Christie and Stefan.

KOSIE HORN

IT CAME as a shock to the rugby community in South Africa that Kosie Horn died on the afternoon of 22 June 2016.

He had been in hospital for just over two weeks with a lung infection and was to be moved from ICU when he suffered a stroke and died. He was 63.

Many people will have experienced his cheerful kindness in his 12-year stint as manager of the Blue Bulls referees and then as the Blue Bulls' training and education manager.

Jacobus Daniel Horn, known to everybody as Kosie, was born on 29 August 1952 in Frankfort on the banks of the Wilge River in the Eastern Free State, but he grew up in Durban, moving there when he was young and going to Dirkie Uys on the Bluff. He played scrumhalf at school and joined the police force in 1971. In 1978 he started refereeing, joining the Durban Referees' Society. The next year the young policeman was transferred to Ladybrand and then Bloemfontein and then on to Pretoria where he stayed till he died.

Horn became a first-league referee in 1979 and from 1985 to 1994 he was a provincial referee, reaching Currie Cup status. In 1994 he moved to Pretoria and the next year stopped active refereeing. For eight years he had been secretary of the Free State Referees' Society and then in 1996 he became the secretary of the Blue Bulls Referees' Society, becoming its first full-time manager in 1998 after taking early retirement from the police force. He ceased to be the referees' manager in 2009 and from then on was the Blue Bulls' training and education manager.

Horn was the wonderful combination of efficiency and unfailing good cheer. You always felt better for contact with him. You looked forward to contact with him, for Kosie was the same cheerful man, unchanged by time.

Kosie Horn died on 22 June 2016, survived by his wife, a son, a daughter and his hero - his grandson.

IGSAAN JABAAR

THE Jabaar family was synonymous with rugby in the Western Province Coloured RFU, which had its headquarters eventually at the Green Point Track. The Muslim community of Cape Town early developed a passion for rugby and the second club formed (in 1883) was Arabian College founded by members of the Awal Mosque in Bo Kaap and the first Jabaar is recorded to have played rugby captained for Arabian College.

The brothers Karriem, Magmoet and Taliep Jabaar all played for Western Province, as did Karriem's three sons - Cassiem, who was one of the best scrumhalves in South Africa in his prime, Taliep and Igsaan, a loose forward.

Like his brothers, Igsaan went to Rahmaniyah Primary. He then went on to Vista High and then studied building at Hewat College. After school he went into the building trade.

Igsaan, like the others of his family, played his club rugby for Caledonian Roses, whose nickname was the RFC, and he played for

Western Province in 1978 and 1979. His playing days over, Igsaan was involved in the administration of Caledonian Roses from 1980 to 1985.

Igsaan Jabaar was born in District Six, Cape Town, on 17 September 1954. He died of cancer in Vincent Pallotti Hospital on 21 July 2016, survived by his wife Ruwayda, his sons Nazmie and Faizel, his daughter Faruz, two granddaughters and two grandsons.

DOUG JEFFERY

THERE seemed little at sport that Doug Jeffery could not do - a strong, fit man, which made his early death all the more surprising.

He was fast and strong, an athlete, a wing with a massive boot, a provincial softball player and a scratch golfer. He came from the Eastern Cape and became a household name in Namibia, even before it was Namibia.

He was born in Port Elizabeth, went to Park Primary and the Technical High School. But it was during his military training in Bloemfontein that his interest in rugby was awakened.

In 1977 Jeffery, playing first for Police and then for Parks in Port Elizabeth, made his debut for Eastern Province and went to the Springbok trials in Pretoria, the first officially racially mixed trials in South African rugby history.

He made the B team in the final trial but there was only one Test that year - against a World XV to celebrate the opening of the new stadium at Loftus Versfeld. Jeffery did not make the Springbok side but he did make the Gazelles team, then the South African Under-24 side from which six players did make the Springbok side.

The next year, 1979, Jeffery made his debut for Orange Free State, playing for Defence club. He played for Free State in 1978, 1979 and a part of 1980. In 1980 Billy Beaumont's Lions toured South Africa and Jeffery played against them twice - for Free State and for the Junior Springboks, both matches won by the Lions. The Free State match was close - 21-17 - and the highlight of the match was Jeffery's try. The Lions kicked on Gysie Pienaar who started a counter-attack. Pienaar gave to Jeffery who, despite a sore ankle, raced some 60 metres down the touchline in front of the Grand Stand to score in the left corner. Jeffery played for Eastern Province from 1980-83, 50 matches in all.

Then he met and married his Namibian wife and off they went to Windhoek where he played for Wanderers and also for South West Africa, as Namibia then was. They played in South Africa's Sport Pienaar competition, then in the Currie Cup B and then in the Currie Cup A, ending third in 1988 behind Northern Transvaal and Western Province. In their season they had victories over Transvaal, Free State and, at Newlands, Western Province. They went on tour to South America, beating Chile 36-15 and Paraguay 110-3.

South West Africa played its last season in the Currie Cup in 1989, for it became independent as Namibia in 1990 when Jeffery got to play a Test. He was 35 years of age when he came off the bench in the first Test in the two-Test series in Windhoek, a match which France won 24-15, one try to nil. Later in the year Jeffery was in the Namibian team that toured England and France and played his last match for Namibia in Bourges when Namibia beat the French Army 12-3.

Golf absorbed his later days and he played for Namibia in amateur golf competitions. His son Roux is a professional golfer. Two of his other sons are also to the fore at sport - Wayne at hockey and Jean-Pierre on the rugby field.

He had trouble with a knee and friends were organising a golf day to get funds for a knee replacement when he suddenly became ill and was placed in intensive care with kidney trouble and then general organ failure.

Douglas Jeffery was born in Port Elizabeth on 8 February 1955. He died in Windhoek on the night of 15 September 2016, survived by his wife, four sons and a daughter.

TIAAN JOUBERT

TIAAN Joubert's death at the age of 42 came as a shock. Born in Johannesburg he shone as a powerful centre for the Bulls in Super Rugby and for the Blue Bulls in the Currie Cup.

After playing for the Golden Lions at the 1991 Craven Week, he started his provincial career there in 1994 before moving to the Leopards for two seasons and then to the South Western Districts Eagles for a year before joining the Blue Bulls in 2000. He stayed. In 2002 he was in the team that won the Currie Cup, beating the Golden Lions 31-7 at Ellis Park. His highest honours were being chosen for South Africa Under-21 in 1994 and for the South African Barbarians in 1999 when they played against Namibia in Windhoek.

Christiaan Hermanus Beyers Joubert was born on 3 December 1973. He was educated at Hoërskool Randburg and then RAU. He was admitted to hospital with pneumonia and suffered a heart attack in hospital in Randburg. He died on 10 September 2016.

BLAKE KERDACHI

BLAKE Kerdachi was in his 16th year and on his way home for Easter from his school's rugby and netball tour to Hong Kong. His death on Good Friday morning was a shock.

Blake was in Grade 11, a talented boy held in great esteem by staff and pupils at Thomas More College in Kloof outside Durban in KwaZulu-Natal. Just before Easter the school sent 36 pupils, the 1st teams at rugby and netball, with five staff to the Far East. At the end of their trip, several contracted flu and their last rugby match was shortened because of bad weather.

The team flew to Dubai from Hong Kong

on the Wednesday, 23 March. Because Blake was ill, his passport was misplaced on the plane and he and a team-mate could not fly the last leg to Johannesburg with the rest of their mates. It took over eight hours for the two passports to be recovered. During this time Blake was not feeling well. On the overnight flight on 24-25 March from Dubai to Johannesburg, Blake took a turn for the worse. When the plane landed, he was rushed to the Arwyp Medical Centre in nearby Kempton Park where surgeons struggled to help Blake to breathe. After several attempts to resuscitate him and a major heart surgery the doctors were unable to save his life.

At a memorial service for Blake at his school, the principal, Allan Chandler, was full of praise of Blake for his virtues and skills. For one thing he led a very active school life in the classroom and on the sports fields, playing rugby at flyhalf, hockey, cricket, soccer, water polo, indoor hockey, softball and golf. Chandler ended his eulogy, saying: "We are going to miss Blake; we are going to miss his gentle disposition, his cheerfulness and quick wit. We are going to miss his commitment; his-never-say-die attitude, and his loyalty to family, friends and school.

Blake Antony Kerdachi was born in Pinetown on 10 September 1999 and died in Kempton Park on 26 March 2016, survived by his parents Antony and Debbie and his sister Rachel.

Blake's funeral service was held at St Dominic's Catholic Church in Hillcrest.

KLIPPIES KRITZINGER

KLIPPIES Kritzinger grew up in the Free State, went to school in Harrismith, and played for Orange Free State at the 1967 Craven Week. He was playing for Durban Collegians when chosen for Natal and then for the 1972 Gazelles who toured Argentina. He also played for the Junior Springboks. Big, strong and remarkably skilled, he also played for several provinces in a nomadic career - Natal Country (Northern Natal), Natal, Transvaal, Free State, Northern Free State and Western Transvaal. And he played club rugby in Northern Transvaal, Boland and Eastern Free State.

He was playing for Transvaal in 1974 when he was chosen for the battered Springboks against the might of the 1974 Lions. He played in the Port Elizabeth Test at eighthman with Gerrie Sonnekus at scrumhalf, a Test with lots of fighting as the Lions revealed their infamous '99' call. Kritzinger joined in and knocked out the great Gordon Brown. He was on the flank with Kleintjie Grobler at eighthman, the fourth Springbok eighthman in four Tests, for the drawn fourth Test at Ellis Park. He then was chosen for the resurrection tour to France later that year, playing in seven matches, including the Tests in Toulouse and Paris, both won by the Springboks. In 1975 he played twice against France in the victories in Bloemfontein and Pretoria.

Then came the All Blacks in 1976 and Kritzinger played in the controversial fourth Test at Ellis Park when the Springboks won 15-14 to take the series 3-1, and the All Blacks believed that they were robbed. It was Kritzinger's only Test in the series and the last he played, as Springbok rugby went into a three-year hibernation.

In 1975 he had moved to the Free State and captained them in the very first match he played for them. Free State gave him his greatest success in provincial rugby. He captained them 23 times in 42 matches and was in their side in 1976 when they beat the All Blacks 15-10 and won the Currie Cup for the first time. They played in four consecutive finals - 1975, 1976, 1977 and 1978. Kritzinger captained them in 1975 and then again in 1976, but not against the All Blacks and not in the victorious Currie Cup Final when they beat Western Province 33-16, for Wouter Hugo captained the side that day. He played the first four matches in 1977 but then was dropped for Hennie Bekker, who was then doing his military training in the Free State, and announced his retirement.

In 1966 and 1967 he represented Free State at athletics and in 1967 became a Springbok athlete when he did the shot putt and discus against West Germany. The next year he was in the Defence Force 4x400 relay team. He was also a deep-sea diving instructor.

Johannes Lodewyk Kritzinger was born in Harrismith on 1 March 1948. His brother became General WG Kritzinger of the South African Defence Force. In his time Klippies was a salesman, a business broker and a garage owner. He was admitted to the Centurion Hospital with the rare Guillain-Barré syndrome, in which the immune system attacks the nervous system, resulting in the weakening of muscles. He did not survive the attack and died on 17 February 2016, survived by his wife Valerie and their children, daughter Hilané and son Johannes Hermanus, names inherited from Klippies's father.

DAVE LANGLEY

DAVE Langley was first of all an athlete. His specialties were long jump and 110m hurdles. In 1969 he was chosen for the Springbok athletics team and the next year was made captain of the team. Just before South Africa was expelled from world athletics, he was able to compete in Europe, Africa and South America. In 1972 he broke the 17-year-old South African long jump record set by Neville Price.

After school at Hoërskool Louis Trichardt, Langley came from what is now Limpopo to Tukkies in Pretoria. There he developed his athletics and also played rugby for the university, naturally on the wing, starting in 1963, the year when Tukkies won the Carlton League, Northern Transvaal's major club competition. The coach that year was Professor Daan Swiegers. And then, just once, he was chosen for Northern Transvaal. That was in 1965, the year the Springboks toured New Zealand.

At Tukkies, Langley obtained an Hons BSc (Agric.) and taught for four years at Affies where he coached the 1st XV. At the time of his death he was on his farm Buchan at Waterpoort near Alldays. His funeral service was held on the next-door farm, Ringer, belonging to his brother Thomas, between Vivo and Alldays.

David Stephanus Langley was born at Alldays on 27 July 1943 and died after a long battle with cancer on 7 June 2016.

JANNIE LE ROUX

JANNIE le Roux was a genial man, a good companion, but beneath the good humour and charm there was the determination of a fighter, at times a street fighter. For nearly 20 years, he was the lively but controversial President of the Transvaal Rugby Union.

Le Roux was born in Johannesburg, went to school at Helpmekaar and then went down to Stellenbosch where he studied law - and played rugby at centre, winning his Matie colours in 1950 when Danie Craven coached the Maties side. Back in Johannesburg he joined Diggers, whose president he was from 1958 to 1963, in the days when Diggers was a powerful club in the Transvaal.

In the 1940s, with the political success of Afrikaner nationalism, there was a concerted effort to remove the English speakers from rugby's positions of power at a time when most rugby presidents were English speaking.

In the Transvaal it was Sandy Sanderson who was the President for 31 years. In 1964 he let it be known that he would not stand again as he was 75. The first effort to oust him was organised by Willem Stork of Diggers, the base of the movement. Le Roux, a Stork disciple, stood for the Presidency in 1965 and won the election with his famous slogan 'Love me or leave me'. With his entry into office all the Sanderson men were dropped and Le Roux surrounded himself with six vice-presidents of his own making.

From time to time much was made of Le Roux's membership of the Broederbond, but he was in fact such a passive member that the Broederbond chastised him for 'lack of interest'. During his time he was the vice-president of the South African Rugby Board, after ousting Kobus Louw in 1973 till he was himself ousted by Fritz Eloff. In 1974 he was the manager of the Springboks on their tour to France. His presidency lasted till 1984 when a palace revolution ousted him.

In Le Roux's presidency Transvaal won the Currie Cup once and shared it once with Northern Transvaal. His dream was the reconstruction of Ellis Park, Transvaal's headquarters. He realised his dream but it turned into a nightmare for the union because of the huge debt (some R37 million) involved and eventually led to the move to oust him, led by Professor Jannie Ferreira, and Springboks Mickey Gerber and Avril Malan.

Their chosen successor was Louis Luyt. Luyt phoned Le Roux on the night before the union's general meeting and told him the plan. Le Roux's response was: "Louis this is a bloody good plan. I hope you will agree to go along. We'll try to muster all our supporters on your side." Le Roux resigned at the meeting, Luyt was unanimously elected, and Ellis Park was saved, standing as a great monument to Jannie le Roux and his dream.

After that Le Roux withdrew from public life, a man who could plan big and push through to get the plan realised, and do it all with a smile and a laugh.

Johannes Zacharias le Roux was born in 1928 and died in his home on his farm in Mbombela, Nelspruit when his heart gave up on Sunday, 31 January 2016, survived by his wife Igna, their sons Jaco and Anton and daughter Leandie and seven grandchildren.

SAKI MANAKAZA

SAKI Manakaza was much involved in rugby administration in Border during a seriously difficult time for the union. His career in provincial rugby administration started in 2004, when he was elected vice-president of the Border Rugby Union under Monwabisi Yako, after which he also served under Cliff Pringle.

Saki Manakaza was born on 2 December 1965 in Ndakana village at Ngqamakwe in the Transkei and died after a long illness in East London on 14 January 2016, survived by his wife Khanyisa and three children.

HENRY MEYER

HENRY Meyer was a passionate man of Heidelberg, a lovely town east of Cape Town, which got its name from the Heidelberg Catechism, which the church used in the 19th century.

Meyer had a great love for the Young Stars Rugby Club for which he played scrumhalf, quick and elusive. He also played for the South Western Districts affiliated to the pre-unity SARU in the late 1970s and early 1980s. After his playing days and when Young Stars became the Heidelberg RFC in 1994, he remained a passionate supporter. He was proud of his club and devoted to it.

The day before he died he was travelling with the club down to Kuilsriver for the annual match between the two clubs.

Henry James Meyer, nicknamed Tok, was born in Heidelberg on 29 April 1956. He went to Steward School in Heidelberg and worked as an artisan. He died suddenly in the Riversdale Hospital on 26 June 2016, survived by his wife Cathleen, their children Henriette, Thelma, Divan, Sydney and Roderick, and 10 grandchildren.

LUKAS MEYER

LUKAS Meyer was at Free State University in 1956 when he played two matches on the wing for Free State, both defeats - at the hands of Transvaal at Ellis Park and then against Natal at Woodburn in Pietermaritzburg, the first time Free State had lost to Natal in a Currie Cup match for 20 years. He played for Kovsies from 1953 to 1956.

Later he became a journalist on Die Volksblad in Bloemfontein and then Die Oosterlig in Port Elizabeth. In his retirement Meyer went to live in Jeffreys Bay.

Lukas Meyer was born on 18 November 1931 and died in Port Elizabeth in February 2016.

TREVOR MILLAR

YOU don't get nicer people than Trevor Millar, unfailingly genial with a ready smile and a happy laugh and always willing to be a helpful friend. His love of rugby and his warmth was remarkable. He was a man without prejudice.

Millar grew up in Ballymena, where rugby is an eager sport, played for Ballymena Academy 1st XV and then moved on to play for Ballymena's club 1st XV for ten seasons. He was a prop. Look at his photos as a small child and meet him in his sixties, and you know he was a prop, born to prop it seems. His brother Sydney was a famous prop and rugby man, from Ireland and the Lions as player, selector, coach and manager, and then as the chairman of the International Rugby Board, as World Rugby then was. Both Syd and Trevor were rugby idealists.

Trevor, a quantity surveyor, came out to Johannesburg for two years in 1965 and then in 1981 he and wife Pat settled in Durban before migrating to Cape Town in 1992. And always he made an ever-increasing circle of friends in the rugby community. If there was a pre-Test lunch at Kelvin Grove, Trevor was there. If there was a club celebration, Trevor was there. If there was an ex-player's funeral, Trevor was there. When Max Baise was publishing his autobiography, Trevor was constructively involved.

Pat described Trevor's death as "the way he would have wanted it". As a birthday present to Pat, Trevor arranged a voyage around the world. Their first leg took them from Cape Town to Fremantle on the Queen Elizabeth where they disembarked and stayed with Pat's brother and his family in Perth. Trevor went to bed one night and died peacefully in his sleep. Pat brought his body home and a memorial service was held at the Rondebosch United Church. Sydney and Enid Millar were there and so was a huge crowd.

Trevor Millar was born in Ballymena, Northern Ireland, on 13 May 1944. He died in Perth, Australia, on 17 February 2016, survived by wife Pat, daughters Caroline and Mandy, and three grandchildren.

DERRICK MINNIE

DERRICK Minnie was a gentleman, a highly successful gentleman in his family life, business life and sporting life.

He was possibly most widely known in his sporting life. As a player her was successful: Eastern Province colours for rugby, athletics (captain of the team) and volleyball. He played his club rugby for the famous Crusaders club in Port Elizabeth.

His playing days over, Minnie started out on a lifetime of service to rugby in the important background activities of the game - as the coach and a selector of Eastern Province teams. He was the chairman of Eastern Province selectors in the 1970s.

At the same time he was building an excellent business career in the packaging industry. This entailed hard work on his part, starting with a night-school matric after earlier schooling at Pearson High School and then an MBA. By 1976 he was the general manager of Kohler Corrugated, and then the managing director of Bumleys and the operations director of Kohler Paper. In 1988 he left Port Elizabeth to become the CEO of Kohler Packaging Ltd. Then in 1993 he became the managing director of Mondi Ltd, then the executive chairman of Mondipak and the deputy chairman of Mondi Limited, certainly a powerful player in South Africa's packaging industry. He was a member of several boards, including NB, Relyant Retail Ltd, Anglo American Industrial Corporation Ltd, Alex White Holdings Ltd and Profurn Ltd.

When he moved to Johannesburg his rugby involvement continued. He coached Benoni RFC, Eastern Transvaal and Transvaal, preserving all of the sportsman's good humour and balance.

Nicholas Derrick Minnie was born in Port Elizabeth on 14 October 1939. He died in Johannesburg on 10 November 2016, survived by his wife Rose and their children Craig, Tracey, Rachel, Cathryn, Nicholas and Sarah. There was a memorial service at the Bryanston Methodist Church.

FRANS MULLER

FRANS Muller was a man of the South Western Districts who moved to Port Elizabeth and the Eastern Province. He played rugby for the Olympics Club in Port Elizabeth as a scrum-half or a centre and played for Eastern Province Under-20, till injury struck and he took up refereeing.

A determined and thoughtful man with a good feel for the game, fully aware of the referee environment, he was bound to do well at refereeing. And he had Jimmy Smith-Belton, the other great referee in the Eastern Province at the time, to keep him determined and ambitious. He went to the top in this difficult art, becoming South Africa's 41st Test referee.

Muller won the Eastern Province Referees' prestige trophy, awarded for the referee who showed the most progress and promise, in his first year of refereeing. After he stopped refereeing he became a life member of SA Referees.

Muller had a long and glorious career as a top referee. He was just breaking into the top echelons when Quintus van Rooyen wrote in the SA Rugby Annual on refereeing in 1978, the year Muller went to Craven Week in icy Middelburg (Mpumalanga): "Just behind him [Steve Strydom] was young Fransie Muller (Eastern Province) who refereed the second meeting between Transvaal and Northern Transvaal brilliantly.... A lot will be heard of Muller."

Included in his 176 first-class matches in South Africa, Muller was twice appointed to Lion Cup Finals - in 1985 and again in 1988 when injury forced him to leave the field to be replaced by Gerrit Coetzer.

His Test career started in 1976 when he refereed the match between the SA Rugby Football Federation and the SA African Rugby Board. Then came the Jaguars in 1982 - a team chosen from South American countries, mostly from Argentina, as a means of getting round the boycott of South African rugby. There were two Tests between the Springboks and the Jaguars in 1982. Steven Strydom refereed the first one, which the Springboks won handsomely. Muller refereed the second in Bloemfontein when the Jaguars, spearheaded by Hugo Porta turned the tables and won 21-12 with Porta scoring all 21 points. (The next South African referee to handle a Test involving the Springboks was Jonathan Kaplan in 2007 when they played Namibia at Newlands.) In 1984 Muller was the referee when England played the SA Rugby Association in East London.

In 1985 Steve Strydom became the first South African referee to take charge of a Five Nations match. The next was Fransie Muller in 1988 when he refereed two matches - Scotland vs France and France vs Ireland.

During the 1991 season Muller retired from refereeing. He served on the Referees' Society committee from the 1970s as a committee member, the secretary, the appointments co-ordinator, the vice-chairman and treasurer and from 2000 as chairman and treasurer of the Society in succession to Smith-Belton, a post he held till 2014. During his time as chairman he continued to help with the assessing of referees and in 2003 was chosen by the International Rugby Board (now World Rugby) as an assessor at the Rugby World Cup in Australia.

Fransie Muller was a loyal man - loyal to his union, his church and his family. For years and years he ran the finances of the NG Kerk in Adcockvale and was actually on his way to deposit money for church staff when he dropped dead, this after he had worked on the books at home the night before.

His heart had troubled him for over 25 years. Twice he had bypass operations and also had a pacemaker inserted. After a triple bypass

late in his refereeing career, he recovered from the operation and went back to refereeing Currie Cup rugby.

Muller worked for years in civil administration before retiring at the compulsory age of 63 from the Nelson Mandela Bay Municipality.

Frans Muller was born in George on 4 February 1940. He went to Hoërskool Outeniqua before heading to Port Elizabeth. He died in Port Elizabeth on Friday, 25 February 2016. He is survived by Stephanie, his wife of 41 years, son Gerald and daughter Shoneé and three granddaughters. The funeral was at the NG Kerk in Adcockvale on 2 March 2016. The tribute was given by Dominee Marius Cornelissen, a former rugby referee who is the father of Muller's son-in-law.

LOFTY NEL

SOUTH Africans enjoy ironic nicknames: Tiny Neethling and even bigger Tiny Naudé and Boy Louw with Speedy Wilson at fullback. But Lofty was not ironic. He was 1,93 metres tall - much taller 50 years ago than it is amongst modern giants. It is the same height that Schalk Burger is now.

Nel was a warrior on the field and a gregarious gentleman off the field, a man who gave rather than received and was still playing the game when he was 40 - because he loved it and more than that loved the camaraderie that went with it.

After he retired from his job with SA Breweries, he went to live in Fairy Glen, Pretoria, close to his son and a daughter and their children, taking a great interest in the games the grandchildren played. And he still followed rugby with interest.

His only son, Pieter, was a fine three-quarter, playing for South African Schools in 1983 and touring Wales with the team before going on to the University of Pretoria and good career with Northern Transvaal, as the Blue Bulls then were.

Father Lofty was born in Pretoria and went to school at Hoërskool Jan van Riebeeck in Randfontein. He was a rep for Breweries, married to jukskei Springbok Hester Nel, née Müller, the nephew of Hennie Nel who captained Natal and Northern Transvaal.

Lofty was playing for West Rand when first chosen for Transvaal in 1957. He played 22 matches for the province until 1960, when he became a Springbok. Later he played for Western Transvaal and, when living in Witbank, for South Eastern Transvaal, ending his provincial career in 1970 - the year he ended his Springbok career.

His international career has a unique achievement. He is the only Springbok - we are talking of pre-professional days - to have played against three successive All Black teams - 1960, 1965 and 1970. He also played against the Wallabies in 1963 and 1965 - 11 Tests all told, eight against the All Blacks and three against

OBITUARIES

the Wallabies. His immediate opponent for the All Blacks in 1960 was the mighty fisherman, Peter Jones, and in 1965 and again in 1970 it was Brian Lochore. Nel was warrior enough to stand up to opposition of that calibre.

Even after he had 'retired' he would still turn out for his club from time to time when needed, till he was 40.

Johannes Arnoldus Nel, always called Lofty, was born in Pretoria on 11 August 1935. He died in Pretoria on 18 July 2016. It was a peaceful death for a peaceful man. He went to take a shower where he was found sitting peacefully but dead, presumably of a heat attack. He is survived by his wife Hester, son Pieter, daughters Dina and Hester, and grandchildren.

PIET NEL

PIET Nel was one of those schoolmasters everybody needs, a man who gives his enthusiastic best without regard to comfort, certainly not a time-watcher.

For 35 loyal years he taught at Hoërskool Wessel Maree in the Free State. For 28 of those years he coached the 1st XV. For the last 12 years he was the principal of the school.

He had a huge love of rugby and it went beyond the boundaries of his school. He coached Northern Free State teams, including the Craven Week team, he was a schools selector from 1989 to 2000, he was the manager of the Northern Free State Schools Union from 1988 to 2002 and in 2002 and 2003 he was the vice-president of the Northern Free State Rugby Union.

He was the principal when, in February 2016, he was diagnosed with cancer. He died on 21 April 2016 in Bloemfontein where he was in hospital, survived by Alta, his wife of 45 years, their son Philip, their daughter Tania and three grandsons.

COLIN NELSON

WESTERN Province came to Port Elizabeth to play Eastern Province in 1957. For Eastern Province it was their greatest rugby desire to beat Western Province. It provided Colin Nelson with his most memorable moment on the rugby field. Western Province were passing the ball as usual with their elegant swing passes when Nelson took a chance. He leapt forward, intercepted and ran 50 metres down the Crusader Field to score a try, still remembered 60 years later.

In 1958 the French came on tour to South Africa. They became the first team to win a series against the Springboks since 1896 and they did so by drawing a Test and then winning one. They won a series without scoring a try. Their non-Test matches were mostly against combined teams, and Colin Nelson was on the wing for Border-Eastern Province-North Eastern Districts at the Border Rugby Union Ground in East London when France won 16-9.

Nelson was an Old Boy of Grey High school of Port Elizabeth. After school he played for Olympics, the oldest rugby club in the Eastern Province, which no longer exists, and between 1956 and 1958 on the wing for Eastern Province.

Colin Nelson was born in Port Elizabeth on 11 March 1935. He worked for Ford in Port Elizabeth and died in Port Elizabeth on 9 January 2016, survived by two daughters.

DRIES NIEMANDT

DRIES Niemandt was a man who served. He served his community and he served rugby, and both his community and rugby were better off and grateful for his service and leadership. He was really keen on sport, above all rugby.

As a player Niemandt played for Simmer & Jack, a mining club as many of Transvaal's major clubs were. It later became Germiston Simmer. Later he moved to Kempton Park which became his home and where he made his greatest contribution. He played rugby for Kempton Park, he refereed rugby, and he coached at the club, before graduating to Transvaal teams as an age-group coach and a selector and then as a senior selector and team manager. This provided an introduction to administration, first as a representative for Kempton Park.

In 1974 Niemandt was elected to the executive of the Transvaal Rugby Union whose president was Jannie le Roux. He became the senior vice-president of the Union and then, when he retired from administration, he was elected an honorary life vice-president of the Union, now called the Golden Lions Rugby Union.

Niemandt had graduated from the University of Pretoria with a BComm degree and later did an MBA. He thrived as a businessman, became a director of Rentmeester Assurance Limited and several other companies, he was the trustee of two pension funds, the chairman of the Afrikaanse Handelsinstituut and the chairman of other boards of civic institutions.

Niemandt also applied his enthusiasm and energy to the civic needs of his town, Kempton Park. He served on the city council, promoted sport in the town, improved facilities and became the long-serving mayor of Kempton Park. In his honour there is the Dries Niemandt Precinct, which includes the Barnard Stadium, the Kempton Park Golf Course, and several other recreation facilities. In 1991 he was made a freeman of the city of Kempton Park.

Then Niemandt settled to the less frantic life of a farmer, proud of his Simmentaler cattle on his stud near Swartruggens.

Andries Dewald Niemandt was born in Zeerust on 6 June 1929. He died in Pretoria on 2 April 2016, survived by his wife Hannie, his son Nelus and his daughter Nita, six grandchildren and one great-grandchild. Hannie was his second wife after the death of his first wife, Thea.

OBITUARIES

FERDI NIEUWOUDT

FERDI Nieuwoudt played fullback for Rustenburg, Police and Pretoria clubs and for Northern Transvaal in 33 matches from 1948 to 1955. Then in 1957 he played for Natal. In 1954 he was the vice-captain of Pretoria RFC when they won the Carlton League. In later life he played bowls.

Nieuwoudt matriculated from Hoërskool Rustenburg and obtained a diploma in public administration from Pretoria University. He was employed in the department of water affairs, whose deputy director he was when he retired. He worked on with all sorts of handyman jobs, starting with the building of a guesthouse on his brother-in-law's farm in Limpopo and including the building of the house that he and his wife lived in for 20 years before heading for a retirement village in Kempton Park. After retirement he suffered his first stroke in 2009. His second stroke in 2012 affected his speech and memory.

Henri Ferdinand Nieuwoudt was born in Heilbron on 23 January 1929. He died of kidney failure in Pretoria on 8 November 2015, survived by his second wife Corrie, stepchildren Gerhard and Amalia, two grandsons, two granddaughters and two great-grandsons. His two sons both predeceased him, both in motor accidents - Anton in 1974 and Louis in 1999.

DAAN NOLTE

DAAN Nolte was a passionate rugby man who gave a great deal to rugby over a lifetime. In fact he made an enthusiastic contribution to cricket and athletics as well, but his main bent was rugby football. In the end his efforts were coloured by his conservative political attitude but there was still no doubting his commitment and his leadership abilities.

Nolte, as a primary-school teacher, was in a great position to develop interest in many things as he did. He himself was educated on his parents' farm Stompiesfontein that is not far from Delmas in Mpumalanga and at Heidelberg Volkskool. Then he went on to Potchefstroom Teachers' Training College to qualify as a primary-school teacher and gradually improved himself through Unisa and ended with a BA and an Hons BCom.

In 1955 Nolte started teaching in Delmas and became increasingly involved in the school and its extramural activities. At the same time the energetic man became involved in farming on Stompiesfontein. Later he bought the farm Steenkoolspruit in Devon in Gauteng, about 25km west of Delmas. His farming interests would develop in fine fashion. He was also the principal of Laerskool Devon and then of Laerskool Eendracht in Pretoria.

At the Training College he played for and captained the 1st XV and the 1st XI. Then when he started teaching he played for and captained Delmas's town team. More and more he became involved in schools rugby

administration - in primary schools and then high schools, as coach and selector. He became the coach of the Eastern Transvaal Currie Cup team and had a serious stroke in 1977 while coaching them. He later served on the union's executive and later for years was the president of the Eastern Transvaal Rugby Union. He was also a popular member of the South African Rugby Board.

In 1980 the Craven Week was opened to all races for the first time. This annoyed AP Treurnicht, once a provincial scrumhalf and once a Dutch Reformed Church dominee who became a cabinet minister but in anger at the opening of Craven Week led others with him in forming the Conservative Party. At the 1987 general election, two members of the SA Rugby Board committee, Nolte and Boetie Malan, stood for the Conservative Party. Nolte won Delmas but Malan was beaten in Cradock. Both were later required to resign as their party's policy on race conflicted with that of the SA Rugby Board.

Nolte then became involved in the formation of a body called Afrikaner Volkseie Sport, whose president, then honorary president then patron he became. He was especially involved in the Bokkieweek, which he started.

Nolte's farming interests grew from Stompiesfontein and Steenkoolspruit with its seed production and huge dairy. He had a highly successful Brahmin stud, a farm with red Afrikaners up in Messina in Limpopo, which he converted into a game farm, and a farm in the Klaserie District, which he later sold. After a stroke in 1972 he pulled back a bit and moved to the farm Witklipbank near Witbank where he developed a merino stud, Elton.

Daniel Gideon Hugo Nolte was born on 11 December 1931 and died on 30 November 2015 and was buried from the Afrikaanse Protestantse Kerk in Delmas, survived by Ina, his wife of 47 years, their children Danie and Laetitia, four granddaughters and three great-grandchildren. Their daughter Stephanie died in 1999.

ARRIE OBERHOLZER

ARRIE Oberholzer was a talented man who expressed his talents in many ways, mostly as a team man. He played and worked as a team man and was a team man in his contribution to the welfare of others.

Born in South West Africa, as Namibia then was, he was educated in Pretoria and then settled in Lichtenburg in what was Western Transvaal where he played and worked with distinction.

After schooling at Affies (Afrikaanse Seuns Hoërskool), he went to the University of Pretoria and left Tukkies with a BA LLB in 1953. From 1954 to 1990 he practised as a attorney in Lichtenburg.

Oberholzer's sport was rugby football. He played fullback and flyhalf for Lichtenburg from 1954 to 1961 and for Western Transvaal

OBITUARIES

from 1955 to 1961. In those years Lichtenburg was a part of Western Transvaal but in 1975 the western part of Western Transvaal was formed into a union named Stellaland, named after the short-lived Boer Republic of the same name. Oberholzer was involved in the foundation of the new union, and selected and coached their team. He was the coach in 1987 when Stellaland beat Western Province League 22-10 in the Sport Pienaar Final. In 1988 Oberholzer became the vice-president and manager of Stellaland. In 1990 he became the president of Stellaland and was elected to the executive committee of the South African Rugby Board. He then succeeded Alex Kellermann as the general manager of the SA Rugby Football Union in the delicate time of unification, a position he held till he retired in 1995, the year of the World Cup in South Africa. After all that, farming in the Klerksdorp District must have seemed exceedingly quiet.

Arnold Jacobus Oberholzer was born in Keetmanshoop on 29 May 1932. He died in Klerksdorp on 17 June 2016, survived by his wife Dolla, their two sons Arnold and Anton and five grandchildren.

SAREL PELSER
HIS family called him Bekker, his mother's maiden name that should have been his third name but his father forgot it when registering it. But his friends called him Sarel, who, at the time of his death, was the oldest living Free State player. He was two years younger than his legendary brother, Pa Pelser.

Pa played for Transvaal, Sarel for Free State, and twice they played against each other, both times in 1954. Transvaal won 13-11 at Ellis Park and Free State won 19-12 in Welkom. On both occasions Pa captained Transvaal. In all, when he was playing for Welkom in the North West Sub-union of the Free State, Sarel played 10 matches for Free State, making his debut when they beat Natal 24-8 in a Currie Cup match in Bethlehem. Like his older brother, he was a flank.

Sarel went farming in the Ellisras district of what is now Limpopo, his farm named Nooitverwacht. Later he joined Vleissentraal in Pretoria and retired as its assistant manager.

Sarel Christoffel Pelser was born in Rustenburg on 14 November 1925 and died in Pretoria on 28 June 2016.

HENNIE PIENAAR
HENNIE Pienaar, whose inevitable nickname was Pine or more elegantly Pinos, was a proper prop - tough, durable and able to play on both sides of the front row, a man who stood up to the best that South Africa, New Zealand, Great Britain and Ireland, and France had to offer in a first-class career that lasted for 13 seasons.

After leaving school in 1950, Pienaar immediately joined the police force and played for Diggers from 1957 to 1960, years in which

it ruled Transvaal club rugby. In that team he propped the scrum in 11 matches, including a match for the Transvaal XV against Wilson Whineray's All Blacks. The All Blacks won 9-3.

Then Hennie Pienaar, policeman, was transferred to Carletonville and played for Goldfields West and from 1960 to 1969 for Western Transvaal. Altogether he played 13 seasons of tough rugby. In 1962 he played against the B&I Lions and in 1967 against the French, both at Olën Park in Potchefstroom. The Lions won 11-6 and France won 38-11.

After Brigadier Pienaar retired from the police force he went farming near Nylstroom, now called Modimolle. Then he and his wife Joey, a writer of cookery books, moved into the splendid Koro Creek Golf Estate at Modimolle.

Hendrik Jacobus Pienaar was born on 19 August 1931. He died on 23 November 2016, after developing breathing problems and being taken to a hospital in Pretoria. He is survived by Joey, their two sons and two daughters, nine grandchildren and seven great-grandchildren. At his funeral service in the NG Kerk Waterberg, his son-in-law Dominee Charl Bredell preached.

PAAL PRETORIUS
THE first time Paarl Pretorius played for Free State, in 1956, he was just over 19 years old, one of the youngest ever. He went on to play 14 times for Free State. He was, as his nickname suggests, a lock, his partner in that first match against South Western Districts one Louis Luyt. His last match was in 1965, but then for five years he was not chosen. Then in 1965 he played in all seven matches, ending with a 14-13 win over Transvaal.

After his schooling at Hoërskool Sentraal in Bloemfontein, Pretorius graduated from the University of the Free State in 1959, where he played his rugby. He then played for Old Collegians in Bloemfontein and joined the South African Defence Force. He rose up through the ranks and ended as Brigadier Pretorius, Director of Physical Training and Sport in the South African Defence Force with General Magnus Malan as his immediate superior and with his office at army headquarters in Pretoria.

Sarel Pretorius was born in Wesselbron on 8 October 1936 and died in Bloemfontein in August 2016 after a battle with cancer.

PIET PRETORIUS
PIET Pretorius, known as Vleis, played for Northern Natal when it was an independent union, formed in 1973 and lasting till 1995 after which it was back as part of KwaZulu-Natal. In all Pretorius played lock 64 times for the union from 1976 to 1985, a long provincial career. The Union's best year was 1976 when they reached the Sport Pienaar final, losing 21-9 to South West Africa.

Pretorius played his club rugby for Vryheid.

His death at a young age came as a shock, though he had had heart trouble and had undergone a heart transplant in 2014. An automotive machinist, he retired to beautiful St Helena Bay, the first place in South Africa where Vasco de Gama landed.

Rudolf Gerhardus Petrus Pretorius was born in Pinetown on 8 May 1953. He died of a heart attack in St Helena Bay on 17 November 2016, survived by his wife Helena and their two sons Pierre and JC. JC played for the Sharks Under-21 and for the Leopards at eighthman.

MARTIN RIDDLES
Energetic Martin Riddles played inside centre for Heidelberg and SARU's South Western Districts in the 1970s and 1980s. He was so eager in chasing the ball that they nicknamed him Hond, out of admiration. He was born in Heidelberg, went to school there, lived there, worked there as an artisan, played there and raised a family of 10 children there. Martin John Riddles was born on 8 July 1953. He died in the Riversdale Hospital on 13 October 2015, survived by his wife Elizabeth, eight sons, two daughters and five grandchildren.

BRIAN SCHABRAM
BRIAN Schabram was one of the best members a rugby team could have - an excellent scrumhalf with an enormous sense of fun. He was the life and soul of any gathering and the gathering would be laughing happily. Rugby dinners in Natal will be quieter and less fun at his passing.

He was also an astonishingly good scrumhalf for Durban Collegians between 1951 and 1965 and for Natal between 1955 and 1965, with a break till he came back to the game in 1961.

Many found it strange that he was never a Springbok because his combination with the great Keith Oxlee was excellent. In fact he did go to trials once - in 1964. That was in Durban before the Test there against Wales.

The trials were a flop for him. The story goes that on the night before the first match, he and two established Springboks slipped out on the town. In the early hours of the morning they decided to head for home and persuaded a friendly policemen to drive them back to the hotel. The policeman had his dog in the back and when they got to the hotel, the dog started barking and out came Danie Craven and Frank Mellish, chairman of the SA Rugby Board and the chairman of selectors. The next morning Scharbie and his two chums left the trials, never to return.

Schabram was also a good cricketer. He was invited to join Leicestershire but his brother had died and his parents would not let him go.

Schabram was at Newcastle High in Northern Natal. He left in 1949 to take up an apprenticeship on the Railways. He later left the Railways and joined Amalgamated Packaging Industries, Hypak, as a salesman. In 1967 he became sales manager, a position he held for 30 years, after which he stayed on as a part-timer till he retired in 2005, aged 73.

Brian Stuart Schabram was born on 25 September 1932. He died peacefully in Alberlito Hospital in Ballito on 14 October 2016. He had had a successful hip replacement but other complications related mostly to age meant he had a few stays in hospital before dying peacefully with family present. His funeral service was held at the North Durban Presbyterian Church in Sunningdale. He was married twice, first to Jean in 1956 and then to Alice in 1978. He is survived by Alice, son Stuart, daughters Sandra and Carla, six grandchildren and a great-grandchild.

DAVID SMIT
FOUR friends set sail from Lambert's Bay on the West Coast. It was their regular fishing trip, one they had been looking forward to as they had not been out for a month while the boat was being refurbished. Despite the refurbishing things went wrong, Hottie Pretorius's boat capsized and three of them drowned. One of them was David Smit, know as Smitty, who played rugby for Boland. Of the other three, two, Herman Tolken and Hugo Visser, drowned trying to swim ashore, Pretorius made it to shore and the boat later washed up but Smit's body was never found.

After leaving school in Clanwilliam, Smit went to the Wellington Teachers' Training College, at a time when the college was the dominant club in the Boland and which he eventually captained.

Smit was 20 when he was first chosen as an eighthman for Boland in 1973. He played for Boland in 25 matches over eight seasons. Those were tough years for once-powerful Boland as they lost their A Section status in the Currie Cup. In 1976 they were combined with South Western Districts to play the All Blacks, but, except for one player, it was a Boland side that lost 42-6 to Andy Leslie's side.

From Wellington Teachers' Training College, where he met his future wife, Smit went to Moorreesburg where he enthusiastically taught in the primary school. He left teaching and went farming before retiring to Lambert's Bay.

David Erasmus Smit was born in Clanwilliam on 7 July 1952. He died on 8 March 2016 in Lambert's Bay, survived by his wife Edna, their children Ryan and Suzanne.

ANDRE SKINNER
FORMER Northern Transvaal and Transvaal lock, André Skinner, who was diagnosed with cancer of the kidneys, lost an 18-month battle on December 16, 2016.

Skinner was born in Pretoria but educated at Hoërskool Brits. In 1977 he was a lock for Northern Transvaal at the Craven Week in Oudtshoorn, an outstanding lock.

His first-class career kicked off in 1981. That year he first played for Northern Transvaal, captained by Naas Botha, and won the Currie

Cup. Skinner played for the Gazelles and the Junior Springboks. At the time he was playing for Defence. Later he played for Tukkies.

The Gazelles (South Africa Under-23) beat Ireland 18-15 in Pretoria in May and the Junior Springboks beat the South African Barbarians 36-19 in Durban in June. It was a good year for Skinner. His lock partner for the Gazelles was Vleis Visagie and for the Junior Springboks, Hennie Bekker.

In 1985, after 34 matches for Northern Transvaal, Skinner moved across to Transvaal for whom he played 48 times, ending in 1988 when he returned to Pretoria, played for Harlequins and was in the Northern Transvaal team that beat Western Province in the Currie Cup Final 19-18 at Loftus Versfeld. He was in a Currie Cup-winning side in his first year of provincial rugby and his last. He was in a Transvaal team that won the short-lived (1983-92) Lion Cup in 1986 and 1987.

André Skinner was born in Pretoria on 13 January 1959. He contracted cancer of the kidneys and had a battle of some 18 months before dying of organ failure, just after midnight on December 16, 2015, survived by his wife Yolanda, son Marné and daughter Donné. He and Yolanda had a series of bed shops.

NELIE SMITH

NELIE Smith had great rugby achievements in his life - Springbok player, captain, selector and coach.

Cornelius Michael Smith, always called Nelie, was born in Bloemfontein on 8 May 1934. He went to Hoërskool Sentraal in Bloemfontein, played for Orange Free State and had a sports shop in Bloemfontein. He was a Free Stater.

He was at the University of the Orange Free State in 1955 when the great Lions came on their 24-match tour. The match after that great Test at Ellis Park was against Central Universities in Durban. Smith, normally a scrumhalf, played flyhalf that day with Max Prozesky as his scrumhalf. The Lions won 21-14. Smith kicked a penalty goal. In 1957 he played centre for Free State in two matches.

Just before his 22nd birthday, Smith made his debut at scrumhalf for Free State. It was against South West Africa, as Namibia then was, in Windhoek. Free State lost 9-3, but Smith was retained and in their next match they beat Northern Transvaal 8-6 in Bloemfontein. Smith went on to play 60 matches for Free State up to 1965, captaining them 37 times.

Also making his debut with Smith in Windhoek was Sakkie van Zyl who had a very long (121 matches) career for Free State. In 1976 he and Smith would coach the Free State when they first won their Currie Cup.

In that year, too, Smith went on a tour to Europe with the SA Students team and in 1959 he toured South America with an excellent Junior Springbok team.

Smith did not find it an easy journey to the top for the No.1 scrumhalf in the Free State at the time was Popeye Strydom. The Springbok scrumhalves were Dick Lockyear, Piet Uys and then Dawie de Villiers. But 1963 was a good year for Smith.

John Thornett's strong Wallaby side came on a 24-match tour that year. Smith played against them four times. First he captained the Junior Springboks in Springs when they beat the Wallabies 12-5. Two matches later he was a Springbok - chosen for the third Test at Ellis Park. He kicked three penalty goals but, alas, they were the Springboks' only scores in an 11-9 defeat. But then he captained the Free State when they beat the Wallabies 14-8 and was back in the Springbok team that won the fourth Test 22-6, thus sharing the series.

The next year it was the SA Rugby Board's 75th birthday. Wales came and South Africa gave them a 24-3 hiding in Durban on a day when Smith scored a try. They left in May and the French arrived in July. Smith was made captain of the Springboks for the first time in what was perhaps the worst Test ever played in South Africa - a scruffy Test at a scruffy ground in Springs, and the French beat the Springboks 8-6, the first in a list of seven consecutive defeats.

In 1965 the Springboks went to Australasia, and Nelie was named vice-captain to Dawie De Villiers. De Villiers could not play in the Tests against the Wallabies. Smith played and captained the side that lost both Tests. He was captain again when the Springboks lost the first Test in New Zealand. In all he played in seven Tests, four times as a winless captain and only twice in a winning side.

In 1966, with Dirk de Vos established as the Free State scrumhalf, Smith moved to Griquas and played for them four times. This was the end of his playing career.

Smith had a sports shop in Bloemfontein but it did not flourish and he turned to what he did best - coaching rugby. He coached Free State, became the SA Rugby Board's first coaching organiser, coached Stellenbosch University, Old Greys in Bloemfontein, Eastern Province, Northern Free State, Rovigo in Italy and Ballymena in Northern Ireland, but above all he was the Springbok coach - in 1980 when their crowning achievement was the 3-1 defeat of Billy Beaumont's Lions and then again in 1981 when they beat Ireland and then went off on that tense tour of New Zealand.

He coached in several places, including Northern Transvaal with Ernst Dinkelmann, at the South African Rugby Board and in the Eastern Province.

Smith had many tales to tell and worked on lengthy memoirs with the help of Amanda Botha, though it may never see the light of day.

Nelie Smith had a long and uncomfortable illness, dependent on an oxygen tank for breathing. He also had a pacemaker. He died at his home in the Strand on 2 May 2016. His wife Orna predeceased him by 21 years but he is survived by his son Cornelius and his daughters Carin and Annien.

NEIL STEYN

NEIL Steyn was one of the most prominent sports writers in South Africa in his time. He was the sports editor of two newspapers, first Hoofstad and of the Transvaler, where he was for 13 years, ending as assistant editor. (Both newspapers are now defunct.)

He wrote four books - Sesse tot Oorwinning on the Australian cricket tour to South Africa in 1966-67, Weer Wêreldkampioene on the 1976 All Black tour, a biography of the boxing champion Kallie Knoetze and a biography of the Northern Transvaal (now Blue Bulls) hero, Thys Lourens.

Born in the Transvaal, Steyn grew up in the Free State and finished his schooling at Hoërskool Sentraal in Bloemfontein before moving up to the University of Pretoria. He played as a prop for his school's 1st XV, for the Tukkies 1st XV and then for Oostelikes 1st XV, till injury stopped him from playing but not from his enthusiasm for the game.

Neil Johan Steyn was born in Nigel on 4 November 1938. He was living at the Featherwood Retirement Village in Pretoria when he developed painful kidney problems and died in hospital on 30 May 2016, survived by Jeane, his wife of 52 years, Marna who teaches in Moscow, Karien on a farm in Komatipoort and Christa who lives in Pretoria, and nine grandchildren.

TANNIE CILLIE STEYTLER

A LOT of rugby depends on a lot of women, and one of the most dependable was Tannie Cillie Steytler of St John's Ambulance, who started her devoted service to Griqualand West's rugby on 14 May 1963, at a time when St John's and the Noodhulpliga attended to players' injuries at rugby grounds. In Kimberley it was St John's and she was a lot more than a water-and-bandage person.

She became an ardent Griqua supporter. Those were days before TV and sponsorships, when unions battled to save money. Tannie Cillie would wash and iron players' jerseys and shorts, mend them when necessary and work the numbers on. And in 1982 she became Griquas' first full-time rugby administrator with her own office, later claiming with a twinkle in her eye that she was Griquas' first CEO. In 1986 she was an organiser of the centenary of the Griqualand West Rugby Union.

After nearly 50 years of dedicated service she was honoured by being made a Dame of Grace of the Most Venerable Order of the Hospital of Saint John of Jerusalem, a rare honour. She retired from active service in 2011.

Magdalena Cecilia Cilliers Steytler, née Van Heerden, was born in Philipstown in the Karoo on 9 January 1938. She was sick for only a short while before she died on 24 January 2016, survived by her children Henry and Riana, three granddaughters and two great-grandchildren.

MAKHENKESI STOFILE

MAKHENKESI Stofile held many high offices in his life, some of them sporting, some political, some a mixture of both, some religious. He was able to combine politics, sport and religion – a rare feat.

He was a well-educated man: first at Newell High School, founded in 1942 by a Presbyterian minister, George Molefe, in New Brighton, Port Elizabeth, and then at the University of Fort Hare in Alice, a university which has an impressive list of alumni, including Nelson Mandela, Desmond Tutu and Oliver Tambo. At the university Stofile obtained a master's degree in theology. At the time of his death he was the chancellor of the university. In 1983 he also obtained a master's degree at Princeton University in New Jersey, USA.

In 1975 Stofile was ordained a Presbyterian minister.

While at the university Stofile played rugby, as a scrumhalf, sometimes as a wing and sometimes as a hooker, and he was also chosen for Border, an affiliate of the pre-unification SARU. But he is better known for his political actions in the world of rugby. His playing days over, he served for more than 20 years on the administration of the Victoria East Rugby Union, the South Eastern District Rugby Union, and the pre-rugby unity South African Rugby Union.

In 1981 the Springboks toured New Zealand and the USA. It was a highly controversial tour with lots of vigorous action against the tour. Stofile, then known by his middle name, Arnold, went abroad to help organise opposition to the tour, which ended in New Zealand with the flour bomb Test when a protestor flew a light aircraft over Eden Park, dropping bags of flour onto the players below.

In 1985 the All Blacks were due to tour South Africa and again Stofile was active in garnering opposition against the tour, which was stopped on a court decision by Judge Casey. Instead the players came on a rebel tour as the New Zealand Cavaliers in 1986. His efforts caused him to be detained for four months on his return home and in 1986 he was sentenced to 11 years' imprisonment for "terrorism". He was released in a "gesture of goodwill", after serving three years. The next year Nelson Mandela was freed from prison, banned political parties were unbanned, apartheid was ended and there were elections for all in 1994, which made the African National Congress the ruling party in South Africa.

South Africa had 11 provinces each with its own government and Stofile became the premier of the Eastern Cape in 1997, a province with grave problems. From 2004 to 2010 he was the minister of sport and in 2011 he became the ambassador to Germany, a post he

OBITUARIES

held when he died.

Makhenkesi Arnold Stofile was born in Adelaide in the Eastern Cape on 27 December 1944. He died at his home in Alice on 15 December 2016, survived by his wife Nambitha and two daughters. His son predeceased him.

HENNIE VAN DER MERWE

HENNIE van der Merwe, a genial policeman, played a big role in Griqualand West's rugby. After playing for Police in Kimberley, he continued his involvement at club level, coaching Police, and then became in 1976 the convener of selectors for the provincial side.

Van der Merwe was a policeman from 1962 to 1997, first in Kimberley, then in Pretoria where he retired. After his retirement he came back to Kimberley.

Van der Merwe also came onto the executive of the Union, became vice-president and then for four years to 2014 he was the Union's president in succession to Ronnie Bauser. His involvement had much to do with delicacies of politically acceptable unification of rugby and, as he was a policeman, he was happy to listen to people and sympathetic towards those who were less privileged.

Colonel Hendrik Schalk van der Merwe was born in Barkly West, a town on the Vaal River about 35km northwest of Kimberley, on 1 May 1942. His death was sudden. First he had an operation on a leg and then died of colon cancer in the Mediclinic Gariep in Kimberley on 18 May 2016, survived by his wife Theresa, daughters Hanlie and Annalize, son Schalk, and four grandchildren. A memorial service was held in the NG Kerk Du Toitspan in Du Toitspan Road.

RUDI VAN HEERDEN

RUDI van Heerden was a Port Elizabeth man. He was born there, went to school there, lived, worked and played there, built his family there and eventually died there.

His schooling was at Diaz Laerskool and then the relatively new Hoërskool Otto du Plessis. He played for Police for six seasons, from 1971 to 1976. He had a good year in 1975 when he played four matches for Eastern Province, one of them against the French touring team at Boet Erasmus Stadium. France won 18-9 on that robust tour but their prop Gérard Cholley, who was notorious for his violent acts on the rugby field, where he was euphemistically referred to as a enforcer, was sent off late in the second half.

In later life he became a self-employed electrical engineer.

The last five years of Rudi van Heerden's life were tough. He was diagnosed with leukaemia, eventually had a bone-marrow transplant in Pretoria in 2015 with his brother as his donor. For a while things went well but the transplant was not a success.

Rudolf Philippus van Heerden was born on 18 February 1951. He died on 1 May 2016, survived by his wife Susan, their two daughters and three grandchildren - two girls and a boy. His funeral service was at the NG Kerk PE Hoogland.

KOBUS VAN NOORDWYK

A TALL, elegant fullback, probably the greatest match Kobus van Noordwyk played was in 1960 when Wilson's Whineray All Blacks were possibly lucky to draw 6-all with Natal at Kings Park in Durban before a record crowd of 27 000 - a thrilling match, exhausting for players and spectators.

Roy Dryburgh, who captained the Springboks from fullback in the first two Tests in 1960, played on the right wing for Natal against the All Blacks, which allowed Van Noordwyk to play, such was his value to the side. At the end of the All Black tour the South African Barbarians were first formed and played their first match - against Natal. The Barbarians were a mixture of eight Springboks and seven All Blacks. Natal won 28-11. Again Van Noordwyk was at fullback.

Van Noordwyk was really from the Cape – he was born and schooled in Riversdale and came close at one stage to returning to the Cape. Kobus's son Anton talks about the early rugby influence on his father: "Dad's father was a rugby fanatic and a staunch supporter of Western Province and it wasn't uncommon for the family to embark on the long trek to Cape Town to watch their beloved Western Province play at Newlands and to return to Riversdale in the early hours of Sunday morning."

After leaving Hoërskool Langenhoven in Riversdale, Van Noordwyk joined Standard Bank and transfers made him a wanderer. He was in Kroonstad and playing for Kroonstad Wanderers when he was chosen to play for Orange Free State against Eastern Province in Bloemfontein in 1957. That was also Louis Luyt's first match as captain of Free State. Four weeks later they played against Western Province at Newlands. The night before the team left by train for Cape Town, Van Noordwyk and girlfriend invited Louis Luyt out for the evening, providing him with a blind date. Luyt had the car and off they went to pick up the girls, and that is how Louis met Adri and just over a year later they became Mr and Mrs.

In 1959 Van Noordwyk was transferred from Kroonstad to Eshowe and then up to Mtubatuba in Northern Zululand. In that year he made his debut for Natal, against Transvaal at Ellis Park, a match that Natal won 13-12. He played 21 matches for Natal from 1959 to 1963.

In fact Natal rugby was particularly strong in the early 1960s. The 1961 team lost just one match and the 1963 team was unbeaten. Van Noordwyk played his last season for Natal in 1963. He retired after that but remained involved in rugby, serving as a coach, selector and referee in the Zululand region of Natal and at his Mtubatuba Rugby Club.

Van Noordwyk was a keen sportsman. Besides rugby, he played tennis for Free State for two years and golf and tennis for Zululand.

In 1962 he married Nola Holmes and nearly got back to the Cape in 1963. The bank transferred him to Wellington but his father-in-law was so angered that his daughter should be leaving Mtubatuba that Van Noordwyk left the bank and stayed in Mtubatuba and became a successful businessman in Northern Zululand, being involved in food retail and wholesale and later in property investments.

Jacobus van Noordwyk was born in Riversdale on 20 December 1932. He died in Mtubatuba on 18 April 2016. Nola, his wife of 50 years, died in 2012 and he is survived by their three sons, Ray, Anton and Chris, and three grandsons.

Ray coached Durban Collegians successfully and coached the Sharks at Under-21 and Under-19 levels. Anton played club cricket and rugby and manages the family property business in Mtubatuba. Chris played cricket for South African Schools while he was at Kearsney College and then for Northern Transvaal/Titans. He coached the Titans and is still a coaching consultant in Pretoria.

ROOIES VAN WYK

ROOIES van Wyk was one of the big characters of rugby in the Western Cape over a number of years, as player and then as an administrator.

His nickname came from the colour of his hair. The nickname outlasted his hair.

Born in Namaqualand he came to Stellenbosch University in 1960 at the age of 20 to study agriculture and was in Helderberg koshuis. His road to Stellenbosch was not an easy one. After school at Kammieskroom and Garies, which took him to Std 8 (now Grade 10), he worked on the mines at Alexander Bay to get money to study further, became a diesel mechanic and got the important matric certificate.

Van Wyk, too late to play for Maties Under-19, went straight into the senior ranks, played for the famous Maties and became their captain, a big, tough flank forward with a pleasant sense of humour and a ready smile. He played for Western Province from 1964, when he made his debut against Transvaal, to 1968.

In 1964, his first year for Western Province, he played in their famous victory in Pretoria when Jannie Engelbrecht scored two tries with a broken collarbone. Van Wyk, also injured, scored a try near the end. Western Province won the Currie Cup that year and again in 1966.

In April 1965 Van Wyk was one of six Maties to make the final Springbok trials but he did not make the team in that miserable year for South African rugby. In 1965 and 1966 he played for Southern Universities.

When he was lecturing and living at Elsenburg Agricultural College he played for Paarl for five seasons, four as captain. His coach was Wynand Mans, Van Wyk's younger team-mate whose career was ended by an injury. When Mans took up refereeing, Van Wyk coached Paarl and later became the chairman of the club. He also coached Elsenburg and lectured at the Agricultural College.

Van Wyk obtained his doctorate in agriculture with a thesis on formulating diets for growing pigs. He would tell with a chuckle that a pig was just like a human. They gave three pigs the lees of a wine barrel. One went to sleep, one picked a fight and one went in search of a sow!

Involved in agricultural corporations in Caledon and Malmesbury, Van Wyk threw in his lot with Boland and was on the executive and a senior selector in 1984. In 1988 he became the fourth president of the Boland Rugby Union in succession to the former Springbok Flappie Lochner. The next year the Boland Rugby Union celebrated its 50th jubilee with Van Wyk as president. He stayed president till 1995, which means he was the president at the time when rugby in South Africa was finally unified in 1992.

In 1994 he and Bonnie moved to Stellenbosch and he became the president of the Coetzenburg Club. In 2001 he became the vice-president of the Stellenbosch RFC and its chairman from 2002 to 2004. He was then elected a life member of the club.

Gert Nieuwoudt van Wyk was born in the Vanrhynsdorp District, where his parents farmed, on 11 June 1939. He died of cancer in Stellenbosch on 29 November 2016, survived by his wife Bonnie, sons Kotze and Theron, daughter Enees Huisamen, eight grandchildren, amongst them grandsons Hannes and Gerrit Huisamen. In 2016 Hannes played for the EP Kings, Gerrit for the Madibaz in Varsity Cup. They are both locks.

FANIE VERMAAK

FANIE Vermaak was regarded by many as the toughest prop ever to play for South Eastern Transvaal, a province formed out of Eastern Transvaal in 1968 but which no longer exists on its own after it was incorporated into Mpumalanga. He played for the province for 12 seasons, starting when they beat Italy 39-12 in 1973 and ending in 1984. In all he played 60 matches for the Union. He played his club rugby for Witbank.

His most famous exploit was in the semi-final of the 1980 Currie Cup against Northern Transvaal at Loftus Versfeld. Northern Transvaal won 49-8 but lost the tighthead count 10-1 as Vermaak's power enabled Ronnie Cook to outhook Springbok Willie Kahts. Northern Transvaal went on to beat Western Province 39-9 in the final.

That year Vermaak was in the South Eastern Transvaal team that lost 30-27 to the Jaguars of South America. Each side scored four tries; in the two Tests the Springboks scored a total of only four tries.

Vermaak also wrestled for Northern Transvaal in interprovincial competitions.

When Hennie Erasmus, long the president of South Eastern Transvaal and a highly regarded attorney, died in 1999 Vermaak became the union's president and as such a member of the national body's council. Then the national body was called the South African Rugby Football Union. He remained the Union's president till 2003, a financially troubled time for the Union.

Vermaak lived in Witbank most of his live. As a child he lived in a mining village just outside Witbank. He worked on the mines and then went into contract work as an electrician where they did most of the town's electricity installation on new schools and neighbourhoods around Witbank. He later on worked at the municipality of Emalahleni.

Stephanus Johannes Vermaak, who was born in 1950, had heart problems for some time and eventually died in his home in Witbank on 22 November 2016, survived by his wife Alida, their children, Carien and Fanie, and five grandchildren.

KOOS VERMAAK

THERE was a time when several university professors were in top positions in South African rugby - Danie Craven as president of the SA Rugby Board, Peter Booysen as president of the Natal Rugby Union, Fritz Eloff as president of Northern Transvaal, Johan Claassen as president of Western Transvaal and Koos Vermaak, of Eastern Province. It suggests that there was a high level of intellectuality in rugby in those amateur days, when being a president cost the incumbent money, not the union.

Vermaak was a top physicist, universally acknowledged as such, one of the pioneers of semiconductor physics, but his greatest contribution was to his own university - the University of Port Elizabeth, now incorporated into the Nelson Mandela Metropolitan University. He was the university's first head of the physics department.

Involved in the university club and on the executive of the South African Universities Rugby Union, Vermaak became increasingly involved in rugby administration. He served on the executive of the Eastern Province Rugby Union whose president he became in 1988 when Lawton Fourie retired. Vermaak's term was a short two years compared with Fourie's 17 and Trevor Jennings took over. Vermaak had a short term on the executive of the South African Rugby Board before he and Steve Strydom were voted off. This was at a sensitive time as the process of the politically acceptable unification of South Africa's rugby was on the go.

His mind was lively and decisive, not at all the absentminded professor. In his rugby dealings he quickly cut to the quick. At the same time he had a great sense of humour and fun, which made him such good company.

Vermaak matriculated from Hoërskool Erasmus in 1954 and while at the University of Pretoria won Northern Transvaal for athletics, winning the 880 yards and the mile at the South African championships in Kimberley. His master's degree was in mathematics, his doctorate in physics.

Down the years Vermaak had a great deal to do with top physicists in the USA. In 1967 he visited Virginia University in Charlottesville; in 1974 and 1981 he worked with North American Philips in Terrytown, Louisiana; and from 1993 to 2001 he was at Sensors Unlimited, working closely with Princeton University with lasers.

Jacobus Stephanus Vermaak was born in the Middelburg District of Mpumalanga on 15 September 1936 and died in Port Elizabeth on 14 January 2016, survived by Suzette, his wife of 57 years, their four children and nine grandchildren. A memorial service was held in the NG Kerk Summerstrand.

DENNIS VICTOR

OVER 10 seasons Dennis Victor played 18 times at scrumhalf for Northern Transvaal, between 1949 and 1958. But then those were the days of fewer provincial matches and the time when Fonnie du Toit was in his heyday. But he did play in the 1956 Currie Cup final against Natal, a match that Northern Transvaal won 9-8 in Durban. Victor 'made' the first of Northern Transvaal's two tries. The ball went loose behind the Natal scrum and he pounced on it and gave to Willa Esterhuizen, who scored.

Despite his long career, he did not get a chance to play against a major touring team, because tours were few and Du Toit was chosen ahead of him against the All Blacks, the Wallabies and the Lions, while Jimmy Moodie of Western Transvaal was chosen for a combined side against the 1958 French, when Victor was already 31.

At the end of his playing days, Victor coached Defence, who shared the Carlton Cup with Tukkies in 1960.

Victor was certainly adventurous. At the age of 17, he left Selborne College, where he was at school, and joined the Transvaal Scottish. He ended the war in the tanks in Italy.

Back in South Africa Victor wrote matric and then joined the South African Air Force in the communications section. He retired as Colonel Victor in 1982. He then joined Grinel Electronics in Pretoria and retired in 1992 as their marketing and sales manager.

In 1949 Victor married Constance Martin and they had three sons, one of whom predeceased his father. Constance died in 1998. In 2006 he married Ann Gillian Paton, whom he met in the Protea Retirement Village in Centurion.

Dennis Peter Victor was born in East London on 5 July 1927. He died on 14 April 2016, survived by Gillian, Claude and Neville, three grandsons and six great-grandchildren.

ERNEST VILJOEN

THIS is in so many ways a sad tale, the life of this Bloemfonteiner who died a lonely death at the age of 56.

After he left Hoërskool Sand du Plessis, Viljoen went into the army and played rugby for Defence and then Old Collegians. He played his first game at fullback for Free State in 1981 and in all played for them 28 times, which was a remarkable achievement as the incumbent fullback throughout his career was the great Gysie Pienaar, which meant that he got a game only when Pienaar was playing for higher teams or injured.

After his playing days Viljoen coached rugby with his former team-mate, Johan Steyn, whose son became the Springbok Morné Steyn.

In 2007, Viljoen and a Bloemfontein businessman, JC Gie, went to see Johan Steyn with a proposal to provide machinery - claimed to have been imported from Australia through David Campese - to establish carwash businesses. The Steyn investment would be R250,000, which Johan Steyn's wife Marita transferred into Gie's account from her son Morné's account.

The transaction turned out to be a scam and in 2011 Viljoen was sentenced to five years' imprisonment. At the age of 69, Gie, who was involved in bigger scams, received more jail time. In prison Viljoen had become a pastor and completed a degree in theology.

Viljoen was released in January 2016. He was living in a flat, but when his son phoned his cellphone, there was no reply. The son called his uncle who broke into the flat and found his brother Ernest, having had, it seems, a heart attack on the day before.

Ernest Viljoen was born in Bloemfontein on 26 November 1960 and died there on 12 December 2016, survived by his wife Elzabi, a son EJ and a daughter.

TUCKER VORSTER

TUCKER Vorster was a remarkable man, a great achiever at a high level, a man who did lots of things - an academic, a sportsman and an author.

He reached provincial level at rugby, tennis, golf and athletics. And when he died he was 94. His provincial rugby career was started young. He went to Potchefstroom Volkskool and was the flyhalf and hero of their 1st XV, especially in 1939 when Volkies won the Administrator's Cup. He was also the top hurdler in the school. Vorster was 18 when his senior provincial career started - flyhalf for Western Transvaal. Then he moved to the University of Pretoria, at a time when the Northern Transvaal flyhalf was the genius Hansie Brewis. Vorster did well to get two matches for Northern Transvaal in 1943. It was, of course, a tough time for the

world, in the middle of World War II with lots of tension in South Africa between those who volunteered to fight and those who did not. In some parts of South African rugby the tension became a rift.

Vorster left Tukkies with an MSc and in 1950 started lecturing in geography before moving back to Tukkies, this time as a lecturer specialising in climatology. He retired in 1982.

He played flyhalf for Western Transvaal before coming to Pretoria in the 1940s. After retiring from rugby, he took up tennis and represented Northern Transvaal for a number of years. He lectured geography at the University of Pretoria for more than 30 years until he retired in 1982. He became an avid golfer and played off a handicap of 4 for many years. He ended up breaking his age in golf well in excess of 100 times and as a 90-year-old carded four 2s in one round at the Pretoria Country Club (making birdies on all the par threes).

His grandson, Tucker Vorster, played number one for the South African team at the Davis Cup.

Vorster and his wife Elize built a house at Cape St Francis, a village on a headland in the Eastern Cape, the home of the perfect wave, an enticement to surfers. The Vorsters were amongst the first people to build in Cape St Francis. For about three months of the year it was their home. He became one of the great personalities of the town and in particular its beautiful golf club.

Vorster also wrote a novel in the 1970s - Die Baron van Skoonrivier.

Jan Harm Vorster was born in Potchefstroom on 8 June 1922 and died in Pretoria on 2 January 2016, survived by his son Japie and two daughters.

JEAN-JIREH YAMWIMBI

JEAN-JIREH Yamwimbi was chosen to go to the 2016 Craven Week in Durban but died six days before the tournament started. The Falcons decided not to take a replacement out of respect, and went to Durban with 22 players and Jean-Jireh's name still Number 19 on the programme. At Craven Week there was a period of silence to honour JJ, as his friends called him.

JJ was at Rhodesfield Technical High School in Kempton Park and played lock for the 1st XV. In 2015 he had been chosen for the Falcons Under-16 team and played at the Grant Khomo Week.

Some time before Craven Week, while JJ was playing for Rhodesfield he suffered a bang to the head and so did not play for the school side for two weeks. For three weeks he sat out of Falcons preparations for Craven Week and when he went to the training camp in Rustenburg he was not required to take part in contact sessions, but complained of headaches.

Jean-Jireh Yamwimbi was born in Johannesburg on 3 June 1999 and died on 5 July 2016.